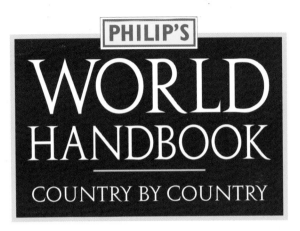

PHILIP'S

# WORLD
# HANDBOOK

## COUNTRY BY COUNTRY

# PHILIP'S

# WORLD HANDBOOK

## COUNTRY BY COUNTRY

**EXECUTIVE EDITOR**
Caroline Rayner

**EDITOR**
Kara Turner

**EXECUTIVE ART EDITOR**
Alison Myer

**COVER DESIGN**
Stewart Cocking

**WORLD FLAGS**
Bosse Norrgård

**WORLD STATISTICS**
Typeset by eMC Design, Bromham,
Bedford, UK


Published in Great Britain in 1995
by George Philip Limited,
an imprint of Reed Books,
Michelin House, 81 Fulham Road, London SW3 6RB,
and Auckland, Melbourne, Singapore and Toronto

Cartography by Philip's

Copyright © 1995 Reed International Books Limited

ISBN 0–540–05891–2 (Paperback)
ISBN 0–540–05892–0 (Hardback)

A CIP catalogue record for this book is available
from the British Library

Printed in Great Britain

# CONTENTS

*See also contents lists for individual sections*

# GENERAL NOTES

## World Gazetteer Statistical Tables

In the country fact-files certain terms have been used which may require some explanation.

**AREA** The area of the whole country, including inland water areas.

**POPULATION** The 1994 United Nations official population estimate is given, which is based on the latest censuses. The population of the cities is taken from the most recent census or the latest estimate (whichever is the more recent), and as far as possible is for the urban agglomeration rather than the strictly defined city proper.

**ETHNIC GROUPS** Only the main ethnic groups are listed and percentages are given wherever

possible. The figures are usually taken from the latest available census results.

**LANGUAGES** The official languages are listed together with any other major languages, with percentages given wherever possible. The figures are usually taken from the latest available census results.

**RELIGIONS** The principal religions are listed, with a breakdown of the main demoninations and percentages provided wherever possible.

**CURRENCY** The currency of each country is given in the format one pound equals 100 pence. Where a country does not have its own currency, the name is given of the country whose currency is used.

## World Statistics Section

In the last few years, some countries have broken up to form separate states while others have united to make a single country. Some statistical data have already been published for these new countries, or, alternatively, interpretations have been drawn from the information that had previously been available. All available figures have been used in the listings, but data for the former larger countries – USSR, Czechoslovakia, Ethiopia and Yugoslavia – have sometimes also been given. The form of names for the new countries follows the convention used in Philip's world atlases, but the region that is generally called Serbia is listed under Yugoslavia (Serbia) and Bosnia-Herzegovina is abbreviated to Bosnia.

The world lists include as many countries
‥ ‥ ͑possible. For certain coun-
ͺ conventional names have
ͺthan some newly-adopted
ͻa for Myanmar, Ivory Coast
ͺand Surinam (Suriname).
ͺtistics for Belgium include

those of Luxembourg, and any historic figures for Pakistan for 1950 will also contain those for Bangladesh.

Wherever possible, in the world statistics, the world total is given, followed by the countries in alphabetical order. Historic data are given for 1950 or 1970 (depending on data availability) as well as figures for the latest available year. All data are taken from official sources. The production statistics include all countries that have at some point produced over one-thousandth part of the world total. The top-ten producers are also indicated, together with their percentage of the world total.

The measure 'tonnes' is used and it is spelled in this way to indicate that the figures shown are in metric tons. The symbol ... indicates that the relevant figures are not available or that they are not applicable to a particular country. The symbol – means that although there was production for a particular year, it was very small.

# WORLD MAPS

## Symbols

——— Principal railways

═══ Motorways

——— Principal roads

▬▬▬ International boundaries

▨▨▨ Internal boundaries

4125 Heights (m)

✿ Principal airports

## Height of Land

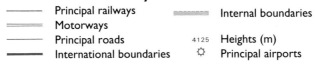

For pages 6, 7, 8, 9

For pages 4, 5, 12, 13, 16, 17, 18, 20, 21, 22, 26, 31, 32, 33

For pages 10, 11, 27, 28, 29, 30, 36

For pages 14, 15, 19, 23, 24, 25, 34, 35

# WORLD : Political

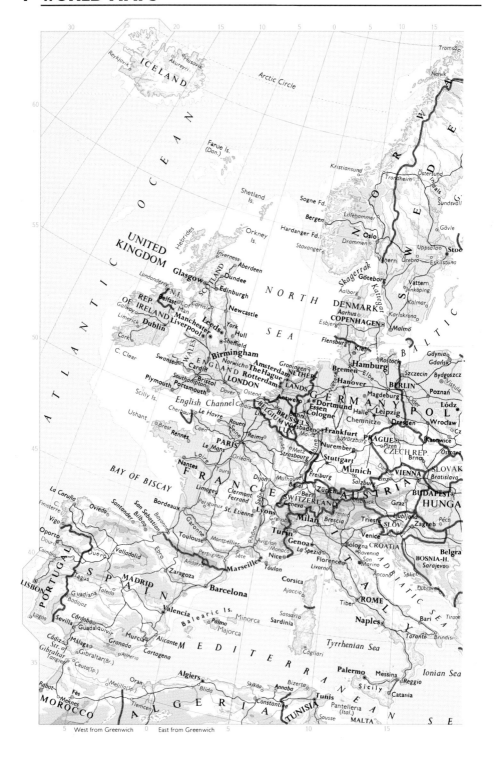

## EUROPE

| 0 | 100 | 200 | 300 | 400 miles |
|---|---|---|---|---|
| 0 | 200 | 400 | 600 | km |

### E.U. Members & Populations

| | | | |
|---|---|---|---|
| Austria | 7,918,000 | Italy | 57,157,000 |
| Belgium | 10,080,000 | Luxembourg | 401,000 |
| Denmark | 5,173,000 | Netherlands | 15,397,000 |
| Finland | 5,083,000 | Portugal | 9,830,000 |
| France | 57,747,000 | Spain | 39,568,000 |
| Germany | 80,278,000 | Sweden | 8,738,000 |
| Greece | 10,416,000 | U.K. | 58,091,000 |
| Ireland | 3,359,000 | | |

COPYRIGHT. GEORGE PHILIP & SON, LTD.

ENGLAND AND WALES

## SCOTLAND

0 ————— 20 ————— 40 ————— 60 miles
0 —— 20 —— 40 —— 60 —— 80 —— 100 km

SHETLAND
Shetland Is.
On same scale

West from Greenwich

# IRELAND

| 0 | 20 | 40 | 60 miles |
| 0 | 20 40 60 | 80 | 100 km |

ATLANTIC

OCEAN

SCOTLAND

NORTHERN IRELAND

REPUBLIC OF IRELAND

West from Greenwich

# FRANCE

| 0 | 20 | 40 | 60 | 80 | 100 miles |
|---|----|----|----|----|-----------|
| 0 | 40 | 80 | 120 | 160 km | |

**FRENCH DEPARTMENTS**

| | | |
|---|---|---|
| A. | 01 | Ain |
| Ai. | 02 | Aisne |
| Al. | 03 | Allier |
| A.H.P. | 04 | Alpes-de-Haute-Provence |
| H.A. | 05 | Hautes-Alpes |
| A.M. | 06 | Alpes-Maritimes |
| Ar. | 07 | Ardèche |
| Ard. | 08 | Ardennes |
| Ari. | 09 | Ariège |
| Aub. | 10 | Aube |
| Aud. | 11 | Aude |
| Av. | 12 | Aveyron |
| B.R. | 13 | Bouches-du-Rhône |
| C. | 14 | Calvados |
| Ca. | 15 | Cantal |
| Ch. | 16 | Charente |
| Ch.M. | 17 | Charente-Maritime |
| Che. | 18 | Cher |
| Co. | 19 | Corrèze |
| | 20 | Corse a) Haute-Corse |
| C.O | 21 | Côte-d'Or b) Corse du |
| Cr. | 22 | Côtes-d'Armor Sud |
| Cr. | 23 | Creuse |
| D. | 24 | Dordogne |
| Do. | 25 | Doubs |
| Dr. | 26 | Drôme |
| E. | 27 | Eure |
| E.L. | 28 | Eure-et-Loir |
| F. | 29 | Finistère Nord et Sud |
| G. | 30 | Gard |
| H.G. | 31 | Haute-Garonne |
| Ge. | 32 | Gers |
| Gi. | 33 | Gironde |
| He. | 34 | Hérault |
| I.V. | 35 | Ille-et-Vilaine |
| I. | 36 | Indre |
| I.L. | 37 | Indre-et-Loire |
| Is. | 38 | Isère |
| J. | 39 | Jura |
| L. | 40 | Landes |
| L.C. | 41 | Loir-et-Cher |
| Lo. | 42 | Loire |
| H.L. | 43 | Haute-Loire |
| L.A. | 44 | Loire-Atlantique |
| Loi. | 45 | Loiret |
| Lot | 46 | Lot |
| L.G. | 47 | Lot-et-Garonne |
| Loz. | 48 | Lozère |
| M.L. | 49 | Main-et-Loire |
| M. | 50 | Manche |
| Ma. | 51 | Marne |
| H.M. | 52 | Haute-Marne |
| May. | 53 | Mayenne |
| M.M. | 54 | Meurthe-et-Moselle |
| Me. | 55 | Meuse |
| Mo. | 56 | Morbihan |
| Mos. | 57 | Moselle |
| N. | 58 | Nièvre |
| No. | 59 | Nord |
| O. | 60 | Oise |
| Or. | 61 | Orne |
| P.C. | 62 | Pas-de-Calais |
| P.D. | 63 | Puy-de-Dôme |
| P.A. | 64 | Pyrénées Atlantiques |
| H.P. | 65 | Hautes Pyrénées |
| P.O. | 66 | Pyrénées (Orientales) |
| B.R. | 67 | Bas Rhin |
| H.R. | 68 | Haut Rhin |
| Rh. | 69 | Rhône |
| H.S. | 70 | Haute Saône |
| S.L. | 71 | Saône-et-Loire |
| S. | 72 | Sarthe |
| Sa. | 73 | Haute-Savoie |
| H.Sa. | 74 | Haute-Savoie |
| | 75 | Paris |
| S.Me. | 76 | Seine-Maritime |
| S.M. | 77 | Seine-et-Marne |
| Yv. | 78 | Yvelines |
| D.S. | 79 | Deux-Sèvres |
| So. | 80 | Somme |
| T. | 81 | Tarn |
| T.G. | 82 | Tarn-et-Garonne |
| V. | 83 | Var |
| Va. | 84 | Vaucluse |
| Ve. | 85 | Vendée |
| Vi. | 86 | Vienne |
| H.V. | 87 | Haute Vienne |
| Vo. | 88 | Vosges |
| Y. | 89 | Yonne |
| | 90 | Belfort |
| Es. | 91 | Essonne |
| | 92 | Hauts-de-Seine |
| | 93 | Seine-St. Denis |
| | 94 | Val-de-Marne |
| | 95 | Val-d'Oise |

**CORSICA**
On same scale

Corse

Bastia

Calvi

Mt. Cinto
2710

Mte. Rotondo
2675

Corse

Ajaccio

Porto
Vecchio

Bonifacio

Str. of Bonifacio

## NETHERLANDS

0    10   20   30   40   50 miles
0      20      40      60    80 km

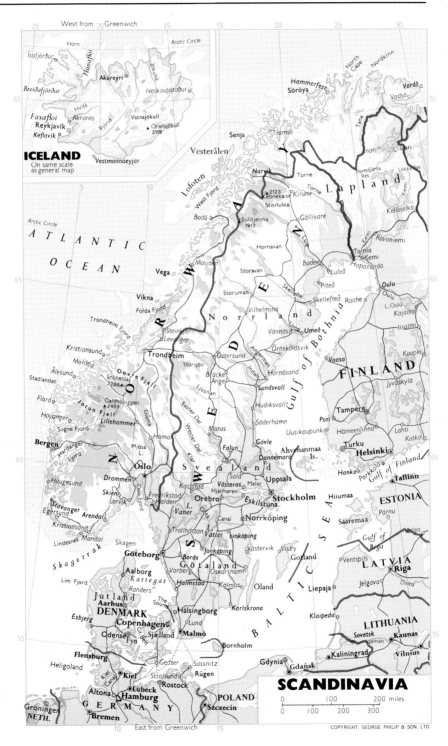

ICELAND
On same scale
as general map

SCANDINAVIA

0        100        200 miles
0     100    200    300

COPYRIGHT. GEORGE PHILIP & SON. LTD.

CENTRAL EUROPE

## ITALY AND S.E. EUROPE

0   50   100   150   200 miles
0   100   200   300 km

MIDDLE EAST

Division between Greeks and Turks in Cyprus; Turks to the north.

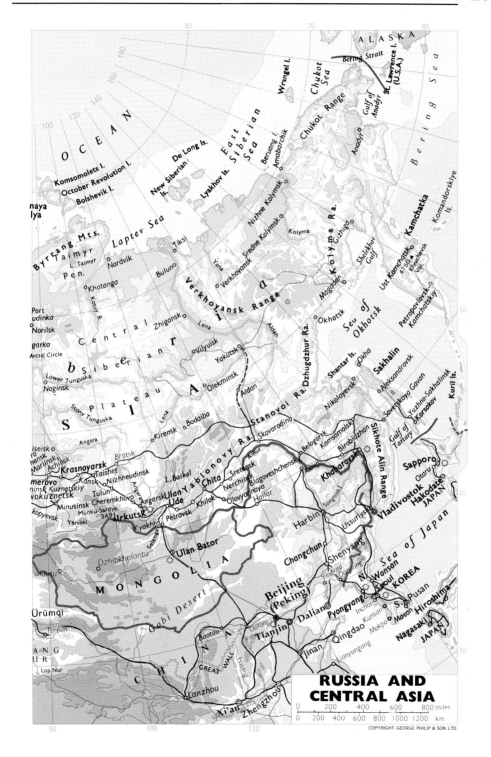

**RUSSIA AND CENTRAL ASIA**

| 0 | 200 | 400 | 600 | 800 miles |
|---|---|---|---|---|

| 0 | 200 | 400 | 600 | 800 | 1000 | 1200 km |

S.W. ASIA

## INDIA, PAKISTAN, SRI LANKA & BURMA

COPYRIGHT GEORGE PHILIP & SON LTD

CHINA

**JAPAN**

REFERENCE TO PREFECTURES

| HOKKAIDO DISTRICT | KANTO DISTRICT | CHUGOKU DISTRICT |
|---|---|---|
| 1 Hokkaido | 17 Gumma | 31 Tottori |
| TOHOKU DISTRICT | 18 Tochigi | 32 Okayama |
| 2 Aomori | 19 Saitama | 33 Shimane |
| 3 Akita | 20 Ibaraki | 34 Hiroshima |
| 4 Iwate | 21 Tokyo | 35 Yamaguchi |
| 5 Yamagata | 22 Chiba | |
| 6 Miyagi | 23 Kanagawa | SHIKOKU DISTRICT |
| 7 Fukushima | | 36 Kagawa |
| | KINKI DISTRICT | 37 Tokushima |
| CHUBU DISTRICT | 24 Hyogo | 38 Ehime |
| 8 Niigata | 25 Kyōto | 39 Kochi |
| 9 Ishikawa | 26 Shiga | |
| 10 Tuyama | 27 Osaka | KYUSHU DISTRICT |
| 11 Fukui | 28 Nara | 40 Fukuoka |
| 12 Gifu | 29 Mie | 41 Saga |
| 13 Nagano | 30 Wakayama | 42 Nagasaki |
| 14 Yamanashi | | 43 Kumamoto |
| 15 Aichi | | 44 Oita |
| 16 Shizuoka | | 45 Miyazaki |
| | | 46 Kagoshima |

**JAPAN**

0    50    100    150    200 miles

0   50  100  150  200  250  300 km

East from Greenwich

# SOUTH-EAST ASIA

## CANADA

Scale:
0 100 200 300 400 500 miles
0 200 400 500 800 km

COPYRIGHT GEORGE PHILIP & SON LTD.

Projection: Bonne

USA

| | 0 | 100 | 200 | 300 | 400 miles |
| 0 | 200 | | 400 | | 600 km |

A  D  A

nnipeg

Cochrane

Arvida

Laurentian Plateau

Quebec

Fredericton

MINNE-

Lake Superior

Thunder Bay

Duluth

Sault Ste. Marie

Sudbury

Trois Rivières

Montreal

Sherbrooke

MAINE

Saint John

SOTA

St. Paul

WISCONSIN

Green Bay

MICHIGAN

Lake Huron

Georgian Bay

Ottawa

Kingston

Toronto

NEW YORK

VERMONT

N.H.

Portland

Manchester

Minneapolis

Mississippi

Ontario

Rochester

Troy

MASS.

Boston

Austin

Saginaw

Hamilton

Buffalo

Albany

R.I.

C. Cod

Providence

Madison

Milwaukee

Grand Rapids

London

Windsor

Lake Erie

Cleveland

Scranton

Newark

New Haven

Sioux City

IOWA

CHICAGO

Detroit

PENNSYLVANIA

NEW YORK

Des Moines

Cedar Rapids

Toledo

Akron

Pittsburgh

N.J.

Philadelphia

Council Bluffs

Illinois

Fort Wayne

OHIO

Columbus

Baltimore

M. D.

Delaware B.

Omaha

Peoria

INDIANA

Dayton

WEST VIRGINIA

Washington

St. Joseph

ILLINOIS

Indianapolis

Cincinnati

Ohio

Richmond

s City

Kansas City

Jefferson City

St. Louis

Louisville

Huntington

VIRGINIA

Topeka

MISSOURI

Evansville

Lexington

Roanoke

Norfolk

Chesapeake B.

KENTUCKY

Oak Ridge

Springfield

Greensboro

Raleigh

C. Hatteras

Tulsa

T  A  T  E  S

Nash-ville

Knoxville

NORTH CAROLINA

Charlotte

M A

ARKANSAS

TENNESSEE

Greenville

SOUTH CAROLINA

Wilmington

Fort Smith

Arkansas

Memphis

Chattanooga

Little Rock

Tennessee

Savannah

Red

Birmingham

Gadsden

Atlanta

Charleston

MISSISSIPPI

GEORGIA

Dallas

Shreveport

Monroe

Jackson

ALABAMA

Columbus

Savannah

Tyler

Montgomery

Albany

S

LOUISIANA

Alabama

Dothan

Jacksonville

ATLANTIC

Beaumont

Baton Rouge

Mobile

OCEAN

Houston

New Orleans

Galveston

Mississippi Delta

Tampa

West Palm Beach

pus Christi

St. Petersburg

FLORIDA

Freeport

BAHAMAS

Everglades

Miami

Nassau

tamoros

Gulf of Mexico

C. Sable

Key West

Florida Strait

Havana

Matanzas

C.   Connecticut
D.   Delaware
M.   Maryland
Mass.  Massachusetts
N.H.  New Hampshire
N.J.  New Jersey
R.I.  Rhode Island

Yucatan Strait

Camagüey

**MEXICO AND THE CARIBBEAN**

0 100 200 300 400 500 miles
0 200 400 600 800 km

ATLANTIC OCEAN

PACIFIC OCEAN

Caribbean Sea

Gulf of Mexico

Gulf of California

Lower California

Tropic of Cancer

West from Greenwich

COPYRIGHT GEORGE PHILIP & SON, LTD.

UNITED STATES

Charleston
Savannah
Jacksonville
Atlanta
Columbus
Montgomery
Birmingham
Mobile
Jackson
Baton Rouge
New Orleans
Houston
Tampa
Miami
C. Sable
Florida
Florida Strait

BAHAMAS
Nassau
Turks & Caicos Is. (Br.)

Dallas
Fort Worth
Austin
San Antonio
Corpus Christi
Matamoros
Tampico
El Paso
Ciudad Juarez
Chihuahua
Hermosillo
Guaymas
Nogales
Mexicali

Piedras Negras
Nuevo Laredo
Monterrey
Saltillo
Torreón
Durango
Mazatlán
Aguascalientes
Guadalajara
León
San Luis Potosí
MEXICO CITY
Puebla
Veracruz
Oaxaca
Acapulco
Coatzacoalcos
Villahermosa
Tuxtla Gutiérrez

Eastern Sierra Madre
Western Sierra Madre
Mexican Plateau

Rio Grande

M E X I C O

Popocatepetl 5452
Orizaba 5700

Yucatan
Yucatan Strait
Merida
Gulf of Campeche
Salina Cruz
G. of Tehuantepec
Revilla Gigedo Is. (Mexico)
C. San Lucas
C. Corrientes

Havana
Sta. Clara
Camagüey
Holguin
Santiago de Cuba
CUBA
Cayman Is. (Br.)

BELIZE
Belmopan
GUATEMALA
Guatemala
San Salvador
EL SALVADOR
HONDURAS
Tegucigalpa
Gulf of Honduras
C. Gracias á Dios
C. Catoche
NICARAGUA
Managua
Chinandega
L. Nicaragua
COSTA RICA
San José
PANAMA
Panamá
G. of Panama
Colón
Darién
G. of Darién

Hispaniola
HAITI
DOMINICAN REP.
Port au Prince
Santo Domingo
JAMAICA
Kingston

PUERTO RICO
Virgin Is.
San Juan
ANGUILLA
ANTIGUA
BARBUDA
ST. KITTS-NEVIS
GUADELOUPE (Fr.)
DOMINICA
MARTINIQUE (Fr.)
ST. LUCIA
ST. VINCENT
THE GRENADINES
BARBADOS
GRENADA
TOBAGO
TRINIDAD & TOBAGO
Port of Spain
NETHERLANDS ANTILLES
Aruba
Curaçao

Greater Antilles
Lesser Antilles

CARACAS
VENEZUELA
Maracaibo
L. of Maracaibo
Barquisimeto
Ciudad Bolívar
Orinoco
Caroni
Caura
Sa. Pacaraima
Apure
Meta
Cúcuta
Bucaramanga
Mérida
Medellín
COLOMBIA
Barranquilla
Cartagena
Sa. Nevada de S. Marta
Magdalena
Cauca

## SOUTH AMERICA

0  200  400  600  800 miles
0  200 400  800  1200 km

CARIBBEAN SEA

Santiago de Cuba
Sierra Maestra
Hispaniola
HAITI DOM.
JAMAICA
Kingston
Port au Prince
REP.
S. Juan
PUERTO RICO
(U.S.)
Leeward Is.
Windward Is.
Venezuela
Curaçao (Neth.)
BARBADOS
NICARAGUA
CANAL ZONE
COSTA RICA
Maracaibo
Barranquilla
G. of
Darien
PANAMA
Cartagena
La Guaira
Port of Spain
TRINIDAD AND TOBAGO
Caracas
Barquisimeto
Orinoco
Ciudad Bolivar
Georgetown
Demerara
Paramaribo
FR. GUIANA
Cayenne
VENEZUELA
Roraima
2810
Sa. Pacaraima
GUYANA
SURINAM
Sa. de Tumucumaque
Pereira
Manizales
Medellín
Bogotá
Cali
COLOMBIA
Papayán
Casiquiare
Macapá
Amazon
Pará
Equator
ECUADOR
Quito
Chimborazo
6267
Cotopaxi
5897
Guayaquil
Cuenca
C. Pariña
Piura
Marañón
Iquitos
Putumayo
Japurá
Solimões
Negro
Benjamin Constant
Manaus
Amazon
Santarém
Marajó I.
Belém
São Luis
Teresina
Fortaleza
C. de São Roque
Natal
Imperatriz
Chiclayo
Trujillo
S. Antonio Falls
Branco
Rooseveit
Madeira
Purus
Tapajós
Xingu
Tocantins
Araguaya
Parnaiba
Pernambuco
João Pessoa
Recife
C. Branco
Paulistana
São Francisco
PERU
Callão
Lima
Huancayo
Cuzco
Juliaca
Ucayali
Ampú
8550
Plateau of Mato Grosso
Cuyabá
Goiânia
Brasília
Barreiros
Salvador
Alagoinhas
Aracaju
Maceió
BRAZIL
Highlands
Pisco
Arequipa
Mollendo
Tacna
Arica
Iquique
BOLIVIA
La Paz
Cochabamba
Oruro
Santa Cruz
Sucre
Potosi
Corumbá
Paraguay
Ribeirão Prêto
Uberaba
Liberato
Montes Claros
Piracpora
Belo Horizonte
Ilhéus
Vitória de Conquista
Cardveiros
Tropic of Capricorn
Antofagasta
Taltal
Pilcomayo
PARAGUAY
Asunción
Iguaçu Falls
Campinas
São Paulo
Santos
Ribeirão Prêto
Campos
Niteroi
Rio de Janeiro
C. Frio
Juan Fernández (Chile)
La Serena
Ojos del Salado
6863
Tucumán
Corrientes
Uruguay
Paraná
Santa Maria
Blumenau
Curitiba
Pôrto Alegre
Uruguaiana
Bagé
Lagoa dos Patos
Rio Grande do Sul
Aconcagua
Viña del Mar
Valparaiso
ARGENTINA
Córdoba
Mendoza
Rosario
Santiago
Santa Fé
Paraná
Pelotas
Rocha
URUGUAY
Montevideo
ATLANTIC
Talca
Concepción
Mercedes
Buenos Aires
Rio de la Plata
La Plata
Azul
Mar del Plata
Pta. Mogotes
Temuco
Colorado
Santa Rosa
Valdivia
Osorno
Negro
Bahia Blanca
Puerto Montt
Chiloé
Piedma
G. of San Matias
Chubut
Rawson
Chonos Arch.
Comodoro Rivadavia
G. of San Jorge
O C E A N
PACIFIC
O C E A N
ANDES
CHILE
Rio Gallegos
Punta Arenas
Magellan's Str.
Falkland Is. (Br.)
Stanley
Tierra del Fuego
Staten I.
C. Froward
C. Horn
South Georgia (Br.)
Drake Passage

90  80  70 West from 60 Greenwich 50

# AUSTRALIA

```
0    100    200    300    400    500 miles
0       200    400    600    800 km
```

**PAPUA NEW GUINEA**

Ede
Wau
G. of Papua
Mt. Victoria
4073
Port Moresby
Rigo

Torres Strait
Prince of Wales I.
Cape York

D'Entrecasteaux Is.

Louisiade Arch.

Bougainville
Choiseul

**SOLOMON**
Santa Isabel
**ISLANDS**
Malaita
Indispensible Str.

S. Cristóbal

of
Weipa
**Cape York Peninsula**
Coleman
Cooktown
Wellesley Is.

Chillagoe
Mt. Bartle Frere 1611
Normanton
Innisfail
Cairns
Burketown
Croydon
Norman
Townsville
oweal
Isa
Cloncurry
Charters Towers
Bowen
Hughenden
Mackay
Selwyn
Dajarra
Winton

**QUEENSLAND**

Longreach
Emerald
Mt. Morgan
Rockhampton
Gladstone
Windorah
Bundaberg
Birdsville
Maryborough
Fraser I.
Charleville
Gympie
Darling
Toowoomba
Brisbane
Cunnamulla
Ipswich
Dirranbandi
Tibooburra
L. Callabonna
Bourke
Walgett
Moree
Grafton
Coffs Harbour

**Coral Sea**

**PACIFIC OCEAN**

Chesterfield Is.

Bird I.
Cato I.

**NEW SOUTH WALES**

Wilcannia
Cobar
Broken Hill
Menindee
Dubbo
Peterborough
Roto
Newcastle
Murray River
Mildura
Bathurst
**SYDNEY**
Gawler
Cootamundra
Wollongong
**Adelaide**
Canberra
Goulburn
Jervis B.
Basin
CAP. TERR.
Queanbeyan
Batemans B.
Snowy Mts.
Kosciusko 2230
Bombala

**VICTORIA**
Ararat
Stawell
Wangaratta
Ballarat
**MELBOURNE**
Colac
Geelong
King I.
Bass Strait
Furneaux Group
Burnie
Devonport
Scottsdale
Strahan
Queenstown
**Launceston**
**TASMANIA**
Hobart
P. Davey
Storm B.
S.E. Cape
Tasman Penin.
P. Arthur

**NEW ZEALAND**

North C.
Doubtless B.
Kaipara Harb.
**Auckland**
Great Barrier I.
Devonport
Thames
**North Island**
Hamilton
Tauranga
B. of Plenty
North Taranaki Bight
Rotorua
East C.
New Plymouth
Gisborne
Pateo
Hawke Bay
Wanganui

**NEW ZEALAND**
Karamea B.
Nelson
Blenheim
**Wellington**
Westport
Campbell
**South Island**
Ross
Waiau
Mt. Cook 3753
Christchurch
Mt. Aspiring 3035
Lyttelton
Southern Alps
Canterbury Plains
Milford Sd.
Oamaru
Kingston
Port Chalmers
Otago Harb.
**Dunedin**
Bluff
Invercargill
Stewart I.
Bluff Harb.
Southwest C.

Chatham Is.
(N.Z.)

**NEW ZEALAND**
on same scale

COPYRIGHT. GEORGE PHILIP & SON. LTD

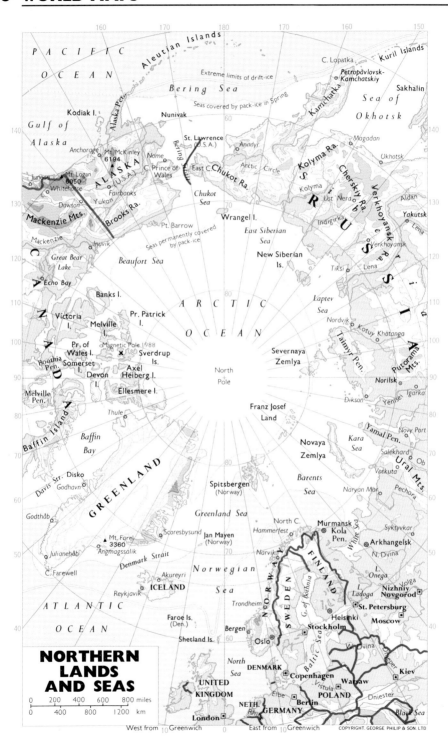

**NORTHERN
LANDS
AND SEAS**

0    200   400   600   800 miles
0      400    800    1200 km

COPYRIGHT GEORGE PHILIP & SON LTD

# WORLD
# FLAGS

*See pages 43–58 for detailed explanations of each flag's meaning and origin.*

**AFGHANISTAN**

**ALBANIA**

**ALGERIA**

**AMERICAN SAMOA**

**ANDORRA**

**ANGOLA**

**ANGUILLA**

**ANTIGUA & BARBUDA**

**ARGENTINA**

**ARMENIA**

**ARUBA**

**ASCENSION**

**AUSTRALIA**

**AUSTRIA**

**AZERBAIJAN**

**AZORES**

**BAHAMAS**

**BAHRAIN**

**BANGLADESH**

**BARBADOS**

**BELARUS**

**BELGIUM**

**BELIZE**

**BENIN**

**BERMUDA**

**BHUTAN**

BOLIVIA

BOSNIA-HERZEGOVINA

BOTSWANA

BRAZIL

BRUNEI

BULGARIA

BURKINA FASO

BURMA (MYANMAR)

BURUNDI

CAMBODIA

CAMEROON

CANADA

CANARY ISLANDS

CAPE VERDE

CAYMAN ISLANDS

CENTRAL AFRICAN REP

CHAD

CHILE

CHINA

COLOMBIA

COMOROS

CONGO

COSTA RICA

CROATIA

CUBA

CYPRUS

CZECH REPUBLIC

DENMARK

DJIBOUTI

DOMINICA

DOMINICAN REPUBLIC

ECUADOR

EGYPT

EL SALVADOR

EQUATORIAL GUINEA

ERITREA

ESTONIA

ETHIOPIA

FALKLAND ISLANDS

FAROE ISLANDS

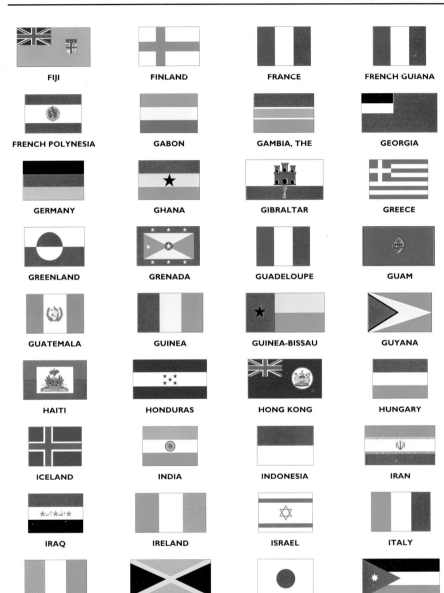

| | | | |
|---|---|---|---|
| FIJI | FINLAND | FRANCE | FRENCH GUIANA |
| FRENCH POLYNESIA | GABON | GAMBIA, THE | GEORGIA |
| GERMANY | GHANA | GIBRALTAR | GREECE |
| GREENLAND | GRENADA | GUADELOUPE | GUAM |
| GUATEMALA | GUINEA | GUINEA-BISSAU | GUYANA |
| HAITI | HONDURAS | HONG KONG | HUNGARY |
| ICELAND | INDIA | INDONESIA | IRAN |
| IRAQ | IRELAND | ISRAEL | ITALY |
| IVORY COAST | JAMAICA | JAPAN | JORDAN |
| KAZAKHSTAN | KENYA | KIRIBATI | KOREA, NORTH |

| KOREA, SOUTH | KUWAIT | KYRGYZSTAN | LAOS |

| LATVIA | LEBANON | LESOTHO | LIBERIA |

| LIBYA | LIECHTENSTEIN | LITHUANIA | LUXEMBOURG |

| MACAU | MACEDONIA | MADAGASCAR | MADEIRA |

| MALAWI | MALAYSIA | MALDIVES | MALI |

| MALTA | MARSHALL ISLANDS | MARTINIQUE | MAURITANIA |

| MAURITIUS | MEXICO | MICRONESIA, FED. STATES | MOLDOVA |

| MONACO | MONGOLIA | MONTSERRAT | MOROCCO |

| MOZAMBIQUE | NAMIBIA | NAURU | NEPAL |

| NETHERLANDS | NETHERLANDS ANTILLES | NEW CALEDONIA | NEW ZEALAND |

NICARAGUA

NIGER

NIGERIA

NORTHERN MARIANAS

NORWAY

OMAN

PAKISTAN

PALAU

PANAMA

PAPUA NEW GUINEA

PARAGUAY

PERU

PHILIPPINES

PITCAIRN ISLANDS

POLAND

PORTUGAL

PUERTO RICO

QATAR

RÉUNION

ROMANIA

RUSSIA

RWANDA

ST CHRISTOPHER & NEVIS

ST HELENA

ST LUCIA

ST VINCENT & THE GRENADINES

SAN MARINO

SÃO TOMÉ & PRÍNCIPE

SAUDI ARABIA

SENEGAL

SEYCHELLES

SIERRA LEONE

SINGAPORE

SLOVAK REPUBLIC

SLOVENIA

SOLOMON ISLANDS

SOMALIA

SOUTH AFRICA

SPAIN

SRI LANKA

| | | | |
|---|---|---|---|
|  SUDAN | SURINAM | SWAZILAND | SWEDEN |
| SWITZERLAND | SYRIA | TAIWAN | TAJIKISTAN |
| TANZANIA | THAILAND | TOGO | TONGA |
| TRINIDAD & TOBAGO | TRISTAN DA CUNHA | TUNISIA | TURKEY |
| TURKMENISTAN | TURKS & CAICOS ISLANDS | TUVALU | UGANDA |
| UKRAINE | UNITED ARAB EMIRATES | UNITED KINGDOM | UNITED STATES OF AMERICA |
| URUGUAY | UZBEKISTAN | VANUATU | VATICAN CITY |
| VENEZUELA | VIETNAM | VIRGIN ISLANDS, BRITISH | VIRGIN ISLANDS, US |
| WALLIS & FUTUNA ISLANDS | WESTERN SAMOA | YEMEN | YUGOSLAVIA |
| ZAÏRE | ZAMBIA | ZIMBABWE | UNITED NATIONS |

## AFGHANISTAN

After many changes since the late 1970s, a new flag was introduced in 1992 based on the colours used by the Mujaheddin during the civil war. The flag bears the new national arms which show wheatsheaves and the *shahada*, the Muslim statement of faith, above a mosque.

## ALBANIA

The name of the country means 'land of the eagle'. Following the formation of a non-Communist government in March 1992, the star that had been placed above the eagle's head in 1946 was removed.

## ALGERIA

Featuring traditional Islamic symbols and colours, this design dates back to the early 19th century. Used by the liberation movement that fought against French rule after 1954, it was adopted on independence in 1962.

## AMERICAN SAMOA

A flag was introduced in 1960 for this American dependency. It shows the American eagle holding two typically Samoan objects: a war-club and a fly-whisk, both symbols of a chief's authority. The colours used on the flag are those of the American flag.

## ANDORRA

Andorra is traditionally said to have been granted independence by Charlemagne in the 9th century, after the Moorish Wars. The flag, adopted in 1866, sometimes features the state coat of arms on the obverse in the yellow band.

## ANGOLA

The flag is based on that of the Popular Movement for the Liberation of Angola during the struggle for independence from Portugal (1975). The emblem, incorporating a half gearwheel and a machete, symbolizes Angola's socialist ideology.

## ANGUILLA

This flag came into use in 1993 and, since Anguilla is a British dependency, the British Blue Ensign is flown. The three dolphins depicted on the shield represent strength, unity and endurance, while the white stands for peace and the blue for the sea.

## ANTIGUA AND BARBUDA

The design of the flag was decided in a competition in 1967. The V depicted in the design denotes victory and the golden sun symbolizes the dawning of a new era. The black represents African heritage and the soil, blue is for hope and red for the dynamism of the people.

## ARGENTINA

The 'celeste' and white stripes, symbol of independence since 1810 around Buenos Aires, became the national flag in 1816 and influenced other Latin American countries. A yellow May Sun, only used on the state flag, was added two years later.

## ARMENIA

The flag used in the period 1918–22 was re-adopted on 24 August 1990. The colours represent the blood shed in the past (red), the land of Armenia (blue) and the unity and courage of the people (orange).

## ARUBA

The flag of this Dutch overseas territory was introduced in 1976. The four points of the star represent the area's four main language groups.

## ASCENSION

As a dependency of St Helena, Ascension uses her flag, which shows the shield from her coat of arms in the fly of the British Blue Ensign.

## AUSTRALIA

Showing its historical link with Britain, Australia's flag, adopted in 1901, features the British Blue Ensign. The five stars in the fly represent the Southern Cross constellation and the larger star, known as the Commonwealth Star, symbolizes the six states and the territories.

## AUSTRIA

According to legend, the flag's colours date from the battle of Ptolemais in 1191, when the only part of the Duke of Bebenberg's tunic not bloodstained was under his swordbelt. The design was officially adopted in 1918.

## AZERBAIJAN

This flag was instituted on 5 February 1991. The blue stands for the sky, the red for freedom and the green for the land and the Islamic religion; the crescent and star symbolize Islam, and the points of the star represent the eight races of Azerbaijan.

**AZORES**
The flag dates from 1979 and shows the hawk (*açor*) after which the islands are named, below an arc of nine stars (one for each island).

**BAHAMAS**
The black hoist triangle symbolizes the unity of the Bahamian people and their resolve to develop the island's natural resources. The golden sand and blue sea of the islands are depicted by the yellow and aquamarine stripes.

**BAHRAIN**
The flag dates from about 1932, with the white section a result of the British request that it be included in the flags of all friendly Arab states around the Arabian Gulf. Red is the traditional colour of Kharijite Muslims. The serrated edge was added to distinguish between the colours.

**BANGLADESH**
Bangladesh adopted this flag in 1971 following the break from Pakistan. The green represents the fertility of the land, while the red disc, as the sun of independence, commemorates the blood shed in the struggle for freedom.

**BARBADOS**
The flag was adopted on independence in 1960. The trident had been part of the colonial badge of Barbados and was retained as the centre to its flag, maintaining the link between old and new. The gold stripe represents the beaches and the two blue stripes the sea and the sky.

**BELARUS**
On 19 September 1991 the old flag of Belarus, previously adopted in 1917, was restored. The white and red derive from the ancient coat of arms, also used by Latvia.

**BELGIUM**
The colours of Belgium's flag derive from the arms of the province of Brabant which rebelled against Austrian rule in 1787. It was adopted as the national flag in 1830

when Belgium gained independence from the Netherlands.

**BELIZE**
The badge shows loggers bearing axes and oars, tools employed in the industry responsible for developing Belize. The motto underneath reads '*Sub Umbra Floreo*' ('flourish in the shade') and the tree is a mahogany, the national tree.

**BENIN**
This flag, showing the red, yellow and green Pan-African colours, was first used after independence from France in 1960 and has now been readopted. While Benin was a Communist state after 1975, another flag, showing a red Communist star, was used.

**BERMUDA**
Instead of the customary British Blue Ensign, the Red Ensign with the shield from Bermuda's badge is on the fly. The shield depicts a red lion holding another shield in which the shipwreck of the *Sea Venture* in 1609 is shown.

**BHUTAN**
The striking image on Bhutan's flag is explained by the name of this Himalayan kingdom in the local language, *Druk Yil*, which means 'land of the dragon'. The saffron colour stands for royal power and the orange-red for Buddhist spiritual power.

**BOLIVIA**
Dating from liberation in 1825, the tricolour has been used as both national and merchant flag since 1888. The red stands for Bolivia's animals and the army's courage, the yellow for mineral resources and the green for its agricultural wealth.

**BOSNIA-HERZEGOVINA**
The flag was adopted when independence was declared in April 1992 and has a shield recalling the ancient Bosnian monarchy of pre-Turkish times. The fleur-de-lis is thought to be derived from the lily specific to Bosnia, *Lilium bosniacum*.

**BOTSWANA**
Botswana's flag dates from independence

from Britain in 1966. The white-black-white zebra stripe represents the racial harmony of the people and the coat of the zebra, the national animal. The blue symbolizes the country's most vital need – rainwater.

## BRAZIL
The sphere bears the motto 'Order and Progress' and its 27 stars, arranged in the pattern of the night sky over Rio de Janeiro, represent the states and federal district. Green symbolizes the nation's rainforests, and the yellow diamond represents its mineral wealth.

## BRUNEI
The yellow background represents the flag of the Sultan, with the black and white stripes standing for his two main advisers (*wazirs*). The arms contain the inscription in Arabic 'Brunei, Gate of Peace' and a crescent, the symbol of Islam.

## BULGARIA
The Slav colours of white, green and red were used in the Bulgarian flag from 1878. The national emblem, incorporating a lion (a symbol of Bulgaria since the 14th century), was first added to the flag in 1947, but the crest is now only added for official occasions.

## BURKINA FASO
Formerly Upper Volta, this country adopted a new name and flag in 1984, replacing those used since independence from France in 1960. The colours are the Pan-African shades of Burkina Faso's neighbours, representing the desire for unity.

## BURMA (MYANMAR)
The colours were adopted following independence from Britain in 1948. The socialist symbol, added in 1974, includes a ring of 14 stars for the country's states. The gearwheel represents industry and the rice plant agriculture.

## BURUNDI
Burundi adopted this unusual design when it became a republic in 1966. The three stars symbolize the nation's motto 'Unity, Work, Progress'. Green represents hope for the future, red the struggle for independence, and white the desire for peace.

## CAMBODIA
As well as being associated with Communism and revolution, red is the traditional colour of Cambodia. The silhouette is the historic temple of Angkor Wat. The blue symbolizes the water resources which are so vital.

## CAMEROON
Cameroon's flag employs the Pan-African colours, as used by many former African colonies. The design, with the yellow liberty star, dates from 1975 and is based on the tricolour adopted in 1957 before independence from France in 1960.

## CANADA
The British Red Ensign was used from 1892 but became unpopular with Canada's French community. After many attempts to find a more acceptable design, the present flag – featuring the simple maple leaf emblem – was finally adopted in 1965.

## CANARY ISLANDS
As a Spanish Autonomous Region, the Canary Islands have their own arms and flag. This flag was adopted in 1982 on the basis of colours used by the dominant political movement. The arms can be added in the centre.

## CAPE VERDE
This new flag was adopted in September 1992 to replace the red-yellow-green one adopted in 1975. The flag was adopted to symbolize the end of the rule of the *Partido Africano da Independencia de Cabo Verde* and the election of the Movement for Democracy.

## CAYMAN ISLANDS
As a British Dependency, the Cayman Islands fly the Blue Ensign with a white roundel, depicting the islands' coat of arms in the fly. The coat of arms shows an English heraldic lion, with the blue and white wavy lines representing the sea.

## CENTRAL AFRICAN REPUBLIC
The national flag of the Central African Republic, adopted in 1958, combines the green, yellow and red of Pan-African unity with the blue, white and red of the flag of the country's former colonial ruler, France.

## CHAD

Adopted in 1959, Chad's colours are a compromise between the French and Pan-African flags. Blue represents the sky, the streams of the south and hope, yellow the sun and the Sahara Desert in the north, and red represents national sacrifice.

## CHILE

Inspired by the US 'Stars and Stripes', the flag was designed by an American serving with the Chilean Army in 1817 and adopted that year. White represents the snow-capped Andes, blue the sky and red the blood of the patriots.

## CHINA

Red, the traditional colour of both China and Communism, was chosen for the People's Republic flag in 1949. The large star represents the Communist Party programme; the small stars represent the four principal social classes.

## COLOMBIA

The colours – showing the (yellow) land of the nation separated by the (blue) sea from the tyranny of Spain, whose rule the people fought with their (red) blood – are shared by Ecuador and Venezuela. It was first used in 1806.

## COMOROS

Since independence in 1975 a flag depicting a crescent and four stars has been flown. This latest design, adopted in 1978, shows the crescent representing the Muslim faith, and the stars representing the four islands, on a plain green background, representing Islam.

## CONGO

The People's Republic of the Congo was created in 1970, ten years after it achieved independence from France, becoming Africa's first Communist state. Marxism was officially abandoned in 1990 and this new flag was adopted.

## COSTA RICA

Dating from 1848, Costa Rica's national flag is based on the blue-white-blue sequence of the flag of the Central American Federation (*see Guatemala*), which is itself based on the Argentinian flag, but with an additional red stripe in the centre.

## CROATIA

The red, white and blue flag was originally adopted in 1848. During the Communist period a red star appeared in the centre, but this was replaced by the present arms, which symbolize the various parts of the country.

## CUBA

First designed in 1849, Cuba's flag, the 'Lone Star' banner, was not officially adopted until the island finally gained its independence from Spain in 1901. The red triangle represents people's bloody struggle for independence.

## CYPRUS

Featuring a map of the island with two olive branches, this has been the official state flag since independence from Britain in 1960. However, Cyprus is now divided and the separate communities fly the Greek and Turkish flags.

## CZECH REPUBLIC

On independence in January 1993, the Czech Republic adopted the flag of the former Czechoslovakia. It features the red and white of Bohemia with the blue of Moravia and Slovakia, the colours of Pan-Slavic liberation.

## DENMARK

The Dannebrog ('the spirit of Denmark') flag is said to represent King Waldemar II's vision of a white cross against a red sky before the Battle of Lyndanisse in 1219, and is possibly the oldest national flag in continuous use.

## DJIBOUTI

Djibouti's flag was adopted on independence from France in 1977, though its use by the independence movement had begun five years earlier. The colours represent the two principal peoples in the country: the Issas (blue) and the Afars (green).

## DOMINICA

Dominica adopted its flag on independence from Britain in 1978 and slightly amended it in 1981. The parrot, from the coat of arms, is the national bird, the sisserou, and the stars represent the ten island parishes.

## DOMINICAN REPUBLIC

This flag dates from 1844, when the country

finally gained its independence from both Spain and Haiti. The design developed from Haiti's flag, adding a white cross and re-arranging the position of the colours.

## ECUADOR
Shared in different proportions by Colombia and Venezuela, Ecuador's colours were used in the flag created by the patriot Francisco de Miranda in 1806 and flown by Simón Bolívar, whose armies also liberated Peru and Bolivia.

## EGYPT
Egypt has flown a flag of red, white and black (Pan-Arab colours) since 1958 but with various emblems in the centre. The present design, with the gold eagle emblem symbolizing the Arab hero Saladin, was introduced in 1984.

## EL SALVADOR
The original flag, the 'Stars and Stripes', was replaced in 1912 by the current one. The blue and white stripes are a common feature of the flags of Central American countries that gained their independence from Spain at the same time in 1821.

## EQUATORIAL GUINEA
Equatorial Guinea's flag dates from independence from Spain in 1968. Green represents the country's natural resources, blue the sea, red the nation's struggle for independence and the white stands for peace.

## ERITREA
The new flag was hoisted on 24 May 1993 to celebrate independence from Ethiopia. It is a variation on the flag of the Eritrean People's Liberation Front, and shows an olive wreath which featured on the flag of the region between 1952 and 1959.

## ESTONIA
Used for the independent republic of 1918–40, the Estonian flag was readopted in June 1988. The colours are said to symbolize the country's blue skies, its black earth and the snows of its long winter.

## ETHIOPIA
Ethiopia's tricolour was first flown as three separate pennants, one above the other. The combination of red, yellow and green dates from the late 19th century and appeared in flag form in 1897. The present sequence was adopted in 1941.

## FALKLAND ISLANDS
The white roundel in the flag contains the islands' badge which shows the ship *Desire*, which discovered the islands in 1592, and a sheep, representing the main farming activity.

## FAROE ISLANDS
In 1948 the Faroe Islands, which are part of Denmark, adopted a flag combining the local arms with the Danish arms. The cross, like that on other Scandinavian flags, is slightly off-centre. Red and blue are ancient Faroese colours and the white represents the sea's foam.

## FIJI
The Fijian flag, based on the British Blue Ensign, was adopted in 1970 after independence from Britain. The state coat of arms shows a British lion, sugar cane, a coconut palm, bananas and a dove of peace.

## FINLAND
Finland became an independent republic only in 1917 after separation from Russia, then in the throes of the Revolution, and the present flag was adopted soon after. The colours symbolize Finland's blue lakes and white snow.

## FRANCE
The colours of the French flag originated during the Revolution of 1789. The red and blue are said to represent Paris and the white the monarchy. The present design, adopted in 1794, symbolizes republican principles.

## FRENCH GUIANA
The official flag flown over 'Guyane' is the French tricolour. A French possession since 1676 (apart from 1809–17), the territory is treated as part of mainland France, sending representatives to the Paris parliament.

## FRENCH POLYNESIA
The flag was adopted in 1984 and is in the traditional colours of Tahiti, but can only be flown in conjunction with the French tricolour since it is still a French territory. The emblem

in the centre is a native canoe (*pirogue*) against the background of a rising sun over the sea.

## GABON
Gabon's tricolour was adopted on independence from France in 1960. The yellow, now representing the sun, used to be thinner to symbolize the Equator on which the country lies. The green stands for Gabon's forests and blue for the sea.

## GAMBIA, THE
The blue stripe in the flag represents the River Gambia that flows through the country, while the red stands for the sun overhead and the green for the land. The design was adopted on independence from Britain in 1965.

## GEORGIA
The flag was first adopted in 1917 and lasted until 1921. The colours represent the good times of the past and the future (wine-red), the period of Russian rule (black) and the hope for peace (white). It was readopted on independence in 1990.

## GERMANY
The red, black and gold, dating back to the Holy Roman Empire, are associated with the struggle for a united Germany from the 1830s. The horizontal design was officially adopted for the FRG in 1949, and accepted by 'East Germany' on reunification.

## GHANA
Adopted on independence from Britain in 1957, Ghana's flag features the colours first used by Ethiopia, Africa's oldest independent nation. Following Ghana's lead, other ex-colonies adopted them as a symbol of black Pan-African unity.

## GIBRALTAR
The official flag is the Union Jack but this flag has been in use unofficially (on land only) since about 1966. It is a banner of the city arms granted to Gibraltar in 1502 by Spain; the key symbolizes Gibraltar's strategic importance as the gateway to the Mediterranean.

## GREECE
Blue and white became Greece's national colours during the war of independence. Finally adopted in 1970, the stripes represent the battle cry '*Eleutheria i thanatos*' ('Freedom or Death') used during the struggle against Ottoman (Turkish) domination in the war of 1821–9.

## GREENLAND
The flag was introduced in 1985 after a competition to decide a design and can be used on land and at sea. The design is in the Danish colours, with the red depicting the midsummer sun rising over the (white) polar ice.

## GRENADA
Each star represents one of Grenada's seven parishes. The country's traditional cash crop, nutmeg, is depicted in the hoist triangle. The people are represented by the colours red (for unity) and yellow (for friendliness and the sunshine), and the island by the colour green.

## GUADELOUPE
As an overseas department of France, Guadeloupe uses the French tricolour for its flag.

## GUAM
The flag was adopted in 1917. The badge in the centre is based on the island seal and depicts the mouth of the Agana River and a *prao* sailing off Point Ritidian. Guam has been a dependency of the USA since 1898 and flies its flag only with the US 'Stars and Stripes'.

## GUATEMALA
The simple design of Guatemala's flag was adopted in 1871, but its origins date back to the Central American Federation (1823–39) formed with Honduras, El Salvador, Nicaragua and Costa Rica after the break from Spanish rule in 1821.

## GUINEA
Guinea's Pan-African colours, adopted on independence from France in 1958, represent the three words of the national motto, *Travail, Justice, Solidarité*: Work (red), Justice (yellow) and Solidarity (green). The design is based on the French tricolour.

## GUINEA-BISSAU
This flag, using the Pan-African colours, was

adopted on gaining independence from Portugal in 1973. It is based on the one used by the PAIGC political party that led the struggle from 1962, who in turn based it on the flag of Ghana, the first of the African colonies to gain independence.

## GUYANA
This striking design, adopted by Guyana on independence from Britain in 1966, has colours representing the people's energy building a new nation (red), their perseverance (black), minerals (yellow), rivers (white), and agriculture and forests (green).

## HAITI
Although the colours, first used in 1803, are said to represent the country's two communities (the blacks [blue] and the mulattos [red]), the design of Haiti's flag derives from that of France, to which it once belonged. The present version was first used in 1843 and restored in 1986.

## HONDURAS
Officially adopted in 1949, the Honduras flag is based on that of the Central American Federation (*see Guatemala*). Honduras left the organization in 1838, but in 1866 added the five stars to the flag to express a hope for a future federation.

## HONG KONG
Hong Kong has flown the Blue Ensign since 1841 when it became a British dependent territory. The coat of arms dates from 1959, and includes the British lion and the Chinese dragon. In 1997 Hong Kong will revert to Chinese government control.

## HUNGARY
The tricolour became popular in the European revolutions of 1848, though the colours had been in the Hungarian arms since the 15th century. Adopted in 1919, the design was amended in 1957 to remove the state emblem, which had been added in 1949.

## ICELAND
Dating from 1915, the flag became official on independence from Denmark in 1944. It uses the traditional Icelandic colours of blue and

white and is in fact the same as the Norwegian flag, but with the blue and red reversed.

## INDIA
India's flag evolved during the struggle for freedom from British rule. The orange represents the Hindu majority, green the country's many Muslims and white peace. The Buddhist wheel symbol, the blue *charka*, was added on independence in 1947.

## INDONESIA
While the colours date back to the Middle Ages, they were adopted by political groups in the struggle against the Netherlands in the 1920s and became the national flag in 1945, when Indonesia proclaimed its independence.

## IRAN
Iran's flag has been in use since July 1980 after the fall of the Shah and the rise of the Islamic Republic. Along the edges of the stripes is the legend '*Allah Akbar*' ('God is Great') repeated 22 times; in the centre is the new national emblem, representing *Allah* (God).

## IRAQ
Using the four Pan-Arab colours, Iraq's flag was adopted in 1963 at the time of the proposed federation with Egypt and Syria. Iraq retained the three green stars, symbolizing the three countries, even though the union failed to materialize.

## IRELAND
The Irish flag was first used by nationalists in 1848 in the struggle for freedom from Britain and adopted in 1922 after independence. Green represents the Roman Catholics and orange the Protestants, with white representing the desire for peace between the two.

## ISRAEL
The blue and white stripes on Israel's flag are based on the *tallit*, a Hebrew prayer shawl. In the centre is the ancient six-pointed Star of David. The flag was designed in America in 1891 and officially adopted by the new Jewish state in 1948.

## ITALY
When Napoleon invaded Italy in 1796, the

French Republican National Guard carried a military standard of vertical green, white and red stripes. After many changes, it was finally adopted as the national flag after the unification of Italy in 1861.

## IVORY COAST (CÔTE D'IVOIRE)
On independence from France in 1960 this former colony adopted a compromise between the French tricolour and the colours of the Pan-African movement. Orange represents the northern savannas, white peace and unity, and green the forests and agriculture.

## JAMAICA
Jamaica's distinctive flag dates from independence from Britain in 1962. The gold stands for the country's natural resources and sunshine, the green for its agriculture and hope for the future, and black for the nation's hardships.

## JAPAN
The geographical position of Japan in the East is expressed in the name of the country, *Nihon-Koku* (Land of the Rising Sun), and in the flag. Officially adopted in 1870, the simple design had been used by Japanese emperors for many centuries.

## JORDAN
Green, white and black are the colours of the three tribes who led the Arab Revolt against the Turks in 1917, while red is the colour of the Hussein dynasty. The star was added in 1928 with its seven points representing the first seven verses of the Koran.

## KAZAKHSTAN
This flag was adopted on 4 June 1992. The soaring eagle and the golden sun represent the love of freedom and the blue represents the cloudless skies. There is also a hoist-based vertical strip of golden ornamentation.

## KENYA
The Kenyan flag, which dates from independence from Britain in 1963, is based on the flag of the Kenya African National Union, which led the colonial struggle. The Masai warrior's shield and crossed spears represent the defence of freedom.

## KIRIBATI
The flag is a banner of the arms granted to the Gilbert and Ellice Islands in 1937 and was adopted on independence in 1979. Kiribati is the sole Commonwealth country to use an armorial banner; that is, a flag whose design corresponds exactly to the shield of its arms.

## KOREA, NORTH
The Korean Democratic People's Republic has flown this flag since the country split into two separate states in 1948. The colours are those of the traditional Korean standard, but in a new Communist design with a red star.

## KOREA, SOUTH
Adopted in 1950, South Korea's flag is the traditional white of peace. The central emblem signifies nature's opposing forces: the black symbols stand for the four seasons, the points of the compass and the Sun, Moon, Earth and Heaven.

## KUWAIT
Kuwait's national flag dates from 1961, when the country ceased to be a British protectorate and gained its independence. The flag features the four Pan-Arab colours, the black portion having an unusual trapezium shape.

## KYRGYZSTAN
The flag was adopted in March 1992 and depicts a bird's-eye view of a *yurt* within a radiant sun. The *yurt* stands for the ancient nomadic way of life and the rays of the sun for the 40 traditional tribes.

## LAOS
Since 1975 Laos has flown the flag of the Pathet Lao, the Communist movement which won the long struggle for control of the country. The blue stands for the Mekong River, the white disc represents the Moon, and the red is for the unity and purpose of the people.

## LATVIA
The burgundy and white Latvian flag, revived after independence from the USSR in 1991, dates back to at least 1280. According to one legend, it was first made from a white sheet stained with the blood of a Latvian hero who was wrapped in it.

## LEBANON

Adopted on independence in 1943, Lebanon's colours are those of the Lebanese Legion in World War I. The cedar tree, many of which grow in the country's mountains, has been a Lebanese symbol since biblical times.

## LESOTHO

In 1987 this succeeded the flag adopted on independence from Britain in 1966. The white, blue and green represent peace, rain and prosperity – the words of the national motto. The emblem comprises a shield, knobkerrie and ostrich feather sceptre.

## LIBERIA

Liberia was founded in the early 19th century as an American colony for freed black slaves. The flag, based on the US flag, was adopted on independence in 1847, with its 11 red and white stripes representing the 11 men who signed the declaration of independence.

## LIBYA

The simplest of all world flags, Libya's flag represents the nation's quest for a green revolution in agriculture. Libya flew the flag of the Federation of Arab Republics until 1977, when it left the organization.

## LIECHTENSTEIN

The colours of Liechtenstein's flag originated in the early part of the 19th century. The gold crown, often rotated 90° so that the flag can be hung vertically, was added in 1937 to avoid confusion with the flag then used by Haiti.

## LITHUANIA

The flag was created in 1918, at the birth of the independent republic; it was suppressed after the Soviet annexation in 1940, and restored in November 1988. The colours represent Lithuania's rich forests and agricultural wealth.

## LUXEMBOURG

Luxembourg's colours are taken from the Grand Duke's 14th-century coat of arms. The Grand Duchy's flag is almost identical to that of the Netherlands, but the blue stripe is a lighter shade and the flag itself is longer.

## MACAU

Portugal declared Macau independent from China in 1849, and a century later proclaimed it an overseas province. Macau uses the flag of Portugal.

## MACEDONIA

The emblem in the centre of the flag is the device from the war-chest of Philip of Macedon, and is one reason why Greece refuses to recognize independent Macedonia. The flag was introduced in August 1992.

## MADAGASCAR

Madagascar's colours are those of historical flags of South-east Asia, from where the island's first inhabitants came before AD 1000. The present flag was adopted in 1958 when the country first became a republic after French rule.

## MADEIRA

The emblem in the flag is the cross of the Order of Christ, which inspired the colonization of the islands in the 15th century. The flag was adopted in 1978.

## MALAWI

The colours in Malawi's flag come from the flag adopted by the Malawi Congress Party in 1953. The rising sun symbol, representing the beginning of a new era for Malawi and Africa, was added when the country gained independence from Britain in 1964.

## MALAYSIA

The red and white bands date back to a revolt in the 13th century. The star and crescent are symbols of Islam; the blue represents Malaysia's role in the Commonwealth. This flag was first flown after federation in 1963.

## MALDIVES

The Maldives used to fly a plain red flag until the Islamic green panel with white crescent was added early this century. The present design was officially adopted in 1965, after the British left the islands.

## MALI

Adopted on independence from France in 1960, Mali's flag uses the Pan-African colours, employed by the African Democratic Rally, and symbolizing the desire for African unity. Its design is based on the French tricolour.

## MALTA

The colours of Malta's flag, adopted on independence in 1964, are those of the Knights of Malta, who ruled the islands from 1530 to 1798. The George Cross was added in 1943 to commemorate the heroism of the Maltese people during World War II.

## MARSHALL ISLANDS

The flag dates from 1 May 1979 and has two rays which represent the two chains of islands: Ratik (Sunrise) is in orange and Ralik (Sunset) is in white. The 24 points on the star represent the municipalities of the area, all set against the blue of the Pacific Ocean.

## MARTINIQUE

As an overseas department of France, Martinique uses the French tricolour for its flag.

## MAURITANIA

The Mauritanian Islamic Republic's flag features the star and crescent, traditional symbols of the Islamic religion, as is the colour green. It was adopted in 1959, the year before the country gained its independence from France.

## MAURITIUS

The flag of this small island state was adopted on independence from Britain in 1968. Red stands for the struggle for independence, blue for the Indian Ocean, yellow for the bright future, and green for the lush vegetation.

## MEXICO

The stripes on the Mexican flag were inspired by the French tricolour and date from 1821. The emblem of the eagle, snake and cactus is based on an ancient Aztec legend about the founding of Mexico City. The design was adopted for the Olympic year, 1968.

## MICRONESIA, FED. STATES OF

The flag was adopted in 1978 when the country broke away from the US Trust Territory of Micronesia and became the Federated States of Micronesia. The four stars stand for the

four states (Kosrai, Pohnpei, Truk and Yap) that remained in the federation.

## MOLDOVA

The flag and the eagle are based on those of pre-Communist Romania, and the bull's head is the distinctive emblem of Moldova. The flag was adopted in 1990. According to the official description, the tricolour represents 'the past, present and future' of Moldova.

## MONACO

An independent state since AD 980, Monaco has been ruled by the Grimaldi family since 1297. The colours of the flag, officially adopted in 1881, come from the Prince of Monaco's coat of arms, which dates to medieval times.

## MONGOLIA

On Mongolia's flag the blue represents the country's national colour. In the hoist is the Golden Soyonbo, a Buddhist symbol, representing freedom. Within this, the flame is seen as a promise of prosperity and progress.

## MONTSERRAT

The flag is the British Blue Ensign with the arms in a white roundel in the fly. The shield dates from 1909 and shows a black Passion cross rising from the (brown) ground, grasped in the right arm of a female figure in a green robe, representing the Irish origin of the island's immigrants.

## MOROCCO

A red flag had been flown in Morocco since the 16th century and the star-shaped green pentagram, the Seal of Solomon, was added in 1915. This design was retained when Morocco gained independence from French and Spanish rule in 1956.

## MOZAMBIQUE

The green stripe represents the fertile land, the black stripe Africa and the yellow stripe mineral wealth. The badge on the red triangle contains a rifle, hoe, cogwheel and book, which are all Marxist symbols of the struggle against colonialism.

## NAMIBIA

Namibia adopted its flag after independence

from South Africa in 1990. The red and white colours symbolize human resources, while the green, blue and the gold sun represent the natural resources, mostly minerals.

**NAURU**
The flag represents the geographical location of Nauru, south of the Equator in the middle of the Pacific Ocean. The 12 points of the star stand for the traditional tribes, and the flag was adopted on independence in 1968.

**NEPAL**
This Himalayan kingdom's uniquely shaped flag was adopted in 1962. It came from the joining together in the 19th century of two triangular pennants – the royal family's crescent moon emblem and the powerful Rana family's sun symbol.

**NETHERLANDS**
The Dutch national flag dates from 1630, during the long war of independence from Spain that began in 1568. The tricolour became a symbol of liberty and inspired many other revolutionary flags around the world.

**NETHERLANDS ANTILLES**
The flag was originally introduced in 1959 with six white stars in the centre, but these were reduced to five in 1986 when Aruba became a separate territory. Each star represents one of the five islands that make up the territory.

**NEW CALEDONIA**
New Caledonia has been a French possession since 1853. It became a French Overseas Territory in 1958 and therefore uses the French tricolour as its flag.

**NEW ZEALAND**
Like Australia, New Zealand flies a flag based on the British Blue Ensign. Designed in 1869 and adopted in 1907 on acquiring Dominion status, it displays four of the five stars of the Southern Cross constellation.

**NICARAGUA**
Nicaragua's flag, adopted in 1908, is identical to that of the Central American Federation to which it once belonged. Except for a differ-

ence in the shading of the blue and the motif, it is the same as the flag of El Salvador.

**NIGER**
Niger's flag was adopted shortly before independence in 1960. The circle represents the sun, the orange stripe the Sahara Desert in the north, the green stripe the grasslands of the south, divided by the (white) River Niger.

**NIGERIA**
This design was selected after a competition to find a new national flag in time for independence in 1960. The green represents the country's forests and the white is for peace.

**NORTHERN MARIANAS**
The sea-blue flag of this island group shows a grey latte stone, a Polynesian *taga*, surrounded by a wreath of flowers and shells. The flag was originally adopted in 1972 and the wreath was added in 1989. The latte stone represents the old traditions of the Chamorro people.

**NORWAY**
Norway's flag has been used since 1898, though its use as a merchant flag dates back to 1821. The design is based on the Dannebrog flag of Denmark, which ruled Norway from the 14th century to the early 19th century.

**OMAN**
Formerly Muscat and Oman, the state's flag was plain red – the traditional colour of the people who lived in the area. When Oman was established in 1970, the state arms of sword and dagger were added with stripes of white and green.

**PAKISTAN**
This flag was adopted when Pakistan gained independence from Britain in 1947. The green, the crescent moon and five-pointed star are traditionally associated with Islam. The white stripe represents the other religions.

**PALAU (BELAU)**
The flag dates from 1980 when Palau became a republic and depicts a full moon over the blue Pacific Ocean. The moon stands for national unity and destiny and the blue sea for the achievement of independence.

## PANAMA

The Panamanian flag dates from the break with Colombia in 1903. Blue stands for the Conservative Party, red for the Liberal Party and white for the hope of peace. The red star represents law and order and the blue star represents 'public honesty'.

## PAPUA NEW GUINEA

When Papua New Guinea became independent from Australia in 1975 it adopted a flag which had been used for the country since 1971. The design includes a local bird of paradise, the *kumul*, in flight and the stars of the Southern Cross constellation.

## PARAGUAY

Paraguay's tricolour is a national flag with different sides. On the obverse the state emblem, illustrated here, displays the May Star to commemorate liberation from Spain (1811); the reverse shows the treasury seal – a lion and staff, with the words 'Peace and Justice'.

## PERU

Flown since 1825, the flag's colours are said to have come about when the Argentine patriot General José de San Martin, arriving to liberate Peru from Spain in 1820, saw a flock of red and white flamingos flying over his army.

## PHILIPPINES

The eight rays of the large sun represent the eight provinces that led the revolt against Spanish rule in 1898 and the three smaller stars stand for the three main island groups. The flag was adopted on independence from the USA in 1946.

## PITCAIRN ISLANDS

A flag for local use was granted to Pitcairn in 1984. The flag is the British Blue Ensign with the whole arms in the fly. The arms were first used in 1969.

## POLAND

The colours of Poland's flag were derived from the 13th-century coat of arms of a white eagle on a red field, which still appears on the Polish merchant flag. The flag's simple design was adopted when Poland became a republic in 1919.

## PORTUGAL

Portugal's colours, adopted in 1910 when it became a republic, represent Henry the Navigator (green) and the monarchy (red). The armillary sphere – an early navigation instrument – reflects Portugal's leading role in world exploration.

## PUERTO RICO

Puerto Rico fought with Cuba for independence from Spain and their flags are almost identical (the red and blue colours are transposed). The island is a dependent territory of the USA and the flag, adopted in 1952, is flown only with the US 'Stars and Stripes'.

## QATAR

The flag was adopted in 1971. The maroon colour is said to result from the natural effect of the sun on the traditional red banner, while the white was added after a British request in 1820 that white should be included in the flags of friendly states in the Arabian Gulf.

## RÉUNION

As a French Overseas Department, Réunion uses the French tricolour as its flag.

## ROMANIA

Romania's colours come from the arms of the provinces that united to form the country in 1861, and the design was adopted in 1948. The central state coat of arms, added in 1965, was deleted in 1990 after the fall of the Communist Ceausescu regime.

## RUSSIA

Distinctive Russian flags were first instituted by Peter the Great, based on those of the Netherlands. This flag became the official national flag in 1799 but was suppressed in the Bolshevik Revolution. It was restored in 1991.

## RWANDA

Adopted in 1961, this tricolour in the Pan-African colours features the letter 'R' to distinguish it from Guinea's flag. Red represents the blood shed in the 1959 revolution, yellow for victory over tyranny, and green for hope.

## ST CHRISTOPHER AND NEVIS

The colours represent fertility (green), sunshine (yellow), the independence struggle (red) and the African heritage (black); the two stars stand for hope and liberty. The flag was adopted on independence from Britain in 1983.

## ST HELENA
Since 1984 the British dependent territory of St Helena, with its dependencies of Ascension Island and the Tristan da Cunha group, has used the shield from its new coat of arms in the fly of the British Blue Ensign. The main part of the shield shows a ship sailing towards the island.

## ST LUCIA
This Caribbean island became an Associated State of Great Britain in 1967, and adopted this modern-looking flag. It is a symbolic representation of St Lucia itself: the black volcanic hills of the island rising steeply from the blue ocean.

## ST VINCENT AND THE GRENADINES
On independence from Britain in 1979, St Vincent adopted this tricolour, but with the islands' coat of arms in the centre. In 1985 this was replaced by the present three green diamonds representing the islands as the 'gems of the Antilles'.

## SAN MARINO
The tiny republic of San Marino, enclosed completely within the territory of Italy, has been an independent state since AD 885. The flag's colours – white for the snowy mountains and blue for the sky – derive from the state coat of arms.

## SÃO TOMÉ AND PRÍNCIPE
Adopted on independence from Portugal in 1975, this variation of the familiar Pan-African colours had previously been the emblem of the national liberation movement. The two black stars represent the two islands that comprise the country.

## SAUDI ARABIA
The inscription on the Saudi flag above the sword means 'There is no God but Allah, and Muhammad is the Prophet of Allah'. The only national flag with an inscription as its main feature, the design was adopted in 1938.

## SENEGAL
Apart from the green five-pointed star, which symbolizes the Muslim faith of the majority of the population, Senegal's flag is identical to that of Mali. It was adopted in 1960 when the country gained its independence from France.

## SEYCHELLES
The flag dates from 1977 following a *coup d'état* by the People's Progressive Front, and diagrammatically shows the Indian Ocean (in white) surrounding the islands of the group and the resources contained in it. Green represents agriculture and red stands for revolution and progress.

## SIERRA LEONE
The colours of Sierra Leone's flag, adopted on independence from Britain in 1961, come from the coat of arms. Green represents the country's agriculture, white stands for peace and blue for the Atlantic Ocean.

## SINGAPORE
Adopted in 1959, this flag was retained when Singapore broke away from the Federation of Malaysia in 1963. The crescent stands for the nation's ascent and the stars for democracy, peace, progress, justice and equality.

## SLOVAK REPUBLIC
The horizontal tricolour which the Slovak Republic adopted in 1992 dates from 1848. The red, white and blue colours are typical of Slavonic flags. The three blue mounds in the shield represent the traditional mountains of Slovakia: Tatra, Matra and Fatra.

## SLOVENIA
The Slovene flag, based on the flag of Russia, was originally adopted in 1848. During the Communist period a red star appeared in the centre. This was replaced in June 1991 after independence, with the new emblem showing an outline of Mt Triglav.

## SOLOMON ISLANDS
Adopted on independence in 1978, the five white stars represent the five main islands, while the colours stand for the forests (green) and waters (blue) lit by the sun (yellow).

## SOMALIA

In 1960 British Somaliland united with Italian Somalia to form present-day Somalia and the flag of the southern region was adopted. It is based on the colours of the UN flag with the points of the star representing the five regions of East Africa where Somalis live.

## SOUTH AFRICA

This new flag was adopted in 1994, after the country's first multiracial elections were held. The colours are a combination of the ANC colours (black, yellow and green) and the traditional Afrikaner ones (red, white and black).

## SPAIN

The colours of this flag date back to the old kingdom of Aragon in the 12th century. The present design, in which the central yellow stripe is twice as wide as each of the red stripes, was adopted during the Civil War in 1938.

## SRI LANKA

This flag was adopted in 1951, three years after 'Ceylon' gained independence from Britain. The lion banner represents the ancient Buddhist kingdom and the stripes the island's minorities – Muslims (green) and Hindus (orange).

## SUDAN

The design of Sudan's flag is based on the flag of the Arab revolt used in Syria, Iraq and Jordan after 1918. Adopted in 1969, it features the Pan-Arab colours and an Islamic green triangle symbolizing material prosperity and spiritual wealth.

## SURINAM

Adopted on independence in 1975, Surinam's flag features the colours of the main political parties, the yellow star symbolizing unity and a golden future. The red is twice the width of the green, and four times that of the white.

## SWAZILAND

The kingdom has flown this distinctive flag, whose background is based on that of the Swazi Pioneer Corps of World War II, since independence from Britain in 1968. The emblem has the weapons of a warrior – ox-hide shield, two *assegai* (spears) and a fighting stick.

## SWEDEN

While this national flag has been flown since the reign of King Gustavus Vasa in the early 16th century, it was not officially adopted until 1906. The colours were derived from the ancient state coat of arms dating from 1364.

## SWITZERLAND

Switzerland's square flag was officially adopted in 1848, though the white cross on a red shield has been the Swiss emblem since the 14th century. The flag of the International Red Cross, based in Geneva, derives from this Swiss flag.

## SYRIA

In the Pan-Arab colours, the flag of Syria is the one adopted in 1958 by the former United Arab Republic. At various times in their history Egypt and Syria have shared the same flag, but since 1980 Syria has used this design.

## TAIWAN

In 1928 the Nationalists adopted this design as China's national flag and used it in the struggle against Mao Tse-tung's Communist army. When forced to retreat to Taiwan (then Formosa) in 1949, the flag went with them.

## TAJIKISTAN

The new flag was adopted early in 1993 and denotes a gold crown of unusual design under an arc of seven stars.

## TANZANIA

In 1964 Tanganyika united with the island of Zanzibar to form the United Republic of Tanzania and a new flag was adopted. The colours represent agriculture (green), minerals (yellow), the people (black), water and Zanzibar (blue).

## THAILAND

The two red-and-white stripes are all that remains of Thailand's traditional red-on-white elephant emblem, removed from the flag in 1916. The blue stripe was added in 1917 to show solidarity with the Allies in World War I.

## TOGO

Togo's Pan-African colours stand for agriculture and the future (green), mineral wealth and the value of hard work (yellow), and the blood shed in the struggle for independence from France in 1960 (red), with the white star for national purity.

## TONGA
Introduced in 1862 by Taufa'ahau Tupou, the first king of all Tonga, the flag represents the Christian faith of the islanders. The red cross, similar to the methodist badge and the Red Cross flag, illustrates the Tongans' adherence to the Christian religion.

## TRINIDAD AND TOBAGO
The islands of Trinidad and Tobago have flown this flag since independence from Britain in 1962. Red stands for the people's warmth and vitality, black for their strength, and white for their hopes and the ocean surf.

## TRISTAN DA CUNHA
The flag is the British Blue Ensign with the shield from the arms in the fly. A new coat of arms was introduced in 1984.

## TUNISIA
The Tunisian flag features the crescent moon and five-pointed star, traditional symbols of Islam. It originated in about 1835 when the country was still officially under Turkish rule and was adopted after independence from France in 1956.

## TURKEY
Although the crescent moon and the five-pointed star are symbols of Islam, their presence on Turkey's flag dates from long before the country became a Muslim state. The flag was officially adopted when the republic was founded in 1923.

## TURKMENISTAN
The flag dates from 1992 and depicts a typical Turkmen carpet design and a crescent and five stars. The stars and the five elements of the carpet represent the country's traditional tribes.

## TURKS AND CAICOS ISLANDS
In the British Blue Ensign is a gold roundel containing the islands' badge which shows a conch shell, a spiny lobster and a turks head cactus, all of which are found on the islands.

## TUVALU
The flag is based on the British Blue Ensign, but in a lighter blue, and has nine yellow stars representing the geographical position of the nine main islands. It was adopted on independence in 1978.

## UGANDA
Adopted on independence in 1962, Uganda's flag is that of the party which won the first election. The colours represent the people (black), the sun (yellow), and brotherhood (red); the country's emblem is a crested crane.

## UKRAINE
The colours of the Ukraine flag, first adopted in 1848, are heraldic in origin. The flag was used in the period 1918–20 and was re-adopted in 1991.

## UNITED ARAB EMIRATES
When seven small states around the Gulf combined to form the United Arab Emirates in 1971, this flag was agreed for the new nation. It features the Pan-Arab colours, first used in the Arab revolt against the Turks from 1916.

## UNITED KINGDOM
The first Union flag, combining England's cross of St George and Scotland's cross of St Andrew, dates from 1603 when James VI became James I of England. The Irish emblem, the cross of St Patrick, was added in 1801 to form the present flag.

## UNITED STATES OF AMERICA
The 'Stars and Stripes' has had the same basic design since 1777, during the War of Independence. The 13 stripes represent the original colonies that rebelled against British rule, the 50 stars the present states of the Union.

## URUGUAY
Displayed since 1830, the stripes represent the nine provinces of Uruguay on independence from Spain two years earlier. The blue and white and the May Sun derive from the flag originally employed by Argentina.

## UZBEKISTAN
This flag replaced the Soviet-style flag on 18 November 1991. The blue recalls the blue flag

of Timur (a former ruler), the white peace, the green nature and the red vitality. The crescent moon is for Islam and the 12 stars represent the months of the Islamic calendar.

## VANUATU
The device in the triangle is a boar's tusk surrounding two crossed fern leaves, the emblems of war and peace. The flag is in the colours of the Vanuaaku Pati, the dominant political party at the time of independence in 1980.

## VATICAN CITY
Since the 13th century, the emblem on the flag has represented the Vatican's role as the headquarters of the Roman Catholic Church. Consisting of the triple tiara of the Popes above the keys of heaven given to St Peter, it was adopted in 1929.

## VENEZUELA
The seven stars on the tricolour represent the provinces forming the Venezuelan Federation in 1811. The proportions of the stripes are equal to distinguish it from the flags of Colombia and Ecuador.

## VIETNAM
First used by the forces of Ho Chi Minh in the liberation struggle against Japan in World War II, this was adopted as the national flag of North Vietnam in 1945. It was retained when the two parts of the country reunited in 1975.

## VIRGIN ISLANDS, BRITISH
In the British Blue Ensign is the green badge of the islands, which shows a vestal virgin dressed in white and carrying a lamp. On either side of her are rows of lamps. Below the shield is a gold scroll bearing the motto *Vigilate* ('Be Alert').

## VIRGIN ISLANDS, US
The flag was adopted in 1921 and is based on the seal of the USA. The three arrows grasped by the eagle stand for the three main islands. The emblem appears between the initial letters of the islands' name, 'V' and 'I', in blue.

## WALLIS AND FUTUNA ISLANDS
As a French Overseas Territory, the Wallis

and Futuna Islands use the French tricolour as their flag.

## WESTERN SAMOA
The red and white are traditional colours used in Samoan flags of the 19th century. The design of the flag, in use since 1948 (14 years before independence), links Samoa with other nations of the southern hemisphere by its inclusion of the Southern Cross constellation.

## YEMEN
The design of Yemen's flag, incorporating the Pan-Arab colours, dates from 1990 when the Yemen Arab Republic (in the north and west) united with the People's Democratic Republic of Yemen (in the south and east).

## YUGOSLAVIA
Only the republics of Serbia and Montenegro now remain in Yugoslavia. The same flag is still used with its colours identifying it as a Slavic state which was once part of the Austro-Hungarian empire. It used to have a red star in the centre, but this was dropped in 1992.

## ZAÏRE
The Pan-African colours of red, yellow and green were adopted for Zaïre's flag in 1971. The central emblem symbolizes the revolutionary spirit of the nation.

## ZAMBIA
The flag's colours are those of the United Nationalist Independence Party, which led the struggle against Britain. The flying eagle represents freedom. The design was adopted on independence in 1964.

## ZIMBABWE
Adopted in 1980, Zimbabwe's flag is based on the colours of the ruling Patriotic Front. Within the white triangle is the soapstone bird national emblem and a red star, symbolizing the party's socialist policy.

## UNITED NATIONS
Adopted in 1947, this flag bears the UN emblem in white, which is a map of the world as viewed from above the North Pole, surrounded by olive branches of peace.

# WORLD
# GAZETTEER

# CONTENTS

*Numbers in brackets refer to the World Maps page on which the country is principally named. Where a nation is too small to appear on the maps at the chosen scales, its position may be determined by the locator map accompanying the text.*

# CONTENTS 61

## AFGHANISTAN

accounts, but nearer 6 million according to the UN Commissioner – fled the country altogether, predominantly to Pakistan. This latter estimate, the UN stated in 1990, was around 42% of the world total of displaced persons.

Nearly three-quarters of Afghanistan is mountainous, comprising most of the Hindu Kush and its foothills, with several peaks over 6,400 m [21,000 ft], and much of the rest is desert or semi-desert. However, the restoration of the Helmand canals has brought fertility to the far south-west, and the sweet waters of the Hamun support fish and cattle; the plains of the north, near the borders with Turkmenistan, Uzbekistan and Tajikistan, yield most of the country's limited agriculture.

### ECONOMY AND RESOURCES

The most profitable crop may well be opium, from poppies grown in the hills of the Pathans adjoining Pakistan's North-West Frontier province. With the Islamic Revolution in Iran and the crackdown in the 'Golden Triangle' of Laos, Burma and Thailand, Pakistan became the world's biggest source of heroin (the derivative drug); but while US pressure saw the Pakistani government start to control production on its side of the border, it could do little to stem the flow from Afghanistan – a prime source of revenue for the Mujaheddin's fight against occupying Soviet forces in the 1980s.

The war, which cost over a million Afghanis their lives, left what was an already impoverished state almost totally crippled. Before the Soviet invasion Afghanistan had one of the world's poorest records for infant mortality, literacy, women's rights and a host of other measurements, but the occupation also reduced the economy to ruins. Before the 1978 Marxist revolution Afghanis abroad sent home remittances worth some $125 million, and tourism brought in about $50 million; now all that had gone. Based on natural gas, exports were not helped by the decision of the USSR to cap the wells in 1989.

The greatest problem, however, was the one of refugees. Some 2 million people had moved into crowded cities and towns to avoid the Russian shelling, but far more – somewhere between 3 million and 5 million, by most

### HISTORY AND POLITICS

Landlocked Afghanistan has always been in a critical position in Asia: the Khyber Pass was both the gateway to India and the back door to Russia. Since earliest times it has been invaded by Persians, Greeks, Arabs, Mongols, Tartars and the British, who finally failed in their attempts to create a buffer state between India and Russia and bowed to Afghan independence after the Third Afghan War in 1921. The latest invaders, entering the country on Christmas Day 1979, were 80,000 men of the Soviet army.

The Russian forces were sent in support of a Kremlin-inspired coup that removed a revolutionary council set up after the ousting of the pro-Soviet government of Mohammed Daud Khan. Killed in that 1978 coup – the Saur Revolution – Daud Khan had been in power since 1953, first as prime minister and then, after he toppled the monarchy in 1972, as founder, president and prime minister of a fiercely pro-Soviet single-party republic.

The Saur Revolution and subsequent Soviet occupation led to a bitter and protracted civil war, the disparate Muslim tribes uniting behind the banner of the Mujaheddin ('holy warriors') to wage an unrelenting guerrilla war financed by the US and oiled with the co-operation of Pakistan. Despite their vastly superior weaponry and resources, the Soviet forces found it impossible to control the mountain-based rebels in a country the size of Texas, and Afghanistan quickly threatened to turn into an unwinnable war – Moscow's 'Vietnam'.

President Gorbachev began moves to end the conflict soon after coming to power in 1985, and in 1988 a cease-fire was agreed involving both Afghanistan and Pakistan, its main overt ally. In February 1989 the Soviet troops withdrew, leaving the cities in the hands of the pro-Moscow government and the countryside under the control of the Mujaheddin; the civil war intensified, however, fuelled by internecine and traditional feuds as well as the battle for the country's government, before a fragile cease-fire was agreed in 1991 with a view to talks the following year. However, the divisions remained and the nation returned to its familiar patchwork pattern of feuding tribal fiefdoms, with little control over the countryside being exercised from Kabul. In the spring of 1992, after a prolonged onslaught by the Mujaheddin, the government in Kabul finally surrendered, bequeathing an uncertain future to the country. [*Map page 22*] ∎

**AREA** 652,090 sq km [251,772 sq mls]
**POPULATION** 18,879,000
**CAPITAL (POPULATION)** Kabul (1,424,400)
**GOVERNMENT** Islamic republic
**ETHNIC GROUPS** Pashtun ('Pathan') 52%, Tajik 20%, Uzbek 9%, Hazara 9%, Chahar 3%, Turkmen 2%, Baluchi 1%
**LANGUAGES** Pashto, Dari (Persian), both official
**RELIGIONS** Islam (Sunni Muslim 74%, Shiite Muslim 25%)
**CURRENCY** Afghani = 100 puls

# ALBANIA

**B**y far Europe's poorest country, Albania is also one of the most isolated, separated physically and culturally from even its closest neighbours, Greece and Yugoslavia. The Albanian language has no close affinities with other European languages, and until 1990 the political system, priding itself on being the last fortress of true Marxism-Leninism, emphasized the country's remoteness.

Geographical obstacles have reinforced Albania's linguistic and political isolation. The mountainous interior forms a barrier to penetration from the east. The main ranges, which rise to almost 2,000 m [6,500 ft] are continuations of the Dinaric Alps; these run from north-west to south-east, rising steeply from the coastal lowlands that border the Adriatic Sea.

## ECONOMY AND RESOURCES

Limestone is the most common type of rock, although in the central area there are igneous masses rich in mineral ores, including copper, iron, nickel and chrome. Albania relies heavily on exports of chrome for foreign exchange, and is the world's eighth largest producer, contributing 2.8% of the total in 1993.

Although the country has adequate energy resources – including petroleum, brown coal and hydroelectric potential as well as useful minerals – Albania remains one of the least industrialized countries in Europe, and transport is poorly developed. Horses and mules are widely used in rural areas, and there are no rail links with other countries. Most people still live by farming, with maize, wheat, barley, sugar beet and fruits predominant, though the country has always found it a difficult task feeding a population with a growth rate of 2.1% – the highest in Europe.

## HISTORY AND POLITICS

Albania declared independence in 1912, after five centuries under the rule of the Ottoman Turks. A legacy of this period is the fact that, until the government closed all religious establishments in 1967, some 70% of Albanians were Muslims. Though not official, the figure is likely to be the same today.

At the end of World War II, an Albanian People's Republic was formed under the Communist leadership who had led the partisans against the Germans. Pursuing a modernization programme on rigid Stalinist lines, the regime of Enver Hoxha has at various times associated politically and often economically with Yugoslavia (up to 1948), the USSR (1948–61) and China (1961–77) before following a fiercely independent policy.

Hoxha's successor, Ramiz Alia, continued the dictator's austere policies after his death in 1985, but by the end of the decade even Albania was affected by the sweeping changes in Eastern Europe, and in 1990 the more progressive wing of the Communist Party (led by Alia) won the struggle for power. They instituted, somewhat reluctantly, a wide programme of reform, including the legalization of religion, the encouragement of foreign investment, the introduction of a free market for peasants' produce, and the establishment of pluralist democracy. A president and the 140-member Assembly are elected under a system of proportional representation by universal adult suffrage, for a period of four years.

In the elections of April 1991, the Communists comfortably retained their majority, but two months later the government was brought down by a general strike and an interim coalition 'national salvation' committee took over; this fragile 'government of stability' in turn collapsed after six months, when the Democrats withdrew their support. Elections in the spring of 1992 brought to an end the last Communist regime in Europe when Dr Sali Berisha, the Democratic Party leader, was elected by parliament as Albania's first non-Communist president.

Meanwhile, the country had descended into chaos and violence, triggered by food shortages. Tens of thousands of unwelcome refugees fled the civil unrest to Greece and Italy, and in some places control rested with local bandits and brigands. In neighbouring Yugoslavia (itself in the throes of disintegration), the large Albanian population in the 'autonomous province' of Kosovo were in conflict with the Serbian authorities.

After a lifetime of Orwellian state control, a backward country was being catapulted without real government into modern industrialized Europe – and towards a Western world preoccupied with recession. At the end of 1993, a UN report put the annual income per capita figure for Albania at around US$820 – alongside many a struggling nation in what is still called the Third World. [*Map page 17*] ■

AREA 28,750 sq km [11,100 sq mls]
POPULATION 3,414,000
CAPITAL (POPULATION) Tirana (251,000)
GOVERNMENT Multiparty republic
ETHNIC GROUPS Albanian 98%, Greek 1.8%, Macedonian, Montenegrin, Gypsy
LANGUAGES Albanian (official)
RELIGIONS Many people say they are non-believers; of the believers, 65% follow Islam, and 33% Christianity (Orthodox 20%, Roman Catholics 13%)
CURRENCY Lek = 100 qindars

# ALGERIA

After Sudan, Algeria is the biggest political unit in the Middle East and Africa, and the world's 11th largest nation. However, over 90% of the country's 27.3 million inhabitants live in the Mediterranean coastlands. The vast Saharan territories, covering over 2 million sq km [772,200 sq mls], or about 85% of the total area, are very sparsely populated; most of the inhabitants are concentrated in the oases, which form densely-populated 'islands' separated by vast empty areas. The majority of the population speak Arabic, but there is a significant Berber-speaking indigenous minority in the mountainous north-east.

## ECONOMY AND RESOURCES

European settlers acquired over a quarter of the cultivated land, mainly in north-western Algeria, and rural colonization transformed the plains, producing cash crops.

Oil was discovered in the Algerian Sahara in 1956 and Algeria's natural gas reserves are among the largest in the world. The country's crude-oil refining capacity is the biggest in Africa. Since independence in 1962, revenues from oil and gas, which provide 65% of all revenue and account for over 90% of exports, have enabled the government to embark on an ambitious economic development programme, with rapid industrialization. Industrial developments include iron and steel plants, food processing, chemicals and textiles, while Algeria is one of the few African nations to have its own car-manufacturing facility, producing about a third of its commercial vehicles. In addition there is an array of production allied to the oil and gas reserves: oil refineries, petrochemical plants and gas liquefication units. While most of the larger industries are nationalized, much of the light industry remains under private control.

Though agriculture has suffered by comparison, about 30% of Algerians are farmers. Arable land accounts for only 3% of the total land area, but the rich northern coastlands

## THE ATLAS MOUNTAINS

Extending from Morocco into northern Algeria and Tunisia, the Atlas is a prominent range of fold mountains. Its highest peak and the highest in North Africa, Jebel Toubkal (4,165 m [13,670 ft]), is one of a jagged row – the High Atlas – in central Morocco; the lesser ranges cluster on either side and to the east, generally with a north-east to south-west trend.

In Morocco there are the Anti-Atlas in the south-west, the Middle Atlas in the centre of the country, and the Er Rif mountains near the Mediterranean coast. In Algeria the range includes the Saharan Atlas and, further north, the Tell or Maritime Atlas. Heavily glaciated during the Ice Age, the highest Atlas ranges are now capped with patches of permanent snow and alpine tundra. North-facing slopes receive good winter rainfall, and are forested with pines, cedars, and evergreen and cork oaks. Tablelands between the ranges provide high pastures and rich soils for farming. The southern and eastern ranges are drier and covered with semi-desert scrub, providing rough pastures and poor cultivation.

Formerly linked to Spain during short spells of geological history, the Atlas Mountains support both European and African plants and animals. While the Algerian bear and wild ass and the Barbary lion, once plentiful, are now extinct, small populations of deer, closely akin to European red deer, graze with Barbary sheep and Dorcas gazelles among the high peaks, and Barbary apes may steal crops.

produce wheat, barley, vines and olives – as well as early fruit and vegetables for the European markets, notably France and Italy. Further south, dates are an important product, but in the mountains the primary occupation of the Berber population is the rearing of sheep, cattle and goats.

### HISTORY AND POLITICS

Like its neighbours Morocco and Tunisia, Algeria experienced French colonial rule and settler colonization. Algeria was the first Maghreb country to be conquered by France and the last to receive independence, following years of bitter warfare between nationalist guerrillas and the French armed forces.

In January 1992, with the Islamic fundamentalist FIS on course for electoral victory, the government cancelled the second round and declared a state of emergency, effectively ending Algeria's four-year flirtation with Western-style democracy. In June 1992 the FIS assassinated President Boudiaf and has since been waging a relentless terrorist campaign (including the murder of foreigners) which has led to the death of over 3,000 people. [*Map page 32*] ∎

**AREA** 2,381,700 sq km [919,590 sq mls]
**POPULATION** 27,325,000
**CAPITAL (POPULATION)** Algiers (1,722,000)
**GOVERNMENT** Socialist republic
**ETHNIC GROUPS** Arab, Berber, French
**LANGUAGES** Arabic (official), Berber, French
**RELIGIONS** Sunni Muslim 98%, Christianity (mainly Roman Catholic)
**CURRENCY** Algerian dinar = 100 centimes

# AMERICAN SAMOA

American Samoa is a group of five volcanic islands and two atolls covering a land area of 200 sq km [77 sq mls] in the South Pacific, with Tutuila the largest. Swain Island to the north also comes under its administration, taking the total population to about 53,000. More than twice that number of American Samoans live in the US. Though the US naval base at Pago Pago closed in 1951, the American influence in the territory is still vital, giving substantial grants and taking 90% of exports, almost exclusively canned tuna. Most of the land is bush or jungle, and agriculture is limited.

The Samoan Islands were divided in 1899, with British consent, between Germany and the US along a line 171° west of Greenwich. American Samoa is now a self-governing 'unincorporated territory of the US'. While Pago Pago – the recipient of about 5,000 mm [200 in] of rain a year – is the capital, the seat of government is to the east at Fagatogo. There is little prospect of Samoan reunification: the American islands enjoy a standard of living some ten times as high as their neighbours in Western Samoa. [*Map page 2*] ■

**AREA** 200 sq km [77 sq mls]
**POPULATION** 53,000
**CAPITAL (POPULATION)** Pago Pago (3,519)
**GOVERNMENT** Self-governing 'unincorporated territory of the US'
**ETHNIC GROUPS** Samoan 90%, Caucasian 2%, Tongan 2%
**LANGUAGES** Samoan, English
**RELIGIONS** Christianity
**CURRENCY** US currency

# ANDORRA

Perched near the eastern end of the high central Pyrenees, Andorra consists mainly of six valleys (the Valls) that drain to the River Valira. These deep glaciated valleys lie at altitudes of 1,000–2,900 m [3,280–9,500 ft]. In the north a lofty watershed forms the frontier with France and is crossed by a road over the Envalira Pass at 2,400 m [7,870 ft]; to the south the land falls away down the Valira Valley to the Segre Valley in Spain, again followed by the same vital highway. In the colder months the Envalira Pass often becomes snowbound.

The climate is severe in winter and pleasantly cool in summer when, because the valleys lie in a rain-shadow, slopes above 1,400 m [4,600 ft] often suffer from drought and need irrigation. Some agriculture is possible on the slopes: sheep and cattle are grazed, and crops grow in terraced fields.

Andorra has five main sources of income: stock rearing and agriculture, especially tobacco; the sale of water and hydroelectricity to Catalonia; fees from radio transmission ser-

vices; tourism, based in winter on skiing; and the sale of duty-free goods and of postage stamps. Of these, tourism and duty-free sales are by far the most important – every year up to 10 million visitors come to Andorra to shop, and to witness this rare surviving example of a medieval principality.

The rights of the co-principality or *seigneurie* have been shared since 1278 between the Spanish Bishop of Urgel and the French Comte de Foix. The latter's lordship rights passed to the French government, now represented by the prefect of the adjoining *département* of the Eastern Pyrenees. The Andorrans pay a small annual sum to the bishop and the prefect, and each co-prince is represented in their Council by a *viguier*; but in most other respects the co-principality governs itself. In 1993, a new democratic constitution was adopted. [*Map page 18*] ■

**AREA** 453 sq km [175 sq mls]
**POPULATION** 65,000
**CAPITAL (POPULATION)** Andorra la Vella (20,437)
**GOVERNMENT** Co-principality
**ETHNIC GROUPS** Spanish 46%, Andorran 28%, Portuguese 11%, French 8%, British 2%
**LANGUAGES** Catalan (official)
**RELIGIONS** Christianity (Roman Catholic 90%)
**CURRENCY** French and Spanish currency

# ANGOLA

More than 13 times the size of its former colonial ruler, Portugal, Angola is southern Africa's largest state, extending through 13° of latitude. Most of the country is part of the huge plateau which makes up the interior of southern Africa. In the west is a narrow coastal plain, and in the northeast, several rivers flow northwards to the Zaïre (Congo) River. In the south, some rivers, including the Cubango (Okavango) and Cuanda, flow south-eastwards into the interior of Africa.

There is a strong cooling effect from the cold offshore Benguela Current, and climate and vegetation vary from desert on the south coast to equatorial and montane conditions in the centre and north.

## ECONOMY AND RESOURCES

Potentially, Angola is one of Africa's richest countries. The country has exceptionally varied agricultural output, while the coastal waters are rich in fish. Oil reserves are important both on the coast and offshore near Luanda and in the enclave of Cabinda (which is separated from Angola by a strip of land belonging to Zaïre), and hydroelectric power and irrigation developments are substantial. Diamonds, a major export (Angola is one of the world's largest producers), come from the north-east, and there are unexploited reserves of copper, manganese and phosphates. The country has a growing manufacturing sector.

## HISTORY AND POLITICS

Bantu-speaking peoples from the north settled in Angola around 2,000 years ago. In the late 15th century, Portuguese navigators, seeking a route to Asia around Africa, explored the coast and, in the early 16th century, the Portuguese set up bases. Portugal established Luanda in 1575, and Angola's capital is the oldest European-founded city in Africa south of the Sahara. As a centre of the slave trade, some 3 million captives from Angola passed through it to the Americas, and the depopulation dislocated local life for many generations.

After the decline of the slave trade, Portuguese settlers began to develop the land, and the Portuguese population increased greatly in the 20th century. In the 1950s, local nationalists began to demand independence, and in 1956 the MPLA (Popular Movement for the Liberation of Angola) was founded with support from the Mbundu and mestizos. The MPLA led a revolt in Luanda in 1961, but this was put down by Portuguese troops.

Other opposition groups now developed. In the north, the Kongo set up the FNLA (Front for the Liberation of Angola), while, in 1966, the people of the south, including many Ovimbundu, formed UNITA (National Union for the Total Independence of Angola). The Portuguese agreed to grant independence to Angola in 1975, but the rival nationalist forces began a struggle for power. The MPLA formed the government, but UNITA troops, opposed to the MPLA's socialist policies, and with support from South Africa, began a long civil war, which continued into the 1990s. A peace treaty was signed in 1991 and elections were held in 1992. But after a victory for the MPLA, which had renounced its socialist policies, the civil war broke out again. [*Map page 33*] ■

> **AREA** 1,246,700 sq km [481,351 sq mls]
> **POPULATION** 10,674,000
> **CAPITAL (POPULATION)** Luanda (1,544,000)
> **GOVERNMENT** Multiparty republic
> **ETHNIC GROUPS** Ovimbundu 37%, Mbundu 22%, Kongo 13%, Luimbe-Nganguela 5%, Nyaneka-Humbe 5%, Chokwe, Luvale, Luchazi
> **LANGUAGES** Portuguese (official)
> **RELIGIONS** Christianity (Roman Catholic 69%, Protestant 20%), traditional beliefs 10%
> **CURRENCY** Kwanza = 100 lwei

# ANGUILLA

Deriving its name from its 'discovery' in 1493 by Columbus – *anguil* is Spanish for eel – Anguilla is indeed long and thin, a low coral atoll covered with poor soil and scrub, measuring 96 sq km [37 sq mls].

Of the 8,000 population – largely of African descent, English-speaking and of various Christian denominations – nearly a quarter live in the capital of The Valley. The main source of revenue is now tourism, though lobster accounts for half of exports, while many Anguillans send home earnings from the UK and USA. Sadly, 80% of the island's coral has now disappeared through the effects of tourism – namely, pollution and the sale of coral as souvenir items.

First colonized by Britain in 1690 and long administered with St Kitts and Nevis, the island was subject to intervention by British troops in 1969 to restore legal government following its secession from the self-governing federation in 1967. Its position as a separate UK dependent territory was confirmed in 1971 and formalized in 1980. [*Map page 30*] ■

# ARGENTINA

**AREA** 96 sq km [37 sq mls]
**POPULATION** 8,000
**CAPITAL (POPULATION)** The Valley (2,000)
**GOVERNMENT** British dependency
**ETHNIC GROUPS** Mainly of African descent
**LANGUAGES** English and Creole
**RELIGIONS** Christianity
**CURRENCY** Eastern Caribbean dollar

# ANTIGUA AND BARBUDA

A ntigua is untypical of the Leeward Islands in that despite its height – rising to 405 m [1,328 ft] – it has no rivers or forests; Barbuda, by contrast, is a well-wooded low coral atoll.

Both islands rely heavily on tourism, though some attempts at diversification (notably Sea Island cotton) have been successful. Other activities include livestock rearing, mixed market gardening and fishing. Antigua's white-owned sugar industry – accounting for most of exports in the 1960s – was closed down in 1971. Only 1,400 people live on the game reserve island of Barbuda, where lobster fishing is the main occupation, and none on the rocky island of Redondo. Antigua and Barbuda are strategically situated islands linked by Britain after 1860; gaining internal self-government in 1967 and independence in 1981. [*Map page 30*] ■

**AREA** 440 sq km [170 sq mls]
**POPULATION** 65,000
**CAPITAL (POPULATION)** St John's (36,000)
**GOVERNMENT** Multiparty constitutional monarchy
**ETHNIC GROUPS** Mainly of African descent
**LANGUAGES** English, local dialects
**RELIGIONS** Christianity
**CURRENCY** Eastern Caribbean dollar

L argest of the Spanish-speaking countries of Latin America, but still less than a third of the size of Brazil, Argentina forms a wedge-shaped country from the Tropic of Capricorn to Tierra del Fuego. The western boundary lies high in the Andes, including basins, ridges and peaks of 6,000 m [19,685 ft] in the north. South of latitude 27°S the ridges merge into a single high cordillera, the highest point being Aconcagua at 6,960 m [22,834 ft], the tallest mountain in the western hemisphere; south of 39°S the Patagonian Andes are lower, but include glaciers and volcanoes. Eastern Argentina is a series of alluvial plains, stretching from the Andean foothills to the sea. The Gran Chaco in the north slopes gradually towards the valley of the Paraná River, from the high desert in the foothills to lowland swamp forest.

Further south are the extensive pampas grasslands, damp and fertile near Buenos Aires, drier but still productive elsewhere. Southwards again the pampas give way to the less hospitable plateaux of Patagonia, areas of mixed volcanic, alluvial and glacial debris that form a harsh, windswept landscape. The climate varies dramatically from hot and humid in the north of the country to bitterly cold, damp and stormy in the extreme south.

**ECONOMY AND RESOURCES**
Argentina is one of the richest of South America's countries in terms of natural resources, and its population – though remarkably urban, with 85% living in towns and cities – is not growing at anything like the rates seen in most of Africa and Asia. The population, predominantly European and mainly middle class, nevertheless relies on an economic base that is agricultural: Argentina's farming industry exports wheat, maize, sorghum and soya beans as well as enormous quantities of meat, and produces sugar, oilseed, fruit and vegetables for home consumption. The chief industries, too, are based

on food products, and the government aims to switch to manufacturing from agricultural processing. The manufacturing base is around Buenos Aires, where more than a third of the population live, and there is a strong computer industry.

Minerals are largely undeveloped, though coal and natural gas are exploited and the country is approaching self-sufficiency in petroleum production, mainly from Patagonia and the north-west. Other areas yet to be explored are the mining of copper and uranium and, on a more rural level, fishing and forestry.

## HISTORY AND POLITICS

Formerly a dependency of Peru, Argentina ('land of silver') was settled first in the north-west around Salta and San Miguel de Tucumán with strong links to Lima. This area is unusual today in retaining a largely mestizo (mixed Indian and Spanish) population, a remnant of colonial times. In 1776 Argentina, Uruguay, Paraguay and southern Bolivia were disengaged from Peru to form a separate viceroyalty, with its administrative centre in Buenos Aires. After a long war of independence the United Provinces of the Rió de la Plata achieved self-government under Simón Bolivar, but Uruguay, Bolivia and Paraguay separated between 1814 and 1828; it took many years of warfare and turbulence before Argentina emerged as a national entity in 1816, united and centred on Buenos Aires.

Early prosperity, based on stock-raising and farming, was boosted from 1870 by a massive influx of European immigrants, particularly Italians and Spaniards for whom the Argentine was a real alternative to the USA. They settled lands recently cleared of Indians and often organized by huge land companies. Britain provided much of the capital and some of the immigrants; families of English and Welsh sheep farmers, still speaking their own languages, are identifiable in Patagonia today. Development of a good railway network to the ports, plus steamship services to Europe and refrigerated vessels, helped to create the strong meat, wool and wheat economy that carried Argentina through its formative years and into the 20th century.

A military coup in 1930 started a long period of military intervention in the politics

---

### THE PAMPAS

*Pampa* is a South American Indian word describing a flat, featureless expanse: the pampas of South America are the broad, grassy plains – equivalent to the temperate grasslands of the North American prairies, the Central Asian steppes or the South African veld – that stretch between the eastern flank of the Andes and the Atlantic Ocean. Geologically, they represent outwash fans of rubble, sand, silt and clay, washed down from the Andes by torrents and redistributed by wind and water. Fine soils cover huge expanses of pampas, providing good deep soils in the well-watered areas, but scrub and sandy desert where rainfall and groundwater are lacking.

Originally the pampas were covered with indigenous bunch-grasses, with scattered stands of trees in the well-watered areas. Pampas deer, guanaco, viscachas and cavys were the main grazers, and the pampas fauna included the maned wolf, hairy armadillo and a wealth of bird life including the rhea, the South American ostrich.

Early Spanish settlers introduced horses and cattle, and later the best areas of pampas were enclosed for cattle ranching and cultivation. Now the pampas are almost entirely converted to rangelands growing turf grasses (vehicles have mostly replaced the gauchos) or to huge fields producing alfalfa, maize, wheat and flax.

---

of the country. The period from 1976 – the so-called 'dirty war' – saw the torture, wrongful imprisonment and murder ('disappearance') of up to 15,000 people by the military, and up to 2 million people fled the country. In 1982 the government, blamed for the poor state of the economy, launched an ill-fated invasion of the Falkland Islands (Islas Malvinas), a territory they had claimed since 1820. Britain regained possession later that year by sending an expeditionary force, and President Galtieri resigned. Constitutional rule was restored in 1983 under President Raúl Alfonsín, though the military remained influential.

The country's economic problems – with

their classic Latin American causes of reliance on certain commodities, big borrowing ($62 billion foreign debt) and maladministration – were inherited by his Peronist successor, Carlos Menem, in 1989. His austerity programme took Argentina through inflation rates of 3,084% and 2,314% down to 85% in 1991 – stable money by previous standards. His policies of economic liberalization and reduction of state involvement may work. [*Map page 31*] ■

AREA 2,766,890 sq km [1,068,296 sq mls]
POPULATION 34,182,000
CAPITAL (POPULATION) Buenos Aires (11,256,000)
GOVERNMENT Federal republic
ETHNIC GROUPS European 85%, Mestizo, Amerindian
LANGUAGES Spanish (official)
RELIGIONS Christianity (Roman Catholic 92%, Protestant 2%)
CURRENCY Peso = 10,000 australs

# ARMENIA

The smallest of the 15 republics of the former Soviet Union, Armenia was also one of the weakest. It is a rugged, wooded and mountainous country landlocked between traditionally hostile neighbours. Most of Armenia consists of a rugged plateau, criss-crossed by long faults and subject to earthquakes. Fast-flowing rivers have cut deep gorges in the plateau. The highest point is Mt Aragats, at 4,090 m [13,419 ft] above sea level. The lowest land is in the north-west, where the capital Yerevan is situated, and the north-east. The largest lake is Ozero (Lake) Sevan.

The height of the land – which averages 1,500 m [4,920 ft] above sea level – helps to give Armenia severe winters and cool summers. The highest peaks are snow-capped, but the total yearly rainfall is generally low, between about 200 mm and 800 mm [8 in to 31 in].

## ECONOMY AND RESOURCES

Armenia has few natural resources (though lead, copper and zinc are mined), limited industry, and registered the poorest agricultural output per head in the Union; the country's main products are wine, tobacco, olives and rice, the main occupation the rearing of livestock. Much of the west is recovering from the devastating earthquake of 1988, in which some 55,000 people died. Its vulnerability is heightened by the lack of support for its conflict with Azerbaijan over the area of Nagorno-Karabakh, and its heavy reliance for energy on the other former Soviet republics.

## HISTORY AND POLITICS

Originally a much larger independent kingdom centred on Mt Ararat, the legendary resting place of Noah's Ark, Armenia had already been established for more than 1,000 years when it became the first country in the world to make Christianity (Armenian Apostolic) the official state religion in the 4th century. Later, the area came under first Arab and then Turkish control. By the early 16th century, Armenia was part of the Turkish Ottoman empire.

In the 19th century, Armenians suffered great hardships under Turkish rule, and in the 1890s the Turks slaughtered hundreds of thousands of Armenians. Then, during World War I, 600,000 Armenians were killed and 1.75 million deported to Syria and Palestine by the Turks, who feared the Armenians would support Russia.

At the end of World War I, in 1918, an independent Armenian republic was set up in the area held by Russia, though the western part of historic Armenia remained in Turkey, and another area was held by Iran. In 1920, Armenia became a Communist republic and, in 1922, it became, with Azerbaijan and Georgia, part of the Transcaucasian Republic within the Soviet Union. However, in 1936, the three territories became separate Soviet Socialist Republics.

Armenia has long disputed the status of an area called Nagorno-Karabakh, which lies inside Azerbaijan, because the majority of the people there were Armenians. After the break-up of the Soviet Union in 1991, fighting broke out between Armenia and Azerbaijan, and in 1992 Armenia occupied the land between its eastern border and Nagorno-Karabakh. The fierce fighting led to large movements of Armenians and Azerbaijanis. A cease-fire was finally agreed in 1994, with Armenia in control of about 20% of Azerbaijan's land area. [*Map page 22*] ■

**AREA** 29,800 sq km [11,506 sq mls]
**POPULATION** 3,548,000
**CAPITAL (POPULATION)** Yerevan (1,254,000)
**GOVERNMENT** Multiparty republic
**ETHNIC GROUPS** Armenian 93%, Azerbaijani 3%, Russian 2%, Kurd 2%
**LANGUAGES** Armenian (official)
**RELIGIONS** Christianity (mainly Armenian Apostolic)
**CURRENCY** Dram = 100 couma

# ARUBA

A dry, flat limestone island and the most western of the Lesser Antilles, Aruba measures 193 sq km [75 sq mls]. The country has a population of 62,000, a third living in the capital of Oranjestad. About half the people are of Arawak Indian stock; on most Caribbean islands, the Amerindian population was extirpated by genocide, disease or transportation.

While tourism and the production of petrochemicals and fertilizers are important, over half of the country's export earnings still come from beverages and tobacco, while foodstuffs account for over half of imports.

Incorporated into the Netherlands Antilles in 1845, and part of the self-governing federation from 1954, Aruba held a referendum in 1977, which supported autonomy. The 1983 Constitutional Conference agreed that Aruba's separate status should least for ten years from 1986, after which time the islands would become fully independent. In March 1994 this decision was overturned when

Aruba decided it would remain within the Kingdom of the Netherlands ■

**AREA** 193 sq km [75 sq mls]
**POPULATION** 69,000
**CAPITAL (POPULATION)** Oranjestad (20,000)
**GOVERNMENT** Self-governing Dutch territory
**ETHNIC GROUPS** Mixed European/Caribbean Indian 80%
**LANGUAGES** Dutch, Papiamento, English, Spanish
**RELIGIONS** Christianity
**CURRENCY** Aruban florin = 100 cents

# ASCENSION

A scension stands in isolation on the Mid-Atlantic Ridge, a triangular volcanic island of 88 sq km [34 sq mls], with a single high peak, Green Mountain (859 m [2,817 ft]), surrounded by hot low-lying ash and lava plains. The island is 1,130 km [700 mls] north-west of St Helena and is famous for turtles, which land on the beaches from January to May to lay their eggs.

The mountain climate is cool and damp enough to support a farm, which supplies vegetables for the local community. Administered from St Helena since 1922, its inhabitants are British, St Helenian or American, many of them involved in telecommunications, satellite research and servicing an important mid-ocean airstrip. [*Map page 33*] ■

**AREA** 88 sq km [34 sq mls]
**POPULATION** 1,500
**CAPITAL (POPULATION)** Georgetown (1,500)
**GOVERNMENT** Dependent territory of the UK
**ETHNIC GROUPS** No native ones
**LANGUAGES** English
**RELIGIONS** Christianity
**CURRENCY** St Helena pound = 100 pence

# AUSTRALIA

Whether Australia is the world's largest island or its smallest continental land mass – or both, or neither, depending on the school of geography – it is primarily a land of low to medium altitude plateaux that form monotonous landscapes extending for hundreds of kilometres. The edges of the plateaux are more diverse, particularly in the east where deep gorges and waterfalls create rugged relief between the Great Divide and the coast. In the north-west, impressive gorge scenery is found in the Hamersley Range and Kimberley area.

The western half of Australia is formed of ancient rocks. Essentially an arid landscape of worn-down ridges and plateaux, with depressions occupied by sandy deserts and occasional salt lakes, this area has little surface water.

The eastern sixth of the continent, including Tasmania, forms the Eastern Highlands, the zone of greatest relief, greatest rainfall, most abundant vegetation and greatest population. Peaks in this region include Mt Kosciusko, at 2,230 m [7,316 ft] Australia's highest. Much of this area shows signs of volcanic activity in the relatively recent geological past, and these young basalts support nutrient-rich soils in contrast to the generally well-weathered, nutrient-poor soils of nearly all the remainder of Australia.

Between the western plateaux and Eastern Highlands lie the Carpentaria, central and Murray lowlands. The central lowlands drain to the great internal river systems supplying Lake Eyre, or to the Bulloo system, or through great inland deltas to the Darling River. The parallel dune ridges of this area form part of a great continent-wide set of dune ridges extending in a huge anti-clockwise arc, eastwards through the Great Victoria Desert, northwards through the Simpson Desert and westwards in the Great Sandy Desert. All these, though inhospitable, are only moderately arid, allowing widespread if sparse vegetation cover.

## Vegetation
On the humid margins of the continent are luxuriant forests. These include the great jarrah forests of tall eucalyptus hardwoods in the extreme south-west of Western Australia; the temperate rainforests with the Antarctic beech found in Tasmania and on humid upland sites north through New South Wales to the Queensland border; and the tropical and subtropical rainforests found in the wetter areas along the east coast, from McIllwraith Range in the north to the vicinity of Mallacoota Inlet in the south. Some of these rainforest areas are maintained as managed forests, others are in national parks, but most of the original cover has been cleared for agriculture, particularly for dairying and cattle-fattening, and for sugar and banana cultivation north of Port Macquarie.

The most adaptable tree genus in Australia is the *Eucalyptus*, which ranges from the tall flooded gum trees found on the edges of the rainforest to the dry-living mallee species found on sand plains and interdune areas. Acacia species, especially the bright-yellow flowered wattles, are also adapted to a wide range of environments. Associated with this adaptation of plants is the wide variety of animal adaptations, with 277 different mammals, about 400 species of reptiles and some 700 species of birds.

Aborigines arriving from Asia over 40,000 years ago brought the dingo, which rapidly replaced the Tasmanian wolf, the largest marsupial predator, and preyed on smaller animals. Fires, lit for hunting and allowed to burn uncontrolled, altered much of the vegetation, probably allowing eucalyptus forests to expand at the expense of the rainforest. However, the Aborigines understood their environment, carefully protecting vital areas of natural food supply, restricting the use of certain desert waterholes which tradition taught would be reliable in a drought, and developing a resource-use policy which was aimed at living with nature.

European settlement after 1788 upset this ecological balance, through the widespread clearing of coastal forests, overgrazing of inland pastures and introduction of exotic species, especially the destructive rabbit. But Europeans also brought the technology which enabled the mineral, water and soil resources of Australia to be developed.

## ECONOMY AND RESOURCES

Much of Australia's growth since the beginning of European settlement has been closely related to the exploitation of mineral resources, which has led directly to the founding, growth and often eventual decline of the majority of inland towns. Broken Hill and Mount Isa are copper-, lead-, zinc- and silver-producing centres, while Kalgoorlie, Bendigo, Ballarat and Charters Towers all grew in the 19th-century gold rushes. Today, less glamorous minerals support the Australian economy. In Western Australia, the great iron-ore mines of Mount Tom Price, Mount Newman and Mount Goldsworthy are linked by new railways to special ports at Dampier and Port Hedland. Offshore are the oil and gas fields of the north-west shelf.

In the east, the coal mines of central Queensland and eastern New South Wales are linked by rail to bulk loading facilities at Sarina, Gladstone, Brisbane, Newcastle, Sydney and Port Kemble, which enable this high-grade coking coal to be shipped to worldwide markets and by 1986 had made Australia the biggest exporter (15% of export earnings). Bauxite mining has led to new settlements at Nhulunby and Weipa on the Gulf of Carpentaria, with associated refineries at Kwinana, Gladstone and Bell Bay.

Rum Jungle, south of Darwin, became well known as one of the first uranium mines, but now deposits further east in Arnhem Land are being developed. Meanwhile, new discoveries of ore bodies continue to be made in the ancient rocks of the western half of Australia. Natural gas from the Cooper Basin, just south of Innamincka on Cooper Creek, is piped to Adelaide and Sydney, while oil and gas from the Bass Strait and brown coal from the Yallourn-Morwell area have been vital to the industrial growth of Victoria. Fossil fuels are supplemented by hydroelectric power from major schemes in western Tasmania and the Snowy Mountains and smaller projects near Cairns and Tully in north Queensland.

Australia's mineral wealth is phenomenal. In 1993 it produced over 40% of the world's diamonds, around 13% of gold and iron ore,

## THE GREAT BARRIER REEF

When coral is alive it sways gently in the sea's currents, but when it dies it forms hard coral 'limestone' rock. The beautiful Great Barrier Reef, off the coast of Queensland in the Coral Sea and the world's biggest, is a maze of some 2,500 reefs exposed only at low tide, ranging in size from a few hundred hectares to 50 sq km [20 sq mls], and extending over an area of 250,000 sq km [100,000 sq mls].

The section extending for about 800 km [500 mls] north of Cairns forms a discontinuous wall of coral through which narrow openings lead to areas of platform or patch reefs. South of Cairns, the reefs are less continuous, and extend further from the coast. Between the outer reef and the coast are many high islands, remnants of the mainland; coral cays, developed from coral sand on reefs and known locally as low islands, are usually small and uninhabited, exceptions being Green Island and Heron Island.

A major tourist attraction comprising over 400 types of coral and harbouring more than 1,500 species of fish, the modern reefs have evolved in the last 20,000 years, over older foundations exposed to the atmosphere during former low sea levels. Coral is susceptible to severe damage from tropical cyclones and, increasingly, to attack by the crown-of-thorns starfish. Much is now protected as the Great Barrier Reef Marine Park (the world's largest protected sea area), but the existence of oil around and beneath the reef is a great long-term threat to its ecological stability.

8% of silver, 7% of aluminium, nickel, magnesium and uranium, 5% of zinc and lead (down from 14% in 1989), and was the world's biggest exporter of mineral sands. Inspite of these statistics however, by 1991 the country was experiencing its worst recession since the 1920s.

### Agriculture

Apart from the empty and largely unusable desert areas in Western Australia and the Simpson Desert, extensive cattle or sheep production dominates all of Australia north and west of a line from Penong in South Australia, through Broken Hill in New South Wales to Bundaberg in Queensland, and east of a line from Geraldton to Esperance in Western Australia. Cattle and sheep populations in this zone are sparse, individual pastoral holdings are large, some over 400,000 hectares [1 million acres], and towns are both small and far apart.

Some Aborigines retain limited tracts of land in Arnhem Land and on the fringes of the deserts where they live by hunting and gathering, but nearly all Aborigines now live close to government settlements or mission stations. Many are employed as stockmen and seasonal agricultural workers, while thousands of others have migrated to country towns and the major cities.

The intensive pastoral and agricultural zones support the bulk of the sheep and cattle of Australia, and wool, mutton and beef production is still the basic industry. The country is the world's largest producer of wool and third in lamb and mutton. Wheat is cultivated in combination with sheep raising over large tracts of the gentle inland slopes of the coastal ranges.

Along the east coast are important cattle-fattening, dairy and sugar-cane industries, the latter significant on the east coast from Brisbane to Cairns. Irrigated areas also support cotton, rice, fruit and vegetable crops, largely for consumption within Australia. Wine production around Perth, Adelaide, central Victoria and eastern New South Wales has expanded in recent decades, producing vintages of international renown.

### HISTORY AND POLITICS

European settlement in Australia began in 1788 as a penal colony in New South Wales, spreading quickly to Queensland and Tasmania. During the 19th century the continent became divided into the states of New South Wales, Queensland (1859), South Australia (1836), Tasmania (1825), Victoria (1851) and Western Australia (1829), with the area now forming the Northern Territory being under the control of South Australia. During this colonial period the state seaport capitals of Sydney, Brisbane, Adelaide, Hobart, Melbourne and Perth became established as

## MARSUPIALS

Marsupials are mammals that give birth to their young at an early stage of development and attach them to their milk glands for a period, often inside a pouch (marsupium). Once widespread around the world, they have mostly been ousted by more advanced forms, but marsupials of many kinds continue to flourish in the isolation of Australia, New Guinea and South America.

Best known are the big red and grey kangaroos that range over the dry grasslands and forests of Australia. Standing up to 2 m [6.5 ft] tall, they are browsers and grazers that now compete for food with cattle and sheep; many hundreds are killed each year. Bounding at speed they can clear fences of their own height. Wallabies – small species of the same family – live in the forests and mountains.

Australia has many other kinds of marsupials, though several have died out since the coming of Europeans. Tree-living koalas live exclusively on eucalyptus leaves. Heavily-built wombats browse in the undergrowth like large rodents, and the fierce-sounding Tasmanian Devils are mild scavengers of the forest floor. There are also many tiny mouse-like, shrew-like, and mole-like species that feed on insects, seeds or honey.

the dominant manufacturing, commercial, administrative and legislative centres of their respective states – a position none of them has since relinquished.

In 1901, the states came together to create the Commonwealth of Australia with a federal constitution. Trade between the states became free, and external affairs, defence and immigration policy became federal responsibilities, though health, education, transport, mineral, agricultural and industrial development remained firmly in the hands of each state. Only gradually did powers of taxation give the federal government the opportunity to develop national policies.

The federal capital established at Canberra, in the new Australian Capital Territory, grew from a tiny settlement in 1911 to become a great seat of administration and learning, and the largest inland regional commercial centre. The federal government's territorial responsibilities also include the Northern Territory, self-governing since 1978.

Immigration has changed the ethnic character of Australia since about 1960. Australian society now has Greek, Italian, Yugoslav, Turkish, Lebanese and South-east Asian communities alongside the longer-established Aboriginal, British, Irish, Chinese, Dutch and German communities, though the culture remains strongly British in flavour. Almost 60% of the total Australian population live in Sydney, Melbourne, Adelaide, Brisbane, Perth and Hobart. Migration within the states from inland rural areas to capital cities or coastal towns leaves many rural communities with an ageing population, while the new mining centres have young populations. The most rapid growth outside new mining centres is occurring in coastal towns through migration on retirement and attempts to establish an alternative lifestyle by leaving the big cities.

Soon after 1788, small-scale manufacturing began to supply domestic goods and machinery to the colonial community. Inevitably manufacturing grew in the colonial seaport capitals, especially Sydney and Melbourne, which now have over 60% of all manufacturing industry (though only 40% or so of the total population).

Under the Australian Constitution, the federal government has control over interstate and overseas transport, with the state governments responsible for regulation within their own borders. Seven railway systems thus exist, each state system focusing on its capital city, with the Commonwealth Railways responsible for the Trans-Australian, Central Australian and Northern Territory routes. The notorious differences in gauges between the states have been partially overcome by the construction of the standard-gauge links from Brisbane to Sydney, Sydney to Melbourne, and Sydney to Perth via Broken Hill. The completion of the Tarcoola-Alice Springs route will provide the basic strategic standard-gauge rail network for Australia.

Railways are vital for bulk freight, especially mineral ores, coal and wheat. Among the busiest of the railways are the iron-ore lines

## AUSTRALIAN TERRITORIES

Australia is responsible for a number of territories outside the seven states. In the Indian Ocean Britain transferred to Canberra sovereignty of Heard Island and McDonald Island (both 1947), and further north the Cocos (Keeling) Islands (1955) and Christmas Island (1958). The federal government also has jurisdiction over the Ashmore and Cartier Islands in the Timor Sea, the Coral Sea Islands Territory, and Norfolk Island in the southwest Pacific – while Lord Howe Island and Macquarie Island are administered by New South Wales and Tasmania respectively. Of all these, only the Cocos Islands (700), Christmas Island (2,300), Norfolk Island (2,000) and Lord Howe Island (300) have permanent populations.

Australia is also in charge of the largest sector of Antarctica, a continent protected from military and nuclear pollution under international agreement since 1991. A member of ANZUS since 1951, Australia has reviewed its own defence position since New Zealand banned US Navy nuclear warships in 1985.

in the north-west of Western Australia. Most cattle and sheep, however, are carried by 'road trains' – a powerful unit pulling several trailers. A rapidly improving highway system links all major cities and towns, providing easy mobility for a largely car-owning population. Some journeys are still difficult, especially when floods wash away sections of road or sand-drifts bury highways. Although 90% of all passenger transport is by road, air services cope with much interstate travel.

Australia is also well served by local broadcasting and television. The radio remains a lifeline for remote settlements dependent on the flying doctor or aerial ambulance, and for many others when floods or bush fires threaten isolated communities.

The worldwide economic depression of the late 1980s was mirrored in Australia by a deterioration in the country's hitherto buoyant export of agricultural products and its worst unemployment for 60 years. It was against this background that the Labour Prime Minister, Bob Hawke, was elected for an unprecedented fourth term, but in 1991 the worsening economic situation forced his replacement by Paul Keating. Under Keating's administration the key issue of Australia's trade relations, following the extension of the European Community and the success of the Pacific Rim economies, came to the fore, as did the associated question of the country's national identity. With Britain joining the EEC, Australia had looked increasingly to the Pacific Rim countries, and especially to Japan, for its trade. However, fears of a flood of Japanese investment cloaked deeper concerns for many ordinary 'Aussies'. [*Map pages 34–5*] ■

**AREA** 7,686,850 sq km [2,967,893 sq mls]
**POPULATION** 17,847,000
**CAPITAL (POPULATION)** Canberra (310,000)
**GOVERNMENT** Federal constitutional monarchy
**ETHNIC GROUPS** White 95%, Aboriginal 1.5%, Asian 1.3%
**LANGUAGES** English (official)
**RELIGIONS** Christianity (Roman Catholic 26%, Anglican 24%, other 20%), Islam, Buddhism, Judaism
**CURRENCY** Australian dollar = 100 cents

# AUSTRIA

A mountainous country, more Alpine even than Switzerland and with over 35% forested, Austria has two-thirds of its territory and rather less than a third of the population within the eastern Alps, which extend in a series of longitudinal ridges from the Swiss border in the west almost to Vienna in the east. The longitudinal valleys between the ridges accommodate much of the Alpine population, but are less effective than might be expected as routes of internal communication. Transverse routes, for example the Linz-Klagenfurt and Vienna-Semmering, are vital internal links across the eastern Alps to

the valleys and basins of Steiermark and Kärnten. The rail and motorway routes over the 1,371 m [4,500 ft] Brenner Pass are more intensively used, but these benefit neighbours rather than Austria.

## ECONOMY AND RESOURCES
Austria's lowlands include a section of the northern Alpine foreland, which narrows eastwards towards Vienna and contains the Danube basin. This is Austria's most important east-west route with rail, motorway and river navigation leading through Vienna to Budapest and beyond. Another important lowland is the Burgenland, a rich farming area bordering the eastern Alps and facing southeast towards Hungary.

Unlike Switzerland, Austria has important heavy industries based in large part on indigenous resources. The mountains are a major source of hydroelectric power. Oil and natural gas occur predominantly in the Vienna Basin and are supplemented by imports from the former Soviet republics and from German refineries. Germany, sharing many cultural links as well as language, remains by far the most important trading partner. Minerals occur in the eastern Alps, notably iron ore in Steiermark (Styria); iron and steel production is located both at Donawitz (near Leoben) in the mountains, and also in the Alpine foreland which has become a major centre of metal, chemical engineering and vehicle manufacturing industries. Various industrial plants are also established around Vienna.

The capital stands at a major European crossroads where the Danube is joined by the Moravian Gate route from the northern lowlands of Europe, and by the Alpine route through the Semmering Pass. A city of political as well as cultural and artistic importance, Vienna is home to OPEC, the International Atomic Energy Agency and the UN Industrial Development Organization, among others, and contains one-fifth of Austria's population.

## HISTORY AND POLITICS
A federal republic comprising nine states (*Länder*) – including the capital, Vienna – Austria's present boundaries derive from the

Versailles Treaty of 1919, which dissolved the Austro-Hungarian Empire. It was absorbed by the German Reich in 1938, occupied by the Allies in 1945 and recovered its full independence in 1955.

Like most European countries, Austria experienced low population growth or even a slight reduction in the 1960s and 1970s. Within the country, decline has been greatest in the east, while the west has gained from a higher birth rate, and also from the settlement of refugees and the industrialization of the Tirol since World War II.

Austria's neutrality was enshrined in the constitution in 1955, but unlike Switzerland it has not been frightened to take sides on certain issues. A member of EFTA since 1960, in 1994 two-thirds of the population voted in favour of joining the EU and on 1 January 1995 Austria, along with Finland and Sweden, became a member. The EU now has15 member countries. [*Map page 15*] ■

---

**AREA** 83,850 sq km [32,374 sq mls]
**POPULATION** 7,918,000
**CAPITAL (POPULATION)** Vienna (1,560,000)
**GOVERNMENT** Federal republic
**ETHNIC GROUPS** Austrian 93%, Yugoslav 2%, Turkish, German
**LANGUAGES** German (official)
**RELIGIONS** Christianity (Roman Catholic 78%, Protestant 6%), Islam
**CURRENCY** Schilling = 100 Groschen

---

# AZERBAIJAN

T he Azerbaijani Republic is a country, facing the Caspian Sea to the east, in south-western Asia. It includes an area called the Nakhichevan Autonomous Republic (population 300,000), which is completely cut off from the rest of Azerbaijan by Armenian territory. The Caucasus Mountains border Russia in the north. Another highland region, including the Little Caucasus Mountains and part of the rugged Armenian plateau, is in the

south-west. Between these regions lies a broad plain drained by the River Kura which flows into the Caspian Sea.

Azerbaijan has hot summers and cool winters. The rainfall is low on the plains, ranging from about 130 mm to 380 mm [5 in to 15 in] per year. The annual rainfall is much higher in the highlands and on the subtropical south-eastern coast.

## ECONOMY AND RESOURCES

Though much of Azerbaijan is semi-arid – there is also a large tract below sea level – it nevertheless grows crops such as cotton, grains, rice and grapes, with fishing also important, though the Caspian Sea has become increasingly polluted. With its economy in disarray since the break-up of the Soviet Union, Azerbaijan now ranks among the world's 'lower-middle-income' countries.

Oil is still the mainstay of Azerbaijan's revenue. It was being collected by the Caspian Sea near Baku over 1,000 years ago, and burning natural gas leaking from the ground gave the area its name, 'Land of eternal fire'. Today, along with industries both traditional (carpets, timber, iron) and modern (cement, aluminium, chemicals), it makes the country's economy a viable one. Under Communism, most property and economic activity were under government control, but the government is now encouraging private enterprise.

## HISTORY AND POLITICS

In ancient times, the area which is now Azerbaijan was invaded many times. In AD 642, Arab armies introduced Islam. But most modern Azerbaijanis are descendants of Persians and Turkic peoples, who migrated to the area from the east by the 9th century. The area later came under Mongol rule between the 13th and 15th centuries, and then the Persian Safavid dynasty.

In the 18th century, Russia began to expand. By the early 19th century, Azerbaijan was under Russian rule. After the Russian Revolution of 1917, attempts were made to form a Transcaucasian Federation made up of Armenia, Azerbaijan and Georgia. When this failed, Azerbaijanis set up an independent state. But Russian forces occupied the area in 1920. In 1922, the Communists set up a

Transcaucasian Republic consisting of Armenia, Azerbaijan and Georgia under Russian control, then in 1936 the three areas became separate Soviet Socialist Republics within the Soviet Union.

In the late 1980s, the government of the Soviet Union began to introduce reforms, giving the people more freedom, and when the Soviet Union was voted out of existence in 1991, Azerbaijan became an independent nation.

Since independence, economic progress has been slow, partly because of civil unrest in Nagorno-Karabakh, a region within Azerbaijan, where the majority of the people are Christian Armenians. In 1992, Armenia occupied the area between its eastern border and Nagorno-Karabakh, while ethnic Armenians took over Nagorno-Karabakh. This conflict led to large migrations of Armenians and Azerbaijanis. A cease-fire was agreed in 1994, with about 20% of Azerbaijan territory under Armenian control. [*Map page 22*] ■

**AREA** 86,600 sq km [33,436 sq mls]
**POPULATION** 7,472,000
**CAPITAL (POPULATION)** Baku (1,149,000)
**GOVERNMENT** Federal multiparty republic
**ETHNIC GROUPS** Azerbaijani 83%, Russian 6%, Armenian 6%, Lezgin, Avar, Ukrainian, Tatar
**LANGUAGES** Azerbaijani (official)
**RELIGIONS** Islam
**CURRENCY** Manat = 100 gopik

# AZORES

Part of the Mid-Atlantic Ridge, the Azores are nine large and several small islands situated about 1,200 km [745 mls] west of Lisbon. They can be divided into three widely separated groups: São Miguel (759 sq km [293 sq mls] out of a total area of 2,247 sq km [868 sq mls]) and Santa Maria are the most easterly; 160 km [100 mls] to the north-west is the central cluster of Terceira, Graciosa,

São Jorge, Pico and Faial; another 240 km [150 mls] to the north-west are Flores and the most isolated significant island of Corvo.

Of relatively recent volcanic origin, the islands are mostly mountainous, with high cliffs and narrow beaches of shell gravel or dark volcanic sand. The highest mountain (and Portugal's highest) is Pico Alto, a volcanic cone of 2,351 m [7,713 ft].

The name Azores means 'islands of the hawks' and birds of prey are a common sight.

## ECONOMY AND RESOURCES
Well watered with an equable, temperate climate and fertile soils, the economy of the Azores is based predominantly on agriculture, although tourism is playing an increasingly important part. All flat or slightly sloping land is cultivated with with food crops or vines. Small-scale farming and fishing are the main occupations, with fruit, wine, tea, tobacco and canned fish exported (mostly to Portugal).

## HISTORY AND POLITICS
The islands were discovered in the 15th century by Portuguese navigators and were later settled by Flemish knights. There were no indigenous people and the present population of 238,000 is mostly of Portuguese stock, although later settlers of Moorish origin from the Algarve and the Alentejo, Jewish farmers from the Minho and Bretons have all left their cultural mark on the islands. Since 1976 they have been governed as three districts of Portugal – Angra do Heroísmo, Ponta Delgada and Horta – making up an autonomous region represented by five members in the Portuguese Parliament. The capital is Ponta Delgada on the island of São Miguel, which hosts more than half the total population. [*Map page 2*] ■

**AREA** 2,247 sq km [868 sq mls]
**POPULATION** 238,000
**CAPITAL (POPULATION)** Ponta Delgada (21,000)
**GOVERNMENT** Portuguese Autonomous Region
**ETHNIC GROUPS** Portuguese
**LANGUAGES** Portuguese
**RELIGIONS** Christianity
**CURRENCY** Portuguese currency

# BAHAMAS

# BAHRAIN

The Bahamas consists of a coral-limestone archipelago of 29 inhabited low-lying islands, plus over 3,000 uninhabited cays, reefs and rocks, centred on the Grand Bahama Bank off eastern Florida and Cuba. The island of San Salvador was the first landfall in the New World of Christopher Columbus on 12 October 1492.

Over 90% of its 3.6 million visitors a year are Americans, and tourism now accounts for more than half the nation's revenues, involving over 40% of the total workforce. Offshore banking, financial services and a large 'open registry' merchant fleet also offset the imports (including most foodstuffs), giving the country a relatively high standard of living. Nassau and Freeport have commercial shipping ports and international airports, Freeport being the country's leading industrial centre. The remainder of the non-administrative population works mainly in traditional fishing and agriculture, notably citrus fruit production, but fresh vegetables, meat and eggs are produced for the domestic market. Rum is produced for export in the distillery on the island of New Providence.

Though the Bahamas is an independent democracy, it is also élitist. It has developed close ties with the USA since independence from Britain in 1973. However, relations with the USA were strained when the country was used as a tax haven for drug traffickers in the 1980s, with government ministers implicated in drug-related corruption. [*Map page 30*] ■

> AREA 13,880 sq km [5,359 sq mls]
> POPULATION 272,000
> CAPITAL (POPULATION) Nassau (172,196)
> GOVERNMENT Constitutional monarchy
> ETHNIC GROUPS Black 73%, Mulatto 14%, White 13%
> LANGUAGES English, English Creole 80%
> RELIGIONS Christianity 95%
> CURRENCY Bahamian dollar = 100 cents

The country is made up of 35 small islands, the largest of which is called Bahrain, located in the Arabian Gulf close to the coast of Saudi Arabia. Bahrain island is about 48 km [30 mls] long and 16 km [10 mls] wide at its broadest.

This relatively liberal state led the region in developing oil production after discovery in 1932. When production waned in the 1970s it diversified into other sectors: its aluminium-smelting plant is the Gulf's largest non-oil industrial complex, and the moves into banking, communications and leisure came when the cosmopolitan centre of Beirut was plunging into chaos. Banking now accounts for some 15% of GDP, while oil takes as much as 20% – though far more of government revenues. Most of the land is barren, but soil imports have created some fertile areas.

Bahrain does have problems, however. Tension between the Sunni and majority Shiite population (the latter favouring an Islamic republic) has been apparent since before independence, and during the First Gulf War Iran responded to Bahrain's support for Iraq by reiterating its claims to the territory. In 1986 a rumbling dispute began with Qatar over claims to a cluster of oil-rich islands, reefs and sandbars; the disagreement was taken by Qatar to the International Court of Justice in 1991. [*Map page 22*] ■

> AREA 678 sq km [262 sq mls]
> POPULATION 549,000
> CAPITAL (POPULATION) Manama (or Al Manamah, 152,000)
> GOVERNMENT Monarchy (emirate) with a cabinet appointed by the Emir
> ETHNIC GROUPS Bahraini Arab 68%, Persian, Indian and Pakistani 25%, other Arab 4%, European 3%
> LANGUAGES Arabic
> RELIGIONS Islam 85%, Christianity 7%
> CURRENCY Bahrain dinar = 1,000 fils

# BANGLADESH

**B**attered by a relentless cycle of flood and famine, and plagued by political corruption and a succession of military coups, Bangladesh is perhaps Asia's most pitiful country, once known as Golden Bengal (Sonar Bangla) for its treasures but gradually plundered and now pushed near to the bottom of the Third World pile. It is – apart from statistically irrelevant city-states and small island countries – the most crowded nation on Earth: the 1994 figure was a density of some 818 people per sq km [2,119 per sq ml], well ahead of the next realistic rival Taiwan (574 per sq km [1,486 per sq ml]) and far greater than Europe's contender Belgium (330 per sq km [854 per sq ml]), which in any case has a much larger urban proportion. The world's tenth biggest population – a figure expected to increase by another 30 million or more by the year 2000 – lives on an area of precarious flat lowlands smaller than the US states of Illinois or Iowa.

Apart from a south-eastern fringe of forested ridges east of Chittagong, Bangladesh consists almost entirely of lowlands – mainly the (greater) eastern part of the large delta formed jointly by the Ganges and Brahmaputra. The western part (now West Bengal, in India) is largely the 'dying delta' – its land a little higher and less often flooded, its deltaic channels seldom flushed by floodwaters. In contrast, the heart of Bangladesh, following the main Ganges channel and the wide Brahmaputra, is the 'active delta'. Frequently flooded, with changing channels that are hazardous to life, health and property, the rivers also renew soil fertility with silt washed down from as far away as the mountains of Nepal and Tibet. Indeed, while deforestation in the Himalayan foothills has caused enough silt to form new 'islands' for the burgeoning Bangladeshi population, it has also led to the blocking of some waterways (60% of the country's internal trade is carried by boat), danger to fish stocks, and the increased risk of flooding.

## ECONOMY AND RESOURCES

The alluvial silts of the 'active delta' yield up to three rice crops a year as well as the world's best jute, and though Bangladesh is now only the third largest producer in a declining market, high-quality fibre is exported to India; jute and cotton are processed also in post-independence mills, for example at Narayanganj. There is a large hydroelectric plant at Karnaphuli reservoir, and a modern paper industry using bamboo from the hills. Substantial reserves of coal await exploitation, but a more realistic development may be the construction of a canal 320 km [200 mls] long to transfer water from the flooding Brahmaputra to the Ganges, in order to increase supplies to India's drought-affected areas. The scheme, like so many others, has run into political problems and mutual suspicion that dog the area.

## HISTORY AND POLITICS

Bangladesh was until 1971 East Pakistan, the oriental wing of the Muslim state set up by the partition of British India in 1947. Separated by 1,600 km [1,000 mls] of India from the politically-dominant, Urdu- and Punjabi-speaking western province, the easterners felt the victims of ethnic and economic discrimination. In 1971 resentment turned to war when Bengali irregulars, considerably aided and abetted by Indian troops, convened the independent state of 'Free Bengal', with Sheikh Mujibur Rahman as head of state.

The Sheikh's assassination in 1975 – during one of four military coups in the first 11 years of independence – led finally to a takeover by General Zia Rahman, who created an Islamic state before himself being murdered in 1981. General Ershad took over in a coup the following year and resigned as army chief in 1986 to take up the civilian presidency, lifting martial law; but by 1990 protests from supporters of his two predecessors toppled him from power and, after the first free parliamentary elections since independence, a coalition government was formed in 1991.

The new authority faced not only the long-term problems of a debt-ridden, aid-reliant country where corruption is a way of life: it also had to deal with the consequences of the worst cyclone in living memory and, from

## THE DELTA CYCLONES

Most of Bangladesh is almost unbelievably low and flat, and the people of the coastal fringes are all too familiar with the cyclones from the Bay of Bengal. Even so, 1991 brought the worst in memory: the official death toll was a staggering 132,000 (it may well have been higher), and more than 5 million people, almost all of them poor peasants already living on or below the poverty line, were made homeless.

The cyclone caused inestimable damage to the area around Chittagong: crops and fields were inundated with sea water; herds of cattle and goats and flocks of poultry were decimated; dykes were breached and trees ripped up; wells filled up with salt water. The struggling survivors were victims of dysentery and cholera, dehydration and malnutrition. However generous, aid rarely reached the most needy, as it was sifted and filtered down the line despite the efforts of charity administrators. Corrupt practices, like cyclones, are endemic to Bangladesh; funds allocated for concrete cyclone-proof shelters, for example, were appropriated by individuals and government officials.

As with most natural disasters – earthquakes, volcanic eruptions, tidal waves, landslips – the cyclones usually affect countries that are least equipped to deal with them and least able to withstand the losses inflicted.

widespread. However, Bangladesh's biggest problem remains a single one: it has far too many people. [*Map page 23*] ■

**AREA**  144,000 sq km [55,598 sq mls]
**POPULATION**  117,787,000
**CAPITAL (POPULATION)**  Dhaka (6,105,000)
**GOVERNMENT**  Multiparty republic
**ETHNIC GROUPS**  Bengali 98%, tribal groups
**LANGUAGES**  Bengali (official)
**RELIGIONS**  Islam 87%, Hinduism 12%, Buddhism, Christianity
**CURRENCY**  Taka = 100 paisas

# BARBADOS

The most eastern Caribbean country, and first in line for the region's seasonal hurricanes, Barbados is underlain with limestone and capped with coral. Mt Hillaby (340 m [1,115 ft]), the highest point, is fringed by marine terraces marking stages in the island's emergence from the sea. The wet season stretches from June to November, but annual rainfall varies spatially – the higher interior receiving the most. Soils are fertile and deep, easily cultivated except in the eroded Scotland district of the north-east.

Sugar production, using African slave labour, began soon after Barbados became British in 1627. Cane plantations take up most of the cropped land (over half the total), but at 17% now contributes far less than previously to exports. Manufactures now constitute the largest exports, though tourism is the growth sector and the leading industry (432,000 visitors in 1990, 28% from the US and 23% from the UK), and is the most likely future for this relatively prosperous but extremely overcrowded island; at 607 per sq km [1,535 per sq ml], it is one of the most densely populated rural societies in the world (45% urban).

Despite political stability (the island became an independent state within the Commonwealth in 1966) and advanced welfare and education services, emigration (as from many

1992, the increasing prospect of war with Burma, triggered by Rangoon's treatment of the Rohingyas, its Muslim minority. As far back as 1978 Bangladesh took in some 300,000 Rohingyas fleeing persecution, and while most went back, the emigrants of the 1990s are unlikely to follow suit.

Meanwhile, both nations amassed troops on a border that snakes its way through misty hills, mahogany forests and rubber plantations. Defence spending is already too high, and funds should go on other areas: for example, Bangladesh's hospital capacity (one bed for each 5,000 population) is the world's worst. As in West Bengal, an urban educated élite holds the real power, and corruption is

West Indian countries) is high, notably to the US and UK. [*Map page 30*] ∎

AREA 430 sq km [160 sq mls]
POPULATION 261,000
CAPITAL (POPULATION) Bridgetown (6,700)
GOVERNMENT Constitutional monarchy
ETHNIC GROUPS Black 92%, White 3%, Mulatto 3%
LANGUAGES English (official), Creole
RELIGIONS Christianity (Protestant 65%, Roman Catholic 4%)
CURRENCY Barbados dollar = 100 cents

# BELARUS

The Republic of Belarus ('White Russia') is a landlocked country in Eastern Europe, formerly part of the Soviet Union. The land is low-lying and mostly flat. In the south, much of the land is marshy. This area contains Europe's largest marsh and peat bog, the Pripet (Prypyat) Marshes. A hilly region extends from north-east to south-west through the centre of the country, which includes the highest point in Belarus, situated near the capital, Minsk. This hill reaches a height of only 346 m [112 ft] above sea level.

Forests cover about a third of the country, but farmland and pasture have replaced most of the original forest. The colder north has such trees as alder, birch and pine, whereas ash, oak and hornbeam grow in the warmer south. The climate of Belarus is affected by the moderating influence of the Baltic Sea and continental conditions to the east. Winters are cold and the summers are warm.

## ECONOMY AND RESOURCES

The World Bank classifies Belarus as an 'upper-middle-income' economy. Like other former republics of the Soviet Union, it faces many problems in working to turn a government-run economy into a free-market one. Though mainly agricultural – 46% of the land is used efficiently for flax, potatoes,

cereals, dairying, pigs and peat digging – it also has the largest petrochemical complex in Europe and the giant Belaz heavy-truck plants; these, however, like its many light industries, are heavily reliant on Russia for electricity and raw materials, including steel. More relentlessly integrated into the Soviet economy than any republic, Belarus was also the most dependent on trade, at nearly 70%.

## HISTORY AND POLITICS

Slavic people settled in what is now Belarus about 1,500 years ago. In the 9th century, the area became part of the first East Slavic state, Kievan Rus. Mongol armies overran the area in the 13th century, and, later, Belarus became part of Lithuania. In 1569, Lithuania, including Belarus, became part of Poland. In the 18th century, Russia took over most of eastern Poland, including Belarus, yet the people kept their individuality. Belarus became an independent republic in 1918, but Russia invaded the country and in 1919 a Communist state was set up. In 1922, Belarus became a founder republic of the USSR.

Most observers were surprised when this most conservative and Communist-dominated of parliaments declared independence on 25 August 1991, forcing the Party president to stand down. The quiet state of the European Soviet Union, it played a supporting role in its deconstruction and in the creation of the CIS; the latter's first meeting was in Minsk – now its capital. However, in a referendum in May 1995, the people voted for economic integration with Russia and adopted Russian as an official language. It was also agreed that the former Soviet flag for Belarus would eventually be restored. [*Map page 5*] ∎

AREA 207,600 sq km [80,154 sq mls]
POPULATION 10,163,000
CAPITAL (POPULATION) Minsk (1,613,600)
GOVERNMENT Multiparty republic
ETHNIC GROUPS Belarussian 80%, Russian 13%, Polish 4%, Ukrainian 3%, Jewish 1%
LANGUAGES Belarussian, Russian
RELIGIONS Christianity (mainly Belarussian Orthodox, with Roman Catholics in the west and Evangelicals in the south-west)
CURRENCY Belarussian rouble = 100 kopeks

# BELGIUM

Physically Belgium may be divided into the uplands of the Ardennes and the lowland plains, which are drained by the Meuse to the Rhine through the Netherlands, and by the Schelde through Antwerp to the North Sea. The Ardennes, rising in Belgium to about 700 m [2,296 ft] at the highest point, is an area predominantly of moorland, peat bogs and woodland.

Lowland Belgium has varied soils, including some poor-quality sands in the Campine (Kempenland) area near the Dutch frontier, supporting only heaths and woodland. But in general careful cultivation, sound husbandry and attention to drainage have provided good soils; lowland farming is prosperous, with a strong emphasis on grain crops, potatoes and other vegetables, hops, sugar and fodder beet, with hay.

Few hedges exist in the farmed landscape and the holdings are small with intensive cultivation. Traditionally many factory workers of the towns also had a smallholding. There is a small area of polders near the coast, in all less than 500 sq km [200 sq mls], which is rich agricultural land. Outside the towns the density of rural settlement is high.

## ECONOMY AND RESOURCES

No minerals other than coal exist in significant quantities and the Belgian emphasis on manufacturing is based on the import of raw materials. The Ardennes includes the country's most productive coalfield (the Campine) in the Sambre-Meuse Valley, centred on the cities of Charleroi and Liège. Charleroi is a coal-mining and metallurgical city while Liège is the centre of the iron industry. The Campine coalfield continues into the Netherlands and Germany, but production has declined in recent years as uneconomic mines have been closed.

Still of major importance, however, is the textile industry, which has existed in the towns of Flanders from medieval times and in its

## THE GREAT DIVIDE

Belgium has always been an uneasy marriage of two peoples: the majority Flemings, speaking a very close relative of Dutch, and the Walloons, who speak French (rather than the old Walloon variation of French). The dividing line between the two communities runs east-west, just south of Brussels, with the capital itself officially bilingual.

Since the inception of the country, the Flemings have caught up and overtaken the Walloons in cultural influence as well as in numbers of people. In 1932 the Belgian government was designated bilingual, and in 1970 the country was effectively splintered into four parts. In the far eastern frontier areas German is the official language; Brussels remained bilingual but its province of Brabant divided; and the other eight provinces were split into four Fleming and four Walloon – with only the dominant language being official.

Belgium has three governments: the national authority in Brussels, and regional assemblies for both Flanders and Wallonia. During the 1980s, as power gradually devolved from the centre to the regions in crucial aspects of education, transport and the economy, the tension between the 'Germanic' Flemings and the 'Latin' Walloons increased in government.

The various coalitions of Dutch- and French-speaking Christian Democrats and Socialists – which had held together for more than a decade under the astute stewardship of Prime Minister Wilfried Martens – was seriously undermined by the results of the emergency election of November 1991, with many experts predicting the break-up of the national state into two virtually independent nations before the end of the century – leaving Brussels (ironically the focal point of European integration) as a political island.

modern form includes a wide range of products. It is associated particularly with Ghent and Bruges, though these are equally renowned for their medieval architecture. Industry has been diversified and some manufactures, such as glass, are well known in the international market.

It is this part of the country that makes Belgium not only one of Europe's most crowded nations – with 330 people per sq km [856 per sq ml] – but the most 'urban' of any reasonably sized independent state, with an official figure of 97%.

Belgium's main port is Antwerp, much modernized since 1956. The main industrial centres are served by ship canals, including one of 29 km [18 mls] from Ghent to Terneuzen. Constructed in 1825–7, it can take ships of as much as 61,000 tonnes in capacity. There are canals to Bruges from the North Sea at Zeebrugge, and also to Brussels, both completed in 1922. Barges of 1,372 tonnes capacity can use the 125 km [79 mls] Albert Canal to Liège, opened in 1939, and the Meuse and Sambre are being widened and deepened to take barges of similar capacity. Comparable improvements are being made in the River Schelde between Antwerp and Ghent, and in the Brussels-Charleroi Canal. The North Sea ports of Ostend and Zeebrugge cater for overseas trade.

Now, as in past centuries, the lowlands of Belgium, and particularly the city of Brussels (headquarters of the European Union, of which Belgium was a founder member), remain a major focus of commercial and political life in Europe.

### HISTORY AND POLITICS

Throughout a chequered and stormy history as the 'cockpit of Europe', Belgium's fine cities, including Brussels, Ghent and Bruges, have maintained their churches and public buildings, though some have been rebuilt after wars. Following the Napoleonic Wars, from 1815, Belgium and the Netherlands were united as the 'Low Countries', but in 1830, a famous year of ferment in Europe, a National Congress proclaimed independence from the Dutch and in 1831 Prince Leopold of Saxe-Coburg was 'imported from Germany' to become king.

At the Treaty of London in 1839 (which the Netherlands also signed), Britain, France and Russia guaranteed the independence of Belgium – and the famous 'scrap of paper' was upheld when Germany invaded Belgium

in August 1914. For nearly four years the fields of Flanders became the battlefield of Europe.

The division between Belgium and the Netherlands rests on history and sentiment rather than on any physical features. Belgium is predominantly a Roman Catholic country, while the Netherlands is traditionally Protestant (though about 34% of the population are Roman Catholic). Both were neutral in foreign policy, but in 1940 they were invaded by Nazi Germany and remained under occupation until September 1944.

Since the end of World War II economic progress has been marked, for the geographical advantages Belgium possesses have given it a position of significance in Europe, especially in the EU. The unity of the people, however, is less secure, and in the early 1990s there were growing signs that the fragile alliance which had preserved the nation for so long – and under such arduous circumstances – was beginning to crack.

Of the country's universities, Louvain (Catholic and Belgium's oldest, dating from 1426) provides courses in both Flemish and French; of the universities founded in the 19th century, Ghent (1816) is Flemish and Liège (1817) is French-speaking. At Brussels' Free University (founded in 1834) the courses are mainly in French, but provision is made for Flemish speakers. Gradually, the grievances of the Flemish speakers have been removed and in 1974 regional councils were established for Flanders, Wallonia and the Brussels district. [*Map page 11*] ∎

AREA  30,510 sq km [11,780 sq mls]
POPULATION  10,080,000
CAPITAL (POPULATION)  Brussels (Bruxelles or Brussel, 954,000)
GOVERNMENT  Federal constitutional monarchy
ETHNIC GROUPS  Belgian 91% (Fleming 55%, Walloon 32%), Italian, French, Dutch, Turkish, Moroccan
LANGUAGES  Dutch, French, German (all official)
RELIGIONS  Christianity (Roman Catholic 86%), Islam
CURRENCY  Belgian franc = 100 centimes

# BELIZE

L arger than El Salvador but with only a fraction of its population, Belize is a sparsely populated enclave on the Caribbean coast of Central America, whose head of state is Britain's monarch. A governor-general represents the monarch, while an elected government, headed by a prime minister, actually rules the country.

Behind the swampy coastal plain in the south, the land rises to the low Maya Mountains, which reach a height of 1,120 m [3,674 ft] at Victoria Peak. Northern Belize is mostly low-lying and swampy. The main river, the River Belize, flows across the centre of the country. Offshore lies the world's second biggest coral reef after the Great Barrier Reef.

Belize has a humid tropical climate. Temperatures are high throughout the year and the average yearly rainfall ranges from 1,300 mm [51 in] in the north to over 3,800 mm [150 in] in the south, with February to May the driest months. Hurricanes may sometimes hit the coast, and it was the hurricane damage to Belize City in 1961 that led to the decision to move the capital to Belmopan in 1970.

## ECONOMY AND RESOURCES
The World Bank classifies Belize as a 'lower-middle-income' developing country. Its economy is based on agriculture, and sugar cane is the chief commercial crop and export. Other crops include bananas, beans, citrus fruits, maize and rice. Forestry, fishing and tourism are other important activities, but there are few manufacturing industries.

## HISTORY AND POLITICS
Between about 300 BC and AD 1000, Belize was part of the Maya empire, which extended into Mexico, Guatemala, Honduras and El Salvador. But this civilization had declined long before Spanish explorers reached the coast in the early 16th century.

Spain claimed the area, although no Spaniards settled there. Instead, Spain ruled the area as part of Guatemala. Shipwrecked British sailors founded the first European settlement in the area in 1638. Over the next 150 years, Britain gradually took control of Belize, using slaves to open up the territory. Spain's last attempt to reassert its rule by force was defeated in 1798. In 1862, the area, then known as British Honduras, became a British colony. The country was renamed Belize in 1973 and it became fully independent in 1981.

Guatemala, which had claimed Belize since the early 19th century, objected to the country becoming independent and British troops remained in the country to prevent a possible invasion. In 1983, Guatemala reduced its claim to the southern fifth of Belize, and in the early 1990s improvements in relations with Guatemala, which finally agreed to recognize Belize's independence in 1992, led Britain to announce its decision to withdraw its troops by the end of 1993. [*Map page 30*] ∎

> **AREA** 22,960 sq km [8,865 sq mls]
> **POPULATION** 210,000
> **CAPITAL (POPULATION)** Belmopan (5,000)
> **GOVERNMENT** Constitutional monarchy
> **ETHNIC GROUPS** Mestizo (Spanish-Indian) 44%, Creole (mainly African American) 30%, Mayan Indian 11%, Garifuna (Black-Carib Indian) 7%, White 4%, East Indian 3%
> **LANGUAGES** English (official)
> **RELIGIONS** Christianity (Roman Catholic 58%, Protestant 29%), Hinduism 2%
> **CURRENCY** Belize dollar = 100 cents

# BENIN

P reviously called Dahomey (the name of an old cultured kingdom centred on Abomey), Benin, one of Africa's smallest countries, extends some 620 km [390 mls] north to south, although the coastline is a mere 100 km [62 mls] long. Lagoons line the coast, and the country has no natural harbours. The harbour at Cotonou, Benin's main port and chief commercial centre, is artificial.

Behind the lagoons is a flat plain partly covered by rainforests. About 80 km [50 mls] inland, there is a large marshy depression. In central Benin, the land rises to low plateaux. The highest land is in the north-west. Northern Benin is covered by savanna (grassland with scattered trees), the habitat of such animals as buffaloes, elephants and lions. The north has two national parks, the Penjari and the 'W', which Benin shares with Burkina Faso and Niger.

### ECONOMY AND RESOURCES

Today's dominant tribe in Benin is the Fon, who (with the Yoruba) occupy the more populous and fertile south, mostly as subsistence farmers, growing yams, cassava, sweet potatoes and vegetables. In the central parts and some of the north are the Bariba, renowned for their horsemanship, and the Somba, while some Fulani still follow the increasingly precarious nomadic lifestyle in the far north, the least populated of the regions.

Benin has little to sell, its main exports being palm-oil produce, cotton and groundnuts, with the timber from the central rainforest belt depleting rapidly. Fees from Niger's transit trade through Cotonou are an important additional source of revenue, but illegal trade with Nigeria is also rife. Offshore oil began production in 1982, but output peaked three years later and the industry has since been hampered by low prices.

### HISTORY AND POLITICS

After the Dutch expelled the Portuguese from the Gold Coast in 1642, they established their West African headquarters at Ouidah where, until 1961, there was a tiny Portuguese enclave. Several million slaves were shipped from here, mainly to Brazil, where Dahomean customs survive today among blacks there. Because of early European contact, and through returned ex-slaves, coastal Benin early acquired an educated élite, as did Senegal, Sierra Leone and Gabon.

Rival tribal kingdoms flourished in this part of Africa for centuries until the French began establishing their presence from around 1850, creating a colony (Dahomey) in 1892 and formally making the country part of French West Africa in 1904. Before that, from the 13th century, the area had been the western part of the kingdom (or empire) of Benin, centred on the Nigerian city of that name and famous for its life-size brass heads and plaques and for its ruler, the Oba, from the 15th century. Situated east of Lagos, Benin City is now capital of the Nigerian state of Bendel.

Following independence from France in 1960, the country experienced a series of coups and power struggles, going through 11 changes of government in 12 years. Then, during the military single-party regime of General Mathieu Kerekou, who in 1974 introduced 'scientific socialism' (and the following year dropped the name Dahomey), Benin found itself sitting awkwardly as a Marxist state between the market-oriented economies of Togo and Nigeria. Kerekou officially abandoned his path in 1989, and in 1990 he was forced to concede multiparty elections in a referendum. He was roundly beaten in March 1991, when the country enjoyed a relatively peaceful return to democracy for the first time in nearly two decades. [*Map page 32*] ■

AREA 112,620 sq km [43,483 sq mls]
POPULATION 5,246,000
CAPITAL (POPULATION) Porto-Novo (179,000)
GOVERNMENT Multiparty republic
ETHNIC GROUPS Fon, Adja, Bariba, Yoruba, Fulani, Somba
LANGUAGES French (official)
RELIGIONS Traditional beliefs 60%, Christianity 23%, Islam 15%
CURRENCY CFA franc = 100 centimes

# BERMUDA

Comprising about 150 small islands, the coral caps of ancient submarine volcanoes rising over 4,000 m [13,000 ft] from the ocean floor, Bermuda is situated 920 km [570 mls] east of Cape Hatteras in North

Carolina. Some 20 are inhabited, the vast majority of the population living on the biggest island of Great Bermuda, 21 km [13 mls] long and connected to the other main islands by bridges and causeways. The capital, Hamilton, stands beside a deep harbour on Great Bermuda.

## ECONOMY AND RESOURCES
The pleasant climate, coral sand beaches, historic buildings and pastel-coloured townships attract nearly 505,500 tourists each year, mainly from the USA; but if tourism is the mainstay of the economy, the islands are also a tax haven for overseas companies and individuals. Food and energy needs dominate imports, while (legal) drugs and medicines account for over 50% of exports – though services are the main earners, offsetting a large deficit and giving the islanders an annual per capita income of US$27,800 (1994), the third highest in the world.

## HISTORY AND POLITICS
Uninhabited when discovered by the Spaniard Juan Mermúdez in 1503, the islands were taken over by the British more than a century later (following a shipwreck) and slaves brought in from Virginia to work the land. Today over 60% of the population is of African descent.

Bermuda remains Britain's oldest colony, but with a long tradition of self-government; the parliament dates from 1603. Ties with the US are strong, however, and in 1941 part of the islands was leased for 99 years by Washington for naval and air bases. The government is in regular discussions with the US, UK and Canada over constitutional change, but public opinion continues to oppose moves towards independence ■

---

# BHUTAN

Geographically, a smaller and even more isolated version of Nepal, the remote mountain kingdom of Bhutan faces many of the same problems and hopes for many of the same solutions – notably the harnessing of hydroelectric power from the Himalayas: India has already built one plant and commissioned two more from King Jigme Singye Wangchuk.

The world's most 'rural' country (less than 6% of the population live in towns and over 90% are dependent on agriculture), Bhutan produces mainly rice and maize as staple crops and fruit and cardamom as cash crops. Timber is important, too, though outweighed by cement and talcum in earning foreign exchange. Despite these activities, plus tourism and stamps, the World Bank ranks Bhutan as one of the world's poorest countries. Aircraft and diesel fuels are its main imports, supplying crucial contacts.

Like Nepal, Bhutan was subject to a series of pro-democracy demonstrations in 1990, but because the protesters were mainly Hindus there has been little political progress in this predominantly Buddhist country. The Hindu minority, mostly Nepali-speakers, maintain they are the victims of discrimination, denied basic rights such as religious freedom and the ownership of property. The monarch is head of both state and government, though foreign affairs are under Indian guidance following a treaty of 1949. [*Map page 23*] ■

---

**AREA** 53 sq km [20 sq mls]
**POPULATION** 63,000
**CAPITAL (POPULATION)** Hamilton (3,440)
**GOVERNMENT** British dependency
**ETHNIC GROUPS** Black 61%, White 37%
**LANGUAGES** English
**RELIGIONS** Christianity (Anglican 37%, Roman Catholic 14%, other Christian 25%)
**CURRENCY** Bermuda dollar = 100 cents

---

**AREA** 47,000 sq km [18,147 sq mls]
**POPULATION** 1,614,000
**CAPITAL (POPULATION)** Thimphu (30,340)
**GOVERNMENT** Constitutional monarchy
**ETHNIC GROUPS** Ngalops, Sharchops, Nepalese
**LANGUAGES** Dzongkha (official, a Tibetan dialect), Sharchop, Bumthap, Nepali and English
**RELIGIONS** Buddhism 75%, Hinduism 25%
**CURRENCY** Ngultrum = 100 chetrum

# BOLIVIA

By far the larger of South America's two landlocked countries, Bolivia is made up of a wide stretch of the Andes and a long, broad Oriente – part of the south-western fringe of the Amazon basin. The western boundary is the High Cordillera Occidental, crowned by Sajama at 6,542 m [21,464 ft] and many other volcanic peaks. To the east lies the Altiplano, a high plateau which in prehistoric times was a great lake. Eastwards again rises the Cordillera Real, where Illimani, a glacier-covered peak of 6,462 m [21,200 ft], forms a backdrop to La Paz (The Peace), the world's highest capital. In the transmontane region to the north and east lies the huge expanse of the Oriente – foothills and plains extending from the semi-arid Chaco of the south-east through the savanna-like *llanos* of the centre to the high, wetter forests of the northern plains.

## ECONOMY AND RESOURCES

Today Bolivia is the poorest of the South American republics, though it has abundant natural resources with large reserves of petroleum, natural gas and many mineral ores. Lack of investment both in these areas and in the agricultural sector does not help the comparatively poor development, but new irrigation schemes in the south-western Oriente may improve local production of staple foods. Over half the working population is engaged in agriculture, but mining still contributes significantly to the country's wealth. However, Bolivia, once the world's leading tin producer, now ranks fifth with 7.6% of the total. Today's main export may well be coca and refined cocaine; the government, with US help and cooperation with neighbours, is trying to stifle the growing industry.

The collapse of the tin market was linked to the record inflation of 1985 – figures vary between 12,000% and over 20,000%, and the 1980–8 average was the world's worst at 483% – though the rates were more stable by the end of the decade.

## THE ALTIPLANO

A high, rolling plateau 3,600 m [12,000 ft] above sea level on the Peruvian border of Bolivia, the Altiplano stretches 400 km [250 mls] north to south between the eastern and western cordilleras of the Andes. Surrounded by high, snow-capped peaks, at its north end lies Lake Titicaca, the highest navigable body of water in the world and according to Indian legend the birthplace of the Inca civilization. To the south are smaller lakes, and extensive salt flats representing old lake beds. Though tropical in latitude the Altiplano is cold, windswept and bleak, by any standards a harsh environment, yet over half the population of Bolivia, including a high proportion of native Indians, make it their home.

The natural vegetation is grassland merging at high levels to *puna* – small bushes and trees forming a harsh scrubland. Summer rains and winter snows bring enough moisture to support grass, and the Altiplano is grazed by guanaco and vicuña as well as many smaller herbivores – chinchillas, viscachas and guinea-pigs. Llama and alpaca, domesticated from guanaco-like ancestors, are herded to provide meat and wool for the peasant farmers. Small and tough, the local people are physiologically adapted for life at high altitude, with more blood, more oxygen-carrying haemoglobin and more efficient lungs than the Indians of the foothills.

## HISTORY AND POLITICS

In pre-Conquest days Bolivia was the homeland of the Tiahuanaco culture (7th to 11th centuries AD) and was later absorbed into the Inca empire; Quechua, the Inca language, is still spoken by large Amerindian minorities that constitute the highest proportion of any South American country. Famous for its silver mines, the high Andean area was exploited ruthlessly by the Spanish *conquistadores*; the mine at Potosí, discovered in 1545, proved the richest in the world, and Upper Peru (today's highland Bolivia) was for two centuries one of the most densely populated of Spain's American colonies. In 1824 the local population seized their independence, naming the country after Simón Bolívar, hero of other South American wars of independence. When the era of silver passed, the economy flagged and the country began to lose ground to its neighbours. The Pacific coast was lost to Chile and Peru in 1884 and large tracts of the Oriente were ceded to Brazil (1903) and Paraguay (1935). Bolivia is renowned for its political volatility: it has suffered 192 coups in 156 years from independence to 1981. Since 1982, however, it has had democratically elected governments. [*Map page 31*] ■

---

**AREA** 1,098,580 sq km [424,162 sq mls]
**POPULATION** 7,237,000
**CAPITAL (POPULATION)** La Paz (1,126,000)
**GOVERNMENT** Multiparty republic
**ETHNIC GROUPS** Mestizo 31%, Quechua 25%, Aymara 17%, White 15%
**LANGUAGES** Spanish, Aymara, Quechua (all official)
**RELIGIONS** Christianity (Roman Catholic 94%)
**CURRENCY** Boliviano = 100 centavos

---

# BOSNIA-HERZEGOVINA

---

The Republic of Bosnia-Herzegovina is one of the five republics to emerge from the former Federal People's Republic of Yugoslavia. Much of the country is mountainous or hilly, with an arid limestone plateau in the south-west. The River Sava, which forms most of the northern border with Croatia, is a tributary of the River Danube. Because of the country's odd shape, the coastline is limited to a short stretch of 20 km [13 mls] on the Adriatic coast.

Mediterranean conditions, with sunny, dry summers and mild, moist winters, prevail only near the coast. Inland, the weather becomes more severe, with hot, dry summers and bitterly cold, snowy winters. The north has the most severe weather, where forests of beech, oak and pine are found. The south has bare limestone landscapes, interspersed with farmland and pasture, which together cover nearly half of the country.

## ECONOMY AND RESOURCES

The economy of Bosnia-Herzegovina, the least developed of the six republics of the former Yugoslavia apart from Macedonia, was shattered by the war in the early 1990s. Before the war, manufactures were the main exports, including electrical equipment, machinery and transport equipment, and textiles, while farm products included fruits, maize, tobacco, vegetables and wheat. There are reserves of coal and iron ore.

## HISTORY AND POLITICS

Slavs settled in the area that is now Bosnia-Herzegovina around 1,400 years ago. In the late 15th century, the area was taken by the Ottoman Turks. Austria-Hungary gained temporary control over Bosnia-Herzegovina in 1878, formally taking over the area in 1908. In 1914, World War I began when Austria-Hungary's Archduke Francis Ferdinand was assassinated in Sarajevo.

In 1918, Bosnia-Herzegovina became part of the Kingdom of the Serbs, Croats and Slovenes, which was renamed Yugoslavia in 1929. Germany occupied the area during World War II. But from 1945, Communist governments ruled Yugoslavia as a federation containing six republics, one of which was Bosnia-Herzegovina. In the 1980s, the country faced problems as Communist policies proved unsuccessful and differences arose between the country's ethnic groups.

In 1990, free elections were held in Bosnia-Herzegovina and non-Communists won a majority. A Muslim, Alija Izetbegovic, was elected president. In 1991, Croatia and Slovenia, other parts of the former Yugoslavia, declared themselves independent. In 1992, Bosnia-Herzegovina held a vote on independence – most Bosnian Serbs boycotted the vote, while the Muslims and Bosnian Croats voted in favour.

Many Bosnian Serbs, opposed to independence, now started a war against the non-Serbs. They soon occupied more than two-thirds of the land. In their 'ethnic cleansing' campaign, heavily-equipped Bosnian Serb militias drove Muslims from towns they had long inhabited. By early 1993, the Muslims controlled less than a third of the former federal republic, and even the capital, Sarajevo, was disputed territory under constant shellfire. The war was later extended when Croat forces seized other parts of the country.

In 1993 and 1994, the United Nations tried to find a way of ending the war by dividing Bosnia-Herzegovina into self-governing provinces, under a unified, multi-ethnic central government. But attempts to produce a map of provincial boundaries met with failure. [*Map page 16*] ■

> **AREA** 51,129 sq km [19,745 sq mls]
> **POPULATION** 3,527,000
> **CAPITAL (POPULATION)** Sarajevo (525,980)
> **GOVERNMENT** Transitional
> **ETHNIC GROUPS** Muslim 49%, Serb 31%, Croat 17%
> **LANGUAGES** Serbo-Croatian
> **RELIGIONS** Islam 40%, Christianity (Serbian Orthodox 31%, Roman Catholic 15%, Protestant 4%)
> **CURRENCY** Dinar = 100 paras

# BOTSWANA

**M**ore than half of the land area is occupied by the Kalahari Desert, with much of the rest taken up by saltpans and swamps. Although the Kalahari extends into Namibia and South Africa, Botswana accounts for the greater part of this vast dry upland. It is, however, not a uniform desert: occasional rainfall allows growth of grasses and thorny scrub, enabling the area's sparse human population of about 100,000 – mostly nomadic Bantu herdsmen – to graze their cattle.

## ECONOMY AND RESOURCES

When it became independent in 1966, Botswana was one of the world's poorest countries, with cattle as the only significant export. The country was transformed by the mining of vast diamond resources, starting at Orapa in 1971, and, despite a protracted drought, expanding output in the 1980s made the economy the fastest growing in sub-Saharan Africa, paving the way for wide-ranging social programmes. Indeed, by 1993 Botswana was producing some 15% of the world's total.

Politically stable under Seretse Khama, the country's main target became diversification, not only to reduce dependence on diamonds (85% of export earnings) and on South African imports, but also to create jobs for a rapidly expanding population. Copper has been mined at Selebi-Pikwe since 1974, but the emphasis in the 1990s is on tourism: 17% of Botswana's huge area (the world's highest figure) is assigned to wildlife conservation and game reserves, and more than half a million visitors a year are drawn to them.

## HISTORY AND POLITICS

The earliest inhabitants of the region were the San, who are also called Bushmen. They had a nomadic way of life, hunting wild animals and collecting wild plant foods. The Tswana, who speak a Bantu language, now form the majority of the population. They are cattle owners, who settled in eastern Botswana more than 1,000 years ago. Their arrival led the San to move into the dry Kalahari region. Today, the San form a tiny minority of the population. Most of them live in permanent settlements and work on cattle ranches.

Britain ruled the area as the Bechuanaland Protectorate between 1885 and 1966. When the country became independent, it adopted the name of Botswana. Since then, unlike many African countries, Botswana has been a stable multiparty democracy. [*Map page 33*] ■

> **AREA** 581,730 sq km [224,606 sq mls]
> **POPULATION** 1,443,000
> **CAPITAL (POPULATION)** Gaborone (133,470)
> **GOVERNMENT** Multiparty republic
> **ETHNIC GROUPS** Tswana 75%, Shona 12%, San (Bushmen) 3%
> **LANGUAGES** English (official), Setswana (national language)
> **RELIGIONS** Traditional beliefs 50%, Christianity 50%
> **CURRENCY** Pula = 100 thebe

# BRAZIL

By any standard Brazil is a big country. Fifth largest in the world, it covers nearly 48% of South America. Structurally, it has two main regions. In the north lies the vast Amazon basin, once an inland sea and now drained by a river system that carries one-fifth of the Earth's running water. In the centre and south lies the sprawling bulk of the Brazilian Highlands, a huge extent of hard crystalline rock deeply dissected into rolling uplands. This occupies the heartland (Mato Grosso), and the whole western flank of the country from the bulge to the border with Uruguay.

The Amazon River rises in the Peruvian Andes, close to the Pacific Ocean, and many of its tributaries are of similar origin. Several are wide enough to take boats of substantial draught (6 m [20 ft]) from the Andean foothills all the way to the Atlantic – a distance of 5,000 km [3,000 mls] or more.

The largest area of river plain lies in the upper part of the basin, along the frontier with Bolivia and Peru. Downstream the flood plain is relatively narrow, shrinking in width to a few kilometres where the basin drains between the Guiana Highlands in the north and the Brazilian Highlands in the south. Overall only 1–2% of the Amazon Valley is alluvial flood plain; away from this the soils are heavily leached and infertile, and liable to be washed away by tropical rainstorms if the protective canopy of forest is felled: this, unfortunately, is happening at an increasingly alarming rate.

The undulating plateau of the northern highlands also carries poor soils; here rainfall is seasonal, and the typical natural vegetation is a thorny scrub forest, used as open grazing for poor cattle herds. Further south scrub turns to wooded savanna – the *campo cerrado* vegetation that covers 2 million sq km [770,000 sq mls] of the interior plateau. It extends into the basin of the Paraná River and its tributaries, most of which start in the coastal highlands and flow west, draining ultimately into the Plate estuary. The Mato Grosso, on the border with Bolivia, is part of this area and still largely unexplored. The north-eastern uplands are poor farming country; dry for at least half the year, they occasionally suffer long periods of drought.

Conditions are better in the south, with more reliable rainfall. The south-east includes a narrow coastal plain, swampy in places and with abundant rainfall throughout the year; behind rises the Great Escarpment (820 m [2,700 ft]), first in a series of steps to the high eastern edge of the plateau. Over 60% of Brazil's population live in four southern and south-eastern states that account for only 17% of the total area.

## ECONOMY AND RESOURCES

For many decades following the early settlements, Brazil was mainly a sugar-producing colony, with most plantations centred on the rich coastal plains of the north-east. Later the same areas produced cotton, cocoa, rice and other crops. In the south, colonists penetrated the interior in search of slaves and minerals, especially gold and diamonds; the city of Ouro Prêto in Minas Gerais was built, and Rio de Janeiro grew as the port for the region.

During the 19th century São Paulo state became the centre of a huge coffee-growing industry; and while the fortunes made in mining helped to develop Rio de Janeiro, profits from coffee were invested in the city of São Paulo. Immigrants from Italy and Germany settled in the south, introducing farming into the fertile valleys in co-existence with the cattle ranchers and gauchos whose herds dominated the plains.

The second half of the 19th century saw the development of the wild rubber industry in the Amazon basin, where the city of Manaus, with its world-famous opera house, served as a centre and market; though Manaus lies 1,600 km [1,000 mls] from the mouth of the Amazon, rubber collected from trees in the hinterland could be shipped out directly to world markets in ocean-going steamers. Brazil enjoyed a virtual monopoly of the rubber trade until the early 20th century, when Malayan plantations began to compete, later with massive success.

Vast mineral resources exist, particularly in Minas Gerais and the Amazon area; they include bauxite, tin, iron ore, manganese,

## THE AMAZON

Though not the world's longest river – 6,430 km [3,990 mls] – the Amazon is easily the mightiest, discharging some 180,000 cu m/sec [6,350,000 cu ft/sec] into the Atlantic, more than four times the volume of its nearest rival, the Zaïre. The flow is so great that silt discolours the water up to 200 km [125 mls] out to sea, and the river accounts for a fifth of the world's total river discharge into the oceans.

The Amazon starts its journey in the Andes of Peru – only 150 km [95 mls] from the Pacific – at Lake Villafro, head of the Apurimac branch of the Ucayali, which then flows north to join the other main headstream, the Marañón. Navigable to ocean-going vessels of 6,000 tonnes up to the Peruvian jungle port of Iquitos, some 3,700 km [2,300 mls] from the sea, it then flows east, briefly forming the Peru-Colombian border – before entering Brazil. Here it becomes the Solimões before joining the Negro (itself 18 km [11 mls] wide) at Manaus, where river levels can vary by over 15 m [50 ft] in a year.

Along with more than 1,000 significant tributaries, seven of which are more than 1,600 km [1,000 mls] long, the Amazon drains the largest river basin in the world – about 7 million sq km [2.7 million sq mls] – nearly two-fifths of South America and an area more than twice the size of India. This vast river system provides a crucial network of communications through the otherwise impenetrable jungle: the total is around 43,000 km [27,000 mls].

For nearly half its length the Amazon flows through the world's largest and most important rainforest (*selva*) – a mantle of 6.5 million sq km [2.5 million sq mls] covering an area larger than the whole of Western Europe.

chrome, nickel, uranium, platinum and industrial diamonds. Brazil is the world's leading exporter of iron ore and there are reserves of at least 18,000 million metric tons including the world's biggest at Carajás. Discoveries of new reserves of minerals are frequently

being made. The world's largest tin mine is situated in the Amazon region, 50% of the world's platinum is in Brazil, and 65% of the world's supply of precious stones are produced within the country.

The demand for energy has increased rapidly over the years and over a quarter of imports are for crude petroleum. An alternative energy was developed from 1976 made from sugar cane and cassava called ethanol (combustible alcohol) with the aim of reducing demand for petroleum, and in the eight years to 1987, some 3.5 million cars were manufactured to take this fuel; falling oil prices later made this uneconomic. Large investments have been made in hydroelectricity – 93% of the country's electricity is now from water – and the Itaipú HEP station on the Paraná, shared with Paraguay, is the world's largest.

Brazil is one of the world's largest farming countries, and agriculture employs 35% of the population and provides 40% of her exports. The main agricultural exports are coffee, sugar, soya beans, orange juice concentrates, beef, cocoa, poultry, sisal, tobacco, maize and cotton. While Brazil is no longer the leading exporter of coffee – a position now held by Colombia – the country is the world's biggest producer, as it is for sugar cane, bananas, oranges, sisal and castor oil.

The manufacturing industry includes the production of steel, chemicals, machinery, vehicles, pharmaceuticals, cement, timber, paper, shipping and consumer goods. There is also offshore oil production, and nearly 70% of the country's output comes from the continental shelf. The Amazon basin is gradually being opened for the controversial exploitation of forests and mines, with Santarém a new focus of agriculture in a frontier land. There are 35 deep-water ports in Brazil, and the two main oil terminals at São Sebastião and Madre de Jesus are being expanded. Though river transport now plays only a minor part in the movement of goods, for many years rivers gave the only access to the interior, and there are plans to link the Amazon and the Upper Paraná to give a navigable waterway across central Brazil.

A network of arterial roads is being added and these are replacing the 19th-century railways which have been used to take primary products to markets on the coast. Road transport now accounts for 70% of the movement of freight and 97% of passenger traffic.

## POPULATION

In 1872 Brazil had a population of about 10 million. By 1972 this had increased almost tenfold, and 1994 saw a figure of 159.1 million Brazilians – with a projected increase to 179.5 million by the end of the century. Of the economically active population (55 million in 1985), 15 million were engaged in agriculture, 9 million in the service industries, 8 million in manufacturing, 5 million in the wholesale and retail trade, and 3 million in construction.

On 21 April 1960, Rio de Janeiro ceased to be the capital and inland the new city of Brasilia, built from 1956 onwards, in many ways encapsulated both the spirit and the problems of contemporary Brazil – a sparkling, dramatic, planned city, deliberately planted in the unpopulated uplands of Goías as a gesture of faith; modern, practical and beautiful, but still surrounded by the shanties of poverty and – beyond them – the challenge of an untamed wilderness.

So much of the nation's wealth is still held by the élites of the cities, particularly those of the south-east, and despite grandiose development plans aimed at spreading prosperity throughout the country, the interior remains poor and underpopulated.

Although possessing great reserves, Brazil has not made the big jump from developing to developed country. The boom of 'the miracle years' from 1968 to 1973, when the economy grew at more than 10% per annum, was not sustained. Indeed, falls in commodity prices and massive borrowing to finance large and often unproductive projects have combined to make Brazil the world's biggest debtor nation; despite paying back $69 billion between 1985 and 1991 – a huge drain on any economy – there was still over $120 billion owed. Inflation during 1990 was nearly 3,000% – down to under 400% in 1991 – and mismanagement and corruption still afflicted administration. In August 1993, an attempt to control the monthly inflation of over 30% was made by the introduction of a new currency, the Cruzeiro real. While Brazil does not have

## THE AMAZON RAINFOREST

The world's largest and ecologically most important rainforest was still being destroyed at an alarming rate in the late 1980s, with somewhere between 1.5% and 4% disappearing each year in Brazil alone. Opening up the forest for many reasons – logging, mining, ranching, peasant resettlement – the Brazilian authorities did little in real terms when confronted with a catalogue of indictments: decimation of a crucial world habitat; pollution of rivers; destruction of thousands of species of fauna and flora, especially medicinal plants; and the brutal ruination of the lives of the last remaining Amerindian tribes.

Once cut off from the world by impenetrable jungle, hundreds of thousands of Indians have been displaced in the provinces of Rondonia and Acre, principally by loggers and landless migrants, and in Para by mining, dams for HEP and ranching for beef cattle. It is estimated that five centuries ago the Amazon rainforest supported some 2 million Indians in more than 200 tribes; today the number has shrunk to a pitiful 50,000 or so, and many of the tribes have disappeared altogether.

A handful have been relatively lucky – the Yanomani, after huge international support, won their battle in 1991 for a reserve three times the size of Belgium – but for the majority their traditional lifestyle has vanished forever.

the huge population growths of many African and Asian countries, it does have poverty on a large scale.

### HISTORY AND POLITICS

Brazil was 'discovered' by Pedro Alvarez Cabral on 22 April 1500 and gradually penetrated by Portuguese settlers, missionaries, explorers and prospectors during the 17th and 18th centuries. Many of the semi-nomadic Indians indigenous to the country were enslaved for plantation work or driven into the interior, and some 4 million African slaves were introduced, notably in the sugar-growing areas of the north-east.

## RIO DE JANEIRO & SÃO PAULO

Much of Brazil's population is concentrated in a relatively small and highly developed 'corner' in the south-east of the country. Rio de Janeiro, discovered by the Portuguese in 1502, lies in a magnificent setting, stretching for 20 km [12 mls] along the coast between mountain and ocean, its superb harbour overlooked by Sugar Loaf Mountain and, on Corcovado, the famous statue of Christ. Though no longer the capital, it remains the focus of Brazil's cultural life, attracting visitors with the world's greatest pre-Lent festival at carnival time.

São Paulo, its early growth fuelled by the coffee boom of the late 19th century, is the most populous city in the southern hemisphere and rivals Mexico City as the world's fastest growing and largest conurbation. Estimates state that the 1985 total of 15.5 million will increase to 22.1 million by the year 2000. In both cities the yawning gap between rich and poor is all too evident, the sprawling shanty towns (*favelas*) on the fringes standing in sharp contrast to sophisticated metropolitan centres.

Little more than a group of rival provinces, Brazil began to unite in 1808 when the Portuguese royal court, seeking refuge from Napoleon, transferred from Lisbon to Rio de Janeiro. The eldest surviving son of King Joãs VI of Portugal was chosen as 'Perpetual Defender' of Brazil by a national congress. In 1822 he proclaimed the independence of the country and was chosen as the constitutional emperor with the title Pedro I. He abdicated in 1831 and was succeeded by his son, Pedro II, who ruled for nearly 50 years and whose liberal policies included the gradual abolition of slavery (1888).

A federal system was adopted for the United States of Brazil in the 1881 constitution and Brazil became a republic in 1889. Until 1930 the country experienced strong economic expansion and prosperity, but social unrest in 1930 resulted in a major revolt and from then until 1945 the country was under the control of President Vargas, who established a strong corporate state similar to that of fascist Italy, although Brazil entered World War II on the side of the Allies. Democracy, often corrupt, prevailed from 1956 to 1964 and from 1985; between were five military presidents of illiberal regimes.

A new constitution came into force in October 1988 – the eighth since independence from the Portuguese in 1822 – which transferred powers from the president to congress and paved the way for a return to democracy in 1990. Today the country comprises 23 states, each with its own directly elected governor and legislature, three territories and the Federal District of Brasília. [*Map page 31*] ■

**AREA** 8,511,970 sq km [3,286,472 sq mls]
**POPULATION** 159,143,000
**CAPITAL (POPULATION)** Brasília (1,596,000)
**GOVERNMENT** Federal republic
**ETHNIC GROUPS** White 53%, Mulatto 22%, Mestizo 12%, African American 11%, Japanese 1%, Amerindian 0.1%
**LANGUAGES** Portuguese (official)
**RELIGIONS** Christianity (Roman Catholic 88%, Protestant 6%)
**CURRENCY** Cruzeiro real = 100 centavos

# BRUNEI

Comprising two small enclaves on the coast of northern Borneo, Brunei rises from humid plains to forested mountains over 1,800 m [6,000 ft] high along the Malaysian border.

Formerly a British protectorate, and still a close ally of the UK, the country was already rich from oil (discovered by Shell in 1929) when it became independent in 1983. Today oil and gas account for 70% of GDP and even more of export earnings – oil 41%, gas 53% – though income from the resultant investments overseas exceeds both. Imports are dominated by machinery, transport equipment, manufactures and foodstuffs. Brunei is, however, currently undergoing a drive towards agricultural self-sufficiency. The revenues have made Sultan Hassanal Bolkiah (crowned 1968) allegedly the world's richest man, and given his people the second highest income per capita in Asia after Japan. There is no income tax system in Brunei and citizens enjoy free cradle-to-the-grave welfare. All government employees (two-thirds of the workforce) are banned from political activity, and the Sultan and his family retain firm control. [*Map page 26*] ∎

---

**AREA** 5,770 sq km [2,228 sq mls]
**POPULATION** 280,000
**CAPITAL (POPULATION)** Bandar Seri Begawan (46,000)
**GOVERNMENT** Absolute monarchy with an advisory council
**ETHNIC GROUPS** Malay 69%, Chinese 18%, Indian
**LANGUAGES** Malay and English (both official), Chinese
**RELIGIONS** Islam 63%, Buddhism 14%, Christianity 10%
**CURRENCY** Brunei dollar = 100 cents

---

# BULGARIA

The Balkan Mountains (Stara Planina), which rise to heights of over 2,000 m [6,500 ft], stretch across the centre of the country, from the eastern coastal areas bordering the Black Sea to the west, separating two lowland areas: the Danubian lowlands to the north and the Maritsa Valley to the south. The climate is one of hot summers and fairly cold winters.

## ECONOMY AND RESOURCES
With fertile soils but few natural resources, Bulgaria's economy has a distinct agricultural bias, with half the population still earning their living from the land. The most productive agriculture occurs in the two lowland areas – the hills sloping down to the Danube, where wheat, barley and maize are the chief crops,

and the warmer central valley of the River Maritsa, where grains, cotton, rice, tobacco, fruits and vines are grown.

In the south-facing valleys overlooking the Maritsa plains, the main crops are plums, vine and tobacco. A particular feature of this area is the rose fields of Kazanluk, from which attar of roses is exported worldwide to the cosmetics industry.

South and west of the Maritsa Valley are the Rhodopi Mountains, containing lead, zinc and copper ores. There are also rich mineral veins of both iron and non-ferrous metals in the Stara Planina, north of the capital and chief industrial city, Sofia.

## HISTORY AND POLITICS
The most subservient of the former Eastern bloc satellites, Bulgaria's links with Russia date back to 1878, when the Tsar's forces liberated the country from five centuries of Ottoman (Turkish) rule. In the period after World War II, and especially under President Zhivkov from 1954, Bulgaria became all too dependent on its overseer; nearly two-thirds of its trade (much of it subsidized) was conducted with the USSR – including most of its energy requirements.

Predictably, Bulgaria was the last and least publicized of the Eastern European countries to fall. In 1990 the Communist Party held on to power under increasing pressure by ousting Zhivkov, renouncing its leading role in the nation's affairs, making many promises of social and economic reform and changing its name to the Socialist Party before winning the first free elections since the war – unconvincingly and against confused opposition. With better organization the Union of Democratic Forces defeated the old guard the following year and began the unenviable task of making the transition from central planning to a free-market economy.

The new government inherited a host of problems – inflation, food shortages, rising unemployment, strikes, large foreign debt, limited Western interest, a declining traditional manufacturing industry, reduced demand at home and abroad, increased prices for vital raw materials, and a potential drop in the recently growing revenue from tourism. In addition there was the nagging worry of a sizeable Turkish minority disaffected with mismanaged attempts at forced assimilation. [*Map page 17*] ■

**AREA** 110,910 sq km [42,822 sq mls]
**POPULATION** 8,818,000
**CAPITAL (POPULATION)** Sofia (1,221,000)
**GOVERNMENT** Multiparty republic
**ETHNIC GROUPS** Bulgarian 86%, Turkish 10%, Gypsy 3%, Macedonian 3%, Armenian, Romanian, Greek
**LANGUAGES** Bulgarian (official)
**RELIGIONS** Christianity (Eastern Orthodox 87%), Islam 13%
**CURRENCY** Lev = 100 stotinki

# BURKINA FASO

As large as Italy, and with just over 10 million inhabitants, landlocked Burkina Faso ('land of upright men') is nevertheless overpopulated: low, seasonal and erratic rainfall, thin, eroded soils, desertification and a dearth of other natural resources combine to keep it one of the poorest and most agrarian states in the world, heavily reliant on aid.

## ECONOMY AND RESOURCES
The Mossi people, who are the majority tribe, live around Ouagadougou, the capital; another major group, the Bobo, dwell around the second city of Bobo Dioulasso. Both grow cotton and millet, guinea corn (sorghum) and groundnuts for food, and collect shea nuts for cooking oil. Nomadic Fulani keep cattle. Though small surpluses of all these products are sold overseas and to the better-off countries to the south, especially the Ivory Coast, remittances sent home by migrants working in those countries probably provide most of Burkina Faso's foreign income. Manganese mining could be developed in the far northeast, though this would necessitate an extension, 340 km [210 mls] long, to the railway from Abidjan which is already 1,145 km [715 mls] long. Another hope lies in eliminating the

simulium fly, whose bite causes blindness. This would permit settlement and farming of the valleys, which have the most fertile and best watered lands. Among these is the 'W' national park, shared with Niger and Benin.

## HISTORY AND POLITICS
Burkina Faso (known until 1984 as Upper Volta) is the successor to Mossi, an early West African state dating from 1100. Plagued by numerous coups and political assassinations, the country tasted democracy in December 1991 for the first time in more than a decade when the military regime of Blaise Compaore granted elections. However, 20 opposition parties combined to produce a boycott involving 76% of the electorate (claiming that it was a ploy to legitimize the military rule), and the government registered a hollow victory. [*Map page 32*] ■

**AREA** 274,200 sq km [105,869 sq mls]
**POPULATION** 10,046,000
**CAPITAL (POPULATION)** Ouagadougou (634,000)
**GOVERNMENT** Multiparty republic
**ETHNIC GROUPS** Mossi 48%, Mande 9%, Fulani 8%, Bobo 7%
**LANGUAGES** French (official)
**RELIGIONS** Traditional beliefs 45%, Islam 43%, Christianity 12%
**CURRENCY** CFA franc = 100 centimes

# BURMA (MYANMAR)

Geographically, the country has three main regions. The core area is a great structural depression, largely drained by the Chindwin and Irrawaddy rivers. Its coastal zone has a wet climate, but the inner region between Prome and Mandalay constitutes a 'dry zone', sheltered from the south-west monsoon and with an annual rainfall of less than 1,000 mm [40 in].

To the west lie the fold mountains of the Arakan Yoma, while to the east rises the great

Shan Plateau. In the south-east, running down the isthmus that takes Burma on to the Malay Peninsula, are the uplands of the Tenasserim, with hundreds of islands dotted along the coast of the Andaman Sea.

## ECONOMY AND RESOURCES

Once a green and gentle land, rich in agriculture and timber and blessed with many natural resources from precious stones to oil, Burma has become one of the three poorest countries in Asia.

More than 60% of the country is forested, rubber plantations augmenting the indigenous teak. In the dry zone, which was the original nucleus of the Burmese state, small-scale irrigation has long been practised in the narrow valleys, and rice, cotton, jute and sugar cane are important crops. Until 1964 Burma was the world's leading exporter of rice, and the crop still accounts for more than 40% of Burma's meagre export earnings. This central area was also the base of Burmah Oil, hosting the small fields that once made the country the British Empire's second largest producer. Even today it has sufficient oil and gas to meet most of Burma's needs.

## HISTORY AND POLITICS

British since 1895, Burma was separate from India as a crown colony in 1937. A battleground for Japanese and British troops in World War II, it became an independent republic in 1948 and left the Commonwealth. Military dictatorship came in 1962 and a one-party state in 1974, both headed by General Ne Win, leader of the Burma Socialist Programme Party.

The party's rigid combination of state control, Buddhism and isolation, under the banner 'The Burmese Way to Socialism', had disastrous results, the country plunging quickly from prosperity to poverty. Politically, too, Burma was in a perilous state, with over a third of the country in rebel hands.

In the south-east the guerrillas of two Karen liberation movements control large tracts of mountains near the Thai border; in the north and east the Burmese Communist Party holds sway in most of Kachin and a good deal of Shan; here also, at the western end of the 'Golden Triangle', the authorities try to contain the local warlords' trafficking in opium. Another flashpoint is in the west, where Rohinya, the Muslim minority, have been persecuted by the army and repeatedly pushed over the border with Bangladesh in tens of thousands.

Burma spends more than 35% of its budget on 'defence' – much of it on the brutal suppression of political opposition and of human rights. In 1990, the coalition NLD won over 80% of the votes in a multiparty election conceded by the regime following violent demonstrations, but the ruling junta simply refused to accept the result – keeping its leader, Nobel Peace Prize winner Aung San Suu Kyi, under house arrest until July 1995. The powerless opposition were forced to renounce the result and agree to a new and no doubt again ineffective agenda for a return to democracy.

Meanwhile, the country continued to crumble, if with great charm; despite the hideous regime a black market flourishes behind the crumbling colonial façade of Rangoon, once a rival to Bangkok and Singapore. Though some visitors make the trips round the attractions of Rangoon, Mandalay and Pagan, tourism is hardly encouraged by the suspicious government, and most of the country is still closed to foreigners.

A change of name – the title Union of Myanmar was officially adopted in 1989 – has not changed the political complexion of a desperate nation. Burma remains an anomaly, holding out almost friendless against the tide of democratic and diplomatic changes that swept the world in the late 1980s and early 1990s. It seems that, even with some form of conciliation, it will not long survive as a geopolitical entity. [*Map page 23*] ∎

**AREA** 676,577 sq km [261,228 sq mls]
**POPULATION** 45,555,000
**CAPITAL (POPULATION)** Rangoon (or Yangon, 2,513,000)
**GOVERNMENT** Military regime
**ETHNIC GROUPS** Burman 69%, Shan 9%, Karen 6%, Rakhine 5%, Mon 2%, Chin 2%
**LANGUAGES** Burmese (official)
**RELIGIONS** Buddhism 89%, Christianity 5%, Islam 4%
**CURRENCY** Kyat = 100 pyas

# BURUNDI

The Republic of Burundi is the fifth smallest country on the mainland of Africa. It is also the second most densely populated after its northern neighbour Rwanda. Part of the deep Great Rift Valley, which runs throughout eastern Africa into south-western Asia, lies in western Burundi. It includes part of Lake Tanganyika.

East of the Rift Valley are high mountains, reaching 2,670 m [8,760 ft], composed partly of volcanic rocks. In central and eastern Burundi, the land descends in a series of steplike grassy plateaus.

Grasslands cover much of the country. The land was formerly mainly forest, but farmers have cleared most of the trees. Soil erosion is a serious problem, and in some areas new forests are being planted to protect the soil against the rain and wind.

## ECONOMY AND RESOURCES

Burundi is one of the world's ten poorest countries. About 92% of the people are farmers, who mostly grow little more than they need to feed their families. The main food crops are beans, cassava, maize and sweet potatoes. Cattle, goats are sheep are raised, while fish, caught in Lake Tanganyika, are an important supplement to the diets of local people. The main cash crops are coffee, which accounts for over 80% of the exports, tea and cotton. Manufacturing is on a small scale, with most of the factories based in Bujumbura.

## HISTORY AND POLITICS

The Twa, a pygmy people, were the first known inhabitants of Burundi. About 1,000 years ago, the Hutu, a people who speak a Bantu language, gradually began to settle the area, pushing the Twa into remote areas. From the 15th century, the Tutsi, a cattle-owning people from the north-east, gradually took over the country. The Hutu, although greatly outnumbering the Tutsi, were forced to serve the Tutsi overlords.

Germany conquered the area that is now Burundi and Rwanda in the 1890s. The area, called Ruanda-Urundi, was taken by Belgium during World War I. In 1961, the people of Urundi voted to become a monarchy, while the people of Ruanda voted to become a republic. The two territories became fully independent as Burundi and Rwanda in 1962.

After 1962, the rivalries between the Hutu and Tutsi led to periodic outbreaks of fighting. The Tutsi monarchy was overthrown in 1966 and Burundi became a republic. But massacres of thousands of people still occurred as the Tutsi and Hutu fought for power. The worst recent manifestation was in 1972, when the murder of the deposed king in an attempted coup led to the massacre of more than 100,000 Hutu, but some 20,000 were also killed in 1988. As in Rwanda, the indigenous pygmoid Twa people now comprise a tiny proportion of a burgeoning population. The first democratic presidential election, which a Hutu won, took place in 1993. [*Map page 33*] ■

AREA 27,830 sq km [10,745 sq mls]
POPULATION 6,209,000
CAPITAL (POPULATION) Bujumbura (235,000)
GOVERNMENT Republic
ETHNIC GROUPS Hutu 85%, Tutsi 14%, Twa (pygmy) 1%
LANGUAGES French and Kirundi (both official)
RELIGIONS Christianity 85% (Roman Catholic 78%), traditional beliefs 13%
CURRENCY Burundi franc = 100 centimes

# CAMBODIA

The heartland of Cambodia is a wide basin drained by the Mekong River, in the centre of which lies the Tonlé Sap ('Great Lake'), a former arm of the sea surrounded by a broad plain. From November to June, when rains are meagre and the Mekong low, the lake drains to the south and away to the sea. During the rainy season and period of high river water in June to October the flow reverses, and the lake more than doubles its area to become the largest freshwater lake in Asia.

To the south-west stand low mountain chains, while the northern rim of the country is bounded by the Phanom Dangrek uplands, with a prominent sandstone escarpment. Three-quarters of the country is forested, and 90% of the population live on the fertile plains, mostly in small village settlements; Phnom Penh, the capital of Cambodia, is the only major city.

### ECONOMY AND RESOURCES
The wealth of 'the gentle kingdom' rested on abundant fish from the lake and rice from the flooded lowlands, for which an extensive system of irrigation channels and storage reservoirs was developed.

In a short period of stability during the late 1950s and 1960s the country developed its small-scale agricultural resources and rubber plantations – it has few workable minerals or sources of power – remaining predominantly rural but achieving self-sufficiency in food, with some exports. However, civil war and the Khmer Rouge regime have left Cambodia devastated.

### HISTORY AND POLITICS
The Tonlé Sap lowlands were the cradle of the great Khmer Empire, which lasted from 802 to 1432; its zenith came in the reign of Suryavarman II (1113–50), who built the great funerary temple of Angkor Wat: together with Angkor Thom, the 600 Hindu temples form the world's largest group of religious buildings.

Cambodia was under French rule from 1863 as part of French Indo-China, achieving independence in 1954. This was followed by years of internal political struggles, involvement in the Vietnam War, a destructive civil war and a four-year period of ruthless Khmer Rouge dictatorship, under which Pol Pot ordered the genocide of somewhere between 1 million and 2.5 million people. After the overthrow of Pol Pot in 1979 by Vietnam there was a civil war between their puppet government of the People's Republic of Kampuchea (Cambodia) and the government of Democratic Kampuchea, a coalition of Prince Sihanouk – deposed by a US-backed coup in 1970 – Son Sann's Khmer People's Liberation Front and the Khmer Rouge, who from 1982 claimed to have abandoned their Communist ideology. It was this strange tripartite government in exile that was recognized by the United Nations.

Denied almost any aid, Cambodia continued to decline, but it was only the withdrawal of Vietnamese troops in 1989, sparking a fear of a Khmer Rouge revival, that forced a settlement. In October 1991, following numerous failures, a UN-brokered peace plan for elections by 1993 was accepted by all parties concerned, and a glimmer of real hope returned to the beleaguered people of Cambodia. However, peace was fragile and there was the massive problem of hundreds of thousands of refugees camped over the border in Thailand – itself plunged into turmoil in the spring of 1992. [*Map page 26*] ■

AREA 181,040 sq km [69,900 sq mls]
POPULATION 9,968,000
CAPITAL (POPULATION) Phnom Penh (800,000)
GOVERNMENT Constitutional monarchy
ETHNIC GROUPS Khmer 94%, Chinese 3%, Cham 2%, Thai, Lao, Kola, Vietnamese
LANGUAGES Khmer (official)
RELIGIONS Buddhism 88%, Islam 2%
CURRENCY Riel = 100 sen

# CAMEROON

Half the size of neighbouring Nigeria, Cameroon has only a seventh of the population. It is, nevertheless, a remarkably diverse country, stemming from more than 160 ethnic groups (each with their own language) and a colonial past involving several European countries. The mountainous borderlands between Nigeria and Cameroon lie on a line of crustal weakness dating from the break-up of the supercontinent, Gondwana-land. Mostly volcanic, the mountains include Mt Cameroon (4,070 m [13,350 ft]) which is occasionally active. There is desert to the north, dense tropical rainforest in the south and dry savanna in the intermediate area.

## ECONOMY AND RESOURCES
Despite oil production passing its peak in the 1980s and likely to stop before the end of the century, and despite patchy industrial development, Cameroon is one of tropical Africa's better-off nations, with an annual income per person of $850 and rare self-sufficiency in food. This relative prosperity rests partly on diverse but well-managed agriculture, with extensive plantations of palm, rubber, bananas and other crops in the south-west dating from colonial times. Douala is Cameroon's main port for exports of cocoa, coffee (the chief cash crops) and aluminium, and for the transit trade of neighbours, while Kribi exports timber. Aluminium is produced at Edéa, using hydroelectric power generated from the Sanaga River, and a railway is being built to the north.

## HISTORY AND POLITICS
The word Cameroon is derived from the Portuguese *camarões* – prawns fished by Portuguese explorers' seamen in coastal estuaries – but European contact dates mainly from German rule as a protectorate after 1884. After World War I the country was divided according to League of Nations mandates between France (mainly) and Britain. The French Cameroons became independent in 1960, while following a 1961 plebiscite the north of the British Cameroons voted to merge with Nigeria and the south federated with the new independent state; this became unitary in 1972 and a republic in 1984. Though Cameroon is officially bilingual, the government and public sector are dominated by French-speakers – a fact that continues to upset the rest of the population.

The austerity programme of President Paul Buja, initiated in 1987, appeared to reap rewards by the end of the decade, but there was widespread unrest at the repressive regime (one-party politics was introduced in 1966 by Buja's mentor and predecessor Ahmadou Ahidjo, who had been president since independence). Elections were held in 1992, but disputes over the results led Buja to declare a state of emergency. [*Map page 32*] ■

AREA 475,440 sq km [183,567 sq mls]
POPULATION 12,871,000
CAPITAL (POPULATION) Yaoundé (750,000)
GOVERNMENT Multiparty republic
ETHNIC GROUPS Fang 20%, Bamileke and Mamum 19%, Duala, Luanda and Basa 15%, Fulani 10%
LANGUAGES French and English (both official)
RELIGIONS Christianity (Roman Catholic 35%, Protestant 18%), traditional beliefs 25%, Islam 22%
CURRENCY CFA franc = 100 centimes

# CANADA

A vast confederation of ten provinces and two territories, Canada is the world's second largest country after Russia, and with an even longer coastline (250,000 km [155,000 mls]). Sparsely populated, it has huge areas of virtually unoccupied mountains, forests, tundra and polar desert in the north and west.

To the east lie the Maritime provinces of Newfoundland, Nova Scotia, New Brunswick and Prince Edward Island, and the predominantly French-speaking province of Québec; clustered about the Gulf of St Lawrence, they are based on ancient worn-down mountains – the northern extension of the Appalachians – and the eastern uptilted edge of the even older Canadian Shield. The central province of Ontario borders the Great Lakes, extending north across the Shield to Hudson Bay. Further to the west come the prairie provinces of Manitoba, Saskatchewan and Alberta; like Québec and Ontario, these include fertile farmlands in the south, where most of the population is to be found, and lake-strewn forest on the subarctic wastelands to the north.

South-western Alberta includes a substantial block of the Rocky Mountains, with peaks rising to over 4,000 m [13,120 ft] in Banff, Yoho and Kootenay National Parks. The westernmost province of British Columbia is mountainous, a land of spectacular forests, lakes and fjords, with sheltered valleys harbouring rich farmland. The huge northern area includes the relatively small and mountainous Yukon Territory in the west, bordering Alaska, and the much more extensive Northwest Territories stretching from the 60th parallel to the northern tip of Ellesmere Island.

## ECONOMY AND RESOURCES

Though the population of Canada expanded rapidly from Confederation onwards, it remained predominantly rural for many generations; only in recent decades have Canada's cities grown to match those of the USA. At Confederation in 1867 about 80% was rural, and only Montréal had passed the 100,000 population mark, with just six towns over 25,000. Not until the end of World War II did the rural and urban elements stand in balance, and today the situation is reversed: 76% of Canada's population is urban.

The metropolitan areas of Toronto and Montréal jointly contain a quarter of the total, and together with Vancouver account for over 30% of the entire population. By contrast the urban centres of Newfoundland and the Maritimes have been relatively stable.

### Agriculture and industry

Although farming settlements still dominate the landscape, if not the economy, abandonment of farmland is a serious problem in the eastern provinces, where the agrarian economy – except in such favoured areas as the Annapolis Valley, Nova Scotia – has always been marginal. Through the St Lawrence lowlands and Ontario peninsula farms are more prosperous and rural populations are denser, thinning again along the north shores of the Great Lakes. On the prairies mechanization of grain farming long ago minimized the need for labour, so population densities remain low; the mixed farming communities on the forest margins are often denser. The Pacific coast population is generally concentrated in such

## SAINT-PIERRE ET MIQUELON

The last remaining fragment of the once-extensive French possessions in North America, Saint-Pierre et Miquelon comprises eight islands (total area 242 sq km [93 sq mls]) off the south coast of Newfoundland.

The population of 6,300 (the vast majority of whom live on Saint-Pierre, the rest on Miquelon) depend mainly on fishing – the cause of territorial disputes with Canada.

Settled by Frenchmen in the 17th century and a colony from 1816, it became an overseas department in 1976, thus enjoying – like Martinique, Guadeloupe, Guiana and Réunion – the same status as the departments in Metropolitan France. In 1985, however, it became a 'territorial collectivity' (a status already held by Mayotte in the Indian Ocean), sending one representative to the National Assembly in Paris and one to the Senate.

rich farming areas as the Okanagan and lower Frazer River basins.

Industry, often dependent on local development of power resources, has transformed many remote and empty areas of Canada. Newfoundland's Labrador iron-ore workings around Schefferville are powered by the huge hydroelectric plant at Churchill Falls, one of the largest of its kind in the world. Cheap hydroelectric power throughout Québec and Ontario, coupled with improved transmission technology, has encouraged the further development of wood pulp and paper industries, even in distant parts of the northern forests, and stimulated industry and commerce in the south. Canada is by far the world's leading producer and exporter of paper and board. Mining, too, has helped in the development of these provinces; Sudbury, Ontario, supplies about 20% of the Western world's nickel, while Canada is one of the leading producers of zinc and uranium.

In the prairie provinces, small marketing, distribution and service centres have been transformed by the enormous expansion of the petrochemical industry; the mineral-rich province of Alberta produces 90% of the country's oil output, and the boom towns of Alberta, Edmonton and Calgary have far outpaced the growth of the eastern cities during recent decades. By contrast – lacking hydrocarbons, depending mainly on farming, logging and pulping for their prosperity – the settlements of Pacific Canada have on the whole grown slowly, with the notable exception of Vancouver.

**The northlands**
Canada's northlands, virtually uninhabited apart from small Inuit communities, have an immense, though localized, potential for development. Though the soils are poor and the climate is unyielding, mineral wealth is abundant under the permanently frozen subsoils. Already a major producer of uranium, zinc and nickel, the north also holds vast reserves of copper, molybdenum, iron, cadmium, and other metals of strategic importance; sulphur, potash and asbestos are currently being exploited, and natural gas and petroleum await development beyond the Mackenzie River delta.

Much of this immense mineral wealth will remain in the ground until the high costs of extraction and transportation can be justified. Also, pressure for legislation to protect the boreal forest and tundra against unnecessary or casual damage is rapidly growing – a trend which one day may also curb the massive timber industry.

**HISTORY AND POLITICS**
Norse voyagers and fishermen were probably the first Europeans briefly to visit Canada, but John Cabot's later discovery of North America, in 1497, began the race to annex lands and wealth, with France and Britain the main contenders.

Jacques Cartier's discovery of the St Lawrence River in 1534 gave France a head start; from their settlements near Québec explorers, trappers and missionaries pioneered routes deeply penetrating the northern half of North America. With possible routes to China and the Indies in mind, Frenchmen followed the St Lawrence and Niagara rivers deep into the heartland of the continent, hoping for the riches of another El Dorado.

Discovering the Great Lakes, they then moved north, west and south in their search

for trade. From the fertile valley of the upper St Lawrence, French influence spread north beyond the coniferous forests and over the tundra. To the west and south they reached the prairies – potentially fertile farming country – exploring further to the Rockies and down the Ohio and Mississippi rivers. By 1763, after the series of wars that gave Britain brief control of the whole of North America, French-speaking communities were already scattered widely across the interior. Many of the southern settlements became American after 1776, when the USA declared independence from Britain, and the northern ones became a British colony.

British settlers had long been established on the Atlantic coast, farming where possible, with supplementary fishing. In the 1780s a new wave of English-speaking settlers – the United Empire Loyalists – moved north from the USA into Nova Scotia, New Brunswick and Lower Canada. With further waves of immigration direct from Britain, English speakers came to dominate the fertile lands between Lakes Huron and Erie. From there they gradually spread westwards.

Restricted to the north by intractable coniferous forests and tundra, and to the south by the USA, the settlers spread through Québec into Upper Canada – now Ontario, the only province along the Canadian shores of the Great Lakes. Mostly English-speaking and retaining British traditions, they continued westwards to establish settlements across the narrow wedge of the northern prairie, finally crossing the Rockies to link with embryo settlements along the Pacific coast. So the fertile lowlands of the St Lawrence basin and the pockets of settlement on the Shield alone remained French in language and culture. The bulk of Canada, to east and west, became predominantly British.

Canada's varied topography and immense scale inhibited the development of a single nation; to promote Canadian unity across so wide a continent has been the aim of successive governments for more than two centuries. The union of British Upper Canada and French Lower Canada was sealed by the Confederation of 1867, when as the newly-named Provinces of Ontario and Québec they were united with the Maritime core of Nova

## THE TUNDRA

Beyond their habitable southern rim, the northlands of Canada and Alaska are bleak and bare; in the subarctic zone conifers stretch across the continent, but northwards the boreal forest thins and dies out, replaced with tundra. Glaciation has scoured the rocks bare, and soils have had insufficient time to form; the surface thaws in summer, but subsoils remain frozen. Winters are long and bitterly cold, summers brief and cool. Even in the south the season of plant growth is only 70–80 days. Precipitation is light – usually less than 250 mm [10 in] a year, and most of it snow; except where it drifts, the snow seldom lies deep, but it provides cover for vegetation and burrowing animals. The tundra is covered with low grasses, lichens, mosses and spindly shrubs, providing food for migrating reindeer and resident hares, voles, lemmings and other small browsers and grazers. Their numbers are augmented each summer by hosts of migrant birds that fly in from temperate latitudes to feed on the vegetation and insects.

Scotia and New Brunswick. Three years later the settlement on the Red River entered the Confederation as Manitoba, and in the following year the Pacific colonies of Vancouver Island and British Columbia, now united as a single province, completed the link from sea to sea. Prince Edward Island joined in 1873, the prairie provinces of Alberta and Saskatchewan in 1905, and Newfoundland in 1949.

Though self-governing in most respects from the time of the Confederation, Canada remained technically subject to the British Imperial parliament until 1931, when the creation of the British Commonwealth made the country a sovereign nation under the crown.

With so much of the population spread out along a southern ribbon of settlement, 4,000 km [2,500 mls] long but rarely more than 480 km [300 mls] wide, Canada has struggled constantly to achieve unity. Transcontinental communications have played a critical role. From the eastern provinces the Canadian Pacific Railway crossed the Rockies to reach

Vancouver in 1885. Later a second rail route, the Canadian National, was pieced together, and the Trans-Canada Highway links the extreme east and west of the country symbolically as well as in fact. Transcontinental air routes link the major centres, and local air traffic is especially important over trackless forests, mountains and tundra. With radio and telephone communications, all parts of the confederation are now linked, though the vastness is intimidating and the country spans six time zones: at noon in Vancouver it is already 3:00 pm in Toronto, and 4:30 pm in St Johns, Newfoundland.

A constant hazard to Canadian nationhood is the proximity of the USA. Though benign, with shared if dwindling British traditions, the prosperous giant to the south has often seemed to threaten the very survival of Canada through economic dominance and cultural annexation. The two countries have the largest bilateral trade flow in the world.

A real and growing threat to unity is the persistence of French culture in Québec province – a lasting political wedge between the western prairie and mountain provinces and the eastern Maritimes. Urbanization and 'Americanization' have fuelled a separatist movement that seeks to turn the province into an independent French-speaking republic. This issue may obscure a wider and more fundamental division in Canadian politics, with the development of a Montréal-Toronto axis in the east, and a Vancouver-Winnipeg axis in the west. [*Map page 27*] ∎

**AREA** 9,976,140 sq km [3,851,788 sq mls]
**POPULATION** 29,141,000
**CAPITAL (POPULATION)** Ottawa (921,000)
**GOVERNMENT** Federal multiparty constitutional monarchy
**ETHNIC GROUPS** British 34%, French 26%, German 4%, Italian 3%, Ukrainian 2%, Native American (Amerindian/Inuit) 1.5%, Chinese, Dutch
**LANGUAGES** English and French (both official)
**RELIGIONS** Christianity (Roman Catholic 47%, Protestant 41%, Eastern Orthodox 2%), Judaism, Islam, Hinduism, Sikhism
**CURRENCY** Canadian dollar = 100 cents

# CANARY ISLANDS

T he Canary Islands comprise an archipelago of seven large islands and numerous small volcanic islands situated in the Atlantic off southern Morocco, the nearest within 100 km [60 mls] of the mainland. The 'inshore' islands of Lanzarote and Fuerteventura are low-lying, while the western group, including Gran Canaria and Tenerife, are more mountainous, the volcanic cone of Pico de Teide rising to 3,718 m [12,198 ft]. The islands, totalling 7,273 sq km [2,807 sq mls] in area, have a subtropical climate, pleasantly dry at sea level but damp on higher ground.

## ECONOMY AND RESOURCES

Soils are fertile, supporting farming and fruit growing, mainly by large-scale irrigation. Bananas, sugar, coffee and citrus fruits are the main crops at lower levels, and temperate cereals, potatoes, tomatoes and vines grow in the cooler, damper air of the hills. Much of the produce is exported to Western Europe for the early spring market. The principal industries include food and fish processing, boat-building and crafts.

Known to ancient European civilizations as the Fortunate Islands, the picturesque Canaries are today a major destination for both winter and summer tourists. The average January temperature being 17.9°C [64°F] rising to 24.4°C [76°F] in July. There are four national parks on the islands, noted for their interesting Mediterranean and African flora and volcanic formations.

## HISTORY AND POLITICS

Claimed by Portugal in 1341, the Canary Islands were ceded to Spain in 1479 and since 1927 have been divided into two provinces under the name of their respective capitals, Las Palmas de Gran Canaria (with a population of 342,000 Spain's eighth biggest city) and Santa Cruz de Tenerife. The former province (56% of the area) comprises Gran Canaria, Lanzarote, Fuerteventura and

numerous islets, and the latter (44%) comprises the islands of Tenerife, La Palma, Gomera and Hierro. [*Map page 32*] ■

AREA 7,273 sq km [2,807 sq mls]
POPULATION 1,494,000
CAPITAL (POPULATION) Las Palmas (342,000)/Santa Cruz (189,300)
GOVERNMENT Spanish autonomous region
ETHNIC GROUPS Spanish
LANGUAGES Spanish
RELIGIONS Christianity (mainly Roman Catholic)
CURRENCY Spanish currency

# CAPE VERDE

A n archipelago of ten large and five small islands, divided into the Barlavento (windward) and Sotavento (leeward) groups, Cape Verde lies 560 km [350 mls] off Dakar in Senegal. They are volcanic and mainly mountainous, with steep cliffs and rocky headlands; the highest, Fogo, rises to 2,829 m [9,281 ft] and is active. The islands are tropical, hot for most of the year and mainly dry at sea level.

## ECONOMY AND RESOURCES

Higher ground is cooler and more fertile, producing maize, groundnuts, coffee, sugar cane, beans and fruit when not subject to the endemic droughts that have killed 75,000 people since 1900. Poor soils and lack of surface water prohibit development.

Cape Verde's meagre exports comprise mainly bananas and tuna fish, but it has to import much of its food. The only significant minerals are salt and *pozzolana*, a volcanic rock used in making cement. Much of the population's income comes from foreign aid and remittances sent home by the 600,000 Cape Verdeans who work abroad – nearly twice the native population; in the last severe drought (1968–82), some 40,000 emigrated to Portugal alone. Tourism is still in its infancy –

only 2,000 visitors a year – lagging well behind the Azores, Madeira and the Canaries.

The economic problems experienced by the Cape Verdeans are compounded by tens of thousands of Angolan refugees.

## HISTORY AND POLITICS

Portuguese since the 15th century – and used chiefly as a provisioning station for ships and an assembly point for slaves in the trade from West Africa – the colony became an overseas territory in 1951 and independent in 1975. Linked with Guinea-Bissau in the fight against colonial rule, its Socialist single-party government flirted with union in 1980, but in 1991 the ruling PAICV was soundly trounced in the country's first multiparty elections by a newly legalized opposition, the Movement for Democracy. [*Map page 32*] ■

---

**AREA** 4,030 sq km [1,556 sq mls]
**POPULATION** 381,000
**CAPITAL (POPULATION)** Praia (61,800)
**GOVERNMENT** Multiparty republic
**ETHNIC GROUPS** Mulatto 71%, Black 28%, White 1%
**LANGUAGES** Portuguese (official), Crioulo
**RELIGIONS** Christianity (Roman Catholic 97%, Protestant 2%)
**CURRENCY** Cape Verde escudo = 100 centavos

---

# CAYMAN ISLANDS

---

The Cayman Islands comprise three low-lying islands covering 259 sq km [100 sq mls], south of Cuba, with the capital George Town (population 14,000, in a total of 30,000) on the biggest, Grand Cayman.

The main activities used to be farming and fishing until the 1960s, when an economic revolution transformed them into the world's biggest offshore financial centre, offering a secret tax haven to 18,000 companies and 450 banks. The flourishing luxury tourist industry (predominantly from US sources)

now accounts for more than 70% of its official GDP and foreign earnings, while a property boom has put beachfront prices on Grand Cayman among the world's highest. An immigrant labour force, chiefly Jamaican, constitutes about a fifth of the population – similar to European and black groups; the rest are of mixed descent.

A Crown Colony since 1959, the Cayman Islands are a dependent territory of Britain. [*Map page 30*] ■

---

**AREA** 259 sq km [100 sq mls]
**POPULATION** 30,000
**CAPITAL (POPULATION)** George Town (14,000)
**GOVERNMENT** British dependency
**ETHNIC GROUPS** Mulatto 40%, White 20%, Black 20%
**LANGUAGES** English (official)
**RELIGIONS** Christianity
**CURRENCY** Cayman Is dollar = 100 cents

---

# CENTRAL AFRICAN REPUBLIC

---

The Central African Republic is a remote, landlocked country enclosed by Chad, Sudan, Zaïre, Congo and Cameroon. It lies on an undulating plateau, which is mostly between 600 m and 800 m [1,970 ft to 2,620 ft] above sea level. This plateau divides the headwaters of two river systems. In the south, the rivers flow into the navigable Ubangi (Oubangi) River. This river itself flows into the Zaïre (Congo) River. The Ubangi and its tributary the Bomu form much of the country's southern border. In the north, most rivers are headwaters of the Chari (Shari) River. This river flows into Lake Chad to the north.

Rainforest is confined to the south-west, with tongues of forest extending along the rivers. But wooded savanna covers much of the country, with more open grasslands in the north. The country has many forest and savanna animals, including buffaloes, elephants, lions, leopards and many kinds of birds. About 6% of the land is protected in national parks and reserves. But tourism is on a small scale, because of the remoteness of the country.

## ECONOMY AND RESOURCES
The World Bank classifies Central African Republic as a 'low-income' developing country. More than 80% of the people are farmers, and most of them produce little more than they need to feed their families. The main food crops are bananas, maize, manioc, millet and yams. Coffee, groundnuts, cotton, timber and tobacco are produced for export, mainly on commercial plantations.

Diamonds, the only major mineral resource, are the most valuable single export. Manufacturing is on a small scale, with products including beer, cotton fabrics, footwear, leather, soap and sawn timber. Central African Republic's development has been impeded by its remote position, its poor transport system and its untrained workforce. The country depends heavily on aid, especially from France.

## HISTORY AND POLITICS
Little is known of the early history of the area. Between the 16th and 19th centuries, the population was greatly reduced by the slave trade and the country is still thinly populated today. Although it is larger than France, France has 18 times as many people.

France set up an outpost at Bangui in 1899 and ruled the country as a colony from 1894. Known as Ubangi-Shari, France ruled the country for most of the time as part of French Equatorial Africa, a vast area which also included Chad, Congo and Gabon. The country became fully independent in 1960.

Central African Republic became a one-party state in 1962, but army officers seized power in 1966. The head of the army, Jean-Bedel Bokassa, made himself emperor in 1976. The country was renamed the Central African Empire, but after a brutal and tyrannical reign, he was overthrown by a military group in 1979. The monarchy was abolished and the country again became a republic.

In March 1981, the country became a multiparty democracy, but the army took over

in September and banned all political parties. The country adopted a new, multiparty constitution in 1991, and elections were held in 1993. [*Map page 32*] ∎

| | |
|---|---|
| **AREA** | 622,980 sq km [240,533 sq mls] |
| **POPULATION** | 3,235,000 |
| **CAPITAL (POPULATION)** | Bangui (597,000) |
| **GOVERNMENT** | Multiparty republic |
| **ETHNIC GROUPS** | Banda 29%, Baya 25%, Ngbandi 11%, Azande 10%, Sara 7%, Mbaka 4%, Mbum 4% |
| **LANGUAGES** | French (official), Sango (the most common language) |
| **RELIGIONS** | Traditional beliefs 57%, Christianity 35%, Islam 8% |
| **CURRENCY** | CFA franc = 100 centimes |

# CHAD

Chad is Africa's largest landlocked country, and twice the size of France, its former ruler. In the Saharan northern third of the country, a sparse nomadic Arabic population lives in a harsh, hot desert containing extensive tracts of mobile dunes (Erg du Djourab), and the volcanic Tibesti Mountains. The wetter southern portions of the country are covered by wooded savanna.

## ECONOMY AND RESOURCES
Chad is a sprawling, strife-torn, desperately poor state with no industries except for the processing of agricultural products. Over 90% of the population make a living from crop cultivation, notably cotton, or by animal herding.

In the south, crops of cotton, groundnuts, millet and sorghum are grown – drought permitting – by settled black cultivators. A central bank of thorn bush (Sahel) provides pasturage for migratory cattle and herds of game, though drought and desertification have combined to wreak havoc here in recent years.

Lake Chad is the focal point of much of the country's drainage, affecting two-thirds of the country. However, most water feeding the lake comes from the rivers Chari and Logone, the only large perennial water courses in the country and now only streams. Agriculture and population are concentrated along their valleys and in the vicinity of Lake Chad, now shrinking fast – some estimates state that the water area is only 20% of its size in 1970, and the levels much lower; and while fishing is locally important, catches are less each year. Dried fish is still exported, but sales of cotton, meat and other animal products provide most exports.

## HISTORY AND POLITICS

Since independence Chad has been plagued by almost continuous civil wars, primarily between the Muslim Arab north and the Christian and animist black south, but also with many subsidiary ethnic conflicts. In 1973 Colonel Gaddafi's Libya, supporters of the Arab faction, occupied the mineral-rich Aozou Strip in the far north and has held it virtually ever since.

Libya tried incursions further south in 1983 – to back the forces of the previously separate state of Bourkou-Ennedi-Tibesti – and in 1987, to support one of many abortive coups against a succession of repressive governments in Ndjamena; the former ended in agreement on 'joint withdrawal', the latter in crushing victory for French and Chadian forces.

Diplomatic relations were restored with Libya in 1988, but Chad's massive commitments in maintaining control in the drought-afflicted country as well as on several of its borders – in addition to an impossible foreign debt – make it one of the terminally ill nations of Africa. [*Map page 32*] ■

---

AREA 1,284,000 sq km [495,752 sq mls]
POPULATION 6,183,000
CAPITAL (POPULATION) Ndjamena (530,000)
GOVERNMENT Transitional
ETHNIC GROUPS Bagirmi, Kreish and Sara 31%, Sudanic Arab 26%, Teda 7%, Mbum 6%
LANGUAGES French and Arabic (both official)
RELIGIONS Islam 40%, Christianity 33%, traditional beliefs 27%
CURRENCY CFA franc = 100 centimes

---

# CHILE

Extending in an extraordinary shape down the west coast of South America from latitude 17° 30'S, well inside the tropics, to 55° 50'S at Cape Horn, Chile falls into three parallel zones based on the longitudinal folding of the Andes, whose high peaks form the boundaries with Bolivia and Argentina. It is the world's 'thinnest' country, 25 times as long as it is wide.

From the Bolivian border in the north down as far as 27°S runs an extension of the high plateau of Bolivia. Several volcanic peaks of more than 6,000 m [19,680 ft] mark the edge of the western cordilleras. South of Ojos del Salado the ranges narrow and steepen, then gradually reduce in height as they approach Cape Horn.

The parallel coastal ranges create a rolling, hilly belt, rising to 3,000 m [10,000 ft] or more in the north but generally much lower. Between this belt and the Andes runs the sheltered and fertile central valley, most clearly marked southwards from Santiago; over 60% of the population live in a stretch of land 800 km [500 mls] long here. Punta Arenas (population 125,000 in 1991), on the Straits of Magellan, is the southernmost city in the world.

Climatically Chile divides readily into a desert north (the Atacama Desert, where no recorded rain fell for almost 400 years), a warm-temperate centre and a cool-temperate south.

## ECONOMY AND RESOURCES

Chile's economy continues to depend on agriculture, fishing and, particularly, mining: the country is the world's second largest copper producer (13% of total) and copper accounts for nearly half of all export earnings. Magellanes, the southernmost region that includes Cape Horn and Tierra del Fuego (shared with Argentina), has oilfields that produce about half the country's needs. When the military took over in 1973 inflation was running at about 850%, despite government controls, and Pinochet reintroduced a market economy and abandoned agricultural reform. Economic decline began in 1981 – brought about, in part, by low world prices for minerals and primary products in general – but with great application the situation has improved. Though there is still political tension and manufacturing industry remains subject to heavy competition, there were encouraging signs of a full recovery as the country entered the 1990s.

## HISTORY AND POLITICS
A Spanish colony from the 16th century, Chile developed as a mining enterprise in the north and a series of vast ranches, or *haciendas*, in the fertile central region. After Chile finally freed itself from Spanish rule in 1818 mining continued to flourish in the north, and in the south Valparaiso developed as a port with the farmlands of the southern valley exporting produce to the settlers of California and Australia.

The first Christian Democrat president was elected in 1964, but in 1970 he was replaced by President Allende; his administration, the world's first democratically elected Marxist government, was overthrown in a CIA-backed military coup in 1973 and General Pinochet took power as dictator, banning all political activity in a strongly repressive regime. A new constitution took effect from 1981, allowing for an eventual return to democracy, and free elections finally took place in 1989. President Aylwin took office in 1990, but Pinochet secured continued office as commander-in-chief of the armed forces. [*Map page 31*] ∎

AREA 756,950 sq km [292,258 sq mls]
POPULATION 14,044,000
CAPITAL (POPULATION) Santiago (5,343,000)
GOVERNMENT Multiparty republic
ETHNIC GROUPS Mestizo 92%, Amerindian 7%
LANGUAGES Spanish (official)
RELIGIONS Christianity (Roman Catholic 81%, Protestant 6%)
CURRENCY Chilean peso = 100 centavos

# CHINA

By far the most populous country in the world, the People's Republic of China also ranks as the third largest country after Russia and Canada, being marginally bigger than the USA. Before the development of modern forms of transport, the vast size of China often hampered efficient communication between the centre of the country and the peripheries. Distances are huge. By rail, the distance from Beijing (Peking) to Guangzhou (Canton) is 2,324 km [1,450 mls].

One of the main determining influences on the evolution of Chinese civilization had been the geographical isolation of China from the rest of the world. Surrounded to the north, west and south by forests, deserts and mountain ranges, and separated from the Americas by the vast expanse of the Pacific Ocean, China until modern times was insulated from frequent contact with other civilizations, and its culture and society developed along highly individual lines.

### Landscape and relief
The Chinese landscape is like a chequerboard in which mountains and plateaux alternate with basins and alluvial plains. There are two intersecting systems of mountain chains, one trending from north-north-east to south-south-west, the other from east to west. Many mountain areas have been devastated by soil erosion through indiscriminate tree-felling. The agricultural wealth of China is all in the lowlands of the east – where the vast majority of the population lives.

The chequerboard pattern includes an extraordinary variety of landscapes. Manchuria, in the far north, comprises a wide area of gently undulating country, originally grassland, but now an important agricultural area. The loess lands of the north-west occupy a broad belt from the great loop of the Huang He (Hwang Ho) into Shanxi and Henan provinces. Here, valley sides, hills and mountains are blanketed in loess – a fine-grained unstratified soil deposited by wind during the last glaciation. Within this region, loess deposits occur widely in the form of plateaux that are deeply incised by gorges and ravines.

By contrast with the loess lands, the landscape of the densely populated North China Plain is flat and monotonous. Settlement is concentrated in walled villages while large fields are the product of post-1949 land consolidation schemes. Further south the Yangtze delta is a land of large lakes. Water is a predominant element of the landscape – the low-lying alluvial land with its irrigated ricefields is traversed by intricate networks of canals and other man-made works, many of which date back several centuries.

Far inland in the Yangtze basin, and separated from the middle Yangtze valley by precipitous river gorges, lies the Red basin of Sichuan (Szechwan). To the north, west and south, the basin is surrounded by high mountain ranges. The mountains of the Qin Ling ranges, in particular, protect the basin from cold winter winds. With its mild climate and fertile soils, the Red basin is one of the most productive and densely populated regions of China. Ricefields, often arranged in elaborate terraces, dominate the landscape.

Other distinctive landscapes of southern China include those of north-eastern Guizhou province, where limestone spires and pinnacles rise vertically above small, intensively cultivated plains, and the Guangdong coastal lowlands, with their villages in groves of citrus, bananas, mangoes and palms.

## The Huang He and the Yangtze

The two major rivers of China are the Huang He and the Yangtze Kiang (Chang Jiang), the world's seventh and third longest. The Huang He, or Yellow River (so called from the large quantities of silt which it transports), is 4,840 km [3,005 mls] long. Also known as 'China's Sorrow', it has throughout history been the source of frequent and disastrous floods. In 1938, dykes along the Huang He were demolished in order to hamper the advance of the Japanese army into northern China, and the river was diverted so as to enter the sea to the south of the Shandong peninsula. In the catastrophic floods which followed, nearly 900,000 lives were lost and

## TIBET

With an average elevation of 4,500 m [14,750 ft] – almost as high as Europe's Mont Blanc – and an area of 1.2 million sq km [460,000 sq mls], Tibet is the highest and most extensive plateau in the world. It is a harsh and hostile place, and most of its population of just over 2 million people live in the relatively sheltered south of the country, where the capital, Lhasa, is situated.

Since the 7th century, Tibet has been deeply influenced by Buddhist beliefs, and for much of its history was ruled by Buddhist priests – lamas – as a theocracy. The Dalai Lama, a title passed on in successive incarnations from a dying elder to a newborn junior, usually dominated from Lhasa. Between 1720 and 1911 Tibet was under Chinese control, and in 1950 Tibet was reabsorbed by a resurgent Red China; after an unsuccessful uprising in 1959, the Dalai Lama fled to Delhi and a brutal process of forced Chinese acculturation began: in 1961, a report of the International Commission of Jurists accused China of genocide. An 'Autonomous Region of Tibet' was proclaimed in 1965, but during the 1966–76 Cultural Revolution, many Tibetan shrines and monasteries were destroyed.

54,000 sq km [21,000 sq mls] of land was inundated. Since 1949, the incidence of flooding has declined sharply, largely as a result of state investment in flood-prevention schemes.

The Yangtze, China's largest and most important river, is 6,380 km [3,960 mls] long, and its catchment basin is over twice as extensive as that of the Huang He. Unlike the Huang He, the Yangtze is navigable. During the summer months, ocean-going vessels of 10,000 tonnes may reach Wuhan, and 1,000-tonne barges can go as far upstream as Chongqing. Despite the post-1949 improvement of roads and railways, the Yangtze remains an important transport artery.

## Climate and weather

Although the Chinese subcontinent includes a wide variety of relief and climate, it can be divided into three broad regions. Eastern

China is divided into two contrasting halves, north and south of the Qin Ling ranges, while the third region comprises the mountains and arid steppes of the interior.

**Northern China:** Rainfall is light and variable throughout northern China, and is generally insufficient for irrigated agriculture. In winter, temperatures fall to between −1°C and −8°C [30°F and 18°F] and bitterly cold winds blow eastwards across the North China Plain from the steppes of Mongolia. The summer temperatures, by contrast, are little different from those of southern China, and may reach a daily average of 28°C [82°F]. The growing season diminishes northwards and in northern Manchuria only 90 days a year are free of frost.

**Southern China:** The area to the south of the Qin Ling ranges receives heavier and more reliable rainfall than the north, and winter temperatures are generally above freezing point. Summer weather, especially in the central Yangtze valley, is hot and humid. At Nanjing, temperatures as high as 44°C [111°F] have been recorded. The far south of China, including Guangdong province and the island of Hainan, lies within the tropics.

**The interior:** While the Qin Ling ranges are an important boundary between the relatively harsh environments of the north and the more productive lands of the south, a second major line, which follows the Da Hinggan Ling mountains and the eastern edge of the high Tibetan plateau, divides the intensively cultivated lands of eastern China from the mountains and arid steppes of the interior. In the north, this boundary line is marked by the Great Wall of China. Western China includes the Dzungarian basin, the Turfan depression, the arid wastes of the Takla Makan Desert, and the high plateau of Tibet.

## ECONOMY AND RESOURCES

**Northern China:** Despite advances in water conservation since World War II, aridity and unreliability of rainfall restrict the range of crops that can be grown. Millet, maize and winter wheat are the staple crops of the North China Plain, while coarse grains and soya beans are cultivated in Manchuria.

**Southern China:** Inland, the mild climate and fertile soils of the Red basin make this an important agricultural region. Rice production is dominant but at lower altitudes the climate is warm enough to allow the cultivation of citrus fruits, cotton, sugar cane and tobacco, of which China is the world's biggest producer. The far south enjoys a year-round growing season. Irrigated rice cultivation is the economic mainstay of southern China. Double cropping (rice as a main crop followed by winter wheat) is characteristic of the Yangtze valley; along the coast of Guangdong province two crops of rice can be grown each year, and in parts of Hainan Island the annual cultivation of three crops of rice is possible; the country produces more than 35% of the world total. Crops such as tea, mulberry and sweet potato are also cultivated, and in the far south sugar cane, bananas, and other tropical crops are grown.

**The interior:** Although aridity of climate has hampered agriculture throughout most of western China, oasis crops are grown around the rim of the Takla Makan Desert, and farming settlements also exist in the Gansu corridor to the north of the Qilian mountains.

## Communist China

Under Communist rule the mass starvation, malnutrition and disease which afflicted China before World War II were virtually eliminated, and living standards greatly improved, particularly in the countryside. One of the salient features of the centrally planned economy was the organization of the rural population into 50,000 communes – self-sufficient units of varying size which farm the land collectively. Communes also ran rural industries, and are responsible for the administration of schools and clinics. Through the communes, labour has been organized on a vast scale to tackle public works schemes such as water conservation, flood control and land reclamation.

Living standards improved markedly, with life expectancy doubling and education improving, though the GNP per capita figure remained that of a poor Third World nation – some 1.5% that of Japan. The agricultural communes were not notably successful, and since peasants have been freed from petty bureaucracy, harvests of grain crops went up by over 40% in the decade from 1976.

Although food supply has generally kept

abreast of population growth, the size and growth rate of the Chinese population has always given cause for concern. By the early 1980s, the population was growing at 1.3% per year, a net annual increase of about 13 million people; government penalties and incentives over the size of family have met with some success, but between 1988 and 2000 it was expected to grow by 187 million – slightly less than the prediction for India, but more than the 1988 totals for Indonesia or Brazil.

Only 10% of the land area of China is cultivable, but environmental constraints are such that there is little prospect of meeting increased food demand by reclaiming land for agriculture. Future growth in food supply must come from continued intensification of land use and gains in yields.

Although China is an agricultural country, government planners, especially since the death of Mao Tse-tung in 1976, have emphasized the need to industrialize. China has sufficient resources in coal, iron ore and oil to support an industrial economy, but it is deficient in capital and industrial technology.

Beijing, the capital city of China, is a governmental and administrative centre of prime importance. Several buildings of outstanding architectural interest, such as the former imperial palace complex (once known as the Forbidden City) and the Temple and Altar of Heaven, have been carefully preserved and are now open to the public. In the 19th and early 20th centuries, with a large community of foreign merchants, Shanghai grew rapidly as a major banking and trading centre. Since 1949, the city has lost its former commercial importance, but it remained China's largest and has emerged as a major centre for the manufacture of iron and steel, ships, textiles and a wide range of engineering products.

## HISTORY AND POLITICS

Early Chinese civilization arose along the inland margins of the North China Plain, in a physical setting markedly harsher (especially in terms of winter temperatures) than the environments of the other great civilizations of the Old World. The Shang dynasty, noted for its fine craftsmanship in bronze, flourished in northern China from 1630 to 1122 BC. Shang civilization was followed by many centuries of

## THE GREAT WALL OF CHINA

The world's longest fortification, the Great Wall was begun in the 3rd century BC and extended throughout Chinese history; most of the present wall was constructed during the Ming Dynasty, between 1368 and 1644. Its purpose was ostensibly to protect the Chinese Empire from northern nomadic raiders, though (like Egypt's pyramids) it also served as a make-work project for hundreds of thousands of otherwise unemployed labourers.

The wall's total length is at least 6,400 km [4,000 mls]; recently, archaeologists discovered what may be another 1,000 km [600 mls]. Only a few small sections, renovated largely as tourist attractions, remain in good repair. Contrary to legend, the Great Wall is not visible from the Moon, nor even from very high altitudes. Despite its great length, its flat top is no more than 4 m [13 ft] wide.

political fragmentation, and it was not until the 3rd century BC that China was unified into a centrally administered empire. Under the Ch'in dynasty (221 to 206 BC) the Great Wall of China was completed, while Chinese armies pushed southwards beyond the Yangtze, reaching the southern Chinese coast in the vicinity of Canton.

In succeeding centuries there was a gradual movement of population from the north to the warmer, moister, and more productive lands of the south. This slow migration was greatly accelerated by incursions of barbarian nomads into north China, especially during the Sung dynasty (AD 960 to 1279). By the late 13th century the southern lands, including the Yangtze valley, probably contained around 75% of the Chinese population.

During the Han, T'ang and Sung dynasties, a remarkably stable political and social order evolved within China. The major distinguishing features of Chinese civilization came to include Confucianism, whereby the individual was subordinated to family obligations and to state service, the state bureaucracy, members of which were recruited by public examination, and the benign rule of the emperor – the

'Son of Heaven'. Great advances were made in the manufacture of porcelain, silk, metals and lacquerware, while gunpowder, the compass, and printing were among several Chinese inventions which found their way to the West in medieval times. Nevertheless, the economy of pre-modern China was over-whelmingly agricultural, and the peasant class accounted for most of the population.

Despite the geographical diversity and great size of its territory, China during pre-modern times experienced long periods of unity and cohesion rarely disturbed by invasion from outside. Two important dynasties, the Yuan (1279–1368) and the Ch'ing (1644–1912), were established by the Mongols and Manchus respectively, but, almost invariably, alien rulers found it necessary to adopt Chinese methods of government, and the Chinese cultural tradition was preserved intact.

In the 18th century, China experienced a rapid acceleration in the rate of population growth, and living standards began to fall. By the early 19th century, the government was weak and corrupt, and the country suffered frequent famines and political unrest. British victory in the Opium War (1839–42) was followed by the division of China into spheres of influence for the major Western imperialist powers, and by the establishment of treaty ports, controlled by Western countries, along the Chinese coast and the Yangtze.

Meanwhile, the disintegration of imperial China was hastened by peasant uprisings such as the Taiping rebellion (1850–64), and by the defeat of China in the Sino-Japanese War of 1894–5. Belated attempts were made to arrest the decline of the Chinese empire, but in 1912, and following an uprising in Wuhan, the last of the Chinese emperors abdicated and a republic was proclaimed.

Although the republican administration in Beijing was regarded as the legitimate government, real power rested with army generals and provincial governors. Rival generals, or warlords, raised private armies and plunged China into a long and disastrous period of internal disorder. Alternative solutions were offered by two political parties – the Kuomintang (or Chinese Nationalist Party) formed by Sun Yat-sen and later led by Chiang Kai-shek, and the Communist Party.

In 1931, Japan seized Manchuria, and in 1937 full-scale war broke out between the two countries. In the bitter fighting which followed, the Communists, under Mao Tsetung, gained the support of the peasantry and proved adept practitioners of guerrilla warfare.

The defeat of Japan in 1945 was followed by a civil war which cost 12 million lives: the Communists routed the Kuomintang armies, forcing them to take refuge on the island of Taiwan, and the People's Republic of China was officially proclaimed on 1 October 1949.

## Communist China

The establishment and consolidation of the Communist regime were carried at a huge human cost: it is now estimated that about one million so-called 'counter-revolutionaries' were executed in 1949 and 1950. The Great Leap Forward, the radical economic programme started in 1958, which emphasized ideological purity, ended in failure. In 1966 Mao Tsetung initiated the Great Proletarian Cultural Revolution, another attempt to reassert revolutionary principles: students calling themselves Red Guards took to the streets, denouncing and often persecuting officials and intellectuals. Eventually order had to be restored by the Army and after Mao's death in 1976, more pragmatic policies were adopted. Under the leadership of Deng Xiaoping, far-reaching economic reforms were implemented and China opened itself to foreign investment. However, pressure for political reforms has been resisted and pro-democracy student demonstrations were brutally crushed in Tiananmen Square in 1989. [*Map page 24*] ■

AREA  9,596,960 sq km [3,705,386 sq mls]
POPULATION  1,208,841,000
CAPITAL (POPULATION)  Beijing (or Peking, 9,750,000)
GOVERNMENT  Single-party Communist Republic
ETHNIC GROUPS  Han (Chinese) 92%, 55 minority groups
LANGUAGES  Mandarin Chinese (official)
RELIGIONS  More than half the people say they are atheists; Buddhism, Taoism, Islam
CURRENCY  Renminbi yuan = 10 jiao or 100 fen

# COLOMBIA

The Andes cross Colombia from south to north, fanning out into three ranges with two intervening valleys. In the west the low Cordillera Occidental rises from the hot, forested Pacific coastal plain. Almost parallel to it, and separated by the Cauca Valley, is the much higher Cordillera Central; the high peaks of this range, many of them volcanic, rise to over 5,000 m [16,400 ft].

To the east, across the broad valley of the Magdalena River, lies the more complex Cordillera Oriental, which includes high plateaux, plains, lakes and basins; the capital city, Bogotá, is situated on one of the plateaux, at a height of 2,610 m [8,563 ft]. North-west of the mountains lies the broad Atlantic plain, crossed by many rivers. The Andean foothills to the east, falling away into the Orinoco and Amazon basins and densely covered with rainforest (albeit rapidly diminishing), occupy about two-thirds of the total area of the country. Less than 2% of the population, mainly cattle rangers and Indians, live east of the mountains.

## ECONOMY AND RESOURCES
Little of the country is under cultivation, but much of the land is very fertile and is coming into use as roads improve. The range of climate for crops is extraordinary and the agricultural colleges have different courses for 'cold-climate farming' and 'warm-climate farming'. The rubber tree grows wild and fibres are being exploited, notably the *fique*, which provides all the country's requirements for sacks and cordage. Colombia is the world's second biggest producer of coffee, which grows mainly in the Andean uplands, while bananas, cotton, sugar and rice are important lowland products. Colombia imports some food, though the country has the capacity to be self-sufficient. Drugs, however, may be the biggest industry: it was reported in 1987 that cocaine exports earn Colombia more than its main export, coffee.

## Industry
Colombia was the home of El Dorado, the legendary 'gilded one' of the Chibcha Indians, but today the wealth is more likely to be coal or oil. The country has the largest proven reserves of coal in Latin America (18 billion tonnes) and is South America's biggest exporter. Gold, silver, iron ore, lead, zinc, mercury, emeralds (90% of world production) and other minerals are plentiful, and hydroelectric power is increasingly being developed. Petroleum is an important export and source of foreign exchange; large reserves have been found in the north-eastern areas of Arauca and Vichada. Early in 1992 BP stepped up its exploration programme among speculation that its new finds, north-east of Bogotá, were among the world's biggest.

There is compulsory social security funded by employees, employers and the government, but the benefits are far from evenly spread. Education spending accounts for nearly 20% of the national budget.

Attempts are being made to broaden the industrial base of the economy to counter the decline in domestic demand and the recession being experienced by Colombia's neighbours. Foreign investment will be essential, but to achieve this the Liberal government – convincing winners in the 1991 elections – must first defeat the drug barons and the habitual violence that pervades the nation.

## HISTORY AND POLITICS
Christopher Columbus sighted the country that would bear his name in 1499, and the Spanish conquest of the territory began ten years later. The nation gained independence from Spain following a decade of conflict in 1819, and since the 19th century the two political parties, the pro-clerical, centralizing Conservatives and the anti-clerical, federal-oriented Liberals, have regularly alternated in power. Their rivalry led to two brutal civil wars (1899–1902 and 1949–57), in which some 400,000 people lost their lives: the 1950s conflict, known as *La Violencia*, claimed 280,000 of them. In 1957 the two parties agreed to form a coalition, and this fragile arrangement – threatened by right-wing death squads, left-wing guerillas and powerful drug cartels – lasted until the Liberal President

## THE DRUGS TRADE

Colombia is notorious for its illegal export of cocaine, and several reliable estimates class the drug as the country's most lucrative source of foreign exchange. In addition to the indigenous crop, far larger amounts of leaf are smuggled in from Bolivia and Peru for refining, processing and 're-export'. US agencies estimated that in 1987 retail sales of South American cocaine totalled $22 billion – earning about $2 billion in foreign exchange for the producers to reinvest in their own countries, often in property. Violence, though focused on the drug capitals of Medellín and Cali, is endemic, with warfare between rival gangs and between producers and the authorities an almost daily occurrence.

In 1990, as part of US President George Bush's $10.6 billion 'war on drugs', the governments of Colombia, Bolivia and Peru joined forces with the US Drug Enforcement Agency in a concentrated attempt to clamp down on the production and distribution of cocaine. But while early results from Bolivia were encouraging – voluntary eradication quadrupled in a month in Chapare, where over 80% of the country's crop was grown – the situation in Colombia if anything hardened, despite the brave attempts of politicians, administrators and police in many areas to break the socio-economic stranglehold of the drug cartels. A major problem was the support the warlord barons received from their peasant tenant farmers, who knew that no 'legal' crop or occupation would produce the revenue guaranteed by coca, no matter what initial incentives were offered. In addition, the growers of the Upper Huallaga Valley, the world's biggest coca-growing area, enjoyed the protection of the left-wing 'Shining Path' guerrillas.

Virgilio Barco Vargas was elected by a record margin in 1986. Even by the violent standards of South America, however, Colombia remains politically unstable. [*Map page 31*] ■

**AREA** 1,138,910 sq km [439,733 sq mls]
**POPULATION** 34,545,000
**CAPITAL (POPULATION)** Bogotá (4,921,000)
**GOVERNMENT** Multiparty republic
**ETHNIC GROUPS** Mestizo 58%, White 20%, Mulatto 14%, Black 4%, mixed Black/Indian 3%, Amerindian 1%
**LANGUAGES** Spanish (official)
**RELIGIONS** Christianity (Roman Catholic 93%)
**CURRENCY** Peso = 100 centavos

# COMOROS

The Comoros are three large mountainous islands and several smaller coral islands, lying at the northern end of the Mozambique Channel. Njazidja (formerly Grande Comoro) rises to an active volcano; Nzwami (Anjouan) is a heavily eroded volcanic massif; Mwali (Mohéli) is a forested plateau.

With fertile though porous soils, the islands were originally forested; now they are mostly under subsistence agriculture and produce cash crops such as coconuts, coffee, cocoa and spices, vanilla accounting for 78% of exports.

Formerly French, the Comoros became independent (without the agreement of France) following a referendum in 1974. One of the world's poorest countries, it is plagued by lack of resources and political turmoil.

**Mayotte**, the easternmost of the large islands (population 101,000), voted to remain French in the 1974 referendum, and in 1976 became a Territorial Collectivity. [*Map page 33*] ■

**AREA** 2,230 sq km [861 sq mls]
**POPULATION** 630,000
**CAPITAL (POPULATION)** Moroni (22,000)
**GOVERNMENT** Federal Islamic republic
**ETHNIC GROUPS** Mainly mixture of Arab, Bantu and Malagasy peoples
**LANGUAGES** Arabic (official), Comorian (Swahili and Arabic dialect), French
**RELIGIONS** Islam 86%, Roman Catholic 14%
**CURRENCY** CFA franc = 100 centimes

# CONGO

The Republic of Congo is located on the River Congo (Zaïre) in west-central Africa. The Equator runs through the centre of the country. Congo has a narrow coastal plain on which its main port, Pointe Noire, stands. Behind the plain are uplands through which the River Niari has carved a fertile valley. The central part of the country consists of high plains. The north contains large swampy areas in the valleys of rivers that flow into the River Congo and its large tributary, the Oubangi (Ubangi).

Although astride the Equator, only the near-coastal Mayombe ridges and the east-central and northern parts of the Congo basin have a truly equatorial climate and vegetation. The areas around Brazzaville, the capital, and those north and west of it are drier, with savanna vegetation except where tributaries of the River Congo flood widely.

## ECONOMY AND RESOURCES

Because of the huge areas of dense forest more than half the population live in towns – a high proportion for Africa – though subsistence agriculture, mainly for cassava, occupies a third of the fast-growing workforce. Oil is by far the country's main source of income (as Africa's fifth largest producer). Palm-oil produce and timber are valuable exports but the timber industry, in relative decline, has always been hampered by poor transport – despite the spectacular Congo-Ocean railway from Brazzaville (formerly the capital of French Equatorial Africa) to Pointe Noire, the nation's only significant port.

## HISTORY AND POLITICS

Between the 15th and 18th centuries, part of Congo probably belonged to the huge Kongo kingdom, whose centre lay to the south. But the Congo coast became a centre of the European slave trade. The European exploration of the interior took place in the late 19th century, and the area came under French protection in 1880. It was later governed as part of a larger region called French Equatorial Africa and the country remained under French control until 1960.

Congo became a one-party state in 1964 and a military group took over in 1968. In 1970, Congo became Africa's first declared Communist state, but its Marxist-Leninist ideology did not prevent the government seeking Western help in exploiting the vast off-shore oil deposits. Marxism was abandoned in 1990 and the regime announced the planned introduction of a multiparty system. Following a referendum in favour of a new constitution, elections were held in 1992 and Pascal Lissouba was elected president. Other elections were held in 1993. [*Map page 33*] ■

**AREA** 342,000 sq km [132,046 sq mls]
**POPULATION** 2,516,000
**CAPITAL (POPULATION)** Brazzaville (938,000)
**GOVERNMENT** Multiparty republic
**ETHNIC GROUPS** Kongo 52%, Teke 17%, Mboshi 12%, Mbete 5%
**LANGUAGES** French (official)
**RELIGIONS** Christianity (Roman Catholic 54%, Protestant 25%, African Christian 14%), traditional beliefs 5%
**CURRENCY** CFA franc = 100 centimes

# COSTA RICA

Three mountain ranges form the skeleton of the country. In the south-east the Talamanca ranges rise to 3,837 m [12,585 ft] in Chirripó Grande; further north and west the Central Cordillera includes volcanic Irazú (3,432 m [11,260 ft]) and Poas (2,705 m [8,875 ft]), both active in recent decades; Miravalles (2,020 m [6,627 ft]) is one of four active volcanoes in the Cordillera de Guanacaste.

## ECONOMY AND RESOURCES

Agriculture is the mainstay of the economy,

the most important crop being coffee, which has been grown in the interior since 1850; in this century bananas have become a second major resource, and together they supply nearly half of Costa Rica's overseas earnings. Timber and fishing are also important. The capital, San José, stands in the fertile Valle Central, in the economic heartland of the country. Drier Guanacaste, in the far north-west, is an important cattle-raising region.

### HISTORY AND POLITICS

Christopher Columbus reached the Caribbean coast in 1502 on his fourth and final voyage to the Americas and rumours of treasure (Costa Rica means 'rich coast') soon attracted many Spaniards to settle in the country. Spain ruled the country until 1821, when the Spanish Central American colonies broke away to join Mexico in 1822. In 1823, the Central American states broke with Mexico and set up the Central American Federation. Later, however, this large union broke up and Costa Rica became fully independent in 1838.

From the late 19th century, Costa Rica experienced a number of revolutions, with periods of dictatorship and periods of democracy. In 1948, following a revolt, the armed forces were abolished. Since 1948, Costa Rica has enjoyed a long period of stable democracy, which many in Latin America admire and envy – of the republics of the isthmus, it has the best educational standards, a long life expectancy, the most democratic system of government, the highest per capita gross domestic product, and the least disparity between the poor and the rich. Its neutral stance has enabled the country to play the role of broker in many regional disputes. [*Map page 30*] ■

---

**AREA** 51,100 sq km [19,730 sq mls]
**POPULATION** 3,347,000
**CAPITAL (POPULATION)** San José (296,625)
**GOVERNMENT** Multiparty republic
**ETHNIC GROUPS** White 85%, Mestizo 8%, Black and Mulatto 3%, East Asian (mostly Chinese) 3%
**LANGUAGES** Spanish (official)
**RELIGIONS** Christianity (Roman Catholic 81%)
**CURRENCY** Colón = 100 céntimos

---

# CROATIA

The Republic of Croatia was one of the six republics that made up the former Communist country of Yugoslavia, until it became independent in 1991. The region bordering the Adriatic Sea, with many islands offshore, is called Dalmatia. It includes the coastal ranges, which contain large areas of bare limestone, reaching 1,913 m [6,276 ft] at Mt Troglav. Other highlands lie in the north-east. Most of the rest of the country consists of the fertile Pannonian plains, which are drained by Croatia's two main rivers, the Drava and the Sava.

The coastal area has a typical Mediterranean climate, with hot, dry summers and mild, moist winters. Inland, the climate becomes more continental. Winters are usually bitterly cold, while temperatures often soar to 38°C [100°F] in the summer months.

### ECONOMY AND RESOURCES

The wars of the early 1990s disrupted Croatia's economy, which had been quite prosperous before the disturbances. Tourism on the Dalmatian coast had been a major industry. Croatia also had major manufacturing industries, and manufactures remain the chief exports, including cement, chemicals, refined oil and oil products, ships, steel and wood products. Major farm products include fruits, livestock, maize, soya beans, sugar beet and wheat.

### HISTORY AND POLITICS

Slav people settled in the area around 1,400 years ago. In 803, Croatia became part of the Holy Roman Empire and the Croats soon adopted Christianity. Croatia was an independent kingdom in the 10th and 11th centuries, but in 1102 the king of Hungary also became king of Croatia, creating a union that lasted 800 years.

In 1526, part of Croatia and Hungary came under the Turkish Ottoman empire, while the rest of Croatia came under the Austrian

Habsburgs. In 1699, however, all of Croatia came under Habsburg rule. In 1867, the Habsburg empire became the dual monarchy of Austria-Hungary.

Following the defeat of Austria-Hungary in World War I, Croatia became part of the new Kingdom of the Serbs, Croats and Slovenes, which was renamed Yugoslavia in 1929. Germany occupied Yugoslavia during World War II – Croatia was proclaimed independent, but it was really ruled by the invaders.

After the war, the Communists took power with Josip Broz Tito as the country's leader. Despite ethnic differences between the people, Tito held Yugoslavia together until his death in 1980. In the 1980s, economic and ethnic problems, including a deterioration in relations with Serbia, threatened the country's stability. Then, in the 1990s, Yugoslavia split up into five separate nations, one of which was Croatia, officially declaring its independence in 1991.

After Serbia supplied arms to Serbs living in Croatia, war broke out between the two republics, causing great damage and loss of life. The vital tourist industry (Croatia accounted for 80% of the Yugoslav total in 1990) was also devastated, with the fine medieval city of Dubrovnik on the Dalmatian coast a prime casualty. As a result of the fighting, Croatia lost more than 30% of its territory. But in 1992, the United Nations sent a peacekeeping force to Croatia, which effectively ended the war with Serbia.

In 1992, when war broke out in Bosnia-Herzegovina, Croatian troops at first gave support to the Muslims against Serbian attacks. But, later, Croatian forces took some areas of Bosnia-Herzegovina, expelling Muslims from the areas they occupied. [*Map page 16*] ■

AREA  56,538 sq km [21,824 sq mls]
POPULATION  4,504,000
CAPITAL (POPULATION)  Zagreb (931,000)
GOVERNMENT  Multiparty republic
ETHNIC GROUPS  Croat 78%, Serb 12%, Bosnian, Hungarian, Slovene
LANGUAGES  Serbo-Croatian
RELIGIONS  Christianity (Roman Catholic 77%, Eastern Orthodox 11%), Islam 1%
CURRENCY  Kuna = 100 lipas

# CUBA

As large as all the other Caribbean islands put together, Cuba is only 193 km [120 mls] across at its widest, but stretches for over 1,200 km [750 mls] from the Gulf of Mexico to the Windward Passage. Though large, it is the least mountainous of all the Greater Antilles. The plains run the length of the island from Cape San Antonio in the far west of Guantánamo Bay in the south-east (site of an anomalous US naval base), broken by three sets of mountains which occupy no more than a quarter of the country.

## ECONOMY AND RESOURCES
The undulating fringes of the mountainous areas provide some of the best tobacco lands, while the higher areas also produce coffee as a cash crop. Sugar cane, however, remains by far the most important cash crop, as it has done throughout the century, and Cuba is the world's third largest producer behind the giants of Brazil and India, producing 74 million tonnes in 1991. It uses over 1 million hectares [2.5 million acres], more than half the island country's cultivated land, and accounts for more than 75% of exports.

Before the 1959 revolution, the cane was grown on large estates, many of them owned by US companies or individuals, but after these were nationalized the focus of production shifted eastwards to Guayabal, with the Soviet Union and Eastern European countries replacing the USA as the main market. Cattle raising and rice cultivation have also been encouraged to help diversify the economy, while Cuba is also a significant exporter of minerals, notably nickel. In 1993, oil production satisfied 40% of domestic requirements.

## HISTORY AND POLITICS
Cuba, apart from a brief occupation by the British in 1762–3, remained a Spanish colony from its discovery by Columbus in 1492 (he thought it was part of India) until 1898. It was then under American military

rule until independence in 1902. Since the revolution that deposed the right-wing dictator Fulgencio Batista and brought Fidel Castro to power in 1959 – when 600,000 people fled the island, many of them to Florida – rural development has been fostered in a relatively successful bid to make the quality of life more homogeneous throughout the island. Havana, the chief port and capital, was particularly depopulated.

Cuba's relationship with the US, which secured its independence from Spain but bolstered the corrupt regimes before the revolution, has always been crucial. In 1961, US-backed 'exiles' attempted to invade at the Bay of Pigs, and relations worsened still further the following year when the attempted installation of Soviet missiles on Cuban soil almost led to global war. A close ally of the USSR, Castro has encouraged left-wing revolutionary movements in Latin America and aided Marxist governments in Africa, notably in Angola, while emerging as a Third World leader.

The rapid political changes in Eastern Europe and the USSR from 1989 to 1991 left Cuba isolated as a hardline Marxist state in the Western Hemisphere, and the disruption of trade severely affected the economy of a country heavily dependent on subsidized Soviet oil and aid. Early in 1992 Cuban state radio called for an end to the 30-year-old trade embargo imposed by the US government. Economic difficulties have forced the government to introduce free-market reforms to guard against worsening shortages of food and fuel, but despite the political uncertainty Fidel Castro was re-elected as President of the Council of State for a further five-year term in 1993. [Map page 30] ■

**AREA** 110,860 sq km [42,803 sq mls]
**POPULATION** 10,9602,000
**CAPITAL (POPULATION)** Havana (2,119,000)
**GOVERNMENT** Socialist republic
**ETHNIC GROUPS** White 66%, Mulatto 22%, Black 12%
**LANGUAGES** Spanish (official)
**RELIGIONS** Christianity (Roman Catholic 40%, Protestant 3%)
**CURRENCY** Cuban peso = 100 centavos

# CYPRUS

A small but strategically situated Mediterranean island, Cyprus is a detached fragment of the mainland mountains to the east. In the south, the broad massif of Troodos, rich in minerals, is a classic example of an ophiolite, or intrusive dome of ancient suboceanic rocks. The northern coast is backed by the long limestone range of Kyrenia.

## ECONOMY AND RESOURCES
The central plain between Morphou and Famagusta is fertile and well irrigated and grows fruits, flowers and early vegetables. The former forests were cut mainly in classical times to fuel the copper smelteries; *Kypros* is the Greek for copper.

The Greek Cypriot sector has prospered from tourism, British bases, invisible earnings and specialized agriculture, as well as increased manufacturing. The more agriculturally based north has done rather less well: the 'Turkish Republic of Northern Cyprus' is recognized only by Ankara and relies heavily on financial aid from Turkey.

## HISTORY AND POLITICS
Turks settled in the north of the island during Ottoman rule, from 1571 to 1878, when Cyprus came under British administration. In the 1950s Greek Cypriots, led by Archbishop Makarios (later President), campaigned for union with Greece (Enosis), while the Turks favoured partition. After a guerrilla campaign by EOKA a power-sharing compromise was reached and in 1960 the island became a republic.

This fragile arrangement broke down in 1963, however, and the following year the UN sent in forces to prevent more intercommunal fighting. In 1968 the Turkish Cypriots set up an 'autonomous administration' in the north, but in 1974, following a coup by Greek-born army officers that deposed Makarios, Turkey invaded the mainland and took control of the northern 40% of the country, displacing 200,000 Greek Cypriots. The UN has since supervised an uneasy partition of the island. All attempts at federation have failed. [*Map page 19*] ■

**AREA** 9,250 sq km [3,571 sq mls]
**POPULATION** 734,000
**CAPITAL (POPULATION)** Nicosia (or Lefkosia,169,000)
**GOVERNMENT** Multiparty republic
**ETHNIC GROUPS** Greek Cypriot 81%, Turkish Cypriot 19%
**LANGUAGES** Greek and Turkish (both official)
**RELIGIONS** Christianity (Greek Orthodox), Islam
**CURRENCY** Cyprus Pound = 100 cents

# CZECH REPUBLIC

With 61% of the total land area of the former Czechoslovakia, the Czech Republic is the larger of its two successor states. In the west, Bohemia is a diamond-shaped area, surrounded by ranges of mountains that enclose a basin drained by the River Elbe and its tributaries. In the centre lies Prague, the historic capital city. Moravia, in the middle of the country, is divided from Bohemia by plateau land known as the Moravian Heights. Central Moravia is a lowland, with the industrial city of Brno, home of the Bren gun, at its heart.

## ECONOMY AND RESOURCES

The Czech Republic is the most highly industrialized of the former Soviet satellites, but agriculture remains strong and well developed, with high yields of most crops suited to the continental climate, including barley, fruit hops, maize, potatoes, sugar beet, vegetables and wheat. Food-processing industries, including brewing, are important in the western provinces. The mountains are rich in minerals, including iron ore, lead, zinc and uranium, while in western Bohemia there are also reserves of hard coal and lignite. Manufactures include such products as chemicals, iron and steel and machinery, but the country also has light industries making such things as glassware and textiles for export.

## HISTORY AND POLITICS

Created after World War I and reorganized as a federation in 1969, Czechoslovakia was formally broken up on 1 January 1993, when the eastern Slovak Republic became independent in its own right. The Czech Republic is itself composed of two units, both Czech-speaking, mainly Protestant in religion and with a common history as provinces of the Austrian part of the Austro-Hungarian empire, ruled from Vienna.

Czechoslovakia's 'velvet revolution' of 1989 was Eastern Europe's smoothest transition, toppling the old Communist regime by 'people power' and soon replacing it with a multiparty system that elected a government headed by President Vaclav Havel, the country's best-known playwright and noted dissident (with Charter 77, part of the coalition Civic Forum). It was all very different from 1968, when in the 'Prague Spring' Soviet forces suppressed an uprising supporting Alexander Dubcek's brave attempts at rekindling democracy and breaking the stranglehold of the party bosses.

As elsewhere in Central and Eastern Europe, the road to a free-market economy was not easy. The burdens that plagued the former Soviet satellites were all too obvious – large budget deficit, over-reliance on other Communist countries for trade, increasingly obsolete industrial capacity – and so were the immediate results: inflation, falling production, strikes and unemployment.

Politically, too, there were difficulties. Pragmatic concerns soon dulled the euphoria of democratization and indeed Civic Forum split over the pace of economic reform. Principles of the new constitution were still the subject of controversy in 1992, when resurgent Slovak nationalism forced the parliamentary vote that ended the old Czechoslovak federation – unnecessarily, according to most Czechs and a substantial minority of Slovaks. But the Czech economy, with a serviceable foreign debt and a skilled and adaptable workforce, was in far better shape than that of, say, Poland, while the break-up was, for the most part, amicable. Border adjustments were negligible and negotiated calmly; after the separation, Czechs and Slovaks maintained a customs union and other economic ties, and there was no sign of the bitter hatreds that were causing so much bloodshed in Yugoslavia. [*Map page 16*] ■

**AREA** 78,864 sq km [30,449 sq mls]
**POPULATION** 10,295,000
**CAPITAL (POPULATION)** Prague (or Praha, 1,216,000)
**GOVERNMENT** Multiparty republic
**ETHNIC GROUPS** Czech 81%, Moravian 13%, Slovak 3%, Polish, German, Silesian, Gypsy, Hungarian, Ukrainian
**LANGUAGES** Czech (official)
**RELIGIONS** Christianity (Roman Catholic 39%, Protestant 4%)
**CURRENCY** Czech koruna = 100 halura

# DENMARK

T he smallest of the Scandinavian countries (but the second largest in population), Denmark consists of the Jutland (Jylland) peninsula, which is an extension of the North German Plain, and an archipelago of 406 islands, of which 89 are inhabited. The coastline – about 7,300 km [4,500 mls] – is extremely long for the size of the country. The largest and most densely populated of the islands is Zealand (Sjaelland), which lies close to the coast of southern Sweden. In the early 1990s this will be connected to the most important island – Fünen (Fyn) – by the Storebaeltstunnel. Copenhagen (København), the capital city, lies on the narrow strait, The Sound, which leads from the Kattegat to the Baltic Sea.

Structurally, Denmark is part of a low-lying belt of sedimentary rocks extending from north Germany to southern Sweden, which are geologically much younger than the rest of Scandinavia. The surface is almost entirely covered by glacial deposits, but the underlying strata are exposed as the 122 m [400 ft] chalk cliffs on the island of Møn. Nowhere in Denmark, however, is higher than 173 m [568 ft] and the country averages just 98 m [30 ft]. Along the west coast of Jutland, facing the North Sea, are lines of sand dunes with shallow lagoons behind them.

## ECONOMY AND RESOURCES
Denmark has few mineral resources and no coal, though there is now some oil and natural gas from the North Sea. A century ago this was a poor farming and fishing country, but Denmark has now been transformed into one of Europe's wealthiest industrial nations. The first steps in the process were taken in the late 19th century, with the introduction of co-operative methods of processing and distributing farm produce, and the development of modern methods of dairying and pig- and poultry-breeding. Denmark became the main supplier of bacon, eggs and butter to the growing industrial nations of Western Europe. Most of the natural fodder for the animals is still grown in Denmark – three-quarters of the land is cultivated and more than 60% is arable – with barley as the principal crop.

Although less than 5% of the working population is actively engaged in farming, the scientific methods used and the efficient co-operative marketing system ensure that output remains high. Over a third of Denmark's exports are of food products, with Britain and Germany the chief customers.

From a firm agricultural base, Denmark has developed a whole range of industries. Some – brewing, meat canning, fish processing, pottery, textiles and furniture-making – use Danish products, while others – shipbuilding, oil refining, engineering and metal-working – depend on imported raw materials. The famous port of Copenhagen is also the chief industrial centre and draw for more than a million tourists each year. At the other end of the scale there is Legoland, the famous miniature town of plastic bricks, built at Billand, north-west of Vejle in eastern Jutland. It was here, in a carpenter's workshop, that Lego was created before it went on to become the world's best-selling construction toy – and a prominent Danish export. The country is also the world's biggest exporter of insulin.

## HISTORY AND POLITICS

Control of the entrances to the Baltic – the Great and Little Belts and The Sound – contributed to the power of Denmark in the Middle Ages, when the kingdom dominated its neighbours and expanded its territories to include Norway, Iceland, Greenland and the Faroe Islands. The link with Norway was broken in 1814, and with Iceland in 1944, but Greenland and the Faroes retain connections with Denmark. The granite island of Bornholm, off the southern tip of Sweden, also remains a Danish possession.

Denmark is a generally comfortable mixture of striking social opposites. The Lutheran tradition and the cradle of Hans Christian Andersen's fairy-tales co-exist with open attitudes to pornography and one of the highest illegitimacy rates in the West (44%). A reputation for caring and thorough welfare services – necessitating high taxation – is dented somewhat by the world's highest recorded suicide rate.

It is, too, one of the 'greenest' of the advanced nations, with a pioneering Ministry of Pollution that has real power to act: in 1991 it became the first government anywhere to fine industries for emissions of carbon dioxide, the primary 'greenhouse' gas. At the same time, Danes register Europe's highest rate of deaths from lung cancer.

Denmark gets on well with its neighbours and partners. On 1 January 1973, along with Britain and Ireland, it joined the EEC – the first Scandinavian country to make the break from EFTA – but it still co-operates closely on social, cultural and economic matters with its five Scandinavian partners in the Nordic Council. Having voted by a slender majority to reject the treaty of Maastricht in 1992, the Danes reversed this decision in a second referendum held in May 1993.

**Bornholm** is a Danish island well away from the rest of the country and far nearer to the southern tip of Sweden (40 km [25 mls]) than to Copenhagen (168 km [104 mls]). A separate administrative region, it was occupied by Germany in World War II but liberated by the Russians, who returned it to Denmark in 1946.

Measuring 558 sq km [227 sq mls], Bornholm is composed mainly of granite and has poor soils, but deposits of kaolin (china clay) spawned a pottery industry. The principal town and ferry port is Rønne, the fishing port Neksø. Fishing and fish processing, agriculture (mainly cattle rearing) and tourism are the main sources of income – the last-named reliant partly on the island's fine examples of fortified churches. [*Map page 13*] ■

AREA **43,070 sq km [16,629 sq mls]**
POPULATION **5,173,000**
CAPITAL (POPULATION) **Copenhagen (1,337,000)**
GOVERNMENT **Parliamentary monarchy**
ETHNIC GROUPS **Danish 97%**
LANGUAGES **Danish (official)**
RELIGIONS **Christianity (Lutheran 91%, Roman Catholic 1%)**
CURRENCY **Danish krone = 100 øre**

# DJIBOUTI

The Republic of Djibouti is a small country in eastern Africa, occupying a strategic position where the Red Sea meets the Gulf of Aden, which leads into the Indian Ocean. Djibouti lies around an inlet of the Gulf of Aden, called the Gulf of Tadjoura. Behind the coastal plain on the northern side of the Gulf of Tadjoura is a highland region, the Mabla Mountains, rising to 1,783 m [5,850 ft] above sea level. Djibouti also contains, at Lake Assal, the lowest point on land in Africa (155 m [509 ft] below sea level).

Djibouti has one of the world's hottest and driest climates. Summer days are exceptionally hot, with temperatures regularly exceeding 42°C [100°F]. The sparse rainfall on the coast is most likely to occur in winter. On average, it rains only on 26 days every year. Inland, where the rainfall is slightly higher on highland areas, rain is more likely between April and October.

A few areas of woodland occur in the mountains north of the Gulf of Tadjoura, where the average annual rainfall reaches about 500 mm [20 in]. But the main vegetation in Djibouti is scrub or dry grassland. The shortage of pasture and surface water makes life difficult for the people, most of whom are nomads who wander in search of pasture.

## ECONOMY AND RESOURCES

Djibouti is a poor country. Its economy is based mainly on money it gets for use of its port and the railway that links it to Addis Ababa. Djibouti is a free trade zone and it also has an international airport. The country has no major resources and manufacturing is on a very small scale. The only important activity is livestock raising and half of the people are pastoral nomads. Most of the food the country needs has to be imported.

## HISTORY AND POLITICS

Islam was introduced into the area which is now Djibouti in the 9th century AD. The conversion of the Afars led to conflict between them and the Christian Ethiopians who lived in the interior. By the 19th century, the Issas, who are Somalis, had moved north and occupied much of the traditional grazing land of the Afars. France gained influence in the area in the second half of the 19th century and, in 1888, they set up a territory called French Somaliland. The capital of the territory, Djibouti, became important when the Ethiopian emperor Menelik II decided to build a railway to it from Addis Ababa. This made Djibouti the main port handling Ethiopian trade, though Djibouti lost trade when Eritrea was federated with Ethiopia in 1952, giving Ethiopia another port, Assab, on the Red Sea.

In 1967, the people voted to retain their links with France, though most of the Issas were opposed and favoured independence. The country was renamed the French Territory of the Afars and Issas, but it was named Djibouti when it became fully independent in 1977.

Djibouti became a one-party state in 1981, but a new constitution was introduced in 1992, permitting four parties which must maintain a balance between the ethnic groups

in the country. However, in 1992 and 1993, tensions between the Afars and Issas flared up when Afars launched an uprising which was eventually put down by government troops. [*Map page 32*] ∎

> **AREA** 23,200 sq km [8,958 sq mls]
> **POPULATION** 566,000
> **CAPITAL (POPULATION)** Djibouti (290,000)
> **GOVERNMENT** Multiparty republic
> **ETHNIC GROUPS** Issa 47%, Afar 37%, Arab 6%
> **LANGUAGES** Arabic and French (both official)
> **RELIGIONS** Islam 96%, Christianity 4%
> **CURRENCY** Djibouti franc = 100 centimes

# DOMINICA

Dominica is a mountainous, forested island of 751 sq km [290 sq mls], volcanic in origin, with an indented coastline edged with steep cliffs. The climate is tropical with heavy rainfall.

The population of 71,000 is over 90% African and 6% mixed, with small Asian and white minorities and a settlement of about 500 mainly mixed-blood Carib Indians. Predominantly Christian (75% Roman Catholic), most people speak the local French *patois*, though English is the official language. Nearly 30% of the islanders live in the capital, Roseau, and its suburbs.

Though rich soils support dense vegetation, less than 10% is cultivated; bananas and coconut-based soaps and cigars are the chief exports, although fishing, forestry and food-processing industries are being encouraged. Much food is imported, and future prospects for a relatively poor Caribbean island depend a good deal on the development of the island as a luxury tourism destination.

Discovered by Christopher Columbus in 1493, Dominica has been an independent republic (the Commonwealth of Dominica) since 1978, after 11 years as a self-governing colony of the UK. Britain and France fought long over the island, its ownership decided in 1805 by a ransom of £12,000 (then US$53,000). [*Map page 30*] ■

AREA 751 sq km [290 sq mls]
POPULATION 71,000
CAPITAL (POPULATION) Roseau (21,000)
GOVERNMENT Multiparty republic
ETHNIC GROUPS Of African descent
LANGUAGES English (official), French patois
RELIGIONS Christianity (Roman Catholic 75%, Protestant 15%)
CURRENCY East Caribbean dollar = 100 cents

# DOMINICAN REPUBLIC

Second largest of the Caribbean nations in both area and population, the Dominican Republic shares the island of Hispaniola with Haiti, occupying the eastern two-thirds. Of the steep-sided mountains that dominate the island, the country includes the northern Cordillera Septentrional, the huge Cordillera Central (rising to Pico Duarte, at 3,175 m [10,417 ft] the highest peak in the Caribbean), and the southern Sierra de Bahoruco. Between them and to the east lie fertile valleys and lowlands, including the Vega Real and the coastal plains where the main sugar plantations are found. Typical of the area, the Republic is hot and humid close to sea level, while cooler and fresher conditions prevail in the mountains; rainfall is heavy, especially in the north-east.

## ECONOMY AND RESOURCES
In the 1980s, growth in industry (exploiting vast hydroelectric potential), mining (nickel, bauxite, gold and silver) and tourism have augmented the traditional agricultural economy based on sugar (still a fifth of exports), coffee, cocoa, tobacco and fruit. There are a growing number of light processing industries producing beer, peanut oil, soap, paint, glass products, textiles and other products.

## HISTORY AND POLITICS
Columbus 'discovered' the island and its Amerindian population (soon to be decimated) on 5 December 1492; the city of Santo Domingo, now the capital and chief port, was founded by his brother Bartholomew four years later and is the oldest in the Americas. For long a Spanish colony, Hispaniola was initially the centrepiece of their empire but later it was to become its poor relation. In 1795 it became French, then Spanish again in 1809, but in 1821 (then called Santo Domingo) it won independence. Haiti held the territory from 1822 to 1844, when on restoring sovereignty it became the Dominican Republic.

Growing American influence culminated in occupation from 1916 to 1924, followed by a long period of corrupt dictatorship. Since a bitter war was ended by US military intervention in 1965, a precarious fledgling democracy has survived violent elections under the watchful eye of Washington. This highly Americanized Hispanic society is, however, far from stable. [*Map page 30*] ■

AREA 48,730 sq km [18,815 sq mls]
POPULATION 7,684,000
CAPITAL (POPULATION) Santo Domingo (1,601,000)
GOVERNMENT Multiparty republic
ETHNIC GROUPS Mulatto 73%, White 16%, Black 11%
LANGUAGES Spanish (official)
RELIGIONS Christianity (Roman Catholic 93%)
CURRENCY Peso = 100 centavos

# ECUADOR

Ecuador's name comes from the Equator, which divides the country unequally; Quito, the capital, lies just within the southern hemisphere. The country has three distinct regions – the coastal plain (Costa), the Andean uplands (Sierra), and the eastern alluvial plains of the Oriente.

The coastal plain, which averages 100 km

[60 mls] wide, is a hot, fertile area of variable rainfall. Recently cleared of forests and largely freed of malaria, it is now good farmland where banana farms, coffee and cocoa plantations and fishing are the main sources of income, with the country's commercial centre of Guayaquil a flourishing port.

The Andes form three linked mountain ranges across the country, with several of the central peaks rising above 5,000 m [16,400 ft]. Quito, an old city rich in art and architecture from a colonial past, has a backdrop of snow-capped mountains, among them Cotopaxi – at 5,896 m [19,340 ft] the world's highest active volcano – and Chimborazo (6,267 m [20,556 ft]). The Oriente, a heavily forested upland, is virtually unexploited except for recent developments of oil and natural gas.

## ECONOMY AND RESOURCES

Ecuador's economy was based on the export of bananas, for which the country was world leader, and is still the biggest exporter, but this changed from 1972 when oil was first exploited with the opening of the trans-Andean pipeline linking with the tanker-loading port of Esmeraldas. Petroleum and derivatives account for about 40% of export earnings, after peaking at 66% in 1985. A shortage of power limits much development in the manufacturing industry – even in the mid-1980s only 60% of the population had use of electricity. During the 1970s, the manufacture of textiles, cement and pharmaceuticals grew, as did food processing, but there is little heavy industry. Fishing has been affected by the warm water current (El Niño) and there is now an emphasis on greater investment and using much more new technology.

Changes in demand for oil and an earthquake in March 1987, which disrupted much of industry, led the government to suspend payment of interest on its overseas debt, then cancel all debt repayment for the rest of the year. A strict economic recovery programme was put into place and a rescheduling of debt payments agreed in 1989.

## HISTORY AND POLITICS

The Inca people of Peru conquered much of what is now Ecuador in the late 15th century, introducing their language, Quechua, which is widely spoken today. But in 1533 Spanish forces defeated the Incas and took control of Ecuador. The country became independent in 1822, following the defeat of a Spanish force in a battle near Quito. Ecuador then became part of Gran Colombia, a confederation with Panama, Colombia and Venezuela, but left in 1830. Between 1830 and 1947 there were no less than 14 constitutions.

In the 19th and 20th centuries, Ecuador suffered from political instability, while successive governments failed to tackle the social and economic problems of the country. A war with Peru in 1941 led to a loss of territory, but the area taken by Peru is still claimed by Ecuador. After seven years of military rule elections took place in 1979 and democracy was restored (voting is compulsory for all literate citizens over the age of 18); civilian governments have ruled since then.

**The Galápagos Islands** lie scattered across the Equator, 970 km [610 mls] west of Ecuador (of which they form a province). They consist of six main islands and over 50 smaller ones; all are volcanic, some of them active, but only four of the islands are inhabited.

Discovered by the Spanish in 1535 but annexed by Ecuador in 1832, the archipelago became famous after the visit of Charles Darwin in 1835, when he collected crucial evidence for his theory of natural selection. The islands contain a large variety of unique endemic species of flora and fauna, including giant tortoises and marine iguanas. Though 90% of the land area is devoted to a national park (which attracted 42,000 visitors in 1992), most of the 10,000 inhabitants derive their livelihood from fishing and farming. [*Map page 31*] ■

---

**AREA**  283,560 sq km [109,483 sq mls]
**POPULATION**  11,220,000
**CAPITAL (POPULATION)**  Quito (1,101,000)
**GOVERNMENT**  Multiparty republic
**ETHNIC GROUPS**  Mestizo (mixed White and Amerindian) 40%, Amerindian 40%, White 15%, Black 5%
**LANGUAGES**  Spanish (official)
**RELIGIONS**  Christianity (Roman Catholic 92%)
**CURRENCY**  Sucre = 100 centavos

# EGYPT

Bul for the River Nile, which brings the waters of the East African and Ethiopian Highlands to the Mediterranean, Egypt would scarcely be populated, for 96% of the present population lives in the Nile Valley and its rich delta.

The vast majority of the country, away from the Nile, is desert and semi-desert. Egypt's deserts are not uniform, but offer varied landscapes. Beyond the Gulf of Suez and the Suez Canal the Sinai Peninsula in the south is mountainous and rugged; it contains the highest of Egypt's mountains – Gebel Katherina (2,637 m [8,650 ft]) – and is almost entirely uninhabited. The Eastern Desert, between the Nile and the Red Sea, is a much dissected area and parts of the Red Sea Hills are over 2,000 m [6,560 ft]; water is obtained from the light rainfall, from occasional springs, and from beneath dry stream beds. Except for a few mining settlements along the coast, this area is not suitable for permanent settlement and is occupied mostly by nomads.

The Western Desert includes almost three-quarters of Egypt and consists of low vales and scarps, mainly of limestones. Over its stony and sandy surfaces great tank battles were fought in World War II. A number of depressions in the desert surface fall below sea level, the most notable being the Qattâra Depression (–133 m [–435 ft]) – a waste of salt lakes and marshes. There are a number of oases, the most important being Khârga, Dakhla, Farâfra, Baharîya and Siwa. By drawing on deep-seated artesian waters, it is hoped to expand the farming area of the first four of these as a contribution to the solution of Egypt's present population problem. Except at the oases, the desert is virtually uninhabited.

## ECONOMY AND RESOURCES

The Nile Valley was one of the cradles of civilization, and Egypt has the longest-known history of any African country. The depend-

able annual flooding of the great river each summer and the discovery of the art of cultivating wheat and barley fostered simple irrigation techniques and favoured co-operation between the farmers. Stability and leisure developed arts and crafts, city life began and the foundations were laid of writing, arithmetic, geometry and astronomy. Great temples and pyramid tombs within the valley remain as memorials to this early civilization – and a magnet for nearly 2 million tourists every year.

Today, even more than in the past, the Egyptian people, living within a desert, depend almost entirely on the waters of the Nile. These are extremely seasonal, and control and storage have become essential during this century. For seasonal storage the Aswan Dam (1902) and the Jebel Awliya Dam in Sudan (1936) were built. The Aswan High Dam (1970), sited 6.4 km [4 mls] above the Aswan Dam, is the greatest of all. Built with massive Soviet aid, it holds back 25 times as much as the older dam and permits year-round storage. Through this dam the Egyptian Nile is now regulated to an even flow throughout the year. The water that has accumulated behind the dam in Lake Nasser (about 5,000 sq km [1,930 sq mls]) is making possible the reclamation of more desert land, the intensification of agriculture and the cultivation of crops that need more water, such as rice for export. The dam is also a source of hydroelectric power and aids the expansion of industry. However, 50,000 Nubians had to be resettled and the regulation of the river's flow has led to some unforeseen environmental problems.

## Industry

The traditional Egypt of the *galabiyah*-clad peasant toiling on his tiny plot of land is slowly changing. Pressure of population on the limited amount of farmland is leading to an expansion of industry as an alternative way of life, and Egypt is today one of the most industrialized countries of Africa.

Most of this industrial development has come about since World War II. Textiles, including the spinning, weaving, dyeing and printing of cotton, wool, silk and artificial fibres, form by far the largest industry. Other manufactures derive from local agricultural and mineral raw materials, and include sugar refining, milling, oil-seed pressing, and the manufacture of chemicals, glass and cement. There are also iron-and-steel, oil-refining and car-assembly industries, and many consumer goods such as radios, TV sets and refrigerators are manufactured. The main cities of Cairo and Alexandria – the capital is the largest city in Africa – are also Egypt's major industrial centres.

The Suez Canal, which opened in 1869 and is 173 km [107 mls] long, is still an important trading route. Though it cannot take the large modern cargo vessels, oil tankers and liners, it still carries around 17,500 vessels a year between the Mediterranean and the Red Sea.

## HISTORY AND POLITICS
The British-built Suez Canal was nationalized in 1956 by the Egyptian president, Gamal Abdel Nasser, who from 1954 until his death in 1970 was the leader of Arab nationalism. In 1952 the army had toppled the corrupt regime of King Farouk, the last ruler of a dynasty dating back to 1841. Egypt had previously been part of the Ottoman empire (from 1517), though British influence was paramount after 1882 and the country was a British protectorate from 1914 to 1922, when it acquired limited independence.

Egypt was involved in two wars against Israel (in 1967 and 1973) but Nasser's successor broke with the rest of the Arab world to sign a peace treaty with Israel in 1979. He was assassinated in 1981. Egypt joined the allied forces against Saddam Hussein in the 1991 Gulf War. In recent years, the country has experienced a rising tide of Islamic fundamentalism which has included terrorist attacks on foreign tourists. [*Map page 22*] ■

AREA 1,001,450 sq km [386,660 sq mls]
POPULATION 61,636,000
CAPITAL (POPULATION) Cairo (or El Qâhira, 6,800,000)
GOVERNMENT Republic
ETHNIC GROUPS Egyptian 99%
LANGUAGES Arabic (official), French, English
RELIGIONS Islam (Sunni Muslim 94%), Christianity (mainly Coptic Christian 6%)
CURRENCY Egyptian pound = 100 piastres

# EL SALVADOR

The only Central American country without a Caribbean coast, El Salvador is also the smallest and the most densely populated; pressure on agricultural land, combined with civil war, has led to widespread emigration. The Pacific coastal plain is narrow and backed by a volcanic range averaging about 1,200 m [4,000 ft] in altitude. El Salvador has over 20 volcanoes, some of which are still active, and crater lakes occupying a fertile central plain 400 m to 800 m [1,300 ft to 2,600 ft] above sea level. Urban and rural populations in this belt together account for 60% of the country's total.

## ECONOMY AND RESOURCES
This fertile zone also produces 90% of the coffee and tobacco, and most of the maize and sugar – the foundations of the agricultural economy, with coffee usually accounting for over half the total value of exports. The towns are centres of manufacturing for the domestic market. In May 1992 El Salvador, Guatemala and Honduras created a fre trade zone.

Inland, the frontier with Honduras is marked by mountain ranges which reach heights of 2,000 m [6,560 ft]; previously forested and empty, they are now attracting migrants desperate for agricultural land.

## HISTORY AND POLITICS
El Salvador was plagued by conflict from the early 1970s and by full-blown civil war from 1980, when the political left joined revolutionary guerrillas against the US-backed extreme right-wing government. During the next 12 years, more than 75,000 people were killed (most of them civilians) and hundreds of thousands were made homeless as the regime received $4 billion in aid from the US in abetting the 55,000-strong Salvadorean Army and notorious death squads.

After 19 months of UN-mediated talks, the two sides agreed complicated terms at the end of 1991. A cease-fire took effect in February

1992, but the country remained in disarray, with unemployment, for example, standing at more than 50% of the workforce. [*Map page 30*] ■

> **AREA** 21,040 sq km [8,124 sq mls]
> **POPULATION** 5,641,000
> **CAPITAL (POPULATION)** San Salvador (1,522,000)
> **GOVERNMENT** Republic
> **ETHNIC GROUPS** Mestizo (mixed White and Amerindian) 89%, Amerindian 10%, White 1%
> **LANGUAGES** Spanish (official)
> **RELIGIONS** Christianity (Roman Catholic 94%)
> **CURRENCY** Colón = 100 centavos

# EQUATORIAL GUINEA

The Republic of Equatorial Guinea consists of a mainland territory which makes up 90% of the land area, called Mbini (or Rio Muni), between Cameroon and Gabon, and five offshore islands in the Bight of Bonny, the largest of which is Bioko. The island of Annobon lies 560 km [350 mls] south-west of Mbini.

Mbini consists mainly of hills and plateaux behind the coastal plains. Its main river, the Lolo (formerly Mbini), rises in Gabon and flows across Mbini. Bioko is a volcanic island with fertile soils; Malabo's harbour is part of a submerged volcano.

The climate is hot and humid. Bioko is mountainous, with the land rising to 2,850 m [9,350 ft] and hence it is particularly rainy, though there is a marked dry season between December and February. Mainland Mbini has a similar climate, though the rainfall diminishes inland. The dense rainforests contain valuable trees, including mahogany, okoumé and African walnut, while mangrove forests border much of the coast. Bioko is more varied, with grasslands at higher levels.

## ECONOMY AND RESOURCES
Plantations of coffee and cocoa have been established on the mountainous and volcanic islands, similar to many Caribbean islands.

Mainland Mbini, which accounts for over 90% of the country's land area, is very different, lower and thinly peopled, less developed, and with fewer foreign enterprises, except in forestry (especially okoumé and mahogany production) and palm oil. Coffee and cocoa are also grown, though the economy relies heavily on foreign aid.

## HISTORY AND POLITICS
At the turn of the 15th century the Papacy awarded Africa and Asia to Portugal, and the Americas west of 50°W to Spain. The latter sought a source of slaves in Africa, and in 1778 the Portuguese ceded the islands of Fernando Poó (Bioko) and Annobon (Pagalu), together with rights on the mainland, Mbini (Rio Muni), against Spanish agreement to Portuguese advance west of 50°W in Brazil.

Guinea, a name which derives from an ancient African kingdom, was once used to describe the whole coastal region of West Africa. Equatorial Guinea was granted partial autonomy from Spain in 1963, and gained full independence in 1968. Thanks to its cocoa plantations, Equatorial Guinea once boasted the highest per capita income in West Africa. But after independence, the bloody 11-year dictatorship of President Francisco Macías Nguema left the economy in ruins. He was overthrown in 1979 and a group of officers, led by his nephew, Lt.-Col. Teodoro Obiang Nguema Mbasago, set up a Supreme Military Council to rule the country. In 1991, the people voted to set up a multiparty democracy and elections were held in 1993. [*Map page 33*] ■

> **AREA** 28,050 sq km [10,830 sq mls]
> **POPULATION** 389,000
> **CAPITAL (POPULATION)** Malabo (37,000)
> **GOVERNMENT** Multiparty republic (transitional)
> **ETHNIC GROUPS** Fang 83%, Bubi 10%, Ndowe 4%
> **LANGUAGES** Spanish (official)
> **RELIGIONS** Christianity (mainly Roman Catholic) 89%, traditional beliefs 5%
> **CURRENCY** CFA franc = 100 centimes

# ERITREA

# ESTONIA

Eritrea consists of a low coastal plain in the south and mountain ranges in the north. It was Ethiopia's third largest province but only seventh in terms of population. However, the capital, Asmara (Asmera), was the country's second city (358,000) after Addis Ababa.

The economy was devastated by the war of independence. Industries such as textiles and footwear are being rebuilt and so are the ports of Massawa and Assab (Aseb). The main crops are cotton, coffee and tobacco.

The far northern province of Ethiopia bordering the Red Sea, Eritrea was an Italian colony from the 1880s until 1941, when it passed to British military administration. In accordance with a UN resolution, it was given to Ethiopia in 1952, becoming an autonomous region within the Federation of Ethiopia and Eritrea. This became a unitary state ten years later, when the region was effectively annexed by Haile Selassie.

The Eritrean People's Liberation Front (EPLF) then pressed for independence with an unrelenting guerrilla campaign in what became Africa's longest war. Like their counterparts in Tigre and the Oromo movement in Wollo and Gondar, they held large tracts of the countryside for years while government forces occupied the towns. With the fall of the Mengistu regime in 1991, the EPLF gained agreement on independence for Eritrea, guaranteeing access to the Red Sea by making Assab a free port. Independence was formally declared on 24 May 1993. [*Map page 32*] ∎

AREA  94,000 sq km [36,293 sq mls]
POPULATION  3,437,000
CAPITAL (POPULATION)  Asmera (358,000)
GOVERNMENT  Military government
ETHNIC GROUPS  Tigre, Afar, Beja, Saho, Agau
LANGUAGES  Arabic, English, Tigrinya, Tigre, Saho, Agail, Afar
RELIGIONS  Coptic Christianity 50%, Islam 50%
CURRENCY  Ethiopian birr = 100 cents

Smallest of the three Baltic states, and the least populous of any of the 15 former Soviet republics, Estonia is bounded on the north by the Gulf of Finland and on the west by the Baltic Sea. The country comprises mostly flat, rock-strewn, glaciated lowland, with over 1,500 lakes, and has more than 800 offshore islands, by far the biggest being Saaremaa and Hiiumaa. The largest lake, Chudskoye Ozero (Lake Peipus), forms much of the border with Russia in the east.

## ECONOMY AND RESOURCES

Over a third of the land is forested, and the timber industry is among the country's most important industries, alongside metalworking, shipbuilding, clothing, textiles, chemicals and food processing. The last is based primarily on extremely efficient dairy farming and pig breeding, but oats, barley and potatoes suit the cool climate and average soils. Fishing is also a major occupation.

Like the other two Baltic states, Latvia and Lithuania, Estonia is not endowed with natural resources, though its shale is an important mineral deposit: enough gas is extracted by processing to supply St Petersburg, Russia's second largest city.

## HISTORY AND POLITICS

The ancestors of the Estonians, who are related to the Finns, settled in the area several thousand years ago. German crusaders, known as the Teutonic Knights, introduced Christianity in the early 13th century, and by the 16th century, German noblemen owned much of the land in Estonia. In 1561, Sweden took the northern part of the country and Poland the south. From 1625, Sweden controlled the entire country, until it was handed over to Russia in 1721.

Estonian nationalists campaigned for their independence from around the mid-19th century. Finally, Estonia was proclaimed independent in 1918. In 1919, the government began to break up the large estates and distribute land among the peasants.

Then, in 1939, Germany and the Soviet Union agreed to take over parts of eastern Europe. In 1940, Soviet forces occupied Estonia, but they were driven out by the Germans in 1941. Soviet troops returned in 1944 and Estonia became one of the 15 Soviet Socialist Republics of the Soviet Union. The Estonians strongly opposed Soviet rule and many were deported to Siberia.

Political changes in the Soviet Union in the late 1980s led to renewed demands for freedom. In 1990, the Estonian government declared the country independent and, finally, the Soviet Union recognized this act in September 1991, shortly before the Soviet Union was dissolved. Estonia adopted a new constitution in 1992, when multiparty elections were held for a new national assembly. In 1994, Russia completed the withdrawal of its troops from Estonia. [*Map page 13*] ∎

---

**AREA** 44,700 sq km [17,300 sq mls]
**POPULATION** 1,541,000
**CAPITAL (POPULATION)** Tallinn (499,000)
**GOVERNMENT** Multiparty republic
**ETHNIC GROUPS** Estonian 62%, Russian 30%, Ukrainian 3%, Belarussian 2%, Finnish 1%
**LANGUAGES** Estonian (official)
**RELIGIONS** Christianity (Lutheran, with Orthodox and Baptist minorities)
**CURRENCY** Kroon = 100 sents

---

# ETHIOPIA

---

Ethiopia's main feature is a massive block of volcanic mountains, rising to 4,620 m [15,150 ft] and divided into Eastern and Western Highlands by the Great Rift Valley. Steep escarpments face each other across the rift, opening northwards to form the southern and eastern boundaries of the high Welo plateau. The Eastern Highlands fall away gently to the south and east. The Western Highlands, generally higher and far more extensive and deeply trenched, are the sources of the Blue Nile and its tributaries. Off their north-eastern flank, close to the Red Sea, lies the Danakil Depression, an extensive desert that falls to 116 m [380 ft] below sea level.

Giant thistles, red-hot pokers and lobelia are characteristic of the montane vegetation. In the desert of the Rift Valley the Danakil tend their diminishing herds, as do the Somali pastoralists on the dry Ogaden plain to the south-east.

## ECONOMY AND RESOURCES

In the lower areas of both highlands tropical cereals, oil seeds, coffee and cotton were the dominant crops before the wrecking of the rural economy, while at higher altitudes temperate cereals, pulses and fruits are produced.

Ethiopia was thrust before the attention of the world late in 1984 by unprecedented television pictures of starving millions – victims not only of famine but also of more than two decades of civil war and a Marxist government determined to enforce hardline economic and social policies. While that regime was finally toppled in 1991, and aid continued to pour in from the richer nations, the accumulative effects of drought (beginning in 1972, but with three merciless ones in the 1980s) combined with administrative mismanagement had left the nation destitute.

## HISTORY AND POLITICS

Coptic Christianity reached the northern kingdom of Aksum in the 4th century, surviving there and in the mountains to the south when Islam spread through the rest of north-east Africa. These core areas also survived colonial conquest; indeed Ethiopia (previously known as Abyssinia) itself became a colonial power between 1897 and 1908, taking Somali and other peoples into its feudal Empire. Invaded by Italy in 1935, Ethiopia became independent again six years later when British troops forced the Italians out.

Emperor Haile Selassie ('the Lion of Judah'), despite promising economic and social reforms following a two-year drought, was deposed after his 44-year rule by a revolutionary military government in 1974. A month later, Ethiopia was declared a socialist state: foreign investments and most industries were nationalized and a programme of land collectivization was started, sweeping away the feudal aristocracy. Though the ideology changed, it was still centralized, bureaucratic despotism, proving to be as inefficient as the old system.

By 1977 President Mengistu had assumed control, and with massive Soviet military and financial aid pursued interlocking policies of eliminating rival left-wing groups, suppressing secessionist movements (in Eritrea, Tigre, Wollo, Gondar and Ogaden) and instituting land reform, including the forced resettlement of millions from their drought-afflicted homelands. His period of 'Red Terror' killed tens of thousands of innocent people. Collectivist agriculture failed to cope with deforestation, overgrazing and the effects of drought, while for 14 years more than 60% of the national budget was spent on defence and 'security'. The Marxist government, plagued by Somali incursions (into Ogaden in 1978, and lasting for ten years), as well as internal rebellions, drained vital resources from the economy.

After a decade of unparalleled disaster driven by drought, Mengistu was finally put to flight in 1991 as Addis Ababa was taken by forces of the EPRDF (Ethiopian People's Revolutionary Democratic Front) – an unstable alliance of six separate rebel organizations. The EPRDF announced a caretaker coalition government and plans for multiparty elections, but the administration faced one of the most daunting tasks in the Third World. Relief organizations estimated that of the 25 million people facing starvation in Africa, some 6 million were Ethiopians. In 1993, Eritrea became independent of Ethiopia. [*Map page 32*] ∎

---

**AREA** 1,128,000 sq km [435,521 sq mls]
**POPULATION** 53,435,000
**CAPITAL (POPULATION)** Addis Ababa (2,213,000)
**GOVERNMENT** Transitional regime
**ETHNIC GROUPS** Amhara 38%, Galla (Oromo) 35%, Tigre 9%, Gurage 3%, Ometo 3%
**LANGUAGES** Amharic (official)
**RELIGIONS** Christianity (Ethiopian Orthodox 53%, other Christian 5%), Islam 31%, traditional beliefs 11%
**CURRENCY** Birr = 100 cents

---

# FALKLAND ISLANDS

Comprising two main islands and over 200 small islands, the Falkland Islands lie 480 km [300 mls] from South America. Windswept, virtually treeless, covered with peat moorland and tussock grass, the rolling landscape rises to two points of about 700 m [2,300 ft] – Mt Usborne in East Falkland and Mt Adam in West Falkland. Over half the population lives in (Port) Stanley, the capital situated in a sheltered inlet on East Falkland.

## ECONOMY AND RESOURCES
The economy is dominated by sheep farming, almost the only industry, with over 40% of exports comprising high-grade wool, mostly to Britain. The UK government is also funding a fishing development programme and helping with tourism: the islands are rich in subarctic wildlife, including penguins, seals and numerous birds, notably the albatross. Since the war with Argentina there has been a large British garrison.

## HISTORY AND POLITICS
Discovered in 1592 by the English navigator John Davis, the Falklands were first occupied nearly 200 years later – by the French (East) in 1764 and the British (West) in 1765. The French interest, bought by Spain in 1770, was assumed by Argentina when it gained independence in 1806, and the Argentinians retained their settlements there. The British, who had withdrawn on economic grounds back in 1774, had never relinquished their claim, and in 1832 they returned to the islands to dispossess the Argentine settlers and start a settlement of their own – one that became a Crown Colony in 1892.

The prospect of rich offshore oil and gas deposits from the 1970s aggravated the long-standing dispute, and in 1982 Argentine forces invaded the islands (*Islas Malvinas* in Spanish) and expelled the governor. Two months later – after the loss of 725

Argentinians and 225 Britons – the UK regained possession. Anglo-Argentine diplomatic relations were restored in 1990, but the UK refuses to enter into discussions on sovereignty.

**South Georgia** and **South Sandwich Island**, to the east, ceased to be Falklands dependencies in 1985, though they are administered via Stanley. They have had no permanent population since the closure of the whaling station at Leith in 1966. [*Map page 31*] ■

AREA 12,170 sq km [4,699 sq mls]
POPULATION 2,120
CAPITAL (POPULATION) Stanley (1,557)
GOVERNMENT British dependency
ETHNIC GROUPS British
LANGUAGES English
RELIGIONS Christianity
CURRENCY Falkland pound = 100 pence

# FAROE ISLANDS

The Faroes are a group of rocky islands situated in the North Atlantic 450 km [280 mls] from Iceland, 675 km [420 mls] from Norway and 300 km [185 mls] from the Shetlands. Like Iceland, they are composed mainly of volcanic material. They were dramatically moulded by glacial action and the landscape forms a forbidding setting for the Faroese farming and fishing settlements. Away from the villages and scattered hamlets, high cliffs are home to millions of seabirds. Winters are mild for the latitude but the summers are cool. It is usually windy and often overcast or foggy. The people speak Faroese, a Scandinavian language official (alongside Danish) since 1948. Of the 22 islands, 17 are inhabited.

## ECONOMY AND RESOURCES
Sheep farming on the poor soils is the principal occupation but salted, dried, processed and frozen fish, fishmeal and oil – from cod, whiting, mackerel and herring – comprise the chief exports. Faroese motor vessels are found in all the deep-sea fishing grounds of the North Atlantic and the capital, Tórshavn, has ship-repairing yards. Denmark, Norway and Britain are the country's main trading partners.

Since 1940 the currency has been the Faroese króna, which is freely interchangeable with the Danish krone.

## HISTORY AND POLITICS
The Faroe Islands have been part of the Danish kingdom since 1386 and from 1851 they sent two representatives to the Danish parliament. Their own elected assembly, dating from 1852, secured a large degree of self-government as a region within the Danish realm in 1948.

The islands left the European Free Trade Association (EFTA) when Denmark switched membership to the European Economic Community (EEC) on 1 January 1973, but did not join the community – though they do have a special associate status allowing for free industrial trade. [*Map page 4*] ■

AREA 1,400 sq km [541 sq mls]
POPULATION 47,000
CAPITAL (POPULATION) Tórshavn (14,601)
GOVERNMENT Danish self-governing region
ETHNIC GROUPS Of Scandinavian descent
LANGUAGES Faroese (official), Danish
RELIGIONS Christianity (mainly Lutheran)
CURRENCY Danish currency & Faroese króna

# FIJI

By far the most populous of the Pacific nations, Fiji comprises more than 800 Melanesian islands, of which the larger ones are volcanic, mountainous and surrounded by coral reefs, while the rest are low coral atolls. About 100 islands are permanently inhabited. Easily the biggest are Viti (10,430 sq km [4,027 sq mls]), with the capital of Suva on its south coast, and Vanua Levu, which is just over half the size of the main island.

## ECONOMY AND RESOURCES

The islands' economy is basically agricultural, with sugar cane (45% of exports), copra and ginger the main cash crops, and fish and timber also exported. However, nearly 20% of revenues are generated by sales of gold. The main trading partners are the UK and Australia for exports, and the US, New Zealand and Australia for imports.

## HISTORY AND POLITICS

Fiji suffers today from its colonial past. It was a British colony from 1874 until 1970, when it became an independent state and a member of the Commonwealth. The Indian workers brought in by the British for the plantations in the late 19th century now outnumber the native Fijians, but have been until recently second-class citizens in terms of electoral representation, economic opportunity and land ownership. The constitution adopted on independence in 1970 was intended to ease racial tension, but two military coups in 1987 overthrew the recently elected (and first) Indian-majority government, suspended the constitution and set up a Fijian-dominated republic outside the British Commonwealth.

The country finally returned to full civilian rule in 1990; but with a new constitution guaranteeing Melanesian political supremacy, many Indians had already emigrated before the elections of 1992, taking their valuable skills with them. The turmoil of the late 1980s also had a disastrous effect on the growing tourist industry – and by the time the situation stabilized, most of the Western countries that provide the foreign visitors were already in deep recession. [*Map page 3*] ∎

---

**AREA** 18,270 sq km [7,054 sq mls]
**POPULATION** 771,000
**CAPITAL (POPULATION)** Suva (71,600)
**GOVERNMENT** Republic
**ETHNIC GROUPS** Indian 49%, Fijian 46%
**LANGUAGES** English, Bauan, Hindustani
**RELIGIONS** Christianity 53%, Hinduism 38%, Islam 8%
**CURRENCY** Fiji dollar = 100 cents

---

# FINLAND

Located almost entirely between latitudes 60°N and 70°N, Finland is the most northerly state on the mainland of Europe, though Norway's county of Finnmark actually cuts it off from the Arctic Ocean. A third of its total area lies within the Arctic Circle, a far higher proportion than for its two large Scandinavian partners.

The climate of the northern province of Lappi (Lapland) is not as severe as in places which lie in similar latitudes, such as Canada and Siberia, because of the North Atlantic Drift. This influence keeps the Arctic coasts of Europe free from ice all year round.

Finland enjoys a short but warm summer, with average July temperatures at Helsinki of 17°C [63°F] and 13°C [55°F] in Lapland. Because of the high latitudes, summer days are extremely long; indeed, in the Arctic region there is virtually no night throughout the month of June.

Winters are long and cold (Helsinki's January average is –6°C [21°F]) and the days are short. In severe winters the sea freezes for several miles offshore and ice-breakers have to be used to keep the ports open. Snowfall is not heavy, however, and rail and road transport is seldom badly disrupted, even in Lapland.

## Landscape

Geologically, Finland is made up of a central plateau of ancient crystalline rocks, mainly granites, schists and gneisses, surrounded by lowlands composed of recent glacial deposits. In the 600 million years between the formation of these ancient rocks and the last Ice Age, the surface of the land was worn down to a peneplain, and most of central and southern Finland is below 200 m [650 ft]. However, the roots of an old mountain system running north-west to south-east can still be traced across Lapland and along Finland's eastern border with Russia. Peaks of over 1,000 m [3,000 ft] occur in northern Lapland, near the Swedish and Norwegian borders.

A tenth of the land surface is covered by lakes. Concentrated in the central plateau, they are in most cases long, narrow and shallow, and aligned in a north-west to south-east direction, indicating the line of movement of the ice-sheet which scoured out their basins. The number of lakes varies from 60,000 to 185,000, depending on the source of the information and the definition used; but whatever the exact figure may be, they dominate the landscape of the southern half of Finland and contribute to its austere beauty. The Saimaa area in the south-east, near the Russian frontier, is Europe's largest inland water system.

Although under increasing threat from pollution caused by wood processing and fertilizers as well as acid rain, the lakes are still rich in fish – mainly trout, salmon, pike and perch – and provide a prime source of recreation for large numbers of Finnish people.

## ECONOMY AND RESOURCES

More than two-thirds of Finland is covered by lakes and forest – a fact that accounts for almost everything from the composition of its exports to the brilliance of its rally car drivers. Forests occupy almost 60% of the land surface, the main trees being pine, spruce and birch. Forest-based products – wood pulp, sawn timber, paper and board – still constitute 40% of Finland's exports, but since World War II engineering, shipbuilding and metallurgical industries have greatly expanded. Whilst a member of EFTA, Finland saw its economy grow at a faster rate than that of Japan during the 1980s. In 1992 Finland formally applied to become a member of the European Union, and in 1994 the Finnish people voted in favour of membership of the EU on 1 January 1995.

## HISTORY AND POLITICS

Between 1150 and 1809 Finland was under Swedish rule, and one of the legacies of this period is a Swedish-speaking minority of 6.5% of the total population. In some localities on the south and west coasts, Swedish speakers are in a majority and Åland, an island closer to the Swedish coast than to Finland, is a self-governing province. Many towns in Finland use both Finnish and Swedish names; for

example, Helsinki is Helsingfors and Turku is Åbo in Swedish. Finnish bears little relation to Swedish or any Scandinavian language, and is closest to Magyar, the native tongue of Hungary. Since 1945, Finland has managed to retain its neutrality and played an important role in the setting up of the CSCE. Finnish politics are dominated by multiparty coalitions. [*Map page 13*] ■

## THE LAPPS

Hunters, fishermen and herdsmen living in Arctic Europe, approximately 35,000 Lapps are scattered between Norway (with 20,000), Sweden and Finland, with a small group in Russia. Physically, the short, dark Lapps – or Samer, as they call themselves – are noticeably different from other Scandinavians, though their language, Saarme, is related to Finnish. They probably originated in northern Russia at least 2,000 years ago, and may have been the original inhabitants of Finland. Until the 17th century, when they first learned to domesticate reindeer, they lived entirely by hunting and fishing; thereafter, many followed a semi-nomadic life, driving their herds each summer from their winter settlements at the edge of the forest to the high pastureland.

Industrialization, especially mining and hydroelectric development and the associated roads, has badly affected nomadic herding, and it now occupies only about 10% of Lapps. Most live in fixed settlements in coastal areas, and a steady trickle migrate south, assimilating themselves into modern Scandinavian society.

---

**AREA** 338,130 sq km [130,552 sq mls]
**POPULATION** 5,083,000
**CAPITAL (POPULATION)** Helsinki (977,000)
**GOVERNMENT** Multiparty republic
**ETHNIC GROUPS** Finnish 93%, Swedish 6%
**LANGUAGES** Finnish and Swedish (both official)
**RELIGIONS** Christianity (Evangelical Lutheran 88%)
**CURRENCY** Markka = 100 penniä

# FRANCE

Although replaced by the Ukraine as Europe's biggest 'country' in 1991, France remains a handsomely proportioned runner-up, well ahead of Spain and more than twice the area of the entire United Kingdom. Yet the nation possesses space as well as size, and while the growth of cities in the years since World War II has been spoken of in terms of crisis (*la crise urbaine*), urban expansion is a problem only in a few special areas, notably Paris and its immediate surroundings. In general, France has stayed predominantly rural.

## Frontiers

Frontiers are a natural concern of continental European countries, but of France's 5,500 km [3,440 mls] almost half consists of sea coast and another 1,000 km [620 mls] winds through the mountains of the Pyrenees and the Alps. In general the Pyrenees frontier follows the crest line of the major hills, rather than the watershed between rivers flowing north into France or south into Spain. There are few easy crossings through the Pyrenees into Spain, but good coastal routes exist on the west from Bayonne into the Basque country, and on the east from Perpignan to Gerona.

In the south-east of France, Savoie and the county of Nice were ceded by Italy at the Treaty of Turin in 1860 and in the following year the Prince of Monaco gave Menton and a neighbouring area to France. The cession of Savoie meant that France's territory extended to the summit of Mont Blanc, the highest mountain in Europe outside the Caucasus.

It also gave France part of the shores of Lake Geneva. Geneva itself is Swiss, but French territory lies within walking distance, and special customs arrangements exist so that people from the French countryside may use the city's trading facilities. North of Geneva the frontier runs through the Jura Mountains to Basle on the Rhine where France, Germany and Switzerland meet. Though Basle itself is in Switzerland, its airport is in France. North

of Basle, for 160 km [100 mls] the border between France and Germany follows the Rhine. Alsace and Lorraine, west of the river, were sought by both countries for centuries, and after the Franco-Prussian War in 1870–1 the whole of Alsace and part of Lorraine were returned to Prussia. This frontier remained until the Treaty of Versailles following World War I, but in World War II it was violated again by the Germans – their third invasion of France in 70 years. The frontiers from the Rhine to the North Sea were defined in their present form during the 18th century. Local government in France was reorganized during the French Revolution. In 1790 Turgot defined the *départements* as areas in which everyone could reach the central town within one day.

## Landscape

**Highland France:** Most of France lies less than 300 m [1,000 ft] above sea level, but there are several distinctive upland areas. The most impressive are the Alps and the Pyrenees, but they also include the ancient massifs of Brittany and the Central Plateau, the Vosges and that part of the Ardennes which is within France.

The Alps are formed of complex folded rocks of intricate structure, with relief made even more complicated by the successive glaciations of the Ice Age. Areas of permanent snow exist on Mont Blanc and many other high peaks, and visitors to the upper Arve valley at Chamonix, St-Gervais and other holiday centres have easy access to glaciers. The Alps are visited by tourists throughout the year – in winter for skiing, and in summer for walking on the upland pastures (the original 'alps'). In the French Alps, as in the other alpine areas, hydroelectricity has become universal both for general home use and for industry. The Pyrenees, though comparable to the Alps, lack arterial routes.

The Breton massif includes part of Normandy and extends southwards to the neighbourhood of La Rochelle. In general physical character it is a much dissected hilly area. The Massif Central is more dramatic: it covers one-sixth of France between the Rhône-Saône valley and the basin of Aquitaine, and its highest summits rise to more than 1,800 m

[5,900 ft]; striking examples are Mont du Cantal and Mont Dore (1,866 m [6,200 ft]). Volcanic activity of 10–30 million years ago appears in old volcanic plugs. Earlier rocks include limestones, providing poor soils for agriculture, and coal measures which have been mined for more than a century at St-Étienne and Le Creusot. The Vosges and the Ardennes are forested areas of poor soil.

**Lowland France:** Although France has striking mountain areas, 60% of the country is less than 250 m [800 ft] above sea level. Fine rivers, including the Rhône, Garonne, Loire and Seine, along with their many tributaries, drain large lowland areas. From the Mediterranean there is a historic route northwards through the Rhône-Saône valley to Lyons and Dijon. North-westwards there is the famous route through the old towns of Carcassonne and Toulouse to Bordeaux on the Gironde estuary, into which the Garonne and the Dordogne flow. This is the basin of Aquitaine, bordered by the Massif Central to the north and the Pyrenees to the south. It is not a uniform lowland – there are several hilly areas and on the coast a belt of sand dunes, the Landes, extending for 200 km [125 mls] from Bayonne to the Gironde estuary.

From Aquitaine there is an easy route to the north, followed by the major railway from Bordeaux to Poitiers, Tours, Orléans and Paris. This lowland is called the Gate of Poitou, though in place of the word 'gate' the French say *seuil* or 'threshold', which is perhaps more appropriate. Crossing the threshold brings the traveller to the Paris basin, in the heart of which is the great city itself.

The ancient centre of Paris lies on the Ile de la Cité, where the Seine was easily crossed. The Paris basin is a vast area floored by sedimentary rocks. Those that are resistant to erosion, including some limestones and chalks, form upland areas. The Loire, with its many tributaries in the south-west of the basin, and the Seine, with its numerous affluents (notably the Yonne, Aube, Marne, Aisne and Oise), offer easy routes between the upland areas.

## ECONOMY AND RESOURCES

The lowlands of France are warmer than those of England in summer; the cooler winters of the north, with more frost and snow than on the lowlands of England, have little adverse effect on agriculture. Rainfall is moderate, with a summer maximum in the north and a winter maximum in the areas of Mediterranean climate to the south.

Modern improvements in agriculture include the provision of irrigation during the summer in the south. This has transformed many areas in the Rhône and Durance valleys, and also the coastal lands such as the Crau, south-east of Arles. Without irrigation this was a stony, steppe-like area; now it supports vast flocks of sheep and has fine hay crops, cut three times a year. Further west in the Camargue, on the Rhône delta, rice is grown with the help of irrigation and there are other areas of rice production close to the Mediterranean. Water comes either from canals, leading into ditches through the fields, or by sprinkler systems from a network of underground pumps; one water point can supply 4 hectares [10 acres].

France's agricultural revolution is far from complete. There are areas where modern technology has made large reclamation schemes possible, but there are still many independent peasant farmers, making a living that is a meagre reward for the labour expended, even with the generous terms of the EU's Common Agricultural Policy (CAP). The younger generation tend to regard emigration to the towns as a more promising way of life.

**Alpine areas:** In the alpine areas of France, including the Pyrenees, farms are far more numerous on hillslopes having good exposure to sunlight (the *adret*) than on those less favoured (the *ubac*). There are fine upland pastures, apparently retaining their fertility through centuries of use, which provide summer feed for cattle. Although there is still traditional farming in these areas, many people have diversified or emigrated. Some find work in tourist resorts, and many of the old timber-built houses have been bought by people from the cities as holiday homes. The future of peasant farming in mountain areas is a problem that France shares with Switzerland, Austria and Spain.

**Mediterranean France:** From the French Riviera lowlands extend northwards through the Rhône and Saône valleys and westwards through Languedoc to the neighbourhood of

Narbonne. This is the area of Mediterranean climate, having most rain in winter, with wheat, vines and olives as the traditional crops. Wheat is well suited to a Mediterranean climate, for it grows best with a cool, moist period followed by one that is warm and dry; in 1993 France was the world's fifth largest producer. Vines need summer warmth – with temperatures of at least 18°C [64°F] for the greater part of the growing season, and dryness, but not to an excessive degree, during the 70 days from the opening of the buds to maturity. The olive is the traditional tree of the Mediterranean climate. Originally a native of Egypt, through the centuries it was planted first in the eastern and later in the western Mediterranean. The ripe, dark purple fruits contain oil, used for cooking; green, unripe olives are commonly used as appetizers.

These three crops are familiar in the south but with them are many more, including maize (the country is the world's fifth largest producer) and a wide range of vegetables. Not all the rural land in Mediterranean France is continuously cultivated for agriculture, for in places it is interspersed with rocky outcrops unsuited to cultivation but covered with *maquis* or pines. Farmers have made fertile the patches of good soil and adequate moisture, and the general landscape is a mixture of rough hills and limestone pavements surrounding rich areas of cultivation.

**Aquitaine:** To the west, Aquitaine is not a uniform lowland; the agricultural land is interspersed by hills and plateaux that are generally wooded or left as heathland. It is nevertheless a richly productive area, with arable farming for cereal crops, maize and vegetables, and also pastures for cattle. Aquitaine is also a celebrated wine-producing area, with enormous fields laid out as vineyards. Many of the old farms have disappeared, and even whole villages have been abandoned, for example in the Dordogne, as vines have replaced other, less remunerative crops. Much of the wine is consumed on the home market as the normal *vin ordinaire*, mostly red but including some less favoured whites.

The famous claret-producing area around Bordeaux includes the Médoc, between the Gironde estuary and the sea: here also are the districts that produce white table wines,

## CORSICA

Annexed by France from Genoa in 1768 – just months before the birth of Napoleon Bonaparte, its most famous son – Corsica is 168 km [105 mls] from France and just 11 km [7 mls] from Sardinia, which is Italian territory. Corsica is divided into two *départements* of France, with its administrative centre at Ajaccio on the west coast. Roughly oval in shape, it is 190 km [118 mls] long and half as wide.

Most of the island is formed of rugged mountains, with more than 40 peaks over 2,000 m [6,500 ft] and some reaching over 2,900 m [9,500 ft]. Varied ancient rocks, much metamorphosed, make up these mountains. Only a quarter of Corsica provides rough grazing for sheep and goats; another quarter is in forests with evergreen oak and cork oak to 650 m [2,000 ft], then chestnuts with beech followed by pines to the treeline, between 1,600 and 2,000 m [5,000–6,000 ft]. In winter there is heavy snow on the mountains, causing severe flooding in the numerous short rivers.

Only 2% of the island is cultivated, mainly in the valleys, on terraced hillsides or on the discontinuous fringe of alluvial lowland along the coasts. Fishing is a primary activity and industries include tunny and lobster canning, chiefly at Ajaccio and Bastia, the two main towns – though tourism is now the main earner. Separatist terrorist movements are still sporadically active in some areas.

such as graves and sauternes. Aquitaine can in fact boast a wide range of red and white wines; several of them, though well known locally, are not exported because the quantity produced is small, and possibly because they do not travel well. Cognac and Armagnac wines are suited to brandy distillation.

**Northern France:** Northwards from Aquitaine through the lowland Gate (*seuil*) of Poitou, the winters become cooler, with rain in the summer as well as the winter months. Though the summers are cooler in the Paris basin than in Aquitaine, vines flourish on favoured slopes facing south, and many fine

French wines come from these northern areas.

As a whole, the Paris basin is agriculturally rich, with varied soils. The last Ice Age has left many areas of drifts and wind-blown soils, here as elsewhere in Europe providing land of great fertility. Between the valleys of the Paris basin lie the *pays*, low plateaux, each with its own characteristic. Some, such as the Beauce, with fertile soils, are suited to crops; others, such as the Sologne, have poor, sandy soils, hard to cultivate and best suited to forest. Local farmers have for centuries adjusted their activity to the qualities of the soil, and now use their specialized production as a basis both for trade with other areas, and for sale in the towns. Despite all the profound changes in French life, the variety of agriculture and land use in the Paris basin remains clear – few areas of the world have so neat a division into units as the *pays* of France.

Finally, to the west of the Paris basin there is the area of ancient rocks covering Brittany and its margins. This area, regarded as archaic but picturesque, has small farms with fields divided by wooded hedges to give a sheltered *bocage* landscape. Rich in medieval churches, old customs and even costumes, it was never of great economic significance. Like Cornwall, in the far south-west of England, it had its own language (still used) and is part of the traditional Celtic west of Europe. There is now increasing pressure for local autonomy in Brittany, expressed particularly in efforts to improve agriculture by upgrading pastures, removing hedges to enlarge fields for animals and cultivation, developing market gardening, and encouraging industrial growth in the towns. Fishing remains a valued resource, while tourism (both from France and neighbouring Europe) brings additional prosperity to Brittany.

Agriculture remains a valued resource in the French economy – for example, France accounts for almost 6% of the world's barley and wheat (more of the latter than Canada), and agriculture contributes 17% of export earnings – and politicians make this clear both in Paris and outside France. But there are many changes. In general these appear to reflect the opinion of the American geographer, Isaiah Bowman, that 'man takes the best and lets the rest go'. Poor land is abandoned, perhaps for forest, but promising areas are made rich through investment. Improvements such as drainage, irrigation and scientific fertilization in some areas counterbalance the decline in agriculture elsewhere, such as in the Alps and the Pyrenees. Loss of people from the land does not indicate a decline in agricultural production but rather an improvement in agricultural efficiency, and the freedom of people, no longer tied to the land, to seek, and generally to find, alternative and more satisfying employment.

**Forests**

Forests cover one-fifth of France. Most of them are on soils of poor quality, including the sands in parts of the Paris basin, the Vosges and the Landes between Bordeaux and the Spanish frontier, the poor limestones of Lorraine and the clay-with-flints of Normandy. Some of the great forests were planted by landowners as parts of their estates, like those of Fontainebleau and Rambouillet near Paris; others were planted as barriers between former kingdoms, such as those between Normandy and Picardy.

The greatest single forested area in France is the Landes, which covers 10,000 sq km [3,860 sq mls]. This is mainly coniferous forest, interspersed only here and there by farms. Since 1956, attempts have been made to reclaim and replant the extensive areas devastated by fire, and to substitute a more varied rural economy for the exclusive exploitation of the pine forests. In the Alps and the Pyrenees about a quarter of the land is covered with forest.

In France, some two-thirds of all the woodlands are comprised of deciduous trees, compared with less than a third in Germany, and about 60% of the country's timber requirements, especially for paper pulpmaking, has to be imported. Since World War II various laws have been passed to encourage the production of softwood.

Farms revert to waste when they are no longer cultivated, and become impenetrable thickets of vegetation. Through most of France this vegetation is known as *maquis*, from the shelter it gives to fugitives: the term *maquis* was given in World War II to the resistance forces in hiding. In dry summers the risk

## THE VINEYARDS

While behind Italy in production of both grapes and wine, France remains the drink's spiritual home as well as its greatest per capita consumer. Vines are grown south of a line from Nantes to the Ardennes. In the northern areas they occur on sites with specially favourable climatic qualities, notably good southerly exposure to sunshine; in the southern areas the vine covers a high proportion of the agricultural land.

The threat of disease, the need to preserve the quality of particular named vines, and the necessity of maintaining the export trade, all involve government control. Different soils and varying types of grape, combined with local traditions of treating them, produce a wide range of wines, most of which are consumed locally. In the export market clarets from the Bordeaux area, burgundies from the Rhône valley south of Dijon, and champagne, an aerated wine from the *pays* of the same name in the Paris basin, are all well known, but there are many other lesser-known wines of which smaller quantities are exported. The quality of the vintage varies each year according to climatic conditions.

of fire is considerable, especially in the south.

### RESOURCES AND INDUSTRY

France is a declining but still significant producer of iron ore (mostly from Lorraine), and several other minerals are also mined, including bauxite, potash, salt and sulphur. There are old coalfields in the north-east, but the output of these does not meet the country's needs. France instead switched to new sources of energy, including experiments with solar power in the Pyrenees and the world's first major tidal power station on the Rance estuary in Brittany, but more significantly utilizing the water of the mountains for hydro-electric power (24% of output) and mined uranium – seventh largest producer in the world, with 5% of world production – to create the most nuclear-based output of any nation (73% by the early 1990s).

Since World War II, the marked industrial expansion in France has been accompanied by a change in the distribution of population. Before the war France was regarded as a country with a fairly even distribution of population between town and country, but from the late 1940s there was a spectacular increase in the urban population. In the first postwar planning period, 1947–53, industrial production rose by 70%, agricultural production by 21% and the standard of living by 30%.

During the following years there was further expansion, particularly in the chemical and electrical industries. In the period of the third plan, 1958–61, the success of export industries became notable, especially in such products as automobiles, aircraft and electrical goods. In this period, too, natural gas was discovered at Lacq, and such industries as chemicals and aluminium smelting prospered. However, traditional industries, such as textiles and porcelain, are still important, and despite technological innovation and success, France is still weak in 'high-tech' areas compared to Japan, the USA and several European rivals.

Nevertheless, the country's postwar transition to a prosperous, dynamic society with more relaxed attitudes has been rapid and pronounced. French life has been, and still is, focused to a remarkable degree on Paris, where traditional luxury industries, such as perfumes, thrive alongside commerce, light industry, heavy industry and services of all kinds. Virtually all the major commercial enterprises of France have their headquarters in Paris – and Paris and district now has almost a fifth of the total population.

The other important industrial centres are on and around the mining areas, and at or near the major ports where imported raw materials are used: Fos, west of Marseilles, for example, and the steel complex at Dunkerque. The aims of modern planning include the development of regional prosperity, based on such centres as Lyons, Marseilles, Toulouse, Nantes, Lille, Nancy and Strasbourg, home to the European parliament. While the industrial attraction of the Paris area remains powerful and population growth continues to exceed that of the second largest urban area, the district around Lyons, the traditional centralization of France is showing signs of weakening and governments of both complexions have sought to reduce state power both in local affairs and the economy.

Modern economic planning in France has been pursued at a time of great difficulty, which included the loss of the colonial territories in North Africa and South-east Asia, as well as the period of unrest in the 1960s, not only in the universities but throughout the country. Consumer industries have prospered, but some critics say that there is still inadequate provision for social services, including housing. Since World War II there has been agitation about the poor standard of housing throughout France, both rural and urban, much of it obsolete and without basic amenities. Rapid urban growth, which still continues, has resulted in overcrowding and even the growth of poor shanty towns to house immigrants, especially those from Spain and North Africa. The 4 million underprivileged workers from the Maghreb countries could prove to be one of the nation's most testing problems in the 1990s.

Achieving expansion and prosperity over the whole country has not been easy. In France, as in most other countries, there remains a disparity between the richer and poorer areas; for France this is between the east and the west, the richest of all being in closest touch with the great industrial complexes of Germany and the Benelux countries. Though often devastated in European wars, this always emerges in peacetime as one of the most prosperous corners of France.

## HISTORY AND POLITICS

Celtic Gaul was conquered by Caesar in 57–52 BC and was under Roman rule until Clovis I, king of the Franks, defeated the Romans in 486. After the death of Charlemagne, whose empire extended over a large area of Europe, France became a separate kingdom (843). By the 14th century, however, nearly half of France belonged to the English king. This led to the Hundred Years' Wars (1337–1453), at the end of which the English were driven out of France. Francis I, in the 16th century, continued to strengthen and centralize the powers of the crown, and in the 17th century, the French monarchy, under Louis XIV, experienced its golden age, when the arts flourished at the court of Versailles.

However, the country's economic problems and social changes brought about the French Revolution of 1789 and the abolition of feudalism. Following a period of corrupt and inefficient government, Napoleon seized power in 1799 and eventually crowned himself 'Emperor of the French' in 1804. His rule was as absolute as that of previous monarchs but he established a modern and efficient administration. Defeated in foreign wars, Napoleon had to abdicate in 1814. Constitutional monarchy, restored in 1814, gave way to the Second Empire in 1848 and the Third Republic after France's defeat in the Anglo-Prussian War in 1871.

France suffered huge human losses during World War I when the fighting went on inconclusively for nearly four years on the western front. Germany was eventually defeated and had to sign the Treaty of Versailles which returned Alsace and Lorraine (ceded in 1871) to France. In 1939, Hitler invaded Poland and France and Britain declared war on Germany. France was soon overrun by German forces and in June 1940, Marshal Pétain signed an armistice. He was put in charge of a puppet government in Vichy, initially controlling less than half of the country, but by 1942, the whole of France was occupied.

Meanwhile, General de Gaulle had formed an alternative 'Free French' government in London and rallied the various resistance movements around him. France was liberated by the Allied forces in 1944. The Fourth Republic (1946–58) was a period marked by political instability and colonial wars, first in Indo-China and then in Algeria. As a result of the latter, de Gaulle was called back to power in 1958. He brought in a new constitution which defined the new institutions of the Fifth Republic and in particular gave greater powers to the president. He then proceeded to grant independence to all remaining colonies and to modernise the French economy in the context of the developing European integration (France was a founder member of the European Steel and Coal Committee in 1951 and of the EEC in 1957). He also reasserted the independence of France's foreign policy. However, growing discontent with the regime led to a students' and workers' revolt in 1968 and de Gaulle's resignation in 1969. His right-wing successors, Pompidou and Giscard d'Estaing, continued his policies. In May 1981, the French elected François Mitterand as the first Socialist president of the Fifth Republic and he won a second mandate in 1988. Jacques Chirac succeeded him as president following elections in May 1995. [*Map pages 10–11*] ■

AREA 551,500 sq km [212,934 sq mls]
POPULATION 57,747,000
CAPITAL (POPULATION) Paris (9,319,000)
GOVERNMENT Multiparty republic
ETHNIC GROUPS French 93%, Arab 3%, German 2%, Breton 1%, Catalan 1%
LANGUAGES French (official)
RELIGIONS Christianity (Roman Catholic 86%, other Christians 4%), Islam 3%
CURRENCY Franc = 100 centimes

# FRENCH GUIANA

The smallest country in South America, French Guiana has a narrow coastal plain comprising mangrove swamps and marshes, alternating with drier areas that can be cultivated; one such is the site of the capital, Cayenne. Inland, a belt of sandy savanna rises to a forested plateau.

## ECONOMY AND RESOURCES

The economy is very dependent on France, both for budgetary aid and for food and manufactured goods. The French have also built a rocket-launching station near the coast at Kourou. Timber is the most important natural resource; bauxite and kaolin have been discovered but are largely unexploited. Only 104 sq km [40 sq mls] of the land is under cultivation, where sugar, cassava and rice are grown. Fishing, particularly for shrimps, much of which are exported, is a leading occupation, and tourism, though in its infancy, has as main attractions the Amerindian villages of the interior and the lush tropical scenery.

## HISTORY AND POLITICS

A French settlement was established in 1604 by a group of merchant adventurers, and after brief periods of Dutch, English and Portuguese rule the territory finally became permanently French in 1817. In 1946 – a year after the closure of Devil's Island, the notorious convict settlement – its status changed to that of an overseas department of France, and in 1974 it also became an administrative region.

An independence movement developed in the 1980s, but most people want to retain their links with France and continue to obtain financial aid in order to develop their territory. [*Map page 31*] ■

AREA 90,000 sq km [34,749 sq mls]
POPULATION 141,000
CAPITAL (POPULATION) Cayenne (41,660)
GOVERNMENT Overseas department of France
ETHNIC GROUPS Creole 42%, Chinese 14%, French 10%, Haitian 7%
LANGUAGES French (official)
RELIGIONS Christianity (Roman Catholic 80%, Protestant 4%)
CURRENCY French currency

# FRENCH POLYNESIA

French Polynesia consists of 130 islands, totalling only 4,000 sq km [1,544 sq mls] but scattered in five groups over a large area of ocean halfway between Australia and South America. The Society Islands comprise the Leewards, of which the best known is Bora-Bora, and the Windwards, which include Moorea and Tahiti – the largest island and home to the capital of Papeete. Along with the Marquesas, most of the Tubuais and the smaller Gambier islands, these islands are of volcanic origin with steep-sided mountains; the Tuamotus are low-lying coralline atolls.

## ECONOMY AND RESOURCES

The relatively high standard of living comes

largely from the links with France, including a substantial military presence. The other factor which changed the islands' economy from subsistence agriculture and fishing is tourism; in 1988 this earned about half as much as all visible exports. After petroleum re-exports, the main earners are cultured pearls, vanilla and citrus fruits. Almost half the territory's trade is with France, and it shares a currency (the Pacific franc) with New Caledonia and Wallis and Futuna.

## HISTORY AND POLITICS
The tribal chiefs of Tahiti eventually agreed to a French protectorate in 1843, and by the end of the century France controlled all of the present islands. They formed an overseas territory from 1958, sending two deputies and a senator to Paris, and in 1984 gained increased autonomy with a territorial assembly. There are, however, sporadic calls for independence. The French government began stationing military personnel there in 1962, and have carried out nuclear testing at Mururoa. [*Map page 2*] ∎

**AREA** 4,000 sq km [1,544 sq mls]
**POPULATION** 215,000
**CAPITAL (POPULATION)** Papeete (79,000)
**GOVERNMENT** Overseas territory of France
**ETHNIC GROUPS** Polynesian 70%, French 10%, Chinese 7%
**LANGUAGES** French (official), Tahitian
**RELIGIONS** Christianity (Protestant 47%, Roman Catholic 40%)
**CURRENCY** CFP franc = 100 centimes

# GABON

The Gabonese Republic lies on the Equator in west-central Africa. In area, it is a little larger than the United Kingdom, with a coastline 800 km [500 mls] long. Behind the narrow, partly lagoon-lined coastal plain, the land rises to hills, plateaux and mountains divided by deep valleys carved by the River Ogooué and its tributaries. The Ogooué, which rises in Congo, reaches the sea near Port Gentil. This seaport lies on an island in the river's estuary near Cape Lopez, Gabon's most westerly point.

Most of Gabon has an equatorial climate, with high temperatures and humidity throughout the year. The rainfall is heavy and the skies are often cloudy. The capital, Libreville, is marginally drier between June and August, when winds blow outwards from the land towards the sea.

Dense rainforest covers about 75% of the country, but, in the east and south, the rainforest gives way to savanna grasslands. The forests contain abundant animals, with antelopes, including the rare bongo and sitatonga, buffaloes, chimpanzees, elephants and gorillas. Gabon has several national parks and wildife reserves.

## ECONOMY AND RESOURCES
Figures for GNP suggest that Gabon is one of Africa's richest states, but this is misleading: though rich in natural resources, the country has a small population, to whom the wealth has not yet spread.

With much of the country densely forested, valuable timbers were the main exports until 1962. Since then, minerals have been developed, as so often in Africa, by foreign companies whose profits leave the country. First came oil and gas from near Port Gentil (oil still provides over 65% of export earnings). Then the world's largest deposit of manganese was mined at Mouanda, near Franceville, although originally the ore had to be exported through the Congo by a branch of the Congo-Ocean railway. Gabon is the world's fourth biggest producer of manganese and has about a quarter of the world's known reserves. Lastly, there is uranium from nearby Mounana; Gabon, Niger and the Central African Republic are France's main sources of uranium. The Trans-Gabon railway was completed in 1987 to provide the country's own outlet for the manganese and uranium, and to open new areas to forestry.

Apart from cocoa and coffee which are grown in the north near Mbini, farming of all kinds is rare and engages only 1% of the land area, the Gabonese preferring to work in other economic activities and the towns. Most food has to be imported.

## HISTORY AND POLITICS
The name Gabon is derived from the name given by a Portuguese explorer in the 16th century to an estuary which he thought resembled a hooded and sleeved cloak, *gabāo* in Portuguese. In the 19th century the French Navy suppressed the local slave trade, and landed freed slaves at the base called Libreville – where, as in the British counterpart of Freetown, in Sierra Leone, an educated élite established itself.

Gabon became a one-party state in 1968 and though multiparty elections were held in 1990 (the first for 26 years, following widespread demonstrations that required French military intervention), there were allegations of government fraud. The Gabonese Democratic Party, formerly the only party, won a majority in the National Assembly. [*Map page 33*] ∎

AREA 267,670 sq km [103,347 sq mls]
POPULATION 1,283,000
CAPITAL (POPULATION) Libreville (418,000)
GOVERNMENT Multiparty republic
ETHNIC GROUPS Fang 36%, Mpongwe 15%,
Mbete 14%, Punu 12%
LANGUAGES French (official)
RELIGIONS Christianity (Roman Catholic
65%, Protestant 19%, African churches 12%),
traditional beliefs 3%, Islam 2%
CURRENCY CFA franc = 100 centimes

# GAMBIA, THE

The Republic of The Gambia is the smallest country in mainland Africa, consisting of a narrow strip of land bordering the River Gambia. The Gambia is almost entirely enclosed by Senegal, except along the short Atlantic coastline. The land is low-lying, and near the sea the land is flat and the soils are salty. The middle river is bordered by terraces, called *banto faros*, which are flooded after heavy rains. The upper river flows through a deep valley which the river has cut into a sandstone plateau.

The Gambia has hot, humid summers, but the winter temperatures (November to May) drop to around 16°C [61°F]. In winter, dry north-easterly winds blow over the country, but in the summer, moist south-westerlies bring rain, which is heaviest on the coast but diminishes inland.

Mangrove swamps line the river banks from the coast through to the centre of the country. But savanna used to cover most of the land until it was largely cleared for farming. The Gambia is rich in birdlife. Crocodiles and hippopotamuses live in the River Gambia.

## ECONOMY AND RESOURCES
Except for the capital Banjul, which is also the major port, no town has a population of more than 10,000, and all the large settlements are on the river, which provides the principal means of communication.

Rice is grown in swamps and on the floodplains of the river (though not enough to feed the country's modest population), with millet, sorghum and cassava on the higher ground. Groundnuts still dominate the economy and provide 90% of export earnings, but a successful tourist industry has now been developed: whether northern Europeans looking for sunshine or black Americans tracing their ancestry, the number of visitors rose from a few hundred at independence to more than 90,000 in 1990.

## HISTORY AND POLITICS
Portuguese mariners reached The Gambia's coast in 1455 when the area was part of the large Mali empire. In the 16th century, Portuguese and English slave traders operated in the area, and English traders bought rights to trade on the River Gambia in 1588.

In 1664, the English established a settlement on an island in the river estuary, and in 1765 the British founded a colony called Senegambia, which included parts of The Gambia and Senegal. Britain handed this colony over to France in 1783.

In 1816, Bathurst (now Banjul) was founded as a base for Britain's anti-slavery operations. But control of inland areas was made difficult by wars between local Muslims and non-Muslims. In the 1860s and 1870s, Britain and France discussed the exchange of The Gambia for some other French territory, but no agreement was reached and Britain made The Gambia a British colony in 1888. It remained under British rule until it achieved full independence in 1965. In 1970, The Gambia became a republic. But in July 1994, a military group overthrew the president, Sir Dawda Jawara, who fled into exile.

One major political issue concerns relations between the English-speaking Gambians and their French-speaking Senegalese neighbours. In 1981, an attempted coup in The Gambia was defeated with the help of Senegalese troops. In 1982, The Gambia and Senegal set up a defence alliance, the Confederation of Senegambia. But this move towards closer co-operation ended in 1989, when the Confederation was dissolved. [*Map page 32*] ∎

---

**AREA** 11,300 sq km [4,363 sq mls]
**POPULATION** 1,081,000
**CAPITAL (POPULATION)** Banjul (150,000)
**GOVERNMENT** Military regime
**ETHNIC GROUPS** Mandinka (also called Mandingo or Malinke) 40%, Fulani (also called Peul) 19%, Wolof 15%, Jola 10%, Soninke 8%
**LANGUAGES** English (official)
**RELIGIONS** Islam 95%, Christianity 4%, traditional beliefs 1%
**CURRENCY** Dalasi = 100 butut

---

# GEORGIA

---

Positioned between Russia and Turkey, Georgia comprises four main areas: the Caucasus Mountains (Bolshoi Kavka) in the north, including Mt Elbrus (5,633 m [18,841 ft]) on the Russian border; the Black Sea coastal plain in the west; the eastern end of the mountains of Asia Minor to the south; and a low plateau in the east, protruding into Azerbaijan. Separating the two mountain sections is the crucial Kura valley, in which the capital Tbilisi stands.

The Black Sea plains have hot summers and mild winters, when temperatures seldom drop below freezing point. The rainfall is heavy, but inland Tbilisi has moderate rainfall, with the heaviest rains in spring and early summer. Summers are hot but winters are colder than in the west. Snow covers the highest mountains throughout the year.

## ECONOMY AND RESOURCES
The largest of the three Transcaucasian republics, Georgia is rich in citrus fruits and wine (notably in the Kakhetia region), tea (the main crop), tobacco, wheat, barley and vegetables, while perfumes are made from flowers and herbs and, in Imeretia, silk is a flourishing industry. Almost 40% forested, it also has a significant stake in timber. It has large deposits of manganese ore, but despite reserves of coal and huge hydroelectric potential, most of its electricity is generated in Russia and the Ukraine.

## HISTORY AND POLITICS
Mostly Orthodox Christians, Georgians have a strong national culture and a long literary tradition based on their own language and alphabet. Land of the legendary 'Golden Fleece' of Greek mythology, the area was conquered by the Romans, Persians and Arabs before establishing autonomy in the 10th century, but Tartars, Persians and Turks invaded before it came under Russian domination around 1800. Renowned for their longevity, the population's most famous product was Josef Stalin, born in Gori, 65 km [40 mls] north-west of Tbilisi.

Always a maverick among the Soviet republics, Georgia was the first to declare independence after the Baltic states (April 1991), but did not officially join the CIS until parliament ratified the decree in March 1994. When Gorbachev resigned, the democratically elected leader of Georgia, Zviad Gamsakhurdia, found himself holed up in Tbilisi's KGB headquarters, under siege from rebel forces representing widespread disapproval of his policies, from the economy to the imprisonment of political opponents. In January he fled the country (now ruled by a military council), returning to lead resistance from his home territory in the west, though to little effect. He committed suicide at the end of 1993. A charismatic, highly individual president, Gamsakhurdia had also been in conflict with the Ossetian minority in one of the republic's three autonomous regions (Abkhazia in the north-west, South Ossetia in north-central Georgia, and Adzharia (Ajaria) in the south-west), who feared being swamped in a new independent nation. In March 1992 former Soviet foreign minister Edvard Shevardnadze agreed to become chairman of the ruling council. [*Map page 22*] ▪

**AREA** 69,700 sq km [26,910 sq mls]
**POPULATION** 5,450,000
**CAPITAL (POPULATION)** Tbilisi (1,279,000)
**GOVERNMENT** Multiparty republic
**ETHNIC GROUPS** Georgian 70%, Armenian 8%, Russian 6%, Azerbaijani 6%, Ossetian 3%, Greek 2%, Abkhazian 2%, other 3%
**LANGUAGES** Georgian (official)
**RELIGIONS** Christianity (Georgian Orthodox 65%, Russian Orthodox 10%, Armenian Orthodox 8%), Islam 11%
**CURRENCY** Lari

# GERMANY

On reunification, West and East Germany moved from the ninth and 15th biggest countries in Europe (in terms of area) to a combined fourth – still much smaller than France, Spain and Sweden – but with the independence of the Ukraine the following year dropped back to fifth. It is, nevertheless, 12th in the world in terms of population.

Germany extends from the North Sea and Baltic coasts in the north to the flanks of the central Alps in the south. The country includes only a narrow fringe of Alpine mountains, with the Zugspitze (2,963 m [9,721 ft]) the country's highest peak. There is, however, a wide section of the associated Alpine foreland bordering Switzerland and Austria, stretching northwards from the foothills of the Alps to the Danube. The foreland is largely covered by moraines and outwash plains which, with many lakes, including the Bodensee (shared with Switzerland), are relics of the glacial age, and are reminders of the many glaciers that once emerged from the Alpine valleys.

The central uplands of Europe are more amply represented, occupying a broad swathe of Germany. Four types of terrain are found. Block mountains are remnants of pre-Alpine fold mountains shattered and reshaped by the later earth movements. The Harz, Thüringer Wald and Erzgebirge (Ore Mountains) massifs rise above a varied scarpland terrain, notably the Thüringian Basin, which has the fertile Erfurt lowland at its heart.

Tectonic uplift was greatest in the south, close to the Alps, producing the Schwarzwald (Black Forest) and Böhmerwald. Between these great blocks of forested mountains are open basins of sedimentary rocks, their resistant bands picked out by erosion as in the magnificent scarp of the Schwäbische Alb, overlooking the Neckar basin.

A third kind of country is provided by down-faulted basins filled with softer deposits of more recent age, notably the Upper Rhine plain between Basle and Mainz. Earth movement and eruptions produced a fourth element, such volcanic mountains as the Vogelsberg and the hot and mineral springs that gave rise to the famous spas. Here is Germany at its most picturesque, with baronial castles on wooded heights, looking down over vineyards to clustered villages of half-timbered houses, whose occupants still cultivate open-field strips as they have done for centuries.

The northern lowlands, part of the great North European Plain, owe their topography mainly to the retreat of the ice-sheets. The most recent moraines, marked by forested ridges that may include good boulder-clay soils, are restricted to Schleswig-Holstein. The rest of the lowland is covered with leached older moraine and sandy outwash, so that in many places soils are poor. The glacial period also left behind loess, windblown dust deposited along the northern edge of the central uplands and in basins within them, providing some of the country's best soils for wheat, malting barley and sugar beet. This belt broadens in the lowland of Saxony around Halle and Leipzig.

The coast is also the product of glaciation and subsequent changes. The low Baltic shore is diversified by long, branching inlets, formed beneath the ice of the glacial period and now beloved by yachtsmen, while inland the most recent moraines have left behind a confused terrain of hills and lakes, but also areas of good soil developed on glacial till. The movement of water around the edge of the ice-sheets carved stream trenches (*Urstromtäler*), south-east to north-west; these are now in part occupied by the present rivers, and have also proved convenient for canal construction. The North Sea is fringed by sandy offshore islands, the products of a beach bar now breached by the sea.

## ECONOMY AND RESOURCES

Over a quarter of Germany is forested, with particular concentration in the Alps, the massifs of the central uplands, and the poorer areas of the northern lowland. It is amazing that this economically most advanced country has some of Europe's smallest farms, particularly characteristic of southern Germany. Most are used for arable-based mixed farming, with minor livestock enterprises. In the warmer basins tobacco, vegetables and, increasingly, maize are grown. Vineyards and orchards clothe the slopes of the Rhine and its tributaries. Much larger wheat and sugar-beet farms with important livestock enterprises are characteristic of the loess soils on the northern edge of the central uplands. The Bavarian Alpine foreland in the south, and Schleswig-Holstein in the north, are other areas of above-average farm size. The sandy northern lowland, which used to support a poor agriculture based on rye, potatoes and pigs, increasingly specializes in intensive meat and poultry production. Dairy specialization is typical of the milder north-west and the Alpine fringes.

Because of the generally small size of holdings many farmers seek a supplementary income outside agriculture – often a halfway stage to giving up agriculture altogether. Persons employed in agriculture, who were a quarter of the employed population of the FRG in 1950, accounted for well below 10% on reunification four decades later. With this movement out of agriculture, the average size of holding is steadily but all too slowly rising.

In the GDR, by contrast, all agricultural holdings were brought into 'co-operatives', many of over 500 hectares [1,236 acres] and some up to ten times that size. The East German government's version of the collective farm proved much more efficient than the equivalent in many other Communist states, however, and the economic outlook was quite promising prior to reunification.

### Minerals and energy

Germany is the most important coal producer of continental Western Europe, though output from the Ruhr, Saar and Aachen fields has dropped since the mid-1950s, owing mainly to competition from oil. Some oil and gas is home-produced, mainly extracted from fields beneath the northern lowland, but most of the oil consumed in Germany is delivered by pipeline from Wilhelmshaven, Europoort and the Mediterranean to refineries in the Rhineland and on the Danube.

Brown coal (lignite) is excavated between Cologne and Aachen, but the former GDR (East Germany) was unique in depending for energy supply on this source of low calorific value, economically mined in vast open pits. The older centre of mining was in the lowland of Saxony, between Halle and Leipzig, but the main area of expansion is now in Niederlausitz, south of Cottbus. Brown coal is increasingly reserved for electricity generation, although atomic plants built on the coast and principal rivers are expected to be of increasing importance (at present 34% of the total for the former FRG), with hydroelectric stations concentrated in the Bavarian Alps. Energy needs and feedstock for the important chemical industry around Halle are met by oil brought by pipeline from the former Soviet republics or by tanker through Rostock. The other mineral resource of value is potash, mined south of the Harz; Germany is the world's third largest producer. The non-ferrous metallic ores of the Harz and other massifs of the central uplands are no longer of great significance, while high-grade imported iron ores have proved more economic than the

## THE REUNIFICATION

In 1945, a devastated Germany was divided into four zones, each occupied by one of the victorious powers: Britain, France, the USA and the Soviet Union. The division was originally a temporary expedient (the Allies had formally agreed to maintain German unity), but the Russians published a constitution for the German Democratic Republic in 1946. The split solidified when the Russians rejected a currency reform common to all three Western zones. The German Federal Republic – 'West Germany' – was created in 1949.

Throughout the years of the Cold War, as NATO troops faced Warsaw Pact tanks across the barbed wire and minefields of the new frontier, the partition seemed irrevocable. Although both German constitutions maintained hopes of reunification, it seemed that nothing short of the total war both sides dreaded could bring it about. The West, with three-quarters of the population, rebuilt war damage and prospered. The East was hailed as the industrial jewel of the Soviet European empire, though some of its people were prepared to risk being shot to escape westwards.

By the late 1980s it was clear that the Soviet empire was crumbling. In the autumn of 1989, thousands of East Germans migrated illegally to the West across the newly open Hungarian border and mass demonstrations in East German cities followed. At first, the government issued a stream of threats, but when it became clear that there would be no Soviet tanks to enforce its rule, it simply packed up. With the frontiers open, it became clear that the 'successful' East German economy was a catastrophic shambles, a scrapyard poisoned by uncontrolled pollution, with bankruptcy imminent. The choice facing German leaders in 1990 was starkly simple: either unite East and West, or accept virtually the entire Eastern population as penniless refugees.

The West German government acted quickly, often bullying the weaker Easterners. The Western Deutschmark became the common currency and on 3 October 1990 – more than 45 years after Germany had lost the war – the country was formally reunited. The costs of bringing the East up to the standards of the West are high, and Germans will be paying them for years to come. But there had been no other possible choice.

---

home ores found predominantly in the districts of Siegen and Peine-Salzgitter.

### SETTLEMENT AND INDUSTRY

From Neolithic times the core settlement areas of Germany were the fertile lowlands – areas like the northern edge of the central uplands in Lower Saxony and Westphalia, the Upper Rhine plain, the Main and Neckar basins, and the Alpine foreland. From these core areas land-hungry medieval peasants advanced to clear large areas of forest in the uplands, and also streamed eastwards to settle in lands beyond the Elbe and Saale.

The fragmentation of the Holy Roman Empire into a swarm of competing states had a positive side in the founding and fostering by local rulers, large and small, of a dense system of towns, among them future regional capitals like Hanover, Stuttgart or Munich (München). The contrast with the 'French desert' created by Parisian centralization is striking.

When industrial growth came in the 19th century, heavy industry naturally concentrated in the Ruhr and Saar coalfields, but thanks to the railways other production could disperse widely to these existing towns. Since 1945 the Ruhr and Saar coalfields have been undergoing a difficult period of conversion, owing to the problems of the now declining coal, steel and heavy engineering industries. Western Europe's largest industrial region, stretching from Duisburg to Dortmund, the Ruhr ('the forge of Germany') has seen its mines for top-grade coking coal cut from 145 to less than 20 and has been forced to diversify – the western end into petrochemicals based on the Rhine ports and pipelines, the eastern part into lighter and computer-based industry.

By contrast, towns away from the coalfields, especially the great regional capitals of southern Germany, have flourished with the inauguration of modern industries (motor vehicles, electrical equipment, electronics), the growth of administrative and office work, and the division among a number of cities of capital functions formerly concentrated in Berlin.

As an advanced industrial country of Western type, the role of East Germany within the Communist-bloc states was to provide technically advanced equipment, receiving in return supplies of raw materials and semi-finished products such as steel. Because of industrial inertia, the location of the important machine-building industry had not greatly changed since capitalist times, being heavily concentrated in and around the southern cities of Leipzig, Chemnitz (then Karl-Marx-Stadt) and Dresden. Other centres were Magdeburg and East Berlin, which was also the leading producer of electrical equipment.

The GDR inherited a traditional strength in precision and optical industries, mostly located in Thüringia (such as the famous Zeiss works at Jena), the base for important developments in industrial instrumentation and electronics. The government tried to steer some major new developments into the rural north and east of the country, including ship-building at Rostock – also the site of a new ocean port, to avoid the use of facilities in the FRG – oil refining and chemicals at Schwedt, and iron smelting and steel rolling in the town of Eisenhüttenstadt.

While the inner parts of the greatest cities have tended to lose population, their suburbs and satellites have exploded across the surrounding countryside, forming vast urban areas of expanding population. In the west and south of the country, an axis of high population growth and high density stretches from the Rhine-Ruhr region (largest of all but checked in expansion by the problems of Ruhr industry), through the Rhine-Main (Frankfurt), Rhine-Neckar (Mannheim-Ludwigshafen) and Stuttgart regions to Munich. In the east and north plains the densely populated areas are more isolated, centred on the cities of Nuremberg, Hanover, Bremen, Hamburg, Dresden, Leipzig and, of course, Berlin.

Since 1950 there has been a tendency for the West's population to drift towards the more attractive south. Urban population losses have in part been made up by immigrant workers (nearly 2.5 million at their peak

## BERLIN

Like defeated Germany itself, Berlin was formally divided between the four victorious powers – despite the fact that it was located in Prussia, 160 km [100 mls] inside Soviet-occupied eastern Germany. In June 1948, in an attempt to bring the whole city under their control, the Soviets closed all road and rail links with the West. The Western Allies supplied the city by a massive airlift; in October 1949 the blockade was abandoned, but Berlin's anomalous situation remained a potential flashpoint, and provoked a series of diplomatic crises – mainly because it offered an easy escape route to the West for discontented East Germans.

In August 1961, alarmed at the steady drain of some of its best-trained people, the East German authorities built a dividing wall across the city. Over the years, the original improvised structure – it was thrown up overnight – became a substantial barrier of concrete and barbed wire, with machine-gun towers and minefields; despite the hazards, many still risked the perilous crossing, and hundreds of would-be refugees – often youngsters – died in the attempt.

The Berlin Wall, with its few, heavily-guarded crossing points, became the most indelible symbol of the Cold War, the essential background to every spy thriller. When the East German government collapsed in 1989, the Wall's spontaneous demolition by jubilant Easterners and Westerners alike became the most unambiguous sign of the Cold War's ending.

When East Germany joined the West, it was agreed that Berlin would become the formal capital of the unified state in the year 2000 – until that time, both Berlin and the quiet, Rhineland city of Bonn were to be joint capitals.

in the early 1970s, with Turkey the principal source), increasingly joined by their families to supplement a German native population – which at the end of the 1960s entered a period of negative growth.

Germany's wary neighbours, fearing that a

nation suddenly swollen to nearly 80 million through reunification could swamp Europe, could rest easy. According to a report from the Institute of German Economy, published in 1992, there will be 20 million fewer Germans alive than today by the year 2030, and on current trends the number of young people below the age of 15 will drop from 13.7 million in 1990 to 10 million in 2010. The findings suggested that, as a result, the country would need at least 300,000 new immigrants a year to fill the gap in its labour market.

**Communications**
Germany has the advantage of the superb Rhine waterway, which from its Alpine sources cuts right across the central uplands to the North Sea. A combination of summer snow-melt from the Alps and autumn-spring rainfall in the central uplands gives it a powerful and remarkably even flow – if increasingly polluted. Although traffic is at its most intensive between Rotterdam and the Rhine-Ruhr region, where Duisburg is the largest inland harbour of Europe, standard 1,250-tonne self-propelled barges can reach Basle. The Rhine-Main-Danube waterway has also opened a through route to Eastern Europe and the Black Sea, while for north German traffic the Mittelland Canal, following the northern edge of the central uplands, opens up links to the north German ports and Berlin. Unusually for Europe, Germany's rivers and canals carry as much freight as its roads.

Hamburg is Germany's biggest seaport, followed by Bremen with its outport, Bremerhaven. All German ports suffer by being too far from the main centre of European population and economic activity in the Rhinelands; the Belgian and Dutch ports are at a great advantage being closer.

Germany was the first European country to build motorways (Hitler's *Autobahns*, built in the 1930s), and also enjoys an efficient if highly subsidized railway network. Both are crucial to a country which, on reunification, increased its land borders from nine to ten countries. Air travel, too, both internal and international, is increasingly important.

**HISTORY AND POLITICS**
The German Empire that was created under

Prussian dominance in 1871, comprising four kingdoms, six grand duchies, five duchies and seven principalities, and centred on the great imperial capital of Berlin, was to last for fewer than 75 years. Even at its greatest extent it left large areas of Europe's German-speaking population outside its boundaries, notably in Austria and large parts of Switzerland. Following the fall of Hitler in 1945, a defeated Germany was obliged to transfer to Poland and the Soviet Union 114,500 sq km [44,200 sq mls] situated east of the Oder and Neisse rivers, nearly a quarter of the country's pre-war area. The German-speaking inhabitants were expelled – as were most German-speaking minorities in the countries of Eastern Europe – and the remainder of Germany was occupied by the four victorious Allied powers.

The dividing line between the zones occupied by the three Western Allies (USA, UK and France) and that occupied by the USSR rapidly hardened into a political boundary dividing the country. In 1948 West Germany was proclaimed as the independent Federal Republic of Germany (FRG), with a capital at Bonn (deemed 'provisional' pending hoped-for German reunification), and measuring 248,000 sq km [96,000 sq mls]. East Germany became the German Democratic Republic (GDR), a Soviet satellite of 108,000 sq km [41,700 sq mls]. Berlin was similarly divided, the three western sectors of an enclave of occupation becoming 480 sq km [186 sq mls] embedded in the territory of the GDR, of which the Soviet-occupied East Berlin was deemed to be capital.

**Administration**
The system of powerful federal states (*Länder*) created in the FRG after World War II remained remarkably stable, though huge disparities of size have remained in spite of various reform proposals. Bavaria has by far the largest area, and North Rhine-Westphalia, with the Rhine-Ruhr region at its heart, has the largest population, over a fifth of the German total. At the other extreme are the 'city states' of Bremen and Hamburg, though Saarland is also small.

In 1990 the ten *Länder* of the FRG (excluding the enclave of West Berlin) were joined by the five rejuvenated old states of the GDR –

Brandenburg, Mecklenburg-West Pomerania, Saxony, Saxony-Anhalt and Thüringia – plus the new 'united' Berlin. The East German organization had been very different, the country politically divided into 15 administrative districts (*Bezirke*) under the control of the central government in East Berlin.

### The cost of unification

The stability of the federal system may well come under considerable strain in the early years of the reunited Germany. The phenomenal and sustained rise of the FRG from the ashes of World War II to become the world's third biggest economy and its largest exporter – the so-called *Wirtschaftswunder*, or 'economic miracle', accomplished with few natural resources – was already levelling out before the financial costs of reunification (such as the 'two-for-one' Deutschmark for Ostmark deal for GDR citizens) became apparent.

While East Germany had achieved the highest standard of living in the Soviet bloc, it was well short of the levels of advanced EC countries. Massive investment was needed to rebuild the East's industrial base and transport system, and that meant increased taxation. In addition, the new nation found itself funnelling aid into Eastern Europe (Germany led the EC drive for recognition of its old allies Slovenia and Croatia) and then into the former Soviet republics. All this took place against a background of continued downturn in world trade: in February 1992 the German government officially announced the calculation of negative growth – it averaged 8% a year in the 1950s – and the German economy, on paper at least, was 'in recession'.

The costs could be social, too. If Westerners resent added taxes and the burden of the GDR, and if the Easterners resent the overbearing, patronizing attitudes of the old FRG, there could be cultural as well as economic polarization. In 1992 there was the spectacle – not seen in 18 years – of several public sector strikes. More likely, however, are a revived German sense of identity bordering on hegemony, even a swing to the 'right', and a revival of Fascism.

Reunification soon appeared in the early 1990s to be the beginning rather than the end of a chapter in German history. At the very least, it would be a more complicated, expensive and lengthy undertaking than anyone was prepared to envisage as the Berlin Wall came crumbling down. [*Map pages 14–15*] ■

**AREA** 356,910 sq km [137,803 sq mls]
**POPULATION** 80,278,000
**CAPITAL (POPULATION)** Berlin (3,446,000)/Bonn (296,000)
**GOVERNMENT** Federal multiparty republic
**ETHNIC GROUPS** German 93%, Turkish 2%, Yugoslav 1%, Italian 1%, Greek, Polish, Spanish
**LANGUAGES** German (official)
**RELIGIONS** Christianity (Protestant, mainly Lutheran 45%, Roman Catholic 37%), Islam 2%
**CURRENCY** Deutsche Mark = 100 pfennig

# GHANA

The Republic of Ghana faces the Gulf of Guinea in West Africa, just north of the Equator. Behind the thickly populated southern coastal plains, which are lined by lagoons, lies a plateau region in the south-west. Northern Ghana is drained by the Black and White Volta rivers which flow into Lake Volta. This lake, which has formed behind the Akosombo Dam, is one of the world's largest artificially created lakes.

Rainforests grow in the south-west. To the north, the forests merge into savanna (tropical grassland with some woodland). More open grasslands dominate in the far north. Temperatures and humidity are uniformly high all year round.

### ECONOMY AND RESOURCES

The Akosombo Dam below Lake Volta provides power to smelt imported alumina into aluminium, and for the main towns, mines and industries in the Takoradi-Kumasi-Tema triangle, the most developed part of the country. To build the dam, a second deep-water port was developed at Tema, east of Accra, the capital. Tema is now Ghana's main port for imports and for cocoa export.

Cocoa has been the leading export since 1924, and until the late 1970s Ghana was the world's leading producer. However, neighbouring Ivory Coast has now overtaken Ghana both in this and in forestry production. In turn, Ghana has attempted to expand the fishing, tourism and agricultural industries.

Unlike the Ivory Coast, Ghana has long been a producer of minerals – gold has been exploited for a thousand years. The area within a radius of 100 km [60 mls] of Dunkwa produces 90% of Ghana's mineral exports. However, production of most minerals is currently static or declining. The few remaining gold mines, with the notable exception of Obuasi, are now scarcely economic. Manganese production was recently revived to meet a new demand in battery manufacture, but the country's substantial reserves of bauxite remain undeveloped while imported alumina is used in the Tema aluminium smelter. Industrial diamonds contribute modestly to Ghana's economy. Offshore oil was discovered in 1978 but has yet to be commercially developed.

## HISTORY AND POLITICS

Formerly known appropriately as the Gold Coast, Ghana's post-colonial name recalls the state which lay north of the upper Niger from the 8th to the 13th centuries, and from whose population some of today's Ghanaians may well be descended.

In 1957 Ghana was the first tropical African country to become independent of colonial rule, and until 1966 was led by Dr Kwame Nkrumah, a prominent Third World spokesman and pioneer of Pan-African Socialism.

Nkrumah's overthrow was followed by a succession of coups and military governments, with Flight-Lieutenant Jerry Rawlings establishing himself as undoubted leader in 1981. While his hardline regime has steadied the economy, political progress has been token: an agreement to change the constitution to a pluralist democracy and set up a consultative assembly (in place of his ruling Provisional National Defence Council) was approved by a referendum in April 1992, but was seen by opponents as merely window-dressing. Only 29% of the electorate voted in the 1992 elections and Rawlings, now president, remains firmly in control. [*Map page 32*] ■

**AREA** 238,540 sq km [92,100 sq mls]
**POPULATION** 16,944,000
**CAPITAL (POPULATION)** Accra (965,000)
**GOVERNMENT** Multiparty republic
**ETHNIC GROUPS** Akan 54%, Mossi 16%, Ewe 12%, Ga-Adangame 8%, Gurma 3%
**LANGUAGES** English (official)
**RELIGIONS** Christianity 62% (Protestant 28%, Roman Catholic 19%), traditional beliefs 21%, Islam 16%
**CURRENCY** Cedi = 100 pesewas

# GIBRALTAR

The Rock, as it is popularly known, guards the north-eastern end of the Strait of Gibraltar and lies directly opposite the very similar peninsula of Ceuta, one of two remaining Spanish enclaves in Morocco (the other is Melilla). Only 23 km [14 mls] separate Ceuta and Gibraltar. The Rock, 6.5 sq km [2.5 sq mls] in area, occupies a narrow peninsula consisting largely of a ridge thrusting south along the eastern side of Algeciras Bay, terminating in the 30 m [100 ft] cliffs of Europa Point. It shelters a spacious anchorage and harbour from east winds with long artificial break-waters and quays constructed of stone tunnelled from the ridge. On the north there is a low, flat sandy plain used for an airport.

Shrubs, partly wild olives, clothe the more precarious slopes and provide shelter for the only wild monkeys in Europe. Considerable areas of the summit are used as catchments for drinking water, supplemented by diesel-powered seawater distillation.

## ECONOMY AND RESOURCES

Houses cover the slope facing the harbour and spread around two flattish beaches on the south, leaving the precipitous eastern slopes uninhabited except near Catalan Bay. The built-up area has an excellent road network but the topography prohibits cultivation and the Gibraltarians rely on the port, the ship-repairing yards, the military and air bases, and on tourism for their livelihood. About 2,400 merchant ships and numerous pleasure craft call at Gibraltar annually and the low import duties, excellent tourist facilities and almost rainless summers make it a popular shopping and holiday centre.

## HISTORY AND POLITICS

Local rock carvings demonstrate that Gibraltar has been inhabited since Neolithic times. Greeks and Romans also settled here, but the first sure date for colonization is AD 711 when Tariq ibn Zaid, a Berber chieftain, occupied it. Although taken over by Spaniards for a short while in the 14th century, it remained Moorish until 1462. An Anglo-Dutch naval force captured it in 1704 and it was formally recognized as a British possession at the Treaty of Utrecht in 1713. In spite of long sieges and assaults – not to mention pressure from Spain – it has remained British ever since, becoming a strategically vital naval dockyard, a commercial port and a base for reconnaissance aircraft.

The 28,000 Gibraltarians are of British, Spanish, Maltese, Portuguese and Genoan descent. Though bilingual in Spanish and English, they remain staunchly pro-British. In 1966, following a long-standing claim, the Spanish government called on Britain to give 'substantial sovereignty' of Gibraltar over to Spain and closed the border (1.2 km [0.74 mls]) to all but pedestrian traffic. In a 1967 referendum the residents voted overwhelmingly to remain under British control, and in 1969 they were granted the status of a self-governing dependency.

Spain closed the frontier completely, preventing thousands of Spaniards from reaching their daily work. The border was reopened fully by Spain in 1985 following British agreement that, for the first time, they would discuss the sovereignty of Gibraltar; but despite being fellow members of NATO (Spain joined in 1982) and the EU (Spain joined on 1 January 1986), there has been no progress towards British compliance with the UN General Assembly's resolution for an end to Gibraltar's 'colonial status' by 1 October 1996. [*Map page 18*] ■

---

**AREA** 6.5 sq km [2.5 sq mls]
**POPULATION** 28,000
**CAPITAL (POPULATION)** Gibraltar Town (28,000)
**GOVERNMENT** British dependency
**ETHNIC GROUPS** British, Spanish, Maltese, Portuguese
**LANGUAGES** English, Spanish
**RELIGIONS** Christianity (mainly Roman Catholic)
**CURRENCY** Gibraltar pound = 100 pence

---

# GREECE

Mainland Greece consists of a mountainous peninsula which projects 500 km [312 mls] into the Mediterranean from the south-west corner of the Balkans, and an 80 km [50 ml] coastal belt along the northern shore of the Aegean Sea.

Nearly a fifth of the total land area of Greece is made up of its 2,000 or so islands, found mainly in the Aegean Sea to the east of the main peninsula but also in the Ionian Sea to the west; only 154 of these islands are inhabited, but they account for over 11% of the population. Some of the islands of the Dodecanese group in the eastern Aegean lie just 16 km [10 mls] off the coast of Turkey, and northern Corfu in the Ionian Islands is separated from the Albanian coast by a narrow channel.

The principal structural feature of Greece are the Pindos Mountains, which extend south-eastwards from the Albanian border to cover most of the peninsula. The island of Crete is also structurally related to the main Alpine fold mountain system to which the Pindos range belongs. Its highest peak, Mt Ida, is 2,456 m [8,057 ft] high. In these ranges limestone rocks predominate, though many of the Aegean Islands are of similar formation to the Rhodopi Massif in the north and made up of crystalline rocks.

## ECONOMY AND RESOURCES

With so much of Greece covered by rugged mountains, only about a third of the area is suitable for cultivation, yet 40% of the population depend for their living on agriculture. The average farm size is under 4 hectares [10 acres], though on a few areas of flat land, mostly around the Aegean coasts in Macedonia and Thrace, large estates can be found.

The chief crops are typical of Mediterranean lands – wheat, olives, vines, tobacco and citrus fruits. Most villagers keep a few domestic animals, particularly sheep and goats. The mountain pastures are poor, in the main consisting of scrubland, and many areas have been stripped of what tree cover they once had by goats (notoriously destructive of growing trees), and by the need for wood for ships, house building and charcoal burning.

Greece has been described as a land of mountains and of the sea. Nowhere in Greece is more than 80 km [50 mls] from the sea, and most of the towns are situated on the coast. Greater Athens, which consists of the capital city and its seaport, Piræus, has a third of the total population and has grown six-fold since 1945. Thessaloniki (Salonica), the second city, is also a seaport, serving not only northern Greece but also southern Yugoslavia. Greece's mountainous terrain makes communication on land difficult, but the country has the world's largest merchant fleet (measured by ownership, not national registry), and shipbuilding and repairs are still important industries, while fishing provides a crucial supplement to the diet of a people who have difficulty wresting a living from their poor if beautiful homeland.

Greece is poorly endowed with industrial raw materials. There are deposits of iron ore, bauxite, nickel and manganese, but no coal and very small amounts of oil. The possibilities for hydroelectric development are severely limited because of the irregularity of the streams, many of which dry up entirely during the long summer drought. Thus Greece must import most of its sources of energy – mainly oil and coal. Industrial activity is largely

## CRETE

The island of Crete was the home of the seafaring Minoan civilization, which flourished in the period 3500–1100 BC and left behind a wealth of archaeological sites and artefacts. Most southerly and by far the largest of the Greek islands, Crete has a milder, more maritime climate than the mainland. The rugged, harbourless south coast, backed by steep limestone mountains, is the more inhospitable side, with winter gales adding to the hazards of navigation.

Most of the population of 536,980 live in the lowlands of the north, about a quarter of them in Iráklion (the capital) and Khania. About a quarter of the island is under crops; agriculture, tourism and small-scale mining are the main sources of income. Though Greek-speaking, Cretans differ in outlook and culture from the mainlanders; they suffered long occupation by Venetians and then by Turks, remaining under Turkish rule until 1898, 70 years after mainland Greece had been liberated.

concerned with the processing of agricultural produce – fruit and vegetables, canning, the production of wine and olive oil, cigarette manufacture, textiles and leather processing. Greece is one of the world's major producers of dried fruits; the word 'currant' is derived from the name of the Greek town of Corinth that lies on the narrow isthmus connecting the southern peninsula of the Pelopónnisos to the mainland. A canal, built in 1893 and 4.8 km [3 mls] long, cuts through the isthmus, linking the Gulf of Corinth with the Aegean.

The tourist industry is vital – in 1992 there were nearly 9.8 million visitors. Overseas visitors are attracted by the warm climate, the beautiful scenery, especially on the islands, and also by the historical sites which survive from the days of classical Greece. However, a number of factors have combined to limit the importance of tourism in recent years, including the emergence of cheaper rivals like Turkey and Tunisia, the recession in Western countries and the appalling pollution in Athens – by some measures the most polluted city in Europe outside the former Eastern bloc, with 60% of the nation's total manufacturing capacity.

## HISTORY AND POLITICS

In the great days of classical Greece, during the thousand years before Christ, Greek colonies were established all round the shores of the Mediterranean and Black Seas. For a brief period in the 4th century BC, Alexander the Great built an empire which extended from the Danube, through Turkey and the Middle East to the Indus Valley of northern India. Even more important were the great contributions to philosophy, sculpture, architecture and literature made by the early Greeks.

The great epic poems of Greece – the *Iliad* and the *Odyssey* – speak of the exploits of ancient Greek seafarers who travelled around the Mediterranean. Today Greeks are still great seamen and wanderers, and large communities are to be found in the USA, Australia, Canada and Latin America. Since 1960 many Greek migrants have found work in Germany, and the admission of Greece to the EC (on 1 January 1981) has given further opportunities for Greeks to find work in Western Europe. The gap in economic strength and performance between Greece and most of its EU partners remains wide, but the prospect of a single market may help to overcome the traditional obstacles of partisan, often volatile politics, an inflated, slow-moving government bureaucracy, and a notorious 'black economy'. In February 1994 the government imposed a trade embargo on the Former Yugoslav Republic of Macedonia over its alleged territoiral claim on northern Greece. [*Map page 17*] ■

---

**AREA** 131,990 sq km [50,961 sq mls]
**POPULATION** 10,416,000
**CAPITAL (POPULATION)** Athens (3,097,000)
**GOVERNMENT** Multiparty republic
**ETHNIC GROUPS** Greek 96%, Macedonian 2%, Turkish 1%, Albanian, Slav
**LANGUAGES** Greek (official)
**RELIGIONS** Christianity (Eastern Orthodox 97%), Islam 2%
**CURRENCY** Drachma = 100 lepta

---

# GREENLAND

Recognized by geographers as the world's largest island (the Australian mainland being considered a continental land mass), Greenland is almost three times the size of the second largest, New Guinea. However, more than 85% of the land is covered in continuous permafrost, an ice-cap with an average depth of about 1,500 m [5,000 ft], and though there are a few sandy and clay plains in the ice-free areas, settlement is confined to the narrow rocky coasts. The few towns, including the capital of Godthåb (Nuuk), are on the southwest coast, warmed by the southerly currents of the Atlantic; on the east side, a northerly current from the Arctic chills the pack-ice and makes it inaccessible for most of the year.

## ECONOMY AND RESOURCES

The economy still depends substantially on subsidies from Denmark, which remains its chief trading partner. The main rural occupations are sheep rearing and fishing – with shrimps, prawns and molluscs contributing over 60% of exports. The only major manufacturing is fish canning, which has drawn many Eskimos to the towns; few now follow the traditional life of nomadic hunters. Most Greenlanders (a mixture of Inuit Eskimo and Danish extraction) live precariously between the primitive and the modern; in the towns rates of alcoholism, venereal disease and suicide are all high. Yet the nationalist mood prevails, buoyed by abundant fish stocks, lead and zinc from Uummannaq in the north-west, untapped uranium in the south, possible oil in the east – and the increase in organized, often adventure-oriented tourism.

## HISTORY AND POLITICS

The first recorded European to visit this barren desert was Eirike Raudi (Eric the Red), a Norseman from Iceland who settled at Brattahlid in 982. It was he who named the place Greenland – to make it sound attractive to settlers. Within four years, more than 30 ships had ferried pioneers there, founding a colony which would last five centuries.

Greenland became a Danish possession in 1380 and, eventually, an integral part of the Kingdom of Denmark in 1953. After the island was taken into the EC in 1973 – despite a majority vote against by Greenlanders – a nationalist movement developed and in 1979, after another referendum, a home rule was introduced, with full internal self-government following in 1981. Then, in 1985, Greenland withdrew from the EC, halving the Community's territory.

Independence is a daunting task, as the Danes point out: the island is nearly 50 times the size of the mother country with only 1% of the population – figures which make Mongolia, the world's least densely populated country, look almost crowded. [*Map page 36*] ∎

AREA 2,175,600 sq km [839,999 sq mls]
POPULATION 58,000
CAPITAL (POPULATION) Godthåb (or Nuuk, 12,000)
GOVERNMENT Self-governing division of Denmark
ETHNIC GROUPS Greenlander 86%, Danish 14%
LANGUAGES Eskimo dialects, Danish
RELIGIONS Christianity (mainly Lutheran)
CURRENCY Danish currency

# GRENADA

The most southern of the Windward Islands, the country of Grenada also includes the Southern Grenadines, principally Carriacou. It is mainly mountainous, with lush vegetation. Grenada is known as 'the spice island of the Caribbean' and is the world's leading producer of nutmeg, its main crop. Cocoa, bananas and mace also contribute to exports, but attempts to diversify the economy from an agricultural base have been largely unsuccessful. In the early 1990s

there were signs that the tourist industry was finally making a recovery after the debilitating events of 1983.

Formally British since 1783, Grenada became a self-governing colony in 1967 and independent in 1974. Then, in 1979, it went Communist after a bloodless coup when Maurice Bishop established links with Cuba. After Bishop was executed by other Marxists in 1983, the US (supported by some Caribbean countries) sent in troops to restore democracy, and since the invasion the ailing economy has been heavily reliant on American aid. [*Map page 30*] ∎

AREA 344 sq km [133 sq mls]
POPULATION 92,000
CAPITAL (POPULATION) St George's (35,700)
GOVERNMENT Constitutional monarchy with a bicameral legislature
ETHNIC GROUPS Black 84%, Mixed 12%, East Indian 3%, White 1%
LANGUAGES English, French patois
RELIGIONS Christianity (Roman Catholic 64%, Protestant 34%)
CURRENCY East Caribbean dollar = 100 cents

# GUADELOUPE

Slightly the larger of France's two overseas departments in the Caribbean, Guadeloupe comprises seven islands including Saint-Martin and Saint-Barthélemy to the northwest. Over 90% of the area, however, is taken up by Basse-Terre, which is volcanic – La Soufrière (1,467 m [4,813 ft]) is the highest point in the Lesser Antilles – and the smaller Grande-Terre, made of low limestone; the two are separated by a narrow sea channel called Rivière-Salée (Salt River).

The commercial centre of Pointe-à-Pitre (population 25,300) is on Grande-Terre. Food is the biggest import (much of it from France), bananas the biggest export, followed by wheat flour, sugar, rum and aubergines.

French aid has helped create a reasonable standard of living, but despite this and thriving tourism – the majority of it from France and the USA – unemployment is high.

Though sharing an identical history to Martinique, Guadeloupe has a far stronger separatist movement, which sporadically resorts to acts of terrorism.

**St Martin** is administered as two separate parts: the northern two-thirds (Saint-Martin, French and administered as part of Guadeloupe), and the southern third (St Maarten, Dutch and part of the Netherlands Antilles federation). Located 260 km [162 mls] north of Guadeloupe, the island is just 88 sq km [34 sq mls] in total. [*Map page 30*] ■

> **AREA** 1,710 sq km [660 sq mls]
> **POPULATION** 421,000
> **CAPITAL (POPULATION)** Basse-Terre (14,000)
> **GOVERNMENT** Overseas department of France
> **ETHNIC GROUPS** Mixed (Black and White) 90%
> **LANGUAGES** French
> **RELIGIONS** Christianity (Roman Catholic 95%)
> **CURRENCY** French currency

# GUAM

T he largest of the Marianas, measuring 541 sq km [209 sq mls], Guam is composed mainly of a coralline limestone plateau, with mountains in the south, hills in the centre and narrow coastal lowlands in the north of the island. Though parts are highly developed along American lines, there are also traditional villages, beautiful beaches and dense jungles. Almost half the population of 147,000 are Chamorro – of mixed Indonesian, Spanish and Filipino descent – and another quarter Filipino, but 20% of the total population is composed of US military personnel and their families.

## ECONOMY AND RESOURCES

Textiles, beverages, tobacco and copra are the main exports, but most food is imported. As a Pacific tourist destination, it is second only to Hawaii; in 1990 visitors' receipts were $550 million. All this helps to give Guamanians a relatively high standard of living, with an annual per capita income of over $6,000.

## HISTORY AND POLITICS

Populated for over 3,000 years, charted by Magellan in 1521, colonized by Spain from 1668, but ceded to the US after the 1896–8 war and occupied by the Japanese 1941–4, it is today – as a 'self-governing unincorporated territory' – of huge strategic importance to Washington, and a third of its usable land is occupied by American naval and airforce establishments. In 1979, a referendum overwhelmingly backed a return of much of the military land to civilian use, and a 1982 vote showed clear support for the Commonwealth status enjoyed by the Northern Marianas. [*Map page 26*] ■

> **AREA** 541 sq km [209 sq mls]
> **POPULATION** 147,000
> **CAPITAL (POPULATION)** Agana (50,800)
> **GOVERNMENT** US territory
> **ETHNIC GROUPS** Chamorro 47%, Filipino 25%, American 20%
> **LANGUAGES** Chamorro, English
> **RELIGIONS** Christianity (Roman Catholic 98%)
> **CURRENCY** US currency

# GUATEMALA

M ost populous of the Central American countries, Guatemala's Pacific coastline, two and a half times longer than the Caribbean coast, is backed by broad alluvial plains, formed of material washed down from the towering volcanoes that front the ocean. These include extinct Tajumulco (4,217 m [13,830 ft]), the highest peak in Central America.

A heavily-dissected plateau, the Altos, forms the core of the country; beautiful lakes such as the Atitlán mark its junction with the mountains. This area, with comfortable temperatures for living and maize cultivation, is both a focus of dense rural settlement and also the site of the capital – earthquake-prone Guatemala City. The north-eastern third of the country is the Petén, a flat, low-lying limestone wilderness on the Yucatan Peninsula. Once a centre of Mayan civilization, it contains many remarkable archaeological remains, in particular Tikal and Uaxactún.

## ECONOMY AND RESOURCES
The plains have been used for commercial-scale agriculture only since the 1950s, when malaria was brought under control and roads were built; cattle and cotton are now more important than the traditional banana crop. Lower mountain slopes, up to about 1,500 m [5,000 ft], yield most of the country's best coffee, above that maize and beans are grown.

## HISTORY AND POLITICS
Guatemala was under Spanish rule from 1524 to 1821, when it became independent. The republic is divided into 22 departments. While Indians are in the majority, society and government are run on autocratic, often repressive lines by the mestizos of mixed Indian and European stock. The Indians were the principal victims of the army's indiscriminate campaign against left-wing URNG guerrillas in the early 1980s – the acceleration of a policy in place since the 1950s.

The 'low-intensity' civil war that followed was still smouldering when a UN-mediated cease-fire became operative in neighbouring El Salvador in February 1992. This influence, allied to the government's sudden recognition of Belizean independence in 1991 (Guatemala had claimed the entire territory), would benefit a nation whose 'defence' spending takes 15% of the budget, and whose record on human rights is appalling. As in El Salvador, Washington's stance is vitally important: in keeping with all the Central American republics (except Nicaragua), the US is crucial to the economy – in Guatemala's case, accounting for more than 40% of trade.

In March 1994 a human rights agreement was reached, allowing for the establishment of a UN observer mission in the country. [*Map page 30*] ■

AREA 108,890 sq km [42,042 sq mls]
POPULATION 10,322,000
CAPITAL (POPULATION) Guatemala City (2,000,000)
GOVERNMENT Republic
ETHNIC GROUPS Amerindian 45%, Ladino/Mestizo (mixed Hispanic and Amerindian) 45%, White 5%, Black 2%, others including Chinese 3%
LANGUAGES Spanish (official)
RELIGIONS Christianity (Roman Catholic 75%, Protestant 25%)
CURRENCY Guatemalan quetzal = 100 centavos

# GUINEA

The Republic of Guinea faces the Atlantic Ocean in West Africa. A flat, swampy, mangrove-fringed plain borders the coast, behind which the land rises to a plateau region called Fouta Djalon. Dense forests occupy the western foothills of the Fouta Djalon. The Upper Niger plains, named after one of Africa's longest rivers, the Niger, which rises there, are in the north-east. The Sénégal and Gambia rivers also start in north-eastern Guinea. In the south-east lie the Guinea Highlands, which reach 1,752 m [5,748 ft] at Mt Nimba on the border with Ivory Coast and Liberia.

## ECONOMY AND RESOURCES
Two-thirds of the population are employed in agriculture and food processing. Bananas, palm oil, pineapples and rice are important crops on the wet Atlantic coastal plain, where swamps and forests have been cleared for agricultural development, while in the drier interior cattle are kept by nomadic herdsmen.

Guinea's natural resources are considerable: it has some of the world's largest reserves of high-grade bauxite, and the three large mines account for some 80% of export earnings. The Aredor diamond mine has also been very profitable since opening in 1984, and there is great potential for iron ore mining and hydroelectric power.

## HISTORY AND POLITICS

Guinea was the first independent state of French-speaking Africa. France granted the troublesome territory independence in 1958 following a rise in nationalism after World War II, and for more than a quarter of a century Guinea was ruled by the repressive regime of President Ahmed Sékou Touré, who isolated Guinea from the West and leaned towards the Eastern bloc for support.

Though reconciled with France in 1978, it was not until after the military coup following Touré's death in 1984 that economic reforms began to work (it is estimated that up to a quarter of the population left for neighbouring countries during Touré's presidency). After his death, military leaders took over. Colonel Lansana Conté became president and his government introduced free enterprise policies. In 1993, Conté won a presidential election. [*Map page 32*] ■

---

**AREA** 245,860 sq km [94,927 sq mls]
**POPULATION** 6,501,000
**CAPITAL (POPULATION)** Conakry (705,000)
**GOVERNMENT** Multiparty republic
**ETHNIC GROUPS** Fulani 40%, Malinke 26%, Susu 11%, Kissi 7%, Kpelle 5%
**LANGUAGES** French (official)
**RELIGIONS** Islam 85%, traditional beliefs 5%, Christianity 2%
**CURRENCY** Guinean franc = 100 cauris

---

# GUINEA-BISSAU

The Republic of Guinea-Bissau is a small country in West Africa, where the land is mostly low-lying, with a broad, swampy coastal plain and many flat offshore islands, including the Bijagós Archipelago. These islands were probably once joined to the mainland but the coast has been submerged in recent geological time – this submergence has created broad river estuaries. The land rises in the east where there are low plateaux, but the highest land (up to 310 m [1,017 ft]) is found near the border with Guinea.

Mangrove forests grow along the coasts and estuaries, while dense rainforest covers much of the coastal plain. Inland, the forests thin out and merge into savanna, with open grassland on the highest ground. The country has a rich birdlife. Wild animals include buffaloes, crocodiles, gazelles and leopards.

## ECONOMY AND RESOURCES

Guinea-Bissau is a poor country. Agriculture employs more than 80% of the people, but most farmers produce little more than they need to feed their families. Major crops include beans, coconuts, groundnuts, maize, palm kernels and rice, the staple food.

Fishing is also important – the main port is Bissau – and fish, including shrimps, make up about one third of the country's exports. Groundnuts and coconuts together make up about 40% of the exports. Livestock are raised and some hides and skins are exported. Guinea-Bissau has some undeveloped mineral deposits (there are bauxite deposits in the south), but the country has few manufacturing industries.

## HISTORY AND POLITICS

Historians know little of the early history of the area, which lay near the edge of the medieval West African empires of Ghana and Mali. The coast was first visited by Portuguese navigators in 1446. Between the 17th and early 19th centuries, the Portuguese used the coast as a slave-trade base. Some slaves were taken to Brazil and others to the Cape Verde Islands where they were forced to work on Portuguese plantations.

Portugal appointed a governor to administer Guinea-Bissau and the Cape Verde Islands in 1836, but in 1879, the two territories were separated and Guinea-Bissau became a colony, then called Portuguese Guinea. But development was slow, partly because the territory did not attract settlers on the same scale as Portugal's much healthier African colonies of Angola and Mozambique.

In 1956, African nationalists in Portuguese Guinea and Cape Verde founded the African Party for the Independence of Guinea and Cape Verde (PAIGC). Because Portugal seemed determined to hang on to its overseas territories, the PAIGC began a guerrilla war in 1963. By 1968, it held two-thirds of the country. In 1972, a rebel National Assembly, elected by the people in the PAIGC-controlled area, voted to make the country independent as Guinea-Bissau. In 1974, Guinea-Bissau became independent, followed in 1975 by Cape Verde.

In 1974, Guinea-Bissau faced many problems arising from its under-developed economy and its lack of trained people to work in the administration. One objective of the leaders of Guinea-Bissau was to unite their country with Cape Verde. But army leaders overthrew Guinea-Bissau's government in 1980. The Revolutionary Council, which took over, did not favour unification with Cape Verde and instead concentrated on national policies. It followed a socialist programme, introducing some reforms. For example, it reduced adult illiteracy from 97% to 64% between 1974 and 1990. Other reforms concerned women who were now encouraged to play a full part in national development.

In 1991, the country abolished the law making the PAIGC the country's only political party. Opposition parties were then formed, with ten opposition parties legalized since November 1991. Legislative elections to a new 100-seat legislature were held in July 1994 and won by the PAIGC. [*Map page 32*] ∎

AREA 36,120 sq km [13,946 sq mls]
POPULATION 1,050,000
CAPITAL (POPULATION) Bissau (125,000)
GOVERNMENT Multiparty republic
ETHNIC GROUPS Balante 27%, Fulani (or Peul) 23%, Malinke (Mandingo or Mandinka) 12%, Mandyako 11%, Pepel 10%
LANGUAGES Portuguese (official)
RELIGIONS Traditional beliefs 54%, Islam 38%, Christianity 8%
CURRENCY Guinea-Bissau peso = 100 centavos

# GUYANA

The vast interior, covering 85% of the land area, includes low forest-covered plateaux, the wooded Rupununi savannas, meandering river valleys, and the spectacular Roraima Massif on the Venezuela-Brazil border. The coastal plain is mainly artificial, reclaimed from the tidal marshes and mangrove swamps by dykes and canals. It is largely uninhabited and 95% of the population live within a few kilometres of the coast, leaving the interior virtually empty.

## ECONOMY AND RESOURCES

Land reclamation for sugar and cotton planting began in the 18th century under Dutch West India Company rule, using slave labour, and continued through the 19th century after the British took over, with indentured Asian labour replacing slaves after emancipation. Today sugar remains the main plantation crop, with production largely mechanized, most of it in the lower Demerara River area.

The Asian community, however, which makes up about half the total Guyanan population, is involved in rice growing. Bauxite mining and alumina production are well-established industries, combining with sugar production to provide 80% of the country's overseas earnings. But neither sugar nor rice provide year-round work and unemployment remains a stubborn problem. The economy, which is 80% state-controlled, entered a prolonged economic crisis in the 1970s, and in the early 1980s the situation was exacerbated by the decline in the production and the price of bauxite, sugar and rice.

Following unrest, the government sought to replace Western aid by turning for help to socialist countries. During the late 1980s Western aid and investment were again sought, but by 1989 the social and economic difficulties had led to the suspension of foreign assistance.

## HISTORY AND POLITICS

The 'land of many waters' was settled by the

Dutch between 1616 and 1621. The territory was ceded to Britain in 1814, and in 1831 British Guiana was formed. Independent since 1966, Guyana – the only Englishspeaking country in South America – became a republic in 1970. Forbes Burnham was the first prime minister after independence. Under a new constitution adopted in 1980, the powers of the president were increased, and Burnham became president until his death in 1985. He was succeeded by Hugh Desmond Hoyte, but Hoyte was defeated in presidential elections in 1992 by an Asian Indian Cheddi Jagan, who had been prime minister prior to independence. [*Map page 31*] ■

AREA 214,970 sq km [83,000 sq mls]
POPULATION 825,000
CAPITAL (POPULATION) Georgetown (188,000)
GOVERNMENT Multiparty republic
ETHNIC GROUPS Asian Indian 49%, Black 36%, Mixed 7%, Amerindian 7%, Portuguese, Chinese
LANGUAGES English (official)
RELIGIONS Christianity (Protestant 34%, Roman Catholic 18%), Hinduism 34%, Islam 9%
CURRENCY Guyana dollar = 100 cents

# HAITI

Occupying the western third of Hispaniola, the Caribbean's second largest island, Haiti is mainly mountainous with a long, indented coast. Most of the country is centred around the Massif du Nord, with the narrow Massif de la Hotte forming the southern peninsula. In the deep bight between the two lies the chief port and capital, Port-au-Prince.

## ECONOMY AND RESOURCES

Haiti has few natural resources and most of the workforce is engaged on the land, with coffee the only significant cash crop. Two-thirds of the population, however, lives at or below the poverty line, subsisting on small-scale agriculture and fishing. Measures have been taken to increase productivity, such as the Artibonite valley irrigation scheme, and the planting of tropical fruit and vegetables has been encouraged.

## HISTORY AND POLITICS

Ceded to France in 1697, a century before the rest of Hispaniola, Haiti developed as a sugar-producing colony. Once the richest part of the Caribbean, it is now the poorest nation in the Western Hemisphere. For nearly two centuries, since a slave revolt made it the world's first independent black state in 1804, it has been bedevilled by military coups, government corruption, ethnic violence and political instability, including a period of US control from 1915 to 1934.

The violent regime of François Duvalier ('Papa Doc'), president from 1957 and declaring himself 'President for Life' in 1964, was especially brutal, but that of his son Jean-Claude ('Baby Doc'), president from 1971, was little better; both used their murderous private militia, the Tontons Macoutes, to conduct a reign of terror. In 1986 popular unrest finally forced Duvalier to flee the country, and the military took over.

After another period of political chaos and economic disaster – not helped by the suspension of US aid between 1987 and 1989 – the country's first multiparty elections were held in December 1990, putting in office a radical Catholic priest, Father Jean-Bertrand Aristide, on a platform of sweeping reforms. But with the partisans of the old regime, including the Tontons Macoutes, still powerful, the military took control in September 1991, forcing Aristide to flee (to the USA) after only seven months of government. Tens of thousands of exiles followed in the ensuing weeks, heading mainly for the US naval base at Guantánamo Bay, in Cuba, in the face of a wave of savage repression, but the American government returned the 'boat people' to Port-au-Prince. Military intervention (as in Panama in 1989) was considered by the Organization of American States, but they instead imposed a trade embargo, inflicting further hardship on an already impoverished Haitian population.

However, in 1994, the US sent in troops to restore democracy and reinstate Aristide as president once again. He returned to Haiti on 15 October 1994. [*Map page 30*] ∎

---

AREA 27,750 sq km [10,714 sq mls]
POPULATION 7,035,000
CAPITAL (POPULATION) Port-au-Prince (1,144,000)
GOVERNMENT Transitional government
ETHNIC GROUPS Black 95%, Mulatto 5%
LANGUAGES French (official) 10%, Haitian Creole 88%
RELIGIONS Christianity (Roman Catholic 75%), Voodoo
CURRENCY Gourde = 100 centimes

---

# HONDURAS

S ome 80% of Honduras is mountainous, with peaks of more than 2,500 m [8,000 ft] in the west. The state has a short frontage, 124 km [80 mls] long, on the Pacific Ocean in the Gulf of Fonseca. Most of Honduras has a seasonal climate, relatively dry between November and May.

Second largest of the Central American countries, Honduras has a small population: indeed, it is five times as large as neighbouring El Salvador – its opponent in the 'Soccer War' of 1969, triggered by illegal Salvadorean immigration – but has fewer people.

## ECONOMY AND RESOURCES

The mountain ranges are metalliferous: lodes of gold drew the first Spanish *conquistadores* to found Tegucigalpa, the capital, in 1524, and silver is still an important export. Mining contributes more to the economy than it does in any other Central American state.

The limited lowlands around the Gulf form some of the prime cotton lands of the country. Traditional cattle ranching, employing cowboys, is as much in evidence as agriculture. The aromatic pine forests of the east are being consumed by new paper mills on the hot, rain-soaked Caribbean coast. The lower alluvium-filled valleys of the rivers draining into the Caribbean have been reclaimed and the forest replaced by orderly banana plantations. Honduras was the original 'banana republic' – the world's leading exporter in the interwar years. Today it remains an important crop, accounting for nearly a quarter of exports, with production dominated by two US companies, though coffee is now the largest earner. Dependent on these cash crops, the country is the least industrialized in the region.

It is also the most reliant on the US for trade – quite a claim in Central America: 56% of its imports and 49% of its exports are with the Americans.

## HISTORY AND POLITICS

After a short civil war in the 1920s a series of military regimes ruled Honduras until 1980, when civilians took over; the country has since had a series of democratically elected pro-American centre-right governments, but with the military retaining considerable influence.

Aid from the US is crucial, partly in return for services rendered; strategically important to Washington, Honduras allowed the US-backed 'Contra' rebels to operate from its territory against the Communist revolutionary Sandinista government in Nicaragua throughout the 1980s, and in 1990 – following the Sandinistas' defeat in the elections – signed a peace agreement with the pro-American government of Violeta Chamorro. Less enthusiastically, the Honduran Army also collaborated with US efforts to defeat left-wing guerillas in El Salvador. [*Map page 30*] ∎

---

AREA 112,090 sq km [43,278 sq mls]
POPULATION 5,493,000
CAPITAL (POPULATION) Tegucigalpa (679,000)
GOVERNMENT Republic
ETHNIC GROUPS Mestizo 90%, Amerindian 7%, Black (including Black Carib) 2%, White 1%
LANGUAGES Spanish (official)
RELIGIONS Christianity (Roman Catholic 85%, Protestant 10%)
CURRENCY Honduran lempira = 100 centavos

# HONG KONG

The 1,071 sq km [413 sq mls] that comprise the British colony of Hong Kong consist of Hong Kong Island itself, 235 smaller islands, the Kowloon peninsula on the Chinese province of Guangdong and the 'New Territories' adjoining it. Hong Kong Island is largely hilly, but the highest point in the colony is Tai Mo Shan at 957 m [3,140 ft] in the New Territories. Much land reclamation has taken place along the rugged coast, particularly in the harbour area, where sites backfilled with the island's refuse have provided the foundations for many of the skyscrapers which form Hong Kong's distinctive skyline.

## ECONOMY AND RESOURCES

The colony has few natural resources: most of its food, water and raw materials have to be brought in, principally from China. Its prosperity rests on the ingenuity, acumen and hard work of the people.

The economy of Hong Kong is based on manufacturing (textiles, electronics, watches and plastic goods), banking and commerce, with the sheltered waters between Kowloon and Victoria providing one of the finest natural deep-water harbours in the world. Thus, when the Chinese resume control of the colony, they will inherit the world's biggest container port, its biggest exporter of clothes and its tenth biggest trader. Hong Kong's economy has been so successful since World War II that its huge neighbour will be increasing its export earnings by more than a quarter.

Certainly, the entrepreneurial spirit is still strong as time ticks away to the changeover: in 1992 Hong Kong embarked on its scheme for a new airport to replace the dangerous Kai Tak – the world's largest civil engineering project and due for opening in 1997, with final completion in 2040. Nevertheless, with the future still uncertain, the economy has recently shown signs of slowing as some businessmen drifted elsewhere and some services shifted to rivals such as Singapore.

## HISTORY AND POLITICS

Hong Kong was acquired by Britain in three stages. The island itself, containing the city of Victoria, was ceded in 1842; Kowloon, on the mainland, came under its control in 1860; and the New Territories, between Kowloon and the Chinese border, were leased in 1898.

On 1 July 1997 the Crown Colony and its possessions will return to the Chinese government. Under a 1984 accord, China agrees to allow the territory to enjoy full economic autonomy and pursue its capitalist path for at least another 50 years. In 1988, a Draft Basic Law, drawn up by an Anglo-Chinese committee, was published for discussion. However, the events of Tiananmen Square in 1989 and the limitations on democratic representation suggested in the basic law have caused anxiety and resentment among many Hong Kong citizens. Negotiations between Britain and China to safeguard the interests of the inhabitants are still continuing. [*Map page 24*] ■

**AREA** 1,071 sq km [413 sq mls]
**POPULATION** 5,838,000
**CAPITAL (POPULATION)** Victoria (part of Hong Kong Island – population 1,251,000)
**GOVERNMENT** UK appointed governor
**ETHNIC GROUPS** Chinese 98%, others 2% (including European)
**LANGUAGES** English and Chinese (official)
**RELIGIONS** Buddhism majority, Confucism, Taoism, Christianity, Islam, Hinduism, Sikhism, Judaism
**CURRENCY** Hong Kong dollar = 100 cents

# HUNGARY

Hungary has two large lowland areas – the aptly-named Great Plain (Nagyalföld) which occupies the south-eastern half of the country and is dissected by the country's two main rivers, the Danube and the Tisa, and the Little Plain (Kisalföld) in the north-west. Between them a line of hills runs south-west to north-east from Lake Balaton to the Slovak border. Balaton (72 km [45 mls] long), the largest lake in central Europe, is a favourite holiday resort.

The Hungarian Plains have some of the most fertile agricultural land in Europe, especially in the areas covered by a mantle of loess (a windblown deposit dating from the Ice Age), but there are also infertile areas of marsh, sand and dry steppeland, where crop growing gives way to grazing. In the region to the north-west of the Great Plain, known as Hortobagy and the only remaining steppe in Europe outside the former USSR, it is still possible to see Europe's last remaining cowboys – the *gulyas* – riding on horseback to round up their cattle. But the expanse of dry steppeland where this way of life is practised is dwindling as irrigation schemes are introduced, and ranching gives way to the growing of wheat, tobacco and rice.

The continental climate, with its spring rains, long, hot summers and cold winters, favours crops such as wheat, maize, sunflowers and vines. Rainfall is around 63 cm [25 in] in the west, but falls to under 50 cm [20 in] in the east.

## ECONOMY AND RESOURCES

Hungary has reserves of gas, but is poorly endowed with natural resources, bauxite being one of the few plentiful minerals. Industries have been built up on the basis of imported raw materials, mainly from the former USSR. The main industrial centres are in the north, around the towns of Miskolc and Budapest (home to a fifth of the population) where iron and steel, engineering and chemicals predominate. Aluminium is manufactured north of Lake Balaton.

Hungary's move away from the classic Eastern European reliance on heavy industry and agriculture would be easier than, say, that of Poland, and many joint ventures with Western capital were inaugurated in the first months of the new democracy, bringing in not only high-tech expertise but also much-needed managerial skills. Hungary has the edge in tourism, too – by the late 1980s the number of annual visitors was already outstripping its own population.

The lack of energy resources, however, remains a concern, and the government began

## THE DANUBE

With around 300 tributaries and a length of 2,850 km [1,750 mls], the Danube is Europe's second longest river. Rising from a source in the Black Forest in south-west Germany, it flows east and south through Austria, the Slovak Republic, Hungary and Yugoslavia, and forms a large part of the Romanian-Bulgarian frontier before entering the Black Sea through a wide, swampy delta on the border between Romania and the Ukraine. Navigable as far upstream as Ulm in Bavaria, the Danube links the three capitals of Vienna, Budapest and Belgrade. It has long been one of Europe's main commercial waterways, and with the ending of the Cold War and the consequent divisions between East and West, it is likely to be of growing importance.

pursuing an ambitious programme to increase its nuclear capacity from the 1988 figure of 49% of electricity generation. Even as a relative success, Hungary's progress has its cost, with inflation around 25–30% and unemployment doubling in 1991 alone to 700,000 – around 14% of the workforce.

## HISTORY AND POLITICS

As a large part of the Austro-Hungarian empire, Hungary enjoyed an almost autonomous position within the Dual Monarchy from 1867, but defeat in World War I saw nearly 70% of its territory apportioned by the Treaty of Versailles to Czechoslovakia, Yugoslavia and Romania. Some 2.6 million Hungarians live in these countries today. The government hoped to regain lost land by siding with Hitler's Germany in World War II, but the result was the occupation of the Red Army and, in 1949, the establishment of a Communist state. The heroic Uprising of 1956 was put down by Soviet troops and its leader, Imre Nagy, was executed.

President János Kádár came to power in the wake of the suppression, but his was a relatively progressive leadership, introducing an element of political freedom and a measure of economic liberalism. Before the great upheavals of 1989 Hungary had gone further than any Eastern European Soviet satellite in decentralization and deregulation.

However, failure to tackle the underlying economic problems led in 1988 to some of his own Socialist Workers Party members exerting pressure for change. In 1989 the central committee agreed to a pluralist system and the parliament, previously little more than a rubber-stamp assembly, formally ended the party's 'leading role in society'. In 1990, in the first free elections since the war, Hungarians voted into office a centre-right coalition headed by the Democratic Forum.

Unlike its more static neighbours, the new government of Prime Minister Jozsef Antall was able to press on with a rapid transition to a full market economy. The region's first stock market was set up, Budapest was chosen as the European Union's first regional office and Hungary – a founder member of the now defunct Warsaw Pact – applied to join NATO. [Map pages 16–17] ▪

> **AREA** 93,030 sq km [35,919 sq mls]
> **POPULATION** 10,161,000
> **CAPITAL (POPULATION)** Budapest (2,016,000)
> **GOVERNMENT** Multiparty republic
> **ETHNIC GROUPS** Magyar (Hungarian) 98%, Gypsy, German, Croat, Romanian, Slovak
> **LANGUAGES** Hungarian (official)
> **RELIGIONS** Christianity (Roman Catholic 64%, Protestant 23%, Orthodox 1%), Judaism 1%
> **CURRENCY** Forint = 100 fillér

# ICELAND

Situated far out in the North Atlantic Ocean, Iceland is not only the smallest but also the most isolated of the independent Scandinavian countries. Though politically part of Europe, the island (nearer to Greenland than to Scotland) arises geologically from the boundary between Europe and America – the Mid-Atlantic Ridge. It is indeed a product of the ridge, formed almost entirely by volcanic outpourings at a point where the Earth's crust is opening at a rate measurable in centimetres per year.

A central zone of recently active volcanoes and fissures crosses Iceland from Axarfjörður in the north to Vestmannaeyjar in the south, with a side-branch to Reykjanes and an outlying zone of activity around the Snaefellsnes peninsula in the west. During the thousand years that Iceland has been settled, between 150 and 200 eruptions have occurred in the active zones, some building up substantial volcanic cones. Between 1104 and 1970 Mt Hekla, in the south-west, erupted at least 15 times. Its earliest outpourings of ash devastated local farms, some of which have recently been excavated.

A huge eruption in 1783 destroyed pasture and livestock on a grand scale, causing a famine that reduced the Icelandic population by a quarter. More recent eruptions include the formation of a new island – Surtsey – off the south-west coast in 1963, and the partial devastation of the town of Vestmannaeyjar-Karpstadur, on neighbouring Heimaey, ten years later. Paradoxically, Iceland is also an island of glaciers and ice-sheets, with four large ice-caps occupying 11% of the surface and several smaller glaciers.

## ECONOMY AND RESOURCES

Since the country was formerly pastoral, with most of the population scattered in farms and small hamlets, the standard of living depended on the vicissitudes of farming close to the Arctic Circle. Now the economy is based on deep-sea fishing; fish and fish products make up 70% of exports. About a fifth of the land is used for agriculture, but only 1% is actually cultivated for root crops and fodder. The rest is used for grazing cattle and sheep. Self-sufficient in meat and dairy products, Iceland augments its main exports with clothing such as sheepskin coats and woollen products.

Geothermal and hydroelectric power provide cheap energy for developing industries, including aluminium smelting and hot-house cultivation; and most houses and offices in Reykjavík, the capital, are heated geothermally. About a quarter of the workforce is engaged in the production of energy and manufacturing – processing food and fish, making cement and refining aluminium from imported bauxite. The population is concentrated mainly in settlements close to the coast, over half of them in or near Reykjavík. Living standards currently compare with those of other Scandinavian countries. In some respects they are better: Iceland boasts the lowest infant mortality rate in the world and the highest life expectancy outside Japan.

## HISTORY AND POLITICS

Colonized by Viking and British farmers in the 9th century, Iceland became a dependency first of Norway, then of Denmark, though mainly self-governing with a parliament (*Althing*) dating from AD 930. This is thought to be the world's first parliament in the modern sense, and is certainly the oldest. Recognized as a sovereign state from 1918, the country was united with Denmark through a common sovereign until 1944, when Iceland became a republic. The Icelandic language has close affinities to Anglo-Saxon and differs little today from when it was introduced in the ninth century. [*Map page 13*] ∎

**AREA** 103,000 sq km [39,768 sq mls]
**POPULATION** 266,000
**CAPITAL (POPULATION)** Reykjavík (101,000)
**GOVERNMENT** Multiparty republic
**ETHNIC GROUPS** Icelandic 94%, Danish 1%
**LANGUAGES** Icelandic (official)
**RELIGIONS** Christianity (Evangelical Lutheran 92%, other Lutheran 3%, Roman Catholic 1%)
**CURRENCY** Icelandic króna = 100 aurar

# INDIA

A diamond-shaped country – the world's seventh largest – India extends from high in the Himalayas through the Tropic of Cancer to the warm waters of the Indian Ocean at 8°N. Almost 919 million people live here in the world's second most populous state – and its largest democracy.

## Landscape

Geographically, India can be divided into three parts – the mountainous north, the great alluvial plains of the Brahmaputra and Ganges, and the plateaux and lowlands that occupy the southern area, including the Deccan and most of the peninsula. Each provides an astonishing range of scenery – a picture intensified by the variety of peoples, cultures and activities within them.

**The mountainous north:** The Himalayan foothills make a stunning backdrop for northern India, rising abruptly from the plains in towering ranks. Harsh dry highlands, sparsely occupied by herdsmen, stretch northwards to the everlasting snows of the Karakoram. Below lie alpine meadows, lakes and woodlands, often grazed in summer by seasonally migrant flocks from lower villages. The high plateau of Meghalaya ('abode of the clouds') is damp and cool; nearby Cherrapunji has one of the highest rainfalls in the world.

**The plains:** The great plains form a continuous strip from the Punjab eastwards. Among the most densely populated areas of India (the state of Uttar Pradesh has a population larger than Nigeria, Pakistan or Bangladesh), these lowlands support dozens of cities and smaller settlements – notably Agra, with its Red Fort and Taj Mahal, and the sacred cities of Allahabad and Varanasi (Benares).

Downstream from Tinpahar ('three hills'), near the Bangladeshi border, the Ganges begins its deltaic splitting into distributary streams, while still receiving tributaries from the north and west. The Sundarbans – mangrove and swamp forests at the seaward margin of the Ganges delta – extend eastwards into Bangladesh.

South-west from the Punjab plains lies the Thar or Great Indian Desert, its western fringes in Pakistan but with a broad tract of dunes in the north-eastern lowlands in Rajasthan, India's largest state. The desert ranges from perennially dry wastelands of shifting sand to areas capable of cultivation in wet years. As the name Rajasthan implies, this state was once (until 1950) a land of rajahs and princes, palaces and temples; some of the buildings – including universities – endowed by these private benefactors remain important in Jodhpur, Jaipur, Ajmer, Udaipur and other cities. Rajasthan rises in a series of steps to a jagged, bare range of brightly coloured sandstone ridges, the Aravallis, that extend north-eastwards and end at Delhi.

Between the Gulfs of Khambhat and Kachchh is the low peninsular plateau of Kathiawar, whose declining deciduous forests still harbour small groups of tribal peoples, and indeed the last of India's native lions. Between this and the Pakistan border stretches the desert salt marsh of the Rann of Kachchh, once an arm of the Arabian Sea and still occasionally flooded by exceptionally heavy rains.

South-east of the Aravallis is an area of transition between the great plains of the north and the uplands and plateaux of peninsular India. First come the Chambal badlands (wastelands south of Agra, now partly reclaimed), then rough hill country extending south-eastwards to Rewa. The River Sone provides a lowland corridor through the hills south of Rewa, and an irrigation barrage provides water for previously arid lands west of Gaya. Eastwards again the hills are forested around Ambikapur and Lohardaga.

**Peninsular India:** South of the Chambal River and south of Indore (a princely capital until 1950), the sandy plateau of the north gives way to forested hills, split by the broad corridors of the Narmada and Tapi rivers. Tribal lands persist in the Satpura Range, and the Ajanta Range to the south is noted for primitive cave paintings near Aurangabad. From here to the south volcanic soils predominate. The Ghats are edged with granite, gneiss, sandstone and schist, and clad in heavy rainforest.

## ECONOMY AND RESOURCES

In total, around 50% of India is cultivated, 22% is forested and 20% is classified as desert, wasteland or urban.

**The mountainous north:** The fertile Vale of Kashmir has emerald-green rice terraces, walnut and plane trees, and apple and apricot orchards around half-timbered villages. It is crossed by ancient trackways once used as trade routes by mule and yak trains, now military roads to the garrisons of the north. The wet, forested eastern Himalayas of Assam are ablaze with rhododendrons and magnolias,

## KASHMIR

Until Indian independence in August 1947, Kashmir's mainly Muslim population was ruled, under British supervision, by a Hindu maharaja. Independence obliged the maharaja to choose between Pakistan or India; hoping to preserve his own independence, he refused to make a decision. In October, a rag-tag army of Pathan tribesmen invaded from newly created Pakistan. Looting industriously, the Pathans advanced slowly, and India had time to rush troops to the region. The first Indo-Pakistan war resulted in a partition that satisfied neither side, with Pakistan holding one-third and India the remainder, with a 60% Muslim population. Despite promises, India has refused to allow a plebiscite to decide the province's fate. Two subsequent wars, in 1965 and 1972, failed to alter significantly the 1948 cease-fire lines.

In the late 1980s, Kashmiri nationalists in the Indian-controlled area began a violent campaign in favour of either secession to Pakistan or local independence. India responded by flooding Kashmir with troops and accusing Pakistan of intervention. By 1992, at least 3,000 Kashmiris had died. India stood accused of repression, and there was little sign of a peaceful end to the conflict.

and terraced for buckwheat, barley and rice growing. Tropical oaks and teaks on the forest ridges of Nagaland, Manipur and Mizoram, bordering Burma, alternate with rice patches and small towns; on the hilltops dry cultivation of rice is practised, in plots cleared for a few years' cultivation and then left fallow.

**The plains:** Heavily irrigated by canals engineered in the late 19th century, the rich alluvial soils have provided prosperity for Sikh and Jat farmers of the Punjab and Haryana. Here are grown winter wheat and summer rice, cotton and sugar cane with sorghum in the drier areas, the successful agriculture forming a foundation for linked industrial development. Many small market towns are thriving and the fine plans for the joint state capital of Chandigarh, devised by Le Corbusier, have been fully realized.

Somewhat similar landscapes extend eastwards to the plains surrounding Delhi, India's third largest city on the west bank of the Jumna (Yamuna) River. An ancient site, occupied for over 3,000 years, it now includes the Indian capital New Delhi, designed by Sir Edwin Lutyens and built from 1912. Old city and new lie at a focal point of road and rail links, and like many Indian cities rapidly became overcrowded. To the east again are the lowlands of Uttar Pradesh, crisscrossed by the Ganges and Jumna rivers and their many tributaries. Slightly wetter, but less irrigated, these plains are farmed less for wheat and rice than for spiked millet and sorghum, though maize and rice cultivation increase again in the wetter areas towards the state of Bihar.

Along the Nepal border the *terai* or hillfoot plains, formerly malaria-infested swamp forest, have now been cleared and made healthy for prosperous farming settlements. West Bengal consists largely of the rice- and jute-growing lands flanking the distributary streams that flow south to become the Hooghly, on which Calcutta is built. The Ganges-Kobadak barrage now provides irrigation for the north of this tract, while improving both water supply and navigation lower down the Hooghly. South and west of the Aravallis lie the cotton-growing lands of tropical Gujarat; Ahmadabad is its chief city. Industrial development becomes important around the coalfields of the Damodar Valley, centred on Asansol and the developing steel town of Jamshedpur.

**Peninsular India**: Bombay, India's second largest city, lies on the coastal lowlands by a broad estuary, among ricefields dotted with low lava ridges. Fishing villages with coconut palms line the shore, while inland rise the stepped, forested slopes and pinnacles of peninsular India's longest mountain chain, the Western Ghats (Sahyadri).

East of the Ghats, on rich black soils well watered by the monsoons, stretch seemingly endless expanses of cotton and sorghum cultivation. Arid in late winter and spring, and parched by May, they spring to life when the rains break in late May or June. The sleepy market towns follow a similar rhythm, full of activity when the agricultural cycle demands,

and relaxing under the broiling sun when the time for activity is past.

South from the holiday beaches of Goa (formerly a Portuguese enclave, still Portuguese in flavour), past busy Mangalore, Calicut and Cochin to the state capital of Kerala, Trivandrum, the coast becomes a kaleidoscope of coconut groves and fishing villages, ricefields, scrublands, cashew orchards and tapioca plantations.

To the east the peninsula is drier, with rolling plateaux given over to the production of millet, pulses and other dry crops. Sugar, rice and spices are grown where simple engineering provides tanks, stopped with earth or masonry dams, to save the summer rains; now canals perform the same task. Bangalore and Hyderabad, once sleepy capitals of princely states, are now bustling cities, respectively capitals of Karnataka and Andhra Pradesh.

**Communications and development**

A vital memorial from colonial times is the railway network – a strategic broad-gauge system fed by metre-gauge subsidiaries, with additional light railways, for example to the hill-stations of Simla (in Himachal Pradesh), Darjeeling (between Nepal and Bhutan) and Ootacamund (in Tamil Nadu). Among developments since independence are the fast and comfortable intercity diesel-electric trains, but steam-engines remain the main workhorses in a coal-rich country.

The road system also has strategic elements from the Mogul and British past, now rationalized into a system of national highways. Main roads are passable all year round, and feeder-roads are largely all-weather dirt roads taking traffic close to most of India's 650,000 villages. The well-served international airports are linked with good, cheap internal services, widely used by passengers from a broad social spectrum, including pilgrims and tourists.

At independence India was already established as a partly industrialized country, and has made great strides during a succession of five-year plans that provided explicitly for both nationalized and private industry. The Damodar coalfield around Asansol has been developed, and new fields opened. The Tata family's steel city of Jamshedpur, itself now diversified by other industries, has been complemented by new state plants and planned towns at Durgapur and other places, in collaboration with Britain, Germany and the former Soviet Union. Major engineering factories have been built at Bangalore, Vishakhapatnam and elsewhere (including the ill-fated Bhopal), and oil refineries set up at Barauni in the north-east, and near Bombay for new fields recently developed in the north-west. Several nuclear power stations are in operation, and the massive potential of hydroelectric power is being exploited. Small-scale industry is also being encouraged. Industrial estates have had mixed success, but do well in places like Bangalore where there are enough related industries to utilize interactions.

In the countryside a generation of effort in community and rural development is starting to achieve results, most obviously where the Green Revolution of improved seeds and fertilizers has been successful, for example in the wheatlands of the Punjab and Haryana, or where irrigation has been newly applied and brought success. In such areas it can be argued that the gap between landless labourers and prosperous farmers widens when new methods bring greater yields; but this is one of many social problems that beset a complex, diverse society which appears to be always on the verge of collapse into chaos, but despite its size, burgeoning population and potential for division manages to remain intact.

## HISTORY AND POLITICS

India's earliest settlers were widely scattered across the subcontinent in Stone Age times. The first of its many civilizations developed in the Indus Valley about 2600 BC, and in the Ganges Valley from about 1500 BC. By the 4th and 3rd centuries BC Pataliputra (modern Patna) formed the centre of a loosely-held empire that extended across the peninsula and beyond into Afghanistan. This first Indian empire broke up after the death of the Emperor Asoka in 232 BC, to be replaced by many others, both transient and lasting, during the centuries that followed. The Portuguese who crossed the Indian Ocean in the late 15th century, and the British, Danes, French and Dutch who soon followed them, found a subcontinent divided in itself and ripe for plundering.

## THE HIMALAYAS

The Earth's highest mountain range, with an average height of 6,100 m [20,000 ft], the Himalayas are structurally part of the high plateau of Central Asia. The range stretches over 2,400 km [1,500 mls] from the Pamirs in the north-west to the Chinese border in the east. There are three main ranges: Outer, Middle and Inner; in Kashmir, the Inner Himalayas divide into five more ranges, including the Ladakh Range and the Karakorams. The world's highest mountain, Mt Everest (8,848 m [29,029 ft]), is on the Tibet-Nepal border; the next highest is K2 (8,611 m [28,251 ft]) in the Karakorams, and there are a further six peaks over 8,000 m [26,250 ft].

The name comes from the Nepalese words *him* ('snows') and *alya* ('home of'), and the mountains are much revered in Hindu mythology as the abode of gods. Recently, the hydroelectric potential of the range has inspired more secular reverence: enormous quantities of energy could be tapped, although certainly at some cost to one of the world's most pristine environments.

As a result of battles fought both in Europe and in India itself, Britain gradually gained ascendancy over both European rivals and local factions within the subcontinent; by 1805 the British East India Company was virtually in control, and the British Indian Empire (which included many autonomous states) was gradually consolidated. Power was transferred from the East India Company to the British Crown after the Sepoy Rebellion in 1857. Organized opposition to Britain's rule began before World War I and reached a climax after the end of World War II. In August 1947 the Indian subcontinent became independent, but divided into the separate states of India, a mainly Hindu community, and Pakistan, where Muslims formed the vast majority. In the boundary disputes and reshuffling of minority populations that followed perhaps a million lives were lost – and events since then have done little to promote good relations between the two states.

## Languages and religions

India is a vast country with enormous problems of organization. It has over a dozen major languages, each with a rich literature, and many minor languages. Hindi, the national language, and the Dravidian languages of the south (Tamil, Telugu and Malayalam) are Indo-European; in the north and east occur Sino-Tibetan tongues, and in forested hill refuges are found residual Austric languages. Racial stocks, too, are mixed, with dark tribal folk in forest remnants, Mongoloids in the north and east, and often lighter-coloured skins and eyes in the north-west – and in the higher castes throughout the country.

The mosaic of religion also adds variety – and potential conflict. Hinduism is all-pervasive (though the state is officially secular), and Buddhism is slowly reviving in its country of origin (the Buddha was born on the border of India and Nepal about 563 BC). Buddhism's near-contemporary Mahavira and Jainism, with common elements including stress against destruction of any form of life, are strong in the merchant towns around Mt Abu in the Aravalli hills north of Ahmadabad. Islam contributes many mosques and tombs to the Indian scene; the Taj Mahal is the most famous, but there are many more.

The forts of Delhi, Agra and many other northern cities, and the ghost city of Fatehpur Sikri, near Agra, are also Islamic relics of the Mogul period (1556–1707). Despite the formation of Pakistan, India retains a large Muslim minority of about 76 million. Now it is the turn of the Punjab's militant Sikhs, claiming to represent their population of 13 million, who seek separation. Christian influences range from the elaborate Catholic churches and shrines remaining from Portuguese and French settlement, to the many schools and colleges set up by Christian denominations and still actively teaching; there are also notable church unions in both south and north India. The British period of rule left its own monuments; Bombay and Calcutta both have some notable Victoriana, and New Delhi is a planned city of the Edwardian period.

## Recent history

During the Cold War period, under Nehru's leadership, India played a prominent role in the Third World as one of the leading non-aligned nations. This, however, did not prevent a border dispute with China in 1962, during which Chinese troops invaded Indian territory, and in 1965 an undeclared war with Pakistan over Kashmir. Internally India continued to suffer from religious and communal conflict and separatist pressures.

Indira Gandhi (Nehru's daughter), elected as prime minister in 1966, resorted to emergency powers between 1975 and 1977, using press censorship and mass imprisonment of opponents to impose her policies. Defeated in the 1977 elections, she nevertheless managed to regain office in 1980. In June 1984, in response to an increasingly militant campaign for Sikh autonomy, Indian troops stormed the Golden Temple of Amritsar, a holy shrine and centre of Sikh extremism. A few months later Indira Gandhi was assassinated by a Sikh member of her personal guard. Her son, Ranjiv Gandhi, succeeded her as prime minister but lost the 1989 elections following accusations of incompetence and corruption. He too was murdered, during the 1991 electoral campaign.

In recent years autonomous pressures in Kashmir and Punjab have increased, and conflict between Hindus and Muslims has dramatically sharpened. The destruction of a mosque in Ayodhya by Hindu extremists in December 1992 led to widespread rioting and a series of bombings in Calcutta and Bombay during 1993 which killed over 300 people.

**Sikkim**, after Goa the smallest of India's 25 self-governing states, was a Buddhist kingdom before being ruled by Britain from 1866 and protected by India from 1950 to 1975, when following a plebiscite it joined the Union. On the border with Nepal is Mt Kanchenjunga, at 8,598 m [28,028 ft] the world's third highest peak. The state is the world's biggest producer of cardamom (a spice).

**Indian islands**. The Andaman and Nicobar Islands, in the Bay of Bengal, became an Indian state in 1950 and now form one of the country's seven Union territories (with a population of 280,660); a similar status is held by the Lakshadweep (Laccadive) Islands, off the Malabar Coast, where 10 of the 36 coral atolls are inhabited (population 51,707). [*Map page 23*] ■

| | |
|---|---|
| **AREA** | 3,287,590 sq km [1,269,338 sq mls] |
| **POPULATION** | 918,570,000 |
| **CAPITAL (POPULATION)** | New Delhi (part of Delhi, 294,000) |
| **GOVERNMENT** | Multiparty federal republic |
| **ETHNIC GROUPS** | Indo-Aryan (Caucasoid) 72%, Dravidian (Aboriginal) 25%, other (mainly Mongoloid) 3% |
| **LANGUAGES** | Hindi 30% and English (both official), Telugu 8%, Bengali 8%, Marati 8% Urdu 5% and many others |
| **RELIGIONS** | Hinduism 83%, Islam (Sunni Muslim) 11%, Christianity 2%, Sikhism 2%, Buddhism 1% |
| **CURRENCY** | Indian rupee = 100 paisa |

# INDONESIA

With the break-up of the Soviet Union in 1991, Indonesia moved up from the fifth to the fourth most populous nation on Earth. It is also the world's largest archipelago, with 13,677 islands (less than 6,000 of which are inhabited) scattered over an enormous area of tropical sea. However, three-quarters of the area is included in the five main centres of Sumatra, Java, Kalimantan (southern Borneo), Sulawesi (Celebes) and Irian Jaya (the western end of New Guinea), which also include over 80% of the people; more than half the population live on Java alone, despite its being only 7% of the land area.

Most of the big islands stand on continental shelves and have extensive coastal lowlands, though Sulawesi and the chain of islands between Java and Irian Jaya rise from deep water. All are mountainous, for this is an area of great crustal activity. Along the arc formed by Sumatra, Java and the Lesser Sunda Islands stand over 200 volcanoes, about 70 of which – including Krakatoa (Pulau Rakata) in the Sunda Strait – have erupted within the last two

centuries, usually with memorable violence. Java alone has over 120 volcanoes, 14 of which exceed 3,000 m [10,000 ft].

The natural vegetation of the tropical lowlands is rainforest, which also spreads up into the hills. Much of this has now been cleared by shifting cultivators and replaced by secondary growth, though forest is still the dominant vegetation on most of the less populated islands.

## ECONOMY AND RESOURCES

About a tenth of the land area is under permanent cultivation, mostly rice, maize, cassava and sweet potato, and Indonesia remains essentially an agricultural nation. There are also large plantations of rubber, sugar cane, coffee and tea. Accessible parts of the rainforest are being exploited at an alarming rate for their valuable timber; native forest in Sumatra is now virtually restricted to reserves and national parks, though mountain forests, less vulnerable because they are more isolated, still remain over wide areas. Many of the coasts are lined with mangrove swamps, and several accessible islands are stunningly beautiful; tourism is one of the country's fastest growing sectors.

The population of Indonesia is complex and varied. There is a wide range of indigenous peoples, speaking some 25 different languages and over 250 dialects. Four of the world's major religions – Islam, Hinduism, Christianity and Buddhism – are well represented, though followers of Islam are in the great majority and Indonesia is the world's most populous Muslim nation.

General Suharto's military regime, with US technical and financial assistance, has brought a period of relatively rapid economic growth, supported by an oil boom that by 1970 accounted for 70% of export earnings – a figure that shrank to less than 50% by 1990. Self-sufficiency in rice and a degree of population control also helped raise living standards, though Java's overcrowding remained a problem, and in 1986 a 'transmigration programme' was initiated to settle large numbers of Javanese on sparsely populated islands, notably (and notoriously) on Irian Jaya.

While the Javanese dominate Indonesian affairs, most of the country's wealth – oil, timber, minerals and plantation crops – comes

## EAST TIMOR

Invaded by Indonesian troops in 1975, East Timor has effectively remained its 21st state despite numerous UN condemnatory resolutions. The end of the Cold War has done little to ease the people's plight; Australia still does not recognize their right to self-determination, while the Western powers leave the problem to the ineffectual UN.

East Timor was a neglected, coffee-growing Portuguese colony for 300 years before Lisbon promised independence in 1974. The 1975 free elections were won by Fretilin, the left-wing nationalists who had fought the empire for years, but the following month Indonesia occupied the territory. Their policies of deportation, resettlement, harassment, torture, bombings, summary executions and massacres – including one filmed by a British film crew in 1991 – have resulted in the deaths of a third of the population (still officially 630,000) and the encampment of 150,000 or more, according to Amnesty International. At the same time, 100,000 Indonesians have been settled in a country rich in sandalwood, marble and coffee, with oil reserves of 5 billion barrels.

Fretilin's fighters, who returned to the hills in 1975, have since kept up a sporadic and dispersed campaign, while the population – mostly Catholic – await international help. In practice, however, East Timor stays closed to the world.

from other islands. Establishing better relations with the West and its ASEAN (Association of South-east Asian Nations) neighbours, the government has now deregulated much of the economy.

### HISTORY AND POLITICS

The first important empire in the region was centred at Palembang in south-eastern Sumatra. This was the great maritime power of Sri Vijaya, which held sway from the 8th to 13th centuries over the important trade routes of the Malacca and Sunda Straits. During the 14th century it was replaced by the kingdom of Madjapahit, centred on the fertile lands of east-central Java. From the 16th century onwards, European influences grew, the area coming progressively under the domination and ruthless exploitation of the Dutch East India Company. Freedom movements starting in the early 20th century found their full expression under Japanese occupation in World War II, and Indonesia declared its independence on the surrender of Japan in 1945. After four years in intermittent but brutal fighting, the Dutch finally recognized the country as a sovereign state in 1949 under Achmed Sukarno, leader of the nationalist party since 1927.

Sukarno's anti-Western stance and repressive policies plunged his country into chaos, while costly military adventures drained the treasury. In 1962 he invaded Dutch New Guinea (Irian Jaya) and between 1963 and 1966 he attempted to destabilize the fledgling Federation of Malaysia by incursions into northern Borneo. Throughout his dictatorship Indonesia seemed to be permanently on the edge of disintegration, government forces fighting separatist movements in various parts of the country. In 1967 Sukarno was toppled by General Suharto, following the latter's suppression of a two-year allegedly Communist-inspired uprising that cost 80,000 lives.

Corruption and nepotism remain rife and power is firmly in the hands of Golkar, the military-backed coalition which thwarts the aspirations of the two permitted political parties. The army, perhaps correctly, continues to regard itself as the only protector of stability in a country that has proved almost impossible to govern. [*Map page 26*] ∎

**AREA** 1,904,570 sq km [735,354 sq mls]
**POPULATION** 191,170,000
**CAPITAL (POPULATION)** Jakarta (1980 census = 7,886,000; 1993 estimate = 9,000,000)
**GOVERNMENT** Multiparty republic
**ETHNIC GROUPS** Javanese 39%, Sundanese 16%, Indonesian (Malay) 12%, Madurese 4%, more than 300 others
**LANGUAGES** Bahasa Indonesian (official)
**RELIGIONS** Islam 87%, Christianity 10% (Roman Catholic 6%), Hinduism 2%, Buddhism 1%
**CURRENCY** Rupiah = 100 sen

# IRAN

The Islamic Republic of Iran is a large country in south-western Asia. The barren central plateau covers about half of the country. It includes the Dasht-e-Kavir (Great Salt Desert) and the Dasht-e-Lut (Great Sand Desert). The Elburz (or Alborz) Mountains north of the plateau contain Iran's highest point, Damavand. West of the plateau are the Zagros Mountains, beyond which the land descends to plains bordering the Gulf. Forests of such trees as beech and oak cover about a tenth of Iran, mainly in the Caspian Sea region and the Zagros Mountains. Much of Iran has a severe, dry climate, with hot summers and cold winters, though the climate in the lowlands is generally milder.

## ECONOMY AND RESOURCES

The most populous and productive parts of Iran lie at the four extremities – the fisheries, ricefields and tea gardens of the Caspian shore in the foothills of the earthquake zone to the north, the sugar plantations and oilfields of Khuzestan to the south (target of the Iraqi invasion in 1980), the wheat fields of Azerbaijan in the west, and the fruit groves of the oases of Khorasan and Seistan in the east. In between are the deserts of Kavir and Lut, and the border ranges which broaden in the west into the high plateaux of the Zagros, the summer retreats of the tribes of Bakhtiars and Kurds.

The cities of the interior depend on ingenious arrangements of tunnels and channels for tapping underground water, and these have been supplemented by high dams, notably at Dezful. The burgeoning capital of Tehran is the crossing-point of the country's two great railways, the Trans-Iranian from the Gulf to the Caspian and the east-west track from Mashhad to Tabriz.

## HISTORY AND POLITICS

Called Persia until 1935, the country retained its Shah – thanks first to British and later American support – until 1979, when the emperor's extravagantly corrupt regime (a single-party affair from 1975) was toppled by a combination of students, middle-class professionals and, above, all, clerics offended by the style and pace of Westernization.

The despotism was replaced with another: that of a radical fundamentalist Islamic republic inspired by the return of exiled leader Ayatollah Khomeini. The revolution created a new threat to the conservative Arabs of the Gulf and beyond, who saw it as a dangerous call to challenge the flimsy legitimacy of their own oil-rich governments. The effect would rumble round the Muslim world: 12 years later, in far-off Algeria, the Islamic Salvation Front won the democratic elections.

Many Arab states were less hostile, however, and despite Iranian backing of a series of international terrorist attacks and hostage-takings linked to the Palestinian issue, their regime won respect for the steadfast way they fought the Iraqis from 1980–8, when hundreds of thousands of zealous young Shiite men died defending their homeland.

The war left Iran's vital oil production at less than half the level of 1979 (though still seventh highest in the world and supported by the largest known gas reserves outside Russia), and the government began to court the Western powers. Its stance during the Second Gulf War (albeit predictable) and a tempering of the militant position to one of peace-broker on international issues – led by President Rafsanjani – encouraged many powers to re-establish closer links with a country whose role took on even greater significance with the Muslim republics of the former Soviet Union to the north gaining independence from Moscow in 1991. [*Map page 22*] ∎

| | |
|---|---|
| **AREA** | 1,648,000 sq km [636,293 sq mls] |
| **POPULATION** | 65,758,000 |
| **CAPITAL (POPULATION)** | Tehran (6,476,000) |
| **GOVERNMENT** | Islamic republic |
| **ETHNIC GROUPS** | Persian 46%, Azerbaijani 17%, Kurdish 9%, Gilaki 5%, Luri, Mazandarani, Baluchi, Arab |
| **LANGUAGES** | Farsi (or Persian, official) |
| **RELIGIONS** | Islam 99% |
| **CURRENCY** | Rial |

# IRAQ

The country includes a hilly district in the north-east, and in the west a substantial slice of the Hamad or Syrian Desert; but essentially it comprises the lower valleys and combined deltas of the Tigris and Euphrates. Rainfall is meagre, but the alluvium is fertile and productive when supplied with water. The western desert is nomad country, with good winter grazing, and from here the tribes move in summer with their flocks to the banks of the Euphrates.

## ECONOMY AND RESOURCES

The north-east of Iraq includes part of the Zagros Mountains, where fruits and grains grow without the help of irrigation. The Kirkuk oilfield is the country's oldest and largest, and nearby the Lesser Zab River has been impounded behind a high dam. The population here includes many Turks, settled in the times of Ottoman rule, and Kurdish tribes akin to those in Iran.

Upstream of Ramadi and Samarra, the Jazirah stands too high for irrigation, though the swamp of Tharthar is used to store the excess flow of the River Euphrates through a diversionary channel from Samarra. This is dry-farming country or pasture. In the north near the Syrian frontier the block mountain of Sinjar is an oasis of fertility, with an unorthodox Yezidi population (a religious sect).

Downstream of the Jazirah lies Iraq proper, the deltaic plains which, with skill and effort, can be drained and irrigated. The rivers rise rapidly in spring as the snows melt around their sources in Turkey, and are full enough for irrigation throughout the summer. Lower down, a barrage on the Euphrates at Hindiyah and another on the Tigris at Kut control canals which irrigate land reclaimed from the great swamp.

In addition to the Kirkuk oilfield, which exports by pipeline through Syria and Lebanon, there are reserves of oil near Mosul, Khanaqin and Basra. The main seaport,

Basra, is connected to the Gulf by the crucial Shatt-al-Arab Waterway, shared with Iran and the ostensible cause of the First Gulf War (Iran-Iraq War).

## HISTORY AND POLITICS

Absorbed into the Ottoman (Turkish) empire in the 16th century, Iraq was captured by British forces in 1916 and after World War I became a virtual colony as a League of Nations mandated territory run by Britain. The Hashemite dynasty ruled an independent kingdom from 1932 (British occupation 1941–5), but in 1958 the royal family and premier were murdered in a military coup that set up a republic. Ten years later, after struggles between the Communists and Pan-Arab Baathists, officers for the latter seized control. From 1969 the vice-president of this single-party government was Saddam Hussein, who in a peaceful transfer of power became president in 1979. The next year he invaded neighbouring Iran.

### The Gulf Wars

Supplied with financial help and arms by the West, the Soviets and conservative Arab countries, all of whom shared a fear of the new Islamic fundamentalism in Iran, Saddam amassed the fourth largest army in the world by 1980. His attack on Iran was meant to be a quick, land-grabbing, morale-boosting victory. Instead it led to an eight-year modern version of Flanders which drained Iraqi resolve (over a million men were killed or wounded, many of them fighting fellow Shiites), and nearly crippled a healthy if oil-dependent economy that had, despite colossal defence spending, financed a huge development programme in the 1970s. Even then, Iraq was still the world's sixth biggest oil producer in 1988, and Saddam's repellent regime continued to enjoy widespread support from Western countries.

If Iraq was hit by this long war, it was decimated by the Second Gulf War. In August 1990 Saddam, having accused Kuwait of wrecking Baghdad's economy by exceeding its oil quota and forcing prices down, ordered the invasion of Kuwait, then annexed it as an Iraqi province. It gave him more oil and far better access to the Gulf. Unlike a decade before, the international community were almost unani-

## THE KURDS

With between 15 and 17 million people dispersed across the territories of five countries – Turkey (8 million), Iran, Iraq, Syria and Armenia – the Kurds form the world's largest stateless nation, and they are likely to remain so. The 1920 Treaty of Sévres, a postwar settlement designed to dismember the old Ottoman Empire, proposed a scheme for Kurdish independence, but it was never implemented.

Neither Arab nor Turk, the Kurds are predominantly Sunni Muslims, and in the past have provided more than their fair share of Islam's leaders: indeed, Saladin, the near-legendary nemesis of the Crusaders, was a Kurd. Now, as in the past, the Kurds are an agricultural people; many earn their living by pastoralism, a way of life that pays little attention to borders or the governments that attempt to control them. Since World War II, they have suffered consistent repression by most of their titular overlords. Turkey has regularly used armed force against Kurdish nationalists; an uprising in Iran was put down in 1979–80; and during the Iran-Iraq war of the 1980s, Iraqi forces regularly used chemical weapons – as well as more orthodox brutality – against Kurdish settlements.

The defeat of Iraqi dictator Saddam Hussein by Coalition forces in 1991 inspired another massive uprising; but Saddam's badly weakened army still proved quite capable of murdering Kurdish women and children on a scale that provoked a limited Western intervention. The outcome, though, was upwards of 1.5 million Kurds living in refugee camps, with the dream of an independent Kurdistan no nearer realization.

mous in their condemnation of the invasion, and following the imposition of sanctions a multinational force – led by the USA but backed primarily by Britain, France and Saudi Arabia – was dispatched to the Gulf to head off possible Iraqi moves on to Saudi oilfields.

After Saddam failed to accede to repeated UN demands to withdraw his troops, the Second Gulf War began on 16 January 1991

with an Anglo-American air attack on Baghdad, and in late February a land-sea-air campaign freed Kuwait after just 100 hours, Iraq accepting all the terms of the UN cease-fire and Coalition troops occupying much of southern Iraq. This did not prevent the brutal suppression of West-inspired revolts by Shiites in the south and Kurds in the north, millions of whom fled their homes. International efforts were made to help these refugees, some of whom had fled to Iran and others, less successfully, to Turkey.

Saddam Hussein, though surviving in power, was left an international leper in charge of a pitiful country. Much of the infrastructure had been destroyed in the war, disease was rife and food scarce, trade had virtually ceased and oil production was near a standstill. Sanctions, war damage and mismanagement have combined to cause economic chaos and personal hardship, and normal life is unlikely to return until the establishment of a regime acceptable to the rest of the international community; that, in turn, means the end of Saddam. [*Map page 19*] ∎

AREA 438,320 sq km [169,235 sq mls]
POPULATION 19,925,000
CAPITAL (POPULATION) Baghdad
(3,841,000)
GOVERNMENT Republic
ETHNIC GROUPS Arab 77%, Kurdish 19%, Turkmen 2%, Persian 2%, Assyrian
LANGUAGES Arabic (official), Kurdish (official in Kurdish areas)
RELIGIONS Islam 96%, Christianity 4%
CURRENCY Iraqi dinar = 20 dirhams = 1,000 fils

# IRELAND

Geographically, Ireland is the whole island west of Britain; the Republic of Ireland (Eire, or the Irish Free State until 1949) comprises the 26 counties governed from Dublin, and Northern Ireland (Ulster) is the six counties that remained part of the United Kingdom from 1921, when the Free State was granted dominion status within the British Commonwealth. Today, the word 'Ireland' is used as political shorthand for the Republic – which occupies some 80% of the island of Ireland.

The original four provinces of Ireland gradually emerged as major divisions from Norman times. Three counties of the present Republic (Donegal, Cavan and Monaghan), together with the six counties which now make up Northern Ireland, formed the old province of Ulster; Connacht, in effect the land beyond the River Shannon, includes the five counties of Leitrim, Sligo, Roscommon, Galway and Mayo; Munster comprises Clare, Limerick, Tipperary, Kilkenny, Waterford, Cork and Kerry; and Leinster consists of the heart of the central lowland and the counties of the south-east (Wicklow, Wexford and Carlow) between Dublin and Waterford harbour.

Physically, the main outlines of Ireland are simple. In the western peninsulas of Donegal and Connacht ancient rocks were folded to form mountain chains running north-east to south-west; good examples are the fine Derryveagh range of Co. Donegal and the Ox Mountains of Co. Sligo. The highest peaks, for example Errigal, 752 m [2,466 ft], are generally of quartzite, a metamorphosed sandstone. The same trend is seen also in the long range, including the Wicklow Mountains, between Dublin Bay and Waterford harbour in the south-east, and in the Slieve Bloom of the central lowland. The fine east-west ranges of the south, extending from Waterford to the western peninsulas, and the islands of Kerry and West Cork, were formed at a later period. Much of lowland Ireland is floored by rocks contemporary with the coal measures in England, and these also form some uplands like those around Sligo. Unfortunately these rocks contain little coal; some is mined in the Castlecomer area of Co. Kilkenny, and near Lough Allen in the upper Shannon Valley.

The basalt lavas that poured out in the north-east of Ireland, forming the desolate Antrim Plateau with its fine scenic cliffs on the famous Coast Road, and the Giant's Causeway, are more recent. Irish soils, however, are largely derived from glacial deposits, and the famous peat bogs result from the drainage patterns that emerged as the ice-sheets of the Ice Age dispersed. Peat remains the main indigenous fuel source, but reserves may not last long into the 21st century.

## ECONOMY AND RESOURCES

Agriculture has been the traditional support of the Irish people, though fishing, home crafts and local labouring have been extra sources of livelihood in the poorer western areas. There is a marked contrast between the richest and the poorest agricultural areas. In the eastern central lowland and the south-east, particularly the lowland areas of Wicklow and Wexford, there are large farms, with pastures supporting fine-quality cattle, sheep and in some areas racehorses. From Wexford, too, rich farmlands extend westwards to the counties of Tipperary and Limerick, and from Waterford to Cork and Killarney. Many of the farms specialize in dairying.

North of the Shannon, in Clare and east Galway, there is intensive sheep and some cattle production. To the north farming is mixed, with dairying, meat production, and in some cases specialization on crops such as potatoes and barley. Little wheat is grown; oats are better suited to the damp summer climate.

Farming in much of Ireland is now relatively prosperous, aided by EU grants. The number of people working on the land continues to decline, but that is due to the introduction of machinery, the union of small farms into larger holdings, and the increased opportunities of finding employment in the towns, with overseas emigration still an alternative. The tradition of emigration dates back to the great famine of 1846–51, when over a million people fled to Britain and the USA.

Ireland is economically far more prosperous than it was in 1845, when the population of the island numbered 8.5 million. Industrialization only really happened in the north-east, especially Belfast, leaving the Free State an agrarian country from the 1920s. As a result, it has something of a 'Third World' profile: rural (though almost 29% of the population lives in and around Dublin), dependent on tourism and, increasingly, high-tech industries such as electronics and pharmaceuticals. Prosperity in the 1960s was followed by a slowdown in growth – when government spending was high – but with a new spirit of economic co-operation, the 1990s appeared to have reversed the trend.

The poorer western areas have been aided by government grants and the development of local industries, including the tourist industry. Home industries flourish, especially tweed manufacture. The fishing industry, though never meeting expectations, is increasingly prosperous. The poor west, known from 1891 as the 'congested areas', is not depopulated as in some comparable areas of Scotland, though discarded houses are taken over as holiday cottages. Many problems have been at least partially solved and the EU has been a source of help, making the Republic feel part of a wider world than the British Isles.

## HISTORY AND POLITICS

The Anglo-Irish Treaty of 1921 established southern Ireland – Eire – as an independent state, with the six northern Irish counties, and their Protestant majority, remaining part of the United Kingdom (though Eire's constitution claimed authority over the whole island). Northern Ireland (Ulster) was granted local self-government from the Stormont parliament in Belfast. However, the Protestant majority (roughly two-thirds of the population) systematically excluded the Catholic minority from power and often from employment, despite occasional attacks from the near-moribund IRA – the Irish Republican Army, which had done most of the fighting that led to Eire's independence.

In 1968, inspired by the Civil Rights movement in the southern states of the USA, northern Catholics launched a civil rights movement of their own. But Protestant hostility threatened a bloodbath, and in August 1969 British Prime Minister Harold Wilson deployed army units to protect Catholics from Protestant attack.

Within a short period, the welcome given by Catholics to British troops turned to bitterness; the IRA and many of the Catholic minority came to see them as a hostile occupying force, and there were deaths on both sides. Protestant extremists were quick to form terrorist organizations of their own. In 1971, the British introduced internment without trial for suspected IRA terrorists, removing some of the main security risks from the streets but provoking violent protest demonstrations. In 1972, British troops killed 13 demonstrators in Londonderry, claiming to have been fired upon: the claims were vigorously denied by the demonstrators.

In an attempt to end the alienation of the Catholics, Britain negotiated an agreement with some Protestant politicians to share power in an executive composed of both communities, but the plan collapsed after dissatisfied Protestants staged a general strike. The British government responded by suspending the Stormont parliament and ruling Northern Ireland direct from Westminster. The failure of power-sharing encapsulated the British policy dilemma in Ulster: the Catholics, or most of them, wanted to join the Irish Republic; the Protestants, virtually without exception, did not. Each side bitterly distrusted the other, and long years of sectarian killing only increased the distrust.

The violence continued throughout the 1970s and 1980s, despite a series of political initiatives that included an Anglo-Irish agreement giving the Republic a modest say in Ulster's affairs. Among the conflict's victims over the following years were Earl Mountbatten and several senior British politicians, as well as soldiers, policemen, terrorists and thousands of ordinary men and women. Armed troops patrolling the streets and almost daily reports of sectarian murders became a way of life. But with the increasing war-weariness of the people, a joint declaration on Northern Ireland was agreed between the British and Irish prime ministers in December 1993. This first step towards a lasting peace was followed in 1994 by a declared cease-fire by the IRA and Loyalist paramilitary groups. [*Map page 9*] ■

AREA 70,280 sq km [27,135 sq mls]
POPULATION 3,539,000
CAPITAL (POPULATION) Dublin (1,024,000)
GOVERNMENT Multiparty republic
ETHNIC GROUPS Irish 94%
LANGUAGES Irish and English (both official)
RELIGIONS Christianity (Roman Catholic 93%, Protestant 3%)
CURRENCY Irish pound (Punt) = 100 pence

# ISRAEL

Within the 1949 borders, the country is made up of four areas: the highlands of Galilee in the north, the valleys of Jezreel and the Jordan, the arid hills of Judaea, a thin coastal plain and the Negev Desert. To the east lies part of the Great Rift Valley which runs through East Africa as far south as Mozambique. In Israel, the Rift Valley contains the River Jordan, the Sea of Galilee and the Dead Sea.

In general, the country is most fertile in the north, and becomes progressively more desert-like towards the south.

## ECONOMY AND RESOURCES

In the north of Israel, Galilee is rolling hill country with good rainfall and a rich black soil weathered from basalt. Both here and in the hills of Judaea, new pine woods have been established to fix the soil and hold the water. The Upper Jordan Valley is excellent farmland, with rich and fertile soils reclaimed from the swamps of Lake Huleh.

The valley of Jezreel, with a deep alluvial soil washed down from Galilee, is intensively tilled with market gardens. South of the promontory of Carmel, the coastal plain of Sharon is excellent fruit-growing country, but needs irrigation, especially in its southern stretches. Here the drifting dunes have been fixed with grass and tamarisk and reclaimed for pasture.

## The Negev Desert

Between Sinai and the Rift Valley, the great wedge of desert plateau known as the Negev accounts for about half the total territory of Israel. Its bedrock is widely covered with blown sand and loess, which will grow tomatoes and grapes in profusion if supplied with fresh water. The object of the Jordan-Western Negev scheme, the most ambitious of Israel's irrigation enterprises, has been to direct through canals and culverts all the water that can be spared from the Upper Jordan and the

## JERUSALEM

Though held sacred by all of the world's three great monotheisms, Jerusalem's religious importance has brought the city little peace. King David's capital in the 11th century BC, with the building of the great Temple of Solomon, it became the cult centre of Judaism. The Temple was destroyed by the Assyrians and rebuilt in the 6th century, re-assuming its importance until AD 70, when Jerusalem, Temple and all, was destroyed by Roman legions during the great Jewish Revolt against the Empire. Later, a rebuilt Jerusalem became a great centre of Christian pilgrimage. In the 7th century, the city was captured by the expanding armies of Islam, and for Muslims, too, Jerusalem (al-Quds in Arabic) is also a holy place: it was visited by the Prophet Muhammad during the 'Night Journey' re-counted in the Koran, and Muslims also believe that it was from Jerusalem that the Prophet ascended to paradise. The great mosque known as the Dome of the Rock was built on the site of the Jewish Temple.

During the Israeli War of Independence, Arab and Jew fought bitterly for possession of the city: neither could oust the other and until 1967 it was divided by bristling fortifications, with the Wailing Wall, the only surviving part of the old Temple, firmly under Arab control. In the Six Day War, Israeli soldiers at last captured all of the city, to universal Jewish rejoicing and Arab lamentation.

streams and drainage channels of the coastal plain southwards to the desert.

The Negev south of Be'er Sheva is pioneer territory, with new towns mining oil, copper and phosphates, factories using the potash and salt of the Dead Sea, and farms experimenting with solar power and artificial dew. Carob trees have been planted for fodder, and dairy farms and plantations of bananas and dates have been established with the aid of the artesian springs of the rift valley or Araba. Elat on the Gulf of Aqaba is an increasingly successful tourist town and Israel's sea outlet to Africa and most of Asia. From here, a pipeline takes imported oil to the refinery at Haifa.

## THE PALESTINIANS

The sorrowful modern history of the Palestinians began in 1948, when the birth of Israel transformed most of their former territory into a foreign state; some 700,000 fled, most finding no better homes than refugee camps in Jordan, Lebanon and Egypt's Gaza Strip. After the 'Six Day War' in 1967, most Palestinians not already refugees found themselves living under enemy occupation. Since 1964, the Palestine Liberation Organization has existed to free them by 'armed struggle', but the PLO's adoption of international terrorism as a tactic alienated many potential allies, as did their alliance with Saddam Hussein during the 1991 Gulf War. The 1987 *intifada* brought much world support, but by late 1991, when peace talks with Israel at last began, almost half the Palestinian population were still classified as refugees. After long and difficult negotiations, Israel and the PLO finally signed a historic treaty in September 1993: the PLO recognized the state of Israel and Israel granted the Palestinians self-rule in the Gaza Strip and Jericho.

To supplement the facilities of Haifa, Israel built a deep-sea port at Ashdod to replace the old anchorage at Jaffa (Yafo).

### Industry
Israel has become the most industrialized country in the Near East. Iron is smelted at Haifa and converted to steel at the foundries of Acre. Chemicals are manufactured at Haifa and at plants by the Dead Sea. With the aid of a national electricity grid, factories for textiles, ceramics and other products have been widely established in country towns, including the new foundations of Dimona and Mizpe Ramon in the Negev. Some railways were inherited from the British, but most commercial movement is now along the road network. Despite its expansion, Israel remains vulnerable on many fronts: reliance on huge US aid (the world's biggest per capita movement); terrorism and international pressure over Palestine; hostile neighbours and huge defence spending; massive influx of immigrants, often overqualified and notably now from the former Soviet republics; and a lack of natural resources forcing dependence on imported raw materials.

### HISTORY AND POLITICS
In 1948 the new Jewish state of Israel comprised the coastal plain, the vale of Esdraelon (Jezreel) behind Haifa, the foothills in the south, most of the hill country of Samaria, and half of Jerusalem with a corridor to the west. It was also the intention of the UN that Israel should acquire either Galilee in the north or the Negev Desert in the south, but in the event both these regions were included. The rest of Palestine, mainly Judaea and the Rift Valley west of the river, was added to Jordan, but as a result of the Six Day War in 1967, its administration as the 'West Bank' was taken over by Israel along with East Jerusalem. At the same time the Israelis also occupied the Gaza Strip (Egypt) and the Golan Heights (Syria).

In October 1973, Egypt and Syria launched attacks against Israel in an unsuccessful attempt to regain territories. Egypt and Israel eventually signed a peace treaty in 1979: Israel agreed to withdraw from the Sinai and Egypt recognized Israel.

In 1982, Israeli forces invaded Lebanon to destroy PLO strongholds in that country and only left in 1985. From 1987 onwards, Palestinian resistance to Israeli occupation of the Gaza Strip and the West Bank became more and more widespread and violent. In the 1990s, increased international pressure eventually led to the signing of a treaty in 1993 between Israel and the PLO. A framework document for peace with Jordan was signed in July 1994. [*Map page 19*] ∎

AREA 26,650 sq km [10,290 sq mls]
POPULATION 5,458,000
CAPITAL (POPULATION) Jerusalem (544,200)
GOVERNMENT Multiparty republic
ETHNIC GROUPS Jewish 82%, Arab and other 18%
LANGUAGES Hebrew and Arabic (both official)
RELIGIONS Judaism 82%, Islam 14%, Christianity 2%, Druse and others 2%
CURRENCY New Israeli shekel = 100 agorat

# ITALY

Despite more than a century of common language, religion and cultural traditions, great differences remain in the ways of life of people in different parts of Italy. These can partly be explained in terms of geography. The long, narrow boot-shaped peninsula, with coastal lowlands on either side of the central Apennines, extends so far south that its toe, and the neighbouring island of Sicily, are in the latitudes of North Africa. Southern Sicily is as far south (36°N) as Tunis and Algiers, while the northern industrial city of Milan (45.5°N) is nearer to London than it is to Reggio in Calabria, the extreme south of peninsular Italy. Given their markedly disparate social and historical backgrounds, the long period of isolation that preceded the unification and widely differing climates, it is hardly surprising that northern and southern Italy retain their independence of character and culture.

**The Alps and Apennines:** Italy's topographical structure is determined mainly by the events of the Alpine period of mountain building, when the main ranges of the Alps and the Apennines were uplifted together. There are traces of earlier periods in the central Alps, between Mont Blanc (4,807 m [15,771 ft]) on the French border and Monte Rosa (4,634 m [15,203 ft]) on the Swiss border, and in the Carnic Alps in the north-east. Here ancient crystalline rocks predominate, although many of the higher peaks are formed from limestone. The Dolomite Alps, famous for their climbing and skiing resorts, have given their name to a particular form of magnesian limestone.

Generally lower than the Alps, the Apennines reach their highest peaks – almost 3,000 m [9,800 ft] – in the Gran Sasso range overlooking the central Adriatic Sea near Pescara. The most frequently occurring rocks are various types of limestone.

Italy is well known for volcanic activity and earthquakes. Three volcanoes are still active – Vesuvius, near Naples, renowned for its burial

## VESUVIUS

Rising steeply from the Plain of Campania, behind the Bay of Naples, the massive cone of Vesuvius forms one of a family of southern Italian volcanoes, clustered in an area of crustal weakness. Others include the nearby island of Ischia, Stromboli and Vulcano of the Lipari Islands, and Etna in eastern Sicily.

Ischia's volcanoes last erupted in the 14th century. Stromboli and Vulcano are currently active, emitting lava and gases, and Etna has a long record of eruptions from 475 BC to the present day. In April 1992 an eruption threatened to destroy a village on Etna's slopes.

Vesuvius, which probably arose from the waters of the bay some 200,000 years ago, has been intermittently active ever since; over 30 major eruptions have been recorded since Roman times. However, its slopes are forested or farmed, the fertile volcanic soils producing good crops during the quiescent periods between eruptive spells. There are many settlements on its flanks, and laboratories for volcanic and seismic studies.

The most famous eruption of Vesuvius occurred in AD 79, when the flourishing Roman port of Pompeii and nearby town of Stabiae were engulfed in a rain of ashes. Excavations begun in 1748 have revealed streets, shops, houses, frescos, statues, and many other artefacts of Roman times – even the bread in the bakery.

of Pompeii in AD 79, Etna in Sicily, and Stromboli on an island in the south Tyrrhenian Sea. Traces of earlier volcanism are to be found throughout the country. Ancient lava flows cover large areas, and where they have weathered they produce fertile soils. Mineral deposits, such as the iron ores of Elba and the tin ores of the Mt Annata area, are often associated with earlier volcanic intrusions. Italy is still subject to earthquakes and volcanic eruptions. During the 20th century disasters have occurred at Messina (1908 – the worst in Europe in recent times, with more than 80,000 deaths), Avezzano (1915), Irpinia (1930), Friuli (1976) and Naples (1980).

**Lombardy:** The great triangular plain of Lombardy, lying between the northern Alps and the Apennines, is drained by the River Po, which flows west to east, rising in the Ligurian Alps near the French frontier and flowing across a delta into the Gulf of Venice.

**Central Italy:** Between the Po Valley and the River Tiber, Central Italy is a transitional zone between the industrially developed north and the poor, agrarian south. It contains Rome, which has survived as a capital city for over 2,000 years, Florence and Bologna. Almost all Italians are brought up as Roman Catholics; since a 1985 agreement between church and state, Catholic religious teaching is offered, but not compulsory, in schools. The Vatican, in theory an independent state, is in fact an enclave of Rome.

## ECONOMY AND RESOURCES

**The Apennines:** The slopes are covered by thin soils and have been subjected to severe erosion, so that in many areas they are suitable only for poor pasture. Between the mountains, however, are long narrow basins, some of which contain lakes. Others have good soils and drainage and provide a basis for arable farming.

**Lombardy:** The Lombardy plains are the most productive area of Italy, both agriculturally and industrially. There is no shortage of water, as in the areas further south, although some places are served by irrigation canals. Crops include maize, wheat, potatoes, tomatoes, rice and mulberries – these associated with the development of the silk industry. In the Alpine valleys above the Lombardy plain vines are cultivated.

Industry and urban life in Lombardy is long established. Textiles – silk, cotton, flax and wool – metal-working and food processing all began long before the modern industrial period. Large-scale Italian industry was slower to develop than in Britain and Germany, partly because of the lack of coal, but in Lombardy this has been offset by the availability of hydroelectric power from the Alpine rivers, and by the development of a natural gas field in the area of the Po delta. Oil and gas are also imported by pipeline from Austria. Italy is more dependent on imported energy than any European country, nearly 60% of it oil, though

## VENICE

The city of Venice originally grew up on a group of over 100 small islands, lying in a lagoon sheltered from the open Adriatic Sea by a sandbar. It now also includes the mainland industrial suburbs of Mestre and Marghera, where two-thirds of the city's population live. Causeways carry road and rail links to the mainland, but cars are not allowed in the old city. Boats of all types, from the traditional gondolas to the diesel-powered water-buses, use the canals which form the 'streets' of Venice.

Venice was once the capital of an imperial republic which, until overthrown by Napoleon in 1797, controlled much of the trade of the Adriatic and the eastern Mediterranean. The heart of the city is around St Mark's Square, where stand the cathedral and the Palace of the Doges (Dukes) who once ruled the republic.

The unique site and the rich art treasures attract about 2 million tourists a year, providing a living for tens of thousands of Venetians who cater for them; tourists, too, help to support such craft industries as glass-blowing, for which the city is famous. For Expo 2000 the figure is expected to be over 250,000 a day, imposing a massive strain on a city already suffering from erosion, subsidence and pollution.

Algeria remains a major supplier of gas through the Transmed pipeline via Tunisia.

Engineering and metal-working are now the most important industries, centred on Milan and, in Piedmont, on Turin. Lombardy remains dominant, however; the most densely populated region, it accounts for a third of Italy's GDP and some 30% of export earnings, and in the 1992 election the separatist party made huge gains at the expense of established rivals.

**Central Italy:** The area has a glorious history of artistic and literary achievement, but with its limited resources, steep slopes and difficult communications it has been left behind in economic development by the more favoured lowlands of the north, and relies heavily on tourism for regional income.

## SICILY

The triangular-shaped island of Sicily lies in a strategic position between the two basins of the Mediterranean, and has had a stormy history as successive powers wishing to dominate the Mediterranean have sought to conquer it. A beautiful island, with both natural and man-made attractions to interest the millions of tourists, it is nevertheless in a low state of economic development and its people are among the poorest in Europe.

There is some industrial development around the ports of Palermo, Catania, Messina and Syracuse, based on imported materials or on oil and natural gas found off-shore during the 1960s. The only other local industrial materials are potash, sulphur and salt. However, a large proportion of the inhabitants still live by peasant farming, supplemented by fishing and work in the tourist industry.

There are few permanent streams on Sicily, as the island experiences an almost total drought in summer, and agriculture is severely restricted by the availability of water. Citrus fruits, vines and olives are among the chief crops. On coastal lowlands such as those around Catania, Marsala and Palermo, wheat and early vegetables are grown. The rapid growth in the population and the strong family ties which exist among Sicilians have, however, led to a situation in which too many people are trying to make a living from tiny parcels of land.

**The Mezzogiorno:** The south of Italy, known as the Mezzogiorno, is the least developed part of the country. It displays, in less severe form, many of the characteristics of the developing countries of the Third World. Its people depend for their livelihood on Mediterranean crops produced on small peasant farms too small to lend themselves to modern techniques, although there are some large estates.

Over a third of the people are still in agriculture, with unemployment three or more times that of the north. Though the eight regions of the Mezzogiorno cover some 40% of the land area (including Sicily and Sardinia) and contain more than a third of the country's population, they contribute only about a quarter of the GDP.

The birth rate is much higher than in the north, and there is a serious problem of overpopulation which is partly eased by large-scale, often temporary, migration to the cities of the north and to Italy's more developed partners in the EU, as well as more permanent migration overseas. Migration often exacerbates the problems of the Mezzogiorno, however, as it tends to take away the younger, more active members of society, leaving behind an ageing population.

There are also serious urban problems, caused by the rapid growth of cities such as Naples and Reggio as young people leave the rural areas to live in the slums. As one of Italy's major ports, Naples imports oil, coal, iron ore, chemicals and cotton to provide the raw materials for manufacturing industries. In recent years great efforts have been made by a government-sponsored agency, the *Cassa di Mezzogiorno*, to found new factories in the Naples area, but they have had little effect on the mass poverty and unemployment of the region.

### HISTORY AND POLITICS

In 1800, present-day Italy was made up of several political units, including the Papal States, and a substantial part of the north-east was occupied by Austria. The struggle for unification – the Risorgimento – began early in the century, but little progress was made until an alliance between France and Piedmont (then part of the kingdom of Sardinia) drove Austria from Lombardy in 1859. Tuscany, Parma and Modena all joined Piedmont-Lombardy in 1860, and the Papal States, Sicily, Naples (including most of the southern peninsula) and Romagna were brought into the alliance. King Victor Emmanuel II was proclaimed ruler of a united Italy in Turin the following year, Venetia was acquired from Austria in 1866, and Rome was finally annexed in 1871. Since that time Italy has been a single state, becoming a republic following the abolition of the monarchy by popular referendum in 1946.

Regions like Tuscany, Umbria and Lazio have retained considerable autonomy from

## SARDINIA

Just a little smaller than Sicily, but with less than a third of its population, Sardinia's isolation from the mainstream of Italian life is due partly to its physical position, 480 km [300 mls] from the Italian coast, but the rugged, windswept terrain and lack of resources have also set it apart.

The chief crops on the lowlands are wheat, vines, olives and vegetables, and there are rough pastures for sheep on the scrub-covered hills. Fishing for tuna provides an important source of income for the ports of the west coast. Sardinia is rich in minerals, including lead, zinc, iron ore and lignite, and the island is an increasingly popular tourist destination.

Rome, with control over health and education, for example, and other devolved powers. Indeed five regions enjoy more autonomy than the rest: French-speaking Valle d'Aosta, in the north-west of the country; Trentino-Alto Adige, the largely German-speaking area in the far north; Friuli-Venézia Giulia in the north-east; and the two island provinces of Sardinia and Sicily.

### North and south

Since unification the population has doubled, and though the rate of increase is notoriously slow today, the rapid growth of population, in a poor country attempting to develop its resources, forced millions of Italians to emigrate during the first quarter of the 20th century. Italy's short-lived African empire enabled some Italians to settle overseas, but it did not substantially relieve the population pressure. Now there are immigrant Italians to be found on all the inhabited continents. Particularly large numbers settled in the USA, South America and Australia, and more recently large numbers of Italians have moved for similar reasons into northern Europe.

The problems of the Mezzogiorno, including especially those of the Naples area and Sicily, arise partly from geographical limitations and partly from historical circumstances. They are no longer a problem only for Italy,

for the stability and prosperity of Italy is a matter of concern for the rest of Europe, and in particular for the countries of the EU, of which Italy was a founder member. The continuing gulf between north and south has a disturbing effect on the economic and political health of Italy, a country whose people have contributed so much to the civilization of Europe.

Overall, however, Italy has made enormous progress since the devastation of World War II, particularly given its few natural resources. However, social problems, corruption at high levels of society, and a succession of weak coalition governments all contributed to instability. A referendum in April 1993 saw 82% of Italians voting to replace the system of proportional representation for the senate with one of majority voting. In 1994, new political groupings emerged. A right-wing coalition was formed, but its leader, Silvio Berlusconi, a multi-millionaire owner of television and publishing businesses, was forced to resign in December. In 1995, Lamberto Dini, a former banker, was appointed as the new prime minister. [*Map page 16*] ∎

AREA 301,270 sq km [116,320 sq mls]
POPULATION 57,157,000
CAPITAL (POPULATION) Rome (2,791,000)
GOVERNMENT Multiparty republic
ETHNIC GROUPS Italian 94%, German, French, Greek, Albanian, Slovene, Ladino
LANGUAGES Italian (official) 94%, Sardinian 3%
RELIGIONS Christianity (Roman Catholic) 83%
CURRENCY Lira = 100 centesimi

# IVORY COAST

The Republic of the Ivory Coast is officially known as the Côte d'Ivoire. The south-east coast is bordered by sand bars that enclose lagoons, on one of which the chief port and former capital of Abidjan is situated. But the south-western coast is lined by rocky cliffs. Behind the coast is a coastal plain, but the land rises inland to high plains. The highest land is an extension of the Guinea Highlands in the north-west, along the borders with Liberia and Guinea. The rivers run in a generally north-south direction.

The Ivory Coast has a hot and humid tropical climate, experiencing high temperatures throughout the year. The south has two distinct rainy seasons: May to July, and October to November. Inland, the rainfall decreases. In contrast, northern Ivory Coast has a dry season and only one rainy season.

### ECONOMY AND RESOURCES

There are substantial forests in the south where the basic resources of coffee, cocoa and timber are produced, as well as the lesser crops of bananas and pineapples. However, the depletion of the rainforest, as in much of West Africa, has been rapid. The Guinea savanna lands of the centre and north are much less fertile, producing small amounts of sugar, cotton and tobacco that now support developing industries, and food crops important to a rapidly growing market in Abidjan. Like Kenya, which is economically comparable, the Ivory Coast has few worked minerals, but manufacturing industries are developing.

In terms of such indices as GNP and international trade figures, the relatively stable Ivory Coast is one of Africa's most prosperous countries. This show of prosperity was initiated by the Vridi Canal, opened in 1950, which made Abidjan a spacious and sheltered deep-water port – a rarity in an area of Africa renowned for barrier reefs. The Ivory Coast's free-market economy has proved attractive to foreign investors, especially French firms, and France has given much aid, particularly for basic services and education. It has also attracted millions of migrant West African workers. In 1960, the Ivory Coast freed itself economically from support of seven other countries in the French West African Federation. The country is the world's largest exporter of cocoa and Africa's biggest producer of coffee. It has few worked minerals, but its manufacturing industries are developing.

Outward prosperity is visually expressed in Abidjan, but across the country there are great social and regional inequalities. In 1983, the National Assembly agreed to move the capital from Abidjan to Yamoussoukro, site of the world's biggest church (consecrated by Pope John Paul II in 1990) and the president's birthplace. But economic setbacks in the 1980s delayed the completion of the capital and government offices remained in Abidjan until 1990. Further efforts are being made to develop other towns and the relatively backward north. A second port to Abidjan has been developed since 1971 at San Pedro in the west of the country.

### HISTORY AND POLITICS

Ivory Coast became a French colony in 1893 and gained independence in 1960. Under the patriarchal rule of President Felix Houphouët-Boigny, it became one of the most prosperous of the tropical African nations. Pressure from demonstrations by students and workers in 1990 led to the country's first multiparty presidential election. Houphouët-Boigny, at the time already Africa's longest-ruling head of state, was returned to power. He died in 1993, and his successor as president was Henri Konan Bédié. [*Map page 32*] ∎

AREA 322,460 sq km [124,502 sq mls]
POPULATION 13,780,000
CAPITAL (POPULATION) Yamoussoukro (126,000)
GOVERNMENT Multiparty republic
ETHNIC GROUPS Akan 41%, Kru 17%, Voltaic 16%, Malinke 15%, Southern Mande 10%
LANGUAGES French (official)
RELIGIONS Islam 38%, Christianity 28%, traditional beliefs 17%
CURRENCY CFA franc = 100 centimes

# JAMAICA

T hird largest of the Caribbean islands and the most populous in the English-speaking 'West Indies', Jamaica has a central range culminating in Blue Mountain Peak (2,256 m [7,402 ft]), from which it declines westwards. Called Xaymaca ('land of wood and water') by the Arawak Indians, half the country lies above 300 m [1,000 ft] and moist south-east trade winds bring rain to the mountains, windward slopes receiving up to 500 cm [200 in] in a normal year; hurricanes may bring exceptionally heavy rains during the later part of the wet season, which extends from May to October – as well as devastation, as with Hurricane Gilbert in 1988.

The 'cockpit country' in the north-west of the island is an inaccessible limestone area of steep broken ridges and isolated basins. These offered a refuge to escaped slaves prior to emancipation in 1838.

## ECONOMY AND RESOURCES
In various parts of the island the limestone has weathered to bauxite, an ore of aluminium. Bauxite overlies a quarter of the island; mined since 1952, most is exported as ore, about one-fifth as alumina, making Jamaica the world's third producer and accounting for over 38% of exports. Tourism and bauxite production, Jamaica's two most important industries, comprise almost two-thirds of foreign earnings. In 1992 the island had over 1.5 million visitors, spending more than US$850 million. Garment manufacture, bananas and illegal marijuana are also important elements of an economy hampered by large foreign debts.

Sugar, a staple product since the island became British in 1655, first made Jamaica a prized imperial possession, and the African slaves imported to work the plantations were the forefathers of much of the present population. But the plantations disappeared and the sugar market collapsed in the 19th century; today sugar contributes only about 10% of the country's foreign earnings.

Michael Manley's democratic socialist experiment in the 1970s was followed by a modest growth in the 1980s; but unemployment and underemployment are currently rife, and many Jamaicans leave their country each year to work abroad, mainly in the USA, Canada and the UK.

## HISTORY AND POLITICS
Jamaica gained independence from Britain in 1962. Since then government has been con-trolled alternatively by the socialist People's National Party and the conservative Jamaican Labour Party (led by Edward Seaga). The PNP won the general election held in March 1993. [*Map page 30*] ∎

**AREA** 10,990 sq km [4,243 sq mls]
**POPULATION** 2,429,000
**CAPITAL (POPULATION)** Kingston (588,000)
**GOVERNMENT** Constitutional monarchy
**ETHNIC GROUPS** Black 76%, Afro-European 15%, East Indian and Afro-East Indian 3%, White 3%
**LANGUAGES** English (official), English Creole, Hindi, Spanish, Chinese
**RELIGIONS** Christianity (Protestant 70%, Roman Catholic 8%)
**CURRENCY** Jamaican dollar = 100 cents

# JAPAN

The Japanese archipelago lies off the Asian mainland in an arc extending from 45°N to 30°N, occupying a latitudinal range comparable to the Atlantic seaboard of the USA from Maine to Florida. Four large and closely grouped islands (Hokkaido, Honshu, Shikoku and Kyushu) constitute 98% of the nation's territory, the remainder being made up of some 4,000 smaller islands, including the Ryukyus, which lie between Kyushu and Taiwan. Japan is a medium-sized country, smaller than France but larger than Italy.

The Japanese islands occupy a zone of instability in the Earth's crust, and earthquakes and volcanic eruptions are frequent. Throughout Japan, complex folding and faulting has produced an intricate mosaic of landforms, in which mountains and forested hills alternate with small inland basins and coastal plains. The pattern of landforms is further complicated by the presence of several volcanic cones and calderas. The highest mountain in Japan, the majestic cone of Fuji-san (3,776 m [12,388 ft]), is a long-dormant volcano which last erupted in 1707.

In the mountains, fast-flowing torrents, fed by snowmelt in the spring and by heavy rainfall during the summer, have carved out a landscape of deep valleys and sharp ridges. In central Japan, dense mixed forests of oak, beech and maple blanket mountain slopes to an altitude of 1,800 m [5,900 ft]; further north in Hokkaido, boreal forests of fir and spruce predominate. In central Honshu, the Japan Alps with their snow-capped ridges provide spectacular mountain scenery.

Small intensively cultivated coastal plains, separated from one another by rugged mountain spurs, make up most of Japan's lowlands. None of the plains is extensive: the Kanto plain, which is the largest, covers an area of only 13,000 sq km [5,000 sq mls]. Most of the coastal plains are formed of material deposited by rivers, but their soils have been altered and improved by centuries of careful cultivation.

### ECONOMY AND RESOURCES

Japan is a predominantly mountainous country and only 16% of the land is cultivable. Although Japan lacks extensive habitable areas, the population is nevertheless the eighth largest in the world. A limited area of agricultural land must therefore support many people, and Japan is now one of the most densely populated countries in the world – with an ever-ageing profile.

The main centres of population and industry are concentrated within a narrow corridor stretching from the Kanto plain, through the coastlands of the Setonaikai, to northern Kyushu. This heavily urbanized zone contains nine cities with populations of over a million and three great industrial regions, centring respectively on Tokyo, Osaka and Nagoya. The capital Tokyo, which will be overtaken by Mexico City as the world's most populous metropolis by 2000, forms the nucleus of a large and congested conurbation.

### The Japanese boom

In 1945 Japan lay in ruins, with its major cities in ashes – two of them dangerously radioactive. Its smouldering ports were choked with the sunken remnants of its merchant marine, and its people were demoralized. Less than two generations later, the Japanese economy was second only to that of the USA. Its high-tech products dominated world markets, while Japanese banks and private investors owned huge slices of industry and real estate on every continent.

The far-sighted American Occupation authorities deserve some of the credit. Realizing that industrial recovery could only go hand in hand with political development, they wrote Japan a new constitution. As a link with the past, the emperor kept his place, but as a constitutional monarch answerable to a democratically elected Diet, with women given full voting rights for the first time. Trade unions, with the right to strike, were established, and land reform eliminated politically subservient tenants: by 1950, 90% of farmland was owner-cultivated. Great industrial conglomerates were broken into smaller units, and education was enormously expanded.

The Korean War in 1950 gave the slowly recovering Japanese economy a tremendous boost. Japanese factories, well paid in US dollars, provided much of the steel, vehicles and other equipment the war demanded. When the Occupation formally ended in 1952, Japan was clearly on the way up. The US military presence, guaranteed by treaty, continued, but caused no resentment: on the contrary, safe beneath the US defence umbrella, Japan could devote its resources to productive industry, not armaments.

The Japanese owed the first stage of their transformation to the Americans; the rest, they did themselves. Carefully planned economic policies, directed by the Ministry of Trade and Industry – nicknamed 'Japan Inc.'s Corporate Headquarters' – directed investment to key industries. First, the metal, engineering and chemical industries were rationalized and modernized – and in the 1950s and 1960s, efficient Japanese steel-makers consistently undersold their rivals, while producing better-quality steel. 'Made in Japan', once a sneering joke to describe shoddy goods, was taking on an entirely new commercial meaning.

Japan's major weakness was its near-total lack of natural resources; but foresight and planning made up for them. After the 1970s oil crisis, it was clear that the costs of heavy industry were going to rise unprofitably high; besides, the pollution they had brought was reaching dangerous levels. MITI switched resources to automobiles and electronics. Soon, Japan began to capture and dominate these markets, too.

By the 1980s, Japan's trading partners were becoming seriously alarmed. Noting that trade with Japan was largely a one-way traffic – Japan's home market is still notoriously hard to penetrate – they built protective walls of tariffs and duties. Japan responded with its usual flexibility: it bought factories within its rivals' walls, and traded from there. The Tokyo stock market even survived a serious 'crash' in the spring of 1992 – testament to the strength of the national economy.

## HISTORY AND POLITICS

Early Japan was peopled by immigrants arriving in successive waves from Korea and elsewhere on the Asian mainland. The earliest zone of settlement included northern Kyushu and the coastlands of the Setonaikai (Inland Sea). By the 5th century AD, Japan was divided amongst numerous clans, of which the largest and most powerful was the Yamato. Shinto, a polytheistic religion based on nature worship, had already emerged, as had the Japanese imperial dynasty.

During the next three centuries Chinese cultural and political influences entered Japan. These included Buddhism, the Chinese script, and Chinese methods of government and administration. At a later stage, Confucianism was also imported. Early cities, modelled on the capital of T'ang-dynasty China, were built at Nara (710) and at Kyoto (794); the latter city remained the seat of the imperial court until 1868.

The adoption of the Chinese system of centralized, bureaucratic government was relatively short-lived. From the early 12th century onwards, political power passed increasingly to military aristocrats, and government was conducted in the name of the emperor by warrior leaders known as *shoguns*. Civil warfare between rival groups of feudal lords was endemic over long periods, but under the rule of the Tokugawa *shoguns* (1603 1867), Japan enjoyed a great period of peace and prosperity; society was feudal and rigidly stratified, with military families (the feudal lords and their retainers, or *samurai*) forming a powerful élite.

In the 1630s, Japan embarked on a lengthy phase of enforced isolation from the rest of the world. This policy of seclusion could not be maintained indefinitely. In 1853, Commodore Perry of the US Navy arrived in Japan and demanded that ports be opened to Western trade. The capitulation of the *shogun* to Perry's demands prepared the way for the overthrow of the Tokugawa government, and with the Meiji Restoration of 1868 imperial rule was resumed.

Under Western-style government, a programme of modernization began. Industrialization proceeded swiftly, and after victories in the Sino-Japanese War (1894–5) and the Russo-Japanese War (1904–5), Japan began to build up an overseas empire which included the colonies of Taiwan and Korea. The growing strength of the Japanese military was demonstrated by the army's seizure of Manchuria in 1931. During the 1930s, and especially after the outbreak of war between Japan and China in 1937, militarist control of the government of Japan grew steadily. In 1941, the launching of a surprise attack on the American naval base of Pearl Harbor in Hawaii took Japan – and drew the USA – into World War II.

From its defeat in 1945 to 1952, Japan was administered by US forces. Many liberal reforms were enacted, and under the new constitution the power of the emperor was much reduced, with sovereignty formally vested in the people. The current system of government is a constitutional monarchy with the emperor as head of state and the prime minister as head of government. In spite of recent political scandals, the Liberal Democrats have continued to dominate the Japanese political scene. [*Map page 25*] ■

---

**AREA** 377,800 sq km [145,869 sq mls]
**POPULATION** 124,815,000
**CAPITAL (POPULATION)** Tokyo (11,927,000)
**GOVERNMENT** Constitutional monarchy
**ETHNIC GROUPS** Japanese 99%, Chinese, Korean, Ainu
**LANGUAGES** Japanese (official)
**RELIGIONS** Shintoism 93%, Buddhism 74%, Christianity 1% (most Japanese consider themselves to be both Shinto and Buddhist)
**CURRENCY** Yen = 100 sen

# JORDAN

The Hashemite Kingdom of Jordan is an Arab country in south-western Asia. The Great Rift Valley in the west contains the River Jordan and the Dead Sea, which Jordan shares with Israel. The Great Rift Valley runs south through East Africa to Mozambique. East of the Rift Valley is the Transjordan plateau, where most Jordanians live. To the east and south of the county lie vast areas of desert. Jordan has a short coastline on an arm of the Red Sea, the Gulf of Aqaba.

The city of Amman has a much lower rainfall and longer dry season than the Mediterranean lands to the west. The Transjordan plateau, on which Amman stands, is a transition zone between the Mediterranean climate zone to the west and the true desert climate to the east. Parts of the western plateau have a scrub vegetation, much like that in Mediterranean lands. Jordan also has areas of dry grassland, though few plants grow in the eastern deserts.

## ECONOMY AND RESOURCES
Jordan is not blessed with the natural resources enjoyed by some Middle East countries – whether oil or water – and a limited agricultural base is supported by mining of phosphates and potash, the main exports. The World Bank classifies Jordan as a 'lower-middle-income' developing country and the country's economy depends substantially on aid. Because of the dry climate, under 6% of the land is farmed or used as pasture. Major crops include barley, citrus fruits, grapes, olives, vegetables and wheat. Jordan has an oil refinery and manufactures include cement, pharmaceuticals, processed food, fertilizers and textiles.

## HISTORY AND POLITICS
After World War I, the Arab territories of the Ottoman empire were divided by the League of Nations and the area east of the River Jordan ('Transjordan') was awarded to Britain

as part of Palestine, becoming a separate emirate in 1923. When the mandate ended in 1946 the kingdom became independent, as Jordan, and two years later (in the first Arab-Israeli War) it acquired the West Bank region, which was officially incorporated into the state in 1950.

This crucial area, including Arab Jerusalem, was lost to Israel in the 1967 war, and Jordan has since carried the burden of Palestinian refugees on its own limited territory. In the 1970s the guerrillas using Jordan as a base became a challenge to the authority of King Hussein's government, and after a short civil war the Palestinian leadership fled the country. In 1988 Hussein suddenly renounced all responsibility for the West Bank – a recognition that the PLO, and not long-suffering Jordan, was the legitimate representative of the Palestinian people, though Palestinians, nevertheless, still formed a majority of the population.

The country's position was further undermined by the 1991 Gulf War, when despite official neutrality the pro-Iraq, anti-Western stance of the Palestinians did nothing to improve prospects of trade and aid deals with Europe and the US, Jordan's vital economic links with Iraq having already been severed. Another factor was the expulsion and return of large numbers of Palestinians and Jordanians from crucial jobs in Kuwait, Saudi Arabia and other wealthy Gulf states. There were, however, signs of political progress: in 1991 the ban on political parties was removed and martial law was lifted after 21 years. Multiparty elections were held in 1993. In October 1994, Jordan and Israel signed a peace treaty ending a state of war which had been going on for over 40 years. The treaty restored some land in the south to Jordan. [*Map page 19*] ∎

**AREA** 89,210 sq km [34,444 sq mls]
**POPULATION** 5,198,000
**CAPITAL (POPULATION)** Amman (1,272,000)
**GOVERNMENT** Constitutional monarchy
**ETHNIC GROUPS** Arab 99%, of which roughly half are Palestinians
**LANGUAGES** Arabic (official)
**RELIGIONS** Islam 93%, Christianity 5%
**CURRENCY** Jordanian dinar = 1,000 fils

# KAZAKHSTAN

A lthough a modest second in size behind Russia among the former Soviet republics, Kazakhstan is a colossal country – more than two and a half times the combined area of the other four Central Asian states, over four times the size of Ukraine (Europe's largest 'whole' state), bigger than any nation in Africa and indeed ninth in the world.

This new nation, stretching from near the Volga River in the west to the Altai Mountains in the east, comprises mainly vast plains with a (mineral-rich) central plateau. North to south, the steppe gradually gives way to desert.

## ECONOMY AND RESOURCES
Kazakhstan has emerged as a powerful entity, wealthier and more diversified than the other Asian republics. Irrigation schemes have led to the fertilization of large areas between the Aral Sea and Lake Balkhash, a rich fishing ground. Though its agriculture is traditionally associated with livestock rearing, Kazakhstan accounted for 20% of the cultivated area of the Soviet Union and in 1993 produced 6.2% of the world's total barley and wheat output.

Well endowed with oil and gas, it also has good deposits of coal, iron ore, bauxite, copper, nickel, tungsten, zinc, silver and gold. Though not industrialized by Western standards, it is growing in oil refining, metallurgy, engineering, chemicals, food processing and textiles, the last mostly dependent on home-grown cotton and high-quality native wool.

## HISTORY AND POLITICS
The first extension of the Russian Empire in Central Asia, the area's 'khanates' were gradually subdued or bought off from the 18th century, though rural resistance persisted well into the Soviet era. It was Kazakhstan that gave Mikhail Gorbachev his first ethnic problem when, in 1986, nationalist riots erupted after a Russian replaced a Kazakh as the republic's Party leader, and in 1991 it led the Central Asian states into the new Common-

wealth; indeed, the meeting that finally buried the Soviet Union was held in Alma-Ata, testimony to Kazakhstan's rank as number three in the hierarchy – an estimate helped by its 1,800 nuclear warheads.

It was not always so. Successive Soviet regimes used the huge republic as a dumping-ground and test-bed. Stalin exiled Germans and other 'undesirables' there, and Khrushchev experimented with his (largely catastrophic) Virgin Lands Programme; the Soviet missile- and rocket-launching site was located at Baykonur, north-east of the Aral Sea (shrunk by 70% after disastrous Soviet irrigation projects dried up its two feeder rivers), and the USSR's first fast-breeder nuclear reactor was built at Mangyshlak, on the Caspian Sea.

Kazakhstan could provide the 'new order' with a valuable bridge between East and West, between Islam and Christianity; it is the only former Soviet republic where its ethnic population is almost outnumbered by another group (the Russians), and its (Sunni) Muslim revival is relatively muted. Such divisions can of course have the opposite effect, leading to ethnic tensions and cruelties. [*Map page 20*] ■

**AREA** 2,717,000 sq km [1,049,150 sq mls]
**POPULATION** 17,027,000
**CAPITAL (POPULATION)** Alma-Ata
(1,147,000)
**GOVERNMENT** Multiparty republic
**ETHNIC GROUPS** Kazakh 40%, Russian 38%,
German 6%, Ukrainian 5%, Uzbek, Tatar
**LANGUAGES** Kazakh (official); Russian, the
former official language, is widely spoken
**RELIGIONS** Mainly Islam, with a Christian
minority
**CURRENCY** Tenge

# KENYA

B isected by the Great Rift Valley, the Kenya Highlands were formed by volcanoes and lava flows rising from 1,500 m

[4,900 ft] to the snow-capped peak of Mt Kenya at 5,199 m [17,000 ft]. The greater part of the country, however, comprises plains cut across old crystalline rocks, except where sedimentary strata extend across the Tana Basin and into the Somali Republic.

**ECONOMY AND RESOURCES**
Some 80% of the people crowd into about 15% of the plains in the south-west of the country, where average rainfalls of over 750 mm [30 in] a year support dense farming populations. Corn meal is the staple diet, but Kenya is one of the few African nations also supporting a dairy industry. The Kikuyu and other tribes practise small-scale farming on the

fertile volcanic soils on the eastern flanks of the Highlands from Limuru to Nyeri, Meru and Embu.

The western Highlands descend to the equally populous Lake Victoria basin around Kakamega and Kisii, focusing on Kisumu. Nakuru and Eldoret are farming centres originally settled by Europeans. The modern capital city of Nairobi is within this core area of Kenya, from which derive most of the exports of tea, coffee, pyrethrum and sisal, with soda ash from the Magadi alkaline lake.

A second concentration of population occurs along the coast adjacent to Mombasa, Kenya's second city and a port that also serves Uganda via Nairobi. There are ancient towns

## AIDS AND POVERTY IN AFRICA

The Acquired Immune Deficiency Syndrome was first identified in 1981, when American doctors found otherwise healthy young men succumbing to rare infections. By 1984, the cause had been traced to the Human Immunodeficiency Virus (HIV), which can remain dormant for many years and perhaps indefinitely; only half of those known to carry the virus in 1981 had developed AIDS ten years later. By the early 1990s, AIDS was still largely restricted to male homosexuals or needle-sharing drug users in the West. However, the disease is spreading fastest among heterosexual men and women in the Third World.

Africa is the most severely hit. In 1991 a World Health Organization (WHO) conference in Dakar, Senegal, was told that AIDS would kill more than 6 million Africans in the coming decade. In the same period, 4 million children would be born with the disease, and millions more would be orphaned by it. In Uganda, an estimated million people are thought to be carrying the virus. The total number of AIDS cases in adults and children reported to the WHO up to the end of 1994 was 1,025,073, but the WHO estimates the real figure is in excess of 4.5 million, of which an estimated 70% are in Africa. Trained people are desperately needed to help the continent's future development. Africans are also more than usually vulnerable to HIV and AIDS infection, partly because of urbanization and sexual freedom. In addition, most are poor and many are undernourished; many more suffer from various debilitating, non-fatal diseases. Their immune systems are already weak, making them less likely to shrug off exposure to the HIV virus, and more likely to develop AIDS.

Thus in Africa, a pregnant mother with HIV has a one-in-two chance of passing the virus to her child; in the West, the child of a similarly afflicted mother has only one chance in eight of contracting the infection. African poverty also means that victims have virtually no chance of receiving any of the expensive drugs developed to prolong the lives of AIDS sufferers. Even if researchers succeed in developing an AIDS vaccine, it is likely to be well beyond the reach of countries whose health budget is seldom much more than $2 a year for each citizen; there are few refrigerators to store such a vaccine, and few needles to administer it safely.

Africa faces millions of individual human tragedies. Yet even so, AIDS-related deaths are unlikely to impinge significantly on continental population growth. At its current rate of increase – 2.97% per annum – Africa by the year 2000 will have acquired more than 243 million extra people – more than 40 times the number of predicted deaths from AIDS. And AIDS is only the newest scourge Africa must suffer. Malaria, measles, a host of water-borne infections and simple malnutrition will kill far more Africans during the same period.

and ruins, and an Islamic Swahili culture. These now co-exist with an international tourist industry that is Kenya's third biggest source of foreign exchange. By contrast, the extensive semi-arid interior plains contain widely scattered pastoral peoples such as the Masai, Turkana and Galla.

By the standards of tropical Africa, Kenya has a stable and safe economy, even allowing for the traditionally thriving black market and usual reliance on aid. The country could nevertheless be in danger from two explosions, one in AIDS and the other, by contrast, in sheer numbers of people. Though relatively sparse in terms of density, Kenya's extraordinarily high birth rate of 4.2% is expected to produce an increase of 82% in its population between 1988 and 2000 – a figure exceeded only by Haiti. By 1990 it was already registering the world's 'youngest' profile, with more than 52% of the total under 15 years of age.

## HISTORY AND POLITICS

The 1990s brought signs, too, of increasing political problems as Daniel arap Moi, the president since 1978 and successor to the moderate Jomo Kenyatta, found his authoritarian one-party regime under threat. In December 1991, after months of pressure and government defections, he was forced to concede the principle of pluralist democracy – not seen since 1969. The president (a Kalenjin in a country whose affairs have always been dominated by the Kikuyu) was re-elected in multiparty elections in December 1992, though there were many allegations of vote-rigging. [*Map page 33*] ■

AREA 580,370 sq km [224,801 sq mls]
POPULATION 27,343,000
CAPITAL (POPULATION) Nairobi (1,429,000)
GOVERNMENT Multiparty republic
ETHNIC GROUPS Kikuyu 21%, Luhya 14%, Luo 13%, Kamba 11%, Kalenjin 11%
LANGUAGES Swahili and English (both official)
RELIGIONS Christianity (Roman Catholic 27%, Protestant 19%, others 27%), traditional beliefs 19%, Islam 6%
CURRENCY Kenyan shilling = 100 cents

# KIRIBATI

The Republic of Kiribati comprises three groups of coral atolls – 16 Gilbert Islands, eight Phoenix Islands and 11 of the Line Islands – plus the higher and volcanic Banaba. Comprising 728 sq km [281 sq mls], they are scattered over 5 million sq km [2 million sq mls] of the Pacific, straddling both the Equator and the International Date Line.

## ECONOMY AND RESOURCES

Little of the coral islands rises above 4 m [13 ft], though coconuts, bananas, papayas, and breadfruits are harvested, with taro (babai) laboriously cultivated in deep pits to provide the staple vegetable. Following the exhaustion of Banaba's phosphate deposits in 1980, the main exports are copra (63%), fish and fish preparations (24%), but Kiribati remains heavily dependent on foreign aid.

## HISTORY AND POLITICS

Kiribati was known as the Gilbert Islands until independence in 1979. Together with the Ellice Islands (which broke away as Tuvalu in 1975), the Gilberts were a British protectorate from 1892 and a colony from 1916; they were occupied by the Japanese in World War II, and recaptured after the battle for Tarawa in 1943.

The future, both medium-term economic and long-term environmental (due to possible rising sea levels from global warming) is bleak, compounded by an overcrowding problem that has forced the resettlement of some 4,700 people in the 1990s. [*Map page 3*] ■

AREA 728 sq km [281 sq mls]
POPULATION 77,000
CAPITAL (POPULATION) Tarawa (24,000)
GOVERNMENT Multiparty republic
ETHNIC GROUPS Micronesian
LANGUAGES English (official), Gilbertese
RELIGIONS Christianity (Roman Catholic 48%, Protestant 45%)
CURRENCY Australian currency

# KOREA, NORTH

Mountains and rugged hills occupy most of the Korean peninsula, and only 20% of the surface area is suitable for cultivation. The interior of North Korea is a harsh environment, characterized by long and severe winters, during which lakes and rivers regularly freeze over. High forested mountains, cut by river gorges, lie along the borders of North Korea and Manchuria. Further south, a chain of bare, eroded mountains runs for almost the entire length of the peninsula, parallel with and close to the eastern coast.

## ECONOMY AND RESOURCES
The most productive land in the peninsula occurs along the southern coast, where winters are relatively mild. While South Korea contains the best rice lands in the peninsula, most mineral resources, including coal – which supplies 70% of the country's energy needs – and iron ore, are concentrated in North Korea. Though the North has nearly 55% of the land area, it has only just over a third of the total Korean population.

While the Communist regime's collectivist agriculture programme has been reasonably successful – around 90% of cultivated land is under the control of co-operative farms – most of its effort went into the development of heavy industry, a decision which, after initial success, left the economy lagging well behind the 'sunrise' countries of the region, which moved quickly into electronics and computers. Defence, too, continues to be a significant drag on the economy.

## HISTORY AND POLITICS
The Stalinist regime of North Korea installed by the Soviet Union after World War II – and supported by China during the Korean War of 1950–3 – has been a total dictatorship revolving around the extraordinary and dynastic personality cult of Kim Il Sung and his nominated heir, Kim Jung Il, whom the president also designated his successor as supreme commander of the army. The world's most durable Communist ruler, Kim Il Sung imposed on North Korea his own brand of Marxism-Leninism, resting on the principles of self-reliance and party supremacy, and created a forbidding society virtually closed to foreigners and with few international friends.

As the Cold War ended and the Soviet satellites strived for a new age, North Korea remained isolated from the momentous events taking place outside. In 1991, however, there were quite sudden signs of progress (*see South Korea*), with unexpected breakthroughs appearing to end confrontation on the peninsula. However, the sudden death of the 'Great Leader' on 8 July 1994, at a time of increasing uncertainty surrounding North Korea's nuclear capabilities, cast a cloud of unease over the region as a whole. [*Map page 24*] ■

> **AREA** 120,540 sq km [46,540 sq mls]
> **POPULATION** 23,483,000
> **CAPITAL (POPULATION)** Pyongyang (2,639,000)
> **GOVERNMENT** Single-party people's republic
> **ETHNIC GROUPS** Korean 99%
> **LANGUAGES** Korean (official)
> **RELIGIONS** Traditional beliefs 16%, Chondogyo 14%, Buddhism 2%, Christianity 1%
> **CURRENCY** North Korean won = 100 chon

# KOREA, SOUTH

The Republic of Korea, as South Korea is officially known, occupies the southern part of the Korean peninsula. Mountains cover most of the country apart from the narrow coastal lowlands. The western coastlands, where the capital and main industrial city, Seoul, is situated, is a region of low-lying hills and plains dotted with farms. The southern coast is another major farming region. Many islands are found along the west and south coasts. The largest island is Cheju-do, which contains South Korea's highest peak, rising to 1,950 m [6,398 ft].

Like North Korea, South Korea is chilled in winter by cold, dry winds blowing from central Asia. Snow often covers the mountains in the east, but the summers are hot and wet, especially in July and August, when it rains, on average, every other day.

## ECONOMY AND RESOURCES

The story of South Korea since the civil war had been a very different one from the North, though it was hardly a Far Eastern oasis of liberalism. While land reform based on small-holdings worked well enough to produce some of the world's highest rice yields (and self-sufficiency in food grains), the real economic miracle came in industrial expansion from the early 1960s. Initiated by a military government – one of several bouts of army rule since the inauguration of the republic – and based on slender natural resources, the schemes utilized cheap, plentiful but well-educated labour to transform the economy and make South Korea one of the strongest countries in Asia. The original manufacturing base of textiles remains important, but South Korea is now a world leader in footwear, shipbuilding, and a host of other activities, including consumer electronics, toys and vehicles.

Seoul, hiding its pollution and housing shortages as best it could, celebrated the country's growth by hosting the 1988 Olympic Games: from a population of 1.4 million in 1950, it had reached 10.5 million by 1985. The dynamism of the country must now be linked to more liberal policies – and less spending on defence. The economy was growing, too: at nearly 9% a year from 1960 to 1990. South Korea has now opened up the possibility of trade links with China, which, though Communist, is desperate to broaden its economic possibilities, while approaches are being made to bodies to recognize the country's achievements and net status. A major breakthrough occurred in 1991 when both North and South Korea were admitted as full members of the United Nations.

## HISTORY AND POLITICS

For centuries the Koreans were very much a united people, an independent kingdom – 'Land of the Morning Calm' – knitted together by race, language and culture. Then, in

## THE KOREAN WAR

Hastily divided in 1945 between a Soviet-occupied North and an American-occupied South, Korea was considered by most Western strategists an irrelevance to the developing Cold War. But when the heavily-armed North invaded the South in June 1950, US President Truman decided to make a stand against what he saw (mistakenly) as Moscow-organized aggression. A Soviet boycott of the UN allowed American troops – assisted by contingents from Britain, Canada, France and other allies – to fight under the UN flag, and under General Douglas MacArthur they went on the offensive. American seapower permitted a landing far behind North Korean lines, and soon the Northerners were in retreat.

With some misgivings, Truman ordered his forces north of the 38th parallel, the former partition line. But as US troops neared the Chinese frontier in November 1950, hundreds of thousands of Chinese 'volunteers' surged across the Yalu River and threatened to overwhelm them. They retreated far southwards in disarray, until a 1951 counter-attack slowly pushed back up the country and the combatants became entrenched along the 38th parallel in a bitter war of attrition that endured until an armistice was negotiated in 1953. Not until 1991, almost 40 years later, were North and South able to agree to a tentative non-aggression pact.

1910, came annexation by Japan and its harsh colonial rule, followed after World War II with division by the Allied powers into the Soviet (North) and American (South) zones of occupation each side of the 38th parallel. In 1948 the Soviets established a Communist regime in the North, the Americans a republic in the South, and the country – especially after the civil war of 1950–3 – seemed permanently partitioned. With a handful of interruptions, the two governments retained their hostile positions on the artificial frontier for nearly four decades; then, in 1991, the sides began to talk.

They first came together over a combined table-tennis team, yet only ten months later they had signed a full-blown non-aggression pact. In January 1992, following New Year messages from both presidents talking of unification, they signed a nuclear weapons agreement, setting up a joint control committee. While German-style reunification still seems a remote possibility in the near future deep suspicion remains on both sides, and much depends on the events in North Korea following the death of Kim Il Sung in 1994 – it was a remarkable breakthrough from such institutionalized positions. [*Map page 24*] ■

**AREA** 99,020 sq km [38,232 sq mls]
**POPULATION** 44,563,000
**CAPITAL (POPULATION)** Seoul (or Soul, 10,628,000)
**GOVERNMENT** Multiparty republic
**ETHNIC GROUPS** Korean 99%
**LANGUAGES** Korean (official)
**RELIGIONS** Buddhism 28%, Christianity (Protestant 19%, Roman Catholic 6%)
**CURRENCY** South Korean won = 100 chon

# KUWAIT

Most of the country is a flat desert, extremely dry and hot. Kuwait has large reserves of oil and natural gas. The impressive if unevenly distributed prosperity built by the ruling Sabah family since oil was first commercially produced in 1946 was suddenly and brutally undermined by the Iraqi invasion of 1990. Occupying troops were soon expelled by a US-led multinational force – but not before they had set fire to more than 500 oil wells (causing unprecedented pollution) and destroyed almost all industrial and commercial installations in Kuwait.

Kuwait's revenge over the devastation was directed mainly at the large contingent of Palestinian, Jordanian and Yemeni immigrant workers (seen as pro-Iraq) on whom the economic progress of the country had been based for more than two decades. Reconstruction for this former British protectorate (the country

gained independence in 1961) was expected to cost hundreds of billions of dollars, but the high proportion of foreign investments made during the good years had produced massive funds to get it under way. Predictably, in a country with virtually no meaningful agricultural activity, oil would be the key to recovery. [*Map page 19*] ■

**AREA** 17,820 sq km [6,880 sq mls]
**POPULATION** 1,633,000
**CAPITAL (POPULATION)** Kuwait City (189,000)
**GOVERNMENT** Constitutional monarchy
**ETHNIC GROUPS** Kuwaiti Arab 40%, non-Kuwaiti Arab 38%, various Asian 21%
**LANGUAGES** Arabic 78%, Kurdish 10%, Farsi 4%
**RELIGIONS** Islam 92%, Christianity 6%
**CURRENCY** Kuwaiti dinar = 1,000 fils

# KYRGYZSTAN

The Republic of Kyrgyzstan, or Kirghizia as it is also known, is a landlocked country between China, Tajikistan, Uzbekistan and Kazakhstan. The country is mountainous, with spectacular scenery. The highest mountain, Pik Pobedy in the Tian Shan range, reaches 7,439 m [24,406 ft] above sea level in the east. Less than a sixth of the country is below 900 m [2,950 ft]. The largest of the country's many lakes is Ozero Issyk-Kul (Ysyk Köl) in the north-east. Its shoreline is 1,609 m [5,279 ft] above sea level.

The lowlands have warm summers and cold winters. But the altitude influences the climate in the mountains, where January temperatures plummet to –28°C [–18°F]. Because of its remoteness from the sea, much of Kyrgyzstan has a low annual rainfall.

## ECONOMY AND RESOURCES
Kyrgyzstan has a strong agricultural economy. Much of the lower land is used as pasture for sheep, pigs, cattle, goats, horses and yaks –

pastoralism is the traditional livelihood of the Mongoloid Kyrgyz, though few nomads remain – while irrigated land produces a wide range of crops from sugar beet and vegetables to rice, cotton, tobacco, grapes and mulberry trees (for silkworms). The main manufacturing industry is textiles and there are huge reserves of uranium, mercury and gold.

## HISTORY AND POLITICS

The area that is now Kyrgyzstan was populated in ancient times by nomadic herders. Mongol armies conquered the region in the early 13th century. They set up areas called *khanates*, ruled by chieftains, or *khans*. Islam was introduced in the 17th century.

China gained control of the area in the mid-18th century, but, in 1876, Kyrgyzstan became a province of Russia. Russia encouraged settlement by Russians, Ukrainians and others, a policy which was resented by the local people whose grazing land was reduced in area. In 1916, Russia put down a rebellion and many local people fled to China.

In 1917, Communist leaders seized control of Russia, and in 1922, when the Soviet Union was formed, Kyrgyzstan became an autonomous *oblast* (self-governing region). In 1936, it became a Soviet Socialist Republic in the Soviet Union, and under Communism, nomads were forced to live on government-run farms. The government tried to suppress some local customs, including religious worship, but Communist rule also led to improvements in such fields as health and education.

Following the break-up of the Soviet Union in 1991, and despite its geographical isolation on the borders of China's Xinjiang provinces and its conventionally strong links with Moscow, Kyrgyzstan has pursued very aggressive 'European' policies towards Western-style capitalist democracy in the period since independence was declared in August 1991. Its young president, Askar Akayev, has introduced rapid privatization, nurtured pluralism, and encouraged trade and investment links with OECD countries. In addition, he has established good relations with China, a suspicious neighbour and potential foe. However, the large Russian minority (in positions of power under the Soviet regime), disenchanted Uzbeks and an influx of Chinese Muslim immigrants have the potential for an ethnic tinderbox. [*Map page 20*] ∎

AREA  198,500 sq km [76,640 sq mls]
POPULATION  4,667,000
CAPITAL (POPULATION)  Bishkek (628,000)
GOVERNMENT  Multiparty republic
ETHNIC GROUPS  Kyrgyz 52%, Russian 22%, Uzbek 13%, Ukrainian 3%, German 2%, Tatar 2%
LANGUAGES  Kyrgyz
RELIGIONS  Islam
CURRENCY  Som = tyiyn

# LAOS

The Lao People's Democratic Republic is a landlocked country in South-east Asia. Mountains and plateaux cover much of the country. The highest point is Mount Bia, which reaches 2,817 m [9,242 ft] in central Laos. Most people live on the plains bordering the River Mekong and its tributaries. This river, one of Asia's longest, forms much of the country's north-western and south-western borders. A range of mountains, called the Annam Cordillera, runs along the eastern border with Vietnam.

Laos has a tropical monsoon climate. Winters are dry and sunny, with winds blowing from the north-east. Temperatures rise until April, when the wind directions are reversed and moist south-westerlies reach Laos, heralding the start of the wet monsoon season.

## ECONOMY AND RESOURCES

Laos is one the world's poorest countries. Agriculture employs about 76% of the people, as compared with 7% in industry and 17% in services. The River Mekong is the main artery, as the country has no railways. Up to 85% of the sparse population work on collective farms at subsistence level, growing mainly rice, although timber and coffee are both exported. But the most valuable export is electricity, which is produced at hydroelectric power stations on the River Mekong and is exported to Thailand. Laos also produces opium – in the early 1990s, Laos was thought to be the world's third biggest source of this illegal drug.

## HISTORY AND POLITICS

From the 9th century AD, Lao and Thai people set up a number of small states ruled by princes. But the area that is now Laos was united in 1353, in a kingdom called Lan Xang ('land of a million elephants'). Around 1700, the region was divided into three separate kingdoms. France made Laos a protectorate in the late 19th century and ruled it as part of French Indo-China, a region which also included Cambodia and Vietnam. Laos became a member of the French Union in 1948 and an independent kingdom in 1954.

After independence, Laos suffered from instability caused by a long struggle power between royalist government forces and a pro-Communist group called the Pathet Lao. Civil war broke out in 1960 and continued off and on into the 1970s. The Pathet Lao finally took control of Laos in 1975 and the king abdicated. Laos was greatly influenced by the dominant Communist government in Vietnam, which had used Laos as a great supply line during the Vietnam War (1957–75).

From the late 1980s, along with other Communist countries, Laos began a programme of economic reforms, including the encouragement of private enterprise and opening up trade links with neighbours (notably China and Japan). But there were few indications that the Communist government was prepared to introduce political reforms and some measure of democracy. [*Map page 26*] ■

AREA  236,800 sq km [91,428 sq mls]
POPULATION  4,742,000
CAPITAL (POPULATION)  Vientiane (377,000)
GOVERNMENT  Single-party republic
ETHNIC GROUPS  Lao 67%, Mon-Khmer 17%, Thai 8%, Man 5%
LANGUAGES  Lao (official)
RELIGIONS  Buddhism 58%, traditional beliefs 34%, Christianity 2%, Islam 1%
CURRENCY  Kip = 100 at

# LATVIA

The Republic of Latvia is one of three states on the south-eastern corner of the Baltic Sea which were ruled as parts of the Soviet Union between 1940 and 1991. Latvia consists mainly of flat plains separated by low hills, composed of glacial moraine deposited in the last Ice Age. The country's highest point is only 311 m [1,020 ft] above sea level, and small lakes and peat bogs are common. The country's main river, the Daugava, is also known as the Western Dvina.

Forests cover about 40% of the county. Pine and spruce forests are widespread, but mixed forests with alder, aspen and birch also occur. About 27% of the land is under crops, while 13% is used for grazing livestock.

## ECONOMY AND RESOURCES

Like its Baltic neighbours, Latvia contains much of the former Soviet Union's less traditional, 'clever' industries, while Ventspils is an important conduit for the export of Russian oil and gas. Latvia is the most urbanized of the Baltic states, with over 70% of the population living in cities and towns.

In the 1990s, however, it faced many problems in transforming its government-run economy into a free-market one. The country lacks any significant natural resources apart from its land and forests, and it has to import many of the materials needed for its most valuable activity, manufacturing. In addition, Latvia produces only about a tenth of the electricity it needs. The rest has to be imported from Belarus, Russia and Ukraine. Manufactured products cover a wide range, including electronic goods, farm machinery, fertilizers, processed food, plastics, radios, vehicles and washing machines.

## HISTORY AND POLITICS

The ancestors of most modern Latvians settled in the area about 2,000 years ago. But between the 9th and 11th centuries, the region was attacked by Vikings from the west and

## THE BALTIC STATES

The three Baltic republics have always found it hard to establish their nationhood, though their cultures have proved resilient. Estonia and Latvia survived 1,000 years of rule by Danes, Swedes, Lithuanians and Poles before becoming part of the Russian Empire in 1721; Lithuania, once a powerful medieval empire, was united with Poland in 1385 but also came under Russian control in 1795.

Nationalist movements grew in all three countries in the late 19th century, and in 1920, following German occupation, the Soviet Union granted them the status of independent democratic republics. However, all had Fascist coups by the time Hitler assigned them to Stalin in the notorious secret pact of 1939.

After three years of occupation by (Nazi) Germany, incorporation into the USSR was confirmed by plebiscite in 1944. On declaring independence in 1990, the Baltic states claimed this was fraudulent and that their countries were never legally part of the Soviet Union. Referenda supported this view, and on 6 September 1991 the transitional States Council of the Soviet Union recognized them as independent sovereign states. All three were United Nations members by the end of the year.

Under Soviet rule, many Russian immigrants settled in Latvia and many native Latvians (Letts) feared that the Russians would become the dominant ethnic group. In the late 1980s, when reforms were being introduced in the Soviet Union, Latvia's government ended absolute Communist rule and made Latvian the official language. In 1990, it declared the country to be independent, an act which was finally recognized by the Soviet Union in September 1991.

Latvia held its first free elections to its parliament in 1993. Voting was limited only to citizens of Latvia on 17 June 1940 and their descendants. This meant that about 34% of Latvian residents were unable to vote. In 1994, Latvia adopted a law restricting the naturalization of non-Latvians, including many Russian settlers, who are not allowed to vote or to own land. [*Map page 13*] ■

AREA 64,589 sq km [24,938 sq mls]
POPULATION 2,583,000
CAPITAL (POPULATION) Riga (917,000)
GOVERNMENT Multiparty republic
ETHNIC GROUPS Latvian 53%, Russian 34%, Belarussian 4%, Ukrainian 3%, Polish 2%, Lithuanian, Jewish
LANGUAGES Latvian (official)
RELIGIONS Christianity (including Lutheran, Russian Orthodox and Roman Catholic)
CURRENCY Lats = 10 santimi

Russians from the east, while in the 13th century German invaders took over, naming the country Livland, or Livonia in Latin.

From 1561, the area was partitioned between various groups, including Poles, Lithuanians and Swedes. In 1710, the Russian Peter the Great conquered Riga, and Latvia was soon under Russian rule. Nationalist movements developed in the 19th century and, just after the end of World War I (1914–18), Latvia declared itself independent. However, in 1939, Germany and the Soviet Union made a secret agreement to divide up parts of eastern Europe, and in 1940 Soviet troops invaded Latvia, which became part of the Soviet Union. German forces seized Latvia in 1941, but Soviet troops returned in 1944.

# LEBANON

The Republic of Lebanon is a country on the eastern shores of the Mediterranean Sea. The country's narrow coastal plain contains the main cities, including Beirut (Bayrut) and Tripoli (Tarabulus). Behind the coastal plain are the rugged Lebanon Mountains, which rise to 3,088 m [10,131 ft]. Another range, the Anti-Lebanon Mountains, form the eastern border with Syria. Between the two ranges is the Beqaa Valley, a fertile farming region.

The coast of Lebanon experiences the hot, dry summers and mild, wet winters that are typical of many Mediterranean lands. Inland, onshore winds bring heavy rain to the western slopes of the mountains in winter, with snow at the higher altitudes. Lebanon was famous in ancient times for its cedar forests in the mountains (as depicted on their flag), but these have been largely cut down. Forest and woodland now cover only about 8% of the land.

### ECONOMY AND RESOURCES
Lebanon's economy, devastated by civil war, is gradually being rebuilt. The main agricultural crops include citrus and other fruits, olives, sugar beet and tobacco, and the principal industries are textiles, electrical goods, processed food and chemicals. The previously thriving financial and commercial sectors are being developed once again.

### HISTORY AND POLITICS
For three decades after its independence from the French mandate in 1944 Lebanon was a relatively peaceful and prosperous country by Middle East standards. An association with France going back a century – before that the country was part of the Ottoman empire – had bequeathed a distinct Gallic flavour, though with so many racial and religious groups the population was truly cosmopolitan; Beirut, the dominant city, was a centre of international commerce (the Lebanese are descendants of the Phoenicians, legendary traders and businessmen).

All that changed suddenly after March 1975 when this beautiful country saw sporadic conflict spiral into violent civil war between Christians, Muslims and Druses. The complex politics of the next 14 years proved almost unfathomable as Lebanon sank into a seemingly permanent state of ungovernable chaos. Bombing, assassination and kidnapping became routine as numerous factions and private militias – Maronite, Druse, Sunni and Shia groups (including fundamentalists backed by Iran) – fought for control. The situation was complicated by a succession of interventions by Palestinian liberation organizations, Israeli troops, the Syrian Army, Western and then UN forces, as the country became a patchwork of occupied zones and 'no-go' areas.

The core religious confrontation has deep roots: in 1860 thousands of Maronites (aligned to the Catholic Church) were murdered by Druses (so tangential to other Islamic sects that they are now not regarded as Muslims), and Muslim tolerance of Christian power after independence lasted only until 1958. Though not directly involved, Lebanon was destabilized by the Arab-Israeli War of 1967, and the exile of PLO leadership to Beirut in 1970.

By 1990 the Syrian Army had crushed the two-year revolt of Christian rebels against the Lebanese government. Since then, the Lebanese Army has regained control of many areas and the government has been able to start the process of reconstruction. However, Israeli-backed forces continue to occupy the south of the country (claimed to be a base for Palestinian terrorists), while the fundamentalist Hezbollah still controls much of the Beqaa Valley in the north. [*Map page 19*] ∎

---

**AREA** 10,400 sq km [4,015 sq mls]
**POPULATION** 2,915,000
**CAPITAL (POPULATION)** Beirut (1,500,000)
**GOVERNMENT** Multiparty republic
**ETHNIC GROUPS** Arab (Lebanese 80%, Palestinian 12%), Armenian 5%, Syrian, Kurdish
**LANGUAGES** Arabic (official)
**RELIGIONS** Islam 58%, Christianity 27%, Druse
**CURRENCY** Lebanese pound = 100 piastres

---

# LESOTHO

---

Consisting mainly of a high mountainous plateau deeply fretted by the headwaters of the Orange (Oranje) River, Lesotho declines altitudinally from east to west, with the highest ridges, over 3,000 m [9–10,000 ft], developed on basaltic lavas. This treeless zone with its steep valleys has an excess of water, making it boggy in summer, frozen in winter. It is, nevertheless, overpopulated. All of this contrasts with the lower narrow western belts of the foothills and lowlands, stretching southwards from Butha-Buthe to Mohale's Hoek. Here the dominant rock is sandstone.

## ECONOMY AND RESOURCES

The physical environment, and being surrounded on all sides by South Africa, provides major economic problems for the country. Most of the population are involved in subsistence agriculture, battling for a living against steep slopes and thin soils. The only urban and industrial development lies at Maseru, but the trend is still for people to drift to the small towns or to find employment in the gold and coal mines of South Africa. The country's scenery is conducive to tourism and the altitude allows winter sports; however, massive capital investment, especially in roads, would be necessary to develop this potential.

## HISTORY AND POLITICS

Formerly a British protectorate (known as Basutoland), Lesotho became independent in 1966, joining the Commonwealth as a constitutional monarchy. However the constitution was suspended in 1970 and the prime minister, Chief Jonathan, was deposed by an army coup in 1986. In 1990 the ruling Military Council replaced King Moshoeshoe II with his son, Letsie III, but its own leader, Major-General Lekhanya, was in turn overthrown by a coup in 1992. This led to the first elections for 23 years being held in 1993. A civilian prime minister was voted in and a new constitution restoring multiparty democracy was adopted. The military were opposed to the new government and in August 1994 launched a coup attempt, propelling the country into a constitutional crisis. [*Map page 33*] ■

AREA   30,350 sq km [11,718 sq mls]
POPULATION   1,996,000
CAPITAL (POPULATION)   Maseru (109,000)
GOVERNMENT   Constitutional monarchy
ETHNIC GROUPS   Sotho 99%
LANGUAGES   Sesotho and English (both official)
RELIGIONS   Christianity 93% (Roman Catholic 44%), traditional beliefs 6%
CURRENCY   Loti = 100 lisente

# LIBERIA

Liberia is a sparsely populated country with a swampy and humid coastal strip, 500 km [311 mls] long, bordering the Atlantic Ocean. Behind this the land rises to plateaus and low mountains in the interior with large tracts of inaccessible tropical rainforest. A number of rivers flow across the country generally from the north-east to the south-west. The most important rivers are the Cavally (or Cavalla), which forms the border with Ivory Coast, and the St Paul which reaches the Atlantic Ocean near the capital, Monrovia.

Liberia has a tropical climate with high temperatures and humidity throughout the year. Rainfall is abundant, with two especially wet periods, namely May to July and October to November. The rainfall generally increases from east to west across the country.

## ECONOMY AND RESOURCES

Liberia is popularly known for its 'flag of convenience' (used by about one-sixth of the world's commercial shipping), and for large American-owned rubber plantations.

There has been an open-door policy towards foreign entrepreneurs, and the economy has developed rapidly following the exploitation of large iron-ore deposits by foreign companies, mainly American. Though diamonds and gold have long been worked, iron ore accounts for about half the value of all exports. The economy is a mixture of large foreign-owned corporations operating mines and plantations, and of various indigenous peoples who still exist largely as very poor shifting subsistence cultivators.

## HISTORY AND POLITICS

West Africa's oldest independent state, Liberia lacks a legacy of colonial administration. The country was founded in the early 19th century as an American colony for freed black slaves wanting to return to Africa from the USA.

In 1989 Liberia was plunged into vicious civil war when a force led by Charles Taylor invaded from the Ivory Coast. The president, Samuel Doe, who had seized power in 1980, was later assassinated and a jigsaw of conflicts developed between his successor, Amos Sawyer, Taylor and other rebel forces, including those led by Prince Johnson. Peacekeeping troops from five West African countries arrived in October 1990, but despite several agreements fighting continued into 1991. By mid-1993, an estimated 150,000 people had died and hundreds of thousands were homeless. In July 1993, a cease-fire was agreed, but elections scheduled for 1994 were postponed when more fighting occurred. [*Map page 32*] ■

AREA 111,370 sq km [43,000 sq mls]
POPULATION 2,941,000
CAPITAL (POPULATION) Monrovia (425,000)
GOVERNMENT Multiparty republic
ETHNIC GROUPS Kpelle 19%, Bassa 14%, Grebo 9%, Gio 8%, Kru 7%, Mano 7%
LANGUAGES English (official)
RELIGIONS Christianity 68%, Islam 14%, traditional beliefs and others 18%
CURRENCY Liberian dollar = 100 cents

# LIBYA

The Socialist People's Libyan Arab Jamahiriya, as Libya is officially called, is a large country in North Africa. Most people live on the Mediterranean coastal plains in the north-east and north-west. The Sahara, the world's largest desert which occupies 95% of Libya, reaches the Mediterranean coast along the Gulf of Sidra (Khalij Surt). The Sahara is mostly uninhabited except around scattered oases, where date palms provide protection from the hot sun. The land rises towards the south, reaching 2,286 m [7,500 ft] at Bette Peak on the border with Chad.

The plains in the north-east and north-west experience a Mediterranean climate, with hot, dry summers and mild winters with some rain. Inland, the average yearly rainfall drops to 100 mm [4 in] or less.

## ECONOMY AND RESOURCES

When it became independent in 1951, Libya was one of the poorest countries in the world, with few known natural resources and a largely nomadic population. This bleak picture changed dramatically after 1959 with the discovery of vast reserves of oil and natural gas.

With growing revenues from petroleum and gas exports, important highways were built to link the different regions across the desert, and considerable investment was made in housing, education and health provision. Today the country's income per head is twice that of its nearest rivals on the African continent – Algeria, Gabon and South Africa. But despite a high population growth rate (6.5%), agricultural development and industrialization still rely heavily on immigrant workers.

## HISTORY AND POLITICS

A former Turkish possession and Italian colony, the kingdom of Libya gained independence from British and French military administration in 1951. But, in 1969, a military group headed by Colonel Muammar Gaddafi deposed King Idris and set up a military government. Under Gaddafi, the government took control of the economy and used money from oil exports to finance welfare services and development projects.

Gaddafi has attracted international criticism for his support for radical movements, such as the PLO and various terrorist groups. In 1986, his policies led the US to bomb installations in the capital and in Benghazi. Libya has several long-running disputes with its neighbours, notably Chad, where it sent troops to intervene in a civil war. In 1994, the International Court of Justice ruled against Libya's claim for territory in the Aozou Strip in northern Chad. [*Map page 32*] ■

AREA 1,759,540 sq km [679,358 sq mls]
POPULATION 5,225,000
CAPITAL (POPULATION) Tripoli (990,000)
GOVERNMENT Single-party socialist state
ETHNIC GROUPS Libyan Arab and Berber 89%, others 11%
LANGUAGES Arabic (official)
RELIGIONS Islam
CURRENCY Libyan dinar = 1,000 dirhams

# LIECHTENSTEIN

# LITHUANIA

The tiny state of Liechtenstein stands at the end of the eastern Alps between Austria and Switzerland, where the Rhine cuts its way northwards out of the Alpine chains. The capital, Vaduz, is situated on the Oberland plateau above the fields and meadows of the Rhine Valley, and rising numbers of tourists (there were as many as 72,000 overnight visitors in 1992) are arriving at its royal castle, intrigued by the notion of this miniature state.

While Liechtenstein is best known abroad for its postage stamps – an important source of income – it is as a haven for international companies, attracted by extremely low taxation and the strictest (most secretive) banking codes in the world, that the state has generated the revenue to produce the highest GDP per capita figure on record. Since World War II there has also been an impressive growth in specialized manufacturing – the product of a judicious mixture of Swiss engineers, Austrian technicians, Italian workers and international capital.

Liechtenstein became an independent principality within the Holy Roman Empire in 1719 and since then has always managed to escape incorporation into any of Europe's larger states. Liechtenstein has been in customs and currency union with Switzerland since 1923, which also provides overseas representation; and although many Swiss regard it as their 27th canton, it retains full sovereignty in other spheres. [*Map page 15*] ▪

---

**AREA** 157 sq km [61 sq mls]
**POPULATION** 30,000
**CAPITAL (POPULATION)** Vaduz (4,919)
**GOVERNMENT** Principality
**ETHNIC GROUPS** Alemmanic 95%
**LANGUAGES** German, Alemannic dialects
**RELIGIONS** Christianity (Roman Catholic 87%, Protestant 8%)
**CURRENCY** Swiss currency

---

Largest and most populous of the Baltic states, Lithuania is also the most homogeneous, some 80% of its population being staunch Catholics who speak the native language and are proud of their history and culture. The country consists mostly of a low, glaciated but fairly fertile central lowland. In the east, towards the border with Belarus, is an area of forested sandy ridges, dotted with lakes.

## ECONOMY AND RESOURCES

Livestock rearing (cattle, pigs and poultry) was highly intensified under the Soviet collective system. Crops grown are very similar to those of Estonia, and although there are also widespread forests and significant peat reserves, Lithuania remains pitifully short of any significant natural resources.

A range of industries, among them many of the most advanced programmes in the former Soviet Union, include timber, metalworking, textiles, building materials, fertilizers, fibres and plastics, computers and instruments and food processing. Craftsmen still make jewellery from amber, a semiprecious fossilized resin found in abundance along the Baltic coast.

## HISTORY AND POLITICS

From 1988 it was Lithuania which led the 'Balts' in their drive to shed Communism and regain their nationhood; in March 1990 it became the first of the 15 constituent Soviet republics to declare itself an independent, non-Communist country, resulting in the occupation of much of its capital by Soviet troops and an economic blockade not suffered by the other states of the Union. The successful crusade was led by the emotional president, Vytautus Landsbergis, whose crucial role in the process of 'deconstruction' – and that of his people – was somewhat overshadowed by the figure of Boris Yeltsin and the mighty Russian Federation.

After independence, Lithuania faced numerous problems as it sought to change its Communist-run economy into a private enterprise one. In 1992, the Democratic Labour Party, containing many ex-Communists, won a general election, and in 1993 Algirdas Brazauskas, a former Communist Party chairman, became president. However, Lithuania's strongest links were with Western Europe and finally, in 1993, the last Soviet troops withdrew from the country.

While Lithuania, in concert with the other Baltic states, seeks to establish closer ties with the rest of Europe – a US$2.5 billion highway is planned, linking the three capitals with Warsaw – it also has simmering ethnic problems of its own. Its significant Polish population, largely self-governing under the Soviets, now fear 'Lithuanization', while the majority resent the pro-Union stance taken by Poles and Russians during their fight for freedom. [*Map page 13*] ■

AREA 65,200 sq km [25,200 sq mls]
POPULATION 3,706,000
CAPITAL (POPULATION) Vilnius (593,000)
GOVERNMENT Multiparty republic
ETHNIC GROUPS Lithuanian 80%, Russian 9%, Polish 7%, Belarussian 2%
LANGUAGES Lithuanian (official)
RELIGIONS Christianity (mainly Roman Catholic)
CURRENCY Litas = 100 centai

# LUXEMBOURG

The Grand Duchy of Luxembourg is one of the smallest and oldest countries in Europe. The north is mountainous, belonging to an upland region which includes the Ardennes in Belgium and Luxembourg, well wooded and famed for its deer and boar. This scenic region contains the country's highest point, at 565 m [1,854 ft] above sea level. The southern two-thirds of Luxembourg is a rolling plateau called the Bon Pays.

Luxembourg has a temperate climate characterized by warm summers and autumns in the south. Winters can sometimes be severe, especially in the Ardennes region.

## ECONOMY AND RESOURCES
Stock rearing is important, and crops include grains, potatoes, roots and fruit, and vines in the Moselle valley. There is also a prosperous iron and steel industry based on rich iron-ore deposits. Luxembourg also has many high technology industries, producing electronic goods and computers. Other major activities include tourism and financial services.

## HISTORY AND POLITICS
Declaring itself a Grand Duchy in 1354, Luxembourg is the only one out of hundreds of independent duchies, which once comprised much of continental Europe, to survive and become a full member of the United Nations.

In 1922, Luxembourg formed an economic union with Belgium, extended in 1944 to include the Netherlands under the composite name of Benelux. Luxembourg is a founder member of NATO (1949) and the EEC (1957), and is perhaps best known to Europeans as the host for the European Investment Bank, the Secretariat of the European Parliament, the European Monetary Co-operation Fund and the Court of European Communities.

Though Luxembourg's population is barely a thousandth of the EU total, it remains a relatively important player in Western European commerce and politics. [*Map page 11*] ■

AREA 2,590 sq km [1,000 sq mls]
POPULATION 401,000
CAPITAL (POPULATION) Luxembourg (76,000)
GOVERNMENT Constitutional monarchy (Grand Duchy)
ETHNIC GROUPS Luxembourger 71%, Portuguese 10%, Italian 5%, French 3%, Belgian 3%, German 2%
LANGUAGES Letzeburgish (Luxembourgian – official), French, German
RELIGIONS Christianity
CURRENCY Luxembourg franc = 100 centimes

# MACAU

# MACEDONIA

Macau (also known as Macao) comprises a peninsula at the head of the Canton (Pearl) River, 64 km [40 mls] west of Hong Kong and connected to China by a narrow isthmus, and the islands of Coloane and Taipa.

One of the principal economic activities is tourism (in 1990 there were nearly 6 million visitors, 81% from Hong Kong), but there is no airport – most visitors arrive via Hong Kong. The territory, with a population that is 98% Chinese, is also heavily reliant on the Chinese mainland for food, water and raw materials. Macau's major industry is textile manufacturing, which accounts for 62% of all exports, but revenue from gambling is also important to the economy.

A Portuguese colony from 1557 and for 200 years one of the great trading centres for silk, gold, spices and opium, Macau was overtaken in importance by Hong Kong in the 19th century. When China re-established diplomatic relations with the colonial power in 1979, the coastal enclave was redefined as 'Chinese territory under Portuguese administration', and in 1987 the powers agreed that the territory will return to China on 20 December 1999 as a Special Administrative Region of that country – an agreement based on the 'one country, two systems' principle used by China and Britain to settle the future of Hong Kong in 1984. Macau will continue to persue capitalist policies after 1999. [*Map page 24*] ∎

AREA 16 sq km [6 sq mls]
POPULATION 398,000
CAPITAL (POPULATION) Macau (395,000)
GOVERNMENT Overseas territory of Portugal
ETHNIC GROUPS Chinese 95%, Portuguese 3%
LANGUAGES Cantonese, Portuguese
RELIGIONS Buddhism 45%, Christianity
CURRENCY Pataca = 100 avos

The Former Yugoslav Republic of Macedonia is a country in south-eastern Europe, which was once one of the six republics that made up the former Federal People's Republic of Yugoslavia. Macedonia is landlocked between Albania, Greece and Bulgaria, its northern frontier dangerously contiguous with Serbia's troubled Kosovo region.

Geologically, most of the country forms part of the Balkan Mountains, a well-wooded region of ancient, rounded crystalline rocks. The highest point is Mt Korab, which reaches 2,764 m [9,068 ft] above sea level on the border with Albania. The country suffers periodic earthquakes, the capital Skopje, was devastated as recently as 1963. Most of the country is drained by the River Vardar and its many tributaries. In the south-west, Macedonia shares two large lakes – Ohrid and Prespa – with Albania and Greece.

## ECONOMY AND RESOURCES

Already one of the most undeveloped regions of the former Yugoslavia, the new republic has suffered from an economic blockade imposed by Greece. The leading sector of the economy is manufacturing and manufactures dominate the exports. Manufactures include cement, chemicals, iron and steel, textiles and tobacco products. Macedonia mines coal, but it has to import all its oil and natural gas. Chromium, copper, iron ore, lead, manganese, uranium and zinc are also mined.

Agriculture employs under 10% of the population. Major crops include cotton, fruits, maize, tobacco and wheat, and livestock rearing and forestry are also important. The country's farmers fulfil Macedonia's basic food needs.

## HISTORY AND POLITICS

Until the 20th century, Macedonia's history was closely tied to that of a larger area, also called Macedonia, which included parts of northern Greece and south-western Bulgaria.

Between the 14th and 19th centuries, Macedonia was ruled by the Turkish Ottoman empire. Between 1912 and 1913, the region was divided between Serbia, which controlled the north and centre, Bulgaria which took a small area in the east, and Greece which gained the south. At the end of World War I (1914–18), Serbian Macedonia became part of the Kingdom of the Serbs, Croats and Slovenes, which was renamed Yugoslavia in 1929. After World War II (1939–45), a Communist government under President Josip Broz Tito took power in Yugoslavia.

Tito died in 1980, and in the early 1990s the country broke up into five separate republics. Macedonia declared its independence in September 1991. Greece, however, objected to the use of the name 'Macedonia' which it considered to be a territorial claim on the Greek province of the same name. It also objected to a symbol on the Macedonian flag, the currency and a reference in the constitution to the desire to reunite the three parts of the old Macedonia.

As a result, Macedonia adopted a new clause in its constitution rejecting any Macedonian claims on Greek territory and, in 1993, the United Nations accepted the new republic as a member under the name of The Former Yugoslav Republic of Macedonia (FYROM). By the end of 1993, all the countries of the European Union, except for Greece, were establishing diplomatic relations with the FYROM. But Greek hostility continued. In early 1994, Greece banned Macedonian use of the Greek port of Thessaloniki, which normally handles 75% of Macedonia's foreign trade and 100% of its vital oil imports. [*Map page 17*] ∎

---

**AREA** 24,900 sq km [9,600 sq mls]
**POPULATION** 2,142,000
**CAPITAL (POPULATION)** Skopje (563,000)
**GOVERNMENT** Multiparty republic
**ETHNIC GROUPS** Macedonian 65%, Albanian 21%, Turkish 5%, Romanian 3%, Serb 2%
**LANGUAGES** Macedonian
**RELIGIONS** Christianity (mainly Eastern Orthodox, with Macedonian Orthodox and Roman Catholic communities), Islam
**CURRENCY** Denar = 100 paras

---

# MADAGASCAR

The world's fourth largest island, Madagascar is virtually a semi-continent, bigger than France and immensely varied, physically, ecologically and culturally. There are extensive rugged areas so that soils are often poor and farming unrewarding, and the coasts are hostile, with little natural shelter. The north and east are hot and wet, and subject to cyclones. The west is drier, and the south and south-west are arid.

Separated from the African mainland for more than 50 million years, Madagascar developed a distinct flora and fauna – over 150,000 plant and animal species are unique to the islands. Before the coming of people some 3,000 years ago, nearly all the island was variously forested, and although up to 90% of it was cleared for agriculture, a strange collection of animals survived in the remnants – among them 40 species of chameleons, pygmy hippos, elephant birds and the renowned lemurs. But with so much of the forest gone, Madagascar is today one of the most eroded places in the world and its unique wildlife is seriously under threat.

## ECONOMY AND RESOURCES

Also unique to the island is its mixture of peoples, derived from several continents. Those on the west side are of Bantu origin, drawn from southern Africa via the Comoros Islands 'bridge'. Those of the centre and east (the Merina or Hova people) came first from Indonesia, as early as 2,000 years ago, with later waves arriving during the 7th to 15th centuries. Other Asians followed, all rice growers, reverent to cattle, with language and funeral rites similar to those in South-east Asia. They had a monarchy until French occupation in 1895. In the south, the Betsileo are more mixed Bantu-Indonesian, as are other groups, yet all feel 'Malagasy' rather than African or Asian. Many other immigrant groups, including Europeans, Chinese and Indians, have also settled.

Both landscapes and agriculture (dominantly rice with cattle and pigs) in the central highlands are south Asian in character; the east coast and northern highlands are more African, with fallow farming of food crops and cultivation of coffee, sugar, essential oil plants and spices for export – the country produces 60% of the world's vanilla. In the dry west and south nomadic pastoralism is important, and rice is grown by irrigation. Significant minerals are graphite, chromite and mica. Air transport is important, with a network of over 60 airports and airstrips.

## HISTORY AND POLITICS
The government which took power on independence in 1960 continued Madagascar's links with France, but a resurgence of nationalism in the 1970s was followed by the emergence of Didier Ratsiraka, who seized power in 1975 and established a dictatorial one-party socialist state. Under a new constitution approved in 1992, Ratsiraka, whose incompetence had plunged Madagascar into poverty, was defeated in elections in 1993 by the opposition leader, Albert Zafy. [*Map page 33*] ■

AREA 587,040 sq km [226,656 sq mls]
POPULATION 14,303,000
CAPITAL (POPULATION) Antananarivo (802,000)
GOVERNMENT Republic
ETHNIC GROUPS Merina 27%, Betsimisaraka 15%, Betsileo 11%, Tsimihety 7%, Sakalava 6%
LANGUAGES Malagasy (official), French, English
RELIGIONS Christianity 51%, traditional beliefs 47%, Islam 2%
CURRENCY Malagasy franc = 100 centimes

# MADEIRA

Madeira is the largest of the group of picturesque volcanic islands of that name lying 550 km [350 mls] from the Moroccan coast and 900 km [560 mls] south-

west of the Portuguese capital, Lisbon. Porto Santo and the uninhabited Ilhas Selvagens and Desertas complete the group, with a total area of 813 sq km [314 sq mls], of which Madeira itself contributes 745 sq km [288 sq mls].

With a warm temperate climate, adequate rainfall and good soils, Madeira was originally forested, but early settlers cleared the uplands for plantations. Farming is still the main occupation, producing sugar cane, wines, vegetables and both temperate and tropical fruits. The main exports are grapes (mainly for Madeira wine), bananas and sugar. Handicrafts and, increasingly, tourism are additional sources of revenue.

Known to the Genoese in the 14th century but colonized by the Portuguese from the 15th century onwards, the islands have since 1976 formed an autonomous region of Portugal. [*Map page 32*] ■

AREA 813 sq km [314 sq mls]
POPULATION 253,000
CAPITAL (POPULATION) Funchal (45,000)
GOVERNMENT Portuguese autonomous region
ETHNIC GROUPS Portuguese
LANGUAGES Portuguese
RELIGIONS Christianity (mainly Roman Catholic)
CURRENCY Portuguese currency

# MALAWI

The Republic of Malawi is a landlocked country in southern Africa. It includes part of Lake Malawi, which is drained in the south by the River Shire, a tributary of the River Zambezi. Lake Malawi, which is called Lake Nyasa in Tanzania and Mozambique, lies on the floor of the Great African Rift Valley. This huge gash in the Earth's crust extends from Mozambique to south-western Asia. The land is mostly mountainous. The highest peak, Mulanje, reaches 3,000 m [9,843 ft] in the south-east. Malawi's unusual shape (nowhere is it more than 160 km [100 mls] wide) derived from a 19th-century missionaries' and traders' route up the Zambezi, Shire and Lake Nyasa (Malawi).

## ECONOMY AND RESOURCES

The country is relatively poor in natural resources, and compared with its neighbours has a high population density, placing excessive pressure on the land. This problem was inflamed during the 1980s, when Malawi became the main host to nearly a million refugees from neighbouring Mozambique, putting an intolerable burden on an already weak economy, despite massive aid packages.

Industrial and urban development are extremely limited. Most of the commercial activity centres on agriculture, which provides over 90% of Malawi's domestic exports. Tea and tobacco, mostly from large estates, are the principal export crops, while basic foodstuffs such as maize are largely derived from small, quasisubsistence peasant holdings which occupy most of the farmland. Malawi has a long history as an exporter of labour migrants, and large numbers of Malawians still work or seek work abroad, notably in South Africa.

## HISTORY AND POLITICS

Malawi's recent history has been dominated by one man: Dr Hastings Kumuzu Banda. Already 62 years old, he led the country (formerly Nyasaland) to independence in 1964, and two years later declared a one-party republic with himself as president for life from 1971. His autocratic regime was different from most of black Africa in being conservative and pragmatic, hostile to socialist neighbours but friendly with South Africa.

At first his austerity programme and agricultural policies seemed to have wrought an economic miracle, but the 1980s sealed a swift decline and a return to poverty. As well as a million refugees Malawi faced another immediate problem – the world's worst recorded national incidence of AIDS. Malawi means 'the land lake where the sun is reflected in the water like fire', but the reality for most of the people has been a good deal less romantic.

In June 1993, 63% of voters chose a multi-party system in a referendum, with Dr Banda remaining as president, but in further elections

in May 1994, Banda and his party, the Malawi Congress Party, were defeated. Bakili Muluzi was elected president. [*Map page 33*] ■

**AREA** 118,480 sq km [45,745 sq mls]
**POPULATION** 8,823,000
**CAPITAL (POPULATION)** Lilongwe (223,318)
**GOVERNMENT** Multiparty republic
**ETHNIC GROUPS** Maravi (Chewa, Nyanja, Tonga, Tumbuka) 58%, Lomwe 18%, Yao 13%, Ngoni 7%
**LANGUAGES** Chichewa and English (both official)
**RELIGIONS** Christianity (Protestant 34%, Roman Catholic 28%), traditional beliefs 21%, Islam 16%
**CURRENCY** Kwacha = 100 tambala

# MALAYSIA

The Malay Peninsula is dominated by fold mountains with a north-south axis. There are seven or eight ranges, with frequently exposed granite cores. The most important is the so-called Main Range, which runs from the Thai border to the south-east of Kuala Lumpur, attaining 2,182 m [7,159 ft] at its highest point, Gunong Kerbau. South of the Main Range lies the flat and poorly drained lowland of Johor, which is punctuated by isolated hills, often rising over 1,060 m [3,500 ft]. The small rivers of Malaya have built up a margin of lowland around the coasts.

Northern Borneo has a mangrove-fringed coastal plain, up to 65 km [40 mls] wide, backed by hill country averaging 300 m [1,000 ft] in height. This is dominated by the east-west fold mountains of the interior, which rise from 1,400 m to 2,300 m [4,500 to 7,500 ft]; the most striking is the granite peak of Mt Kinabalu (4,101 m [13,455 ft]) in Sabah, Malaysia's highest mountain. The natural vegetation of most of Malaysia is lowland rainforest and its montane variants. The Malaysian forests, which are dominated by the dipterocarp family of trees, are the richest in species of all the world's forests. Unfortunately, few undisturbed areas remain, mostly in such national parks such as the Gunong Mulu in Sarawak and the Kinabalu in Sabah.

## ECONOMY AND RESOURCES

The traditional mainstays of the economy – rice, plus exports of rubber, palm oil and tin (Malaysia is among the world's biggest producers of all three) – have been supplemented by exploitation of other natural resources, notably oil and timber, though the pace of the latter is causing widespread unrest among environmentalists. Exports are now safely diverse, from Sarawak's pepper to the new Proton 'national car', and with a growing tourist industry in support, Malaysia seems set to join Japan and the four 'little dragons' as a success story of postwar eastern Asia.

## HISTORY AND POLITICS

The new country of Malaysia was born in 1963 by the joining of the Federation of Malaya (independent from Britain since 1957), the island state of Singapore and the colonies of Sarawak and North Borneo (renamed Sabah). In 1965 Singapore seceded to become an independent nation, and the present federation comprises 11 states and a federal territory (Kuala Lumpur) on the Malay Peninsula, and two states and a federal territory (Labuan) in northern Borneo. The regions are separated by some 650 km [400 mls] of the South China Sea.

An early golden age of Malay political power came in the 15th century with the rise of the kingdom of Malacca, which controlled the important sea routes and trade of the region. In 1414, the ruler of Malacca accepted the Islamic faith, which remains the official religion of Malaysia today. The country is, however, characterized by great ethnic, religious and cultural diversity, with Malays of many different origins, Chinese and Indians (mainly brought in by the British to work the tin mines and rubber plantations), Eurasians, Europeans and a number of aboriginal peoples, notably in Sabah and Sarawak.

This patchwork has caused tensions, particularly between the politically dominant Muslim Malays and the economically dominant, mainly Buddhist, Chinese, but while

riots did break out in 1969, it has never escalated into serious armed conflict; nor has it prevented remarkable economic growth that has, according to World Bank ratings, made Malaysia an upper middle-income country. By the early 1990s, it was playing a leading role in regional affairs, especially through its membership of ASEAN (Association of South-east Asian Nations). [*Map page 26*] ■

> **AREA** 329,750 sq km [127,316 sq mls]
> **POPULATION** 19,695,000
> **CAPITAL (POPULATION)** Kuala Lumpur (938,000)
> **GOVERNMENT** Federal constitutional monarchy
> **ETHNIC GROUPS** Malay and other indigenous groups 62%, Chinese 30%, Indian 8%
> **LANGUAGES** Malay (official)
> **RELIGIONS** Islam 53%, Buddhism 17%, Chinese folk religionist 12%, Hinduism 7%, Christianity 6%
> **CURRENCY** Ringgit (Malaysian dollar) = 100 cents

# MALDIVES

The archipelago of the Maldives comprises over 1,190 small low-lying islands and atolls (202 of them inhabited), scattered along a broad north-south line starting 650 km [400 mls] west-south-west of Cape Comorin. Coral reefs, probably built on a foundation of extinct submarine volcanoes, the Maldives are strategically significant as mid-ocean islands. Adequately watered and covered with tropical vegetation, the islands' crops are coconuts, bananas, mangoes, sweet potatoes and spices, but much food is imported – as are nearly all capital and consumer goods. Fish are plentiful in lagoons and open sea; bonito and tuna are leading exports together with copra and coir. Tourism, however, has now displaced fishing as the mainstay of the economy, though its future depends much on political stability.

The islands were settled from Sri Lanka

about 500 BC. For a time under Portuguese and later Dutch rule, they became a British protectorate in 1887, administered from Ceylon but retaining local sultanates. Independence was granted in 1965, and the last sultan deposed in 1968. A coup against the authoritarian nationalist government was put down with Indian troops in 1988. [*Map page 3*] ■

| | |
|---|---|
| **AREA** | 298 sq km [115 sq mls] |
| **POPULATION** | 246,000 |
| **CAPITAL (POPULATION)** | Malé (55,130) |
| **GOVERNMENT** | Republic |
| **ETHNIC GROUPS** | Mixture of Sinhalese, Indian and Arab |
| **LANGUAGES** | Divehi (Sinhala dialect) |
| **RELIGIONS** | Islam |
| **CURRENCY** | Rufiyaa = 100 laaris |

# MALI

The Republic of Mali is a landlocked country in northern Africa. The land is generally flat, with the highest land in the Adrar des Iforhas on the border with Algeria. This highland region in the northern desert contains many wadis (dry valleys), where rivers once flowed. But today, the only permanent rivers and streams are in the south. The main rivers are the Sénégal, which flows westwards to the Atlantic Ocean, and the Niger, which makes a large turn, called the Niger Bend, in south-central Mali.

Northern Mali is part of the Sahara, with a hot, practically rainless climate, but the south has enough rain for farming. The dry grasslands in central and south-eastern Mali are part of a region called the Sahel. During long droughts, the northern Sahel dries up and becomes part of the Sahara. Southern Mali, which is covered by savanna, is the most densely populated part of the country.

## ECONOMY AND RESOURCES

Water (or the lack of it) dominates the life of the people and most of the country's popula-

tion is concentrated along the Sénégal and Niger rivers, which provide water for stock and irrigation and serve as much-needed communication routes. The Niger and its tributaries support a fishing industry that exports dried fish to neighbouring Ivory Coast, Burkina Faso and Ghana.

With the exception of small areas in the south of the country, irrigation is necessary for all arable crops. The savanna grasslands and highland areas in the Sahelian south-east are free of tsetse fly (carrier of sleeping sickness), and large numbers of sheep and cattle are traditionally kept in the area, though grazing lands have been decimated by a series of catastrophic droughts. Northern Mali is entirely poor desert, inhabited only by Tuareg and Fulani nomads.

Millet, cotton and groundnuts are important crops on the unirrigated lands of the south, while rice is intensively grown with irrigation. A large irrigation scheme has been developed near Ségou which produces rice, cotton and sugar cane, and there are many other smaller schemes. Industry is confined mainly to one commercial gold mine, salt production and embryonic manufacturing – shoes, textiles, beer and matches.

## HISTORY AND POLITICS

In the 14th century it was the centre of a huge West African Malinka empire based on the legendary city of Timbuktu (Tombouctou). A French colony between 1893 and 1960, Mali was then governed by a radical Socialist government for the first eight years of independence, before this was overthrown by a bloodless coup under General Moussa Traoré. His repressive military, single-party regime did little for the country – despite successful pressure from aid donor nations to liberalize the planned economy – and in 1987 the World Bank classified Mali as the world's fourth poorest country; they were still in the bottom 20 in 1993. In 1985 the government had been involved in a border dispute with neighbouring Burkina Faso; the International Court of Justice finally granted Mali 40% of its claimed land.

Student-led protests finally ended Traoré's 23-year reign in 1991. Following a referendum in 1992, elections were held, in which Alphar

Oumar Konare became Mali's first democratically elected president. [*Map page 32*] ■

> **AREA** 1,240,190 sq km [478,837 sq mls]
> **POPULATION** 10,462,000
> **CAPITAL (POPULATION)** Bamako (646,000)
> **GOVERNMENT** Multiparty republic
> **ETHNIC GROUPS** Bambara 32%, Fulani (or Peul) 14%, Senufo 12%, Soninké 9%, Tuareg 7%, Songhai 7%, Malinké (Mandingo or Mandinke) 7%
> **LANGUAGES** French (official)
> **RELIGIONS** Islam 90%, traditional beliefs 9%, Christianity 1%
> **CURRENCY** CFA franc = 100 centimes

# MALTA

**M**alta lies in the centre of the Mediterranean, roughly halfway between Gibraltar and Suez, 93 km [58 mls] south of Sicily and 290 km [180 mls] from North Africa. Its strategic importance arises from its position, and from its possession of magnificent natural harbours – notable among them Grand Harbour and Marsamxett; these lie on either side of the rocky peninsula on which stands the capital, Valletta.

## ECONOMY AND RESOURCES
Malta and the neighbouring islands of Comino and Gozo have few natural resources (apart from splendid building stone), and with no rivers and sparse rainfall there are only limited possibilities for agriculture. Yet they constitute one of the world's most densely populated states, with two-thirds of the people living in the 'conurbation' of districts around Valletta. The native islanders are of mixed Arab, Sicilian, Norman, Spanish, English and Italian origin. Maltese and English are spoken, the former universally, although it was not written until the present century.

From the Napoleonic period until after World War II, the Maltese economy depended on agriculture (which still involves nearly half the workforce), and the existence of British military bases. Before the last garrison left in 1979 Malta had already obtained independence, and was developing export-oriented industries and 'offshore' business facilities that would replace the income from the military and naval connections. Germany became its chief trading partner ahead of the UK and Italy, though Libya supplies most of its oil.

Year-round tourism, taking advantage of the mild Mediterranean winters and the hot, dry summers, brings over a million visitors annually, of whom 50% are British. The skill of the dockyard workers is still world-famous, however, and with help from overseas, Malta is developing a new port, wharf and storage facilities. The other main industries include electronics, textiles, foodstuffs and clothing.

## HISTORY AND POLITICS
A former British colony, Malta became independent in 1964, and in 1974 it became a republic. In 1979, Britain's military agreement with Malta expired and it ceased to be a military base when all British forces withdrew. In the 1980s, the Maltese people declared their country to be neutral. But in the 1990s, Malta applied to join the EU. [*Map page 4*] ■

> **AREA** 316 sq km [122 sq mls]
> **POPULATION** 364,000
> **CAPITAL (POPULATION)** Valletta (102,000)
> **GOVERNMENT** Multiparty republic
> **ETHNIC GROUPS** Maltese 96%, British 2%
> **LANGUAGES** Maltese and English (both official)
> **RELIGIONS** Christianity (Roman Catholic 99%)
> **CURRENCY** Maltese lira = 100 cents

# MARSHALL ISLANDS

**T**he country comprises over 1,250 islands and atolls – including the former US nuclear testing sites of Bikini and Enewetak – totalling just 181 sq km [70 sq mls]. The population, mainly Micronesian, Protestant and

English-speaking, is 52,000, with nearly half living in the capital of Dalap-Uliga-Darrit on Majuro island.

The economy, based on agriculture and tourism, is very heavily supported by aid from the US, which still retains a missile site on the largest island, Kwajalein. Self-governing since 1979, the Marshall Islands became a republic 'in free association with the USA' in 1986, moving from Trust Territory status to a sovereign state responsible for its own foreign policy, but not (until 2001) for its own defence and security. [*Map page 3*] ■

**AREA** 181 sq km [70 sq mls]
**POPULATION** 52,000
**CAPITAL (POPULATION)** Dalap-Uliga-Darrit (20,000)
**GOVERNMENT** Republic 'in free association with the USA'
**ETHNIC GROUPS** Micronesian
**LANGUAGES** English, Marshallese dialects, Japanese
**RELIGIONS** Christianity (mainly Protestant)
**CURRENCY** US currency

# MARTINIQUE

Martinique comprises three groups of volcanic hills and the intervening lowlands. The highest peak is Mt Pelée (1,397 m [4,583 ft]), notorious for its eruption of 1902, when in minutes it killed all the inhabitants of St Pierre (estimated at about 28,000) except one – a prisoner who was saved by the thickness of his cell.

## ECONOMY AND RESOURCES
Bananas, rum and pineapples are the main agricultural exports, but tourism (mainly French and American) is the biggest earner; transport equipment and food, chiefly from France, are the main imports. The industrial sector includes cement, food processing and oil refining, using Venezuelan crude; oil products account for 14% of exports. French

government expenditure is higher than on Guadeloupe, at some 70% of GDP, helping provide jobs and retain a better standard of living than its northern compatriot.

## HISTORY AND POLITICS
Martinique was 'discovered' by Columbus in 1493, colonized by France from 1635 and, apart from brief British interludes, has been French ever since. It became an overseas department in 1946 – with the same status and representation as *départements* – and was made an administrative region in 1974. The island has a less vociferous independence movement than Guadeloupe – though in the 1991 elections the separatists made substantial gains, winning 19 of the 41 seats. [*Map page 30*] ■

**AREA** 1,100 sq km [425 sq mls]
**POPULATION** 375,000
**CAPITAL (POPULATION)** Fort-de-France (100,000)
**GOVERNMENT** Overseas department of France
**ETHNIC GROUPS** Of African descent, Mixed, White
**LANGUAGES** French, Creole patois
**RELIGIONS** Christianity (mainly Roman Catholic)
**CURRENCY** French currency

# MAURITANIA

The Islamic Republic of Mauritania in north-western Africa is nearly twice the size of France – but France has more than 26 times as many people. Part of the world's largest desert, the Sahara, covers northern Mauritania and most Mauritanians live in the south-east. The land is mostly flat or gently rolling, with low rocky plateaux and areas of drifting sand dunes in the interior. The highest point, Kediet Ijill, reaches 915 m [3,002 ft] above sea level and is rich in the mineral haematite (an iron ore).

The amount of rain and the length of the

rainy season increase from north to south. Much of the land is desert, with dry north-east and easterly winds throughout the year. In the summer, south-westerly winds bring rain to the south of the country.

Savanna vegetation characterizes the far south. Here, such trees as baobabs and palms dot the landscape. To the north, the savanna merges into the dry grasslands of the Sahel, where trees are rare. But most of Mauritania is desert and plants grow only around oases or in wadis (dry valleys) beneath which some water continues to flow.

## ECONOMY AND RESOURCES

Apart from oasis settlements such as Atar and Tidjikdja, the only permanent arable agriculture is in the south, concentrated in a narrow strip along the Sénégal River. Crops of millet, sorghum, beans, peanuts and rice are grown, often using the natural late-summer floods for irrigation. When the Sénégal River Project is complete, large areas should be developed for irrigated crops of rice, cotton and sugar cane.

Many people are still cattle herders who drive their herds from the Sénégal River through the Sahel steppelands in tandem with the seasonal rains. In good years the country's livestock outnumber the human population by about five to one, but the ravages of drought and the development of the mining industries in the 1980s – allied to traditional overgrazing – have reduced the nomadic population from three-quarters to less than a third of the national total.

Off the Atlantic coast, the cold Canaries Current is associated with some of the richest fishing grounds in the world. The national fishing industry is still evolving and over 100,000 tonnes of fish are landed and processed each year, mainly at the major fishing port of Nouadhibou (Port Étienne); the potential catch is estimated at 600,000 tonnes.

As the Atlantic coast in the south of the country lacks good harbours, a port and capital city have been constructed at Nouakchott. This now handles a growing proportion of the country's trade, including exports of copper mined near Akjoujt. Exported minerals, particularly high-grade iron ores, worked from the vast reserves around Fdérik, provide the country with most of its foreign revenue, though animal products, gum arabic and dates are also among the exports. Apart from the main north-south highway and routes associated with mineral developments, land communications consist of rough tracks.

## HISTORY AND POLITICS

From the 4th to the 16th centuries, parts of Mauritania belonged to two great African empires – ancient Ghana and Mali. Portuguese explorers arrived in the 1440s but European contact did not begin in the area until the 17th century when trade in gum arabic, a substance obtained from the acacia tree, became important.

France set up a protectorate in Mauritania in 1903 and the country became a territory of French West Africa and a French colony in 1920. French West Africa was a huge territory, which included present-day Benin, Burkina Faso, Guinea, Ivory Coast, Mali, Niger and Senegal, as well as Mauritania. In 1958, Mauritania became a self-governing territory in the French Union and it became fully independent in 1960.

In 1961, Mauritania's political parties were merged into one by the president, Mokhtar Ould Daddah, who made the country a one-party state in 1965. In 1976, Spain withdrew from Spanish (now Western) Sahara, a territory bordering Mauritania to the north. Morocco occupied the northern two-thirds of this territory, while Mauritania took the rest. But Saharan guerrillas belonging to POLISARIO (the Popular Front for the Liberation of Saharan Territories) began an armed struggle for independence. In 1978, military leaders overthrew Ould Daddah and set up a military regime.

The rulers in Nouakchott surrendered their claims to the southern part of the Western Sahara in 1979. The following year slavery was formally abolished – though some estimates put the number of 'Haratines' (descendants of black slaves) still in bondage as high as 100,000. Unlike several of the former colonial territories of West and Central Africa, Mauritania was not affected by the wave of democratization that toppled military and single-party regimes from the late 1980s. However, in 1991, the country adopted a new constitution when the people voted to create a multiparty government. Multiparty elections, held in 1992, were won by Maaouiya Sidi Ahmed Taya, former president of the military government. [*Map page 32*] ■

**AREA** 1,025,220 sq km [395,593 sq mls]
**POPULATION** 2,217,000
**CAPITAL (POPULATION)** Nouakchott (393,000)
**GOVERNMENT** Multiparty Islamic republic
**ETHNIC GROUPS** Moor (Arab-Berber) 70%, Wolof 7%, Tukulor 5%, Soninke 3%, Fulani 1%
**LANGUAGES** Arabic and French (both official)
**RELIGIONS** Islam 99%
**CURRENCY** Ouguiya = 5 khoums

# MAURITIUS

Mauritius consists of the main island, Rodruigues (formerly a dependency), situated 800 km [500 mls] to the east of Madagascar, 20 nearby islets and the dependencies of the Agalega Islands and the tiny Cargados Carajas shoals (St Brandon). The beautiful main island, fringed with coral reefs, rises to a high lava plateau. Good rainfall (up to 5,000 mm [200 in] a year) and steep slopes have combined to give fast-flowing rivers, now harnessed for limited hydroelectric power.

Similar to Réunion in climate and soils, its vast plantations produce sugar cane (now declining but with derivatives like molasses still accounting for over 40% of exports), tea and tobacco, while home consumption centres around livestock and vegetables. To some extent the decline in sugar has been offset by the growth in tourism (374,600 visitors in 1993) and the expansion of textiles and clothing (nearly half of exports), especially woollen knitwear.

French from 1715 and British from 1810, the colony gained independence within the Commonwealth in 1968. The islands suffer from increasing tensions between the Indian majority – descended from contract workers

brought in to tend the plantations after the end of slavery in 1834 – and the Creole (mixed Afro-French) minority. The country became a republic in March 1992. [*Map page 3*] ■

**AREA** 1,860 sq km [718 sq mls]
**POPULATION** 1,104,000
**CAPITAL (POPULATION)** Port Louis (144,000)
**GOVERNMENT** Republic
**ETHNIC GROUPS** Indian 56%, Creole 30%, European 4%
**LANGUAGES** English, Creole, French
**RELIGIONS** Hinduism 52%, Christianity 26%, Islam
**CURRENCY** Mauritius rupee = 100 cents

# MEXICO

Mexico is a land of great physical variety. The northern, emptier, half is open basin-and-range country of the Mesa Central. The land rises southwards from the Rio Grande (Rio Bravo del Norte) at the US border, averaging about 2,600 m [8,500 ft] above sea level in the middle, where it is crowned by many snow-capped volcanic cones, Orizaba (5,750 m [18,865 ft]) in the east being the highest. Though an active earthquake zone, this is the most densely settled part of the country. The Mesa Central ends equally dramatically in the west, where the Sierra Madre Occidental rise to over 4,000 m [13,120 ft], and in the east, where the Sierra Madre Oriental form a backcloth to the modest coastal plain bordering the Gulf of Mexico. In the far north-west is the isolated, 1,220 km [760 ml] mountain-cored peninsula of Baja California.

Mountains dominate southern Mexico, broken only by the low, narrow isthmus of Tehuantepec, which is crossed by railways and roads linking the Gulf ports with Salina Cruz on the Pacific. The flat, low-lying limestone Yucatan peninsula in the south-east is an exception in a country where half the land is over 1,000 m [3,280 ft] above sea level, and a quarter has slopes of over 25 degrees. Deserts characterize the north-west of the country and tropical rainforest is the natural vegetation of the Tehuantepec region; over 70% of the country is arid or semi-arid and irrigation is mandatory for agriculture.

## ECONOMY AND RESOURCES

Agriculture occupies half the population but contributes less than a third of the economic product contributed by manufacturing, with metals also important. Fresh petroleum discoveries during the 1970s from massive reserves in Tabasco and Campeche have turned Mexico into the world's fourth biggest producer, much of it exported to the USA, but the economy is now very diverse with food processing, textiles, forestry and tourism all making significant progress. Only an estimated 15–20% of the nation's mineral wealth has been exploited, with precious metals comprising almost half the value of the total known mineral reserves.

The world's largest and most populous Spanish-speaking nation, Mexico has a faster-growing population than any other big country: between 1960 and 1980 it doubled, growing at an unprecedented 3.5% a year. It is thus an astonishingly young society; the average Mexican is a 17-year-old, and 75% of the people are under 30.

The combination of a stable and very high birth rate (now about 27 per thousand) and a declining and now low death rate (about five per thousand) is the main cause of this population explosion. Mexico City (population 1 million in 1930, 8.7 million in 1970, 15.0 million in 1990) is already the most populous in the Americas and estimated to be the world's largest by 2000, overtaking both Tokyo and São Paulo.

## HISTORY AND POLITICS

While the century after independence in 1821 was characterized by political chaos, climaxing in the violent revolution of 1910–21, the post-revolutionary period was steady by Latin American standards, with the PRI in power for more than six decades from 1929 and instituting crucial land reforms in the 1930s. The economy has been dominated by this regime

### PRE-COLUMBIAN CIVILIZATIONS

The pre-Columbian civilizations of Central America flourished for centuries before the Spanish conquest and this heritage plays a strong role in fostering Mexican national identity today.

The Olmecs, the classical cultures of Teotihuacan, the Zapotecs and the Toltecs all left remarkable architectural monuments in the Mexican landscape, but the two outstanding cultures were those of the Maya and the Aztecs. The Maya civilization was the most brilliant, flourishing from the 3rd to the 10th centuries in an area extending from the Yucatan peninsula to Honduras. The Maya were mathematically advanced and had a sophisticated calendar.

The Aztec empire was at its height when Mexico succumbed to the Spanish *conquistadores* in 1519. Originally an insignificantly nomadic tribe, the Aztecs invaded the settled lands of central Mexico in the 13th century and founded their island-city of Tenochtitlán in Lake Texcoco in 1325. During the 15th century they conquered neighbouring states and drew tribute from an empire which extended from the Pacific to the Gulf of Mexico and into northern Central America.

Many of the great pre-Columbian centres survive as archaeological sites today. The stepped pyramid, the rectangular courtyard and the symbolic ornamental masonry are particularly characteristic of the architecture.

since oil was nationalized in 1938, enjoying huge growth in the 1970s, when living standards rose considerably, but running into massive debt crises in the 1980s.

Mexico has since pursued the idea of a trading area with Canada and the US, but rural-urban migration and high unemployment remain the biggest domestic problems. Above all, there is the emigration across the world's busiest border: hundreds of thousands of Mexicans cross into the USA each year, many of them staying as illegal immigrants. In June 1993 Mexico joined the OECD, the first new member for some 20 years, and negotiated an economic alliance called NAFTA (North

American Free Trade Agreement) with the United States and Canada, which took effect on 1 January 1994. [*Map page 30*] ■

**AREA** 1,958,200 sq km [756,061 sq mls]
**POPULATION** 91,858,000
**CAPITAL (POPULATION)** Mexico City (15,048,000)
**GOVERNMENT** Federal republic
**ETHNIC GROUPS** Mestizo 60%, Amerindian 30%, European 9%
**LANGUAGES** Spanish (official)
**RELIGIONS** Christianity (Roman Catholic 90%, Protestant 5%)
**CURRENCY** Peso = 100 centavos

# MICRONESIA

Comprising the bulk of the Carolines, the Federation – despite a land area of just 705 sq km [272 sq mls] – stretches across more than 3,200 km [2,000 mls] of Pacific, with the Equator as the southern boundary. The 607 islands divide into four groups and range from mountains to low atolls. Over half the land area is contributed by the main island, Pohnpei, on which Palikir is situated.

The cultures of the 'FSM', both Micronesian and Polynesian, are diverse, and four main languages are spoken in line with the four states of Yap, Truk, Pohnpei and Kosrae – though English is official.

## ECONOMY AND RESOURCES
While some areas are highly Americanized, the traditional way of life has survived in others, based on subsistence farming and fishing. Copra is the main crop and phosphate is also exported, while tuna-fishing brings in revenue from American, Japanese and Korean fleets. The FSM remains heavily dependent on US aid however.

## HISTORY AND POLITICS
The FSM became a sovereign state in 1986, when they entered into 'free association with

the USA' – they had been a US Trust Territory since 1947 – and were formally admitted as an independent member of the UN in September 1991. [*Map page 26*] ■

**AREA** 705 sq km [272 sq mls]
**POPULATION** 121,000
**CAPITAL (POPULATION)** Palikir (Pohnpei Island = 33,000)
**GOVERNMENT** Federal republic
**ETHNIC GROUPS** Micronesian, Polynesian
**LANGUAGES** English, local languages
**RELIGIONS** Christianity
**CURRENCY** US currency

# MOLDOVA

The Republic of Moldova, or Moldavia as it is also called, is a small country sandwiched between Ukraine and Romania. It was formerly one of the 15 republics that made up the Soviet Union. Much of the land is hilly and the highest areas are near the centre of the country, where the highest point, 429 m [1,407 ft] above sea level, is situated. A large plain covers southern Moldova. The main river is the Dniester (Dnestr or Nistru), which flows through the eastern part of the country.

Moldova has warm summers and fairly cold winters, when temperatures dip below freezing point. Forests of hornbeam, oak and other trees grow in the north and centre of the country, and in the drier south the land was originally grassy steppe, though most of this region is now used for farming. Rich pasture lies along the rivers.

## ECONOMY AND RESOURCES
Though barred from the Black Sea by an arm of the Ukraine, Moldova is well off. Fertile lands and a tolerant climate provide vines, tobacco and honey as well as more conventional produce, while light industry – based mainly on food processing and household appliances – is expanding. Moldova has no major natural resources and imports materials

and fuels for its industries. Exports include food, wine, tobacco, textiles and footwear.

## HISTORY AND POLITICS
In the 14th century, the Moldovans formed a state called Moldavia, which included parts of Romania and Bessarabia. The Ottoman Turks took the area in the 16th century, but in 1812 Russia took over Bessarabia. In 1861, Moldavia and Walachia united to form Romania. Russia retook southern Bessarabia in 1878.

After World War I (1914–18), all of Bessarabia was returned to Romania, but the Soviet Union did not recognize this act. From 1944, the Moldovan Soviet Socialist Republic was part of the Soviet Union. In 1989, the Moldovans asserted their independence by making Romanian the official language and, at the end of 1991, when the Soviet Union broke up, Moldova became an independent country. In 1992, however, fighting occurred between Moldovans and Russians in Trans-Dniester, the land east of the River Dniester .

Moldova held its first multiparty elections in 1994. The people also rejected a proposal to unite with Romania. [*Map page 17*] ■

AREA 33,700 sq km [13,010 sq mls]
POPULATION 4,420,000
CAPITAL (POPULATION) Chişinau (or Kishinev, 667,000)
GOVERNMENT Multiparty republic
ETHNIC GROUPS Moldovan 65%, Ukrainian 14%, Russian 13%, Gagauzi 4%, Jewish 2%, Bulgarian
LANGUAGES Moldovan (Romanian) – official
RELIGIONS Christianity (Eastern Orthodox)
CURRENCY Leu = 100 bani

increased in size by 20% since its land reclamation programme began in 1958. Monaco falls into four districts: vacation-oriented Monte Carlo; the old town of Monaco-Ville, with the royal palace and cathedral; the shops, banks and smart houses of La Condamine; and the light industries and marinas of Fontvieille.

A densely populated city-state, Monaco derives its considerable income almost entirely from services: banking, finance, and above all tourism; this is based not just on its climate but also on the famous casino. Monégasques are not allowed to gamble there, but there is ample compensation in paying no state taxes.

Monaco has been ruled by the Grimaldi dynasty since 1297, though in 1815 (with the Treaty of Vienna) it came under the protection of the kingdom of Sardinia; the greater part, including Menton, was annexed by France in 1848 and the remainder came under its protection in 1861 – a situation that essentially survives today within a customs union. The present monarch, Prince Rainer III (ascended 1949), drew up a new liberalizing constitution in 1962. [*Map page 11*] ■

AREA 1.5 sq km [0.6 sq mls]
POPULATION 31,000
CAPITAL (POPULATION) Monaco (31,000)
GOVERNMENT Constitutional monarchy under French protection
ETHNIC GROUPS French 47%, Monégasque 16%, Italian 16%
LANGUAGES French, Monégasque
RELIGIONS Christianity (mainly Roman Catholic)
CURRENCY French currency

# MONACO

The world's smallest nation outside Rome, and by far its most crowded, the tiny principality of Monaco – comprising a rocky peninsula and a narrow stretch of coast – has

# MONGOLIA

Worthy of its harsh, isolated reputation, Mongolia is the world's largest landlocked country and the most sparsely populated. Despite its traditional nomads, more than half the population live in towns, a quarter of them in Ulan Bator, a modern city built in the postwar Soviet mould. Geographically Mongolia divides into two contrasting regions, north and south of a line joining the mountains of the Altai, Hangayn and Hentiyn ranges.

In the north, pastures support herds of cattle and wheat is grown, especially where black earth soils occur. In the far north-west, boreal forests blanket the slopes. The southern half of the country has a strong continental climate with meagre, variable rainfall. In these semi-desert steppelands, salt lakes occupy shallow depressions, poor scrub eventually giving way to the arid wastes of the Gobi Desert.

### ECONOMY AND RESOURCES
Mongolia is a land of nomadic pastoralists – less than 1% of the land is cultivated – and huge herds of sheep, goats, yaks, camels and horses form the mainstay of the traditional economy. Herdsmen's families inhabit *ghers* (*yurts*), circular tents covered in felt, and subsist on a diet of milk, cheese and mutton.

Textiles and food processing were developed, with aid from the USSR and COMECON, and mineral deposits such as flourspar, copper, molybdenum and coking coal were exploited. In the late 1980s minerals overtook the agricultural sector as the country's main source of income.

### HISTORY AND POLITICS
Outer Mongolia broke away from China following the collapse of the Ch'ing dynasty in 1911, but full independence was not gained until 1921 – with Soviet support in what was the world's second Socialist revolution. In 1924 a Communist People's Republic was proclaimed and the country fell increasingly under Soviet influence.

In recent years, Mongolia has followed the path of other less remote Soviet satellites, reducing the presence of Soviet troops (1987–9), introducing pluralism (the country's first multiparty elections were held in 1990), launching into privatization and a free-market economy in 1991, and early in 1992 adopting a new constitution eschewing Communism and enshrining democracy. In June 1993, Mongolians voted in their first direct presidential election, electing Pun Salmaagiyn

Ochirbat as president. The pace of change was frantic after seven decades of authoritarian rule – Mongolia still owes Moscow $15 billion – and like the newly independent republics of the former Soviet empire, the Mongolians will not find the transition easy. [*Map page 21*] ■

| | |
|---|---|
| **AREA** | 1,566,500 sq km [604,826 sq mls] |
| **POPULATION** | 2,363,000 |
| **CAPITAL (POPULATION)** | Ulan Bator (575,000) |
| **GOVERNMENT** | Multiparty republic |
| **ETHNIC GROUPS** | Khalkha Mongol 79%, Kazakh 6% |
| **LANGUAGES** | Khalkha Mongolian (official) |
| **RELIGIONS** | Lamaistic Buddhism was once the main religion; reliable recent information is unavailable |
| **CURRENCY** | Tugrik = 100 möngös |

# MONTSERRAT

The Emerald Isle, as it is also known, lies 43 km [26.7 mls] south-west of Antigua. Although tourism is the mainstay of the island's economy (25% of national income), it is well supported by exports of electronic equipment, Sea Island cotton, fruit and vegetables; unusually for the Caribbean, Montserrat is almost self-sufficient in food. Discovered by Columbus in 1493 and colonized from 1632 by Britain, which brought in Irish settlers, Montserrat (though still a UK dependent territory) has been self-governing since 1960 ■

| | |
|---|---|
| **AREA** | 102 sq km [39 sq mls] |
| **POPULATION** | 11,000 |
| **CAPITAL (POPULATION)** | Plymouth (3,500) |
| **GOVERNMENT** | Dependent territory of the UK |
| **ETHNIC GROUPS** | Black, European |
| **LANGUAGES** | English |
| **RELIGIONS** | Christianity |
| **CURRENCY** | East Caribbean dollar = 100 cents |

# MOROCCO

More than a third of Morocco is mountainous. The High (*Haut*) Atlas contains the highest peak, Djebel Toubkal, at 4,165 m [13,665 ft]. Other ranges include the Anti Atlas in the south, the Middle (*Moyen*) Atlas, and the Rif Atlas (*Er Rif*) in the far north. Between the Atlas Mountains and the narrow western coastal plain lies a broad plateau. There are fertile plains in the west and south-west, while in the south-east the country extends into the Sahara Desert. The Sahara region is barren, but cedars, firs and junipers swathe the mountain slopes.

The Atlantic coast of Morocco is cooled by the Canaries Current. Inland, summers are hot and dry, and winters are mild. In winter, between October and April, south-westerlies from the Atlantic bring moderate rainfall, and snow often falls on the High Atlas Mountains.

## ECONOMY AND RESOURCES

Since independence a large proportion of the once-important European and Jewish communities have departed. To the difficulties accompanying reunification were added the burdens of a fast-growing population – nearly half the people are under 15 years old – high unemployment and a lack of trained personnel and capital. Yet Morocco has considerable potential for economic development: the country possesses large cultivable areas, abundant water supplies for irrigation and hydro-electric power, and diverse mineral resources including deposits of iron ore, lead and zinc.

Two principal ways of life exist in the mountains – peasant cultivation and semi-nomadic pastoralism. In contrast to these, modern economic development is found in the Atlantic plains and plateaux. The major irrigation schemes created during the colonial period are situated here, resulting in the intensive agricultural production of citrus fruits, grapes, vegetables, wheat and barley. More than half of the population is involved in agriculture.

Phosphates, of which Morocco is the world's leading exporter and third largest producer, are mined around Khouribga as well as in Western Sahara. These are the vital raw material for fertilizers. But the country's modern industry is concentrated in the Atlantic ports, particularly in Casablanca, which is the largest city, chief port and the major manufacturing centre.

The biggest growth industry, however, is tourism, based on the Atlantic beaches, the Atlas Mountains and the rich, international history of cities like Casablanca, Tangier, Agadir, Marrakech, Rabat and Fès (Fez), famed not only for its hat but also as the home of the University of Kairaouin – founded in 859 and the oldest educational institution in the world. Morocco is Africa's biggest tourist destination, attracting more than 3.2 million visitors in 1991.

## HISTORY AND POLITICS

The name Morocco is derived from the Arabic *Maghreb-el-Aksa* ('the farthest west'). Over the centuries the country's high mountains have acted as a barrier to penetration, so that Morocco has been much less affected by outside influences than Algeria and Tunisia. Morocco was the last North African territory to succumb to European colonialism; not until 1912 did the Sultan of Morocco accept the French protectorate, in a settlement that gave Spain control of the Rif Mountains and several enclaves along the coast (of which Ceuta and Melilla remain under Spanish administration).

In 1956 France and Spain gave up their protectorate as Morocco became independent, and in 1958 the international zone of Tangier was incorporated in a unified Morocco, which became an independent kingdom. Ruled since 1961 by the authoritarian and nationalistic regime of King Hassan II, Morocco is today one of only three kingdoms left on the continent of Africa, though the king's grip showed signs of slipping during the unsettled 1980s. He has pressed Morocco's claims for Western Sahara, but the cost of the struggle to contain the Saharan nationalist guerrillas has drained the country's resources.

**Western Sahara** is a former Spanish possession (and the province of Spanish Sahara from

1960) occupying the desert lands between Mauritania and the Atlantic coast; with an area of 266,000 sq km [102,700 sq mls] it is more than half the size of Morocco. Most of the indigenous population are Sahrawis, a mixture of Berber and Arab, almost all of whom are Muslims. The capital is El Aaiún, which has a population of 97,000.

Rich in phosphates – it has the world's largest known deposits of phosphate rock – the country has since the mid-1970s been the subject of considerable conflict, with the Rabat government claiming the northern two-thirds as historically part of 'Greater Morocco'. While Morocco has invested heavily in the two-thirds or so of Western Sahara it controls, the rich earnings from the phosphate exports could finance more economic, social and educational programmes. In 1991, more than 170,000 Sahrawi refugees were living in camps around Tindouf, in western Algeria.

A cease-fire was agreed in 1991 between the Rabat government and the Sahrawi liberation movement, POLISARIO (the Popular Front for the Liberation of Saharan Territories), who are still in dispute over part of Western Sahara. In the early 1990s the peace, overseen by the United Nations, remained fragile. [*Map page 32*] ■

AREA 446,550 sq km [172,413 sq mls]
POPULATION 26,448,000
CAPITAL (POPULATION) Rabat (893,000)
GOVERNMENT Constitutional monarchy
ETHNIC GROUPS Arab 70%, Berber 30%
LANGUAGES Arabic (official)
RELIGIONS Islam 99%, Christianity 1%
CURRENCY Moroccan dirham = 100 cents

# MOZAMBIQUE

The Republic of Mozambique borders the Indian Ocean in south-eastern Africa. The coastal plains are narrow in the north but broaden in the south, making up nearly half of the country. Inland lie plateaux and hills,

which make up another two-fifths of Mozambique, with highlands along the borders with Zimbabwe, Zambia, Malawi and Tanzania. The coast is fringed by sand dunes and swamps, with coral reefs offshore. The only natural harbour is at the capital, Maputo, in the far south.

Mozambique has a tropical climate, though Maputo lies just outside the tropics. Due to the warm, southwards-flowing Mozambique (Agulhas) Current, Maputo has hot and humid summers, though winters are mild and fairly dry. Inland, the temperatures and the humidity are a little lower.

Whilst palm trees are common on the coast, inland patches of rainforest contain trees such as ebony and ironwood. On the whole however, savanna is the most widespread vegetation type.

## ECONOMY AND RESOURCES
Only the inner borderlands are high; because of this and its remoteness from Portugal, Mozambique attracted few European settlers. Agriculture is still based around subsistence crops, such as maize and groundnuts, but in the northern foothills farmers also grow cotton and cashew for export. On the alluvial flats of Mozambique's coastal plains are plantations of coconut, sisal and sugar. There is some light industry based mainly in Beira and Maputo. At the limit of navigation on the River Zambezi is Africa's biggest dam, Cabora Bassa, whose power goes largely to South Africa. Large deposits of coal, copper, bauxite and offshore gas have yet to be exploited.

Mozambique forms a transit route for much of the overseas trade of Swaziland, Zimbabwe and Zambia, involving mainly the ports of Maputo, Beira and Nacala-Velha, just north of the town of Moçambique. Rail, port and handling services provide employment and substantial revenues.

## HISTORY AND POLITICS
Like other former ex-Portuguese African countries, Mozambique arose from the search for a route round Africa to the riches of Asia; Vasco da Gama and his successors established forts at Beira (Sofala), Quelimane and Moçambique Island. Dutch conquest of Portuguese Asia in the 17th century, and

subsequent concentration by the Portuguese on the slave trade from West Africa to the Americas, resulted in decay of Mozambique settlements. However, being so little affected by the slave trade, and acting as a refuge in wars, Mozambique was never depopulated to the extent of Angola, and still maintains a higher population on a smaller area.

When the Portuguese rulers and settlers abruptly abandoned Mozambique in 1975 at independence, they left behind a country totally unprepared for organizing itself – the literacy rate, for example, was less than 1%. The Marxist-Leninist government of Samora Machel's FRELIMO movement (Front for the Liberation of Mozambique), which had been fighting the colonial regime for more than a decade, tried to implement ambitious social policies, but erratic administration, along with a series of natural disasters, reduced the economy to ruins by the mid-1980s.

From the 1970s progress was also severely hampered by the widespread activities of the Mozambique National Resistance (MNR, or RENAMO), backed first by Rhodesia and later by South Africa. RENAMO soon controlled huge areas of the countryside – convoys could only cross the 'Tete Corridor' escorted by Zimbabwean and Malawian forces – forcing more than a million refugees to flee, the vast majority of them going to poor Malawi; by 1988 almost half of all Mozambique's population was reliant on external aid.

Well before Machel was mysteriously killed in a plane crash inside South Africa in 1986, his government had been opening up the country to Western investment and influence – a policy continued by his successor, President Joaquim Chissano. In 1989 FRELIMO formally abandoned its Marxist ideology, and the following year agreed to end one-party rule and hold talks with the rebels. Despite South Africa's withdrawal of official assistance, the talks dragged on without a permanent cease-fire and hostilities continued to dog the country. Relief agencies estimated in 1991 that up to 3 million people had been displaced by the war – and that as many again faced starvation. A peace agreement between FRELIMO and RENAMO was finally reached and a cease-fire took effect in October 1992. The demobilization of government and RENAMO forces took place in 1994 and UN troops were stationed in the country. Multiparty elections were held in 1994. [*Map page 33*] ■

---

**AREA** 801,590 sq km [309,494 sq mls]
**POPULATION** 15,527,000
**CAPITAL (POPULATION)** Maputo (1,070,000)
**GOVERNMENT** Multiparty republic
**ETHNIC GROUPS** Makua 47%, Tsonga 23%, Malawi 12%, Shona 11%, Yao 4%, Swahili 1%, Makonde 1%
**LANGUAGES** Portuguese (official)
**RELIGIONS** Traditional beliefs 48%, Christianity (Roman Catholic 31%, other 9%), Islam 13%
**CURRENCY** Metical = 100 centavos

---

# NAMIBIA

---

Namibia is a country of enormous physical and social diversity. Fringing the southern Atlantic coastline is the arid Namib Desert, virtually uninhabited, separated by a major escarpment from a north-south spine of mountains which culminate in the Khomas Highlands near Windhoek. This rugged spine, built of thick schists and quartzites, rises to 2,483 m [8,150 ft] in the peak of Moltkeblik. To the east, the country occupies the fringes of the Kalahari Desert.

## ECONOMY AND RESOURCES
Though 60% of the population is engaged in agriculture, and offshore the Benguela Current feeds some of the Atlantic's richest fishing grounds, over 60% of Namibia's income comes from exports of minerals – notably uranium (3% of the world total) and diamonds (in 1993 the world's seventh largest producer). There are also large gasfields and good prospects for oil.

## HISTORY AND POLITICS
Apart from the British enclave of Walvis Bay, Namibia was (as South West Africa) a German protectorate from 1884 before being

occupied by the Union of South Africa at the request of the Allied powers in 1915. Granted a League of Nations mandate in 1920, South Africa refused to place the territory under UN trusteeship after World War II, and in 1966 the mandate was cancelled. However, South Africa continued to exploit Namibia, even though in 1971 the International Court of Justice ruled that its occupation of the country was illegal; the main nationalist movement, SWAPO, began a guerrilla campaign supported by Cuba and Angola, but it was not until March 1990, following increasing international pressure, that the country eventually won its independence and joined the Commonwealth.

The status of Walvis Bay, the crucial deep-water port and military base, was in doubt at independence, but on 28 February 1994 South Africa renounced all claims and it was returned to Namibia. [*Map page 33*] ■

**AREA** 825,414 sq km [318,694 sq mls]
**POPULATION** 1,500,000
**CAPITAL (POPULATION)** Windhoek (115,000)
**GOVERNMENT** Multiparty republic
**ETHNIC GROUPS** Ovambo 50%, Kavango 9%, Herero 7%, Damara 7%, White 6%, Nama 5%
**LANGUAGES** English (official)
**RELIGIONS** Christianity 90% (Lutheran 51%)
**CURRENCY** Namibian dollar = 100 cents

# NAURU

$A$ low-lying coral atoll of just 21 sq km [8 sq mls] located halfway between Australia and Hawaii, 40 km [25 mls] south of the Equator, Nauru is the world's smallest republic. The climate is hot and wet, though the rains can fail.

## ECONOMY AND RESOURCES
A plateau rising to over 60 m [200 ft], surrounded by a belt of fertile, cultivated land, has provided the island with rich deposits of high-grade phosphate rock, exported to the

Pacific Rim countries for fertilizer. The industry, nationalized in 1970, accounts for over 98% of exports, and though Nauru is only just inside the world's top 20 producers this is enough to furnish the population with an average national income of US$20,000 – a similar figure to Canada or Denmark – giving them exemption from taxes and free education and welfare. The 7,000 native people – of mixed Micronesian and Polynesian origin, speaking a hybrid Nauruan language and predominantly Christian (mainly Protestant) – are supplemented by more than 3,000 migrant workers from less endowed Pacific islands.

Nauru's economic future is, nevertheless, uncertain, since the phosphates are likely to be exhausted by the end of the century. The government is planning to derive new revenues from shipping and air services, as well as developing the island as a Pacific tax haven.

## HISTORY AND POLITICS
Discovered by Britain in 1798, the island was under the control of Germany (1888), Australia (1914), Japan (1942) and Australia again (UN trusteeship from 1946) before it gained independence in 1968 ■

**AREA** 21 sq km [8 sq mls]
**POPULATION** 11,000
**CAPITAL (POPULATION)** Yaren District (559)
**GOVERNMENT** Democratic republic
**ETHNIC GROUPS** Nauruan 58%, other Pacific groups 26%
**LANGUAGES** Nauruan, English
**RELIGIONS** Christianity
**CURRENCY** Australian currency

# NEPAL

$O$ ver three-quarters of Nepal lies in a mountain heartland located between the towering Himalayas, the subject of an inconclusive boundary negotiation with China in 1961, and the far lower Siwalik Range overlooking the Ganges plain. Its innumerable valleys are home to a mosaic of peoples, of Indo-European and Tibetan stock, with a wide range of cultures and religions, and exercising fierce clan loyalties. This heartland, some 800 km [500 mls] from west to east, is divided between the basins of three main rivers — the Ghaghara, Gandak and Kosi. Between the last two, on a smaller river flanked by lake deposits, stands Katmandu, the royal and parliamentary capital, surrounded by emerald ricefields and orchards. The provincial centre of Pokhara is in a similar valley tributary to the Gandak, north of Nuwakot.

Nepal's most famous assets are the mountains, now an increasing tourist attraction bringing vital revenue to the country. Everest (8,848 m [29,029 ft]) and Kanchenjunga (8,598 m [28,208 ft]) are the tallest peaks of a magnificent range, giving a backdrop that dominates every vista in Nepal.

## ECONOMY AND RESOURCES

South of the Siwalik Range, the formerly swampy and malarious *terai*, or hillfoot plain, is now an economic mainstay, with new farming settlements growing rice, wheat, maize, jute and sugar. Development is encouraged by the *terai* section of the Asian Highway and new roads to India and Tibet.

The authorities now hope for more than increased tourism. Today's plan is for the Himalayas to be tapped for their colossal hydroelectric potential, to supply the factories of industrial India; Nepal's goal is to become the powerhouse of the region. If the scheme envisaged by the government and the World Bank proceeds, the first stage would be under way by the mid-1990s at Chisapani Gorge. Once completed, the 267 m [878 ft] dam would house the second-largest HEP plant in the world, generating more than the total of Britain's nuclear stations combined. There would be environmental costs, including the displacement of 70,000 people, but the result would be valuable and renewable 'clean' power.

Financing such schemes – at $6 billion Chisapani alone is nearly twice the total gross national product – is a huge problem for a country which ranks alongside Laos as the poorest in Asia. With Chinese Tibet to the north and India to the south, the nation is already heavily reliant on Indian trade and co-operation – a fact emphasized when border restrictions operated in the late 1980s. Devoid of coast, independent trade links and mineral resources, Nepal has remained an undeveloped rural country, with more than 90% of the adult population (only one in four of whom can read) working as subsistence farmers. In addition, indiscriminate farming techniques have led to deforestation – in turn causing the erosion of precious soils.

## HISTORY AND POLITICS

While tourism is now encouraged, it was only in 1951 that Nepal was opened up to foreigners. Before that it had been a patchwork of feudal valley kingdoms, and though these were conquered by the Gurkhas in the 18th century – forming the present country – local leaders always displayed more allegiance to their clans than to the state. From the mid-19th century these families (notably the powerful Rana) reduced the power of the central king, but in 1951 the monarchy was re-established. A brief period of democracy ended with the return of autocratic royal rule in 1960 under King Mahendra, but after mass demonstrations and riots his son, Birendra, despite attempts at stalling, was forced to concede a new constitution incorporating pluralism and basic human rights in 1990 and the hierarchical system of *panchayats* (rubber-stamping local councils) was over. In May 1991 the first democratic elections for 32 years took place with 10 million voters, and were won by the left-of-centre Nepali Congress Party. Though the birthplace of Buddha (Prince Siddhartha Gautama, *c.* 563 BC), Nepal remains a predominantly Hindu country. [*Map page 23*] ■

AREA 140,800 sq km [54,363 sq mls]
POPULATION 21,360,000
CAPITAL (POPULATION) Katmandu (419,073)
GOVERNMENT Constitutional monarchy
ETHNIC GROUPS Nepalese 58%, Bihari 19%, Tharu 4%, Tamang 4%, Newar 3%
LANGUAGES Nepali
RELIGIONS Hinduism 90%, Buddhism 5%, Islam 3%
CURRENCY Nepalese rupee = 100 paisa

# NETHERLANDS

Often, and inaccurately, called Holland – this refers only to the two north-western provinces – the Netherlands is the most crowded country of any size in Europe. The daunting figures for density are only an average however: the east and south are relatively sparsely populated, while the figure for the province of Zuid-Holland is 1,080 people per sq km [2,800 per sq ml].

The greatest concentration of population is in the towns and cities of Randstad Holland, a horseshoe of urban areas 50 km [31 mls] in diameter, with Dordecht at the centre of the loop. This area, dominant in the Dutch economy, includes most of the major cities, including (clockwise) Hilversum, Utrecht, Dordecht, Rotterdam, The Hague (home of the International Court of Justice), Leiden, Haarlem and Amsterdam, the last still the centre of Dutch cultural life despite being overtaken in size by Rotterdam. Nearly all of this crucial area, rich in history and culture, lies well below sea level.

To anyone travelling through the Netherlands, the density of people is obvious, for the fields are smaller, the villages more tightly concentrated with small neat houses, and the land is cultivated more intensively. Over much of the countryside rivers are at a higher level than the surrounding farmland, with villages sited above the flood level.

Since 1900 almost 3,000 sq km [1,160 sq mls] have been added to the nation's territory by reclaiming land from the sea. The largest and most famous project has been the reclamation of the Zuiderzee, begun in 1920. The major sea barrage of 32 km [21 mls] was completed in 1932, and by 1967 four large 'island' areas were finished, providing some 1,814 sq km [700 sq mls] of former seabed for both cultivation and for planned towns and villages. A controversial fifth area, Markerwaard, is under way, leaving the Ijsselmeer, a freshwater lake, the only remnant of the original inlet.

Without the protection of dykes and sand dunes along the coast, more than two-fifths of the Netherlands (the 'Low Countries') would be flooded. Constant pumping – formerly by windpumps (as most picturesque 'windmills' were) and steam pumps, but now by automated motor pumps – lifts surplus water from ditches to canals at a higher level, and from canals to the rivers, particularly the rivers Lek and Waal, which take the waters of the Rhine to the sea, and the Maas (Meuse in France and Belgium).

The dunes that line much of the coast are carefully guarded against erosion by planting marram grass and, where possible, trees. There are massive dykes to guard the farmland and towns, but inspite of sea defence systems, periodic flooding does affect parts of the country. In 1953 the exceptionally high tides at the end of January broke through coastal dykes and sand dunes, causing widespread devastation. In January 1995, catastrophic flooding once again affected low-lying areas following a period of heavy rainfall and around 250,000 people had to be evacuated.

## ECONOMY AND RESOURCES

The use of land in the Netherlands varies. In the west, near Haarlem, the concentration on bulb farming is marked in soils of clay mixed with sand. There, too, glasshouse cultivation, combined on many holdings with the growing of flowers and vegetables out-of-doors, is widespread. The Dutch grow and sell more than 3 billion flowers every year. Much of the produce is exported, some of it by air to London and other north European cities. Some soils are better suited to pastoral farming, with milk, cheese and butter production. Gouda has a famous cheese market, and the well-known round, red-coated Edam cheeses come from northern areas. In the areas above sea level, farming is varied, with a combination of cattle and crops, including fruit.

Industry and commerce provide support for the greater part of the Dutch population. Mineral resources include china clay, which is abundant and natural gas from the North Sea. The emphasis of modern industry is on oil, steel, electrical engineering and chemicals.

In the area south of Rotterdam a vast port and industrial area, Europoort, has been developed since 1958. Together with Rotter-

## THE DUTCH POLDERS

Polders are artificial farmlands reclaimed from water. The first were formed in Holland and Zeeland about a thousand years ago, when settlers on marshlands found that they could protect their land by building dykes of earth, brushwood (around which mud would accumulate) and stones. The effort was vast, but dry land was created and protected against floods from rivers and high tides. Sluices were made in the dykes to let out surplus water; marshes and peat bogs were gradually drained and the water pumped out to major rivers and canals by windpumps. These were largely replaced in the mid-19th century by steam-pumps.

Today some of the most profitable farmland in the Netherlands is polderland, much of it 6–7 m [about 20 ft] below sea level. Within some of the polders the farmland is divided into hundreds of strips separated by water channels and accessible only by boat. Modern polders, including those of the Zuiderzee, have large fields of great fertility. With modern technology the level of water in each polder can be controlled from central pumping stations. Many older settlements are on dykes, or patches of land known to lie above the highest flood levels. The Dutch engineers have, over the centuries, exported their expertise to many areas, most notably the Fens in eastern England.

dam's own facilities, the complex is the largest and busiest in the world. The Dutch are skilled at languages, to which a considerable part of the teaching time is given even in primary schools. This is essential to the country's prosperity, for now as in past centuries the Dutch control a main outlet for the commerce of Europe in the port of Rotterdam, with the Rhine Valley and a wider area as its hinterland. The main export markets are the EU partners – Germany, Belgium, the UK and France – while strong trade links with Indonesia recall the Dutch colonial age.

### HISTORY AND POLITICS
The country came into being as the United Provinces of Netherlands when it declared its independence from Spain in 1581. In the 17th century, the Dutch republic experienced a golden era of economic prosperity, naval pre-eminence, religious tolerance and artistic achievement. It succeeded in building an empire with colonies in the Americas, Africa and Asia. But it became part of the Napoleonic Empire and had to reassert its independence in 1813.

The constitution of 1814 instituted a hereditary constitutional monarchy which is still in place today. The country maintained its neutrality during World War I, but in 1940 was invaded by German forces. In 1949 the Netherlands abandoned its neutrality and joined NATO.

Since the end of World War II, it has been at the heart of European construction, as a founder member of Benelux, the ECSC and the EEC. The granting of independence to its former colonies has led to large-scale immigration to the Netherlands with all the attendant social and economic problems. The Dutch political system (based on proportional representation) encourages the existence of numerous political parties. [*Map page 12*] ∎

AREA 41,526 sq km [16,033 sq mls]
POPULATION 15,397,000
CAPITAL (POPULATION) Amsterdam (1,091,338)
GOVERNMENT Constitutional monarchy
ETHNIC GROUPS Netherlander 95%, Indonesian, Turkish, Moroccan, German
LANGUAGES Dutch (official)
RELIGIONS Christianity (Roman Catholic 34%, Dutch Reformed Church 17%, Calvinist 8%), Islam 3%
CURRENCY Guilder (florin) = 100 cents

# NETHERLANDS ANTIILLES

The Netherlands Antilles consists of two very different island groups – Curaçao and Bonaire, off the coast of Venezuela, and

Saba, St Eustatius and the southern part of St Maarten, at the northern end of the Leeward Islands, some 800 km [500 mls] away. Curaçao is the largest island, accounting for nearly 45% of the total of 993 sq km [383 sq mls] and 80% of the population.

The people – mainly mulatto, Catholic and Creole-speaking – are well off by Caribbean standards, enjoying the benefits of an economy buoyed by tourism, offshore banking and oil refining from Venezuela (mostly for export to the Netherlands), more than the traditional orange liqueur. The soil is generally too poor however, to permit large-scale agriculture.

With Aruba, the Netherlands Antilles formed part of the Dutch East Indies, in 1954 attaining internal self-government as constitutional equals with the Netherlands and Surinam. Curaçao is politically dominant in the federation ■

---

**AREA** 993 sq km [383 sq mls]
**POPULATION** 197,000
**CAPITAL (POPULATION)** Willemstad (50,000)
**GOVERNMENT** Self-governing Dutch territory
**ETHNIC GROUPS** Of African descent 85%, European
**LANGUAGES** Dutch, Papiamento (a dialect of Spanish, Portuguese, Dutch and English), English
**RELIGIONS** Christianity
**CURRENCY** Guilder = 100 cents

---

# NEW CALEDONIA

M ost southerly of the Melanesian countries, New Caledonia comprises the main island of Grande Terre and the dependencies of the Loyalty Islands (Iles Loyauté), Ile des Pins and the Bélep archipelago. The remaining islands (many of them coral atolls) are all small and uninhabited.

## ECONOMY AND RESOURCES
New Caledonia's economy is dominated by a single commodity, nickel, which accounts for

over 83% of export earnings. The world's largest producer in the 1960s, it has slipped to sixth place – though still with a healthy 5% of the total world share and with reserves estimated at more than a third of the known world total. Other exports are copra and coffee.

## HISTORY AND POLITICS
A French possession since 1853 and overseas territory from 1958, New Caledonia today has a fundamental split on the question of independence from Paris. The Kanaks, the indigenous Melanesian people (but numbering under half the total), on the whole support it; the less numerous French settlers (many of whom fled Algeria after it gained independence) are passionately against it. An agreement for increased autonomy – supposedly leading to independence – has helped to ease tension between the two camps, but the future of the former colony looks cloudy. Another independence referendum (one was held in 1987) has been promised for 1998. Much may depend on finance: France provides a third of the government budget, but separatists have purchased (from its French owner) the islands' largest nickel mine. [*Map page 3*] ■

---

**AREA** 19,000 sq km [7,334 sq mls]
**POPULATION** 178,000
**CAPITAL (POPULATION)** Nouméa (98,000)
**GOVERNMENT** French overseas territory
**ETHNIC GROUPS** Melanesian 43%, European 37%
**LANGUAGES** French, Melanesian and Polynesian dialects
**RELIGIONS** Christianity (Roman Catholic 60%, Protestant 30%)
**CURRENCY** CFP franc = 100 centimes

---

# NEW ZEALAND

G eologically part of the Circum-Pacific Mobile Belt of tectonic activity, New Zealand is mountainous and partly volcanic. Many of the highest mountains – the Southern for example – were thrust up from the seabed in the past 10 to 15 million years, representing only the latest in a long series of orogenies. Much of the North Island was formed by volcanic action even more recently, mainly in the past 1 to 4 million years. Minor earthquakes are common, and there are several areas of volcanic and geothermal activity, especially in the North Island.

Its youth makes New Zealand a rugged country with mountains always in sight and about 75% of the total land area above the 200 m [650 ft] contour. The North Island has many spectacular but low ranges with peaks of 1,200 to 1,500 m [4,000 to 5,000 ft], made up of folded sedimentary rocks that form good soils. The Coromandel Range and hilly Northland peninsula are softer and more worn, with few peaks over 800 m [12,600 ft].

Overlying these older rocks in the centre and north are massive spreads of lava, pumice and volcanic tuffs, formed during the past 1 to 3 million years. The great central plateau is dominated by three slumbering volcanoes – Ruapehu (2,797 m [9,176 ft], the North Island's highest peak), Ngauruhoe and Tongariro. Further north, extensive fields of lava and ash cones lie across the base of the Northland peninsula, forming a firm, rolling site for the suburbs of Auckland, New Zealand's largest city.

The far larger South Island is also mainly mountainous, with an alpine backbone extending obliquely from north-east to south-west. The highest peaks form a central massif, the Southern Alps, clustered around Mt Cook, at 3,764 m [12,349 ft] New Zealand's highest mountain. From this massif, which is permanently ice-capped, glaciers descend on either flank, and on the east the outwash fans of glacier-fed rivers form the Canterbury Plains – South Island's only extensive lowland. In the far south-west (Fjordland), the coast is indented by deep, steeply-walled sounds that wind far into the forested mountains.

## ECONOMY AND RESOURCES

From 1844, when the first Merinos were introduced from Australia, New Zealand became predominantly a land of sheep, the grassy lowlands (especially in the South Island) providing year-round forage. Huge flocks were

built up, mainly for wool and tallow production. From the lowlands they expanded into the hills – the 'high country' which was cleared of native bush and sown with European grasses for pasture. More than half the country is still covered with evergreen forest. The North Island proved more difficult to turn into productive farmland, only later proving its value for dairying.

New Zealand's early prosperity was finally established when the export of frozen mutton and lamb carcasses began in 1882. Soon a steady stream of chilled meat and dairy products – and later of fruit – was crossing the oceans to established markets in Britain, and the country is still the world's second biggest producer of lamb. Wheat and other cereals were also grown. High productivity was maintained by applications of fertilizers, mainly based on rock-phosphate mined on Nauru.

New Zealand is a prosperous country, with a high standard of living for a refreshingly harmonious multiracial population. Since 1907 a self-governing Dominion, it long relied on British markets for the export of agricultural produce, and has generally strong ties and affinities with Britain. Though agricultural products are still the main exports, the economy has diversified considerably since World War II, including fish, timber and wood pulp. Iron ores, coal and small amounts of gold are among the few valuable minerals, recently boosted by natural gas and petroleum. Geothermal and hydroelectric power are well developed, and timber and forest products are finding valuable overseas markets. Despite the country's isolation, a promising tourist industry is also developing, based on the scenic beauty, abundance of game animals, and relatively peaceful and unhurried way of life.

However, the idyll was showing signs of cracking from the 1970s, beginning when the UK joined the EEC and New Zealand's exports to Britain shrank from 70% to 10%. Along with a re-evaluation of its defence position, the country has had to rethink its previous 'safe' economic strategy – cutting subsidies to farmers, privatization, seeking new markets in Asia – and, like Australia and most fellow members of the OECD, find a way to survive the recession of the late 1980s and early 1990s.

### HISTORY AND POLITICS

New Zealand was discovered by Abel Tasman in 1642 and charted thoroughly by James Cook in 1769–70. Both explorers recorded the presence of Maoris – Polynesians who hunted and farmed from well-defended coastal settlements, who were themselves relatively recent arrivals on the islands. Sealing gangs and whalers were New Zealand's first European inhabitants, closely followed by missionaries and farmers from Britain and Australia. By the early 1830s about 2,000 Europeans had settled there.

In 1840 Britain took possession, in a treaty which gave rights and privileges of British subjects to the Maori people. The following decades saw the arrival of thousands of new settlers from Britain, and by mid-century there were over 30,000. Though their relationships with the Maoris (who at this stage outnumbered them two to one) were generally good, difficulties over land ownership led to warfare in the 1860s. Thereafter the Maori population declined while European numbers continued to increase.

New Zealand fought in World War I as an ally of Britain, and during World War II

## THE MAORIS

'Strong, raw-boned, well-made, active people, rather above than under the common size ... of a very dark brown colour, with black hair, thin black beards, and ... in general very good features.' So Captain James Cook described the Maoris he met in New Zealand in 1770. Of Polynesian stock, the Maoris settled (mainly in North Island) from about AD 800 to 1350. A warlike people, living in small fortified settlements, they cultivated kumaras (sweet potatoes) and other crops, hunted seals and moas (large flightless birds, now extinct) and gathered seafoods.

The Maoris befriended the early European settlers; readily accepting British sovereignty, Christianity and pacification, they rebelled only as more and more of their communal land was bought for the settlers' use. Given parliamentary representation from 1876, they eventually integrated fully. Now Maoris form about 9% of New Zealand's population, still living mostly in North Island. Though socially and politically equal in every way to whites, they are still over-represented in the poorer, unskilled sections of the population, separated more by poverty and lack of opportunity than by colour from the mainstream of national life.

forged close links with Australia and the USA. Although it sent troops to support the Americans in the Vietnam war, the country has since adopted a much more independent foreign policy. [*Map page 35*] ∎

**AREA** 270,990 sq km [104,629 sq mls]
**POPULATION** 3,531,000
**CAPITAL (POPULATION)** Wellington (326,000)
**GOVERNMENT** Constitutional monarchy
**ETHNIC GROUPS** New Zealand European 74%, New Zealand Maori 10%, Polynesian 4%
**LANGUAGES** English and Maori (both official)
**RELIGIONS** Christianity (Anglican 21%, Presbyterian 16%, Roman Catholic 15%, Methodist 4%)
**CURRENCY** New Zealand dollar = 100 cents

# NICARAGUA

L argest and least densely populated of the Central American countries, Nicaragua's eastern half is almost empty. With over 750 cm [300 in] of rain in some years, it is forested and rich in a tropical fauna including crocodiles, turtles, deer, pumas, jaguars and monkeys. Cut off from the populous west of Nicaragua, it was for two centuries the British protectorate of the Miskito Coast, with Bluefields (San Juan del Norte) as the largest settlement.

Inland, the plain gives way to mountain ranges broken by basins and fertile valleys. In the west and south they overlook a great depression which runs from the Gulf of Fonseca south-eastwards and contains lakes Managua and Nicaragua. Nicaragua (8,264 sq km [3,191 sq mls]) is the largest lake in Central America; though only 20 km [12.5 mls] from the Pacific, it drains to the Caribbean by the navigable San Juan River and formed an important route across the isthmus before the Panama Canal was built.

Forty volcanoes, many active, rise above the lakes; San Cristóbal (1,745 m [5,725 ft]) is the highest, still-smoking Momotombo the most spectacular. Earthquakes are common and the capital Managua was vitually destroyed in 1931 and 1972.

## ECONOMY AND RESOURCES
In the early 1990s, Nicaragua faced many problems in rebuilding its shattered economy. Agriculture is the main activity, employing nearly half of the people. Coffee, cotton, sugar and bananas are grown for export, while rice is the main food crop. The country has some copper, gold and silver, but mining is under-developed. Most manufacturing industries are based in and around Managua.

## HISTORY AND POLITICS
Christopher Columbus reached Nicaragua in 1502 and claimed the land for Spain, which ruled Nicaragua until 1821. In the mid-19th century, Nicaragua was ravaged by civil war, but by the early 20th century the United States had considerable influence in the country, and in 1912 US forces entered the country. From 1927 to 1933, rebels under General Augusto César Sandino tried to drive the US forces out of the country. In 1933, the US marines set up a Nicaraguan army, called the National Guard. Its leader, Anastasio Somoza Garcia, had Sandino murdered in 1934. From 1937, Somoza ruled Nicaragua as a dictator.

In the mid-1970s, many people began to protest against the Somoza dictatorship, and in 1979, after a 17-year campaign, the long domination of the corrupt Somoza family (who controlled 40% of the economy) was ended by a popular uprising led by the Sandinista National Liberation Front (named after General Sandino), which went on to win democratic power in 1985. Meanwhile, the US government, which opposed the Sandinista regime, claiming that it was a Communist dictatorship, trained and supplied Contra guerrillas from bases in Honduras and imposed a trade embargo, pushing Nicaragua into increasing dependence on Cuba and the former Soviet Union.

A cease-fire agreed in 1989 was followed the next year by electoral defeat for Daniel José Ortega Saavedra's Sandinistas at the hands of the US-backed coalition of Violeta Barrios de Chamorro. But while the two sides were forced into working uneasily together to try and put the country back on its feet with the benefit of conditional US aid, fighting frequently broke out between former Contra rebels and ex-Sandinistas, most notably away from the capital. Some progress towards peace and disarmament had been made by the summer of 1994. [*Map page 30*] ∎

**AREA** 130,000 sq km [50,193 sq mls]
**POPULATION** 4,275,000
**CAPITAL (POPULATION)** Managua (682,000)
**GOVERNMENT** Multiparty republic
**ETHNIC GROUPS** Mestizo 77%, White 10%, Black 9%, Amerindian 4%
**LANGUAGES** Spanish (official)
**RELIGIONS** Christianity (Roman Catholic 91%, others 9%)
**CURRENCY** Córdoba = 100 centavos

# NIGER

The title Niger, derived from the Tuareg word *n'eghirren* (meaning 'flowing water') is something of a misnomer for the country that bears the river's name. West Africa's great waterway runs through only the extreme south-west of what is, apart from its fertile southern strip, a desolate territory of hot, arid sandy and stony basins.

The monotony of the northern 60% of the country is broken by the jagged peaks of the Aïr Mountains, rising to 2,022 m [6,634 ft] from the desert plains; here rainfall is sometimes sufficient to permit the growth of thorny scrub. The southern part of the country includes the most fertile areas of the Niger basin around Lake Chad.

## ECONOMY AND RESOURCES

In the north, severe droughts since the 1970s have crippled the traditional lifestyle of the nomads in the area, grazing their camels, horses, cattle and goats, and whole clans killed as the Sahara slowly makes its way south.

The same period has seen the growth of uranium mining by the government in conjunction with the French Atomic Energy Commission, and this has now overtaken groundnuts as Niger's chief export, despite the drop in world demand during the 1980s. Tin and tungsten are also mined here, but reserves of other minerals, including iron ore, manganese and molybdenum, remain largely untouched. Over 95% of Niger's population however still derive their living from agriculture and trading.

The southern part of the country has also been affected by drought; but here desertification, linked to overgrazing, climbing temperatures as well as water shortage, is a wider problem. The crucial millet and sorghum crops – often grown by slash-and-burn techniques – have repeatedly failed, and migration to the already crowded market towns and neighbouring countries is widespread. The capital, Niamey, a mixture of tra-

## THE SAHARA DESERT

The world's biggest desert, the Sahara's 9,065,000 sq km [3,500,000 sq mls] stretch from the Atlantic to the Red Sea and amount to almost a third of the African continent. To the north, it is bordered by the Mediterranean; to the south, it merges with the Sahel, a zone of sparse vegetation and irregular rainfall. On average, the Sahara receives less than 100 mm [4 in] of rain annually, though a scattering of oases fed by underground water support small, sedentary communities and nomadic herdsmen alike; the region as a whole has around a million inhabitants. Daytime shade temperatures frequently reach 50°C [122°F]; at night, because heat quickly escapes through the cloudless skies, temperatures can fall below freezing point. Over 70% of the Sahara's area is covered with coarse gravel and rock, rising in its high central plateau to mountains of 3,000 m [10,000 ft] or more, mostly of volcanic origin. About 15% is made up of plains of shifting sand, including the Great Western Erg, a sand sea of more than 78,000 sq km [30,000 sq mls] in Algeria, where winds of 50 km/h [30 mph] or more regularly whip up sandstorms, dark walls 1.5 km [1 ml] high and up to 500 km [300 mls] wide.

The Sahara was not always a desert: as recently as 15,000 years ago, during the last Ice Age, even the Great Western Erg was green and fertile, well stocked with grazing animals and a paradise for the humans of the era, who left behind numerous cave paintings of successful hunts. At present, though, the Sahara is growing southwards at the expense of the marginal Sahel lands – an expansion caused by long-term drought exacerbated by overpopulation and overgrazing.

ditional African, European colonial and modern Third World, is the prime destination for migrants travelling in search of food and work.

South of Niamey is the impressive 'W' national park, shared with Burkina Faso and Benin. The wooded savanna landscape – offering protection to elephants, buffaloes, crocodiles, cheetahs, lions and antelopes –

is intended to attract growing numbers of tourists in the 1990s.

## HISTORY AND POLITICS

Nomadic Tuaregs settled in the Aïr Mountains about 1,000 years ago, and by the 15th century they had built up an empire based on Agadez. At around the same time, the Zerma-Songhai people founded the Songhai empire along the River Niger. The Songhai conquered the Tuaregs, but in the late 16th century Songhai was defeated by a Moroccan army.

Later on, the Hausa and then the Fulani set up kingdoms in the area. France became involved in Niger in the late 19th century and ruled Niger as part of French West Africa from 1900–58. The country became an autonomous republic in 1958, and in 1960 it became fully independent.

Food shortages and the destruction of the traditional nomadic lifestyle of some of Niger's people have caused political instability. In 1974, a group of army officers, led by Lt.-Col. Seyni Kountché, overthrew the country's first president, Hamani Diori, and seized control of the government. Civilian rule was restored in 1989 after Kountché's death. In 1992, a referendum was held, in which 89% of the people voted for a new, multiparty constitution. Elections were held in 1993. [Map page 32] ■

AREA 1,267,000 sq km [489,189 sq mls]
POPULATION 8,846,000
CAPITAL (POPULATION) Niamey (398,000)
GOVERNMENT Multiparty republic
ETHNIC GROUPS Hausa 53%, Djerma-Songhai 21%, Tuareg 11%, Fulani (or Peul) 10%
LANGUAGES French (official)
RELIGIONS Islam 98%
CURRENCY CFA franc = 100 centimes

# NIGERIA

Four times the size of the United Kingdom, whose influence dates from 1861, Nigeria is tropical Africa's most important country.

The landscape varies from the savanna of the north – much of it under threat of desertification – through mountains and tropical rainforests to the coastal lands on the Gulf of Guinea. The coast has huge expanses of fine sandy beaches, interspersed with mangrove swamps where rivers join the ocean. Much of the country's coast is formed by the Niger delta, behind which lie thousands of creeks and lagoons.

## ECONOMY AND RESOURCES

Before roads were constructed, the inland waterways provided crucial transport, and boats and canoes still carry both people and cargoes between towns and villages in the area. Here the heavy rains allow the production of yams, cassava, maize and vegetables, with rice grown on the patches of land beside rivers and on large stretches of irrigated land where streams do not flood in the wet seasons.

Farther north, in the forest belt, the hills rise towards the Jos Plateau – famous for its holiday resorts – and in the east towards the steep valleys and wooded slopes of the Cameroon Highlands. These areas produce Nigeria's important tree crops – cocoa, rubber, hardwoods and palm oil. North of the Jos Plateau, parkland gives way to grassland, but the savanna becomes increasingly dry and some areas are now little more than semi-arid scrub.

Northern Nigeria is reliant on one precarious wet season, while the south enjoys two. Poor-quality millet and sorghum are the staples, with cotton and groundnuts the main cash crops. Where desertification has not taken hold, livestock are still important – enjoying the absence of the tsetse fly that afflicts the area of moist vegetation in the south of the country.

Nigeria is unique in Africa south of the Sahara for the numerous pre-colonial towns of the south-west (such as Ibadan) and the north (such as Kano). Domestic trade between these and Nigeria's very varied regions was developed in pre-colonial days, and is now intense.

The country is in the top 15 producers of world oil, but there are many other resources (albeit dwarfed in exports by oil), including cocoa in the south-west, timber, rubber and palm oil in the south-centre and east, and cotton and groundnuts in the north.

## THE SAHEL

The Sahel is a wide band of scrub and savanna grassland stretching from Mauritania and northern Senegal in the west through parts of Mali, Burkina Faso, Benin and Niger to southern Chad in the east, and including much of northern Nigeria. To the north is the Sahara, the world's largest desert; to the south are the rainforests of tropical West and Central Africa. Though used mainly for pasture, the whole area has irregular and unpredictable rainfall and suffers frequently from drought and the resultant famine. Attention was first drawn to the desperate plight of the region by the Sahelian famine of 1973, when hundreds of thousands died.

Over the past 30 years, the Sahara has gradually encroached southwards in the world's most blatant example of 'desertification'. The causes are many and interwoven. As well as declining rainfall, there are the pressures of a growing population; herdsmen overgrazing the land with their cattle, sheep and goats; overcultivation by farmers; cutting of ground cover, mainly for fuelwood; and poor or faulty irrigation techniques, where limited water supplies are wasted and the land left too saline or alkaline to support crops.

Ironically, the problem was aggravated in the previous two decades, when above-average rainfall encouraged the expansion of settlement and the cultivation of cash crops into marginal land. Experts estimate that as much as two-thirds of the world's pasture and grazing lands are now in danger from desertification. Africa, and notably the Sahel, is the worst affected: in places the Sahara has advanced more than 350 km [200 mls] in just two decades. The process is containable – even reversible – if the land is allowed to recover and the soil rejuvenated through tree planting, terracing and proper irrigation under careful and consistent management with sufficient funds. But these conditions are rarely found: pressures of population, lack of finance and changing policies all mean that such techniques have not been applied anywhere in the Sahel on a substantial scale.

Nigeria's foreign exchange earnings from oil, the country's prime source of income, were halved in a year. Oil production had begun in the 1950s and risen steadily to a peak of 2.4 million barrels a day in the early 1980s. Foreign exchange earnings peaked in 1980 at $26 billion, but by the end of the decade this figure had shrunk to $9 billion. At the same time the foreign debt, constantly shuffled and rescheduled, had blossomed to some $36 billion, easily Africa's largest. In seven years the annual income of the average Nigerian has shrunk from $1,120 (among the top three on the continent) to a meagre $270, a figure below even that of some poor neighbours. In 1991 the World Bank officially reclassified Nigeria as a low-income rather than middle-income country.

In the early 1990s there were, nevertheless, signs of a recovery, with agriculture (50% of the population still rely on farming) and some areas of manufacturing growing quickly.

There are over 88 million Nigerians, making it by far the most populous African state; one in every six Africans is Nigerian. It is also the second most populated country of the Commonwealth, and eleventh in the world. Natural wealth and substantial armed forces give Nigeria a commanding position in Africa, and its oil and gas reserves are a focus of worldwide interest.

### HISTORY AND POLITICS

European contact dates back to the 15th century. A federation of 31 states, many of which are larger than most African states, Nigeria includes many tribal groups, the largest being the Yoruba of the south-west, the Ibo of the east, and the Hausa, Fulani and Kanuri of the north. The north is predominantly Muslim, and the Islamic influence is increasing in the south, where most people are pagan or Christian. With so many diversities, including those of religion and a developing social system, Nigeria suffers internal stresses and national unity is often strained.

Though blessed with many natural resources, Nigeria has had an uneasy path since independence in 1960 (becoming a full republic in 1963). Democratically elected governments have found it an impossible task to unify and stabilize an unruly jigsaw of more than 250 ethnic and linguistic groups, and civilian administrations have ruled for only ten years since the departure of the British.

An unwieldy tripartite federal structure first introduced in 1954 proved unable to contain rivalries after independence and in 1966 the first Prime Minister, Abubaka Tafawa Balewa, and many other leaders were assassinated in a military coup. A counter-coup brought General Yakubu Gowon to power, but a vicious civil war ensued from 1967 when the Eastern Region (Biafra), dominated by the Christian Ibo, attempted to secede from the union after the slaughter of thousands of their tribe in the north by Muslim Hausa – and wrangles over increasing oil revenues.

## DEMOCRACY IN AFRICA

The great flush of liberty that followed decolonization in the 1950s and 1960s did not bring the rewards of peace, prosperity and self-government that many early African nationalists had envisaged. Instead, within a few years, most of the newly-independent African nations had been transformed into corrupt and incompetent dictatorships, at best authoritarian one-party states, usually heavily reliant on Western or Soviet subsidies and often plagued by guerrilla fighting and banditry. Governments were changed, if at all, by means of a coup d'état.

In the late 1980s, however, new hope reached the world's poorest continent. Everywhere, it seemed, dictators were succumbing peacefully to popular demands for multiparty elections and many long-running civil wars were coming to an end. By the early 1990s, some form of democracy was in place in 80% of African nations.

But democracy has no easy answer to Africa's chronic problem: its poverty, and the continuing collapse in world prices for most African commodities. In some instances Western-style democracy may even prove to be impossible, as in Algeria, where in 1992 the military intervened to prevent power passing to elected Islamic fundamentalists, who had sworn to destroy the system that would have given them their victory.

Hundreds of thousands died (most from starvation) before Biafra admitted defeat early in 1971. The federation was gradually splintered from three to 21 full states (now 31) to try to prevent one area becoming dominant. Gowon was overthrown in 1975, but another attempt at civilian rule (1979-83) also ended in a military takeover. The latest coup, a bloodless affair in 1985, brought General Ibrahim Babangida to office, and he immediately faced the crucial problems of falling oil prices and mounting foreign debts. In 1989, Babangida promised to introduce civilian rule by 1992. Elections did take place in July 1992 though the two permitted parties were both created by the Armed Forces Ruling Council and genuine pluralism still seemed a long way off. However, presidential elections held in 1993 and declared invalid by the military government did lead to the resignation of Babangida. A transitional council is preparing a return to civilian rule. Whatever the regime, Nigeria's biggest worry could simply be numbers: on the trends of the 1980s the total population could be more than 300 million by the year 2025. [*Map page 32*] ■

**AREA** 923,770 sq km [356,668 sq mls]
**POPULATION** 88,515,000
**CAPITAL (POPULATION)** Abuja (federal capital, 306,000)
**GOVERNMENT** Federal republic
**ETHNIC GROUPS** Hausa 21%, Yoruba 21%, Ibo (or Igbo) 19%, Fulani 11%, Ibibio 6%
**LANGUAGES** English (official)
**RELIGIONS** Christianity (Protestant 26%, Roman Catholic 12%, others 11%), Islam 45%
**CURRENCY** Naira = 100 kobo

# NORTHERN MARIANAS

The Northern Mariana Islands comprise all 17 Mariana Islands except Guam, the most southerly, forming a mountainous and volcanic chain extending northwards with a total land area of 477 sq km [184 sq mls].

The population of 47,000 is concentrated on three of the six inhabited islands, with Saipan and the capital town of Susupe accounting for 19,000. Tourism appears to be the key to the future: the number of foreign visitors rose from 130,000 in 1984 to over 435,400 in 1990.

Part of the US Trust Territory of the Pacific from 1947, its people voted in a 1975 UN plebiscite for Commonwealth status in union with the USA. Washington approved the change in 1976, granting US citizenship, and internal self-government followed in 1978. [*Map page 26*] ■

**AREA** 477 sq km [184 sq mls]
**POPULATION** 47,000
**CAPITAL (POPULATION)** Saipan (19,000)
**GOVERNMENT** Commonwealth in union with the USA
**ETHNIC GROUPS** Chamorro, Micronesian, Spanish
**LANGUAGES** English, Chamorro
**RELIGIONS** Christianity (mainly Roman Catholic)
**CURRENCY** US currency

# NORWAY

O ne of the world's most distinctly shaped countries, the kingdom of Norway occupies the western part of the Scandinavian peninsula, from North Cape at latitude 71°N to Lindesnes at 58°N, a north-south distance of over 1,600 km [1,000 mls]. It covers an area far larger than Poland, yet has a population of less than 4.4 million, most of whom live in the southern part of the country, where the capital, Oslo, is situated.

Nowhere in Norway is far from the sea. At the widest point it is only 430 km [270 mls] from west to east, and near the Arctic port of Narvik the Swedish border comes to within 6.5 km [4 mls] of the Norwegian coast. A third of Norway lies within the Arctic Circle, but the climate is not as severe as might be expected because the Norwegian coast benefits from the moderating effects of the warm waters of the North Atlantic Drift. Even on the Arctic coast, the ports of Hammerfest and Kirkenes remain unfrozen in most winters.

## Landscape

Norway is a rugged, mountainous country in which communication is difficult. The Norwegian landscape is dominated by rolling plateaux, the *vidda*, generally 300 m to 900 m [1,000 ft to 3,000 ft] high, above which some peaks rise to as much as 1,500 m to 2,500 m [5,000 ft to 8,000 ft] in the area between Oslo, Bergen and Trondheim. In the far north the summits are around 1,000 m [3,000 ft] lower.

The highest areas retain permanent ice-fields, as in the Jotunheim Mountains above Sognefjord. The Norwegian mountains have been uplifted during three mountain-building episodes during the last 400 million years, and they contain rocks of the earliest geological periods. Intrusions of volcanic material accompanied the uplifting and folding, and there are great masses of granites and gneisses – the source of Norway's mineral wealth. There are few large areas of flat land in the country, but in the east the *vidda* are broken by deep valleys of rivers flowing to the lowlands of south-east Norway, focused on Oslo. In glacial times the whole country was covered by the great northern ice-cap. When it melted about 10,000 years ago it left behind large deposits of glacial moraine, well represented around Oslo in the Raa moraines. Soils of better quality are used for crops and meadows, while the less productive sands and gravels remain forested.

## The coast and the islands

The configuration of the coast – the longest in Europe – helps to explain the ease with which the Norwegians took to the sea in their early history and why they have remained a seafaring nation since. The *vidda* are cut by long, narrow, steep-sided fjords on the west coast, shaped by the great northern ice-cap. The largest of these, Sognefjord – 203 km [127 mls] long and less than 5 km [3 mls] wide – is the longest inlet in Europe and the best known fjord, though not the most spectacular.

Along the coast there are hundreds of

islands, the largest group of which, the Lofoten Islands, lie north of the Arctic Circle. These islands, known as the *skerryguard*, protect the inner coast from the battering of the Atlantic breakers, and provide sheltered leads of water which the coastal ferries and fishing boats can navigate in safety.

Until recently, communications along the coast were easier by boat than by land. Oslo is linked to the south by rail and a line reaches north to Bodö at latitude 67.5°N. Roads are difficult to build and costly to maintain, and are often blocked by snow in winter and spring (snow accumulates to March).

There are still several hundred ferries which carry cars across the fjords, but much money has been invested in the building of a north-south trunk road, with bridges across the fjords, to avoid the constant use of ferries. Air transport is of increasing importance and many small airstrips are in use, bringing remote communities into contact with the populated south.

## ECONOMY AND RESOURCES

With two-thirds of the country comprising barren mountains, snowfields or unproductive wastes, and one-fifth forested, less than 3% of the land can be cultivated. The barrenness of the soil, the heavy rainfall, winter snows and the short growing season restrict agriculture, especially in the north, though in the long days of summer good crops of hay, potatoes, quick-growing vegetables and even rye and barley are grown. Near the coast, farming is restricted to the limited areas of level or gently-sloping ground beside the sheltered fjords. Cattle and sheep use the slopes above them in the summer but are fed in stalls during the winter. Everywhere fish is caught in the local waters.

The sea has always been a major influence in Norwegian life. A thousand years ago Viking sailors from Norway roamed the northern seas, founding colonies around the coasts of Britain, Iceland and even North America. Today fishing, shipbuilding and the management of merchant shipping lines are of vital importance to the Norwegian economy, and its merchant ships, most of which seldom visit the home ports, earn profits which pay for a third of the country's imports.

Iron and lead ores are found in the north,

copper in central Norway and titanium in the south. The extent of Norway's mineral resources is not fully known, and prospecting is still revealing new deposits. Oil and natural gas deposits in the seabed of the North Sea have made a great contribution to the Norwegian economy in recent years, and comprise more than half of the country's export earnings. Statfjord B (816,000 tonnes) is the world's biggest oil platform. Exploitation of all these reserves provides more than enough for the country's needs.

There is no coal in mainland Norway, although some is found in the islands on the Svalbard archipelago in the Arctic Ocean. The lack of coal has been partly compensated for by the development of hydroelectricity, begun in the early 20th century, when the waterfalls of rivers flowing down the steep slopes above the fjords were first harnessed. Later, inland sites were developed, the greatest concentration is in the Rjukan Valley, 160 km [100 mls] west of Oslo. Today Norway (which owns five of the world's highest waterfalls) derives 99.6% of its electricity from water power.

The availability of cheap electricity made possible the rapid growth of the wood-pulp, paper and chemical industries, and later stimulated the metal-working industries. Many of the industrial sites are on the shores of remote fjords, where cheap electricity and deep-water access for the import of raw materials and for the export of finished products are the determining factors in choosing the location. The aluminium and chemical industries of the south-west coast are typical.

Metal-working has developed in the far north since World War II. After primary treatment iron is exported from Kirkenes to a smelter at Mo-i-Rana, on the coast just south of the Arctic Circle, which uses coal imported from Svalbard. The port of Narvik was connected by rail to the Swedish system in 1903, so that Swedish iron ore could be sent from an ice-free port to supply the iron smelters of Germany and other continental markets. This trade remains important today.

Rapid industrial development since World War II has transformed the Norwegian economy, and has ensured that the Norwegians are among the most prosperous people in Europe. Few people are very wealthy – taxation rates are high – but few are very poor, and an advanced welfare state (common to all the Scandinavian countries) provides good services even to the most isolated or rural communities. The great majority of people own their houses, and many families have second homes on the shores of fjords and lakes. Today's Norwegians are also more generous than their Viking ancestors: the nation is by far Europe's biggest donor of foreign aid per capita, with a figure of 1.1% of GNP – well above the OECD (Organization for Economic Co-operation and Development) target of 0.7%.

The pre-war economy, dependent on forestry, farming, fishing and seafaring, is still important, but the numbers employed in these industries are dwindling as more and more people move into the new industries and services in the growing towns. There are still few large towns, and all six of those with more than 50,000 population are on the coast. The largest are Oslo, Bergen and Trondheim.

## HISTORY AND POLITICS

After having been united with Denmark (1381–1814) and Sweden (1814–1905), Norway became independent in 1905. In 1940, although neutral at the time, it was occupied by German troops. At the end of World War II Norway abandoned its neutrality. Unlike its neighbours, Sweden and Finland, which have remained neutral, Norway is a member of NATO (North Atlantic Treaty Organization). However, it refused to join the EEC when Britain, Ireland and Denmark decided to enter (on 1 January 1973), and in November 1994 the Norwegian people again voted against joining the European Union. Norway is, however, a member of the Nordic Council and remains a member of EFTA, along with Iceland, Switzerland and Leichtenstein.

**Svalbard** is an archipelago of 62,920 sq km [24,295 sq mls] – half as big again as Denmark – sitting halfway between the North Pole and the Arctic Circle. Despite this exposed, northerly position, the climate is tempered by the relatively mild prevailing winds from the Atlantic. By far the largest island is Spitzbergen (or Vestspitzbergen), the former

## SCANDINAVIA

There are several possible definitions of the term Scandinavia. In the narrow geographical sense it refers to the peninsula shared by Norway and Sweden; in a broader cultural and political sense it includes the five countries of the Nordic Council – Norway, Sweden, Denmark, Finland and Iceland. All except Finland have related languages, and all have a tradition of parliamentary democracy: Finland and Iceland are republics, while the others are constitutional monarchies.

There are also strong historical links between them, beginning in the 8th century when their ancestors, the Norsemen, colonized large parts of northern Europe. All have at different times been governed together, Sweden and Finland separating in 1809, Norway and Sweden in 1905, and Denmark and Iceland as recently as 1944.

Because of their northerly position, and their exposure to Atlantic weather systems, the Scandinavian states have a cool, moist climate not favourable to crops. However, because of the long hours of daylight in the northern summer, some surprisingly good crops are grown north of the Arctic Circle.

The Scandinavians were once among the poorest peoples of Europe, but during the last century they have become among the richest, making full use of their limited natural resources, and also seizing the opportunities which their maritime position gave them to become major shipping and fishing nations.

also being used as the name of the whole group of islands.

The rival claims on the islands by the Norwegians, the Dutch and the British lost their importance in the 18th century with the decline of whale hunting, but were raised again in the 20th century with the discovery of coal. A treaty signed in Paris by 40 parties in 1920 finally recognized Norwegian sovereignty in return for mining rights, and in 1925 the islands were incorporated officially into the kingdom of Norway.

Coal remains the principal product and main occupation, with mines run by Norway and the former Soviet Union, both of which produce similar amounts of coal. Soviet citizens outnumbered Norwegians by more than 2 to 1 in 1988, when the total population was 3,646. By 1993 the population was 2,977.

Following the success of the North Sea projects, there is now prospecting in Svalbard for oil and natural gas. There are several meteorological stations and a research station, and other residents work on the extensive national parks and nature reserves. An airport opened in 1975 near Longyearbyen, the capital that is named after an American (J.M. Longyear), who in 1905 was the first man to mine coal on Svalbard.

**Jan Mayen** is a volcanic island of 380 sq km [147 sq mls], north-north-east of Iceland but actually closer to the east coast of Greenland. Mountainous and partly covered by glaciers, its dominant feature is the volcano of Beerenberg (2,277 m [7,470 ft]), which had been dormant but became active again in 1970.

The island was named in 1614 after the Dutch whaling captain Jan Jacobsz May, but 'discovered' by Henry Hudson in 1608. Though uninhabited, it was used by seal trappers and other hunters, and in 1921 Norway established a meteorological and radio station. In 1929 it was annexed into the kingdom of Norway, and today the only residents are the 30 or so staff at a weather station.

**Bjørnøya** (Bear Island) lies halfway between Svalbard and the Norwegian mainland, on the cusp of the Norwegian Sea and Barents Sea. Measuring 179 sq km [69 sq mls], it is uninhabited but remains the centre of important cod fisheries; after a long dispute over territorial rights it was internationally recognized as part of Norway in 1925. [*Map page 13*] ■

AREA 323,900 sq km [125,050 sq mls]
POPULATION 4,318,000
CAPITAL (POPULATION) Oslo (746,000)
GOVERNMENT Constitutional monarchy
ETHNIC GROUPS Norwegian 97%
LANGUAGES Norwegian (official), Lappish, Finnish
RELIGIONS Christianity (Lutheran 88%)
CURRENCY Norwegian krone = 100 øre

# OMAN

The Sultanate of Oman occupies the southeastern corner of the Arabian peninsula. It also includes the tip of the Musandam peninsula, overlooking the strategic Strait of Hormuz. This area is separated from the rest of Oman by the United Arab Emirates. A narrow, fertile plain, the Al Batinah, borders the Gulf of Oman in the north. The plain is backed by the Al Hajar Mountains. In the south, the land is barren and rocky and includes part of the bleak Rub 'al Khali desert.

## ECONOMY AND RESOURCES

Backward compared to its oil-rich Gulf neighbours to the west until 1970, the country has since been enjoying an expanding economy based on oil reserves far larger than expected when production began modestly in 1967.

Petroleum now accounts for more than 90% of government revenue – and because of Oman's detached situation the industry was not hit by the lack of confidence that afflicted the Gulf states in the 1991 war. Huge natural gas reserves were discovered in 1991 that were equal in size to all the finds of the previous 20 years. There are also some copper deposits.

But agriculture still provides a living for half of the people. Major crops include alfalfa, bananas, coconuts, dates, limes, tobacco, vegetables and wheat. Some farmers raise camels and cattle, and fishing, especially for sardines, is also important. But Oman has to import food to feed its people.

## HISTORY AND POLITICS

In ancient times, Oman became an important trading area on the main route between the Gulf and the Indian Ocean. Islam was introduced in the 7th century AD and Arab-Muslim culture remains the unifying force in Oman.

Portuguese sailors captured several seaports in Oman, including Muscat, in 1507, but Arabs expelled the Portuguese in 1650. In the 1740s, the Al Bu Said family took power in Oman, and this family has ruled Oman ever since. In 1798, Oman signed the first of several treaties of friendship with Britain. Then, in the late 19th and early 20th centuries, war broke out between the Sultan's forces and peoples from the interior who wanted a religious leader to take over the government. Conflict broke out again in the 1950s and again, in the south, between 1964 and 1975, but the rebels were put down with the aid of British troops.

Oil was discovered in 1964 and the country became fully independent in 1971. Since Sultan Said bin Taimur was deposed in 1970 by his son, Qaboos bin Said – with British collusion – Oman has made substantial strides, particularly after the end of the civil war against Yemen-backed separatist guerrillas in the southern province of Dhofar (Zufar). An absolute ruler – as his family heads have been since 1749 – Qaboos has tended to forego the usual prestigious projects favoured by wealthy Arab leaders, in favour of social programmes. Even so, by 1992 an estimated 65% of adults could not read or write, and defence and internal security were taking a large proportion of the annual budget. Ties with Britain remain close and Oman is also an ally of the United States, allowing it to use air and naval bases during emergencies. [*Map page 22*] ∎

AREA 212,460 sq km [82,031 sq mls]
POPULATION 2,077,000
CAPITAL (POPULATION) Muscat (250,000)
GOVERNMENT Monarchy with a consultative council
ETHNIC GROUPS Omani Arab 74%, Pakistani 21%
LANGUAGES Arabic (official)
RELIGIONS Islam 86%, Hinduism 13%
CURRENCY Omani rial = 1,000 baiza

# PAKISTAN

West of the Indus delta, the arid coastal plain of Makran rises first to the Coast Range, then in successive ridges to the north –

stark, arid, deforested and eroded. Between the ridges lie desert basins like that containing the saltmarsh of Hamun-i-Mashkel on the Iranian border. Ridge and basin alternate through Baluchistan and the earthquake zone round Quetta, the *daman-i-koh* ('skirts of the hills') are still irrigated by the ancient tunnels called *karez* or *qanats*, which facilitate the growing of cereals and fruit.

North again stretches the famous North-West Frontier province, pushing up between the towering Hindu Kush and Karakoram, with K2 on the border with China the world's second highest mountain standing at 8,611 m [28,251 ft]. East of Peshawar lies Kashmir, which Pakistan controls to the west of the 1947 cease-fire line, and India to the east.

## ECONOMY AND RESOURCES

As Egypt is the gift of the Nile, so Pakistan is the gift of the Indus and its tributaries. Despite modern industrialization, irrigated farming is vital to this Islamic state, both in Punjab, the 'land of the five rivers' – Indus, Jhelum, Beas, Ravi and Sutlej – and downstream on the dry plains flanking the Indus between Khairpur and Hyderabad. The HEP stations at Tarbela (on the Indus) and Mangla (on the Jhelum) are among the world's biggest earth- and rock-filled dams.

Like most developing countries, Pakistan has increased both mineral exploitation and manufacturing industry. To the small oil and coalfield near Rawalpindi has now been added a major resource of natural gas between Sukkur and Multan. Karachi, formerly the capital and developed in the colonial period as a wheat port, is now a considerable manufacturing centre, principally textiles; so is the cultural centre, Lahore, in the north. The well-planned national capital of Islamabad, begun in the 1960s, is still growing to the north-east of Rawalpindi, with the serrated outline of the Murree Hills – refuge for the wealthier citizens on weekends – as a backdrop to the architecture of the new city.

The world's seventh most populous country, Pakistan is likely to be overtaken by Bangladesh – its former partner separated by 1,600 km [1,000 mls] of India – by the end of the century.

'West' Pakistan's economy has done better

than poor Bangladesh, while reserves of some minerals (notably bauxite, copper, phosphates and manganese) have yet to be exploited. Yet there are huge problems: dependence on textiles, an increasingly competitive area, and on remittances from Pakistani workers abroad, especially in the Middle East (the main source of foreign income); a chronic trade deficit and debt burden; massive spending on defence and security; growing drug traffic through the North-West Frontier; and the added pressure of some 5 million Afghan refugees who fled the civil war in their homeland. However, the fall of Kabul to Afghan Mujaheddin rebels in the spring of 1992 brought the prospect of an improvement in Pakistan's refugee problem – though it also raised the possibility of renewed Pathan nationalism.

## HISTORY AND POLITICS

The 1947 cease-fire ended war and appalling internecine slaughter that followed the grant of independence from Britain, when the old Indian empire was divided between India and Pakistan – Hindu and Muslim states. The Kashmir problem was partly religious – a mainly Muslim population ruled by a Hindu maharaja who acceded to India – but there was also an underlying strategic issue: five rivers rising in or passing through Kashmir or the neighbouring Indian state of Himachal Pradesh are vital to Pakistan's economy, and could not be left in the hands of possible enemies.

In 1971, East Pakistan broke away from the western wing of the nation and formed the new state of Bangladesh, following a bitter civil war and Indian military intervention, but neither country state has enjoyed political stability or sound government.

Pakistan has been subject to military rule and martial law for much of its short life, interspersed with periods of fragile democracy resting on army consent. During one such, in 1988, Benazir Bhutto – daughter of the president executed after his government (the country's first elected civilian administration) was overthrown by the army in 1977 – was freely elected prime minister, the first female premier in the Muslim world. Two years later she was dismissed by the president following accusations of nepotism and corruption, but

managed to return to power following her party's success in elections held in October 1993. [*Map page 23*] ■

**AREA** 796,100 sq km [307,374 sq mls]
**POPULATION** 136,645,000
**CAPITAL (POPULATION)** Islamabad (204,000)
**GOVERNMENT** Federal republic
**ETHNIC GROUPS** Punjabi 60%, Sindhi 12%, Pushtun 13%, Baluch, Muhajir
**LANGUAGES** Urdu (official)
**RELIGIONS** Islam 97%, Christianity, Hinduism
**CURRENCY** Pakistan rupee = 100 paisa

# PALAU (BELAU)

The republic of Palau comprises an archipelago of six Caroline groups, totalling 26 islands and over 300 islets varying in terrain from mountain to reef and totalling 458 sq km [177 sq mls].

Eight of the islands are permanently inhabited, including Peleliu (Beleliu) and Angaur – guarding the passage between the Indian and Pacific Oceans and the scene of fierce battles between American and occupying Japanese forces in World War II. Most of the largely Catholic population speak the official Palauan (Belauan), but English is widely used. The present capital is Koror (population 9,000 – over half the national total), site of one of the few deep-water harbours in the Pacific, on the island of the same name; a new capital is being built in the east of Babelthuap, the largest island, where coastal plains surround a high jungle interior.

## ECONOMY AND RESOURCES

Agriculture is still largely at subsistence level, with copra the main export crop, but luxury tourism is growing, based strongly on scuba-diving and sea fishing. The country relies heavily on US aid – indeed Washington has pursued a policy of deliberate indebtedness – and the US government is by far the largest employer on the islands.

## HISTORY AND POLITICS

The last remaining member of the four states that comprised the US Trust Territory of the Pacific, established under UN mandate in 1947 – thanks to sustained American skulduggery – Palau (Belau) voted to break away from the Federated States of Micronesia in 1978, and a new self-governing constitution became effective in 1981. The territory then entered into 'free association with the USA', providing sovereign-state status, but in 1983 a referendum rejected the proposal, since Washington refused to accede to a 92% vote in a 1979 referendum that declared the nation a nuclear-free zone. The result was a stalemate with the UN Trusteeship still technically in force, that was until 1 October 1994, when full independence was declared. [*Map page 26*] ∎

| | |
|---|---|
| **AREA** | 458 sq km [177 sq mls] |
| **POPULATION** | 17,000 |
| **CAPITAL (POPULATION)** | Koror (9,000) |
| **GOVERNMENT** | Independent republic |
| **ETHNIC GROUPS** | Palauan (mixture of Polynesian, Melanesian and Malay) |
| **LANGUAGES** | Palauan (official), English |
| **RELIGIONS** | Christianity (mainly Roman Catholic) |
| **CURRENCY** | US currency |

# PANAMA

Less than 60 km [37 mls] wide at its narowest point, the isthmus of Panama not only links Central and South America but also, via its famous Canal, the Atlantic and Pacific Oceans. Most of the country, including some 750 offshore islands, lies below 700 m [2,300 ft], sweltering daily in tropical heat and high humidity, with heavy downpours marking the May to December rainy season. The mountain ranges trend north-west to south-east slightly against the lie of the country, and fragment the lowlands. The eastern region and the Caribbean coast are covered in dense tropical rainforests.

## ECONOMY AND RESOURCES

Basins and valleys between the ranges support pockets of agriculture, and rainforests have been cleared for production of bananas, coffee, cocoa and sugar cane, for cattle ranching and for subsistence crops of rice, maize and beans. To the east, in Darien, the thick jungle remains largely undisturbed and still home to a few indigenous Indian tribes.

Many Panamanians live within about 20 km [12 mls] of the Canal Zone, a quarter of them in the capital city and 80% of the country's GDP originates here. This includes revenues from free trade, the open-registry merchant fleet (some 12,000 ships), and 'offshore' finance facilities. With exports of bananas (25% of total), shrimps (19%) and mahogany, not to mention income from tourism and substantial US aid, these have given Panama the highest standard of living in Central America.

The Panama Canal is 82 km [51 mls] long from deep water at either end, 65 km [40 mls] long from coast to coast. Three sets of locks at each end lift vessels to the elevated central section 26 m [85 ft] above sea level, which includes Gatun Lake and the Gaillard Cut, 13 km [8 mls] through the continental divide.

## HISTORY AND POLITICS

Though an American-built railway crossed the isthmus in 1855, it was a French company under Ferdinand de Lesseps that began cutting the Canal in 1880, but engineering problems and deaths from disease stopped operations after ten years. In 1903 the province of Panama declared independence from Colombia and granted the USA rights in perpetuity over a Canal Zone, 16 km [10 mls] wide. Work on the present Canal began a year later, and it was finally opened for shipping in 1914. In 1980 there were some 13,000 transits through the Canal – over 36 ships per day – carrying twice the total cargo of 1960. Now running close to capacity, the Canal cannot take fully-laden ships of over about 80,000 tonnes (thus excluding most large tankers) and an alternative Panama Seaway is under discussion. From 1979 sovereignty of the Canal Zone was restored to Panama, and the Canal itself will follow suit in 1999.

Panama's government has changed many

times since independence. In 1983, General Manuel Antonio Noriega became Panama's leader. In 1988, two US grand juries in Florida indicted Noriega on charges of drug trafficking. In 1989, Noriega was apparently defeated in a presidential election, but the government declared the election invalid. After the killing of a US marine, US troops entered Panama and arrested Noriega, who was convicted by a Miami court of drug offences in 1992. Elections in 1994 were won by the Democratic Revolutionary Party, led by Pérez Balladares. [*Map page 30*] ■

**AREA** 77,080 sq km [29,761 sq mls]
**POPULATION** 2,585,000
**CAPITAL (POPULATION)** Panama City (584,000)
**GOVERNMENT** Multiparty republic
**ETHNIC GROUPS** Mestizo 60%, Black and Mulatto 20%, White 10%, Amerindian 8%, Asian 2%
**LANGUAGES** Spanish (official)
**RELIGIONS** Christianity (Roman Catholic 84%, Protestant 5%), Islam 5%
**CURRENCY** Balboa = 100 cents

# PAPUA NEW GUINEA

Forming part of Melanesia, Papua New Guinea is the eastern section of the island of New Guinea, plus the Bismarck Archipelago and the copper-rich island of Bougainville – geographically, though not politically, part of the Solomons. The backbone of the main island is a high cordillera of rugged fold mountains, averaging between 2,500 to 4,600 m [8,000 to 15,000 ft] in height and covered with tropical montane 'cloud' forest.

Isolated valleys and intermontane basins run parallel with the main ranges. Fertile with alluvium and volcanic materials, these are the sites of isolated settlements, even today linked only by light aircraft. The capital city, Port Moresby, is not linked by road to any other major centre, and communication with the highlands depends on the country's 400 airports and airstrips.

## ECONOMY AND RESOURCES

The traditional garden crops of the 'highlanders' include kaukau (sweet potato), sugar cane, bananas, maize, cassava and nut-bearing pandans. Pigs are kept mainly for status and ritual purposes. In the lowlands, taro is the staple food, although yams and sago are also important. The main cash crops are coconuts, coffee, cocoa and rubber.

While 80% of the population still live by agriculture, minerals (notably copper, gold and silver) have provided an important share of the country's exports, encouraging 'PNG' to reduce its dependence on Australian aid. Most of the copper comes from the world's biggest mine at Panguna, on Bougainville.

## HISTORY AND POLITICS

Although the first European contact came as early as 1526, it was only in the late 19th century that permanent German and British settlements were established. After World War II, the UN Trust Territory of New Guinea and the Territory of Papua were administered by Australia. Self-government came in 1973, with full independence in 1975.

Demands by the Bougainville islanders for a greater share of the earnings from the copper mine spiralled into a separatist struggle by 1989 – followed by the closure of the mine, a declaration of independence by the secessionists and a blockade of the island by the government. Despite a peace accord of 1991, the position was still unchanged after three years – with the 'revolution' passing into the hands of criminal gangs. [*Map page 26*] ■

**AREA** 462,840 sq km [178,703 sq mls]
**POPULATION** 4,205,000
**CAPITAL (POPULATION)** Port Moresby (174,000)
**GOVERNMENT** Constitutional monarchy
**ETHNIC GROUPS** Papuan 84%, Melanesian 15%
**LANGUAGES** English (official)
**RELIGIONS** Christianity (Protestant 58%, Roman Catholic 33%, Anglican 5%), traditional beliefs 3%
**CURRENCY** Kina = 100 toea

# PARAGUAY

Alandlocked nation, Paraguay is bounded mainly by rivers – the Paraná (South America's second longest) in the south and east, the Pilcomayo in the south-west, and the Paraguay and Apa rivers in the north-west. The middle reach of the Paraguay, navigable for vessels of 1,700 tonnes to Asunción, 1,610 km [1,000 mls] from the sea, divides the country unequally. The eastern third, an extension of the Brazilian plateau at a height of 300 m to 600 m [1,000 ft to 2,000 ft] is densely forested with tropical hardwoods. The western two-thirds is the Northern Chaco, a flat, alluvial plain rising gently from the damp, marshy Paraguay river valley to semi-desert scrubland along the western border.

## ECONOMY AND RESOURCES

During Stroessner's dictatorship (1954–89), there was considerable economic growth, particularly in the 1970s, and great emphasis was placed on developing hydroelectricity: by 1976 Paraguay was self-sufficient in electric energy and by 1990 the country was producing 99.9% of its electricity from water power. This was achieved by the development of two major projects – Acaray and Itaipú (the world's largest HEP project, inaugurated in 1984). In 1984 another complex on the Paraná river at Yacyreta was begun in conjunction with Argentina, and is due for completion in 1998. Yacyreta has the world's longest dam.

## HISTORY AND POLITICS

Paraguay was settled in 1537 by Spaniards attracted by the labour supply of the native Guarani Indians – and the chance of finding a short cut to the silver of Peru. Forming part of the Rio de la Plata Viceroyalty from 1766, Paraguay broke free in 1811 and achieved independence from Buenos Aires in 1813. For over a century the country struggled for nationhood, torn by destructive internal strife and conflict with neighbouring states: in 1865–70, war against Brazil, Argentina and Uruguay cost the country more than half its 600,000 people and much of its territory. At a time when most other South American countries were attracting European settlers and foreign capital for development, Paraguay remained isolated and forbidding. Some territory was regained after the Chaco Wars against Bolivia in 1929–35, and in 1947 a period of civil war was followed by political and economic stability.

In 1954 General Stroessner seized power and assumed the presidency. His regime was a particularly unpleasant variety of despotism, and he ruled with an ever-increasing disregard for human rights during nearly 35 years of fear and fraud before being deposed by his own supporters in 1989. The speeches about reform from his successor, General Andrés Rodríguez, sounded somewhat hollow, but at the end of 1991 Paraguayans did indeed go to the polls to elect a constituent assembly which would frame a new constitution incorporating a multiparty system. Free multiparty elections held in 1993 resulted in the instalment of Juan Carlos Wasmosy, Paraguay's first civilian president since 1954. [*Map page 31*] ■

AREA 406,750 sq km [157,046 sq mls]
POPULATION 4,830,000
CAPITAL (POPULATION) Asunción (945,000)
GOVERNMENT Multiparty republic
ETHNIC GROUPS Mestizo 90%, Amerindian 3%
LANGUAGES Spanish and Guaraní (both official)
RELIGIONS Christianity (Roman Catholic 96%, Protestant 2%)
CURRENCY Guaraní = 100 céntimos

# PERU

Largest of the Andean states, Peru spread over coastal plain, mountains and forested Amazon lowlands in the interior.

The coastal plain is narrow and generally

arid, cooled by sea breezes from the offshore Humboldt Current. Occasionally it suffers violent rainstorms, associated with shifts in the pattern of surface waters. Rivers that cut through the foothills provide water for irrigated agriculture, mainly of cotton, rice and sugar cane. The middle slopes of the Andes – the Quechua, at heights of 2,000 m to 3,500 m [6,500 ft to 11,500 ft] – are warm-temperate and fairly well watered. These areas supported the main centres of Indian population in the Inca empire, and are just as well suited to densely populated rural settlements today.

Above stand the higher reaches of the Andes, extending westwards in cold inhospitable tablelands at 4,000 m to 4,800 m [13,000 ft to 15,700 ft], cultivated up to 4,200 m [13,700 ft] by peasant farmers and grazed by their sheep, alpacas, llamas and vicuñas. The snowy peaks of the high Andes rise to over 6,000 m [19,500 ft]. Though close to the Pacific Ocean, most of the rivers that rise here eventually drain into the Amazon. Their descent to the lowlands is through the *montaña*, a near-impenetrable maze of valleys, ridges and plains, permanently soaked by rain and thickly timbered. Beyond extend the Amazon lowlands – hot, wet and clad mainly in dense tropical rainforest. Occupying half the country, they are thinly inhabited by native Indians.

## ECONOMY AND RESOURCES

Lima was developed as the Spanish colonial capital, and through its port of Callao passed much of the trade of the Spanish settlers; 19th-century exports included guano (bird-droppings, valuable as an agricultural fertilizer) from the offshore islands, and wild rubber. Peru gained independence from Spain in 1824, but difficulties of communication, political strife, earthquakes and other natural disasters, and a chronically unbalanced economy have dogged the country's development.

Today Peru faces many economic, social and political problems. Agricultural production has failed to keep up with population, so wheat, rice, meat and other staple foods are imported. Cotton, coffee and sugar are exported. Peru is the leading producer of coca, the shrub used in the illegal production of cocaine, and earnings were thought to be in excess of

## THE ANDES

Created 200 million years ago by the collision of the Nazca plate and the land mass of South America – and still moving at about 12.5 mm [0.5 in] each year – the Andes mountain system extends along the entire west side of the continent from the coast of the Caribbean to Tierra del Fuego for over 6,400 km [4,000 mls], making it the world's longest chain.

The Andes is the highest mountain range outside the Himalayas and Argentina's Cerro Aconcagua, at 6,960 m [22,834 ft], is the highest peak outside Asia. Argentina shares with Chile four of the ten highest summits. In the middle section there are two main chains and elsewhere three, with the breadth exceeding 800 km [500 mls] to the north of latitude 20°S. Altogether the range has 54 peaks over 6,100 m [20,000 ft].

Many of South America's great rivers, including the Orinoco, Negro, Amazon and Madeira, rise in the Andes, and the range is home to the continent's largest lake, Titicaca, which lies on the Peru-Bolivia border at 3,812 m [12,506 ft]. The Andes contains numerous volcanoes and is subject almost everywhere to violent earthquakes. Many volcanoes are still active and Cotopaxi in north-central Ecuador is usually regarded as the world's highest (5,896 m [19,457 ft]).

The condor, symbol of the mountains and the world's largest vulture, is now down to a few hundred, despite attempts by several Andean countries – backed by the United States – to increase its dwindling numbers.

In 1910 the Andes were tunnelled, linking Chilean and Argentine railways by the tunnel, 3 km [2 mls] long, at an altitude of 3,200 m [10,500 ft], north of Aconcagua.

US$3 billion in the 1980s. An agreement was reached in February 1990 with the USA to stop the planting of coca in some areas and instead to plant oil palms, but success has been limited and much still finds its way to Colombia for processing and re-export.

Peru once had the largest fish catch in the world and there are 70 canning factories. Anchoveta was the main target, but fishing

## THE INCA CIVILIZATION

The empire of the Incas, centring on Cuzco in the Peruvian highlands, developed from millennia of earlier Andean civilizations that included the Chavin, the Nazca and the Tiahuanaco. The Incas began their conquests about AD 1350, and by the end of the 15th century their empire extended from central Chile to Ecuador. Perhaps some 10 million people owed allegiance to it when it fell to the Spanish *conquistadores* in 1532.

The empire was military and theocratic, with the sun as the focus of worship. Temples and shrines, built of huge, laboriously shaped, closely fitting but uncemented blocks (the Incas had no metal tools), were created for sun worship; the Sun Temple at Cuzco had a circumference of 350 m [1,148 ft], and many other buildings were equally massive. The people were skilled farmers, using elaborate irrigation systems and terraced fields.

Gold and silver were particularly valued by the Incas for ornamentation. They were prized also by the *conquistadores*, who looted them from every corner of the empire and quickly set the Indians to mining more. The Incas had no written script: buildings and terracing – notably those of 'the lost city' of Machupicchu north-west of Cuzco – and delicate ornaments form their main memorials, though fragments of Inca culture and beliefs remain among the Quechua-speaking peoples of Peru and Bolivia.

was halted from 1976 until 1982 because of depleted stocks. In 1983 a warm current known as 'El Niño' ruined the fishing but recovery followed from 1986.

Several metals are exported, including silver, zinc and lead, with copper the most important earner. However, industrial unrest has reduced production dramatically. Exports of oil are growing, providing much-needed foreign capital for industrial development, now forthcoming after a lull following limited debt repayment in 1985. Peru's inflation rate – a staggering 7,480% in 1990 – settled down to a modest 200% or so in 1991, the year that many state industries were liberalized.

## HISTORY AND POLITICS

Amerindian people probably reached the area about 12,000 years ago. Several civilizations developed in the Andes region. By about AD 1200, the Inca were established in southern Peru. In 1500, their empire extended from Ecuador to Chile. The Spanish adventurer Francisco Pizarro visited Peru in the 1520s. Hearing of Inca riches, he returned in 1532. By 1533, he had conquered most of Peru.

In 1820, the Argentinian José de San Martín led an army into Peru and declared the country to be independent. But Spain still held large areas. In 1823, the Venezuelan Simón Bolívar led another army into Peru, and in 1824 one of his generals defeated the Spaniards at Ayacucho. The Spaniards surrendered in 1826, but Peru suffered much instability throughout the 19th century and into the 20th century.

In 1980, when civilian rule was restored, a left-wing group called the *Sendero Luminoso*, or the 'Shining Path', began guerrilla warfare against the government. In 1990, Alberto Fujimori, son of Japanese immigrants, became president. In 1992, he suspended the constitution and the guerrilla leader, Abimael Guzmán, was arrested, but instability continued. A new constitution was introduced in 1993, giving increased power to the president, who faced many problems in rebuilding the shattered economy.

To add to Peru's problems, the country suffered the worst cholera outbreak in the Americas this century early in 1991, with some 2,500 deaths. Trading partners were reluctant to import vulnerable Peruvian food products. [*Map page 31*] ∎

**AREA** 1,285,220 sq km [496,223 sq mls]
**POPULATION** 23,331,000
**CAPITAL (POPULATION)** Lima (Lima-Callao, 6,415,000)
**GOVERNMENT** Transitional republic
**ETHNIC GROUPS** Quechua 47%, Mestizo 32%, White 12%, Aymara 5%
**LANGUAGES** Spanish and Quechua (both official)
**RELIGIONS** Christianity (Roman Catholic 93%, Protestant 6%)
**CURRENCY** New sol = 100 centavos

# PHILIPPINES

The Republic of the Philippines consists of 7,107 islands, of which, 2,770 are named and about 1,000 permanently inhabited, with the two largest, Luzon and Mindanao, making up over two-thirds of the total area. The country lacks extensive areas of lowland and most of the islands are characterized by rugged interior mountains, the highest of which are Mt Apo (2,954 m [9,691 ft]) in Mindanao and Mt Pulog (2,929 m [9,610 ft]) in Luzon. There are over 20 active volcanoes in the islands, including Mt Apo and Mt Pinatubo, which erupted violently in 1991.

## ECONOMY AND RESOURCES

The most important lowland region is the central plain of Luzon, a key rice-producing area and a major zone of population concentration, including the Manila Bay area. The most impressive man-made sight, however, is the spectacular series of irrigated rice terraces that contour the mountain slopes in the northern interior of Luzon. These have been constructed by Igorot tribesmen, descendants of some of the earliest people to colonize the Philippines. Elsewhere in the islands, and especially on Cebu, Leyte and Negros, maize is the staple foodstuff, reflecting the Philippines' former contacts with Spanish America. Another link is Roman Catholicism; over 80% of the population are Catholic, and named after King Philip II of Spain, the country is the only predominantly Christian nation of any size in Asia.

The economy, lacking any exploitable natural resources, remains weak, and levels of unemployment and emigration among Filipinos are high.

## HISTORY AND POLITICS

Following three centuries of harsh Spanish rule the islands were ceded to the US in 1898 after the Spanish-American War. Though the Philippines gained independence from the USA in 1946, ties have remained strong, notably during the corrupt regime of President Ferdinand Marcos (1965–86), though in 1991 the Philippines government announced the closure of Subic Bay naval base, the largest in Asia, by the end of 1992.

Marcos was overthrown by the 'people power' revolution that brought to office Corazon Aquino, widow of the opposition leader assassinated in 1983. The political situation remained volatile however, with Communist and Muslim Nationalist rebels undermining stability. Mrs Aquino did not stand in the presidential elections in 1992. Her successor was General Fidel V. Ramos. [*Map page 26*] ■

---

**AREA** 300,000 sq km [115,300 sq mls]
**POPULATION** 66,188,000
**CAPITAL (POPULATION)** Manila (or Metro Manila, 6,720,000)
**GOVERNMENT** Multiparty republic
**ETHNIC GROUPS** Tagalog 30%, Cebuano 24%, Ilocano 10%, Hiligaynon Ilongo 9%, Bicol 6%, Samar-Leyte 4%
**LANGUAGES** Pilipino (Tagalog) and English (both official)
**RELIGIONS** Christianity (Roman Catholic 84%, Philippine Independent Church or Aglipayan 6%, Protestant 4%), Islam 4%
**CURRENCY** Philippine peso = 100 centavos

---

# PITCAIRN ISLANDS

A British dependent territory of four islands (48 sq km [19 sq mls]), Pitcairn is situated halfway between New Zealand and Panama in the Pacific Ocean.

Subsistence gardening and fishing are the main activities. The islanders also derive some income from wood carvings and postage stamps, as well as from outside investment.

Uninhabited until 1790, Pitcairn was occupied by nine mutineers from HMS *Bounty* and some men and women from Tahiti. In 1856 some 194 of its people moved at their own request to Norfolk Island, though 43 of them returned between 1859 and 1864. The present population of 70, all living in Adamstown on Pitcairn, come under the administration of the British High Commission in Wellington and use the New Zealand dollar. [*Map page 2*] ■

**AREA** 48 sq km [19 sq mls]
**POPULATION** 70
**CAPITAL (POPULATION)** Adamstown (70)
**GOVERNMENT** British dependent territory
**ETHNIC GROUPS** English, Tahitian
**LANGUAGES** English
**RELIGIONS** Seventh-Day Adventists
**CURRENCY** New Zealand currency

# POLAND

Poland consists mostly of lowlands that form part of the Northern European Plain. On its southern borders are the Tatra Mountains, a section of the Carpathian range. The geographical location of Poland has had a strong influence on the country's stormy history. On many occasions powerful neighbours – notably Russia and Germany – have found it all too easy to invade and occupy the land. The most recent frontier changes came at the end of World War II – in which the country lost 6 million people, or a massive 17% of the total population – when Poland gave up territory to the USSR, and in compensation gained parts of Germany as far as the River Oder.

**ECONOMY AND RESOURCES**
As a result of these changes Poland lost poor agricultural land in the east and gained an important industrial region in the west, including, in the south-west, Silesia and the former German city of Breslau (now called Wroclaw), in the north-west the Baltic port of Stettin (now Szczecin), and in the north the other port of Danzig (now Gdansk). Acquisition of a length of Baltic coastline (there was only a narrow access corridor where the Poles developed the port of Gdynia as a competitor with Danzig) gave Poland a chance to develop

maritime interests. Now a major fishing nation, Poland's fleets operate worldwide.

Before World War II Poland was primarily an agricultural country, with 65% of the population dependent on farming, but the postwar industrialization drive under Communism reduced this proportion to about 30%, most of them still on privately owned farms. Poland is still, however, a major supplier of agricultural produce: nearly two-thirds of the land surface is farmed, about half of this area supporting crops of rye and potatoes. Oats, sugar beet, pigs and dairy produce are also important.

Poland's industrial development since World War II has been striking. Coal, lignite, sulphur, lead and zinc are the main mineral products, though Poland is also Europe's top producer of copper and silver. Underground salt deposits form the basis of important chemical industries. Most of Poland's industrial energy is derived from coal, but oil and natural gas are being developed, and hydroelectric power is being produced in increasing amounts from the Carpathians. Heavy industries include manufacture of steel and cement, and many secondary products. Many of Poland's newer industries remain almost wholly reliant on gas and oil from various parts of the former Soviet Union – a difficult position in a changing world.

Poland's reliance on heavy industry, much of it state-controlled and unprofitable, proved to be a major obstacle in the country's 'fast-track' route from Communism to capitalism that followed the pioneering triumph of democratic forces in 1989. The old industries needed drastic measures – re-equipping, restructuring and diversifying – but this could be achieved only with huge assistance from the West; Poland received nearly 70% of all Western credits to Eastern Europe between 1989 and 1991, adding to an already unserviceable foreign debt. Rising inflation (1,000% at one stage) and unemployment however, coupled with a drastic drop in living standards (the economy shrank by 10% in 1991), led to a resurgence of militant unionism.

**HISTORY AND POLITICS**
Under the banner of the independent trade union Solidarity, based originally in the Gdansk shipyards and led by Lech Walesa,

Poland was the first of the Soviet satellites to challenge and bring down its Communist regime. The example set by the Poles (even though they were to be the last Eastern European country to implement full democracy in October 1991), proved an inspiration not only to the other European Socialist states, but also to the peoples of the Baltic republics.

Elected national president a year earlier, Lech Walesa found it difficult to form a stable government after the 1991 elections – the country's first truly democratic ballot since before World War II – with the new constitution producing a parliament representing no less than 29 different parties. Solidarity itself had not lived up to its name, dividing in 1990 over personality clashes and the speed of reform, seemingly unable to reconcile an innate conflict between its two roles – on the one hand forming 35% of a government implementing severe economic measures and, on the other, a trade union trying to protect the interests of its members. Indeed, Poland's transition to a free market proved more painful than that of Czechoslovakia and Hungary. Despite being the pioneer of the process it seemed weighed down by its very size, a prisoner of its postwar past. [*Map pages 4–5*] ■

**AREA** 312,680 sq km [120,726 sq mls]
**POPULATION** 38,341,000
**CAPITAL (POPULATION)** Warsaw (1,655,000)
**GOVERNMENT** Multiparty republic
**ETHNIC GROUPS** Polish 98%, Ukrainian 1%
**LANGUAGES** Polish (official)
**RELIGIONS** Christianity (Roman Catholic 94%, Orthodox 2%)
**CURRENCY** Zloty = 100 groszy

# PORTUGAL

The most westerly of Europe's 'mainland' countries, Portugal occupies an oblong coastland in the south-west of the Iberian peninsula, facing the Atlantic Ocean. Here the Meseta edge has splintered and in part foundered to leave upstanding mountain ranges, particularly in the Serra da Estrêla and its continuation just north of the River Tagus (Tejo), and in the Serra de Monchique.

Portugal has two conurbations with over a million inhabitants. Lisbon, the capital, is the chief centre of the country's financial, commercial and industrial concerns and has a fine sheltered harbour in the large Tagus estuary. Oporto, the main centre for the densely-populated north, has an ocean outport. These two cities still dominate the nation, but during recent decades tourism and rapid residential growth have transformed the subtropical coastline of the Algarve, and have led to a substantial increase in its population.

## ECONOMY AND RESOURCES
The mild, moist airflow from the Atlantic encourages good tree growth. Forests reach a height of at least 1,300 m [4,260 ft] in the north and over a quarter of the country is forested. Pines form the most common species, especially on the sandy 'litorals' near the coast, where large plantations provide timber as well as resin and turpentine. Cork oaks abound in the Tagus valley and farther south; Portugal is the world's leading producer of the cork that is derived from their bark.

A wide variety of fruits is cultivated, including olives, figs and grapes. Portugal is home to some of the world's greatest vineyards and in 1991 ranked eigth in the world, producing 991,000 tonnes of wine. Most of the grapes are grown north of the Tagus, where the most celebrated speciality is port wine from the Douro valley near the Portuguese-Spanish frontier. The grape juice is transported by boat down the Douro to Vila Nova, where it is fortified and stored for export. The lower parts of the Douro and Minho basins produce famous sparkling vinhos verdes, while the vineyards near the Tagus estuary are noted for white table wines and brandy. In the south the Algarve, with its greater sunshine and aridity, specializes more in liqueurs and muscatels.

The Portuguese economy relies heavily on agriculture and fishing, which together employ over a quarter of the national workforce. These industries are mostly undercapitalized and still rather primitive by European standards, although they provide valuable exports.

In the rainy north the pressure of overpopulation has created fragmented and tiny agricultural holdings (*minifundia*); in the drier south large holdings (*latifundia*) tend to create monoculture with below-average yields and seasonal unemployment. Recently there has been some investment in irrigation.

The main general crops are food cereals and vegetables, including a wide variety of the beans that form a frequent and favourite item of the Portuguese diet. Maize and rye predominate in the north, and wheat, barley and oats in the south. Of the many farm animals, the pig deserves special mention as the forager of the heavy yield of acorns from the cork and evergreen oaks.

Portugal's long coastline provides an important supplementary source of livelihood and of foreign tourist currency. The shallow lagoons yield shellfish, especially oysters; the coastal waters supply sardines, anchovy and tunny; the deep-sea fisheries, long frequented by Portuguese sailors, bring hake, mackerel, halibut and, above all, cod.

While much of Portuguese industry is concerned with the products of farming, fishing and forestry, the manufacture of textiles and ceramics is also widespread. Modern engineering, associated with a complete iron and steel plant, has been established at Seixal near Lisbon. There is some small-scale mining for copper ores and wolfram (a tungstate of iron and manganese, from which tungsten is obtained), but a relative shortage of power resources is a problem. A small quantity of poor-quality coal is mined annually, and this is supplemented with foreign imports. Great efforts have been made to develop hydroelectric power stations in the north, but Portugal remains the poorest member of the EU since switching economic allegiance from EFTA on 1 January 1986.

**HISTORY AND POLITICS**
Portugal first established its independence in 1128. It formed an alliance with England in 1373, which has lasted. In the 15th century, Portugal built an empire with colonies in South America, Africa, India and the Far East, and became a major naval power. Occupied by French forces during the Napoleonic wars, it was liberated by British troops in 1811.

A republic was proclaimed in 1910 and the following two decades saw a great deal of political instability. This led to the dictatorship of Prime Minister Antonio Salazar which was to last from 1932 to 1968. Salazar engaged in long and expensive colonial wars against emerging independence movements, particularly in Angola and Mozambique. General dissatisfaction with Salazar's policies (largely continued by his successor, Caetano) finally culminated in a bloodless coup by left-wing army officers on 25 April 1974. They soon granted independence to the former colonies and attempted to establish a radical socialist regime. This was rejected by Portuguese voters in the 1976 elections and by 1979 the centre right parties were in power and civilian government was fully restored in 1982. Portugal was a founder member of NATO (in 1949) and joined the EC in 1986, at the same time as Spain. [*Map page 18*] ■

**AREA** 92,390 sq km [35,672 sq mls]
**POPULATION** 9,830,000
**CAPITAL (POPULATION)** Lisbon (2,561,000)
**GOVERNMENT** Multiparty republic
**ETHNIC GROUPS** Portuguese 99%, Cape Verdean, Brazilian, Spanish, British
**LANGUAGES** Portuguese (official)
**RELIGIONS** Christianity (Roman Catholic 95%, other Christians 2%)
**CURRENCY** Escudo = 100 centavos

# PUERTO RICO

Easternmost of the major Greater Antilles, Puerto Rico is mountainous in the interior, with a narrow coastal plain. Cerro de Punta (1,338 m [4,389 ft]) is the highest peak.

**ECONOMY AND RESOURCES**
Flat ground for agriculture is scarce, mainly devoted to cash crops like sugar, coffee, bananas and, since the arrival of Cuban refugees, tobacco, as well as tropical fruits, vegetables and various spices.

However, the island is now the most industrialized and urban nation in the Caribbean – nearly half the population lives in the San Juan area – with chemicals constituting 36% of exports and metal products (based on deposits of copper) a further 17%. Manufacturing, dominated by US companies attracted by tax exemptions, and tourism are now the two growth sectors in a country where the standard of living (while low in US terms) is nevertheless the highest in Latin America outside the island tax havens, and rising.

## HISTORY AND POLITICS
Puerto Rico ('rich port') was discovered in 1493 by Colombus and was a Spanish possession until ceded to the USA in 1898. It became a self-governing Commonwealth in free association with the USA after a referendum in 1952. Though this gave the island a considerable measure of autonomy, American influence stretches well beyond its constitutional roles in defence and immigration.

Debate over the exact status of the country subsided in the 1970s, the compromise apparently accepted as a sensible middle way between the extremes of being the 51st state of the US or completely independent, but resurfaces with the boom years. A referendum in December 1991 narrowly rejected a proposal to guarantee 'the island's distinct cultural identity' – a result interpreted as a move towards statehood. Meanwhile, free access to the US has relieved the growing pressure created by one of the greatest population densities in the New World, with New York City traditionally the most popular destination; the immigrants, however, are not always welcome. [*Map page 30*] ■

AREA  8,900 sq km [3,436 sq mls]
POPULATION  3,646,000
CAPITAL (POPULATION)  San Juan (1,816,000)
GOVERNMENT  Self-governing Commonwealth in free association with the USA
ETHNIC GROUPS  Spanish 99%, African-American, Indian
LANGUAGES  Spanish, English
RELIGIONS  Christianity (mainly Roman Catholic)
CURRENCY  US currency

# QATAR

The State of Qatar is an Arab Emirate which occupies a peninsula jutting out from the Arabian peninsula into the Gulf. The low-lying land is mostly stony desert, with some barren salt flats. Much of the country's drinking water supply is distilled sea water.

Qatar derives its high standard of living from oil and gas. Oil was first discovered in 1939 and accounts for about 90% of Qatar's exports. Money from oil has been used to create manufacturing industries and to develop agriculture and fishing. But despite diversification into cement, steel and fertilizers, oil and gas still account for over 80% of revenues. The economy of the country is heavily dependent on the immigrant workforce, notably from India and poorer Middle East states.

Once part of the Ottoman empire, Qatar signed a protection treaty with Britain in 1916. Having failed to set up a federation of emerging new states in the area, it declared its independence in 1971. [*Map page 22*] ■

AREA  11,000 sq km [4,247 sq mls]
POPULATION  540,000
CAPITAL (POPULATION)  Doha (217,000)
GOVERNMENT  Constitutional absolute monarchy
ETHNIC GROUPS  Southern Asian 34%, Qatari 20%
LANGUAGES  Arabic
RELIGIONS  Islam 92%, Christianity, Hinduism
CURRENCY  Qatar riyal = 100 dirhams

# RÉUNION

Réunion is the largest of the Mascarene islands, lying east of Madagascar and south-west of Mauritius and composed of a rugged, mountainous forested centre surrounded by a fertile coastal plain. The volcanic mountains rise in spectacular scenery to the peak of the sporadically active Piton des Neiges (3,070 m [10,076 ft]). Réunion receives heavy rainfall from the cool south-east trade winds in winter, while the summers can be oppressively hot and humid.

The lowlands are intensely cultivated with huge plantations of sugar cane; providing 75% of exports (plus rum 3%), this remains the island's only significant industry, though vanilla, perfume oils and tea also produce revenue. Local consumption revolves around vegetables, maize and livestock. Tourism is a big hope for the future, following the success of Mauritius, but unemployment is high and France still subsidizes the islands heavily in return for its use as the main military base in the area. The people of the island – which has a very varied and potentially explosive ethnic mix – are divided on its status; as in the other overseas departments (Guadeloupe, Martinique and French Guiana), there is increasing pressure on Paris for independence, especially from the young underprivileged population. In 1991 several people were killed in outbreaks of civil unrest. [*Map page 3*] ■

---

**AREA** 2,510 sq km [969 sq mls]
**POPULATION** 644,000
**CAPITAL (POPULATION)** Saint-Denis (122,875)
**GOVERNMENT** French overseas department
**ETHNIC GROUPS** Mixed 64%, East Indian 28%, Chinese 2%, East African 1%
**LANGUAGES** French, Creole
**RELIGIONS** Christianity (mainly Roman Catholic), Islam
**CURRENCY** French currency

---

# ROMANIA

O n three sides Romania has clearly defined natural boundaries – the Danube in the south, the Black Sea coast, 200 km [125 mls]

long, in the east, and the River Prut in the north-east – but in the west the frontier with Hungary crosses the Hungarian Plain, cutting across several tributaries of the River Tisa.

Romania is dominated by a great arc of high fold mountains, the Carpathians, which curve round the plateaux of Transylvania in the heart of the country. South and east of the Carpathians are the plains of the lower Danube. The southern arm of the fold mountains, rising to 2,538 m [8,327 ft], is known as the Transylvanian Alps, the legendary home of Count Dracula. Where these meet the Danube, on the border with Yugoslavia, the river has cut a deep gorge – the Iron Gate (Portile de Fier) – whose rapids over 160 km [100 mls] long have been tamed by the construction of a huge barrage. In the east the Danube delta area has more than 3,000 glaciated lakes and some of Europe's most celebrated expanses of wetland.

There is a great contrast between the fairy-tale landscape of wooded hills in Transylvania and the Carpathians, and the wheat and maize fields of the Danubian lowlands.

## ECONOMY AND RESOURCES

Romania is still a strong agricultural country, with an export surplus of cereals, timber, fruits and wine, though the agrarian workforce shrank from 75% in 1950 to less than 30% in 1984. In 1991 the country ranked sixth in maize production and tenth in wine.

Under Ceausescu there was a great drive to develop industries, based on the abundant oil and gas resources of areas on the flanks of the Transylvanian Alps. The copper, lead, zinc and aluminium industries use domestic supplies, mainly found in the Bihor Massif in Transylvania, but the iron and steel industry, especially the new plant at Galati at the head of the Danubian delta, relies on imported ores.

Bucharest, the capital, lies between the Danube and the Carpathians. An important industrial centre, its manufactures include vehicles, textiles and foodstuffs.

## HISTORY AND POLITICS

Ceausescu's 24-year rule was one of the Communist world's most odious. Corrupt and self-seeking, he had nevertheless won plaudits from the West for his independent stance against Soviet control – including a knighthood from Queen Elizabeth II. Coming to power in 1965, he accelerated the party policy of distancing the country from Moscow's foreign aims while pursuing a strict Stalinist approach on the domestic front. The remorseless industrialization and urbanization programmes of the 1970s caused a severe debt problem, and in the 1980s he switched economic tack, cutting imports and diverting output to exports. But while Romania achieved the enviable status of a net creditor, its people – brainwashed by incessant propaganda – were reduced from sufficiency to subsidence to shortage, with food and energy both savagely rationed. Meanwhile, with many of his relatives in positions of power, Ceausescu built ghetto-like 'agro-industrial' housing complexes, desecrating some of the country's finest architecture and demolishing thousands of villages in the process.

The army-backed revolt of 1989 began in the western province of Transylvania, following the suppression of demonstrations in Timisoara by the notorious *Securitate* (secret police). It culminated only days later in the execution of the dictator Nicolae Ceausescu and his wife on Christmas Day, on charges of genocide and corruption. A provisional government of the National Salvation Front (founded only on 22 December) took control; much of the old administrative apparatus was dismantled, the Communist Party was dissolved and religion was re-legalized. In May 1990, under Ion Iliescu, the NSF won Romania's first free elections since the war by a huge majority – a result judged flawed but not fraudulent by international observers.

The NSF, however, contained many old-guard Communists, and its credibility sank further when Iliescu used miners to curb anti-government demonstrations. Strikes and protests continued, not only against the new authorities but also against the effects of a gradual but nevertheless marked switch to a market economy: food shortages, rampant inflation and rising unemployment. In addition, foreign investment was sluggish, deterred by the political instability. During 1991 the struggle between the two factions of the NSF – conservative President Iliescu (a former Ceausescu Politburo member) and reformist

Prime Minister Petre Roman – personified the split that existed right across a country in desperate need of unity.

Another problem appeared with the new independent status of Moldova. The republic has a vociferous Romanian minority in the large area of Bessarabia, handed over to the USSR as part of the Hitler-Stalin pact of 1940 and not returned by the Red Army in 1945. The new mood in the former Soviet Union rekindled the concept of *Romania Mare* ('Greater Romania').

A new constitution, approved in 1991, made the country a democratic republic. Elections held under this constitution in 1992 again resulted in victory for Ion Iliescu, whose party was renamed the Party of Social Democracy in 1993. In March 1994 a coalition government was formed, but the government still faces many problems as it tries to reform the economy. [*Map page 17*] ■

---

**AREA** 237,500 sq km [91,699 sq mls]
**POPULATION** 22,922,000
**CAPITAL (POPULATION)** Bucharest (2,064,000)
**GOVERNMENT** Multiparty republic
**ETHNIC GROUPS** Romanian 89%, Hungarian 7%, Gypsy 2%
**LANGUAGES** Romanian (official)
**RELIGIONS** Christianity (Romanian Orthodox 87%, Roman Catholic 5%, Greek Orthodox 4%)
**CURRENCY** Leu = 100 bani

---

# RUSSIA

---

It is an indication of the sheer size of the former Soviet Union that, having shed very nearly a quarter of its area with the departure of the 14 republics in 1991, the Russian Federation remains by far the largest country in the world, still getting on for twice the size of Canada, China or the USA. This territorial immensity brings a number of disadvantages – it is awkward to administer, large investments have to be made in the transport system and the long borders are difficult to defend – but set against these are the benefits that derive from the diversity of environments and cultures and the abundance of resources in the country's vast expanses, many of which are relatively untouched.

**Landscape**

Diversity certainly characterizes Russia's landforms, for within the country's borders are to be found rugged peaks and salt flats, glaciers and deserts, marshes and rolling hills as well as broad level plains. In the west the North European Plain, underlain by the ancient peneplained rocks of the Russian platform, occupies the greater part of European Russia as well as much of Ukraine and all of Belarus and the Baltic nations. On the eastern side of the plain are the Ural Mountains: popularly seen as the divide between Europe and Asia, the Urals are low and rounded with few peaks rising above 1,600 m [5,248 ft]. The eastern slopes of the Urals merge into the West Siberian lowland, the largest plain in the world, with extensive low-lying marshes. Still further to the east the Siberian platform, similar in origin to the Russian platform, underlies the Central Siberian Plateau. The relief of this plateau is a good example of a peneplain, with its rolling uplands rising 500 to 700 m [1,640 to 2,300 ft] and deeply incised river valleys.

The extensive plains of Russia are surrounded on the south and east by mountain ranges of geologically recent origin: the Caucasus, rising to over 5,000 m [16,400 ft] on the borders of Georgia and Azerbaijan; the Altai and Sayan, extending into Mongolia; and, beyond Lake Baykal and the Lena River, the East Siberian ranges at the easternmost tip of the Asian land mass. The Kamchatka peninsula is still geologically unstable – part of the 'Pacific Rim' – and volcanic eruptions and earthquakes occur fairly often. Much of Russia's landscape bears the imprint of the last Ice Age in the form of chaotic drainage systems, extensive marshlands, lakes and moraines in the lowland areas and cirques and U-shaped valleys in the mountains. Today large areas remain ice-bound, while more than half the total area has permafrost – permanently frozen ground which may extend

## TRANS-SIBERIAN RAILWAY

The world's longest line, the Trans-Siberian Railway runs for 9,310 km [5,785 mls] from Moscow to Vladivostok and Nakhodka on the Sea of Japan. The Siberian section, beginning at Chelyabinsk in the southern Urals, was built between 1881 and 1905, with an extension round Lake Baykal completed in 1917. The line has played a crucial role in opening up Siberia for settlement and industrialization, and most of the major cities and towns are served by it. Today the lifeline is largely double-track and electrified; the whole journey from capital to coast (involving 92 stops in eight time zones) takes over seven days. A spur of 3,200 km [2,000 mls], opened in 1984, passes north of Lake Baykal to reach Sovetskaya Gavan, opposite the island of Sakhalin.

hundreds of metres in depth. In the permafrost of East Siberia prehistoric woolly mammoths have been found in near-perfect condition.

The rivers that flow across the Russian plains are among the longest and most languid in the world. Drainage in European Russia forms a radial pattern with the hub in the Central Uplands west of Moscow. The Volga flows from this area for 3,700 km [2,300 mls] south to the landlocked Caspian Sea, the world's largest inland body of water. In Siberia the main rivers flow north to the Arctic – among them the Yenisey-Angara, the Ob-Irtysh and the Lena, respectively the fifth, sixth and 11th longest in the world. Shifting channels and irregular flow make these rivers difficult to navigate and they are ice-bound in winter. In the east Lake Baykal (Oz Baykal) acts as a holding reservoir for the Yenisey.

**Natural regions**

Extending latitudinally across Russia, and corresponding to the major climatic belts, are a series of sharply differentiated natural zones – from north to south the tundra, the taiga, the mixed forests and the steppe. The dominant natural zones can also be seen as vertical bands in the mountainous regions.

**Tundra:** This zone forms a continuous strip north of the Arctic Circle from the Norwegian border to Kamchatka. Climatic conditions here restrict plant growth and soil formation so that the region well deserves its name 'bald mountain top', the meaning of the word 'tundra' in Lapp. Stunted shrubs, mosses, lichens and berry-bearing bushes growing in thin, infertile soils form the vegetation cover, supporting various hardy creatures – including the herds of reindeer which for centuries have formed the basis of the local tribes' economy.

**Taiga:** Extending south from the boundary with the tundra and occupying about 60% of the country are the coniferous forests that make up the taiga – larger than the Amazonian rainforest. Different species of tree dominate in different parts of the taiga, but throughout the most common are firs, pines and the silver birch. Soils under the forest are podzols, a Russian term meaning 'ashy-grey underneath'. These soils are acidic and usually unsuitable for cultivation unless fertilized. A major source of wealth in the taiga has always been its large population of fur-bearing animals such as ermine, sable and beaver – and it was the quest for furs that first lured man into this inhospitable environment.

**Mixed forest:** In the west and east the coniferous forests merge into zones of mixed forest – wide in European Russia but contracting towards the east to form a narrow finger which peters out beyond the Urals. The mixed forest contains both coniferous species and broadleaves such as oak, beech, ash, hornbeam and maple. Today much of the natural vegetation has been cleared for farming, despite the fact that the soils require heavy application of fertilizers to be productive. From early times the mixed forest has been the focus of settlement for the Russians and has supported large numbers of people.

**Steppe:** Sandwiched between the forests to the north and the semi-deserts and deserts of the Central Asian republics to the south is the steppe zone. Hardly any natural vegetation remains in the steppe today as vast expanses have been brought under the plough. The soils of the steppe are chernozems, black-earths, and they are among the most fertile in the world. Before conversion into farmland the steppe consisted of extensive grasslands which

## LAKE BAYKAL

With a lowest point of 1,620 m [5,315 ft], Oz Baykal in southern Siberia is the world's deepest lake. Also the largest in Eurasia – at 636 km [395 mls] long by an average width of 48 km [30 mls] it measures some 31,500 sq km [12,160 sq mls], more than the area of Belgium – it is so deep that it is the world's largest body of fresh water and indeed contains no less than a fifth of the fresh water contained in all the world's lakes. Its volume of 23,000 cu km [5,520 cu mls] is as much as the five Great Lakes of North America combined.

Situated in a deep tectonic basin, and fed by 336 rivers and streams, it acts as a reservoir for only one river: the Angara, which flows north to join the Yenisey. Though renowned for the purity of its water and its endemic lifeforms (65% of its 1,500 animal species and 35% of its plant species are unique to Baykal), industrial plants, including mining but notably cellulose factories at the southern end, have caused increasing pollution since the 1960s.

The graben fault that hosts the arc-shaped lake was caused by gigantic upheavals in the Earth's crust some 80 million years ago. When the climate turned wetter, about 25 million years ago, the lake began to fill – and it is still getting larger. When the *sarma* wind blows from the north-west, it generates waves more than 5 m [16.5 ft] high. Located 80 km [50 mls] from the Mongolian border, Lake Baykal drains an area of 540,000 sq km [208,500 sq mls] – an area 13% greater than that drained by all five of North America's Great Lakes.

in the north were interspersed with trees. The vast majority of the steppeland of the former Soviet Union, however, falls in the Ukraine and Kazakhstan.

## ECONOMY AND RESOURCES

Russia's physical environment offers varied opportunities for exploitation. The vast stretches of forest make it the world's largest possessor of softwoods, but although the most extensive stands are found in Siberia, felling has been concentrated in the European part of the country, where the wood is of high quality and is more readily accessible.

The rivers, lakes and seas have yielded marine and freshwater products from early days. In the 11th century fishing villages were already established on the northern coast of European Russia for whaling, sealing and fishing. Today fish catches are large on the Pacific coast while, among the freshwater varieties, the sturgeon continues to be valued for its famous caviar.

Because of the widespread occurrence of poor soils and harsh climatic conditions, agriculture is confined to a relatively small area of the country. Most of the arable is in the steppe and forest-steppe and from the time this was first ploughed it has been used for grains. More than half of the output that made the USSR the world's top producer of barley, oats and rye, and second in wheat, came from Russian land. On the Black Sea coast, sub-tropical conditions allow the cultivation of crops exotic to the rest of the country, including wines, tea and citrus fruits.

Mineral and energy resources are abundant and formed the basis of the former USSR's powerful industrial economy. The most notable mineral deposits are found on the Kola peninsula by the Barents Sea, in eastern Siberia and the far east where spectacular discoveries of gold, lead, zinc, copper and diamonds have been made. Iron ore is found in most regions – the Soviet Union produced a quarter of the world total – but the most recently opened field is at Kursk, south of Moscow. Energy resources are varied. Estimates show Russia to have sufficient coal to last several hundred years, while oil and natural gas deposits are projected to last for several decades, with the main fields in the Volga-Urals region and western Siberia. Before 'deconstruction' the USSR was by far the world's leading producer of oil and gas, and Russia itself was responsible for over 90% of oil output and nearly 80% of gas. Large hydropower complexes have also been built on many rivers, though the development of nuclear energy remains under review following the tragic disaster of Chernobyl (in the Ukraine) in 1986.

## THE KURIL ISLANDS

A chain of 56 windswept volcanically active islands extending 1,200 km [750 mls] between the end of Russia's Kamchatka Peninsula and the tip of Japan's northern island of Hokkaido, the Kurils separate the Sea of Okhotsk from the Pacific Ocean. Totalling 15,600 sq km [6,000 sq mls] but sparsely peopled, they were discovered by the Dutch in 1634, divided between Russia and Japan in the 18th century and ceded to Japan in 1875. At the end of World War II they were seized by Stalin, giving his fleets ice-free northern access to the Pacific. The Japanese, however, still regard the southern section – Etorofu, Kunashir, Shikotan and the Habomai islets – as theirs, referring to them as the 'northern territories' and allotting 7 February as a national day in their honour.

Though there are rich fishing grounds in the territorial waters and the possibility of mineral wealth, it is indeed a matter of honour rather than economics for Tokyo. The Soviets offered to return Shikotan and the Habomai islands in 1956, but the Japanese held out for all four, and the offer was withdrawn. While the advent of Gorbachev and glasnost made little difference, the deconstruction of the Soviet Union has: Boris Yeltsin's Russia, desperate for Japanese aid and co-operation, found the islands a stumbling block to assistance. However, over half the population who have moved there since 1945 are Russian, and in a 1991 poll the islanders voted 4–1 to remain under Moscow's control – even though various bridge-building exercises were being initiated towards Japan.

## Population

The state that the Communists inherited in 1917 was not merely large; it was also made up of peoples of very diverse ethnic, religious and cultural backgrounds. Among the varied peoples – speaking over 100 languages – the Slavs, consisting of the Russians, Ukrainians and Belarussians, were the most numerous. Other groups include the Turkik and Persian people of Central Asia, the Caucasians, the

Baltic peoples, Finno-Ugrians, Mongols and many others. Under Soviet rule the ethnic diversity of the state was recognized in the existence of federal republics (of very disparate size), and autonomous republics and regions were set up to recognize smaller ethnic groups.

Although all parts of Russia are inhabited, even the most remote, the greatest concentration of people has traditionally been in the European part of the country. It was here that in the centuries before the Revolution the first Russian towns with their fortresses (*kremlins*) and onion-domed churches were founded. Outside this settled core there were towns and cities which the Russians acquired during their expansion or themselves established on the frontiers. In central Asia the Russians took over what had once been a flourishing urban civilization, gaining towns such as Bukhara (Bukhoro), Samarkand (Samarqand) and Khiva all now in Uzbekistan.

After the Revolution, changes took place in the distribution of population so that the former pattern of a small highly populated core and 'empty' periphery began to break down. Today the settled area extends into Siberia and, in a narrow band, across to the Pacific Ocean. As a result, a far higher proportion of the Russian population is to be found east of the Urals than before the Revolution, even before World War II. This redistribution has been actively encouraged by a regime committed to a policy of developing the east. Migration to the towns and cities has also been marked since 1917 so that the greater part of the Russian population is now urban (in 1990 it was 74%). Some of these urban settlements have been built from scratch during Soviet times and are to be found in the more remote regions of the country. Norilsk, for example, was founded in the 1930s north of the Arctic Circle near to important mineral deposits. The most famous city is the capital Moscow (Moskva); like the other cities of the North European Plain, it is a mixture of the old and the new, but it is also a mixture of European and Asian styles and cultures.

While Russian cities and towns have been the site of vigorous building programmes, villages all over the country have changed ittle. In the forests, people still live in the traditional wooden hut (*izba*), while in the steppe agricultural workers' dwellings are often of wattle and daub. Electricity has been introduced and in most villages a range of other services is now provided, though some still do not have a modern sanitation system or running water.

## ECONOMIC DEVELOPMENT

The Soviet government transformed the USSR from an underdeveloped country into the second most powerful industrial nation of the world. At the time of the Revolution (1917) most industrial development was concentrated in a few centres in the European part of the country: Moscow, St Petersburg and, in the Ukraine, the Donbas. Also, much was financed by foreign investment and the development of major industrial sectors was unbalanced. On taking power the Communist Party vowed to develop industry rapidly and to introduce it into the backward regions of the country. As in many other parts of the world, Soviet industrialization was initially based on the iron and steel industry. In Stalin's drive of the 1930s, heavy national investment went into expanding production in the already existing industrial areas of European Russia and establishing the industry in central and eastern Russia; new large integrated steel mills were built in the southern Urals and on the Kuzbas coalfield in western Siberia. Later the industry was introduced into the Kazakh republic on the Karaganda coalfield. Most recently a new plant has been established at Kursk in European Russia.

The shift away from coal as a basis for industrial development to alternative energy sources has taken place later in the countries of the former Soviet Union than in many other countries. Since the 1960s, however, petroleum and natural gas industries have begun to develop rapidly and the same is true of industries based on hydroelectricity; HEP has been especially important in building up industry in eastern Siberia, where massive installations on the River Angara provide the energy for aluminium production.

Although the introduction of large-scale industry into formerly backward parts of the country has helped to even out levels of development, regional imbalances in production in the territories of the old Soviet Union

## COMMONWEALTH OF INDEPENDENT STATES

After 74 years, the Union of Soviet Socialist Republics slipped into history a week ahead of schedule on Christmas Day 1991, when Mikhail Gorbachev resigned the leadership of what had become a nation only on paper. His offices in the Kremlin were occupied by Boris Yeltsin, first President of the Russian Federation and driving force behind the 'deconstruction' of the Soviet Union.

Though far from substituted, the USSR was in part replaced by the Commonwealth of Independent States, born in Minsk on 8 December 1991 when Russia, Ukraine and hosts Belarus – between them responsible for 73% of the Soviet population, nearly 80% of its grain production and over 85% of its industrial output – signed a declaration effectively ending the former superpower's life both as a geopolitical entity and as a force in international relations. Two weeks later, in the Kazakhstan capital of Alma-Ata, they were joined by Moldova, Armenia, Azerbaijan and the five Asian republics; missing were the three Baltic states (already *de facto* independent nations), and Georgia: Georgia finally joined in March 1994. Azerbaijani and Moldovan membership effectively lapsed because of non-ratification until September 1993 and April 1994 respectively. The declaration from the 11 governments covered subjects as diverse as international borders, human rights, ethnic minorities, non-interference and international law, while setting up committees on foreign affairs, defence, finance, transport and security.

These remarkable events, spread over less than three weeks, could be traced back to 1985 and the appointment of Gorbachev as General Secretary of the Communist Party. His unprecedented policies of *glasnost* (openness) and *perestroika* (restructuring) were to have a devastating effect in a very short time. The domestic impact was equally dramatic, the republics of the USSR ridding themselves of doctrinaire Communism, adopting pluralism and declaring themselves independent of Moscow. In 1991, the entire system through which the Soviet Union had functioned for seven decades came crumbling down in the course of one calendar year.

The first signs of actual disintegration of the USSR came in January 1991 in Lithuania, and within weeks all three Baltic states had voted for independence, Georgia following in March. Over the next few months Gorbachev tried continually to establish consensus on a new Union treaty and economic reform, but when Yeltsin became directly elected President of Russia in June, his federation took the lead in opposing the Soviet president's increasingly personal and decree-based rule as he attempted to find a middle way between the old guard and the progressives.

While the new laws had produced far-reaching effects on the political and social lives of Soviet citizens, the parallel restructuring of the economy patently failed – not least because the movement to a market economy was constantly hindered by party bureaucrats, factory managers, collective farm chairmen and many others who were unwilling to see the erosion of their positions.

In August, hardline Communist leaders ousted Gorbachev – detaining him in his Crimean *dacha* – and a small emergency committee took control of the Soviet Union. Resistance, bravely led by Yeltsin, centred on Moscow, and after three days the coup collapsed. Gorbachev returned to his post in the Kremlin, but his already tenuous position, now undermined by events, was further weakened by the worst harvest for a decade, an energy crisis that included a coal-miners' strike, and the collapse of the Soviet Central Bank.

On 21 December Gorbachev was told by the Alma-Ata protocol that his services were no longer required; outmanoeuvred by Yeltsin and overtaken by events, he resigned on Christmas Day, and the tricolour flag of Russia replaced the hammer and sickle on the Kremlin. Two days later, the Chamber of Deputies of the Supreme Soviet, the USSR's parliament, formally voted itself out of existence, and the Soviet Union was clinically dead.

remain large. The pre-revolutionary foci of development continued to attract a large proportion of available investment and retained

their leading position in Soviet industry. This effectively means Russia, and of the regions developed since the Revolution only western

Siberia can be said to have a well-developed mature industrial structure today. Other parts of Russia and the former Soviet Union, especially the non-Russian republics in the south, still have relatively weak industrial economies. For example, in 1989 the Russian Federation produced nearly 60% of both crude steel and agricultural machinery. In both cases the Ukraine was a respectable second (35% and 30%), but the next republic was below 5%.

While overall industrial production forged ahead, agriculture was the 'Achilles' heel' of the Soviet economy, and in several years from the middle 1960s foreign grain had to be imported. Since 1965 there has been a notable improvement in yields but even so output and consumption per capita can only just keep ahead of increases in population. Western commentators often ascribed the poor performance of agriculture to concentration on farms which are too large and too impersonal to be efficient.

Soviet farms were of two types, collective (*kolkhozi*) and state (*sovkhozi*). The former were, according to the official definition, democratically-run producers' co-operatives which, in return for a grant of land, delivered some of their produce to the state. In theory free to run their affairs, they were always subject to considerable government interference. The equally large state farms were state owned and managed. Until the 1950s they were relatively uncommon because they were expensive to run, but in the last two decades their number increased. While the greater part of total Soviet agricultural output came from collective and state farms, a large share of market garden produce and some livestock products originated on the so-called personal plots of farm workers.

In both agriculture and industry the Soviet government pursued large-scale projects. Campaigns, as they were called in the former USSR, were at times launched to rapidly increase the output of chemicals or machinery, for example. A much-publicized campaign in agriculture was launched in the 1950s to bring into cultivation thousands of hectares of hitherto fallow land east of the Ural Mountains. As a result of this project, much of it in Kazakhstan and called the Virgin Lands Campaign, the sown land of the nation doubled in the space of a few years. Following some initial difficulties, and the ensuing withdrawal from some of the more marginal land, the Virgin Lands are now a principal grain-producing region.

In the drive for economic development, the Soviet government at first neglected the consumer sector. Growth rates in textiles, food industries and wood processing, for example, lagged behind those for iron and steel production. The paucity of consumer goods, often compounded by gross inefficiencies in the state distribution system, was obvious in the size of the queues that formed whenever scarce products came on sale. Another indication is the existence of a flourishing black market.

During Stalin's rule a conscious policy to restrict foreign trade and maximize self-sufficiency was pursued. With the formation of Comecon, the Eastern trading block, after World War II and the realization that much of Western technology would be useful to its own continued development, the USSR revised trade policy. By the 1980s the Soviet Union was trading with most countries of the world, although the Soviet share of total turnover was small. Once again, Russia had the lion's share: while only 15% of its output went to other Soviet republics in 1989, the nearest rivals were Ukraine and Kazakhstan (32%), while six republics recorded a dependency of more than 60% and another four a figure of more than 50%.

## HISTORY AND POLITICS

The present size of Russia is the product of a long period of evolution. In early medieval times the first Slavic state, Kievan Rus, was formed at the junction of the forest and steppe in what is now the Ukraine. As the centuries wore on other states were formed further to the north. All were eventually united under the principality of Muscovy. In the 13th century Mongol hordes from the east penetrated the forests and held sway over the Slavic people there, extracting tribute from them.

It was only in the 16th century that the Mongol yoke was thrown off as the Slavs, under Ivan the Terrible, began to advance across the steppes. This signalled the beginning of a period of expansion from the core area of Slavic settlement to the south, east and west. Expansion across Siberia was rapid and the first Russian settlement on the Pacific, Okhotsk, was established in 1649. Progress across the open steppe, the realm of tribal horsemen, was slower but by 1696 Azov, the key to the Black Sea, was secured. A series of struggles in the 17th and 18th centuries against the Swedes and Poles resulted in the addition of the Gulf of Finland, the Baltic coast and part of Poland to the growing Russian empire, and in the 19th century the Caucasus, Central Asia and new territories in the Far East were added. In the 20th century the gains and losses of area through war, treaties and secret deals have been comparatively small, if at times dramatic.

Russia has been a centralized state throughout its history. A major landmark in the country's history, and indeed in the history of the world, was the 1917 Revolution, when the Tsarist order was overthrown and a Communist government established under Lenin – replacing one form of totalitarianism with another. The years from 1917 witnessed colossal changes in the political, social and economic structure of the country, the most dramatic and far-reaching of which took place from the 1930s when Stalin instituted central planning of the economy, collectivized agriculture and began a period of rapid industrialization. After Stalin's death in 1953, Soviet leaders modified some policies but they remained true to the general principles of Communism until the radical approach of Gorbachev changed the face of Russia – and in the process most of the Communist world.

**A new country**

Given its size and resources it may be thought that Russia would not need the Commonwealth of Independent States, its economic strength (properly managed) making it more than viable as a major nation and a natural successor internationally to the Soviet Union; indeed it inherited the USSR's mantle on the UN Security Council and its diplomatic missions worldwide, while applying for membership of CSCE and even NATO.

But Russia, despite its size, fears isolation. With the Eastern European countries and the Baltic states fully independent, the three Caucasus republics unstable, the Asian republics (whose fast-growing populations suggest that by 2000 Russia will lose its majority in the CIS) looking increasingly to their Islamic neighbours, and even Mongolia converting to democracy and the free market, Russia has little control of the former 'buffer zones'. Though large and powerful, it has always felt under siege, and better that the buffers were partners rather than opponents. In any case, at least in the medium term, the Commonwealth states had to live with the structure created by the Soviet system – and that meant interdependency.

Despite Gorbachev's best and at times brave efforts, the Russian President Boris Yeltsin inherited an economy in crisis, bogged down by lumbering and often obstructive bureaucracy, inept use of resources and a cumbersome, inefficient transport system, of which the state airline Aeroflot (the world's largest) was a prime example. Though the West preferred aid, the impressive-sounding amounts were relatively small, and the final solution would have to lie with the Russians themselves.

After the abolition of price controls sent the cost of basic commodities rocketing, 1992 and 1993 saw food shortages worsen and unemployment rise. Like Eastern Europe, the Russians found it difficult to stabilize their economy, its citizens paying a high price for the introduction of Western-style democratic capitalism. However, in spite of these difficulties, the people backed Yeltsin's programme of reforms in a referendum in April 1993. In October 1993, Yeltsin used the army to crush a parliamentary rebellion and in elections held in December 1993 won backing for his proposed new constitution giving the president extensive powers. However, these elections also saw the emergence as a significant political force of Zhironovsky's extreme nationalist party and the bitter struggle between conservatives and reformers showed no sign of abating.

Neither is the nation homogenous. Several autonomous regions – including Karelia, Komi, North Ossetia, Tatarstan, Gorno-Altay, Bashkortostan, Buryatia and the vast Sakha (formerly Yakutia) – declared independence in the last months of Soviet control. They could well pursue their policy (although some have been dissuaded by the war in Chechenia), effectively reducing Russia's size and influence in the region. [*Map pages 20–1*] ∎

> **AREA** 17,075,000 sq km [6,592,000 sq mls]
> **POPULATION** 147,370,000
> **CAPITAL (POPULATION)** Moscow (8,957,000)
> **GOVERNMENT** Federal multiparty republic
> **ETHNIC GROUPS** Russian 82%, Tatar 4%, Ukrainian 3%, Chuvash 1%, more than 100 other nationalities
> **LANGUAGES** Russian (official)
> **RELIGIONS** Christianity (mainly Russian Orthodox, with Roman Catholic and Protestant minorities), Islam, Judaism
> **CURRENCY** Russian rouble = 100 kopecks

# RWANDA

The Republic of Rwanda is a small, land-locked African country, bordered by Uganda, Tanzania, Burundi and Zaïre. Lake Kivu and the River Ruzizi form the boundary in the west. These two features lie in the Great African Rift Valley. Overlooking the valley in western Rwanda are high, volcanic mountains of the Mufumbiro Range, reaching 4,507 m [14,787 ft] above sea level in the north-west.

Kigali stands on the central plateau of Rwanda. Here, temperatures are moderated by the altitude. The rainfall is abundant, but much heavier rain falls on the western mountains. The floor of the Great Rift Valley is warmer and drier than the rest of the country.

Rainforests occur in the west of the country. These forests contain many plant and animal species, including mountain gorillas. Forests once also covered eastern Rwanda, but they have been largely cut down to create farmland. The cleared land has been badly eroded by the heavy rain.

## ECONOMY AND RESOURCES

Rwanda is by far the most densely populated state in Africa – in 1994 there were 295 people per sq km [762 people per sq mls] – and the steep slopes are intensively cultivated. Most people are poor farmers, who produce little more than they need to feed their own families. Some cattle are raised, and food crops include bananas, beans, cassava and sorghum. The country's most valuable crop is coffee, which accounts for more than 70% of Rwanda's exports. Some tea, tungsten, pyrethrum, which is used to make insecticides, and tin are other products which are exported. Rwanda has few manufacturing industries, and when conditions permit there is a large movement into neighbouring countries for employment.

## HISTORY AND POLITICS

Rwanda was merged with Burundi by German colonialism in 1899, making Ruanda-Urundi part of German East Africa. Belgium occupied it during World War I, and then administered the territory under a League of Nations mandate, later (1946) a UN trusteeship. In 1959 it was again divided into two, Rwanda finally achieving full independence in 1962, the same year as Burundi.

As in Burundi, there are deep social and cultural divisons between the farming majority and the traditional, nomadic owners of cattle. Several decades of ethnic strife climaxed in 1990 when a rebel force of Tutsi 'refugees' invaded from Uganda and occupied much of the north before being repulsed by French, British and Zaïrian troops brought in by the Hutu-dominated Rwanda government. The problems stem from the revolution of 1959, when the Hutu overthrew the aristocratic Tutsi minority rulers in one of the most violent clashes in modern African history. In February 1991, in return for its neighbours granting Tutsi refugees citizenship, Rwandan leaders agreed to the principle of a return to democracy, but the violence continued into 1992, and erupted again in 1994 with appalling loss of life (500,000 people were massacred in three months), following the dual assassination of the presidents of both Rwanda and Burundi when their aircraft was hit by a rocket as it approached the airport at Kigali. Tens of thousands of refugees fled to neighbouring countries, placing a great strain on those countries' resources as well as the aid agencies trying to remedy the situation. [*Map page 33*] ■

AREA  26,340 sq km [10,170 sq mls]
POPULATION  7,750,000
CAPITAL (POPULATION)  Kigali (232,730)
GOVERNMENT  Republic
ETHNIC GROUPS  Hutu 90%, Tutsi 9%, Twa 1%
LANGUAGES  French and Kinyarwanda (both official)
RELIGIONS  Christianity 74% (mainly Roman Catholic), traditional beliefs 17%, Islam 9%
CURRENCY  Rwandan franc = 100 centimes

# ST CHRISTOPHER & NEVIS

The federation comprises two well-watered volcanic islands, mountains rising on both to around 1,000 m [3,300 ft], and about 20% forested.

Thanks to fine beaches, tourism (88,264 visitors in 1992) has replaced sugar, nationalized in 1975 and still producing 57% of exports, as the main exchange earner. Industries include electronic equipment, footwear, batik and sugar derivatives; the main agricultural products are cotton, copra, palm oil, bananas, cocoa and tropical vegetables.

The first West Indian islands to be colonized by Britain (1623 and 1628), St Christopher and Nevis became independent in 1983. St Christopher is usually shortened to St Kitts; Nevis derives its name from Columbus (1493), to whom the cloud-covered peaks were reminiscent of Spanish mountains (*nieves* meaning snow). [*Map page 30*] ■

AREA  360 sq km [139 sq mls]
POPULATION  41,000
CAPITAL (POPULATION)  Basseterre (15,000)
GOVERNMENT  Constitutional monarchy
ETHNIC GROUPS  Of African descent
LANGUAGES  English
RELIGIONS  Christianity
CURRENCY  East Caribbean dollar = 100 cents

# ST HELENA

St Helena is an isolated rectangular, slab-sided island of old volcanic rocks, well off the main line of the Mid-Atlantic Ridge and measuring 122 sq km [47 sq mls]. A tableland deeply dissected by valleys, it has steep cliffs and ridges, and there is relatively little flat ground available. Standing in the trade winds, St Helena has a cool tropical maritime climate, dry at sea level but moist enough for limited farming on the heights.

The population of about 6,000, mainly of East Indian descent, produce potatoes and other vegetables and raise cattle, sheep and goats on smallholdings. Cultivable land is scarce and many are unemployed.

St Helena, a British colony since 1834 and the administrative centre for six of the UK's South Atlantic islands, is heavily dependent on subsidies. [*Map page 33*] ■

AREA  112 sq km [47 sq mls]
POPULATION  6,000
CAPITAL (POPULATION)  Jamestown (1,500)
GOVERNMENT  Dependent territory of the UK
ETHNIC GROUPS  Mixed European (British), Asian and African
LANGUAGES  English
RELIGIONS  Christianity
CURRENCY  St Helenian pound = 100 pence

# ST LUCIA

A mountainous, forested island of extinct volcanoes – graphically represented on its flag – St Lucia boasts a huge variety of plant and animal life. To the south of its highest point of Mt Gimie (949 m [3,114 ft]) lies the Qualibou, an area containing 18 lava domes and seven craters. In the west are the dramatic Pitons, rising to over 750 m [2,460 ft].

Though not poor, St Lucia is still overdependent on bananas, a crop easily hit by hurricane and disease. It is supported by coconuts and cocoa, and the free port of Vieux Fort has attracted modern industries. Cruise liners deliver tourists to Castries, and the Grande Cul de Sac Bay to the south is one of the deepest tanker ports in the Americas, used mainly for trans-shipment of oil.

First settled by the British in 1605, St Lucia changed hands between Britain and France 14 times before finally being ceded formally in 1814. Internally self-governing as 'Associated State of the UK' from 1967, it gained full independence within the Commonwealth in 1979. [*Map page 30*] ■

**AREA** 610 sq km [236 sq mls]
**POPULATION** 141,000
**CAPITAL (POPULATION)** Castries (56,000)
**GOVERNMENT** Constitutional monarchy
**ETHNIC GROUPS** Of African descent 90%, Mixed 6%, East Indian 3%
**LANGUAGES** English, French patois
**RELIGIONS** Christianity (Roman Catholic 90%, Protestant 7%, Anglican)
**CURRENCY** East Caribbean dollar = 100 cents

# ST VINCENT & THE GRENADINES

St Vincent is a mountainous, volcanic island that boasts luxuriant vegetation. Soufrière (1,178 m [3,866 ft]), which last erupted in 1979, is one of two active volcanoes in the eastern Caribbean – Mt Pelée is the other.

Bananas account for 38% of exports, but the island is also the world's biggest producer of arrowroot (for medicines and computer paper). Less prosperous than its Commonwealth neighbours, there are nevertheless prosperous pockets, notably Mustique and Bequia, where beautifully clean waters have fostered tourism.

St Vincent and the Grenadines comprise the main island (constituting 89% of the area and 95% of the population) and the Northern Grenadines, of which the largest are Bequia, Mustique and Canouan. 'Discovered' in 1498, St Vincent was settled in the 16th century and became a British colony with the Treaty of Versailles in 1783, after a century of conflict with France, often supported by the Caribs – the last of whom were deported to Honduras after the Indian War of 1795–7. The colony became self-governing in 1969 and gained independence as part of the Commonwealth in 1979. [*Map page 30*] ■

**AREA** 388 sq km [150 sq mls]
**POPULATION** 111,000
**CAPITAL (POPULATION)** Kingstown (26,500)
**GOVERNMENT** Constitutional monarchy
**ETHNIC GROUPS** Of African descent
**LANGUAGES** English, French patois
**RELIGIONS** Christianity
**CURRENCY** East Caribbean dollar = 100 cents

# SAN MARINO

Surrounded by Italy, the tiny independent state of San Marino – the world's smallest republic – lies 20 km [12 mls] south-west of the Adriatic port of Rimini. Most of the territory consists of the limestone mass of Monte Titano (725 m [2,382 ft]), around which are clustered wooded mountains, pastures, fortresses and medieval villages. The republic is named after St Marinus, the stonemason saint who is said to have first established a community here in the 4th century AD.

Nearly all the inhabitants live in the medieval fortified city of San Marino, which is visited by over 2 million tourists a year. The chief occupations are tourism (which accounts for 60% of total revenues), limestone quarrying and the making of wine, textiles, ceramics and paints.

San Marino has a friendship and co-operation treaty with Italy dating back to 1862; the ancient republic uses Italian currency, but issues its own stamps, which contribute a further 10% to state revenues. The *de facto* customs union with Italy makes San Marino an easy conduit for the illegal export of lira and certain kinds of tax evasion for Italians. The state is governed by an elected council and has its own legal system. In 1957 a bloodless takeover replaced the Communist-Socialist regime that had been in power from 1945. It has no armed forces, and police are 'hired' from the Italian constabulary. [*Map page 16*] ■

AREA 61 sq km [24 sq mls]
POPULATION 23,000
CAPITAL (POPULATION) San Marino (2,395)
GOVERNMENT Republic
ETHNIC GROUPS San Marinese, Italian
LANGUAGES Italian (official)
RELIGIONS Christianity (Roman Catholic)
CURRENCY Italian currency & San Marino lira = 100 centisimi

# SÃO TOMÉ & PRÍNCIPE

These mountainous, volcanic and heavily forested Atlantic islands some 145 km [90 mls] apart, comprise little more than twice the area of Andorra, with São Tomé the larger and more developed of the two. The highest point is Pico de São Tomé which stands at 2,024 m [6,640 ft].

A Portuguese colony since 1522, the islands were suddenly granted independence in 1975, and the cocoa plantations that formed the platform for the economy quickly deteriorated under a one-party hardline socialist state. Reliance on the Soviet Union was lessened from the mid-1980s and the cocoa industry revived – as well as diversification into palm oil, pepper and coffee and the encouragement of tourism.

In 1990 Marxism was abandoned altogether and, following the lead from many mainland African nations and pressure from Portugal (the main trading partner) and France (the major aid donor), São Tomé held multiparty

elections in 1991 – won by the opposition. [*Map page 33*] ■

AREA 964 sq km [372 sq mls]
POPULATION 130,000
CAPITAL (POPULATION) São Tomé (43,420)
GOVERNMENT Multiparty republic
ETHNIC GROUPS Mainly descendants of slaves
LANGUAGES Portuguese, Fang
RELIGIONS Christianity (mainly Roman Catholic)
CURRENCY Dobra = 100 centimos

# SAUDI ARABIA

The heart of the state – the largest in the Middle East but over 95% desert – consists of the province of Najd, within which are three main groups of oases. Najd is enclosed on its east side by a vast arc of sandy desert which broadens out into the two great dune-seas of Arabia, the Nafud in the north, and in the south the Rub 'al Khali, or 'Empty Quarter', the largest expanse of sand in the world. Here are found most of the country's Bedouin nomads, still deriving a living as traders and herdsmen.

To the west, Najd is separated from the border hills of the Red Sea by fields of rough basaltic lava. Particularly in its southern section towards the border with Yemen, this coastal strip is quite well supplied with water, and a high storage dam has been built inland from Jizan.

## ECONOMY AND RESOURCES
The hills of Asir which back the coastal plain benefit from the summer monsoon, and are extensively terraced to grow grain and orchard trees. For the most part, however, lack of water is a big problem. Saudi Arabia relies heavily on desalination plants and has the world's biggest on the shores of the Gulf – vulnerable to the oil pollution resulting from the 1991 war against Iraq.

The eastern province, by the shores of the

## MECCA

The holiest city of Islam, Mecca was an important centre of pilgrimage long before the birth of the Prophet Muhammad. Its chief sanctuary, then as now, was the Ka'ba, a square building housing a remarkable and much venerated black stone of probable meteoric origin, said to have been given to the patriarch Abraham by the Archangel Gabriel.

In 632, shortly before his death, the Prophet undertook his own final pilgrimage to the city; the pilgrimage to Mecca – the Hajj – remains the fifth of the Five Pillars of Islam, and every Muslim is expected to make it at least once in a lifetime. Mecca is also part of the Second Pillar, the duty of prayer, for it is towards the Ka'ba (now enclosed by Mecca's Great Mosque) that the world's Muslims face five times daily when they pray.

At the beginning of the 20th century, Mecca was a provincial town in the Ottoman empire; now, with a population of over 618,000, it is the administrative capital of the Western Province of Saudi Arabia. Its chief business remains, as ever, the Hajj, with upwards of 1.5 million pilgrims visiting annually. Non-Muslims (infidels) are to this day excluded from the city.

Gulf, is known as the Hasa. Near its chief city of Hufuf in particular, the long underground seepage of water from the Hejaz, the western mountains, breaks out in the artesian springs of the oases. This region contains the country's great oilfields including Ghawar, the world's largest. The oil port of Az Zahran is linked with Riyadh by the only railway; asphalt roads and, increasingly, air travel are the country's main means of transport.

The world's largest producer and exporter of oil in 1992, Saudi Arabia used the enormous revenues (peaking at more than $100 billion a year after the 400% price hikes of 1973) to launch a colossal industrial and domestic development programme: some $250 billion was spent on the plan for 1980–5, requiring over a million foreign workers. A strictly Muslim society suddenly boasted some of the most advanced architecture and facilities in the world, as well as introducing an array of social and educational benefits.

## HISTORY AND POLITICS

During and shortly after World War I, the Saudis of Najd (central Arabia) extended their territory at the expense of the Rashidis and Hashemites, and consolidated their control over the greater part of the Arabian peninsula. The frontiers with neighbours to the south and east remained ill-defined, but this mattered little until its vast reserves of oil (the world's largest) were tapped after World War II; since then some disputes have been settled, notably the division of the Gulfshore Neutral Zone with Kuwait. Progress has not always been smooth. In the mid-1980s world oil prices slumped dramatically, disrupting many of the projects begun in the boom years. Meanwhile, expenditure on defence is high even by the profligate standards of the region. The country's position as the West's staunchest Middle East ally has often conflicted with its role as the guardian of Islam's holy places – hundreds of thousands make the pilgrimage to Mecca every year – and despite large donations to poorer Arab nations (Saudi Arabia is by far the world's biggest donor by percentage of GNP), its commitment to their cherished cause of a Palestinian state has at times appeared relatively weak.

While supporting Iraq against Shiite Iran in the First Gulf War, Saudi Arabia then invited Western forces in to protect it against possible Iraqi aggression following the invasion of Kuwait in 1990, playing a significant role in the quick victory of the Allies over Saddam Hussein. [*Map page 22*] ∎

**AREA** 2,149,690 sq km [829,995 sq mls]
**POPULATION** 17,451,000
**CAPITAL (POPULATION)** Riyadh (or Ar Riyad, 2,000,000)
**GOVERNMENT** Absolute monarchy with consultative assembly
**ETHNIC GROUPS** Arab (Saudi 82%, Yemeni 10%, other Arab 3%)
**LANGUAGES** Arabic (official)
**RELIGIONS** Islam 99%, Christianity 1%
**CURRENCY** Saudi riyal = 100 halalas

# SENEGAL

The Republic of Senegal is on the north-west coast of Africa. The volcanic Cape Verde (Cap Vert), on which Dakar stands, is the most westerly point in Africa. Plains cover most of Senegal, though the land rises gently in the south-east. Wind-blown sand dunes are common in the north and on the coast. The main rivers are the Sénégal, which forms the northern border, and the Casamance in the south. The River Gambia flows from Senegal into The Gambia, a small country almost enclosed by Senegal.

The capital, Dakar, has a tropical climate with a short rainy season between June and September, when moist winds blow from the south-west. During the dry season, hot north-easterly winds blow from the Sahara. Temperatures are higher inland, while the rainfall is greatest in the south.

Desert and semi-desert cover much of the north-east, but in central Senegal dry grasslands and scrub predominate. The far south is a region of savanna, with forests along the rivers. Although large areas in the south have been cleared for farming, some areas are protected. The largest sanctuary is the Niokolo-Kobo Wildlife Park, which is rich in animal species. Mangrove swamps border parts of the southern coast.

## ECONOMY AND RESOURCES

Dakar, once the administrative centre for France's federation of West African colonies, has large modern docks and is the nation's major industrial centre. In the north-east of the country, Fulani tribesmen eke out a spartan existence by keeping herds of cattle on the scrub and semi-desert vegetation. In contrast, in the wetter and more fertile south, savanna bushlands are cultivated and cassava, sorghum and rice are grown. About half of the cultivated land produces groundnuts, a crop that still dominates the country's economy and exports. The only other major exports are phosphates, although tourism is becoming an increasingly important source of revenue.

In an attempt to diversify and stabilize the economy, the government is encouraging fishing and tourism, and is involved with Mali and Mauritania in a major scheme to increase irrigated crop production.

## HISTORY AND POLITICS

The name derives from the Zenega Berbers, who invaded from Mauritania in the 14th century, bringing Islam with them. On gaining independence in 1960, Senegal had a well-planned capital, a good road network and a top-heavy administration, all legacies from its role as the administrative centre for French West Africa. Its first president, Léopold Sédar Senghor, was a noted African poet. He continued in office until 1981, when he was succeeded by the prime minister Abdou Diouf.

One of the few African countries to remain stable and democratic through the 1980s, Senegal nevertheless struggles economically, is prone to drought and reliant on aid. Federations with Mali (1959–60) and Gambia (1981–9) were unsuccessful, and since 1989 there have been violent, though sporadic, clashes with Mauritania, such as the border dispute in 1992.

Senegal was the only African colony where French citizenship was granted to the people, and indeed the Senegalese were encouraged to become 'black Frenchmen'. As a result many of the Wolof – the largest tribe group and traditionally savanna farmers – are now city dwellers in Dakar, dominating the political, economic and cultural life of the country. Strangely, today's quality of life is for most Senegalese little better than their neighbours'. [*Map page 32*] ∎

**AREA** 196,720 sq km [75,954 sq mls]
**POPULATION** 8,102,000
**CAPITAL (POPULATION)** Dakar (1,382,000)
**GOVERNMENT** Multiparty republic
**ETHNIC GROUPS** Wolof 44%, Fulani-Tukulor 24%, Serer 15%
**LANGUAGES** French (official)
**RELIGIONS** Islam 94%, Christianity (mainly Roman Catholic) 5%, traditional beliefs and others 1%
**CURRENCY** CFA franc = 100 centimes

# SEYCHELLES

# SIERRA LEONE

The Seychelles are a compact group of four large and 36 small granitic islands, plus a wide scattering of coralline islands (14 of them inhabited) lying mainly to the south and west of the four main islands; 82% of the land area is composed of the four main islands which host 98% of the population, the vast majority on lush and mountainous Mahé.

With a beautiful tropical oceanic climate the Seychelles produce copra, cinnamon and tea, but the islands are not self-sufficient in food and rice has to be imported. The economy is based on two activities, fishing and tourism. Canned fish account for a third of exports, and deep-sea tuna fishing is carried out by foreign fleets under licence. Luxury tourism (the main foreign exchange earner) is growing in importance. In 1990, there were 103,770 visitors to the islands.

Proclaimed a French territory from 1756 and British from 1814, the islands gained independence in 1976. A year later a political coup set up a one-party Socialist state that several attempts have failed to remove. But multiparty democracy was restored when elections were held in 1992.

Formerly part of the British Indian Ocean Territory (BIOT), Farquhar, Desroches and Aldabra (famous for its unique wildlife) were returned to the Seychelles in 1976. BIOT now includes only the Chagos Archipelago, with Diego Garcia, the largest island, supporting a US naval base. [*Map page 3*] ■

**AREA** 455 sq km [176 sq mls]
**POPULATION** 73,000
**CAPITAL (POPULATION)** Victoria (24,325)
**GOVERNMENT** Multiparty republic
**ETHNIC GROUPS** Mixture of African, Asian and European
**LANGUAGES** English, French, Creole
**RELIGIONS** Christianity (Roman Catholic 90%, Anglican 8%)
**CURRENCY** Seychelles rupee = 100 cents

The coast of Sierra Leone ('lion mountain') contains several deep estuaries in the north, with lagoons in the south. The most prominent feature is the mountainous Freetown (or Sierra Leone) peninsula. North of the peninsula is the River Rokel estuary, West Africa's best natural harbour. Behind the coastal plain with its mangrove swamps, the land rises to plateaux and mountains. The highest peak, Loma Mansa, reaches 1,948 m [6,391 ft] near the north-eastern border.

## ECONOMY AND RESOURCES

At independence from Britain in 1961, three-quarters of the population were employed in subsistence agriculture, yet rice had to be imported, and only small surpluses of palm kernel, coffee and ginger were produced.

Revenue from the export of minerals, namely diamonds and iron-ore, has been important since the 1930s, although rutile (titanium ore) is now the country's most important export.

The main centres for the production of coffee, cocoa, and timber products are in the south-east of the country near Kenema. Rice and palm oil are produced throughout Sierra Leone, except in the drier north, where groundnuts and cattle herding are more important. The government has established large-scale mechanized rice cultivation in the bolilands of the north-west, the seasonally-flooded riverine grasslands of the south-east and the mangrove swamps near Port Loko, in an effort to boost rice production.

Apart from mills processing palm oil and rice, most factories are in or near the capital, Freetown. The government is doing all it can to aid Sierra Leone's growing tourist industry and modern hotels have been established along the coast near Freetown.

## HISTORY AND POLITICS

Portuguese sailors reached the coast in 1460, and in the 16th century the area became a source of slaves. In 1787, Freetown was founded as a home for freed slaves. The British made the Sierra Leone peninsula a colony in 1808, and in 1896 they declared the interior a protectorate. Sierra Leone became independent in 1961.

After independence, Sierra Leone became a monarchy. Its head of state was the British monarch, who was represented in the country by a governor-general. But after a military government took power in 1968, Sierra Leone was made a republic in 1971. Then, in 1991, a majority of the people voted for the restoration of multiparty democracy. In 1992, a military group overthrew the government and seized power. [*Map page 32*] ■

---

**AREA** 71,740 sq km [27,699 sq mls]
**POPULATION** 4,402,000
**CAPITAL (POPULATION)** Freetown (470,000)
**GOVERNMENT** Single-party republic
**ETHNIC GROUPS** Mende 35%, Temne 37%, Limba 8%,
**LANGUAGES** English (official)
**RELIGIONS** Traditional beliefs 51%, Islam 39%, Christianity 9%
**CURRENCY** Leone = 100 cents

---

# SINGAPORE

---

Singapore comprises the main island itself and an additional 54 much smaller islands lying within its territorial waters. The highest point on the main island is Bukit Timah (176 m [577 ft]). The position of Singapore at the southernmost point of the Malay Peninsula, controlling the Strait of Malacca, has throughout history been one of enormous strategic importance.

## ECONOMY AND RESOURCES

Singapore is one of the world's most remarkable commercial and industrial experiments. It is, in effect, a city-state, its downtown thick with skyscrapers, one of the most densely populated countries in South-east Asia and an economy based on its vast port, manufacturing and commercial and financial services.

The port began its modern expansion as a conduit for shipping out tin and rubber from Malaya. Today, easily the world's busiest, it handles nearly 70 million tonnes a year, much of it entrepôt (re-export) trade but also involving significant amounts of materials for and from its own thriving industries.

The positive strategy of industrialization, first labour- and later skill-intensive, has given Singapore an outstanding average growth of 7% a year and has made it the richest of Asia's four 'little dragons'.

## HISTORY AND POLITICS

When Sir Stamford Raffles established British influence in 1819, leasing the island and its muddy Malay fishing village for the East India Company, there were only 150 inhabitants. This had not always been so; 'Singapura' (the city of the lion) was an important settlement in the 14th century, but had been destroyed in the rivalry between the great kingdoms of Madjapahit (Java) and Siam. The modern city, originally planned by Raffles, remained under British rule until self-government in 1959. In 1963, Singapore became part of the Federation of Malaysia, but seceded in 1965 to become a fully independent nation.

The success of Singapore owes much to the vision and dynamism of Lee Kuan Yew, prime minister from independence in 1959 to 1990, who despite having a predominantly Chinese population in a Malay region made his ambitious policies work. The cost, however, was a lack of genuine democracy, his regime increasingly bordering on a one-party dictatorship; his attitude, essentially, was that Singapore could not afford the luxury — or danger — of political debate. Impressive though the new city may be, most Singaporeans live in massive apartment blocks reminiscent of postwar Eastern Europe, with most aspects of their lives rigidly controlled and much of their former culture buried forever beneath a Western façade.

Lee's groomed successor, Goh Chok Tong, seemed set to continue his policies with equal vigour, turning Singapore into the hub of an expanding region. Despite its political stance, it was in the vanguard of nations opening up links with the reticent Communist countries of Laos, Vietnam and North Korea in the post-*perestroika* era.

The future of his party's wealthy establishment appeared secure, with its sights set on replacing Hong Kong as eastern Asia's second financial and commercial centre after Tokyo. The feeling nevertheless persisted that Singapore's crucial tertiary activity would give it little to fall back on in the face of a deep and lasting world recession. [*Map page 26*] ■

**AREA** 618 sq km [239 sq mls]
**POPULATION** 2,821,000
**CAPITAL (POPULATION)** Singapore City (2,818,000)
**GOVERNMENT** Multiparty republic
**ETHNIC GROUPS** Chinese 78%, Malay 14%, Indian 7%
**LANGUAGES** Chinese, Malay, Tamil and English (all official)
**RELIGIONS** Buddhism, Taoism and other traditional beliefs 54%, Islam 15%, Christianity 13%, Hinduism 4%
**CURRENCY** Singapore dollar = 100 cents

# SLOVAK REPUBLIC

The Slovak Republic, or Slovakia, is a new nation which emerged on 1 January 1994, following the division of the former Czechoslovakia into two states. The land is mainly mountainous, consisting of part of the Carpathian range that divides it from Poland. The highest peak, reaching 2,655 m [8,711 ft], is on the northern boundary in the scenic Tatra Mountains.

By contrast, the south is a fertile lowland, drained by the River Danube, which forms part of the southern border with Hungary – Bratislava, the new nation's chief city, lies in the south and has become the fourth European capital (Vienna, Budapest and Belgrade are the others) to lie on the river. Several rivers flow from the mountainous north into the Danube river basin.

## ECONOMY AND RESOURCES

Before 1948, Slovakia's economy was based on farming, but Communist governments developed manufacturing industries, producing such things as chemicals, machinery, steel and weapons. Since the late 1980s, the non-Communist governments have tried to hand over state-run businesses to private ownership. In mid-1994 the new government speeded up the privatization process.

Manufacturing employs about 33% of the workforce. Bratislava and Kosice are the chief industrial cities, but the armaments industry is based on Martin, in the north-west.

Farming employs about 12% of the people. Major crops include barley, grapes for wine-making, maize, sugar beet and wheat. Cattle, pigs and sheep are also raised.

## HISTORY AND POLITICS

While the Czechs prospered and flourished under Austrian rule, Slovakia was subject to Hungarian authority for centuries. Its people suffered from enforced 'Magyarization' and their development was stifled. Divisions were exacerbated from 1939 when, after the proclamation of a pro-German Fascist regime in Slovakia, Hitler's troops invaded the Czech lands of Bohemia and Moravia. But, even in Communist Czechoslovakia, the Slovaks were in no sense a persecuted minority; their post-1989 independence movement was driven more by the desire to revive their distinct culture than by serious ethnic grievances. Elections in 1992 led to a victory for the Movement for a Democratic Slovakia, led by a former Communist and staunch nationalist, Vladimir Meciar. In September 1992, the Slovak National Council voted to create a separate, independent Slovak Republic on 1 January 1994.

Following independence, the new Slovak Republic maintained close links with its former partner: around 400,000 Slovak workers cross the frontier to work each week, while about 200,000 are still resident in the Czech Republic. Conversely, 60,000 Czechs live in Slovakia, but at between 500,000 and 600,000, the nation's most substantial minority is Hungarian. Predictably, Slovak independence has raised national aspirations among its Magyar-speaking community, mostly in its southern regions; such ethnic tensions as exist, though, are likely to be settled pragmatically and not by violence. [*Map page 17*] ■

---

**AREA** 49,035 sq km [18,932 sq mls]
**POPULATION** 5,333,000
**CAPITAL (POPULATION)** Bratislava (441,450)
**GOVERNMENT** Multiparty republic
**ETHNIC GROUPS** Slovak 86%, Hungarian 11%, small groups of Czech, German, Gypsy, Polish, Russian and Ukrainian
**LANGUAGES** Slovak (official)
**RELIGIONS** Christianity (Roman Catholic 60%, Protestant 6%, Orthodox 3%)
**CURRENCY** Slovak koruna = 100 halura

---

# SLOVENIA

---

The Republic of Slovenia was one of the six republics which made up the former Yugoslavia. The most northern of the republics, much of the land is mountainous, rising to 2,863 m [9,393 ft] at Mt Triglav in the Julian Alps (Julijske Alpe) in the north-west. Central and eastern Slovenia contain hills and plains drained by the Drava and Sava rivers. The central limestone area, called the Karst region, is characterised by underground rivers and deep caves. The Postojna caves near Ljubljana are the largest in Europe.

The short Slovenian coast has a mild Mediterranean climate, but inland the climate is more continental with snow-capped mountains in winter. Eastern Slovenia has cold winters and hot summers.

## ECONOMY AND RESOURCES

The reform of the formerly government-run economy and the fighting in areas to the south have caused problems for Slovenia, and in 1992 the World Bank classified Slovenia as an 'upper-middle-income' developing country. Manufacturing is the leading activity and manufactures are the leading exports, including chemicals, machinery and transport equipment, metal goods and textiles. Agriculture

employs 8% of the people. Fruits, maize, potatoes and wheat are major crops, while many farmers raise cattle, pigs and sheep. Other important sources of income are wine-making and Alpine tourism (1.4 million tourists in 1991).

Slovenia has access to the Adriatic through the port of Koper, near the Italian border, giving it a flourishing transit trade from land-locked central Europe.

## HISTORY AND POLITICS

The ancestors of the Slovenes, the western branch of a group of people called the South Slavs, settled in the area around 1,400 years ago. From the 13th century until 1918, Slovenia was ruled for most of the time by the Austrian Habsburgs. In 1918, Slovenia became part of the Kingdom of the Serbs, Croats and Slovenes. This country was renamed Yugoslavia in 1929. During World War II, Slovenia was invaded and partitioned between Italy, Germany and Hungary, but after the war, Slovenia again became an integral part of Yugoslavia.

From the late 1960s, some Slovenes demanded independence, but the central government opposed the break-up of the country. In 1990, when Communist governments had collapsed throughout Eastern Europe, a non-Communist coalition government was elected. Slovenia subsequently declared itself independent. This led to fighting between Slovenes and the federal army, but Slovenia did not become a battlefield like other parts of the former Yugoslavia. The European Community recognized Slovenia's independence in 1992 and elections were held. A coalition government led by the Liberal Democrats was set up as a result. [*Map page 15*] ■

---

**AREA** 20,251 sq km [7,817 sq mls]
**POPULATION** 1,942,000
**CAPITAL (POPULATION)** Ljubljana (323,000)
**GOVERNMENT** Multiparty republic
**ETHNIC GROUPS** Slovene 88%, Croat 3%, Serb 2%, Bosnian 1%
**LANGUAGES** Slovene (official)
**RELIGIONS** Christianity (mainly Roman Catholic)
**CURRENCY** Tolar = 100 stotin

# SOLOMON ISLANDS

The double chain of Pacific islands forming the Solomons (and the southerly extension of Vanuatu) extends for some 2,250 km [1,400 mls] and represents the drowned outermost crustal fold on the borders of the ancient Australian continent. New Caledonia lies on an inner fold, nearer the mainland. The main islands, all of volcanic origin, are Guadalcanal, Malaita, New Georgia, San Cristóbal, Santa Isabel and Choiseul.

The northern Solomons have a hot and wet tropical oceanic climate, but further south the islands tend to experience an increasingly long cool season.

## ECONOMY AND RESOURCES

The coastal plains are used for the subsistence farming that sustains about 90% of the population. While coconuts (giving copra and palm oil) and cocoa are important exports, tuna fish is the biggest earner and lumbering the main industry, with Japan the main market for both. Significant phosphate deposits are also mined on Bellona Island and marine shells are exoported. Plagued by a population growth of 3.5% – half the total is under 20 – the Solomons' progress is faltering, with development hampered by the mountainous and densely forested environment of the six main islands; transport is often impossible between scattered settlements. The economy was also hit by a devastating cyclone in 1986.

## HISTORY AND POLITICS

Occupied by the Japanese during World War II, the islands were the scene of fierce fighting, notably the battle for Guadalcanal, on which the capital Honiara lies. Known as the British Solomons, the islands won full independence in 1978. The country is a constitutional monarchy, with the Queen as head of state, represented locally by a Governor-General. Though currently a stable parliamentary monarchy, political activity is turbulent, and it is likely that a federal republican structure will

be introduced to the country during the 1990s. [*Map page 35*] ∎

> AREA  28,900 sq km [11,158 sq mls]
> POPULATION  366,000
> CAPITAL (POPULATION)  Honiara (34,000)
> GOVERNMENT  Constitutional monarchy
> ETHNIC GROUPS  Melanesian 94%, Polynesian 4%
> LANGUAGES  Many Melanesian languages, English
> RELIGIONS  Christianity
> CURRENCY  Solomon Islands dollar = 100 cents

# SOMALIA

Somalia is more than twice as large as Italy (which formerly ruled the southern part of the country). The northern section, formerly British Somaliland and the literal 'Horn of Africa', is the highest and most arid, rising to 2,408 m [7,900 ft]; the mountains are an easterly projection of the Ethiopian Highlands, wooded with box and cedar. The east and south have some 500 mm [20 in] rainfall on the coast. Dunes have diverted one of the country's two rivers, the Scebeli, to the south, making it available for irrigation. The inland plain is arid with grass and thorn bush.

## ECONOMY AND RESOURCES

Most Somali are subsistence farmers or nomadic herdsmen. Expatriate Somali living in southern Djibouti, Ogaden (eastern Ethiopia) and north-east Kenya are mostly pastoralists, who move across borders in an increasingly desperate search for pasture, fuelwood and water. Bananas are a major export, especially to Italy. The country's economy has suffered badly from drought and the effects of the civil war.

## HISTORY AND POLITICS

The Somali Republic became independent in 1960. The Somali, though belonging to separate tribes or clans, are conscious of being one people and members of one of Africa's rare nation states. The quest for a reunification of all the Somali peoples led to conflict with neighbouring countries, notably Ethiopia and the Ogaden war of 1978, which has continued intermittently and has caused thousands of Somali refugees to flee across the border.

Somalia relied heavily on Soviet aid until Ethiopia went Marxist and sought massive help from Moscow; the revolutionary socialist government of President Siyad Barre, which had seized power and suspended the constitution in 1969, then became increasingly reliant on Italian support and US aid.

Grievances against the repressive regime, spearheaded by secessionist guerrillas in the north, reached their peak in 1991 with the capture of Mogadishu. Free elections and independence for the north-east part of the country, as the Somaliland Republic, were promised after the cease-fire and Barre's fall from power, but vicious factional fighting continued not only in the capital but also in many rural areas. The Western nations virtually abandoned Somalia to its fate, with thousands dying every week in interclan bloodletting and through starvation. One of the world's poorest countries was plunged into anarchy. The situation deteriorated further into 1992, despite UN attempts at mediation and several cease-fires. Much of Mogadishu was reduced to rubble, violence spread to country areas, and tens of thousands of refugees fled to northern Kenya and eastern Ethiopia. In 1993, the United Nations intervened and sent in a task force of US Marines to protect and oversee the distribution of food aid. The US troops withdrew in 1994. [*Map page 32*] ■

**AREA** 637,660 sq km [246,201 sq mls]
**POPULATION** 9,077,000
**CAPITAL (POPULATION)** Mogadishu (or Muqdisho, 1,000,000)
**GOVERNMENT** Single-party republic, military dominated
**ETHNIC GROUPS** Somali 98%, Arab 1%
**LANGUAGES** Somali and Arabic (both official), English, Italian
**RELIGIONS** Islam 99%
**CURRENCY** Somali shilling = 100 cents

# SOUTH AFRICA

Geologically very ancient, South Africa has only scant superficial deposits of sediments less than 600 million years old. Geological history has had a great effect on all aspects of the country's development – on its landforms, patterns of population, industrial growth and agricultural potential.

The country is divisible into two major natural zones – the interior and the coastal fringe – the interior in turn consisting of two major parts. Most of Northern Cape province and the Orange Free State are drained by the Orange River and its important right-bank tributaries which flow with gentle gradients over level plateaux, varying in height from 1,200–2,000 m [4,000–6,000 ft]. The Northern Transvaal is occupied by the Bushveld, an area of granites and igneous intrusions, drained by rivers which flow northwards to the Limpopo river.

The coastal fringe is divided from the interior by the Fringing Escarpment, a feature that makes communication within the country very difficult. In the east the massive basalt-capped rock wall of the Drakensberg, at its most majestic near Mont-aux-Sources and rising to over 3,000 m [over 10,000 ft], overlooks the KwaZulu-Natal and Eastern Cape coastlands. In the west there is a similar divide between the interior plateau and the coastlands, though this is less well developed. The Fringing Escarpment also runs along the south coast, where it is fronted by many independent mountain ranges with an east-west alignment.

South Africa's economic and political development is closely related to these physical components.

## ECONOMY AND RESOURCES

Stretching from the Northern Transvaal's western border with Botswana, running in a horseshoe to the north of Pretoria and then southwards through KwaZulu-Natal and Eastern Cape province, are the former so-called 'homelands' – territories occupied almost exclusively by Africans. From the outset the Africans operated a form of mixed agriculture, giving them subsistence but little more. The men were cattle-keepers and warriors, the women tilled the plots, in a culture based on extensive holdings of communal land. European farming was also based on extensive holdings but incorporated individual land rights. Not surprisingly, conflict arose from the juxtapositioning of the two groups, and with the discovery of valuable minerals – gold in the Banket deposits of the Witwatersrand, diamonds in the Kimberlite pipes of the Cape, platinum in the Bushveld and coal in the Northern Transvaal and KwaZulu-Natal – both were drastically affected.

South Africa still produces over 30% of the world's gold, and today chrome, uranium, nickel and many others may be added to the list. Exploitation of southern Africa's minerals led to trade with overseas markets and the development of major urban complexes. Johannesburg grew the fastest; its growth encouraged the expansion of Durban and to a large extent caused Cape Town and Port Elizabeth to flourish. The appearance of a capitalist, market-oriented economy caused even greater divergence between white and black. The politically-dominant whites reproduced a European economy and, after the transfer of political power, developed strong links with Britain.

The African farmers gained little from the mineral boom. With their constant needs for new grazing grounds, frustrated by the white farmers, and with taxes to pay, they had little alternative but to seek employment in the cities and mines, and on European-owned farms; the African areas became labour pools. Migrant labour became the normal way of life for many men, while agriculture in the Native Reserves (so designated early in the 20th century) stagnated and even regressed, with yields decreasing and soil erosion becoming widespread and of increasing severity.

Small groups of Africans took up urban life in 'locations' which became a typical feature of all towns whatever their size. Separated by a *cordon sanitaire* of industry, a river or the railway line from the white settlement, these townships with their rudimentary housing, often supplemented by shanty dwellings and

without any real services, mushroomed during World War II and left South Africa with a major housing problem in the late 1940s. Nowhere was this problem greater than in the Johannesburg area, where it was solved by the building of a vast complex of brick boxes, the South-Western Townships (SOWETO).

## HISTORY AND POLITICS

The country was first peopled by negroids from the north, who introduced a cattle-keeping, grain-growing culture. Entering by the plateaux of the north-east, they continued southwards into the well-watered zones below the Fringing Escarpment of present-day KwaZulu-Natal and Eastern Cape province. Moving into country occupied by Bushmanoid peoples they absorbed some of the latter's cultural features, especially the 'clicks' so characteristic of the modern Zulu and Xhosa languages. By the 18th century these Bantu-speaking groups had penetrated to the south-east in the region of the Kei and Fish rivers.

Simultaneously with this advance, a group of Europeans was establishing a victualling point for the Dutch East India Company on the site of modern Cape Town. These Company employees, augmented by Huguenot refugees, eventually spread out from Cape Town, beginning a movement of European farmers throughout southern Africa and bringing about the development of the Afrikaners.

The advance of the Europeans was channelled in the south by the parallel coastal ranges, so that eventually black and white met near the Kei River. To the north, once the Fringing Escarpment had been overcome, the level surface of the plateaux allowed a rapid spread northwards. From this colonizing process, aided by an implanting of British people in the south-east and near Durban, the present disposition of black-dominated and white-dominated lands arose.

The contrast in prosperity between South African whites and blacks is nowhere more visibly expressed than in their respective urban areas. The white areas could be 'Anytown' in North America; skyscrapers, multitrack roads, large department stores and well-tended suburbs. The black towns could only be South African: though rudimentary in what they offer, they have been rigidly planned.

A further problem is posed by the Coloured people – descendants of mixed-race marriages – and the Asiatics, who are mainly descendants of Indians brought in several generations ago to work in the sugar-cane fields of Natal.

## The Rise and Fall of Apartheid

From its 1948 institution, *apartheid* – 'separate development' – meant not only racial segregation but also massive racial discrimination. Over the next generation, a whole body of apartheid law was created. Key measures deprived blacks of political rights except in 'homelands' – modest tracts of poor land. Whites were guaranteed exclusive ownership of most of the country's best land, and most blacks, with no right of residence outside homelands few had ever seen, found themselves foreigners in their own country, obliged to carry passes at all times and subject to the authority of an aggressive police force.

The African National Congress, the main black political organization, was banned, and black opposition was brutally suppressed. South Africa's racial policies led to increasing isolation from the rest of the world, and by the 1980s the country was considered a pariah by other nations.

Changing demographic patterns – the blacks were outnumbering whites by more and more every year – combined with international sanctions made apartheid increasingly unsupportable. The 1989 election of liberal Nationalist President F.W. de Klerk brought dramatic change. In 1990, Nelson Mandela, leader of the banned African National Congress (ANC), was released from jail to the negotiating table, after serving 28 years as a political prisoner, and in 1991 de Klerk announced his intention to dismantle the entire structure of apartheid. In 1992, an all-white referendum gave him a mandate to move quickly towards a multiracial democratic system.

Under a new constitution, the first multiracial elections were held in April 1994, resulting in a massive victory for the ANC (62.7% of the vote, the National Party in second place gained just 20.4% of the vote) and the election of Nelson Mandela as the country's first black president. The four former provinces of South Africa have been replaced by nine new regions, each with its own Prime Minister. [*Map page 33*] ■

**AREA** 1,219,916 sq km [470,566 sq mls]
**POPULATION** 40,555,000
**CAPITAL (POPULATION)** Cape Town (legislative, 1,912,000), Pretoria (administrative, 1,080,000), Bloemfontein (judicial, 300,000)
**GOVERNMENT** Multiparty republic
**ETHNIC GROUPS** Black 76%, White 13%, Coloured 9%, Asian 2%
**LANGUAGES** Afrikaans, English, Ndebele, North Sotho, South Sotho, Swazi, Tsonga, Tswana, Venda, Xhosa, Zulu (all official)
**RELIGIONS** Christianity 68%, Hinduism 1%, Islam 1%
**CURRENCY** Rand = 100 cents

# SPAIN

A global position between coastal northwest Europe and Africa, and between the Mediterranean countries of the Old World and the Americas, made Spain a great crossroads. Yet the lofty Pyrenean barrier in the north weakened land contacts with the rest of Europe, while the narrow Strait of Gibraltar in the south encouraged African contacts, lending truth to the old cliché that 'Africa begins at the Pyrenees'.

## Landscape

Spain occupies most of the Iberian peninsula. Its chief physical feature is the vast central plateau, the Meseta, which tilts gently towards Portugal. A harsh and often barren area, the plateau is crossed by the Central Sierras, a mountain chain running north-west to south-east. This central divide separates two mountain basins: Old Castile in the north and New Castile in the south.

On the north-eastern and southern edges of the Meseta are large triangular lowlands. In the north these drain to the Ebro, in the south to the Guadalquivir, the largest river wholly in Spain. Beyond the Ebro trough the land rises

## BALEARIC ISLANDS

The Islas Baleares group contains five larger islands (Majorca, Minorca, Ibiza, Formentera, Cabrera) and 11 rocky islets, together covering 5,014 sq km [1,936 sq mls] and spread over 350 km [218 mls].

Majorca (Mallorca), by far the largest island, has limestone ridges on the north-west and south-east with a plain covered with flat-bedded, very fertile marine sediments between them. Minorca (Menorca), the second largest, has limestone plains and small outcrops of crystalline rocks, but nowhere rises above 358 m [1,175 ft].

The typical sunny Mediterranean climate supports an equally typical vegetation. Shrub-growth (*matorral* or *garrigue*) still clothes the highest areas and is grazed by sheep and goats. The rainier upper slopes of the hills have been terraced for olives, carobs and vines, while the lower slopes are under market-garden crops. The level lowlands are planted with wheat and barley, usually in rotation with beans. Generally, almonds, apricots and carobs are more important here than vines and citrus fruits. The rural economy is essentially peasant with a high degree of self-sufficiency.

Like most Mediterranean islands the Balearics were settled early. Archaeological remains exist from 1,000 BC (Bronze Age) to the Roman period and include boat-shaped burial mounds (*navetas* or *naus*) and conical stone towers (*talayots*) thought to be refuges from piratical raiding parties. Ibiza town and Port Mahon were originally settled from Carthage. During recent times the islands were repeatedly occupied by the British, French and Spanish and remained finally a province of Spain. Each different occupation has left its mark, and Port Mahon has fine buildings representing all these changes of ownership.

Today the population lives mainly either in agricultural villages some way inland or in small ports around the coast. Power resources and raw materials for manufacture are scarce, apart from agricultural products; textile manufacture (wool and cotton) and food processing are the only widespread factory occupations. Handicrafts flourish in response to the tourism that now dominates the whole economy.

Palma, the capital of Majorca and of the Balearic province, continues to grow rapidly. It has a fine harbour with regular sailings to Barcelona, Alicante and Valencia for passengers and the export of Balearic surpluses of almonds, grain, textiles and vegetables. It is also a regular port of call for Mediterranean cruise ships and its airport, one of the busiest in Spain, deals with well over a million visitors annually. Manacor, the only other large centre on Majorca, is an agricultural market town near limestone caves and subterranean lakes that attract numerous tourists. Port Mahon is the capital of Minorca, and Ibiza town the capital of that small island.

---

to the Pyrenees, which form the Franco-Spanish border, and continue westwards in the Cantabrian Mountains. Similarly, the Mediterranean flank of Andalusia rises to a lofty cordillera (mountain chain) that culminates in the snowy Sierra Nevada (peaking at 3,478 m [11,400 ft]). The Mediterranean side of the Meseta has summits of about 2,000 m [6,560 ft] but then drops sharply to narrow coastal plains.

Spain has perhaps the widest range of climate of any country in Western Europe. The most striking contrast is between the humid north and north-west and the mainly arid remainder of the country. Large areas of the country are barren or steppeland, and

about a fifth is covered by *matorral*, a Mediterranean scrub like the French *maquis*.

### Vegetation

Spain is unique in Europe for the quantity and variety of her plant species, a reflection of varied local environments, a position as a land bridge between Africa and Europe, and a long colonial history during which time many foreign plants were introduced. Generally, moisture-loving plants flourish north of the Central Sierras and drought-enduring species south of them.

The vegetation falls into three broad categories: forest, *matorral* and steppe. Forests (almost 10% of the land surface) are today mainly confined to the rainier north and north-west, with beech and deciduous oak common. Towards the drier south and east, Mediterranean pines and evergreen oaks take over, and forests resemble open parkland. Widespread clearance for fuel and cultivation and grazing by sheep, goats and cattle have turned large areas into *matorral* or shrub.

This low bush growth, often of aromatic evergreen plants, may be dominated over large tracts by one species, such as rosemary, thyme or broom. Where soils are thin and drought prevalent, *matorral* gives way to steppe, mainly of alfalfa and *esparto* grasses.

### Population

The population of Spain is most dense on the coastlands and lowlands around the Meseta. Madrid, in the heart of the tableland, forms a grand exception. The capital stands on the small Manzanares River, a tributary of the Tagus, and has a long history dating from early Roman times. The Moors first provided it with clean drinking water and Philip II made it the seat of the national government in 1561. A fine metropolis, it has flourished during the decades since the Civil War (1936–9) and now accommodates about 10% of the total population of continental Spain. The second Spanish city, Barcelona, is a great commercial and industrial centre; in all ways the core of Catalonia, it was given a huge boost by the staging of the summer Olympics in 1992.

The other major cities include Bilbao, the Basque capital and chief urban area of the north coast, long noted for its metallurgy; Cádiz, an important naval centre; Seville, the river port and regional capital of Andalusia; Valencia and Murcia, the largest of the Mediterranean *huerta* cities; Zaragoza, the expanding centre for the Ebro lowland, noted for food processing and engineering; and Málaga, the fast-growing nucleus of the Costa del Sol. Toledo, which was the national capital before Madrid, ranks far below these conurbations in size, but, protected as a national monument, is the finest medieval city that survives almost intact from the golden age of Spain.

### ECONOMY AND RESOURCES

Despite the problems of aridity and poor soils,

agriculture occupies nearly a third of the national workforce. Irregular river regimes and deeply incised valleys make irrigation difficult and expensive and, on the higher and drier regions, tracts favourable for cultivation are often isolated by expanses of low fertility where only a meagre livelihood can be wrested from the soil. There are, too, problems connected with the size of farms. In semi-arid Spain large estates (*latifundios*) abound with much seasonal employment or share-cropping, while in the rainy north-west and north excessive fragmentation of small farms (*minifundios*) has proved uneconomic.

It is against this picture of difficulties that the great progress made since 1939 by the Instituto Nacional de Colonización (INC) must be viewed. The institute, by means of irrigation, co-operative farming schemes, concentration of landholdings, agricultural credit schemes and technical training, has resettled over a quarter of the land needing reorganization and reclamation. But, generally, crop yields are still comparatively modest and agricultural techniques remain backward.

**Stock rearing:** Large areas of farmland are used solely or partly for pastoral purposes, which are of great economic importance. Spain has about 20 million sheep, mainly of the native merino type which produces a fine fleece. The Mesta, an old confederation of sheep-owners, controls the seasonal migrations on to the summer pastures on the high sierras. Areas too rocky and steep for sheep are given over to goats while cattle, apart from working oxen, are mostly restricted to regions with ample grass and water – for example the north and north-west. Pigs are bred in the cattle districts of the north, and are also kept to forage the acorns in the large tracts of evergreen oaks in the south. Many working animals are kept, and fighting bulls are bred on the marshes (*marismas*) at the mouth of the Guadalquivir.

**Arable crops:** The typical arable crops are the classical Mediterranean trio of wheat, olive and vine, with maize important in rainier districts and vegetables and citrus fruits where there is irrigation water. Wheat occupies a third of the cropland and is usually followed in rotation by leguminous pulses or fallow, grazed and so manured by sheep.

In dry areas barley, oats and rye, grown for fodder, replace wheat, and in the wetter north maize dominates both for grain and feed. Rice is harvested in Murcia, Valencia and the Ebro Valley and Spain follows Italy for rice production in Europe.

**Fruit growing:** Fruits occupy a high and honoured place in Spain's agricultural economy. The olive crop, mainly from large estates in Andalusia, makes Spain one of the world's chief producers of olive oil. Vines cover about 10% of the cultivated land and only Italy and France exceed the Spanish output of wine. Sherry (from Jérez) is renowned and there are other fine wines such as the vintages of Rioja.

For citrus fruit Spain easily outstrips other European producers, the bulk of the crop being Seville oranges destined largely for Britain for making marmalade. Large quantities of other fruits, especially apricots and peaches, are grown with vegetables in irrigated market gardens (*huertas*) and orchards (*vegas*).

Some of the *huertas* are devoted to industrial crops such as cotton, hemp, flax and sugar beet, while most richer soils in Andalusia are entirely given over to cotton. The poorer steppes yield *esparto* (a strong grass) for paper-making.

Maps of modern Spain clearly indicate the tremendous progress made recently in water reservation and river regulation on all the major rivers. Large new reservoirs have been constructed on the Miño, Duero, Tajo, Guadiana, Guadalquivir and other main rivers as well as numerous dams on the lesser water-courses. The INC, which directs this work, aims at bringing 70,000 hectares [173,000 acres] a year under irrigation as well as undertaking all kinds of land reclamation, drainage, reforestation, settlement schemes and farm co-operative planning.

## Mining and Industry

Spain is lamentably short of its own supplies of solid and liquid fuels and in an average year produces only small quantities of poor-quality coal (mainly from Asturias at Oviedo near Gijón), and some lignite from a field south of Barcelona. Small deposits of petroleum found near Burgos and at the mouth of the Ebro have not yet proved economic to develop. Some use is made of nuclear power but the main developments have been in hydroelectricity, especially in Catalonia and the northern coastlands.

In contrast to fossil fuels, workable mineral ores are widespread. High-quality iron ores, with substantial reserves, occur in Vizcaya, Santander and Granada. Bilbao, the chief ore-exporting port, has an important integrated iron and steel plant; so have Oviedo, Gijón and several other towns on the north coast, and smaller enterprises are found at Sagunto and Zaragoza.

Many localities yield non-ferrous ores in sufficient quantity to broaden the base of Spain's metallurgical industries. The chief workings are for copper at Río Tinto, lead and silver at Linares and Peñarroya (near Pueblonovo), and mercury at Almadén; in addition, manganese, titanium and sulphur are produced in small quantities and considerable amounts of potassium salts come from the region of Catalonia.

The major Spanish manufacturing industries are based on agriculture rather than minerals. Textiles, including cotton, wool, silk, jute and linen lead the industrial sector. Barcelona, Catalonia's great industrial, financial and commercial centre, is surrounded by a ring of satellite textile towns, some of which specialize in spinning, as at Manresa and Ribas, and others in weaving, as at Sabadell and Granollers.

Cotton fabrics form the chief single product and supply a wide market, especially at home and in Latin America. Barcelona has a wide variety of light industries, while the heavy metallurgical sectors are located in the cities of the north coast. Madrid has become an important centre for consumer goods, particularly electric appliances.

Food-processing industries are concentrated in the north-east, the chief being flour-milling, sugar refining and oil-pressing. Fish canning and processing are widespread in the coastal towns and the Galicians and Basques are skilled fishermen.

## Tourism and communications

The relative absence of closely-packed industrial plants and industrial pollution, the historical attractions of the relics of a long history dating from the Greeks and Arabs, and the dry warm sunny climate of the Mediterranean south and east have fostered tourism, the greatest of all Spain's non-agricultural industries. In 1992 39.6 million people visited Spain and the Costa Brava and Costa del Sol are internationally famous as tourist destinations.

Equally significant is the great increase in the number of those who came to live permanently or for most of the year in the picturesque coastlands with warm winters and subtropical vegetation.

The prime communication routes in Spain focus on Madrid, which has radial links to the peripheral cities. First-class highways radiate to the main ports and good roads connect all the major towns; but minor roads are seldom tarred and for so large a country relatively few vehicles are registered.

Railways likewise converge on Madrid with minor networks round the regional capitals and main ports. The tracks are not of standard European gauge, about 75% being broad gauge and the remainder narrow. The chief land communications with France run at either end of the Pyrenees and are supplemented by several high-level transmontane rail and road routes.

Air travel focuses on Madrid airport and, particularly for tourism, on 40 other civil airports, many of them with busy international services. The large coastal and ocean-going traffic involves 230 Spanish ports, but the bulk of the overseas trade passes through the modernized harbours – in particular Bilbao, Barcelona, Cartagena, Cádiz and Gijón.

## HISTORY AND POLITICS

First settled by Iberians, Basques and Celts, Spain later became a Roman province until it was invaded by the Visigoths in the 5th century. They established a Christian kingdom and were only displaced by the Moors in 711. The Christian reconquest, started in 962, eventually led to the unification of the kingdoms of Castile and Aragon in 1469 and the fall of the last Moorish enclave (Granada) in 1492, the year in which Columbus reached America. In the 16th century, Spain extended its colonies in the Americas and the Far East. In the aftermath of the Napoleonic Wars, the Spanish king, Ferdinand VII, was restored by British forces in 1814. By 1830, most of

Spain's American colonies had gained independence and in 1898, Cuba, the Philippines and Puerto Rico were lost to the US as a result of the Spanish-American War.

Spain's neutrality in World War I strengthened support for the republican parties and, in reaction to a period of dictatorship by General Primo de Rivera (1923–30), the elections of 1931 produced a republican majority. This led to the abdication of Alphonso XII and the proclamation of a republic. A left-wing Popular Front government was elected in 1936, which provoked a military rebellion led by General Francisco Franco. The ensuing civil war lasted for three years and cost about a million lives. Backed by fascist Italy and Germany, Franco eventually defeated the republican government forces and went on to establish a dictatorship based on corporatism.

Although officially neutral in World War II, Spain's close relations with the fascist powers caused it to be expelled from the United Nations. In 1969, Prince Juan Carlos was named by Franco as his successor and he became king on Franco's death in 1975. He quickly set about restoring democracy: political parties were legalized in 1976 and an election, the first since 1936, was held in 1977. A new constitution, approved by referendum in 1978, established a democratic parliamentary monarchy, and in the same year Catalonia and the Basque country were granted autonomy. Basque extremists, however, have continued their struggle for full independence. In 1981, Juan Carlos was instrumental in putting down an attempted coup by right-wing army officers. Spain joined NATO in 1982 and the EC in 1986. Felipe González Márquez of the PSOE (Socialist Party) has been prime minister since 1982. [*Map page 18*] ∎

**AREA** 504,780 sq km ([194,896 sq mls]
**POPULATION** 39,568,000
**CAPITAL (POPULATION)** Madrid (3,121,000)
**GOVERNMENT** Constitutional monarchy
**ETHNIC GROUPS** Castilian Spanish 72%, Catalan 16%, Galician 8%, Basque 2%
**LANGUAGES** Castilian Spanish (official), Catalan, Galician, Basque
**RELIGIONS** Christianity (Roman Catholic 97%)
**CURRENCY** Peseta = 100 céntimos

# SRI LANKA

Known as Ceylon until 1972, when it became a Socialist republic, Sri Lanka has been described as 'the pearl of the Indian Ocean'; the island is also its crossroads.

From its mountain core to the coral strand stretches the 'wet zone' of south-western Sri Lanka, supporting cool, grassy downs, rainforests and tea-gardens near the ancient religious centre of Kandy, and evergreen forest and palm-fringed beaches in the lowlands from Colombo to east of Galle. White Buddhist shrines and peasant cottages dot the cultivated land among coconut palms, rice paddies, sugar-cane plantations and spice gardens. In contrast are the much drier zones of the north and east.

## ECONOMY AND RESOURCES

While light industry has gone some way to diversifying an agricultural base dependent on tea, rubber and coconuts, Sri Lanka's economic progress since independence – when it was a relatively prosperous state – has been plagued by civil war and communal violence.

## HISTORY AND POLITICS

First inhabited by forest-dwelling negroid Veddas, it was settled later by brown-skinned Aryans from India. These are now dominant in the population, though diluted by successive waves of incomers. Long-resident Tamils farm in the northern limestone peninsula of Jaffna, and Arab *dhow* sailors and merchants settled in the ports. After Vasco da Gama's contact with India in the 15th century came new traders and colonists – first Portuguese, then Dutch, then British (in control from 1796 to 1948) – and new immigrant Tamils were brought in from south-east India to intensively farm the plantations.

Conflict between the Sinhalese Buddhist majority and the Tamil Hindu minority, has led to disorder in 1958, 1971 and 1977; since 1983 the conflict has been virtually continuous as Tamil guerrillas have fought for an inde-pendent homeland in the north (Eelam), with Jaffna the capital.

An Indian-brokered cease-fire in 1987 allowed an Indian peacekeeping force in, but it failed to subdue the main terrorist group, the Tamil Tigers, and withdrew in March 1990. Between then and the start of 1992 more than 12,000 people died in renewed clashes between the predominantly Sinhalese government forces and the rebels, despite an agreement on Tamil autonomy. In 1993, the country's president was assassinated by a suspected Tamil separatist. Many civilians, too, have lost their lives, and the conflicts have stemmed the flow of foreign tourists.

In addition, the authorities were dogged by a rumbling rebellion of the left-wing Sinhalese nationalist movement (JVP) in the south. Banned in 1983, the JVP escalated their campaign after the Indo-Sri Lankan pact of 1987, but their guerrillas were virtually broken by an offensive initiated by the new government – elected democratically after a delay of some six years in 1988. [*Map page 23*] ■

**AREA** 65,610 sq km [25,332 sq mls]
**POPULATION** 18,125,000
**CAPITAL (POPULATION)** Colombo (1,863,000)
**GOVERNMENT** Multiparty republic
**ETHNIC GROUPS** Sinhalese 74%, Tamil 18%, Sri Lankan Moor 7%
**LANGUAGES** Sinhala and Tamil (both official)
**RELIGIONS** Buddhism 69%, Hinduism 16%, Islam 8%, Christianity 7%
**CURRENCY** Sri Lankan rupee = 100 cents

# SUDAN

The Sudan is the largest state of Africa. It consists essentially of vast clay plains and sandy areas, parts of the Nile basin and the Sahara, but it presents two very different landscapes. The extreme north is virtually uninhabited desert; to the south, where the desert gives way to semi-desert, nomads move over age-old tribal areas. During the rainy season the plain becomes a vast reed-covered swamp and the Nilotic cattle-rearing tribes (Shilluk and Dinka) move to the dry ridges and islands until the floods abate.

The belt across the centre of the country holds most of the population. Here low rainfall, supplemented by wells and small reservoirs for irrigation, allows subsistence farming, but the bulk of the population lives adjacent to the Blue and White Niles. This is the predominantly Arab part of the Sudan, where 70% of the population live.

### ECONOMY AND RESOURCES
Near the Blue and White Niles, and relying on them for irrigation, are a number of modern mechanized farming schemes, headed by the famous if fallible Gezira Scheme, one of the first of its kind in the world. Crops grown are cotton and oilseed for export, sugar cane and sorghum for local consumption. Despite once being 'the bread-basket of Africa', schemes like Gezira have failed to realize the full agricultural potential.

### HISTORY AND POLITICS
The Sudan, formerly an Anglo-Egyptian Condominium, has suffered from an amalgam of the plagues which, in various combinations, have afflicted of post-colonial Africa. The so-called plagues are ethnic, religious and ideological division; political repression and instability; intermittent civil war, with high spending on 'defence'; economic crisis and massive foreign debt which, to service, would cost three times as much as export earnings; prolonged drought (punctuated by flash floods such as those in 1988, which left 1.5 million people homeless); and an influx of famine-stricken refugees since the 1980s.

The 17-year-old civil war that ended in 1972 was rekindled in 1983 by the (largely effective) pressure from extremists for the reinstatement of fundamental Sharic law. The renewed rivalries of the Arab north and the non-Muslim south – a pattern mirrored in neighbouring Chad, which shares many of Sudan's problems – have caused the deaths of hundreds of thousands of people and the decimation of a traditional way of life in an area already prone to drought and severe food shortages. Despite attempts to restore order, the fighting continued into the 1990s.

While the power in the land rests in the north with the military council in Khartoum – a city laid out in the pattern of the British flag at the confluence of the White Nile and Blue Nile – there seems little hope of a return to democracy, and the possibility of the south seceding remains a distinct if distant one. [*Map page 32*] ■

> **AREA** 2,505,810 sq km [967,493 sq mls]
> **POPULATION** 27,361,000
> **CAPITAL (POPULATION)** Khartoum (561,000)
> **GOVERNMENT** Military regime
> **ETHNIC GROUPS** Sudanese Arab 49%, Dinka 12%, Nuba 8%, Beja 6%, Nuer 5%, Azande 3%
> **LANGUAGES** Arabic (official)
> **RELIGIONS** Islam 73%, traditional beliefs 17%, Christianity (Roman Catholic 4%, Protestant 2%)
> **CURRENCY** Sudanese dinar = 10 pounds

# SURINAM

Surinam has a coastline of 350 km [218 mls] of Amazonian mud and silt, fringed by extensive mangrove swamps. Behind lies an old coastal plain of sands and clays, bordering a stretch of sandy savanna. The heavily forested interior uplands further to the south are part of the Guiana Highlands, whose weathered soils form the basis of the crucial bauxite industry.

### ECONOMY AND RESOURCES
Surinam's hot, steamy climate grows an abundance of bananas, citrus fruits and coconuts for export, with rice and many other tropical commodities for home consumption. Plantations were initially worked by African slaves, later by Chinese and East Indian indentured labour. Bauxite and its derivatives, shrimps and bananas are the main exports, but though 92% of the land is covered by forest –

the world's highest figure – at present little is commercially exploited.

## HISTORY AND POLITICS

Although Spaniards visited as early as 1499, Surinam was first settled by British colonists in 1651. In 1667 it was ceded to Holland in exchange for Nieuw-Amsterdam, now New York, and was confirmed as a Dutch colony, called Dutch Guiana, in 1816.

Surinam gained independence in 1975 and since then the country has experienced a great deal of political instability, mainly due to racial tension. In 1980 there was a military coup and later, in 1982, after the execution of 15 opposition leaders and the banning of all political parties, the Netherlands broke off relations and suspended all aid. Relations were resumed in 1988 following elections.

Another military coup occurred in 1990, but further elections were held in 1991, and Ronald Venetiaan, leader of a coalition group called the New Front, became president. In 1992, a peace agreement was negotiated with the *boschneger*, descendants of African slaves, who had launched a struggle against the government in 1986. [*Map page 31*] ■

---

**AREA** 163,270 sq km [63,039 sq mls]
**POPULATION** 438,000
**CAPITAL (POPULATION)** Paramaribo (200,970)
**GOVERNMENT** Multiparty republic
**ETHNIC GROUPS** Asian Indian 37%, Creole (mixed White and Black), 31%, Indonesian 14%, Black 9%, Amerindian 3%, Chinese 3%
**LANGUAGES** Dutch (official)
**RELIGIONS** Christianity (Roman Catholic 23%, Protestant 19%), Hinduism 27%, Islam 20%
**CURRENCY** Surinam guilder = 100 cents

---

# SWAZILAND

A lthough the smallest country in sub-Saharan Africa, Swaziland nevertheless reveals strong scenic contrasts. From west to east the country descends in three altitudinal steps: the Highveld, average altitude 1,200 m [4,000 ft], and the Middleveld, lying between 350 and 1,000 m [1,000 and 3,500 ft], are made of old, hard rocks; the Lowveld, average height 270 m [900 ft], is of softer shales and sandstones in the west, and basalts in the east. Shutting the country in on the east are the Lebombo Mountains (800 m [2,600 ft]). Rivers rising in South Africa completely traverse these belts; their valleys provide communication lines and are sources of perennial water, important for irrigation.

## ECONOMY AND RESOURCES

In the late 19th century European colonists settled and today the main economic features result from basic differences in occupational structures between 'black' and 'white' Swazi. Those derived from European stock are involved in commerce, industry and, predominantly, the production of exports such as sugar, citrus fruits and wood pulp as well as cereals and cattle. The majority indigenous Swazi are still mostly engaged in subsistence farming based on maize, with fragmented land-holdings and a dispersed settlement pattern. As a result there are few large towns, but the population remains far better off than in Lesotho, with which it is often compared, somewhat unrealistically.

Swaziland is part of a customs union which includes South Africa, but for overseas trade the country relies largely on the port of Maputo (in Mozambique), to which it is linked by the only railway. During the 1980s this was frequently inoperative because of the war in Mozambique – while Swaziland was also burdened with a flow of refugees. The kingdom would no doubt rather have tourists: there are already more than 258,000 a year.

## HISTORY AND POLITICS

According to tradition, in the 18th century, a group of Bantu-speaking people, under the Swazi chief Ngwane II, crossed the Lebombo range and united with local African groups to form the Swazi nation. Under attack from Zulu armies, the Swazi people were forced to seek British protection in the 1840s. Gold was discovered in the 1880s and many Europeans sought land concessions from the king, who did not realize that in doing this he was losing control of the land.

In 1894, Britain and the Boers of South Africa agreed to put Swaziland under the control of the South African Republic (the Transvaal). But at the end of the Anglo-Boer War (1899–1902), Britain took control of the country. In 1968, when Swaziland became fully independent as a constitutional monarchy, the head of state was King Sobhuza II.

In 1973, Sobhuza suspended the constitution and took over supreme power in 1976. He banned political parties in 1978, though the people elected the 80 members of an electoral college, from which are chosen representatives to serve in parliament.

Sobhuza died in August 1982 after a reign of 82 years. In 1983, one of his sons, Prince Makhosetive (born in 1968), was chosen as his heir. In April 1986, he was installed as king, taking the name Mswati III. In 1993, Swaziland held its first-ever multiparty elections. [*Map page 33*] ■

**AREA** 17,360 sq km [6,703 sq mls]
**POPULATION** 832,000
**CAPITAL (POPULATION)** Mbabane (38,300)
**GOVERNMENT** Monarchy
**ETHNIC GROUPS** Swazi 84%, Zulu 10%, Tsonga 2%
**LANGUAGES** Siswati and English (both official)
**RELIGIONS** Christianity (Protestant 37%, indigenous African churches 29%, Roman Catholic 11%), traditional beliefs 21%
**CURRENCY** Lilangeni = 100 cents

# SWEDEN

The kingdom of Sweden is the largest of the Scandinavian countries in terms of both population and area. It occupies the eastern half of the Scandinavian peninsula, extending southwards to latitude 55°N and having a much smaller Arctic area than either Norway or Finland.

The eastern coast, stretching 1,600 km [1,000 mls] along the shores of the Baltic Sea and the Gulf of Bothnia, extends from the mouth of the Torne River, which forms the border with Finland, to Ystad in the south. Sweden also has a coastline facing west along the shores of the Kattegat – the strait that separates Sweden and the Jutland peninsula, which is part of Denmark.

## Landscape

Sweden's share of the Scandinavian peninsula is less mountainous than that of Norway. The northern half of the country forms part of the Baltic or Fenno-Scandian Shield, a stable block of ancient granites and gneisses which extends round the head of the Gulf of Bothnia into Finland. This part of Sweden contains most of the country's rich mineral wealth. The shield land is an area of low plateaux which rise gradually westwards.

South of the plateaux area there is a belt of lowlands between the capital city, Stockholm, and the second city, Göteborg (Gothenburg). These lowlands contain several large lakes, the chief of which are Mälar, near Stockholm, and the larger Vänern and Vättern, which are situated in the middle of the lowland belt. These are all that remains of a strait which, in glacial times, connected the Baltic with the Kattegat. Changes in land and water level during the later stages of the Ice Age led to the breaking of this connection. Now linked by canals, these lakes form an important water route across the country.

Sweden's topography was greatly affected by the Ice Age: the long, narrow lakes which fill the upper valleys of many of the rivers of northern Sweden have been shaped by the action of ice. They are the relics of a much larger lake system which was fed by water from the melting ice-sheet and provide excellent natural reservoirs for hydroelectric stations. Some of the most fertile soils in Sweden were formed from material deposited in the beds of such glacial lakes. Elsewhere, glacial moraines and deposits of boulder clay are other reminders of the impact of the Ice Age.

## Climate

The high mountains which form the spine of the Scandinavian peninsula shut off the modifying influence of the Atlantic weather systems from northern Sweden. This area therefore has colder, drier winters than the seaward side, but also enjoys warmer and drier summers. On the Norrland plateau annual rainfall is less than 508 mm [20 in], July temperatures average 15°C [59°F] and the long summer days of the high northern latitudes make summertime pleasant – although the long winters are dark and cold. The Gulf of Bothnia is affected by ice between November and April, creating problems for shipping.

The southern part of Sweden, between the Kattegat and the Baltic, is open to Atlantic influences and has milder winters than the northern areas, but summers are cooler and wetter. Göteborg has average winter temperatures of 0°C [32°F], compared with Stockholm's –3°C [27°F], whilst at Haparanda, at the head of the Gulf of Bothnia, the coldest month of February has an average temperature of –12°C [10°F]. In summer, however, there is little difference between north and south, most areas having between 15°C and 20°C [59°F to 68°F].

## ECONOMY AND RESOURCES

There are extensive coniferous forests throughout northern Sweden; indeed, half the country's land area is covered with trees. In the south the original cover of mixed deciduous woodland has been cleared for agriculture from the areas of better soil, the typical landscape now being farmland interspersed with forest. This is usually spruce or pine, often with birch – the national tree.

There are better opportunities for agriculture in Sweden than elsewhere in Scandinavia. Cereal crops, potatoes, sugar beet and vegetables are grown for human consumption in Skåne and in central Sweden, but by far the greatest area of cultivated land is given over to the production of fodder crops for cattle and sheep. Dairy farming is highly developed, and Sweden is self-sufficient in milk, cheese and butter production..

Many farmers have left the land since World War II, attracted by the higher wages and more modern lifestyle of the towns. Sweden has been able to create a high standard of living based on industry – despite the fact that, apart from the large iron-ore deposits, many of the essential fuels and raw materials have to be

## ÅLAND

Swedish settlers colonized various coastal tracts of Finland from the 12th century, and the 6.5% of the Finnish population who are Swedish-speaking include all the 25,000 people of Åland, the group of more than 6,500 islands situated between the two countries in the Gulf of Bothnia.

Although the inhabitants voted to secede to Sweden in a 1917 referendum, the result was annulled in 1921 by the League of Nations for strategic reasons and Åland (as Ahvenanmaa) remains a Finnish province. However, the islands were granted considerable autonomy and still enjoy a large degree of 'home rule' with their own flag, postage stamps and representation at the annual assembly of the Nordic Council.

Boasting many important relics of the Stone, Iron and Bronze Ages, the province's income derives mainly from fishing, farming and, increasingly, from tourism.

imported: the development of hydroelectricity however, has made up for the lack of oil and coal. Most of the iron ore obtained from the mines at Kiruna and Gällivare in Arctic Sweden is exported via Narvik and Lulea to Europe, mainly to Germany.

Sweden is famous for high-quality engineering products such as ball bearings, match-making machinery, agricultural machines, motor vehicles (Saab and Volvo), ships, aircraft and armaments (Bofors). In addition to these relatively new industries, the traditional forest-based industries have been modernized. Sweden is among the world's largest exporters of wood pulp and paper and board – as well as Europe's biggest producer of softwood.

## HISTORY AND POLITICS

The bulk of the population lives in the lakeland corridor between Stockholm and Göteborg, or around the southern city of Malmö. These citizens, by virtue of their working hard, peaceful past, now enjoy a standard of living that is in many ways the envy of most other Western countries. Sweden has by far the highest percentage figure for public spending in the OECD, with over 70% of the national budget going on one of the widest-ranging welfare programmes in the world.

In turn, the tax burden is the world's highest (some 57% of national income) and some Swedes are beginning to feel that the 'soft' yet paternalistic approach has led to overgovernment, depersonalization and uniformity. The elections of September 1991 saw the end of the Social Democrat government – in power for all but six years since 1932 – with voters swinging towards parties canvassing lower taxation. Other attractive policies appeared to include curbs on immigration and diversion of Third World aid (Sweden spends well above the OECD per capita average each year) to the newly independent Baltic states.

Other changes were in the wind, too. A founder member of the European Free Trade Association (EFTA) – Stockholm played host to the inaugural meetings in 1960 – Sweden nevertheless applied for entry to the EC in 1991. And in 1994 the people voted to join the European Union on 1 January 1995.

Sweden remains the key state in Scandinavia: its long experience of peace and stability, and a wide industrial base built on efficiency and quality, together with its strategically central position and relatively large population, form the most important power among the Nordic nations.

However, it is possible that it will be vulnerable to forces largely beyond its control. Like its neighbours, Sweden suffers from forest-killing acid rain generated mostly by the UK and Germany, and after the shock waves from Chernobyl in 1986 the government was also forced to reconsider its electricity-generating programme, now 52% dependent on nuclear power. [*Map page 13*] ■

---

**AREA** 449,960 sq km [173,730 sq mls]
**POPULATION** 8,738,000
**CAPITAL (POPULATION)** Stockholm (1,503,000)
**GOVERNMENT** Constitutional monarchy
**ETHNIC GROUPS** Swedish 91%, Finnish 3%
**LANGUAGES** Swedish (official), Finnish
**RELIGIONS** Christianity (Lutheran 89%, Roman Catholic 2%)
**CURRENCY** Swedish krona = 100 öre

---

# SWITZERLAND

Nearly 60% of Swiss territory is in the Alps, of which two notable peaks are on the Italian border: the Matterhorn (4,478 m [14,700 ft]) and the Monte Rosa (4,634 m [15,200 ft]). The Alps are drained by the upper Rhine tributaries and by the Rhône Valley via Lac Léman (Lake Geneva). Numerous lakes add to the scenic attraction of the permanently snow-capped mountains.

## ECONOMY AND RESOURCES

The Alps have become one of the great tourist attractions of the world. As a result, around 200,000 people work in the hotel and catering industries. Nationally, unemployment is very low by world standards.

Despite its lingering image as a predominantly pastoral country, Switzerland is a very advanced country, providing its citizens with a per capita income which is by far the highest of the reasonably sized economies, and is outstripped only by neighbouring Liechtenstein. The reasons for Switzerland's high standard of living include neutrality in two World Wars, plentiful hydroelectric power, a central geographical position within Europe and rich mineral deposits, including uranium (40% of the electricity is now nuclear-derived) and iron ore. It would also be unfair, however – as in the case of Germany and Japan – not to include hard work, a sense of purpose and organizational ability in the list of attributes.

Agriculture is efficient, with both arable and pastoral farming; a wide range of produce is grown throughout the country, including maize and other cereals, fruits, vegetables, and grapes for the local wine industry. The mountain pastures are still used for summer grazing, though most of the famous migrations of herds and herders up the mountains in summer no longer take place. Industry is progressive and prosperous, in particular mechanical and electrical engineering, metallurgy, chemicals and textiles. Watch- and clock-making is perhaps the most famed of all Swiss industries,

## THE ALPS

Thrust upwards by continental collision 25 or 30 million years ago, the Alps are Europe's principal mountain range. They stretch for over 1,000 km [600 mls] between north-eastern Italy and Austria and include Europe's highest mountain, Mont Blanc (4,807 m [15,771 ft]). The Alpine watershed is the source of many great European rivers, including the Rhine and the Po.

Despite the nine major passes that cross them, the mountains were seen by their pastoralist inhabitants and travellers alike as a troublesome obstacle until the 19th century, when interest in mountaineering, originally an English craze, gave puzzled locals new employment as guides. Six tunnels, including one under Mont Blanc, now make access very easy, and tourism has become a mass industry built around modern winter sports.

Alpine agriculture, once the mainstay of mountain life, is currently in decline, but skiing and summer tourism have brought new prosperity. Throughout the 1980s, the Alps attracted up to 50 million visitors a year, most intent on skiing some of the 40,000 runs that have been created for them. Unfortunately, the impact of mass skiing on the fragile Alpine environment is serious. Thousands of hectares of high forest have been bulldozed to create smooth pistes, denuding the slopes of scarce topsoil as well as creating perfect conditions for massive avalanches: in 1987, more than 60 people were killed by summer mudslides, and almost 50 towns and villages were damaged, some of them severely.

The remaining Alpine forests are under threat from industrial air pollution. Acid rain, formed from dissolved sulphur dioxide, is destroying trees at an alarming rate: in some districts, two-thirds have been affected, and many will never recover. In 1994, the Swiss voted to ban foreign lorries using alpine roads. This will be phased in over 10 years.

and it remains a very important source of income for the national economy.

In addition to agricultural and industrial strength Switzerland also has a world trade in banking and insurance, concentrated particularly in Zürich, while its revenues are boosted both by tourism and its position as the head-quarters for numerous international bodies. Geneva alone hosts EFTA, GATT and the International Red Cross (which was first formed there in 1864), as well as ten UN agencies that include WHO, ILO and the High Commission for Refugees, and over 140 others: Basle, for example, is home to the Bank for International Settlements (the central banks' bank).

### HISTORY AND POLITICS

Ironically, Switzerland has remained stubbornly outside the UN – a policy reiterated by a referendum held in 1986. As Europe started moving towards greater economic and political union, Switzerland announced in May 1992 that it would be applying to join the EU; but a December 1992 referendum rejected this proposal. However, in June 1993, Switzerland decided to establish by 1995 a 600-man battalion for use in the UN peacekeeping force.

Switzerland is a multilingual patchwork of 26 cantons, each of which has control over housing and economic policy. Six of the cantons are French-speaking, one Italian-speaking, one with a significant Romansch-speaking community (*Graubünden*), and the rest speak German. It nevertheless remains a strongly united country – internationally recognized as a permanently neutral power, politically stable with an efficient reservist army (but no navy), active in good causes, and shrewdly trading with most of the countries of the world. [*Map page 15*] ∎

AREA 41,290 sq km [15,942 sq mls]
POPULATION 7,131,000
CAPITAL (POPULATION) Bern (299,000)
GOVERNMENT Federal republic
ETHNIC GROUPS German 64%, French 19%, Italian 8%, Yugoslav 3%, Spanish 2%, Romansch 1%
LANGUAGES French, German, Italian and Romansch (all official)
RELIGIONS Christianity (Roman Catholic 46%, Protestant 40%)
CURRENCY Swiss franc = 100 centimes

# SYRIA

The northern part of the former Ottoman province of the same name, Syria stretches from the Mediterranean to the Tigris, and from the southern edge of the Kurdish plateau in the north to the heart of the Hamad or stony desert in the south.

The Orontes River flows northwards along the Great Rift Valley, through alternating gorges and wide valleys which have been reclaimed by drainage and irrigation. Near Hamah and Hims the ranges of Lebanon and Anti-Lebanon are relatively low, but further south the Anti-Lebanon rises to the Heights of Hermon, whose snows water the gardens of the capital, Damascus, on the eastern side. In the far south, by the frontier with Jordan, the volcanic mass of Mount Hauran supports a group of oases around the town of Suwayda. The Golan Heights, in the south-west, are occupied by Israel.

## ECONOMY AND RESOURCES

Aleppo, the second city of Syria, is set in a well-watered agricultural area. Further east the steppe becomes progressively drier. This

## THE MIDDLE EAST CONFLICT

Arab-Jewish hostility in the Middle East dates from the so-called Balfour Declaration of 1917, when an embattled British government proposed a 'Jewish national home' in the then Turkish imperial province of Palestine without prejudicing the 'existing rights' of the overwhelmingly Arab (Christian and Muslim) population. After World War I, Palestine became a League of Nations mandate under British control; throughout the 1920s, a trickle of Jewish immigrants inspired rioting without noticeably affecting the population balance. But the rise of Nazism in Europe brought floods of Jewish refugees, and Arab-Jewish violence became endemic.

In 1947 the recently formed United Nations proposed a formal partition of the land, which was accepted by the Jews and rejected by the Palestinians. Even before the British announced they would withdraw in May 1948, 150,000 Arab refugees had fled. On 14 May, the day the British quit, the independence of a new State of Israel was declared. Egypt, Lebanon, Syria, Transjordan and Iraq at once launched an invasion, later joined by Yemen and Saudi Arabia. But by the 1949 cease-fire, Israel had beaten them off and controlled more territory than the UN partition plan had allocated the Jews. Jerusalem remained a divided city, half controlled by Israel, half by the armies of Transjordan, later the kingdom of Jordan. An uneasy peace descended, with sporadic border clashes; hundreds of thousands of Palestinians lost their homes. In 1956, full-scale war erupted once more when Israel joined with Britain and France in an attack on Egypt. Egypt's armies were badly mauled, but Israel's borders remained unchanged. In 1967, Israel responded to an Egyptian maritime blockade – and public threats from Syria and Egypt – with a pre-emptive strike that left it in control of the Sinai peninsula, the Gaza Strip, the 'West Bank' of the Jordan and all of Jerusalem. But real peace was no nearer: Israel had acquired an Arab population of several million. Palestinian freedom fighters – 'terrorists' to their enemies – began a worldwide campaign, including aircraft hijacking, to broadcast their people's plight.

A 1973 Egyptian attack across the Suez Canal, backed by Syria, came close to over-running Sinai, but Israeli counterattacks recovered much of the lost territory. Egypt's partial victory eventually led to the 1979 Camp David accord, by which Israel returned Sinai in exchange for Egyptian recognition of Israel's right to exist. Egypt was excoriated by its former Arab allies, and Palestinian terrorism continued. From 1987 onwards, a low-intensity Palestinian uprising (the *intifada*) began, which was repressed by Israel. Finally, on 13 September 1993, the Israeli prime minister Itzhak Rabin officially recognized the PLO, and Yasser Arafat, leader of the PLO, renounced terrorism and recognized the state of Israel, leading to an agreement signed by both sides in Washington. The agreement provided for limited Palestinian self-rule in the Gaza Strip and in the West Bank city of Jericho.

was traditionally winter pasture for the nomads who moved in from their summer homes in the mountains of Lebanon, but in recent years, thanks to techniques of dry-farming with machinery, it has become a prosperous farming zone, devoted almost exclusively to cotton and cereals. The water from the Euphrates barrage, which produces 70% of the country's electricity, will extend agriculture in this region. Syria has only one large harbour, at Latakia.

Syria has struck oil in the 'panhandle' by the Tigris in the far north-east, and a pipeline has been laid from there to the Mediterranean. Another pipeline crosses the desert further south from the Kirkuk fields in Iraq to the sea-terminal at Baniyas.

## HISTORY AND POLITICS

President Assad's repressive but stable regime, in power since 1970, was heavily reliant on Arab aid, but Syria's anti-Iraq stance in the 1991 Gulf War will almost certainly result in greater Western assistance to the improving economy. Though small compared to Egypt or Saudi Arabia, Syria's position (both historical and geographical) makes the country a key player in the complicated power game of Middle East politics. [*Map page 19*] ■

AREA 185,180 sq km [71,498 sq mls]
POPULATION 14,171,000
CAPITAL (POPULATION) Damascus (or Dimashq, 1,451,000)
GOVERNMENT Multiparty republic
ETHNIC GROUPS Arab 89%, Kurd 6%
LANGUAGES Arabic (official)
RELIGIONS Islam 90%, Christianity 9%
CURRENCY Syrian pound = 100 piastres

# TAIWAN

High mountain ranges, which extend for the entire length of the island, occupy the central and eastern parts of Taiwan, and only a quarter of the island's surface area is cultivated. The central ranges rise to altitudes of over 3,000 m [10,000 ft], and carry dense forests of broadleaved evergreen trees such as camphor and Chinese cork oak. Above 1,500 m [5,000 ft], conifers such as pine, larch and cedar dominate.

## ECONOMY AND RESOURCES

With its warm, moist climate – the island sits astride the Tropic of Cancer – Taiwan provides a highly favourable environment for agriculture, and the well-watered lands of the western coastal plain produce heavy rice crops. Sugar cane, sweet potatoes, tea, bananas and pineapples are also grown. Recently, however, agriculture has declined as industrial output has risen.

Taiwan produces a wide range of manufactured goods, including colour television sets, electronic calculators, footwear and ready-made clothing, and is the world's leading ship-breaker. Taipei, the capital, is a modern and affluent city, as well as being an important administrative and cultural centre.

Less than half the size of Ireland or Tasmania, but supporting nearly 21 million people, Taiwan has been a remarkable success story, averaging nearly 9% growth every year from 1953 to the 1990s.

## HISTORY AND POLITICS

Ceded by the Chinese empire to Japan in 1895, Taiwan was surrendered by the Japanese Army to General Chiang Kai-shek's Nationalist Chinese government in 1945. Beaten by Mao Tse-tung's Communists, some 2 million Nationalists and their leader fled the mainland to the island in the two years before 1949. The influx was met with hostility by the 8 million Taiwanese, and the new regime was imposed with force.

Boosted by US help, Chiang's government set about ambitious programmes for land reform and industrial expansion, the latter taking Taiwan into the world's top 20 nations by 1980 and providing high living standards. The island, nevertheless, remained politically isolated, losing its UN seat to Communist China in 1971, and being diplomatically abandoned by the US in 1979, when Washington switched recognition to Beijing. Though few countries take seriously Taipei's claim to be the sole legitimate government of China, the country administers a number of islands off the mainland, notably Quemoy (Jinmen) and Matsu (Mazu).

In 1987, the authoritarian regime lifted martial law after nearly 40 years, a native Taiwanese became president in 1988, and in 1991 came the country's first full general election. Technically still at war with Beijing, there have been signs that the thaw of the Cold War might reach the island. [*Map page 24*] ■

AREA 36,000 sq km [13,900 sq mls]
POPULATION 20,659,000
CAPITAL (POPULATION) Taipei (2,718,000)
GOVERNMENT Multiparty republic
ETHNIC GROUPS Taiwanese (Han Chinese) 84%, mainland Chinese 14%
LANGUAGES Mandarin Chinese
RELIGIONS Buddhism 43%, Taoism 21%, Christianity 7%, Confucianism
CURRENCY New Taiwan dollar = 100 cents

# TAJIKISTAN

The Republic of Tajikistan is one of the five central Asian republics that formed part of the former Soviet Union. Only 7% of the country is below 1,000 m [3,280 ft], while almost all of eastern Tajikistan is above 3,000 m [9,840 ft]. The highest point is Communism Peak (Pik Kommunizma) which reaches 7,496 m [24,593 ft]. The main ranges are the westwards extension of the Tian Shan range in the north and the snow-capped Pamirs in the south-east. Earthquakes are common throughout the country.

Tajikistan is a landlocked country with a continental climate. The summers are hot and dry in the lower valleys, but winters are long and bitterly cold in the mountainous areas.

## ECONOMY AND RESOURCES

The World Bank classifies Tajikistan as a 'low-income' developing country. Agriculture,

mainly on irrigated land in the north-west (there are 43,000 km [26,720 mls] of irrigation channels in total), is the principal activity and cotton is the chief product. Other crops include fruits, grains, vegetables and mulberry trees (for silkworms), as well as eucalyptus and geraniums for the perfume industry. The country has large hydroelectric power resources and it produces aluminium. Otherwise, manufacturing is mostly on a small scale. The country's main exports are aluminium, cotton, fruits, vegetable oils and textiles.

## HISTORY AND POLITICS

The ancestors of the people of Tajikistan were Persians who had settled in the area by 2,500 years ago. The area was conquered many times; one important group of invaders were the Arabs via whom Islam was introduced in the 7th century. From the 9th century onwards, the Tajiks lived under the control of various feudal emirates until, in the late 19th century, Russia conquered part of Tajikistan, and it extended its rule after the Russian Revolution of 1917. By 1920, all of Tajikistan was under Russian control.

In 1924, the area was ruled as part of the Uzbek Soviet Socialist Republic. But in 1929 it was expanded, taking in areas containing Uzbeks, and it became the Tajik Soviet Socialist Republic within the Soviet Union. Under Communism, all features of Tajik life were strictly controlled and religious worship was discouraged, though certain aspects of life were improved, such as health and education.

While the Soviet Union began to introduce reforms in the 1980s, many Tajiks demanded freedom. In 1989, the Tajik government made Tajik the official language instead of Russian, and in 1990 it stated that its local laws overruled Soviet laws. Tajikistan became fully independent in 1991, after the break-up of the Soviet Union. As the poorest of the former Soviet republics, Tajikistan faced many problems in trying to reorganize its economy along free-enterprise lines.

In 1992, civil war broke out between the government, which was run by former Communists, and an alliance of democrats and Islamic forces. The government maintained control, but it relied heavily on aid from the Commonwealth of Independent States, the organization through which most of the former republics of the Soviet Union have kept in contact, but sporadic fighting continues in many parts. [*Map page 22*] ■

AREA 143,100 sq km [55,520 sq mls]
POPULATION 5,933,000
CAPITAL (POPULATION) Dushanbe (602,000)
GOVERNMENT Transitional democracy
ETHNIC GROUPS Tajik 62%, Uzbek 24%, Russian 8%, Tatar, Kyrgyz, Ukrainian, German
LANGUAGES Tajik (official)
RELIGIONS Islam
CURRENCY Tajik rouble = 100 kopeks

# TANZANIA

From the islands of Zanzibar and Pemba, Tanzania extends across the high plateau of eastern Africa, mostly above 1,000 m [3,000 ft], to the rift valleys filled by lakes Tanganyika and Nyasa (Malawi). The Northern Highlands flank branches of the eastern rift valley, containing the strongly alkaline Lake Natron and lakes Eyasi and Manyara, and dominated by the ice-capped extinct volcano of Kilimanjaro which, at 5,895 m [19,340 ft], is the highest mountain in Africa. The Southern Highlands overlook Lake Nyasa at the southern end of the rift system.

## ECONOMY AND RESOURCES
Tanzania's population is dispersed into several concentrations mostly on the margins of the country, separated by sparsely inhabited savanna woodland (*miombo*). Attempts to develop the *miombo* woodlands have been hindered by sleeping sickness, drought and poor soils. Along the coast and on self-governing Zanzibar and other islands are old cities and ruins of the historic Swahili-Arab culture, and the major ports and railway termini of Dar es Salaam and Tanga. Rail connections enable Dar es Salaam to act as a port for Zambia and, by ferry across Lake Tanganyika, for eastern

Zaïre. Local products include sisal and cashew nuts with cloves from Zanzibar and Pemba, and there are some fine beach resorts.

Tanzania received 202,000 visitors in 1992, less than a third of Kenya's total, but there are hopes that this figure will rise. Certainly, the country has many of the prerequisites for a successful tourist industry. There are 17 national parks and reserves – among them the Selous, the largest game reserve in the world; the celebrated Serengeti; and the Ngorongoro crater, renowned for its abundant wildlife. In addition, there are important archaeological sites such as Olduvia Gorge, west of the Serengeti, where in 1964 Louis Leakey, the famous British archaeologist and anthropologist, discovered the remains of humans some million years old.

The Northern Highlands centre on Moshi and support intensive agriculture, exporting coffee, tea and tobacco. This contrasts with the nomadic Masai pastoralists of the surrounding plains whose traditional lifestyle is based on shifting cultivation. Tea also comes from the Southern Highlands. South of Lake Victoria is an important cotton-growing and cattle-rearing area, focusing on Mwanza. The most important minerals are diamonds.

## HISTORY AND POLITICS
Tanzania was formed in 1964 when mainland Tanganyika – which had become independent from Britain in 1961 – was joined by the small island state of Zanzibar. For 20 years after independence Tanzania was run under the widely admired policies of self-help (*ujamaa*) and egalitarian socialism pioneered by President Julius Nyerere. While his schemes produced relatively high levels of education and welfare for Africa, economic progress was stifled not only by lack of resources and falling world commodity prices but also by inefficient state corporations and corrupt bureaucracies. As a result the country ranks little better than war-torn states like Ethiopia and the Somali Republic in terms of income, and is almost as dependent on foreign financial aid.

Nyerere stepped down as president in 1985, but retained the (only) party leadership and considerable influence for another five years. In the meantime his successor, Ali Hassan Mwinyi, was attempting to liberalize the economy – if not the political system. In 1992 he amended the constitution to allow multiparty politics, provided the parties were not formed on tribal or racial grounds. [*Map page 33*] ■

**AREA** 945,090 sq km [364,899 sq mls]
**POPULATION** 28,846,000
**CAPITAL (POPULATION)** Dodoma (203,833)
**GOVERNMENT** Multiparty republic
**ETHNIC GROUPS** Nyamwezi and Sukuma 21%, Swahili 9%, Hehet and Bena 7%, Makonde 6%, Haya 6%
**LANGUAGES** Swahili and English (both official)
**RELIGIONS** Christianity (mostly Roman Catholic) 34%, Islam 33% (99% in Zanzibar), traditional beliefs and others 33%
**CURRENCY** Tanzanian shilling = 100 cents

# THAILAND

M eaning 'Land of the Free' (*Muang Thai*), and known as Siam until 1939, Thailand is comparable in size to France or Spain. The country is centred on the valley of the River Chao Phraya that flows across the central plain extending from the Gulf of Siam to the foothills of the northern mountains. Bounded in the west by the narrow mountain range that borders Burma, and in the east by lower hills separating the plain from the higher Khorat Plateau (Cao Nguyen Khorat), the central plain is Thailand's rice bowl; it presents long vistas, with extensive ricefields, canals and rivers that provide the main routeways, with villages raised on stilts. Northern Thailand is a region of fold mountains, with agriculturally rich intermontane basins.

The capital city, Bangkok, stands at the southern edge of the plain, near the mouth of the Chao Phraya; with a seaport and international airport it is the transport centre of the country. Ornate Buddhist temples stand side by side with modern concrete buildings, and the growing city population is already over a tenth of the total. Founded as a royal capital in

1782, this 'Venice of the East' is rich in examples of Thai culture, including fantastic statues of Buddha. The name Bangkok refers only to the Thon Buri side of the River Chao Phraya; the proper term is Krung Thep ('city of angels' – like Los Angeles). Today, it is a sprawling metropolis with high levels of traffic congestion, struggling to absorb the waves of migrants who pour in from rural areas in search of work.

### ECONOMY AND RESOURCES

The hill forests produce teak and other valuable timbers. Thailand's highest mountain, Doi Inthanon (2,575 m [8,514 ft]), and the high hills surrounding it are the home of many hill tribes who live by shifting cultivation of dry rice and opium poppies; Chiengmai, the beautiful northern capital, lies in this area. The Khorat Plateau to the east is a sandstone region of poor soils supporting savanna woodlands; glutinous rice and cassava (the country has overtaken Brazil as the world's leading producer) are its main crops. The long southern part of Thailand, linked to the Malay Peninsula by the Isthmus of Kra, is a forested region of rolling hills, producing tin ore and plantation rubber.

Thailand has long been famous for rice production; though fifth in the world league, it is the biggest exporter and it is still the country's best agricultural earner, despite the increasing importance of several other commodities including rubber, tapioca products and sugar. Wolfram, forest products and fisheries are also being exploited. Offshore oil and gas were discovered in the late 1970s, and crude oil production began in 1983. Industries remain largely underdeveloped, but manufacturing based on cheap labour is expanding rapidly in textiles, clothing, electrical goods and food processing, contributing more to GDP than agriculture since 1984, while local crafts in the villages help to provide overseas income, as does tourism. In 1992 Thailand received nearly 5.4 million visitors – Burma received just 11,400 – and since 1982 tourism has been the main foreign exchange earner.

### HISTORY AND POLITICS

Thailand is the only South-east Asian country that has not been colonized, or occupied by foreign powers, except in war. An absolute monarchy until 1932, when the king graciously surrendered to a bloodless coup that set up a provisional constitution, Thailand has seen a more stable recent history than most of its unfortunate neighbours, though for most of the next 40 years it was dominated by military rulers. Forced into alliance with Japan in World War II, the Thais aligned themselves firmly to the USA after 1945 – a policy that has brought much military, technical and financial aid.

Despite continuing army involvements and interventions – the bloodless coup of 1991, claimed to be protecting King Rama IX and promising a swift return to civilian democracy, was the 17th takeover in half a century – and despite the presence of Cambodian refugees and its use by various camps as a political conduit and military springboard for intentions in South-east Asia, Thailand's subtle and pragmatic approach to life has seen the country prosper. In a system often referred to as 'semi-democracy', constitutional rule propped up by the pillars of military, monarch, bureaucracy and religion, Thailand has managed (not without criticism) to avoid the dreadful events that have afflicted the rest of mainland South-east Asia since the end of World War II – though in May 1992 the unelected leadership found itself under serious pressure. Hundreds died in protests against the takeover as prime minister by the head of the army, and an uneasy peace was restored only after his removal and an appeal for order from the King. Elections were held later in 1992 and a civilian government under Prime Minister Chuan Leekpai took office. The new government has committed itself to reducing the political power of the military. [*Map page 26*] ■

**AREA** 513,120 sq km [198,116 sq mls]
**POPULATION** 58,183,000
**CAPITAL (POPULATION)** Bangkok (5,876,000)
**GOVERNMENT** Constitutional monarchy
**ETHNIC GROUPS** Thai 80%, Chinese 12%, Malay 4%, Khmer 3%
**LANGUAGES** Thai (official)
**RELIGIONS** Buddhism 94%, Islam 4%, Christianity 1%
**CURRENCY** Baht = 100 statang

# TOGO

The Republic of Togo is a long, narrow country in West Africa. From north to south, it extends about 500 km [311 mls], but its coastline on the Gulf of Guinea is only 64 km [40 mls] long and it is only 145 km [90 mls] at its widest point. Crossing the country from south-west to north-east, the Togo-Atacora Mountains in southern Togo, which rise to 986 m [3,235 ft], overlook a plateau. The land descends to a densely populated coastal plain in the south. In the north lies another plateau, which descends northwards to the border with Burkina Faso.

The main wet season is from March to July, with a minor wet season in October and November, but temperatures are high throughout the year. The central mountains are cooler and rainier than the capital Lomé, on the coast, while the far north is hot with a single rainy season.

Behind the sandy coastal plain, with its many palm trees, are areas of grassland with clumps of hardwood trees. Some rainforest grows in central Togo, but the north is savanna country with many animal species, including antelopes, buffaloes, elephants, leopards and lions.

## ECONOMY AND RESOURCES

The major forests and cash crops are in the south-west. The railway inland from the coast stops at Blitta, in central Togo, and the road is the only means of keeping the poorer, drier northern parts of this awkwardly shaped country in touch with the more developed areas of the south, including the capital and main port of Lomé and the important phosphate mining area, with its port of Kpémé. Phosphates, coffee and cocoa are the important exports, but major food crops are cassava, yams, maize and sorghum-millets.

## HISTORY AND POLITICS

As Togoland, the country was colonized by Germany in 1884 and then occupied by

Franco-British troops during World War I. It was partitioned between the two powers under a League of Nations mandate in 1922, with British Togoland later becoming part of Ghana and the larger eastern French section gaining independence as Togo in 1960.

Local rivalries, especially between northerners and southerners, are important political factors and, in 1963, a group of army officers from the north assassinated the president, a southerner. In 1967, Gnassingbé Eyadéma, one of the officers responsible for the 1963 coup, took power and suspended the constitution, though constitutional government was restored in 1980. Following strikes and protests, the principle of multiparty elections was conceded in March 1991, but by the end of the year there were violent clashes between the army and the new civilian government, with old rivalries between Eyadéma's northern Kabre people and the dominant Ewe tribe re-emerging to block the path to stable democratization. Multiparty elections for parliament took place in 1994 and a coalition government was formed. [*Map page 32*] ■

> **AREA** 56,790 sq km [21,927 sq mls]
> **POPULATION** 4,010,000
> **CAPITAL (POPULATION)** Lomé (500,000)
> **GOVERNMENT** Multiparty republic
> **ETHNIC GROUPS** Ewe-Adja 43%, Tem 4%, Kabre 22%, Gurma 16%
> **LANGUAGES** French (official), Ewe, Kabre
> **RELIGIONS** Traditional beliefs 50%, Christianity 35%, Islam 15%
> **CURRENCY** CFA franc = 100 centimes

Nuku'alofa, site of the royal palace. Vava'u (15,000) in the north is the next most populous. Predominantly Christian, the people speak Tongan, though English is also official.

Most Tongans live off their own produce, including coconuts, yams, tapioca, groundnuts and fish. While the government owns all land, men are entitled to rent areas to grow food – a policy now under pressure with a burgeoning young population. The main exports are coconut oil products and bananas, with New Zealand the main trading partner. Tourism is becoming increasingly important, with 23,000 visitors to the islands in 1992.

Tonga is an absolute monarchy. Since 1965 the ruler has been Taufa'ahau Tupou IV, latest in a line going back a thousand years, who presided over the islands' transition from British protectorate to independent Commonwealth state in 1970. His brother is prime minister on a council that has hereditary chiefs as well as elected representatives; there are no parties. The country has remained peaceful, enhancing the name given by Captain James Cook in the 1770s – the Friendly Islands. [*Map page 2*] ■

> **AREA** 750 sq km [290 sq mls]
> **POPULATION** 98,000
> **CAPITAL (POPULATION)** Nuku'alofa (29,000)
> **GOVERNMENT** Constitutional monarchy
> **ETHNIC GROUPS** Polynesian
> **LANGUAGES** Tongan, English
> **RELIGIONS** Christianity
> **CURRENCY** Pa'anga = 100 seniti

# TONGA

# TRINIDAD & TOBAGO

The archipelago comprises over 170 islands, 36 of which are inhabited, covering 750 sq km [290 sq mls] in a mixture of low coralline and higher volcanic outcrops that fall into three distinct belts. Nearly two-thirds of the population live on the largest island of Tongatapu, 29,000 of them in the capital of

Furthest south of the West Indies, Trinidad is a rectangular island situated just 16 km [10 mls] off Venezuela's Orinoco delta. Tobago is a detached extension of its Northern Range of hills, lying 34 km [21 mls] to the north-east. Trinidad's highest point is Cerro Aripe (940 m [3,085 ft]) in the rugged, forested Northern Range; the capital, Port of

Spain (in the county of St George, one of the eight counties of Trindad), nestles behind the hills on the sheltered west coast.

## ECONOMY AND RESOURCES

Both islands are valued for their agricultural produce, including sugar, coffee, cocoa, rubber and citrus fruits, but the main source of income is oil. First exploited in 1867, it has been the lifeblood of the nation's economy, giving the island a relatively high standard of living, and (with petrochemicals) still accounts for over 70% of exports. Falling prices in the 1980s had a severe effect, only partly offset by the growth of tourism and continued revenues from asphalt, which occurs naturally, and gas.

## HISTORY AND POLITICS

'Discovered' by Columbus in 1498, Trinidad was later planted for sugar production by Spanish and French settlers before becoming British in 1797. Black slaves worked the plantations until emancipation in 1834, when Indian and Chinese indentured labourers were brought in. Tobago came under British control in 1814, joining Trinidad to form a single colony in 1899. Independence came in 1962 and a republic was established in 1976, though Tobago would like internal self-government.

A potentially volatile ethnic mix, often overcrowded, Trinidad experienced a sharp political change in 1986, when after 30 years the People's National Movement was voted out and the National Alliance for Reconstruction coalition took office. After five years of instability, the PNM was returned by a landslide in December 1991, but it faced mounting economic problems. [*Map page 30*] ■

AREA  5,130 sq km [1,981 sq mls]
POPULATION  1,292,000
CAPITAL (POPULATION)  Port of Spain (51,000)
GOVERNMENT  Republic
ETHNIC GROUPS  Black 43%, East Indian 40%, Mixed 16%, White 1%, Chinese 1%
LANGUAGES  English
RELIGIONS  Christianity 49%, Hinduism 24%, Islam 9%
CURRENCY  Trinidad and Tobago dollar = 100 cents

# TRISTAN DA CUNHA

Tristan da Cunha is the largest of four scattered islands towards the southern end of the Mid-Atlantic Ridge, a volcanic cone of 2,060 m [6,760 ft], ringed by a lava plain that drops steeply to the sea; a narrow strip of flat ground accommodates the only settlement of about 330 inhabitants. The climate is mild and damp with frequent storms. The island was evacuated 1961–3 following a volcanic eruption. The Nightingale and Inaccessible Islands are small, uninhabited islands nearby; Gough Island, 400 km [250 mls] to the southeast, is a steep, craggy, forest-covered island some 13 km [8 mls] long; its only settlement is a meteorological and radio station.

The islanders grow potatoes and rear sheep and cattle for their own use.

Like Ascension to the north, all the islands are administered as dependencies of St Helena. [*Map page 2*] ■

AREA  104 sq km [40 sq mls]
POPULATION  330
CAPITAL (POPULATION)  Edinburgh (330)
GOVERNMENT  Dependent territory of the UK
ETHNIC GROUPS  No native ones
LANGUAGES  English
RELIGIONS  Christianity
CURRENCY  English currency

# TUNISIA

Smallest of the three Maghreb countries that comprise north-west Africa, Tunisia consists of the eastern end of the Atlas Mountains together with the central steppelands to the south, which are separated from the country's Saharan sector by the vast low-lying saltpans of Chott Djerid. In the north the lower Medjerda Valley and the low-lying plains of Bizerte and Tunis were densely colonized.

Mountainous northern Tunisia has a Mediterranean climate, with dry, sunny summers, and mild wet winters. The average yearly rainfall decreases to the south; in the north rainfall can be in excess of 900 mm [36 in], whereas at Gafsa in south-central Tunisia, the average annual rainfall is only 150 mm [6 in].

## ECONOMY AND RESOURCES
Agriculture is important to the Tunisian economy, employing 40% of the population. Major irrigation schemes have been carried out in recent years and these lowlands, which produce cereals, vines, citrus fruits, olives and vegetables, represent the country's most important agricultural area. New industries, sometimes coupled with tourism, have transformed a number of coastal towns, including Sfax, Monastir and Sousse. By comparison, the interior has been neglected.

## HISTORY AND POLITICS
Tunisia has a long and rich history. It was the first part of the region to be conquered by the Phoenicians, Romans (Carthage is now a suburb of Tunis) and later the Arabs and Turks, and each successive civilization has left a marked impression on the country. Consequently, Tunisia has acquired a distinct national identity and culture, with a long tradition of urban life.

In 1881, France established a protectorate over Tunisia and ruled the country until 1956. The new parliament immediately abolished the monarchy and declared Tunisia to be a republic in 1957, with the nationalist leader, Habib Bourguiba, as president.

In 1975, Bourguiba was elected president for life. His government introduced many reforms, including votes for women. But problems arose, such as unemployment among educated groups and fears that Western influences, introduced by tourists, might damage traditional Muslim values. Finally, the prime minister, Zine el Abidine Ben Ali, removed Bourguiba from office in 1987 and succeeded him as president. He was elected in 1989 and 1994. His party dominated the Chamber of Deputies, though some seats were reserved for the opposition parties. [*Map page 16*] ■

**AREA** 163,610 sq km [63,170 sq mls]
**POPULATION** 8,733,000
**CAPITAL (POPULATION)** Tunis (1,395,000)
**GOVERNMENT** Multiparty republic
**ETHNIC GROUPS** Arab 98%, Berber 1%, French and others
**LANGUAGES** Arabic (official)
**RELIGIONS** Islam 99%
**CURRENCY** Tunisian dinar = 1,000 millimes

# TURKEY

L ying in two continents, Turkey comprise the broad peninsula of Asia Minor, together with its 'roots' around Lake Van, and in Europe that part of Thrace (Thraki) which lies to the east of the lower Maritsa River. The straits separating the European part (roughly 5% of the total area of the country) and the Asiatic part of Turkey have been of strategic importance for thousands of years. The Dardanelles, joining the Aegean Sea to the Sea of Marmara, are 1.6 km [1 ml] wide at their narrowest point; the Bosphorus, linking the Sea of Marmara to the Black Sea, measures just 640 m [2,100 ft] at one point and is spanned by two suspension bridges at Istanbul.

## ECONOMY AND RESOURCES
The heart of the country is the high karst plateau of Anatolia, semi-desert around the central salt lake, but mainly sheep country. The Taurus ranges afford summer grazing for the plateau flocks, and also timber. The northern Pontic ranges are better wooded, with fertile plains.

The valleys of the Gediz and Cürüksu, which open westwards from the plateau to the Aegean, export tobacco and figs, while the deltaic plain around Adana grows abundant cotton. The very high and thinly-peopled plateaux and ranges to the east of the Euphrates produce chrome (in 1993 Turkey was the world's fourth largest producer), copper and oil.

Istanbul, the former imperial capital of Byzantium and Constantinople, which controls the straits between the Black Sea and the Mediterranean, is the country's chief port and commercial city, but the function of capital has been transferred to the more centrally-placed town of Ankara. Turkey, with a rapidly growing population, now has one of the best railway networks in the Middle East, and though lacking in large resources of mineral oil has built up a thriving industrial economy based on imported oil, on coal (from Zonguldak), and above all on hydroelectric power. Though still important, agriculture has been overtaken by manufacturing, particularly textiles and clothing.

## HISTORY AND POLITICS

Constantinople's huge Ottoman empire had been in decline for centuries when alliance with Germany in World War I ended in the loss of all non-Turkish areas. Nationalists led by Mustafa Kemal – known later as Atatürk ('father of the Turks') – rejected peace proposals favouring Greece and after a civil war set up a republic. Turkey's present frontiers were established in 1923, when Atatürk became president, and until 1938 he ruled as a virtual dictator, secularizing and modernizing the traditional Islamic state.

Between 1960 and 1970 the government was overthrown three times by military coups; civilian rule returned in 1983 and since then democracy has been relatively stable, though the country's human rights record remained poor. In June 1993, Turkey's first woman prime minister, Tansu Çiller, was elected. Since 1984 Turkey has been fighting armed guerrillas of the Kurdish Workers Party in the south-east of the country where Kurds are the majority population.

The economic progress that partnered political stability in the mid-1980s – growth averaged more than 7% a year – encouraged Turkey to apply for EU membership in 1987, but the response from Brussels was unenthusiastic. Turkey's disputes with Greece – notably over Ankara's invasion of northern Cyprus in 1974, but also over claims to territory and mineral rights in the Aegean – plus the

country's poor human rights record and low standard of living were all factors. Although Turkey has been a NATO member since 1952, and is an associate member of the EU, this was likely to remain the EU's position for some time – while the emergence of Islamic fundamentalism raised new doubts about Turkey's 'European' identity and stance.

Situated at one of the world's great geo-political crossroads, the nation seemed destined to remain sandwiched between Europe and the Middle East. Turkey, nevertheless, has a two-way traffic in people with Western Europe: while tourism was a boom industry in the late 1980s (often at the expense of Greece), with 2.5 million visitors a year visiting the country, these were outnumbered by Turkish men working (or seeking work) in EU cities, the majority of them in Germany. [*Map page 22*] ■

**AREA** 779,450 sq km [300,946 sq mls]
**POPULATION** 60,771,000
**CAPITAL (POPULATION)** Ankara (3,022,000)
**GOVERNMENT** Multiparty republic
**ETHNIC GROUPS** Turkish 86%, Kurdish 11%, Arab 2%
**LANGUAGES** Turkish (official)
**RELIGIONS** Islam 99%
**CURRENCY** Turkish lira = 100 kurus

# TURKMENISTAN

The Republic of Turkmenistan is one of the five central Asian republics which once formed part of the former Soviet Union. Most of the land is low-lying, with mountains lying on the southern and south-western borders. In the west lies the salty Caspian Sea. A depression called the Kara Bogaz Gol Bay contains the country's lowest point, at 31 m [102 ft] below sea level. Most of Turkmenistan is arid and the Karakum, Asia's largest sand desert, covers about 80% of the country.

Turkmenistan has a continental climate.

The average annual rainfall varies from 80 mm [3 in] in the desert to 300 mm [12 in] in the southern mountains. The summers are hot, but in winter the temperatures sometimes drop well below freezing point.

The vegetation in Turkmenistan is sparse and practically non-existent in the sandy areas. But plants grow around desert oases and in the mountains, where trees such as almond, fig and walnut can be found.

## ECONOMY AND RESOURCES

As much Middle Eastern as Central Asian, the scant population of Turkmenistan is found mainly around irrigated oases and along the Kara-Kum canal, growing cereals, cotton and fruit, and rearing karakul lambs. Apart from astrakhan rugs and food processing, industry is largely confined to mining magnesium, sulphur and salt and the production of natural gas. The country is dependent on trade with other former Soviet republics for more than 75% of its GDP, much of which is subsidized.

## HISTORY AND POLITICS

Just over 1,000 years ago, Turkic people settled in the lands east of the Caspian Sea and the name 'Turkmen' comes from that time. Mongol armies conquered the region in the 13th century and Islam was introduced in the 14th century.

Russia took over the area in the 1870s and 1880s. After the Russian Revolution of 1917, came under Communist rule and, in 1924, the area became the Turkmen Soviet Socialist Republic. The Communists strictly controlled all aspects of life, discouraging religious worship in particular, though at the same time they improved such services as education, health, housing and transport.

In the 1980s, when the Soviet Union began to introduce reforms, the Turkmen began to demand more freedom, and in 1990 the Turkmen government stated that its laws over-ruled Soviet laws. In 1991, Turkmenistan became fully independent after the break-up of the Soviet Union and joined the UN. But the country kept ties with Russia through the Commonwealth of Independent States (CIS) which it joined in January 1994.

In 1992, Turkmenistan adopted a new constitution, allowing for the setting up of political parties, providing that they were not ethnic or religious in character. But, effectively, Turkmenistan remained a one-party state and in 1992, Saparmurad Niyazov, the former leader of the Communist Party (renamed the Democratic Party), was the only candidate. Faced with many economic problems, Turkmenistan began to look south rather than to the CIS for support. As part of this policy, it joined the Economic Co-operation Organization which had been set up in 1985 by Iran, Pakistan and Turkey. [*Map page 22*] ■

AREA  488,100 sq km [188,450 sq mls]
POPULATION  4,010,000
CAPITAL (POPULATION)  Ashgabat (or Ashkhabad, 407,000)
GOVERNMENT  Single-party republic
ETHNIC GROUPS  Turkmen 72%, Russian 10%, Uzbek 9%, Kazakh 3%, Tatar
LANGUAGES  Turkmen (official)
RELIGIONS  Islam
CURRENCY  Manat

# TURKS & CAICOS IS

A group of 30 islands (eight of them inhabited), lying at the eastern end of the Grand Bahama Bank, north of Haiti, the Turks and Caicos are composed of low, flat limestone terrain with scrub, marsh and swamp providing little agriculture.

Tourism has recently overtaken fishing (chiefly lobsters) as the main industry, with direct flights from Miami feeding the new airport on the main tourist island of Providenciales. Offshore banking facilities are also expanding, though harmed in the mid-1980s by allegations of ministerial drug-trafficking and organized crime.

Previously claimed by France and Spain, they have been British since 1766, administered with Jamaica from 1873 to 1959 and a separate Crown Colony since 1973. Around a third of the 14,000 population, mainly of mixed Afro-European descent, lives in the capital of Cockburn Town on the island of Grand Turk. [*Map page 30*] ■

**AREA** 430 sq km [166 sq mls]
**POPULATION** 14,000
**CAPITAL (POPULATION)** Cockburn Town (4,000)
**GOVERNMENT** Dependent territory of the UK
**ETHNIC GROUPS** Of African descent
**LANGUAGES** English
**RELIGIONS** Christianity
**CURRENCY** US currency

1978, three years after separation from the Gilbert Islands – a decision supported by a large majority in a referendum held in 1974. [*Map page 3*] ■

**AREA** 24 sq km [9 sq mls]
**POPULATION** 9,000
**CAPITAL (POPULATION)** Fongafale (2,810)
**GOVERNMENT** Constitutional monarchy
**ETHNIC GROUPS** Polynesian
**LANGUAGES** Tuvaluan, English
**RELIGIONS** Christianity
**CURRENCY** Australian currency

# TUVALU

# UGANDA

None of Tuvalu's nine coral atolls – total area 24 sq km [9 sq mls] – rises more than 4.6 m [15 ft] out of the Pacific, and though the climate is uniformly pleasant, poor soils restrict vegetation to coconut palms, breadfruit trees and bush. The government has tried to publicize the country's vulnerability to the possible effects of global warming, namely sea-level rise, which would have a detrimental affect on many Pacific island communities.

The population of 9,000 (a third of whom live on the main island of Funafuti, where the capital Fongafale is situated) survive by subsistence farming, raising pigs and poultry, and by fishing. Copra is the only significant export crop, but most foreign exchange comes from the sale of elaborate postage stamps to the world's philatelists. Tuvalu however, remains largely dependent on foreign aid.

The population, once far higher, was reduced from about 20,000 to just 3,000 in the three decades after 1850, by Europeans abducting the inhabitants to work in the plantations of other Pacific island territories. An estimated 1,500 Tuvaluans still work overseas, mainly in Nauru.

Tuvalu became an independent constitutional monarchy within the Commonwealth in

Extending from Lake Victoria to the western arm of the Great African Rift Valley and beyond, the Republic of Uganda is a land of lakes (sources of the White Nile) originating from the tilting and faulting associated with the rift valley system. On the western side of the country, the Ruwenzori block has been uplifted to 5,109 m [16,762 ft], while the eastern frontier bisects the large extinct volcano of Mt Elgon (4,321 m [14,176 ft]).

In the south rainfall is abundant in two seasons, and patches of the original rainforest (covering 25% of land area) remain. To the north, one rainy season each year supports a savanna of trees and grassland.

**ECONOMY AND RESOURCES**
In the south, most of the forest has been cleared from the densely settled areas, notably in the historic kingdoms of Buganda and Busoga. Here the banana is a staple of diet, and coffee, tea and sugar are cash crops; Uganda is the world's eighth largest coffee producer. Here, too, are the capital Kampala, and the industrial centre of Jinja, adjacent to the huge Owen Falls hydroelectric plant. The western areas, the former kingdoms of Bunyoro, Toro and Ankole, depend more on cattle rearing.

In the north, population is generally less

dense, and farmers grow finger-millet and sorghum, with cotton and tobacco as cash crops. Tsetse fly inhibits cattle-keeping in some areas, which have become game parks, but the dry north-east (Karamoja) supports nomadic pastoralists. Blessed with an equable climate, fertile soils and varied resources, from freshwater fish to copper, Uganda could have lived up to Churchill's colonial description as 'the pearl of Africa'. Instead, independence soon brought two decades of disaster with almost ceaseless internal conflict and a shattered economy.

## HISTORY AND POLITICS

Little is known of the early history of Uganda. When Europeans first reached the area in the 19th century, many of the people were organized in kingdoms, the most powerful of which was Buganda, the home of the Baganda people. Britain took over the country between 1894 and 1914 and ruled it until independence in 1962. In 1967, Uganda became a republic and Buganda's Kabaka (king), Sir Edward Mutesa II, was made president. But tensions between the Kabaka and the prime minister, Apollo Milton Obote, led to the dismissal of the Kabaka in 1966.

Between the break from Britain in 1962 and the takeover by Yoweri Museveni in 1986, the country suffered a succession of linked civil wars, violent coups, armed invasions and tribal massacres. The worst of several bad periods was the sordid regime of Idi Amin, who in 1971 ousted Obote – then president of a one-party state – and in an eight-year reign of terror killed up to 300,000 people as all political and human rights were suspended. Amin was finally removed when he tried to annex part of Tanzania and President Nyerere ordered his troops to carry on into Uganda after they had repelled the invaders.

Obote returned to power, but the bloodshed continued and he was ousted again in 1985. The following year, 1986, brought in Yoweri Museveni, who achieved some success in stabilizing the situation as a prelude to a return to democracy. But he faced a problem not known to his predecessors: Uganda's AIDS explosion. Some estimates suggest that by the end of 1991 more than a quarter of the children under five were infected with the HIV virus.

In 1993, Museveni restored the traditional kingdoms, including Buganda where a new Kabaka was crowned. Museveni also held national elections in 1994, though political parties were not permitted. Museveni's supporters won a majority. [*Map page 33*] ■

**AREA** 235,880 sq km [91,073 sq mls]
**POPULATION** 20,621,000
**CAPITAL (POPULATION)** Kampala (773,000)
**GOVERNMENT** Republic in transition
**ETHNIC GROUPS** Baganda 18%, Banyoro 14%, Teso 9%, Banyan 8%, Basoga 8%, Bagisu 7%, Bachiga 7%, Lango 6%, Acholi 5%
**LANGUAGES** English and Swahili (both official)
**RELIGIONS** Christianity (Roman Catholic 40%, Protestant 29%), traditional beliefs 18%, Islam 7%
**CURRENCY** Uganda shilling = 100 cents

# UKRAINE

Ukraine is the second largest country in Europe after Russia. It formed most of the south-western part of the former USSR which broke up in 1991. The country is mostly flat, with higher land in the west, south and south-east. The southern border is formed by the Black Sea.

The western Ukraine comprises the fertile uplands of Volhynia, with the Carpathians cutting across the far western corner of the country. The north is mostly lowlands, with the Dnepr River (Dnieper or Dnipro) at its heart, which include marshes and the state capital of Kiev (Kiyev or Kyyiv) in addition to arable land. This area, however, suffered most from the Chernobyl nuclear disaster of 1986, with huge tracts of land contaminated by radioactivity.

In the centre of the republic, south of Kiev and west of Kirovograd (Kirovohrad), are the rich lands with fertile chernozem soils. In the south are dry lowlands bordering the Black Sea and the Sea of Azov, with Odessa (Odesa) the main port. Still further south is the

Crimean peninsula, a favourite tourist area for Russians as well as Ukrainians.

Woodland with such trees as ash, oak and pine grows in the north, while pine forests swathe the slopes of the Carpathians and Crimean mountains. Grassy steppe once covered central Ukraine, but much of it has now been ploughed up for farmland.

## ECONOMY AND RESOURCES

The main industrial cities are in the east, clustered round the coalfields and iron-ore mines of the vital Donets Basin. Ukraine's main industries are coal mining, iron and steel, agricultural machinery, petrochemicals and plastics, but there are also numerous food-processing plants based on agricultural output that includes wheat, rye, oats, maize, barley, flax, sugar beet, hops, soya, sunflower seeds, potatoes and other vegetables, meat, dairy produce and cotton. In 1993 Ukraine was the world's leading producer of sugar beet (12% of the world total) and second largest producer of barley (8%), behind Russia. Though traditionally 'the granary of the Soviet Union', Ukraine is neither the largest nor the most efficient overall producer of grain; Russia producers twice as much, and the agricultural output per capita of Belarus is some 65% higher than that of its southern neighbour.

Minerals are important to the economy; Ukraine dominated world manganese production in 1993 (with 32% of the total) and was in the top ten for iron, iron-ore and steel. In 1991 it produced nearly a quarter of the total USSR coal output. Not blessed with huge reserves of oil, the Kiev government signed an agreement in February 1992 to secure future supplies from Iran.

## HISTORY AND POLITICS

In the 9th century AD, the East Slavs founded a civilization called Kievan Rus, with its capital at Kiev. Russians took over the area in 980 and the region became prosperous, but in the 13th century, Mongol armies ravaged the area. Later, the region was split into small kingdoms and large areas fell under foreign rule. In the 17th and 18th centuries, parts of Ukraine came under Polish and Russian rule, but Russia gained most of Ukraine in the late 18th century. In 1918, Ukraine gained its independence, but in 1922 it was incorporated into the Soviet Union.

Millions of people died in the 1930s as the result of Soviet policies. Millions more died during the Nazi occupation between 1941 and 1944. In 1945, the Soviet Union took control of parts of Ukraine that had been in Czechoslovakia, Poland and Romania. In the 1980s, however, Ukrainian people demanded more say over their affairs.

Following the break-up of the Soviet Union in 1991, Ukraine's declaration of independence from Moscow was ratified by referendum on 1 December 1991, when Leonid Kravchuk, the former Communist Party ideological secretary, was voted president by direct poll over five rivals. A week later, in Minsk, Kravchuk helped Boris Yeltsin create the basis for the Commonwealth of Independent States, and in the early months of 1992 Ukraine and Russia reached agreement on a number of potentially explosive issues, not least in the military field, with resolutions on nuclear weapons, the Red Army and the distribution of the Black Sea fleet.

The country, however, will not be seen as Russia's sidekick. While it suffered many of the economic agonies endured by its massive neighbour – notably chronic food shortages and the hyperinflation that followed the abolition of price controls – Ukraine set out from the beginning to be a fully-fledged and large independent nation. While Russia assumed the diplomatic powers of the Soviet Union, Ukraine already had a seat at the UN – a reward granted in 1945 for the appalling devastation caused by the German invasion in 1941 and its aftermath – and would seek separate representation on bodies such as the CSCE and OECD. [*Map page 5*] ■

**AREA** 603,700 sq km [233,100 sq mls]
**POPULATION** 51,465,000
**CAPITAL (POPULATION)** Kiev (2,643,000)
**GOVERNMENT** Multiparty republic
**ETHNIC GROUPS** Ukrainian 73%, Russian 22%, Jewish 1%, Belarussian 1%, Moldovan
**LANGUAGES** Ukrainian 73% (official), Russian
**RELIGIONS** Christianity (mostly Ukrainian Orthodox)
**CURRENCY** Karbovanet

# UNITED ARAB EMIRATES

# UNITED KINGDOM

The Emirates are bounded in the north by the Persian Gulf and cover 83,600 sq km [32,278 sq mls] exluding over 100 offshore islands. Though mainly low-lying desert and salt marshes, there is a range of sandy hills (the Hajar Mountains) in the east of the country.

When British forces withdrew from the Persian Gulf in 1971, six of the seven British-run Trucial States – Abu Dhabi, Ajman, Dubai, Fujairah, Sharjah and Umm al-Qaiwain – opted to form the United Arab Emirates (UAE), with Ras al-Khaimah joining in 1972. It could have been a federation of nine, but Bahrain and Qatar chose independence. Traditional values, sustained by the control of the emirs, remain strong in the UAE, inspite of a large expatriate workforce.

The UAE is the Gulf's third largest oil producer after Saudi Arabia and Iran, producing an average of 3 million barrels per day in 1993. The revenue from its oil and gas (50% of GDP) has enabled the government to invest in health, education and social services: the UAE has the highest GNP per capita figure in Asia, after Japan. Abu Dhabi has by far the largest population of the Emirates and is easily the biggest oil producer.

As well as oil and gas, manufacturing and finance play an important part in the economy. In addition, the UAE is becoming a more attractive place for tourists – in 1991 there were 189 hotels and 348,000 visitors. [*Map page 22*] ■

**AREA** 83,600 sq km [32,278 sq mls]
**POPULATION** 1,861,000
**CAPITAL (POPULATION)** Abu Dhabi (or Abu Zaby, 243,000)
**GOVERNMENT** Federation
**ETHNIC GROUPS** Arab 87%, Indo-Pakistani 9%, Iranian 2%
**LANGUAGES** Arabic, English
**RELIGIONS** Islam
**CURRENCY** UAE dirham = 100 fils

The British Isles stand on the westernmost edge of the continental shelf – two large and several hundred small islands for the most part cool, rainy and windswept. Despite physical closeness to the rest of Europe (32 km [20 mls] at the nearest point – little more than the distance across London), Britain is curiously isolated, with a long history of political independence and social separation from its neighbours. In the past the narrow seas served the islanders well, protecting them against casual invasion, while Britons in turn sailed to explore and exploit the rest of the world. Now with increasing co-operation within the EU, this insularity is rapidly breaking down.

The islands are confusingly named. 'Great Britain', the largest in Europe and eighth largest in the world – so named to distinguish it from 'Little Britain' (Brittany, in France) – includes the kingdoms of England and Scotland and the principality of Wales; Ireland was once a kingdom, but is currently divided into the Province of Northern Ireland, under the British Crown, and the politically separate Republic of Ireland. Great Britain, Northern Ireland, and many off-lying island groups from the Scillies to the Shetlands, together make up the United Kingdom of Great Britain and Northern Ireland, commonly known as the UK. Even isolated Rockall, far out in the Atlantic Ocean, is part of the UK, but the Isle of Man and the Channel Islands are separate but direct dependencies of the Crown, with a degree of political autonomy and their own taxation systems.

## Climate

Despite a subarctic position Britain is favoured climatically. Most other maritime lands between 50°N and 60°N – eastern Siberia, Kamchatka, the Aleutian Islands, southern Alaska, Hudson Bay and Labrador – are cold throughout the year, with long winters, ice-bound coasts and a short growing season. Britain's salvation is the North Atlantic Drift or Gulf Stream, a current of surface water that brings subtropical warmth from the southern Atlantic Ocean, spreading it across the continental shelf of Western Europe and warming the prevailing westerly winds.

The growing season, indicated roughly by the number of months in which mean air temperature exceeds 6°C [42°F], ranges from less than four months in the Scottish Highlands to nine months or more on the south-west coast. Most of lowland Britain has a growing season of seven to eight months, enough to ensure the prosperity of arable farmers in most years.

Britain's reputation for cloudiness is well merited. Mean duration of sunshine throughout the year is about 5 hours daily in the south, and only 3.5 hours daily in Scotland. At the height of summer only the south-west receives more than 7.5 hours of sunshine per day. In winter only the south coast, the Severn Estuary, Oxfordshire and a sliver of south-eastern Essex receive more than 1.5 hours per day, while many northern areas receive less than half an hour daily.

Despite a reputation for rain Britain is fairly dry. More than half of the country receives less than 750 mm [30 in] annually, and parts of Essex have less than 500 mm [20 in] per year. The wettest areas are Snowdonia with about 5,000 mm [200 in], Ben Nevis and the north-western highlands with 4,300 mm [172 in], and the Lake District with 3,300 mm [132 in].

The British climate is far from static. It was warmer at the time of the Domesday Survey (1086) when vineyards flourished as far north as York, and it cooled throughout the Middle Ages, when Arctic pack-ice was reported off Shetland and Eskimos are said to have visited northern Scotland in their kayaks. Cooling continued into the mid-19th century, followed by a long period of warming up to World War II and a succession of warm summers in the 1980s and 1990s.

### Population and immigration

Despite insularity the British people are of mixed stock. The earliest immigrants – land-hungry farmers from the Continent – were often refugees from tribal warfare and unrest. The Belgic tribesmen escaping from Imperial Rome, the Romans themselves (whose troops included Spanish, Macedonian and probably

## THE CHANNEL ISLANDS

Lying 16 km to 48 km [10 mls to 30 mls] from the French coast, the Channel Islands are a British dependency covering an area of only 200 sq km [78 sq mls]. The largest are Jersey with 115 sq km [45 sq mls] and 84,000 inhabitants, and Guernsey, with 78 sq km [30 sq mls] and 59,000 people. The other islands – Alderney, Sark and others – are small, with fewer than 3,000 residents.

The only part of the Duchy of Normandy retained by the English Crown after 1204, and the only part of Britain occupied by the Germans in World War II, the islands have their own legal system and government, with lower taxation than that of Britain. This, combined with a favourable climate and fine coastal scenery, has attracted a considerable number of wealthy residents, notably retired people, and established Jersey and Guernsey as offshore financial centres.

The main produce is agricultural, especially early potatoes, tomatoes and flowers for Britain, and the countryside has a vast number of glasshouses. The soil is now fertile, having been made so by the farmers' skilful use of seaweed and other fertilizers. Jersey and Guernsey cattle are famous breeds, introduced to many countries. Holiday-makers visit the islands in large numbers during the summer months, travelling by air or by the various passenger boats, especially from Weymouth. English is the official language but French is widely spoken.

North African mercenaries), the Angles, Saxons, Jutes, Danes and Normans, all in turn brought genetic variety; so too did the Huguenots, Sephardic and Ashkenazim Jews, and Dutch, French and German businessmen who followed them. Latterly the waves of immigrants have included Belarussians, Poles, Italians, Ukrainians and Czechs – most, like their predecessors, fugitives from European wars, overcrowding, intolerance and unrest.

During the 19th century Britain often took in skilled European immigrants through the front door while steadily losing her own sons and daughters – Scots and Irish peasants in

## THE ISLE OF MAN

Covering 590 sq km [227 sq mls], the Isle of Man sits in the Irish Sea almost equidistant from County Down and Cumbria, but actually nearer Galloway in Scotland. The uplands, pierced by the corridor valley from Douglas to Peel, extend from Ramsey to Port Erin. Mainly agricultural, with some fishing and a few light industries, the island is now largely dependent on tourism, with the annual Tourist Trophy (motorcycle) races attracting many visitors. Douglas, the capital, has over a third of the island's total population of 70,000. Like the Channel Islands, the Isle of Man is a dependency of the British Crown with its own legislative assembly, legal system and tax controls – leading to a position as a financial centre and tax shelter.

particular – through the back. Most recent arrivals in Britain are immigrants from crowded and impoverished lands once part of the British Empire, notably the West Indies, West Africa, India and Pakistan. These and their descendants now make up about 4% of the population of Britain.

Under Roman rule the population of the British island numbered half to three-quarters of a million. By the time of the Domesday Survey it had doubled, and it doubled again by the end of the 14th century. The Black Death of the late 15th century killed one in every three or four, but numbers climbed slowly; at the Union of 1707 some 6 million English and Welsh joined about 1 million Scots under a single parliament. By 1801 the first national census revealed 8.9 million in England and Wales, 1.6 million in Scotland; Ireland missed the first two ten-year counts, but probably numbered about 5 million. In 1821 the total British population was 21 million, in 1851 31 million, and in 1921 47 million. Fortunately the rate of increase has now declined, but some parts of Britain, notably the south-east and the conurbations, are among the most heavily populated areas of the world.

### ENGLAND
Visitors to England are often amazed at the

variety of the landscape. Complex folding, volcanic activity, glaciation and changes in sea level have all left their mark. From Northumberland to the Trent, the Pennines extend southwards as an upland with rolling hills, plateaux and fine valleys, many known as 'dales'. The range includes two western outliers – the Forest of Rossendale north of Manchester, and the Forest of Bowland in north Lancashire. To either side lie the lowlands of Lancashire and Yorkshire.

The Eden Valley separates the northern Pennines from Cumbria, which includes the Lake District. This is England's most striking mountain mass, a circular area of peaks, deep valleys, splendid lakes and crags. The loftiest peak is Scafell, 978 m [3,210 ft]. In the southwest Exmoor is a fine sandstone upland, and Dartmoor a predominantly granite area with many prominent tors. Elsewhere are isolated hills, small by world standards but dramatic against the small-scale background of Britain.

Much of the English lowland consists of chalk downlands, familiar to continental visitors who enter England through Folkestone or Dover as the famous chalk cliffs. These are the exposed coastal edge of the North Downs, whose scarped northern slope forms a striking feature in the Croydon area of Greater London. The North Downs continue westwards through Surrey to the Hampshire Downs, then south and east as the South Downs, emerging at another coastal landmark – Beachy Head.

There is a northwards extension of downland through the Berkshire and Marlborough Downs to the Chilterns then north again into East Anglia to disappear under the edge of the fens near Cambridge. Formerly forested, the downlands were cleared early for pasture and agriculture, and now provide a rich and varied mixture of woodlands, parklands, fields and mostly small settlements.

Older rocks, predominantly limestones, form the ridge of the Cotswold Hills, and the rolling, hilly farmlands of Leicestershire, the Lincoln Edge (cut by the River Witham at Lincoln), and finally the North York Moors. In these older rocks are rich iron deposits, mined in Cleveland to supply ores for the steel towns of the Tees Estuary until 1964, and still mined in the Midlands.

England is drained by many fine rivers, of which the greatest are the Thames, the Severn, the fenland Ouse, the Trent, and the great Yorkshire Ouse that receives its tributaries from the many picturesque valleys – the Dales – of the Pennine flank. There are many smaller rivers, and a large number of the old towns that dot England were built at their crossing points – generally where dry ground existed above marshes and gave firm sites for building. Chester, for example, was founded on a patch of sandstone beside the Dee; one of the four gates of the Roman town is still called the Watergate. York, too, was built on firm ground by a river crossing, as was Manchester. London arose on the site chosen by the Romans for the first convenient crossing place of the Thames, formerly a much broader and shallower river.

## WALES

United with England in 1535, Wales still preserves a sense of individuality – a separateness resting on history and sentiment rather than any clear boundary in the countryside. Although only 20% of the population speak Welsh, 75% of the inhabitants do so in the western counties of Gwynedd and Dyfed. The national sentiment is not only expressed through language, but also through literature, the arts (especially music), sport and political life. Cardiff, the capital, grew rapidly during the 19th century with the iron and steel industry and coal mining, but no Welsh town is centrally placed for the whole country; meetings of the boards representing the colleges of the University of Wales – Cardiff, Swansea, Lampeter, Aberystwyth and Bangor – take place at Shrewsbury, an English border town.

Wales is predominantly hilly and mountainous, although two-thirds of the rural area is farmland and one-third moorland. The most famous of the highland areas is Snowdonia, now a National Park covering 2,138 sq km [825 sq mls] from Snowdon to Cader Idris. But there are fine upland areas in central Wales, on both sides of the upper Severn Valley which cuts through them to the Dovey Valley and the coastal lowlands facing Cardigan Bay. South of the Severn, in the counties of Powys and Dyfed, the uplands dominate the landscape, and in the Brecon Beacons, south of the Usk Valley on which the old town of Brecon is situated, they provide another National Park, of 1,303 sq km [500 sq mls]. Many of the uplands and high lakes are sources of water for English towns, including Liverpool and Birmingham.

## SCOTLAND

Scotland is a generally cool, hilly and, in the west, wet country occupying about a third of Great Britain. Physically, it can be divided into three parts: the Highlands and Islands, bounded by the edge of the mountains from Stonehaven to the mouth of the Clyde; Central Scotland – sometimes called the Central Lowlands, though it is interspersed by a number of hill ranges; and the Southern Uplands, defined in the north by a geological fault extending from Dunbar to Girvan, and in the south by the border with England.

**The Highlands and Islands:** More than half of Scotland's area is in the Highlands and Islands. These are divided by the Great Glen, from Fort William to Inverness, with its three lochs – Lochy, Oich and Ness (where the monster is prone to appear in the tourist season) – linked by the Caledonian Canal. Much of the whisky for which Scotland is famous is produced in the Highlands, notably near the River Spey. The north-western part of the Highlands has splendid scenery – deep, glaciated valleys dominated by mountains, and only limited areas of farmland, much of it now abandoned.

Ben Nevis, at 1,343 m [4,406 ft] dominating the town of Fort William, is the highest summit in the British Isles, and a number of peaks in the Cairngorms, including Ben Macdhui (1,311 m [4,300 ft]), are of almost equal height.

**The Central Lowlands:** This area includes several ranges of rolling uplands – the Sidlaw Hills north of Dundee, the Ochils south of Perth, and the Pentlands extending in a south-westerly direction from the suburbs of Edinburgh.

**The Southern Uplands:** Though less spectacular than the Highlands, these include many fine hills, rolling moorlands and rich valleys. From the summit of Merrick (843 m [2,764 ft]) in Galloway the Highlands can be seen to the north, the plateau of Northern

Ireland to the west, and the Lake District, the Pennines and the Isle of Man to the south.

## ECONOMY AND RESOURCES

### ENGLAND

**Agriculture:** England has a rich variety of soils, derived both locally from parent rocks and also from glacial debris or 'drift'. During the 12,000 and more years since the ice retreated, soils have been enriched, firstly by such natural processes such as flooding and the growth of forests, latterly by the good husbandry of many generations of farmers. Husbandry improved particularly from the 18th century onwards; the Industrial Revolution was accompanied by an agricultural revolution that resulted in massive increases in crop yields and in the quality of livestock.

Through the 18th and 19th centuries farming became more scientific and more specialized; as the demands from the towns grew, so did the ability of English farmers to meet increasing markets for food. The eastern counties, particularly East Anglia and Holderness (now part of Humberside), became the granaries of England, while the rich, wet grasslands of the west and the Midlands turned pastoral – Cheshire cheese is a famous product of this specialization. There were other local products – the hops of Kent and Hereford, the apples of Worcester, and the fine wools that continued to be the main product of the chalk downlands. In south Lancashire potatoes and vegetables became major crops for sale in the markets of the growing northern industrial towns; market gardening and dairying on a small scale developed near every major settlement, taking advantage of the ready market close at hand.

Scenically, England still gives the impression of being an agricultural country. Less than 10% of the area is rough moorland, about 5% is forest, and about another 10% is urban or suburban, leaving roughly three-quarters under cultivation of one kind or another. Yet only 3% of the working population is currently employed in agriculture, a figure that has declined drastically in recent years. Loss of rural populations has been an inevitable result of agricultural rationalization and improvements in farming methods, although many of

## NORTH SEA OIL

The discovery of gas and oil in the North Sea in the 1960s – exploitation began a few years later – transformed Britain from an oil importer into the world's fifth largest exporter within a decade. Natural gas from the new fields rapidly replaced coal gas in the British energy system, and by 1981 the country was self-sufficient in oil. In the peak production year of 1986, the British sector of the North Sea produced 128.6 million tonnes of crude oil, accounting for over 20% of UK export earnings; in 1989, North Sea output amounted to 3% of total world production. In 1991, remaining reserves were estimated at 4 billion barrels – little more than four years' production at 1986 levels.

In taxes and royalties, North Sea oil gave an immense fillip to British government revenue, contributing more than £76 billion since 1979, and protecting the balance of payments despite severe industrial decline. There was much discussion as to the best use for this windfall money, which would taper away during the 1990s and vanish altogether in the next century; but it certainly helped finance substantial tax cuts during the controversial years of Mrs Thatcher's government. The sight of North Sea oil wealth flowing south to the Westminster treasury also provoked nationalist resentment in Scotland, off whose coast most of the oil rigs (and much of the gas) are located.

those who lost their jobs were being supported at little more than subsistence level.

**Industry and urbanization:** England had important reserves of coal, the major fields being on either side of the Pennines (Yorkshire, Lancashire, Northumberland and Durham), and in the Midlands (Derbyshire and Nottinghamshire). These coalfields and extensive reserves of iron ore – now largely defunct – were the basis of the Industrial Revolution of the 18th century, and the associated industrial growth of the 19th century, which together resulted in major changes in the English landscape.

Areas which previously had only small populations rose to industrial greatness. Perhaps the most striking example was Teesside where, following the exploitation of the Cleveland iron ores, the town of Middlesbrough grew from a small port (7,000 population in 1851) to a large manufacturing centre. Today Middlesbrough and its neighbouring settlements have almost 400,000 inhabitants. Similarly, small mill villages in Lancashire and Yorkshire grew into large towns while the West Midlands pottery towns and villages coalesced into the urban areas of Stoke-on-Trent.

Although the coalfields of the north saw the greatest local expansion of population, London and England's other major ports, such as Liverpool and Bristol, also developed as export markets flourished. These developments were accompanied by significant improvements in communications. From the 1840s town growth was rapid, and by the end of the 19th century 80% of the population was urban. While the working-class population was mainly housed in slums, the prosperity of the commercial and professional classes was reflected in the Victorian 'villas' that, in varying degrees of splendour, appeared in select areas of the towns.

This phase of expansion continued until World War I. By the 1930s, however, there were signs that the prosperity of many older and industrial mining areas was threatened and efforts were made to bring new industries to areas of particularly high unemployment, such as the Northumberland and Durham coalfield, West Cumberland, and the South Wales coalfield. In all of these, whole areas had become virtually derelict because their coal was exhausted, or no longer in demand.

The main areas of industrial growth since World War I have been around London and also in the West Midlands. A number of towns, for example Coventry, experienced extremely rapid growth. The introduction of conscious planning had the aim of controlling industrial expansion and preventing the indiscriminate growth of some towns, for example Oxford and Cambridge.

Today, England is a significant steel producer and most of the steel produced is used in other British industries such as shipbuilding and vehicle manufacture – although, as elsewhere in Western Europe, all three industries are currently facing considerable difficulties. Highly-skilled engineering industries are also important and centres include Birmingham, Wolverhampton and Manchester. Textiles are still a major industry, with cotton goods being produced mainly in Lancashire and woollens and worsteds in Yorkshire. Similarly, pottery is still important in the Midlands – though, like most manufacturing in Britain, it is losing out to service industries.

**Planning:** After World War II the need for replanning England to take account of the industrial areas was generally accepted. The existence of conurbations where towns had grown into one another was recognized by their listing in the 1951 census, which included Greater London, the West Midlands (Birmingham and the Black Country), South-east Lancashire with North-east Cheshire (Greater Manchester), Merseyside and Tyneside. Prolonged discussion followed on the best form of new administrative structure needed in England, and ultimately, in 1974, the new scheme of local government emerged. Many county boundaries were changed but one alteration of particular significance was the definition of some new counties based on the major industrial areas.

In creating the new administrative units of Tyne and Wear, Cleveland, West Yorkshire, South Yorkshire, Greater Manchester and West Midlands, and in redefining Greater London on more generous lines, the planners at last recognized the realities of population distribution in England. Many towns are developing new industrial areas – the 'industrial estates', housing light industries on their outskirts – and since 1945 government-sponsored 'new towns' have arisen in many parts of the country, in an attempt to stem the further growth of London and existing conurbations.

London has several satellite new towns – Basildon, Harlow, Stevenage and Milton Keynes, for example, most of them founded on small existing settlements. In the north are Washington, Peterlee and Aycliffe, built around old mining villages, with new industries invited in on favourable terms. Powers to develop new towns fortunately go hand-in-hand with powers to protect the remaining countryside against casual despoilment. Agricultural land, particularly at hazard, may be protected by local planning authorities, and new building kept within bounds.

**Conservation:** In an age when increased prosperity has spread leisure and the means of travel to millions of people, new emphasis has been placed on recreation. One result is the National Parks, another the many scenic areas under the control of the Countryside Commission and other national bodies. In these areas there are special provisions for conserving the beauty of the English countryside, and creating amenities that help people enjoy them. Though it is never the intention that National Parks be kept as rural museums, with all development stifled, the siting of new buildings, roads and electricity cables is carefully controlled, and national need must be shown before mining and other disruptive activities can be justified.

The Forestry Commission, too, has a mandate to provide amenity sites in its forests, and to landscape new plantings in ways that provide timber, but also maintain the natural beauty of the area concerned.

## WALES

**Mining and industry:** Some writers on Wales regard the uplands as the country's real heartland, with their sheep pastures and forested valleys, interspersed by farming villages and small towns. But over half the population live in the industrialized area of South Wales, which includes the mining valleys of Gwent, Mid Glamorgan and West Glamorgan – all of which ceased to extract coal by the 1990s – and the towns of Newport, Cardiff and Swansea with their traditional heavy-metal industries and newer factories for light industry. All are ports, and Cardiff now has many central buildings for the whole of Wales, including the National Museum and the Welsh Office.

No other area of Wales is so heavily dominated by mining and industry as Deeside. Flint and the Wrexham areas are also industrialized, with coalfields now in decline and modern light industries taking their place.
**Tourism:** Just as the railways stimulated economic growth in South Wales from the 1840s, so on the North Wales coast they stimulated the growth of holiday and residential towns, notably Rhyl, Colwyn Bay and Llandudno.

These attracted English residents, many of them retired people from Lancashire, and the holiday industry boomed. In the motoring age it developed further, so that almost every beach and coastal village had its guest houses, holiday cottages, caravan parks and camping sites. Now tourism has spread to virtually the whole of Wales. In Anglesey, many small places have devoted visitors who favour sailing as well as walking and sea bathing, while this is true also of many ports of the Welsh mainland coast. The south-west, formerly Pembrokeshire but now part of Dyfed, has fine scenery, forming the Pembrokeshire National Park with a coast path 268 km [167 mls] long.

Wales is rich in scenic attractions. The landscape is dominantly agricultural, with mixed farming, notably for dairying, cattle and sheep. Many upland farmers combine agriculture with the tourist trade, providing guest houses or camping centres. Forestry plantations exist in many upland valleys but the main characteristic of the countryside is farmland.

## SCOTLAND

**The Highlands and Islands:** The financial returns from crofting (small-scale tenant farming) were meagre, and many old croft cottages have become holiday homes. Forests now cover many of the valleys; some of the mountains are deer parks, owned by landlords and let to visitors for seasonal shooting. Railways reach the western coast at Mallaig and Kyle of Lochalsh, from which there are boat services to Skye – to be augmented by a controversial bridge – and the Outer Hebrides. Roads are in part single track with passing places, although they are gradually being improved. At the various villages there are hotels, guest houses and other accommodation for visitors, and the main commercial occupations are fishing and home weaving. The traditional weaving of Harris tweeds in the Hebrides is now industrially organized, with much of the work done in workshops. Skye has splendid climbing in the Cuillin Hills, and the numerous rivers and lakes are favoured by fishermen. Here, as in the rest of the Highlands, efforts to improve local industries have had some success.

The highland area east of the Great Glen is a richer country, flanked on the east by the lowlands around Aberdeen, which extend into

Buchan and then westwards to Moray Firth around Inverness. This is sound farming country, famous for pedigree cattle, and from these lowlands tongues of farmland extend into the valleys of the Dee, Don, Spey and others. Aberdeen and Fraserburgh are major fishing centres. Aberdeen has become increasingly prosperous with the oil extraction from the North Sea.

Little known in the past, the Cairngorms have now been developed for winter skiing and summer climbing and fishing. There are still deer forests in the uplands but much of the country is used for sheep farming and tourism. Fort William and a few other centres have industry based on local hydroelectricity – aluminium smelting, for example – but Oban is the main holiday centre on the west coast.

In the north, the Orkney Islands are connected to Thurso (Scrabster) by boat and also to Aberdeen. Fishing and farming are the mainstays of the economy, with a successful specialization in egg production. The Shetlands have a far harsher environment, with craggy hills and limited areas suited to farming, though fishing is prominent, notably at Lerwick. The oil industry has brought great, if temporary, prosperity to some places in these islands.

**The Central Lowlands:** Most of Scotland's population and industrial activity occurs in this central area, and here too are its two largest cities – Glasgow on innumerable small glacial hills (drumlins) in the Clyde Valley, and the capital Edinburgh on splendid volcanic ridges, dominated by Arthur's Seat.

Clydeside is still the greatest industrial area of Scotland. Textile industries, engineering and shipbuilding were the basis of the prosperity of Glasgow and its neighbouring towns, which in time grew into one another and held more than a third of Scotland's total population. There is now a wide range of industries in Central Scotland including electronics, printing, brewing and carpet-making.

Edinburgh, with its port of Leith, remained much smaller than Glasgow, with only half its population, but is still the administrative centre, and the seat of the main law courts and the National Museum and Library, as well as of many cultural organizations. A favoured centre for retirement in Scotland, it has an increasing tourist trade, particularly during the Edinburgh Festival in the summer. Much of the central area is rich farmland, especially to the east of Edinburgh.

**The Southern Uplands:** The Tweed with its numerous tributaries and – further west – the Esk, Annan, Nith, Ken and Cree provide sheltered valleys for farming, and there is splendid agricultural country in Galloway, where dairying has been particularly successful. Cattle rearing with crop production is more general in the drier east, where many farms specialize in meat production. The hills are used for sheep rearing. Some of the towns, notably Hawick and Galashiels, are prominent in the textile industry and have a large export trade.

Although tourism is relatively less important than in the Highlands, many people come to see the historic centres, such as Melrose and Dryburgh Abbey. To the west, in Galloway, there has been a policy of afforestation on the poorer soils, and several centres have been opened as small museums and educational sites. The coast attracts tourists and Forest Parks, such as that at Glen Trool close to Merrick, have been well laid out for visitors. In the west the towns are small, but there is heavy traffic to Stranraer, the port for the shortest sea crossing to Larne in Northern Ireland.

[*For the geography of Northern Ireland, see pages 173–4.*]

## HISTORY AND POLITICS

Whilst Caesar made brief forays into England in 55 and 54 BC, the country was only made part of the Roman Empire in AD 43. Roman rule lasted until the beginning of the 5th century, after which the country experienced invasions by various Germanic tribes, in particular the Angles and Saxons. The subsequent history of Anglo-Saxon England from the 8th to the 11th centuries was marked by resistance to Vikings from Scandinavia. The last successful invasion was that of the Normans, culminating in their victory at the Battle of Hastings (1066) and the crowning of William the Conqueror as king of England. In 1215, King John was forced by his barons to accept limits on his authority when he signed the Magna Carta, a declaration which included a guarantee to a fair trial. The following period saw the emergence of something approaching a parliamentary system. The Hundred Years War with France ended in 1453 with England's defeat and was followed by a long civil war (War of the Roses, 1455–85).

The coming to power of the Tudors ushered in an age of prosperity and modernization. Under Elizabeth I, England became a major naval power and established colonies in America. Literature and the arts flourished. The 'Glorious Revolution' of 1688 established the sovereignty of parliament, which continued to be strengthened during the 18th century. The Industrial Revolution made Britain one of the wealthiest nations in the world and was followed by a great expansion of the Empire under the reign of Queen Victoria (1837–1901).

Britain suffered huge losses, both human and economic, during World War I. The Irish Easter Rising of 1916 led to the partition of Ireland in 1921. In World War II, Britain played a major part in the defeat of Germany. The post-war Labour government of Clement Attlee brought in measures which laid the foundation for the 'welfare state'. During the 1950s and 1960s, most remaining British colonies became independent and joined the Commonwealth. After much internal debate, Britain joined the EEC in 1973. From 1979 onwards, Conservative governments, first led by Margaret Thatcher and from 1990 by John Major, broke from the 'consensus politics' that had dominated post-war Britain and set about privatizing most public sector industries and drastically reducing the scope of the 'welfare state'. [*Map pages 6–9*] ■

AREA  243,368 sq km [94,202 sq mls]
POPULATION  58,091,000
CAPITAL (POPULATION)  London (6,933,000)
GOVERNMENT  Constitutional monarchy
ETHNIC GROUPS  White 94%, Asian Indian 1%, Pakistani 1%, West Indian 1%
LANGUAGES  English (official)
RELIGIONS  Christianity (Anglican 57%, Roman Catholic 13%, Presbyterian 7%, Methodist 4%, Baptist 1%), Islam 1%, Judaism, Hinduism, Sikhism
CURRENCY  Pound sterling = 100 pence

# UNITED STATES OF AMERICA

The world's fourth largest country – and third most populous – the United States of America fills the North American continent between Canada and Mexico and also includes Alaska and the archipelago of Hawaii. Geographically, the main part (of 48 states) falls readily into an eastern section, including the Appalachian Mountains and eastern coastal plain; a central section, including the Mississippi basin and the broad prairie plains from the Dakotas to Texas; and a western section, including the Rocky Mountains and Pacific coastlands.

## The East

Eastern North America is crossed by a band of low, folded mountains: though nowhere much above 2,000 m [6,500 ft], they long formed a barrier to settlers. In the north are the Adirondacks, a southern extension of the ancient granite shield of Canada, rising to 1,629 m [5,344 ft]. From Maine to Alabama runs a broad range of sedimentary mountains, the Appalachians. Younger than the Adirondacks (though much older than the Rockies), the Appalachians separate the Atlantic coastlands of the east from the Great Lakes and low plateaux of Ohio, Kentucky and Tennessee.

North-east of New York City lie the six New England states – the fertile wooded country that, at least in summer, made the early settlers feel at home. To the south the coastal plain widens, to be split by the drowned estuaries of the Susquehanna and Potomac rivers, draining into Chesapeake Bay. From Virginia south to Florida smaller rivers drain eastwards, across a much broader plain, many of them entering coastal sounds with offshore sand bars and islands.

In New York State a major spillway cuts through the mountains between the Adirondacks and Appalachians, linking the Great Lakes with the Hudson Valley and the Atlantic Ocean. This is the line of the famous Erie Canal route, the most used of several that gave the early settlers access to the Ohio country beyond the mountains. Other routes led to Pittsburgh and, through the southern part of the Appalachians, into Tennessee. Central Ohio, Indiana and Illinois, which once formed America's Northwest Territory, are rolling uplands and plains, smoothed by glaciation in the north but more rugged in the south, and drained by the rambling Ohio River.

**Vegetation:** The original vegetation of eastern America, on either flank of the mountains, was broadleaf deciduous forest of oak, ash, beech and maple, merging northwards into yellow birch, hemlock and pine. In the drier Mid-west these immense woodlands turned to open country. Patchy grasslands covered northern Indiana and southern Illinois; central Illinois was forested along most watercourses, with prairie blue-stem grasses on the drier interfluves. Around the southern Appalachians mixed oak, pine and tulip-tree dominated; pines covered the coastal plains to the south and east with bald cypress in northern Florida. Spruce blanketed the highlands from northern Maine to the Adirondacks; spruce, tamarack and balsam fir covered the high Appalachians.

Most of this original forest is now gone, but there is still enough left – and some regenerating on abandoned farmland – to leave the mountains a blaze of colour each autumn. Despite more than 300 years of European settlement, the overall impression of eastern America, seen from the air, is still one of dense semi-continuous forests, except in the extensive farmlands north of the Ohio.

### The Central States

Within the 1,400 km [875 mls] from the Mississippi to the foothills of the Rockies, the land rises almost 3,000 m [9,850 ft], though the slope is often imperceptible to the traveller. From the Gulf of Mexico northwards to Minnesota and the Dakotas the rise is even less noticeable, though the flatness is occasionally relieved by the outcrops of uplands – the Ozarks of northern Arkansas, for example. In summer nothing bars the northwards movement of hot moist air from the Gulf of Mexico, nor in winter the southwards movement of dry, cold air from the Arctic. These air masses produce great seasonal contrasts of climate, exacerbated by storms, blizzards and tornadoes. Westwards from the Mississippi the climate grows progressively drier.

The plains are crossed by a series of long, wide rivers, often of irregular flow, that drain off the Rockies: the Missouri, the Platte, the Arkansas, the Canadian and the Red. In contrast to the Ohio, which enabled travellers to pass downstream and so westwards to the Mississippi, these rivers of the plains provided little help to settlers moving westwards, due to their seasonal variations in flow and the effort which was needed to move upstream when floods gave them depth.

**Vegetation:** West of the margins of the Mississippi tall blue-stem prairie grasses once extended from the Canadian border to southern Texas. Only along the watercourses were there trees – cottonwood and willow in the north, merging into oak and hickory further south. Westwards the prairie grasslands thinned to the bunch grass and needle grass of the Great Plains in a belt from central North Dakota to western Oklahoma; locally favoured areas such as western Nebraska had patches of broadleaf evergreens amidst shrubs and a variety of grasses.

West of about meridian 100°W a variety of short grasses stretched from Montana and the Dakotas southwards to north-west Texas: in the far south, on the Mexican border, low xerophytic shrubs were an indicatation of the increasing aridity. Higher ground, for example the Black Hills of south-western South Dakota, supported stands of pine.

### The West

The western USA is a complex mountain and plateau system, rich in scenic beauty and natural history, bordered by a rugged coast that starts in the semi-deserts of the south and ends in the rain-soaked forests of the north. Americans appreciate their far west; for long the final frontier of a youthful, expanding nation, it is still the goal of tens of thousands of immigrants each year and the vacation dream of many more: tourism is the most widespread industry.

**Landscape and vegetation:** Topographically the west is a land of high mountain ranges divided by high plateaux and deep valleys. The grain of the country runs north-west to south-east, at a right-angle to the crustal pressures that produced it, and the highest mountains – the Rocky Mountains of a thousand legends – form a spectacular eastern flank. The southern Rockies of Colorado and New Mexico, remnants of an ancient granite plateau, are carved by weathering into ranges of spectacular peaks; Colorado alone has over 1,000 mountains of 3,000 m [10,000 ft] or more. Rising from dry, sandy, cactus-and-sagebrush desert, their lower slopes carry grey piñon pines and juniper scrub, with darker spruce, firs and pines above. At the timber line grow gnarled bristlecone pines, some 3,000 and more years old. Between the ranges, 'parks' of mixed forest and grassland support deer and other game in summer grazing. To the southwest are the dry, colourful sandstones of the Colorado Plateau, dotted with cactus and deeply gouged by the Colorado River; to the north lies the Wyoming Basin, a rangeland of rich volcanic soil that once grazed herds of bison, and now supports sheep and cattle.

The central Rocky Mountains, towering over western Wyoming, Idaho and Montana, include a number of snow-capped peaks of more than 4,000 m [13,000 ft]; their eastern outliers, the Bighorn Mountains, rise 3,000 m [10,000 ft] almost sheer above the surrounding grasslands. These are the Rockies of the tourists; each year thousands of people visit the many national parks and reserves in the splendid heartland of the Cordilleras. The scenery is matchless, the forests, grasslands, alpine tundras and marshes are ecologically fascinating, and the wild animals are reasonably accessible. There is every chance for tourists to see bison, wapiti, mule deer, moose, black and brown bears, beavers and a host of smaller mammals and birds.

West of the Rockies, beyond the dry plateau scrublands of Arizona, Utah and Nevada, a double chain of mountains runs parallel to the coast from Mexico to Canada. In the arid, sun-baked south they form the desert landscape on either side of the Gulf of California. At Los Angeles they merge, parting again to form the Sierra Nevada and the Coastal Ranges that face each other across the Great Valley of central California. They rejoin in the Klamath Mountains, then continue north on either side of a broad valley – to the west as a lowly coastal chain, to the east as the magnificently forested Cascade Range. By keeping rain away from the interior, these mountains create the arid landscapes of the central Cordilleras.

**Climate and agriculture:** In the damp winters and dry summers of southern California the coastal mountains support semi-desert scrub; the Sierra Nevada, rising far above them, is relatively well-watered and forested. In the early days of settlement the long, bone-dry summers made farming – even ranching – difficult in the central valley of California. But the peaks of Sierra Nevada, accumulating thick snow in winter, now provide a reservoir for summer irrigation. Damming and water channelling have made the semi-deserts and dry rangelands bloom all over southern and central California, which now grows temperate and tropical fruits, vegetables, cotton and other thirsty crops in abundance – despite severe drought from the late 1980s.

Through northern California and Oregon, where annual rainfall is higher and summer heat less intense, the coastal mountains are clothed in forests of tall cedars and firs; notable among them are stands of giant redwood cedars, towering well over 100 m [330 ft]. In coastal Washington Douglas firs, grand firs, Sitka spruce and giant arborvitae are the spectacular trees, rivalling the giant redwoods. Forests of giant conifers cover the Cascade Range too, providing the enormous stocks of timber on which the wealth of the American north-west was originally based.

## ECONOMY AND RESOURCES

### The East
**Settlement and development:** The eastern USA is the heartland of many of America's rural and urban traditions. In the 19th century European immigrants poured through the ports of Boston, New York, Philadelphia and Baltimore. Many stayed to swell the cities, which grew enormously. Others moved across the mountains to populate the interior and start the farms that fed the city masses. As raw materials of industry – coal and iron ore especially – were discovered and exploited, new cities grew up in the interior. Some were based on old frontier forts: for example, Fort Duquesne became Pittsburgh

## ALASKA

In 1867 the USA bought Alaska from the Tsarist government of Russia for a mere $7 million. More extensive than the southwestern lands acquired from Mexico, Alaska remained a territory for over 90 years, becoming America's largest state in 1959. Geographically it forms the north-western end of the Western Cordilleras; peaks in the main Alaska Range rise to over 6,000 m [20,000 ft], and the southern 'panhandle' region is a drowned fjordland backed by ice-capped mountains. A gold rush in the 1880s stimulated the subsequent development of other mineral resources – most notably copper and, especially, oil. Alaska is the first real test of the USA's resolve to balance economic development and conservation; the six largest US national parks are in Alaska. Some farming is possible on the southern coastal lowlands; the interior tablelands are tundra-covered and rich in migrant birds and mammals.

Today the pattern is much the same, though prosperity has increased throughout the east. The densest concentrations of industry and population lie in the north-east, especially in central New England. New York remains an important financial hub, while Washington, DC, now part of a vast, sprawling megalopolis, loses none of its significance as the centre of federal government. The south-eastern states remain relatively rural and thinly populated, though they are increasingly popular with the retired, notably Florida.

### The Central States
**Settlement and development:** Over 30 major tribes of native Indians used these vast and varied plains. Some – the Mandan, the Omaha and the Kansa along the Missouri River, for example – were settled farmers, while on the drier western plains the Blackfoot, Crow, Arapaho, Kiowa and Comanche were nomadic, following the buffalo, the game and the pasture.

European influences revolutionized their lives. By 1800 the horse, introduced from the south by the Spanish, made the Indian population of about 100,000 mobile as never before. Then English- and French-speaking trappers and traders from the east brought firearms: the mounted Indian with a gun became too efficient a hunter, and rapidly depleted his food supply. Behind the traders came white settlers, killing off the buffalo and crowding in other native peoples that they had driven from homelands in the south-east. As railways, cattle trails and the fences of the ranchers crossed the old hunting grounds, Indian farmers and hunters alike lost their traditional lands and livelihoods to the European intruders, and the plains settlement was virtually completed by the late 19th century.

The coming of the railways after the Civil War of the 1860s not only doomed the remnant Indian societies, but also introduced long and often bitter competition between different types of European farming. The dry grasslands that once supported the buffalo could just as well support herds of cattle on the open range, raised to feed the eastern cities. So the range lands often became crop farms. In the dry years that followed soil deterioration and

and Fort Dearborn became the city of Chicago.

Railways spread over the booming farmlands, linking producer and consumer. Huge manufacturing cities, vast markets in their own right, developed along the Great Lakes as people continued to arrive – firstly from abroad, but latterly from the countryside, where mechanization threw people off the land into the cities and factories. In less than a hundred years between the late 18th and 19th centuries the Ohio country passed from Indian-occupied forests and plains to mechanized farmlands of unparalleled efficiency, virtually becoming the granary of the Western world, and spawning some of its greatest and wealthiest industrial centres.

While the north boomed, the warmer southern states slipped into rural lethargy; becoming overdependent on cotton cultivation, they remained backward and outside the mainstream of American prosperity. Though fortunes were made on the rich cotton estates of the south-east, Tennessee and the southern Appalachians spelled rural poverty for many generations of settlers.

erosion began, becoming a major problem in the early decades of the present century.

With their markets in the cities of the east and in Europe, the plains farmers were caught in a vice between the desiccation of their farms and the boom and slump of their markets. By the 1930s agricultural depression led to massive foreclosing on mortgaged lands, and when the dust storms of eroded topsoil came the people were driven away – the 'Okies' of Woody Guthrie and John Steinbeck who fled to California. Much farmed land subsequently reverted to ranching.

Farming prospects improved during the later 1930s, when the New Deal brought better price structures. New approaches to farming practice, including dry farming (cropping only one year out of several), contour ploughing, diversification beyond basic grains, and widespread irrigation that was linked to the creation of a vast network of dams and reservoirs, all transformed the plains. Nevertheless, these areas are marginal to semi-desert, remaining highly susceptible to periodic changes in precipitation over a wide area: thus a poor snowfall on the Rockies may mean insufficient water for irrigation the following summer. Coupled with worldwide fluctuations in the cereals market (on which Mid-West farmers still depend heavily), farming on the plains remains very risky.

**The growth of industry:** In the Gulf Coast states, petroleum provides a radically different basis for prosperity. Since the exploitation of oil reserves in the early years of the century Oklahoma, Texas and Louisiana have shifted from a dependence on agriculture (notably wheat, cattle, rice and sugar production) to the refining and petrochemical industries. Oil has transformed Dallas-Fort Worth into a major US conurbation, now larger than the twin cities of Minneapolis-St Paul, which were once the chief urban focus of the agricultural economy of the upper Mississippi. At the meeting of the High Plains and the Rocky Mountains, Denver changed from a small elevated railhead town to a wealthy state capital (and further to a smog-ridden metropolis) in response to mineral wealth and the growth of aerospace industries.

Further north the cities of the central USA are great trading centres, dependent on local

## HAWAII

Most recent and most southerly of the United States, Hawaii is an archipelago of eight large and over 100 smaller volcanic islands in the mid-Pacific, 3,850 km [2,400 mls] south-west of California. Only on the main island are there currently active volcanoes. High rainfall, warmth and rich soils combine to provide a wealth of year-round vegetation; originally forested, the islands are still well covered with trees and shrubs, but now provide commercial crops of sugar cane, cereals, forage for cattle, and a wide range of fruit and vegetables.

Originally settled by Polynesians and visited by James Cook in 1778, Hawaii became a port-of-call for trans-Pacific shipping and a wintering station for New England whalers, but retained its independent status until annexed by the USA in 1898. Only about 2% of its people are full-blooded Polynesians; the rest are of Chinese, Japanese, Korean, Philippine and Caucasian origins, including many immigrants from mainland USA.

About 80% live on the islands of Oahu, over half of them in the capital city of Honolulu. Agriculture, fishing and food processing are the main industries, though defence and tourism are also important to the state's economy.

agriculture for their prosperity. Wholesaling and the trans-shipping of produce have been crucial since the days of the railheads, but cities like St Louis, Kansas City and Chicago have been able to diversify far beyond their original role to become major manufacturing centres. Chicago, for example, is the main mid-western focus of the steel industries. Nowadays the interstate freeway system supplements and has partly replaced the railway networks, and air passenger traffic has increased rapidly.

From the air the landscape between the Mississippi and the Rockies is one of quilted farmlands and vast reservoirs, blending into wheatlands with extensive grasslands. Almost all the original vegetation is long gone, and most people now live in the cities, but the landscape still reflects the critical importance of agriculture past and present.

## The West

**Settlement and development:** The Indian cultures of western America included hunting, fishing, seed-gathering and primitive irrigation farming. Some were semi-nomadic, others settled, living mostly in small, scattered communities. The first European colonists, spreading northwards from New Spain (Mexico) in the 1760s, made little impact on the Indians. But their forts and missions (which included San Diego, Los Angeles and San Francisco) attracted later settlers who proved more exploitative. From the 1840s pressures increased with the arrival of land-hungry Americans, both by sea and along wagon trails from the east. After a brief struggle, the south-west was sold to the USA; almost immediately the gold rushes brought new waves of adventurers and immigrants.

The Oregon coast, though visited by Spanish, British and Russian mariners in search of furs from the 16th century onwards, was first settled by American fur traders in 1811. Immigration began during the 1830s, the famous Oregon Trail across Wyoming and Idaho from the Mississippi coming into full use during the 1840s. After the establishment of the 49th parallel as the boundary between Canada and the USA, Oregon Territory (including Washington, Idaho and part of Montana) became part of the USA. Here in the north-west the forests and rangelands were equally vital to Indians and to settlers, and many battles were fought before the Indians were subdued and confined in tribal reserves.

Now the wagon trails are major highways, the staging posts, mission stations and isolated forts transformed into cities. Gold mining, once the only kind of mining that mattered, has given way to the delving and processing of a dozen lesser metals, from copper to molybdenum. Fish canning, food processing, electronics and aerospace are major sources of employment. The movie industry is based in Los Angeles, but the city now has a broad economy based on high-technology industries. The mountain states – once far behind in economic development – have caught up with the rest of the USA.

## ECONOMY

The years following the Civil War (1861–5) saw the firm establishment of the USA as the world's leading industrial society. Still attracting enormous numbers of emigrants from Europe, its agricultural and industrial output grew at unprecedented rates to the end of the century and beyond.

**Agriculture:** Stimulated by education, research and new, sophisticated machinery, agriculture developed into a highly mechanized industry for food production and processing. Chicago's agricultural machinery industries transformed the farmers' lives with mass-produced ploughs, tractors, seed drills, reapers and binders. Only a generation after the pioneering days, farmers found themselves tightly integrated into an economic system with such factors as mortgages, availability of spare parts, freight prices and world markets at least as crucial to the success of their efforts as climate and soil.

To the east of the western mountains farming was established in a zonal pattern which remains intact – though much modified – today, a pattern reflecting both the possibilities offered by climate and soils, and the inclinations and national origins of the settlers who first farmed the lands. In the north, from Minnesota to New England, lies a broad belt where dairy farming predominates, providing milk, butter and cheese for the industrial cities. Spring wheat is grown further west, where the climate is drier. The eastern and central states from Nebraska to Ohio form the famous Corn Belt – immensely productive land, formerly prairie and forest, where corn (maize) is the main crop.

Now much extended by the development of new, more tolerant strains, corn production has spread into neighbouring belts on either side. No longer principally human food, except in the poorer areas of the south, corn is grown mainly for feeding to cattle and pigs, and other livestock, which in turn supply the meat-packing industries.

Southwards again, from Oklahoma and Kansas to Virginia, stretches a broad belt of mixed farming where winter wheat and corn alternate as the dominant cereals. In the warmer southern states lies the former Cotton Belt, where cotton and tobacco were once the most widespread crops; both are now concentrated into small, highly-productive areas where mechanical handling is possible, and the bulk of the land is used for a wide variety of other crops ranging from vegetables to fruit and peanuts.

Throughout American farming there has been a tendency to shift from small-scale operations to large, from labour-intensive to mechanized, and from low-capital to high-capital investment. The main centres of production are now concentrated in the western plains: much of the land originally farmed by the Pilgrim Fathers and other early settlers is now built over, or has reverted to attractive second-growth forest. By concentrating effort in this way, America has become a leading producer of meat, dairy foods, soya beans, corn, oats, wheat, barley, cotton, sugar and many other crops, both for home consumption and export.

**Resources and industry:** The spread of prosperity throughout a very broad spectrum of the community generated new consumer industries, to satisfy the demands of a large middle class for ever-increasing standards of comfort and material welfare. America became the pioneer of massive-scale industrial production of everything from thumbtacks to automobiles. With almost every raw material needed for production available within its own boundaries, or readily gained through trading with close neighbours, its mining and extractive industries have been heavily exploited from the start.

For several generations coal formed the main source of power and the basis of industrial prosperity. Anthracite from eastern Pennsylvania, good bituminous and coking coals from the Appalachians, Indiana, Illinois, Colorado and Utah are still in demand, and enormous reserves remain. Oil, first drilled in Pennsylvania in 1859, was subsequently found in several major fields underlying the Mid-West, the eastern and central mountain states, the Gulf of Mexico, California and Alaska. Home consumption of petroleum products has grown steadily: though the US remains a major producer, it is also by far the world's greatest consumer, and has for a long while been a net importer of oil. Natural gas too is found in abundance, usually in association with oil, and is moved to the main consumer

areas through an elaborate, transcontinental network of pipes.

Today the USA is a major producer of iron and steel, mica, molybdenum, uranium and many other primary materials, and a major consumer and exporter of a wide range of manufactured goods, from chemicals and industrial machinery, to paper and electronic equipment. But though the USA remains the world's greatest economic power, its position as leading industrial nation was being threatened by Japan into the 1990s.

**Population:** The USA has one of the most diverse populations of any nation in the world. Until about 1860, with the exception of the native Indians and the southern blacks, the population was largely made up by immigrants of British (and Irish) origin, with small numbers of Spanish and French. After the Civil War, however, there was increasing immigration from the countries of central and south-eastern Europe – Italy, the Balkans, Poland, Scandinavia and Russia. This vast influx of Europeans, numbering about 30 million between 1860 and 1920, was markedly different in culture and language from the established population. More recently there have been lesser influxes of Japanese, Chinese, Filipinos, Cubans and Puerto Ricans, with large numbers of Mexicans (many of them illegal) from across the southern border. Although there are strong influences and pressures towards Americanization, these minority groups have tended to establish distinct social and cultural enclaves within US society as a whole.

The major westwards movement of population through the last century was replaced after 1900 by more subtle but no less important shifts of population away from rural areas and into the cities. Today there is further movement from the old, industrial centres and the tired, outmoded cities that flourished early in the century, away from the ageing buildings and urban dereliction, especially in the north and east, to new centres elsewhere.

The cities that gain population are mostly peripheral, on the Great Lakes and the coasts. The south is especially favoured for its warmth (particularly by retired people) and its closeness to the major source of energy in the USA – petroleum. Development of southern petrochemical and electronic industries has helped to relieve rural poverty and given new economic life, though partly at the expense of the north. However, Chicago and the eastern conurbations – New York, Boston, Philadelphia, Baltimore and Washington – still remain pre-eminent as centres of US commercial, as well as political, life.

Since its earliest inception from the 13 colonies, the USA has led the world in industrial, economic and social innovation, creating problems through sheer ebullience and solving them – more or less – through inventiveness and enterprise, and with massive, wealth-bringing resources of energy and materials. The United States today continues to enjoy one of the highest material standards of living ever known, and continues to produce what may well be its greatest asset of all – a highly skilled, literate and imaginative population.

## HISTORY AND POLITICS

Leif Ericson was the first European to visit North America, around AD 1000, but the Vikings left no permanent settlements. However, about 1 million Native Americans lived in North America when Christopher Columbus reached the New World in 1492.

The first permanent European settlement in the present-day United States was founded by Spain in 1565 at Saint Augustine, Florida. Jamestown, Virginia became the first permanent English settlement in 1607. African slaves were brought to Virginia in 1619.

During the 18th century, England, France and Spain became dominant colonial powers in North America. Great Britain gained much French territory during the French and Indian War (1756–63), but policies introduced after the war led to increasing colonial resentment of British rule. The American Revolution began in 1775, and the Continental Congress issued the Declaration of Independence on 4 July 1776. American forces, aided by France, defeated the British at the Battle of Yorktown in 1781, and in 1783 the Treaty of Paris recognized American independence.

The Constitution of the United States was approved in 1787, and ratified by all thirteen original states by 1790. The Louisiana Purchase in 1803 nearly doubled the size of the US. The War of 1812, waged against Britain, increased the nation's confidence in foreign affairs, culminating in the Monroe doctrine of 1823. Rapid westward expansion led to the acquisition of Texas in 1845 and the Oregon Territory in 1846. A huge expanse of western territory, including California was won in the Mexican-American War of 1846–8.

Conflict over slavery between the industrialized North and the agricultural South led to the American Civil War (1861–5). Slavery was abolished after the North won, while the South entered Reconstruction.

The late 19th century was marked by a huge influx of European immigrants and rapid industrial and economic development. The last Native American tribes were defeated and forced into reservations as territorial expansion continued. The US bought Alaska from Russia in 1867. Guam, the Philippines and Puerto Rico were won in the Spanish-American War of 1898, and Hawaii was annexed the same year. The Panama Canal Zone was seized in 1903.

US isolationism ended in 1917 with entry into World War I, confirming America's status as a world power. The economic boom of the 1920s was followed by the crash of 1929 and the Great Depression. The New Deal offered slight improvement during the years of the Depression, but the Japanese bombing of Pearl Harbor on 7 December 1941 led to the US entry into World War II, which fuelled economic recovery. The US ended the war in August 1945 by dropping atomic bombs on Hiroshima and Nagasaki.

Post-war tensions between the US and the USSR led to the Cold War. US forces fought in Korea (1950–3) and Vietnam (1965–73) to stop the spread of Communism. Domestic anti-Communist hysteria peaked during the 1950s. Civil rights campaigns and growing dissatisfaction with US involvement in Vietnam marked the 1960s. Riots erupted in several cities as a result of protests against social conditions and race relations. Then, at the end of the 1960s, in July 1969, US astronauts landed on the Moon.

The Watergate scandal (1973–4) altered many Americans' perception of the federal government. The economy suffered during the late 1970s, culminating in the recession of 1981–2, but a sustained recovery beginning in 1983 lasted the rest of the decade.

The fall of Communism and the division of the Soviet Union left the US as the world's sole remaining superpower, as evidenced by its leadership during the Gulf War. However, lingering domestic problems remained, including simmering race relations and increasing urban violence. Long-term economic prospects were buoyed by the conclusion of the North American Free Trade Agreement with Canada and Mexico, which went into effect in 1994. [*Map pages 28–9*] ■

AREA 9,372,610 sq km [3,618,765 sq mls]
POPULATION 260,631,000
CAPITAL (POPULATION) Washington, DC (3,924,000)
GOVERNMENT Federal republic
ETHNIC GROUPS White 80%, African American 12%, other races 8%
LANGUAGES English (official), Spanish, more than 30 others
RELIGIONS Christianity (Protestant 53%, Roman Catholic 26%, other Christian 8%), Islam 2%, Judaism 2%
CURRENCY US dollar = 100 cents

# URUGUAY

After Surinam, the Eastern Republic of Uruguay, as Uruguay is officially known, is the smallest South American state. It is a low-lying rolling country of tall prairie grasses and riparian woodlands – the highest point, Mirador Nacional, which lies south of Minas, is only 501 m [1,644 ft] above sea level. The Atlantic coast and River Plate estuary are fringed with lagoons and sand dunes; the centre of the country is a low plateau, rising in the north towards the Brazilian border. The River Uruguay forms the western boundary, and is navigable as far as the falls at Salto, 300 km [186 mls] from the Plate. The climate is temperate with warm summers and mild winters, moderated by the prevailing easterly winds which blow in from the sea.

## ECONOMY AND RESOURCES

Meat processing, pioneered at Fray Bentos in the 1860s, was the start of a meat-and-hide export industry that, boosted by railways to Montevideo and later by refrigerated cargo ships, established the nation's fortunes. Today a modern and moderately prosperous country, Uruguay still depends largely on exports of animal products – mostly meat, wool and dairy produce – for her livelihood.

Farming is thus the main industry, though four out of five Uruguayans are urban-living and almost half live in the capital. Moreover, although more than 90% of Uruguay's land could be used for agriculture, only 10% of it is currently under cultivation. The manufacturing industry today is largely centred on food processing and packing, though with a small domestic market the economy has diversified into cement, chemicals, leather, textiles and steel. Uruguay's trading patterns are changing, too, in an attempt to avoid reliance on Brazil and Argentina, and in 1988 trade agreements with China and the USSR were signed. With inadequate supplies of coal, gas and oil, the nation depends on HEP (90%) for its energy, and exports electricity to Argentina.

## HISTORY AND POLITICS

Originally little more than the hinterland to the Spanish base at Montevideo, Uruguay formed a buffer area between northern Portuguese and western Spanish territories. Though independent in 1828, internal struggles and civil war intervened before the country developed a basis for prosperity. European immigrants settled the coast and the valley of the River Uruguay, farming the lowlands and leaving the highlands for stock rearing.

Since 1828 Uruguay has been dominated by two political parties – Colorados (Liberals) and Blancos (Conservatives) – and from 1904 has been unique in constitutional innovations aimed at avoiding a dictatorship. The early part of the 20th century saw the development of a pioneering welfare state which in turn encouraged extensive immigration. From 1973 until 1985, however, the country was under a strict military regime accused of appalling human rights abuses. In 1989 the country had its first fully free presidential and legislative elections for eighteen years, which were won by the Blancos. President Lacalle's first task was to try and reduce the dependency on events in Brazil and Argentina, Uruguay's huge neighbours. [*Map page 31*] ■

**AREA** 177,410 sq km [68,498 sq mls]
**POPULATION** 3,167,000
**CAPITAL (POPULATION)** Montevideo (1,384,000)
**GOVERNMENT** Multiparty republic
**ETHNIC GROUPS** White 86%, Mestizo 8%, Mulatto or Black 6%
**LANGUAGES** Spanish (official)
**RELIGIONS** Christianity (Roman Catholic 66%, Protestant 2%), Judaism 1%
**CURRENCY** Uruguay peso = 100 centésimos

# UZBEKISTAN

The Republic of Uzbekistan is one of the five republics in Central Asia which were once part of the Soviet Union. Plains cover most of western Uzbekistan, with highlands in the east, and there is a populous eastern spur jutting into Kyrgyzstan. The main rivers, the Amu Darya and Syr Darya, drain into the Aral Sea. So much water has been taken from these rivers to irrigate the land that the Aral Sea has shrunk from 66,900 sq km [25,830 sq mls] in 1960 to 33,642 sq km [12,989 sq mls] in 1993. The dried-up lake area has become desert, like much of the rest of the country.

Uzbekistan has a continental climate. The winters are cold, but temperatures soar in the summer months. The west is extremely arid, with an average annual rainfall of about 200 mm [8 in], but parts of the highlands in the east have three times as much rain.

## ECONOMY AND RESOURCES
The World Bank classifies Uzbekistan as a 'lower-middle-income' developing country, and the government still controls most of the economic activity. The country produces coal, copper, gold, oil and natural gas, and in 1993 was the world's third largest producer of

uranium. Manufactures include agricultural machinery, chemicals, processed food and textiles. Agriculture is important and cotton is the main crop, though various fruits and rice are also grown. Cattle, sheep and goats are raised. Uzbekistan's exports include cotton, gold, textiles, chemicals and fertilizers.

## HISTORY AND POLITICS
Turkic people first settled in the area that is now Uzbekistan about 1,500 years ago, and Islam was introduced in the 7th century AD. Mongols invaded the land in the 13th century and, in the late 14th century, the Mongol Turk Tamerlane ruled a great empire from Samarkand (Samarqand). Turkic Uzbek people invaded in the 16th century and gradually the area was divided into states known as *khanates*. A large part of eastern Uzbekistan is taken up by the Kara-Kalpak Autonomous Region, annexed to the Uzbek Soviet Socialist Republic (as it was then known) in 1936.

Russia conquered the area in the 19th century. After the Russian Revolution of 1917, the Communists took over and, in 1924, set up the Uzbek SSR. Under Communism, all aspects of Uzbek life were controlled and religious worship was discouraged, but education, health, housing and transport were improved. The Communists also increased cotton production, but caused great environmental damage in doing so.

In the 1980s, when reforms were being introduced in the Soviet Union, the people demanded more freedom. In 1990, the government stated that its laws overruled those of the Soviet Union. On 1 September 1991, Uzbekistan declared its independence after the break-up of the Soviet Union and this was confirmed in a referendum in December. Uzbekistan has kept its links with Russia through the Commonwealth of Independent States and has established new cultural and political ties with Turkey.

On 29 December 1991, Islam Karimov, leader of the People's Democratic Party (formerly the Communist Party), was elected president. Many opposition leaders have since been arrested. Karimov has asserted that economic reform will be slow in order to avoid internal disruption. In 1994 the government approved a six-year plan for the transfer of the

Uzbek language from its present Turkik form to a Latin script. [*Map page 20*] ∎

**AREA** 447,400 sq km [172,740 sq mls]
**POPULATION** 22,349,000
**CAPITAL (POPULATION)** Tashkent (2.094,000)
**GOVERNMENT** Socialist republic
**ETHNIC GROUPS** Uzbek 71%, Russian 8%, Tajik 5%, Kazakh 4%, Tatar 2%, Kara-Kalpak 2%, Crimean Tatar, Korean, Kyrgyz, Ukrainian, Turkmen
**LANGUAGES** Uzbek (official)
**RELIGIONS** Islam
**CURRENCY** Som = 100 tiyin

# VANUATU

An archipelago of 13 large islands and 70 islets largely of volcanic origin, the majority of the islands are mountainous with coral beaches, reefs and very limited coastal cultivation. Nearly two-thirds of the population live on four islands, 19,000 of them in the capital of Port-Vila, on the island of Efate. The Melanesian people live largely by subsistence farming and fishing, with copra, beef and veal the main exports.

Formerly the New Hebrides and governed jointly by France and Britain from 1906, the islands became an independent republic within the Commonwealth in 1980. The francophone island of Espíritu Santó attempted separation from the anglophone government, and politics have since remained unstable. [*Map page 3*] ∎

**AREA** 12,190 sq km [4,707 sq mls]
**POPULATION** 165,000
**CAPITAL (POPULATION)** Port-Vila (19,310)
**GOVERNMENT** Multiparty republic
**ETHNIC GROUPS** Melanesian 94%, French 4%
**LANGUAGES** Bislama, English, French
**RELIGIONS** Christianity
**CURRENCY** Vatu = 100 centimes

# VATICAN CITY

The world's smallest nation – a walled enclave on the west bank of the River Tiber in the city of Rome – the Vatican City State exists to provide an independent base for the Holy See, governing body of the Roman Catholic Church and its 950 million adherents round the world. It consists of 44 hectares [109 acres], including St Peter's Square, with a resident population of about 1,000 – including the country's only armed force of 100 Swiss Guards. The population is made up entirely of unmarried males – and the birth rate is zero.

The Vatican is sustained by investment income and voluntary contributions. The popes have been prominent patrons of the arts, and the treasures of the Vatican, including Michelangelo's frescoes in the Sistine Chapel, attract tourists from all over the world. Similarly, the Vatican library contains a priceless collection of manuscripts from both pre-Christian and Christian eras.

The Vatican City State is all that remains of the extensive Papal States which, until 1870, occupied most of central Italy. In 1929 Benito Mussolini recognized the independence of the Vatican City in return for papal recognition of the kingdom of Italy.

The Vatican City has its own newspaper, police and railway station, and issues its own stamps and coins. It's radio station, *Radio Vaticana*, broadcasts in 34 languages.

The popes have lived in the Vatican since the 5th century, apart from a brief period at Avignon in the 14th century ∎

**AREA** 0.44 sq km [0.17 sq mls]
**POPULATION** 1,000
**CAPITAL (POPULATION)** Vatican City (1,000)
**GOVERNMENT** Papal Commission
**ETHNIC GROUPS** Italian, Swiss
**LANGUAGES** Latin (official), Italian
**RELIGIONS** Roman Catholic
**CURRENCY** Italian currency

# VENEZUELA

In the north and north-west of Venezuela, where 90% of the population lives, the Andes split to form two ranges separated by the Maracaibo basin (which surounds the freshwater lake of Maracaibo). At 5,007 m [16,427 ft], snow-capped Merida is the highest of several tall peaks in the area. Above 3,000 m [10,000 ft] are the *paramos* – regions of grassland vegetation where Indian villagers live; temperatures are mild and the land is fertile. By contrast, Maracaibo swelters in tropical heat alongside the oilfields that for half a century have produced Venezuela's wealth.

The mountains running west to east behind the coast from Valencia to Trinidad have a separate geological history and gentler topography. Between the ranges are fertile alluvial basins, with many long-established market towns. Caracas, the teeming capital, was one such town before being expanded and modernized on the back of the 1970s oil boom. It now has to accommodate a rapidly swelling population and is fringed with the shanties of hopeful immigrants from poor rural areas.

South of the mountains are the *llanos* of the Orinoco – mostly a vast savanna of trees and grasslands that floods, especially in the west, during the April-to-October rains. This is now cattle-raising country. The Orinoco itself rises on the western rim in the Guiana Highlands, a region of high dissected plateaus made famous as the site of Arthur Conan Doyle's *Lost World*, and dense tropical forest makes this still a little-known area. Mount Roraima, the highest peak, rises to 2,810 m [9,217 ft] at the conjunction of the border with Guyana (with whom Venezuela has a grumbling territorial dispute – as it does with Colombia) and Brazil.

## ECONOMY AND RESOURCES

Cerro Bolívar, where iron ore is mined and fed to the steel mills of Ciudad Guayana, is a new industrial city built on the Orinoco since 1960. The smelting is powered by hydroelectricity from the nearby Caroni River, and a new deep-water port allows 60,000-tonne carriers to take surplus ore to world markets. Modern developments in a primeval setting typify the changes that Venezuela is undergoing.

Oil made Venezuela a rich country, but the wealth was always distributed very unevenly and concentrated in the cities – hence the rapid urbanization that made 17 out of every 20 Venezuelans a city dweller and left enormous areas of the country unpopulated. Before the coming of oil, Venezuela was predominantly agricultural.

Commercially-viable reserves of oil were found in Venezuela in 1914, and by the 1930s the country had become the world's first major oil exporter – the largest producer after the USA. The industry was nationalized in 1976 but by 1990 there were signs of dangerous dependence on a single commodity controlled by OPEC and in plentiful supply, while the large foreign debt saw austerity measures that triggered a violent reaction from many Venezuelans.

The oil-producing region around Maracaibo covers an area of 77,700 sq km [30,000 sq mls] and produces three-quarters of the nation's total. Exploration for oil is also being carried out offshore in the Caribbean. Before the development of the oil industry Venezuela was predominantly an agricultural country, but 85% of export earnings are now from oil and some of the profits from the industry help to fund developments in agriculture and other industries, including the exploitation of natural gas. Gold, nickel, iron ore, copper and manganese are also found and aluminium production has increased following further discoveries of bauxite; aluminium has now replaced iron ore as the second most important export earner. Manufactures include cement, steel, chemicals, food processing, shipbuilding and vehicles.

Agriculture can supply only 70% of the country's needs. Only 5% of the arable land is cultivated and much of that is pasture. The chief crops are sugar cane, coffee, bananas, maize and oranges; there is also substantial dairy and beef production. It is thought that more than 10,000 head of cattle are smuggled into Colombia each month. The reverse is almost certainly the case for cocaine, where Venezuela acts as a

## ANGEL FALLS

Called Cherun-Meru by the local Indians, and first known to Europeans in 1910, the world's highest waterfall was 'rediscovered' in 1937 when an American airman called Jimmy Angel flew his small plane into the Guiana Highlands in eastern Venezuela in search of gold – but found instead a natural wonder nearly 20 times the height of Niagara, plunging down from the plateau of Auyán Tepuí, the 'Devil's Mountain'.

In 1949 an expedition confirmed Angel's report and today light aircraft follow his route to take tourists to falls that tumble a total of 979 m [3,212 ft] on the Rio Carrao, a tributary of the Caroni. The cataract is broken only by a single ledge, the main drop measuring 807 m [2,648 ft].

increasing its prosperity further in a world economic upturn – but to avoid political problems the government must learn to distribute the benefits more widely to its citizens. [*Map page 31*] ■

AREA 912,050 sq km [352,143 sq mls]
POPULATION 21,378,000
CAPITAL (POPULATION) Caracas (2,784,000)
GOVERNMENT Federal republic
ETHNIC GROUPS Mestizo 67%, White 21%, Black 10%, Amerindian 2%
LANGUAGES Spanish (official)
RELIGIONS Christianity (Roman Catholic 94%)
CURRENCY Bolívar = 100 céntimos

# VIETNAM

conduit to the US for its Andean neighbours.

Venezuela is still the richest country in South America but now plans to diversify away from the petroleum industry, and foreign investment is being actively encouraged.

**HISTORY AND POLITICS**
Sighted by Columbus in 1498, the country was visited by Alonzo de Ojeda and Amerigo Vespucci in 1499, when they named it Venezuela ('Little Venice'). It was part of the Spanish colony of New Granada until 1821 when it became independent, first in federation with Colombia and Ecuador and then, from 1830, as a separate independent republic under the leadership of Simón Bolívar. Between 1830 and 1945 the country was governed mainly by dictators; after frequent changes of president, a new constitution came into force in 1961 and since then a fragile civilian-rule democracy has been enjoyed, resting on widespread repression and corruption – almost endemic in South America. Two military coup attempts were defeated by President Pérez who then resigned in May 1993 after charges of corruption. The new president is Rafael Caldera.

Demographically stable, with a growing middle class and a proven record in economic planning, Venezuela has every chance of

A land of mountains, coastal plains and deltas, Vietnam is perhaps Asia's most strangely shaped country. In the north the coastal lands widen into the valley and delta of the Hongha (Red) River and the valley of the Da. This region has long been the main cultural focus of the country, and it was the original core of the Annamite empire which came into being with the revolt against Chinese rule in AD 939.

In the south of the country, the coastal plains open out into the great delta of the Mekong, the world's ninth longest river at 4,500 km [2,795 mls]. For most of their length the coastal lowlands are backed in the west by the steep and deeply dissected mountains of the Annamite Chain, and to the north the country is dominated by the plateaux of Laos and Tongking, often characterized by an intensely craggy, inhospitable karstic (limestone) landscape. The mountain areas are the home of many different hill peoples.

**ECONOMY AND RESOURCES**
Vietnam's huge standing army of 1.2 million (plus reserves of 3 million) remains a great drain on a desperately poor nation subsisting on agriculture: rice, cassava, maize, sweet

## CONFLICT IN INDO-CHINA

Vietnamese conflict dates back at least to 1939, when the Viet Minh coalition of nationalists, including Communists, began agitating for independence from France; by 1945, with experience in anti-Japanese resistance behind them, they would not accept a quiet return to colonial administration after the Japanese collapse. Proclaiming the Democratic Republic of Vietnam, within months they were fighting French troops sent from Europe. Gradually, the Viet Minh, increasingly dominated by a well-organized Communist leadership under Ho Chi Minh, began to overwhelm the French. The US, alarmed by the Viet Minh's Communism, provided weaponry and logistical support, but Presidents Truman and Eisenhower both refused to allow American military aid. The climax came in May 1954, when a besieged French army surrendered at Dien Bien Phu. At a subsequent peace conference at Geneva, the French abandoned their colony. The country was partitioned between a Communist north, its capital in Hanoi, and a non-Communist south, administered from Saigon. The Geneva accord assumed Vietnamese elections would follow, and included an explicit proviso: the division was 'provisional, and should not in any way be interpreted as constituting a political or territorial boundary'.

Still anxious to avoid military engagement, the US poured aid into the South, the supposedly Democratic Republic of Vietnam. In fact, as US intelligence reports repeatedly explained to the White House, the republic was far from democratic, and its ruling élite was quite incapable of running the country, far less inspiring its people's loyalty; most of them would vote Communist if the elections were ever held. The elections were postponed, on the grounds that Communist violence would prevent a fair outcome – probably true, but giving Hanoi justification for a guerrilla campaign in the South, spearheaded by the Viet Cong, heirs to the Viet Minh tradition.

The newly elected President Kennedy decided to make a stand against Communism in Vietnam, despite the cautious counsel of his most experienced diplomats. American aid was backed up by military advisers, then combat units. The Viet Cong continued to make headway. After Kennedy's assassination in 1963, President Johnson increased the military commitment. US aircraft blasted Vietnam with more explosives than had been used in all of World War II; American casualties began to rise – more than 50,000 would die – and with them the tide of anti-war sentiment back home. By 1968, Johnson was convinced that the war could not be won; he stood down from power. Under his successor, Richard Nixon, the war continued, drawing neighbouring Cambodia into the cauldron. Yet real military progress remained as elusive as ever.

Finally, in 1972, a peace treaty was signed. The Americans withdrew; in 1975 North Vietnamese troops rolled across the 'provisional' border, and the country was reunited. To delay a Communist victory by less than 20 years, the Americans had paid a high price in prestige abroad and political discord at home. The Vietnamese had paid vastly higher in lives. And although Vietnam triumphed in a subsequent 1979 war against its former Chinese allies, political repression and economic disaster caused its people to risk their lives by the thousand in seaborne escapes – the refugee 'Boat People' – during the 1980s.

potatoes and the world's largest population of ducks. Despite the industries of the north, based on natural resources, the economy needs to diversify along the pattern of the 'sunrise' countries of eastern Asia.

## HISTORY AND POLITICS

Vietnam already had a long and turbulent history before the French, following decades of missionary involvement and a military campaign lasting 25 years, made it a French protectorate in 1883, later joined by Laos and Cambodia in the French Indo-Chinese Union. Freedom movements starting early in the 20th century made little headway until the end of World War II, when Communist-led guerrillas under Ho Chi Minh, having fought the Japanese occupation, declared Vietnam once again united and free. There followed a long war against the French (1946–54), which resulted in a Communist-dominated north centred on Hanoi and non-Communist south, divided at the 17th parallel of latitude. A second and more ferocious conflict between the north and south, involving heavy deployment of US troops – the 'Vietnam War' – began in the early 1960s and engulfed the whole region before the ceasefire in 1973. In 1975, after a relatively brief campaign between north and south, Vietnam was united under a Communist government. Vietnamese forces then invaded Cambodia in 1978 and were involved in a border war with China in 1979.

Such a recent history left Vietnam exhausted, 2 million of its people died in the American war alone and the countryside was devastated; the problems facing the reunified nation's Communist government in 1976 were enormous. Doctrinaire policies and further aggravation of the Western powers in Cambodia did not help its economic and political isolation, and in 1978 there started the sad saga of the 'Boat People' – peasants fleeing hardship and perhaps persecution in Vietnam to find a new life in Hong Kong and elsewhere; after being put into camps, many were forcibly repatriated years later.

The Hanoi regime softened its position in many ways from the late 1980s, efforts being made to establish diplomatic and trading ties with important international clients and aid donors, Soviet assistance having dwindled following the break-up of the USSR. In the 1990s Vietnam began to introduce reforms; to this end, a new constitution was adopted in June 1992 which reaffirmed Communist Party rule but also formalized free market reforms, including encouragement for foreign investment and some form of private enterprise. [*Map page 26*] ■

**AREA** 331,689 sq km [128,065 sq mls]
**POPULATION** 72,931,000
**CAPITAL (POPULATION)** Hanoi (3,056,000)
**GOVERNMENT** Socialist republic
**ETHNIC GROUPS** Vietnamese 87%, Tho (Tay), Chinese (Hoa), Tai, Khmer, Muong, Nung
**LANGUAGES** Vietnamese (official)
**RELIGIONS** Buddhism 55%, Christianity (Roman Catholic 7%)
**CURRENCY** Dong = 10 hao or 100 xu

# VIRGIN IS, BRITISH

**M**ost northerly of the Lesser Antilles, they comprise four notable low-lying islands and 36 islets and cays. The largest island, Tortola, contains over three-quarters of the total population of 18,000, a third of whom live in the capital Road Town.

Though an increasing rival to the Caymans and the Turks and Caicos in terms of offshore banking, tourism remains the main source of income, the 320,000 visitors produce 75% of the economic activity. Agriculture is limited by the low rainfall and poor soils and most food has to be imported. Rum is the chief export.

Like their larger American neighbours, the British Virgin Islands were 'discovered' by Columbus in 1493. Dutch from 1648 but British since 1666, they are now a British dependency enjoying (since 1977) a strong measure of self-government. [*Map page 30*] ■

**AREA** 153 sq km [59 sq mls]
**POPULATION** 18,000
**CAPITAL (POPULATION)** Road Town (6,330)
**GOVERNMENT** British dependent territory
**ETHNIC GROUPS** African American 90%
**LANGUAGES** English
**RELIGIONS** Christianity (Protestant 86%)
**CURRENCY** US currency

# VIRGIN IS, US

**T**he US Virgin Islands were first Spanish, then Danish and then, for a sum of US$25 million, American from 1917 – Washington wishing to protect the approaches to the Panama Canal. As an 'unicorporated territory', the residents have been US citizens since 1927. The 68 islands (dominated by the three largest – St Thomas, St Croix and St John) host a population of 104,000, most of them split between St Croix and St Thomas, home of the capital Charlotte Amalie. Tourism is the main industry, notably cruise ships and day-trippers from the US. The islands have the highest density of hotels and 'condominiums' in the Caribbean. [*Map page 30*] ■

---

**AREA** 340 sq km [130 sq mls]
**POPULATION** 104,000
**CAPITAL (POPULATION)** Charlotte Amalie (12,330)
**GOVERNMENT** US territory
**ETHNIC GROUPS** Black 80%, White 15%
**LANGUAGES** English, Spanish, Creole
**RELIGIONS** Christianity (Baptist 42%)
**CURRENCY** US currency

---

# WALLIS & FUTUNA IS

---

The smallest and poorest of France's three Pacific overseas territories, the Wallis and Futuna Islands comprise three main islands and numerous islets. Futuna and uninhabited Alofi, main constituents of the Hoorn group, are mountainous; the much larger Uvea, the chief island of the Wallis group, is hilly with coral reefs. Uvea contains 60% of the population, 850 of them in the capital of Mata-Utu.

French aid remains crucial to an economy based mainly on tropical subsistence agriculture; the main crops being cassava, copra, yams and bananas.

In a 1959 referendum the Polynesian islanders voted overwhelmingly in favour of change from a dependency to an overseas territory ■

---

**AREA** 200 sq km [77 sq mls]
**POPULATION** 19,000
**CAPITAL (POPULATION)** Mata-Utu (850)
**GOVERNMENT** French overseas territory
**ETHNIC GROUPS** Polynesian
**LANGUAGES** French, Wallisian, Futunian
**RELIGIONS** Christianity
**CURRENCY** CFP franc =100 centimes

---

# WESTERN SAMOA

---

Western Samoa comprises two large islands, seven small islands (two of which, Apolima and Manono, are inhabited) and a number of islets. The main islands of Upolu and Savai'i both have a central mountainous region, heavily forested and divided by fast-flowing rivers, surrounded by narrow coastal lowlands and coral reefs. Upolu, the most fertile island, contains two-thirds of the population. The climate is tropical and hurricanes are liable to occur from time to time.

### ECONOMY AND RESOURCES
The traditional lifestyle still thrives, with over 60% of the workforce engaged in agriculture, chiefly tropical fruits and vegetables, and in fishing. The main exports are coconut oil, taro and cocoa, with New Zealand the main trading partner. Many of the 38,000 tourists a year visit the home of Robert Louis Stevenson – now the official residence of King Malietoa Tanumafili II.

### HISTORY AND POLITICS
The cradle of Polynesian civilization, Western Samoa first gained independence in 1889, but ten years later became a German protectorate. Administered by New Zealand from 1920, the island achieved independence as a parliamentary monarchy in 1962, following a plebiscite. New Zealand handles relations with governments and organizations outside the Pacific islands zone. The first elections using universal suffrage were held in 1991. [*Map page 2*] ■

---

**AREA** 2,840 sq km [1,097 sq mls]
**POPULATION** 169,000
**CAPITAL (POPULATION)** Apia (32,860)
**GOVERNMENT** Constitutional monarchy
**ETHNIC GROUPS** Samoan, mixed European and Polynesian
**LANGUAGES** Polynesian, English
**RELIGIONS** Christianity
**CURRENCY** Tala = 100 sene

# YEMEN

The Republic of Yemen faces the Red Sea and the Gulf of Aden in the south-western corner of the Arabian peninsula. Behind the narrow coastal plain along the Red Sea, the land rises to a mountain region called High Yemen. Beyond the mountains, is the Rub 'al Khali Desert. There are other mountains along the Gulf of Aden, while to the east lies a fertile valley called the Hadramawt.

The climate in Sana is moderated by the altitude of more than 2,000 m [6,000 ft] – temperatures are much lower than in Aden, which is at sea level. In August, south-west monsoon winds bring thunderstorms, but most of Yemen has a desert climate.

## ECONOMY AND RESOURCES
The production of oil, first discovered in 1984, was little affected by either the Gulf War or the civil war of 1994, yet in spite of this income Yemen remains one of the poorest countries in the world. Subsistence agriculture is the chief occupation with sorghum, millet and sesame being the main crops. Exports include cotton, coffee and animal hides.

## HISTORY AND POLITICS
The optimism that greeted unification of the two Yemeni countries – the Yemen Arab Republic (or North Yemen) and the People's Democratic Republic of Yemen (or South Yemen) – in May 1990 proved short-lived; support for Iraq in the Gulf War, publicized by a vote on the UN Security Council, wrought swift revenge from Iraq's Arab enemies on the ending of hostilities, with Kuwait and Saudi Arabia expelling vast numbers of Yemeni workers. This not only removed the main source of earnings for a homeland already struggling with a weak economy, but it also jeopardized hopes of much-needed foreign aid from rich Gulf nations and the West. Saudi Arabia alone forced the repatriation of some 800,000 immigrants.

The process of marrying the disparate needs of a traditional state (an independent kingdom since 1918) and the failed Marxist regime based in the South Yemen capital of Aden (formerly a vital British staging post) has proved difficult. Though a good deal smaller than the South, the North provided over 65% of the population. In May 1994 civil war erupted between the north and south, with President Saleh (a northerner) attempting to remove the vice-president (a southerner). The war ended in July 1994 following the capture of Aden by Northern forces. [*Map page 32*] ◼

AREA 527,970 sq km [203,849 sq mls]
POPULATION 13,873,000
CAPITAL (POPULATION) Sana (427,000)
GOVERNMENT Multiparty republic
ETHNIC GROUPS Arabs 96%, Somali 1%
LANGUAGES Arabic (official)
RELIGIONS Islam
CURRENCY North–Yemeni riyal = 100 fils; South–Yemeni dinar = 1,000 fils (in use during transition period)

# YUGOSLAVIA

The Federal Republic of Yugoslavia consists of Serbia and Montenegro, two of the six republics which made up the country of Yugoslavia until it broke up in 1991 and 1992. Behind the short coast along the Adriatic Sea lies a mountainous region, including the Dinaric Alps and part of the Balkan Mountains. The Pannonian Plains make up northern Yugoslavia. This fertile region is drained by the River Danube and its tributaries; the river enters neighbouring Romania through a scenic gorge called the 'Iron Gate'.

The coastal regions experience a Mediterranean climate, but the interior highlands have bitterly cold winters and cool summers. Belgrade, in the north, has hot summers and cold winters. Summer is the wettest season, but there is also plenty of sunshine.

Forests of beech, hornbeam and oak, together with firs and pines at higher levels, cover about a quarter of the country and farmland and pasture cover more than half.

## ECONOMY AND RESOURCES

The main industries are steel, textiles, food processing and wood products. They are mostly located around Belgrade, the capital. Agriculture remains an important activity, major crops include maize, wheat, tobacco and sugar beet, while many farmers rear cattle, pigs and sheep. Since 1991 the economy has been very badly affected by civil wars and UN-imposed trade sanctions.

## HISTORY AND POLITICS

By 1992 Yugoslavia was an almost figmentary state, the discredited and politically impotent rump of the southern Slav union created under Allied pressure after World War I. Known from 1918 as the State of the Serbs, Croats and Slovenes, and from 1929 as Yugoslavia ('land of the south Slavs'), the unity of the state was always under constant threat from nationalist and ethnic tensions. The most serious friction was between the Serbs, with around 35% of the population the largest single group, and the neighbouring Croats with 20%; but Muslims, Slovenes, Macedonians, Montenegrins, Albanians and Hungarians also chafed against each other. Potential flashpoints existed not only where sections of the Yugoslav patchwork met, but within each patch itself.

In the interwar period the country was virtually a 'Greater Serbia', and after Hitler invaded in 1941 Yugoslavs fought both the Germans and each other. The Communist-led Partisans of 'Tito' (Josip Broz, a Croat) emerged victorious in 1945, re-forming Yugoslavia as a republic on the Soviet model. The postwar Tito dictatorship kept antagonisms out of sight, but in 1990, a decade after his death, the first free elections since the war saw nationalist victories in four out of the six republics that made up the federation.

The formal secession of Slovenia and Croatia in June 1991 began an irreversible process of disintegration. Slovenia, the most ethnically homogeneous of Yugoslavia's component republics, made the transition almost bloodlessly; but the Serbian-dominated federal army launched a brutal campaign against the Croats, whose territory included a large and vociferous Serbian minority. The most destructive conflict in Europe since 1945 continued until January 1992, when the cease-fire finally held. The fighting then moved to Bosnia-Herzegovina, declared independent in 1992 and at once the theatre of a multilateral civil war involving Serbs, Croats and ethnic Bosnian Muslims.

Expelled from the United Nations in 1992, 'Yugoslavia' thereafter included only Montenegro and Serbia, Serbia's President Slobodan Milosevic, bolstered by his people's military successes in Croatia and Bosnia, controlled most remaining federal resources and was frequently at loggerheads with an impotent federal premier.

However, Serbia had problems of its own: international sanctions struck at an already war-ravaged economy, while in its supposedly autonomous Kosovo region in the south-east, many Albanian-speaking people favour self-government or even unification with Albania. [*Map page 17*] ■

AREA 102,173 sq km [39,449 sq mls]
POPULATION 10,763,000
CAPITAL (POPULATION) Belgrade (1,137,000)
GOVERNMENT Federal republic
ETHNIC GROUPS Serb 62%, Albanian 17%, Montenegrin 5%, Hungarian, Muslim, Croat
LANGUAGES Serbo-Croatian (official)
RELIGIONS Christianity (mainly Serbian Orthodox, with Roman Catholic and Protestant minorities), Islam
CURRENCY Yugoslav new dinar = 100 paras

# ZAÏRE

The Republic of Zaïre is the world's 12th largest country. Much of the country lies within the drainage basin of the huge River Zaïre, which was formerly called the River Congo. Mountains rise in the south and east where Zaïre's borders run through lakes Tanganyika, Kivu, Edward and Mobutu Sese

Seko (recently renamed Lake Albert). These lakes all lie on the floor of an arm of the Great African Rift Valley.

The Equator passes through northern Zaïre. The equatorial region has high temperatures and high rainfall throughout the year, though in the subtropical south, where Lubumbashi is situated, there is a marked wet and dry season. Dense rainforests grow in northern Zaïre, but, to the south, the forests merge into savanna.

## ECONOMY AND RESOURCES

In colonial days, palm and rubber plantations were developed in the equatorial Congo Basin (the world's second largest river drainage system), with mining on the Congo-Zambezi watershed and coffee-growing on the Congo-Nile watershed in the north-east. The Congo (Zaïre) River was developed as a major artery, its rapids and falls by-passed by railways – including the Boyoma (Stanley) railway, the world's most voluminous, and an important railway built from the river port of Kinshasa to the coastal port of Matadi.

Minerals from the 'Copperbelt' in the far south-eastern province of Shaba (formerly Katanga), and refined on the spot, provide much of Zaïre's export income, though shortages of skilled workers and spare parts, gross misgovernment, illegal trade, and dislocation of railway links through Angola, Zimbabwe and Mozambique because of war have all affected revenues.

Most outstanding of many minerals are copper and cobalt, with copper accounting for more than half the country's export earnings, but manganese, tin, gold and diamonds are also important. 'Strategic minerals', including cadmium, also emanate from Shaba. Industry was already substantial at independence, and the massive hydroelectric developments at Inga, below Kinshasa, which supplies power to the mining town of Kolwezi in Shaba, some 1,725 km [1,800 mls] to the south-east, should provide for further expansion under new government policies.

With its massive mineral reserves Zaïre should be among the wealthiest of African nations, but it remains a low-income nation and well inside the world's bottom 20 according to World Bank figures. While transport and communications are difficult in a huge country still dominated by dense rainforest, the reasons for Zaïre's plight are almost wholly man-made.

## HISTORY AND POLITICS

Formerly made up of several African kingdoms, more recently a Belgian colony, Zaïre and her peoples suffered successively from the slave trade and then the brutal methods and corruption of the Congo Free State (1884–1908), the personal possession of King Leopold II, before Belgium assumed administration until independence was granted in 1960. The country's huge size and small population stretched Belgium's modest resources.

Belgium left the country politically unprepared for its sudden withdrawal, and within days of independence the army mutinied and the richest province, Shaba (Katanga), tried to secede. Then called the Congo, the country invited the UN to intervene, but the appallingly violent civil war lasted three years. In 1965 General Mobutu seized control in a period of sustained confusion and remained in power into the 1990s, declaring a one-party state in 1967 and renaming the nation Zaïre in 1971 as part of a wide-ranging Africanization policy that also brought conflict with the Christian churches.

Mobutu's long dictatorship was a catalogue of repression, inefficiency and corruption in government and unrest, rebellion and poverty among the people, with impenetrably inconsistent policies wreaking havoc in the economy even during the various mineral booms of the 1970s and 1980s, and confused by alternating periods of nationalization and privatization. His reign was one of orchestrated chaos.

On the whole, he was supported by the West, notably France, Belgium and the USA, who valued his strategic minerals and his support to the UNITA rebels in Angola and wanted Zaïre outside the Soviet sphere of influence. But with the end of the Cold War that support evaporated: indeed, the US soon pushed hard for reform. This, combined with increasing protests, finally forced Mobutu in 1990 to concede limited multiparty elections for the summer of 1991. But the new elected leaders faced complete chaos in Kinshasa as thousands rioted against inflation spiralling towards 2,000% a year. French and Belgian troops were sent in to restore order and evacuate European nationals (many of whom had done very well from the regime), while Mobutu – who, according to the US State Department, enjoyed a personal wealth of about $5 billion, around the same figure as the nation's debts – tried desperately to cling to power. The signs were that Zaïre would soon become one of the alarming flashpoints of Africa again. [*Map page 33*] ■

**AREA** 2,344,885 sq km [905,365 sq mls]
**POPULATION** 42,552,000
**CAPITAL (POPULATION)** Kinshasa (3,804,000)
**GOVERNMENT** Single-party republic
**ETHNIC GROUPS** Luba 18%, Kongo 16%, Mongo 14%, Rwanda 10%, Azandi 6%, Bangi and Ngale 6%, Rundi 4%, Teke, Boa, Chokwe, Lugbara, Banda
**LANGUAGES** French (official)
**RELIGIONS** Christianity (Roman Catholic 48%, Protestant 29%, indigenous Christian churches 17%), traditional beliefs 3%, Islam 1%
**CURRENCY** Zaïre = 100 makuta

# ZAMBIA

A vast expanse of high plateaux in the interior of south-central Africa, most of Zambia (formerly Northern Rhodesia) is drained by the Zambezi and two of its major tributaries, the Kafue and the Luangwa. The latter and the central section of the Zambezi occupy a low-lying rift valley bounded by rugged escarpments. Lake Kariba, formed by damming in 1961 and the second largest artificial lake in Africa, occupies part of the floor of this valley. Like the hydroelectric power it generates, the lake is shared with Zimbabwe, though power from the Kafue River now supplements supplies from Kariba. The magnificent Victoria Falls are similarly shared between the two countries. Much of northern Zambia is drained to the Atlantic Ocean by headwaters of the River Zaïre, including the Chambeshi, which loses itself within the vast swamps of the Bangweulu Depression.

## ECONOMY AND RESOURCES

Zambia is one of the world's largest producers of copper, but despite efforts to diversify, the economy remains stubbornly dependent (95% of export earnings in 1989) on this one mineral. The Copperbelt, centred on Kitwe, is the dominant urban region while the capital, Lusaka, provides the other major growth pole. Rural-urban migration has increased markedly since independence in 1964 – Zambia has 'black' southern Africa's highest proportion of town-dwellers – but work is scarce.

Commercial farming, concentrated in central regions astride the railway, and mostly maize, frequently fails to meet the needs of the growing urban population, but as a landlocked country heavily dependent on international trade, Zambia relies on its neighbours for access to ports via Zimbabwe, Mozambique and South Africa. Alternatives, notably a railway, highway and oil pipeline to Dar es Salaam, have been developed, but Zambia continues to have serious transport problems compounded by lack of finances.

## HISTORY AND POLITICS

European contact with Zambia began in the 19th century, when the explorer David Livingstone crossed the River Zambezi. In the 1890s, the British South Africa Company, set up by Cecil Rhodes (1853–1902), the British financier and statesman, made treaties with local chiefs and gradually took over the area. In 1911, the Company named the area Northern Rhodesia. In 1924, Britain took over the government of the country.

In 1953, Britain formed a federation of Northern Rhodesia, Southern Rhodesia (now Zimbabwe) and Nyasaland (now Malawi). But local Africans opposed this step, because they believed that it concentrated power in the hands of the European minority. The federation was dissolved just ten years later in 1963 and Northern Rhodesia became independent as Zambia in 1964.

The leading opponent of British rule, Kenneth Kaunda, became president in 1964. His government enjoyed reasonable income until the copper crash of the mid-1970s, but his collectivist policies failed to diversify the economy (before or after) and neglected agriculture. In 1972, he declared the United Nationalist Independence Party (UNIP) the only legal party, and it was nearly 20 years before democracy returned. In the 1991 elections (conceded by Kaunda after intense pressure in 1990), he was trounced by union leader Frederick Chiluba of the Movement for Multiparty Democracy (MMD) – Kaunda's first challenger in 27 years of post-colonial rule. Chiluba inherited a foreign debt of $4.6 billion – one of the world's biggest per capita figures. [*Map page 33*] ■

AREA 752,614 sq km [290,586 sq mls]
POPULATION 9,196.000
CAPITAL (POPULATION) Lusaka (982,000)
GOVERNMENT Multiparty republic
ETHNIC GROUPS Bemba 34%, Tonga 16%, Malawi 14%, Lozi 9%
LANGUAGES English (official)
RELIGIONS Christianity (Protestant 34%, Roman Catholic 26%, African Christians 8%), traditional beliefs 27%
CURRENCY Kwacha = 100 ngwee

# ZIMBABWE

T he Republic of Zimbabwe is a landlocked country in southern Africa. Most of the country lies on a high plateau between the Zambezi and Limpopo rivers between 900 m and 1,500 m [2,950 ft to 4,920 ft] above sea level. The main land feature is the High Veld, a ridge crossing Zimbabwe from north-east to south-west. Bordering the High Veld is the Middle Veld, the country's largest region. Below 900 m [2,950 ft] is the Low Veld. The highest land is in the east near the Mozambique border.

In summer, between October and March, the weather is hot and wet, but in winter the daily temperatures vary greatly. Frosts have been recorded between June and August. The climate also varies according to the altitude – the Low Veld is much warmer and drier than the High Veld.

## ECONOMY AND RESOURCES
Zimbabwe's relatively strong economy – founded on gold and tobacco but now far more diverse – evolved its virtual self-sufficiency during the days of international sanctions against Smith's white minority regime. After 1980 there was a surge in most sectors, with successful agrarian policies enabling the nation to supply less endowed well-off neighbours with food in good years and the exploitation of the country's rich and varied mineral resources. However, a fast-growing population will exert pressure on both land and resources of all kinds in the 1990s. In 1992, the country suffered a terrible drought and had to appeal for foreign aid.

## HISTORY AND POLITICS
Formerly Rhodesia (and Southern Rhodesia before 1965), Zimbabwe was nurtured by Britain as a 'white man's country'. When Ian Smith declared UDI in 1965, there were some 280,000 Europeans there. Guerrilla action against the Smith regime soon escalated into a full-scale civil war, eventually forcing a move to black majority rule in 1980. The rift that followed independence, between Robert Mugabe's ruling ZANU and Joshua Nkomo's ZAPU, was healed in 1989 when they finally merged after nearly three decades and Mugabe renounced his shallow Marxist-Leninist ideology. In 1990 the state of emergency that had lasted since 1965 was finally allowed to lapse – three months after Mugabe had secured a landslide election victory. [*Map page 33*] ■

AREA 390,579 sq km [150,873 sq mls]
POPULATION 11,002,000
CAPITAL (POPULATION) Harare (1,189,000)
GOVERNMENT Multiparty republic
ETHNIC GROUPS Shona 71%, Ndebele 16%, other Bantu-speaking Africans 11%, Europeans 2%
LANGUAGES English (official)
RELIGIONS Christianity 45%, traditional beliefs 40%
CURRENCY Zimbabwe dollar = 100 cents

# WORLD TOWNS & CITIES

**Aachen** (Aix-la-Chapelle) Town in western Germany, in North Rhine-Westphalia. Ancient regional centre near border with Netherlands and Belgium, with noted cathedral; place of coronation for Holy Roman Emperors until 1531. In coal mining area; textiles, electronic engineering and food industries. [50° 47'N  6° 4'E]

**Abéché** Town in east-central Chad; capital of Ouaddaï Prefecture. On main road to Sudan. Old market centre for desert nomad caravans. Groundnuts important. [13° 50'N  20° 35'E]

**Aberdeen** Capital of Grampian region, north-east Scotland, between mouths of rivers Don and Dee. Important commercial centre, especially for North Sea oil industry. Centre of Scottish fishing industry. Textiles, paper manufacture. University. Resort. [57° 9N  2° 6'W]

**Abidjan** Former capital and chief port of Ivory Coast, on lowland side of lagoon. Vridi Canal cuts through sand bar; deep-water harbour built 1951. Exports cocoa, coffee, bananas, pineapples. Processes agricultural and forest products; textiles, car assembly; fish canneries. [5° 26'N  3° 58'W]

**Abu Dhabi** Capital of Abu Dhabi and federal capital of the United Arab Emirates. Sited on island in Arabian Gulf, linked to mainland by Maqta Bridge. Modern city, large port; oil related industries. [24° 28'N  54° 22'E]

**Abuja** Official capital of Nigeria, south of original town of this name which is now called Sulaija. Replaced Lagos as the federal capital and seat of government in December 1991. [9° 16'N  7° 2'E]

**Accra** City and port, capital of Ghana, on Gulf of Guinea. Commercial and route centre near narrowest part of coastal plain. Light industry. Focus of air routes. Exports cocoa, manganese, gold. [5° 35'N  0° 6'W]

**Ad Dammam** Main oil port of Saudi Arabia, on the Arabian Gulf. End of railway from Riyadh. Cement plant. [26° 25'N  50° 6'E]

**Adapazari** Town in north-west Turkey, on the River Sakarya. Railway junction; agricultural and trade centre. Important silk and linen industries. [40° 48'N  30° 25'E.]

**Addis Ababa** City and capital of Ethiopia. Rich agricultural area. Terminus of railway line from Djibouti. Large market. Altitude c. 2,400 m [8,000 ft]. [9° 2'N  38° 42'E]

**Adelaide** Seaport, capital of South Australia. The site was selected by Colonel William Light, the first Surveyor-General of South Australia. The vineyards of the Barossa Valley are nearby. [34° 52'N 138° 30'E]

**Aden** Seaport in southern Yemen, on Gulf of Aden. Formerly the national legislative capital of the People's Democratic Republic of Yemen (South Yemen), prior to unification with the Yemen Arab Republic (North Yemen) in 1990. Linked to Mediterranean by Red Sea and Suez Canal. Imports crude oil, foodstuffs; exports petroleum products, fuel oils, fish. Distribution trade for neighbouring territories: cotton, grain, coffee, hides, consumer goods. [12° 45'N 45° 0'E]

**Agadez** Town in central Niger, south of Aïr Massif, on the route from Algiers to Kano. Old caravan centre. Market for nomads; leather and wool goods. Uranium deposits to north at Anlit. [16° 58'N 7° 59'E]

**Agadir** Town on north-west (Atlantic) coast of Morocco. Resort, with fine beaches, rebuilt south of the older city destroyed by an earthquake in 1960. [30° 28'N 9° 55'W]

**Agra** City in south-west Uttar Pradesh state, northern India, on the River Yamuna. Former seat of the Moghul empire, in the 16th–17th centuries. Site of the Taj Mahal. Important wheat market. Famous for carpets, also gold and silver embroidery. [27° 17'N 77° 58'E]

**Ahmadabad** City in Gujarat state, western India, on the River Sabarmati. Founded in 1411 by Ahmed Shah. Judicial capital of state; state capital Gandhinagar to north-east. Textiles, especially fine cotton; handicrafts, especially gold and silver ware. Oilfields nearby. Fine mosque. [23° 0'N 72° 40'E]

**Ahvaz** Commercial town, railway junction and port of western Iran, 129 km [80 mls] north-east of Abadan. The modern town is built over an ancient city. Oil-based industries predominate. [31° 20'N 48° 40'E]

**Ajaccio** Capital of the island of Corsica, to south-east of France. Resort, fishing port and commercial centre. The birthplace of Napoleon. [41° 55'N 8° 40'E]

**Ajmer** Ancient walled town in Rajasthan state, north-west India, on main road and railway to Delhi. Place of Muslim pilgrimage. 12th-century artificial lake. Railway workshops. [26° 28'N 74° 37'E]

**Aksum** Town in north-west Ethiopia, on low-lying hills overlooking the plain. End of desert caravan route. Capital of ancient Axumite empire and legendary site of Ark of Covenant. [14° 5'N 38° 40'E]

**Aktyubinsk** (Aqtöbe) Capital of Aktyubinsk Oblast in north-west Kazakhstan. Chemical, food and metallurgical industries, especially nickel. [50° 17'N 57° 10'E]

**Akureyri** Town in north Iceland at head of Eyjafjördhur, longest fjord in Iceland. Fishing and shipping industries. Tourist centre, especially for winter sports. [65° 40'N 18° 6'W]

**Al Dhahran** Major port on The Gulf in east Saudi Arabia. Business centre adjacent to Dammam in extensive oil region; University of Petroleum and Minerals. [26° 10'N 50° 7'E]

**Al Hufuf** Oasis in the Najd, Saudi Arabia. Caravan route from Riyadh to the United Arab Emirates; great mosque and active market. [25° 20'N 49° 34'E]

**Al Manamah** Port and capital of Bahrain, at northern end of Bahrain Island. Centre for oil industry; boatbuilding, fishing. Modern city. [26° 12'N 50° 38'E]

**Albany** Port and capital of New York state, north-east USA, at junction of Hudson and Mohawk rivers. Centre of large manufacturing region; textiles, paper and printing, electrical engineering. [42° 39'N 73° 45'W]

**Albany** Port and regional centre in Western Australia. Site of first settlement in state in 1826. [35° 1'S 117° 58'E]

**Albi** Town in southern France. Capital of Tarn *département*. Focus of 12th–13th century

Albigensian heresy. Noted 13th–14th century brick cathedral. Traditional textile industry; glass and chemicals. [43° 56'N  2° 9'E]

**Ålesund**  Seaport in Norway on west coast. Has largest fishing harbour in Norway. Centre of cod and herring fisheries; base for Arctic sealers. [62° 28'N  6° 12'E]

**Alexandria**  City and major Mediterranean seaport of Egypt to west of Nile Delta. Founded 332 BC. Ancient seat of learning. 17th-century mosque. Resort with sandy beaches. [31° 0'N  30° 0'E]

**Algiers**  Capital of Algeria, on the Mediterranean coast. Major port of Barbary States until early 19th century. Fine harbour. Modern city built on hills with many suburbs. Tourist trade. [36° 42'N  3° 8'E]

**Alicante**  Town in south-east Spain. Capital of Alicante province. Commercial centre and port in rich agricultural area (vines, almonds, olives); aluminium, cement and salt industry. Resort. [38° 23'N  0° 30'W]

**Alice Springs**  Town in southern part of Northern Territory, Australia. Transport centre for cattle and minerals. On Stuart Highway north-south link, Darwin to Port Augusta; airport. Tourist centre. [23° 40'S  133° 50'E]

**Allahabad**  Town in southern Uttar Pradesh state, northern India, near confluence of Yamuna and Ganges rivers. Holy city for Hindus, on main routes from Delhi to Calcutta. [25° 25'N  81° 58'E]

**Alma-Ata** (Almaty)  Capital of Kazakhstan. Spacious modern town in scenic surroundings; miscellaneous industries. Academic and scientific centre. Famous for its apple orchards. [43° 15'N  76° 57'E]

**Almadén**  Town in south-central Spain, in Ciudad Real. Ancient centre of mercury mining area in Sierra Morena, with leading world production. [38° 49'N  4° 52'W]

**Altdorf**  Town in central Switzerland between the St Gotthard Pass and Lake Lucerne.

Capital of Uri Canton. Known for statue of William Tell. [46° 2'N  8° 6'E]

**Amiens**  Town in northern France, on River Somme. Capital of Somme *département*. Has a magnificent cathedral begun in 1220. Large textile, footwear and food processing industries. [49° 54'N  2° 16'E]

**Amman**  Capital of Jordan, 40 km [25 mls] north-east of the Dead Sea. Historic city. Exports building stone, phosphates and vegetables. [31° 57'N  35° 52'E]

**Amritsar**  Town in west Punjab state, in northern India. Founded in 1577. Centre of the Sikh religion. Golden Temple is covered in gilded copper. Woollen and silk industries and carpet manufacturing. [31° 35'N  74° 57'E]

**Amsterdam**  Port in north-west Netherlands, in Noord Holland. Historic, commercial and cultural centre, known for its concentric canals and diamond industries. Shipbuilding, marine engineering industries; also aircraft, food and printing. [52° 23'N  4° 54'E]

**Anchorage**  Port in Alaska, north-west USA, at head of Cook Inlet. Commercial centre and Alaska's largest town, virtually ice-free. Destroyed by an earthquake in 1964. Base for oil development. Offshore oil production. Salmon processing. [61° 13'N  149° 54'W]

**Ancona**  Seaport in eastern Italy, on a peninsula of the Adriatic Sea. Capital of The Marches. Commercial centre and fishing port; shipbuilding, textile industry, musical instruments manufactured. [43° 37'N  13° 30'E]

**Andijon**  Capital of Andijon Wiloyat, a region in eastern Uzbekistan. Engineering and food industries; cotton produced; oil and gas reserves to the east. [41° 10'N  72° 15'E]

**Angarsk**  Major new town in Siberia, Russia, east of Lake Baykal. Rapidly expanding town, with spacious, planned layout. Oil refining industry. [52° 30'N  104° 0'E]

**Angmagssalik**  Trading post and settlement on east coast of Greenland, 95 km [60 mls] south of the Arctic Circle, on Denmark Strait. US air base; important meteorological and radio station. [65° 40'N 37° 20'W]

**Angoulême** Town in west France. Capital of Charente *département*. Historic defensive centre. Large paper industry; brewing, agricultural engineering. [45° 39'N 0° 10'E]

**Ankara** Capital of Turkey, in central Turkey. Republic proclaimed here in 1923. Cultural and administrative centre. Mausoleum of Kemal Ataturk; also notable archaeological remains and museum. [39° 57'N 32° 54'E]

**Annapolis** Capital of Maryland, eastern USA. Centre of agricultural area on Chesapeake Bay. Oldest US State House (1772); site of Naval Academy. Vegetables, fish processing. [38° 59'N 76° 30'W]

**Annecy** Town in south-east France. Capital of Haute-Savoie *département*. Picturesque regional and tourist lakeside centre. Metal industries, especially ball bearings; traditional bell-founding. [45° 55'N 6° 8'E]

**Antalya** Seaport in southern Asiatic Turkey, on Mediterrranean. Founded 2nd century BC. St Paul sailed from here to Antioch on his first missionary journey. [36° 52'N 30° 45'E]

**Antananarivo** Capital of Madagascar in centre of highland area. Location of Queen's Palace, an ancient monument of the Merina kingdom. Cotton and paper mills, vehicle assembly, fertilizer plant. [18° 55'S 47° 31'E]

**Antigua** Town in south-central Guatemala. Site of former capital, destroyed by an earthquake in 1773. Coffee and sugar industries. [14° 34'N 90° 41'W]

**Antrim** Capital of Antrim District, eastern Northern Ireland. Market and linen manufacturing centre on north-east shore of Lough Neagh. [54° 43'N 6° 13'W]

**Antwerp** (Antwerpen) City and port in northern Belgium at head of Scheldt estuary. Capital of Antwerp province. Historic, commercial and cultural centre with noted

cathedral. Manufacturing industries; as well as non-ferrous metals, diamond processing, petrochemical, car assembly and shipbuilding industries. [51° 13'N 4° 25'E]

**Anuradhapura** Town in north-central Sri Lanka. On site of capital of ancient kingdom (founded *c.* 437 BC). Many ancient ruins. Pilgrimage centre to sacred Buddhist Bo Tree. Rice-growing area. [8° 22'N 80° 28'E]

**Anzio** Fishing port and resort in west-central Italy, in Lazio, on Mediterranean. Ancient city. Birthplace of Nero. Allied landing in 1944. [41° 28'N 12° 37'E]

**Aosta** Town in north-west Italy. Capital of Valle d'Aosta. Ancient regional and ecclesiastical centre with many Roman remains. Important steel industry and tourist centre. [45° 43'N 7° 20'E]

**Apia** Capital of Western Samoa, an island group in the Pacific Ocean. Chief port on the northern coast of the volcanic island of Upolu. [13° 50'S 171° 50'W]

**Appenzell** Town in north-east Switzerland. Capital of Inner Rhoden, half canton of Appenzell. Centre of dairying, with characteristic wooden houses. [47° 20'N 9° 25'E]

**Aracaju** Port and capital of Sergipe state, on the coast of Brazil between Recife and Salvador. Industry: sugar refining, cotton mills; exports sugar, cotton, hides, rice and coffee. [10° 55'S 37° 4'W.]

**Arad** Town in western Romania on River Mures. Industrial and commercial centre in agricultural area; products include spirits, machinery, tiles. [46° 10'N 21° 20'E]

**Arequipa** City of southern Peru. Built on site of ancient Inca city. Important commercial centre. Steel, nylon, plastics, soap. Tourist centre. [16° 20'S 71° 30'W]

**Arica** Seaport in desert region of north-central Chile. The port for La Serena. Market town; copper; winter station of Chilean army. [18° 32'S 70° 20'W]

**Arlon** Town in south-east Belgium, in the Ardennes. Capital of Arlon district, Luxembourg province. Roman town, with many remains. Food industries. [49° 42'N  5° 49'E]

**Armagh** Capital of County Armagh and Armagh District, in the south of Northern Ireland. Important ancient ecclesiastical centre and the site of the first church of St Patrick. [54° 22'N  6° 40'W]

**Arnhem** Town in eastern Netherlands at edge of Veluwe. Capital of Gelderland. Commercial and route centre, known for battle of 1944. Chemical, textile, tin-smelting and shipbuilding industries. [51° 58'N  5° 55'E]

**Arras** Town in northern France. Capital of Pas-de-Calais *département*. Market and manufacturing centre, famous for its tapestry. Industries include agricultural equipment and sugar processing. [50° 17'N  2° 46'E]

**Arusha** Town in north-east Tanzania. Railway terminus; on international road from Cairo to Cape Town. Agricultural products: coffee, wheat, sisal and sugar. Important textile industry. Starting point for safaris into National Parks. [3° 20'S  36° 40'E]

**Aschaffenburg** Town in central Germany on River Main in Bavaria. Regional centre with palace at foot of Spessart. Precision instruments industry. [49° 58'N  9° 8'E]

**Ashdod** Port and commercial centre in southern Israel with deep-water harbour. Ancient Philistine city. [31° 49'N  34° 35'E]

**Ashkhabad** (Ashgabat) Capital of Turkmenistan, near border with Iran. Rebuilt to withstand earthquakes since 1948 disaster. Silk, cotton and carpets.[38° 0'N  57° 50'E]

**Asmara** (Asmera) Capital of Eritrea. Ancient ruins. Textiles. Altitude 2,300 m [7,600 ft] above sea level. [15° 19'N  38° 55'E]

**Assisi** Town in north-central Italy, in Umbria. Walled town and place of pilgrimage associated with St Francis and St Clare. Tourist centre. [43° 4'N  12° 36'E]

**Astrakhan** Town in Russia, on Volga delta, inland from Caspian Sea. Major fishing port. [46° 25'N  48° 5'E]

**Asunción** Capital of Paraguay, situated on the east bank of the Paraguay River. Important transport centre; textiles, food products, footwear. [25° 0'S  57° 30'N]

**Aswân** Town in upper valley of River Nile in Egypt, near first cataract. Aga Khan mausoleum. Nearby Aswân Dam and the Aswân High Dam, opened in 1971, and forming Lake Nasser to south. [24° 4'N  32° 57'E]

**Ath Thawrah** New town in northern Syria, on the Euphrates River. Associated with Lake Assad, reservoir completed in 1970s for agricultural irrigation and hydroelectric power. [35° 50'N  38° 30'E]

**Athens** (Athínai) Capital of Greece and of department of Attica on Attica peninsula. Ancient centre of Greek civilization, with many antiquities, including the Acropolis (Parthenon, Propylaea, Erechtheion), the Olympieion, Hadrian's Arch, and many important museums. [37° 58'N  23° 46'E]

**Atlanta** Capital of the state of Georgia and largest city of south-east USA. Commercial, manufacturing and route centre, especially for air traffic. Important car- and aircraft-assembly industry; food production; printing and publishing. [33° 45'N  84° 23'W]

**Auckland** Town on Tamaki Isthmus, North Island, New Zealand. Original capital 1840–52. Many extinct volcanoes in vicinity. Main industrial and commercial area of New Zealand. Extensive suburbs. Intensive dairy and farming hinterland. [36° 52'S  174° 46'E]

**Augsburg** Town in southern Germany, in Bavaria. Ancient trading centre, formerly important for banking. Known for the Fuggerei, an old city quarter, established in 1519. Large textile industry; also electrical engineering. [48° 21'N  10° 54'E]

**Aurangabad** Town in Maharashtra state, west-central India, on Deccan plateau.

Administrative centre. Caves nearby with sculptures. Centre for visiting Ellora and Ajanta cave temples; wall paintings at Ajanta. [19° 50'N  75° 23'E]

**Avignon** Town in south-east France on Rhône River. Capital of Vaucluse *département*. Papal residence in 14th century; famous for its bridge. Centre of wine producing area; canning; textile industry. [43° 57'N  4° 50'E]

**Ávila** Town in central Spain. Capital of Ávila province. Highest Spanish provincial capital at 1,128 m [3,700 ft]. Famous for 11th-century walls. Birthplace of St Teresa. Textile and food industries. [40° 39'N  4° 43'W]

**Ayacucho** Tourist centre in Andes, south-central Peru. Silver and lead mines nearby. Capital of Ayacucho province. Site of last great battle in the war of independence (1824) nearby. [13° 0'S  74° 0'W]

**Az Zarqa** (Zarca)  Second largest town in Jordan, north-east of Amman. Refining, tanning. Route centre. [32° 10'N  35° 37'E]

**Baalbek** Town in central Lebanon. It is near the site of the vast ruins of the ancient city of Heliopolis. Unique Phoenician, Roman, Greek and Arab remains. [34° 0'N  36° 12'E]

**Babylon** Extensive remains of ancient city in central Iraq, near Euphrates River, and the modern town of Al Hillah. Hanging Gardens of Babylon were an ancient wonder of the world. [32° 40'N  44° 30'E]

**Badajoz** Town in south-east Spain near Portuguese border. Capital of Badajoz province. Site of many battles. Fertilizer and textile industries. [38° 50'N  6° 59'W]

**Baden Baden** Town in south-western Germany, in Baden-Württemberg. International resort, spa and conference centre in wine producing area. [48° 45'N  8° 15'E]

**Baden** Town in north-central Switzerland in Aargau canton on Limmat River. Historic defensive centre and spa. Engineering, especially railway industry. [47° 28'N  8° 18'E]

**Badulla** Town in south-central Sri Lanka, in highland area. Important tea-growing region. Approached by railway through spectacular scenery. [7° 1'N  81° 7'E]

**Baghdad** Capital of Iraq, at the head of shallow-draft navigation on the Tigris River. Important transport centre with railway and airline systems; also textile industry and tobacco products. [33° 20'N  44° 30'E]

**Bahawalpur** Town in eastern Pakistan, on Sutlej River, crossed by fine railway bridge. Commercial and light industrial centre. Textiles manufactured. [29° 24'N  71° 40'E]

**Bahía Blanca** Naval port on the coast of central Argentina. Industries include oil refining, meat-packing, tanning and flour milling. Exports include hides, grain and wool. [38° 35'S  62° 13'W]

**Baku** Capital of Azerbaijan. Major port on Caspian Sea, notable for extensive oil industry. Founded in 8th century and rich in historic monuments. [40° 25'N  49° 45'E]

**Baltimore** Seaport in Maryland, eastern USA. Major commercial, industry and educational centre. Large steel, shipbuilding and food industries; aircraft parts, car assembly, chemicals. [39° 17'N  76° 37'W]

**Bamako** Capital of Mali, on River Niger in south-west near Guinea border. Founded by French in 1883. River port and administrative centre. Niger navigable south to Kouroussa. Dam for irrigation. [12° 34'N  7° 55'W]

**Bamian** Ancient city in north-east Afghanistan, in valley north of Koh-i-Baba mountain range. Ruins of great towers and cave dwellings. Two Buddhist figures (AD 630) nearby. [35° 0'N  67° 0'E]

**Bandar Seri Begawan** Capital of Brunei in north-west of Borneo, 20 km [12 mls] from mouth of Brunei River. Formerly Brunei Town. [4° 52'N  115° 0'E]

**Bandung** Indonesian city in west-central Java. Headquarters of several government departments. Produces aircraft, ammunition, quinine. Tourist centre. [6° 54'S 107° 36'E]

**Banff** Town in south-west Canada, in Alberta. Tourist centre for the Rocky Mountains and the large national and forest parks nearby. [51° 10'N 115° 34'W]

**Bangalore** Capital of Karnataka state, in southern India, on the Deccan plateau. Railway junction. Industry centre; machine tools; aircraft industry; electronics; porcelain; textiles. Tata Institute of Science. Kular goldfields to east. [12° 59'N 77° 40'E]

**Bangkok** Port and capital of Thailand, on the Chao Phraya River about 32 km [20 mls] above its mouth on Gulf of Thailand. Also serves Laos. Industries include textiles, building materials, motor and radio assembly. Exports include teak, rice. Famous floating market. [13° 45'N 100° 35'E]

**Bangui** Capital of the Central African Republic, on the River Ubangi at the head of navigation from Brazzaville. On a main north-south African route. Sawmills and textile mills; produces cotton. [4° 23'N 18° 35'E]

**Banjul** Port and capital of the Gambia. Situated on eastern tip of St Mary's Island on estuary of Gambia River. Founded in 1819 as military post to help stamp out slave trade. Exports groundnuts. [13° 28'N 16° 40'W]

**Barcelona** City in north-east Spain. Capital of Barcelona province and Catalonia region. Focus of Catalan separatism and culture. Seat of governemnt in Civil War 1936–9. Famous for its wide avenues, cathedral, palaces, 15th-century university. Leading Spanish seaport and commercial and manufacturing centre. Textile, transport equipment, paper and chemical industries. [41° 21'N 2° 10'E]

**Barisal** Town in Bangladesh, south of Dacca on the delta of the Ganges and Brahmaputra Rivers. Suffers from cyclones and tidal waves. Industries include boat-building and wood working; as well as the manufacture of bricks and soap. Exports rice, jute, oilseed and grain products. [22° 5'N 90° 20'E]

**Barranquilla** Port in northern Colombia, on Magdalena River. Accessible to ocean-going vessels. Industries include chemicals and pharmaceuticals; products include flour, rubber goods and footwear. [11° 0'N 74° 50'W]

**Basel** Town in north-west Switzerland on the border with France and Germany, comprising the half-canton of Basel Stadt. Historic commercial centre, noted for banking, and a port at the head of navigation on the Rhine. Large pharmaceutical industry; machinery; and food processing. [47° 35'N 7° 35'E]

**Basra** Port in south-west Iraq, 110 km [70 mls] from the Arabian Gulf on the Shatt al Arab Waterway. Exports dates, cereal, wool and oil. [30° 30'N 47° 50'E]

**Basse-Terre** Town and port, administrative capital of the French Overseas Department of Guadeloupe, Lesser Antilles in the West Indies. [16° 0'N 61° 44'W]

**Bassein** Port in lower Burma, 113 km [70 mls] from mouth of Bassein River, 151 km [94 mls] east of Rangoon. Exports rice and manufactures pottery. [16° 45'N 94° 30'E]

**Bastia** Largest town and port of Corsica, on east coast. Fishing, food and tobacco processing. Resort. [42° 40'N 9° 30'E]

**Bata** Main town and port of Mbini, mainland Equatorial Guinea, on Gulf of Guinea. Timber exports. [1° 57'N 9° 50'E]

**Bath** City in Avon, south-west England. Ancient spa with famous Roman baths and Pump Room (1795). Planned Georgian centre. Annual Festival. University (1966). Electrical engineering. [51° 22'N 2° 22'W]

**Baton Rouge** Capital of Louisiana, southern USA, on Mississippi River. Important river port. Commercial, industrial and route centre at northern end of 161 km [100 mls] petrochemical complex. Food processing; aluminium smelter. [30° 27'N 91° 1'W]

**Bayeux** Town in northern France, in Calvados *département*. Historic and regional centre, famous for tapestry depicting Norman conquest of England. [49° 17'N 0° 42'W]

**Béchar** Settlement in western Algeria, near the frontier with Morocco. The town is at the start of the important trans-Saharan route to the south. [31° 38'N 2° 18'W]

**Beijing** (Peking) Capital and municipality of north China. Contains historic walled city dating from Kublai Khan, and old imperial palace of Mings and Manchus, formerly 'Forbidden City', now museum and major tourist attraction. Red Square, scene of political meetings and demonstrations. Residential and educational development to west. Industry concentrated to east. [39° 55'N 116° 20'E]

**Beira** (Bayrut) Important river port in Mozambique. Terminus of rail links to Zimbabwe, Zambia and Malawi; handles trade for interior. Timber, rice, sugar and bananas. [19° 50'S 34° 52'E]

**Beirut** Port and capital of Lebanon, situated on a promontory. Engineering, food processing and textiles; several universities and colleges. Economy disrupted by sectarian war (1975–91). [33° 53'N 35° 31'E]

**Belém** Chief port of the River Amazon basin, on the River Para. Located south of the mouths of the Amazon, in northern Brazil. Exports include timber, nuts, rubber, rice and jute. [1° 20'S 48° 30'W]

**Belfast** Capital of Northern Ireland, on Belfast Lough at mouth of River Lagan. Major commercial and industrial centre in area of 16th- and 17th-century English and Scottish settlement. Shipbuilding, aircraft machinery, textile industries. [54° 35'N 5° 56'W]

**Belfort** Historic fortress town in eastern France. Capital of Belfort *département*. Important route centre between the Vosges and Jura mountains. Large engineering industries; textiles. [47° 38'N 6° 50'E]

**Belgrade** Capital of the former Yugoslavia (inside Serbia) and now the capital of what remains of Yugoslavia (namely Serbia and

Montenegro). River port at the confluence of the Danube and Sava rivers. Strategic site occupied by Romans, Huns, Byzantines, Turks, Hungarians and Serbians. Industrial, cultural and communications centre. Various industries. [44° 50'N 20° 37'E]

**Belize** City Town and port, former capital of Belize, on Caribbean coast. Exports sugar, bananas, citrus fruits, fish, forestry products. [17° 25'N 88° 0'W]

**Belmopan** Town, since 1970 the capital of Belize, in Central America, 80 km [50 mls] inland to west of Belize City, the former capital. [17° 13'N 88° 48'W]

**Belo Horizonte** City in east Brazil, 354 km [220 mls] north of Rio de Janeiro. Capital of Minas Gerais state. Centre of agricultural and mining area producing iron, manganese, cotton and cattle and iron and steel. Also diamond-cutting and chemical industries. [19° 55'S 43° 56'W]

**Benghazi** (Banghazi) Town in Cyrenaica province, on eastern part of Mediterranean coast of Libya. First settled by Greeks. Rapid population growth since Saharan oil discoveries. [32° 11'N 20° 3'E]

**Benin City** Town and administrative centre in southern Nigeria to west of Niger delta. Site of ancient city dating back to 10th century. River port of Sapele to south. Rubber and palm oil production. [6° 20'N 5° 31'E]

**Bergen** Seaport in south-west Norway. Former Hanseatic port. Birthplace of Grieg. Fishing, shipbuilding industry. Area of highest rainfall in Norway. [60° 23'N 5° 20'E]

**Berlin** City in and joint capital of Germany, formerly enclave in East Germany since 1945 with wall dividing East and West Berlin, until reunification between East and West Germany in 1990. Due to take over as capital in 2000. Major commercial and cultural centre. Large electrical and precision engineering industry; printing and publishing. [52° 32'N 13° 24'E]

**Bern** Capital of Switzerland and of Bern

canton. Picturesque and historic defensive centre in loop of Aare River. Known for its clock tower, bear pit and many museums. Textiles; chocolate; printing and publishing industry. Tourist centre. [46° 57'N  7° 28'E]

**Besançon** Town in eastern France at the foot of the Jura Mountains. Capital of Doubs *département*. Historic fortress. Centre of the French watch and clock industries. Also textiles and brewing. [47° 15'N  6° 2'E]

**Bethlehem** (Bayt Lahm) Town in the West Bank, formerly part of Jordan, under Israeli administration since 1967. Located 8 km [5 mls] south-south-west of Jerusalem. Reputed birthplace of Christ. [31° 43'N  35° 12'E]

**Bhadgaon** (Bhaktapur) Hindu religious town 13 km [8 mls] east of Kathmandu in Nepal. Many temples. [27° 41'N  85° 26'E]

**Bhopal** Town and capital of Madhya Pradesh state, central India. Situated on a small lake and enclosed by a wall. Site of the Palace of the Nawab. Large mosque. Location of major industrial disaster in 1984 in which *c.* 2,500 people died. [23° 20'N  77° 30'E]

**Bialystok** Town in north-eastern Poland. Industrial centre specializing in textiles; railway. Baroque town hall. [53° 10'N  23° 10'E]

**Birmingham** City, capital of West Midlands, west-central England. Important commercial, manufacturing and route centre with many canals. Major metal-working industry, arms, cars; chocolate (Bournville 'model' estate established 1879); traditional jewellery manufacturing. [52° 30'N  1° 55'W]

**Bishkek** Capital of Kyrgyzstan. Formerly known as Frunze. Long history; academic centre. Rapidly expanding, largely on planned 20th-century layout. [42° 54'N  74° 46'E]

**Bissau** Capital and port of Guinea-Bissau, on northern shore of River Geba. Once centre of slave trade. [11° 45'N  15° 45'W]

**Bizerta** Town and port on northern coast of Tunisia. Originally fortified Phoenician port,

former French naval base. Orchard area. Exports minerals and agricultural products. [37° 15'N  9° 50'E]

**Blackpool** Town in Lancashire, north-west England. Major seaside resort on western Fylde coast. Famed for tower and illuminations. [53° 48'N  3° 3'W]

**Bloemfontein** Capital of Orange Free State, South Africa. Seat of Appeal Court and administrative centre of South Africa. To the north-west are the rich gold-fields centred on Welkom. Centre of major maize producing area. [29° 6'S  26° 7'E]

**Blois** Town in central France on Loire River. Capital of Loir-et-Cher *département*. Has noted château. Centre of wine- and vegetable producing area. [47° 35'N  1° 20'E.]

**Bobo Dioulasso** Town in south-west Burkina Faso. Former capital (of Upper Volta), on railway from Ouagadougou to Abidjan, Ivory Coast. Road junction. Market centre for groundnuts, cotton and cattle. Some industry. [11° 8'N  4° 13'W.]

**Bogor** Town in west-central Java, Indonesia. Palace, former residence of the Governor-General. Rubber factory; textiles, footwear. In area producing tea, coffee, rice, sugar and rubber. Botanical gardens. [6° 34'S  106° 45'E]

**Bogotá** Capital of Colombia. Situated in basin of the Cordillera Oriental over 2,700 m [8,860 ft] above sea level. Tobacco, chemicals, food processing. [4° 34'N  74° 0'W]

**Bologna** Town in northern Italy. Commercial and route centre with oldest European university (established AD 425); trade fair. Railway engineering, agricultural machinery, food industries. [44° 30'N  11° 20'E]

**Bombay** Port and capital of Maharashtra state, western India. Portuguese colony founded on islands off coast of Arabian Sea. Ceded to British in 1661. Fine harbour; navy headquarters. Industrial centre, especially cotton mills, motor vehicles. Exports cotton. Famous for jewellery, wood-carving and lacquer work.

In May 1995, Hindu nationalists changed the name to Mumbai, but this has not been widely adopted. [18° 55'N 72° 50'E]

**Bonn** Joint capital of Germany (with Berlin until the year 2000, when Berlin will take over as the capital), in North Rhine-Westphalia, on west bank of River Rhine. Birthplace of Beethoven. Printing and publishing; furniture industry. [50° 43'N 7° 6'E]

**Bordeaux** Seaport in south-west France at head of Gironde estuary. Capital of Gironde *département*. Commercial centre of famous wine producing region, with large traditional wine trade. Industries include food processing, chemicals and aircraft engineering. Tourist centre. [44° 50'N 0° 36'W]

**Boston** Seaport and capital of Massachusetts, in north-eastern USA. Commercial and educational centre of New England. American Revolution began here. Important electrical engineering industries, especially electronics and transport equipment. Printing and publishing; important wool market; textiles; fishing. [42° 22'N 71° 4'W]

**Bouaké** City in central Ivory Coast. Market centre on plateau; forest to south, savanna to north. On railway from Abidjan to Burkina Faso. Light industry. [7° 40'N 5° 2'W]

**Boulogne-sur-Mer** Seaport in northern France, in Pas-de-Calais *département*. Leading French fishing port and cross-channel ferry port. [50° 42'N 1° 36'E]

**Brasília** Capital of Brazil, built for this purpose in 1960 on a tributary of the Tocantins River, in east-central Brazil. Modern architecture; main employment is in government service. [15° 47'S 47° 55'W]

**Bratislava** Town in Slovak Republic near Austrian and Hungarian borders. Dates back to 9th century; capital of Hungary 1541–1784. 13th-century Gothic cathedral, Church of the Franciscans, Parliament House; Slovak University. Significant as river port and railway centre, with trade in wine and grain and extensive industry. [48° 10'N 17° 17'E]

**Brazzaville** Capital of Congo, on north shore of Pool Malebo on Congo (Zaïre) River opposite the city of Kinshasa. Former capital of French Equatorial Africa. Rail/river transport. Light industry. [4° 09'S 15° 12'E]

**Bremen** Port in north west Germany at head of Weser estuary. Capital of Bremen Land and oldest German maritime city. Important raw materials trade. Important industries include steel, shipbuilding, food processing and aircraft engineering. [53° 4'N 8° 47'E]

**Brest** Capital of Brest Oblast in Belarus. As Brest-Litovsk, was famous for 1918 treaty between the former USSR and Germany. [52° 10'N 23° 40'E]

**Bridgetown** Town and port, capital of Barbados, West Indies, on west coast. Exports sugar, rum and molasses. Tourist centre. [13° 5'N 59° 30'W]

**Brisbane** Seaport, capital of Queensland, Australia. Founded as penal settlement in 1824. Fine setting between edge of uplands and coast. Warm, temperate climate. Port and heavy industry lie along Brisbane River below city centre. Oil refining. [27° 25'S 153° 2'E]

**Bristol** Capital of Avon, south-west England. Historic commercial centre and former important city-port on River Avon. John and Sebastian Cabot sailed to Newfoundland from here in 1497. Aircraft and confectionery industries. [51° 26'N 2° 35'W]

**Brno** Town in south-eastern Czech Republic. Has 16th-century town hall and 15th-century cathedral. Centre of textile industry, also manufacturing hardware, chemicals, beer, leather. [49° 10'N 16° 35'E]

**Bruges** (Brugge) Capital of West Flanders, in north-west Belgium. Historic textile trade centre, associated with Hanseatic League. Known for canals and traditional lace-making. Electrical engineering industry. Tourist centre. [51° 13'N 3° 13'E]

**Brussels** (Brussel, Bruxelles) Capital of Belgium on Senne River. Commercial and cultural centre. Headquarters of many international bodies, including European Union executive and NATO. Steel, car assembly, pharmaceuticals and publishing industries. Famed for its lace. [50° 51'N  4° 21'E]

**Bucharest**  Capital of Romania on Dimbovita River near Bulgarian border. Residence of rulers of Wallachia from 14th century and capital of Romania since 1861. Major industrial and commercial centre, also focus of ecclesiastical and cultural life. Flour milling, oil refining, tanning; metal goods, textiles and chemicals. [44° 27'N  26° 10'E]

**Budapest**  Capital of Hungary, comprising the towns of Buda and Pest, united in 1872. Has 19th-century Basilica of St Stephen and 13–15th century Coronation Church of St Matthias. Commercial, industrial, political and financial centre. Trades in grain, wine, cattle and hides. Also flour milling, brewing, iron and steel, engineering, telecommunications, precision instruments and clocks; large oil refineries. [47° 29'N  19° 5'E]

**Buenos Aires**  Capital and chief seaport of Argentina on the Rio de la Plata. Industries include meat processing, flour milling and brewing; also local natural gas and petroleum products. Main exports grain, beef and wool. [34° 40'S  58° 20'W]

**Bujumbura**  Capital of Burundi and lake port at northern end of Lake Tanganyika. Capital of former Ruandi-Urundi. Near River Ruzizi hydroelectric scheme. Industry centre; railway to Tanzania and Zaïre. Airport. Exports coffee, cotton and tea. [3° 16'S  29° 18'E]

**Bukhara**  (Bukhoro)  Capital of Bukhara Oblast in southern Uzbekistan. Ancient cultural centre of central Asia with many historic buildings. [39° 48'N  64° 25'E]

**Bulawayo**  Town in south-west Zimbabwe. On main railway to South Africa through Botswana and route centre for agricultural area. Centre for sugar refining. Asbestos mining to the east. [20° 7'S  28° 32'E]

**Burgos**  Town in northern Spain. Capital of Burgos province and first capital of Old Castile. Famous cathedral. Iron founding, ceramics and photographic equipment industries. [42° 21'N  3° 41'W]

**Bursa**  Town in north-western Turkey and capital of ancient Bithynia. Greek and Armenian archbishopric. Famous for silk, gold and silver work, carpets, tapestry and wood products. [40° 15'N  29° 5'E]

**Caernarfon**  Market town in Gwynedd, north-west Wales. Ancient defensive centre with large, well-preserved castle (built 1285–1322) at south-west end of Menai Straits. [53° 8'N  4° 17'W]

**Caerphilly**  Market town in Mid Glamorgan, south Wales. Regional centre north of Cardiff. Former major cheese producer. Site of an unusual large 13th-century 'concentric' castle. [51° 34'N  3° 13'W]

**Cagliari**  Seaport in Italy, capital of Sardinia, on south coast. Ferry and fishing port; university. Food, chemicals and cement industries. Tourist centre. [39° 15'N  9° 06'E]

**Cairns**  Port in Queensland, Australia. Bulk sugar port and tourist centre for Great Barrier Reef. [16° 57'S  145° 45'E]

**Cairo**  City, capital of Egypt to south of Nile delta. Largest city in Africa. Founded AD 640; university (AD 972). Many fine mosques and historic buildings. Modern 'Tower of Cairo'. [30° 1 N  31° 14'E]

**Calais**  Seaport in northern France, in Pas-de-Calais *département*. Historic defensive centre; leading French cross-channel ferry port. Textile industry. [50° 57'N  1° 56'E]

**Calcutta**  Port, capital of West Bengal state and second largest city in India, on Hooghly river. West of Ganges Delta, near Bangladesh border on east. Warren Hastings was first Governor of British India here in 1772. Commercial centre. Industries include textiles, especially jute; sugar refining, paper. Exports: jute, tea, coal. Massive overcrowding problem. [22° 36'N  88° 24'E]

**Calgary** Town in south-west central Canada in Alberta. Important commercial centre for oil and natural gas industry. Meat-packing, grain milling, manufacture industries. Famous for ranching. [51° 5'N 114° 10'W]

**Callao** Seaport in western Peru. Handles most of Peru's imports and a quarter of the country's exports. Fishing, meat-packing, flour milling, brewing, sugar refining, metal goods. [12° 0'S 77° 0'W]

**Cambridge** Capital of Cambridgeshire, eastern England; market and ancient university town on River Cam, south of Fens. First college founded 1284; many beautiful buildings, including King's College Chapel. Electronics and engineering industries. [52° 13'N 0° 8'E]

**Canberra** Capital of Australia, in the northeast of the Australian Capital Territory in the Great Dividing Range. Seat of government. [35° 15'S 149° 8'E]

**Canea** Seaport in Greece, on north-west coast of Crete. Capital of Canea department and (since 1841) of Crete. Flourishing city under Venetians. [35° 30'N 24° 4'E]

**Cannes** Seaport in south-east France on the Côte d'Azur in Alpes-Maritimes *département*. Fashionable resort established in the mid-19th century. Annual international film festival in April–May. [43° 32'N 7° 1'E]

**Canterbury** Cathedral city in Kent, southeast England. Ancient regional centre; metropolitan city of Christian Church since AD 597, with magnificent cathedral associated with St Thomas à Becket. University of Kent. Major tourist centre. [51° 17'N 1° 5'E]

**Canton** City in south-east China and capital of Guangdong province. Foreign trade with Europe since 1516. Centre of river trade up Xi Jiang River; trunk rail from north and to Hong Kong. Sugar refining, newsprint, cement, shipbuilding and chemical industries. [23° 5'N 113° 10'E]

**Cap Haïtien** Town in Haiti, West Indies, on north coast. Centre of region of first settlement and former capital. Sugar and sisal in lowland area, coffee and cocoa on hill slopes. [19° 40'N 72° 20'W]

**Cape Coast** Town on coast of Ghana, west of Accra. Former capital of British colony. Administrative and educational centre. Historic buildings. [5° 5'N 1° 15'W]

**Cape Town** Seaport, capital of Western Cape province and joint capital, with Pretoria and Bloemfontein, of South Africa. Situated on fine site on bay of south-west coast of South Africa, with Table Mountain in background. Founded in 1652. Legislative and commercial centre and seat of government, with many resorts around Cape Peninsula. [33° 55'S 18° 22'E]

**Caracas** Capital of Venezuela, in the north. Lies in basin at 900 m [3,000 ft]; its port is La Guaira. Commercial centre for oil. Textiles, glassware, pharmaceuticals, chemicals, food processing; universities. [10° 30'N 66° 55'W]

**Carcassonne** Town in southern France. Capital of Aude *département*. 11th–13th century castle and walled town. Market centre in wine producing area. [43° 13'N 2° 20'E]

**Cardiff** Capital of South Glamorgan, south Wales, and of Wales since 1955. Port at mouth of River Taff; commercial and educational centre with many parks. Includes cathedral city of Llandaff. Once major steam coal exporter; now iron and grain imports, with large flour industry. [51° 28'N 3° 11'W]

**Carlisle** Capital of Cumbria, north-west England. Commercial and manufacturing centre on Eden River, at western end of Hadrian's Wall. At forefront, in the past, of Anglo-Scottish border disputes. Industries: agricultural equipment; textiles and food, especially dairy products. [54° 54'N 2° 55'W]

**Cartago** Town in central Costa Rica, at the base of the Irazu volcanic peak. Capital of Costa Rica until 1823. Route centre. Coffee and cattle area. [9° 50'N 83° 55'W]

**Casablanca** Major port and commercial city

on north-west coast of Morocco. Serves wide hinterland. Fish processing, textiles. Export of phosphates important. [33° 36'N 7° 36'W]

**Cassino** Town in central Italy, in Lazio. Ancient cultural and defensive centre with abbey established by St Benedict AD 529. Town and abbey rebuilt after destruction in 1944. [41° 30'N 13° 50'E]

**Castellón de la Plana** Town in eastern Spain and capital of Castellón province. Centre of citrus and wine producing area. Also sugar and olive processing; rope and tile industries. [39° 58'N 0° 3'W]

**Cayenne** Capital of French Guiana, on an island off the Atlantic coast of South America. Penal colonies from 1854 to 1938. Exports shrimps and gold. [5° 5'N 52° 18'W]

**Ceanannus Mór** (Kells) Town in County Meath, Leinster province, in east of Republic of Ireland. Regional centre at site of monastery established by St Columba in 6th century; known for 8th–9th century illuminated Book of Kells. [53° 42'N 6° 53'W]

**Cebu** Second largest city in the Philippines, and capital of Cebu Island, on its east coast. One of the most important ports in Far East and Pacific area. Industry includes manufacturing cement and pottery; exports hemp, copra, cement. [10° 18'N 123° 54'E]

**Cekhira** Oil port on Gulf of Gabès, eastern Tunisia linked by pipeline from oilfields near Edjeleh, in the Sahara. [34° 20'N 10° 5'E]

**Ceuta Town** Spanish possession on northern peninsula of Morocco, separated from Gibraltar by narrow strait. [35° 52'N 5° 18'W]

**Chandigarh** City in India below Siwalik Hills and capital of both Punjab and Haryana states. Modern planned city, built in the 1950s; planned by Le Corbusier after partition in 1947, when the old capital of Punjab came within Pakistan. [30° 43'N 76° 47'E]

**Chardzhou** Town in eastern Turkmenistan. Transport centre with rail link, on Amudarya

River. Textile industry. [39° 06'N 63° 34'E]

**Charleston** Seaport in South Carolina, in south-eastern USA. Commercial centre, naval and air base. Preserved colonial city. Wood processing, fertilizer and shipbuilding industries. [32° 46'N 79° 56'W]

**Chartres** Town in northern France. Capital of Eure-et-Loire *département*. Famous for its 12th-century cathedral with stained glass. [48° 29'N 1° 30'E]

**Chelyabinsk** City in southern Urals, Russia. Route centre, with many light and heavy industry, notably iron and steel, mostly based on local raw materials, including lignite and a rich variety of metals. Rapid recent expansion. [55° 10'N 61° 24'E]

**Chengdu** Capital of Sichuan province in central south-west China. Major industrial centre on the north-west edge of the Sichuan (Red) Basin. Electronic industry and instrument making. [30° 38'N 104° 2'E]

**Cherbourg** Port in north-west France on north coast of Cotentin Peninsula. Transatlantic and cross-channel ferry port. Shipbuilding industry. [49° 38'N 1° 37'W]

**Chernovtsy** (Chernivtsi) Town in Ukraine, capital of Chernovtsy (Chernivtsi) Oblast. Attractively planned in 19th century; agricultural industries. [48° 15'N 25° 52'E]

**Cheyenne** Capital of Wyoming, in western USA. Commercial and route centre; livestock market and large rodeo. [41° 8'N 104° 49'W]

**Chiang Mai** Town in north-east Thailand, in fertile valley of Ping River, surrounded by mountains. Railway terminus. Centre of peak trade. Famous temple. [18° 48'N 98° 59'E]

**Chiba** City and capital of Chiba prefecture in Honshu, Japan. Industrial centre on east Tokyo Bay. Giant shipyard, oil refining, aluminium, iron and steel. [35° 30'N 140° 7'E]

**Chicago** City in Illinois, in north-central USA, at south-western end of Lake Michigan.

Major commercial, industrial, cultural and route centre. Grew as a processing centre for meat and grain; now steel products are as important. Locomotives, rolling stock, aircraft parts, machinery; oil refining, chemicals, printing and publishing. [41° 53'N 87° 38'W]

**Chihuahua**  Town in northern Mexico and capital of Chihuahua state. Administrative and mining centre; silver and zinc mines in area. Timber, cattle and meat-packing industries are important. [28° 40'N 106° 03'W]

**Chimkent**  (Shymkent) Capital of Kazakhstan, in the south, in the Syrdarya basin. Founded in 12th century. Now has varied heavy and light industry. [42° 8'N 69° 36'E]

**Chittagong**  Seaport in Bangladesh, 16 km [10 mls] from the Bay of Bengal on the Karnafuli River, 217 km [135 mls] south-east of Dacca. Industries include engineering, chemicals, flour, rice, oil and timber milling. Soap, candles and bricks are manufactured. Exports include tin, rice, jute, sugar and oilseed. [22° 19'N 91° 48'E]

**Chongjin**  Capital of province of North Hamgyong in North Korea, on the east coast, about 220 km (140 mls) south-west of Vladivostok, Russia. Chief port and industrial centre. Manufacture of steel, pig-iron and matches. Fish processing industry. Exports include timber, iron, fish and cotton textiles. [41° 47'N 129° 50'E]

**Christchurch**  Town in South Island, New Zealand, on River Avon on east coast. Major commercial and manufacturing centre. Important for wheat, grain, wool and lamb. [43° 33'S 172° 47'E]

**Cirebon**  Port on the northern coast of Java in Indonesia. Handicrafts centre. The Chinese temple is one of the oldest in Indonesia. [6° 45'S 108° 32'E]

**Cochin**  Port on Arabian Sea coast, Kerala state, southern India. Earliest European settlement in India (by Portuguese in 1502). Coir industry and fishing industry are important. [9° 59'N 76° 22'E]

**Coimbra**  Town in central Portugal. Ancient regional and cultural centre with university established 1308; first capital of Portugal. Textile, tanning industry. [40° 15'N 8° 27'W]

**Coleraine**  Port in County Londonderry, in the north of Northern Ireland. Manufacturing and university centre near mouth of River Bann. Clothing, especially shirts, engineering and food industries. [55° 8'N 6° 40'W]

**Cologne**  Town in western Germany, in North Rhine-Westphalia on west bank of River Rhine. Historic regional centre of the Rhineland, with famous cathedral and reconstructed old town. In major lignite-mining area. Large engineering industry especially cars; rolling stock; petrochemicals. Known for Eau de Cologne. [50° 56'N 6° 58'E]

**Colombo**  Capital of Sri Lanka, on west coast. Portuguese settlers in 16th century; Dutch 1656; succeeded by British 1796. Artificial harbour. International port and commercial centre. Exports tea, rubber, coconut products. Tourist trade along coastal area, especially to south. [6° 56'N 79° 58'E]

**Colón**  Town in Panama at Caribbean end of Panama Canal, Central America. Commercial centre. Cristóbal, twin town nearby, is port of entry for Canal. Railway to Panama City. [9° 20'N 79° 54'W]

**Compiègne**  Town in northern France, in Oise *département*. Site of imprisonment of Joan of Arc and of signing of armistice of 1918 and French surrender in 1940. [49° 24'N 2° 50'E]

**Conakry**  Port, capital of Guinea, situated on south coast. Founded 1889 on island at end of rocky peninsula. Still centre for administration and commerce. Textiles. Exports iron ore and bauxite. [9° 29'N 13° 49'W]

**Constantine**  City in northern Algeria, east of Algiers. Ancient fortified Arab city built above gorge; on main routes. [36° 25'N 6° 42'E]

**Conwy**  Walled town at the mouth of River Conwy in Gwynedd, north-west Wales. Well-preserved 13th-century castle. Market centre and yachting resort. [53° 17'N 3° 50'W]

**Copenhagen** Capital of Denmark on east coast of Zealand. Industrial, commercial and educational centre. Largest shipbuilding yards in Scandinavia, with extensive harbour. Major industries are electrical equipment, textiles, chemicals, porcelain and glassware. Tourist attractions include Tivoli Gardens and Amalienborg Palace. [55° 41'N 12° 34'E]

**Córdoba** City in central Argentina in agricultural area. Commercial centre. Hydroelectric power for manufacturing glass and cement. Also engineering and textiles. Astronomical observatory. [31° 20'S 64° 10'W]

**Córdoba** Town in southern Spain. Capital of Córdoba province. Ancient provincial capital of Romans and Moors, and noted cultural centre with magnificent mosque. Traditional silver and leather industry; copper smelting, electrical equipment, cement. Tourist centre. [37° 50'N 4° 50'W]

**Corinth** Town in southern Greece. Rebuilt after a destructive earthquake in 1928. Nearby to the south-west lie the important ruins of ancient Corinth, at the acropolis of the Acrocorinth. Nearby Corinth Canal built in 1893. [37° 56'N 22° 55'E]

**Corinto** Main port of Nicaragua, on Pacific coast. Railway connections to León, Managua and Granada. Exports coffee, cotton, sugar, timber, hides. [12° 30'N 87° 10'W]

**Cork** Capital of County Cork in Munster province, Republic of Ireland. Important commercial, manufacturing and route centre; port at mouth of River Lee with large meat-exporting trade. Car assembly, textiles, oil refining industry. University; cathedrals. [51° 54'N 8° 30'W]

**Cotonou** Port and commercial centre on the coast of Benin. Deepwater harbour built in 1964. Exports include oil palm products, groundnuts, coffee, as well as products from Niger. [6° 20'N 2° 25'E]

**Coventry** City in the West Midlands, west-central England. Commercial, industrial and route centre, south-east of Birmingham. First English car built here, 1898. Large car and aero-engine industry. Known for new cathedral, built 1951. [52° 25'N 1° 31'W]

**Cremona** Town in northern Italy, in Lombardy. Strong musical traditions; famous for violin-making (especially Stradivarius), with international school. Noted cheese industry; petrochemicals. [45° 8'N 10° 2'E]

**Cumaná** Port in northern Venezuela and the oldest European settlement in South America. Major fishing port. Exports include tobacco, coffee and cocoa. [10° 30'N 64° 5'W]

**Curitiba** City in southern Brazil, about 113 km [70 mls] from the coast. Capital of Paraná state. Trading centre for coffee, timber and maté. Paper making and furniture industries. [25° 20'S 49° 10'W]

**Cuzco** Town in central Peru, in a valley of the Andes. Former capital of Inca Empire; many ruined Inca sites. [13° 32'S 72° 0'W]

**Czestochowa** Town in south-central Poland. Place of pilgrimage to the 'Weeping Virgin' image. Textiles, iron and steel industries. [50° 49'N 19° 7'E]

**Dakar** Port, capital of Senegal, on Cape Verde peninsula. Founded in 1857, formerly capital of French West Africa and naval base. Phosphates, fish canning and textiles. Exports groundnuts. [14° 34'N 17° 29'W]

**Dalian** Port in Liaoning province, north-east China. Strategic port formerly under Russian and Japanese control, on a peninsula into the Yellow Sea. Industries include soyabean processing, shipbuilding. [38° 53'N 121° 37'E]

**Dallas** City in Texas, southern USA. Commercial centre, especially for cotton, banking and insurance. Textile and textile machinery industries; also petrochemicals, aircraft parts and assembly, and car industries. Major airport. [32° 47'N 96° 49'W]

**Damascus** Capital of Syria, situated on the

edge of an oasis. Commercial and craft centre; metal-working, silk weaving, sugar refineries. Said to be the oldest continuously inhabited city in the world. [33° 30'N 36° 18'E]

**Dar es Salaam** Seaport and former capital of Tanzania, on central part of coast. Oil refinery; textiles, cement and meat-canning industries. [6° 50'S 39° 12'E]

**Darjeeling** Town and hill station in West Bengal state, northern India. Spectacular views of snowcapped Mt Kangchenjunga; Mt Everest in distance. Famous for tea production. [27° 03'N 88° 18'E]

**Darkhan** Town in north central Mongolia. New industrial centre, established 1961 on main north-south railway line. One of three centres designated administratively as cities; the others are Ulan Bator and Erdenet. [49° 30'N 105° 58'E]

**Darwin** Capital of Northern Territory, Australia. Port and administrative centre on peninsula in north-west. Originally named Palmerston. Export of minerals from hinterland, especially uranium from Rum Jungle area. Suffered badly in typhoon in 1974. [12° 25'S 130° 51'E]

**Dawson** Town in north-west Canada in Yukon Territory. Declining goldmining centre of Klondike region and site of 1896–9 Gold Rush. Tourist centre. [64° 10'N 139° 30'W]

**Dehra Dun** Town in Uttar Pradesh state, north India, in foothills of the Himalayas. Railway terminus and transport centre. Agricultural research and administrative centre. Military academy. [30° 20'N 78° 4'E]

**Delft** Town in the western Netherlands, in Zuid Holland. Picturesque, historic market centre. Traditional porcelain manufacturing; cable and textile industries. [52° 1'N 4° 22'E]

**Delhi** City in Delhi Union Territory, northern India, and gateway to Ganges plain on Yamuna river. Major route centre. Old city with Great Temple, an immense mosque and Moghul Imperial Palace; ancient capital for various Hindu and Muslim dynasties and Moghuls before British rule. New Delhi incorporated as capital of British India 1931–47 and now capital of Republic of India. [28° 38'N 77° 17'E]

**Derby** Capital of Derbyshire, north-central England. Ancient commercial, industrial and route centre. Known for Crown Derby pottery. Important engineering industries, especially car and aero-engines, rolling stock; synthetic textiles. [52° 55'N 1° 28'W]

**Detroit** Port in Michigan, northern USA, across Detroit River from Windsor in Canada. Major commercial and manufacturing centre and port for car industry. Manufactures 25% of all US vehicles. Large River Rouge integrated complex: raw materials from docks to finished cars. Also aircraft, rolling stock, chemical industries. [42° 20'N 83° 3'W]

**Dhaka** (Dacca) Capital of Bangladesh, on Burhi Ganga River. Former Moghul capital in early 17th century; centre of Muslim rule in 18th century. International airport. Industry includes chemicals, jute and cotton milling. Fertilizers, glass and electrical goods. Exports jute, hides, tea. [23° 43'N 90° 26'E]

**Dijon** Town in eastern France. Capital of Côte-d'Or *département*. Ancient regional centre of Burgundy. Annual food fair and large wine trade. Famed for its mustard. Cycle and chemical industries. [47° 20'N 5° 3'E]

**Djibouti** Capital of the Republic of Djibouti. Port and terminus of the railway from Ethiopia. Exports hides and skins, also coffee and oilseed. [11° 30'N 43° 05'E]

**Dodoma** Capital of Tanzania, replaced Dar es Salaam in 1974. Route centre. Noted for cattle rearing. [6° 8'S 35° 45'E]

**Doha** Capital of Qatar, on Arabian Gulf. Commercial centre and seaport; modern city. Herb and camel market. [25° 15'N 51° 35'E]

**Donetsk** Capital of Donetsk Oblast in the Ukraine. Main industrial centre of the Donbas region (Donets Basin). Formerly named

Yuzovka after an industrialist, Hughes, then called Stalino. [48° 0'N 37° 45'E]

**Douala** City and main port of Cameroon, 32 km [20 mls] up Wouri river. Market centre. Railway north to N'kongsamba and south-east to Yaoundé. Light industry. [4° 0'N 9° 45'E]

**Douglas** Capital of Isle of Man, England. Commercial centre and biggest resort, on east coast of island. Craft, fishing industry; aero-engineering. [54° 9'N 4° 29'W]

**Dover** Historic Channel port in Kent, south-east England. Large castle, started 11th century. Busiest UK passenger port. Famed for white cliffs. [51° 7'N 1° 19'E]

**Dresden** Town in eastern Germany. Noted for Baroque architecture. Allied bombing in World War II destroyed many fine buildings and art collections. Manufactures electrical equipment, precision tools, optical and musical instruments. Dresden china is made at Meissen. [51° 2'N 13° 45'E]

**Dubai** Capital of Dubai, United Arab Emirates. Port with largest harbour in Middle East; major dry dock. Economy based on oil and important distributary trade. Fishing. [25° 18'N 55° 20'E]

**Dublin** (Baile Atha Cliath) Capital of Irish Republic and of County Dublin in Leinster province on east coast. Commercial city, cultural and route centre and port on Dublin Bay at mouth of River Liffey. Many Georgian squares. Large brewing industry; food, tobacco processing, textiles, transport equipment. Tourist centre. Two universities (Trinity College founded 1591). [53° 20'N 6° 18'W]

**Dun Laoghaire** Ferry port in County Dublin, Leinster province in the east of the Republic of Ireland. Seaside resort and residential centre on the south side of Dublin Bay. Headquarters of Irish yachting association. [53° 17'N 6° 9'W]

**Dundee** Port and capital of Tayside region, eastern Scotland, north of Firth of Tay. Commercial, manufacturing and route centre.

Traditional jute industry; engineering; wood and food processing, especially jam. Ship-building is important, especially for the North Sea oil industry. [56° 29'N 3° 0'W]

**Dunedin** Town on Otago Harbour, south east coast of South Island, New Zealand. First Scottish settlers in 1848. Sea-borne trade now from Port Chalmers. Exports wool, meat and dairy produce from farming hinterland. [45° 50'S 170° 33'E]

**Dunkirk** Port in northern France near Belgian border, in Nord *département*. Scene of Allied evacuation 1940. Shipbuilding and oil refining industries. [51° 2'N 2° 20'E]

**Durango** Town in Mexico, on a plateau east of the Sierra Madre Occidental, and capital of Durango state. Important iron reserves nearby; also silver and lead. Administrative centre and route focus. Western films made in area. [24° 3'N 104° 39'W]

**Durban** City and major port in Natal province, South Africa, on the east coast. Industrial centre with soap, textiles, paper and oil refining industries. Exports include agricultural products, especially maize, and coal. [29° 49'S 31° 1'E]

**Durham** Capital of County Durham, north-east England. Ancient and picturesque city on the River Wear, with university (1832), Norman cathedral (1093–1133) and castle (1069). Centre of former coal-mining region; Miners Gala in July. Carpets and organ manufacturing. [54° 47'N 1° 34'W]

**Durrës** Seaport in western Albania on Adriatic coast. Outlet for Tiranë. Trade in grain, olive oil, and tobacco. Petroleum storage and shipbuilding facilities; railway terminus. [41° 19'N 19° 28'E]

**Dushanbe** Capital of Tajikistan. Formerly called Stalinabad. Many educational establishments. Cotton and silk industries are important. [38° 33'N 68° 48'E]

**Düsseldorf** Town in western Germany and river port on Rhine. Capital of North Rhine-

Westphalia. Financial and fashion centre of Ruhr industrial area. Large chemical and metal industry, especially non-ferrous metal smelting; engineering. [51° 15'N 6° 46'E]

**Dzhambul** (Zhambyl) Capital of Dzhambul Oblast in Kazakhstan. Long historic associations with Islam. Notable for chemicals, such as superphosphates. [42° 54'N 71° 22'E]

**Dzhezkazgan** (Zhezqazghan) Capital of Dzhezkazgan Oblast in central Kazakhstan, and local industrial centre. Notable for its huge copper reserves. [47° 44'N 67° 40'E]

**Edinburgh** Cathedral city, capital of Scotland and of Lothian region. Important commercial, cultural, educational, manufacturing and route centre; port (Leith) on Firth of Forth. Built on hills with historic Old Town sloping east from Castle Rock and Georgian New Town sloping towards the Forth. Noted International Festival of the Arts. Engineering, food processing, brewing, paper, printing and publishing industries. Important tourist centre. [55° 57'N 3° 12'W]

**Edmonton** Town in south-west Canada. Capital of Alberta. Centre of Canadian oil industry and extensive pipeline system. Major commercial and route centre. Meat-packing, grain milling; chemicals; manufacturing industry. [53° 30'N 113° 30'W]

**Eindhoven** Town in south-east Netherlands in the region of Noord Brabant. Important manufacturing centre; site of leading light bulb industry; electronics, car assembly and milk products. [51° 26'N 5° 28'E]

**El Aaiún** Capital of Western Sahara (a former Spanish province), under occupation by Morocco since 1976. [27° 9'N 13° 12'W]

**El Escorial** Town in central Spain near Madrid. Magnificent palace and monastery built for Philip II. [40° 35'N 4° 7'W]

**El Ferrol** Seaport in eastern Spain, in La Coruña province. Birthplace of Franco. Shipbuilding industry. Naval base; 18th-century planned centre. [43° 29'N 8° 15'W]

**El Paso** City in Texas, southern USA, on the Rio Grande opposite Ciudad Juárez in Mexico. Important commercial, manufacturing and route centre. Oil refining, copper smelting, clothing, meat-packing and leather industries. [31° 45'N 106° 29'W]

**Elat** Seaport in southern Israel at the head of the Gulf of Aqaba (Red Sea). Israel's leading oil port. Fishing resort and developing tourist resort. [29° 30'N 34° 56'E]

**Elvas** Town in south-east Portugal, near the border with Spain. Historic defensive centre, famous for its ramparts, aqueduct and plum orchards. [38° 50'N 7° 10'W]

**Ely** Cathedral city in Cambridgeshire, eastern England. Regional centre on an island site in the Great Ouse River until the Fens were drained. Magnificent cathedral established in AD 673. [52° 24'N 0° 16'E]

**Encarnación** Port on the Paraná River, in the extreme south-east of Paraguay. Railway terminus; sawmilling and tanning. Exports include timber, cattle, rice, cotton, tobacco and maté. [27° 15'S 55° 50'W]

**Entebbe** Town on northern shore of Lake Victoria, Uganda. Former administrative centre. Major airport. [0° 4'N 32° 28'E]

**Épernay** Town in north-east France, in Marne *département*. It is the centre, with Rheims, of the champagne wine industry. Famous for its extensive cellars in chalk hills. [49° 3'N 3° 56'E]

**Epidauros** Spa town in southern Greece, in Argolis. Site of the Sanctuary of Asclepius, god of medicine. Renowned also for its ancient theatre. [36° 46'N 23° 0'E]

**Erdenet** New town in north-central Mongolia, 320 km [200 mls] north-west of Ulan Bator. Large mining centre on copper and molybdenum deposits. Connected to Russian rail network. [44° 13'N 111° 10'E]

**Eskisehir** Town in central western Turkey. A spa town with sulphur springs. Centre of

Turkish meerschaum industry, based on local deposits. [39° 50'N  30° 5'E]

**Evora**  Town in southern Portugal. Ancient market centre of Alentejo region; walled town with many preserved buildings. Cork, leather and craft industries [38° 33'N  7° 57'W]

**Fairbanks**  Town in Alaska, north-western USA. Transport centre: railhead, terminus of Alaska Highway and air base. Commercial centre for central Alaska; coal mining. [64° 51'N  147° 43'W]

**Faro**  Seaport in southern Portugal. Commercial centre of the Algarve region; resort and fishing port with canning, cork and salt industries. [37° 2'N  7° 55'W]

**Fergana**  (Farghona)  Capital of Fergana Oblast in Uzbekistan. Centre of the large Fergana Valley oasis, known principally for cotton and silk. [40° 23'N  71° 19'E]

**Fez**  City in northern Morocco. Cultural and religious centre; sacred city of Islam, with many ancient buildings. University reputed to be oldest in the world. Famous mosque. [34° 0'N  5° 0'W]

**Florence**  Town in north-central Italy and capital of Tuscany. Important historical, commercial and cultural centre known for its beauty; associated with Medicis, Dante and many painters including Giotto and Botticelli; site of Uffizi Museum. Important tourist centre. Engineering, leather and jewellery industries. [43° 47'N  11° 15'E]

**Florianópolis**  Port in southern Brazil, on Santa Catarina Island, joined to the mainland by very long steel suspension bridge. Capital of Santa Catarina state. Excellent harbour. Exports sugar, fruit and tobacco; considerable coastal trade. [27° 30'S  48° 30'W]

**Fontainebleau**  Town south of Paris, France, in Seine-et-Marne *département*. Resort with famous palace. [48° 24'N  2° 40'E]

**Fort Portal**  Town in western Uganda. Base for exploring Ruwenzori Mountains and Ituri

equatorial forest, home of the pygmy people. Located on the main road from Kampala. Tea area. [0° 40'N  30° 20'E]

**Fort-de-France**  Town and port, and capital of Martinique, in the West Indies. Formerly Fort Royal. The main exports include sugar and rum. [14° 36'N  61° 2'W]

**Fortaleza**  Port, capital of Ceará state in north-east Brazil. Industry, sugar refining, flour milling; exports sugar, coffee, cotton, hides. [3° 45'S  38° 35'W]

**Frankfurt-am-Main**  Town in central Germany, in Hesse. Birthplace of Goethe. Leading financial and air transport centre, with important trade fairs. Electrical instruments, machinery, printing and publishing and chemicals industries. [50° 7'N  8° 40'E]

**Freetown**  Port and capital of Sierra Leone. Situated on tip of hilly peninsula, with natural harbour on Rokel River estuary. First settlement for freed slaves from US, 1787. Famous Fourah Bay College, founded 1827. Main exports: diamonds, palm kernels and iron ore. [8° 30'N  13° 17'W]

**Fribourg**  Town in west Switzerland. Capital of Fribourg canton and centre of Swiss Catholicism; university and noted cathedral. Electrical and agricultural equipment, cheese and chocolate industries. [46° 49'N  7° 9'E]

**Funchal**  Seaport in and capital of Madeira (Portugal) on south-east coast. Commercial centre; wine trade; sugar and fish processing industries. Resort. [32° 38'N  16° 54'W]

**Fuxin**  City of Liaoning province, eastern China. Rapidly developing coal-mining and power producing centre. Largest strip mine in China nearby. [42° 5'N  121° 48'E]

**Gaborone**  Capital of Botswana. Built in 1965, at altitude 1,006 m [3,300 ft]. On railway between Zimbabwe and South Africa. Light industry. [24° 45'S  25° 57'E]

**Galway**  Capital of County Galway, Connacht province, in the west of the Republic of

Ireland, between Lough Corrib and Galway Bay. University and cathedral centre with clothing, grain and agricultural equipment industries. Tourist centre. [53° 16'N 9° 4'W]

**Gao** Historic market town in eastern Mali, on the River Niger. Road and river route centre and southern terminus of a trans-Saharan route. [18° 0'N 1° 10'W]

**Gaya** Town in Bihar state, east India, above the southern edge of the Ganges Plain. Important railway centre. Place of pilgrimage for Hindus to the Vishnupad Temple. Export and trade of rice. [24° 47'N 85° 4'E]

**Gaza** Coastal town in the Gaza Strip, administered by Israel since 1967. Reputed to be the ancient Philistine city whose temple was destroyed by Samson. [31° 29'N 34° 28'E]

**Gdansk** Seaport in northern Poland on Baltic Sea. Founded in Middle Ages; Free City between the World Wars. Shipbuilding, food processing. [54° 22'N 18° 40'E]

**Geneva** Town in western Switzerland comprising large part of Geneva canton. Commercial centre and headquarters of many international organizations including Red Cross, UN agencies. Traditional haven from persecution; at centre of Reformation, associated especially with Calvin. Watch, clock and jewellery industries. [46° 12'N 6° 9'E]

**Genoa** Seaport in north-west Italy. Capital of Liguria. Historic commercial centre with long seafaring tradition (birthplace of Columbus). Leading Italian port and oil terminal, with large shipbuilding industry; steel, machinery and textiles. [44° 24'N 8° 56'E]

**Georgetown** Capital of Guyana and chief port at the mouth of the Demerara River. Exports include bauxite, sugar, rice and diamonds. [6° 50'N 58° 12'W]

**Ghent** Town and river port in west Belgium. Capital of East Flanders. Historic, commercial, cultural and manufacturing centre of horticultural area. Cathedral. Textile industry, petrochemicals, steel. [51° 2'N 3° 42'E]

**Gifu** Capital of Gifu prefecture in central Honshu, Japan. Manufacturing centre, silk and paper goods. Centre of cormorant fishing on the Nagara. [35° 30'N 136° 45'E]

**Giza** Suburb of Cairo on west bank of River Nile in Egypt. Famous for the pyramids and the Sphinx in the area. [30° 0'N 31°.10']

**Glasgow** Port on River Clyde and capital of Strathclyde region, western Scotland. Major Scottish commercial and industrial centre. Shipbuilding, aircraft engines, textiles, food processing, distilling, textiles, printing and publishing. [55° 52'N 4° 14'W]

**Godthåb** Small seaport and capital of Greenland at the entrance to Davis Strait in the south-west. First Danish colony in Greenland, established 1728. Fish processing. [64° 10'N 51° 35'W]

**Gonder** Town and regional centre to the north of Lake Tana in north-west Ethiopia. Ancient walled imperial city with Italian influences, formerly the capital. Several old palaces. [12° 39'N 37° 30'E]

**Göteborg** Seaport and second largest town of Sweden on the south-west coast. Iron and steel, shipbuilding, oil refining, timber, textiles and fishing industries. Many museums and parks. [57° 43'N 11° 59'E]

**Gouda** Town in western Netherlands, in Zuid Holland. Market centre of dairying area, famous for its cheese. [52° 1'N 4° 42'E]

**Granada** Town in southern Spain. Was the last stronghold of Moors. Cultural centre, known for its palaces. Centre of rich agricultural area. Textiles and footwear industry. [37° 10'N 3° 35'W]

**Grasse** Town in south-east France, in Alpes-Maritimes *département*. Centre of renowned area growing flowers and herbs for the perfume industry. [43° 38'N 6° 56'E]

**Graz** Town in south-east Austria. Capital of Styria. Historic regional and defensive centre, with noted university and cathedral. Industries include transport equipment, textiles and food processing. [47° 4'N  15° 27'E]

**Grenoble** Town in south-east France. Capital of Isère *département*. Historic, regional, route and university centre of Isère Valley. Traditional glove industry; textiles, electrical engineering, cement and petrochemicals. Major tourist centre. [45° 12'N  5° 42'E]

**Groningen** Town in north-east Netherlands. Capital of Groningen province. Market town; centre of natural gas production region. Food, tobacco and light engineering industries. [53° 15'N  6° 35'E]

**Groznyy** Capital of the Republic of Chechenia in southern Russia, since 1994 the location of a civil war between Russian and Chechen forces. Oilfields and related industries disrupted by war. [43° 20'N  45° 45'E]

**Guadalajara** City in western Mexico, north of Lake Chapola, Mexico's largest lake. Capital of Jalisco state. Route centre with an important market. Various light industries. [20° 40'N  103° 20'W]

**Guatemala City** Capital of Guatemala, on plateau in south-central area. Damaged by 1976 earthquake. Light industry. Volcanic peaks to south. [14° 40'N  90° 20'W]

**Guayaquil** Chief port of Ecuador. Sugar refining, tanning and iron-working industries. Major exports include bananas, cocoa and coffee. [2° 15'S  79° 52'W]

**Guernica** Town in northern Spain, in Vizcaya province. Destroyed by German bombers in 1937, during Civil War. Regional centre with former Basque parliament and 1,000-year-old oak. [43° 19'N  2° 40'W]

**Gujranwala** Town in north-east Pakistan. Centre of Sikh power until second Sikh war with British (1848–9). On main road and rail route from Lahore to Rawalpindi. Textile industry. [32° 10'N  74° 12'E]

**Gujrat** Town in north-east Pakistan, near Chenab River. Site of battle which ended second Sikh war (1849). Renowned gold and silver inlay work. [32° 40'N  74° 2'E]

**Guryev** (Atyrau) Capital of Guryev Oblast in Kazakhstan. Old Caspian fishing port, now centre of the oil industry. [47° 8'N  51° 59'E]

**Gwalior** Town in Madhya Pradesh state, north-central India, on southern edge of the River Ganges plain. Ancient fort and 15th-century palace of Tomar dynasty. Manufactures cotton textiles. [26° 12'N  79° 10'E]

**Gyandzha** (Gäncä) Second largest town of Azerbaijan, formerly known as Kirovabad. Much historic architecture. Industry based on local agricuture: silk and agricultural machinery. [40° 39'N  46° 20'E]

**Györ** Town and river port in north-west Hungary. Has 12th-century cathedral. Commercial and industrial centre; manufactures railway carriages and diesel machinery. [47° 41'N  17° 40'E]

**Haarlem** Town in north-west Netherlands. Capital of Noord Holland. Historic commercial and cultural centre at northern end of intensive bulb-growing area. Traditional textile industry. [52° 23'N  4° 39'E]

**Hague, The** Capital of the Netherlands and of Zuid Holland. Commercial and residential centre with resort, Scheveningen, at North Sea coast. Site of International Court of Justice. [52° 7'N  4° 17'E]

**Haifa** Chief seaport of Israel, at the foot of Mount Carmel. Oil refining; manufacturing; naval base. [32° 46'N  35° 0'E]

**Haiphong** City in Vietnam, on the Red River delta, south-east of Hanoi and 8 km [5 mls] from the Gulf of Tongking. Manufactures cement, textiles, phosphates, plastics. Exports minerals and rice. [20° 47'N  106° 41'E]

**Halifax** Seaport and capital of Nova Scotia on the south-east coast of Canada. Ice-free port and naval base (established 1749). Fishing industry. Commercial centre of Atlantic provinces. [44° 38'N  63° 35'W]

**Hamburg** Second largest city, leading port and Land of Germany. Historic trading centre at confluence of Alster and Elbe Rivers. Important shipbuilding, engineering, oil refining, food, brewing, printing and publishing industries. [53° 33'N 10° 0'E]

**Hameenlinna** Town in southern Finland, on Lake Vanajavesi. Terminus of motorboat service to Tampere. Birthplace of Sibelius. Swedish castle dates from 12th–13th centuries. [61° 0'N 24° 28'E]

**Hamhung** Capital of southern Hamgyong province in North Korea. Important industrial town, centre of pre-war aluminium industry; oil refineries and chemical plants; fertilizers and textiles. [39° 54'N 127° 30'E]

**Hamilton** Town on Waikato River in central area of North Island, New Zealand. Important road and rail junction. Regional centre for dairy and fat lamb farming. Agricultural research centre. [37° 47'S 175° 19'E]

**Hammerfest** Town on the northern coast of Norway, most northerly in Europe. Tourist centre for observation of midnight sun. Fish producs, furs exported. [70° 39'N 23° 41'E]

**Hangzhou** Capital of Zhejiang province, eastern China. River port on Fuchan Jiang River and southern terminus of Grand Canal. [30° 18'N 120° 11'E]

**Hanoi** River port and capital of the Republic of Vietnam, on the Red River 100 km [60 mls] from the Gulf of Tongking. Rail and industrial centre; international airport. Engineering, rice milling, tanning and brewing; textiles, leather goods and matches manufactured. [21° 5'N 105° 55'E]

**Harare** Capital of Zimbabwe, in the east-central region. Formerly Salisbury. Altitude 1,524 m [5,000 ft]. Important route centre. Bacon, flour, tobacco and leather goods. Citrus fruits in Magoe area to north. Sugar refining. [17° 43'S 31° 2'E]

**Hartford** Capital of Connecticut, north-east USA. Commercial centre, most notably for insurance. Large aircraft industry, especially jet engines; metal goods, especially guns. [41° 45'N 72° 42'W]

**Hassi Messaoud** Settlement at oil well area on margins of Great Eastern Erg in north-east Algeria. Oil and gas pipelines to Mediterranean coast. [31° 43'N 6° 8'E]

**Havana** City and port, capital of Cuba, West Indies, on Gulf of Mexico. Founded in 1515. Manufactures cigars from fine tobacco grown in west. Other light industries. Exports tobacco, sugar, rum, coffee. [23° 7'N 82° 25'W]

**Hebron** Town in the West Bank (formerly part of Jordan administered by Israel since 1967) to south-west of Jerusalem. Rich agricultural valley; industry includes glass making and tanning. Believed to have been the home of Abraham. [31° 32'N 35° 6'E]

**Heidelberg** Town in south-west Germany, in Baden-Württemberg. Cultural centre with oldest German university (1386) and famous castle. Printing and publishing, car parts industry. [49° 23'N 8° 41'E]

**Helsingør** Seaport in Denmark at narrowest point of Øresund on Jutland peninsula. Dominated by Kronborg Castle. Old market and garrison town, with ferry links to Helsingborg in Sweden. [56° 2'N 12° 35'E]

**Helsinki** Capital of Finland on southern coast. Main industrial, commercial and cultural centre. University, also scientific and cultural institutes. Important for manufacture of timber products, machinery and textiles. [60° 15'N 25° 3'E]

**Herat** Old town in north-west Afghanistan. Route centre with roads into Iran and the former USSR; ancient trade route to India and Iran. Earthworks, palaces, mosques and tombs. Many times destroyed by invaders and rebuilt. [34° 20'N 62° 7'E]

**Hiroshima** City and capital of Hiroshima prefecture in south Honshu, Japan. Important industrial centre; motor vehicles, shipbuilding. Largely destroyed by explosion of first atomic bomb, 6 August 1945. [34° 24'N 132° 30'E]

**Ho Chi Minh City** (Saigon) Important river port and the largest city in Vietnam, on the Saigon River, 55 km [34 mls] from the South China Sea. Centre of light industry, including rice milling, brewing, distilling and textile manufacturing. [10° 58'N 106° 40'E]

**Hobart** Port and capital of Tasmania, Australia, on the River Derwent estuary in the south-east. Fine natural harbour, surrounded by hills. Hydroelectric power important for diversified industry in surrounding area. Exports apples. [42° 50'S 147° 21'E]

**Hohhot** Capital of Inner Mongolian Autonomous Region of China. Rail link with Beijing. Commercial centre of Mongol herding lands. [40° 52'N 111° 40'E]

**Honiara** Capital of Solomon Islands, west Pacific Ocean, on north coast of island of Guadalcanal. Administrative centre, situated in driest part of island. [9° 27'S 159° 57'E]

**Honolulu** Capital of Hawaii, USA, on Oahu Island in mid-Pacific Ocean. Commercial and transport centre of islands, with large airport and port. Important tourist and defence industry; also sugar cane and pineapple processing. [21° 19'N 157° 52'W]

**Houston** Port in Texas, southern USA, at head of Houston Ship Canal on Gulf of Mexico. Commercial, cultural and manufacturing centre of oil and gas region. Major petrochemical industry and equipment manufacturer, especially pipes and drilling gear. Site of NASA Space Center. [29° 46'N 95° 22'W]

**Hradec Králové** Town in northern Czech Republic at confluence of Adler and Elbe rivers. University and Gothic cathedral (1312). Textiles, musical instruments, furniture and metal-work. [50° 15'N 15° 50'E]

**Huancayo** Town in central Peru, in the Andes. Trading centre for maize, wheat, alfalfa famous Indian market. [12° 5'S 75° 12'W]

**Hyderabad** City in south-east Pakistan, on

Indus River at lowest bridging point. Railway centre. Textiles, glass, leather. Famous for embroideries. [25° 23'N 68° 24'E]

**Iasi** Town in north-east Romania. Commercial and cultural centre. Archbishopric, university and national theatre; home of many churches and palaces. [47° 10'N 27° 40'E]

**Ibadan** Administrative centre in south-west of Nigeria. On main road and rail routes linking interior with port of Lagos. Cocoa and palm kernels are main products of area. Light industry; textiles. [7° 22'N 3° 58'E]

**Iloilo** Town and port beside Iloilo Strait in south-east of island of Panay in the Philippines. Commercial, manufacturing and cultural centre. Exports include rice, sugar and copra. [10° 45'N 122° 33'E]

**Inch'on** City on the Yellow Sea coast of South Korea. Capital of Kyonggi province and the port for Seoul, restricted by wide tidal variation. Exports rice, dried fish, soyabeans. Manufactures steel, glass, textiles and chemicals. [37° 27'N 126° 40'E]

**Indianapolis** Capital of Indiana, north-central USA. Important commercial and route centre. Large aircraft, car engine and parts industries; electronics and pharmaceuticals. Food processing, especially meat-packing and grain milling. [39° 46'N 86° 09'W]

**Innsbruck** Town in western Austria at the foot of the Karwendel Mountains. Capital of Tirol. Noted tourist and route centre. University and cathedral town with many historic buildings. [47° 16'N 11° 23'E]

**Invercargill** Town on southern coast of South Island, New Zealand. Chief commercial centre for Southland Plain. Harbour at Bluff. Meat-freezing, grain and wool industries. [46° 24'S 168° 24'E]

**Inverness** Capital of Highland region, northern Scotland. Commercial centre in agricultural area at head of Moray Firth. Sea and canal port. Distilling, textiles; service centre for North Sea oil. [57° 29'N 4° 12'W]

**Inyanga** Regional centre in eastern Zimbabwe, serving farming area. Tea production. Centre for east highlands holiday area, including national park. [18° 12'S 32° 40'E]

**Ioannina** Town in north-west Greece on the shore of Lake Ioanninon. Notable 11th-century citadel. Famous for fine jewellery and crafts. [39° 40'N 20° 51'E]

**Ipoh** Capital of Perak in Malaysia. Commercial centre of Kinta Valley tin-mining area; also extensive rubber plantations. Chinese rock temples. [4° 35'N 101° 5'E]

**Iquitos** Port on Amazon River, north Peru. Commercial centre for vast area; head of navigation for ocean-going steamers. Exports nuts, timber, rubber. [3° 45'S 73° 0'W]

**Iráklion** Seaport in Greece, largest city in Crete, on north-central coast. Manufactures soap and leather goods. [35° 20'N 25° 12'E]

**Irkutsk** Town in eastern Siberia, Russia. Major industrial and transport centre of the region. Long history; some old buildings. [52° 18'N 104° 20'E]

**Islamabad** Capital of Pakistan. Modern planned city in north-east, just north-west of Rawalpindi. Rawal Dam and reservoir within capital for water supply. [33° 40'N 73° 10'E]

**Istanbul** City in Turkey on both sides of Bosporus. Largest town and former capital of Turkey. Founded as Byzantium by Greeks *c.* 660 BC, changed to Constantinople AD 330 and Istanbul in 1930. Capital of Byzantine Empire until 1453. Seat of Ottoman Empire until 1922. Industrial, commercial, cultural and tourist centre. Many churches and mosques, and fine examples of Byzantine art and architecture. [42° 0'N 21° 0'E]

**Izmir** Seaport in western Turkey. Settlements date back to 3rd millennium BC. Site of ancient Smyrna. Largest port in Asian Turkey. Exports grapes, figs, opium, raisins, carpets and silk. [38° 25'N 27° 8'E]

**Jaffna** Town in northern Sri Lanka, on south lagoon coast of Jaffna peninsula. Portuguese occupation 1617; Dutch 1658; remains of forts. Salt produced in area; caustic soda manufactured. [9° 45'N 80° 2'E]

**Jaipur** Walled city, capital of Rajasthan state, north-west India. Founded 1727. Commercial and route centre. Maharajah's Palace of former Jaipur state. Textiles. [27° 0'N 75° 50'E]

**Jakarta** Seaport in north-west Java, capital of and largest city in Indonesia. Communications, trade and industrial centre. University of Indonesia. [6° 9'S 106° 49'E]

**Jammu** Town in southern Jammu and Kashmir state in north Indian subcontinent, on Tawi river, tributary of Chenab river. Winter capital of state. [32° 43'N 74° 54'E]

**Jebel Dhanna** Major new port, oil terminal and industrial centre on southern Arabian Gulf in western Abu Dhabi, United Arab Emirates. [24° 11'N 52° 35'E]

**Jerez de la Frontera** Town in south-west Spain. Capital of Cádiz province. Centre of sherry producing area; noted for horsebreeding; distilling industry. [36° 41'N 6° 7'W]

**Jericho** Town in Jordan, in the valley of the River Jordan, 22 km [14 mls] east-north-east of Jerusalem. Site of important ancient city; below sea level. [31° 25'N 35° 27'E]

**Jerusalem** Town partly in Israel and partly in Jordanian territory administered by Israel since 1967. Sited on two rocky hills 56 km [35 mls] from the Mediterranean coast. Holy city of Jews, Muslims and Christians; site of many holy places; churches, synagogues and mosques. Tourist area. [3° 47'N 35° 10'E]

**Jidda** Major seaport of Hijaz in western Saudi Arabia. Originally founded AD 647, on Red Sea. Financial and commercial centre; chief port for Mecca. [21° 29'N 39° 10'E]

**Jinja** Town in Uganda, north of Lake Victoria, 80 km [50 mls] east of Kampala. Route centre and industrial area. Owen Falls hydroelectric power station nearby. Textiles, brewing, tobacco and copper smelting (ore from Kilembe). [0° 25'N  33° 12'E]

**Jinzhou**  Old Manchurian city of Liaoning province, north-eastern China. Now centre of industrial district, with chemicals and electronics industry. Originally developed by the Japanese in the 1930s. [41° 7'N  121° 6'E]

**Jodhpur**  Walled town in Rajasthan state, north-west India, on edge of Thar Desert. Old trading centre. Once capital of Manwar state. Textiles. [26° 23'N  73° 8'E]

**Johannesburg**  City in the province of Pretoria, Witwatersrand and Vereeniging (PWV), South Africa, lying 1,829 m [6,000 ft] above sea level. Centre of gold-mining area of Witwatersrand. Important industrial area to south, which produces coal; huge iron-and-steel works nearby. [26° 10'S  28° 2'E]

**Johor**  Baharu City, capital of Johor in Malaysia, southern end of Malay Peninsula. Area produces rubber, rice and pineapples. Fine Sultan's Palace. [1° 29'N  103° 46'E]

**Jönköping**  Town in southern Sweden at southern end of Lake Vättern. Centre of Sweden's match-making industry; paper and textile industries. [57° 45'N  14° 10'E]

**Jos**  Town on Jos Plateau in central Nigeria. Assob Waterfalls nearby to south. Commercial centre for tin-mining area. [9° 53'N  8° 51'E]

**Juneau**  Ice-free port and capital of Alaska, north-western USA. Commercial centre in gold-mining area. Sawmilling and salmon-processing industries. [58° 18'N  134° 25'W]

**Kabul**  Capital of Afghanistan, at 2,100 m [6,900 ft], on Kabul River. Commands passes through mountains into Pakistan. Manufactures marble-ware, glass. [34° 28'N  69° 11'E]

**Kabwe**  Town in central Zambia. Important lead and zinc mining centre for the surrounding region. [14° 30'S  28° 29'E]

**Kaduna**  Town in north-central Nigeria, on Kaduna River. Formerly capital of northern Nigeria. Shiroro HEP Dam on Kaduna River to south. Administrative centre; railway junction. Cotton and textiles. [10° 30'N  7° 21'E]

**Kaesong**  Ancient city in North Korea, near the border with South Korea, north-west of Seoul. Famous for its porcelain. Trade in ginseng for medicinal use. [31° 58'N  126° 35'E]

**Kainji**  New town in western Nigeria on Niger River, south of important Kainji Dam and Reservoir. Main road connections to south and east. [9° 42'N  4° 37'E]

**Kalgoorlie**  Town (with Boulder) in southern Western Australia state on the Trans-Australian Railway. Developed in 1893. Gold and nickel mining in the 'Golden Mile' area to the south. [30° 40'S  121° 22'E]

**Kaliningrad**  Capital of Kaliningrad Oblast, a detached enclave of Russia on the Baltic coast. Former German name Konigsberg; a Baltic shipbuilding port. Population largely composed of army personnel. [54° 42'N  20° 32'E]

**Kampala**  Capital of Uganda, north of Lake Victoria. Fine site, built on several low hills. Route centre. Light industry. Makerere University oldest in east Africa. Small port, Port Bell, on lake. [0° 20'N  32° 30'E]

**Kandy**  Town in central Sri Lanka, on small lake. Former capital of old kingdom of Kandy (1592–1815). Ceded to British 1815. Centre of tea trade. Buddhist Temple of the Tooth. Old palace. [7° 18'N  80° 43'E]

**Kano**  City in northern Nigeria, in highly populated area. Commercial centre grown up around old walled town of Hausa people. Road and rail centre. Important groundnuts trade. [12° 2'N  12° 30'E]

**Kanpur**  City in central Uttar Pradesh state, northern India, on the River Ganges. Formerly known as Cawnpore; scene of massacre during Indian Mutiny (1857). Important industrial centre. [26° 28'N  80° 20'E]

**Kaohsiung**  Port in south-west Taiwan. Southern terminus of main railway. Chief market centre for south. Duty-free export-processing zone. Textiles, cement, aluminium, oil refineries. [22° 38'N 120° 18'E]

**Karachi** City and seaport in Pakistan, west of River Indus delta on edge of desert area. Former capital (1947 59). Commercial and route centre; shipbuilding and repairing. Important airport. [24° 53'N 67° 0'E]

**Karaganda** (Qaraghandy) Capital of Karaganda Oblast and chief industrial centre of Kazakhstan. Coal mining, steel works. Large urban agglomeration. [49° 50'N 79° 10'E]

**Karlskrona** Seaport and chief naval base of Sweden on south-eastern coast. Important fishing and china industries. Ice-free harbour. [56° 10'N 15° 35'E]

**Kathmandu** (Katmandu) Capital of Nepal, in valley of Himalayas. Communications and transport centre. Many temples and palaces. [27° 45'N 85° 20'E]

**Katowice** Town in south-central Poland, part of a heavy industrial area which, as Upper Silesia, was part of Germany until 1921. [50° 17'N 19° 5'E]

**Kawasaki** City in east-central Honshu, Japan. Industrial suburb between Tokyo and Yokohama, important for heavy industry. 12th-century temple. [35° 35'N 139° 42'E]

**Kazan** Capital of the Tatarstan Republic, Russian, west of the Urals. Major transport centre with a wide variety of heavy industry. [55° 48'N 49° 3'E]

**Kecskemét** Town in south-east Hungary. Trade centre for fruit-growing area, with associated industry of distilling, preserving fruit and eggs and the manufacture of agricultural implements. [46° 57'N 19° 42'E]

**Kemerovo** City in southern Siberia, Russia. Centre of the Kuzbas industrial zone; coal and associated industries. [55° 20'N 86° 5'E]

**Kemi** Seaport in west Finland at head of Gulf of Bothnia. Large harbour. Centre of the Finnish timber industry with many sawmills. Industries include the manufacture of cellulose and fishing. [65° 44'N 24° 34'E]

**Kenema** Town in eastern Sierra Leone. Administrative centre and focus of diamond and forest trade. Alluvial diamonds mainly from Sewa River; cocoa. [7° 50'N 11° 14'W]

**Kermanshah** City in western Iran. Centre of fertile grain producing area on caravan routes. Sugar and oil refineries. [34° 19'N 47° 4'E]

**Kharkov** (Kharkiv) Capital of Kharkov Oblast in the Ukraine. Long-established route focus and centre of vehicle and aircraft industry. Attractive centre despite wartime destruction. [49° 58'N 36° 20'E]

**Khartoum** Capital of Sudan, between White and Blue Nile. Communications centre. Cotton industry. [15° 31'N 32° 35'E]

**Kherson** Capital of Kherson Oblast in the Ukraine. A Black Sea port on the River Dnieper (Dnipro, Dnepr), now a popular resort. [46° 35'N 32° 35'E]

**Khmelnitskiy** (Khmelnytskyy) Capital of Khmelnitskiy Oblast in Ukraine. Named after a 17th-century revolutionary. Agricultural and food-processing centre. [49° 23'N 27° 0'E]

**Khorramshahr** Port in western Iran. Situated at the confluence of the Shatt-al-Arab river and the Karun river near the frontier with Iraq. Oil-refining centre and major trading port, exporting cotton, dates, hides and skins. [30° 29'N 48° 15'E]

**Khudzhand** Formerly Leninabad, capital of Khudzhand Oblast in Tajikistan. Town with a long, violent history. Cotton, silk and food processing. [40° 14'N 69° 40'E]

**Khulna** City in Bangladesh, on the Ganges delta 129 km [80 mls] south-west of Dacca. Rice, flour and cotton milling. Jute, newsprint, hardboard; boatbuilding. [22° 45'N 89° 34'E]

**Kielce** Town in south-east Poland, with a wide variety of industry including marble and glassworks; as well as iron, lead and zinc mining industries. [50° 52'N  20° 42'E]

**Kiev** (Kiyev, Kyyiv)  Capital of Ukraine and of Kiev Oblast, on the River Dnieper (Dnipro, Dnepr). Major industrial and transport centre. Founded 1,500 years ago; notable for its many architectural features, especially churches and monasteries. [50° 30'N  30° 28'E]

**Kigali**  Capital of Rwanda. Commercial centre, with airport. Trade in cattle and hides. Centre of resurgence of ethnic violence in the 1990s between the Hutu and Tutsi ethnic groups. [1° 59'S  30° 4'E]

**Kilindini**  Modern port on western side of Mombasa Island, Kenya. Exports: coffee, cotton, sisal, tea, soda ash. Also handles traffic from Uganda and north-eastern Tanzania. [4° 4'S  39° 40'E]

**Kimberley**  Market and industrial centre in Orange Free State, South Africa. Centre of diamond-mining industry since diamond rush of 1870s. [28° 43'S  24° 46'E]

**Kingston**  Capital of Jamaica, in the West Indies, on the south coast. Modern port facilities with deep water harbour. Commercial centre. Light industries including textiles. Railway to Montego Bay in the north-west and to Port Antonio, chief banana port, in the north-east. [18° 0'N  76° 50'W]

**Kinshasa**  Capital of Zaïre on River Zaïre at Pool Malebo (Stanley Pool). River port, linked by railway to Matadi at river mouth. Hydroelectricity from Inga Dam downstream. River navigable up to Kisangani. Commercial centre; textiles, brewing and various industries. [4° 20'S  15° 15'E].

**Kirkuk**  Town in north-central Iraq. Agricultural and market centre. Sheep-raising area; crops include grain and fruit. Centre of important oilfield with pipelines to Syria and Lebanon. [35° 30'N  44° 21'E]

**Kirkwall**  Capital of Orkney, Scotland, on Mainland, the largest island. Noted for 12th-century cathedral built during Norse rule.

Port, commercial and service centre, especially for oil industry. [58° 59'N  2° 59'W]

**Kirovograd** (Kirovohrad)  Capital of Kirovograd Oblast in the Ukraine. Industry based on local agriculture, sugar, meat, and agricultural machinery. [48° 35'N  32° 20'E]

**Kiruna**  Most northerly town in Sweden. Centre of Swedish iron-ore industry; on the Lappland railway. [67° 52'N  20° 15'E]

**Kisangani**  Town on River Zaïre in central Zaïre. River navigation west to Kinshasa. Upstream are famous Boyoma Falls. Railway link south to Ubundi. [0° 35'N  25° 14'E]

**Kishinev** (Chişinau)  Capital of Moldova in eastern Europe. Belonged to Romania for part of 20th century. Large food, tobacco and wine industries. [47° 0'N  28° 50'E]

**Kitakyushu**  Seaport in northern Kyushu, Japan. Formed in 1963 by merging of Kokura, Moji, Tobata, Wakamatsu and Yawata on Shimonoseki Strait. [33° 56'N  130° 50'E]

**Kitwe**  A modern, expanding town in the Copper Belt area of central Zambia. Third largest town in Zambia. [12° 54'S  28° 13'E]

**Klagenfurt**  Town in southern Austria. Capital of Carinthia. Historic defensive, route and tourist centre. Leather, wood processing industries. [46° 38'N  14° 20'E]

**Klaipeda**  Historically notable Baltic seaport in western Lithuania. Fishing and timber industries; oil exporting. [55° 43'N  21° 10'E]

**Knossos**  Ancient city of Greece in northern Crete, south-east of Iráklion. Centre of Cretan Bronze Age culture and Minoan civilization. [35° 16'N  25° 10'E]

**Kobe**  Seaport city, capital of Hyogo prefecture in southern Honshu, Japan. Industrial centre; port facilities second only to Yokohama in importance. Iron and steel, shipbuilding, rubber, aircraft. Exports oil, tea, camphor, cotton. Devastating earthquake killed 5,000 in 1995. [34° 45'N  135° 10'E]

**Kofu**  Capital of Yamanashi prefecture in central Honshu, Japan. Agricultural centre for vegetables and fruit, especially grapes. Important market for silk fabrics, raw silk and cocoons. [35° 40'N  138° 30'E]

**Kolwezi**  Town in Shaba province in southern Zaïre, 1,443 m [4733 ft] above sea level. Important cobalt and copper mines, and mineral processing. [10° 40'S  25° 25'E]

**Kosice**  Town in eastern Slovak Republic. Episcopal city; 14th-century Gothic cathedral. Manufactures include tobacco, textiles and wine. [48° 42'N  21° 15'E]

**Kowloon**  Town on Kowloon peninsula on mainland of south-east China, part of the British Crown Colony (until 1999) of Hong Kong and separated from the island by Hong Kong harbour. Major trading and industrial centre. [22° 20'N  114° 15'E]

**Kozhikode** (Calicut)  Town and ancient port in Kerala state, south-west India, on Malabar Coast of Arabian Sea. Noted for cotton cloth – hence 'calico'. [11° 15'N  75° 43'E]

**Kraków**  Town in south Poland. Historic architecture: castle, cathedral and university. Heavy industrial centre (iron and steel, engineering); salt mines. [50° 4'N  19° 57'E]

**Krasnovodsk** (Krasnowodsk)  City in the west of Turkmenistan on the Caspian Sea. Caspian train and ferry port; oil and cotton exports. [40° 0'N  52° 52'E]

**Krasnoyarsk**  Capital of Krasnoyarsk Kray in Siberia, Russia. Large reservoir and power station. Gold-mining centre, timber, furs, shipbuilding, heavy industry. [56° 8'N  93° 0'E]

**Kremenchug** (Kremenchuk)  Industrial town on the River Dnieper in Ukraine. Large Kremenchug reservoir and power station nearby. Timber, textiles, iron ore. [49° 5'N  33° 25'E]

**Krems**  Town in north-east Austria on the northern bank of the River Danube. Capital of Lower Austria. Centre of Weinviertel wine industry. [48° 25'N  15° 36'E]

**Kronshtadt**  Historic naval base, fortress and shipbuilding port on an island in the Gulf of Finland, Russia. [60° 5'N  29° 45'E]

**Kuala Lumpur**  City and capital of Malaysia, 40 km [25 mls] inland from the south-west coast of the Malay Peninsula. On the railway from Singapore to Bangkok. A commercial and railway centre, it grew around the tin and later rubber industry. [3° 9'N  101° 41'E]

**Kuching**  Town and capital of Sarawak in Malaysia. Port on River Sarawak with ferry connections to Malay Peninsula. Rice and sago milling. [1° 33'N  110° 25'E]

**Kulyab** (Kulob)  Capital of the re-established Kulyab Oblast in Tajikistan. Textile industry, notably cotton. [37° 55'N  69° 50'E]

**Kumasi**  City in south-west Ghana. Commercial centre serving cocoa producing area. Distribution, education and route centre. National Cultural Centre. [6° 41'N  1° 38'W]

**Kunming**  Capital of Yunnan province, south-central China. Major transport centre in mountainous area. Copper smelter and iron and steel plant. [25° 1'N  102° 41'E]

**Kursk**  City in western Russia, south of Moscow. Large iron-ore deposits (the 'Kursk Magnetic Anomaly'). [51° 42'N  36° 11'E]

**Kustanay** (Qostanay)  Capital of Kustanay Oblast in northern Kazakhstan. Large iron-ore deposits nearby. Artificial fibres and food processing. [53° 10'N  63° 35'E]

**Kutaisi**  Ancient town in western Georgia. Some important old buildings survive despite unsettled history. Silk, wine and tobacco industries. [42° 19'N  42° 40'E]

**Kuwait**  City Capital of Kuwait at head of Arabian Gulf. Good harbour and considerable trade. Traditional industry of pearling and fishing eclipsed by oil-related industries; petrochemical plants. [20° 30'N  48° 0'E]

**Kyoto**  City, capital of Kyoto prefecture in western Honshu, Japan. Ancient capital of

Japan, famed for its many temples and historical buildings. Cultural and religious centre; Imperial University (1897) and medical school. Now also important manufacturing city: electrical equipment, aircraft, chemicals. Many craft industries: pottery, bronze, porcelain, silk, velvet. [35° 0'N 135° 45'E]

**Kyrenia** Seaport in northern Cyprus at foot of coastal mountain range. Town supposedly founded 10th century BC. Byzantine castle. [35° 20'N 33° 20'E]

**La Chaux de Fonds** Town in north-western Switzerland in Jura Mountains, in Neuchâtel canton. Centre of Swiss watch- and clock-making in Jura. [47° 7'N 6° 50'E]

**La Coruña** Seaport in north-west Spain. Capital of La Coruña province. Armada sailed from here 1588. Fishing industries, engineering, oil refining, glass. [43° 20'N 8° 25'W]

**La Paz** Administrative capital of Bolivia, in valley at foot of Mt Illimani, in the Andes near the Peruvian border. The highest capital in the world at 3,657m [12,000 ft]. Principal industrial and trading centre of Bolivia; manufactures electrical appliances, furniture, chemicals, textiles, glass. [16° 20'S 68° 10'W]

**La Paz** Capital of Baja California Sur (Lower California) state, Mexico, on eastern side of the peninsula, on Gulf of California. Important pearl industry. [24° 10'N 110° 20'W]

**Lagos** Former capital and main seaport of Nigeria, on natural harbour. Oldest settlement, founded on slave trade, on lagoon island of Lagos; spread to other islands and mainland. Industrial centre. Exports mainly oil, cocoa, groundnuts. [6° 25'N 3° 27'E]

**Lahore** City in northern Pakistan. Was the capital of Mogul, then Sikh, empires. Industrial route, cultural and educational centre. Badshahi Mosque is world's largest. Tomb of the Sikh ruler Ranjit Singh. Railway engineering. [31° 32'N 74° 22'E]

**Lalitapur** Market town 3 km [2 mls] south of Kathmandu in Nepal. An ancient city that was the capital of the first king of Nepal; numerous temples. [27° 40'N 85° 20'E]

**Larnaca** Seaport in south-east Cyprus, on site of ancient city of Cilcium. Exports wine, fruit, olive oil, brandy, soap and tobacco products. Tourist area. [34° 54'N 33° 39'E]

**Las Palmas** Capital of Las Palmas province on Gran Canaria Island and largest town of the Canary Islands (Spain). Commercial centre and port; food processing, iron founding, machinery and textile industries. Important tourist centre. [28° 7'N 15° 26'W]

**Las Vegas** Resort in Nevada, western USA. Major gaming and hotel centre. Manufactures gaming equipment. Magnesium smelting. [36° 10'N 115° 9'W]

**Latakia** Seaport of western Syria. Centre of rich agricultural region. Traditional and still important export is tobacco; also asphalt, eggs, cereals, pottery. [35° 30'N 35° 45'E]

**Lausanne** Town in western Switzerland on site steeply sloping to Lake Geneva. Capital of Vaud canton. Ancient ecclesiastical and educational centre; noted cathedral and university. Commerical centre with annual fair. Resort. [46° 32'N 6° 38'E]

**Le Havre** Port in northern France at mouth of Seine estuary, in Seine-Maritime *département*. Important transatlantic and cross-channel traffic. Oil-refining industry; shipbuilding, food processing. [49° 30'N 0° 5'E]

**Leeds** Capital of West Yorkshire, northern England. Important commercial, manufacturing and route centre; known for its large Victorian town hall. Major clothing industry, engineering, especially transport and factory equipment. [53° 48'N 1° 34'W]

**Leeuwarden** Town in northern Netherlands. Capital of Friesland. Centre of intensive dairying region, with large cattle market. Butter and cheese industries. [53° 15'N 5° 48'E]

**Leh** Town in east Jammu and Kashmir state, north Indian subcontinent, on River Indus, at

3,500 m [11,500 ft]. Trade centre. Meteorological observatory. Starting point of expeditions into Himalayas. [34° 9'N  77° 35'E]

**Leiden**  Town in north-west Netherlands, in Zuid Holland. Historic university town and former textile-trading port at southern end of bulb-growing area. Printing industry. Birth place of Rembrandt. [52° 09'N  4° 30'E]

**Leipzig**  Town in eastern Germany. Ancient buildings, including 15th-century Church of St Thomas. Produces iron and steel, chemicals, paper, plastics, electrical and agricultural machinery. Famous for publishing and industry fairs. [51° 20'N  12° 23'E]

**León**  Town in north-west Spain. Capital of Leon province. In coal-mining area. Walled medieval town; noted 13th–14th century cathedral. Livestock market; chemical industry. [42° 38'N  5° 34'W]

**León**  Town in west of Nicaragua, on lowland west of Lake Managua, near Pacific coast. Former capital, cultural centre. Original town destroyed by earthquake in 1609; ruins near volcano Momotombo. [12° 20'N  86° 51'W]

**Lerwick**  Capital of Shetland Islands, northern Scotland, on east coast of Mainland Island. Commercial centre and fishing port with large processing industries. Most northerly town in the United Kingdom with strong Norse character. Major centre for North Sea oil industry. [60° 10'N  1° 10'W]

**Lhasa**  Capital of Tibet Autonomous Region, China, at 3,658 m [12,000 ft], on Tsangpo River, tributary of Brahmaputra. Dominated by spectacular Potala, former palace monastery of Dalai Lama. [29° 25'N  0° 58'E]

**Libreville**  Port and capital of Gabon. On Gabon River estuary on north coast. Freed slaves put ashore here by French in 19th century. Timber exports important, also cocoa and oil. [0° 25'N  9° 26'E]

**Liège**  Town and river port in eastern Belgium. Capital of Liège province. Commercial, manufacturing and route centre. Major steel producer; also heavy engineering, chemical and glass industries. [50° 38'N  5° 35'E]

**Lille**  Town in north-east France. Capital of Nord *département*. Historic defensive centre with famous Vauban citadel. Leading textile industry. [50° 38'N  3° 3'E]

**Lillehammer**  Town in central Norway. Tourist centre for both winter and summer sports. Winter olympics held here February 1994. [61° 8'N  10° 30'E]

**Lilongwe**  Capital of Malawi in the centre of the country. Declared capital 1975. Modern administrative centre. Tobacco grown in the north. [14° 0'S  33° 48'E]

**Lima**  Capital of Peru, in dry foggy coastal area. Oldest university in South America. Its port is Callao. Oil refining and manufacturing; tanning, furniture, pharmaceutical, textile and vehicle industries. [12° 0'S  77° 0'W]

**Limassol**  Seaport in southern Cyprus. 15th-century castle. Centre for agricultural production of surrounding regions. Exports wine and asbestos. Tourist centre. [34° 2'N  33° 1'E]

**Limerick**  Capital of County Limerick in Munster province, south-west Republic of Ireland. Historic, commercial, manufacturing and route centre; port at head of Shannon estuary. Large food-processing industry, especially bacon, grain, dairy products; clothing. Traditional lace industry. [52° 40'N  8° 38'W]

**Limoges**  Town in west-central France. Capital of Haute-Vienne *département*. Famous for porcelain and shoes. Textiles, car and motorcycle parts. [45° 50'N  1° 15'E]

**Linköping**  Town in south-east Sweden. Important medieval town, with fine Gothic cathedral. Industrial centre for aircraft, cars, textiles and furniture. [58° 28'N  15° 36'E]

**Linz**  Town in northern Austria on the River Danube. Capital of Upper Austria. Commercial and manufacturing centre and river port. Large chemical and steel industries; as well as textile industry. [48° 18'N  14° 18'E]

**Lisbon** Capital of Portugal at mouth of River Tagus. Commercial and route centre with large naval harbour. Site of departure of many voyages of discovery in 15th-17th centuries. Destroyed by earthquake in 1755. Passenger, freight and fishing port. Cork, food, steel and shipbuilding industries. [38° 42'N 9° 10'W]

**Liverpool** Cathedral city and capital of Merseyside, north-west England. Important commercial centre and port with leading UK, Atlantic and export trade. Two cathedrals; Liver and Cunard buildings are famous landmarks. Large food-proccssing industry, especially flour and sugar; car assembly; pulp and paper manufacture. [53° 25'N 3° 0'W]

**Livingstone** Town on River Zambezi in southern Zambia. Railway to Shaba (in Zaïre) led to the development of mineral resources. Sawmilling. Tourist centre for Victoria Falls. [17° 46'S 25° 52'E]

**Ljubljana** Capital of Slovenia. Baroque cathedral, university and 15th-century castle. Main industries are iron foundries and glass mills; publishing industry. [46° 4'N 14° 33'E]

**Lobito** Major port in central part of Angola. Good modern harbour. Terminus of Trans-African Railway. Exports copper, zinc, uranium and cobalt from Shaba (in Zaïre). Fish drying and canning. [12° 18'S 13° 35'E]

**Lod** Town 17 km [10 mls] from Tel Aviv Jaffa, Israel. Reputed birthplace of St George. International airport; railway junction. Electronic equipment. [31° 57'N 34° 54'E]

**Lódz** Town in central Poland. Important textile industry; planned layout development in 19th century. [51° 45'N 19° 27'E]

**Logroño** Town in northern Spain. Capital of Logroño province. Centre of Rioja agricultural region in Ebro Valley. Wine, vegetable, chemical and textile industries. [42° 28'N 2° 27'W]

**Lomé** Capital and chief port of Togo, near the border with Ghana. Main exports are phosphates, cocoa, coffee, palm kernels and cotton. [6° 09'N 1° 20'E]

**London** Capital of United Kingdom of Great Britain and Northern Ireland. Major international financial, cultural and educational centre. Route focus, with leading international airport and largest UK importing port (especially food and raw materials). Manufacturing industries, especially electrical and precision goods, pharmaceuticals, publishing, printing. Major tourist centre: many famous buildings, such as St Pauls Cathedral, Houses of Parliament, Westminster Abbey. [51° 30'N 0° 5'W]

**Londonderry** Port and capital of County Londonderry, in the north of Northern Ireland. Historic walled city near mouth of River Foyle. Scene of famous siege and defeat of James II in 1689. Large clothing industry, especially shirts; as well as distilling and food industries. [55° 0'N 7° 23'W]

**Los Angeles** Port on Pacific coast of southern California, USA. Major agglomeration and tourist centre in oil producing area. Oil-refining and shipbuilding industries; leading centre of aerospace and film industries; clothing, car parts and assembly, paper and printing. Processing centre for local fruit especially citrus, vegetables, dairy products and tuna fish. [34° 4'N 118° 15'W]

**Lourdes** Town in south-west France, in Hautes-Pyrenees *département*. Major pilgrimage and tourist centre, associated with St Bernadette. [43° 6'N 0° 3'W]

**Louvain** Town in Brabant, central Belgium. Historic, regional and commercial centre, with textile trade. Roman Catholic university established 1425. Brewing; electrical and engineering industries [50° 52'N 4° 42'E]

**Luanda** Capital city and port on bay in northern Angola. Founded by Portuguese in 1575 for slave trade; rebuilt 1938. Railway east to Malanje. Cotton and important coffee exporter. [8° 50'S 13° 15'E]

**Luang Prabang** Town in north-central Laos, at junction of Mekong and Kahn rivers. Former royal capital. Hydroelectric power on Dong River to south. Rubber, rice and teak production in area. [19° 52'N 102° 10'E]

**Lübeck**  Seaport in northern Germany, in Schleswig-Holstein. Former capital of the Hanseatic League. Industries include shipbuilding and metal-working. Known for its marzipan. [53° 52'N  10° 41'E]

**Lublin**  Town in south-east Poland. Temporary capital of Poland, 1918 and 1944. Agricultural trade and food-processing centre; new copper reserves nearby. [51° 12'N  22° 38'E]

**Lubumbashi**  City in Shaba province in southern Zaïre. On the main railway system. Important administrative and commercial centre for copper and cobalt mining area. Varied industries. [11° 40'S  27° 28'E]

**Lucerne**  Town in north-central Switzerland, at north-western end of Lake Lucerne. Capital of Lucerne canton. Famous resort with annual music festival. Also known for its wooden bridges. [47° 3'N  8° 18'E]

**Lucknow**  Capital of Uttar Pradesh state, northern India. Famous siege (1857) during Indian Mutiny. Route centre. Carpet and paper manufactured; and railway engineering industry. [26° 50'N  81° 10'E]

**Lugansk**  (Luhansk)  Capital of Lugansk Oblast in Ukraine. Formerly Voroshilovgrad. Many heavy industries; centre of the Donbas industrial region. [48° 38'N  39° 15'E]

**Lund**  Town in southern Sweden. University and 11th-century cathedral. Industrial centre; printing and publishing. [55° 44'N  13° 12'E]

**Lusaka**  Capital of Zambia, on River Kafue in the south. Altitude 1,219 m [4,000 ft]. On main railway and important road junction with Great East road to Malawi. Chemical and brewing industries. [15° 28'S  28° 16'E]

**Luxembourg**  Capital of the Grand Duchy of Luxembourg. International commercial centre, especially for banking, with many European organization headquarters, including EC Court of Justice. [49° 37'N  6° 9'E]

**Luxor**  Town on eastern bank of River Nile in upper Egypt. On site of ancient Thebes;

Temple of Luxor dates from 1417 BC. Karnak nearby. [25° 41'N  32° 38'E]

**Lvov**  (Lviv, Lvyv)  Main city of western Ukraine and capital of Lvov Oblast. Polish between the World Wars; many historic churches. [49° 50'N  24° 0'E]

**Lyon**  River port in eastern France at the confluence of the Rhône and Saône rivers. Capital of Rhône *département*. Ancient commercial, financial and route centre. Major silk industry; chemicals, machinery, and motor vehicles. [45° 46'N  4° 50'E]

**Maastricht**  River port in south-east Netherlands. Capital of Limburg. Historic commercial and route centre. Ceramic, glass and cement industries. Treaty on European Union signed December 1991 (came into force on 1 November 1993). [50° 50'N  5° 40'E]

**Madras**  City and port of Tamil Nadu state, southern India; on Bay of Bengal, with artificial harbour. Founded by British in 1653 as Fort St George. Railway focus. Textiles. Exports cotton and hides. [13° 8'N  80° 19'E]

**Madrid**  Capital of Spain and of Madrid province. Commercial and route centre, established as the capital in 1561. Famous Prado Museum. Luxury goods, printing, transport equipment, chemicals industry. Tourist centre. [40° 25'N  3° 45'W]

**Mainz**  Town in west-central Germany, at confluence of Main and Rhine rivers. Capital of Rhineland-Palatinate. Has noted cathedral and largest German wine market. Site of Gutenberg's development of printing. Chemicals and coffee processing. [50° 0'N  8° 17'W]

**Makhachkala**  Capital of the Dagestan Republic in southern Russia. Caspian Sea port with a wide variety of manufacturing industries; also oil refineries. [43° 0'N  47° 30'E]

**Malabo**  Capital of Equatorial Guinea on northern coast of island of Bioko (Fernando Póo). Cocoa, coffee, copra. [3° 45'N  8° 50'E]

**Málaga**  Seaport in southern Spain. Capital of

Málaga province. Commercial centre of Costa del Sol, known for its wines. Textile and food industries. Resort. [36° 43'N 4° 23'W]

**Malang**   City in south central Java in Indonesia. Centre of a fertile agricultural basin and an important coffee producing area. [7° 59'S 112° 45'E]

**Malmö**   Seaport in south-west Sweden. Train and ferry links with Copenhagen; naval base. Major industries include agricultural products, textiles, shipbuilding and engineering. [55° 36'N 12° 59'E]

**Managua**   Capital of Nicaragua, on southern shore of Lake Managua. Original town destroyed by earthquke in 1931, rebuilt on modern lines, but centre again destroyed by earthquake in 1972. Rebuilt as three satellite towns. Volcano Momotombo to north. Highway to Honduras. [12° 6'N 86° 20'W]

**Manaus**   Port on the Rio Negro near its junction with the Amazon river, northern Brazil. Trading port for products of the Amazon basin; accessible to ocean-going ships. Thermal-electric power plant; oil refinery; notable botanic gardens. [3° 0'S 60° 0'W]

**Manchester**   Capital of Greater Manchester Metropolitan County in north-west England. Important commercial, cultural and industrial centre at east end of Manchester Ship Canal. Traditional centre of cotton textile industry, with important markets and spinning industry. Engineering, especially for the textile, transport and food industries. [53° 30'N 2° 15'W]

**Mandalay**   Second largest city of Burma, on the Irrawaddy River. Capital of the Mandalay Division and commercial centre of Upper Burma. Manufactures matches, silk, gold and silverware. [22° 57'N 96° 4'E]

**Mangyshlak**   (Mangghystau) Capital of Mangyshlak Oblast in Kazakhstan, on the east coast of the Caspian Sea. Notable for its large new oilfields. [44° 30'N 52° 30'E]

**Manila**   Capital of the Philippines, in the south-west of Luzon island in Manila Bay.

Chief port, commercial, cultural and industrial centre. Sugar refining and manufacturing of textiles; exports sugar and manila hemp. [14° 40'N 121° 30'E]

**Manizales**   City in west-central Colombia, in the Cordillera Central. Important coffee-producing centre; textiles, leather goods, beer. [5° 5'N 75° 32'W]

**Maputo**   Capital of Mozambique. Port with fine harbour; railway link to Zimbabwe. Fruit in area and cashew nuts to south along coast. Tourist centre. [25° 58'S 32° 32'E]

**Maracaibo**   Deep-water port in north-west Venezuela, on north-west shore of Lake Maracaibo. Expanded after discovery of oil in 1917. Exports oil, coffee, cocoa and sugar. Manufactures chemicals, textiles, soap and rope. [10° 40'N 71° 30'W]

**Maracay**   City in northern Venezuela, north-east of Lake Valencia. Centre of Venezuelan cattle industry; paper, textiles, chemicals, sugar refining; gas wells. [10° 15'N 67° 28'W]

**Maribor**   Town in Slovenia. Has notable 12th-century cathedral. Market (wine and grain) and manufacturing centre: leather, boots and shoes. [46° 36'N 15° 40'E]

**Marrakesh**   City in foothills of High Atlas Mountains in Morocco. Former capital. Famous market square; ancient mosques; notable high minaret. [31° 9'N 8° 0'W]

**Marseilles**   Port in south-east France. Capital of Bouches-du-Rhone *département*. Important commercial centre and leading French port, with petrochemical industry. Large food-processing industry; fertilizers, ship repairing and marine engineering. [43° 18'N 5° 23'E]

**Mary**   Capital of Mary Oblast in Turkmenistan. Ancient town now a centre of cotton, silk and carpets. [37° 40'N 61° 50'E]

**Maseru**   Capital of Lesotho. Short railway from Maseru north to the Bloemfontein to KwaZulu-Natal line in South Africa. Building materials factory. [29° 18'S 27° 30'E]

**Masvingo** Town in southern Zimbabwe. Oldest European settlement. National park to south, near game reserve. [20° 10'S  30° 49'E]

**Matadi** Chief port of Zaïre, on River Zaïre. Railway to Kinshasa linking to inland waterways. Exports mainly palm oil, rubber, cotton, and coffee. [5° 52'S  13° 31'E]

**Matrah** Important deep-water port adjacent to Muscat, Oman. Warehouse facilities; terminus of caravan routes. Trades in dates and fruit. [23.37 N  58.34 E]

**Mbabane** Capital of Swaziland in the northwest of the country in the Dalgeni Hills. The capital was transferred here from Manzini in 1902. [26° 18'S  31° 6'E]

**Mbuji-Mayi** City in southern Kasai area of Zaïre. Important mining centre for industrial diamonds. [6° 10'S  23° 39'E]

**Mecca** Sacred Muslim city of Hijaz, western Saudi Arabia, in a valley surrounded by low hills. Birthplace of Mohammed and site of the Ka'bah Shrine. Its Red Sea port is at Jiddah to the west. [21° 30'N  39° 54'E]

**Medan** Largest city of Sumatra, in north-east Sumatra, Indonesia, on the Deli River. Communications centre. Centre of fertile region. Exports tobacco, coffee, tea and palm oil. University. [3° 40'N  98° 38'E]

**Medellín** City in west-central Colombia, in the Cordillera Central. Main textile centre of Colombia; coffee market. Chief centre for gold and silver mining. Chemicals, leather, pottery, steel, glass. [3° 15'N  75° 35'W]

**Medina** Inland city in Hijaz, western Saudi Arabia. Sacred Muslim city containing the tomb of Mohammed and other important mosques. Trade in agricultural produce, such as dates, cereals and fruit. [24° 35'N 39° 52'E]

**Melbourne** Capital of Victoria, Australia, on almost enclosed Port Philip Bay. Second largest city in Australia. Established 1835 and greatly expanded from 1850 with discovery of gold. Extensive suburban development. Important manufacturing centre; oil refineries. Rich pastoral hinterland. [37° 50'S 145° 0'E]

**Melilla** Modern commercial city on northern coast of Morocco (Spanish enclave). Administered from Málaga. Since 1863 has had free port status. [35° 21'N  2° 57'W]

**Memphis** River port in Tennessee, southeast USA, on Mississippi River. Commercial, manufacturing and route centre. Major cotton and hardwood markets. Furniture and flooring industries; cotton seed oil, farm equipment. Regarded as birthplace of blues music. Graceland, home of Elvis Presley, nearby. [35° 8'N  90° 3'W]

**Mendoza** City in Argentina, in foot hills of Andes on main route from Argentina to the port Valparaiso in Chile. Commercial centre of an irrigated agricultural and wine-growing region. [32° 50'S  68° 52'W]

**Mérida** Town in Mexico, capital of Yucatán state, in north of Yucatán Peninsula. Founded 1542 on site of Mayan city; many ruins in area. Sisal cultivation. [20° 59'N  89° 39'W]

**Mashhad** City in north-east Iran, near Turkmen and Afghan borders. Important trade centre, dealing in carpets and cotton goods. Tanning, flour milling and rug making industries. A holy city and place of pilgrimage for Shia Muslims. [36° 20'N  59° 35'E]

**Mexico City** Capital of Mexico, situated in south-central part of country on plateau over 3,000 m [7,000 ft] above sea level. Built on site of ancient Aztec capital. Volcanoes of Popocatépetl and Iztaccihuatl to south-east. Major industrial centre. One of the world's largest cities with one of the fastest growing urban populations. [19° 20'N 99° 10'W]

**Miami** Resort in Florida, south-east USA, on Atlantic coast at southern end of peninsula near the Everglades. Commercial centre. Important air-traffic centre; cruise port. Tourist service industry. [25° 47'N 80° 11'W]

**Milan** Town in north-east Italy. Capital of Lombardy. Leading Italian commercial and manufacturing centre, with famous cathedral and opera house (La Scala) and important trade fair. Electrical engineering, publishing industry. [45° 28'N  9° 10'E]

**Minneapolis**  City in Minnesota, north USA, at head of navigation of Mississippi River. Major commercial and route centre. Twin city of St Paul on opposite bank. Focus for grain trade and milling industries; electronics and computer centre, especially for aircraft industry. Oil refining. [44° 59'N  93° 16'W]

**Minsk**  Capital of Belarus and of Minsk Oblast. Major industrial, transport and manufacturing centre. [53° 52'N  27° 30'E]

**Miyazaki**  Seaport, capital of Miyazaki prefecture in south-east Kyushu, Japan. Famous shrine. [31° 56'N  131° 30'E]

**Moçambique**  Town on central part of coast of Mozambique. First Portuguese settlement built in 1504 on an island. [15° 3'S  40° 42'E]

**Mogadishu**  Capital and main port of Somalia, on Indian Ocean. Site of ancient settlement; Arabic influence in old quarter. Exports livestock, sugar. [2° 2'N  45° 25'E]

**Mogilev**  (Mahilyow)  Capital of Mogilev Oblast in Belarus. Founded in 13th century; now an industrial town specializing in synthetic fibres. [53° 55'N  30° 18'E]

**Mokpo**  Seaport on south-west coast of southern Cholla province in South Korea. A deepwater port on the Yellow Sea and the southern terminus of the west coast railway to Seoul. Industrial centre. Cotton ginning, rice milling and fishing. [34° 50'N  126° 25'E]

**Mombasa**  Historic seaport of Kenya. Site of medieval town, built on island. Modern harbour of Kilindi on western side of island, now chief port. Oil refinery. Railway to interior. [4° 2'S  39° 43'E]

**Monaghan**  Capital of County Monaghan, Ulster province, in north Republic of Ireland. Cathedral and market centre with dairy and bacon industries. [54° 15'N  6° 58'W]

**Monrovia**  Port, capital of Liberia, on northern part of coast. Founded in 1822 for freed slaves from USA. Railway to north. Exports rubber and iron ore. [6° 18'N  10° 47'W]

**Montego Bay**  Town and resort on the northwest coast of Jamaica in the West Indies. Fine beaches and tourist facilities. Important deep-sea fishing centre. [18° 30'N  78° 0'W]

**Monterrey**  City in Mexico, east of Sierra Madre Oriental range. Capital of Nuevo León state. Important route and industry centre. Iron, steel and lead. [25° 40'N  100° 30'W]

**Montevideo**  Seaport on the Rio de la Plata and capital of Uruguay. Industrial and cultural centre; meat-packing, tanning, flour milling, wines, soap, footwear and textiles. Exports animal products. Resort. [34° 50'S  56° 11'W]

**Montpellier**  Town in southern France. Capital of Hérault *département*. Ancient university. Large wine market; food, pharmceutical and perfume industry. [43° 37'N  3° 52'E]

**Montreal**  City and port in south-east Canada, in Québec, on St Lawrence Seaway. Mostly French-speaking. Major commercial and manufacturing centre. Grain processing; oil refining; aircraft, railway equipment and clothing industries; publishing and printing. [45° 31'N  73° 34'W]

**Morelia**  Town in Mexico, capital of the state of Michoacan. Altitude 1,900 m [6,235 ft]. Founded in 1541 as a mining settlement named Valladolid. Planetarium opened in 1975. [19° 40'N  101° 11'W]

**Moscow**  Capital of Russia and its largest city. Founded in 12th century, burnt down 1812, though some notable buildings remain, including the Kremlin, the seat of government. Chief political, cultural and transport centre with many industries. [55° 45'N  37° 35'E]

**Mosul**  City on west bank of the Tigris river, northern Iraq. Centre of agricultural and oil-producing area. [36° 15'N  43° 5'E]

**Moulmein**  Seaport in Burma, on the Gulf of

Martaban. Capital of the Tenasserim Division at mouth of the Salween River. Exports rice and teak. [16° 30'N  97° 40'E]

**Mount Isa**  Town in Selwyn Range, in western New South Wales, Australia. Important copper-mining centre. [20° 42'S  139° 26'E]

**Mullingar**  Capital of County Westmeath, in Leinster province, central Republic of Ireland. Cathedral, route and market centre of leading cattle area. Centre of former Kingdom of Meath. [53° 31'N  7° 20'W]

**Munich**  City in southern Germany; capital of Bavaria. Major commercial, manufacturing and cultural centre, with many famous buildings including Frauenkirche, Pinakothek and Residenz. Leading brewing industry with Oktoberfest. Electrical engineering, transport equipment, printing and publishing. Tourist centre. [48° 8'N  11° 33'E]

**Murmansk**  Ice-free port on Barents Sea, in the extreme north-west of Russia. It is the country's largest fishing port with important shipyards. [68° 57'N  33° 10'E]

**Muscat**  Capital of Oman, on Gulf of Oman. Former port of some importance; most trade now goes to Matrah. [23° 37'N  58° 36'E]

**Mymensingh**  District capital in Bangladesh, on the Brahmaputra fertile flood plain to north of Dacca. Agricultural centre. Engineering and jute processing. [24° 45'N  90° 24'E]

**Mysore**  Town in Karnataka state, south-west India, in high valley between two ridges. Was capital of former Mysore state. Notable Maharaja's Palace (1897). Commercial centre. Silk weaving. Manufacturing sandalwood oil. [13° 15'N  77° 0'E]

**N'Djamena**  Capital of Chad, at confluence of Logone and Chari rivers in extreme west. Livestock market. [12° 10'N  14° 59'E]

**Naas**  Capital of County Kildare, in Leinster province, east-central Republic of Ireland. Market and horse racing centre east of The Curragh. [53° 12'N  6° 40'W]

**Nagasaki**  Seaport, capital of Nagasaki prefecture in Kyushu, Japan. Centre of Japanese Christianity. Half of city destroyed by second atomic bomb dropped in August 1945. Beautiful natural harbour. Exports coal, cotton goods, raw silk and tea. Manufactures aircraft, ships and electrical equipment. [32° 47'N  129° 50'E]

**Nagoya**  Major port and capital of Aichi prefecture in southern Honshu, Japan. Industrial centre and centre of the Japanese pottery and porcelain industries. Also manufactures aircraft, cars, machine tools, textiles, dyes and chemicals. [35° 10'N  136° 50'E]

**Nairobi**  City and capital of Kenya. Commercial and route centre. Light industry. Tourist trade to national park nearby. Coffee and sisal from Muranga (Fort Hall) area by railway. [1° 17'S  36° 48'E]

**Nakuru**  Town in Rift Valley in Kenya, on Lake Nakuru. Market centre in agricultural region. Pyrethrum extracting. Lake famous for flamingos. [0° 16'S  36° 4'E]

**Nancy**  Town in north-eastern France. Capital of Meurthe-et-Moselle *département*. Noted for 18th-century planned centre. Glass and steel industries. [48° 42'N  6° 12'E]

**Nanking**  Capital of Kiangsu province, eastern China. Former capital of Nationalist China. Manufacturing centre, on south bank of Lower Yellow River, for traditional textiles and porcelain. [32° 2'N  118° 47'E]

**Naples**  Seaport in southern Italy. Capital of Campania. Commercial and manufacturing centre of the south, known for its beauty and site on bay north-west of Vesuvius. Founded by Greeks, with strong cultural tradition. Port, with leading Italian passenger traffic; steel, aircraft and railway engineering, textiles, paper and food industries. [40° 50'N  14° 17'E]

**Narayanganj**  City in Bangladesh, south-east of Dhaka on the Meghna River. Growing industrial area. Power station, boatbuilding, shoe factory, cotton textiles, jute and grain milling. [23° 40'N  90° 33'E]

**Narvik** Seaport in north-west Norway with ice-free harbour. Rail terminus of Lappland railway. Exports iron ore from Sweden. [68° 28'N  17° 26'E]

**Naryn** Capital of Naryn Oblast in Kyrgyzstan. Local administrative centre; large reservoirs and hydroelectric power stations nearby. [41° 26'N  75° 58'E]

**Nashville** Capital of Tennessee, south-east USA. Commercial and manufacturing centre. Major recording industry; textiles, religious publishing and printing. [36° 10'N  86° 47'W]

**Nassau** Capital of the Bahamas, on north-east coast of New Providence Island, West Indies. Tourist centre. [25° 5'N  77° 20'W]

**Nazareth** Town in northern Israel. Junction point of highways from Haifa and Jerusalem to Lake Tiberias. Childhood home of Christ. Textiles, leather goods. [32° 42'N  35° 17'E]

**Ndola** Modern town in northern Zambia. Important centre for Copper Belt. Second largest town in Zambia. [13° 0'S  28° 34'E]

**Negombo** Town and resort on west coast of Sri Lanka, north of Colombo. At mouth of lagoon, with fine beaches. Exports coconuts and cinnamon. [7° 12'N  79° 50'E]

**Neuchâtel** Town in western Switzerland on western shore of Lake Neuchâtel. Capital of Neuchâtel canton. University town with major wine market. Watch and clock research centre. [47° 0'N  6° 55'E]

**New Delhi** Capital of India, in Delhi Union Territory, northern India. Built south of old city of Delhi as capital planned by British; was capital of British India, 1931–47. Tree-lined avenues and gardens. [28° 37'N  77° 13'E]

**New Orleans** Major port in Louisiana, southern USA, on Mississippi river. Important commercial and cultural centre with leading cotton market. Famed for French Quarter Dixieland jazz. Large petrochemical industry; sugar milling, shipbuilding and bauxite-processing industries. [29° 58'N  90° 4'W]

**New Plymouth** Port and regional centre on North Island, New Zealand, in intensively farmed Taranaki lowlands. [39° 4'S  174° 5'E]

**New York** City in New York state, north-east USA, on Manhattan and Long Island at mouth of Hudson River. Major international financial, manufacturing and cultural centre. Transport focus; largest US port, handling especially oil and oil products. Headquarters of UN; World Trade Centre. Clothing, printing and publishing industries; leather goods. Important tourist centre; known as 'Big Apple'. [40° 45'N  74° 0'W]

**Newcastle** Seaport and regional centre in New South Wales, Australia. On edge of important coalfield. Developed from coal-mining village; exports coal. Heavy industry. [33° 0'S  151° 46'E]

**Newcastle upon Tyne** Capital of Tyne and Wear county in north-east England; commercial, cultural and industrial centre of Tyneside conurbation. Route focus; port, especially for coal export; ferry terminal for Scandinavia. Shipbuilding industries; engineering, chemicals and glass. [54° 59'N  1° 37 W]

**Niamey** Capital of Niger, on River Niger near south-west border. Route centre. Agricultural market in productive area. [13° 27'N  2° 6'E]

**Nice** Seaport and resort in south-east France. Capital of Alpes-Maritimes *département*. Route centre and ferry port. Market for horticultural area (noted for mimosa). [43° 42'N  7° 14'E]

**Nicosia** Capital of Cyprus in centre of the island. Enclosed by walls built for defence in 15th century. Ancient buildings including 14th-century cathedral. Varied manufacturing industries. [35° 10'N  33° 25'E]

**Nîmes** Town in southern France. Capital of Gard *département*. Ancient commercial and route centre famed for its Roman amphitheatre and aqueduct. Large textile industry and agricultural machinery. [43° 50'N  4° 23'E]

**Nizhniy Novgorod** Capital of Nizhniy Novgorod Oblast, on Volga River, east of Moscow,

Russia. Formerly called Gorkiy. Developed in mid-20th century into one of the main industrial cities. Light and heavy industries. [56° 20'N 44° 0'E]

**Norilsk** Northernmost town in Russia in a remote part of Krasnoyarsk Kray, near the mouth of the Yenisey River. Coal, uranium and platinum mines. [69° 20'N 88° 6'E]

**Nottingham** Capital of Nottinghamshire, north-central England, on River Trent, south of Sherwood Forest. Commercial and industrial centre. Traditional lace and hosiery; major bicycle manufacturing, tobacco processing, pharmaceuticals. [52° 57'N 1° 10'W]

**Nouakchott** Port and capital of Mauritania, near coast in semi-arid central area. On main north-south trunk road (Morocco-Senegal). Copper exported from Akjoujt area to northeast. [18° 9'N 15° 58'W]

**Nouméa** Capital of New Caledonia, Melanesia, in west Pacific. Large European population. Nickel and chrome exported. [22° 17'S 166° 30'E]

**Novgorod** Capital of Novgorod Oblast in north-west Russia. Historic town with 11th-century cathedral. [58° 30'N 31° 25'E]

**Novosibirsk** Largest city of Siberia, Russia and capital of Novosibirsk Oblast on River Ob. Important industrial, educational and transport centre; vast reservoir and hydroelectric station nearby. Includes Akademgorodok, a scientific research city. [55° 0'N 83° 5'E]

**Nukus** Capital of Karakalpakstan Republic, Uzbekistan, in the region of the Khorezm oasis. Important local administrative centre. [42° 20'N 59° 7'E]

**Nuremberg** Town in south-central Germany in Bavaria. Historic commercial, cultural and manufacturing centre with walled inner town. Large electrical engineering and vehicle industries; toys, confectionery. [49° 26'N 11° 5'E]

**Oaxaca de Juárez** Town in southern Mexico in highland valley area. Capital of Oaxaca state. Archaeological sites nearby. Wheat, oranges, coffee, tobacco. [17° 2'N 96° 40'W]

**Odessa** (Odesa) Historic Black Sea port and resort in the Ukraine. Capital of Odessa Oblast and a major educational centre. Wide range of heavy engineering, including shipbuilding. Possesses catacombs. Associated with 1905 revolution. [46° 30'N 30° 45'E]

**Oklahoma** Capital of Oklahoma state, south-central USA. Commercial and route centre for oil producing, ranching and wheat area. Oilfield and construction machinery, aircraft assembly; air base. Large grain-milling and meat-packing industry. [35° 30'N 97° 30'W]

**Olomouc** Town in eastern Czech Republic. Formerly capital of Moravia. University (1576). Gothic cathedral; 15th-century town hall. Manufacturing, including malt, sugar and starch. [49° 38'N 17° 12'E]

**Omdurman** City in Sudan on Nile, opposite Khartoum. Commercial and industrial centre. Mahdi's tomb. [15° 40'N 32° 28'E]

**Oporto** Seaport in north-west Portugal near mouth of Douro River. Commercial and manufacturing centre, with long-established port wine trade. Textile industries; engineering and ceramics. [41° 8'N 8° 40'W]

**Oran** City and port on Mediterranean coast of Algeria. Former French naval base. Old Moorish city with many mosques. Cereals, wines, fruit and skins. [35° 45'N 0° 39'W]

**Orlando** City in Florida, south-eastern USA. Commercial, manufacturing and route centre of citrus belt, with many lakes to west of Cape Canaveral. Aerospace industry; large fruit- and vegetable-processing industry. Resort based on Disneyland. [28° 33'N 81° 23'W]

**Osaka** Seaport and capital of Osaka prefecture in southern Honshu, Japan. The third largest city of Japan. Manufacturing and heavy industry; metals, machinery. Important commercial and banking centre. Has a fine castle and temples. University dating from 1931. [34° 40'N 135° 30'E]

**Oslo** Capital and largest port of Norway, at northern end of Oslo Fjord. Many fine buildings including Royal Palace and City Hall; Maritime Museum at Bygdøy. Administrative, commercial and cultural centre. Shipbuilding, engineering, wood-pulp, fishing and dairy produce industries. [59° 55'N 10° 45'E]

**Ostend** Seaport and resort in Belgium, on the North Sea, in West Flanders. Ferry terminal. Leading Belgian fishing port and shipbuilding centre. [51° 15'N 2° 54'E]

**Ottawa** Capital of Canada, on Ottawa River in south-east Ontario. Administrative, commercial, cultural and tourist centre. Notable Parliament buildings. [45° 27'N 75° 42'W]

**Ouagadougou** Capital of Burkina Faso, in central position. Modern town on site of capital of Mossi Empire from 15th century. Road centre; terminus of railway from Abidjan, Ivory Coast. [12° 25'N 1° 35'W]

**Oxford** Capital of Oxfordshire, south-central England, on River Thames. Commercial, educational and industrial centre with ancient university, founded in 12th century; many noted buildings, quadrangles and gardens. [5° 45'N 1° 15'W]

**Padang** Seaport city in western Sumatra, Indonesia, and one of the oldest Dutch settlements in Sumatra. The harbour is at Telukbayur (Emmahaven), 8 km [5 mls] away. Exports coal, copra, coffee, rubber, tobacco, tea and palm oil. [1° 0'S 100° 20'E]

**Palembang** City in south-central Sumatra in Indonesia. Important trade and communications centre. Nearby oilfields. Also coal, rubber and coffee. [3° 0'S 104° 52'E]

**Palermo** Seaport in southern Italy, capital of Sicily, on north coast. Ancient commercial centre founded by Phoenicians. Rich agricultural area, Conca d'Oro, with wine, citrus fruits and olive processing. Shipbuilding and repairing industries. [38° 8'N 13° 20'E]

**Palma de Mallorca** Seaport of Spain, capital of Majorca and of Balearic Islands. Com- mercial centre with food and textile industries. International resort. [39° 35'N 2° 39'E]

**Palmerston North** Town and regional centre in south-west lowlands of North Island, New Zealand. Major communications centre. Agricultural and dairy products. Agricultural research centre. [40° 21'S 175° 39'E]

**Panama** Capital of the Republic of Panama, near Pacific end of Panama Canal. Docks at Balboa nearby; railway. Inter-American Highway to Costa Rica begins at Thatcher Ferry Bridge over Canal. [9° 0'N 79° 25'W]

**Papeete** Seaport and capital of French Polynesia, on the north-west coast of Tahiti, south Pacific. Busy harbour, built around a coastal lagoon; exports copra, phosphates, pearl shell and vanilla. Sugar refining and soap manufacturing. [17° 32'S 149° 34'W]

**Paramaribo** Capital of Surinam and river port near the Atlantic. Exports coffee, bauxite, timber and citrus fruits. [5° 50'N 55° 10'W]

**Paris** Capital of France and river port on River Seine. Outstanding French commercial, cultural, route and manufacturing centre; world centre of fashion. Many noted buildings, especially Eiffel Tower, Notre Dame and Arc de Triomphe. Large engineering industry especially cars and aircraft. Clothing, printing. Major tourist centre. [48° 50'N 2° 20'E]

**Pavlodar** Capital of Pavlodar Oblast in northern Kazakhstan. Aluminium, gold, iron ore. Oil refining. [52° 33'N 77° 0'E]

**Pécs** Town in south-west Hungary. Old trade centre of coal-mining region. Uranium deposits. Leather goods, wine, porcelain, tobacco and clothing. [46° 5'N 18° 15'E]

**Pegu** Ancient 6th-century town in Burma, on the Pegu River. Capital of the Pegu Division. Manufactures pottery. [17° 20'N 96° 29'E]

**Périgueux** Town in south-west France, capital of Dordogne *département*. Historic market town known for its truffles and paté; distilling industry. [45° 10'N 0° 42'E]

**Pernik** Town in south-west Bulgaria. Coal-mining town and centre of Bulgaria's heavy industry. Produces iron and steel, and crystal glass. [42° 35'N  23° 2'E]

**Perpignan** Town in southern France, capital of Pyrénées-Orientales *département*. Centre of orchard, vineyard and market gardening area. [42° 42'N  2° 53'E]

**Perth** Capital of Western Australia, on low-lying coastal plain in south-west of state with Darling Range to east. Spreads along both banks of the Swan River. Industrial suburban zone. [31° 57'S  115° 52'E]

**Perugia** Town in central Italy. Capital of Umbria. Ancient university and defensive centre, with confectionery and paper industries. [43° 6'N  12° 24'E]

**Peshawar** Town in north-west Pakistan, commanding the Khyber Pass, on old trade route to Afghanistan. Bazaars. Cereals, rice, sugar cane, cotton, tobacco grown with irrigation from Kabul River. [34° 2'N  71° 37'E]

**Petah Tikva** Industrial centre in central Israel. First modern Jewish settlement in Palestine, 1878. Chemicals, textiles and agricultural machinery. [32° 6'N  34° 53'E]

**Petropavlovsk-Kamchatskiy** Capital of Kamchatka Oblast in far eastern Siberia, Russia. Important fishing port on Pacific Ocean. [53° 3'N  158° 43'E]

**Petrozavodsk** Capital of Karelia Republic in north-west Russia, on Lake Onega. Industries include tractor manufacturing; also an important touring centre. [61° 41'N  34° 20'E]

**Philadelphia** Port in Pennsylvania, eastern USA, on Delaware River. Major commercial and cultural centre. Large oil refining, chemical and machinery industries. Naval base. [39° 57'N  75° 10'W]

**Phnom Penh** Capital of Cambodia, at head of Mekong River delta. Transport centre and river port, with shipping, dried fish, rice and textile industries. [11° 33'N  104° 55'E]

**Phoenix** Capital of Arizona and commercial, route and manufacturing centre for the south-west USA. At northern end of major copper-mining area, in irrigated agricultural region. Large electronics, aircraft and food-processing industries. [33° 27'N  112° 4'W]

**Piraeus** Seaport in south-eastern Greece, south-west of Athens. Industrial and commercial centre; shipbuilding, textiles and oil-refining industries. [37° 57'N  23° 42'E]

**Pisa** Town in west-central Italy, in Tuscany. Former city state and port with ancient university and many fine buildings. Famous for its leaning tower. [43° 43'N  10° 24'E]

**Pittsburgh** City in Pennsylvania, eastern USA, where Allegheny and Monongahela rivers form Ohio River. Commercial, industrial and transport centre. Major steel producer; aluminium and steel rolling; and rolling machinery. Centre of large bituminous coal, natural gas and oilfields. [40° 26'N  80° 0'W]

**Plovdiv** Town in southern Bulgaria. Ruins of 13th-century fortress. Industries include chemicals, textiles, tanning and footwear products. [42° 8'N  24° 44'E]

**Plymouth** Port in Devon, at mouth of River Tamar, in south-west England. Commercial centre for large part of south-west England; naval base (with Devonport). Drake sighted Spanish Armada from Plymouth Hoe, 1588. [50° 23'N  4° 09'W]

**Plzen** Town in western Czech Republic. University, 14th-century cathedral, 16th-century town hall. Manufactures munitions, locomotives, aircraft, electrical motors, leather and Pilsner lager. [49° 45'N  13° 22'E]

**Podgorica** Town in southern Yugoslavia, capital of Montenegro. Agricltural processing and aluminium smelting. [42° 30'N  19° 19'E]

**Pointe Noire** Town and port on coast of Congo. Terminus of railway from Brazzaville. Exports timber; also manganese from Gabon; cotton from Central African Republic. Light industry and fishing. [4° 46'S  11° 53'E]

**Pontianak** Port in western Borneo (Kalimantan), Indonesia. Large trading and distribution centre for west. Exports rubber, copra, forest products and gold. [0° 3'S 109° 15'E]

**Port Elizabeth** Seaport in southern Eastern Cape province, South Africa. Founded by British settlers after the Napoleonic wars. Manufacturing centre, including car industry. Fruit canning and fishing industries. Famous snake park. [33° 58'S 25° 40'E]

**Port Gentil** Port in Gabon, at mouth of navigable Ogooué river. Lumber floated down river, especially valuable akoumé, and then exported. Plywood factory. [0° 40'S 8° 50'E]

**Port Harcourt** Town and port on Bonny River, east of Niger Delta in Nigeria. Railway terminus. Industrial centre; Important oil refining centre, with oil and gas pipelines from delta area. Exports palm products, cocoa, groundnuts. [4° 40'N 7° 10'E]

**Port Laoise** Capital of County Laois in Leinster province, central Republic of Ireland. Market centre in agricultural region; known for its prison. [53° 2'N 7° 20'W]

**Port Moresby** Seaport and capital of Papua New Guinea, on west coast of south-east peninsula of New Guinea. [9° 24'S 147° 8' E]

**Port of Spain** Capital of Trinidad and Tobago, West Indies, on the Gulf of Paria. Principal port and air transport centre for the Caribbean. Produces rum, plastics; oil, sugar, citrus fruits exported. [10° 40'N 61° 31'W]

**Port Pirie** Port in southern South Australia on Spencer Gulf. Developed as main port for lead, silver and zinc ores from Broken Hill mines. [33° 1'S 138° 0'E]

**Port Said** City and chief port in Egypt, at northern end of the Suez Canal. Founded in 1859. Railway to Cairo. Chief export is cotton. [31° 16'N 32° 18'E]

**Port Sudan** Port in Sudan, on Red Sea. Exports cotton, hides. Oil refining; salt works. Coral reefs off coast. [19° 32'N 37° 9'E]

**Port-au-Prince** Port and capital of Haiti, West Indies, on deep bay on west coast. Fine natural harbour. Commercial centre. Sugar industry is important. Light manufacturing development. [18° 40'N 72° 20'W]

**Portalegre** Town in eastern Portugal. Textile centre famous for its tapestries, with many 16th- and 17th-century buildings. Cork industry. [39° 19'N 7° 25'W]

**Portland** River port in Oregon, north-west USA, at confluence of rivers Willamette and Columbia. Commercial and manufacturing centre. Wood processing and lumber equipment industries; electronics, clothing, food processing, fishing. [45° 32'N 122° 37'W]

**Pôrto Alegre** Seaport at the end of the Lagoa dos Patos, south-east Brazil. Capital of Rio Grande do Sul state. Shipyards; meat-packing industries. Exports meat products, wool, rice, tobacco and grapes. [30° 5'S 51° 10'W]

**Porto-Novo** Capital of Benin, situated on a coastal lagoon. Founded by Portuguese in 17th century as slave trade centre. Now administrative centre. [6° 23'N 2° 42'E]

**Portsmouth** Port in Hampshire, southern England. Important naval base and dockyard on north shore of Spithead. Ferryport for Isle of Wight. Nelson's flagship Victory moored here. [50° 48'N 1° 6'W]

**Potosí** Town high in the Andes, south-central Bolivia. At 4,180 m [13,700 ft] is one of the highest towns in the world. Important mining centre for silver, tin, copper lead; manufactures electrical equipment, furniture, iron and steel, and footwear. [19° 38'S 65° 50'W]

**Potsdam** Town in east-central Germany. Has Sans Souci Palace, scene of 1945 conference; noted scientific and technical institutes. Manufactures engines, textiles, chemicals and precision instruments. [52° 23'N 13° 4'E]

**Poznan** Town in west-central Poland, on River Warta. Old city with many ancient buildings surviving or rebuilt. Heavy industrial centre. [52° 25'N 16° 51'E]

**Prague** Capital of Czech Republic on River Vltava. Ancient cultural, historical and political centre; 14th-century town hall, Hradcany Palace (16th–17th century), Charles University (founded 1348), St Vitus Cathedral (begun 1344). Communications centre, with many educational institutes and societies. Manufactures include textiles, chemicals, paper, glass, leather, machinery, and printing and publishing industries. [50° 5'N 14° 22'E]

**Praia** Capital of Cape Verde, on south shore of São Tiago Island, in the eastern Atlantic Ocean. Naval shipyard. [15° 0'N 24° 0'W]

**Pretoria** Inland city to the north of Johannesburg, South Africa, in the province of Pretoria, Witwatersrand and Vereeniging (PWV). Administrative capital of South Africa. Many historic relics, both Afrikaner and British, including President Kruger's house, now a museum. Iron ore in area. Two universities (1873, 1908). [25° 44'S 28° 12'E]

**Providence** Port, capital of Rhode Island, north-eastern USA, at head of Narragansett Bay. Established in 1636 as haven of religious liberty. Textiles; jewellery and silverware industries; oil refining. [41° 49'N 71° 24'W]

**Puebla** Town in highland area of Mexico. Capital of Puebla state. Administrative, route and agricultural centre. Textiles, especially cotton industry. Famous for tiles and onyx ware. [19° 0'N 98° 10'W]

**Pune** City in Maharashtra state, central India, in area west of Ghats mountains on the Mutha and Mula rivers. Railway junction. Military centre, developed by British after 1817. Cotton and paper manufacturing. Aga Khan's palace. [18° 29'N 73° 57'E]

**Punta Arenas** Seaport in southern Chile, on Strait of Magellan. Southern most town in Chile. Exports wool and meat. Military and naval base. [53° 10'S 71° 0'W]

**Pusan** City on the south-east coast of South Korea, developed into a major port under Japanese rule 1910–45. Terminus for the Korean trunk railway. Industries includes railway engineering, shipbuilding, rice milling, textiles and salt refining. Exports rice, fish and soyabeans. [35° 5'N 129° 0'E]

**Pyongyang** City and capital of North Korea, on the right bank of the Taedong River. Hydroelectric power on Yalu River. Industrial centre in an anthracite mining area, manufactures textiles, chemicals, paper and matches. Refines sugar. Remains of ancient walls. [38° 24'S 127° 17'E]

**Qom** Town in north-east central Iran, south-south-west of Tehran, Holy City of Shi'ite Moslems. Centre of grain and cotton regions. Textiles and potteries. [34° 40'N 51° 0'E]

**Quebéc** Town in south-east Canada. Capital of Quebéc province. Long established (1608) administrative and cultural centre; French-speaking. Picturesque old city on two levels. Pulp and paper, food processing and textile mills; shipbuilding. [46° 52'N 71° 13'W]

**Quezon City** City and former capital of the Philippines, adjoining Manila to the north-east. Mainly residential. [14° 38'N 121° 0'E]

**Quito** Capital of Ecuador. Situated on fertile plateau in Andes, 2,890 m [9,480 ft] high; almost on Equator. Textiles, leather goods and carpets. [0° 15'S 78° 35'W]

**Rabat** Capital of Morocco, on north-west coast. Modern city on site of 10th-century *ribat* or fortified monastery. [34° 2'N 6° 48'W]

**Rabaul** Town in north of Gazelle Peninsula of New Britain in Bismarck Archipelago, Papua New Guinea. Administrative centre of Archipelago. Fertile area. Copra and cocoa important. [4° 24'S 152° 8'E]

**Rangoon** Capital of Burma (Myanmar), largest city and chief seaport, 84 km [21 mls] up Rangoon River. Exports rice, cotton and teak. Oil refining, timber working and rice milling. Major airport. [16° 45'N 96° 12'E]

**Rangpur** Town in north-west Bangladesh, north-north-west of Dacca. Market centre for tobacco, jute, rice and oilseed. Railway.

Electrical machinery, carpets, cutlery and bricks manufactured. [24° 42'N  89° 22'E]

**Rawalpindi**  City in northern Pakistan. Temporary capital from 1959 until completion of Islamabad to north-east. On Grand Trunk Road (west-east). Former military station. Railway engineering. [33° 38'N  73° 8'E]

**Recife**  Major seaport in eastern Brazil. Capital of Pernambuco state. Extensive modern port facilities. Exports sugar, cotton, timber and agricultural produce. Airport; naval and military base. [8° 0'S  35° 0'W]

**Regina**  Town in south-central Canada, on Moosejaw Creek. Capital of Saskatchewan. Service and distribution centre for large wheat-growing district. Grain processing, oil refining, steel mills. [50° 27'N  104° 35'W]

**Reykjavik**  Capital of Iceland, in the southwest on a peninsula extending into Faxa Bay. Founded by Vikings in AD 874. Commercial, cultural and industrial centre, with important harbour. Fish processing and shipbuilding industries. [64° 10'N  21° 57'W]

**Richmond**  Port, capital of Virginia, eastern USA at head of navigation of James River. Commercial and cultural centre; was capital of Confederacy. Large tobacco industry; chemicals, wood and food-processing industries; bauxite smelting. [37° 33'N  77° 27'W]

**Riga**  Baltic seaport and capital of Latvia. Industrial and transport centre, with many old churches. Famous resort. [56° 53'N  24° 8'E]

**Rijeka**  Seaport in western Croatia. Hungarian until 1918. Annexed by Italy 1924. Ceded to Yugoslavia 1947. Roman triumphal arch; cathedral (1377). Manufactures ships, torpedoes and machinery. [45° 20'N  14° 21'E]

**Rio de Janeiro**  Principal port of Brazil and capital until 1960. Situated on one of the largest harbours in the world, noted for its scenery. Exports coffee, sugar and iron ore. Major industry associated with large port; one of the leading tourist centres of South America with many seaside resorts. [23° 0'S  43° 12'W]

**Riyadh**  Capital of Saudi Arabia, situated in an oasis in the Najd. Railway to Dammam. Commercial centre with oil processing industries. [24° 41'N  46° 42'E]

**Rome**  Capital of Italy and of Lazio. 'Eternal city' founded by Romulus and Remus on River Tiber; capital of ancient empire with many remains, especially Coliseum, and of Roman Catholic faith. Commercial, educational and tourist centre, with printing, clothing and film industries. [41° 54'N  12° 30'E]

**Rosario**  Argentina's largest inland port on the River Paraná, upstream from the Rio de la Plata. Founded 1725. Railway junction; agricultural trading centre; brewing; manufactures bricks and furniture; exports wheat, meat and hides from the Pampas. [33° 0'S  60° 40'W]

**Roskilde**  Market town in Denmark, in east Zealand. Cathedral is burial place of Danish kings. Industrial centre. [55° 50'N  12° 2'E]

**Rotorua**  Resort in central part of North-Island, New Zealand. On volcanic plateau in famous thermal springs region with many lakes. Local Maori population. Arts and Crafts institute. Resort. [38° 9'S  176° 16'E]

**Rotterdam**  Seaport in Zuid Holland, in south-west Netherlands. Major international port, at Europoort, at outlet of Rhine and Maas (Meuse) rivers. Petrochemicals, shipbuilding, food processing and paper industry. Site of Euromast tower. [51° 55'N  4° 30'E]

**Rovaniemi**  Town in northern Finland at confluence of Kemijoki and Oumasjoki rivers. Capital of Finnish Lappland. Destroyed by fire during World War II and rebuilt to plans of Alvar Aalto. [66° 29'N  25° 41'E]

**Sacramento**  Capital of California, western USA. Commercial manufacturing and route centre of Great Valley. Major food-processing industry, especially rice, peaches, vegetables and nuts. Aerospace industry. Canal link with Pacific. [38° 35'N  121° 29'W]

**St Gallen**  Town in north-east Switzerland and capital of St Gallen canton. Ancient educational centre founded round 7th-century abbey. Major textile centre of Switzerland; linen, embroidery. [47° 26'N  9° 22'E]

**St George's**  Port and capital of Grenada, Windward Islands, West Indies. Founded by French in 1705, British 1783–1974. Picturesque sheltered harbour. [12° 5'N  61° 43'W]

**St John's**  Seaport in eastern Canada. Capital of Newfoundland, on south-east Newfoundland Island. First settled 1593. Fishing port and railhead; industry. [45° 20'N  52° 40'W]

**St Louis**  City and river port in Missouri, central USA, on Mississippi River. Major commercial, route and cultural centre. Large transport industry, especially aerospace and car assembly; brewing; oil refining; chemicals; steel manufacture. [38° 37'N  90° 12'W]

**St Louis**  Town in northern Senegal, at mouth of Senegal River. Founded as French headquarters on Sor island in 1659, and capital 1895–1902. Fishing centre and communications centre for trade. [16° 8'N  16° 27'W]

**St Petersburg**  Second city of Russia. Founded 1703 by Peter the Great; originally named St Petersburg; then Petrograd, then Leningrad. Built on islands separated by River Neva and many canals. Was the capital for two centuries. Major port; industry and transport focus. [59° 55'N  30° 20'E]

**Salamanca**  Town in west Spain, capital of Salamanca province. Grain, leather and fertilizer industries. University town (1215) with famous Roman bridge. [40° 58'N  5° 39'W]

**Thessaloniki**  Town in north-eastern Greece at head of Gulf of Thessaloniki. Industry and communications centre, exports metallic ores, tobacco, hides. Manufactures textiles, chemicals and metal products. [40° 38' N  22° 58'E]

**Salvador**  Seaport and capital of Bahia state, eastern Brazil. Modern port, naval base and dockyard. Tourist centre. [13° 0'S  38° 30'W]

**Salzburg**  Town in eastern Austria, capital of Salzburg province. Commercial and cultural

centre with famous annual music festival associated especially with Mozart (who was born here). Notable buildings. [47° 48'N  13° 2'E]

**Samara**  Capital of Samara Oblast in Russia and old established centre of vast 'Volga Bend' industrial zone. Formerly Kuybyshev. Rapid expansion; oil refining complexes; sulphur. Hydroelectric power from large reservoir nearby. [53° 10'N  50° 10'E]

**Samarkand**  (Samarqand) Ancient city in Uzbekistan. Capital of Samarkand Oblast and an academic centre. Noted for its mosques. Important silk industry. [39° 40'N  66° 55'E]

**San Francisco**  Seaport in California, west USA, on peninsula between San Francisco Bay and the Pacific Ocean. Major commercial and manufacturing centre linked to north by Golden Gate Bridge. Destroyed by earthquake and fire in 1906. Site of Stanford University. Shipbuilding, electronics, fishing, oil refining. Tourist centre. [37° 47'N  122° 25'W]

**San José**  Capital of Costa Rica, in central highland and basin area. Founded in 1737. Route centre. Coffee, cocoa and sugar produced. Light industry. [9° 55'N  84° 2'W]

**San Juan**  Port, capital of Puerto Rico, on north coast. Founded 1510; notable ruins. Oil refinery; ship repairing; sugar; deep-sea fishing. Tourist centre. [18° 28'N  66° 7'W]

**San Luis Potosí**  Town and state capital on central plateau of Mexico. Administration and route centre established in 16th century for San Pedro silver mines. [22° 9'N  100° 59'W]

**San Salvador**  Capital of El Salvador, in south-central area, surrounded by mountains. Destroyed by earthquake in 1854. Commercial and cultural centre. [13° 40'N  89° 10'W]

**San Sebastián**  Seaport in northern Spain, capital of Guipúzcoa province. Commercial centre and resort on Basque coast. Fishing, cement, chemicals. [43° 17'N  1° 58'W]

**Sana**  Capital of Republic of Yemen. Walled city with many mosques, in mountainous area.

Handicrafts and textiles. [15° 24'N  44° 14'E]

**Santa Cruz**  Capital of Santa Cruz de Tenerife province, Tenerife, Canary Islands (Spain). Main manufacturing centre and port. Large exporter of bananas and tomatoes. Tourist centre. [28° 28'N  16° 15'W]

**Santiago**  Capital of Chile, on plain at 518 m [1,700 ft]. Cultural centre and principal industrial city of Chile. Destroyed by an earthquake in 1647. [33° 24'S  70° 40'W]

**Santo Domingo**  Port and capital of Dominican Republic, West Indies, on Caribbean coast. First capital of Spanish South America. 16th-century cathedral; university. Important agricultural area; exports mainly sugar. Some light industry. [18° 30'N  69° 59'W]

**Santos**  Seaport for São Paulo, east Brazil. One of the chief ports of Brazil and world's largest coffee exporting port. One of Brazil's principal seaside resorts. [24° 0'S  46° 20'W]

**São Paulo**  Largest city and principal industrial centre of Brazil. Capital of São Paulo state, west Brazil. Port at Santos. Industries include textiles, chemicals, steel and automobiles. Oil refineries. [23° 32'S  46° 37'W]

**Sarajevo**  Capital of Bosnia-Herzegovina. Scene of assassination of Archduke Franz Ferdinand in 1914, leading to World War I. Centre of Yugoslav Muslims; many mosques. Tobacco, cigars, carpets, silk and pottery. Centre of ethnic war between Serbs, Croats and Muslims since 1991. [43° 52'N  18° 26'E]

**Seattle**  Seaport in Washington, north-west USA, on Puget Sound. Commercial, manufacturing and route centre. Port deals mainly with Far East and Alaska. Major aircraft industry, especially commercial jets. Shipbuilding; wood, fish and grain processing industries. [47° 36'N  122° 20'W]

**Segovia**  Town in north-central Spain. Capital of Segovia province. Ancient defensive centre on spectacular rocky site at 1,000 m [3,280 ft]; famous Roman aqueduct. Traditional wool industry. [40° 57'N  4° 10'W]

**Sekondi-Takoradi**  Twin city on west coast of Ghana. Port (Takoradi) and business centre. Locomotive repair yards and sawmills. Produces timber, cocoa, manganese, bauxite. [4° 58'N  1° 45'W]

**Semipalatinsk**  (Semey) Capital of Semipalatinsk Oblast in east Kazakhstan, on Irtysh (Ertis) River. Meat-packing industry. Centre of a rural steppe region. [50° 30'N  80° 10'E]

**Sendai**  Capital of Miyagi prefecture north Honshu, Japan. Cultural centre, with Tokyo Imperial University (1907) and several technical schools. Trade in salt and fish. Metallurgy, lacquer ware. [38° 15'N  140° 53'E]

**Seoul**  Capital of South Korea. Upstream from mouth of the Han River and its seaport Inch'on. A focal point of transport systems, in the richest and most extensive plain of the country. Industries include tanning, flour milling, railway and metallurgical engineering and textile-based industries. Olympic Games held here in 1988. [37° 31'N  126° 58'E]

**Sevastopol**  Important Black Sea port in the Crimea, southern Ukraine. Razed in two wars; now a popular resort. [44° 35'N  33° 30'E]

**Seville**  Town and river port in south-western Spain. Capital of Seville province and of Andalusia. Commercial and route centre since Roman times, famous for its architecture and Holy Week. Shipbuilding; textile, food-processing, distilling and transport equipment industries. Tourist centre. [37° 23'N  6° 0'W]

**Sfax**  City and port on coastal plain in eastern Tunisia. Important olive-growing area. Olive oil, phosphates, esparto grass and dates exported. [34° 49'N  10° 48'E]

**Shanghai**  City and municipality of east-central China on tributary of the Yangtze River just inland from coast of East China Sea. Heavy industry; iron and steel, chemicals and machine building. Textiles and food processing also important.  [31° 15'N  121° 26'E]

**Sheffield**  City in South Yorkshire, northern England. Commercial and industrial centre on hilly site, east of Pennines. Traditional steel-working industry, famed for cutlery, silver plate; engineering. [53° 23'N 1° 30'W]

**Shenyang**  Capital of Liaoning province, north-east China. On the Hun Ho River, a former Manchu capital. Produces about one quarter of China's machinery. Important metal manufuring centre; textiles, paper, glass and processed foods. [41° 48'N 123° 27'E]

**Shiraz**  Industrial and commercial city in south-west-central Iran, on road from Tehran to Bushehr. Textiles, fertilizers, handicrafts; Tourist centre. [29° 42'N 52° 30'E]

**Saïdi**  Town on coast of Lebanon. Important city of Ancient Phoenicians. Oil pipeline terminus for Saudi Arabia. Oil refining; glass and dye trade. [33° 35'N 35° 25'E]

**Simbirsk**  Capital of Ulyanovsk Oblast in Russia, on River Volga. Formerly Ulyanovsk. Birthplace of Lenin (real name Ulyanov); Lenin museum. [54° 20'N 48° 25'E]

**Skopje**  Capital of the Former Yugoslav Republic of Macedonia in the north on the River Vardar. Largely destroyed by an earthquake in 1963. Road and rail junction. Flour milling, brewing, wine-making, cigarettes, carpets and cement. [42° 1' N 21° 32'E]

**Sligo**  Capital of County Sligo in Connacht province, north-west Republic of Ireland. Regional and cathedral centre; port between Lough Gill and Sligo Bay. Bacon and grain processing. Tourist area. [54° 17'N 8° 28'W]

**Sofia**  Capital of Bulgaria. Founded by the Romans; under Turkish rule for 500 years; passed to Bulgaria in 1877. Cultural, industrial and transport centre. Important railway links with Istanbul. University; many interesting buildings including 19th-century cathedral and 6th-century church of St Sophia. Engineering, chemicals, textiles, metallurgy and food processing. [42° 45'N 23° 20'E]

**Sparta**  Town in southern Greece. Capital of Lakonia. Important city state of ancient Greece. Commercial centre, products include citrus fruits and olive oil. [37° 5'N 22° 25'E]

**Split**  Seaport in southern Croatia on Adriatic Sea. Diocletian's Palace AD 295–306. Commercial and shipping centre. Fisheries and numerous industries. [43° 31'N 16° 26'E]

**Srinagar**  Chief town and summer capital of Jammu and Kashmir state, north India. Area renowned for beautiful scenery. To north-east is scenic Dal Lake, with floating gardens. 8th-century Shankaracharya Temple. Carpet mills, silver, leather, woodwork and cashmere goods. [34° 5'N 74° 50'E]

**Stanley**  Capital and main port of Falkland Islands, south Atlantic Ocean. Seal oil, wool, skins, tallow. Imports: food, electrical machinery, coal, oil and timber. [51° 40'S 59° 51'W]

**Stavanger**  Seaport on south-west coast of Norway, with harbour sheltered by offshore islands. Centre of oil industry. Fish-curing, canning, shipbuilding. [58° 57'N 5° 40'E]

**Stavropol**  Capital of Stavropol Kray in Russia, in the northern Caucasus. Natural gas plant; leather industry. [45° 5'N 42° 0'E]

**Stirling**  Capital of Central region, Scotland. Commercial and route centre in the Forth River valley in rich agricultural area known as Carse of Stirling. Historic strategic centre with castle. Important cattle market. Agricultural equipment industry. [56° 7'N 3° 57'W]

**Stockholm**  Capital and seaport of Sweden, on Baltic coast. Many fine buildings, including City Hall, churches and museums. Important commercial and educational centre. Shipbuilding, timber, iron, paper and textiles. Tourist attractions such as Skansen open-air park and Vasa Museum. [59° 20'N 18° 3'E]

**Stornoway**  Capital of Western Isles region, north-west Scotland, and only town on Isle of Lewis. Centre of Harris tweed industry; fishing port and oilfield equipment manufacture. Tourist centre. [58° 12'N 6° 23'W]

**Strasbourg**  Town in eastern France. Capital of Bas-Rhin *département*. Historic regional centre; canal and river port. Famous cathedral; site of European Parliament. Textiles, engineering, food and printing industries. [18° 35'N  7° 42'E]

**Stuttgart**  Town in south-west Germany. Capital of Baden-Württemberg. River port, commercial and manufacturing centre. Early site of automotive engineering, with noted museum. Electrical engineering, printing, publishing and textiles. [48° 46'N  9° 10'E]

**Sucre**  Legislative capital of Bolivia, founded 1538. Altitude 2,705 m [8,900 ft]. above sea level. Old university (1624) and 17th-century cathedral. Agricultural centre; food processing; oil refining. [19° 0'S  65° 15'W]

**Suez**  City at southern end of Suez Canal in eastern Egypt. Oil refining; fertilizers. Railway to Cairo and Port Said. [29° 58'N  32° 31'E]

**Surabaya**  City in north-east Java in Indonesia. Major seaport and chief naval base; one of the most important trade centres of the Far East. Shipbuilding, oil refining, food processing. Exports: rice, sugar, tobacco, maize, coffee and cassava. [7° 17'S  112° 45'E]

**Surat**  Ancient town and port in Gujarat state, west India, on Gulf of Khambhat. Noted for silks, gold and silver brocades and cotton textiles. [21° 12'N  72° 55'E]

**Suva**  Capital of Fiji, on south-east coast of Viti Levu, Fiji Islands, south-west Pacific. Administrative and manufacturing centre. On major air and sea routes. [18° 6'S  178° 30'E]

**Sverdlovsk**  Capital of Sverdlovsk Oblast and chief city of Urals industrial region, Russia. Large airport and several railways, including Trans-Siberian. Mineralogy museum. Coal, iron, gold and platinum. [56° 50'N  60° 30'E]

**Swansea**  Port, capital of West Glamorgan, Wales. Commercial centre of area with large metals industry. Tin plating, nikel, titanium processing; oil refining. Formerly the world's major coal exporter. [51° 37'N  3° 57'W]

**Sydney**  Seaport and capital of New South Wales, on Jackson Bay in south-east Australia. Largest city in Australia; founded as British convict settlement in 1788. Fine natural harbour with famous bridge and notable Opera House. Administrative, commercial and financial centre, but also important manufacturing centre. [33° 53'S  151° 10'E]

**Taegu**  City and capital of northern Kyongsang province in South Korea, north-north-west of Pusan. In the basin of the Nakkong River at the centre of an agricultural district, it is a commercial city with good rail and road communications. Produces grain, fruit, tobacco and textiles. [35° 50'N  128° 37'E]

**Tainan**  Town in southern Taiwan, on western coast. Former capital and important port. Dutch settled here 1623. Administrative, market and cultural centre. Rice and sugar cane in area. Textile industry. [23° 17'N  120° 18'E]

**Taipei**  City and capital of Taiwan, in extreme north. Seat of Chinese Nationalist Government; administrative and educational centre. Rice-growing area. Food processing and textiles. Tourist centre. [25° 4'N  121° 29'E]

**Tallinn**  Capital of Estonia, on Gulf of Finland. Historic port with many old buildings; 13th-century citadel and the Toomkirik (cathedral) built in the 13th–15th centuries. Transport junction. [59° 22'N  24° 48'E]

**Tangier**  (Tanger)  Historic town on north peninsula of Morocco, overlooking Strait of Gibraltar. Commercial and administrative centre and resort. Site of ancient Phoenician settlement. [35° 50'N  5° 49'W]

**Tarragona**  Seaport in north-eastern Spain. Capital of Tarragona province. Roman capital of Iberia. Wine, distilling and petrochemical industries. [41° 5'N  1° 17'E]

**Tashauz**  (Dashhowuz)  Capital of Tashauz Oblast in the Khorezm Oasis, Turkmenistan. Cotton processing town. [41° 49'N  59° 58'E]

**Tbilisi**  (Tiflis)  Capital of Georgia, in a scenic setting south of the Caucasus, on the River Kura. Founded in 4th century AD. Now a major national, industrial and cultural centre and international air transport focus. World's first funicular railway built here in 1905. Many old buildings. [41° 43'N  44° 50'E]

**Tegucigalpa**  Capital of Honduras, Central America, in southern highlands on Choluteca River. Founded by Spanish in 1524 as a silver-mining centre. Modern town on slopes of Mt El Picacho; other high peaks nearby. Commercial and road centre. [14° 5'N  87° 14'W]

**Tehran**  Capital of Iran, 105 km [65 mls] south of the Caspian Sea, at foot of southern slope of Elburz Mountains. Transport, industrial and cultural centre. Carpets, chemicals and cars. Tourist centre. [35° 44'N  51° 30'E]

**Tel-Aviv-Jaffa**  City in Israel. Founded 1909 by Zionists. Main education and financial centre of the country. [32° 4'N  34° 48'E]

**Thimphu**  Capital of Bhutan, in high valley of Himalayas, 2,600 m [8,500 ft] above sea level. Ricefields in area. Royal Palace built in 1961. [27° 31'N  89° 45'E]

**Thon Buri**  Suburb of Bangkok, southern Thailand, on opposite bank of Chao Phraya River. Former capital. [13° 43'N  100° 29'E]

**Thorshavn**  Capital of the Faroe Islands, on the largest island, Strømø. Ancient fortress; fishing port. Lighthouse. [62° 2'N  6° 47'W]

**Thule**  Settlement on the coast of Hayes Peninsula, north-west Greenland. Danish trading post founded 1910. Seaport open for two to three months per year. American air base and site of ballistic missile early warning system. [77° 40'N  69° 0'W]

**Tianjin**  City in north-east China and independent municipal district. On the Hai He River, 40 km [25 mls] inland, connected to the Yangtze River by the Grand Canal. Industrial and commercial city, with important metallurgical industries. [39° 8'N  117° 10'E]

**Timbuktu**  Historic town to north of Niger River in central Mali. Once Islamic cultural centre and focus of caravan routes. Ancient mosques. Salt brought from old lake beds to north-west. [16° 50'N  3° 0'W]

**Tiranë**  Capital of Albania, most industrialized Albanian town, at edge of fertile coastal plain. Chiefly Muslim. Founded in 17th century by Turks. Market centre for agricultural products. [41° 18'N  19° 49'E]

**Tokyo**  Capital of Japan and of Tokyo prefecture, east-central Honshu. Founded in 1457. Site of the Imperial Palace. Practically destroyed in 1923 by earthquake, tidal wave and fire. Major industrial, commercial and educational centre with varied industries and institutes, including several universities. Has major pollution problems, and marshy site requires expensive reclamation from the sea. Together with Osaka-Kobe-Kyoto, spoken of as the Tokaido megalopolis. [35° 45'N  139° 45'E]

**Toledo**  Town in central Spain. Capital of Toledo province. Ancient cultural and defensive centre with famous cathedral on rocky site. Traditional inlaid metal industry. Tourist centre. [39° 50'N  4° 2'W]

**Toronto**  City and river port in south-east Canada on north-west Lake Ontario. Capital of Ontario province and Canada's largest city. Commercial and manufacturing centre of most populated area of Canada. University (1827), two airports. Food, metal and electrical industries. [43° 39'N  79° 20'W]

**Toulouse**  Town in southern France. Capital of Haute-Garonne *département*. Has ancient university and famous Romanesque church. Aircraft industries, chemicals and food-processing. [43° 37'N  1° 27'E]

**Tralee**  Capital of County Kerry, in Munster province, south-west Republic of Ireland. Regional centre and resort at north-east end of Dingle Peninsula. Important bacon industry. [52° 16'N  9° 42'W]

**Trenton**  Capital of New Jersey, eastern USA, at head of navigation on Delaware River. Manufacturing centre. Large steelworks; consumer goods manufactured. Site of Princeton University. [40° 14'N  74° 46'W]

**Trier**   Town in North Rhine-Westphalia, south-west Germany. Ancient regional and ecclesiastical centre. Site of Roman Porta Nigra. Birthplace of Karl Marx. [49° 45'N  6° 37'E]

**Tripoli**   Capital of Libya and port on western Mediterranean coast, in Tripolitania province. Established by the Phoenicians and developed by the Romans. Ancient city wall. Population growth since Saharan oil discoveries; second largest city in Lebanon. [32° 49'N  13° 7'E]

**Trivandrum**   Capital of Kerala state, southern India, on the Malabar coast. Built on hills. Large temple to Vishnu. Textiles and coconuts; wood carving. [8° 41'N  77° 0'E]

**Trondheim**   Seaport in western Norway at head of the ice-free Trondheim fjord. Shipbuilding. Exports timber, dairy produce and copper from Røros. [63° 36'N  10° 25'E]

**Trujillo**   Town in western Peru. Ruins of pre-Incan city nearby. Commercial and industrial centre for sugar, rice, soap, cocaine, candles and machinery, [8° 6'S  79° 0'W]

**Tselinograd**   (Aqmola)   Capital of Tselinograd Oblast, on the River Ishim in Kazakhstan. Founded 1830. Railway focus; various heavy industries. [51° 10'N  71° 30'E]

**Tunis**   Capital of Tunisia on Gulf of Tunis. Important north coast port; outport La Goulette. Docks linked to sea by canal through Lake of Tunis. Modern town alongside old Arab quarter; fine markets and mosques. Exports: textiles, olive oil, carpets, iron ore and phosphates. [36° 50'N  10° 11'E]

**Turin**   Town in north-east Italy. Capital of Piedmont province. Commercial and manufacturing centre; 17th to 18th-century city with rectangular plan. Major car industry, aircraft engineering and textiles. Noted vermouth manufacture; publishing. [45° 4'N  7° 40'E]

**Turku**   Seaport in south-west Finland at the mouth of the Aurajoki River on the Gulf of Bothnia. Capital of Finland until 1812. Industrial and agricultural centre. Shipbuilding, textiles and tobacco. [60° 30'N  22° 19'E]

**Ujjain**   Town in Madhya Pradesh state, central India, on River Sipra. One of the seven sacred cities of Hindus. [23° 11'N  75° 50'E]

**Ulan Bator**   City and capital of the Mongolian People's Republic, in north-central Mongolia. Focus of several trans-Mongolian roads and camel caravans, and on the main railway from Russia to China. Industries include saddle and knitwear products. Contains almost one quarter of Mongolia's total population. [47° 55'N  106° 53'E]

**Uppsala**   Town in south-west Sweden. Ancient cultural and religious centre, with many Viking remains. Major university town with Gothic cathedral. [58° 9'N  12° 19'E]

**Ushuaia**   Town in south of Tierra del Fuego, southern Argentina. The most southerly town in the world. Lumbering, sheep rearing and fishing all important. [54° 50'S  68° 23'W]

**Ust-Kamenogorsk**   River port and capital of East Kazakhstan Oblast in far eastern Kazakhstan, on right bank of Irtysh River. Chemical industry; lead and zinc mining; hydroelectric and nuclear power. [50° 0'N  82° 36'E]

**Utrecht**   Town in central Netherlands on Amsterdam-Rijnkanaal. Capital of Utrecht province. Important historic, commercial, ecclesiastical and route centre. University (1634); large annual trade fair. Rolling stock and distilling industry. [52° 5'N  5° 8'E]

**Vadodara**   Town in Gujarat state, western India, on coastal plain. Was capital of former state of Baroda. Many fine buildings; cultural centre; Fine Arts School. Railway junction. Textiles. [22° 20'N  73° 10'E]

**Vaduz**   Capital of Liechtenstein, in the Rhine Valley. Commercial centre. 12th-century castle rebuilt after Swabian War in 1499. Textile, and food industries. [47° 8'N  9° 31'E]

**Valencia**   Town in south-east Spain on River Turia. Capital of Valencia province. Ancient city, founded by Greeks, with many fine buildings; Gothic-Baroque cathedral; university (1500). Centre of rich agricultural area, with port at El Grao. Shipbuilding, engineering and textile industries. [39° 27'N  0° 23'W]

**Valladolid**  Town in north-central Spain. Capital of Valladolid province. Former capital of Old Castile. Commercial, manufacturing and route centre, with old university (1346). Agricultural machinery; aluminium industry; grain milling. [41° 38'N  4° 43'W]

**Valletta**  Capital of Malta at the end of a rocky peninsula on the east coast. Many old buildings, including the cathedral and the Auberge de Castille. Commercial and cultural centre. Formerly important as naval base, now an important harbour. New light engineering and food processing industries. Tourism very important. [35° 54'N  14° 31'E]

**Valparaiso**  Principal port of Chile, founded in 1536. Leather goods, vegetable oils and chemicals manufactured. Sugar refining; foundries. Copper, silver nitrate and wheat exported. Naval base. [33° 2'S  71° 40'W]

**Vancouver**  Seaport in south-west Canada in British Columbia. Commercial centre and port at mouth of ice-free Fraser River handling especially grain and wood products. Wood and fish processing, oil refining, brewing and manufacturing industries. Large Chinatown. Tourist area. [49° 15'N  123° 10'W]

**Varanasi**  Ancient town in Uttar Pradesh state, northern India, on River Ganges. Flights of steps (*ghats*) down to river. Holy city of Hinduism; centre of Siva culture. Brasswork famous. [25° 22'N  83° 0'E]

**Venice**  Town and seaport in north-east Italy built on group of small islands; joined to mainland by bridge to Mestre. Former city state and major port, famous for its beauty, especially St Mark's Cathedral and Grand Canal; many canals and bridges. Traditional glass and textile industries. Important tourist centre. [45° 27'N  12° 20'E]

**Veracruz Llave**  Important port in Mexico on Bay of Campeche, Gulf of Mexico, at narrow part of coastal plain. Port for Spanish fleets in 16th and 17th centuries. Oranges,

bananas, coffee, sugar, rice, cattle, pigs, mahogany and vanilla are important products. [19° 10'N  96° 10'W]

**Versailles**  Town in northern France, south-west of Paris. Capital of Yvelines *département*. Site of famous palace built for Louis XIV, which served as a royal palace until 1793. Peace treaty signed 1919. [48° 48'N  2° 8'E]

**Vichy**  Town in central France, in Allier *département*. Spa famous for its bottled water. Pharmaceutical industry. Seat of proGerman government 1940–4. [46° 9'N  3° 26'E]

**Victoria**  Seaport on north-west Hong Kong Island, south-east China  Administrative centre of British colony of Hong Kong, built largely on reclaimed lands. University of Hong Kong. [22° 16'N  114° 13'E]

**Vienna**  Capital of Austria, city and river port on the Danube at edge of Wiener Wald. Major historical, cultural, comercial and manufacturing centre. Former seat of Habsburgs, known especially for music and architecture (including Hofburg, Schönbrunn, Stephansdom). Clothing industry, especially fur; also porcelain, leather and printing industries. Important tourist centre. [48° 12'N  16° 12'E]

**Vientiane**  Town and river port, capital of Laos, on Mekong River, here forming border with Thailand. Administrative and commercial centre. Ferry across Mekong River from Thadeau, 19 km [12 mls] to east, to Nong Khai, Thailand. 'Friendship Bridge' over the Mekong opened in 1994 and links road routes from Singapore to China. Timber, cotton and silk trade. [17° 58'N  102° 36'E]

**Vilnius**  Capital of Lithuania. Formerly Polish. Historic town with castle, cathedral (1977–1801) and old university (1579). Various light industries. One of the largest industrial centres of the former Soviet Baltic region. [54° 38'N  25° 19'E]

**Vladikavkaz**  Capital of the Republic of North Ossetia, northern Caucasus Mountains in Russia. The town was formerly called Ordzhonikidze. Industry based on local non-ferrous metals, including silver. Mountain resort. [43° 0'N 44° 35'E]

**Vladivostok** Capital of Primorye (Maritime) Kray, eastern Russia. Main centre of far east on Sea of Japan. Terminus of Trans-Siberian Railway; major port. [43° 10'N 131° 53'E]

**Volgograd** City and capital of Volgograd Oblast in southern Russia, on Volga River. Formerly called Stalingrad. End of Volga-Don Canal. Scene of World War II decisive battle. Transport centre and river port. Major heavy industry; oil refinery. [48° 40'N 44° 25'E]

**Waco** Town in Texas, southern USA. A regional centre in productive mixed farming area. Food processing, tyre manufacturing. In the headlines in April 1993 when 72 members of the Branch Davidian cult perished in a fire. [31° 33'N 97° 9'W]

**Walvis Bay** Port on coast of Namibia. Administered by South Africa until 1 March 1994 when it was returned to Namibia. Railway connection to South Africa. Mineral exports and fishing. [23° 0'S 14° 28'E]

**Warsaw** Capital of Poland on Vistula River. Under Russian rule from 1815. Became capital of Poland in 1919. Completely rebuilt after destruction in 1944. Major industrial, commercial, academic and educational centre; a focus of eatern European communications of all sorts. Manufactures electrical equipment, chemicals, textiles. Metal-working and sugar-refining industries. [52° 13'N 21° 0'E]

**Washington DC** Capital of the USA on Potomac River. Established 1790 as a planned city. Government and legal services; Library of Congress; research institutes, especially medical. Major tourist centre with many famous landmarks, such as the White House, home of the US President. [38° 54'N 77° 2'W]

**Waterford** Capital of County Waterford, in Munster province, southern Ireland. Port and historic, commercial and manufacturing centre at mouth of River Suir. Noted traditional glass industry; bacon, grain processing and iron founding industries. [52° 16'N 7° 8'W]

**Waterloo** Town in central Belgium, in the region of Brabant. Scene of Napoleon's defeat by Wellington and Blücher in 1815. [50° 43'N 4° 25'E]

**Wellington** Capital of New Zealand, on southern coast of North Island. Founded 1840. Seaport and important commercial centre. Built on steep slopes around harbour with mountains in background. Exports meat, wool and dairy products. [41° 19'S 174° 46'E]

**Willemstad** Port and capital of Netherlands Antilles (Netherlands) on the island of Curaçao, West Indies. Fine deep-water harbour with modern facilities. Ship repairing; bunkering. Oil refinery. [12° 5'N 69° 0'W]

**Willow** Small town in southern Alaska, north-western USA, 110 km [70 mls] north-west of Anchorage. Chosen in 1976 as site of future state capital. [61° 42'N 150° 8'W]

**Windhoek** Capital of Namibia, on central plateau. Railway connection to Walvis Bay on coast and to South Africa. Cattle ranching. Diamonds mined and cut. [22° 35'S 17° 4'E]

**Woomera** Town in South Australia. British and Australian rocket testing station named after Aboriginal spear-throwing device, founded after World War II. [31° 5'S 136° 50'E]

**Wuhan** Metropolis of Hubei province, central China. A tri-city conurbation, consisting of Hankow, Hanyang and Wuchan, at the confluence of the Han Shui and Yangtze rivers, at railway crossing point. Important iron-and-steel plants. [30° 31'N 114° 18'E]

**Xian** Capital of Shanxi province, China. Important route focus in central China. First capital of fuedal China. Terracotta warriors discovered in 1974. Cotton and flour mills; agricultural machinery; mining equipment. Tourist centre. [34° 15'N 109° 0'E]

**Yakutsk** Capital of Sakha (formerly Yakutia) Republic, Russia, on River Lena. Important regional centre for north-eastern Siberia. Timber and fur trade; coal and natural gas nearby. [62° 5'N 129° 50'E]

**Yaoundé** Capital of Cameroon, 270 km [170 mls] inland, in the south-west of the country. Became the capital of French Cameroon in 1921, though it was replaced by Douala between 1940–6. Road and rail centre. Sugar refining; cigarettes. [3° 50'N 11° 35'E]

**Yaroslavl** River port and capital of Yaroslavl Oblast in central Russia, on the River Volga. The oldest town on the Volga. Major centre of heavy industry, chemicals, textiles. Many old churches. [57° 35'N 39° 55'E]

**Yerevan** Capital of Armenia on the River Razdan. One of the world's most ancient cities with many historic buildings; remains of 16th-century Turkish fortress. Important industrial centre, producing diverse manufactured goods. Vodka and wine exported. Rapid post-war expansion. [40° 10'N 44° 31'E]

**Yogyakarta** Important city of south-central Java in Indonesia. Cultural centre in a region of intensive cultivation and dense population. [7° 49'S 110° 22'E]

**Yokohama** Seaport city and capital of Kanagawa prefecture in south-east Honshu, Japan. First Japanese port to be opened to foreign trade in 1858. Manufacturing centre; ranks first in Japanese shipbuilding and important in manufacture of cars and heavy electrical equipment. Oil refining; iron-and-steel industries. [35° 27'N 139° 28'E]

**Ypres** Town in western Belgium, in West Flanders. Historic textile trade centre and defensive site; battles of World War I. Linen and food industries. [50° 51'N 2° 53'E]

**Yuzhno-Sakhalinsk** Capital of Sakhalin Oblast, at southern end of Sakhalin Island in eastern Siberia, Russia. Local industrial and administrative centre. [46° 58'N 142° 45'E]

**Zagorsk** Town north-east of Moscow, Russia. Formerly called Sergiyev Posad. Notable for monastery, centre of the Russian Orthodox Church; also traditional wood crafts. [56° 20'N 38° 10'E]

**Zagreb** Capital of Croatia in the north of the country on the River Sava. Old quarter has medieval architecture. Important cultural and commercial centre. University (1669). Petrochemical industry. [45° 50'N 16° 10'E]

**Zaporozhye** (Zaporizhzhya) River port and capital of Zaporozhye Oblast, south-eastern Ukraine, on River Dnepr (Dnipro, Dnyapro). Founded 1770 as a fortress. Major industrial and transport centre; large early hydroelectric power station (1927). [47° 50'N 35°10'E]

**Zaria** Town on plateau in north-central Nigeria. Includes remains of ancient walled Hausa city. Railway and road centre; cotton growing area. Agricultural research centre nearby. [11° 0'N 7° 40'E]

**Zeebrugge** Seaport in Belgium, in West Flanders. Deep-water container port linked to oil and natural gas terminal. Fishing port and resort. [51° 19'N 3° 12'E]

**Zhengzhou** Capital of Henan province, east-central China. Main rail centre of north China Plain. Major cotton mill industry. Wheat market; food processing. [34° 45'N 113° 34'E]

**Zhitomir** (Zhytomyr) Capital of Zhitomir Oblast in Ukraine. Agricultural trade centre; hops, wheat; woodworking and synthetic textiles. Railway focus. [50° 20'N 28° 40'E]

**Zinder** Town and regional centre in southern Niger. Former capital. Main market for hides and skins; leather and textile industries. Groundnuts important. Route centre: trade with Kano (Nigeria). [13° 48'N 9° 0'S]

**Zouerate** Modern mining settlement in northern Mauritania, east of Fdérik. Terminus of railway to Atlantic port, serving iron-ore mine of Kediet Ijill. [22° 44'N 12° 21'W]

**Zürich** Town in north-east Switzerland at northern end of Zürichsee, at the foot of the Alps. Capital of Zürich canton and largest city in Switzerland. International finance centre, famous for banking. Many old buildings including 11th-century Grossmünster and 13th-century St Peter's Church. Textile and machinery industries. [47° 22'N 8° 32'E]

# WORLD
# STATISTICS

# POPULATION

## POPULATION OF COUNTRIES

*thousands*

| | 1970 | 1980 | 1990 | 2000 Estimate |
|---|---|---|---|---|
| World | 3,697,849 | 4,448,037 | 5,292,195 | 6,260,800 |
| Afghanistan | 13,623 | 16,063 | 16,557 | 26,511 |
| Albania | 2,138 | 2,671 | 3,245 | 3,795 |
| Algeria | 13,746 | 18,740 | 24,960 | 32,904 |
| American Samoa | 27 | 32 | 38 | 39 |
| Andorra | 20 | 32 | 47 | 49 |
| Angola | 5,588 | 7,723 | 10,020 | 13,295 |
| Anguilla | 6 | 7 | 7 | 8 |
| Antigua & Barbuda | 66 | 75 | 76 | 79 |
| Argentina | 23,962 | 28,237 | 32,322 | 36,238 |
| Armenia | 2,520 | 3,067 | 3,335 | 3,608 |
| Aruba | 61 | 64 | 60 | 58 |
| Australia | 12,552 | 14,695 | 16,873 | 18,855 |
| Austria | 7,467 | 7,549 | 7,583 | 7,613 |
| Azerbaijan | 5,172 | 6,165 | 7,134 | 7,987 |
| Bahamas | 171 | 210 | 253 | 295 |
| Bahrain | 220 | 347 | 516 | 683 |
| Bangladesh | 66,671 | 88,219 | 115,593 | 150,589 |
| Barbados | 239 | 249 | 255 | 265 |
| Belarus | 9,040 | 9,650 | 10,260 | 10,811 |
| Belgium | 9,656 | 9,852 | 9,845 | 9,832 |
| Belize | 120 | 145 | 187 | 230 |
| Benin | 2,693 | 3,459 | 4,630 | 6,369 |
| Bermuda | 55 | 56 | 58 | 62 |
| Bhutan | 1,045 | 1,245 | 1,516 | 1,906 |
| Bolivia | 4,325 | 5,570 | 7,314 | 9,724 |
| Bosnia | 3,703 | 4,107 | 4,347 | 4,601 |
| Botswana | 623 | 902 | 1,304 | 1,822 |
| Brazil | 95,847 | 121,286 | 150,368 | 179,487 |
| Brit. Indian Oc. Terr. | 2 | 2 | 2 | 2 |
| British Virgin Is. | 10 | 12 | 13 | 15 |
| Brunei | 133 | 228 | 266 | 333 |
| Bulgaria | 8,490 | 8,862 | 9,010 | 9,071 |
| Burkina Faso | 5,550 | 6,957 | 8,996 | 12,092 |
| Burma | 27,346 | 34,818 | 41,675 | 51,129 |
| Burundi | 3,522 | 4,132 | 5,472 | 7,358 |
| Cambodia | 6,938 | 6,400 | 8,246 | 10,046 |
| Cameroon | 6,610 | 8,653 | 11,833 | 16,071 |
| Canada | 21,324 | 24,043 | 26,521 | 28,488 |
| Cape Verde Is. | 267 | 289 | 370 | 515 |
| Cayman Is. | 11 | 18 | 25 | 35 |
| Central African Rep. | 1,849 | 2,320 | 3,039 | 4,074 |
| Chad | 3,652 | 4,477 | 5,678 | 7,337 |
| Chile | 9,504 | 11,145 | 13,173 | 15,272 |
| China | 830,675 | 996,134 | 1,139,060 | 1,299,180 |
| Christmas Is. | 2.6 | 3 | 3 | 3 |
| Cocos Is. | 0.6 | 0.5 | 1 | 1 |
| Colombia | 21,360 | 26,906 | 32,978 | 39,397 |
| Comoros | 245 | 334 | 460 | 789 |
| Congo | 1,263 | 1,669 | 2,271 | 3,167 |
| Cook Is. | 21 | 19 | 18 | 17 |
| Costa Rica | 1,731 | 2,284 | 3,015 | 3,711 |
| Croatia | 4,411 | 4,588 | 4,770 | 4,822 |
| Cuba | 8,520 | 9,679 | 10,608 | 11,504 |
| Cyprus | 615 | 629 | 701 | 762 |
| Czech Republic | ... | ... | ... | 10,456 |
| Czechoslovakia | 14,334 | 15,311 | 15,667 | 16,180 |
| Denmark | 4,929 | 5,123 | 5,143 | 5,153 |
| Djibouti | 168 | 304 | 409 | 552 |
| Dominica | 71 | 73 | 82 | 87 |
| Dominican Republic | 4,423 | 5,697 | 7,170 | 8,621 |
| Ecuador | 6,051 | 8,123 | 10,587 | 13,319 |
| Egypt | 33,053 | 40,875 | 53,153 | 64,210 |
| El Salvador | 3,588 | 4,525 | 5,252 | 6,739 |
| Equatorial Guinea | 291 | 217 | 352 | 455 |
| Eritrea | ... | ... | ... | 4,218 |
| Estonia | 1,365 | 1,481 | 1,583 | 1,669 |

| | 1970 | 1980 | 1990 | 2000 Estimate |
|---|---|---|---|---|
| Ethiopia | 30,623 | 38,750 | 49,240 | 66,364 |
| Ethiopia (less Eritrea) | ... | ... | ... | 64,032 |
| Falkland Is. | 1.8 | 2 | 2 | 2 |
| Faroe Is. | 39 | 41 | 47 | 49 |
| Fiji | 520 | 634 | 764 | 883 |
| Finland | 4,606 | 4,780 | 4,975 | 5,077 |
| France | 50,772 | 53,880 | 56,138 | 58,145 |
| French Guiana | 48 | 66 | 98 | 130 |
| French Polynesia | 109 | 147 | 206 | 268 |
| Gabon | 504 | 806 | 1,172 | 1,612 |
| Gambia, The | 464 | 641 | 861 | 1,119 |
| Georgia | 4,708 | 5,075 | 5,460 | 5,792 |
| Germany | 77,709 | 78,303 | 79,479 | 76,962 |
| Ghana | 8,612 | 10,736 | 15,028 | 20,564 |
| Gibraltar | 26 | 29 | 30 | 32 |
| Greece | 8,793 | 9,643 | 10,047 | 10,193 |
| Greenland | 47 | 52 | 56 | 60 |
| Grenada | 94 | 107 | 85 | 83 |
| Guadeloupe | 320 | 327 | 343 | 365 |
| Guam | 86 | 108 | 118 | 128 |
| Guatemala | 5,246 | 6,917 | 9,197 | 12,222 |
| Guinea | 3,900 | 4,461 | 5,755 | 7,830 |
| Guinea-Bissau | 525 | 795 | 964 | 1,197 |
| Guyana | 709 | 759 | 796 | 891 |
| Haiti | 4,535 | 5,370 | 6,513 | 8,003 |
| Honduras | 2,627 | 3,662 | 5,138 | 6,846 |
| Hong Kong | 3,942 | 5,039 | 5,851 | 6,336 |
| Hungary | 10,338 | 10,711 | 10,552 | 10,531 |
| Iceland | 204 | 228 | 253 | 274 |
| India | 554,911 | 688,856 | 827,057 | 1,041,543 |
| Indonesia | 120,280 | 150,958 | 179,300 | 218,661 |
| Iran | 28,429 | 38,900 | 54,607 | 68,759 |
| Iraq | 9,356 | 13,291 | 18,920 | 26,339 |
| Ireland | 2,954 | 3,401 | 3,500 | 4,086 |
| Israel | 2,974 | 3,878 | 4,600 | 5,321 |
| Italy | 53,822 | 56,434 | 57,061 | 57,195 |
| Ivory Coast | 5,515 | 8,194 | 11,997 | 17,600 |
| Jamaica | 1,869 | 2,133 | 2,456 | 2,735 |
| Japan | 104,331 | 116,807 | 123,460 | 128,470 |
| Jordan | 2,299 | 2,923 | 4,009 | 5,558 |
| Kazakhstan | 13,110 | 14,939 | 16,742 | 18,332 |
| Kenya | 11,498 | 16,632 | 24,031 | 35,060 |
| Kiribati | 49 | 58 | 66 | 72 |
| Korea, North | 14,619 | 18,260 | 21,773 | 26,117 |
| Korea, South | 31,923 | 38,124 | 42,793 | 46,403 |
| Kuwait | 744 | 1,375 | 1,500 | 2,639 |
| Kyrgyzstan | 2,965 | 3,630 | 4,395 | 5,189 |
| Laos | 2,713 | 3,205 | 4,139 | 5,463 |
| Latvia | 2,374 | 2,543 | 2,684 | 2,813 |
| Lebanon | 2,469 | 2,669 | 2,701 | 3,327 |
| Lesotho | 1,064 | 1,339 | 1,774 | 2,370 |
| Liberia | 1,385 | 1,876 | 2,575 | 3,575 |
| Libya | 1,986 | 3,043 | 4,545 | 6,500 |
| Liechtenstein | 21 | 26 | 28 | 28 |
| Lithuania | 3,148 | 3,439 | 3,737 | 4,007 |
| Luxembourg | 339 | 364 | 373 | 377 |
| Macau | 245 | 287 | 479 | 656 |
| Macedonia | 1,629 | 1,900 | 2,024 | 2,157 |
| Madagascar | 6,742 | 8,785 | 12,004 | 16,627 |
| Malawi | 4,518 | 6,183 | 8,754 | 12,458 |
| Malaysia | 10,853 | 13,763 | 17,891 | 21,983 |
| Maldives | 114 | 154 | 215 | 283 |
| Mali | 5,484 | 6,863 | 8,156 | 12,685 |
| Malta | 326 | 364 | 353 | 366 |
| Martinique | 326 | 326 | 341 | 362 |
| Mauritania | 1,221 | 1,551 | 2,024 | 2,702 |
| Mauritius | 826 | 966 | 1082 | 1,201 |
| Mexico | 52,771 | 70,416 | 86,154 | 107,233 |
| Moldova | 3,595 | 4,001 | 4,365 | 4,500 |
| Monaco | 24 | 26 | 28 | 30 |
| Mongolia | 1,256 | 1,663 | 2,190 | 2,847 |
| Montserrat | 12 | 14 | 12 | 13 |

| | 1970 | 1980 | 1990 | 2000 Estimate | | 1970 | 1980 | 1990 | 2000 Estimate |
|---|---|---|---|---|---|---|---|---|---|
| Morocco | 15,310 | 19,382 | 25,061 | 31,559 | Solomon Is. | 163 | 231 | 320 | 429 |
| Mozambique | 9,395 | 12,095 | 15,656 | 20,493 | Somalia | 3,668 | 5,345 | 7,497 | 9,736 |
| Namibia | 1,016 | 1,306 | 1,500 | 2,437 | South Africa | 22,458 | 28,270 | 35,282 | 43,666 |
| Nauru | 7 | 8 | 9 | 10 | Spain | 33,779 | 37,542 | 39,187 | 40,667 |
| Nepal | 11,488 | 14,858 | 19,143 | 24,084 | Sri Lanka | 12,611 | 14,819 | 17,217 | 19,416 |
| Netherlands | 13,032 | 14,144 | 14,951 | 15,829 | Sudan | 13,859 | 18,681 | 25,203 | 33,625 |
| Netherlands Antilles | 222 | 247 | 188 | 203 | Surinam | 372 | 352 | 405 | 497 |
| New Caledonia | 110 | 142 | 167 | 195 | Swaziland | 419 | 563 | 788 | 1,121 |
| New Zealand | 2,820 | 3,113 | 3,392 | 3,662 | Sweden | 8,043 | 8,310 | 8,444 | 8,560 |
| Nicaragua | 2,053 | 2,771 | 3,871 | 5,261 | Switzerland | 6,187 | 6,319 | 6,609 | 6,762 |
| Niger | 4,165 | 5,586 | 7,731 | 10,752 | Syria | 6,258 | 8,800 | 12,530 | 17,826 |
| Nigeria | 56,581 | 70,000 | 86,000 | 149,621 | Taiwan | 14,676 | 17,805 | 20,100 | 22,000 |
| Niue | 3 | 4 | 3 | 2 | Tajikistan | 2,942 | 3,967 | 5,303 | 6,874 |
| Norfolk Is. | 2 | 2 | 2 | 2 | Tanzania | 13,513 | 18,867 | 25,635 | 39,639 |
| Norway | 3,877 | 4,086 | 4,212 | 4,331 | Thailand | 35,745 | 46,718 | 57,196 | 63,670 |
| Oman | 654 | 984 | 1,502 | 2,176 | Togo | 2,020 | 2,615 | 3,531 | 4,861 |
| Pakistan | 65,706 | 85,299 | 112,050 | 162,409 | Tokelau | 1 | 2 | 2 | 2 |
| Palau (Belau) | 103 | 136 | 142 | 145 | Tonga | 85 | 96 | 95 | 92 |
| Panama | 1,531 | 1,956 | 2,418 | 2,893 | Trinidad & Tobago | 971 | 1,082 | 1,281 | 1,484 |
| Papua New Guinea | 2,422 | 3,086 | 3,874 | 4,845 | Tunisia | 5,127 | 6,384 | 8,180 | 9,924 |
| Paraguay | 2,351 | 3,147 | 4,277 | 5,538 | Turkey | 35,321 | 44,438 | 58,687 | 66,789 |
| Peru | 13,193 | 17,295 | 22,330 | 26,276 | Turkmenistan | 2,189 | 2,860 | 3,668 | 4,479 |
| Philippines | 37,540 | 48,317 | 62,413 | 77,473 | Turks & Caicos | 6 | 6 | 10 | 12 |
| Pitcairn | 0.09 | 0.06 | 0.06 | 0.06 | Tuvalu | 6 | 7 | 9 | 11 |
| Poland | 32,526 | 35,574 | 38,423 | 40,366 | Uganda | 9,806 | 13,120 | 18,794 | 26,958 |
| Portugal | 9,044 | 9,766 | 10,285 | 10,587 | Ukraine | 47,317 | 50,033 | 51,892 | 53,754 |
| Puerto Rico | 2,718 | 3,206 | 3,480 | 3,836 | USSR (former) | 242,766 | 265,546 | 288,595 | 308,363 |
| Qatar | 111 | 229 | 368 | 499 | United Arab Em. | 223 | 1,015 | 1,589 | 1,951 |
| Réunion | 441 | 508 | 598 | 692 | United Kingdom | 55,632 | 56,330 | 57,237 | 58,393 |
| Romania | 20,253 | 22,201 | 23,160 | 24,346 | United States | 205,051 | 227,757 | 249,224 | 266,096 |
| Russia | 130,392 | 138,936 | 148,292 | 155,240 | US Virgin Is. | 62 | 106 | 116 | 135 |
| Rwanda | 3,728 | 5,163 | 7,237 | 10,200 | Uruguay | 2,808 | 2,914 | 3,094 | 3,274 |
| St Christopher-Nevis | 52 | 52 | 44 | 44 | Uzbekistan | 11,973 | 15,975 | 20,515 | 25,224 |
| St Helena | 5 | 6 | 7 | 10 | Vanuatu | 86 | 118 | 158 | 206 |
| St Lucia | 101 | 120 | 150 | 177 | Vatican City | 1 | 1 | 1 | 1 |
| St Pierre et Miquelon | 6 | 6 | 6 | 6 | Venezuela | 10,604 | 15,024 | 19,735 | 24,715 |
| St Vincent & G. | 88 | 99 | 112 | 128 | Vietnam | 42,729 | 53,700 | 66,693 | 82,427 |
| San Marino | 18 | 21 | 23 | 25 | Wallis & Futuna | 9 | 9 | 17 | 26 |
| São Tomé & Príncipe | 74 | 85 | 121 | 151 | Western Sahara | 76 | 135 | 178 | 228 |
| Saudi Arabia | 5,745 | 9,372 | 14,134 | 20,697 | Western Samoa | 143 | 157 | 168 | 171 |
| Senegal | 4,158 | 5,538 | 7,327 | 8,716 | Yemen | 6,332 | 7,675 | 11,282 | 13,219 |
| Seychelles | 52 | 65 | 69 | 75 | Yugoslavia | 20,371 | 22,304 | 23,807 | 24,900 |
| Sierra Leone | 2,656 | 3,263 | 4,151 | 5,437 | Yugoslavia (Serbia) | 8,910 | 9,866 | 10,304 | 11,114 |
| Singapore | 2,075 | 2,300 | 2,700 | 2,997 | Zaire | 19,769 | 26,225 | 35,568 | 49,190 |
| Slovak Republic | ... | ... | ... | 5,513 | Zambia | 4,189 | 5,738 | 8,452 | 12,267 |
| Slovenia | 1,718 | 1,886 | 1,968 | 2,012 | Zimbabwe | 5,260 | 7,126 | 9,709 | 13,123 |

## POPULATION CHANGE

*percentage change in the decade*

| | 1950–60 | 1960–70 | 1970–80 | 1980–90 | 1990–2000 |
|---|---|---|---|---|---|
| World | 20 | 22.5 | 20.3 | 19 | 18.3 |
| Afghanistan | 20.3 | 26.4 | 17.9 | 3.1 | 60.1 |
| Albania | 31 | 32.7 | 24.9 | 21.5 | 16.9 |
| Algeria | 23.4 | 27.3 | 36.3 | 33.2 | 31.8 |
| American Samoa | 10.5 | 28.6 | 18.5 | 18.8 | 2.6 |
| Andorra | 53.9 | 150 | 60 | 46.9 | 4.3 |
| Angola | 16.6 | 16 | 38.2 | 29.7 | 32.7 |
| Anguilla | 20 | 0 | 16.7 | 0 | 14.3 |
| Antigua & Barbuda | 19.6 | 20 | 13.6 | 1.3 | 3.9 |
| Argentina | 20.2 | 16.2 | 17.8 | 14.5 | 12.1 |
| Armenia | 37.9 | 35 | 21.7 | 8.7 | 19 |
| Aruba | 3.5 | 3.4 | 4.9 | –6.3 | –3.3 |
| Australia | 25.5 | 21.7 | 17.1 | 14.8 | 11.7 |
| Austria | 1.6 | 5.9 | 1.1 | 0.5 | 0.4 |
| Azerbaijan | 34.5 | 32.8 | 19.2 | 15.7 | 16.1 |
| Bahamas | 43 | 51.3 | 22.8 | 20.5 | 16.6 |
| Bahrain | 34.5 | 41 | 57.7 | 48.7 | 32.4 |
| Bangladesh | 23.1 | 29.7 | 32.3 | 31 | 30.3 |
| Barbados | 9.5 | 3.5 | 4.2 | 2.4 | 3.9 |
| Belarus | 5.7 | 10.4 | 6.7 | 6.3 | 4.3 |
| Belgium | 5.9 | 5.5 | 2 | –0.1 | –0.1 |
| Belize | 35.8 | 31.9 | 20.8 | 29 | 23 |
| Benin | 9.3 | 20.4 | 28.4 | 33.9 | 37.6 |
| Bermuda | 15.4 | 22.2 | 1.8 | 3.6 | 6.9 |
| Bhutan | 18.3 | 20.4 | 19.1 | 21.8 | 25.7 |
| Bolivia | 23.9 | 26.2 | 28.8 | 31.3 | 33 |
| Bosnia | 21.7 | 14.3 | 10.9 | 5.8 | 5.8 |
| Botswana | 23.7 | 29.5 | 44.8 | 44.6 | 39.7 |
| Brazil | 35.8 | 32 | 26.5 | 24 | 19.4 |
| Brit. Indian Oc. Terr. | 0 | 0 | 0 | 0 | 0 |
| British Virgin Is. | 21.7 | 34.3 | 22.5 | 8.3 | 15.4 |
| Brunei | 95.7 | 47.8 | 71.4 | 16.7 | 25.2 |
| Bulgaria | 8.5 | 7.9 | 4.4 | 1.7 | 0.7 |
| Burkina Faso | 21.8 | 24.7 | 25.4 | 29.3 | 34.4 |
| Burma | 20.7 | 25.6 | 27.3 | 19.7 | 22.7 |
| Burundi | 20 | 19.5 | 17.3 | 32.4 | 34.5 |
| Cambodia | 25 | 27.7 | –8.7 | 28.8 | 21.8 |
| Cameroon | 18.6 | 24.8 | 30.9 | 36.8 | 41.1 |
| Canada | 30.4 | 19.1 | 12.8 | 10.3 | 7.4 |
| Cape Verde Is. | 34.2 | 36.2 | 8.2 | 28 | 39.2 |
| Cayman Is. | 26.7 | 38.2 | 71.4 | 38.9 | 40 |
| Central African Rep. | 16.7 | 20.5 | 25.5 | 31 | 34.1 |
| Chad | 15.3 | 19.2 | 22.6 | 26.8 | 29.2 |
| Chile | 25.2 | 24.8 | 17.3 | 18.2 | 15.9 |
| China | 18.5 | 26.3 | 19.9 | 14.3 | 14.1 |
| Christmas Is. | 170 | –3.7 | 15.4 | 0 | 0 |

| | 1950–60 | 1960–70 | 1970–80 | 1980–90 | *1990–2000* |
|---|---|---|---|---|---|
| Cocos Is. | -41 | 1.7 | -16.7 | 100 | *0* |
| Colombia | 33.4 | 34 | 26 | 22.6 | *19.5* |
| Comoros | 24.3 | 14 | 36.3 | 37.7 | *45.7* |
| Congo | 22.3 | 27.8 | 32.1 | 36.1 | *39.5* |
| Cook Is. | 20 | 16.7 | -9.5 | -5.3 | *-5.6* |
| Costa Rica | 43.4 | 40 | 31.9 | 32 | *23.1* |
| Croatia | 7.5 | 6.5 | 4 | 4 | *4* |
| Cuba | 19.4 | ?? | 13.6 | 9.6 | *8.4* |
| Cyprus | 16 | 7.3 | 2.3 | 11.4 | *8.7* |
| Czechoslovakia | 10.2 | 5 | 6.8 | 2.3 | *3.3* |
| Denmark | 7.3 | 7.6 | 3.9 | 0.4 | *0.2* |
| Djibouti | 33.3 | 110 | 81 | 34.5 | *35* |
| Dominica | 17.6 | 18.3 | 2.8 | 12.3 | *6.1* |
| Dominican Republic | 37.3 | 36.9 | 28.8 | 25.9 | *20.2* |
| Ecuador | 33.3 | 37.1 | 34.2 | 30.3 | *25.8* |
| Egypt | 27.5 | 27.5 | 23.7 | 30 | *20.8* |
| El Salvador | 32.5 | 39.6 | 26.1 | 16.1 | *28.3* |
| Equatorial Guinea | 11.5 | 15.5 | -25.4 | 62.2 | *29.3* |
| Estonia | 10.4 | 12.3 | 8.5 | 6.9 | *4* |
| Ethiopia | 23.6 | 26.6 | 26.5 | 27.1 | *34.8* |
| Falkland Is. | 0 | -14.3 | 11.1 | 0 | *0* |
| Faroe Is. | 12.9 | 11.4 | 5.1 | 14.6 | *4.3* |
| Fiji | 36.3 | 32 | 21.9 | 20.5 | *15.6* |
| Finland | 10.5 | 4 | 3.8 | 4.1 | *2.1* |
| France | 9.2 | 11.1 | 6.1 | 4.2 | *3.6* |
| French Guiana | 24 | 54.8 | 37.5 | 48.5 | *32.7* |
| French Polynesia | 32.3 | 32.9 | 34.9 | 40.1 | *30.1* |
| Gabon | 3.6 | 3.7 | 59.9 | 45.4 | *37.5* |
| Gambia, The | 19.7 | 31.8 | 38.1 | 34.3 | *30* |
| Georgia | 17.9 | 13.2 | 7.8 | 7.6 | *5.8* |
| Germany | 6.3 | 6.9 | 0.8 | 1.5 | *-3.2* |
| Ghana | 38.2 | 27.1 | 24.7 | 40 | *36.8* |
| Gibraltar | 4.3 | 8.3 | 11.5 | 3.4 | *6.7* |
| Greece | 10.1 | 5.6 | 9.7 | 4.2 | *1.5* |
| Greenland | 43.5 | 42.4 | 10.6 | 7.7 | *7.1* |
| Grenada | 18.4 | 4.4 | 13.8 | -20.6 | *-2.4* |
| Guadeloupe | 31 | 16.4 | 2.2 | 4.9 | *6.4* |
| Guam | 13.6 | 28.4 | 25.6 | 9.3 | *8.5* |
| Guatemala | 33.5 | 32.3 | 31.9 | 33 | *32.9* |
| Guinea | 23 | 24.4 | 14.4 | 29 | *36.1* |
| Guinea-Bissau | 7.3 | -3.1 | 51.4 | 21.3 | *24.2* |
| Guyana | 34.5 | 24.6 | 7.1 | 4.9 | *11.9* |
| Haiti | 16.7 | 19.1 | 18.4 | 21.3 | *22.9* |
| Honduras | 38.1 | 35.8 | 39.4 | 40.3 | *33.2* |
| Hong Kong | 55.8 | 28.2 | 27.8 | 16.1 | *8.3* |
| Hungary | 6.9 | 3.5 | 3.6 | -1.5 | *-0.2* |
| Iceland | 23.1 | 15.9 | 11.8 | 11 | *8.3* |
| India | 23.7 | 25.4 | 24.1 | 20.1 | *25.9* |
| Indonesia | 20.9 | 25 | 25.5 | 18.8 | *22* |
| Iran | 27.4 | 31.9 | 36.8 | 40.4 | *25.9* |
| Iraq | 32.7 | 36.6 | 42.1 | 42.4 | *39.2* |
| Ireland | -4.5 | 4.2 | 15.1 | 2.9 | *16.7* |
| Israel | 68 | 40.7 | 30.4 | 18.6 | *15.7* |
| Italy | 6.6 | 7.2 | 4.9 | 1.1 | *0.2* |
| Ivory Coast | 36.9 | 45.2 | 48.6 | 46.4 | *46.7* |
| Jamaica | 16.1 | 14.7 | 14.1 | 15.1 | *11.4* |
| Japan | 12.5 | 10.9 | 12 | 5.7 | *4.1* |
| Jordan | 37 | 35.6 | 27.1 | 37.2 | *38.6* |
| Kazakhstan | 49.1 | 31.2 | 14 | 12.1 | *13.5* |
| Kenya | 33 | 38 | 44.7 | 44.5 | *45.9* |
| Kiribati | 28.1 | 19.5 | 18.4 | 13.8 | *9.1* |
| Korea, North | 10.9 | 35.5 | 24.9 | 19.2 | *20* |
| Korea, South | 22.8 | 27.7 | 19.4 | 12.2 | *8.4* |
| Kuwait | 82.9 | 167.6 | 84.8 | 9.1 | *75.9* |
| Kyrgyzstan | 24.9 | 36.4 | 22.4 | 21.1 | *22.9* |
| Laos | 24 | 24.6 | 18.1 | 29.1 | *32* |
| Latvia | 15.1 | 11.5 | 7.1 | 5.5 | *3.1* |
| Lebanon | 28.7 | 33 | 8.1 | 1.2 | *23.2* |
| Lesotho | 18.5 | 22.3 | 25.8 | 32.3 | *33.6* |
| Liberia | 26.1 | 33.3 | 35.5 | 37.3 | *38.8* |
| Libya | 31.1 | 47.2 | 53.2 | 49.4 | *43* |
| Liechtenstein | 14.3 | 31.3 | 23.8 | 7.7 | *0* |
| Lithuania | 8.3 | 13.3 | 9.2 | 8.7 | *5.3* |
| Luxembourg | 6.1 | 8 | 7.4 | 2.5 | *1.1* |
| Macau | -10.1 | 45 | 17.1 | 66.9 | *37* |
| Macedonia | 13.3 | 17 | 16.6 | 6.5 | *6.6* |
| Madagascar | 25.5 | 27 | 30.3 | 36.6 | *38.5* |
| Malawi | 22.5 | 28 | 36.9 | 41.6 | *42.3* |
| Malaysia | 33.2 | 33.3 | 26.8 | 30 | *22.9* |
| Maldives | 12.2 | 23.9 | 35.1 | 39.6 | *31.6* |
| Mali | 24.3 | 25.3 | 25.1 | 18.8 | *55.5* |
| Malta | 5.4 | -0.9 | 11.7 | -3 | *3.7* |
| Martinique | 27 | 15.6 | 0 | 4.6 | *6.2* |
| Mauritania | 20.1 | 23.2 | 27 | 30.5 | *33.5* |
| Mauritius | 33.9 | 25.2 | 16.9 | 12 | *11* |
| Mexico | 35.7 | 38.8 | 33.4 | 22.4 | *24.5* |
| Moldova | 28.3 | 19.7 | 11.3 | 9.1 | *7.8* |
| Monaco | 4.5 | 4.3 | 8.3 | 7.7 | *7.1* |
| Mongolia | 26 | 31 | 32.4 | 31.7 | *30* |
| Montserrat | -6.9 | -3.3 | 19.7 | -14.3 | *8.3* |
| Morocco | 29.9 | 31.7 | 26.6 | 29.3 | *25.9* |
| Mozambique | 20.4 | 25.9 | 28.7 | 29.4 | *30.9* |
| Namibia | 22.7 | 24.4 | 28.5 | 14.9 | *62.5* |
| Nauru | 28.1 | 70.7 | 14.3 | 12.5 | *11.1* |
| Nepal | 14.9 | 22.2 | 29.3 | 28.8 | *25.8* |
| Netherlands | 13.5 | 13.5 | 8.5 | 5.7 | *5.9* |
| Netherlands Antilles | 18.5 | 15.6 | 11.3 | -23.9 | *8* |
| New Caledonia | 33.9 | 39.2 | 29.1 | 17.6 | *16.8* |
| New Zealand | 24.3 | 18.9 | 10.4 | 9 | *8* |
| Nicaragua | 36 | 37.5 | 35 | 39.7 | *35.9* |
| Niger | 26.2 | 37.5 | 34.1 | 38.4 | *39.1* |
| Nigeria | 28.4 | 33.7 | 23.7 | 22.9 | *22.1* |
| Niue | 25 | -32 | 17.7 | -25 | *-33.3* |
| Norfolk Is. | 0 | 87.5 | 33.3 | 0 | *0* |
| Norway | 9.7 | 8.3 | 5.4 | 3.1 | *2.8* |
| Oman | 22.3 | 29.5 | 50.5 | 52.6 | *44.9* |
| Pakistan | 26.4 | 31.5 | 29.8 | 31.4 | *44.9* |
| Palau (Belau) | 36.8 | 32.1 | 32 | 4.4 | *7.7* |
| Panama | 28.6 | 33.4 | 27.8 | 23.6 | *19.6* |
| Papua New Guinea | 19 | 26.1 | 27.4 | 25.5 | *25.1* |
| Paraguay | 31.3 | 32.5 | 33.9 | 35.9 | *29.5* |
| Peru | 30.1 | 32.8 | 31.1 | 29.1 | *17.7* |
| Philippines | 31.3 | 36.2 | 28.7 | 29.2 | *24.1* |
| Pitcairn Is. | 25 | -40 | -33.3 | 0 | *0* |
| Poland | 19.1 | 10 | 9.4 | 8 | *5.1* |
| Portugal | 5 | 2.5 | 8 | 5.3 | *2.9* |
| Puerto Rico | 6.3 | 15.3 | 18 | 8.5 | *10.2* |
| Qatar | 80 | 146.7 | 106.3 | 60.7 | *35.6* |
| Réunion | 31.9 | 30.1 | 15.2 | 17.7 | *15.7* |
| Romania | 12.9 | 10 | 9.6 | 4.3 | *3.6* |
| Russia | 14.2 | 8.7 | 6.6 | 6.7 | *4.6* |
| Rwanda | 29.3 | 36 | 38.5 | 40.2 | *40.9* |
| St Christopher-Nevis | 19 | -8.8 | 0 | -15.4 | *0* |
| St Helena | 19.1 | 0 | 20 | 16.7 | *42.9* |
| St Lucia | 11.4 | 14.8 | 18.8 | 25 | *18* |
| St Pierre & Miquelon | 4.4 | 16.7 | 7.1 | 0 | *0* |
| St Vincent & G. | 19.4 | 10 | 12.5 | 13.1 | *14.3* |
| San Marino | 15.4 | 20 | 16.7 | 9.5 | *8.7* |
| São Tomé & Príncipe | 6.7 | 15.6 | 14.9 | 42.4 | *24.8* |
| Saudi Arabia | 27.3 | 41 | 63.1 | 50.8 | *46.4* |
| Senegal | 27.5 | 30.5 | 33.2 | 32.3 | *19* |
| Seychelles | 23.5 | 23.8 | 25 | 6.2 | *8.7* |
| Sierra Leone | 15.3 | 18.5 | 22.9 | 27.2 | *31* |
| Singapore | 59.9 | 27 | 10.8 | 17.4 | *11.1* |
| Slovenia | 7.3 | 8.7 | 9.8 | 4.3 | *4.4* |
| Solomon Is. | 18.3 | 32.5 | 41.7 | 38.5 | *34.1* |
| Somalia | 21.1 | 25 | 45.7 | 40.3 | *29.9* |
| South Africa | 27.1 | 29.1 | 25.9 | 24.8 | *23.8* |
| Spain | 8.7 | 10.9 | 11.1 | 4.4 | *3.8* |
| Sri Lanka | 28.8 | 26.5 | 18.4 | 16.2 | *12.8* |
| Sudan | 21.5 | 24.1 | 34.8 | 34.9 | *33.4* |
| Surinam | 34.9 | 28.3 | -5.4 | 15.1 | *22.7* |
| Swaziland | 23.5 | 28.5 | 34.4 | 40 | *42.3* |
| Sweden | 6.6 | 7.5 | 3.3 | 1.6 | *1.4* |
| Switzerland | 14.2 | 15.4 | 2.1 | 4.6 | *2.3* |
| Syria | 30.5 | 37.2 | 40.6 | 42.4 | *42.3* |
| Taiwan | 41.1 | 36 | 21.3 | 12.9 | *9.5* |
| Tajikistan | 36 | 41.2 | 34.8 | 33.7 | *32.8* |
| Tanzania | 27.1 | 34.8 | 39.6 | 35.9 | *54.6* |
| Thailand | 31.9 | 35.4 | 30.7 | 22.4 | *11.3* |
| Togo | 13.9 | 33.4 | 29.5 | 35 | *37.7* |
| Tokelau | 66.7 | -30 | 42.9 | 0 | *0* |
| Tonga | 30 | 30.8 | 12.9 | -1 | *-3.2* |
| Trinidad & Tobago | 32.5 | 15.2 | 11.4 | 18.4 | *15.8* |
| Tunisia | 19.6 | 21.5 | 24.5 | 28.1 | *21.3* |
| Turkey | 32.2 | 28.4 | 25.8 | 32.1 | *13.8* |

| | 1950–60 | 1960–70 | 1970–80 | 1980–90 | 1990–2000 |
|---|---|---|---|---|---|
| Turkmenistan | 31.6 | 37.3 | 30.7 | 28.3 | 25 |
| Turks & Caicos | -5 | -1.8 | 7.1 | 66.7 | 20 |
| Tuvalu | 0 | 20 | 23.3 | 21.6 | 22.2 |
| Uganda | 37.8 | 49.4 | 33.8 | 43.2 | 43.4 |
| Ukraine | 15.9 | 10.6 | 5.7 | 3.7 | 1.3 |
| USSR (former) | 19 | 13.3 | 9.4 | 8.7 | 6.8 |
| United Arab Emirates | 28.6 | 147.8 | 366.2 | 56.6 | 22.0 |
| United Kingdom | 3.5 | 6.2 | 1.3 | 1.6 | 2 |
| United States | 18.7 | 13.5 | 11.1 | 9.4 | 6.8 |
| US Virgin Is. | 18.2 | 94.4 | 71 | 9.4 | 16.4 |
| Uruguay | 13.4 | 10.6 | 3.8 | 6.2 | 5.8 |
| Uzbekistan | 35.6 | 39.9 | 33.4 | 28.4 | 27 |
| Vanuatu | 25 | 32.3 | 37.2 | 33.9 | 30.4 |
| Vatican City | 0 | 0 | 0 | 0 | 0 |
| Venezuela | 49.8 | 41.3 | 41.7 | 31.4 | 25.2 |
| Vietnam | 16 | 23 | 25.7 | 24.2 | 23.6 |
| Wallis & Futuna | 14.3 | 8.8 | 3.5 | 88.9 | 52.9 |
| Western Sahara | 128.6 | 137.5 | 77.6 | 31.9 | 28.1 |
| Western Samoa | 35.4 | 28.8 | 9.8 | 7 | 1.8 |
| Yemen | 21.6 | 20.7 | 21.2 | 47 | 17.2 |
| Yugoslavia | 12.6 | 10.7 | 9.5 | 6.7 | 4.6 |
| Yugoslavia (Serbia) | 12.9 | 10.7 | 10.7 | 4.4 | 4.4 |
| Zaire | 25.7 | 29.1 | 32.7 | 35.6 | 38.3 |
| Zambia | 28.7 | 33.4 | 37 | 47.3 | 45.1 |
| Zimbabwe | 39.6 | 38 | 35.5 | 36.2 | 35.2 |

The estimates for 2000 are those of the UN. They use the medium variants of the population controls.

# BIRTH AND DEATH RATES

*births/deaths per 1,000 population*

| | Birth Rate | | | | | Death Rate | | | | |
|---|---|---|---|---|---|---|---|---|---|---|
| | 1950–55 | 1960–65 | 1970–75 | 1980–85 | 1990–95 | 1950–55 | 1960–65 | 1970–75 | 1980–85 | 1990–95 |
| World | 38 | 35 | 32 | 28 | 26 | 20 | 15 | 12 | 10 | 9 |
| Afghanistan | 48 | 53 | 52 | 49 | 52 | 32 | 30 | 26 | 23 | 22 |
| Albania | 38 | 40 | 32 | 27 | 22 | 14 | 10 | 7 | 6 | 6 |
| Algeria | 51 | 50 | 48 | 41 | 35 | 24 | 19 | 15 | 10 | 7 |
| Andorra | ... | 18 | ... | 15 | 13 | 10 | 6 | 5 | ... | 4 |
| Angola | 50 | 49 | 48 | 47 | 47 | 35 | 30 | 25 | 22 | 19 |
| Anguilla | ... | ... | ... | ... | 25 | ... | ... | ... | ... | 10 |
| Antigua & Barbuda | 35 | 32 | 20 | 15 | 15 | 12 | 9 | 7 | 6 | 5 |
| Argentina | 25 | 23 | 23 | 23 | 20 | 9 | 9 | 9 | 9 | 9 |
| Armenia | ... | ... | ... | ... | 20 | ... | ... | ... | ... | 6 |
| Australia | 23 | 22 | 20 | 16 | 14 | 9 | 9 | 9 | 7 | 8 |
| Austria | 15 | 19 | 14 | 12 | 12 | 12 | 13 | 13 | 12 | 12 |
| Azerbaijan | ... | ... | ... | ... | 25 | ... | ... | ... | ... | 6 |
| Bahamas | 35 | 31 | 28 | 23 | 19 | 12 | 8 | 6 | 5 | 5 |
| Bahrain | 45 | 47 | 36 | 31 | 25 | 16 | 14 | 8 | 5 | 3 |
| Bangladesh | 47 | 47 | 49 | 45 | 41 | 24 | 22 | 21 | 18 | 14 |
| Barbados | 33 | 29 | 21 | 17 | 16 | 13 | 9 | 9 | 9 | 9 |
| Belarus | ... | ... | ... | ... | 15 | ... | ... | ... | ... | 10 |
| Belgium | 17 | 17 | 14 | 12 | 12 | 12 | 12 | 12 | 11 | 12 |
| Belize | 41 | 46 | 40 | 39 | 37 | 12 | 8 | 6 | 5 | 4 |
| Benin | 43 | 48 | 49 | 49 | 49 | 37 | 31 | 26 | 21 | 18 |
| Bermuda | 28 | 26 | 20 | 18 | 16 | 9 | 7 | 7 | 7 | 7 |
| Bhutan | 44 | 42 | 41 | 39 | 38 | 27 | 24 | 21 | 18 | 16 |
| Bolivia | 47 | 46 | 45 | 44 | 41 | 24 | 22 | 19 | 16 | 12 |
| Bosnia | ... | ... | ... | ... | 14 | ... | ... | ... | ... | 6 |
| Botswana | 49 | 53 | 52 | 49 | 44 | 23 | 20 | 17 | 14 | 10 |
| Brazil | 45 | 42 | 34 | 31 | 26 | 15 | 12 | 10 | 8 | 8 |
| British Virgin Is. | 40 | 33 | 26 | 22 | 20 | 11 | 9 | 7 | 6 | 6 |
| Brunei | 54 | 43 | 35 | 32 | 29 | 15 | 8 | 5 | 4 | 3 |
| Bulgaria | 21 | 17 | 16 | 14 | 12 | 10 | 8 | 9 | 11 | 12 |
| Burkina Faso | 51 | 51 | 50 | 47 | 47 | 32 | 27 | 24 | 20 | 17 |
| Burma | 42 | 41 | 38 | 34 | 30 | 24 | 20 | 14 | 11 | 9 |
| Burundi | 49 | 45 | 44 | 47 | 47 | 25 | 22 | 21 | 19 | 16 |
| Cambodia | 45 | 45 | 40 | 46 | 37 | 24 | 20 | 23 | 20 | 15 |
| Cameroon | 44 | 45 | 46 | 47 | 47 | 22 | 24 | 20 | 17 | 13 |
| Canada | 28 | 25 | 16 | 15 | 13 | 9 | 8 | 7 | 7 | 8 |
| Cape Verde Is. | 51 | 49 | 39 | 39 | 41 | 19 | 15 | 12 | 10 | 7 |
| Cayman Is. | 31 | 32 | 28 | 20 | 15 | 7 | 7 | 6 | 6 | 4 |
| Central African Republic | 44 | 43 | 43 | 46 | 45 | 29 | 25 | 22 | 19 | 16 |
| Chad | 45 | 46 | 45 | 44 | 43 | 32 | 29 | 25 | 21 | 18 |
| Chile | 37 | 37 | 28 | 24 | 23 | 14 | 12 | 9 | 6 | 6 |
| China | 45 | 38 | 31 | 19 | 21 | 25 | 17 | 9 | 7 | 7 |
| Christmas Is. | 49 | 26 | ... | ... | 16 | 6 | 5 | 5 | ... | ... |
| Cocos Is. | ... | 30 | 21 | ... | 20 | ... | 9 | 7 | ... | ... |
| Colombia | 47 | 44 | 39 | 29 | 26 | 17 | 12 | 9 | 6 | 6 |
| Comoros | 47 | 52 | 49 | 48 | 47 | 24 | 21 | 18 | 14 | 12 |
| Congo | 44 | 45 | 46 | 46 | 46 | 25 | 22 | 19 | 16 | 13 |
| Cook Is. | 41 | 47 | 32 | 28 | 24 | 19 | 9 | 5 | 5 | 5 |
| Costa Rica | 47 | 45 | 32 | 30 | 26 | 13 | 9 | 5 | 4 | 4 |
| Croatia | ... | ... | ... | ... | 12 | ... | ... | ... | ... | 11 |
| Cuba | 30 | 35 | 27 | 16 | 17 | 11 | 9 | 7 | 6 | 7 |
| Cyprus | 27 | 25 | 18 | 20 | 17 | 11 | 11 | 10 | 8 | 8 |
| Czechoslovakia | 22 | 16 | 18 | 15 | 14 | 11 | 10 | 11 | 12 | 11 |
| Denmark | 18 | 17 | 15 | 10 | 11 | 9 | 10 | 10 | 11 | 11 |
| Djibouti | 50 | 50 | 50 | 48 | 46 | 31 | 27 | 23 | 19 | 16 |
| Dominica | 39 | 43 | ... | 21 | 21 | 17 | 12 | ... | 6 | 5 |
| Dominican Rep. | 51 | 49 | 39 | 34 | 28 | 20 | 15 | 10 | 8 | 6 |
| Ecuador | 47 | 46 | 41 | 35 | 31 | 19 | 14 | 11 | 8 | 7 |
| Egypt | 49 | 45 | 38 | 39 | 31 | 24 | 20 | 16 | 13 | 9 |
| El Salvador | 48 | 48 | 43 | 38 | 36 | 20 | 15 | 11 | 11 | 7 |
| Equatorial Guinea | 42 | 41 | 42 | 43 | 44 | 32 | 28 | 24 | 21 | 18 |
| Estonia | ... | ... | ... | ... | 15 | ... | ... | ... | ... | 12 |
| Ethiopia | 52 | 50 | 48 | 45 | 48 | 32 | 27 | 23 | 24 | 18 |
| Falkland Is. | 23 | 22 | 19 | 15 | 9 | 12 | 11 | 12 | 8 | 6 |
| Faroe Is. | 25 | 23 | 20 | 16 | 18 | 8 | 7 | 7 | 7 | 8 |
| Fiji | 44 | 39 | 32 | 31 | 24 | 14 | 11 | 9 | 8 | 6 |
| Finland | 23 | 18 | 13 | 14 | 12 | 10 | 9 | 10 | 9 | 10 |
| France | 20 | 18 | 16 | 15 | 13 | 13 | 11 | 11 | 11 | 10 |
| French Guiana | 30 | 30 | 29 | 28 | 28 | 16 | 13 | 8 | 7 | 6 |
| French Polynesia | 43 | 45 | 37 | 30 | 28 | 12 | 10 | 9 | 8 | 5 |
| Gabon | 30 | 31 | 31 | 34 | 43 | 27 | 23 | 20 | 18 | 16 |
| Gambia, The | 47 | 51 | 49 | 48 | 45 | 34 | 31 | 27 | 23 | 20 |
| Georgia | ... | ... | ... | ... | 16 | ... | ... | ... | ... | 9 |
| Germany | 16 | 18 | 11 | 11 | 11 | 11 | 12 | 13 | 13 | 12 |
| Ghana | 48 | 48 | 46 | 45 | 44 | 22 | 19 | 16 | 14 | 12 |
| Gibraltar | 23 | 25 | 20 | 18 | 17 | 10 | 9 | 8 | 7 | 7 |
| Greece | 19 | 18 | 16 | 14 | 12 | 7 | 8 | 9 | 9 | 10 |
| Greenland | 44 | 47 | 43 | 28 | 22 | 19 | 9 | 6 | 7 | 8 |
| Grenada | 40 | 39 | 26 | 25 | 25 | 14 | 10 | 8 | 7 | 7 |
| Guadeloupe | 39 | 37 | 29 | 21 | 20 | 13 | 8 | 8 | 7 | 7 |
| Guam | 29 | 26 | 34 | 30 | 27 | 5 | 5 | 4 | 4 | 4 |
| Guatemala | 51 | 48 | 45 | 43 | 39 | 22 | 18 | 13 | 11 | 8 |
| Guinea | 55 | 52 | 52 | 51 | 51 | 34 | 30 | 27 | 24 | 20 |
| Guinea-Bissau | 41 | 40 | 41 | 43 | 43 | 30 | 28 | 27 | 25 | 21 |
| Guyana | 43 | 41 | 35 | 29 | 24 | 18 | 14 | 10 | 9 | 7 |
| Haiti | 44 | 42 | 39 | 37 | 35 | 28 | 22 | 18 | 15 | 12 |
| Honduras | 51 | 51 | 49 | 42 | 37 | 22 | 18 | 14 | 9 | 7 |
| Hong Kong | 38 | 33 | 20 | 17 | 12 | 9 | 6 | 5 | 5 | 6 |
| Hungary | 21 | 14 | 16 | 13 | 12 | 11 | 10 | 12 | 14 | 13 |
| Iceland | 28 | 26 | 21 | 18 | 15 | 8 | 7 | 7 | 7 | 7 |
| India | 44 | 42 | 38 | 35 | 31 | 25 | 19 | 16 | 13 | 10 |
| Indonesia | 43 | 43 | 38 | 32 | 27 | 26 | 22 | 17 | 11 | 9 |
| Iran | 48 | 47 | 44 | 42 | 33 | 25 | 20 | 15 | 10 | 7 |
| Iraq | 49 | 49 | 47 | 44 | 41 | 22 | 19 | 15 | 9 | 7 |
| Ireland | 21 | 22 | 22 | 20 | 18 | 13 | 12 | 11 | 9 | 8 |
| Israel | 33 | 26 | 27 | 24 | 21 | 7 | 6 | 7 | 7 | 7 |
| Italy | 18 | 19 | 16 | 11 | 11 | 10 | 10 | 10 | 10 | 11 |
| Ivory Coast | 53 | 53 | 51 | 50 | 50 | 28 | 24 | 19 | 16 | 13 |
| Jamaica | 35 | 40 | 33 | 27 | 22 | 12 | 9 | 8 | 6 | 6 |
| Japan | 24 | 17 | 19 | 13 | 12 | 9 | 7 | 7 | 6 | 8 |
| Jordan | 47 | 53 | 50 | 38 | 39 | 26 | 22 | 14 | 8 | 5 |
| Kazakhstan | ... | ... | ... | ... | 22 | ... | ... | ... | ... | 8 |
| Kenya | 53 | 53 | 53 | 51 | 47 | 25 | 21 | 17 | 13 | 10 |
| Korea, North | 37 | 41 | 36 | 22 | | 32 | 13 | 8 | 6 | 5 |

| | Birth Rate | | | | | Death Rate | | | | |
|---|---|---|---|---|---|---|---|---|---|---|
| | 1950–55 | 1960–65 | 1970–75 | 1980–85 | 1990–95 | 1950–55 | 1960–65 | 1970–75 | 1980–85 | 1990–95 |
| Korea, South | 32 | 13 | 9 | 6 | 15 | 32 | 13 | 9 | 6 | 6 |
| Kuwait | 45 | 45 | 44 | 35 | 26 | 11 | 9 | 5 | 3 | 2 |
| Kyrgyzstan | ... | ... | ... | ... | 29 | ... | ... | ... | ... | 7 |
| Laos | 46 | 45 | 44 | 45 | 44 | 25 | 23 | 23 | 19 | 15 |
| Latvia | ... | ... | ... | ... | 14 | ... | ... | ... | ... | 12 |
| Lebanon | 41 | 43 | 32 | 29 | 30 | 19 | 13 | 9 | 9 | 8 |
| Lesotho | 42 | 43 | 42 | 42 | 40 | 27 | 23 | 19 | 14 | 11 |
| Liberia | 48 | 50 | 48 | 47 | 47 | 27 | 24 | 20 | 17 | 14 |
| Libya | 48 | 49 | 49 | 46 | 43 | 23 | 18 | 15 | 11 | 8 |
| Liechtenstein | 22 | 22 | 16 | 14 | 13 | 9 | 8 | 8 | 7 | 6 |
| Lithuania | ... | ... | ... | ... | 15 | ... | ... | ... | ... | 10 |
| Luxembourg | 15 | 16 | 12 | 12 | 12 | 12 | 12 | 12 | 11 | 11 |
| Macau | ... | 21 | 11 | ... | 17 | 13 | 8 | 6 | 5 | 3 |
| Macedonia | ... | ... | ... | ... | 17 | ... | ... | ... | ... | 7 |
| Madagascar | 48 | 48 | 46 | 46 | 45 | 27 | 23 | 19 | 15 | 13 |
| Malawi | 52 | 55 | 57 | 57 | 55 | 31 | 28 | 24 | 22 | 19 |
| Malaysia | 45 | 43 | 35 | 32 | 28 | 20 | 13 | 9 | 6 | 5 |
| Maldives | 34 | 37 | 40 | 41 | 41 | 29 | 27 | 20 | 10 | 8 |
| Mali | 53 | 52 | 51 | 51 | 51 | 32 | 29 | 25 | 22 | 19 |
| Malta | 29 | 23 | 18 | 17 | 13 | 10 | 9 | 9 | 9 | 9 |
| Martinique | 40 | 36 | 26 | 18 | 18 | 13 | 9 | 7 | 7 | 7 |
| Mauritania | 48 | 48 | 47 | 47 | 46 | 31 | 28 | 24 | 21 | 18 |
| Mauritius | 47 | 43 | 26 | 22 | 17 | 16 | 9 | 7 | 6 | 6 |
| Mexico | 47 | 46 | 43 | 32 | 27 | 16 | 11 | 9 | 6 | 5 |
| Moldova | ... | ... | ... | ... | 18 | ... | ... | ... | ... | 9 |
| Monaco | 14 | 19 | 8 | ... | 20 | 14 | 16 | 12 | 15 | 17 |
| Mongolia | 44 | 43 | 42 | 38 | 34 | 22 | 17 | 13 | 10 | 8 |
| Montserrat | 32 | 27 | 24 | 20 | 17 | 14 | 10 | 10 | 10 | 10 |
| Morocco | 50 | 50 | 46 | 37 | 33 | 26 | 20 | 16 | 11 | 8 |
| Mozambique | 46 | 47 | 46 | 46 | 44 | 30 | 25 | 22 | 20 | 17 |
| Namibia | 45 | 46 | 45 | 44 | 42 | 25 | 23 | 18 | 14 | 11 |
| Nauru | 27 | 32 | ... | ... | 23 | 7 | 7 | 4 | 5 | 5 |
| Nepal | 46 | 46 | 47 | 43 | 36 | 27 | 25 | 21 | 17 | 13 |
| Netherlands | 22 | 21 | 15 | 12 | 13 | 8 | 8 | 8 | 8 | 9 |
| Neths. Antilles | 35 | 32 | 21 | 19 | 18 | 5 | 5 | 5 | 5 | 6 |
| New Caledonia | 27 | 33 | 33 | 29 | 25 | 10 | 9 | 9 | 7 | 6 |
| New Zealand | 26 | 26 | 21 | 16 | 16 | 9 | 9 | 8 | 8 | 8 |
| Nicaragua | 54 | 50 | 47 | 44 | 39 | 23 | 17 | 13 | 10 | 7 |
| Niger | 54 | 53 | 52 | 52 | 51 | 32 | 28 | 25 | 22 | 19 |
| Nigeria | 51 | 52 | 49 | 49 | 47 | 27 | 24 | 20 | 17 | 14 |
| Niue | 37 | 42 | 29 | 26 | 21 | 15 | 9 | 10 | 7 | 5 |
| Norfolk Is. | 15 | 12 | 11 | 11 | 11 | 14 | 16 | 6 | 7 | 8 |
| Norway | 19 | 17 | 17 | 12 | 13 | 8 | 10 | 10 | 10 | 10 |
| Oman | 51 | 50 | 50 | 48 | 43 | 32 | 26 | 20 | 13 | 6 |
| Pakistan | 50 | 48 | 48 | 50 | 42 | 29 | 22 | 18 | 14 | 11 |
| Palau (Belau) | 29 | 34 | 35 | 33 | 31 | 6 | 7 | 5 | 5 | 4 |
| Panama | 40 | 41 | 36 | 28 | 25 | 13 | 10 | 7 | 5 | 5 |
| Papua New Guinea | 44 | 44 | 41 | 35 | 33 | 29 | 21 | 17 | 13 | 11 |
| Paraguay | 47 | 42 | 37 | 36 | 33 | 9 | 8 | 7 | 7 | 6 |
| Peru | 47 | 46 | 41 | 34 | 29 | 22 | 18 | 13 | 11 | 8 |
| Philippines | 49 | 44 | 37 | 36 | 30 | 20 | 13 | 11 | 9 | 7 |
| Pitcairn Is. | 45 | 8 | 15 | ... | ... | 16 | 10 | ... | ... | ... |
| Poland | 30 | 20 | 18 | 19 | 15 | 11 | 8 | 8 | 10 | 10 |
| Portugal | 24 | 24 | 20 | 15 | 13 | 12 | 11 | 11 | 10 | 10 |
| Puerto Rico | 37 | 31 | 24 | 21 | 18 | 9 | 7 | 7 | 7 | 8 |
| Qatar | 46 | 41 | 31 | 35 | 28 | 22 | 17 | 12 | 5 | 4 |
| Réunion | 39 | 40 | 31 | 24 | 21 | 13 | 10 | 7 | 6 | 6 |
| Romania | 25 | 17 | 19 | 16 | 15 | 12 | 9 | 9 | 10 | 11 |
| Russia | ... | ... | ... | ... | 15 | ... | ... | ... | ... | 10 |
| Rwanda | 47 | 51 | 53 | 52 | 50 | 23 | 21 | 21 | 19 | 16 |

| | Birth Rate | | | | | Death Rate | | | | |
|---|---|---|---|---|---|---|---|---|---|---|
| | 1950–55 | 1960–65 | 1970–75 | 1980–85 | 1990–95 | 1950–55 | 1960–65 | 1970–75 | 1980–85 | 1990–95 |
| St Christopher -Nevis | 37 | 36 | 18 | 24 | 21 | 14 | 11 | 8 | 10 | |
| St Helena | 28 | 28 | 25 | ... | 9 | 9 | 10 | 10 | 8 | |
| St Lucia | 36 | 42 | 39 | 29 | 21 | 15 | 12 | 8 | 6 | |
| St Vincent & G. | 42 | 46 | 30 | 26 | 23 | 16 | 12 | 9 | 7 | |
| Samoa | 37 | 33 | 29 | 30 | 31 | 7 | 5 | 4 | 6 | |
| San Marino | 18 | 18 | 16 | 14 | 10 | 8 | 8 | 8 | 8 | |
| São Tomé & Príncipe | 41 | 50 | 45 | 40 | 35 | 26 | 19 | 11 | 11 | |
| Saudi Arabia | 49 | 49 | 48 | 43 | 42 | 26 | 21 | 17 | 9 | |
| Senegal | 49 | 50 | 49 | 47 | 44 | 28 | 27 | 24 | 19 | |
| Seychelles | 31 | 41 | 32 | 28 | 24 | 12 | 12 | 9 | 9 | |
| Sierra Leone | 48 | 48 | 49 | 48 | 48 | 34 | 32 | 29 | 25 | |
| Singapore | 44 | 34 | 21 | 17 | 16 | 11 | 7 | 5 | 5 | |
| Slovenia | ... | ... | ... | ... | 13 | ... | ... | ... | ... | |
| Solomon Is. | ... | ... | ... | ... | 42 | 15 | 15 | 14 | 12 | |
| Somalia | 49 | 48 | 48 | 53 | 47 | 31 | 27 | 23 | 22 | |
| South Africa | 43 | 42 | 36 | 33 | 31 | 20 | 17 | 13 | 11 | |
| Spain | 20 | 22 | 20 | 13 | 13 | 10 | 9 | 8 | 8 | |
| Sri Lanka | 39 | 35 | 29 | 27 | 21 | 12 | 9 | 8 | 6 | |
| Sudan | 47 | 47 | 47 | 46 | 43 | 27 | 25 | 21 | 17 | |
| Surinam | 44 | 44 | 35 | 29 | 25 | 13 | 10 | 8 | 7 | |
| Swaziland | 50 | 49 | 48 | 47 | 47 | 28 | 23 | 18 | 14 | |
| Sweden | 16 | 15 | 14 | 11 | 13 | 10 | 10 | 10 | 11 | |
| Switzerland | 17 | 19 | 14 | 12 | 12 | 10 | 10 | 9 | 9 | |
| Syria | 47 | 47 | 47 | 46 | 43 | 21 | 17 | 12 | 9 | |
| Taiwan | 45 | 36 | 24 | 21 | 17 | 10 | 6 | 5 | 5 | |
| Tajikistan | ... | ... | ... | ... | 37 | ... | ... | ... | ... | |
| Tanzania | 49 | 52 | 51 | 51 | 50 | 27 | 23 | 19 | 15 | |
| Thailand | 47 | 44 | 35 | 28 | 20 | 19 | 13 | 9 | 8 | |
| Togo | 47 | 48 | 46 | 45 | 45 | 29 | 24 | 19 | 16 | |
| Tokelau | ... | ... | ... | ... | 22 | 14 | 12 | 9 | 8 | |
| Tonga | 37 | 33 | 32 | 31 | 29 | 9 | 4 | 3 | 3 | |
| Trinidad & Tobago | 38 | 38 | 26 | 28 | 23 | 11 | 8 | 7 | 7 | |
| Tunisia | 46 | 47 | 37 | 34 | 27 | 23 | 18 | 12 | 8 | |
| Turkey | 48 | 43 | 35 | 31 | 27 | 24 | 16 | 12 | 9 | |
| Turkmenistan | ... | ... | ... | ... | 33 | ... | ... | ... | ... | |
| Turks & Caicos | 39 | 39 | 30 | 26 | 26 | 13 | 11 | 8 | 6 | |
| Tuvalu | 34 | 28 | 23 | ... | 29 | 19 | 9 | 7 | ... | |
| Uganda | 51 | 49 | 50 | 53 | 52 | 25 | 20 | 19 | 17 | |
| Ukraine | ... | ... | ... | ... | 13 | ... | ... | ... | ... | |
| USSR (former) | 26 | 22 | 18 | 19 | 17 | 9 | 7 | 9 | 11 | |
| United Ar. Em. | 48 | 44 | 33 | 27 | 20 | 23 | 17 | 10 | 4 | |
| United Kingdom | 16 | 18 | 15 | 13 | 14 | 12 | 12 | 12 | 12 | |
| United States | 24 | 22 | 16 | 16 | 14 | 10 | 9 | 9 | 9 | |
| Uruguay | 21 | 22 | 21 | 18 | 17 | 11 | 10 | 10 | 10 | |
| Uzbekistan | ... | ... | ... | ... | 32 | ... | ... | ... | ... | |
| Venezuela | 47 | 44 | 36 | 33 | 28 | 12 | 9 | 7 | 6 | |
| Vietnam | 42 | 41 | 38 | 35 | 30 | 29 | 21 | 14 | 11 | |
| Yemen | 53 | 54 | 55 | 54 | 51 | 32 | 27 | 22 | 18 | |
| Yugoslavia (former) | 29 | 22 | 18 | 17 | 14 | 12 | 9 | 9 | 9 | |
| Yugoslavia (Serbia) | ... | ... | ... | ... | 15 | ... | ... | ... | ... | |
| Zaire | 47 | 47 | 47 | 45 | 45 | 26 | 22 | 19 | 16 | |
| Zambia | 50 | 49 | 49 | 51 | 50 | 26 | 21 | 18 | 15 | |
| Zimbabwe | 52 | 52 | 49 | 43 | 40 | 23 | 19 | 15 | 12 | 9 |

The figures are yearly averages for the period shown.
The figures for 1990–95 are estimates of the UN.

## INFANT MORTALITY

*deaths under one year per 1,000 live births*

| | 1950–55 | 1970–75 | 1990–95 |
|---|---|---|---|
| Afghanistan | 227 | 194 | 162 |
| Albania | 145 | 58 | 32 |
| Algeria | 185 | 132 | 61 |
| Angola | 231 | 173 | 127 |

| | 1950–55 | 1970–75 | 1990–95 |
|---|---|---|---|
| Argentina | 64 | 49 | 29 |
| Armenia | ... | ... | 20 |
| Australia | 24 | 17 | 7 |
| Austria | 53 | 24 | 9 |
| Azerbaijan | ... | ... | 25 |
| Bahamas | 82 | ... | 21 |
| Bahrain | 175 | 55 | 12 |
| Bangladesh | 180 | 140 | 108 |
| Barbados | 132 | 33 | 10 |
| Belarus | ... | ... | 12 |
| Belgium | 45 | 19 | 8 |

| | 1950–55 | 1970–75 | 1990–95 | | 1950–55 | 1970–75 | 1990–95 |
|---|---|---|---|---|---|---|---|
| Benin | 210 | 136 | 85 | Madagascar | 245 | 172 | 110 |
| Bhutan | 197 | 153 | 118 | Malawi | 212 | 191 | 138 |
| Bolivia | 176 | 151 | 93 | Malaysia | 99 | 42 | 20 |
| Bosnia | ... | ... | 15 | Maldives | ... | ... | 73 |
| Botswana | 130 | 95 | 58 | Mali | 213 | 203 | 159 |
| Brazil | 135 | 91 | 57 | Malta | 75 | 22 | 9 |
| Brunei | 112 | 20 | 7 | Martinique | 65 | 35 | 10 |
| Bulgaria | 92 | 26 | 14 | Mauritania | 207 | 160 | 117 |
| Burkina Faso | 226 | 173 | 127 | Mauritius | 99 | 55 | 20 |
| Burma | 183 | 100 | 59 | Mexico | 114 | 71 | 36 |
| Burundi | 166 | 143 | 110 | Moldova | ... | ... | 20 |
| Cambodia | 165 | 181 | 116 | Mongolia | 148 | 98 | 60 |
| Cameroon | 190 | 119 | 86 | Morocco | 180 | 122 | 68 |
| Canada | 36 | 16 | 7 | Mozambique | 205 | 168 | 130 |
| Cape Verde Is. | 129 | 82 | 37 | Namibia | 168 | 134 | 97 |
| Central African Republic | 198 | 132 | 96 | Nepal | 197 | 153 | 118 |
| Chad | 211 | 166 | 122 | Netherlands | 24 | 12 | 7 |
| Chile | 126 | 70 | 19 | New Caledonia | 40 | 38 | 34 |
| China | 195 | 61 | 27 | New Zealand | 26 | 16 | 9 |
| Colombia | 123 | 73 | 37 | Nicaragua | 167 | 100 | 50 |
| Comoros | 180 | 135 | 89 | Niger | 207 | 166 | 124 |
| Congo | 170 | 90 | 65 | Nigeria | 207 | 135 | 96 |
| Costa Rica | 94 | 51 | 17 | Norway | 23 | 12 | 6 |
| Croatia | ... | ... | 10 | Oman | 231 | 145 | 34 |
| Cuba | 82 | 36 | 13 | Pakistan | 190 | 140 | 98 |
| Cyprus | 53 | 29 | 10 | Panama | 93 | 43 | 21 |
| Czechoslovakia | 54 | 21 | 13 | Papua New Guinea | 190 | 105 | 53 |
| Denmark | 28 | 12 | 6 | Paraguay | 106 | 53 | 39 |
| Djibouti | 207 | 154 | 112 | Peru | 159 | 110 | 76 |
| Dominica | 130 | 20 | 17 | Philippines | 100 | 64 | 40 |
| Dominican Republic | 149 | 94 | 57 | Poland | 95 | 27 | 17 |
| Ecuador | 150 | 95 | 57 | Portugal | 91 | 45 | 13 |
| Egypt | 200 | 150 | 57 | Puerto Rico | 63 | 25 | 13 |
| El Salvador | 175 | 110 | 53 | Qatar | 180 | 57 | 26 |
| Equatorial Guinea | 204 | 157 | 117 | Réunion | 141 | 41 | 12 |
| Estonia | ... | ... | 14 | Romania | 101 | 40 | 19 |
| Ethiopia | 190 | 155 | 122 | Russia | ... | ... | 17 |
| Fiji | 88 | 45 | 24 | Rwanda | 160 | 140 | 112 |
| Finland | 34 | 12 | 5 | St Christopher-Nevis | 86 | ... | 24 |
| France | 45 | 16 | 7 | St Lucia | 116 | ... | 18 |
| Gabon | 194 | 132 | 94 | St Vincent & Grenadines | 115 | ... | 22 |
| Gambia, The | 231 | 179 | 132 | São Tomé & Príncipe | ... | 60 | 45 |
| Georgia | ... | ... | 19 | Saudi Arabia | 200 | 120 | 58 |
| Germany | 53 | 20 | 8 | Senegal | 184 | 122 | 80 |
| Ghana | 149 | 107 | 81 | Seychelles | ... | ... | 18 |
| Greece | 60 | 34 | 13 | Sierra Leone | 231 | 193 | 143 |
| Greenland | 120 | ... | 27 | Singapore | 66 | 19 | 7 |
| Grenada | 80 | 40 | 15 | Slovenia | ... | ... | 9 |
| Guadeloupe | 68 | 42 | 12 | Solomon Is. | ... | ... | 50 |
| Guatemala | 141 | 95 | 48 | Somalia | 190 | 155 | 122 |
| Guinea | 222 | 177 | 134 | South Africa | 152 | 110 | 62 |
| Guinea-Bissau | 211 | 183 | 140 | Spain | 62 | 21 | 9 |
| Guyana | 119 | 79 | 48 | Sri Lanka | 91 | 56 | 24 |
| Haiti | 220 | 135 | 86 | Sudan | 185 | 145 | 99 |
| Honduras | 169 | 110 | 57 | Surinam | 89 | 49 | 28 |
| Hong Kong | 79 | 17 | 6 | Swaziland | 160 | 144 | 107 |
| Hungary | 71 | 34 | 17 | Sweden | 20 | 10 | 6 |
| Iceland | 21 | 12 | 5 | Switzerland | 29 | 13 | 7 |
| India | 190 | 135 | 88 | Syria | 160 | 88 | 39 |
| Indonesia | 160 | 114 | 65 | Taiwan | 34 | ... | 6 |
| Iran | 190 | 122 | 40 | Tajikistan | ... | ... | 43 |
| Iraq | 165 | 96 | 56 | Tanzania | 160 | 130 | 97 |
| Ireland | 41 | 18 | 8 | Thailand | 132 | 65 | 24 |
| Israel | 41 | 23 | 10 | Togo | 204 | 129 | 85 |
| Italy | 60 | 26 | 9 | Tonga | 57 | 59 | 23 |
| Ivory Coast | 186 | 129 | 87 | Trinidad & Tobago | 79 | 30 | 14 |
| Jamaica | 85 | 42 | 14 | Tunisia | 175 | 120 | 44 |
| Japan | 51 | 12 | 5 | Turkey | 233 | 138 | 62 |
| Jordan | 160 | 82 | 36 | Turkmenistan | ... | ... | 53 |
| Kazakhstan | ... | ... | 25 | Turks & Caicos | 125 | ... | 13 |
| Kenya | 150 | 98 | 64 | Tuvalu | 123 | ... | 34 |
| Kiribati | 121 | 89 | 59 | Uganda | 160 | 116 | 94 |
| Korea, North | 115 | 47 | 24 | Ukraine | ... | ... | 13 |
| Korea, South | 115 | 47 | 21 | USSR (former) | 73 | 26 | 20 |
| Kuwait | 125 | 43 | 15 | United Arab Emirates | 180 | 57 | 22 |
| Kyrgyzstan | ... | ... | 31 | United Kingdom | 28 | 17 | 8 |
| Laos | 180 | 145 | 97 | United States | 28 | 18 | 8 |
| Latvia | ... | ... | 11 | Uruguay | 57 | 46 | 20 |
| Lebanon | 87 | 48 | 40 | Uzbekistan | ... | ... | 36 |
| Lesotho | 160 | 130 | 89 | Vanuatu | ... | ... | 85 |
| Liberia | 194 | 181 | 126 | Venezuela | 106 | 49 | 33 |
| Libya | 185 | 117 | 68 | Vietnam | 180 | 120 | 54 |
| Lithuania | ... | ... | 10 | Western Samoa | 41 | ... | 47 |
| Luxembourg | 43 | 16 | 9 | Yemen | 231 | 168 | 107 |
| Macedonia | ... | ... | 35 | Yugoslavia | 128 | 45 | 21 |

| | | | |
|---|---|---|---|
| Yugoslavia (Serbia) | ... | ... | *24* |
| Zaire | 182 | 117 | *75* |
| Zambia | 150 | 100 | *72* |
| Zimbabwe | 120 | 93 | *55* |

Infant mortality is the number of deaths per year of children under one year per 1,000 births. The figures are yearly averages for the period shown.

## AGE

*percentage*

| | 1950 | | | | | 1990 | | | | |
|---|---|---|---|---|---|---|---|---|---|---|
| | 0-4 | 5-14 | 15-24 | 25-59 | 60+ | 0-4 | 5-14 | 15-24 | 25-59 | 60+ |
| World | 14 | 21 | 18 | 39 | 8 | 12 | 20 | 19 | 40 | 9 |
| Afghanistan | 20 | 27 | 19 | 31 | 3 | 18 | 24 | 20 | 34 | 5 |
| Albania | 14 | 25 | 19 | 32 | 10 | 11 | 22 | 19 | 40 | 8 |
| Algeria | 16 | 24 | 19 | 35 | 7 | 15 | 28 | 21 | 30 | 5 |
| Angola | 17 | 24 | 19 | 35 | 5 | 18 | 27 | 19 | 32 | 5 |
| Argentina | 11 | 19 | 18 | 44 | 7 | 10 | 20 | 16 | 41 | 13 |
| Armenia | ... | ... | ... | ... | ... | 10 | 20 | 16 | 43 | 11 |
| Australia | 11 | 16 | 15 | 46 | 13 | 7 | 15 | 16 | 46 | 15 |
| Austria | 7 | 15 | 14 | 48 | 15 | 6 | 12 | 15 | 48 | 20 |
| Azerbaijan | ... | ... | ... | ... | ... | 12 | 21 | 18 | 40 | 9 |
| Bahrain | 18 | 25 | 19 | 34 | 5 | 13 | 20 | 15 | 49 | 3 |
| Bangladesh | 15 | 23 | 18 | 38 | 6 | 17 | 27 | 21 | 31 | 5 |
| Barbados | 12 | 21 | 18 | 41 | 9 | 8 | 17 | 19 | 41 | 15 |
| Belarus | ... | ... | ... | ... | ... | 8 | 15 | 14 | 46 | 17 |
| Belgium | 8 | 13 | 15 | 48 | 16 | 6 | 12 | 14 | 48 | 21 |
| Benin | 15 | 21 | 16 | 34 | 14 | 19 | 27 | 19 | 30 | 5 |
| Bhutan | 16 | 24 | 19 | 36 | 6 | 15 | 24 | 19 | 36 | 6 |
| Bolivia | 17 | 25 | 19 | 34 | 5 | 17 | 27 | 19 | 32 | 5 |
| Botswana | 18 | 28 | 20 | 28 | 6 | 20 | 29 | 18 | 27 | 5 |
| Brazil | 17 | 25 | 20 | 34 | 4 | 13 | 23 | 19 | 39 | 7 |
| Bulgaria | 10 | 17 | 19 | 44 | 10 | 6 | 14 | 14 | 47 | 19 |
| Burkina Faso | 18 | 26 | 19 | 33 | 5 | 18 | 26 | 19 | 32 | 5 |
| Burma | 16 | 22 | 18 | 39 | 6 | 13 | 24 | 21 | 36 | 6 |
| Burundi | 16 | 25 | 19 | 35 | 5 | 19 | 27 | 19 | 31 | 5 |
| Cambodia | 17 | 26 | 19 | 34 | 5 | 17 | 18 | 20 | 40 | 5 |
| Cameroon | 16 | 24 | 19 | 36 | 6 | 19 | 27 | 18 | 30 | 5 |
| Canada | 12 | 18 | 16 | 43 | 11 | 7 | 14 | 14 | 49 | 16 |
| Cape Verde Is. | 11 | 24 | 24 | 36 | 7 | 18 | 27 | 22 | 27 | 6 |
| Central African Republic | 14 | 22 | 18 | 38 | 8 | 18 | 27 | 18 | 32 | 6 |
| Chad | 15 | 23 | 18 | 37 | 7 | 17 | 25 | 19 | 33 | 6 |
| Chile | 14 | 23 | 18 | 38 | 7 | 11 | 19 | 19 | 42 | 9 |
| China | 14 | 20 | 18 | 41 | 8 | 10 | 17 | 22 | 42 | 9 |
| Colombia | 18 | 25 | 19 | 33 | 6 | 13 | 24 | 21 | 37 | 6 |
| Comoros | 18 | 26 | 19 | 32 | 5 | 19 | 28 | 20 | 29 | 4 |
| Congo | 16 | 24 | 19 | 36 | 6 | 19 | 27 | 19 | 30 | 5 |
| Costa Rica | 18 | 25 | 19 | 32 | 6 | 13 | 23 | 19 | 38 | 6 |
| Cuba | 13 | 22 | 17 | 40 | 7 | 8 | 14 | 21 | 44 | 12 |
| Cyprus | 14 | 21 | 18 | 39 | 9 | 9 | 17 | 15 | 45 | 14 |
| Czechoslovakia | 10 | 16 | 16 | 47 | 12 | 7 | 16 | 15 | 46 | 17 |
| Denmark | 10 | 17 | 14 | 47 | 13 | 5 | 12 | 15 | 48 | 20 |
| Djibouti | 17 | 24 | 18 | 36 | 5 | 18 | 27 | 18 | 32 | 4 |
| Dominican Rep. | 19 | 26 | 19 | 31 | 5 | 14 | 24 | 21 | 36 | 6 |
| Ecuador | 17 | 25 | 18 | 33 | 7 | 14 | 25 | 21 | 34 | 6 |
| Egypt | 16 | 24 | 19 | 36 | 5 | 15 | 25 | 19 | 36 | 6 |
| El Salvador | 17 | 26 | 19 | 33 | 5 | 16 | 29 | 21 | 29 | 6 |
| Equatorial Guinea | 13 | 21 | 18 | 39 | 9 | 17 | 25 | 18 | 33 | 6 |
| Estonia | ... | ... | ... | ... | ... | 8 | 15 | 14 | 46 | 17 |
| Ethiopia | 18 | 26 | 19 | 32 | 5 | 19 | 27 | 19 | 31 | 5 |
| Fiji | 19 | 28 | 19 | 30 | 5 | 12 | 25 | 19 | 39 | 5 |
| Finland | 13 | 18 | 16 | 44 | 10 | 6 | 13 | 13 | 49 | 18 |
| France | 10 | 13 | 15 | 46 | 16 | 7 | 13 | 15 | 46 | 19 |
| Gabon | 12 | 19 | 17 | 40 | 12 | 15 | 18 | 22 | 37 | 9 |
| Gambia, The | 16 | 23 | 19 | 37 | 5 | 18 | 26 | 18 | 33 | 5 |
| Georgia | ... | ... | ... | ... | ... | 8 | 16 | 15 | 45 | 16 |
| Germany | 7 | 17 | 14 | 51 | 11 | 6 | 10 | 14 | 65 | 6 |
| Ghana | 19 | 27 | 19 | 32 | 4 | 18 | 27 | 19 | 31 | 5 |
| Greece | 10 | 19 | 20 | 42 | 10 | 6 | 14 | 15 | 46 | 20 |
| Guadeloupe | 17 | 22 | 17 | 37 | 7 | 10 | 17 | 20 | 41 | 12 |

| | 1950 | | | | | 1990 | | | | |
|---|---|---|---|---|---|---|---|---|---|---|
| | 0-4 | 5-14 | 15-24 | 25-59 | 60+ | 0-4 | 5-14 | 15-24 | 25-59 | 60+ |
| Guatemala | 18 | 26 | 20 | 31 | 4 | 18 | 28 | 20 | 30 | 5 |
| Guinea | 18 | 25 | 19 | 34 | 4 | 19 | 27 | 19 | 30 | 4 |
| Guinea-Bissau | 15 | 22 | 19 | 38 | 6 | 17 | 24 | 18 | 35 | 7 |
| Guyana | 18 | 23 | 18 | 34 | 7 | 12 | 22 | 23 | 38 | 6 |
| Haiti | 15 | 22 | 17 | 38 | 8 | 15 | 25 | 20 | 34 | 6 |
| Honduras | 18 | 27 | 20 | 32 | 3 | 17 | 28 | 21 | 30 | 5 |
| Hong Kong | 16 | 14 | 23 | 43 | 4 | 6 | 15 | 16 | 50 | 13 |
| Hungary | 9 | 16 | 17 | 47 | 11 | 6 | 14 | 14 | 47 | 19 |
| Iceland | 13 | 18 | 17 | 42 | 11 | 8 | 17 | 17 | 44 | 14 |
| India | 15 | 24 | 19 | 36 | 6 | 13 | 23 | 19 | 37 | 7 |
| Indonesia | 14 | 25 | 20 | 35 | 6 | 12 | 23 | 21 | 37 | 6 |
| Iran | 17 | 22 | 17 | 35 | 8 | 15 | 29 | 20 | 31 | 6 |
| Iraq | 19 | 27 | 19 | 31 | 4 | 18 | 28 | 19 | 30 | 4 |
| Ireland | 11 | 18 | 15 | 41 | 15 | 9 | 19 | 18 | 40 | 14 |
| Israel | 14 | 18 | 17 | 45 | 6 | 11 | 21 | 18 | 39 | 12 |
| Italy | 9 | 17 | 17 | 45 | 12 | 5 | 12 | 16 | 47 | 20 |
| Ivory Coast | 17 | 26 | 20 | 33 | 4 | 20 | 28 | 18 | 30 | 4 |
| Jamaica | 14 | 23 | 19 | 39 | 6 | 11 | 22 | 23 | 35 | 9 |
| Japan | 13 | 22 | 20 | 37 | 8 | 6 | 13 | 15 | 49 | 17 |
| Jordan | 19 | 27 | 17 | 30 | 7 | 17 | 27 | 22 | 29 | 4 |
| Kazakhstan | ... | ... | ... | ... | ... | 11 | 21 | 17 | 42 | 9 |
| Kenya | 17 | 22 | 19 | 35 | 6 | 20 | 30 | 19 | 26 | 4 |
| Korea, North | 16 | 26 | 19 | 34 | 6 | 11 | 18 | 25 | 40 | 7 |
| Korea, South | 16 | 26 | 19 | 34 | 5 | 8 | 18 | 21 | 46 | 8 |
| Kuwait | 15 | 21 | 22 | 37 | 5 | 13 | 23 | 16 | 46 | 3 |
| Kyrgyzstan | ... | ... | ... | ... | ... | 15 | 24 | 18 | 35 | 8 |
| Laos | 16 | 26 | 20 | 34 | 5 | 18 | 26 | 19 | 33 | 5 |
| Latvia | ... | ... | ... | ... | ... | 7 | 15 | 13 | 47 | 18 |
| Lebanon | 14 | 21 | 19 | 36 | 10 | 14 | 22 | 22 | 34 | 8 |
| Lesotho | 16 | 24 | 18 | 34 | 7 | 17 | 26 | 18 | 33 | 6 |
| Liberia | 17 | 25 | 19 | 35 | 5 | 18 | 27 | 19 | 31 | 5 |
| Libya | 17 | 25 | 19 | 32 | 7 | 18 | 28 | 19 | 31 | 4 |
| Lithuania | ... | ... | ... | ... | ... | 8 | 15 | 15 | 47 | 15 |
| Luxembourg | 6 | 14 | 16 | 49 | 15 | 6 | 11 | 13 | 51 | 19 |
| Madagascar | 17 | 25 | 19 | 34 | 5 | 18 | 27 | 19 | 31 | 5 |
| Malawi | 19 | 26 | 19 | 31 | 5 | 21 | 28 | 18 | 29 | 4 |
| Malaysia | 17 | 24 | 18 | 34 | 7 | 15 | 24 | 20 | 37 | 6 |
| Mali | 18 | 26 | 19 | 33 | 4 | 20 | 27 | 19 | 30 | 4 |
| Malta | 15 | 20 | 17 | 38 | 9 | 7 | 16 | 14 | 48 | 14 |
| Martinique | 15 | 22 | 18 | 37 | 8 | 9 | 15 | 19 | 43 | 14 |
| Mauritania | 17 | 25 | 19 | 35 | 5 | 18 | 26 | 19 | 32 | 5 |
| Mauritius | 18 | 27 | 19 | 31 | 5 | 9 | 21 | 19 | 44 | 8 |
| Mexico | 17 | 27 | 19 | 32 | 5 | 13 | 24 | 22 | 35 | 6 |
| Moldova | ... | ... | ... | ... | ... | 10 | 22 | 14 | 41 | 13 |
| Mongolia | 17 | 25 | 19 | 34 | 6 | 16 | 26 | 20 | 34 | 5 |
| Morocco | 18 | 27 | 19 | 32 | 5 | 15 | 25 | 20 | 33 | 6 |
| Mozambique | 17 | 25 | 19 | 35 | 5 | 18 | 26 | 19 | 32 | 5 |
| Namibia | 17 | 24 | 19 | 34 | 6 | 18 | 27 | 18 | 31 | 5 |
| Nepal | 15 | 25 | 20 | 34 | 7 | 16 | 26 | 19 | 34 | 5 |
| Netherlands | 12 | 17 | 16 | 43 | 12 | 6 | 12 | 16 | 49 | 17 |
| New Zealand | 12 | 17 | 14 | 44 | 13 | 8 | 15 | 17 | 45 | 15 |
| Nicaragua | 18 | 26 | 20 | 32 | 4 | 18 | 28 | 20 | 30 | 4 |
| Niger | 18 | 26 | 19 | 33 | 4 | 20 | 28 | 19 | 30 | 4 |
| Nigeria | 19 | 27 | 19 | 31 | 4 | 20 | 28 | 19 | 30 | 4 |
| Norway | 10 | 15 | 13 | 48 | 14 | 6 | 13 | 16 | 44 | 21 |
| Oman | 17 | 25 | 19 | 34 | 5 | 19 | 27 | 17 | 33 | 4 |
| Pakistan | 15 | 23 | 19 | 35 | 8 | 19 | 27 | 19 | 31 | 4 |
| Panama | 17 | 25 | 18 | 35 | 6 | 12 | 23 | 21 | 37 | 7 |
| Papua New Guinea | 15 | 24 | 19 | 35 | 6 | 15 | 25 | 21 | 34 | 5 |
| Paraguay | 16 | 27 | 20 | 32 | 5 | 15 | 25 | 20 | 35 | 5 |
| Peru | 17 | 25 | 19 | 34 | 6 | 13 | 24 | 21 | 36 | 6 |
| Philippines | 18 | 26 | 18 | 33 | 6 | 15 | 25 | 20 | 35 | 5 |
| Poland | 12 | 18 | 19 | 43 | 8 | 8 | 17 | 14 | 46 | 15 |
| Portugal | 11 | 19 | 19 | 42 | 11 | 7 | 15 | 17 | 44 | 18 |
| Puerto Rico | 17 | 27 | 19 | 32 | 6 | 9 | 17 | 19 | 41 | 14 |
| Qatar | 17 | 25 | 19 | 34 | 6 | 14 | 21 | 16 | 46 | 4 |
| Réunion | 16 | 25 | 19 | 36 | 4 | 11 | 22 | 22 | 39 | 8 |
| Romania | 10 | 18 | 20 | 43 | 9 | 8 | 16 | 17 | 44 | 16 |
| Russia | ... | ... | ... | ... | ... | 8 | 14 | 13 | 45 | 20 |
| Rwanda | 19 | 27 | 19 | 31 | 4 | 20 | 29 | 19 | 28 | 4 |
| Saudi Arabia | 17 | 25 | 18 | 34 | 4 | 18 | 27 | 17 | 33 | 4 |
| Senegal | 17 | 26 | 19 | 34 | 6 | 18 | 27 | 19 | 31 | 5 |
| Sierra Leone | 16 | 23 | 19 | 37 | 5 | 18 | 26 | 19 | 32 | 5 |
| Singapore | 16 | 24 | 18 | 38 | 4 | 9 | 15 | 17 | 51 | 9 |
| Somalia | 17 | 24 | 18 | 36 | 5 | 19 | 28 | 17 | 32 | 4 |

| | 1950 | | | | | 1990 | | | | |
|---|---|---|---|---|---|---|---|---|---|---|
| | 0-4 | 5-14 | 15-24 | 25-59 | 60+ | 0-4 | 5-14 | 15-24 | 25-59 | 60+ |
| South Africa | 15 | 23 | 18 | 37 | 6 | 14 | 23 | 19 | 37 | 6 |
| Spain | 10 | 17 | 18 | 44 | 11 | 6 | 14 | 17 | 45 | 18 |
| Sri Lanka | 16 | 25 | 20 | 34 | 6 | 11 | 22 | 19 | 41 | 8 |
| Sudan | 18 | 26 | 19 | 32 | 5 | 18 | 27 | 19 | 31 | 5 |
| Surinam | 17 | 23 | 18 | 34 | 8 | 13 | 21 | 22 | 37 | 7 |
| Swaziland | 18 | 25 | 19 | 33 | 5 | 19 | 28 | 19 | 29 | 5 |
| Sweden | 9 | 15 | 12 | 49 | 15 | 6 | 11 | 14 | 46 | 23 |
| Switzerland | 9 | 15 | 14 | 48 | 14 | 6 | 11 | 14 | 50 | 20 |
| Syria | 17 | 25 | 19 | 33 | 7 | 19 | 29 | 19 | 28 | 4 |
| Taiwan | 19 | 24 | 20 | 34 | 4 | 8 | 20 | 19 | 44 | 9 |
| Tajikistan | ... | ... | ... | ... | ... | 18 | 27 | 18 | 31 | 6 |
| Tanzania | 20 | 27 | 19 | 29 | 5 | 20 | 29 | 19 | 28 | 4 |
| Thailand | 17 | 26 | 20 | 32 | 5 | 10 | 23 | 22 | 39 | 6 |
| Togo | 17 | 24 | 18 | 34 | 7 | 18 | 27 | 19 | 31 | 5 |
| Trinidad & Tobago | 17 | 24 | 16 | 37 | 6 | 12 | 22 | 18 | 40 | 8 |
| Tunisia | 16 | 23 | 18 | 35 | 8 | 14 | 24 | 20 | 35 | 6 |
| Turkey | 15 | 24 | 21 | 35 | 6 | 13 | 22 | 20 | 38 | 7 |

| | 1950 | | | | | 1990 | | | | |
|---|---|---|---|---|---|---|---|---|---|---|
| | 0-4 | 5-14 | 15-24 | 25-59 | 60+ | 0-4 | 5-14 | 15-24 | 25-59 | 60+ |
| Turkmenistan | ... | ... | ... | ... | ... | 16 | 25 | 19 | 34 | 6 |
| Uganda | 19 | 25 | 19 | 32 | 5 | 21 | 29 | 19 | 28 | 4 |
| Ukraine | ... | ... | ... | ... | ... | 7 | 14 | 14 | 46 | 19 |
| USSR (former) | 11 | 20 | 21 | 40 | 9 | 9 | 17 | 15 | 45 | 15 |
| United Ar. Em. | 17 | 26 | 19 | 34 | 8 | 11 | 20 | 13 | 53 | 3 |
| United Kingdom | 9 | 14 | 14 | 49 | 16 | 7 | 12 | 15 | 46 | 21 |
| United States | 11 | 16 | 15 | 46 | 12 | 7 | 14 | 15 | 47 | 17 |
| Uruguay | 10 | 18 | 18 | 43 | 12 | 8 | 17 | 16 | 42 | 17 |
| Uzbekistan | ... | ... | ... | ... | ... | 16 | 26 | 19 | 34 | 5 |
| Venezuela | 19 | 25 | 19 | 34 | 3 | 14 | 24 | 20 | 36 | 6 |
| Vietnam | 13 | 22 | 19 | 40 | 7 | 14 | 25 | 21 | 33 | 7 |
| Yemen | 18 | 25 | 19 | 34 | 6 | 21 | 29 | 20 | 26 | 4 |
| Yugoslavia | 11 | 20 | 21 | 40 | 9 | 7 | 16 | 15 | 47 | 15 |
| Zaïre | 18 | 26 | 19 | 32 | 6 | 19 | 28 | 19 | 31 | 4 |
| Zambia | 19 | 26 | 19 | 32 | 4 | 21 | 28 | 19 | 28 | 4 |
| Zimbabwe | 18 | 27 | 19 | 32 | 5 | 18 | 27 | 21 | 30 | 4 |

This table shows the percentage of the total population in each of the five age-groups for 1950 and 1990.

# LIFE EXPECTANCY

| | 1950–55 | | 1970–75 | | 1990–95 | |
|---|---|---|---|---|---|---|
| | male | female | male | female | male | female |
| Afghanistan | 31 | 32 | 38 | 38 | 43 | 44 |
| Albania | 54 | 56 | 66 | 70 | 70 | 75 |
| Algeria | 42 | 44 | 54 | 56 | 65 | 67 |
| Angola | 29 | 32 | 37 | 40 | 45 | 48 |
| Argentina | 60 | 65 | 64 | 71 | 68 | 75 |
| Armenia | ... | ... | ... | ... | 78 | 73 |
| Australia | 67 | 72 | 68 | 75 | 74 | 80 |
| Austria | 63 | 68 | 67 | 74 | 72 | 79 |
| Azerbaijan | ... | ... | ... | ... | 67 | 75 |
| Bahrain | 50 | 53 | 62 | 65 | 70 | 74 |
| Bangladesh | 38 | 35 | 46 | 44 | 53 | 53 |
| Barbados | 55 | 60 | 67 | 72 | 73 | 78 |
| Belarus | ... | ... | ... | ... | 64 | 75 |
| Belgium | 65 | 70 | 68 | 75 | 72 | 79 |
| Benin | 31 | 34 | 39 | 42 | 46 | 50 |
| Bhutan | 37 | 36 | 43 | 42 | 51 | 49 |
| Bolivia | 39 | 43 | 45 | 49 | 54 | 58 |
| Bosnia | ... | ... | ... | ... | 68 | 73 |
| Botswana | 41 | 44 | 49 | 53 | 58 | 64 |
| Brazil | 49 | 53 | 58 | 62 | 64 | 69 |
| Bulgaria | 62 | 66 | 69 | 74 | 70 | 76 |
| Burkina Faso | 32 | 35 | 40 | 43 | 48 | 51 |
| Burma | 39 | 41 | 51 | 54 | 61 | 64 |
| Burundi | 38 | 41 | 41 | 45 | 48 | 51 |
| Cambodia | 38 | 41 | 39 | 42 | 50 | 52 |
| Cameroon | 35 | 38 | 44 | 47 | 54 | 57 |
| Canada | 67 | 72 | 70 | 77 | 74 | 81 |
| Cape Verde Is. | 47 | 50 | 56 | 59 | 67 | 69 |
| Central African Republic | 33 | 38 | 40 | 46 | 48 | 53 |
| Chad | 31 | 34 | 38 | 41 | 46 | 49 |
| Chile | 52 | 56 | 61 | 67 | 69 | 76 |
| China | 39 | 42 | 63 | 64 | 69 | 73 |
| Colombia | 49 | 52 | 60 | 63 | 66 | 72 |
| Comoros | 40 | 41 | 47 | 48 | 56 | 57 |
| Congo | 36 | 41 | 44 | 49 | 52 | 57 |
| Costa Rica | 56 | 59 | 66 | 70 | 73 | 78 |
| Croatia | ... | ... | ... | ... | 67 | 74 |
| Cuba | 58 | 61 | 69 | 73 | 74 | 78 |
| Cyprus | 65 | 69 | 70 | 73 | 74 | 79 |
| Czechoslovakia | 64 | 68 | 67 | 74 | 69 | 76 |
| Denmark | 70 | 72 | 71 | 76 | 73 | 79 |
| Djibouti | 32 | 35 | 39 | 43 | 47 | 51 |
| Dominican Rep. | 45 | 47 | 58 | 62 | 65 | 70 |
| Ecuador | 47 | 50 | 57 | 61 | 65 | 69 |
| Egypt | 41 | 44 | 51 | 53 | 60 | 63 |
| El Salvador | 44 | 47 | 57 | 61 | 64 | 69 |

| | 1950–55 | | 1970–75 | | 1990–95 | |
|---|---|---|---|---|---|---|
| | male | female | male | female | male | female |
| Equatorial Guinea | 33 | 35 | 39 | 42 | 46 | 50 |
| Estonia | ... | ... | ... | ... | 66 | 75 |
| Ethiopia | 31 | 34 | 39 | 43 | 45 | 49 |
| Fiji | 49 | 52 | 56 | 60 | 64 | 68 |
| Finland | 63 | 70 | 67 | 75 | 72 | 80 |
| France | 64 | 70 | 69 | 76 | 73 | 81 |
| Gabon | 37 | 40 | 43 | 47 | 52 | 55 |
| Gambia, The | 29 | 32 | 36 | 39 | 43 | 47 |
| Georgia | ... | ... | ... | ... | 69 | 76 |
| Germany | 65 | 70 | 68 | 74 | 72 | 78 |
| Ghana | 40 | 44 | 48 | 52 | 54 | 58 |
| Greece | 64 | 68 | 71 | 74 | 74 | 79 |
| Guadeloupe | 55 | 58 | 65 | 71 | 71 | 78 |
| Guatemala | 42 | 42 | 53 | 56 | 62 | 67 |
| Guinea | 31 | 32 | 37 | 38 | 44 | 45 |
| Guinea-Bissau | 31 | 34 | 35 | 38 | 42 | 45 |
| Guyana | 51 | 54 | 58 | 62 | 62 | 68 |
| Haiti | 36 | 39 | 47 | 50 | 55 | 58 |
| Honduras | 41 | 44 | 52 | 56 | 64 | 68 |
| Hong Kong | 57 | 65 | 69 | 76 | 75 | 80 |
| Hungary | 62 | 66 | 67 | 73 | 68 | 75 |
| Iceland | 70 | 74 | 71 | 77 | 75 | 81 |
| India | 39 | 38 | 51 | 49 | 60 | 61 |
| Indonesia | 37 | 38 | 48 | 51 | 61 | 65 |
| Iran | 46 | 46 | 56 | 56 | 67 | 68 |
| Iraq | 43 | 45 | 56 | 58 | 65 | 67 |
| Ireland | 66 | 68 | 69 | 74 | 73 | 78 |
| Israel | 64 | 66 | 70 | 73 | 74 | 78 |
| Italy | 64 | 68 | 69 | 75 | 73 | 80 |
| Ivory Coast | 35 | 38 | 44 | 47 | 53 | 56 |
| Jamaica | 56 | 59 | 67 | 71 | 71 | 76 |
| Japan | 62 | 66 | 71 | 76 | 76 | 82 |
| Jordan | 42 | 44 | 55 | 58 | 66 | 70 |
| Kazakhstan | ... | ... | ... | ... | 64 | 73 |
| Kenya | 39 | 43 | 49 | 53 | 59 | 63 |
| Korea, North | 46 | 49 | 59 | 64 | 68 | 74 |
| Korea, South | 46 | 49 | 59 | 64 | 68 | 74 |
| Kuwait | 54 | 58 | 65 | 69 | 72 | 77 |
| Kyrgyzstan | ... | ... | ... | ... | 65 | 73 |
| Laos | 37 | 39 | 39 | 42 | 50 | 53 |
| Latvia | ... | ... | ... | ... | 64 | 75 |
| Lebanon | 54 | 58 | 63 | 67 | 65 | 69 |
| Lesotho | 34 | 41 | 44 | 53 | 54 | 63 |
| Liberia | 36 | 39 | 46 | 49 | 54 | 57 |
| Libya | 42 | 44 | 51 | 55 | 62 | 65 |
| Lithuania | ... | ... | ... | ... | 67 | 76 |
| Luxembourg | 63 | 69 | 67 | 74 | 72 | 79 |
| Macedonia | ... | ... | ... | ... | 68 | 72 |
| Madagascar | 36 | 39 | 45 | 48 | 54 | 57 |
| Malawi | 36 | 37 | 40 | 42 | 48 | 50 |
| Malaysia | 47 | 50 | 61 | 65 | 69 | 73 |

| | 1950–55 male | female | 1970–75 male | female | 1990–95 male | female | | 1950–55 male | female | 1970–75 male | female | 1990–95 male | female |
|---|---|---|---|---|---|---|---|---|---|---|---|---|---|
| Mali | 31 | 34 | 37 | 40 | 44 | 48 | Slovenia | ... | ... | ... | ... | 67 | 75 |
| Malta | 64 | 68 | 69 | 73 | 72 | 76 | Somalia | 32 | 35 | 39 | 43 | 45 | 49 |
| Martinique | 55 | 58 | 66 | 72 | 73 | 79 | South Africa | 44 | 46 | 51 | 57 | 60 | 66 |
| Mauritania | 32 | 35 | 39 | 42 | 46 | 50 | Spain | 62 | 66 | 70 | 76 | 74 | 80 |
| Mauritius | 50 | 52 | 61 | 65 | 68 | 73 | Sri Lanka | 58 | 56 | 64 | 66 | 70 | 74 |
| Mexico | 49 | 52 | 60 | 65 | 67 | 74 | Sudan | 36 | 38 | 41 | 44 | 51 | 53 |
| Moldova | ... | ... | ... | ... | 65 | 72 | Surinam | 54 | 58 | 62 | 67 | 68 | 73 |
| Mongolia | 41 | 44 | 53 | 55 | 62 | 66 | Swaziland | 34 | 37 | 45 | 50 | 56 | 60 |
| Morocco | 42 | 44 | 51 | 55 | 62 | 65 | Sweden | 70 | 73 | 72 | 78 | 75 | 81 |
| Mozambique | 32 | 35 | 41 | 44 | 47 | 50 | Switzerland | 67 | 72 | 71 | 77 | 75 | 81 |
| Namibia | 38 | 40 | 48 | 50 | 58 | 60 | Syria | 45 | 47 | 55 | 59 | 65 | 69 |
| Nepal | 37 | 36 | 44 | 43 | 54 | 53 | Tajikistan | ... | ... | ... | ... | 67 | 72 |
| Netherlands | 71 | 73 | 71 | 77 | 74 | 81 | Thailand | 45 | 49 | 58 | 62 | 65 | 69 |
| New Zealand | 68 | 72 | 69 | 75 | 73 | 79 | Togo | 35 | 38 | 44 | 47 | 53 | 57 |
| Nicaragua | 41 | 44 | 54 | 56 | 65 | 68 | Trinidad & Tobago | 56 | 59 | 64 | 69 | 70 | 75 |
| Niger | 32 | 35 | 38 | 41 | 45 | 48 | Tunisia | 44 | 45 | 55 | 56 | 67 | 69 |
| Nigeria | 35 | 38 | 43 | 46 | 51 | 54 | Turkey | 42 | 45 | 56 | 60 | 65 | 68 |
| Norway | 71 | 75 | 71 | 78 | 74 | 81 | Turkmenistan | ... | ... | ... | ... | 63 | 70 |
| Oman | 36 | 37 | 48 | 50 | 66 | 70 | Uganda | 39 | 42 | 45 | 49 | 51 | 55 |
| Pakistan | 40 | 38 | 50 | 48 | 59 | 59 | Ukraine | ... | ... | ... | ... | 66 | 75 |
| Panama | 54 | 56 | 65 | 68 | 71 | 75 | USSR (former) | 60 | 69 | 64 | 74 | 67 | 75 |
| Papua New Guinea | 36 | 35 | 48 | 48 | 55 | 57 | United Arab Em. | 47 | 49 | 61 | 64 | 70 | 74 |
| Paraguay | 61 | 65 | 64 | 68 | 65 | 70 | United Kingdom | 67 | 72 | 69 | 75 | 73 | 79 |
| Peru | 43 | 45 | 54 | 57 | 63 | 67 | United States | 66 | 72 | 68 | 75 | 73 | 80 |
| Philippines | 46 | 49 | 56 | 59 | 63 | 67 | Uruguay | 63 | 69 | 66 | 72 | 69 | 76 |
| Poland | 59 | 64 | 67 | 74 | 68 | 76 | Uzbekistan | ... | ... | ... | ... | 66 | 73 |
| Portugal | 57 | 62 | 65 | 71 | 71 | 78 | Venezuela | 54 | 57 | 64 | 69 | 67 | 74 |
| Puerto Rico | 63 | 67 | 69 | 76 | 73 | 79 | Vietnam | 39 | 42 | 48 | 53 | 62 | 66 |
| Qatar | 47 | 49 | 61 | 64 | 68 | 73 | Yemen | 33 | 33 | 43 | 43 | 52 | 52 |
| Réunion | 50 | 56 | 60 | 68 | 68 | 76 | Yugoslavia | 57 | 59 | 66 | 71 | 70 | 76 |
| Romania | 59 | 63 | 67 | 71 | 69 | 74 | Yugoslavia (Serbia) | ... | ... | ... | ... | 68 | 73 |
| Russia | ... | ... | ... | ... | 64 | 74 | Zaire | 38 | 41 | 44 | 48 | 52 | 56 |
| Rwanda | 39 | 42 | 43 | 46 | 49 | 52 | Zambia | 36 | 39 | 46 | 49 | 54 | 57 |
| Saudi Arabia | 39 | 41 | 52 | 56 | 64 | 68 | Zimbabwe | 40 | 43 | 50 | 53 | 59 | 63 |
| Senegal | 36 | 38 | 39 | 41 | 48 | 50 | | | | | | | |
| Sierra Leone | 29 | 32 | 34 | 37 | 41 | 45 | | | | | | | |
| Singapore | 59 | 62 | 67 | 72 | 72 | 77 | | | | | | | |

Life expectancy is the age to which a baby can expect to live with the rate of mortality pertaining at the time of birth. The figures given are averages for the period shown.

## URBAN POPULATION

*percentage of total population*

| | 1950 | 1970 | 1990 | 2000 | | 1950 | 1970 | 1990 | 2000 |
|---|---|---|---|---|---|---|---|---|---|
| Afghanistan | 6 | 11 | 22 | 29 | Burundi | 2 | 2 | 7 | 12 |
| Albania | 20 | 34 | 35 | 40 | Cambodia | 10 | 12 | 12 | 15 |
| Algeria | 22 | 40 | 45 | 51 | Cameroon | 10 | 20 | 49 | 60 |
| Angola | 8 | 15 | 28 | 36 | Canada | 61 | 76 | 76 | 79 |
| Antigua & Barbuda | 46 | 34 | 32 | 39 | Cape Verde Is. | 8 | 19 | 62 | 70 |
| Argentina | 65 | 78 | 86 | 89 | Cayman Is. | 100 | 100 | 100 | 100 |
| Armenia | ... | ... | 70 | ... | Central African Republic | 16 | 30 | 47 | 55 |
| Australia | 75 | 85 | 86 | 86 | Chad | 4 | 11 | 33 | 44 |
| Austria | 49 | 52 | 58 | 61 | Chile | 58 | 75 | 86 | 89 |
| Azerbaijan | ... | ... | 54 | ... | China | 11 | 20 | 21 | 25 |
| Bahamas | 62 | 58 | 59 | 65 | Colombia | 37 | 57 | 70 | 75 |
| Bahrain | 64 | 78 | 83 | 85 | Comoros | 3 | 11 | 28 | 34 |
| Bangladesh | 4 | 8 | 14 | 18 | Congo | 31 | 35 | 42 | 50 |
| Barbados | 34 | 37 | 45 | 51 | Cook Is. | 32 | 30 | 35 | 42 |
| Belarus | ... | ... | 67 | ... | Costa Rica | 34 | 40 | 54 | 61 |
| Belgium | 92 | 94 | 97 | 98 | Croatia | ... | ... | 51 | ... |
| Belize | 57 | 51 | 52 | 58 | Cuba | 49 | 60 | 75 | 80 |
| Benin | 7 | 16 | 42 | 53 | Cyprus | 30 | 41 | 53 | 60 |
| Bermuda | 100 | 100 | 100 | 100 | Czechoslovakia | 37 | 55 | 69 | 74 |
| Bhutan | 2 | 3 | 5 | 8 | Denmark | 68 | 80 | 86 | 89 |
| Bolivia | 38 | 41 | 51 | 59 | Djibouti | 41 | 62 | 81 | 84 |
| Bosnia | ... | ... | 36 | ... | Dominican Republic | 24 | 40 | 60 | 68 |
| Botswana | 0 | 8 | 24 | 33 | Ecuador | 28 | 40 | 57 | 65 |
| Brazil | 36 | 56 | 77 | 83 | Egypt | 32 | 42 | 49 | 55 |
| Brunei | 27 | 62 | 58 | 59 | El Salvador | 37 | 39 | 44 | 50 |
| Bulgaria | 26 | 52 | 70 | 76 | Equatorial Guinea | 16 | 39 | 65 | 71 |
| Burkina Faso | 4 | 6 | 9 | 12 | Estonia | ... | ... | 72 | ... |
| Burma | 16 | 23 | 25 | 28 | Ethiopia | 5 | 9 | 13 | 17 |
| | | | | | Faroe Is. | 18 | 28 | 31 | 36 |
| | | | | | Fiji | 24 | 35 | 44 | 51 |
| | | | | | Finland | 32 | 50 | 68 | 74 |
| | | | | | France | 56 | 71 | 74 | 76 |
| | | | | | French Guiana | 54 | 67 | 75 | 79 |

| | 1950 | 1970 | 1990 | 2000 | | 1950 | 1970 | 1990 | 2000 |
|---|---|---|---|---|---|---|---|---|---|
| French Polynesia | 28 | 56 | 65 | 70 | Nigeria | 10 | 20 | 35 | 43 |
| Gabon | 11 | 26 | 46 | 54 | Niue | 24 | 21 | 23 | 30 |
| Gambia, The | 11 | 15 | 23 | 29 | Norway | 32 | 65 | 74 | 77 |
| Georgia | ... | ... | 56 | ... | Oman | 2 | 5 | 11 | 15 |
| Germany | 72 | 78 | 84 | 86 | Pakistan | 18 | 25 | 32 | 38 |
| Ghana | 15 | 29 | 33 | 38 | Palau (Belau) | 22 | 41 | 60 | 66 |
| Greece | 37 | 53 | 63 | 68 | Panama | 36 | 48 | 55 | 61 |
| Guadeloupe | 42 | 41 | 49 | 55 | Papua New Guinea | 1 | 10 | 16 | 20 |
| Guatemala | 31 | 36 | 42 | 48 | Paraguay | 35 | 37 | 48 | 54 |
| Guinea | 6 | 14 | 26 | 33 | Peru | 36 | 57 | 70 | 75 |
| Guinea-Bissau | 10 | 15 | 20 | 25 | Philippines | 27 | 33 | 42 | 49 |
| Guyana | 28 | 29 | 34 | 42 | Poland | 39 | 52 | 63 | 67 |
| Haiti | 12 | 20 | 30 | 37 | Portugal | 19 | 26 | 33 | 39 |
| Honduras | 18 | 29 | 44 | 52 | Puerto Rico | 41 | 58 | 74 | 79 |
| Hong Kong | 89 | 90 | 93 | 94 | Qatar | 63 | 80 | 90 | 91 |
| Hungary | 37 | 46 | 60 | 67 | Réunion | 24 | 44 | 64 | 70 |
| Iceland | 74 | 83 | 91 | 92 | Romania | 28 | 42 | 50 | 53 |
| India | 17 | 20 | 28 | 34 | Russia | ... | ... | 74 | ... |
| Indonesia | 12 | 17 | 29 | 37 | Rwanda | 2 | 3 | 8 | 11 |
| Iran | 28 | 41 | 55 | 61 | St Christopher-Nevis | 22 | 34 | 49 | 56 |
| Iraq | 35 | 56 | 74 | 79 | St Lucia | 38 | 40 | 46 | 53 |
| Ireland | 41 | 52 | 59 | 64 | St Vincent & Grenadines | 13 | 15 | 21 | 27 |
| Israel | 65 | 84 | 92 | 94 | São Tomé & Príncipe | 13 | 23 | 42 | 51 |
| Italy | 54 | 64 | 69 | 72 | Saudi Arabia | 16 | 49 | 77 | 82 |
| Ivory Coast | 13 | 27 | 47 | 55 | Senegal | 31 | 33 | 38 | 45 |
| Jamaica | 27 | 42 | 52 | 59 | Seychelles | 27 | 26 | 59 | 69 |
| Japan | 50 | 71 | 77 | 78 | Sierra Leone | 9 | 18 | 32 | 40 |
| Jordan | 35 | 51 | 68 | 74 | Singapore | 100 | 100 | 100 | 100 |
| Kazakhstan | ... | ... | 58 | ... | Slovenia | ... | ... | 49 | ... |
| Kenya | 6 | 10 | 24 | 32 | Solomon Is. | 8 | 9 | 11 | 14 |
| Kiribati | 10 | 26 | 36 | 43 | Somalia | 13 | 23 | 36 | 44 |
| Korea, North | 31 | 50 | 67 | 73 | South Africa | 43 | 48 | 59 | 65 |
| Korea, South | 21 | 41 | 72 | 81 | Spain | 52 | 66 | 78 | 83 |
| Kuwait | 59 | 72 | 96 | 97 | Sri Lanka | 14 | 22 | 21 | 24 |
| Kyrgyzstan | ... | ... | 38 | ... | Sudan | 6 | 16 | 22 | 27 |
| Laos | 7 | 10 | 19 | 25 | Surinam | 47 | 46 | 48 | 54 |
| Latvia | ... | ... | 71 | ... | Swaziland | 1 | 10 | 33 | 45 |
| Lebanon | 23 | 59 | 84 | 87 | Sweden | 66 | 81 | 84 | 86 |
| Lesotho | 1 | 9 | 20 | 32 | Switzerland | 44 | 55 | 60 | 62 |
| Liberia | 13 | 26 | 44 | 52 | Syria | 31 | 43 | 52 | 57 |
| Libya | 19 | 36 | 70 | 76 | Taiwan | ... | ... | 75 | ... |
| Liechtenstein | 20 | 21 | 28 | 33 | Tajikistan | ... | ... | 31 | ... |
| Lithuania | ... | ... | 69 | ... | Tanzania | 4 | 7 | 33 | 47 |
| Luxembourg | 59 | 62 | 84 | 87 | Thailand | 11 | 13 | 23 | 29 |
| Macau | 97 | 97 | 99 | 99 | Togo | 7 | 13 | 26 | 33 |
| Macedonia | ... | ... | 54 | ... | Tonga | 13 | 21 | 21 | 25 |
| Madagascar | 8 | 14 | 25 | 32 | Trinidad & Tobago | 23 | 39 | 69 | 75 |
| Malawi | 4 | 6 | 15 | 21 | Tunisia | 31 | 44 | 54 | 59 |
| Malaysia | 20 | 27 | 42 | 50 | Turkey | 21 | 38 | 48 | 54 |
| Maldives | 11 | 14 | 21 | 24 | Turkmenistan | ... | ... | 45 | ... |
| Mali | 9 | 14 | 19 | 23 | Turks & Caicos | 40 | 41 | 51 | 58 |
| Malta | 61 | 78 | 87 | 90 | Uganda | 3 | 8 | 10 | 14 |
| Martinique | 28 | 54 | 75 | 79 | Ukraine | ... | ... | 68 | ... |
| Mauritania | 3 | 14 | 42 | 54 | USSR (former) | 39 | 57 | 68 | 71 |
| Mauritius | 29 | 42 | 42 | 46 | United Arab Emirates | 25 | 42 | 78 | 78 |
| Mexico | 43 | 59 | 73 | 77 | United Kingdom | 84 | 89 | 93 | 94 |
| Moldova | ... | ... | 48 | ... | United States | 64 | 74 | 74 | 75 |
| Monaco | 100 | 100 | 100 | 100 | Uruguay | 78 | 82 | 86 | 87 |
| Mongolia | 19 | 45 | 51 | 55 | Uzbekistan | ... | ... | 40 | ... |
| Montserrat | 22 | 11 | 12 | 16 | Vanuatu | 5 | 14 | 22 | 85 |
| Morocco | 26 | 35 | 49 | 56 | Venezuela | 53 | 72 | 91 | 94 |
| Mozambique | 2 | 6 | 27 | 41 | Vietnam | 12 | 18 | 22 | 27 |
| Namibia | 15 | 34 | 57 | 66 | Western Sahara | 68 | 43 | 57 | 63 |
| Nepal | 2 | 4 | 10 | 14 | Western Samoa | 13 | 20 | 23 | 27 |
| Netherlands | 83 | 86 | 89 | 89 | Yemen | 5 | 10 | 32 | 38 |
| Netherlands Antilles | 49 | 50 | 55 | 61 | Yugoslavia | 22 | 35 | 50 | 58 |
| New Caledonia | 40 | 49 | 81 | 87 | Yugoslavia (Serbia) | ... | ... | 48 | ... |
| New Zealand | 73 | 81 | 84 | 85 | Zaïre | 19 | 30 | 40 | 46 |
| Nicaragua | 35 | 47 | 60 | 66 | Zambia | 9 | 30 | 56 | 65 |
| Niger | 5 | 9 | 20 | 27 | Zimbabwe | 11 | 17 | 28 | 35 |

# CITIES

This list shows the principal cities with more than 500,000 inhabitants (for Brazil, China, India, Japan, Russia and the USA, only cities with more than 1 million inhabitants are included). The figures are taken from the most recent census or estimate available, and as far as possible are the population of the metropolitan area (for example, greater New York, Mexico or London). All the figures are in thousands. For the capitals and largest cities, English conventional name forms have been used (for example, Cairo, Moscow or Rome), but local name forms have been used for the smaller cities (for example, Kraków).

| | Population Thousands |
|---|---|
| **Afghanistan** | |
| Kabul | 1,424 |
| **Algeria** | |
| Algiers | 1,722 |
| Oran | 664 |
| **Angola** | |
| Luanda | 1,544 |
| **Argentina** | |
| Buenos Aires | 11,256 |
| Córdoba | 1,198 |
| Rosario | 1,096 |
| Mendoza | 775 |
| La Plata | 640 |
| San Miguel de Tucumán | 622 |
| Mar del Plata | 520 |
| **Armenia** | |
| Yerevan | 1,254 |
| **Australia** | |
| Sydney | 3,657 |
| Melbourne | 3,081 |
| Brisbane | 1,302 |
| Perth | 1,193 |
| Adelaide | 1,050 |
| **Austria** | |
| Vienna | 1,560 |
| **Azerbaijan** | |
| Baku | 1,149 |
| **Bangladesh** | |
| Dhaka | 6,105 |
| Chittagong | 2,041 |
| Khulna | 877 |
| Rajshahi | 517 |
| **Belarus** | |
| Minsk | 1,613 |
| Gomel | 506 |
| **Belgium** | |
| Brussels | 954 |
| **Bolivia** | |
| La Paz | 1,126 |
| Santa Cruz | 696 |
| **Bosnia-Herzegovina** | |
| Sarajevo | 526 |
| **Brazil** | |
| São Paulo | 9,480 |
| Rio de Janeiro | 5,336 |
| Salvador | 2,056 |
| Belo Horizonte | 2,049 |
| Fortaleza | 1,758 |
| Brasilia | 1,596 |
| Curitiba | 1,290 |
| Recife | 1,290 |
| Nova Iguaçu | 1,286 |
| Pôrto Alegre | 1,263 |
| Belém | 1,246 |
| Manaus | 1,011 |
| **Bulgaria** | |
| Sofia | 1,141 |
| **Burkina Faso** | |
| Ouagadougou | 634 |
| **Burma (Myanmar)** | |
| Rangoon | 2,513 |
| Mandalay | 533 |
| **Cambodia** | |
| Phnom Penh | 800 |
| **Cameroon** | |
| Douala | 884 |
| Yaoundé | 750 |
| **Canada** | |
| Toronto | 3,893 |

| | Population Thousands |
|---|---|
| Montréal | 3,127 |
| Vancouver | 1,603 |
| Ottawa-Hull | 921 |
| Edmonton | 840 |
| Calgary | 754 |
| Winnipeg | 652 |
| Québec | 646 |
| Hamilton | 600 |
| **Central African Republic** | |
| Bangui | 597 |
| **Chad** | |
| Ndjaména | 530 |
| **Chile** | |
| Santiago | 5,343 |
| **China** | |
| Shanghai | 12,320 |
| Beijing (Peking) | 9,750 |
| Tianjin | 7,790 |
| Chongqing | 6,511 |
| Wenzhou | 5,948 |
| Guangzhou | 5,669 |
| Hangzhou | 5,234 |
| Shenyang | 5,055 |
| Dalian | 4,619 |
| Jinzhou | 4,448 |
| Wuhan | 4,273 |
| Qingdao | 4,205 |
| Chengdu | 4,025 |
| Jilin | 3,974 |
| Nanjing | 3,682 |
| Jinan | 3,376 |
| Xi'an | 2,911 |
| Harbin | 2,830 |
| Yingkou | 2,789 |
| Dandong | 2,574 |
| Anshan | 2,517 |
| Nanchang | 2,471 |
| Zibo | 2,460 |
| Lanzhou | 2,340 |
| Lupanshui | 2,247 |
| Fushun | 2,045 |
| Taiyuan | 2,177 |
| Changchun | 2,110 |
| Kunming | 1,976 |
| Tianshui | 1,967 |
| Zhengzhou | 1,943 |
| Fuxin | 1,693 |
| Zigong | 1,673 |
| Fuzhou | 1,652 |
| Liaoyang | 1,612 |
| Zhaozhuang | 1,612 |
| Botou | 1,593 |
| Hepei | 1,541 |
| Guiyang | 1,530 |
| Huainan | 1,519 |
| Tangshan | 1,500 |
| Linyi | 1,385 |
| Qiqihar | 1,380 |
| Tai'an | 1,370 |
| Changsha | 1,330 |
| Shijiazhuang | 1,320 |
| Huaibei | 1,308 |
| Pingxiang | 1,305 |
| Xintao | 1,272 |
| Yangcheng | 1,265 |
| Yulin | 1,255 |
| Dongguang | 1,230 |
| Chao'an | 1,227 |
| Hohhot | 1,206 |

| | Population Thousands |
|---|---|
| Baotou | 1,200 |
| Suining | 1,195 |
| Luoyang | 1,190 |
| Macheng | 1,190 |
| Xintai | 1,167 |
| Yichun | 1,167 |
| Ürümqi | 1,160 |
| Puyang | 1,125 |
| Datong | 1,110 |
| Handan | 1,110 |
| Shaoxing | 1,091 |
| Ningbo | 1,090 |
| Zhongshan | 1,073 |
| Nanning | 1,070 |
| Huangshi | 1,069 |
| Laiwu | 1,054 |
| Leshan | 1,039 |
| Heze | 1,017 |
| Linhai | 1,012 |
| Changshu | 1,004 |
| **Colombia** | |
| Bogotá | 4,921 |
| Cali | 1,624 |
| Medellin | 1,581 |
| Barranquilla | 1,019 |
| Cartagena | 688 |
| **Congo** | |
| Brazzaville | 938 |
| Pointe-Noire | 576 |
| **Croatia** | |
| Zagreb | 931 |
| **Cuba** | |
| Havana | 2,119 |
| **Czech Republic** | |
| Prague | 1,216 |
| **Denmark** | |
| Copenhagen | 1,337 |
| **Dominican Republic** | |
| Santo Domingo | 1,601 |
| **Ecuador** | |
| Guayaquil | 1,508 |
| Quito | 1,101 |
| **Egypt** | |
| Cairo | 6,800 |
| Alexandria | 3,380 |
| El Gîza | 2,144 |
| Shubra el | |
| Kheima | 834 |
| **El Salvador** | |
| San Salvador | 1,522 |
| **Ethiopia** | |
| Addis Ababa | 2,213 |
| **Finland** | |
| Helsinki | 977 |
| **France** | |
| Paris | 9,319 |
| Lyons | 1,262 |
| Marseilles | 1,087 |
| Lille | 959 |
| Bordeaux | 696 |
| Toulouse | 650 |
| Nice | 516 |
| **Georgia** | |
| Tbilisi | 1,279 |
| **Germany** | |
| Berlin | 3,446 |
| Hamburg | 1,669 |
| Munich | 1,229 |
| Cologne | 957 |

| | Population Thousands |
|---|---|
| Frankfurt | 654 |
| Essen | 627 |
| Dortmund | 601 |
| Stuttgart | 592 |
| Düsseldorf | 578 |
| Bremen | 553 |
| Duisburg | 537 |
| Hanover | 517 |
| Leipzig | 503 |
| **Ghana** | |
| Accra | 965 |
| **Greece** | |
| Athens | 3,097 |
| **Guatemala** | |
| Guatemala | 2,000 |
| **Guinea** | |
| Conakry | 705 |
| **Haiti** | |
| Port-au-Prince | 1,144 |
| **Honduras** | |
| Tegucigalpa | 679 |
| **Hong Kong** | |
| Kowloon | 2,031 |
| Hong Kong | 1,251 |
| Tsuen Wan | 690 |
| **Hungary** | |
| Budapest | 2,016 |
| **India** | |
| Bombay | 12,572 |
| Calcutta | 10,916 |
| Delhi | 8,081 |
| Madras | 5,361 |
| Hyderabad | 4,280 |
| Bangalore | 4,087 |
| Ahmadabad | 3,298 |
| Pune | 2,485 |
| Kanpur | 2,111 |
| Nagpur | 1,661 |
| Lucknow | 1,642 |
| Surat | 1,517 |
| Jaipur | 1,015 |
| Kochi | 1,140 |
| Coimbatore | 1,136 |
| Vadodara | 1,115 |
| Indore | 1,104 |
| Patna | 1,099 |
| Madurai | 1,094 |
| Bhopal | 1,064 |
| Vishakhapatnam | 1,052 |
| Varanasi | 1,026 |
| Ludhiana | 1,012 |
| **Indonesia** | |
| Jakarta | 7,886 |
| Surabaya | 2,224 |
| Medan | 1,806 |
| Bandung | 1,567 |
| Semarang | 1,027 |
| Palembang | 787 |
| Ujung Pandang | 709 |
| Malang | 512 |
| **Iran** | |
| Tehran | 6,476 |
| Mashhad | 1,759 |
| Esfahan | 1,127 |
| Tabriz | 1,089 |
| Shiraz | 965 |
| Ahvaz | 725 |
| Qom | 681 |
| Bakhtaran | 624 |

| | Population Thousands | | Population Thousands | | Population Thousands | | Population Thousands |
|---|---|---|---|---|---|---|---|
| **Iraq** | | **Mexico** | | Samara | 1,271 | Donetsk | 1,121 |
| Baghdad | 3,841 | Mexico City | 15,048 | Omsk | 1,193 | Odesa | 1,096 |
| Diyala | 961 | Guadalajara | 2,847 | Chelyabinsk | 1,170 | Zaporizhya | 898 |
| As Sulaymaniyah | 952 | Monterrey | 2,522 | Perm | 1,108 | Lviv | 807 |
| Arbil | 770 | Puebla | 1,055 | Kazan | 1,107 | Kryvyy Rih | 729 |
| Mosul | 644 | León | 872 | Ufa | 1,100 | Mariupol | 523 |
| Kadhimain | 521 | Ciudad Juárez | 798 | Volgograd | 1,031 | Mykolayiv | 515 |
| **Ireland** | | Tijuana | 743 | Rostov | 1,027 | Luhansk | 505 |
| Dublin | 1,024 | Culiacán Rosales | 602 | **Saudi Arabia** | | **United Kingdom** | |
| **Israel** | | Mexicali | 602 | Riyadh | 2,000 | London | 6,933 |
| Tel Aviv– | | Acapulco de Juárez | 592 | Jedda | 1,400 | Birmingham | 1,012 |
| Jaffa | 1,844 | Mérida | 557 | Mecca | 618 | Leeds | 725 |
| Jerusalem | 544 | Chihuahua | 530 | Medina | 500 | Glasgow | 681 |
| **Italy** | | San Luis Potosí | 526 | **Senegal** | | Sheffield | 532 |
| Rome | 2,791 | Aguascalientés | 506 | Dakar | 1,730 | **United States** | |
| Milan | 1,432 | **Moldova** | | **Singapore** | | New York | 18,087 |
| Naples | 1,206 | Chişinau | 667 | Singapore | 2,818 | Los Angeles | 14,532 |
| Turin | 992 | **Mongolia** | | **Somali Republic** | | Chicago | 8,066 |
| Palermo | 734 | Ulan Bator | 575 | Mogadishu | 1,000 | San Francisco | 6,253 |
| Genoa | 701 | **Morocco** | | **South Africa** | | Philadelphia | 5,899 |
| **Ivory Coast** | | Casablanca | 2,409 | Cape Town | 1,912 | Detroit | 4,665 |
| Abidjan | 1,929 | Rabat-Salé | 893 | Johannesburg | 1,726 | Boston | 4,172 |
| **Jamaica** | | Fès | 562 | East Rand | 1,038 | Washington, DC | 3,924 |
| Kingston | 588 | Marrakesh | 549 | Durban | 982 | Dallas | 3,885 |
| **Japan** | | **Mozambique** | | Pretoria | 823 | Houston | 3,711 |
| Tokyo | 11,936 | Maputo | 1,070 | Port Elizabeth | 652 | Miami | 3,193 |
| Yokohama | 3,220 | **Netherlands** | | West Rand | 647 | Atlanta | 2,834 |
| Osaka | 2,624 | Amsterdam | 1,091 | Vereeniging | 540 | Cleveland | 2,760 |
| Nagoya | 2,155 | Rotterdam | 1,069 | **Spain** | | Seattle | 2,559 |
| Sapporo | 1,672 | The Hague | 694 | Madrid | 3,121 | San Diego | 2,498 |
| Kobe | 1,477 | Utrecht | 543 | Barcelona | 1,707 | Minneapolis-SP. | 2,464 |
| Kyoto | 1,461 | **New Zealand** | | Valencia | 753 | St Louis | 2,444 |
| Fukuoka | 1,237 | Auckland | 896 | Seville | 659 | Baltimore | 2,382 |
| Kawasaki | 1,174 | **Nicaragua** | | Zaragoza | 586 | Pittsburgh | 2,243 |
| Hiroshima | 1,086 | Managua | 682 | Málaga | 512 | Phoenix | 2,122 |
| Kitakyushu | 1,026 | **Nigeria** | | **Sri Lanka** | | Tampa | 2,098 |
| **Jordan** | | Lagos | 1,347 | Colombo | 1,863 | Denver | 1,848 |
| Amman | 1,272 | Ibadan | 1,295 | **Sudan** | | Cincinnati | 1,744 |
| Az-Zarqa | 605 | Kano | 700 | Khartoum | 561 | Milwaukee | 1,607 |
| **Kazakhstan** | | Ogbomosho | 661 | Omdurman | 526 | Kansas City | 1,566 |
| Alma-Ata | 1,147 | **Norway** | | **Sweden** | | Sacramento | 1,481 |
| Karaganda | 613 | Oslo | 746 | Stockholm | 1,503 | Portland | 1,478 |
| **Kenya** | | **Pakistan** | | Gothenburg | 734 | Norfolk | 1,396 |
| Nairobi | 1,429 | Karachi | 5,181 | **Switzerland** | | Columbus | 1,377 |
| **Korea, North** | | Lahore | 2,953 | Zürich | 840 | San Antonio | 1,303 |
| Pyongyang | 2,639 | Faisalabad | 1,104 | **Syria** | | Indianapolis | 1,250 |
| Hamhung | 775 | Rawalpindi | 795 | Damascus | 1,451 | New Orleans | 1,239 |
| Chongjin | 754 | Hyderabad | 752 | Aleppo | 1,445 | Buffalo | 1,189 |
| Chinnamp'o | 691 | Multan | 722 | Holms | 518 | Charlotte | 1,162 |
| Sinuiju | 500 | Gujranwala | 659 | **Taiwan** | | Hartford | 1,086 |
| **Korea, South** | | Peshawar | 556 | Taipei | 2,718 | Salt Lake City | 1,072 |
| Seoul | 10,628 | **Paraguay** | | Kaohsiung | 1,396 | **Uruguay** | |
| Pusan | 3,798 | Asunción | 945 | Taichung | 774 | Montevideo | 1,384 |
| Taegu | 2,229 | **Peru** | | Tainan | 690 | **Uzbekistan** | |
| Inchon | 1,818 | Lima-Callao | 6,415 | Panchiao | 543 | Tashkent | 2,094 |
| Kwangju | 1,145 | Arequipa | 635 | **Tajikistan** | | **Venezuela** | |
| Taejon | 1,062 | Trujillo | 532 | Dushanbe | 602 | Caracas | 2,784 |
| Ulsan | 683 | Callao | 515 | **Tanzania** | | Maracaibo | 1,364 |
| Puch'on | 668 | **Philippines** | | Dar es Salaam | 1,361 | Valencia | 1,032 |
| Suwon | 645 | Manila | 6,720 | **Thailand** | | Maracay | 800 |
| Songnam | 541 | Quezon City | 1,667 | Bangkok | 5,876 | Barquisimeto | 745 |
| Chonju | 517 | Davao | 868 | **Togo** | | Ciudad Guayana | 524 |
| **Kyrgyzstan** | | Cebu | 641 | Lomé | 500 | **Vietnam** | |
| Bishkek | 641 | Caloocan | 629 | **Tunisia** | | Ho Chi Minh | 3,924 |
| **Latvia** | | **Poland** | | Tunis | 1,395 | Hanoi | 3,056 |
| Riga | 917 | Warsaw | 1,655 | **Turkey** | | Haiphong | 1,448 |
| **Lebanon** | | Lódz | 847 | Istanbul | 7,309 | **Yugoslavia** | |
| Beirut | 1,500 | Kraków | 751 | Ankara | 3,022 | Belgrade | 1,137 |
| Tripoli | 500 | Wroclaw | 643 | Izmir | 2,665 | **Zaire** | |
| **Libya** | | Poznan | 590 | Adana | 1,430 | Kinshasa | 3,804 |
| Tripoli | 990 | **Portugal** | | Bursa | 1,031 | Lubumbashi | 739 |
| **Lithuania** | | Lisbon | 2,561 | Konya | 1,015 | Mbuji-Mayi | 613 |
| Vilnius | 593 | Oporto | 1,174 | Gaziantep | 760 | Kolwezi | 544 |
| **Macedonia** | | **Romania** | | İçel | 701 | **Zambia** | |
| Skopje | 563 | Bucharest | 2,064 | Kayseri | 588 | Lusaka | 982 |
| **Madagascar** | | **Russia** | | **Uganda** | | **Zimbabwe** | |
| Antananarivo | 802 | Moscow | 8,957 | Kampala | 773 | Harare | 1,189 |
| **Malaysia** | | St Petersburg | 5,004 | **Ukraine** | | Bulawayo | 622 |
| Kuala Lumpur | 938 | Novosibirsk | 1,472 | Kiev | 2,643 | | |
| **Mali** | | Nizhniy Novgorod | 1,451 | Kharkhiv | 1,622 | | |
| Bamako | 746 | Yekaterinburg | 1,413 | Dnipropetrovsk | 1,190 | | |

# ENERGY

*million tonnes of coal-equivalent*

| | Production | | Imports | | Exports | | Consumption per capita | | tonnes of c-e per capita Consumption total |
|---|---|---|---|---|---|---|---|---|---|
| | 1970 | 1990 | 1970 | 1990 | 1970 | 1990 | 1970 | 1990 | 1990 |
| World | ... | 10,876 | ... | 3,516 | ... | 3,525 | ... | 1.93 | 10,285 |
| Afghanistan | 3.44 | 4.15 | 0.33 | 0.9 | 3.08 | 1.37 | 0.05 | 0.22 | 3.64 |
| Albania | 2.65 | 6.31 | 0.03 | 0.25 | 0.12 | 0.08 | 0.6 | 1.26 | 4.07 |
| Algeria | 72.45 | 156.7 | 0.96 | 1.34 | 70.16 | 112.5 | 0.37 | 1.48 | 36.9 |
| American Samoa | 0 | 0 | 0.06 | 0.27 | 0 | 0 | 2.44 | 3.61 | 0.14 |
| Angola | 7.49 | 34.04 | 0.39 | 0.02 | 6.38 | 31.62 | 0.16 | 0.09 | 0.89 |
| Antigua & Barbuda | 0 | 0 | 0.88 | 0.24 | 0.28 | 0.01 | 2 | 1.9 | 0.14 |
| Argentina | 37.29 | 67.55 | 4.53 | 4.03 | 0.15 | 6.5 | 1.58 | 1.83 | 58.98 |
| Australia | 59.65 | 212.21 | 26.8 | 19.16 | 17.2 | 100.05 | 4.83 | 7.53 | 127.05 |
| Austria | 11.15 | 8.23 | 15.48 | 25.03 | 0.84 | 1.37 | 3.27 | 4.06 | 30.81 |
| Bahamas | 0 | 0 | 4.58 | 4.29 | 2.95 | 3.01 | 4.07 | 2.49 | 0.14 |
| Bahrain | 6.03 | 10.39 | 12.64 | 14.51 | 14.31 | 13.04 | 2.64 | 15.59 | 0.05 |
| Bangladesh | ... | 5.54 | ... | 3.39 | 0 | 0 | ... | 0.06 | 8.45 |
| Barbados | 0.01 | 0.13 | 0.47 | 0.51 | 0 | 0.01 | 0.82 | 1.66 | 0.42 |
| Belgium | 11.46 | 7.45 | 64.98 | 85.39 | 12.87 | 26.94 | 5.61 | 5.92 | 58.24 |
| Belize | 0 | 0 | 0.06 | 0.18 | 0 | 0 | 0.49 | 0.65 | 0.12 |
| Benin | ... | 0.42 | ... | 0.26 | 0 | 0.42 | 0.05 | 0.05 | 0.22 |
| Bermuda | 0 | 0 | 0.31 | 0.31 | 0 | 0 | 1.96 | 4.82 | 0.28 |
| Bolivia | 1.76 | 5.6 | 0.02 | 2.94 | 0.86 | 0 | 0.23 | 0.36 | 2.6 |
| Brazil | 18.69 | 80.12 | 28.05 | 57.88 | 1.5 | 5.71 | 0.44 | 0.77 | 115.14 |
| British Virgin Is. | 0 | 0 | 0.01 | 0.02 | 0 | 0 | 0.9 | 1.77 | 0.02 |
| Brunei | 10.07 | 25.26 | 0.02 | 0.05 | 9.79 | 21.48 | 2.18 | 14.94 | 3.97 |
| Bulgaria | 16.15 | 17.81 | 16.58 | 26.99 | 0.4 | 1.2 | 3.77 | 4.3 | 38.78 |
| Burkina Faso | 0 | 0 | ... | 0.26 | 0 | 0 | ... | 0.03 | 0.26 |
| Burma | 1.3 | 2.93 | 0.49 | 0.05 | 0 | 0 | 0.06 | 0.06 | 2.51 |
| Burundi | 0 | 0.02 | 0 | 0.1 | 0 | 0 | 0.01 | 0.02 | 0.11 |
| Cameroon | 0.14 | 12.44 | 0.37 | 0.03 | 0 | 10.3 | 0.07 | 0.24 | 2.89 |
| Canada | 204.98 | 364.55 | 74.8 | 62.15 | 84.45 | 151.34 | 8.81 | 10.26 | 271.98 |
| Cape Verde | 0 | 0 | 0 | 0.05 | 0 | 0 | 0.05 | 0.11 | 0.04 |
| Cayman Is. | 0 | 0 | 0.02 | 0.13 | 0 | 0 | 2.1 | 4.76 | 0.12 |
| Central African Rep. | 0.005 | 0.01 | 0.11 | 0.12 | 0 | 0 | 0.05 | 0.04 | 0.11 |
| Chad | 0 | 0 | 0.09 | 0.14 | 0 | 0 | 0.02 | 0.02 | 0.1 |
| Chile | 6.11 | 7.51 | 4.48 | 9.95 | 0.02 | 0.3 | 1.15 | 1.25 | 16.46 |
| China | 304 | 1,002 | 0.62 | 7.69 | 2.15 | 61.04 | 0.35 | 0.81 | 922.18 |
| Colombia | 21.79 | 58.45 | 0 | 1.91 | 7.99 | 31.99 | 0.61 | 0.77 | 25.42 |
| Comoros | 0 | 0 | 0.01 | 0.03 | 0 | 0 | 0.04 | 0.06 | 0.03 |
| Congo | 0.05 | 11.59 | 0.17 | 0.02 | 0.03 | 10.64 | 0.15 | 0.37 | 0.85 |
| Costa Rica | 0.12 | 0.43 | 0.64 | 1.46 | 0.07 | 0.05 | 0.37 | 0.59 | 1.77 |
| Cuba | 0.24 | 1.27 | 8.74 | 18.58 | 0 | 2.91 | 0.99 | 1.45 | 15.33 |
| Cyprus | 0 | 0 | 0.81 | 2.31 | 0 | 0 | 1.21 | 2.52 | 1.77 |
| Czechoslovakia | 63.75 | 59.33 | 22.21 | 41.05 | 6.69 | 5.91 | 5.39 | 5.59 | 87.65 |
| Denmark | 0.05 | 12.97 | 33.61 | 21.83 | 3.22 | 9.47 | 5.44 | 4.66 | 23.98 |
| Djibouti | 0 | 0 | 1.07 | 0.75 | 0 | 0 | 0.3 | 0.44 | 0.18 |
| Dominica | 0 | 0 | 0.01 | 0.03 | 0 | 0 | 0.18 | 0.37 | 0.03 |
| Dominican Republic | 0.1 | 0.1 | 1.35 | 2.68 | 0 | | 0.32 | 0.37 | 2.62 |
| Ecuador | 0.38 | 22.29 | 1.45 | 0.38 | 0.06 | 14.74 | 0.28 | 0.73 | 7.69 |
| Egypt | 24.55 | 79.52 | 5.89 | 1.23 | 21.36 | 37.02 | 0.26 | 0.74 | 38.57 |
| El Salvador | 0.06 | 0.26 | 0.64 | 1.15 | 0 | 0.08 | 0.19 | 0.25 | 1.3 |
| Equatorial Guinea | 0 | 0 | 0.02 | 0.06 | 0 | 0 | 0.06 | 0.15 | 0.05 |
| Ethiopia | 0.03 | 0.1 | 0.02 | 1.61 | 0 | 0.2 | 0.06 | 0.03 | 1.27 |
| Faroe Is. | 0 | 0 | 0.12 | 0.29 | 0 | 0 | 3.28 | 6.4 | 0.3 |
| Fiji | 0 | 0.04 | 0.45 | 0.6 | 0.02 | 0.12 | 0.45 | 0.56 | 0.01 |
| Finland | 1.18 | 5.63 | 22.46 | 27.22 | 0.3 | 2.12 | 4.07 | 5.93 | 29.51 |
| France | 60.8 | 66.85 | 175 | 191.79 | 14.42 | 25.41 | 3.84 | 3.97 | 222.74 |
| French Guiana | 0 | 0 | 0.05 | 0.28 | 0 | 0 | 0.96 | 2.59 | 0.25 |
| French Polynesia | 0 | 0 | 0.21 | 0.39 | 0 | 0 | 0.82 | 1.47 | 0.3 |
| Gabon | 7.91 | 19.5 | 0.01 | 0.05 | 7.33 | 17.93 | 0.46 | 0.72 | 0.84 |
| Gambia | 0 | 0 | 0.02 | 0.09 | 0 | 0 | 0.05 | 0.11 | 0.09 |
| Germany | 254.96 | 233.36 | 228.64 | 677.66 | 40.2 | 37.23 | 5.4 | 5.75 | 457.3 |
| Ghana | 0.35 | 0.66 | 1.32 | 1.78 | 0.13 | 0.13 | 0.17 | 0.1 | 1.52 |
| Gibraltar | 0 | 0 | 0.24 | 0.72 | 0 | 0 | 0.77 | 0.93 | 0.03 |
| Greece | 2.03 | 11.22 | 10.03 | 30.65 | 0.23 | 9.16 | 1.11 | 3.04 | 30.57 |
| Greenland | 0.02 | 0 | 0.16 | 0.27 | 0 | 0.01 | 3.68 | 4.66 | 0.26 |
| Grenada | 0 | 0 | 0.02 | 0.07 | 0 | 0 | 0.22 | 0.68 | 0.06 |
| Guadeloupe | 0 | 0 | 0.15 | 0.63 | 0 | 0 | 0.45 | 1.43 | 0.49 |

| | Production | | Imports | | Exports | | Consumption per capita | | Consumption total |
|---|---|---|---|---|---|---|---|---|---|
| | 1970 | 1990 | 1970 | 1990 | 1970 | 1990 | 1970 | 1990 | 1990 |
| Guam | 0 | 0 | 1.09 | 0.86 | 0.13 | 0 | 6.49 | 5.98 | 0.71 |
| Guatemala | 0.04 | 0.51 | 1.14 | 1.57 | 0 | 0.09 | 0.19 | 0.19 | 1.73 |
| Guinea | 0 | 0.02 | 0.36 | 0.49 | 0 | 0 | 0.09 | 0.09 | 0.49 |
| Guinea-Bissau | 0 | 0 | 0.03 | 0.11 | 0 | 0 | 0.05 | 0.1 | 0.1 |
| Guyana | 0 | 0 | 0.74 | 0.31 | 0 | 0 | 1.04 | 0.38 | 0.3 |
| Haiti | ... | 0.04 | 0.17 | 0.32 | 0 | 0 | 0.04 | 0.05 | 0.34 |
| Honduras | 0.02 | 0.11 | 1.11 | 0.79 | 0.5 | 0 | 0.23 | 0.19 | 1.73 |
| Hong Kong | 0 | 0 | 5.49 | 17.71 | 0.07 | 3.17 | 0.96 | 1.77 | 10.36 |
| Hungary | 20.66 | 17.2 | 11.72 | 22.41 | 1.53 | 4.7 | 2.81 | 3.28 | 34.66 |
| Iceland | 0.18 | 0.57 | 0.75 | 1.02 | 0 | 0 | 4.11 | 6.23 | 1.58 |
| India | 67.76 | 240.17 | 17.95 | 44.52 | 0.42 | 0.62 | 0.14 | 0.31 | 264.92 |
| Indonesia | 63.91 | 162.88 | 0.5 | 13.52 | 44.78 | 112.44 | 0.12 | 0.3 | 55.42 |
| Iran | 295 | 261.61 | 0 | 10.59 | 257 | 172.96 | 0.96 | 1.65 | 90.34 |
| Iraq | 112 | 150.28 | 0.05 | 0 | 107 | 124.58 | 0.61 | 0.87 | 16.55 |
| Ireland | 1.76 | 4.88 | 7.86 | 10.64 | 1.02 | 0.93 | 2.58 | 3.66 | 13.63 |
| Israel | 7.46 | 0.06 | 1.55 | 16.31 | 0.29 | 1.46 | 2.14 | 3.19 | 14.68 |
| Italy | 25.8 | 32.21 | 182 | 207.66 | 34.89 | 26.84 | 2.65 | 3.68 | 209.85 |
| Ivory Coast | 0.03 | 0.65 | 1.23 | 3.93 | 0.12 | 0.35 | 0.2 | 0.19 | 2.27 |
| Jamaica | 0.02 | 0.02 | 3.04 | 2.25 | 0.22 | 0.09 | 1.21 | 0.83 | 2.04 |
| Japan | ... | 47.65 | ... | 507.06 | ... | 11.49 | ... | 4.15 | 512.11 |
| Jordan | ... | 0.03 | 0.77 | 4.95 | 0 | 0 | 0.27 | 1.82 | 4.34 |
| Kenya | 0.04 | 0.35 | 3.59 | 3.48 | 1.38 | 0.77 | 0.1 | 0.11 | 2.67 |
| Kiribati | 0 | 0 | ... | 0.01 | 0 | 0 | ... | 0.15 | 0.01 |
| Korea, North | 26.63 | 52.4 | 1.92 | 7.67 | 0.09 | 0.05 | 2.05 | 2.76 | 60.07 |
| Korea, South | 9.53 | 18.35 | 13.05 | 102.47 | 0.63 | 4.86 | 0.67 | 2.47 | 105.85 |
| Kuwait | 224 | 96.67 | 0 | 2.73 | 208 | 79.93 | 4.77 | 7.01 | 14.29 |
| Laos | 0 | 0.1 | 0.27 | 0.1 | 0 | 0.06 | 0.09 | 0.04 | 0.15 |
| Lebanon | 0.11 | 0.07 | 3.18 | 4.23 | 0.58 | 0 | 0.68 | 1.52 | 4.11 |
| Liberia | 0.03 | 0.03 | 0.76 | 0.25 | 0 | 0 | 0.48 | 0.09 | 0.24 |
| Libya | 232.37 | 110.52 | 0.7 | 0.01 | 232.03 | 80.06 | 0.67 | 4.72 | 21.46 |
| Luxembourg | 0.11 | 0.1 | 5.84 | 5.01 | 0 | 0.11 | 17.05 | 12.95 | 4.83 |
| Macau | 0 | 0 | 0.09 | 0.5 | 0 | 0 | 0.36 | 1.03 | 0.49 |
| Madagascar | 0.01 | 0.04 | 0.87 | 0.51 | 0.34 | 0.05 | 0.07 | 0.04 | 0.48 |
| Malawi | 0.02 | 0.07 | 0.2 | 0.25 | 0 | 0 | 0.04 | 0.04 | 0.3 |
| Malaysia | 1.5 | 61.45 | 15.09 | 13.53 | 8.53 | 47.26 | 0.56 | 1.51 | 26.95 |
| Mali | 0 | 0.02 | 0.11 | 0.22 | 0 | 0 | 0.02 | 0.02 | 0.22 |
| Malta | 0 | 0 | 0.46 | 0.83 | 0 | 0 | 0.92 | 2.03 | 0.72 |
| Martinique | 0 | 0 | 0.18 | 0.91 | 0 | 0.3 | 0.53 | 1.77 | 0.6 |
| Mauritania | 0 | 0 | 0.2 | 1.35 | 0 | 0 | 0.16 | 0.58 | 1.17 |
| Mauritius | 0.01 | 0.01 | 0.3 | 0.88 | 0 | 0 | 0.33 | 0.49 | 0.54 |
| Mexico | 53.81 | 256.92 | 3.65 | 8.24 | 5.27 | 101.39 | 1.04 | 1.75 | 155.28 |
| Mongolia | 0.72 | 3.07 | 0.37 | 1.06 | 0 | 0.21 | 0.87 | 1.79 | 3.92 |
| Morocco | 0.73 | 0.77 | 2.21 | 9.95 | 0.08 | 0 | 0.19 | 0.37 | 9.21 |
| Mozambique | 0.03 | 0.05 | 1.66 | 0.53 | 0.53 | 0 | 0.14 | 0.03 | 0.49 |
| Nauru | 0 | 0 | 0.03 | 0.07 | 0 | 0 | 4.43 | 6.78 | 0.06 |
| Nepal | 0 | 0.09 | 0.15 | 0.28 | 0 | 0.04 | 0.01 | 0.02 | 0.38 |
| Netherlands | 45.22 | 92.85 | 104 | 133.52 | 58.32 | 109.74 | 4.59 | 7.21 | 107.79 |
| Netherlands Antilles | 0 | 0 | 71.55 | 17.17 | 57.51 | 11.8 | 33.81 | 9.73 | 1.83 |
| New Caledonia | 0.03 | 0.06 | 1.05 | 0.72 | 0 | 0.01 | 9.44 | 4.4 | 0.73 |
| New Zealand | 3.7 | 13.64 | 5.04 | 4.45 | 0.08 | 1.11 | 2.79 | 4.99 | 16.95 |
| Nicaragua | 0.04 | 0.07 | 0.66 | 0.97 | 0 | 0 | 0.32 | 0.26 | 1.01 |
| Niger | ... | 0.16 | 0.09 | 0.32 | 0 | 0 | 0.02 | 0.06 | 0.46 |
| Nigeria | 79.19 | 128.93 | 1 | 4.03 | 74.5 | 110.72 | 0.05 | 0.19 | 20.4 |
| Norway | 7.48 | 171.26 | 16.01 | 6.57 | 3.39 | 144.98 | 4.55 | 6.91 | 29.14 |
| Oman | 24.11 | 52.42 | 0.63 | 0.14 | 24.11 | 46.22 | 0.17 | 3.96 | 5.94 |
| Pakistan | ... | 22.26 | ... | 12.69 | ... | 0.47 | ... | 0.28 | 34.04 |
| Palau (Belau) | 0 | 0 | 0.08 | 0.13 | 0 | 0 | 0.62 | 0.65 | 0.12 |
| Panama | ... | 0.27 | ... | 4.89 | 0 | 0.46 | ... | 0.61 | 1.48 |
| Papua New Guinea | 0.02 | 0.06 | 0.35 | 1.14 | 0 | 0.02 | 0.14 | 0.29 | 1.13 |
| Paraguay | 0 | 0.29 | 0 | 0.78 | 0 | 0.07 | 0 | 0.23 | 0.97 |
| Peru | 6.43 | 11.99 | 2 | 2.29 | 0.34 | 3.06 | 0.61 | 0.49 | 10.57 |
| Philippines | 0.29 | 2.56 | 13.3 | 19.63 | 1.12 | 0.59 | 0.26 | 0.3 | 18.76 |
| Poland | 131 | 140.47 | 15.42 | 35.03 | 28.03 | 27.53 | 3.56 | 3.72 | 142.87 |
| Portugal | 0.99 | 1.31 | 7.85 | 24.05 | 0.69 | 3.36 | 0.74 | 1.87 | 19.21 |
| Puerto Rico | 0.03 | 0.03 | 14.35 | 13.71 | 5.05 | 1.47 | 3.46 | 3.01 | 10.46 |
| Qatar | 26.6 | 36.74 | 0.08 | 0 | 25.29 | 28.56 | 13.26 | 23.69 | 8.72 |
| Reunion | 0.01 | 0.06 | 0.13 | 0.46 | 0 | 0 | 0.31 | 0.84 | 0.5 |
| Romania | 64.85 | 63.54 | 6.18 | 39.68 | 7.65 | 12.94 | 2.99 | 3.73 | 86.83 |
| Rwanda | 0.01 | 0.02 | 0.03 | 0.2 | 0 | 0 | 0.01 | 0.03 | 0.21 |
| São Tomé & Príncipe | 0 | 0 | ... | 0.03 | 0 | 0 | ... | 0.27 | 0.03 |
| Saudi Arabia | 277 | 521.8 | 0.73 | 0.59 | 251 | 391.48 | 0.47 | 6.39 | 90.36 |
| Senegal | 0 | 0 | 2.36 | 1.52 | 0.05 | 0.05 | 0.12 | 0.14 | 1.03 |
| Seychelles | 0 | 0 | 0.03 | 0.21 | 0 | 0 | 0.29 | 1.15 | 0.08 |
| Sierra Leone | 0 | 0 | 0.61 | 0.45 | 0 | 0 | 0.12 | 0.07 | 0.31 |
| Singapore | 0 | 0 | 29.42 | 85.78 | 17.38 | 47.1 | 2.01 | 5.54 | 15.08 |

| | Production | | Imports | | Exports | | Consumption per capita | | Consumption total |
|---|---|---|---|---|---|---|---|---|---|
| | 1970 | 1990 | 1970 | 1990 | 1970 | 1990 | 1970 | 1990 | 1990 |
| Solomon Is. | 0 | 0 | 0.02 | 0.08 | 0 | 0 | 0.11 | 0.24 | 0.08 |
| Somalia | 0 | 0 | 0.11 | 0.04 | 0 | 0 | 0.04 | 0.37 | 0.04 |
| South Africa | 48.52 | 133.71 | 16.61 | 22.47 | 1.84 | 42.98 | 2.19 | 2.6 | 106.25 |
| Spain | 14.12 | 28.94 | 49.75 | 97.83 | 17.94 | 14.41 | 1.47 | 2.53 | 98.97 |
| Sri Lanka | 0.09 | 0.39 | 2.97 | 2.71 | 0.14 | 0.14 | 0.14 | 0.13 | 2.23 |
| St Christopher-Nevis | 0 | 0 | 0 | 0.03 | 0 | 0 | ... | 0.71 | 0.03 |
| St Lucia | 0 | 0 | 0 | 0.08 | 0 | 0 | 0.32 | 0.52 | 0.08 |
| St Pierre & Miquelon | 0 | 0 | 0 | 0.12 | 0 | 0 | 3.2 | 7.33 | 0.04 |
| St Vincent & G. | 0 | 0 | 0 | 0.04 | 0 | 0 | 0.17 | 0.37 | 0.04 |
| Sudan | 0.01 | 0.12 | 2.35 | 1.86 | 0 | 0.05 | 0.15 | 0.06 | 0.22 |
| Surinam | 0.12 | 0.54 | 0.74 | 0.63 | 0 | 0.11 | 2.32 | 1.81 | 0.77 |
| Sweden | 5.14 | 17.36 | 49.06 | 38.48 | 2.78 | 13.27 | 5.77 | 4.74 | 39.99 |
| Switzerland | 3.91 | 6.72 | 20.04 | 23.84 | 1.57 | 3.06 | 3.21 | 3.91 | 25.96 |
| Syria | 6.18 | 33.74 | 1.86 | 1.08 | 5.15 | 19.38 | 0.38 | 1.06 | 13.34 |
| Tanzania | 0.04 | 0.08 | 1.68 | 1.04 | 0.83 | 0.05 | 0.06 | 0.04 | 0.98 |
| Thailand | 0.37 | 16.26 | 7.34 | 26.88 | 0.05 | 1.06 | 0.18 | 0.74 | 41.08 |
| Togo | 0 | 0 | 0.13 | 0.23 | 0 | 0 | 0.06 | 0.06 | 0.22 |
| Tonga | 0 | 0 | 0.01 | 0.04 | 0 | 0 | 0.14 | 0.37 | 0.04 |
| Trindad & Tobago | 13.01 | 18.6 | 23.14 | 1.51 | 27.99 | 10.82 | 4.4 | 6.86 | 8.78 |
| Tunisia | 6.05 | 7.14 | 0.86 | 5.11 | 4.7 | 5.68 | 0.29 | 0.81 | 6.65 |
| Turkey | 11.96 | 24.29 | 6.01 | 40.98 | 0.3 | 3.19 | 0.48 | 1.04 | 58.03 |
| Uganda | 0.09 | 0.07 | 0.64 | 0.4 | 0.04 | 0.02 | 0.07 | 0.02 | 0.45 |
| USSR (former) | 1,216 | 2,357 | 17.04 | 23.93 | 163 | 380.29 | 4.13 | 6.69 | 1,931 |
| United Arab Em. | 55.12 | 180.26 | 0.28 | | 54.8 | 146.57 | 2.52 | 20.18 | 32.07 |
| United Kingdom | 145 | 278.68 | 173 | 115.48 | 28.67 | 103.23 | 4.87 | 4.99 | 286.53 |
| United States | 2,102 | 2,102 | 276 | 588.08 | 74 | 131.05 | 10.82 | 9.96 | 2,482 |
| US Virgin Is. | 0 | 0 | 21.28 | 24.31 | 13.06 | 15.36 | 42.42 | 11.71 | 1.36 |
| Uruguay | 0.15 | 0.78 | 2.85 | 1.96 | 0 | 0.16 | 0.89 | 0.75 | 2.31 |
| Vanuatu | 0 | 0 | 0.04 | 0.06 | 0 | 0 | 0.22 | 0.2 | 0.03 |
| Venezuela | 298 | 198.41 | 0.31 | 0.13 | 258 | 135.71 | 2.24 | 2.84 | 56.06 |
| Vietnam | 3.07 | 9.51 | 9.76 | 4.33 | 0.24 | 4.54 | 0.3 | 0.14 | 9.39 |
| Wake Is. | 0 | 0 | 0.52 | 0.58 | 0 | 0 | 38 | 19 | 0.04 |
| Western Sahara | 0 | 0 | ... | 0.1 | 0 | 0 | ... | 0.52 | 0.09 |
| Western Samoa | 0 | 0 | 0.02 | 0.06 | 0 | 0 | 0.11 | 0.38 | 0.06 |
| Yemen | 0 | 12.09 | 10.05 | 1.11 | 8.19 | 11.51 | 0.18 | 0.17 | 1.57 |
| Yugoslavia | 21.44 | 35.38 | 9.68 | 27.27 | 1.04 | 1.22 | 1.41 | 2.41 | 57.34 |
| Zaïre | 0.49 | 2.88 | 1.48 | 1.52 | 0.19 | 1.69 | 0.07 | 0.07 | 2.35 |
| Zambia | 0.61 | 1.27 | 1.01 | 0.79 | 0 | 0.25 | 0.39 | 0.2 | 1.7 |
| Zimbabwe | 3.61 | 5.39 | 0.7 | 1.17 | 0.54 | 0.16 | 0.71 | 0.65 | 6.31 |

South Africa includes Botswana, Lesotho, Namibia and Swaziland.

# GROSS NATIONAL PRODUCT

| | GNP 1991 | GNP per capita 1991 | GDP share agriculture 1991 | GDP share industry 1991 | GDP share manufacture 1991 | GDP share services 1991 | Average annual rate of change 1980–91 | Consumer price index Jan 1993 |
|---|---|---|---|---|---|---|---|---|
| | *million $US* | *$US* | *%* | *%* | *%* | *%* | *%* | *1980=100* |
| Afghanistan | ... | 450 | 52 | 33 | 25 | 15 | –6 | ... |
| Albania | ... | 1,000 | 33 | 51 | 45 | 16 | 4.5 | ... |
| Algeria | 52,239 | 2,020 | 14 | 50 | 10 | 36 | –0.8 | 374  92 |
| American Samoa | ... | 6,000 | ... | ... | ... | ... | ... | ... |
| Angola | ... | 620 | 13 | 42 | 4 | 45 | 4 | ... |
| Antigua & Barbuda | 355 | 4,770 | 6 | 24 | 3 | 70 | 3.8 | ... |
| Argentina | 91,211 | 2,780 | 15 | 40 | 35 | 45 | –1.5 | 284,555 |
| Armenia | 7,233 | 2,150 | 14 | 71 | 50 | 15 | 2.1 | ... |
| Aruba | ... | 6,000 | ... | ... | ... | ... | ... | ... |
| Australia | 287,765 | 16,590 | 3 | 31 | 15 | 66 | 1.2 | 228 |
| Austria | 157,528 | 20,380 | 3 | 36 | 25 | 61 | 2.1 | 153 |
| Azerbaijan | 12,065 | 1,670 | 31 | 55 | 43 | 14 | 0.4 | ... |
| Bahamas | 3,044 | 11,720 | 4 | 13 | 10 | 83 | 1.3 | 196 |
| Bahrain | 3,679 | 6,910 | 1 | 25 | 18 | 74 | –3.8 | ... |
| Bangladesh | 23,449 | 220 | 36 | 16 | 9 | 48 | 1.9 | 311 |
| Barbados | 1,711 | 6,630 | 7 | 14 | 7 | 79 | 1.3 | 200 |
| Belarus | 32,131 | 3,110 | 26 | 56 | 45 | 18 | 3.3 | ... |
| Belgium | 192,370 | 19,300 | 2 | 30 | 22 | 68 | 2.1 | 166 |
| Belize | 389 | 2,050 | 19 | ... | 25 | ... | 2.5 | 163 |
| Benin | 1,848 | 380 | 37 | 14 | 9 | 49 | –1.1 | ... |
| Bermuda | ... | 25,000 | ... | ... | ... | ... | 2.1 | ... |
| Bhutan | 260 | 180 | 43 | 27 | 10 | 30 | 6.8 | ... |
| Bolivia | 4,799 | 650 | 24 | 30 | 14 | 46 | –2 | 1,468,493  91 |
| Bosnia | ... | ... | 15 | 61 | 54 | 24 | 1.8 | ... |
| Botswana | 3,335 | 2,590 | 5 | 54 | 4 | 41 | 5.8 | 329 |
| Brazil | 447,324 | 2,920 | 10 | 39 | 26 | 51 | 0.4 | 5,212,188 |
| Brunei | ... | 6,000 | 2 | 45 | 9 | 53 | 1.6 | ... |
| Bulgaria | 16,316 | 1,840 | 13 | 63 | 57 | 24 | 1.7 | ... |
| Burkina Faso | 3,213 | 350 | 44 | 20 | 12 | 36 | 1.3 | 108 |
| Burma | ... | 500 | 51 | 12 | 9 | 37 | 1.9 | 502 |
| Burundi | 1,210 | 210 | 55 | 16 | 12 | 29 | 1.4 | 240 |
| Cambodia | 1,725 | 200 | ... | ... | ... | ... | ... | ... |
| Cameroon | 11,320 | 940 | 27 | 22 | 12 | 51 | –0.9 | ... |
| Canada | 568,765 | 21,260 | 3 | 21 | 23 | 76 | 2.1 | 192 |
| Cape Verde Is. | 285 | 750 | 14 | 25 | 5 | 61 | 2.2 | 132 |
| Central African Republic | 1,218 | 390 | 41 | 16 | 8 | 43 | –1.5 | 129 |
| Chad | 1,212 | 220 | 43 | 18 | 16 | 39 | 3.8 | ... |
| Chile | 28,897 | 2,160 | 8 | 30 | 30 | 62 | 1.7 | 950 |
| China | 424,012 | 370 | 27 | 42 | 38 | 31 | 7.8 | ... |
| Colombia | 41,922 | 1,280 | 17 | 35 | 20 | 48 | 1.2 | 1,519 |
| Comoros | 245 | 500 | 41 | 10 | 5 | 49 | –1 | ... |
| Congo | 2,623 | 1,120 | 12 | 37 | 8 | 51 | –0.2 | 204 |
| Costa Rica | 6,156 | 1,930 | 18 | 25 | 19 | 57 | 1 | 1,604 |
| Croatia | ... | ... | 14 | 50 | 43 | 36 | 1.4 | ... |
| Cuba | ... | 1,000 | 12 | 52 | 39 | 36 | 2.1 | ... |
| Cyprus | 6,135 | 8,640 | 7 | 27 | 15 | 66 | 4.9 | 188 |
| Czechoslovakia | 38,427 | 2,450 | 8 | 56 | ... | 36 | 0.4 | 230 |
| Denmark | 121,695 | 23,660 | 5 | 28 | 19 | 67 | 2.1 | 186 |
| Djibouti | ... | 1,000 | 5 | 15 | 7 | 80 | 2.1 | ... |
| Dominica | 175 | 2,440 | 27 | 16 | 7 | 57 | 4.7 | 176 |
| Dominican Republic | 6,807 | 950 | 18 | 25 | 13 | 57 | –0.2 | ... |
| Ecuador | 10,772 | 1,020 | 15 | 35 | 21 | 50 | –0.3 | 5,370 |
| Egypt | 33,068 | 620 | 18 | 30 | 13 | 52 | 2 | 681 |
| El Salvador | 5,697 | 1,070 | 10 | 24 | 19 | 66 | –0.3 | 804 |
| Equatorial Guinea | 142 | 330 | 54 | 7 | ... | 39 | 3.4 | ... |
| Estonia | 6,088 | 3,830 | 26 | 56 | 44 | 18 | 2.1 | ... |
| Ethiopia | 6,144 | 120 | 47 | 13 | 9 | 40 | –1.6 | 220 |
| Fiji | 1,377 | 1,830 | 24 | 21 | 10 | 55 | 0 | 158 |
| Finland | 121,982 | 24,400 | 6 | 34 | 22 | 60 | 2.5 | 206 |
| France | 1,167,749 | 20,600 | 3 | 29 | 21 | 68 | 1.8 | 196 |
| French Guiana | ... | 4,000 | 35 | ... | ... | ... | ... | 211 |
| French Polynesia | ... | 6,000 | 5 | 15 | 7 | 80 | 5.2 | 199 |
| Gabon | 4,419 | 3,780 | 9 | 45 | 6 | 46 | –4.2 | 157 |
| Gambia, The | 322 | 360 | 34 | 12 | 10 | 54 | –0.1 | 595 |
| Georgia | 9,000 | 1,640 | 28 | 54 | 40 | 18 | 2.2 | ... |
| Germany | 1,516,785 | 23,650 | 2 | 39 | 23 | 59 | 2.2 | 141 |
| Ghana | 6,176 | 400 | 53 | 17 | 10 | 30 | –0.3 | 4,853 |
| Gibraltar | ... | 4,000 | ... | ... | ... | ... | ... | 188 |
| Greece | 65,504 | 6,230 | 17 | 27 | 14 | 56 | 1.2 | 850 |
| Greenland | ... | 6,000 | 30 | ... | ... | ... | ... | ... |

| | GNP 1991 | GNP per capita 1991 | GDP share agriculture 1991 | GDP share industry 1991 | GDP share manufacture 1991 | GDP share services 1991 | Average annual rate of change 1980-91 | Consumer price index Jan 1993 | |
|---|---|---|---|---|---|---|---|---|---|
| | million $US | $US | % | % | % | % | % | 1980=100 | |
| Grenada | 198 | 2,180 | 21 | 19 | 5 | 60 | 5.3 | 121 | |
| Guadeloupe | ... | 7,000 | ... | ... | ... | ... | 2.3 | 194 | |
| Guatemala | 8,816 | 930 | 26 | 20 | ... | 54 | -1.8 | 485 | |
| Guinea | 2,669 | 450 | 29 | 35 | 5 | 36 | 3.6 | ... | |
| Guinea-Bissau | 194 | 190 | 46 | 12 | 8 | 42 | 1.3 | ... | |
| Guyana | 233 | 290 | 25 | 31 | 10 | 44 | -4.2 | ... | |
| Haiti | 2,471 | 370 | 31 | 38 | 15 | 31 | -2.4 | 270 | |
| Honduras | 3,010 | 570 | 22 | 27 | 16 | 51 | -0.7 | 318 | |
| Hong Kong | 77,302 | 13,200 | 0 | 25 | 17 | 75 | 5.4 | 275 | |
| Hungary | 28,244 | 2,690 | 10 | 34 | 29 | 56 | 0.7 | 481 | |
| Iceland | 5,814 | 22,580 | 10 | 15 | 18 | 75 | 1.3 | 2,003 | |
| India | 284,668 | 330 | 31 | 27 | 18 | 42 | 3.3 | 307 | |
| Indonesia | 111,409 | 610 | 19 | 41 | 21 | 40 | 3.9 | 133 | |
| Iran | 127,366 | 2,320 | 21 | 21 | 9 | 58 | -1.1 | 328 | |
| Iraq | ... | 2,000 | 25 | 41 | 12 | 34 | 4.4 | 605 | 91 |
| Ireland | 37,738 | 10,780 | 11 | 9 | 3 | 80 | 2.2 | 224 | |
| Israel | 59,128 | 11,330 | 5 | 24 | 19 | 71 | 1.8 | 90,898 | |
| Italy | 1,072,198 | 18,580 | 3 | 33 | 21 | 64 | 2.1 | 284 | |
| Ivory Coast | 8,523 | 690 | 38 | 22 | 21 | 40 | -3.4 | ... | |
| Jamaica | 3,365 | 1,380 | 5 | 40 | 17 | 55 | -0.3 | 420 | |
| Japan | 3,337,191 | 26,920 | 3 | 42 | 25 | 55 | 3.7 | 129 | |
| Jordan | 3,881 | 1,120 | 7 | 26 | 13 | 67 | -3.3 | 226 | |
| Kazakhstan | 41,691 | 2,470 | 34 | 49 | 30 | 17 | 0.9 | ... | |
| Kenya | 8,505 | 340 | 27 | 22 | 12 | 51 | 0.3 | 173 | |
| Kiribati | 53 | 750 | 30 | 8 | 1 | 62 | 0.5 | ... | |
| Korea, North | 22,000 | 1,000 | ... | ... | ... | ... | ... | ... | |
| Korea, South | 274,464 | 6,340 | 8 | 45 | 28 | 47 | 8.8 | 189 | |
| Kuwait | ... | 16,000 | 1 | 56 | 9 | 43 | 0.5 | ... | |
| Kyrgyzstan | 6,900 | 1,550 | 42 | 45 | 33 | 15 | 2.1 | ... | |
| Laos | 965 | 230 | 59 | 17 | 7 | 24 | 1.2 | ... | |
| Latvia | 9,193 | 3,410 | 24 | 55 | 45 | 21 | 2.8 | ... | |
| Lebanon | ... | 2,000 | 8 | 21 | 13 | 71 | -16 | ... | |
| Lesotho | 1,053 | 580 | 14 | 38 | 13 | 48 | 0 | 114 | 90 |
| Liberia | ... | 600 | 37 | 28 | 5 | 35 | 0.5 | ... | |
| Libya | ... | 5,500 | 5 | 50 | 7 | 45 | -2 | ... | |
| Liechtenstein | ... | 33,000 | ... | ... | ... | ... | ... | ... | |
| Lithuania | 10,220 | 2,710 | 32 | 49 | 36 | 19 | 2.5 | ... | |
| Luxembourg | 11,761 | 31,080 | 3 | 41 | 31 | 56 | 3.8 | 108 | |
| Macau | ... | 6,000 | 1 | 34 | 28 | 65 | 6 | 164 | |
| Macedonia | ... | ... | 17 | 60 | ... | 23 | 2 | ... | |
| Madagascar | 2,560 | 210 | 33 | 14 | 12 | 53 | -2.4 | 684 | |
| Malawi | 1,996 | 230 | 35 | 20 | 13 | 45 | 0.1 | 683 | |
| Malaysia | 45,787 | 2,490 | 23 | 42 | 16 | 35 | 2.9 | 112 | |
| Maldives | 101 | 460 | 14 | 53 | ... | 33 | 6.7 | ... | |
| Mali | 2,412 | 280 | 44 | 12 | 11 | 44 | -0.1 | 103 | |
| Malta | 2,598 | 6,850 | 4 | 41 | 27 | 55 | 3.8 | 101 | |
| Martinique | ... | 4,000 | ... | ... | ... | ... | 4 | 212 | |
| Mauritania | 1,026 | 510 | 22 | 31 | 6 | 47 | -1.8 | ... | |
| Mauritius | 2,623 | 2,420 | 11 | 33 | 23 | 56 | 6.1 | 108 | |
| Mexico | 252,381 | 2,870 | 9 | 30 | 22 | 61 | -0.5 | 22,367 | |
| Moldova | 9,529 | 2,170 | 40 | 44 | 34 | 16 | 1.8 | ... | |
| Mongolia | ... | 600 | 16 | 33 | 27 | 51 | ... | ... | |
| Montserrat | ... | 4,000 | 4 | 6 | ... | 90 | ... | ... | |
| Morocco | 26,451 | 1,030 | 19 | 31 | 18 | 50 | 1.6 | 229 | |
| Mozambique | 1,163 | 70 | 37 | 46 | 23 | 17 | -3.6 | ... | |
| Namibia | 2,051 | 1,120 | 10 | 28 | 4 | 62 | -1.5 | ... | |
| Nepal | 3,453 | 180 | 59 | 14 | 5 | 27 | 2.1 | 339 | |
| Netherlands | 278,839 | 18,560 | 4 | 32 | 20 | 64 | 1.5 | 138 | |
| Netherlands Antilles | ... | 6,000 | 1 | 10 | ... | 89 | 2 | 154 | |
| New Caledonia | ... | 4,000 | 25 | 7 | 5 | 68 | ... | 203 | |
| New Zealand | 41,626 | 12,140 | 9 | 27 | 18 | 64 | 0.2 | 287 | |
| Nicaragua | 1,897 | 340 | 30 | 23 | 19 | 47 | -4.6 | ... | |
| Niger | 2,361 | 300 | 38 | 19 | 8 | 43 | -4.1 | 93 | |
| Nigeria | 34,057 | 290 | 37 | 38 | 10 | 25 | -1.7 | 230 | |
| Norway | 102,885 | 24,160 | 3 | 36 | 14 | 61 | 2.2 | 222 | |
| Oman | 8,787 | 5,500 | 4 | 52 | 4 | 44 | 4.5 | ... | |
| Pakistan | 46,725 | 400 | 26 | 26 | 17 | 48 | 3.2 | 210 | |
| Panama | 5,254 | 2,180 | 10 | 11 | 14 | 79 | -1.8 | 124 | |
| Papua New Guinea | 3,307 | 820 | 26 | 35 | 10 | 39 | -0.7 | 199 | |
| Paraguay | 5,374 | 1,210 | 22 | 24 | 18 | 54 | -0.8 | 1,087 | |
| Peru | 38,295 | 1,020 | 8 | 30 | 22 | 62 | -2.6 | 1,062 | |
| Philippines | 46,138 | 740 | 21 | 34 | 26 | 45 | -1.2 | 171 | |
| Poland | 70,640 | 1,830 | 7 | 59 | 50 | 34 | 0.5 | 274 | |

| | GNP 1991 | GNP per capita 1991 | GDP share agriculture 1991 | GDP share industry 1991 | GDP share manufacture 1991 | GDP share services 1991 | Average annual rate of change 1980–91 | Consumer price index Jan 1993 |
|---|---|---|---|---|---|---|---|---|
| | million $US | $US | % | % | % | % | % | 1980=100 |
| Portugal | 58,451 | 5,620 | 9 | 37 | 29 | 54 | 2.7 | 112 |
| Puerto Rico | 22,498 | 6,330 | 1 | 41 | 39 | 58 | 0.9 | 145 |
| Qatar | 6,968 | 16,000 | 2 | 39 | 13 | 59 | -10.9 | ... |
| Réunion | ... | 6,000 | 6 | 17 | 9 | 77 | ... | 197 |
| Romania | 31,079 | 1,340 | 19 | 49 | ... | 32 | -0.1 | ... |
| Russia | 479,546 | 3,220 | 19 | 58 | 45 | 23 | 1.3 | ... |
| Rwanda | 1,930 | 260 | 38 | 22 | 20 | 40 | -2.6 | 203 |
| St Christopher-Nevis | 156 | 3,960 | 10 | 25 | 27 | 65 | 5.8 | ... |
| St Lucia | 380 | 2,500 | 16 | 22 | 17 | 62 | 2.9 | 135 |
| St Vincent & Grenadines | 187 | 1,730 | 17 | 25 | 9 | 58 | 5.2 | 126 |
| São Tomé & Príncipe | 42 | 350 | 31 | 11 | ... | 58 | -3.5 | ... |
| Saudi Arabia | 105,133 | 7,500 | 7 | 52 | 7 | 41 | -4.2 | 99 |
| Senegal | 5,500 | 720 | 20 | 19 | 13 | 61 | 0 | 172 |
| Seychelles | 350 | 5,110 | 7 | 21 | 9 | 72 | 2.5 | 140 |
| Sierra Leone | 904 | 210 | 43 | 14 | 3 | 43 | -1.3 | 64,969 |
| Singapore | 39,249 | 12,890 | 0 | 38 | 29 | 62 | 4.9 | 133 |
| Slovenia | ... | ... | 8 | 62 | 53 | 30 | 1.2 | ... |
| Solomon Is. | 184 | 560 | 35 | 7 | 3 | 58 | 3.5 | 416 |
| Somalia | ... | 150 | 65 | 10 | 5 | 25 | 2.3 | ... |
| South Africa | 90,953 | 2,600 | 5 | 44 | 25 | 51 | 0.9 | 532 |
| Spain | 486,614 | 12,460 | 6 | 39 | 30 | 55 | 2.9 | 278 |
| Sri Lanka | 8,665 | 500 | 27 | 25 | 14 | 48 | 2.5 | 427 |
| Sudan | 10,107 | 450 | 36 | 15 | 9 | 49 | -2.4 | ... |
| Surinam | 1,649 | 3,610 | 11 | 26 | 10 | 63 | -4.5 | 741 |
| Swaziland | 874 | 1,060 | 23 | 40 | 37 | 37 | 3.1 | 125 |
| Sweden | 218,934 | 25,490 | 3 | 34 | 22 | 63 | 1.7 | 235 |
| Switzerland | 225,890 | 33,510 | 4 | 42 | ... | 54 | 1.6 | 156 |
| Syria | 14,234 | 1,110 | 30 | 23 | ... | 47 | -2.1 | 820 |
| Taiwan | 161,000 | 8,000 | 4 | 43 | 34 | 53 | 8 | ... |
| Tajikistan | 5,669 | 1,050 | 37 | 42 | 27 | 21 | -0.1 | ... |
| Tanzania | 2,424 | 100 | 61 | 5 | 4 | 34 | -1.1 | 2,031 |
| Thailand | 89,548 | 1,580 | 12 | 39 | 27 | 49 | 5.9 | 173 |
| Togo | 1,530 | 410 | 33 | 23 | 10 | 44 | -1.7 | 148 91 |
| Tonga | 110 | 1,100 | 41 | 19 | 12 | 40 | 1.5 | 220 |
| Trinidad & Tobago | 4,525 | 3,620 | 3 | 39 | 9 | 58 | -5.2 | 330 |
| Tunisia | 12,417 | 1,510 | 13 | 33 | 17 | 54 | 1.2 | 255 |
| Turkey | 103,888 | 1,820 | 18 | 34 | 24 | 48 | 2.9 | 1,588 |
| Turkmenistan | 6,387 | 1,700 | 43 | 41 | 23 | 16 | 0.7 | ... |
| Uganda | 2,762 | 160 | 51 | 12 | 4 | 37 | 3.3 | ... |
| Ukraine | 121,458 | 2,340 | 28 | 53 | 43 | 19 | 2.3 | ... |
| USSR (former) | 2,700,000 | 9,200 | 23 | 56 | 43 | 21 | 3.3 | ... |
| United Arab Emirates | 32,813 | 19,500 | 2 | 55 | 9 | 43 | -5.8 | ... |
| United Kingdom | 963,696 | 16,750 | 2 | 37 | 30 | 61 | 2.6 | 208 |
| United States | 5,686,038 | 22,560 | 2 | 29 | 25 | 69 | 2.1 | 172 |
| Uruguay | 8,895 | 2,860 | 10 | 32 | 25 | 58 | -0.4 | 46,750 |
| Uzbekistan | 28,255 | 1,350 | 42 | 40 | 26 | 18 | 0.8 | ... |
| Vanuatu | 175 | 1,120 | 34 | 11 | 6 | 55 | -0.2 | 113 |
| Venezuela | 52,775 | 2,610 | 5 | 47 | 16 | 48 | -1.5 | 1,072 |
| Vietnam | ... | 300 | 42 | 35 | 33 | 23 | 2 | ... |
| Western Samoa | 156 | 930 | 51 | 12 | ... | 37 | 5.1 | 320 |
| Yemen | 6,746 | 540 | 22 | 26 | 9 | 52 | 6.7 | ... |
| Yugoslavia | 70,038 | 2,900 | 12 | 48 | ... | 40 | -1.4 | 36,886 |
| Yugoslavia (Serbia) | ... | ... | 18 | 52 | 46 | 30 | 1.8 | ... |
| Zaire | 8,123 | 220 | 30 | 32 | 9 | 38 | -1.6 | ... |
| Zambia | 3,394 | 420 | 16 | 47 | 36 | 37 | -2.9 | 11,092 |
| Zimbabwe | 6,220 | 620 | 20 | 32 | 26 | 48 | 0.2 | ... |

The Gross National Product (GNP) is a measure of a country's total production of goods and services including the net income from overseas. Owing to difficulties in the use of exchange rates and individual nation's methods of calculating the GNP, the figures must be used cautiously. Gross Domestic Product (GDP) is the value of domestic production and excludes net overseas income. Note that manufacturing is also included within the industry total. Services also includes items which cannot be included in the other groups.

The consumer price index is for early 1993 unless stated otherwise in the last column.

# PRODUCTION STATISTICS
## AGRICULTURAL, FOREST AND FISHING PRODUCTS

## BARLEY

thousand tonnes

| | 1950 | 1970 | 1980 | 1990 | 1991 | Rank | % |
|---|---|---|---|---|---|---|---|
| World | 59,267 | 129,036 | 156,649 | 181,946 | 169,385 | | |
| Afghanistan | 269 | 363 | 313 | 216 | 217 | | |
| Algeria | 808 | 470 | 592 | 833 | 1,751 | | |
| Argentina | 656 | 497 | 229 | 330 | 320 | | |
| Australia | 531 | 2,372 | 3,278 | 4,055 | 4,025 | | |
| Austria | 210 | 954 | 1,288 | 1,521 | 1,360 | | |
| Belgium | 254 | 608 | 844 | 625 | 660 | | |
| Brazil | 15 | 26 | 94 | 157 | 188 | | |
| Bulgaria | 332 | 1,108 | 1,439 | 1,387 | 1,495 | | |
| Canada | 4,245 | 10,024 | 11,199 | 13,925 | 12,463 | 3 | 7.4 |
| Chile | 79 | 97 | 103 | 92 | 109 | | |
| China | 12,360 | 6,434 | 3,133 | 3,000 | 3,000 | | |
| Colombia | 50 | 92 | 101 | 100 | 102 | | |
| Czechoslovakia | 1,046 | 2,543 | 3,524 | 4,071 | 3,793 | | |
| Denmark | 1,708 | 5,175 | 6,250 | 4,987 | 4,978 | 9 | 2.9 |
| Egypt | 123 | 93 | 111 | 129 | 110 | | |
| Ethiopia | 720 | 727 | 1,021 | 899 | 965 | | |
| Finland | 201 | 943 | 1,421 | 1,720 | 1,749 | | |
| France | 1,534 | 8,865 | 10,997 | 10,020 | 10,651 | 4 | 6.3 |
| Germany | 1,995 | 7,312 | 13,385 | 13,992 | 14,449 | 2 | 8.5 |
| Greece | 211 | 655 | 838 | 341 | 500 | | |
| Hungary | 654 | 749 | 848 | 1,369 | 1,552 | | |
| India | 2,384 | 2,642 | 2,020 | 1,486 | 1,642 | | |
| Iran | 767 | 1,042 | 1,548 | 3,360 | 3,600 | | |
| Iraq | 722 | 692 | 726 | 1,854 | 520 | | |
| Ireland | 163 | 854 | 1,643 | 1,380 | 1,281 | | |
| Italy | 258 | 326 | 914 | 1,703 | 1,774 | | |
| Japan | 2,020 | 629 | 392 | 346 | 269 | | |
| Korea, North | 155 | 353 | 155 | 150 | 145 | | |
| Korea, South | 846 | 1,589 | 1,059 | 416 | 340 | | |
| Libya | 84 | 70 | 97 | 141 | 145 | | |
| Mexico | 160 | 240 | 486 | 492 | 584 | | |
| Morocco | 1,483 | 2,190 | 1,712 | 2,138 | 3,252 | | |
| Netherlands | 201 | 366 | 265 | 219 | 230 | | |
| New Zealand | 49 | 222 | 254 | 435 | 440 | | |
| Norway | 109 | 545 | 636 | 740 | 680 | | |
| Pakistan | 120 | 97 | 141 | 131 | 140 | | |
| Peru | 208 | 164 | 115 | 80 | 100 | | |
| Poland | 1,061 | 2,162 | 3,563 | 4,217 | 4,257 | 10 | 2.5 |
| Portugal | 96 | 64 | 45 | 79 | 82 | | |
| Romania | 412 | 615 | 2,360 | 2,680 | 2,951 | | |
| Saudi Arabia | 13 | 13 | 8 | 350 | 375 | | |
| South Africa | 41 | 27 | 102 | 262 | 183 | | |
| Spain | 1,909 | 3,922 | 6,571 | 9,415 | 9,141 | 6 | 5.4 |
| Sweden | 231 | 1,836 | 2,323 | 2,123 | 1,869 | | |
| Switzerland | 55 | 147 | 220 | 343 | 357 | | |
| Syria | 321 | 375 | 1,129 | 846 | 950 | | |
| Tunisia | 218 | 126 | 279 | 477 | 721 | | |
| Turkey | 2,270 | 3,720 | 5,480 | 7,300 | 7,800 | 7 | 4.6 |
| USSR (former) | 6,354 | 35,132 | 42,502 | 56,600 | 42,000 | 1 | 24.8 |
| United Kingdom | 2,061 | 8,257 | 10,058 | 7,900 | 7,700 | 8 | 4.5 |
| United States | 5,843 | 9,476 | 8,838 | 9,192 | 10,113 | 5 | 5.9 |
| Uruguay | 23 | 38 | 71 | 133 | 156 | | |
| Yemen | 5 | 157 | 49 | 55 | 22 | | |
| Yugoslavia | 323 | 442 | 726 | 692 | 742 | | |

## BEEF AND VEAL

thousand tonnes

| | 1950 | 1970 | 1980 | 1990 | 1991 | Rank | % |
|---|---|---|---|---|---|---|---|
| World | 20,621 | 38,871 | 44,110 | 51,632 | 51,452 | | |
| Afghanistan | 25 | 66 | 69 | 65 | 65 | | |
| Algeria | 13 | 24 | 44 | 60 | 60 | | |
| Angola | 4 | 40 | 50 | 56 | 57 | | |
| Argentina | 1,972 | 2,503 | 2,933 | 2,610 | 2,640 | 4 | 5.1 |
| Australia | 628 | 997 | 1,683 | 1,677 | 1,760 | 7 | 3.4 |
| Austria | 85 | 155 | 199 | 224 | 220 | | |
| Bangladesh | ... | 141 | 140 | 140 | 142 | | |
| Belgium | 129 | 264 | 306 | 323 | 329 | | |
| Bolivia | 31 | 51 | 88 | 116 | 152 | | |
| Brazil | 1,092 | 1,822 | 2,104 | 2,775 | 2,800 | 3 | 5.4 |
| Bulgaria | 38 | 78 | 117 | 120 | 112 | | |
| Burma | 1 | 67 | 76 | 85 | 86 | | |
| Cameroon | 21 | 35 | 50 | 70 | 70 | | |
| Canada | 503 | 864 | 977 | 924 | 879 | | |
| Chad | 39 | 31 | 30 | 63 | 65 | | |
| Chile | 132 | 165 | 171 | 242 | 240 | | |
| China | 1,330 | 1,433 | 1,680 | 1,102 | 1,302 | 9 | 2.5 |
| Colombia | 281 | 422 | 607 | 795 | 823 | | |
| Costa Rica | 15 | 44 | 80 | 85 | 91 | | |
| Cuba | 179 | 199 | 145 | 141 | 140 | | |
| Czechoslovakia | 181 | 336 | 380 | 404 | 294 | | |
| Denmark | 149 | 193 | 245 | 202 | 212 | | |
| Dominican Republic | 15 | 32 | 49 | 68 | 67 | | |
| Ecuador | 23 | 45 | 79 | 100 | 110 | | |
| Egypt | 130 | 119 | 119 | 222 | 229 | | |
| Ethiopia | 166 | 243 | 214 | 245 | 245 | | |
| Finland | 45 | 109 | 115 | 118 | 122 | | |
| France | 964 | 1,577 | 1,832 | 1,750 | 1,934 | 6 | 3.8 |
| Germany | 662 | 1,633 | 1,890 | 2,112 | 2,183 | 5 | 4.2 |
| Greece | 9 | 86 | 110 | 82 | 80 | | |
| Guatemala | 35 | 57 | 56 | 59 | 53 | | |
| Honduras | 16 | 32 | 61 | 46 | 45 | | |
| Hungary | 96 | 122 | 145 | 101 | 92 | | |
| India | 173 | 66 | 771 | 852 | 857 | | |
| Indonesia | 206 | 133 | 156 | 173 | 192 | | |
| Iran | 50 | 75 | 168 | 230 | 250 | | |
| Iraq | 21 | 46 | 50 | 39 | | | |
| Ireland | 193 | 217 | 384 | 491 | 550 | | |
| Italy | 268 | 1,062 | 1,120 | 1,165 | 1,164 | 10 | 2.3 |
| Ivory Coast | 2 | 39 | 41 | 42 | 45 | | |
| Japan | 61 | 270 | 430 | 549 | 573 | | |
| Kenya | 10 | 131 | 183 | 329 | 326 | | |
| Korea, North | 12 | 22 | 31 | 45 | 53 | | |
| Korea, South | 7 | 37 | 93 | 130 | 130 | | |
| Madagascar | 122 | 114 | 129 | 142 | 142 | | |
| Mali | 27 | 38 | 40 | 71 | 75 | | |
| Mexico | 145 | 450 | 743 | 1,790 | 1,550 | 8 | 3 |
| Mongolia | 74 | 49 | 72 | 66 | 63 | | |
| Morocco | 50 | 91 | 113 | 141 | 145 | | |
| Namibia | 40 | 27 | 33 | 63 | 66 | | |
| Netherlands | 135 | 337 | 420 | 540 | 495 | | |
| New Zealand | 187 | 387 | 502 | 479 | 535 | | |
| Nicaragua | 20 | 59 | 58 | 38 | 38 | | |
| Niger | 33 | 29 | 37 | 21 | 21 | | |
| Nigeria | 113 | 205 | 250 | 282 | 288 | | |
| Norway | 41 | 57 | 73 | 83 | 84 | | |
| Pakistan | 205 | 155 | 184 | 312 | 326 | | |
| Panama | 13 | 35 | 41 | 58 | 60 | | |
| Paraguay | 86 | 124 | 107 | 148 | 160 | | |
| Peru | 65 | 96 | 87 | 117 | 112 | | |
| Philippines | 42 | 73 | 89 | 82 | 78 | | |
| Poland | 178 | 513 | 654 | 725 | 708 | | |
| Portugal | 31 | 87 | 107 | 115 | 108 | | |
| Romania | 101 | 214 | 297 | 176 | 160 | | |
| Somalia | 13 | 45 | 41 | 57 | 57 | | |
| South Africa | 245 | 398 | 590 | 661 | 678 | | |
| Spain | 101 | 296 | 411 | 514 | 490 | | |
| Sudan | 51 | 126 | 246 | 218 | 231 | | |
| Sweden | 118 | 159 | 156 | 146 | 146 | | |
| Switzerland | 75 | 133 | 162 | 164 | 172 | | |
| Tanzania | 95 | 123 | 129 | 195 | 197 | | |
| Thailand | 16 | 89 | 142 | 172 | 179 | | |
| Turkey | 37 | 187 | 209 | 285 | 300 | | |
| Uganda | 40 | 68 | 91 | 77 | 79 | | |
| USSR (former) | 1,726 | 5,508 | 6,720 | 8,800 | 8,200 | 2 | 15.9 |
| United Kingdom | 588 | 921 | 1,063 | 1,001 | 1,019 | | |
| United States | 4,785 | 10,062 | 10,092 | 10,465 | 10,531 | 1 | 20.5 |
| Uruguay | 292 | 338 | 331 | 333 | 350 | | |
| Venezuela | 67 | 208 | 341 | 382 | 370 | | |
| Vietnam | 11 | 33 | 41 | 105 | 110 | | |
| Yugoslavia | 97 | 244 | 333 | 352 | 260 | | |
| Zimbabwe | 39 | 90 | 79 | 78 | 77 | | |

| | 1950 | 1970 | 1980 | 1990 | 1991 | Rank | % |
|---|---|---|---|---|---|---|---|
| Nigeria | 10,422 | 9,473 | 10,833 | 19,043 | 20,000 | 3 | 13 |
| Paraguay | 903 | 1,442 | 1,977 | 3,550 | 3,900 | 8 | 2.5 |
| Peru | 288 | 477 | 453 | 430 | 440 | | |
| Philippines | 290 | 436 | 2,226 | 1,854 | 1,900 | | |
| Rwanda | 300 | 333 | 578 | 550 | 560 | | |
| Senegal | 61 | 159 | 28 | 69 | 69 | | |
| Sri Lanka | 220 | 376 | 520 | 384 | 410 | | |
| Sudan | 87 | 133 | 125 | 6 | 8 | | |
| Tanzania | 900 | 3,373 | 5,547 | 6,922 | 6,266 | 6 | 4.1 |
| Thailand | 269 | 3,208 | 15,128 | 20,701 | 20,300 | 2 | 13.2 |
| Togo | 233 | 562 | 404 | 593 | 500 | | |
| Uganda | 2,024 | 1,058 | 2,122 | 3,339 | 3,350 | | |
| Venezuela | 152 | 317 | 322 | 302 | 310 | | |
| Vietnam | 282 | 960 | 3,238 | 2,525 | 3,000 | | |
| Zaire | 6,000 | 10,232 | 12,942 | 17,600 | 18,227 | 4 | 11.9 |
| Zambia | 135 | 159 | 183 | 260 | 2700 | | |

# CAMELS

*thousand head*

| | 1950 | 1970 | 1980 | 1990 | 1991 | Rank | % |
|---|---|---|---|---|---|---|---|
| World | 10,819 | 15,965 | 17,122 | 19,509 | 19,627 | | |
| Afghanistan | 350 | 300 | 267 | 265 | 266 | | |
| Algeria | 144 | 173 | 150 | 125 | 130 | | |
| Bahrain | ... | 1 | 1 | 1 | 1 | | |
| Burkina Faso | ... | 5 | 6 | 5 | 5 | | |
| Chad | 266 | 397 | 432 | 549 | 565 | 8 | 2.9 |
| China | ... | 693 | 597 | 475 | 463 | 10 | 2.4 |
| Djibouti | 15 | 22 | 51 | 59 | 60 | | |
| Egypt | 165 | 120 | 91 | 197 | 200 | | |
| Ethiopia | 855 | 981 | 980 | 1,050 | 1,050 | 4 | 5.4 |
| India | 638 | 1,110 | 1,050 | 1,450 | 1,490 | 3 | 7.6 |
| Iran | 450 | 135 | 111 | 130 | 130 | | |
| Iraq | 181 | 262 | 72 | 59 | 40 | | |
| Israel | ... | 10 | 11 | 10 | 10 | | |
| Jordan | ... | 13 | 13 | 18 | 18 | | |
| Kenya | 152 | 507 | 608 | 810 | 820 | 7 | 4.2 |
| Kuwait | ... | 10 | 5 | 6 | 6 | | |
| Libya | 324 | 163 | 134 | 140 | 150 | | |
| Mali | 79 | 217 | 230 | 241 | 241 | | |
| Mauritania | 160 | 707 | 734 | 915 | 920 | 6 | 4.7 |
| Mongolia | 741 | 636 | 601 | 558 | 562 | 9 | 2.9 |
| Morocco | 195 | 205 | 157 | 43 | 43 | | |
| Niger | 224 | 340 | 404 | 360 | 360 | | |
| Nigeria | ... | 19 | 17 | 18 | 18 | | |
| Oman | ... | 11 | 41 | 87 | 90 | | |
| Pakistan | 466 | 700 | 844 | 990 | 1,005 | 5 | 5.1 |
| Qatar | ... | 8 | 10 | 22 | 23 | | |
| Saudi Arabia | 265 | 107 | 277 | 389 | 390 | | |
| Senegal | ... | 7 | 7 | 15 | 15 | | |
| Somalia | 2,730 | 4,700 | 5,883 | 6,855 | 6,860 | 1 | 35.5 |
| Sudan | 1,550 | 2,495 | 2,611 | 2,742 | 2,757 | 2 | 14.1 |
| Syria | ... | 10 | 7 | 5 | 5 | | |
| Tunisia | 186 | 233 | 173 | 230 | 230 | | |
| Turkey | ... | 37 | 12 | 2 | 2 | | |
| United Arab Em. | ... | 100 | 57 | 115 | 118 | | |
| USSR (former) | 306 | 248 | 235 | 300 | 300 | | |
| Yemen | 123 | 224 | 158 | 175 | 180 | | |

# CASSAVA

*thousand tonnes*

| | 1950 | 1970 | 1980 | 1990 | 1991 | Rank | % |
|---|---|---|---|---|---|---|---|
| World | 55,200 | 96,760 | 121,472 | 150,768 | 153,689 | | |
| Angola | 1,006 | 1,597 | 1,850 | 1,900 | 1,850 | | |
| Argentina | 344 | 296 | 202 | 140 | 150 | | |
| Benin | 700 | 533 | 631 | 957 | 889 | | |
| Bolivia | 77 | 223 | 204 | 487 | 499 | | |
| Brazil | 12,466 | 29,922 | 24,315 | 24,285 | 24,632 | 1 | 16 |
| Burundi | 700 | 843 | 412 | 569 | 580 | | |
| Cameroon | 1,000 | 637 | 1,273 | 1,200 | 1,230 | | |
| Central Afr. Rep. | 616 | 767 | 920 | 520 | 520 | | |
| Chad | 19 | 140 | 205 | 330 | 342 | | |
| China | ... | 1,938 | 3,390 | 3,216 | 3,320 | | |
| Colombia | 825 | 1,380 | 2,070 | 1,939 | 2,081 | | |
| Congo | 500 | 461 | 631 | 770 | 780 | | |
| Cuba | 179 | 217 | 287 | 300 | 300 | | |
| Dominican Rep. | 148 | 173 | 98 | 127 | 134 | | |
| Ecuador | 18 | 382 | 216 | 134 | 130 | | |
| Gabon | 100 | 155 | 242 | 250 | 250 | | |
| Ghana | 512 | 1,533 | 1,894 | 2,717 | 3,600 | 10 | 2.3 |
| Guinea | 218 | 482 | 480 | 450 | 450 | | |
| Haiti | 104 | 205 | 252 | 300 | 290 | | |
| India | 1,255 | 4,993 | 5,921 | 5,674 | 5,600 | 7 | 3.6 |
| Indonesia | 6,817 | 10,695 | 13,500 | 15,830 | 16,320 | 5 | 10.6 |
| Ivory Coast | 623 | 546 | 1,067 | 1,393 | 1,435 | | |
| Kenya | 350 | 510 | 588 | 650 | 650 | | |
| Liberia | 397 | 264 | 300 | 300 | 300 | | |
| Madagascar | 866 | 1,227 | 1,641 | 2,292 | 2,290 | | |
| Malawi | 545 | 150 | 135 | 145 | 168 | | |
| Malaysia | 350 | 271 | 347 | 410 | 414 | | |
| Mali | 142 | 36 | 59 | 73 | 73 | | |
| Mozambique | 1,860 | 2,549 | 3,100 | 4,056 | 3,690 | 9 | 2.4 |
| Niger | 21 | 182 | 191 | 213 | 216 | | |

# CATTLE

*thousand head*

| | 1950 | 1970 | 1980 | 1990 | 1991 | Rank | % |
|---|---|---|---|---|---|---|---|
| World | 798,153 | 1,094,915 | 1,219,756 | 1,293,641 | 1,294,604 | | |
| Afghanistan | 2,500 | 3,660 | 3,723 | 1,650 | 1,650 | | |
| Algeria | 784 | 872 | 1,356 | 1,427 | 1,443 | | |
| Angola | 1,263 | 2,514 | 3,117 | 3,100 | 3,100 | | |
| Argentina | 42,320 | 48,841 | 55,620 | 50,582 | 50,080 | 7 | 4 |
| Australia | 14,534 | 22,382 | 26,161 | 23,191 | 23,430 | | |
| Austria | 2,207 | 2,440 | 2,553 | 2,562 | 2,584 | | |
| Azerbaijan | ... | ... | 1,800 | ... | 1,800 | | |
| Bangladesh | 19,000 | 25,395 | 25,053 | 23,244 | 23,500 | | |
| Belarus | ... | ... | 6,800 | ... | 7,000 | | |
| Belgium | 2,150 | 2,882 | 3,104 | 3,069 | 3,000 | | |
| Bolivia | 2,227 | 2,298 | 4,570 | 5,538 | 5,600 | | |
| Botswana | 1,019 | 1,660 | 2,906 | 2,696 | 2,500 | | |
| Brazil | 51,305 | 75,658 | 116,645 | 148,000 | 152,000 | 2 | 12 |
| Bulgaria | 1,688 | 1,277 | 1,782 | 1,575 | 1,457 | | |
| Burkina Faso | 1,120 | 2,556 | 2,760 | 2,900 | 2,900 | | |
| Burma | 4,494 | 6,949 | 8,565 | 9,298 | 9,310 | | |
| Burundi | 1,019 | 676 | 614 | 432 | 435 | | |
| Cambodia | 842 | 2,233 | 831 | 2,100 | 2,150 | | |
| Cameroon | 1,540 | 2,308 | 3,521 | 4,697 | 4,700 | | |
| Canada | 7,945 | 11,678 | 13,328 | 12,249 | 12,369 | | |
| Central Afr. Rep. | 306 | 677 | 1,662 | 2,595 | 2,677 | | |
| Chad | 3,260 | 4,500 | 4,360 | 4,297 | 4,400 | | |
| Chile | 2,293 | 2,923 | 3,650 | 3,404 | 3,300 | | |
| China | 46,404 | 63,168 | 52,567 | 79,493 | 81,407 | 5 | 6 |
| Colombia | 14,910 | 20,233 | 24,110 | 24,550 | 24,875 | 10 | 2 |
| Costa Rica | 601 | 1,498 | 2,183 | 1,762 | 1,741 | | |
| Cuba | 4,333 | 6,146 | 5,166 | 4,920 | 4,920 | | |
| Czechoslovakia | 3,966 | 4,253 | 4,935 | 5,129 | 4,923 | | |
| Denmark | 2,998 | 2,855 | 2,970 | 2,241 | 2,220 | | |
| Dominican Rep. | 711 | 1,176 | 1,918 | 2,240 | 2,250 | | |
| Ecuador | 1,467 | 2,391 | 2,987 | 4,359 | 4,200 | | |
| Egypt | 1,356 | 2,108 | 1,906 | 3,463 | 3,500 | | |
| El Salvador | 795 | 1,164 | 1,234 | 1,220 | 1,243 | | |
| Ethiopia | 18,901 | 26,310 | 26,000 | 30,000 | 30,000 | 8 | 2 |
| Finland | 1,700 | 1,907 | 1,747 | 1,363 | 1,315 | | |
| France | 15,606 | 21,669 | 23,825 | 21,419 | 21,446 | | |
| Georgia | ... | ... | 1,600 | ... | 1,300 | | |
| Germany | 14,151 | 19,281 | 20,672 | 20,287 | 19,488 | | |
| Ghana | 374 | 902 | 804 | 1,145 | 1,300 | | |
| Guatemala | 977 | 1,474 | 1,886 | 1,900 | 1,695 | | |
| Guinea | 1,060 | 1,300 | 1,753 | 1,800 | 1,800 | | |
| Haiti | 582 | 800 | 1,000 | 1,450 | 1,400 | | |
| Honduras | 884 | 1,578 | 1,980 | 2,424 | 2,388 | | |
| Hungary | 2,052 | 1,952 | 1,936 | 1,598 | 1,571 | | |
| India | 155,239 | 177,447 | 186,500 | 197,300 | 198,400 | 1 | 15 |
| Indonesia | 4,112 | 6,273 | 6,505 | 10,550 | 10,350 | | |
| Iran | 3,388 | 5,239 | 5,450 | 6,650 | 6,800 | | |
| Iraq | 1,510 | 2,633 | 1,630 | 1,675 | 1,400 | | |
| Ireland | 4,211 | 5,940 | 6,043 | 5,899 | 6,029 | | |
| Italy | 8,281 | 9,436 | 8,697 | 8,746 | 8,647 | | |
| Japan | 2,397 | 3,582 | 4,261 | 4,760 | 4,863 | | |
| Kazakhstan | ... | ... | 8,700 | ... | 9,800 | | |
| Kenya | 5,859 | 8,433 | 10,418 | 13,793 | 13,700 | | |
| Korea, North | 538 | 733 | 945 | 1,300 | 1,350 | | |
| Korea, South | 598 | 1,244 | 1,728 | 2,051 | 2,126 | | |
| Latvia | ... | ... | 1,400 | ... | 1,400 | | |
| Lithuania | ... | ... | 2,200 | ... | 2,300 | | |

| | 1950 | 1970 | 1980 | 1990 | 1991 | Rank | % |
|---|---|---|---|---|---|---|---|
| Madagascar | 5,709 | 8,519 | 10,147 | 10,254 | 10,265 | | |
| Mali | 3,000 | 5,400 | 5,670 | 5,000 | 5,000 | | |
| Mauritania | 514 | 2,250 | 1,262 | 1,350 | 1,360 | | |
| Mexico | 14,489 | 24,668 | 27,706 | 32,054 | 29,847 | 9 | 2 |
| Mongolia | 1,988 | 2,026 | 2,452 | 2,693 | 2,849 | | |
| Morocco | 2,188 | 3,617 | 3,362 | 3,400 | 3,500 | | |
| Mozambique | 699 | 1,274 | 1,400 | 1,380 | 1,370 | | |
| Namibia | 1,492 | 2,500 | 2,403 | 2,087 | 2,131 | | |
| Nepal | 5,507 | 8,292 | 6,003 | 6,281 | 6,350 | | |
| Netherlands | 2,659 | 4,281 | 5,071 | 4,731 | 4,830 | | |
| New Zealand | 4,932 | 8,734 | 8,063 | 8,065 | 8,200 | | |
| Nicaragua | 1,068 | 2,275 | 2,373 | 1,680 | 1,680 | | |
| Niger | 2,818 | 4,077 | 3,343 | 2,200 | 2,200 | | |
| Nigeria | 9,546 | 11,183 | 12,267 | 13,947 | 14,500 | | |
| Norway | 1,204 | 949 | 989 | 953 | 953 | | |
| Pakistan | 11,500 | 14,584 | 15,268 | 17,573 | 17,785 | | |
| Panama | 567 | 1,201 | 1,425 | 1,388 | 1,399 | | |
| Paraguay | 4,600 | 4,433 | 5,966 | 8,254 | 8,260 | | |
| Peru | 2,830 | 3,999 | 3,958 | 4,102 | 3,630 | | |
| Philippines | 710 | 1,653 | 1,885 | 1,629 | 1,677 | | |
| Poland | 6,895 | 10,990 | 12,494 | 10,049 | 8,844 | | |
| Portugal | 878 | 1,252 | 1,332 | 1,335 | 1,375 | | |
| Romania | 4,387 | 4,947 | 6,351 | 6,291 | 5,381 | | |
| Russia | | | 58,100 | | 57,000 | 6 | 4 |
| Senegal | 720 | 2,557 | 2,424 | 2,740 | 2,813 | | |
| Somalia | 1,430 | 3,750 | 4,437 | 5,100 | 4,900 | | |
| South Africa | 11,912 | 11,114 | 13,647 | 13,398 | 13,512 | | |
| Spain | 4,356 | 4,236 | 4,608 | 5,126 | 5,126 | | |
| Sri Lanka | 1,131 | 1,601 | 1,662 | 1,800 | 1,814 | | |
| Sudan | 3,957 | 12,300 | 18,376 | 20,583 | 21,028 | | |
| Sweden | 2,595 | 1,934 | 1,928 | 1,718 | 1,675 | | |
| Switzerland | 1,544 | 1,866 | 2,008 | 1,855 | 1,829 | | |
| Tajikistan | ... | ... | 1,200 | | 1,400 | | |
| Tanzania | 6,356 | 10,141 | 12,616 | 13,047 | 13,138 | | |
| Thailand | 4,608 | 4,470 | 4,228 | 5,669 | 6,052 | | |
| Turkey | 10,121 | 13,235 | 15,467 | 12,173 | 11,377 | | |
| Turkmenistan | ... | ... | ... | | 800 | | |
| Uganda | 2,547 | 3,987 | 5,063 | 4,913 | 5,000 | | |
| Ukraine | ... | ... | 25,400 | | 24,600 | | |
| USSR (former) | 55,778 | 96,707 | 114,748 | 118,400 | 115,600 | 3 | 9 |
| United Kingdom | 10,277 | 12,632 | 13,321 | 11,922 | 11,846 | | |
| United States | 80,569 | 112,321 | 112,152 | 98,162 | 98,896 | 4 | 8 |
| Uruguay | 8,154 | 8,730 | 10,965 | 8,723 | 8,889 | | |
| Uzbekistan | ... | ... | 3,500 | | 4,600 | | |
| Venezuela | 5,769 | 8,292 | 10,527 | 13,272 | 13,368 | | |
| Vietnam | 1,541 | 1,750 | 1,646 | 3,199 | 3,282 | | |
| Yemen | 1,030 | 842 | 973 | 1,175 | 1,180 | | |
| Yugoslavia | 4,866 | 5,143 | 5,467 | 4,705 | 4,527 | | |
| Yugoslavia (Serbia) | ... | ... | ... | | 2,097 | | |
| Zaire | 640 | 968 | 5,063 | 1,550 | 1,600 | | |
| Zambia | 881 | 1,580 | 2,238 | 2,920 | 3,045 | | |
| Zimbabwe | 2,956 | 5,178 | 5,378 | 5,900 | 5,950 | | |

| | 1950 | 1970 | 1980 | 1990 | 1991 | Rank | % |
|---|---|---|---|---|---|---|---|
| Greece | 41 | 142 | 195 | 199 | 207 | | |
| Guatemala | 1 | 11 | 10 | 11 | 11 | | |
| Honduras | 8 | 7 | 8 | 8 | 8 | | |
| Hungary | 5 | 42 | 68 | 80 | 81 | | |
| Iran | 15 | 74 | 107 | 183 | 184 | | |
| Iraq | 13 | 25 | 35 | 34 | 27 | | |
| Ireland | 3 | 30 | 58 | 72 | 75 | | |
| Israel | 7 | 32 | 55 | 76 | 76 | | |
| Italy | 265 | 470 | 608 | 700 | 692 | 5 | 4.9 |
| Japan | ... | 40 | 68 | 81 | 85 | | |
| Jordan | ... | 2.8 | 2 | 29 | 29 | | |
| Lebanon | 5 | 7 | 10 | 7 | 7 | | |
| Mexico | 7 | 77 | 97 | 115 | 115 | | |
| Netherlands | 130 | 284 | 458 | 584 | 614 | 6 | 4.3 |
| New Zealand | 101 | 102 | 93 | 125 | 129 | | |
| Niger | ... | 7.4 | 16 | 11 | 11 | | |
| Norway | 24 | 53 | 71 | 84 | 82 | | |
| Peru | 8 | 36 | 34 | 169 | 169 | | |
| Poland | 13 | 249 | 379 | 333 | 293 | 9 | 2.1 |
| Portugal | 8 | 23 | 38 | 55 | 54 | | |
| Romania | 13 | 83 | 129 | 99 | 102 | | |
| South Africa | 9 | 29 | 31 | 42 | 40 | | |
| Spain | 41 | 80 | 145 | 156 | 155 | | |
| Sudan | ... | 38 | 55 | 65 | 69 | | |
| Sweden | 57 | 64 | 101 | 116 | 113 | | |
| Switzerland | 53 | 87 | 123 | 132 | 132 | | |
| Syria | 11 | 27 | 52 | 65 | 67 | | |
| Turkey | 44 | 94 | 128 | 139 | 141 | | |
| USSR (former) | 229 | 1,006 | 1,520 | 2,064 | 1,845 | 2 | 13 |
| United Kingdom | 44 | 139 | 238 | 312 | 310 | 8 | 2.2 |
| United States | 673 | 1,319 | 2,262 | 3,127 | 3,090 | 1 | 21.8 |
| Uruguay | 5 | 8.4 | 12 | 16 | 17 | | |
| Venezuela | 16 | 28 | 62 | 96 | 92 | | |
| Yemen | ... | 13 | 20 | 23 | 23 | | |
| Yugoslavia | 54 | 99 | 145 | 135 | 135 | | |

# COCOA BEANS

thousand tonnes

| | 1950 | 1970 | 1980 | 1990 | 1991 | Rank | % |
|---|---|---|---|---|---|---|---|
| World | 763 | 1491 | 1,636 | 2,528 | 2,455 | | |
| Bolivia | 2 | 1 | 2 | 4 | 4 | | |
| Brazil | 130 | 183 | 330 | 355 | 345 | 2 | 14.1 |
| Cameroon | 52 | 115 | 120 | 99 | 95 | 8 | 3.9 |
| Colombia | 11 | 20 | 35 | 56 | 59 | 9 | 2.4 |
| Congo | 1 | 2 | 2 | 2 | 2 | | |
| Costa Rica | 5 | 5 | 7 | 5 | 5 | | |
| Cuba | 3 | 1 | 1 | 2 | 2 | | |
| Dominican Rep. | 30 | 32 | 32 | 59 | 50 | 10 | 2 |
| Ecuador | 27 | 57 | 83 | 147 | 136 | 6 | 5.5 |
| Equatorial Guinea | 16 | 25 | 8 | 7 | 7 | | |
| Gabon | 3 | 5 | 4 | 2 | 2 | | |
| Ghana | 253 | 430 | 268 | 295 | 295 | 3 | 12 |
| Grenada | 3 | 3 | 2 | 2 | 2 | | |
| Guatemala | 1 | 1 | 2 | 1 | 1 | | |
| Guinea | ... | ... | 4 | 2 | 2 | | |
| Haiti | 2 | 3 | 3 | 5 | 5 | | |
| Honduras | 0.1 | 1 | 1 | 3 | 3 | | |
| India | 1 | 1 | 2 | 6 | 6 | | |
| Indonesia | 1 | 2 | 11 | 154 | 214 | 5 | 8.7 |
| Ivory Coast | 53 | 195 | 427 | 750 | 710 | 1 | 28.9 |
| Jamaica | 2 | 2 | 2 | 2 | 2 | | |
| Liberia | 1 | 2 | 5 | 4 | 2 | | |
| Madagascar | 0.3 | 1 | 2 | 3 | 3 | | |
| Malaysia | ... | 4 | 38 | 235 | 225 | 4 | 9.2 |
| Mexico | 8 | 27 | 35 | 46 | 39 | | |
| Nigeria | 105 | 261 | 169 | 150 | 115 | 7 | 4.7 |
| Panama | 2 | 1 | 2 | 1 | 1 | | |
| Papua New Guinea | ... | 27 | 30 | 40 | 33 | | |
| Peru | 4 | 2 | 5 | 11 | 11 | | |
| Philippines | 1 | 4 | 4 | 10 | 9 | | |
| Samoa | 3 | 3 | 2 | 1 | 1 | | |
| São Tomé & P. | 8 | 10 | 7 | 3 | 3 | | |
| Sierra Leone | 2 | 5 | 9 | 24 | 24 | | |
| Solomon Is. | ... | 1 | 1 | 3 | 3 | | |
| Sri Lanka | 3 | 2 | 2 | 4 | 4 | | |
| Tanzania | 1 | 2 | 1 | 3 | 3 | | |
| Togo | 4 | 27 | 14 | 9 | 8 | | |
| Trinidad & Tobago | 8 | 4 | 3 | 2 | 2 | | |

# CHEESE

thousand tonnes

| | 1950 | 1970 | 1980 | 1990 | 1991 | Rank | % |
|---|---|---|---|---|---|---|---|
| World | ... | 7,732 | 11,363 | 14,539 | 14,163 | | |
| Afghanistan | ... | 9 | 19 | 18 | 18 | | |
| Albania | 1 | 6 | 11 | 12 | 11 | | |
| Argentina | 95 | 178 | 247 | 270 | 280 | | |
| Australia | 45 | 76 | 144 | 175 | 176 | | |
| Austria | 16 | 59 | 93 | 113 | 113 | | |
| Belgium | 13 | 39 | 47 | 69 | 72 | | |
| Brazil | 24 | 49 | 58 | 60 | 60 | | |
| Bulgaria | 38 | 127 | 163 | 192 | 181 | | |
| Burma | 4 | 12 | 18 | 28 | 29 | | |
| Canada | 48 | 121 | 206 | 286 | 291 | 10 | 2.1 |
| Chile | 10 | 18 | 20 | 32 | 31 | | |
| China | ... | 171 | 75 | 145 | 143 | | |
| Colombia | ... | 39 | 44 | 51 | 51 | | |
| Cuba | 3 | 1 | 11 | 16 | 16 | | |
| Czechoslovakia | 13 | 111 | 173 | 205 | 181 | | |
| Denmark | 69 | 113 | 218 | 295 | 290 | | |
| Ecuador | ... | 10 | 12 | 13 | 13 | | |
| Egypt | 129 | 204 | 240 | 311 | 319 | 7 | 2.3 |
| Finland | 14 | 40 | 72 | 93 | 85 | | |
| France | 252 | 780 | 1,137 | 1,363 | 1,425 | 3 | 10.1 |
| Germany | 193 | 660 | 986 | 1,342 | 1,193 | 4 | 8.4 |

| | 1950 | 1970 | 1980 | 1990 | 1991 | Rank | % |
|---|---|---|---|---|---|---|---|
| Vanuatu | ... | 1 | 1 | 2 | 2 | | |
| Venezuela | 18 | 19 | 16 | 16 | 15 | | |
| Zaire | 1.9 | 6 | 5 | 4 | 4 | | |

## COCONUTS

*thousand tonnes*

| | 1950 | 1970 | 1980 | 1990 | 1991 | Rank | % |
|---|---|---|---|---|---|---|---|
| World | 18,078 | 27,614 | 35,270 | 42,180 | 42,385 | | |
| Bangladesh | 53 | 66 | 75 | 82 | 80 | | |
| Benin | 38 | 20 | 20 | 20 | 20 | | |
| Brazil | 241 | 331 | 507 | 709 | 792 | 10 | 1.9 |
| Burma | 17 | 67 | 95 | 183 | 182 | | |
| Cambodia | 10 | 44 | 28 | 48 | 48 | | |
| China | ... | 53 | 59 | 65 | 67 | | |
| Colombia | 36 | 35 | 64 | 119 | 117 | | |
| Comoros | 60 | 69 | 53 | 50 | 50 | | |
| Dominican Rep. | 29 | 57 | 69 | 140 | 150 | | |
| Ecuador | 13 | 25 | 73 | 42 | 43 | | |
| El Salvador | ... | 30 | 55 | 78 | 78 | | |
| Fiji | 215 | 260 | 217 | 239 | 239 | | |
| French Polynesia | 169 | 178 | 130 | 110 | 110 | | |
| Ghana | 73 | 257 | 225 | 220 | 225 | | |
| Guam | ... | 22 | 30 | 39 | 40 | | |
| Guyana | 44 | 56 | 30 | 48 | 48 | | |
| Haiti | 27 | 24 | 34 | 35 | 35 | | |
| India | 3,656 | 4,472 | 4,192 | 7,207 | 6,550 | 3 | 15.5 |
| Indonesia | 3,614 | 5,892 | 11,200 | 12,550 | 14,000 | 1 | 33 |
| Ivory Coast | 10 | 49 | 156 | 480 | 515 | | |
| Jamaica | 74 | 150 | 176 | 200 | 200 | | |
| Kenya | 65 | 77 | 85 | 75 | 76 | | |
| Kiribati | 45 | 62 | 73 | 42 | 63 | | |
| Madagascar | 9 | 19 | 67 | 84 | 84 | | |
| Malaysia | 1,006 | 1,039 | 1,211 | 1,157 | 1,155 | 6 | 2.7 |
| Martinique | 18 | 2 | 1 | 1 | 1 | | |
| Mexico | 204 | 998 | 851 | 1,091 | 1,101 | 7 | 2.6 |
| Mozambique | 338 | 400 | 453 | 420 | 420 | | |
| New Caledonia | 20 | 21 | 14 | 10 | 10 | | |
| Nigeria | 150 | 86 | 90 | 105 | 105 | | |
| Palau (Belau) | 75 | 101 | 203 | 140 | 140 | | |
| Panama | 50 | 28 | 23 | 19 | 20 | | |
| Papua N. Guinea | 383 | 741 | 835 | 798 | 900 | 9 | 2.1 |
| Philippines | 4,453 | 7,601 | 9,142 | 9,552 | 8,923 | 2 | 21.1 |
| Puerto Rico | 23 | 9 | 9 | 6 | 5 | | |
| St Lucia | 21 | 35 | 34 | 33 | 33 | | |
| Samoa | 122 | 193 | 162 | 138 | 160 | | |
| São Tomé & P. | 41 | 42 | 36 | 42 | 42 | | |
| Seychelles | 53 | 42 | 22 | 10 | 9 | | |
| Solomon Is. | 77 | 184 | 201 | 180 | 210 | | |
| Sri Lanka | 1,975 | 1,963 | 1,692 | 1,924 | 1,800 | 4 | 4.2 |
| Tanzania | 246 | 310 | 310 | 365 | 370 | | |
| Thailand | 413 | 713 | 781 | 1,483 | 1,328 | 5 | 3.1 |
| Togo | 45 | 17 | 14 | 14 | 14 | | |
| Tonga | 100 | 88 | 91 | 25 | 25 | | |
| Trinidad & Tobago | 129 | 105 | 49 | 40 | 40 | | |
| Vanuatu | 135 | 247 | 326 | 357 | 293 | | |
| Venezuela | 74 | 147 | 160 | 177 | 175 | | |
| Vietnam | 80 | 100 | 290 | 940 | 1,000 | 8 | 2.4 |

## COFFEE

*thousand tonnes*

| | 1950 | 1970 | 1980 | 1990 | 1991 | Rank | % |
|---|---|---|---|---|---|---|---|
| World | 2,222 | 4,266 | 5,173 | 6,282 | 6,088 | | |
| Angola | 50 | 216 | 27 | 5 | 6 | | |
| Bolivia | 2 | 11 | 19 | 29 | 30 | | |
| Brazil | 1,077 | 1,197 | 1,475 | 1,463 | 1,497 | 1 | 24.6 |
| Burundi | 7 | 21 | 30 | 34 | 38 | | |
| Cameroon | 9 | 90 | 108 | 102 | 58 | | |
| Central Afr. Rep. | 4 | 10 | 17 | 16 | 17 | | |
| China | ... | 4 | 10 | 33 | 35 | | |
| Colombia | 352 | 483 | 740 | 845 | 870 | 2 | 14.3 |
| Costa Rica | 23 | 82 | 106 | 151 | 158 | | |
| Cuba | 31 | 29 | 21 | 27 | 26 | | |

| | 1950 | 1970 | 1980 | 1990 | 1991 | Rank | % |
|---|---|---|---|---|---|---|---|
| Dominican Rep. | 28 | 44 | 58 | 59 | 46 | | |
| Ecuador | 21 | 60 | 82 | 135 | 114 | | |
| El Salvador | 75 | 139 | 183 | 156 | 149 | | |
| Equat. Guinea | 6 | 7 | 6 | 7 | 7 | | |
| Ethiopia | 27 | 172 | 192 | 206 | 168 | 10 | 2.8 |
| Ghana | 1 | 6 | 2 | 1 | 1 | | |
| Guatemala | 58 | 125 | 167 | 202 | 195 | 7 | 3.2 |
| Guinea | 5 | 9 | 14 | 8 | 8 | | |
| Haiti | 35 | 31 | 39 | 37 | 37 | | |
| Honduras | 13 | 39 | 71 | 118 | 122 | | |
| India | 20 | 82 | 126 | 118 | 173 | 9 | 2.8 |
| Indonesia | 39 | 186 | 295 | 411 | 408 | 3 | 6.7 |
| Ivory Coast | 50 | 243 | 298 | 284 | 240 | 6 | 3.9 |
| Jamaica | 3 | 2 | 2 | 1 | 2 | | |
| Kenya | 11 | 57 | 89 | 105 | 90 | | |
| Liberia | 2 | 5 | 10 | 2 | 2 | | |
| Madagascar | 33 | 63 | 82 | 80 | 80 | | |
| Malawi | 1 | 1 | 1 | 6 | 8 | | |
| Malaysia | 2 | 6 | 6 | 5 | 5 | | |
| Mexico | 63 | 182 | 228 | 440 | 299 | 4 | 4.9 |
| Nicaragua | 20 | 38 | 59 | 43 | 28 | | |
| Nigeria | 1 | 4 | 4 | 1 | 1 | | |
| Panama | 3 | 5 | 7 | 10 | 11 | | |
| Papua New Guinea | ... | 26 | 51 | 67 | 62 | | |
| Paraguay | 1 | 5 | 9 | 18 | 19 | | |
| Peru | 6 | 68 | 90 | 81 | 82 | | |
| Philippines | 4 | 48 | 129 | 134 | 113 | | |
| Puerto Rico | 10 | 12 | 12 | 13 | 13 | | |
| Rwanda | 5 | 14 | 23 | 45 | 43 | | |
| Sierra Leone | 1 | 6 | 11 | 26 | 26 | | |
| Sri Lanka | 1 | 9 | 11 | 8 | 7 | | |
| Tanzania | 14 | 49 | 54 | 52 | 56 | | |
| Thailand | 1 | 1 | 10 | 61 | 55 | | |
| Togo | 3 | 11 | 8 | 9 | 12 | | |
| Uganda | 35 | 215 | 112 | 129 | 180 | 8 | 3 |
| United States | 3 | 1 | 1 | 1 | 1 | | |
| Venezuela | 44 | 60 | 57 | 76 | 66 | | |
| Vietnam | 2 | 5 | 28 | 260 | 285 | 5 | 4.7 |
| Yemen | 5 | 4 | 4 | 7 | 8 | | |
| Zaïre | 21 | 69 | 90 | 120 | 102 | | |
| Zimbabwe | 2 | 2 | 5 | 15 | 14 | | |

## COTTON LINT

*thousand tonnes*

| | 1950 | 1970 | 1980 | 1990 | 1991 | Rank | % |
|---|---|---|---|---|---|---|---|
| World | 7,581 | 12,010 | 14,402 | 18,447 | 20,641 | | |
| Afghanistan | 7 | 25 | 29 | 9 | 12 | | |
| Angola | 6 | 28 | 11 | 11 | 11 | | |
| Argentina | 112 | 114 | 134 | 270 | 290 | 10 | 1.4 |
| Australia | 4 | 27 | 78 | 305 | 433 | 8 | 2.1 |
| Benin | 2 | 9 | 7 | 59 | 67 | | |
| Brazil | 350 | 631 | 555 | 660 | 700 | 6 | 3.4 |
| Bulgaria | 11 | 13 | 5 | 3 | 5 | | |
| Burkina Faso | 3 | 10 | 25 | 77 | 77 | | |
| Burma | 19 | 14 | 20 | 21 | 21 | | |
| Cameroon | 10 | 21 | 32 | 44 | 35 | | |
| Central Afr. Rep. | 12 | 20 | 9 | 13 | 11 | | |
| Chad | 18 | 40 | 30 | 60 | 60 | | |
| China | 786 | 1,988 | 2,627 | 4,508 | 5,663 | 1 | 27.4 |
| Colombia | 8 | 122 | 94 | 140 | 142 | | |
| Egypt | 396 | 520 | 504 | 303 | 294 | 9 | 1.4 |
| El Salvador | 8 | 49 | 57 | 6 | 4 | | |
| Ethiopia | 2 | 13 | 26 | 19 | 19 | | |
| Greece | 21 | 115 | 115 | 209 | 190 | | |
| Guatemala | 2 | 71 | 142 | 41 | 38 | | |
| India | 575 | 1,088 | 1,280 | 1,659 | 1,700 | 5 | 8.2 |
| Iran | 25 | 155 | 82 | 138 | 146 | | |
| Israel | ... | 37 | 83 | 51 | 22 | | |
| Ivory Coast | 1 | 14 | 54 | 116 | 133 | | |
| Korea, North | 10 | 3 | 3 | 9 | 10 | | |
| Korea, South | 22 | 4 | 2 | ... | ... | | |
| Mali | 1 | 22 | 48 | 99 | 115 | | |
| Mexico | 222 | 354 | 352 | 201 | 202 | | |
| Mozambique | 24 | 42 | 17 | 28 | 25 | | |
| Nicaragua | 8 | 80 | 70 | 23 | 30 | | |
| Nigeria | 13 | 62 | 31 | 36 | 45 | | |
| Pakistan | 261 | 595 | 730 | 1,637 | 2,112 | 4 | 10.2 |
| Paraguay | 13 | 10 | 85 | 215 | 259 | | |

| | 1950 | 1970 | 1980 | 1990 | 1991 | Rank | % |
|---|---|---|---|---|---|---|---|
| Peru | 76 | 89 | 86 | 73 | 65 | | |
| South Africa | 3 | 19 | 54 | 53 | 61 | | |
| Spain | 8 | 52 | 58 | 75 | 83 | | |
| Sri Lanka | 1 | 1 | 2 | ... | ... | | |
| Sudan | 67 | 235 | 116 | 83 | 91 | | |
| Syria | 30 | 150 | 126 | 159 | 200 | | |
| Tanzania | 10 | 70 | 53 | 47 | 64 | | |
| Thailand | 7 | 31 | 57 | 32 | 35 | | |
| Togo | 1 | 2 | 7 | 34 | 42 | | |
| Turkey | 119 | 441 | 488 | 611 | 565 | 7 | 2.7 |
| Uganda | 66 | 79 | 5 | 4 | 8 | | |
| USSR (former) | 971 | 2,132 | 2,733 | 2,634 | 2,420 | 3 | 11.7 |
| United States | 3,105 | 2,225 | 3,004 | 3,375 | 3,819 | 2 | 18.5 |
| Venezuela | 4 | 15 | 14 | 31 | 23 | | |
| Zaire | 46 | 21 | 8 | 26 | 26 | | |
| Zambia | 1 | 3 | 6 | 10 | 25 | | |
| Zimbabwe | 1 | 43 | 54 | 67 | 73 | | |

| | 1950 | 1970 | 1980 | 1990 | 1991 | Rank | % |
|---|---|---|---|---|---|---|---|
| Poland | 185 | 387 | 489 | 422 | 380 | | |
| Portugal | 23 | 37 | 62 | 80 | 96 | | |
| Romania | 50 | 165 | 328 | 380 | 370 | | |
| Russia | ... | ... | 2,021 | 2,220 | 2,229 | 5 | 6.3 |
| Saudi Arabia | 2 | 7 | 42 | 160 | 164 | | |
| South Africa | 33 | 115 | 160 | 205 | 191 | | |
| Spain | 138 | 460 | 666 | 621 | 657 | | |
| Sri Lanka | 8 | 20 | 29 | 46 | 48 | | |
| Sudan | 6 | 17 | 32 | 33 | 34 | | |
| Sweden | 84 | 102 | 114 | 117 | 106 | | |
| Switzerland | 27 | 39 | 43 | 35 | 36 | | |
| Syria | 6 | 16 | 69 | 61 | 65 | | |
| Taiwan | 5 | 31.7 | 108 | 216 | 208 | | |
| Tanzania | 8 | 15 | 36 | 38 | 40 | | |
| Thailand | 66 | 117 | 105 | 127 | 128 | | |
| Turkey | 45 | 96 | 217 | 398 | 375 | | |
| Ukraine | ... | ... | 751 | 760 | 765 | | |
| USSR (former) | 684 | 2,250 | 3,759 | 4,540 | 4,400 | 2 | 12.4 |
| United Kingdom | 426 | 878 | 834 | 624 | 646 | | |
| United States | 3,717 | 4,057 | 4,124 | 4,022 | 4,005 | 3 | 11.3 |
| Uzbekistan | ... | ... | 83.2 | 110 | 115 | | |
| Venezuela | 4 | 76 | 129 | 107 | 107 | | |
| Vietnam | 17 | 84 | 55 | 96 | 100 | | |
| Yugoslavia | 43 | 137 | 218 | 228 | 237 | | |
| Yugoslavia (Serbia) | ... | ... | ... | ... | 92 | | |
| Zambia | 2 | 8 | 28 | 34 | 35trf | | |

## EGGS - HEN'S

*thousand tonnes*

| | 1950 | 1970 | 1980 | 1990 | 1991 | Rank | % |
|---|---|---|---|---|---|---|---|
| World | 9,364 | 20,922 | 28,316 | 34,859 | 35,375 | | |
| Argentina | 130 | 182 | 254 | 322 | 324 | | |
| Australia | 116 | 185 | 198 | 188 | 187 | | |
| Austria | 24 | 86 | 97 | 96 | 93 | | |
| Azerbaijan | ... | ... | 40.9 | 46 | 46.2 | | |
| Bangladesh | 12 | 34 | 39 | 49 | 40 | | |
| Belarus | ... | ... | 154 | 170 | 172 | | |
| Belgium | 107 | 229 | 201 | 180 | 185 | | |
| Brazil | 177 | 337 | 765 | 1,300 | 1,400 | 6 | 4 |
| Bulgaria | 36 | 89 | 132 | 135 | 111 | | |
| Burma | 6 | 17 | 31 | 34 | 35 | | |
| Canada | 216 | 328 | 331 | 321 | 320 | | |
| Chile | 13 | 58 | 66 | 91 | 91 | | |
| China | 566 | 3,309 | 2,882 | 6,559 | 6,845 | 1 | 19.3 |
| Colombia | 43 | 95 | 177 | 255 | 267 | | |
| Croatia | ... | ... | ... | ... | 47.9 | | |
| Cuba | 14 | 64 | 99 | 110 | 110 | | |
| Czechoslovakia | 76 | 186 | 243 | 283 | 266 | | |
| Denmark | 117 | 84 | 77 | 82 | 84 | | |
| Ecuador | 5 | 13 | 43 | 56 | 57 | | |
| Egypt | 18 | 55 | 78 | 141 | 128 | | |
| El Salvador | 3 | 23 | 37 | 39 | 39 | | |
| Ethiopia | 39 | 66 | 73 | 79 | 79 | | |
| Finland | 21 | 64 | 78 | 76 | 67 | | |
| France | 411 | 644 | 850 | 902 | 942 | 9 | 2.7 |
| Georgia | ... | ... | 35.1 | 36 | 36.1 | | |
| Germany | 280 | 1,125 | 1,123 | 1,043 | 912 | 10 | 2.6 |
| Greece | 21 | 100 | 123 | 121 | 138 | | |
| Guatemala | 13 | 29 | 40 | 64 | 64 | | |
| Hungary | 51 | 176 | 250 | 260 | 230 | | |
| India | 53 | 262 | 682 | 1,283 | 1,357 | 7 | 3.8 |
| Indonesia | 94 | 32 | 178 | 380 | 400 | | |
| Iran | 34 | 56 | 155 | 270 | 278 | | |
| Iraq | 6 | 10 | 48 | 50 | 35 | | |
| Ireland | 56 | 40 | 35 | 29 | 30 | | |
| Israel | 17 | 74 | 92 | 98 | 106 | | |
| Italy | 274 | 549 | 659 | 702 | 707 | | |
| Japan | 120 | 1,735 | 1,998 | 2,397 | 2,466 | 4 | 7 |
| Kazakhstan | ... | ... | 170 | 190 | 197 | | |
| Kenya | 8 | 12 | 20 | 42 | 42 | | |
| Korea, North | 21 | 55 | 104 | 145 | 148 | | |
| Korea, South | 3 | 131 | 256 | 393 | 489 | | |
| Latvia | ... | ... | 38 | 38 | 38.5 | | |
| Lebanon | 2 | 27 | 41 | 52 | 53 | | |
| Libya | 2 | 2 | 16 | 34 | 35 | | |
| Lithuania | ... | ... | 49.5 | 58 | 59.5 | | |
| Malaysia | 11 | 63 | 122 | 202 | 212 | | |
| Mexico | 77 | 334 | 636 | 1,010 | 1,141 | 8 | 3.2 |
| Moldova | ... | ... | 46 | 51 | 53 | | |
| Morocco | 37 | 44 | 73 | 88 | 93 | | |
| Netherlands | 145 | 268 | 540 | 648 | 646 | | |
| New Zealand | 30 | 52 | 57 | 46 | 46 | | |
| Nigeria | 29 | 102 | 180 | 225 | 225 | | |
| Norway | 23 | 38 | 45 | 51 | 53 | | |
| Pakistan | 6 | 15 | 96 | 220 | 238 | | |
| Peru | 11 | 28 | 60 | 99 | 117 | | |
| Philippines | 38 | 117 | 201 | 286 | 267 | | |

## FISH BY AREA

*thousand tonnes*

| | | 1970 | 1980 | 1989 | 1990 | Rank | % |
|---|---|---|---|---|---|---|---|
| World | | 70,000 | 72,042 | 100,332 | 97,246 | | |
| *Marine areas* | | 60,930 | 64,383 | 86,451 | 82,801 | | |
| 18 | Arctic Sea | 0 | 0 | 0 | 0 | | |
| 21 | Atlantic, NW | 4,239 | 2,867 | 3,086 | 3,221 | 8 | 3.9 |
| 27 | Atlantic, NE | 10,666 | 11,799 | 9,947 | 9,183 | 3 | 11.1 |
| 31 | Atlantic, WC | 1,440 | 1,795 | 1,805 | 1,697 | | |
| 34 | Atlantic, EC | 2,830 | 3,432 | 3,956 | 4,098 | 5 | 4.9 |
| 37 | Mediterranean & Black Sea | 1,120 | 1,649 | 1,716 | 1,489 | | |
| 41 | Atlantic, SW | 1,081 | 1,274 | 2,255 | 2,029 | 10 | 2.5 |
| 47 | Atlantic, SE | 2,460 | 2,170 | 2,096 | 1,530 | | |
| 48 | Atlantic, Antarctic | 0 | 453 | 467 | 393 | | |
| 51 | Indian, W | 1,620 | 2,098 | 3,378 | 3,376 | 7 | 4.1 |
| 57 | Indian, E | 789 | 1,458 | 2,732 | 2,828 | 9 | 3.4 |
| 58 | Indian, Antarctic | 0 | 138 | 31.4 | 35 | | |
| 61 | Pacific, NW | 12,997 | 18,759 | 26,295 | 25,688 | 1 | 31 |
| 67 | Pacific, NE | 2,652 | 1,975 | 3,280 | 3,428 | 6 | 4.1 |
| 71 | Pacific, WC | 4,176 | 5,487 | 7,248 | 7,311 | 4 | 8.8 |
| 77 | Pacific, EC | 902 | 2,417 | 1,758 | 1,519 | | |
| 81 | Pacific, SW | 221 | 382 | 1,063 | 1,031 | | |
| 87 | Pacific, SE | 13,732 | 6,228 | 15,338 | 13,945 | 2 | 16.8 |
| 88 | Pacific, Antarctic | 0 | 3.2 | 1.1 | 0.7 | | |
| Inland waters | | 9,020 | 7,625 | 13,882 | 14,444 | | |
| 1 | Africa | 1,308 | 1,404 | 1,866 | 1,905 | | |
| 2 | N. America | 136 | 146 | 537 | 537 | | |
| 3 | S. America | 249 | 280 | 340 | 333 | | |
| 4 | Asia | 6,251 | 4,673 | 9,618 | 10,197 | | |
| 5 | Europe | 225 | 373 | 479 | 473 | | |
| 6 | Oceania | 2 | 2 | 23 | 24 | | |
| 7 | USSR (former) | 853 | 747 | 1,020 | 975 | | |

The figures include the produce from both inland and marine fishing. In 1990 fish from inland waters accounted for 15% of the world total catch. The figures in both of the tables refer to fish caught in the inland waters or the craft of the country. The flag of the vessel rather than the port of landing is the criteria for assigning the catch to a country. All the figures refer to the live weight of the catch. Whales are not included and are shown in the table entitled Whaling.

## FISH BY NATION

*thousand tonnes*

| | 1948 | 1970 | 1980 | 1989 | 1990 | Rank | % |
|---|---|---|---|---|---|---|---|
| World | 19,600 | 70,000 | 72,042 | 100,332 | 97,246 | | |
| Angola | 113 | 368 | 86 | 111 | 107 | | |
| Argentina | 71 | 215 | 385 | 487 | 556 | | |
| Australia | 39 | 103 | 132 | 176 | 210 | | |
| Bangladesh | ... | 247 | 650 | 844 | 848 | | |
| Belgium | 71 | 53 | 46 | 40 | 42 | | |
| Brazil | 145 | 517 | 818 | 850 | 800 | | |
| Bulgaria | 64 | 92 | 126 | 102 | 56 | | |
| Burma | ... | 432 | 580 | 734 | 744 | | |
| Cambodia | ... | 52 | 52 | 77 | 105 | | |
| Canada | 1,053 | 1,389 | 1,347 | 1,573 | 1,624 | | |
| Chad | ... | 120 | 115 | 110 | 115 | | |
| Chile | 65 | 1,181 | 2,817 | 6,454 | 5,195 | 6 | 5.3 |
| China | 2,500 | 6,868 | 4,235 | 11,220 | 12,095 | 1 | 12.4 |
| Colombia | 15 | 76 | 76 | 98 | 101 | | |
| Cuba | 8 | 106 | 187 | 192 | 188 | | |
| Denmark | 226 | 1,227 | 2,029 | 1,928 | 1,517 | | |
| Ecuador | 3 | 92 | 644 | 740 | 391 | | |
| Egypt | 43 | 72 | 140 | 294 | 313 | | |
| Faroe Is. | 92 | 208 | 275 | 300 | 283 | | |
| Finland | 46 | 81 | 143 | 111 | 97 | | |
| France | 513 | 764 | 789 | 914 | 897 | | |
| Georgia | ... | ... | ... | ... | 104 | | |
| Germany | 414 | 945 | 542 | 411 | 391 | | |
| Ghana | 24 | 172 | 232 | 362 | 392 | | |
| Greece | 34 | 78 | 104 | 139 | 140 | | |
| Greenland | 21 | 40 | 104 | 163 | 138 | | |
| Hong Kong | 34 | 124 | 195 | 243 | 235 | | |
| Iceland | 478 | 734 | 1,515 | 1,505 | 1,508 | | |
| India | 1,000 | 1,756 | 2,442 | 3,641 | 3,791 | 7 | 3.9 |
| Indonesia | 500 | 1,229 | 1,842 | 2,948 | 3,081 | 8 | 3.2 |
| Iran | ... | ... | ... | 44 | 261 | 250 | |
| Ireland | 25 | 79 | 149 | 200 | 231 | | |
| Italy | 183 | 387 | 448 | 551 | 525 | | |
| Ivory Coast | 20 | 58 | 86 | 101 | 109 | | |
| Japan | 2,526 | 9,366 | 10,434 | 11,173 | 10,354 | 3 | 10.6 |
| Kenya | 30 | 34 | 48 | 146 | 142 | | |
| Korea, North | ... | ... | 1,400 | 1,700 | 1,750 | | |
| Korea, South | 294 | 934 | 2,091 | 2,833 | 2,750 | 9 | 2.8 |
| Latvia | ... | ... | ... | ... | 130 | | |
| Lithuania | ... | ... | ... | ... | 317 | | |
| Madagascar | ... | 48 | 50 | 100 | 107 | | |
| Malaysia | 145 | 368 | 737 | 607 | 603 | | |
| Mali | ... | 90 | 80 | 72 | 65 | | |
| Mexico | 68 | 387 | 1,223 | 1,470 | 1,401 | | |
| Morocco | 69 | 256 | 330 | 520 | 566 | | |
| Netherlands | 294 | 301 | 340 | 451 | 438 | | |
| New Zealand | 36 | 59 | 191 | 565 | 565 | | |
| Nigeria | ... | 227 | 480 | 300 | 316 | | |
| Norway | 1,422 | 2,980 | 2,409 | 1,909 | 1,747 | | |
| Oman | ... | 100 | 79 | 118 | 120 | | |
| Pakistan | ... | 158 | 279 | 446 | 479 | | |
| Panama | 1 | 42 | 216 | 189 | 162 | | |
| Peru | 84 | 12,613 | 3,735 | 6,854 | 6,875 | 4 | 7.1 |
| Philippines | 195 | 992 | 1,557 | 2,099 | 2,209 | | |
| Poland | 47 | 469 | 641 | 565 | 473 | | |
| Portugal | 292 | 498 | 279 | 332 | 322 | | |
| Romania | ... | 59 | 174 | 225 | 128 | | |
| Senegal | 70 | 189 | 233 | 288 | 300 | | |
| South Africa | 118 | 1,583 | 615 | 879 | 536 | | |
| Spain | 547 | 1,539 | 1,265 | 1,560 | 1,458 | | |
| Sri Lanka | 24 | 98 | 186 | 205 | 165 | | |
| Sweden | 194 | 295 | 241 | 258 | 260 | | |
| Taiwan | 122 | 613 | 936 | 1,456 | 1,317 | | |
| Tanzania | 30 | 185 | 228 | 377 | 377 | | |
| Thailand | 161 | 1,448 | 1,798 | 2,782 | 2,650 | 10 | 2.7 |
| Turkey | 80 | 184 | 427 | 457 | 382 | | |
| Uganda | 11 | 129 | 166 | 212 | 245 | | |
| Ukraine | ... | ... | ... | ... | 1,100 | | |
| USSR (former) | 1,485 | 7,252 | 9,476 | 11,310 | 10,389 | 2 | 10.7 |
| United Kingdom | 1,206 | 1,099 | 919 | 832 | 811 | | |
| United States | 2,417 | 2,777 | 3,635 | 5,763 | 5,856 | 5 | 6 |
| Uruguay | 4 | 13 | 120 | 122 | 91 | | |
| Venezuela | 92 | 126 | 185 | 329 | 332 | | |
| Vietnam | 200 | 817 | 613 | 868 | 850 | | |
| Yemen | ... | 128 | 94 | 73 | 89 | | |
| Zaire | 18 | 137 | 102 | 166 | 162 | | |

## GRAPES

*thousand tonnes*

| | 1950 | 1970 | 1980 | 1990 | 1991 | Rank | % |
|---|---|---|---|---|---|---|---|
| World | 34,381 | 54,583 | 65,991 | 59,873 | 57,188 | | |
| Afghanistan | 138 | 377 | 468 | 365 | 365 | | |
| Albania | 21 | 62 | 68 | 66 | 52 | | |
| Algeria | 1,738 | 1,263 | 398 | 263 | 260 | | |
| Argentina | 1,586 | 2,636 | 3,230 | 2,600 | 2,000 | 7 | 3.5 |
| Australia | 450 | 620 | 775 | 844 | 915 | | |
| Austria | 132 | 337 | 377 | 427 | 420 | | |
| Brazil | 247 | 528 | 604 | 786 | 619 | | |
| Bulgaria | 504 | 1,128 | 1,029 | 731 | 741 | | |
| Canada | 36 | 69 | 74 | 58 | 68 | | |
| Chile | 473 | 762 | 1,067 | 1,171 | 1,130 | | |
| China | 48 | 155 | 182 | 962 | 1,105 | | |
| Cyprus | 59 | 190 | 208 | 160 | 200 | | |
| Czechoslovakia | 60 | 128 | 189 | 221 | 198 | | |
| Egypt | 79 | 115 | 280 | 585 | 610 | | |
| France | 7,995 | 9,706 | 10,470 | 8,200 | 7,020 | 2 | 12.3 |
| Germany | 324 | 1,049 | 888 | 1,149 | 1,160 | | |
| Greece | 1,124 | 1,569 | 1,504 | 1,192 | 1,300 | | |
| Hungary | 527 | 809 | 788 | 863 | 863 | | |
| India | ... | 219 | 195 | 303 | 314 | | |
| Iran | 254 | 628 | 1,073 | 1,402 | 1,450 | 9 | 2.5 |
| Iraq | 30 | 75 | 220 | 420 | 360 | | |
| Israel | 15 | 69 | 77 | 99 | 96 | | |
| Italy | 7,076 | 10,638 | 12,396 | 8,438 | 9,230 | 1 | 16.1 |
| Japan | 38 | 240 | 328 | 300 | 300 | | |
| Korea, South | 2 | 35 | 61 | 131 | 148 | | |
| Lebanon | 81 | 98 | 142 | 183 | 200 | | |
| Mexico | 40 | 160 | 485 | 463 | 435 | | |
| Morocco | 92 | 213 | 210 | 197 | 200 | | |
| New Zealand | 4 | 14 | 39 | 60 | 62 | | |
| Peru | 54 | 62 | 54 | 45 | 47 | | |
| Portugal | 1,113 | 1,403 | 1,570 | 1,600 | 1,450 | 10 | 2.5 |
| Romania | 623 | 1,020 | 1,518 | 935 | 849 | | |
| Saudi Arabia | ... | 24 | 60 | 103 | 103 | | |
| South Africa | 412 | 820 | 1,202 | 1,463 | 1,470 | 8 | 2.6 |
| Spain | 2,541 | 4,048 | 6,587 | 6,474 | 5,087 | 4 | 8.9 |
| Switzerland | 102 | 129 | 122 | 174 | 178 | | |
| Syria | 172 | 221 | 351 | 423 | 475 | | |
| Tunisia | 105 | 125 | 123 | 89 | 90 | | |
| Turkey | 1,500 | 3,779 | 3,600 | 3,500 | 3,600 | 6 | 6.3 |
| USSR (former) | 753 | 4,220 | 6,648 | 5,600 | 5,400 | 3 | 9.4 |
| United States | 2,670 | 3,325 | 4,549 | 5,135 | 4,944 | 5 | 8.6 |
| Uruguay | 114 | 129 | 108 | 123 | 113 | | |
| Yemen | ... | 21 | 56 | 142 | 145 | | |
| Yugoslavia | 867 | 1,232 | 1,400 | 1,109 | 1,100 | | |

## GROUNDNUTS

*thousand tonnes*

| | 1950 | 1970 | 1980 | 1990 | 1991 | Rank | % |
|---|---|---|---|---|---|---|---|
| World | 9,572 | 18,347 | 18,277 | 23,410 | 23,366 | | |
| Angola | 10 | 20 | 20 | 20 | 20 | | |
| Argentina | 100 | 280 | 451 | 333 | 429 | 9 | 1.8 |
| Australia | 9 | 30 | 48 | 21 | 34 | | |
| Bangladesh | ... | 45 | 28 | 42 | 52 | | |
| Benin | 10 | 47 | 60 | 79 | 69 | | |
| Brazil | 138 | 876 | 433 | 137 | 140 | | |
| Burkina Faso | 51 | 68 | 70 | 140 | 152 | | |
| Burma | 154 | 492 | 390 | 459 | 505 | 7 | 2.2 |
| Burundi | 2 | 21 | 56 | 97 | 98 | | |
| Cambodia | 4 | 21 | 4 | 3 | 3 | | |
| Cameroon | 92 | 206 | 137 | 100 | 110 | | |
| Central Afr. Rep. | 10 | 68 | 123 | 105 | 106 | | |
| Chad | 64 | 95 | 93 | 108 | 115 | | |
| China | 2,114 | 2,634 | 3,501 | 6,433 | 6,060 | 2 | 25.9 |
| Congo | 10 | 17 | 14 | 26 | 27 | | |
| Cuba | 14 | 15 | 15 | 15 | 15 | | |
| Dominican Rep. | 14 | 76 | 40 | 34 | 35 | | |
| Ecuador | 2 | 7 | 14 | 18 | 30 | | |
| Egypt | 18 | 40 | 26 | 31 | 35 | | |
| Ethiopia | 21 | 24 | 27 | 54 | 55 | | |
| Gambia, The | 62 | 129 | 79 | 75 | 85 | | |
| Ghana | 43 | 88 | 125 | 193 | 200 | | |

| | 1950 | 1970 | 1980 | 1990 | 1991 | Rank | % |
|---|---|---|---|---|---|---|---|
| Guinea | 18 | 25 | 83 | 52 | 52 | | |
| Guinea-Bissau | 50 | 36 | 32 | 18 | 20 | | |
| Haiti | 2 | 2 | 35 | 46 | 45 | | |
| India | 3,197 | 5,807 | 5,999 | 7,622 | 7,000 | 1 | 30 |
| Indonesia | 283 | 462 | 723 | 930 | 920 | 5 | 3.9 |
| Israel | 2 | 17 | 22 | 21 | 20 | | |
| Ivory Coast | 15 | 42 | 73 | 134 | 140 | | |
| Japan | 21 | 120 | 61 | 40 | 35 | | |
| Korea, South | I | 8 | 13 | 29 | 30 | | |
| Madagascar | 12 | 42 | 37 | 30 | 30 | | |
| Malawi | ... | 182 | 176 | 39 | 64 | | |
| Mali | 88 | 144 | 136 | 180 | 160 | | |
| Mexico | 55 | 81 | 73 | 133 | 110 | | |
| Morocco | ... | 3 | 34 | 40 | 40 | | |
| Mozambique | 22 | 140 | 83 | 113 | 115 | | |
| Nicaragua | ... | 1 | 21 | 12 | 11 | | |
| Niger | 61 | 223 | 105 | 60 | 60 | | |
| Nigeria | 690 | 1,660 | 466 | 1,166 | 1,219 | 4 | 5.2 |
| Pakistan | 2 | 55 | 60 | 89 | 76 | | |
| Paraguay | 11 | 17 | 34 | 41 | 39 | | |
| Philippines | 19 | 17 | 43 | 35 | 34 | | |
| Senegal | 558 | 794 | 690 | 703 | 700 | 6 | 3 |
| Sierra Leone | 7 | 19 | 12 | 20 | 21 | | |
| South Africa | 93 | 364 | 297 | 111 | 110 | | |
| Spain | 12 | 7 | 5 | 4 | 5 | | |
| Sudan | 19 | 370 | 760 | 123 | 193 | | |
| Syria | 1 | 18 | 18 | 22 | 23 | | |
| Taiwan | 60 | 122 | 86 | 85 | 85 | | |
| Tanzania | 20 | 32 | 54 | 60 | 65 | | |
| Thailand | 60 | 128 | 128 | 162 | 164 | | |
| Togo | 13 | 20 | 25 | 26 | 33 | | |
| Turkey | 7 | 40 | 52 | 63 | 53 | | |
| Uganda | 153 | 207 | 80 | 172 | 173 | | |
| United States | 839 | 1,289 | 1,550 | 1,634 | 2,242 | 3 | 9.6 |
| Vietnam | 8 | 78 | 94 | 218 | 212 | 10 | 0.9 |
| Zaire | 155 | 258 | 334 | 425 | 435 | 8 | 1.9 |
| Zambia | 2 | 24 | 18 | 25 | 45 | | |
| Zimbabwe | 21 | 111 | 101 | 119 | 107 | | |

| | 1950 | 1970 | 1980 | 1990 | 1991 | Rank | % |
|---|---|---|---|---|---|---|---|
| Indonesia | 560 | 666 | 616 | 740 | 750 | | |
| Iran | 358 | 400 | 274 | 270 | 270 | | |
| Iraq | 290 | 98 | 54 | 60 | 48 | | |
| Ireland | 384 | 122 | 69 | 54 | 53 | | |
| Italy | 779 | 292 | 271 | 269 | 280 | | |
| Japan | 1,083 | 159 | 23 | 23 | 24 | | |
| Lesotho | 101 | 103 | 102 | 121 | 122 | | |
| Mali | 60 | 170 | 144 | 62 | 62 | | |
| Mexico | 3,181 | 5,579 | 6,195 | 6,170 | 6,175 | 3 | 10 |
| Mongolia | 2,085 | 2,262 | 2,047 | 2,200 | 2,255 | 8 | 3.7 |
| Morocco | 350 | 380 | 278 | 190 | 190 | | |
| Netherlands | 273 | 95 | 66 | 65 | 65 | | |
| New Zealand | 204 | 75 | 71 | 99 | 100 | | |
| Nicaragua | 150 | 212 | 275 | 250 | 250 | | |
| Niger | 75 | 197 | 253 | 302 | 305 | | |
| Nigeria | 260 | 325 | 250 | 208 | 206 | | |
| Norway | 191 | 36 | 18 | 19 | 19 | | |
| Pakistan | 420 | 385 | 473 | 460 | 461 | | |
| Panama | 138 | 160 | 165 | 156 | 156 | | |
| Paraguay | 302 | 334 | 316 | 335 | 335 | | |
| Peru | 496 | 669 | 650 | 660 | 660 | | |
| Philippines | 210 | 300 | 302 | 200 | 200 | | |
| Poland | 2,673 | 2,573 | 1,787 | 941 | 939 | | |
| Portugal | 87 | 36 | 29 | 26 | 26 | | |
| Romania | 979 | 686 | 564 | 663 | 670 | | |
| Senegal | 25 | 196 | 222 | 400 | 400 | | |
| South Africa | 682 | 258 | 225 | 230 | 230 | | |
| Spain | 686 | 287 | 243 | 241 | 241 | | |
| Sweden | 439 | 60 | 55 | 58 | 58 | | |
| Switzerland | 135 | 53 | 45 | 45 | 49 | | |
| Syria | 101 | 70 | 52 | 41 | 45 | | |
| Thailand | 219 | 172 | 28 | 18 | 18 | | |
| Tunisia | 73 | 96 | 51 | 55 | 56 | | |
| Turkey | 1,136 | 1,103 | 804 | 545 | 513 | | |
| USSR (former) | 12,800 | 7,641 | 5,623 | 5,920 | 5,900 | 4 | 9.6 |
| United Kingdom | 552 | 143 | 147 | 169 | 170 | | |
| United States | 7,757 | 7,667 | 5,053 | 5,400 | 5,650 | 5 | 9.2 |
| Uruguay | 667 | 427 | 493 | 465 | 470 | | |
| Venezuela | 344 | 423 | 478 | 495 | 495 | | |
| Vietnam | 40 | 105 | 123 | 143 | 145 | | |
| Yugoslavia | 1,063 | 1,078 | 630 | 314 | 300 | | |

# HORSES

*thousand head*

| | 1950 | 1970 | 1980 | 1990 | 1991 | Rank | % |
|---|---|---|---|---|---|---|---|
| World | 79,740 | 62,642 | 59,692 | 61,164 | 61,620 | | |
| Afghanistan | 195 | 400 | 403 | 400 | 400 | | |
| Albania | 50 | 43 | 45 | 102 | 100 | | |
| Algeria | 209 | 142 | 173 | 195 | 202 | | |
| Argentina | 7,265 | 3,623 | 3,024 | 3,400 | 3,400 | 6 | 5.5 |
| Australia | 1,055 | 454 | 486 | 310 | 310 | | |
| Austria | 282 | 53 | 43 | 48 | 49 | | |
| Belgium | 257 | 76 | 38 | 21 | 20 | | |
| Bolivia | 158 | 291 | 330 | 320 | 320 | | |
| Brazil | 6,942 | 4,861 | 5,070 | 6,000 | 6,200 | 2 | 10.1 |
| Bulgaria | 511 | 183 | 121 | 115 | 113 | | |
| Burkina Faso | 55 | 88 | 70 | 70 | 70 | | |
| Burma | 12 | 71 | 112 | 120 | 121 | | |
| Canada | 1,580 | 362 | 363 | 415 | 415 | | |
| Chad | 120 | 153 | 166 | 195 | 182 | | |
| Chile | 523 | 478 | 450 | 520 | 520 | | |
| China | 5,503 | 7,300 | 11,144 | 10,294 | 10,174 | 1 | 16.5 |
| Colombia | 1,208 | 1,114 | 1,683 | 1,975 | 1,980 | 9 | 3.2 |
| Costa Rica | 76 | 109 | 113 | 114 | 114 | | |
| Cuba | 410 | 683 | 810 | 629 | 629 | | |
| Czechoslovakia | 613 | 144 | 47 | 42 | 39 | | |
| Denmark | 495 | 45 | 50 | 38 | 38 | | |
| Dominican Rep. | 137 | 184 | 204 | 315 | 320 | | |
| Ecuador | 111 | 242 | 314 | 492 | 512 | | |
| El Salvador | 130 | 79 | 88 | 93 | 93 | | |
| Ethiopia | 1,021 | 1,393 | 1,602 | 2,650 | 2,700 | 7 | 4.4 |
| Finland | 389 | 88 | 33 | 44 | 45 | | |
| France | 2,403 | 691 | 352 | 319 | 322 | | |
| Germany | 2,266 | 411 | 447 | 424 | 491 | | |
| Greece | 259 | 251 | 115 | 50 | 50 | | |
| Guatemala | 166 | 149 | 100 | 113 | 114 | | |
| Haiti | 253 | 335 | 411 | 435 | 435 | | |
| Honduras | 178 | 173 | 165 | 170 | 170 | | |
| Hungary | 665 | 233 | 127 | 77 | 79 | | |
| Iceland | 43 | 34 | 51 | 70 | 69 | | |
| India | 1,514 | 1,010 | 900 | 960 | 965 | 10 | 1.6 |

# MAIZE

*thousand tonnes*

| | 1950 | 1970 | 1980 | 1990 | 1991 | Rank | % |
|---|---|---|---|---|---|---|---|
| World | 134,763 | 278,615 | 423,724 | 479,340 | 478,775 | | |
| Afghanistan | 350 | 707 | 785 | 430 | 420 | | |
| Angola | 285 | 467 | 303 | 180 | 299 | | |
| Argentina | 2,839 | 8,717 | 9,333 | 5,049 | 7,768 | 10 | 1.6 |
| Austria | 120 | 677 | 1,338 | 1,620 | 1,524 | | |
| Benin | 181 | 201 | 289 | 418 | 390 | | |
| Bolivia | 163 | 291 | 422 | 407 | 510 | | |
| Bosnia | ... | ... | ... | ... | 620 | | |
| Brazil | 5,841 | 13,680 | 19,265 | 21,339 | 22,604 | 3 | 4.7 |
| Bulgaria | 720 | 2,436 | 2,626 | 1,221 | 2,718 | | |
| Cameroon | 212 | 283 | 418 | 380 | 450 | | |
| Canada | 388 | 2,487 | 5,901 | 7,157 | 7,319 | | |
| Chile | 68 | 217 | 471 | 823 | 836 | | |
| China | 14,082 | 27,820 | 60,720 | 97,158 | 93,350 | 2 | 19.5 |
| Colombia | 733 | 856 | 868 | 1,213 | 1,274 | | |
| Croatia | ... | ... | ... | ... | 2,100 | | |
| Cuba | 243 | 85 | 95 | 95 | 95 | | |
| Czechoslovakia | 316 | 511 | 800 | 468 | 862 | | |
| Ecuador | 79 | 239 | 247 | 501 | 665 | | |
| Egypt | 1,378 | 2,370 | 3,159 | 4,799 | 5,270 | | |
| El Salvador | 191 | 340 | 517 | 603 | 504 | | |
| Ethiopia | 160 | 909 | 1,224 | 1,636 | 1,590 | | |
| France | 452 | 7,394 | 9,641 | 9,291 | 12,787 | 5 | 2.7 |
| Germany | 20 | 500 | 752 | 1,552 | 1,928 | | |
| Ghana | 168 | 417 | 380 | 553 | 932 | | |
| Greece | 225 | 498 | 1,165 | 1,992 | 1,700 | | |
| Guatemala | 437 | 751 | 947 | 1,293 | 1,150 | | |
| Haiti | 203 | 245 | 179 | 163 | 145 | | |
| Honduras | 211 | 339 | 407 | 559 | 584 | | |
| Hungary | 2,081 | 4,542 | 7,022 | 4,500 | 7,509 | | |
| India | 2,165 | 6,087 | 6,486 | 9,073 | 8,200 | 8 | 1.7 |
| Indonesia | 1,535 | 2,575 | 4,035 | 6,734 | 6,409 | | |
| Italy | 2,306 | 4,601 | 6,590 | 5,864 | 6,208 | | |

| | 1950 | 1970 | 1980 | 1990 | 1991 | Rank | % |
|---|---|---|---|---|---|---|---|
| Ivory Coast | ... | 257 | 352 | 484 | 510 | | |
| Kenya | 591 | 2,292 | 1,714 | 2,630 | 2,250 | | |
| Korea, North | 375 | 1,493 | 3,833 | 4,400 | 4,500 | | |
| Lithuania | ... | ... | ... | ... | 1,400 | | |
| Malawi | 307 | 1,066 | 1,275 | 1,343 | 1,590 | | |
| Mexico | 3,090 | 9,025 | 11,866 | 14,035 | 13,527 | 4 | 2.0 |
| Morocco | 302 | 380 | 245 | 436 | 335 | | |
| Mozambique | 122 | 364 | 383 | 453 | 327 | | |
| Nepal | 829 | 796 | 690 | 1,231 | 1,235 | | |
| Nigeria | 644 | 1,215 | 599 | 1,832 | 1,900 | | |
| Pakistan | 384 | 697 | 925 | 1,185 | 1,190 | | |
| Paraguay | 112 | 197 | 535 | 1,139 | 980 | | |
| Peru | 275 | 605 | 569 | 632 | 669 | | |
| Philippines | 695 | 2,009 | 3,174 | 4,854 | 4,655 | | |
| Portugal | 421 | 599 | 486 | 666 | 677 | | |
| Romania | 2,495 | 7,354 | 11,823 | 6,810 | 10,493 | 6 | 2.2 |
| South Africa | 2,629 | 6,691 | 11,322 | 8,900 | 8,200 | 9 | 1.7 |
| Spain | 520 | 1,804 | 2,227 | 3,086 | 3,151 | | |
| Tanzania | 347 | 817 | 1,762 | 2,445 | 2,332 | | |
| Thailand | 31 | 1,979 | 3,103 | 3,722 | 3,990 | | |
| Turkey | 747 | 1,058 | 1,263 | 2,100 | 2,100 | | |
| Uganda | 121 | 420 | 360 | 584 | 600 | | |
| USSR (former) | 5,751 | 9,993 | 9,076 | 9,900 | 8,500 | 7 | 1.8 |
| United States | 74,308 | 122,649 | 192,084 | 201,508 | 189,867 | 1 | 39.7 |
| Venezuela | 303 | 698 | 547 | 1,002 | 1,100 | | |
| Vietnam | 180 | 272 | 410 | 671 | 652 | | |
| Yugoslavia (Serbia) | ... | ... | ... | ... | 6,000 | | |
| Zaire | 324 | 426 | 604 | 870 | 906 | | |
| Zambia | 45 | 786 | 941 | 1,093 | 1,448 | | |
| Zimbabwe | 167 | 966 | 1,829 | 1,994 | 1,586 | | |

| | 1950 | 1970 | 1980 | 1990 | 1991 | Rank | % |
|---|---|---|---|---|---|---|---|
| Mexico | 1,539 | 3,912 | 6,949 | 6,332 | 6,925 | | |
| Morocco | 271 | 450 | 753 | 980 | 990 | | |
| Netherlands | 5,437 | 8,182 | 11,832 | 11,226 | 11,220 | | |
| New Zealand | 4,720 | 6,112 | 6,586 | 7,700 | 7,973 | | |
| Nigeria | 334 | 313 | 354 | 354 | 360 | | |
| Norway | 1,532 | 1,726 | 1,926 | 1,959 | 1,928 | | |
| Pakistan | 2,800 | 2,070 | 2,189 | 3,320 | 3,449 | | |
| Peru | 237 | 828 | 796 | 777 | 786 | | |
| Poland | 9,091 | 14,951 | 16,250 | 15,832 | 15,050 | 9 | 3.2 |
| Portugal | 219 | 607 | 750 | 1,513 | 1,550 | | |
| Puerto Rico | 151 | 372 | 420 | 402 | 388 | | |
| Romania | 1,900 | 2,774 | 3,987 | 3,242 | 3,150 | | |
| Russia | ... | ... | ... | ... | 55,700 | 3 | 12 |
| Somalia | 65 | 139 | 319 | 530 | 497 | | |
| South Africa | 1,740 | 2,816 | 2,553 | 2,509 | 2,515 | | |
| Spain | 2,191 | 4,427 | 5,984 | 5,825 | 6,200 | | |
| Sudan | 667 | 753 | 1,352 | 2,251 | 2,299 | | |
| Sweden | 4,609 | 2,996 | 3,452 | 3,432 | 3,242 | | |
| Switzerland | 2,483 | 3,172 | 3,653 | 3,866 | 3,850 | | |
| Syria | 80 | 197 | 504 | 771 | 779 | | |
| Tajikistan | ... | ... | ... | ... | 575 | | |
| Tanzania | 356 | 692 | 372 | 459 | 463 | | |
| Turkey | 1,315 | 2,565 | 3,449 | 2,860 | 2,865 | | |
| Ukraine | ... | ... | ... | ... | 24,508 | 7 | 5.3 |
| USSR (former) | 33,228 | 81,967 | 90,557 | 108,700 | 100,000 | 1 | 21.5 |
| United Kingdom | 9,967 | 13,007 | 15,917 | 15,203 | 15,022 | 10 | 3.2 |
| United States | 52,349 | 53,173 | 58,139 | 67,260 | 67,373 | 2 | 14.5 |
| Uruguay | 449 | 744 | 811 | 1,311 | 900 | | |
| Uzbekistan | ... | ... | ... | ... | 3,034 | | |
| Venezuela | 203 | 947 | 1,353 | 1,497 | 1,591 | | |
| Yugoslavia | 1,463 | 2,591 | 4,370 | 4,369 | 4,315 | | |

## MILK - COW'S

thousand tonnes

| | 1950 | 1970 | 1980 | 1990 | 1991 | Rank | % |
|---|---|---|---|---|---|---|---|
| World | 233,025 | 363,193 | 417,347 | 477,565 | 464,468 | | |
| Afghanistan | 238 | 521 | 552 | 340 | 340 | | |
| Algeria | 92 | 292 | 514 | 595 | 596 | | |
| Argentina | 3,758 | 4,527 | 5,311 | 6,400 | 6,200 | | |
| Australia | 5,538 | 7,468 | 5,590 | 6,435 | 6,578 | | |
| Austria | 1,998 | 3,218 | 3,434 | 3,350 | 3,355 | | |
| Azerbaijan | ... | ... | ... | ... | 970 | | |
| Bangladesh | 890 | 678 | 833 | 742 | 750 | | |
| Belarus | ... | ... | ... | ... | 7,457 | | |
| Belgium | 3,323 | 3,971 | 4,042 | 4,020 | 3,900 | | |
| Brazil | 2,581 | 7,317 | 11,378 | 15,000 | 15,300 | 8 | 3.3 |
| Bulgaria | 278 | 1,249 | 1,843 | 2,101 | 1,756 | | |
| Burma | 250 | 400 | 283 | 446 | 456 | | |
| Canada | 7,051 | 8,247 | 7,830 | 7,535 | 7,340 | | |
| Chile | 683 | 1,029 | 1,078 | 1,423 | 1,490 | | |
| China | 2,005 | 3,233 | 1,143 | 4,361 | 4,816 | | |
| Colombia | 1,035 | 2,250 | 2,187 | 3,603 | 3,600 | | |
| Cuba | 460 | 672 | 1,045 | 1,100 | 1,070 | | |
| Czechoslovakia | 3,188 | 4,823 | 5,830 | 6,931 | 5,826 | | |
| Denmark | 4,915 | 4,588 | 5,126 | 4,742 | 4,640 | | |
| Dominican Rep. | 140 | 282 | 427 | 420 | 420 | | |
| Ecuador | 174 | 705 | 924 | 1,539 | 1,505 | | |
| Egypt | 362 | 575 | 648 | 1,060 | 1,140 | | |
| Estonia | ... | ... | ... | ... | 1,208 | | |
| Ethiopia | 344 | 516 | 590 | 748 | 752 | | |
| Finland | 2,414 | 3,401 | 3,236 | 2,730 | 2,477 | | |
| France | 14,578 | 27,467 | 26,720 | 26,561 | 26,600 | 6 | 5.7 |
| Georgia | ... | ... | ... | ... | 602 | | |
| Germany | 15,997 | 29,904 | 31,724 | 31,307 | 29,300 | 4 | 6.3 |
| Greece | 147 | 546 | 666 | 735 | 690 | | |
| Hungary | 1,443 | 1,851 | 2,559 | 2,846 | 2,625 | | |
| India | 7,743 | 7,633 | 13,420 | 27,500 | 27,000 | 5 | 5.8 |
| Iran | 539 | 915 | 1,125 | 1,397 | 1,428 | | |
| Ireland | 2,265 | 3,685 | 4,729 | 5,402 | 5,527 | | |
| Israel | 97 | 447 | 702 | 952 | 965 | | |
| Italy | 7,009 | 9,427 | 10,546 | 10,376 | 10,000 | | |
| Japan | 369 | 4,703 | 6,526 | 8,190 | 8,180 | | |
| Kazakhstan | ... | ... | ... | ... | 5,642 | | |
| Kenya | 120 | 841 | 938 | 2,320 | 2,189 | | |
| Korea, South | 1 | 51 | 449 | 1,752 | 1,848 | | |
| Kyrgyzstan | ... | ... | ... | ... | 1,148 | | |
| Latvia | ... | ... | ... | ... | 1,893 | | |
| Lithuania | ... | ... | ... | ... | 3,157 | | |
| Madagascar | 29 | 32 | 36 | 473 | 472 | | |

## MILLET

thousand tonnes

| | 1950 | 1970 | 1980 | 1990 | 1991 | Rank | % |
|---|---|---|---|---|---|---|---|
| World | 20,000 | 29,417 | 25,610 | 29,896 | 28,970 | | |
| Afghanistan | 10 | 20 | 33 | 26 | 26 | | |
| Angola | ... | 78 | 49 | 63 | 61 | | |
| Argentina | 151 | 168 | 245 | 91 | 65 | | |
| Australia | 7 | 37 | 26 | 38 | 43 | | |
| Bangladesh | 40 | 40 | 40 | 63 | 60 | | |
| Burkina Faso | 221 | 352 | 390 | 449 | 757 | 7 | 2.6 |
| Burma | 56 | 65 | 80 | 126 | 138 | | |
| Burundi | 22 | 26 | 10 | 13 | 12 | | |
| Cameroon | 350 | 343 | 98 | 65 | 63 | | |
| Central Afr. Rep. | 29 | 43 | 11 | 12 | 10 | | |
| Chad | 600 | 615 | 182 | 168 | 302 | | |
| China | 3,000 | 5,473 | 5,790 | 4,576 | 4,501 | 2 | 15.5 |
| Egypt | 1,000 | 847 | 638 | 215 | 200 | | |
| Ethiopia | 190 | 117 | 203 | 273 | 260 | | |
| Gambia, The | 20 | 40 | 26 | 47 | 51 | | |
| Ghana | 100 | 120 | 117 | 75 | 112 | | |
| Guinea | 50 | 50 | 49 | 60 | 60 | | |
| India | 6,064 | 10,182 | 9,189 | 10,462 | 9,000 | 1 | 31 |
| Ivory Coast | 33 | 30 | 37 | 44 | 52 | | |
| Japan | 127 | 12 | 1 | 2 | 1 | | |
| Kenya | 50 | 31 | 84 | 62 | 63 | | |
| Korea, North | 320 | 407 | 66 | 60 | 62 | | |
| Korea, South | 60 | 47 | 4 | 2 | 2 | | |
| Mali | 500 | 784 | 461 | 737 | 792 | 6 | 2.7 |
| Mauritania | 45 | 81 | 3 | 3 | 4 | | |
| Namibia | 16 | 19 | 34 | 58 | 50 | | |
| Nepal | 52 | 128 | 121 | 232 | 220 | | |
| Niger | 400 | 974 | 1,311 | 1,113 | 1,853 | 5 | 6.4 |
| Nigeria | 1,000 | 2,792 | 2,496 | 5,136 | 4,200 | 3 | 14.5 |
| Pakistan | 300 | 300 | 255 | 196 | 200 | | |
| Russia | ... | ... | ... | ... | ... | | |
| Senegal | 300 | 543 | 555 | 514 | 560 | 9 | 1.9 |
| Sudan | 181 | 424 | 436 | 85 | 308 | 10 | 1.1 |
| Syria | 65 | 18 | 16 | 4 | 4 | | |
| Tanzania | 250 | 140 | 360 | 200 | 270 | | |
| Togo | 80 | 121 | 44 | 58 | 70 | | |
| Turkey | 78 | 54 | 21 | 6 | 6 | | |
| Uganda | 510 | 737 | 473 | 564 | 600 | 8 | 2.1 |
| USSR (former) | 1,705 | 2,477 | 1,759 | 3,647 | 3,600 | 4 | 12.4 |
| United States | 100 | 100 | 107 | 140 | 150 | | |
| Yemen | 70 | 70 | 96 | 50 | 20 | | |
| Zaire | 20 | 22 | 24 | 31 | 31 | | |

| | 1950 | 1970 | 1980 | 1990 | 1991 | Rank | % |
|---|---|---|---|---|---|---|---|
| Zambia | 50 | 79 | 22 | 32 | 31 | | |
| Zimbabwe | 50 | 190 | 153 | 143 | 122 | | |

## OLIVES

thousand tonnes

| | 1950 | 1970 | 1980 | 1990 | 1991 | Rank | % |
|---|---|---|---|---|---|---|---|
| World | 4,943 | 7,650 | 9,193 | 9,203 | 10,617 | | |
| Albania | 12 | 33 | 31 | 24 | 18 | | |
| Algeria | 151 | 150 | 154 | 65 | 130 | 9 | 1.2 |
| Argentina | 19 | 70 | 92 | 98 | 98 | 10 | 0.9 |
| Chile | 15 | 12 | 10 | 11 | 11 | | |
| Cyprus | 11 | 14 | 12 | 11 | 11 | | |
| Egypt | 2 | 7 | 5 | 42 | 31 | | |
| France | 27 | 16 | 13 | 8 | 9 | | |
| Greece | 515 | 876 | 1,465 | 1,050 | 1,800 | 3 | 17 |
| Iran | 13 | 10 | 9 | 14 | 10 | | |
| Iraq | 9 | 9 | 3 | 3 | 3 | | |
| Israel | 9 | 13 | 29 | 42 | 20 | | |
| Italy | 1,218 | 2,530 | 2,962 | 913 | 3,250 | 1 | 30.6 |
| Jordan | 28 | 18 | 23 | 64 | 40 | | |
| Lebanon | 32 | 48 | 37 | 62 | 40 | | |
| Libya | 27 | 38 | 139 | 68 | 70 | | |
| Mexico | 10 | 10 | 26 | 15 | 15 | | |
| Morocco | 88 | 329 | 269 | 445 | 440 | 5 | 4.1 |
| Peru | 3 | 9 | 11 | 10 | 10 | | |
| Portugal | 490 | 422 | 271 | 196 | 296 | 7 | 2.8 |
| Spain | 1,602 | 1,897 | 2,025 | 3,369 | 2,891 | 2 | 27.2 |
| Syria | 57 | 110 | 265 | 461 | 201 | 8 | 1.9 |
| Tunisia | 277 | 476 | 521 | 825 | 330 | 6 | 3.1 |
| Turkey | 268 | 438 | 727 | 1,100 | 800 | 4 | 7.5 |
| United States | 46 | 54 | 65 | 119 | 54 | | |
| Yugoslavia | 28 | 10 | 18 | 33 | 18 | | |

## OLIVE OIL

thousand tonnes

| | 1950 | 1970 | 1980 | 1990 | 1991 | Rank | % |
|---|---|---|---|---|---|---|---|
| World | 940 | 1,553 | 1,832 | 1,573 | 2,007 | | |
| Albania | 1 | 4 | 4 | 4 | 3 | | |
| Algeria | 18 | 21 | 19 | 8 | 16 | 9 | 0.8 |
| Argentina | 2 | 17 | 16 | 8 | 9 | | |
| Chile | 2 | 1 | 1 | 1 | 1 | | |
| Cyprus | 2 | 2 | 2 | 2 | 2 | | |
| France | 3 | 2 | 2 | 2 | 2 | | |
| Greece | 115 | 178 | 309 | 188 | 355 | 3 | 17.7 |
| Iran | 1 | 1 | 1 | 2 | 2 | | |
| Israel | 1 | 1 | 2 | ... | | | |
| Italy | 241 | 553 | 635 | 175 | 685 | 1 | 34.1 |
| Jordan | 14 | 3 | 4 | 8 | 11 | 10 | 0.5 |
| Lebanon | 2 | 11 | 7 | 5 | 4 | | |
| Libya | 4 | 7 | 28 | 10 | 10 | | |
| Morocco | 13 | 41 | 28 | 43 | 53 | 6 | 2.6 |
| Portugal | 65 | 70 | 47 | 27 | 26 | 8 | 1.3 |
| Spain | 334 | 419 | 435 | 679 | 608 | 2 | 30.3 |
| Syria | 9 | 23 | 59 | 91 | 43 | 7 | 2.1 |
| Tunisia | 60 | 103 | 101 | 182 | 75 | 5 | 3.7 |
| Turkey | 47 | 86 | 129 | 110 | 96 | 4 | 4.8 |
| Yugoslavia | 4 | 2 | 3 | 6 | 3 | | |

## ORANGES

thousand tonnes

| | 1950 | 1970 | 1980 | 1990 | 1991 | Rank | % |
|---|---|---|---|---|---|---|---|
| World | 12,203 | 25,453 | 36,387 | 52,079 | 55,308 | | |
| Algeria | 215 | 351 | 269 | 184 | 190 | | |
| Argentina | 362 | 892 | 693 | 750 | 740 | | |
| Australia | 123 | 263 | 398 | 492 | 492 | | |

| | 1950 | 1970 | 1980 | 1990 | 1991 | Rank | % |
|---|---|---|---|---|---|---|---|
| Belize | ... | 33 | 37 | 69 | 70 | | |
| Bhutan | ... | ... | 25 | 58 | 62 | | |
| Bolivia | 15 | 53 | 85 | 81 | 96 | | |
| Brazil | 1,316 | 3,084 | 10,243 | 17,506 | 18,942 | 1 | 34 |
| Cambodia | 2 | 41 | 22 | 43 | 45 | | |
| Chile | 63 | 42 | 58 | 102 | 110 | | |
| China | 206 | 727 | 783 | 4,977 | 5,385 | 3 | 9.7 |
| Colombia | | 91 | 233 | 350 | 360 | | |
| Costa Rica | 13 | 59 | 75 | 86 | 86 | | |
| Cuba | 46 | 112 | 251 | 604 | 600 | | |
| Cyprus | 24 | 119 | 36 | 63 | 49 | | |
| Dominican Rep. | 34 | 63 | 68 | 65 | 64 | | |
| Ecuador | 168 | 160 | 521 | 77 | 75 | | |
| Egypt | 263 | 760 | 956 | 1,574 | 1,600 | 8 | 2.9 |
| El Salvador | ... | 38 | 100 | 107 | 107 | | |
| Ghana | 17 | 107 | 100 | 50 | 50 | | |
| Greece | 97 | 418 | 577 | 886 | 703 | | |
| Honduras | 8 | 18 | 38 | 49 | 50 | | |
| India | 226 | 900 | 1,170 | 1,840 | 1,890 | 7 | 3.4 |
| Indonesia | ... | 93 | 322 | 400 | 435 | | |
| Iran | 47 | 65 | 170 | 1,192 | 1,270 | 9 | 2.3 |
| Iraq | ... | 28 | 124 | 180 | 145 | | |
| Israel | 258 | 917 | 866 | 878 | 567 | | |
| Italy | 548 | 1,403 | 1,659 | 1,761 | 1,942 | 6 | 3.5 |
| Jamaica | 54 | 70 | 36 | 60 | 60 | | |
| Japan | 378 | 321 | 352 | 280 | 290 | | |
| Jordan | 1 | 14 | 23 | 54 | 55 | | |
| Lebanon | 47 | 167 | 215 | 250 | 270 | | |
| Libya | 3 | 19 | 62 | 91 | 95 | | |
| Madagascar | 10 | 49 | 59 | 85 | 84 | | |
| Mexico | 480 | 1,377 | 1,811 | 1,064 | 2,175 | 5 | 3.9 |
| Morocco | 158 | 665 | 705 | 771 | 920 | | |
| Nicaragua | ... | 45 | 53 | 66 | 68 | | |
| Pakistan | 135 | 312 | 702 | 1,100 | 1,100 | 10 | 1.9 |
| Panama | 33 | 51 | 43 | 25 | 25 | | |
| Paraguay | 171 | 194 | 280 | 366 | 367 | | |
| Peru | 368 | 246 | 136 | 165 | 165 | | |
| Portugal | 68 | 100 | 94 | 101 | 135 | | |
| Puerto Rico | 30 | 32 | 31 | 29 | 28 | | |
| South Africa | 199 | 533 | 581 | 697 | 689 | | |
| Spain | 975 | 1,884 | 1,657 | 2,561 | 2,504 | 4 | 4.5 |
| Sudan | ... | 35 | 12 | 10 | 15 | | |
| Syria | 3 | 6 | 35 | 171 | 202 | | |
| Thailand | ... | 44 | 54 | 56 | 57 | | |
| Tunisia | 25 | 58 | 113 | 123 | 117 | | |
| Turkey | 66 | 445 | 690 | 739 | 739 | | |
| USSR (former) | 20 | 72 | 261 | 250 | 375 | | |
| United States | 4,509 | 7,302 | 9,519 | 7,083 | 7,258 | 2 | 13 |
| Uruguay | 58 | 42 | 55 | 111 | 121 | | |
| Venezuela | 60 | 205 | 350 | 433 | 432 | | |
| Vietnam | ... | 43 | 80 | 105 | 105 | | |
| Zaire | ... | 126 | 141 | 153 | 155 | | |

Figures for 1950 include tangerines.

## PALM OIL

thousand tonnes

| | 1950 | 1970 | 1980 | 1990 | 1991 | Rank | % |
|---|---|---|---|---|---|---|---|
| World | 1,008 | 1,971 | 4,979 | 11,163 | 11,873 | | |
| Angola | 36 | 40 | 40 | 40 | 40 | | |
| Benin | 34 | 28 | 30 | 40 | 40 | | |
| Brazil | 1 | 7 | 14 | 66 | 70 | | |
| Cameroon | 22 | 63 | 77 | 108 | 105 | | |
| China | ... | 108 | 165 | 133 | 140 | 9 | 1.2 |
| Colombia | ... | 27 | 71 | 252 | 268 | 4 | 2.3 |
| Congo | 4 | 8 | 15 | 17 | 17 | | |
| Costa Rica | ... | 13 | 33 | 60 | 64 | | |
| Ecuador | ... | 6 | 37 | 150 | 157 | 8 | 1.3 |
| Equat. Guinea | 4 | 4 | 5 | 5 | 5 | | |
| Gambia, The | 2 | 2 | 3 | 3 | 3 | | |
| Ghana | 30 | 19 | 21 | 85 | 87 | | |
| Guinea | 10 | 44 | 41 | 50 | 51 | | |
| Guinea-Bissau | 8 | 4 | 5 | 5 | 5 | | |
| Honduras | 1 | 6 | 10 | 78 | 80 | | |
| Indonesia | 114 | 218 | 721 | 2,186 | 2,700 | 2 | 22.7 |
| Ivory Coast | 6 | 46 | 158 | 208 | 218 | 6 | 1.8 |
| Liberia | 40 | 14 | 26 | 30 | 31 | | |
| Malaysia | 49 | 457 | 5,030 | 6,095 | 6,145 | 1 | 51.8 |

| | 1950 | 1970 | 1980 | 1990 | 1991 | Rank | % |
|---|---|---|---|---|---|---|---|
| Nigeria | 422 | 528 | 667 | 820 | 900 | 3 | 7.6 |
| Papua New Guinea | ... | 0.02 | 41 | 114 | 114 | 10 | 1 |
| Paraguay | 1 | 7 | 5 | 4 | 4 | | |
| Peru | ... | ... | 5 | 25 | 23 | | |
| Philippines | ... | 2 | 43 | 45 | 48 | | |
| Senegal | ... | 5 | 6 | 6 | 6 | | |
| Sierra Leone | 35 | 46 | 47 | 56 | 59 | | |
| Solomon Is. | ... | ... | 15 | 23 | 23 | | |
| Thailand | ... | ... | 20 | 226 | 234 | 5 | 2 |
| Togo | 3 | 17 | 20 | 14 | 14 | | |
| Zaire | 172 | 232 | 168 | 180 | 182 | 7 | 1.5 |

# PAPER & PAPER BOARD

*million tonnes*

| | 1961–65 av. | 1970 | 1980 | 1990 | 1991 | Rank | % |
|---|---|---|---|---|---|---|---|
| World | 86.7 | 128 | 170 | 239 | 243 | | |
| Argentina | 0.4 | 0.6 | 0.71 | 1 | 1 | | |
| Australia | 0.6 | 1.1 | 1.43 | 2 | 2 | | |
| Austria | 0.6 | 1 | 1.62 | 2.9 | 3.1 | | |
| Belgium | 0.5 | 1 | 0.86 | 1.2 | 1.2 | | |
| Brazil | 0.7 | 1.2 | 3.36 | 4.8 | 4.9 | | |
| Bulgaria | 0.1 | 0.2 | 0.4 | 0.3 | 0.2 | | |
| Canada | 8.6 | 11.3 | 13.49 | 16.5 | 16.6 | 4 | 6.8 |
| Chile | 0.1 | 0.3 | 0.36 | 0.5 | 0.5 | | |
| China | 2.9 | 4.2 | 6.83 | 17.1 | 18.5 | 3 | 7.6 |
| Colombia | 0.1 | 0.2 | 0.35 | 0.5 | 0.5 | | |
| Czechoslovakia | 0.7 | 1 | 1.19 | 1.3 | 1.1 | | |
| Denmark | 0.2 | 0.3 | 0.23 | 0.3 | 0.4 | | |
| Finland | 2.8 | 4.3 | 5.92 | 8.8 | 8.5 | 7 | 3.5 |
| France | 3 | 4.1 | 5.15 | 7 | 7.4 | 9 | 3 |
| Germany | 4.7 | 7 | 8.82 | 13.2 | 13.5 | 5 | 5.6 |
| Greece | 0.1 | 0.2 | 0.31 | 0.4 | 0.4 | | |
| Hungary | 0.2 | 0.3 | 0.44 | 0.4 | 0.4 | | |
| India | 0.5 | 1 | 0.96 | 2.3 | 2.4 | | |
| Indonesia | 0.01 | 0.02 | 0.23 | 1.4 | 1.7 | | |
| Italy | 1.9 | 3.5 | 4.93 | 5.6 | 5.8 | 10 | 2.4 |
| Japan | 6.4 | 13 | 18.09 | 28.1 | 29.1 | 2 | 12 |
| Korea, South | 0.1 | 0.3 | 1.68 | 4.5 | 5 | | |
| Mexico | 0.4 | 1 | 1.98 | 2.9 | 2.9 | | |
| Netherlands | 1.2 | 1.6 | 1.71 | 2.8 | 3 | | |
| New Zealand | 0.3 | 0.5 | 0.67 | 0.8 | 0.8 | | |
| Norway | 0.9 | 1.4 | 1.37 | 1.8 | 1.8 | | |
| Peru | 0.1 | 0.1 | 0.21 | 0.3 | 0.1 | | |
| Philippines | 0.1 | 0.1 | 0.32 | 0.2 | 0.2 | | |
| Poland | 0.8 | 1 | 1.28 | 1.1 | 1.1 | | |
| Portugal | 0.1 | 0.2 | 0.46 | 0.8 | 0.9 | | |
| Romania | 0.3 | 0.5 | 0.82 | 0.5 | 0.4 | | |
| South Africa | 0.3 | 0.6 | 1.12 | 1.9 | 1.9 | | |
| Spain | 0.5 | 1.3 | 2.57 | 3.4 | 3.6 | | |
| Sweden | 2.7 | 4.4 | 6.18 | 8.4 | 8.4 | 8 | 3.5 |
| Switzerland | 0.6 | 0.7 | 0.91 | 1.3 | 1.2 | | |
| Taiwan | 0.1 | 0.2 | 0.5 | 0.9 | 1 | | |
| Thailand | 0.01 | 0.1 | 0.34 | 0.9 | 1.2 | | |
| Turkey | 0.1 | 0.2 | 0.48 | 0.9 | 0.83 | | |
| USSR (former) | 4 | 6.7 | 8.73 | 10.7 | 9.6 | 6 | 4 |
| United Kingdom | 4.2 | 5 | 3.79 | 4.9 | 5 | | |
| United States | 34.1 | 46.1 | 56.84 | 72 | 72.7 | 1 | 30 |
| Venezuela | 0.1 | 0.3 | 0.5 | 0.6 | 0.6 | | |
| Yugoslavia | 0.3 | 0.6 | 1.1 | 0.9 | 0.7 | | |

# PIGMEAT

*thousand tonnes*

| | 1950 | 1970 | 1980 | 1990 | 1991 | Rank | % |
|---|---|---|---|---|---|---|---|
| World | 16,389 | 38,619 | 54,581 | 69,883 | 70,852 | | |
| Argentina | 151 | 221 | 258 | 216 | 216 | | |
| Australia | 89 | 173 | 217 | 317 | 312 | | |
| Austria | 125 | 263 | 438 | 439 | 429 | | |
| Belgium | 177 | 455 | 669 | 825 | 900 | | |
| Brazil | 351 | 763 | 953 | 1,150 | 1,160 | | |
| Bulgaria | 69 | 160 | 315 | 406 | 366 | | |
| Burma | 8 | 60 | 79 | 80 | 82 | | |
| Canada | 408 | 600 | 979 | 1,133 | 1,110 | | |
| Chile | 42 | 44 | 49 | 123 | 142 | | |
| China | 3,298 | 9,639 | 11,704 | 23,756 | 25,460 | 1 | 35.9 |
| Colombia | 51 | 69 | 98 | 112 | 115 | | |
| Cuba | 36 | 34 | 50 | 89 | 90 | | |
| Czechoslovakia | 399 | 566 | 823 | 913 | 771 | | |
| Denmark | 305 | 722 | 953 | 1,208 | 1,255 | | |
| Ecuador | 7 | 28 | 58 | 65 | 67 | | |
| Finland | 57 | 109 | 171 | 187 | 177 | | |
| France | 811 | 1,388 | 1,775 | 1,871 | 1,820 | 7 | 2.6 |
| Germany | 1,189 | 3,061 | 4,393 | 4,457 | 3,909 | 4 | 5.5 |
| Greece | 19 | 54 | 144 | 148 | 151 | | |
| Hong Kong | 5 | 120 | 178 | 188 | 190 | | |
| Hungary | 194 | 598 | 899 | 1,040 | 1,030 | | |
| India | 24 | 52 | 327 | 360 | 364 | | |
| Indonesia | 35 | 53 | 111 | 302 | 275 | | |
| Ireland | 65 | 147 | 152 | 159 | 168 | | |
| Italy | 233 | 590 | 1,075 | 1,333 | 1,330 | 10 | 1.9 |
| Japan | 46 | 735 | 1,434 | 1,555 | 1,490 | 9 | 2.1 |
| Korea, North | 12 | 54 | 113 | 164 | 161 | | |
| Korea, South | 7 | 80 | 276 | 550 | 530 | | |
| Malaysia | 31 | 76 | 133 | 205 | 195 | | |
| Mexico | 58 | 240 | 467 | 757 | 812 | | |
| Netherlands | 206 | 704 | 1,142 | 1,661 | 1,639 | 8 | 2.3 |
| New Zealand | 39 | 40 | 34 | 43 | 43 | | |
| Nigeria | 13 | 28 | 37 | 128 | 150 | | |
| Norway | 36 | 66 | 83 | 83 | 83 | | |
| Paraguay | 15 | 42 | 85 | 118 | 141 | | |
| Peru | 14 | 64 | 72 | 84 | 91 | | |
| Philippines | 89 | 304 | 415 | 712 | 710 | | |
| Poland | 718 | 1,312 | 1,617 | 1,855 | 1,869 | 5 | 2.6 |
| Portugal | 78 | 98 | 164 | 242 | 236 | | |
| Romania | 28 | 453 | 970 | 920 | 850 | | |
| Singapore | 9 | 25 | 65 | 76 | 78 | | |
| South Africa | 49 | 80 | 87 | 125 | 126 | | |
| Spain | 147 | 468 | 1,115 | 1,789 | 1,850 | 6 | 2.6 |
| Sweden | 165 | 244 | 317 | 293 | 275 | | |
| Switzerland | 83 | 201 | 273 | 270 | 266 | | |
| Thailand | 60 | 210 | 265 | 337 | 340 | | |
| USSR (former) | 1,002 | 4,638 | 5,223 | 6,600 | 6,200 | 3 | 8.8 |
| United Kingdom | 296 | 934 | 929 | 946 | 980 | | |
| United States | 4,904 | 6,227 | 7,248 | 6,965 | 7,258 | 2 | 10.2 |
| Uruguay | 17 | 21 | 18 | 15 | 16 | | |
| Venezuela | 16 | 46 | 76 | 99 | 101 | | |
| Vietnam | 41 | 332 | 323 | 800 | 850 | | |
| Yugoslavia | 151 | 525 | 789 | 817 | 815 | | |

# POTATOES

*thousand tonnes*

| | 1950 | 1970 | 1980 | 1990 | 1991 | Rank | % |
|---|---|---|---|---|---|---|---|
| World | 247,443 | 275,758 | 258,465 | 268,107 | 261,162 | | |
| Algeria | 212 | 253 | 540 | 809 | 1,000 | | |
| Argentina | 1,169 | 2,212 | 1,836 | 2,500 | 2,600 | | |
| Australia | 477 | 782 | 840 | 1,178 | 1,160 | | |
| Austria | 2,270 | 2,787 | 1,356 | 794 | 791 | | |
| Bangladesh | 111 | 842 | 942 | 1,066 | 800 | | |
| Belarus | ... | ... | ... | ... | 8,958 | | |
| Belgium | 2,127 | 1,631 | 1,468 | 1,750 | 1,950 | | |
| Bolivia | 176 | 660 | 794 | 620 | 855 | | |
| Bosnia | ... | ... | ... | ... | 340 | | |
| Brazil | 699 | 1,557 | 2,002 | 2,219 | 2,214 | | |
| Bulgaria | 240 | 378 | 376 | 433 | 503 | | |
| Canada | 1,808 | 2,312 | 2,626 | 2,959 | 2,781 | | |
| Chile | 461 | 707 | 894 | 829 | 844 | | |
| China | 12,090 | 11,029 | 25,415 | 32,031 | 35,533 | 2 | 13.6 |
| Colombia | 506 | 871 | 1,931 | 2,464 | 2,372 | | |
| Croatia | ... | ... | ... | ... | 620 | | |
| Czechoslovakia | 7,055 | 4,864 | 3,388 | 2,534 | 2,713 | | |
| Denmark | 117 | 845 | 913 | 1,483 | 1,511 | | |
| Ecuador | 98 | 560 | 323 | 369 | 337 | | |
| Egypt | 187 | 496 | 1,142 | 1,638 | 920 | | |
| Estonia | ... | ... | ... | ... | 954 | | |
| Ethiopia | 100 | 161 | 301 | 380 | 384 | | |
| Finland | 1,442 | 906 | 629 | 881 | 672 | | |
| France | 13,734 | 8,569 | 6,735 | 5,800 | 6,300 | 9 | 2.4 |
| Georgia | ... | ... | ... | ... | 294 | | |
| Germany | 37,430 | 16,236 | 19,465 | 14,039 | 10,225 | 6 | 3.9 |
| Greece | 385 | 700 | 1,036 | 996 | 1,100 | | |

| | 1950 | 1970 | 1980 | 1990 | 1991 | Rank | % |
|---|---|---|---|---|---|---|---|
| Hungary | 1,976 | 1,874 | 1,504 | 1,226 | 1,226 | | |
| India | 1,547 | 4,482 | 9,377 | 14,770 | 15,254 | 5 | 5.8 |
| Indonesia | 27 | 99 | 217 | 559 | 500 | | |
| Iran | 37 | 417 | 1,269 | 2,475 | 2,500 | | |
| Ireland | 2,903 | 1,450 | 902 | 633 | 650 | | |
| Italy | 2,732 | 3,632 | 2,941 | 2,309 | 2,227 | | |
| Japan | 2,451 | 3,490 | 3,299 | 3,552 | 3,700 | | |
| Kazakhstan | ... | ... | ... | ... | 1,783 | | |
| Kenya | 190 | 206 | 392 | 260 | 300 | | |
| Korea, North | 575 | 960 | 1,535 | 2,100 | 1,975 | | |
| Korea, South | 302 | 598 | 452 | 371 | 416 | | |
| Kyrgyzstan | ... | ... | ... | ... | 324 | | |
| Latvia | ... | ... | ... | ... | 1,016 | | |
| Lithuania | ... | ... | ... | ... | 1,508 | | |
| Madagascar | 79 | 106 | 170 | 272 | 273 | | |
| Malawi | 1 | 85 | 270 | 330 | 340 | | |
| Mexico | 134 | 489 | 993 | 1,236 | 999 | | |
| Moldova | ... | ... | ... | ... | 304 | | |
| Morocco | 56 | 283 | 503 | 880 | 928 | | |
| Nepal | ... | 265 | 279 | 672 | 738 | | |
| Netherlands | 4,679 | 5,367 | 6,329 | 7,036 | 6,735 | 7 | 2.6 |
| New Zealand | 130 | 284 | 209 | 303 | 300 | | |
| Norway | 1,174 | 807 | 524 | 484 | 484 | | |
| Pakistan | 28 | 213 | 412 | 831 | 750 | | |
| Peru | 1,239 | 1,877 | 1,680 | 1,154 | 1,450 | | |
| Poland | 29,641 | 45,012 | 39,508 | 36,313 | 29,038 | 3 | 11.1 |
| Portugal | 1,081 | 1,222 | 1,079 | 1,132 | 948 | | |
| Romania | 1,661 | 2,671 | 4,381 | 3,186 | 1,900 | | |
| Russia | ... | ... | ... | ... | 30,800 | | |
| Slovenia | ... | ... | ... | ... | 385 | | |
| South Africa | 230 | 583 | 747 | 1,247 | 1,250 | | |
| Spain | 3,346 | 4,985 | 5,615 | 5,342 | 5,333 | 10 | 2 |
| Sweden | 1,814 | 1,221 | 1,191 | 1,186 | 1,048 | | |
| Switzerland | 1,021 | 1,016 | 924 | 712 | 725 | | |
| Syria | 34 | 62 | 279 | 398 | 295 | | |
| Turkey | 605 | 1,984 | 2,957 | 4,300 | 4,600 | | |
| Ukraine | ... | ... | ... | ... | 16,765 | | |
| USSR (former) | 80,239 | 93,739 | 76,706 | 63,700 | 64,500 | 1 | 24.7 |
| United Kingdom | 9,443 | 7,359 | 6,601 | 6,504 | 6,700 | 8 | 2.6 |
| United States | 10,681 | 14,483 | 14,923 | 18,239 | 18,970 | 4 | 7.3 |
| Uzbekistan | ... | ... | ... | ... | 336 | | |
| Vietnam | 2 | 103 | 710 | 365 | 281 | | |
| Yugoslavia | 1,486 | 3,020 | 2,646 | 2,172 | 2,180 | | |
| Yugoslavia (Serbia) | ... | ... | ... | ... | 800 | | |

| | 1950 | 1970 | 1980 | 1990 | 1991 | Rank | % |
|---|---|---|---|---|---|---|---|
| Ireland | 28 | 32 | 52 | 93 | 95 | | |
| Israel | 6 | 96 | 153 | 178 | 186 | | |
| Italy | 57 | 619 | 1,007 | 1,104 | 1,105 | 8 | 2.8 |
| Ivory Coast | 4 | 9 | 27 | 46 | 48 | | |
| Jamaica | 0.2 | 16 | 32 | 52 | 53 | | |
| Japan | 10 | 494 | 1,115 | 1,418 | 1,417 | 5 | 3.6 |
| Jordan | 0.3 | 8 | 26 | 49 | 56 | | |
| Kenya | 7 | 16 | 32 | 47 | 47 | | |
| Korea, North | 8 | 20 | 32 | 47 | 48 | | |
| Korea, South | 2 | 46 | 92 | 176 | 203 | | |
| Lebanon | 2 | 21 | 46 | 55 | 59 | | |
| Libya | ... | 2 | 29 | 68 | 70 | | |
| Madagascar | 12 | 35 | 55 | 86 | 88 | | |
| Malaysia | 11 | 53 | 134 | 345 | 352 | | |
| Mexico | 41 | 225 | 440 | 793 | 897 | 9 | 2.2 |
| Morocco | 16 | 30 | 80 | 125 | 130 | | |
| Netherlands | 9 | 297 | 343 | 470 | 499 | | |
| New Zealand | 3 | 17 | 35 | 58 | 58 | | |
| Nigeria | 23 | 73 | 187 | 171 | 176 | | |
| Pakistan | 27 | 14 | 46 | 157 | 182 | | |
| Peru | 4 | 58 | 148 | 245 | 280 | | |
| Philippines | 35 | 103 | 228 | 242 | 237 | | |
| Poland | 33 | 141 | 417 | 332 | 310 | | |
| Portugal | 7 | 54 | 131 | 129 | 131 | | |
| Puerto Rico | 5 | 13 | 28 | 51 | 57 | | |
| Romania | 45 | 128 | 413 | 370 | 350 | | |
| Saudi Arabia | ... | 8 | 46 | 265 | 275 | | |
| Singapore | 3 | 27 | 66 | 66 | 67 | | |
| South Africa | 21 | 107 | 233 | 384 | 394 | | |
| Spain | 66 | 454 | 798 | 836 | 840 | 10 | 2.1 |
| Sweden | 13 | 27 | 44 | 44 | 45 | | |
| Syria | 2 | 14 | 57 | 57 | 62 | | |
| Taiwan | 10 | 22 | 51 | 88 | 90 | | |
| Thailand | 28 | 64 | 373 | 661 | 717 | | |
| Tunisia | 3 | 10 | 40 | 54 | 56 | | |
| Turkey | 18 | 104 | 245 | 270 | 285 | | |
| USSR (former) | 278 | 1,040 | 2,143 | 3,300 | 3,000 | 3 | 7.5 |
| United Kingdom | 95 | 574 | 751 | 1,026 | 1,112 | 7 | 2.8 |
| United States | 2,203 | 5,979 | 6,713 | 10,924 | 11,503 | 1 | 28.9 |
| Venezuela | 3 | 93 | 247 | 332 | 340 | | |
| Vietnam | ... | 70 | 135 | 161 | 168 | | |
| Yemen | 0.9 | 2 | 7 | 57 | 55 | | |
| Yugoslavia | 36 | 138 | 277 | 295 | 293 | | |

## POULTRY MEAT

*thousand tonnes*

| | 1950 | 1970 | 1980 | 1990 | 1991 | Rank | % |
|---|---|---|---|---|---|---|---|
| World | ... | 17,760 | 27,245 | 38,160 | 39,870 | | |
| Algeria | 14 | 28 | 46 | 65 | 69 | | |
| Argentina | 33 | 182 | 321 | 369 | 391 | | |
| Australia | 45 | 128 | 296 | 407 | 416 | | |
| Austria | 3 | 47 | 71 | 87 | 81 | | |
| Bangladesh | ... | 61 | 90 | 74 | 58 | | |
| Belgium | 29 | 116 | 133 | 187 | 190 | | |
| Brazil | 87 | 360 | 1,345 | 2,417 | 2,614 | 4 | 6.6 |
| Bulgaria | 24 | 94 | 151 | 182 | 115 | | |
| Burma | 23 | 16 | 70 | 80 | 83 | | |
| Canada | 142 | 542 | 532 | 745 | 744 | | |
| Chile | 12 | 52 | 105 | 124 | 140 | | |
| China | 1,094 | 1,683 | 1,725 | 3,303 | 3,463 | 2 | 8.7 |
| Colombia | 27 | 46 | 107 | 248 | 257 | | |
| Cuba | 5 | 40 | 74 | 91 | 92 | | |
| Czechoslovakia | 24 | 109 | 192 | 245 | 210 | | |
| Denmark | 23 | 76 | 100 | 131 | 135 | | |
| Dominican Rep. | ... | 28 | 61 | 131 | 138 | | |
| Ecuador | 1 | 9 | 22 | 70 | 75 | | |
| Egypt | 24 | 80 | 120 | 233 | 219 | | |
| Ethiopia | 55 | 54 | 68 | 76 | 77 | | |
| France | 248 | 631 | 1,131 | 1,384 | 1,394 | 6 | 3.5 |
| Germany | 67 | 344 | 531 | 618 | 602 | | |
| Greece | 11 | 71 | 138 | 160 | 161 | | |
| Hong Kong | 0.5 | 21 | 48 | 63 | 65 | | |
| Hungary | 87 | 215 | 346 | 435 | 480 | | |
| India | 45 | 83 | 111 | 334 | 368 | | |
| Indonesia | 37 | 58 | 168 | 486 | 458 | | |
| Iran | 18 | 53 | 180 | 270 | 275 | | |
| Iraq | 1 | 16 | 56 | 192 | 156 | | |

## RAPESEED

*thousand tonnes*

| | 1950 | 1970 | 1980 | 1990 | 1991 | Rank | % |
|---|---|---|---|---|---|---|---|
| World | 2,820 | 6,617 | 11,093 | 24,416 | 27,217 | | |
| Algeria | ... | ... | 34 | 87 | 93 | | |
| Argentina | ... | 2 | 16 | 7 | 80 | | |
| Australia | ... | 31 | 24 | 114 | 140 | | |
| Austria | 5 | 8 | 7 | 97 | 125 | | |
| Bangladesh | 95 | 132 | 225 | 240 | 210 | | |
| Belgium | 5 | 1 | 1 | 18 | 26 | | |
| Canada | 9 | 1,517 | 2,581 | 3,281 | 4,303 | 3 | 15.8 |
| Chile | ... | 72 | 55 | 53 | 58 | | |
| China | 782 | 996 | 2,952 | 6,958 | 7,436 | 1 | 27.3 |
| Czechoslovakia | 25 | 70 | 165 | 380 | 446 | 9 | 1.6 |
| Denmark | 9 | 30 | 204 | 793 | 734 | 8 | 2.7 |
| Ethiopia | 20 | 20 | 19 | 75 | 76 | | |
| Finland | 6 | 9 | 68 | 117 | 95 | | |
| France | 154 | 603 | 871 | 1,973 | 2,286 | 4 | 8.4 |
| Germany | 193 | 370 | 618 | 2,088 | 2,213 | 5 | 8.1 |
| Hungary | 4 | 46 | 71 | 106 | 120 | | |
| India | 815 | 1,629 | 1,864 | 4,125 | 5,152 | 2 | 18.9 |
| Italy | 14 | 5 | 1 | 44 | 35 | | |
| Japan | 129 | 54 | 4 | 2 | 2 | | |
| Korea, South | 4 | 31 | 25 | 7 | 5 | | |
| Mexico | 6 | 6 | 3 | 3 | 3 | | |
| Netherlands | 33 | 22 | 28 | 26 | 25 | | |
| Norway | 5 | 6 | 10 | 9 | 6 | | |
| Pakistan | 175 | 249 | 249 | 233 | 228 | | |
| Poland | 100 | 455 | 434 | 1,206 | 1,043 | 7 | 3.8 |
| Romania | 4 | 3 | 15 | 11 | 9 | | |
| Spain | 4 | 5 | 15 | 30 | 17 | | |
| Sweden | 146 | 218 | 313 | 401 | 350 | | |
| Switzerland | 4 | 19 | 33 | 43 | 50 | | |
| Turkey | 4 | 5 | 20 | 2 | 5 | | |

| | 1950 | 1970 | 1980 | 1990 | 1991 | Rank | % |
|---|---|---|---|---|---|---|---|
| USSR (former) | 63 | 4 | 17 | 506 | 355 | 10 | 1.3 |
| United Kingdom | 3 | 10 | 274 | 1,231 | 1,330 | 6 | 4.9 |
| United States | 1 | 1 | 1 | 44 | 89 | | |
| Yugoslavia | 5 | 13 | 75 | 72 | 40 | | |

| | 1950 | 1970 | 1980 | 1990 | 1991 | Rank | % |
|---|---|---|---|---|---|---|---|
| Philippines | 1 | 19 | 66 | 185 | 201 | 6 | 4 |
| Sri Lanka | 102 | 150 | 137 | 113 | 102 | 8 | 2 |
| Thailand | 104 | 295 | 502 | 1,100 | 1,200 | 3 | 24 |
| Vietnam | 35 | 36 | 44 | 52 | 55 | 10 | 1 |
| Zaire | 10 | 43 | 21 | 10 | 10 | | |

# RICE

thousand tonnes

| | 1950 | 1970 | 1980 | 1990 | 1991 | Rank | % |
|---|---|---|---|---|---|---|---|
| World | 169,575 | 311,469 | 396,259 | 521,703 | 519,869 | | |
| Afghanistan | 331 | 374 | 458 | 333 | 335 | | |
| Argentina | 137 | 347 | 288 | 467 | 347 | | |
| Australia | 63 | 267 | 678 | 924 | 726 | | |
| Bangladesh | 10,000 | 16,540 | 20,125 | 26,778 | 28,575 | 4 | 6 |
| Brazil | 2,921 | 6,847 | 8,533 | 7,419 | 9,503 | 10 | 2 |
| Burma | 5,481 | 8,107 | 12,637 | 13,969 | 13,201 | 7 | 3 |
| Cambodia | 1,635 | 3,016 | 1,160 | 2,500 | 2,400 | | |
| China | 58,188 | 111,599 | 145,665 | 191,197 | 187,450 | 1 | 36 |
| Colombia | 248 | 756 | 1,831 | 2,117 | 1,739 | | |
| Cuba | 164 | 309 | 455 | 447 | 430 | | |
| Ecuador | 135 | 165 | 378 | 840 | 841 | | |
| Egypt | 971 | 2,567 | 2,376 | 3,167 | 3,152 | | |
| Guinea | 208 | 364 | 438 | 500 | 628 | | |
| India | 33,383 | 62,861 | 74,557 | 111,953 | 110,945 | 2 | 21 |
| Indonesia | 9,441 | 19,136 | 29,570 | 45,179 | 44,321 | 3 | 9 |
| Iran | 424 | 1,041 | 1,448 | 2,273 | 2,100 | | |
| Italy | 723 | 858 | 989 | 1,291 | 1,236 | | |
| Ivory Coast | 104 | 335 | 438 | 687 | 690 | | |
| Japan | 12,736 | 16,281 | 13,320 | 13,124 | 12,005 | 8 | 2 |
| Kazakhstan | ... | ... | ... | ... | 579 | | |
| Korea, North | 1,158 | 2,329 | 4,733 | 5,300 | 5,100 | | |
| Korea, South | 3,385 | 5,573 | 6,780 | 7,732 | 7,478 | | |
| Laos | 530 | 870 | 1,025 | 1,491 | 1,400 | | |
| Madagascar | 829 | 1,865 | 2,055 | 2,420 | 2,200 | | |
| Malaysia | 631 | 1,689 | 2,053 | 1,655 | 1,550 | | |
| Mexico | 173 | 390 | 528 | 394 | 354 | | |
| Nepal | 2,460 | 2,297 | 2,361 | 3,502 | 3,600 | | |
| Nigeria | 250 | 352 | 1,027 | 2,500 | 3,185 | | |
| Pakistan | 2,127 | 3,431 | 4,884 | 4,897 | 4,903 | | |
| Peru | 191 | 539 | 580 | 966 | 814 | | |
| Philippines | 2,767 | 5,225 | 7,893 | 9,319 | 9,670 | 9 | 2 |
| Russia | ... | ... | ... | ... | 896 | | |
| Sierra Leone | 274 | 474 | 504 | 504 | 386 | | |
| Spain | 272 | 384 | 435 | 569 | 582 | | |
| Sri Lanka | 479 | 1,463 | 2,093 | 2,538 | 2,397 | | |
| Taiwan | 1,771 | 2,663 | 2,354 | 1,807 | 1,819 | | |
| Tanzania | 62 | 172 | 251 | 740 | 664 | | |
| Thailand | 6,846 | 13,475 | 16,967 | 17,300 | 20,040 | 5 | 4 |
| USSR (former) | 202 | 1,272 | 2,558 | 2,473 | 2,200 | | |
| United States | 1,925 | 3,953 | 6,968 | 7,080 | 7,006 | | |
| Uruguay | 44 | 132 | 289 | 517 | 540 | | |
| Venezuela | 41 | 208 | 638 | 401 | 608 | | |
| Vietnam | 3,815 | 9,752 | 11,812 | 19,225 | 19,428 | 6 | 4 |

# RUBBER - NATURAL

thousand tonnes

| | 1950 | 1970 | 1980 | 1990 | 1991 | Rank | % |
|---|---|---|---|---|---|---|---|
| World | 1,740 | 3,004 | 3,805 | 4,922 | 5,092 | | |
| Bolivia | 1 | 3 | 5 | 4 | 4 | | |
| Brazil | 22 | 24 | 28 | 33 | 35 | | |
| Burma | 10 | 11 | 16 | 15 | 15 | | |
| Cambodia | 16 | 20 | 7 | 38 | 30 | | |
| Cameroon | 2 | 13 | 17 | 38 | 40 | | |
| China | 5 | 5 | 116 | 264 | 280 | 5 | 6 |
| Ghana | 0.4 | 7 | 10 | 4 | 4 | | |
| Guatemala | 8 | 10 | 11 | 18 | 18 | | |
| India | 17 | 90 | 146 | 297 | 330 | 4 | 7 |
| Indonesia | 635 | 838 | 982 | 1,246 | 1,284 | 1 | 25 |
| Ivory Coast | 10 | 11 | 21 | 74 | 74 | 9 | 2 |
| Liberia | 31 | 78 | 81 | 40 | 9 | | |
| Malaysia | 722 | 1,285 | 1,537 | 1,292 | 1,250 | 2 | 25 |
| Nigeria | 14 | 63 | 49 | 88 | 137 | 7 | 3 |
| Papua New Guinea | 2 | 6 | 4 | 4 | 6 | | |

# SHEEP

thousand head

| | 1950 | 1970 | 1980 | 1990 | 1991 | Rank | % |
|---|---|---|---|---|---|---|---|
| World | 773,843 | 1,076,956 | 1,087,985 | 1,215,633 | 1,202,920 | | |
| Afghanistan | 14,000 | 18,900 | 18,667 | 13,500 | 13,500 | | |
| Albania | 1,633 | 1,249 | 1,232 | 1,600 | 1,600 | | |
| Algeria | 3,990 | 7,940 | 13,111 | 13,350 | 13,350 | | |
| Argentina | 52,940 | 42,773 | 31,473 | 28,571 | 27,552 | | |
| Australia | 111,485 | 177,491 | 134,871 | 170,297 | 162,774 | 1 | 14 |
| Azerbaijan | ... | ... | ... | ... | 5,258 | | |
| Bolivia | 7,224 | 6,825 | 9,050 | 12,220 | 12,300 | | |
| Brazil | 14,427 | 17,768 | 18,414 | 20,100 | 20,300 | | |
| Bulgaria | 8,377 | 9,518 | 10,358 | 8,130 | 7,938 | | |
| Burkina Faso | 590 | 1,657 | 1,855 | 3,150 | 3,339 | | |
| Cameroon | 638 | 2,000 | 2,167 | 3,500 | 3,550 | | |
| Canada | 1,176 | 635 | 729 | 759 | 780 | | |
| Chad | 2,000 | 2,200 | 2,620 | 1,964 | 1,983 | | |
| Chile | 5,789 | 6,179 | 6,059 | 6,650 | 6,650 | | |
| China | 31,070 | 78,000 | 101,864 | 113,508 | 112,820 | 3 | 9 |
| Colombia | 1,153 | 1,935 | 2,399 | 2,690 | 2,745 | | |
| Ecuador | 1,724 | 1,897 | 2,310 | 1,420 | 1,250 | | |
| Egypt | 1,254 | 2,000 | 1,691 | 4,806 | 4,900 | | |
| Ethiopia | 9,559 | 24,077 | 23,250 | 22,960 | 23,000 | | |
| Finland | 1,102 | 963 | 107 | 61 | 57 | | |
| France | 7,499 | 10,023 | 11,452 | 11,790 | 11,490 | | |
| Georgia | ... | ... | ... | ... | 1,834 | | |
| Germany | 3,231 | 2,534 | 3,147 | 4,136 | 3,240 | | |
| Ghana | 443 | 1,324 | 1,942 | 2,224 | 2,500 | | |
| Greece | 6,978 | 7,646 | 8,040 | 10,510 | 9,759 | | |
| Hungary | 1,003 | 2,966 | 2,960 | 2,069 | 1,865 | | |
| India | 36,824 | 40,657 | 44,987 | 54,588 | 55,700 | 5 | 5 |
| Indonesia | 2,038 | 3,169 | 4,124 | 5,900 | 5,750 | | |
| Iran | 11,727 | 32,000 | 33,833 | 45,000 | 45,000 | 6 | 4 |
| Iraq | 10,000 | 12,000 | 10,399 | 9,600 | 7,800 | | |
| Ireland | 2,419 | 4,092 | 2,374 | 5,782 | 6,001 | | |
| Italy | 10,187 | 8,097 | 9,120 | 11,569 | 11,575 | | |
| Kazakhstan | ... | ... | ... | ... | 36,223 | | |
| Kenya | 7,240 | 3,935 | 5,100 | 6,516 | 6,550 | | |
| Kyrgyzstan | ... | ... | ... | ... | 10,486 | | |
| Lesotho | 1,561 | 1,610 | 1,183 | 1,460 | 1,470 | | |
| Libya | 1,390 | 2,125 | 5,046 | 5,200 | 5,500 | | |
| Macedonia | ... | ... | ... | ... | 2,297 | | |
| Mali | 4,080 | 5,700 | 6,247 | 5,850 | 5,850 | | |
| Mauritania | 1,065 | 4,427 | 5,098 | 4,200 | 4,200 | | |
| Mexico | 5,041 | 8,687 | 6,484 | 5,846 | 6,003 | | |
| Moldova | ... | ... | ... | ... | 1,282 | | |
| Mongolia | 12,575 | 12,678 | 14,261 | 14,265 | 15,083 | | |
| Morocco | 11,249 | 17,087 | 15,228 | 14,000 | 14,000 | | |
| Namibia | 2,887 | 4,000 | 5,433 | 3,328 | 6,700 | | |
| Nepal | 2,437 | 2,156 | 730 | 892 | 925 | | |
| Netherlands | 404 | 579 | 856 | 1,702 | 1,800 | | |
| New Zealand | 33,871 | 59,708 | 67,393 | 57,852 | 57,000 | 4 | 5 |
| Niger | 1,324 | 2,632 | 2,979 | 2,970 | 2,970 | | |
| Nigeria | 5,200 | 8,083 | 9,000 | 22,104 | 24,000 | | |
| Norway | 1,819 | 1,769 | 2,033 | 2,211 | 2,211 | | |
| Pakistan | 8,000 | 13,096 | 22,580 | 29,239 | 30,160 | 9 | 3 |
| Peru | 17,515 | 16,698 | 14,565 | 12,257 | 11,250 | | |
| Poland | 2,205 | 3,236 | 4,105 | 4,158 | 3,234 | | |
| Portugal | 4,307 | 4,405 | 4,440 | 5,567 | 5,673 | | |
| Romania | 10,519 | 13,964 | 15,766 | 15,435 | 14,062 | | |
| Russia | ... | ... | ... | ... | 55,200 | | |
| Saudi Arabia | 3,572 | 1,960 | 2,888 | 6,492 | 5,692 | | |
| Senegal | 506 | 1,533 | 1,966 | 3,920 | 4,000 | | |
| Somalia | 2,261 | 8,967 | 11,500 | 14,000 | 13,800 | | |
| South Africa | 33,237 | 35,585 | 31,625 | 32,665 | 32,580 | 8 | 3 |
| Spain | 24,489 | 18,712 | 14,721 | 24,037 | 24,500 | | |
| Sudan | 5,560 | 10,300 | 17,628 | 20,168 | 20,700 | | |
| Syria | 2,968 | 5,843 | 9,311 | 14,509 | 15,321 | | |
| Tajikistan | ... | ... | ... | ... | 3,359 | | |
| Tanzania | 2,333 | 2,823 | 3,754 | 3,557 | 3,556 | | |
| Togo | 264 | 589 | 592 | 1,200 | 1,220 | | |
| Tunisia | 2,462 | 3,200 | 4,651 | 5,966 | 6,290 | | |

| | 1950 | 1970 | 1980 | 1990 | 1991 | Rank | % |
|---|---|---|---|---|---|---|---|
| Turkey | 24,282 | 36,470 | 46,199 | 43,647 | 40,553 | 7 | 3 |
| Turkmenistan | ... | ... | ... | ... | 5,083 | | |
| Uganda | 1,063 | 799 | 1,152 | 1,920 | 1,950 | | |
| Ukraine | ... | ... | ... | ... | 8,419 | | |
| USSR (former) | 76,879 | 136,434 | 142,591 | 138,400 | 134,000 | 2 | 11 |
| United Kingdom | 19,945 | 26,332 | 21,643 | 29,521 | 29,954 | 10 | 3 |
| United States | 31,565 | 20,501 | 12,670 | 11,364 | 11,200 | | |
| Uruguay | 23,149 | 19,906 | 19,219 | 25,220 | 25,986 | | |
| Yemen | ... | 2,800 | 3,002 | 3,756 | 3,800 | | |
| Yugoslavia | 10,493 | 9,136 | 7,359 | 7,596 | 7,431 | | |
| Yugoslavia (Serbia) | ... | ... | ... | ... | 3,044 | | |

| | 1950 | 1970 | 1980 | 1990 | 1991 | Rank | % |
|---|---|---|---|---|---|---|---|
| Tunisia | 19 | 27 | 23 | 38 | 40 | | |
| Turkey | 52 | 226 | 253 | 304 | 303 | 6 | 4.3 |
| Uganda | 12 | 4 | 6 | 11 | 11 | | |
| USSR (former) | 494 | 945 | 834 | 970 | 875 | 1 | 12.5 |
| United Arab Em. | 2 | 2 | 4 | 20 | 22 | | |
| United Kingdom | 143 | 221 | 256 | 370 | 382 | 5 | 5.5 |
| United States | 283 | 250 | 143 | 165 | 165 | | |
| Uruguay | 63 | 72 | 37 | 61 | 64 | | |
| Yemen | ... | 15 | 20 | 38 | 38 | | |
| Yugoslavia | 34 | 50 | 59 | 67 | 66 | | |

## SHEEPMEAT

*thousand tonnes*

| | 1950 | 1970 | 1980 | 1990 | 1991 | Rank | % |
|---|---|---|---|---|---|---|---|
| World | 4,255 | 5,708 | 5,663 | 6,934 | 7,006 | | |
| Afghanistan | 80 | 86 | 128 | 115 | 115 | | |
| Albania | 18 | 16 | 17 | 16 | 15 | | |
| Algeria | 34 | 40 | 61 | 71 | 71 | | |
| Argentina | 194 | 181 | 119 | 88 | 85 | | |
| Australia | 332 | 367 | 539 | 628 | 675 | 2 | 9.6 |
| Belgium | 2 | 7 | 6 | 8 | 8 | | |
| Bolivia | 12 | 14 | 20 | 29 | 30 | | |
| Brazil | 32 | 36 | 32 | 41 | 43 | | |
| Bulgaria | 43 | 71 | 63 | 60 | 59 | | |
| Cameroon | 4 | 9 | 8 | 14 | 15 | | |
| Canada | 16 | 8 | 5 | 9 | 9 | | |
| Chad | 9 | 7 | 11 | 8 | 3 | | |
| Chile | 47 | 24 | 16 | 15 | 16 | | |
| China | 220 | 350 | 237 | 548 | 572 | 3 | 8.2 |
| Colombia | 1 | 2 | 9 | 10 | 10 | | |
| Czechoslovakia | 7 | 5 | 6 | 9 | 6 | | |
| Ecuador | 3 | 11 | 8 | 5 | 5 | | |
| Egypt | 36 | 29 | 22 | 67 | 69 | | |
| Ethiopia | 75 | 80 | 82 | 82 | 82 | | |
| Finland | 7 | 1 | 1 | 1 | 1 | | |
| France | 82 | 113 | 170 | 168 | 167 | 10 | 2.4 |
| Germany | 55 | 21 | 43 | 50 | 47 | | |
| Ghana | 3 | 4 | 5 | 6 | 7 | | |
| Greece | 38 | 61 | 81 | 89 | 87 | | |
| Hungary | 8 | 6 | 7 | 4 | 4 | | |
| Iceland | 6 | 12 | 15 | 10 | 10 | | |
| India | 272 | 112 | 115 | 162 | 166 | | |
| Indonesia | 26 | 13 | 23 | 30 | 44 | | |
| Iran | 90 | 145 | 229 | 231 | 240 | 7 | 3.4 |
| Iraq | 25 | 39 | 46 | 22 | 17 | | |
| Ireland | 21 | 44 | 42 | 84 | 90 | | |
| Italy | 47 | 49 | 65 | 81 | 79 | | |
| Jordan | 5 | 5 | 4 | 6 | 6 | | |
| Kenya | 1 | 13 | 18 | 26 | 26 | | |
| Kuwait | ... | 8 | 21 | 27 | ... | | |
| Lebanon | 2 | 11 | 8 | 11 | 11 | | |
| Libya | 8 | 19 | 49 | 51 | 60 | | |
| Mali | 26 | 18 | 24 | 20 | 20 | | |
| Mauritania | 9 | 6 | 7 | 6 | 6 | | |
| Mexico | 10 | 16 | 22 | 25 | 26 | | |
| Mongolia | 150 | 69 | 96 | 112 | 106 | | |
| Morocco | 60 | 47 | 56 | 55 | 55 | | |
| Namibia | 2 | 12 | 17 | 11 | 50 | | |
| Nepal | 16 | 7 | 2 | 3 | 3 | | |
| Netherlands | 6 | 10 | 18 | 14 | 15 | | |
| New Zealand | 324 | 563 | 567 | 535 | 550 | 4 | 7.9 |
| Niger | 18 | 4 | 12 | 13 | 13 | | |
| Nigeria | 72 | 28 | 31 | 75 | 81 | | |
| Norway | 15 | 17 | 20 | 24 | 25 | | |
| Pakistan | 66 | 67 | 122 | 214 | 229 | 9 | 3.3 |
| Peru | 14 | 23 | 21 | 24 | 19 | | |
| Poland | 7 | 22 | 19 | 29 | 20 | | |
| Portugal | 16 | 19 | 19 | 25 | 25 | | |
| Romania | 14 | 62 | 72 | 66 | 69 | | |
| Saudi Arabia | ... | 14 | 34 | 77 | 78 | | |
| Senegal | 4 | 6 | 1 | 13 | 13 | | |
| Somalia | 15 | 11 | 22 | 38 | 37 | | |
| South Africa | 79 | 168 | 133 | 133 | 133 | | |
| Spain | 78 | 123 | 152 | 217 | 230 | 8 | 3.3 |
| Sudan | 22 | 64 | 82 | 70 | 72 | | |
| Syria | 43 | 40 | 80 | 90 | 91 | | |
| Tanzania | 30 | 10 | 10 | 10 | 10 | | |

## SILK

*tonnes*

| | 1950 | 1970 | 1980 | 1990 | 1991 | Rank | % |
|---|---|---|---|---|---|---|---|
| World | 20,860 | 42,146 | 67,968 | 86,474 | 90,872 | | |
| Afghanistan | ... | 45 | 50 | 60 | 60 | | |
| Brazil | 87 | 270 | 1,300 | 1,693 | 1,929 | 6 | 2 |
| Bulgaria | 100 | 253 | 199 | 150 | 150 | | |
| China | 3,600 | 10,258 | 34,199 | 58,051 | 72,667 | 1 | 80 |
| Greece | 90 | 103 | 33 | 11 | 11 | | |
| India | 927 | 2,245 | 4,926 | 11,000 | 11,900 | 2 | 13 |
| Iran | 176 | 145 | 383 | 537 | 537 | 9 | 1 |
| Italy | 1,452 | 321 | 20 | 2 | 2 | | |
| Japan | 11,624 | 20,562 | 15,624 | 6,000 | 6,000 | 3 | 7 |
| Korea, North | ... | 1,400 | 2,700 | 4,200 | 4,400 | 4 | 5 |
| Korea, South | 455 | 2,876 | 3,311 | 1,400 | 1,400 | 7 | 2 |
| Lebanon | 31 | 12 | 5 | 6 | 6 | | |
| Romania | 100 | 106 | 120 | 150 | 150 | | |
| Spain | 36 | 29 | 15 | 15 | 15 | | |
| Thailand | ... | ... | 883 | 1,250 | 1,300 | 8 | 1 |
| Turkey | 150 | 146 | 233 | 270 | 270 | | |
| USSR (former) | 1,855 | 3,009 | 3,625 | 4,094 | 4,100 | 5 | 5 |
| Vietnam | ... | 233 | 246 | 500 | 500 | 10 | 1 |

## SISAL

*thousand tonnes*

| | 1970 | 1980 | 1990 | 1991 | Rank | % |
|---|---|---|---|---|---|---|
| World | 312 | 527 | 377 | 386 | | |
| Angola | 65 | 7 | 1 | 1 | | |
| Brazil | 229 | 234 | 185 | 185 | 1 | 47.9 |
| China | 9 | 20 | 16 | 17 | 6 | 4.4 |
| Cuba | 2 | 5 | 7 | 7 | 10 | 1.8 |
| Ethiopia | 2 | 1 | 1 | 1 | | |
| Haiti | 16 | 12 | 10 | 10 | 7 | 2.6 |
| Indonesia | 5 | 1 | 1 | 1 | | |
| Kenya | 46 | 42 | 40 | 39 | 4 | 10.1 |
| Madagascar | 26 | 15 | 21 | 21 | 5 | 5.4 |
| Mexico | 50 | 86 | 39 | 45 | 2 | 11.7 |
| Morocco | 1 | 1 | 2 | 2 | | |
| Mozambique | 28 | 11 | 1 | 1 | | |
| South Africa | 8 | 6 | 7 | 8 | 9 | 2.1 |
| Tanzania | 198 | 80 | 38 | 40 | 3 | 10.4 |
| Venezuela | 12 | 6 | 8 | 9 | 8 | 2.3 |

## SORGHUM

*thousand tonnes*

| | 1950 | 1970 | 1980 | 1990 | 1991 | Rank | % |
|---|---|---|---|---|---|---|---|
| World | 27,000 | 55,629 | 65,651 | 56,677 | 57,763 | | |
| Argentina | 100 | 3,823 | 5,641 | 2,016 | 2,251 | 7 | 3.9 |
| Australia | 75 | 759 | 1,084 | 946 | 893 | 9 | 1.5 |
| Benin | 50 | 52 | 59 | 99 | 106 | | |
| Brazil | ... | 2 | 172 | 228 | 272 | | |
| Burkina Faso | 370 | 528 | 620 | 751 | 1,113 | 8 | 1.9 |
| Burundi | 60 | 105 | 53 | 64 | 88 | | |
| Cameroon | ... | ... | 301 | 350 | 400 | | |

| | 1950 | 1970 | 1980 | 1990 | 1991 | Rank | % |
|---|---|---|---|---|---|---|---|
| Chad | ... | ... | 210 | 280 | 365 | | |
| China | ... | 8,607 | 7,034 | 5,777 | 5,615 | 3 | 9.7 |
| Colombia | 20 | 153 | 488 | 777 | 738 | | |
| Egypt | ... | ... | 641 | 630 | 655 | | |
| El Salvador | ... | 115 | 144 | 145 | 161 163 | | |
| Ethiopia | 150 | 027 | 1,140 | 707 | 805 | 10 | 1.4 |
| France | 1 | 203 | 332 | 264 | 388 | | |
| Ghana | 79 | 147 | 140 | 136 | 241 | | |
| Guatemala | 12 | 46 | 80 | 87 | 80 | | |
| Haiti | 174 | 210 | 121 | 68 | 70 | | |
| Honduras | 47 | 46 | 49 | 81 | 93 | | |
| India | 5,981 | 8,516 | 11,380 | 11,878 | 10,800 | 2 | 18.7 |
| Italy | 5 | 15 | 73 | 114 | 150 | | |
| Kenya | 50 | 215 | 160 | 145 | 140 | | |
| Korea, North | 10 | 115 | 18 | 15 | 16 | | |
| Lesotho | 23 | 57 | 59 | 28 | 18 | | |
| Malawi | 38 | 78 | 20 | 15 | 19 | | |
| Mali | ... | ... | 341 | 531 | 729 | | |
| Mauritania | ... | ... | 28 | 46 | 59 | | |
| Mexico | 200 | 2,573 | 4,991 | 5,978 | 4,367 | 5 | 7.6 |
| Morocco | 81 | 70 | 20 | 14 | 14 | | |
| Mozambique | 140 | 202 | 181 | 175 | 155 | | |
| Nicaragua | 36 | 57 | 80 | 76 | 70 | | |
| Niger | 215 | 262 | 347 | 286 | 472 | | |
| Nigeria | 1,500 | 3,632 | 3,341 | 4,185 | 4,800 | 4 | 8.3 |
| Pakistan | 239 | 308 | 235 | 239 | 260 | | |
| Rwanda | 80 | 141 | 178 | 151 | 205 | | |
| Saudi Arabia | 14 | 185 | 123 | 81 | 85 | | |
| Senegal | ... | ... | 131 | 147 | 85 | | |
| Somalia | 30 | 132 | 167 | 250 | 145 | | |
| South Africa | 180 | 376 | 540 | 275 | 251 | | |
| Spain | 4 | 168 | 181 | 86 | 108 | | |
| Sudan | 601 | 1,525 | 2,361 | 1,180 | 2,941 | 6 | 5.1 |
| Tanzania | 250 | 156 | 543 | 368 | 480 | | |
| Thailand | 20 | 123 | 237 | 237 | 233 | | |
| Togo | ... | ... | 87 | 115 | 106 | | |
| Uganda | 240 | 337 | 312 | 360 | 380 | | |
| USSR (former) | 56 | 62 | 103 | 150 | 155 | | |
| United States | 3,896 | 19,314 | 19,157 | 14,562 | 14,720 | 1 | 25.5 |
| Uruguay | 10 | 53 | 112 | 59 | 90 | | |
| Venezuela | 3 | 5 | 365 | 376 | 616 | | |
| Yemen | ... | 878 | 616 | 441 | 132 | | |
| Zambia | 122 | 49 | 16 | 20 | 40 | | |
| Zimbabwe | 100 | 98 | 71 | 91 | 68 | | |

# SOYABEANS

*thousand tonnes*

| | 1950 | 1970 | 1980 | 1990 | 1991 | Rank | % |
|---|---|---|---|---|---|---|---|
| World | 16,000 | 43,487 | 85,967 | 108,134 | 103,065 | | |
| Argentina | 4 | 39 | 3,657 | 10,700 | 11,250 | 3 | 10.9 |
| Australia | ... | 5 | 85 | 77 | 70 | | |
| Bolivia | ... | 2 | 49 | 233 | 384 | | |
| Brazil | 83 | 1,547 | 13,468 | 19,888 | 14,771 | 2 | 14.3 |
| Canada | 86 | 257 | 651 | 1,292 | 1,406 | 7 | 1.4 |
| China | 7,200 | 8,131 | 8,266 | 11,008 | 9,807 | 4 | 9.5 |
| Colombia | ... | 114 | 130 | 232 | 194 | | |
| Ecuador | ... | 2 | 32 | 167 | 169 | | |
| Egypt | ... | ... | 110 | 107 | 135 | | |
| France | ... | ... | 19 | 245 | 150 | | |
| India | ... | 2 | 359 | 2,419 | 2,100 | 5 | 2 |
| Indonesia | 270 | 468 | 679 | 1,487 | 1,549 | 6 | 1.5 |
| Iran | ... | 15 | 65 | 105 | 105 | | |
| Italy | ... | ... | ... | 1,751 | 1,325 | 8 | 1.3 |
| Japan | 376 | 128 | 192 | 220 | 260 | | |
| Korea, North | ... | 255 | 340 | 455 | 460 | | |
| Korea, South | 136 | 228 | 243 | 233 | 183 | | |
| Mexico | ... | 252 | 580 | 575 | 718 | | |
| Nigeria | 3 | 61 | 60 | 60 | 65 | | |
| Paraguay | ... | 46 | 616 | 1,795 | 1,304 | 9 | 1.3 |
| Romania | 5 | 102 | 262 | 141 | 179 | | |
| South Africa | ... | ... | 32 | 94 | 126 | | |
| Taiwan | 15 | 65 | 26 | 8 | 8 | | |
| Thailand | 14 | 51 | 111 | 578 | 605 | | |
| Turkey | 2 | 11 | 7 | 162 | 150 | | |
| USSR (former) | 166 | 400 | 494 | 880 | 760 | 10 | 0.7 |
| United States | 7,312 | 31,174 | 54,861 | 52,416 | 54,039 | 1 | 52.4 |
| Yugoslavia | 4 | 5 | 64 | 157 | 147 | | |
| Zimbabwe | ... | ... | 86 | 110 | 97 | | |

# SUGAR

*thousand tonnes*

| | 1950 | 1970 | 1980 | 1990 | 1991 | Rank | % |
|---|---|---|---|---|---|---|---|
| World | 32,296 | 72,176 | 88,632 | 110,823 | 112,224 | | |
| Angola | 47 | 74 | 31 | 25 | 32 | | |
| Argentina | 638 | 985 | 1,584 | 1,351 | 1,594 | | |
| Australia | 913 | 2,511 | 3,243 | 3,536 | 2,800 | | |
| Austria | 104 | 315 | 450 | 451 | 462 | | |
| Bangladesh | ... | 90 | 595 | 200 | 262 | | |
| Barbados | 168 | 146 | 113 | 70 | 67 | | |
| Belgium | 330 | 711 | 994 | 1,120 | 905 | | |
| Belize | 2 | 62 | 101 | 106 | 108 | | |
| Bolivia | 1 | 120 | 250 | 271 | 355 | | |
| Brazil | 1,649 | 5,161 | 8,191 | 7,835 | 8,675 | 3 | 7.7 |
| Bulgaria | 64 | 218 | 165 | 35 | 115 | | |
| Canada | 122 | 130 | 112 | 147 | 152 | | |
| Chile | ... | 217 | 131 | 373 | 359 | | |
| China | 986 | 3,878 | 4,160 | 7,197 | 7,836 | 4 | 7 |
| Colombia | 178 | 710 | 2,117 | 1,589 | 1,617 | | |
| Congo | ... | 78 | 13 | 40 | 40 | | |
| Costa Rica | 26 | 160 | 214 | 230 | 250 | | |
| Cuba | 5,786 | 6,388 | 7,510 | 8,445 | 7,623 | 5 | 6.7 |
| Czechoslovakia | 697 | 731 | 808 | 686 | 714 | | |
| Denmark | 319 | 307 | 493 | 572 | 500 | | |
| Dominican Rep. | 552 | 1,010 | 1,142 | 590 | 656 | | |
| Ecuador | 56 | 258 | 402 | 311 | 319 | | |
| Egypt | 196 | 564 | 666 | 971 | 1,064 | | |
| El Salvador | 28 | 128 | 228 | 213 | 287 | | |
| Ethiopia | ... | 98 | 168 | 186 | 155 | | |
| Fiji | 122 | 329 | 446 | 408 | 389 | | |
| Finland | 20 | 60 | 104 | 168 | 174 | | |
| France | 1,085 | 2,872 | 4,720 | 4,743 | 4,675 | 7 | 4.2 |
| Germany | 1,523 | 2,645 | 3,936 | 4,671 | 4,245 | 8 | 3.8 |
| Greece | ... | 163 | 286 | 312 | 297 | | |
| Guadeloupe | 73 | 154 | 86 | 26 | 53 | | |
| Guatemala | 31 | 191 | 448 | 839 | 918 | | |
| Guyana | 218 | 354 | 291 | 134 | 145 | | |
| Haiti | 53 | 64 | 135 | 35 | 30 | | |
| Honduras | 5 | 60 | 203 | 185 | 186 | | |
| Hungary | 232 | 321 | 511 | 595 | 736 | | |
| India | 1,316 | 4,188 | 13,487 | 11,168 | 12,528 | 1 | 11.2 |
| Indonesia | 287 | 760 | 1,587 | 2,218 | 2,334 | | |
| Iran | 54 | 571 | 630 | 625 | 760 | | |
| Ireland | 93 | 164 | 178 | 245 | 226 | | |
| Italy | 598 | 1,271 | 1,956 | 1,584 | 1,640 | | |
| Ivory Coast | ... | ... | 97 | 154 | 155 | | |
| Jamaica | 279 | 383 | 247 | 209 | 237 | | |
| Japan | 21 | 628 | 789 | 925 | 915 | | |
| Kenya | 15 | 132 | 416 | 467 | 532 | | |
| Madagascar | 16 | 103 | 115 | 118 | 116 | | |
| Malawi | ... | 32 | 140 | 189 | 195 | | |
| Martinique | 40 | 29 | 6 | 6 | 7 | | |
| Mauritius | 443 | 659 | 615 | 624 | 580 | | |
| Mexico | 733 | 2,495 | 2,864 | 3,278 | 3,943 | 10 | 3.5 |
| Morocco | ... | 168 | 364 | 638 | 675 | | |
| Mozambique | 85 | 278 | 189 | 32 | 33 | | |
| Netherlands | 364 | 769 | 1,000 | 1,337 | 1,060 | | |
| Nicaragua | 27 | 147 | 204 | 201 | 225 | | |
| Pakistan | 55 | 557 | 738 | 2,017 | 2,086 | | |
| Panama | 16 | 78 | 184 | 97 | 128 | | |
| Paraguay | 20 | 50 | 85 | 106 | 110 | | |
| Peru | 496 | 782 | 586 | 601 | 550 | | |
| Philippines | 827 | 1,859 | 2,318 | 1,810 | 1,780 | | |
| Poland | 871 | 1,581 | 1,530 | 2,142 | 1,587 | | |
| Puerto Rico | 1,157 | 383 | 158 | 62 | 67 | | |
| Réunion | 116 | 220 | 247 | 191 | 237 | | |
| Romania | 116 | 434 | 595 | 405 | 310 | | |
| St Christopher-N. | 45 | 30 | 37 | 15 | 20 | | |
| South Africa | 555 | 1,629 | 2,011 | 2,289 | 2,152 | | |
| Spain | 315 | 882 | 934 | 1,043 | 1,037 | | |
| Sudan | ... | 85 | 166 | 421 | 470 | | |
| Swaziland | ... | 167 | 317 | 527 | 500 | | |
| Sweden | 285 | 233 | 350 | 429 | 270 | | |
| Switzerland | 27 | 65 | 119 | 160 | 132 | | |
| Taiwan | 520 | 588 | 830 | 475 | 409 | | |
| Tanzania | 10 | 100 | 124 | 108 | 116 | | |
| Thailand | 34 | 436 | 2,134 | 3,506 | 4,006 | 9 | 3.6 |
| Trinidad & Tobago | 151 | 229 | 125 | 118 | 104 | | |
| Turkey | 161 | 700 | 1,178 | 1,946 | 1,957 | | |
| Uganda | 56 | 154 | 14 | 25 | 46 | | |
| USSR (former) | 2,700 | 8,722 | 7,017 | 9,130 | 8,750 | 2 | 7.8 |

| | 1950 | 1970 | 1980 | 1990 | 1991 | Rank | % |
|---|---|---|---|---|---|---|---|
| United Kingdom | 626 | 1,033 | 1,215 | 1,349 | 1,292 | | |
| United States | 2,785 | 5,215 | 5,342 | 6,273 | 6,531 | 6 | 5.8 |
| Venezuela | 60 | 448 | 351 | 499 | 556 | | |
| Vietnam | 1 | 7 | 207 | 376 | 380 | | |
| Yugoslavia | 132 | 440 | 798 | 934 | 663 | | |
| Zambia | ... | 37 | 105 | 147 | 152 | | |
| Zimbabwe | 1 | 155 | 336 | 464 | 329 | | |

This is raw sugar manufactured from beet and cane.

## TEA

*thousand tonnes*

| | 1950 | 1970 | 1980 | 1990 | 1991 | Rank | % |
|---|---|---|---|---|---|---|---|
| World | 639 | 1,341 | 1,858 | 2,533 | 2,576 | | |
| Argentina | ... | 26 | 29 | 43 | 48 | 9 | 1.9 |
| Bangladesh | 22 | 25 | 38 | 39 | 38 | | |
| Bolivia | ... | 1 | 2 | 2 | 3 | | |
| Brazil | 1 | 6 | 10 | 10 | 10 | | |
| Burundi | 1 | 1 | 2 | 4 | 4 | | |
| Cameroon | ... | 1 | 2 | 3 | 3 | | |
| China | 70 | 246 | 334 | 562 | 566 | 2 | 22 |
| Ecuador | ... | 1 | 2 | 1 | 1 | | |
| India | 273 | 416 | 558 | 715 | 730 | 1 | 28.3 |
| Indonesia | 39 | 65 | 104 | 149 | 158 | 5 | 6.1 |
| Iran | 5 | 18 | 32 | 44 | 45 | 10 | 1.7 |
| Japan | 41 | 91 | 101 | 90 | 90 | 8 | 3.5 |
| Kenya | 6 | 38 | 93 | 197 | 204 | 4 | 7.9 |
| Malawi | 7 | 18 | 31 | 39 | 41 | | |
| Malaysia | 2 | 3 | 3 | 5 | 5 | | |
| Mauritius | ... | 4 | 5 | 6 | 6 | | |
| Mozambique | 3 | 17 | 20 | 2 | 2 | | |
| Papua New Guinea | ... | 1 | 8 | 8 | 9 | | |
| Peru | ... | 2 | 2 | 3 | 3 | | |
| Rwanda | ... | 1 | 6 | 13 | 13 | | |
| South Africa | ... | 1 | 8 | 13 | 14 | | |
| Sri Lanka | 140 | 215 | 203 | 238 | 241 | 3 | 9.4 |
| Taiwan | 11 | 28 | 24 | 22 | 21 | | |
| Tanzania | 1 | 9 | 17 | 20 | 21 | | |
| Thailand | ... | 1 | 1 | 5 | 5 | | |
| Turkey | ... | 34 | 80 | 123 | 136 | 6 | 5.3 |
| Uganda | 2 | 18 | 2 | 7 | 8 | | |
| USSR (former) | 21 | 65 | 128 | 136 | 118 | 7 | 4.6 |
| Vietnam | 6 | 10 | 21 | 31 | 32 | | |
| Zaire | ... | 8 | 6 | 3 | 3 | | |
| Zimbabwe | ... | 3 | 9 | 17 | 16 | | |

## TOBACCO

*thousand tonnes*

| | 1950 | 1970 | 1980 | 1990 | 1991 | Rank | % |
|---|---|---|---|---|---|---|---|
| World | 2,851 | 4,603 | 5,575 | 7,076 | 7,662 | | |
| Albania | 2 | 12 | 18 | 15 | 12 | | |
| Algeria | 20 | 5 | 4 | 4 | 5 | | |
| Argentina | 30 | 60 | 61 | 68 | 94 | | |
| Australia | 2 | 18 | 15 | 12 | 14 | | |
| Bangladesh | ... | 43 | 44 | 38 | 36 | | |
| Brazil | 113 | 246 | 397 | 444 | 414 | 4 | 5.4 |
| Bulgaria | 45 | 113 | 138 | 77 | 74 | | |
| Burma | 47 | 53 | 53 | 40 | 40 | | |
| Cambodia | 5 | 12 | 5 | 13 | 14 | | |
| Canada | 62 | 105 | 100 | 63 | 68 | | |
| Chile | 7 | 7 | 6 | 14 | 15 | | |
| China | 132 | 801 | 1,134 | 2,617 | 3,121 | 1 | 40.7 |
| Colombia | 21 | 42 | 52 | 33 | 40 | | |
| Cuba | 32 | 31 | 32 | 44 | 44 | | |
| Czechoslovakia | 8 | 6 | 5 | 5 | 5 | | |
| Dominican Rep. | 18 | 22 | 41 | 19 | 25 | | |
| France | 48 | 45 | 47 | 28 | 27 | | |
| Germany | 24 | 8 | 12 | 10 | 7 | | |
| Greece | 49 | 88 | 125 | 130 | 178 | 9 | 2.3 |
| Guatemala | 2 | 5 | 10 | 7 | 7 | | |
| Honduras | 4 | 6 | 7 | 6 | 7 | | |
| Hungary | 23 | 20 | 21 | 14 | 19 | | |

| | 1950 | 1970 | 1980 | 1990 | 1991 | Rank | % |
|---|---|---|---|---|---|---|---|
| India | 247 | 353 | 458 | 550 | 560 | 3 | 7.3 |
| Indonesia | 64 | 73 | 105 | 150 | 159 | 10 | 2.1 |
| Iran | 12 | 18 | 24 | 25 | 25 | | |
| Iraq | 3 | 15 | 10 | 4 | 2 | | |
| Italy | 76 | 79 | 131 | 194 | 192 | 7 | 2.5 |
| Japan | 90 | 163 | 144 | 78 | 71 | | |
| Kenya | 1 | 2 | 3 | 9 | 10 | | |
| Korea, North | 12 | 40 | 45 | 65 | 66 | | |
| Korea, South | 15 | 60 | 97 | 70 | 73 | | |
| Madagascar | 4 | 5 | 3 | 4 | 4 | | |
| Malawi | 13 | 21 | 53 | 101 | 125 | | |
| Malaysia | 2 | 3 | 8 | 11 | 11 | | |
| Mexico | 35 | 72 | 74 | 62 | 20 | | |
| Morocco | 2 | 3 | 7 | / | / | | |
| Nepal | 6 | 7 | 5 | 7 | 7 | | |
| Nigeria | 11 | 13 | 13 | 9 | 9 | | |
| Pakistan | 68 | 118 | 71 | 68 | 76 | | |
| Paraguay | 8 | 20 | 19 | 5 | 5 | | |
| Philippines | 21 | 58 | 57 | 82 | 79 | | |
| Poland | 25 | 82 | 75 | 59 | 57 | | |
| Portugal | 7 | 10 | 7 | 5 | 6 | | |
| Romania | 17 | 26 | 35 | 32 | 34 | | |
| South Africa | 23 | 35 | 37 | 34 | 35 | | |
| Spain | 19 | 24 | 38 | 36 | 43 | | |
| Sri Lanka | 3 | 9 | 15 | 10 | 11 | | |
| Syria | 6 | 8 | 13 | 13 | 16 | | |
| Tanzania | 2 | 12 | 17 | 14 | 14 | | |
| Thailand | 27 | 77 | 78 | 71 | 71 | | |
| Turkey | 91 | 157 | 204 | 288 | 247 | 5 | 3.2 |
| Uganda | 2 | 5 | 3 | 3 | 4 | | |
| USSR (former) | 157 | 256 | 285 | 260 | 240 | 6 | 3.1 |
| United States | 959 | 819 | 813 | 738 | 753 | 2 | 9.8 |
| Venezuela | 10 | 12 | 16 | 15 | 12 | | |
| Vietnam | 5 | 12 | 20 | 18 | 28 | | |
| Yemen | 1 | 2 | 7 | 7 | 7 | | |
| Yugoslavia | 24 | 46 | 65 | 46 | 46 | | |
| Zaire | 3 | 5 | 7 | 4 | 4 | | |
| Zambia | 3 | 6 | 4 | 4 | 5 | | |
| Zimbabwe | 42 | 63 | 104 | 140 | 178 | 8 | 2.3 |

## WHALING

*number*

| | 1970 | 1980 | 1988 | 1989 | 1990 |
|---|---|---|---|---|---|
| *Minke whale* | | | | | |
| World | ... | 11,828 | 421 | 334 | 432 |
| Brazil | ... | 902 | 0 | ... | ... |
| Greenland | ... | ... | 119 | 73 | 95 |
| Japan | ... | 3,658 | 273 | 241 | 330 |
| Korea, South | ... | 925 | 0 | ... | ... |
| Norway | ... | 2,002 | 29 | 17 | 7 |
| USSR (former) | ... | 3,879 | 0 | ... | ... |
| *Bryde's whale* | | | | | |
| World | 910 | 522 | 0 | ... | ... |
| Japan | ... | 307 | 0 | ... | ... |
| *Sei whale* | | | | | |
| World | 10,466 | 102 | 10 | 2 | ... |
| Iceland | ... | 100 | 10 | ... | ... |
| *Fin whale* | | | | | |
| World | 4,547 | 472 | 77 | 78 | 19 |
| Iceland | ... | 236 | 68 | 68 | ... |
| Denmark | ... | ... | 9 | ... | ... |
| Spain | ... | 219 | 0 | ... | ... |
| *Humpback whale* | | | | | |
| Denmark | 24 | 15 | 0 | ... | ... |
| *Baleen whale* | | | | | |
| World | ... | 217 | 173 | 198 | 192 |
| United States | ... | ... | 23 | 19 | 30 |
| USSR (former) | ... | 178 | 150 | 179 | 162 |
| *Sperm whale* | | | | | |
| World | 22,904 | 2,210 | 8 | ... | ... |
| Japan | ... | 1,192 | 0 | ... | ... |
| Portugal | ... | 330... | ... | ... | ... |
| *Longfin Pilot whale* | | | | | |
| World | ... | 2,820 | 1,705 | 1,262 | 916 |
| Faroe Is. | ... | 2,773 | 1,690 | 1,258 | 916 |
| *Killer whale* | | | | | |
| World | ... | 971 | 0 | 9 | 3 |
| Japan | 0 | 9 | 3 | | |
| *Beluga whale* | | | | | |

|  | 1970 | 1980 | 1988 | 1989 | 1990 |
|---|---|---|---|---|---|
| World | ... | 1,909 | 13 | 1,356 | 1,283 |
| Canada | ... | 774 | 5 | 1,043 | ... |
| Greenland | ... | 889 | 0 | 50 | 1,000 |
| USSR (former) | ... | 236 | 8 | 27 | 44 |
| *Narwhal* |  |  |  |  |  |
| World | 520 | 0 | 362 | 1,200 |  |
| Greenland | ... | 520 | 0 | 342 | 1,200 |
| *Toothed whale* |  |  |  |  |  |
| World | ... | 381 | 128,905 | 163,708 | 102,041 |
| Japan | ... | ... | 48,816 | 52,930 | 41,414 |

# WINE

*thousand tonnes*

|  | 1950 | 1970 | 1980 | 1990 | 1991 | Rank | % |
|---|---|---|---|---|---|---|---|
| World | 18,901 | 28,884 | 34,790 | 29,010 | 27,767 |  |  |
| Algeria | 1,348 | 888 | 274 | 48 | 50 |  |  |
| Argentina | 1,136 | 1,935 | 2,364 | 1,910 | 1,465 | 6 | 5.2 |
| Australia | 145 | 259 | 375 | 445 | 400 |  |  |
| Austria | 92 | 239 | 265 | 317 | 300 |  |  |
| Brazil | 102 | 179 | 258 | 311 | 311 |  |  |
| Bulgaria | 248 | 436 | 455 | 293 | 293 |  |  |
| Canada | 22 | 39 | 45 | 46 | 50 |  |  |
| Chile | 313 | 443 | 591 | 398 | 390 |  |  |
| China | ... | ... | 38 | 90 | 95 |  |  |
| Cyprus | 13 | 45 | 54 | 60 | 60 |  |  |
| Czechoslovakia | 31 | 100 | 139 | 142 | 134 |  |  |
| France | 5,245 | 6,298 | 7,063 | 6,553 | 6,200 | 1 | 22.3 |
| Germany | 232 | 754 | 700 | 949 | 1,015 | 7 | 3.7 |
| Greece | 370 | 454 | 447 | 353 | 450 |  |  |
| Hungary | 316 | 476 | 491 | 547 | 547 |  |  |
| Israel | 6 | 33 | 18 | 13 | 13 |  |  |
| Italy | 4,342 | 6,825 | 8,075 | 5,487 | 5,915 | 2 | 21.3 |
| Japan | 4 | 16 | 55 | 55 | 55 |  |  |
| Mexico | 1 | 17 | 187 | 163 | 145 |  |  |
| Morocco | 64 | 100 | 95 | 30 | 30 |  |  |
| New Zealand | 3 | 18 | 44 | 49 | 49 |  |  |
| Portugal | 817 | 959 | 1,127 | 1,097 | 991 | 8 | 3.6 |
| Romania | 402 | 584 | 880 | 598 | 600 | 10 | 2.2 |
| South Africa | 224 | 489 | 703 | 952 | 963 | 9 | 3.5 |
| Spain | 1,539 | 2,485 | 4,142 | 4,090 | 3,107 | 3 | 11.2 |
| Switzerland | 70 | 91 | 88 | 120 | 124 |  |  |
| Tunisia | 74 | 79 | 60 | 27 | 41 |  |  |
| Turkey | 15 | 44 | 17 | 24 | 24 |  |  |
| USSR (former) | 277 | 2,630 | 3,200 | 1,570 | 1,800 | 4 | 6.5 |
| United States | 904 | 1,183 | 1,678 | 1,585 | 1,490 | 5 | 5.4 |
| Uruguay | 79 | 86 | 70 | 90 | 80 |  |  |
| Yugoslavia | 414 | 603 | 727 | 517 | 500 |  |  |

# WHEAT

*thousand tonnes*

|  | 1950 | 1970 | 1980 | 1990 | 1991 | Rank | % |
|---|---|---|---|---|---|---|---|
| World | 190,000 | 329,033 | 442,768 | 601,723 | 550,993 |  |  |
| Afghanistan | 1,700 | 2,150 | 2,788 | 1,650 | 1,726 |  |  |
| Albania | 89 | 242 | 500 | 450 | 300 |  |  |
| Algeria | 996 | 1,359 | 1,270 | 1,005 | 1,741 |  |  |
| Argentina | 5,175 | 5,873 | 7,993 | 11,014 | 9,000 |  |  |
| Armenia | ... | ... | ... | 310 |  |  |  |
| Australia | 5,161 | 9,014 | 14,486 | 15,402 | 9,633 |  |  |
| Austria | 348 | 912 | 1,025 | 1,404 | 1,341 |  |  |
| Bangladesh | 55 | 103 | 803 | 890 | 1,004 |  |  |
| Belgium | 555 | 848 | 955 | 1,409 | 1,620 |  |  |
| Bosnia | ... | ... | ... | 413 |  |  |  |
| Brazil | 498 | 1,743 | 2,614 | 3,094 | 3,077 |  |  |
| Bulgaria | 1,776 | 2,899 | 3,877 | 5,292 | 4,503 |  |  |
| Canada | 13,443 | 13,901 | 20,287 | 32,708 | 32,822 | 6 | 6 |
| Chile | 942 | 1,296 | 882 | 1,718 | 1,589 |  |  |
| China | 16,000 | 31,005 | 57,965 | 98,232 | 95,003 | 1 | 17.2 |
| Croatia | ... | ... | ... | 1,495 |  |  |  |
| Czechoslovakia | 1,493 | 3,436 | 4,507 | 6,707 | 6,205 |  |  |
| Denmark | 285 | 509 | 678 | 3,953 | 3,629 |  |  |
| Egypt | 1,111 | 1,509 | 1,834 | 4,268 | 4,483 |  |  |
| Ethiopia | 460 | 643 | 470 | 867 | 890 |  |  |
| Finland | 263 | 445 | 267 | 627 | 431 |  |  |
| France | 7,791 | 14,112 | 21,996 | 33,312 | 34,483 | 5 | 6.3 |
| Germany | 3,912 | 8,471 | 11,248 | 15,242 | 16,669 | 8 | 3 |
| Greece | 894 | 1,867 | 2,703 | 1,965 | 2,750 |  |  |
| Hungary | 1,909 | 3,410 | 4,862 | 6,198 | 5,954 |  |  |
| India | 6,087 | 20,859 | 34,599 | 49,850 | 54,522 | 3 | 9.9 |
| Iran | 1,863 | 3,946 | 5,700 | 8,218 | 8,900 |  |  |
| Iraq | 448 | 1,080 | 1,297 | 1,196 | 525 |  |  |
| Ireland | 327 | 375 | 240 | 625 | 703 |  |  |
| Italy | 7,170 | 9,756 | 9,017 | 8,109 | 9,289 |  |  |
| Japan | 1,375 | 557 | 579 | 952 | 860 |  |  |
| Kazakhstan | ... | ... | ... | 16,200 | ... |  |  |
| Mexico | 534 | 2,141 | 2,771 | 3,931 | 4,115 |  |  |
| Morocco | 786 | 1,819 | 1,500 | 3,614 | 4,939 |  |  |
| Nepal | ... | 230 | 444 | 855 | 836 |  |  |
| Netherlands | 324 | 675 | 867 | 1,076 | 916 |  |  |
| New Zealand | 139 | 357 | 325 | 188 | 176 |  |  |
| Pakistan | 3,630 | 6,796 | 10,698 | 14,316 | 14,505 | 9 | 2.6 |
| Poland | 1,833 | 4,925 | 4,197 | 9,026 | 9,269 |  |  |
| Portugal | 499 | 614 | 331 | 296 | 323 |  |  |
| Romania | 2,486 | 4,433 | 5,634 | 7,290 | 5,442 |  |  |
| Russia | ... | ... | ... | 49,600 | ... |  |  |
| Saudi Arabia | 16 | 111 | 150 | 3,600 | 4,000 |  |  |
| South Africa | 555 | 1,461 | 1,882 | 1,702 | 2,245 |  |  |
| Spain | 3,626 | 4,734 | 4,435 | 4,760 | 5,392 |  |  |
| Sudan | ... | 134 | 205 | 408 | 680 |  |  |
| Sweden | 677 | 958 | 1,086 | 2,243 | 1,524 |  |  |
| Switzerland | 260 | 378 | 403 | 563 | 574 |  |  |
| Syria | 761 | 763 | 1,877 | 2,070 | 2,135 |  |  |
| Tunisia | 452 | 520 | 837 | 1,122 | 1,786 |  |  |
| Turkey | 4,770 | 11,423 | 17,054 | 20,000 | 20,400 | 7 | 3.7 |
| Ukraine | ... | ... | ... | 30,370 | ... |  |  |
| USSR (former) | 35,759 | 92,804 | 92,131 | 109,600 | 80,000 | 2 | 14.5 |
| United Kingdom | 2,397 | 4,110 | 8,034 | 14,000 | 14,300 | 10 | 2.6 |
| United States | 31,065 | 40,034 | 66,242 | 74,475 | 53,915 | 4 | 9.8 |
| Uruguay | 469 | 379 | 377 | 539 | 136 |  |  |
| Yugoslavia | 2,171 | 4,760 | 4,624 | 6,359 | 6,530 |  |  |
| Yugoslavia (Serbia) | ... | ... | ... | 4,109 | ... |  |  |

# WOOD - CONIFEROUS*

*million cubic metres*

|  | 1961–65 av. | 1970 | 1980 | 1990 | 1991 | Rank | % |
|---|---|---|---|---|---|---|---|
| World | 959 | 1,081 | 1,190 | 1,400 | 1,295 |  |  |
| Afghanistan | 1.7 | 2.3 | 2.4 | 2.4 | 2.5 |  |  |
| Algeria | 0.7 | 0.8 | 1.1 | 1.5 | 1.5 |  |  |
| Argentina | 0.5 | 0.6 | 0.9 | 2 | 2 |  |  |
| Australia | 1.8 | 2.5 | 4.3 | 7.5 | 7.2 |  |  |
| Austria | 9.4 | 10 | 12.1 | 15 | 14.2 |  |  |
| Belgium | 1.4 | 1.5 | 1.5 | 4 | 3.4 |  |  |
| Brazil | 16.9 | 26.1 | 38 | 46.4 | 46.7 | 5 | 3.6 |
| Bulgaria | 1.5 | 1.5 | 1.2 | 1.1 | 1 |  |  |
| Canada | 89.9 | 111 | 145 | 167 | 164 | 3 | 12.6 |
| Chile | 2.2 | 3.7 | 8 | 11.4 | 11.5 |  |  |
| China | 65.2 | 77.1 | 113 | 135 | 136 | 4 | 10.5 |
| Czechoslovakia | 10.2 | 10.6 | 14.3 | 14.1 | 12.9 |  |  |
| Denmark | 0.9 | 1.3 | 1.2 | 1.5 | 1.5 |  |  |
| Ethiopia | 1.8 | 2.4 | 2.3 | 2.8 | 2.8 |  |  |
| Finland | 34.1 | 32.6 | 39.1 | 35.4 | 27.8 | 8 | 2.1 |
| France | 13.6 | 15 | 18.1 | 23.5 | 23.3 | 9 | 1.8 |
| Germany | 23.3 | 25.1 | 31 | 71 | 33 | 7 | 2.5 |
| Guatemala | 3.1 | 2.8 | 4.9 | 6.4 | 6.6 |  |  |
| Honduras | 2.3 | 2.4 | 2.3 | 2.5 | 2.6 |  |  |
| India | 3.5 | 4.3 | 8 | 10 | 10 |  |  |
| Ireland | 0.2 | 0.3 | 0.3 | 1.6 | 1.6 |  |  |
| Italy | 1.5 | 1.4 | 1.7 | 1.4 | 1.3 |  |  |
| Japan | 34.7 | 26.8 | 21.4 | 19.5 | 19 | 10 | 1.5 |
| Kenya | 0.8 | 1 | 1.4 | 1.8 | 1.9 |  |  |
| Korea, North | 2.7 | 3.1 | 2.4 | 2.7 | 2.8 |  |  |
| Korea, South | 6.5 | 7.3 | 5.6 | 4.3 | 4.3 |  |  |
| Mexico | 5.9 | 7.5 | 9.3 | 11.2 | 11.1 |  |  |
| Mongolia | 1.1 | 2 | 2.2 | 2.2 | 2.2 |  |  |
| New Zealand | 5.5 | 8.4 | 9.7 | 11.5 | 13.5 |  |  |
| Norway | 8.4 | 7.7 | 8.3 | 10.7 | 10 |  |  |
| Pakistan | 0.7 | 1 | 1 | 1.6 | 1.6 |  |  |
| Poland | 14.1 | 15.3 | 16.8 | 13.8 | 12.7 |  |  |
| Portugal | 4 | 4.5 | 5.5 | 6.7 | 6 |  |  |

| | 1961–65 av. | 1970 | 1980 | 1990 | 1991 | Rank | % |
|---|---|---|---|---|---|---|---|
| Romania | 6.4 | 7.3 | 7 | 6.3 | 5.6 | | |
| South Africa | 2.5 | 4 | 6.3 | 7.2 | 6.7 | | |
| Spain | 5.7 | 5.6 | 7.3 | 11.7 | 11.4 | | |
| Swaziland | 0.4 | 0.8 | 1.4 | 1.6 | 1.6 | | |
| Sweden | 40.5 | 53.3 | 41.7 | 45.5 | 44 | 6 | 3.4 |
| Switzerland | 2.8 | 3 | 3.1 | 5 | 3 | | |
| Turkey | 5.8 | 10.4 | 14.2 | 9.4 | 9.4 | | |
| USSR (former) | 301 | 321 | 298 | 321 | 291 | 2 | 22.4 |
| United Kingdom | 1.4 | 1.8 | 2.6 | 5.5 | 5.3 | | |
| United States | 214 | 246 | 263 | 326 | 309 | 1 | 23.9 |
| Yugoslavia | 4.3 | 3.8 | 4.3 | 3.7 | 3.2 | | |

*Statistics refer to roundwood which is timber as it is felled.

## WOOD – NONCONIFEROUS*

*million cubic metres*

| | 1961–65 av. | 1970 | 1980 | 1990 | 1991 | Rank | % |
|---|---|---|---|---|---|---|---|
| World | 1,162 | 1,315 | 1,632 | 1,970 | 1,993 | | |
| Afghanistan | 3.5 | 4.2 | 3.9 | 4 | 4.2 | | |
| Albania | 1.1 | 1.6 | 1.5 | 1.4 | 1.6 | | |
| Angola | 5.9 | 7.3 | 4.3 | 5.4 | 5.5 | | |
| Argentina | 10.4 | 11.2 | 7.3 | 7.4 | 7.4 | | |
| Australia | 12.1 | 11 | 12.6 | 12.4 | 12 | | |
| Austria | 1.6 | 1.8 | 2.3 | 2.5 | 2.5 | | |
| Bangladesh | 7.8 | 9.5 | 23.8 | 31 | 31.7 | | |
| Benin | 1.7 | 2.1 | 3.6 | 4.8 | 4.9 | | |
| Bhutan | ... | ... | 3.2 | 1.5 | 1.6 | | |
| Bolivia | 4.4 | 4.2 | 1.4 | 1.5 | 1.5 | | |
| Brazil | 117 | 132.7 | 145.5 | 179 | 182 | 3 | 9.1 |
| Bulgaria | 3.9 | 3.6 | 2.9 | 3 | 2.7 | | |
| Burkina Faso | 3.5 | 4.1 | 6.6 | 8.6 | 8.8 | | |
| Burma | 13.4 | 15.6 | 18.2 | 23.2 | 23.6 | | |
| Burundi | 0.7 | 0.8 | 3.1 | 4.1 | 4.3 | | |
| Cambodia | 3.6 | 4 | 4.7 | 6 | 6.4 | | |
| Cameroon | 6.4 | 7.6 | 10.2 | 13.3 | 13.5 | | |
| Canada | 9.5 | 10.7 | 13.6 | 14.4 | 14.3 | | |
| Central Afr. Rep. | 1.9 | 2.3 | 3 | 3.5 | 3.4 | | |
| Chad | 2.9 | 3.3 | 1.2 | 1.5 | 1.5 | | |
| Chile | 4.4 | 4 | 5.6 | 7 | 7.1 | | |
| China | 81.4 | 95.2 | 121.2 | 145 | 146.7 | 5 | 7.4 |
| Colombia | 24.9 | 26.6 | 13.9 | 16.1 | 16.3 | | |
| Congo | 1.7 | 2.1 | 2.3 | 3.7 | 3.7 | | |
| Costa Rica | 2 | 2.8 | 3.4 | 4 | 4.1 | | |
| Cuba | 2.2 | 1.8 | 2.8 | 2.6 | 2.6 | | |
| Czechoslovakia | 2.7 | 4 | 4.5 | 3.7 | 3.6 | | |
| Dominican Rep. | 1.7 | 1.8 | 0.5 | 0.6 | 0.6 | | |
| Ecuador | 2.4 | 2.8 | 5.6 | 7.7 | 5.2 | | |
| Egypt | 0.1 | 0.2 | 1.8 | 2.2 | 2.3 | | |
| El Salvador | 2.7 | 2.4 | 3.7 | 4.4 | 4.5 | | |
| Ethiopia | 18.6 | 20.8 | 30.1 | 38.3 | 39.4 | 9 | 2 |
| Finland | 12.1 | 12.5 | 8 | 8.2 | 6.3 | | |
| France | 19.7 | 19.8 | 20.7 | 21.3 | 20.8 | | |
| Gabon | 2.6 | 3 | 3.1 | 4.2 | 4.3 | | |
| Germany | 10.2 | 10.4 | 12.3 | 13.8 | 11.8 | | |
| Ghana | 9.6 | 10.1 | 10.6 | 14.5 | 12.6 | | |
| Greece | 2.5 | 2.3 | 2 | 1.7 | 1.7 | | |
| Guatemala | 0.6 | 4.2 | 1.1 | 1.4 | 1.4 | | |
| Guinea | 2.3 | 2.8 | 3.2 | 3.9 | 4 | | |
| Haiti | 3 | 3.4 | 4 | 4.8 | 5 | | |
| Honduras | 1.3 | 1.7 | 2.6 | 3.6 | 3.7 | | |
| Hungary | 3.7 | 4.8 | 5.8 | 5.6 | 5.6 | | |
| India | 91.2 | 106.5 | 204 | 252.8 | 257.7 | 1 | 12.9 |
| Indonesia | 86 | 107.1 | 144.8 | 165.3 | 171.5 | 4 | 8.6 |
| Iran | 6.5 | 7 | 6.4 | 6.3 | 6.3 | | |
| Italy | 9.8 | 13.7 | 7.3 | 6.6 | 7 | | |
| Ivory Coast | 7.2 | 9 | 11.2 | 11.4 | 11.8 | | |
| Japan | 26 | 23 | 13 | 10 | 9 | | |
| Kenya | 8.8 | 10.3 | 15.7 | 22.6 | 23.4 | | |
| Korea, North | 1.4 | 1.6 | 2 | 2 | 2 | | |
| Korea, South | 2.9 | 3.3 | 3 | 2.1 | 2.1 | | |
| Laos | 2.4 | 2.8 | 2.6 | 3.5 | 3.6 | | |
| Liberia | 1.2 | 1.6 | 3.3 | 4 | 4 | | |
| Madagascar | 3.7 | 5.3 | 6.1 | 8.1 | 8.3 | | |
| Malawi | 3.5 | 4.2 | 5.8 | 8.1 | 8.4 | | |
| Malaysia | 12.9 | 24.1 | 34 | 47.3 | 47 | 8 | 2.4 |
| Mali | 2.3 | 2.7 | 4.1 | 5.6 | 5.7 | | |
| Mexico | 6.7 | 9 | 8.8 | 11.4 | 11.7 | | |

| | 1961–65 av. | 1970 | 1980 | 1990 | 1991 | Rank | % |
|---|---|---|---|---|---|---|---|
| Morocco | 1.8 | 2.2 | 0.9 | 1.1 | 1.60 | | |
| Mozambique | 7.6 | 8.5 | 12.8 | 15.4 | 15.5 | | |
| Nepal | 7.7 | 8.8 | 14 | 18 | 18.4 | | |
| Nicaragua | 1.9 | 1.9 | 2.6 | 3.4 | 3.5 | | |
| Niger | 1.9 | 2.3 | 3.6 | 5 | 5.1 | | |
| Nigeria | 46.6 | 56.9 | 73 | 98.8 | 101.8 | 6 | 5.1 |
| Pakistan | 6.2 | 17.6 | 16.3 | 25 | 25.6 | | |
| Panama | 1.6 | 1.4 | 1.8 | 2 | 2 | | |
| Papua New Guinea | 3.8 | 4.7 | 7 | 8.1 | 8.1 | | |
| Paraguay | 2.4 | 3.7 | 5.8 | 7.2 | 7.2 | | |
| Peru | 4.7 | 5.7 | 8.1 | 7.7 | 8 | | |
| Philippines | 24.9 | 33.7 | 34.8 | 38.4 | 38.7 | 10 | 1.9 |
| Poland | 2.8 | 3.2 | 4 | 3.8 | 4.3 | | |
| Portugal | 1.9 | 2 | 3 | 4.5 | 5.1 | | |
| Romania | 14.8 | 15 | 10.7 | 9.3 | 8.5 | | |
| Rwanda | 3 | 3.7 | 4.8 | 5.6 | 5.6 | | |
| Senegal | 2.1 | 2.5 | 3 | 4 | 4.1 | | |
| Sierra Leone | 2.7 | 2.7 | 2.4 | 3 | 3.1 | | |
| Somalia | 2.4 | 3 | 4.6 | 6.5 | 6.6 | | |
| South Africa | 4.1 | 5.6 | 12.5 | 12.8 | 13 | | |
| Spain | 9.2 | 8.1 | 5.1 | 5.8 | 5.5 | | |
| Sri Lanka | 4 | 4.7 | 7.9 | 9 | 9.1 | | |
| Sudan | 19.7 | 21 | 6.3 | 8.4 | 8.7 | | |
| Sweden | 6 | 6.7 | 7.5 | 8 | 8 | | |
| Switzerland | ... | 1.2 | 1.5 | 1.2 | 1.1 | | |
| Tanzania | 25.9 | 31.4 | 22.6 | 33 | 34.1 | | |
| Thailand | 16 | 18.7 | 30.6 | 34 | 34.2 | | |
| Tunisia | 1.2 | 1.4 | 1.7 | 2.1 | 2.2 | | |
| Turkey | 5.2 | 6.4 | 8.4 | 6.3 | 6.3 | | |
| Uganda | 11.5 | 14 | 10 | 14.2 | 14.8 | | |
| USSR (former) | 65.9 | 64.4 | 58.9 | 65 | 65 | 7 | 3.3 |
| United Kingdom | 1 | 1.5 | 1.3 | 1.1 | 1.1 | | |
| United States | 88.6 | 82 | 146.8 | 183.4 | 184 | 2 | 9.2 |
| Uruguay | 1 | 1 | 2.2 | 3 | 3 | | |
| Venezuela | 5.6 | 7 | 1.2 | 1.3 | 1.3 | | |
| Vietnam | 14.9 | 17.6 | 22.3 | 28.6 | 29.4 | | |
| Yugoslavia | 13.3 | 12.5 | 8.8 | 9 | 8.2 | | |
| Zaire | 12 | 14 | 26.7 | 36.2 | 37.2 | | |
| Zambia | 3.8 | 4.7 | 5 | 6.7 | 7 | | |
| Zimbabwe | 4.5 | 5.4 | 6 | 7.4 | 7.4 | | |

*Statistics refer to roundwood which is timber as it is felled.

## WOOL – GREASY

*thousand tonnes*

| | 1950 | 1970 | 1980 | 1990 | 1991 | Rank | % |
|---|---|---|---|---|---|---|---|
| World | 1,845 | 2,867 | 2,784 | 3,125 | 3,071 | | |
| Afghanistan | 15 | 26 | 23 | 17 | 17 | | |
| Albania | 2 | 2 | 3 | 3 | 2 | | |
| Algeria | 4 | 13 | 20 | 49 | 51 | 10 | 1.7 |
| Argentina | 186 | 169 | 152 | 130 | 115 | 5 | 3.7 |
| Armenia | ... | ... | ... | 3.3 | ... | | |
| Australia | 515 | 899 | 705 | 843 | 841 | 1 | 27.4 |
| Azerbaijan | ... | ... | ... | 11 | ... | | |
| Bolivia | 4 | 7 | 9 | 13 | 13 | | |
| Brazil | 20 | 32 | 32 | 28 | 29 | | |
| Bulgaria | 14 | 29 | 35 | 28 | 25 | | |
| Canada | 4 | 2 | 1 | 1 | 1 | | |
| Chile | 20 | 23 | 21 | 20 | 18 | | |
| China | 45 | 60 | 173 | 239 | 241 | 4 | 7.8 |
| Czechoslovakia | 1 | 4 | 4 | 6 | 1 | | |
| Ecuador | 0.3 | 2 | 3 | 2 | 2 | | |
| Egypt | 2 | 3 | 2 | 2 | 2 | | |
| Ethiopia | 12 | 12 | 12 | 12 | 12 | | |
| Falkland Is. | 2 | 2 | 2 | 3 | 3 | | |
| France | 20 | 20 | 22 | 22 | 22 | | |
| Georgia | ... | ... | ... | 6.4 | ... | | |
| Germany | 11 | 10 | 16 | 21 | 24 | | |
| Greece | 8 | 8 | 10 | 10 | 10 | | |
| Hungary | 4 | 10 | 12 | 7 | 7 | | |
| India | 26 | 37 | 35 | 35 | 32 | | |
| Indonesia | 2 | 5 | 12 | 17 | 17 | | |
| Iran | 15 | 19 | 33 | 32 | 32 | | |
| Iraq | 14 | 16 | 11 | 23 | 15 | | |
| Ireland | 6 | 10 | 10.8 | 17 | 18 | | |
| Italy | 15 | 12 | 13 | 14 | 14 | | |
| Jordan | ... | 3 | 2 | 3 | 3 | | |
| Kazakhstan | ... | ... | ... | 108 | ... | | |

| | 1950 | 1970 | 1980 | 1990 | 1991 | Rank | % |
|---|---|---|---|---|---|---|---|
| Kyrgyzstan | ... | ... | ... | 39 | ... | | |
| Lesotho | 4 | 4 | 3 | 3 | 3 | | |
| Libya | 2 | 4 | 8 | 8 | 8 | | |
| Mexico | 6 | 8 | 7 | 5 | 5 | | |
| Moldova | ... | ... | ... | 3 | ... | | |
| Mongolia | 14 | 19 | 21 | 20 | 21 | | |
| Morocco | 11 | 16 | 14 | 35 | 35 | | |
| Namibia | 7 | 4 | 5 | 2 | 2 | | |
| Nepal | 2 | 4 | 1 | 1 | 1 | | |
| Netherlands | ... | 4.5 | 2 | 4 | 4 | | |
| New Zealand | 179 | 332 | 353 | 309 | 304 | 3 | 9.9 |
| Norway | 3 | 5 | 5 | 5 | 5 | | |
| Pakistan | 11 | 20 | 40 | 61 | 65 | 9 | 2.1 |
| Peru | 9 | 13 | 11 | 10 | 10 | | |
| Poland | 4 | 9 | 12 | 15 | 11 | | |
| Portugal | 10 | 9 | 9 | 9 | 8 | | |
| Romania | 16 | 30 | 37 | 38 | 40 | | |
| Russia | ... | ... | ... | 227 | ... | | |
| Saudi Arabia | ... | 4 | 3 | 3 | 3 | | |
| South Africa | 105 | 137 | 103 | 100 | 104 | 6 | 3.4 |
| Spain | 34 | 33 | 21 | 30 | 30 | | |
| Sudan | 5 | 10 | 15 | 18 | 19 | | |
| Syria | 8 | 14 | 20 | 36 | 38 | | |
| Tajikistan | ... | ... | ... | 4.6 | ... | | |
| Tanzania | ... | ... | 4 | 4 | 4 | | |
| Tunisia | 3 | 5 | 9 | 12 | 12 | | |
| Turkey | 33 | 47 | 61 | 43 | 50 | | |
| Turkmenistan | ... | ... | ... | 16 | ... | | |
| Ukraine | ... | ... | ... | 30 | ... | | |
| USSR (former) | 694 | 412 | 454 | 471 | 447 | 2 | 14.6 |
| United Kingdom | 40 | 47 | 50 | 75 | 75 | 8 | 2.4 |
| United States | 129 | 85 | 48 | 40 | 39 | | |
| Uruguay | 79 | 81 | 68 | 93 | 101 | 7 | 3.3 |
| Yemen | ... | 4.4 | 3 | 4.1 | 4.1 | | |
| Yugoslavia | 15 | 12 | 10 | 10 | 10 | | |
| Zimbabwe | ... | ... | 9 | 1 | 1 | | |

## MINERAL AND MANUFACTURED PRODUCTS

# ALUMINIUM ORE (BAUXITE)

*thousand tonnes*

| | 1948 | 1970 | 1980 | 1990 | 1991 | Rank | % |
|---|---|---|---|---|---|---|---|
| World | 7,810 | 52,650 | 93,300 | 112,692 | 110,803 | | |
| Australia | 6 | 3,294 | 27,179 | 41,391 | 40,503 | 1 | 36.6 |
| Brazil | 15 | 400 | 4,632 | 9,876 | 10,414 | 4 | 9.4 |
| China | ... | 500 | 1,700 | 3,200 | 3,000 | 8 | 2.7 |
| Dominican Rep. | 0 | 1,086 | 511 | 85 | 7 | | |
| France | 804 | 2,992 | 1,925 | 490 | 183 | | |
| Ghana | 133 | 342 | 225 | 381 | 334 | | |
| Greece | 44 | 2,283 | 3,259 | 2,496 | 2,134 | | |
| Guinea | 0 | 2,642 | 13,911 | 17,524 | 17,054 | 2 | 15.4 |
| Guyana | 1,996 | 4,103 | 3,052 | 1,424 | 2,204 | 10 | 2 |
| Haiti | – | 673 | 461 | 0 | 0 | | |
| Hungary | 478 | 2,022 | 2,950 | 2,559 | 2,037 | | |
| India | 21 | 1,370 | 1,785 | 5,277 | 4,835 | 5 | 4.4 |
| Indonesia | 438 | 1,229 | 1,249 | 1,206 | 1,406 | | |
| Iran | 0 | 0 | 0 | 93 | 140 | | |
| Italy | 153 | 225 | 23 | 0 | 9 | | |
| Jamaica | – | 12,106 | 11,978 | 10,937 | 11,609 | 3 | 10.5 |
| Malaysia | 0 | 1,139 | 920 | 398 | 376 | | |
| Romania | 0 | 792 | 450 | 247 | 200 | | |
| Sierra Leone | 0 | 443 | 674 | 1,445 | 1,288 | | |
| Surinam | 1,983 | 6,011 | 4,893 | 3,267 | 3,136 | 7 | 2.8 |
| Turkey | 0 | 51 | 547 | 779 | 530 | | |
| USSR (former) | – | 4,300 | 6,400 | 5,350 | 4,800 | 6 | 4.3 |
| United States | 1,752 | 2,562 | 1,559 | 495 | 50 | | |
| Venezuela | 0 | 0 | 0 | 785 | 1,992 | | |
| Yugoslavia | 144 | 2,099 | 3,138 | 2,951 | 2,542 | 9 | 2.3 |

# YAMS

*thousand tonnes*

| | 1980 | 1990 | 1991 | Rank | % |
|---|---|---|---|---|---|
| World | 23,394 | 20,966 | 23,893 | | |
| Benin | 687 | 967 | 1,206 | 3 | 5 |
| Brazil | 179 | 215 | 215 | 9 | 0.9 |
| Burkina Faso | 71 | 52 | 52 | | |
| Cameroon | 203 | 70 | 80 | | |
| Central African Republic | 153 | 195 | 200 | | |
| Chad | 163 | 240 | 248 | 8 | 1 |
| Colombia | 143 | 28 | 41 | | |
| Ethiopia | 276 | 260 | 261 | 7 | 1.1 |
| Gabon | 80 | 110 | 110 | | |
| Ghana | 614 | 877 | 1,000 | 4 | 4.2 |
| Guinea | 64 | 100 | 106 | | |
| Haiti | 112 | 120 | 110 | | |
| Ivory Coast | 2,079 | 2,528 | 2,559 | 2 | 10.7 |
| Jamaica | 142 | 161 | 186 | | |
| Japan | 144 | 171 | 174 | | |
| Nigeria | 17,000 | 13,624 | 16,000 | 1 | 67 |
| Papua New Guinea | 176 | 210 | 215 | 10 | 0.9 |
| Philippines | 21 | 27 | 28 | | |
| Solomon Is. | 18 | 22 | 22 | | |
| Sudan | 114 | 95 | 128 | | |
| Togo | 498 | 392 | 433 | 5 | 1.8 |
| Tonga | 34 | 33 | 33 | | |
| Venezuela | 33 | 41 | 41 | | |
| Zaïre | 222 | 280 | 300 | 6 | 1.3 |

# ASBESTOS

*thousand tonnes*

| | 1950 | 1970 | 1980 | 1990 | 1991 | Rank | % |
|---|---|---|---|---|---|---|---|
| World | 870 | 4,682 | 4,700 | 3,980 | 3,790 | | |
| Australia | 1.3 | 1 | 92 | ... | ... | | |
| Brazil | 1.5 | 340 | 170 | 232 | 233 | 3 | 6.1 |
| Canada | 650 | 1,508 | 1,323 | 725 | 643 | 2 | 16.7 |
| China | ... | 170 | 132 | 160 | 160 | 5 | 4.2 |
| Cyprus | 8.1 | 29 | 36 | 30 | ... | | |
| Finland | 10.8 | 14 | – | – | – | | |
| Greece | – | – | – | 73 | ... | 9 | 1.9 |
| India | 0.1 | 10 | 34 | 35 | 35 | 7 | 0.9 |
| Italy | 13 | 119 | 158 | 20 | ... | | |
| Japan | 4.8 | 21 | 4 | – | ... | | |
| Korea, South | – | 2 | 10 | ... | ... | | |
| South Africa | 42 | 287 | 268 | 148 | 145 | 6 | 3.8 |
| Swaziland | 29 | 33 | 33 | 35 | ... | 10 | 0.9 |
| Turkey | 0.2 | 3 | 9 | 20 | ... | | |
| USSR (former) | ... | 1,066 | 2,070 | 2,400 | 2,400 | 1 | 63.3 |
| United States | 34 | 114 | 80 | 20 | 33 | 8 | 0.9 |
| Yugoslavia | 2.3 | 12 | 11 | 7 | 7 | | |
| Zimbabwe | 62 | 80 | 251 | 190 | 190 | 4 | 5 |

# CARS

*thousands*

| | 1948 | 1970 | 1980 | 1990 | 1991 | Rank | % |
|---|---|---|---|---|---|---|---|
| World | 4,640 | 22,550 | 28,999 | 35,700 | 34,400 | | |
| Argentina | 0 | 169 | 218 | 114 | 121 | | |
| Australia | 29 | 391 | 316 | 361 | 311 | | |
| Belgium | ... | 734 | 891 | 1,160* | 1,065* | 10 | 3.1 |
| Brazil | 0 | 255 | 652 | 268 | 293 | | |
| Canada | 167 | 923 | 847 | 941 | 890 | | |
| Colombia | 0 | 8 | 32 | 36* | 35* | | |
| Czechoslovakia | 18 | 143 | 186 | 191 | 176 | | |

| | 1948 | 1970 | 1980 | 1990 | 1991 | Rank | % |
|---|---|---|---|---|---|---|---|
| France | 100 | 2,458 | 3,487 | 2,962 | 3,121 | 4 | 9.1 |
| Germany | 33 | 3,655 | 3,688 | 4,618 | 4,270 | 3 | 12.4 |
| India | 0 | 45 | 47 | 221 | 193 | | |
| Indonesia | ... | ... | 43 | 57* | ... | | |
| Iran | 0 | 33 | ... | ... | ... | | |
| Ireland | 14 | 47 | 45 | ... | ... | | |
| Italy | 44 | 1,720 | 1,445 | 1,873 | 1,627 | 6 | 4.7 |
| Japan | 0.4 | 3,179 | 7,038 | 9,948 | 9,756 | 1 | 28.4 |
| Korea, South | 0 | 13 | 58 | 956 | 1,132 | 9 | 3.3 |
| Malaysia | 0 | 21 | 79 | 102* | 152* | | |
| Mexico | ... | 137 | 312 | 614 | 733 | | |
| Netherlands | 2 | 85 | 80 | 124 | 85 | | |
| New Zealand | 10 | 55 | 73 | ... | ... | | |
| Poland | 0 | 65 | 362 | 266 | 167 | | |
| Portugal | 0 | 55 | 22 | 60* | 78* | | |
| Romania | 0 | 23 | 89 | 120 | 74 | | |
| South Africa | ... | 195 | 268 | 221* | ... | | |
| Spain | 0.2 | 455 | 1,048 | 1,736 | 1,830 | 5 | 5.3 |
| Sweden | ... | 272 | 257 | 336 | 269 | | |
| Taiwan | 0 | 9 | 133 | 358 | 405 | | |
| Thailand | 0 | 0 | 24 | 82* | 76* | | |
| Turkey | 0 | 5 | 52 | 167* | 197* | | |
| USSR (former) | 20 | 344 | 1,327 | 1,259 | 1,184 | 8 | 3.4 |
| United Kingdom | 335 | 1,641 | 924 | 1,296 | 1,278 | 7 | 3.7 |
| United States | 3,909 | 8,505 | 6,376 | 6,052 | 5,407 | 2 | 15.7 |
| Venezuela | 0 | 46 | ... | ... | 35 | | |
| Yugoslavia | 0 | 109 | 187 | 292 | 218 | | |

* Assembly only

| | 1948 | 1970 | 1980 | 1991 | 1992 | Rank | % |
|---|---|---|---|---|---|---|---|
| Austria | 3.3 | 3.7 | 2.9 | 2.5 | 2.5 | | |
| Bulgaria | 4.1 | 28.9 | 29.9 | 29 | 28 | | |
| Canada | 1.4 | 3.5 | 6 | 8 | 33 | | |
| China | ... | ... | 9.3 | 119 | 90 | 4 | 6.9 |
| Czechoslovakia | 23.6 | 81.8 | 95.7 | 83 | 70 | 5 | 5.3 |
| Denmark | 2.4 | 0.1 | 0 | 0 | 0 | | |
| France | 1.8 | 2.8 | 2.6 | 2 | 2 | | |
| Germany | 177 | 369 | 388 | 279 | 242 | 2 | 18.5 |
| Greece | 0.1 | 7.7 | 23.5 | 53 | 60 | 7 | 4.6 |
| Hungary | 9.4 | 23.7 | 22.6 | 15 | 14.5 | | |
| India | 0 | 3.5 | 4.5 | 16 | 16 | | |
| Italy | 0.9 | 1.4 | 1.9 | 0.9 | 1.1 | | |
| New Zealand | 1.9 | 1.9 | 0.2 | 0.1 | 0.2 | | |
| Poland | 5 | 32.8 | 30.9 | 69 | 66.8 | 6 | 5.1 |
| Romania | 0.9 | 14.1 | 28.1 | 29 | 33.6 | | |
| Russia | ... | ... | ... | 130 | 123 | | |
| Spain | 1.4 | 2.8 | 15.4 | 14 | 13 | | |
| Thailand | 0 | 0.4 | 1.4 | 13 | ... | | |
| Turkey | 0.7 | 4.5 | 17 | 47 | 45 | 9 | 3.4 |
| Ukraine | ... | ... | ... | 8.7 | 8.5 | | |
| USSR (former) | 58.2 | 145 | 163 | 152 | 142 | 3 | 10.8 |
| United States | 2.8 | 5.4 | 43.4 | 298 | 295 | 1 | 22.5 |
| Yugoslavia | 9.7 | 27.8 | 46.6 | 71 | 39.3 | 10 | 3 |

# COPPER ORE

thousand tonnes

# COAL – BITUMINOUS

million tonnes

| | 1948 | 1970 | 1980 | 1991 | 1992 | Rank | % |
|---|---|---|---|---|---|---|---|
| World | 1,412 | 2,131 | 2,740 | 3,104 | 3,120 | | |
| Australia | 15 | 44 | 78 | 166 | 180 | 5 | 5.8 |
| Belgium | 27 | 11 | 5.3 | 1.1 | 0.2 | | |
| Brazil | 2 | 2.4 | 5.1 | 6.5 | 4.6 | | |
| Canada | 15 | 12 | 31 | 60 | 32 | | |
| Chile | 2 | 1.4 | 1 | 2.6 | 1.9 | | |
| China | 32 | 360 | 590 | 921 | 1,095 | 1 | 35 |
| Colombia | ... | ... | 10 | 23 | 25 | | |
| Czechoslovakia | 17 | 28 | 28 | 20 | 20 | | |
| France | 43 | 37 | 18 | 13 | 11 | | |
| Germany | 103 | 112 | 87 | 70 | 72 | 9 | 2.3 |
| Hungary | 1.2 | 4.2 | 3.1 | 2 | 1.3 | | |
| India | 31 | 74 | 109 | 213 | 213 | 4 | 6.8 |
| Indonesia | ... | 0.1 | 0.3 | 16 | 16 | | |
| Japan | 34 | 40 | 18 | 8.3 | 7.6 | | |
| Kazakhstan | ... | ... | ... | 127 | 123 | | |
| Korea, North | 2.1 | 24 | 19 | 48 | 50 | 10 | 1.6 |
| Korea, South | 0.8 | 12 | 19 | 15 | 12 | | |
| Mexico | ... | ... | 5 | 13 | 13 | | |
| Netherlands | 11 | 4.3 | 0 | 0 | 0 | | |
| Poland | 70 | 140 | 193 | 140 | 132 | 7 | 4.2 |
| Romania | 2 | 6.4 | 9.7 | 4.4 | 3.2 | | |
| Russia | ... | ... | ... | 230 | 218 | | |
| South Africa | 24 | 55 | 116 | 180 | 175 | 6 | 5.6 |
| Spain | 10 | 11 | 13 | 14 | 15 | | |
| Taiwan | 1.6 | 4.5 | 2.6 | 0.4 | 0.3 | | |
| Turkey | 2.7 | 5 | 6.6 | 5.6 | 5.6 | | |
| Ukraine | ... | ... | ... | 128 | 127 | | |
| USSR (former) | 150 | 433 | 493 | 487 | 469 | 3 | 15 |
| United Kingdom | 213 | 145 | 130 | 96 | 87 | 8 | 2.8 |
| United States | 593 | 550 | 715 | 607 | 608 | 2 | 19.5 |
| Vietnam | 0.4 | 3 | 5.3 | 5.5 | 5.5 | | |
| Zimbabwe | 1.7 | 3.4 | 3.1 | 5.2 | 5.2 | | |

| metal content | 1948 | 1970 | 1980 | 1990 | 1991 | Rank | % |
|---|---|---|---|---|---|---|---|
| World | 2,120 | 6,320 | 7,900 | 9,040 | 9,112 | | |
| Albania | – | 7 | 12 | 13.2 | 8 | | |
| Australia | 13 | 142 | 244 | 327 | 320 | 8 | 3.5 |
| Bolivia | 7 | 9 | 2 | 0.2 | 0 | | |
| Botswana | 0 | 0 | 16 | 20.6 | 20.6 | | |
| Brazil | – | 4 | ... | 36.5 | 37 | | |
| Bulgaria | 1 | 43 | 62 | 32.9 | 47.2 | | |
| Burkina Faso | ... | ... | ... | 20.6 | 20.6 | | |
| Canada | 223 | 610 | 716 | 794 | 798 | 4 | 8.8 |
| Chile | 445 | 711 | 1,068 | 1,588 | 1,814 | 1 | 20 |
| China | ... | 100 | 165 | 360 | 350 | 7 | 3.8 |
| Cuba | 15 | 7 | 3 | 2 | 2 | | |
| Cyprus | 11.4 | 17.3 | 4.8 | 0.5 | 0.2 | | |
| Czechoslovakia | ... | 10.7 | 9.3 | 3.6 | 2.6 | | |
| Finland | 20 | 34 | 53 | 12.6 | 11.7 | | |
| Germany | 6 | 10 | 12 | 3.6 | 0 | | |
| India | 8 | 10 | 27 | 51.6 | 50.4 | | |
| Indonesia | – | – | 59 | 170 | 212 | | |
| Iran | – | – | 1 | 74.3 | 97 | | |
| Ireland | ... | 7.7 | 4.3 | 0 | 0 | | |
| Japan | 26 | 120 | 53 | 13 | 12.4 | | |
| Korea, North | 2 | 13 | 12 | 12 | 14 | | |
| Malaysia | – | – | 27 | 24.3 | 25.6 | | |
| Mexico | 59 | 61 | 175 | 291 | 267 | 10 | 2.9 |
| Mongolia | – | – | 44 | 124 | 120 | | |
| Morocco | – | 3 | 8 | 15.3 | 14.2 | | |
| Namibia | 8 | 23 | 39 | 32.5 | 33.9 | | |
| Norway | 15 | 20 | 29 | 19.7 | 17.4 | | |
| Oman | – | – | – | 13.7 | 13.5 | | |
| Papua New Guinea | ... | ... | 147 | 170 | 205 | | |
| Peru | 18 | 206 | 367 | 318 | 381 | 6 | 4.2 |
| Philippines | 2 | 160 | 305 | 181 | 151 | | |
| Poland | – | 83 | 343 | 329 | 320 | 8 | 3.5 |
| Portugal | ... | ... | 1 | 158 | 158 | | |
| Romania | ... | ... | 28 | 32 | 27 | | |
| South Africa | 30 | 148 | 201 | 209 | 193 | | |
| Spain | 4 | 10 | 48 | 15.3 | 10 | | |
| Sweden | 15 | 26 | 43 | 73.5 | 79.9 | | |
| Turkey | 11 | 22 | 21 | 39.8 | 35.5 | | |
| USSR (former) | ... | 925 | 1,130 | 900 | 840 | 3 | 9.2 |
| United States | 757 | 1,560 | 1,181 | 1,587 | 1,631 | 2 | 17.9 |
| Yugoslavia | 41 | 91 | 115 | 119 | 110 | | |
| Zaire | 156 | 387 | 462 | 356 | 235 | | |
| Zambia | 217 | 684 | 610 | 496 | 423 | 5 | 4.6 |
| Zimbabwe | ... | ... | 27 | 14.7 | 13.8 | | |

# COAL – LIGNITE & BROWN

million tonnes

| | 1948 | 1970 | 1980 | 1991 | 1992 | Rank | % |
|---|---|---|---|---|---|---|---|
| World | 316 | 793 | 996 | 1,365 | 1,310 | | |
| Australia | 6.8 | 24.3 | 32.9 | 48 | 51.1 | 8 | 3.9 |

| | 1970 | 1980 | 1990 | 1991 | Rank | % |
|---|---|---|---|---|---|---|
| Spain | 724 | 960 | 967 | 886 | | |
| Sweden | 169 | 180 | 154 | 176 | | |
| Trinidad & Tobago | 75 | 41 | 223 | 232 | | |
| Tunisia | ... | 47 | 206 | 202 | | |
| Turkey | 145 | 672 | 700 | 947 | | |
| USSR (former) | 6,533 | 10,155 | 14,272 | 13,094 | 3 | 15.9 |
| United Arab Em. | ... | ... | 266 | 228 | | |
| United Kingdom | 751 | 1,167 | 1,070 | 980 | | |
| United States | 8,433 | 11,825 | 12,576 | 13,552 | 2 | 16.5 |
| Venezuela | 10 | 145 | 370 | 337 | | |
| Yugoslavia | 360 | 391 | 520 | 461 | | |
| Zimbabwe | 58 | 72 | 72 | 83 | | |

## DIAMONDS

*thousand carats*

| | 1948 | 1970 | 1980 | 1990 | 1991 | Rank | % |
|---|---|---|---|---|---|---|---|
| World | 10,270 | 47,634 | 42,000 | 106,700 | 99,200 | | |
| Angola | 796 | 2,396 | 1,500 | 1,300 | 1,300 | 7 | 1.3 |
| Australia | ... | ... | ... | 36,000 | 36,000 | 1 | 36.3 |
| Botswana | ... | 464 | 5,146 | 17,300 | 16,500 | 3 | 16.6 |
| Brazil | ... | 47 | 667 | 500 | 550 | 10 | 0.6 |
| Central Afr. Rep. | 119 | 494 | 342 | 500 | 500 | | |
| China | ... | ... | 1,000 | 1,000 | 1,000 | 8 | 1 |
| Ghana | 786 | 2,550 | 1,149 | 200 | 200 | | |
| Guinea | 80 | 74 | 38 | 100 | 100 | | |
| Guyana | 37 | 61 | 10 | 8 | 20 | | |
| Liberia | ... | 826 | 298 | 300 | 300 | | |
| Namibia | 201 | 1,865 | 1,560 | 800 | 1,400 | 6 | 1.4 |
| Sierra Leone | 466 | 2,050 | 592 | 700 | 600 | 9 | 0.6 |
| South Africa | 1,382 | 8,112 | 8,520 | 8,500 | 8,200 | 5 | 8.3 |
| Tanzania | 150 | 708 | 270 | ... | ... | | |
| USSR (former) | ... | 14,057 | 10,850 | 15,000 | 13,000 | 4 | 13.1 |
| Venezuela | 76 | 509 | 666 | 80 | 80 | | |
| Zaïre | 5,825 | 14,057 | 10,334 | 24,000 | 19,000 | 2 | 19.2 |

This table does not show synthetic diamond production.

## FERTILIZERS – NITROGENOUS

*thousand tonnes*

| | 1970 | 1980 | 1990 | 1991 | Rank | % |
|---|---|---|---|---|---|---|
| World | 37,825 | 62,766 | 84,640 | 82,270 | | |
| Albania | 36 | 73 | 80 | 73 | | |
| Algeria | 50 | 24 | 88 | 80 | | |
| Australia | 182 | 214 | 230 | 225 | | |
| Austria | 230 | 300 | 230 | 227 | | |
| Bangladesh | 92 | 161 | 678 | 654 | | |
| Belgium | 641 | 743 | 678 | 725 | | |
| Brazil | 78 | 384 | 748 | 737 | | |
| Bulgaria | 523 | 730 | 926 | 915 | | |
| Canada | 772 | 1,755 | 2,706 | 2,683 | 5 | 3.3 |
| Chile | 108 | 101 | 130 | 126 | | |
| China | 2,245 | 10,286 | 14,515 | 14,915 | 1 | 18.1 |
| Colombia | 77 | 42 | 97 | 100 | | |
| Cuba | 2 | 112 | 146 | 140 | | |
| Czechoslovakia | 410 | 705 | 675 | 604 | | |
| Denmark | 77 | 147 | 200 | 185 | | |
| Egypt | 152 | 400 | 678 | 676 | | |
| Finland | 243 | 266 | 278 | 268 | | |
| France | 1,476 | 1,640 | 1,572 | 1,524 | 8 | 1.9 |
| Germany | 1,899 | 2,379 | 1,921 | 1,165 | | |
| Greece | 240 | 311 | 407 | 396 | | |
| Hungary | 374 | 651 | 591 | 470 | | |
| India | 1,054 | 2,164 | 6,747 | 6,993 | 4 | 8.5 |
| Indonesia | 60 | 958 | 2,369 | 2,462 | 6 | 3 |
| Iran | 143 | 71 | 308 | 376 | | |
| Iraq | 26 | 355 | 450 | 409 | | |
| Ireland | 85 | 190 | 297 | 279 | | |
| Italy | 1,046 | 1,335 | 1,169 | 762 | | |
| Japan | 2,199 | 1,202 | 946 | 957 | | |
| Jordan | ... | ... | 109 | 107 | | |
| Korea, North | 230 | 553 | 660 | 660 | | |
| Korea, South | 418 | 688 | 583 | 554 | | |
| Kuwait | 270 | 218 | 386 | 204 | | |
| Libya | ... | ... | 124 | 89 | | |
| Malaysia | 31 | 35 | 249 | 211 | | |
| Mexico | 356 | 739 | 1,498 | 1,366 | 9 | 1.7 |
| Morocco | 5 | 36 | 273 | 344 | | |
| Netherlands | 1,217 | 1,624 | 1,848 | 1,875 | 7 | 2.3 |
| Nigeria | ... | ... | 272 | 284 | | |
| Norway | 396 | 428 | 494 | 509 | | |
| Pakistan | 274 | 580 | 1,156 | 1,120 | | |
| Philippines | 55 | 34 | 127 | 121 | | |
| Poland | 1,147 | 1,290 | 1,643 | 1,303 | 10 | 1.6 |
| Portugal | 150 | 172 | 133 | 126 | | |
| Qatar | ... | 286 | 350 | 343 | | |
| Romania | 874 | 1,707 | 2,035 | 1,249 | | |
| Saudi Arabia | 69 | 152 | 428 | 584 | | |
| South Africa | 248 | 444 | 400 | 430 | | |

## FERTILIZERS – PHOSPHATE

*thousand tonnes*

| | 1970 | 1980 | 1990 | 1991 | Rank | % |
|---|---|---|---|---|---|---|
| World | 23,673 | 34,515 | 39,733 | 38,906 | | |
| Algeria | 38 | 31 | 45 | 50 | | |
| Australia | 900 | 829 | 511 | 270 | | |
| Austria | 139 | 105 | 85 | 70 | | |
| Bangladesh | ... | 33 | 67 | 51 | | |
| Belgium | 780 | 590 | 333 | 353 | | |
| Brazil | 278 | 1,582 | 1,109 | 1,057 | 6 | 2.7 |
| Bulgaria | 126 | 217 | 169 | 47 | | |
| Canada | 738 | 724 | 440 | 348 | | |
| China | 1,031 | 2,367 | 3,808 | 4,196 | 3 | 10.8 |
| Colombia | 40 | 46 | 39 | 40 | | |
| Czechoslovakia | 334 | 361 | 320 | 290 | | |
| Denmark | 97 | 135 | 136 | 81 | | |
| Egypt | 116 | 106 | 217 | 182 | | |
| Finland | 213 | 159 | 183 | 172 | | |
| France | 1,611 | 1,351 | 1,025 | 921 | 7 | 2.4 |
| Germany | 1,395 | 1,056 | 595 | 294 | | |
| Greece | 153 | 170 | 198 | 199 | | |
| Hungary | 161 | 216 | 220 | 109 | | |
| India | 330 | 859 | 1,834 | 2,089 | 4 | 5.4 |
| Indonesia | ... | 220 | 551 | 589 | 9 | 1.5 |
| Iran | 62 | 30 | 50 | 81 | | |
| Iraq | ... | ... | 415 | 207 | | |
| Ireland | 136 | 44 | ... | ... | | |
| Israel | ... | 41 | 180 | 200 | | |
| Italy | 500 | 447 | 266 | 222 | | |
| Japan | 729 | 648 | 445 | 429 | | |
| Jordan | ... | 13 | 277 | 274 | | |
| Korea, North | 105 | 127 | 137 | 137 | | |
| Korea, South | 163 | 494 | 394 | 414 | | |
| Lebanon | 42 | 103 | 15 | 34 | | |
| Mexico | 217 | 201 | 448 | 498 | | |
| Morocco | 154 | 177 | 934 | 1,180 | 5 | 3 |
| Netherlands | 351 | 328 | 378 | 357 | | |
| New Zealand | 421 | 346 | 206 | 168 | | |
| Nigeria | ... | 5 | 44 | 50 | | |
| Norway | 130 | 143 | 230 | 245 | | |
| Pakistan | 8 | 58 | 105 | 105 | | |
| Philippines | 42 | 37 | 191 | 199 | | |
| Poland | 763 | 843 | 946 | 467 | | |
| Portugal | 89 | 102 | 77 | 61 | | |
| Romania | 313 | 687 | 648 | 387 | | |
| Senegal | ... | 25 | 28 | 50 | | |
| South Africa | 340 | 480 | 375 | 380 | | |
| Spain | 576 | 497 | 368 | 326 | | |
| Sweden | 181 | 132 | 108 | 108 | | |
| Tunisia | 194 | 408 | 754 | 657 | 8 | 1.7 |
| Turkey | 125 | 564 | 468 | 525 | 10 | 1.3 |
| USSR (former) | 2,784 | 6,023 | 9,015 | 8,961 | 2 | 23 |
| United Kingdom | 444 | 326 | 172 | 128 | | |
| United States | 5,795 | 9,500 | 9,590 | 10,095 | 1 | 25.9 |
| Venezuela | 10 | 23 | 50 | 57 | | |
| Vietnam | 42 | 33 | 55 | 66 | | |
| Yugoslavia | 231 | 302 | 319 | 262 | | |
| Zimbabwe | 38 | 42 | 38 | 41 | | |

## GOLD

*tonnes*

metal content

| | 1948 | 1970 | 1980 | 1990 | 1991 | Rank | % |
|---|---|---|---|---|---|---|---|
| World | 698 | 1,483 | 1,220 | 1,714 | 1,702 | | |
| Australia | 27.5 | 19.4 | 17 | 243 | 234 | 4 | 13.1 |
| Brazil | 4.1 | 5.6 | 13.8 | 84 | 80 | 7 | 4.5 |
| Canada | 110 | 74.9 | 50.6 | 167 | 177 | 5 | 9.9 |
| Chile | 5.1 | 2 | 6.8 | 33 | 33 | 9 | 1.9 |
| China | ... | ... | 45 | 95 | 110 | 6 | 6.2 |
| Colombia | 10.4 | 6.3 | 15.9 | 33 | 32 | 10 | 1.8 |
| Dominican Rep. | 0 | 0 | 11.5 | 6.5 | ... | | |
| Ecuador | 2.5 | 0.3 | 0.1 | 9.5 | ... | | |
| Fiji | 2.9 | 3.2 | 0.8 | 4.5 | ... | | |
| Ghana | 20.9 | 21.9 | 11 | 17 | 27 | | |
| India | 5.6 | 3.2 | 2.5 | 1.8 | 1.8 | | |
| Indonesia | 6.2 | ... | ... | 13 | 18 | | |
| Japan | 3.1 | 3 | 3.2 | 7.5 | 6 | | |
| Korea, North | ... | ... | 5 | 5 | 5 | | |
| Korea, South | 0.1 | 1.6 | 1.3 | 12 | 12 | | |
| Mexico | 11.4 | 6.2 | 6.1 | 9 | 9 | | |
| New Zealand | 2.9 | 0.4 | 0.2 | 2.4 | ... | | |
| Nicaragua | 6.9 | 3.5 | 1.9 | 0.8 | ... | | |
| Papua New Guinea | 2.7 | 0.7 | 14.7 | 34 | 61 | 8 | 3.4 |
| Peru | 3.5 | 3 | 3.9 | 5.2 | 4 | | |
| Philippines | 6.5 | 18.7 | 20 | 37 | 31 | | |
| South Africa | 360 | 1002 | 673 | 605 | 601 | 1 | 33.7 |
| Sweden | 2.2 | 1.4 | 2 | 3.9 | 3.7 | | |
| Tanzania | 1.8 | 0.2 | 0.3 | 0.2 | ... | | |
| USSR (former) | ... | 195 | 260 | 280 | 242 | 3 | 13.6 |
| United States | 63 | 56.4 | 30.2 | 294 | 300 | 2 | 16.8 |
| Yugoslavia | 0.8 | 1.7 | 3.3 | 4.6 | ... | | |
| Zaire | 9.3 | 5.5 | 2.2 | 3.7 | 2.1 | | |
| Zimbabwe | 16 | 15.6 | 11.4 | 15 | 15 | | |

## IRON AND FERRO-ALLOYS

*thousand tonnes*

| | 1948 | 1970 | 1980 | 1990 | 1991 | Rank | % |
|---|---|---|---|---|---|---|---|
| World | 113,000 | 436,416 | 520,000 | 543,000 | 500,000 | | |
| Algeria | ... | 409 | 669 | 1,500 | 1,500 | | |
| Argentina | 17 | 847 | 1,095 | 2,100 | 2,000 | | |
| Australia | 1,149 | 5,769 | 7,276 | 6,192 | 5,592 | | |
| Austria | 613 | 2,970 | 3,493 | 3,444 | 3,400 | | |
| Belgium | 3,929 | 10,950 | 9,845 | 9,360 | 8,520 | | |
| Brazil | 552 | 4,334 | 14,774 | 21,120 | 23,424 | 6 | 4.7 |
| Bulgaria | ... | 1,251 | 1,583 | 1,140 | 948 | | |
| Canada | 2,140 | 8,424 | 11,185 | 7,344 | 8,268 | | |
| Chile | 14 | 481 | 707 | 732 | 740 | | |
| China | ... | 17,060 | 39,014 | 64,548 | 69,480 | 3 | 13.9 |
| Czechoslovakia | 1,645 | 7,653 | 9,992 | 9,840 | 8,640 | | |
| Egypt | ... | 300 | 650 | 116 | 120 | | |
| Finland | 90 | 1,164 | 2,072 | 2,280 | 2,328 | | |
| France | 6,628 | 19,575 | 19,595 | 14,412 | 14,148 | 8 | 2.8 |
| Germany | 5,857 | 35,985 | 36,513 | 30,324 | 30,024 | 5 | 6 |
| Hungary | 384 | 1,837 | 2,227 | 1,692 | 1,308 | | |
| India | 1,487 | 7,338 | 8,864 | 12,000 | 12,000 | 10 | 2.4 |
| Italy | 525 | 8,529 | 12,411 | 12,024 | 10,992 | | |
| Japan | 836 | 69,728 | 88,907 | 81,360 | 81,144 | 2 | 16.2 |
| Korea, North | 105 | 2,400 | 5,470 | 6,570 | 7,000 | | |
| Korea, South | ... | 35 | 5,686 | 15,528 | 18,744 | 7 | 3.7 |
| Luxembourg | 2,624 | 4,814 | 3,568 | 2,724 | 2,450 | | |
| Mexico | 176 | 2,353 | 5,330 | 3,840 | 3,228 | | |
| Netherlands | 442 | 3,594 | 4,328 | 4,956 | 4,692 | | |
| Norway | 202 | 1,251 | 1,991 | 900 | 864 | | |
| Peru | ... | 86 | 851 | 250 | 250 | | |
| Poland | 1,134 | 7,111 | 11,682 | 8,664 | 6,516 | | |
| Portugal | ... | 314 | 577 | 336 | 252 | | |
| Romania | 186 | 4,210 | 9,013 | 6,492 | 4,644 | | |
| South Africa | 651 | 4,328 | 8,542 | 1,600 | 1,764 | | |
| Spain | 537 | 4,278 | 6,725 | 5,748 | 5,400 | | |
| Sweden | 804 | 2,842 | 2,612 | 2,736 | 2,808 | | |
| Turkey | 100 | 1,176 | 2,048 | 4,824 | 4,500 | | |
| USSR (former) | 13,742 | 85,933 | 102,960 | 110,796 | 90,948 | 1 | 18.2 |
| United Kingdom | 9,453 | 19,023 | 6,413 | 12,492 | 12,060 | 9 | 2.4 |
| United States | 56,166 | 85,303 | 63,748 | 54,924 | 48,504 | 4 | 9.7 |

| | 1948 | 1970 | 1980 | 1990 | 1991 | Rank | % |
|---|---|---|---|---|---|---|---|
| Venezuela | | 510 | 2,450 | 2,400 | 2,400 | | |
| Yugoslavia | 183 | 1,377 | 2,668 | 2,628 | 1,428 | | |
| Zimbabwe | 17 | 250 | 862 | 800 | 800 | | |

## IRON ORE

*million tonnes*

metal content

| | 1948 | 1970 | 1900 | 1990 | 1991 | Rank | % |
|---|---|---|---|---|---|---|---|
| World | 104 | 417 | 520 | 979 | 946 | | |
| Algeria | 1 | 1.5 | 1.9 | 2.9 | 3 | | |
| Angola | – | 3.8 | – | – | – | | |
| Argentina | ... | ... | ... | 0.8 | 0.7 | | |
| Australia | 1.4 | 28.7 | 62.1 | 114 | 122 | 4 | 12.9 |
| Austria | 0.4 | 1.3 | 1 | 2.3 | 2 | | |
| Brazil | 1.1 | 20.4 | 41.2 | 152 | 150 | 3 | 15.9 |
| Bulgaria | – | 0.8 | 0.5 | 1.1 | 0.6 | | |
| Canada | 1.5 | 29.2 | 29.9 | 36.4 | 36.6 | 7 | 3.9 |
| Chile | 1.7 | 6.9 | 5.4 | 7.8 | 8.7 | | |
| China | ... | 24.2 | 32.5 | 169 | 176 | 2 | 18.6 |
| Colombia | ... | 0.5 | 0.2 | 0.6 | 0.6 | | |
| Czechoslovakia | 0.4 | 0.4 | 0.5 | 1.8 | 1.8 | | |
| Egypt | ... | 0.2 | 0.8 | 1.2 | ... | | |
| Finland | – | – | 0.6 | – | – | | |
| France | 7.6 | 17.8 | 9 | 8.7 | 7.5 | | |
| Germany | 1.8 | 1.8 | 0.5 | – | – | | |
| India | 1.5 | 19.7 | 25.8 | 53.7 | 54.7 | 6 | 5.8 |
| Iran | – | ... | ... | 5.5 | 5.5 | | |
| Italy | 0.3 | 0.4 | ... | ... | ... | | |
| Japan | 0.3 | 0.9 | 0.3 | ... | ... | | |
| Korea, North | – | 4 | 3.7 | 9.5 | 9.5 | | |
| Liberia | – | 15.4 | 12.5 | 3 | 1.2 | | |
| Luxembourg | 1 | 1.6 | 0.3 | – | – | | |
| Malaysia | ... | 0.5 | 0.3 | 0.3 | – | | |
| Mauritania | ... | 5.9 | 5.6 | 11.4 | 10 | | |
| Mexico | 0.2 | 2.6 | 5.2 | 8.3 | 7.8 | | |
| Morocco | 0.7 | 0.5 | 0.1 | – | – | | |
| New Zealand | ... | ... | ... | 1.3 | 1.3 | | |
| Norway | 0.1 | 2.6 | 2.5 | 2.1 | 2.3 | | |
| Peru | – | 6.1 | 3.4 | 3.5 | 3.8 | | |
| Poland | 0.2 | 0.7 | 0.1 | ... | ... | | |
| Romania | 0.1 | 0.9 | 0.6 | 0.6 | 0.3 | | |
| Sierra Leone | 0.6 | 1.4 | 0.2 | ... | ... | | |
| South Africa | 0.7 | 5.9 | 16.4 | 30.3 | 28.9 | 8 | 3.1 |
| Spain | 0.8 | 3.5 | 4.4 | 3 | 3.9 | | |
| Swaziland | ... | 1.5 | – | – | – | | |
| Sweden | 8.2 | 19.8 | 17 | 19.9 | 19.3 | 10 | 2 |
| Tunisia | 0.4 | 0.4 | 0.2 | ... | ... | | |
| Turkey | 0.1 | 1.7 | 1.4 | 6.2 | 5.4 | | |
| USSR (former) | 16.2 | 106 | 148 | 236 | 198 | 1 | 20.9 |
| United Kingdom | 3.9 | 3.4 | 0.3 | – | – | | |
| United States | 50.9 | 53.3 | 43.9 | 56.4 | 55.5 | 5 | 5.9 |
| Venezuela | – | 14.1 | 10.4 | 20.1 | 19.9 | 9 | 2.1 |
| Yugoslavia | 0.4 | 1.3 | 1.6 | 4.1 | 2.6 | | |
| Zimbabwe | 0.2 | 0.3 | 0.9 | 0.6 | 0.6 | | |

## LEAD ORE

*thousand tonnes*

metal content

| | 1948 | 1970 | 1980 | 1990 | 1991 | Rank | % |
|---|---|---|---|---|---|---|---|
| World | 1,370 | 3,400 | 3,600 | 3,345 | 3,341 | | |
| Algeria | 1.2 | 8.4 | 2.1 | 1.1 | 4 | | |
| Argentina | 17.8 | 36 | 33 | 23.4 | 24.2 | | |
| Australia | 220 | 459 | 397 | 561 | 579 | 1 | 17.3 |
| Austria | 3.5 | 6 | 5 | 1.5 | 1.2 | | |
| Bolivia | 25.6 | 26 | 17 | 19.9 | 20.8 | | |
| Brazil | ... | 18 | 22 | 9.2 | 8.6 | | |
| Bulgaria | 12.9 | 96 | 100 | 45.2 | 40.6 | | |
| Burma | – | 4 | 6 | 2.3 | 2.7 | | |
| Canada | 172 | 358 | 297 | 241 | 278 | 5 | 8.3 |
| Chile | 6.2 | 1 | 0 | 1.1 | 1.1 | | |
| China | ... | 100 | 160 | 315 | 320 | 4 | 9.6 |
| Congo | 2.7 | ... | 2.5 | – | – | | |

| | 1948 | 1970 | 1980 | 1990 | 1991 | Rank | % |
|---|---|---|---|---|---|---|---|
| Czechoslovakia | ... | 7 | 3 | 3 | 3.4 | | |
| France | 7.7 | 29 | 29 | 1.2 | 1.7 | | |
| Germany | 22.4 | 41 | 32 | 8.6 | 7.3 | | |
| Greece | 1.2 | 10 | 22 | 26.2 | 31.7 | | |
| Greenland | – | ... | 30 | 16.7 | – | | |
| Honduras | 0.1 | 15 | 14 | 4.2 | 8.7 | | |
| India | 0.4 | 3 | 14 | 25.9 | 27.8 | | |
| Iran | ... | 23 | 12 | 9.3 | 15.1 | | |
| Ireland | ... | 63 | 58 | 35.3 | 39.9 | | |
| Italy | 30.4 | 35 | 24 | 15.6 | 14 | | |
| Japan | 6.7 | 64 | 43 | 18.7 | 18.3 | | |
| Korea, North | ... | 70 | 100 | 70 | 80 | 10 | 2.4 |
| Korea, South | 0.3 | 11 | 11 | 18.7 | 15 | | |
| Mexico | 193 | 177 | 145 | 187 | 168 | 7 | 5 |
| Morocco | 28.8 | 85 | 115 | 66.9 | 71.2 | | |
| Namibia | 33.6 | 71 | 48 | 19.4 | 16.1 | | |
| Norway | 0.3 | 3 | 2 | 3 | 3.5 | | |
| Peru | 48.5 | 157 | 189 | 188 | 200 | 6 | 6 |
| Poland | 14.5 | 157 | 189 | 45.4 | 47 | | |
| Romania | 4 | 42 | 23 | 24.7 | 16.2 | | |
| South Africa | 0.1 | ... | 86 | 69.4 | 76.3 | | |
| Spain | 31.2 | 60 | 87 | 61.5 | 49.2 | | |
| Sweden | 23.6 | 78 | 72 | 84.2 | 87 | 8 | 2.6 |
| Thailand | – | 1 | 11 | 22 | 16.7 | | |
| Tunisia | 13.2 | 22 | 9 | 1.8 | 0.8 | | |
| Turkey | 2.6 | 5 | 8 | 12.3 | 15.3 | | |
| USSR (former) | ... | 450 | 580 | 490 | 460 | 3 | 13.8 |
| United Kingdom | 2.3 | 4 | 4 | ... | ... | | |
| United States | 354 | 519 | 550 | 497 | 477 | 2 | 14.3 |
| Yugoslavia | 62.3 | 127 | 121 | 83 | 84.5 | 9 | 2.5 |
| Zambia | 13.2 | 33 | 14 | 11.5 | 9.8 | | |

| | 1948 | 1970 | 1980 | 1990 | 1991 | Rank | % |
|---|---|---|---|---|---|---|---|
| Germany | ... | 68 | 190 | – | – | | |
| Italy | 1,318 | 1,530 | 3 | – | – | | |
| Japan | 50 | 58 | 222 | – | – | | |
| Mexico | 165 | 1,043 | 145 | 735 | 720 | 3 | 19.7 |
| Spain | 782 | 1,570 | 1,721 | 962 | 52 | 7 | 1.4 |
| Turkey | 1 | 324 | 154 | 47 | 26 | 10 | 0.7 |
| USSR (former) | ... | 1,655 | 1,800 | 1,400 | 1,200 | 1 | 32.9 |
| United States | 496 | 941 | 1,058 | 500 | 40 | 8 | 1.1 |
| Yugoslavia | 377 | 533 | – | 37 | 35 | 9 | 1 |

# NATURAL GAS

*thousand terajoules**

| | 1970 | 1980 | 1990 | 1991 | 1992 | Rank | % |
|---|---|---|---|---|---|---|---|
| World | 38,455 | 53,938 | 74,806 | 76,275 | 76,600 | | |
| Afghanistan | 95 | 102 | 110 | ... | ... | | |
| Algeria | 64 | 759 | 1,615 | 1,714 | 1,750 | 7 | 2.3 |
| Argentina | 209 | 326 | 793 | 886 | 925 | | |
| Australia | 56 | 359 | 784 | 908 | 922 | | |
| Austria | 77 | 78 | 46 | 48 | 52 | | |
| Azerbaijan | ... | ... | 323 | 280 | 260 | | |
| Bahrain | 14 | 114 | 201 | 202 | 163 | | |
| Bangladesh | 0 | 45 | 165 | 174 | 186 | | |
| Bolivia | 1 | 80 | 107 | 107 | 100 | | |
| Brazil | 3 | 41 | 147 | 146 | 155 | | |
| Brunei | 8 | 399 | 414 | 425 | 433 | | |
| Burma | 2.2 | 13.3 | 90 | 85 | ... | | |
| Canada | 2,113 | 2,790 | 4,114 | 4,370 | 4,760 | 3 | 6.2 |
| Chile | 48.1 | 27.1 | 9.3 | 7.6 | ... | | |
| China | 144 | 555 | 593 | 599 | 601 | | |
| Colombia | 55.2 | 151 | 275 | 279 | 275 | | |
| Egypt | 3 | 41 | 240 | 275 | 297 | | |
| France | 271 | 289 | 111 | 139 | 134 | | |
| Germany | 479 | 774 | 530 | 613 | 572 | | |
| Hungary | 114 | 237 | 183 | 184 | 173 | | |
| India | 19 | 51 | 441 | 519 | 520 | | |
| Indonesia | 46 | 607 | 1,578 | 1,819 | 1,900 | 6 | 2.5 |
| Iran | 45 | 278 | 934 | 999 | 961 | | |
| Iraq | 30.5 | 50 | 392 | 61.1 | ... | | |
| Ireland | – | 34 | 92 | 95 | 93 | | |
| Italy | 498 | 477 | 648 | 646 | 638 | | |
| Japan | 10 | 85 | 84 | 88 | 89 | | |
| Kazakhstan | ... | ... | 240 | 260 | 180 | | |
| Kuwait | 80 | 133 | 498 | 19 | 97 | | |
| Libya | 79.6 | 134 | 225 | 220 | 230 | | |
| Malaysia | 3 | 10 | 502 | 626 | 667 | | |
| Mexico | 451 | 1,035 | 955 | 948 | 1,000 | | |
| Netherlands | 1,116 | 3,205 | 2,286 | 2,286 | 2,301 | 4 | 3 |
| New Zealand | 4 | 39 | 192 | 207 | 222 | | |
| Nigeria | 4 | 52 | 145 | 111 | 120 | | |
| Norway | – | 1,065 | 1,121 | 1,134 | 1,150 | 9 | 1.5 |
| Pakistan | 96 | 246 | 490 | 523 | 543 | | |
| Poland | 186 | 193 | 134 | 130 | 126 | | |
| Qatar | 39.1 | 176 | 260 | 310 | ... | | |
| Romania | 990 | 1,455 | 959 | 989 | 880 | | |
| Russia | ... | ... | 21,000 | 21,000 | 20,900 | | |
| Saudi Arabia | ... | 49 | 1,101 | 1,452 | 1,500 | 8 | 2 |
| Thailand | – | – | 234 | 254 | 315 | | |
| Trinidad & Tobago | 73 | 146 | 215 | 242 | 242 | | |
| Turkmenistan | ... | ... | 2,800 | 2,800 | 2,000 | | |
| Ukraine | ... | ... | 2,800 | 2,800 | 680 | | |
| USSR (former) | 6,670 | 15,148 | 26,600 | 26,500 | 25,500 | 1 | 33.3 |
| United Arab Em. | 8.9 | 471 | 1840 | 1920 | ... | | |
| United Kingdom | 434 | 1,454 | 1,903 | 1,955 | 1,972 | 5 | 2.6 |
| United States | 22,860 | 19,256 | 19,373 | 19,509 | 19,322 | 2 | 25.2 |
| Uzbekistan | ... | ... | 1,300 | 1,400 | 1,400 | | |
| Venezuela | 382 | 643 | 955 | 1,053 | 1,050 | 10 | 1.4 |
| Yugoslavia | 39 | 75 | 82 | 60 | 59 | | |

* A terajoule is a measure of energy equivalent to 23.88 tonnes of oil or 34.12 tonnes of coal.

# MANGANESE ORE

*tonnes*

| | 1948 | 1970 | 1980 | 1990 | 1991 | Rank | % |
|---|---|---|---|---|---|---|---|
| World | 2,100 | 7,400 | 12,786 | 24,000 | 22,000 | | |
| Angola | 0 | 9 | – | – | – | | |
| Argentina | 1 | 10 | 2 | 2 | ... | | |
| Australia | 2 | 397 | 969 | 2,300 | 1,450 | 6 | 6.6 |
| Botswana | – | 16 | – | – | – | | |
| Brazil | 79 | 830 | 1,027 | 1,850 | 2,000 | 4 | 9.1 |
| Chile | 11 | 11 | 11 | 30 | 30 | | |
| China | ... | 300 | 480 | 2,700 | 2,700 | 3 | 12.3 |
| Czechoslovakia | ... | 14 | 0 | 0 | ... | | |
| Gabon | ... | 729 | 1,073 | 2,200 | 1,800 | 5 | 8.2 |
| Ghana | 314 | 191 | 100 | 260 | 320 | 8 | 1.5 |
| Hungary | 20 | 35 | 25 | 80 | 80 | 10 | 0.4 |
| India | 255 | 616 | 592 | 1,300 | 1,300 | 7 | 5.9 |
| Italy | 7 | 15 | 3 | 9 | ... | | |
| Japan | 19 | 79 | 28 | ... | ... | | |
| Mexico | 24 | 99 | 161 | 450 | 250 | 9 | 1.1 |
| Morocco | 85 | 60 | 65 | 30 | 30 | | |
| Philippines | 12 | 3 | 1 | 1 | ... | | |
| Romania | 18 | 27 | 18 | 65 | 65 | | |
| South Africa | 116 | 1,182 | 4,743 | 3,795 | 3,200 | 2 | 14.5 |
| Spain | 7 | 4 | – | – | – | | |
| Thailand | ... | 8 | 24 | 8 | ... | | |
| Turkey | 4 | 6 | 17 | 7 | ... | | |
| USA | 69 | 47 | 21 | 4 | ... | | |
| USSR (former) | ... | ... | 6,000 | 9,000 | 8,000 | 1 | 36.4 |
| Vanuatu | ... | 12 | – | – | ... | | |
| Yugoslavia | 4 | 5 | 10 | 40 | 40 | | |
| Zaire | 6 | 156 | 3 | ... | ... | | |

# MERCURY

*tonnes*

| | 1948 | 1970 | 1980 | 1990 | 1991 | Rank | % |
|---|---|---|---|---|---|---|---|
| World | 3,250 | 8,810 | 6,818 | 5,514 | 3,652 | | |
| Algeria | 0 | 0 | 841 | 637 | 431 | 4 | 11.8 |
| China | ... | 690 | 800 | 930 | 1,000 | 2 | 27.4 |
| Czechoslovakia | – | 17 | 159 | 126 | 75 | 5 | 2.1 |
| Finland | ... | 3 | 75 | 140 | 74 | 6 | 2 |

# NICKEL ORE

thousand tonnes

metal content

| | 1948 | 1970 | 1980 | 1990 | 1991 | Rank | % |
|---|---|---|---|---|---|---|---|
| World | 144 | 651 | 738 | 881 | 871 | | |
| Albania | ... | ... | 4.8 | 8.5 | 4 | | |
| Australia | – | 18 | 74.3 | 67 | 69 | 4 | 7.9 |
| Botswana | – | – | 15.4 | 19.7 | 20.4 | 10 | 2.3 |
| Brazil | – | 2.9 | 4.3 | 13 | 13.5 | | |
| Canada | 120 | 278 | 185 | 196 | 197 | 2 | 22.6 |
| China | – | – | 11 | 26 | 25 | 9 | 2.9 |
| Colombia | – | – | – | 18.4 | 20.2 | | |
| Cuba | 2.1 | 35.2 | 38.2 | 40.8 | 33.3 | 6 | 3.8 |
| Dominican Rep. | – | – | 18 | 28.7 | 29.1 | 7 | 3.3 |
| Finland | ... | 6.7 | 6.4 | 11.5 | 9.1 | | |
| Germany | ... | ... | 2.7 | 0.9 | – | | |
| Greece | – | – | 13.9 | 18.5 | 18 | | |
| Indonesia | – | 18 | 40.5 | 68.6 | 66.1 | 5 | 7.6 |
| New Caledonia | 3.6 | 138 | 86.6 | 85 | 99.7 | 3 | 11.4 |
| Norway | – | – | 0.6 | 2.2 | 2.3 | | |
| Philippines | ... | ... | 34.9 | 15.8 | 13.8 | | |
| Poland | – | 2 | 1.1 | – | – | | |
| South Africa | 0.5 | 11.6 | 25.7 | 30 | 29 | 8 | 3.3 |
| USSR (former) | 17.5 | 109 | 143 | 212 | 200 | 1 | 23 |
| United States | 0.8 | 17 | 10.2 | 0.3 | 5.5 | | |
| Yugoslavia | – | – | 0.5 | 4.9 | 3.2 | | |
| Zimbabwe | 0 | 10.9 | 14.3 | 12.6 | 12.4 | | |

# OIL - CRUDE

million tonnes

| | 1948 | 1970 | 1980 | 1990 | 1991 | 1992 | Rank | % |
|---|---|---|---|---|---|---|---|---|
| World | 469 | 2,244 | 2,829 | 3,158 | 3,133 | 3,170 | | |
| Algeria | – | 51.2 | 50.6 | 55.2 | 56.4 | 57 | | |
| Angola | – | 4.5 | 7.5 | 24.1 | 25 | 27 | | |
| Argentina | 3.3 | 19.1 | 24.2 | 24 | 24 | 27.9 | | |
| Australia | – | 8.7 | 18.9 | 28.5 | 27.2 | 24.7 | | |
| Azerbaijan | ... | ... | ... | 12.5 | 12 | 11.9 | | |
| Bahrain | – | 3.8 | 2.4 | 2.1 | 2.1 | 1.9 | | |
| Brazil | – | 8 | 9.1 | 33 | 32.7 | 32.5 | | |
| Brunei | 2.7 | 7.4 | 11.5 | 7 | 8 | 9 | | |
| Cameroon | – | 0.1 | 2.9 | 7.9 | 7.5 | 7 | | |
| Canada | 1.7 | 62.9 | 70.3 | 93.7 | 93.9 | 98.2 | 10 | 3.1 |
| China | 0.1 | 24.9 | 106 | 138 | 139 | 142 | 6 | 4.5 |
| Colombia | 3.3 | 10.7 | 6.2 | 21.9 | 21.2 | 22.2 | | |
| Congo | – | – | 2.8 | 7.6 | 7.5 | 8 | | |
| Denmark | – | – | 0.3 | 5.9 | 7.4 | 7.8 | | |
| Ecuador | 0.3 | 0.2 | 11.1 | 15 | 15.5 | 16.7 | | |
| Egypt | 2.1 | 16.3 | 29.7 | 45.5 | 46 | 46.1 | | |
| France | 0.1 | 2.3 | 1.3 | 3 | 2.8 | 2.9 | | |
| Gabon | – | 5.4 | 9 | 13.6 | 14.8 | 14.7 | | |
| Germany | 0.6 | 7.3 | 4.5 | 3.6 | 3.4 | 3.2 | | |
| India | 0.3 | 6.9 | 9.1 | 33.9 | 31.9 | 28.7 | | |
| Indonesia | 4.3 | 42.5 | 78.5 | 70.1 | 74.3 | | | |
| Iran | 25.3 | 166 | 73 | 155 | 162 | 172 | 4 | 5.4 |
| Iraq | 3.4 | 77.1 | 131 | 98.2 | 11.3 | 23.6 | | |
| Italy | – | 1.5 | 1.8 | 4.8 | 4.4 | 4.6 | | |
| Kazakhstan | – | – | 27 | 27 | 28 | 27 | | |
| Kuwait | 6.4 | 136 | 68.8 | 51.8 | 4.4 | 45.6 | | |
| Libya | – | 165 | 88.9 | 64.8 | 72.2 | 73 | | |
| Malaysia | – | – | 14.3 | 30.6 | 32.1 | 32.6 | | |
| Mexico | 8.4 | 21.4 | 95.4 | 142 | 149 | 155 | 5 | 4.9 |
| Netherlands | 0.5 | 1.8 | 1.2 | 3.9 | 3.6 | 3.3 | | |
| Nigeria | – | 53.9 | 102 | 87.8 | 93.6 | 91.6 | | |
| Norway | – | – | 26.3 | 81.9 | 93.4 | 107 | 9 | 3.4 |
| Oman | – | 16.6 | 14.1 | 34.1 | 35.3 | 36.1 | | |
| Pakistan | – | 0.5 | 0.5 | 2.9 | 3.5 | 3.5 | | |
| Peru | 1.9 | 3.6 | 9.9 | 7 | 6 | 6 | | |
| Qatar | – | 18 | 23.5 | 21.2 | 20.5 | 22.6 | | |
| Romania | 4.1 | 13.4 | 12.4 | 7.9 | 6.5 | 6.6 | | |
| Russia | ... | ... | 582 | 544 | 485 | 396 | | |
| Saudi Arabia | 19.1 | 177 | 480 | 326 | 419 | 428 | 2 | 13.5 |
| Syria | – | 4.1 | 8.2 | 21 | 24.5 | 25.2 | | |
| Trinidad & Tobago | 2.9 | 7 | 10.5 | 7.4 | 7.3 | 7.2 | | |
| Tunisia | – | 4.4 | 5.5 | 4.5 | 5.1 | 5.3 | | |
| Turkey | – | 3.4 | 2.2 | 3.8 | 4.4 | 4.3 | | |

| | 1948 | 1970 | 1980 | 1990 | 1991 | 1992 | Rank | % |
|---|---|---|---|---|---|---|---|---|
| USSR (former) | 29.2 | 353 | 603 | 570 | 515 | 450 | 1 | 14.2 |
| United Arab Em. | – | 96.7 | 85.1 | 109 | 124 | 118 | 8 | 3.7 |
| United Kingdom | 0.2 | 0.1 | 80.6 | 91.6 | 91.6 | 94.2 | | |
| United States | 273 | 480 | 427 | 420 | 424 | 417 | 3 | 13.2 |
| Venezuela | 71.7 | 185 | 108 | 123 | 136 | 129 | 7 | 4.1 |
| Vietnam | – | – | – | 2.5 | 3.8 | 5.4 | | |
| Yemen | – | – | 4.2 | 9.5 | 10.9 | 9.1 | | |
| Yugoslavia | – | 2.9 | 4.2 | 3.1 | 2.9 | ... | | |

# PETROLEUM PRODUCTS*

million tonnes

| | 1970 | 1980 | 1990 | 1991 | Rank | % |
|---|---|---|---|---|---|---|
| World | 2,032 | 2,762 | 3,500 | 3,400 | | |
| Algeria | 2.3 | 13 | 38 | 38 | | |
| Argentina | 19.4 | 23.7 | 18.6 | 18.8 | | |
| Australia | 22.1 | 28.2 | 26.1 | 25.8 | | |
| Austria | 5.5 | 8.8 | 7.4 | 7.2 | | |
| Bahamas | 2.3 | 8.3 | ... | ... | | |
| Bahrain | 11.2 | 10.6 | 11 | 11 | | |
| Belgium | 26 | 29.5 | 22.6 | 25.8 | | |
| Brazil | 23.5 | 47.7 | 44 | 41.9 | | |
| Bulgaria | 5.8 | 11.7 | 10 | 10 | | |
| Canada | 57.4 | 98.3 | 64 | 61.6 | 9 | 1.8 |
| Chile | 3.6 | 5 | 5.4 | 5.5 | | |
| China | 21.8 | 64.2 | 84.5 | 87.8 | 4 | 2.6 |
| Colombia | 6.2 | 7.7 | 10 | 10.8 | | |
| Cuba | 4.2 | 5.5 | 6.5 | 6.5 | | |
| Czechoslovakia | 8.7 | 16.1 | 9.7 | 8.5 | | |
| Denmark | 9.4 | 6.2 | 7.2 | 7.6 | | |
| Ecuador | 1.1 | 4.5 | 5.8 | 5.9 | | |
| Egypt | 3.2 | 13.4 | 21.7 | 22.3 | | |
| Finland | 7 | 10.9 | 8.7 | 9.2 | | |
| France | 88.5 | 103 | 63.1 | 21.2 | | |
| Germany | 105.1 | 115.8 | 82.2 | 83 | 5 | 2.4 |
| Greece | 4.6 | 13.1 | 14.7 | 13.3 | | |
| Hungary | 5 | 8.9 | 6 | 5.8 | | |
| India | 14.3 | 19.4 | 37.2 | 36.9 | | |
| Indonesia | 10.4 | 23.8 | 31.5 | 32.2 | | |
| Iran | 24.2 | 32.9 | 33.5 | 35.7 | | |
| Iraq | 3.3 | 8.2 | 15.8 | 11.9 | | |
| Israel | 5 | 5.6 | 7 | 7 | | |
| Italy | 104 | 85.4 | 76.5 | 77.4 | 7 | 2.3 |
| Japan | ... | 185 | 137 | 147 | 3 | 4.3 |
| Korea, South | 8.8 | 22 | 33.2 | 44.5 | | |
| Kuwait | 17 | 17.8 | 24 | 5 | | |
| Libya | 0.4 | 5.3 | 12.3 | 12.5 | | |
| Malaysia | 4 | 5.6 | 8.9 | 8.9 | | |
| Mexico | 21.1 | 56.1 | 58 | 60.8 | 10 | 1.8 |
| Morocco | 1.4 | 3.8 | 4.5 | 4.4 | | |
| Netherlands | 51.6 | 51.9 | 43.3 | 46.2 | | |
| Neths. Antilles | 45.6 | 26.1 | 10 | 10 | | |
| New Zealand | 2.7 | 2.7 | 3.6 | 3.4 | | |
| Nigeria | 0.9 | 6.2 | 11.6 | 11.3 | | |
| Norway | 5.5 | 7.5 | 11.3 | 10.7 | | |
| Pakistan | 4 | 3.9 | 5.1 | 5.9 | | |
| Peru | 4.1 | 7.2 | 7.5 | 7.5 | | |
| Philippines | 8.1 | 8.8 | 9.9 | 9.3 | | |
| Poland | 6.1 | 12.8 | 9.8 | 9.3 | | |
| Portugal | 3.3 | 7.1 | 9.4 | 8.5 | | |
| Puerto Rico | 9.4 | 10.2 | 4.5 | 4.5 | | |
| Romania | 14 | 24.6 | 19.6 | 12.4 | | |
| Saudi Arabia | 25.5 | 36.9 | 62.9 | 65.6 | 8 | 1.9 |
| Singapore | 10.7 | 25.1 | 30 | 30 | | |
| South Africa | 7.7 | 12.7 | 14 | 14 | | |
| Spain | 29.3 | 44.2 | 42.1 | 43.7 | | |
| Sweden | 10.4 | 16.7 | 15.6 | 13.9 | | |
| Switzerland | 4.9 | 4.4 | 2.7 | 4.2 | | |
| Syria | 1.7 | 5.1 | 10.8 | 11.2 | | |
| Taiwan | 5.9 | 20.3 | 20 | 20 | | |
| Thailand | 3.2 | 7.2 | 12 | 12 | | |
| Trinidad & Tobago | 21.7 | 11.5 | 4.3 | 5.3 | | |
| Turkey | 6.8 | 11.4 | 19.2 | 19 | | |
| USSR (former) | 246 | 396 | 450 | 450 | 2 | 13.2 |
| United Arab Em. | 0 | 5 | 13 | 13 | | |
| United Kingdom | 90.6 | 77.6 | 75.8 | 78.8 | 6 | 2.3 |
| United States | 496 | 677 | 572 | 571 | 1 | 16.8 |
| US Virgin Is. | 13.1 | 22.5 | 11 | 11 | | |
| Venezuela | 60.6 | 46.3 | 44.1 | 48.7 | | |

| | 1970 | 1980 | 1990 | 1991 | Rank | % |
|---|---|---|---|---|---|---|
| Yemen | 6.3 | 1.9 | 3.5 | 3.5 | | |
| Yugoslavia | 6.4 | 13.7 | 11 | 9.5 | | |

\* The principal products are aviation gasolene, fuel oils, diesel oil, jet fuel, kerosene liquefied petroleum gas, motor gasolene and residual fuel oil.

## RUBBER - SYNTHETIC

*thousand tonnes*

| | 1960 | 1970 | 1980 | 1990 | 1991 | Rank | % |
|---|---|---|---|---|---|---|---|
| World | 2,439 | 5,055 | 6,515 | 7,300 | 7,000 | | |
| Argentina | ... | 39 | 33.4 | 57.6 | 44.76 | | |
| Australia | 11.4 | 41.9 | 46.2 | 41 | 37 | | |
| Belgium | 0 | 50 | 115 | 125 | 114 | | |
| Brazil | 10.1 | 96.4 | 287 | 252 | 232 | 8 | 3.3 |
| Bulgaria | 0 | 6 | 30 | ... | ... | | |
| Canada | 168 | 218 | 256 | 213 | 160 | | |
| China | ... | ... | 250 | 315 | 335 | 5 | 4.8 |
| Czechoslovakia | 0 | 64.2 | 79.3 | 69 | 43 | | |
| Finland | ... | ... | ... | 29 | 30 | | |
| France | 17.5 | 343 | 528 | 520 | 469 | 4 | 6.7 |
| Germany | 218 | 442 | 540 | 524 | 504 | 3 | 7.2 |
| India | 0 | 30.3 | 22.5 | 52 | 55 | | |
| Italy | 67 | 155 | 250 | 300 | 300 | 6 | 4.3 |
| Japan | 18.6 | 760 | 1,161 | 1,426 | 1,368 | 2 | 19.5 |
| Korea, South | 0 | 5.1 | 75.5 | 184 | 181 | 10 | 2.6 |
| Mexico | 43.7 | 90.8 | 132 | 119 | 107 | | |
| Netherlands | 12 | 200 | 212 | 240 | 223 | 9 | 3.2 |
| Poland | 20.2 | 61.7 | 118 | 103 | 79 | | |
| Romania | ... | 61.2 | 150 | 102 | 61 | | |
| South Africa | 0 | 28.6 | 38.7 | 46 | 36 | | |
| Spain | ... | 38.6 | 81.1 | 66 | 63 | | |
| Sweden | ... | 7.8 | 13.2 | ... | ... | | |
| Turkey | 0 | 0 | 23 | 39 | 34 | | |
| United Kingdom | 138 | 345 | 227 | 298 | 274 | 7 | 3.9 |
| United States | 1,757 | 2,436 | 2,302 | 2,114 | 2,190 | 1 | 31.3 |
| Yugoslavia | 0 | 6.2 | 7.4 | ... | ... | | |

## SHIPS

### Merchant vessels launched

*thousand gross registered tons*

| | 1948 | 1970 | 1980 | 1990 | 1991 | Rank | % |
|---|---|---|---|---|---|---|---|
| World | 2,308 | 21,690 | 15,397 | 14,680 | 15,897 | | |
| Argentina | 0 | 18 | 60 | 37 | 53 | | |
| Australia | 9 | 54 | 8 | 30 | 15 | | |
| Belgium | 52 | 155 | 99 | 110 | 120 | | |
| Brazil | 0 | 100 | 615 | 698 | 669 | 8 | 4.2 |
| Bulgaria | ... | 53 | 152 | 129 | 132 | | |
| Canada | 102 | 33 | 80 | 1 | 15 | | |
| China | ... | ... | ... | 340 | 495 | | |
| Denmark | 99 | 514 | 227 | 108 | 82 | | |
| Egypt | ... | 9 | 6 | 20 | 11 | | |
| Finland | 7 | 222 | 198 | 350 | 314 | | |
| France | 138 | 960 | 328 | 182 | 155 | | |
| Germany | ... | 2,021 | 802 | 502 | 780 | 4 | 4.9 |
| Greece | ... | 73 | 22 | 19 | 21 | | |
| India | ... | 29 | 74 | 144 | 147 | | |
| Indonesia | ... | ... | ... | 15 | 67 | | |
| Ireland | 0 | 28 | 7 | ... | ... | | |
| Italy | 112 | 598 | 168 | 826 | 680 | 7 | 4.3 |
| Japan | ... | 10,476 | 7,288 | 5,030 | 5,245 | 1 | 33 |
| Korea, South | ... | ... | 629 | 1,795 | 2,422 | 2 | 15.2 |
| Netherlands | 142 | 461 | 125 | 137 | 105 | | |
| Norway | 47 | 639 | 319 | 111 | 99 | | |
| Peru | ... | 35 | 17 | 14 | 15 | | |
| Poland | 5 | 463 | 395 | 425 | 603 | 10 | 3.8 |
| Portugal | 4 | 16 | 167 | 24 | 96 | | |
| Romania | ... | ... | 31 | ... | 1,033 | 3 | 6.5 |
| Singapore | ... | 6 | 27 | 102 | 97 | | |
| Spain | 22 | 926 | 509 | 482 | 651 | 9 | 4.1 |
| Sweden | 246 | 1,711 | 338 | 40 | 41 | | |
| Taiwan | 0 | 217 | 572 | 1,211 | 741 | 5 | 4.7 |
| Turkey | ... | 11 | 14 | 207 | 205 | | |

| | 1948 | 1970 | 1980 | 1990 | 1991 | Rank | % |
|---|---|---|---|---|---|---|---|
| United Kingdom | 1,176 | 1,237 | 244 | 284 | 265 | | |
| United States | 126 | 338 | 558 | 18 | 63 | | |
| Yugoslavia | 6 | 393 | 123 | 798 | 691 | 6 | 4.3 |

## SILVER

*tonnes*

*metal content*

| | 1948 | 1970 | 1980 | 1990 | 1991 | Rank | % |
|---|---|---|---|---|---|---|---|
| World | 5,000 | 9,393 | 11,101 | 14,834 | 14,241 | | |
| Argentina | 212 | 64 | 73 | 76 | 70 | | |
| Australia | 313 | 855 | 767 | 1,143 | 1,180 | 6 | 8.3 |
| Bolivia | 235 | 186 | 190 | 311 | 337 | 9 | 2.4 |
| Brazil | ... | 11 | 45 | 60 | 50 | | |
| Bulgaria | ... | ... | 24 | 54 | 37.3 | | |
| Burma | 14 | 17 | 30 | 3.4 | 5.3 | | |
| Canada | 529 | 1,376 | 1,070 | 1,502 | 1,338 | 4 | 9.4 |
| Chile | 27 | 74 | 299 | 655 | 674 | 8 | 4.7 |
| China | ... | 25 | 60 | 150 | 180 | | |
| Czechoslovakia | ... | ... | 35 | 26 | 28 | | |
| Dominican Rep. | ... | ... | 48 | 22.9 | 22 | | |
| Finland | 5 | 23 | 48 | 30 | 30.3 | | |
| France | 15 | 150 | 74 | 20.5 | 23.6 | | |
| Germany | 94 | 205 | 85 | 28 | 7.2 | | |
| Greece | 1 | ... | 60 | 63 | 70 | | |
| Honduras | 100 | 119 | 22 | 31 | 43 | | |
| India | 0.4 | 2 | 11 | 32.2 | 31.9 | | |
| Indonesia | ... | 9 | 22 | 67 | 80 | | |
| Iran | ... | ... | ... | 38 | 48 | | |
| Ireland | ... | 62 | 20 | 8.8 | 10.5 | | |
| Italy | 21 | 33 | 43 | 11 | 13.6 | | |
| Japan | 94 | 343 | 268 | 150 | 171 | | |
| Korea, North | ... | 22 | 290 | 280 | 300 | 10 | 2.1 |
| Korea, South | 1 | 53 | 63 | 16.4 | 3 | | |
| Malaysia | ... | ... | 22 | 12.6 | 13.4 | | |
| Mexico | 1,789 | 1,332 | 1,557 | 2,399 | 2,290 | 1 | 16.1 |
| Morocco | 15 | 21 | 98 | 241 | 234 | | |
| Namibia | 12 | 38 | 105 | 93 | 92 | | |
| New Zealand | 7 | ... | 23 | 4.8 | 11 | | |
| Nicaragua | ... | 7 | 16 | 1.1 | 1 | | |
| Papua New Guinea | 1 | 1 | 37 | 115 | 125 | | |
| Peru | 289 | 1,239 | 1,315 | 1,781 | 1,769 | 3 | 12.4 |
| Philippines | 6 | 53 | 61 | 45.1 | 34.9 | | |
| Poland | ... | ... | 766 | 832 | 867 | 7 | 6.1 |
| Portugal | ... | ... | ... | 2 | 43 | 42.6 | |
| Romania | 20 | 25 | 28 | 24 | 17 | | |
| South Africa | 36 | 110 | 232 | 161 | 171 | | |
| Spain | 11 | 51 | 178 | 270 | 208 | | |
| Sweden | 35 | 123 | 166 | 225 | 253 | | |
| Thailand | ... | ... | ... | 20.5 | 20 | | |
| USSR (former) | ... | 1,182 | 1,550 | 1,380 | 1,270 | 5 | 8.9 |
| United States | 1,220 | 1,400 | 1,006 | 2,125 | 1,848 | 2 | 13 |
| Yugoslavia | 47 | 106 | 149 | 105 | 92 | | |
| Zaire | 118 | 53 | 79 | 84 | 50 | | |
| Zambia | 5 | 48 | 24 | 18.5 | 14.2 | | |
| Zimbabwe | 3 | 2 | 30 | 21.2 | 20.3 | | |

## STEEL

*thousand tonnes*

| | 1948 | 1970 | 1980 | 1991 | 1992 | Rank | % |
|---|---|---|---|---|---|---|---|
| World | 155,800 | 593,791 | 690,000 | 730,000 | 710,000 | | |
| Argentina | 122 | 1,859 | 2,556 | 2,976 | 2,700 | | |
| Australia | 1,245 | 6,874 | 7,895 | 6,216 | 6,456 | | |
| Austria | 648 | 4,079 | 4,624 | 4,404 | 3,900 | | |
| Belgium | 6,373 | 12,609 | 12,321 | 11,292 | 10,332 | | |
| Brazil | 483 | 5,390 | 7,940 | 22,608 | 23,904 | 9 | 3.4 |
| Bulgaria | 0 | 1,800 | 2,565 | 1,620 | 1,600 | | |
| Canada | 2,903 | 11,198 | 15,901 | 23,844 | 25,992 | 7 | 3.7 |
| Chile | 30 | 547 | 695 | 804 | 810 | | |
| China | 800 | 17,790 | 37,120 | 70,560 | 82,000 | 4 | 11.5 |
| Czechoslovakia | 2,621 | 11,480 | 15,225 | 12,072 | 10,900 | | |
| Denmark | ... | ... | 734 | 636 | 588 | | |
| Egypt | 0 | 304 | 500 | 2,600 | 2,500 | | |

| | 1948 | 1970 | 1980 | 1991 | 1992 | Rank | % |
|---|---|---|---|---|---|---|---|
| Finland | 103 | 1,167 | 2,509 | 2,892 | 3,084 | | |
| France | 7,236 | 23,773 | 23,176 | 18,432 | 18,000 | | |
| Germany | 5,866 | 5,093 | 51,146 | 38,784 | 36,876 | 5 | 5.2 |
| Greece | ... | 435 | 935 | 984 | 1,000 | | |
| Hungary | 770 | 3,108 | 3,766 | 1,860 | 1,560 | | |
| India | 1,277 | 6,286 | 9,427 | 16,392 | 18,100 | 10 | 2.5 |
| Indonesia | ... | ... | 360 | 3,000 | 3,100 | | |
| Iran | ... | ... | 566 | 2,200 | 2,900 | | |
| Italy | 2,125 | 17,277 | 26,501 | 25,032 | 24,800 | 8 | 3.5 |
| Japan | 1,715 | 93,322 | 111,395 | 109,644 | 98,100 | 2 | 13.8 |
| Korea, North | 115 | 2,200 | 3,500 | 7,000 | 7,000 | | |
| Korea, South | 8 | 481 | 5,760 | 26,808 | 27,800 | 6 | 3.9 |
| Luxembourg | 2,624 | 5,462 | 4,620 | 3,384 | 3,072 | | |
| Mexico | 292 | 3,846 | 7,003 | 7,716 | 8,400 | | |
| Netherlands | 334 | 5,042 | 4,959 | 5,172 | 5,436 | | |
| Norway | 74 | 869 | 853 | 444 | 456 | | |
| Poland | 1,955 | 11,750 | 18,648 | 10,440 | 11,000 | | |
| Portugal | ... | ... | 382 | 576 | 600 | | |
| Romania | 353 | 6,517 | 13,175 | 7,116 | 5,300 | | |
| Saudi Arabia | ... | ... | 50 | 1,800 | 1,900 | | |
| South Africa | 596 | 4,674 | 8,976 | 8,940 | 9,200 | | |
| Spain | 624 | 7,394 | 12,563 | 12,564 | 12,600 | | |
| Sweden | 1,276 | 5,494 | 4,231 | 4,236 | 4,416 | | |
| Switzerland | 120 | 524 | 929 | 1,000 | 1,000 | | |
| Taiwan | 18 | 607 | 3,651 | 11,000 | 10,800 | | |
| Turkey | 102 | 1,312 | 1,700 | 9,300 | 10,344 | | |
| USSR (former) | 18,639 | 115,889 | 147,941 | 139,920 | 112,000 | 1 | 15.8 |
| United Kingdom | 15,116 | 28,316 | 11,277 | 16,632 | 16,100 | | |
| United States | 80,413 | 119,309 | 101,456 | 87,444 | 91,596 | 3 | 12.9 |
| Venezuela | ... | 927 | 1,784 | 3,108 | 3,400 | | |
| Yugoslavia | 368 | 2,228 | 2,306 | 4,500 | 4,500 | | |
| Zimbabwe | 9 | 250 | 804 | 1,000 | 1,000 | | |

# TIN ORE

*thousand tonnes*

*metal content*

| | 1948 | 1970 | 1980 | 1990 | 1991 | Rank | % |
|---|---|---|---|---|---|---|---|
| World | 154 | 186 | 236 | 209 | 179 | | |
| Argentina | 0.3 | 2.3 | 0.4 | 0.1 | – | | |
| Australia | 1.9 | 8.9 | 11.6 | 7.4 | 5.7 | 9 | 3.2 |
| Bolivia | 38 | 30.1 | 27.5 | 17.3 | 16.8 | 5 | 9.3 |
| Brazil | 0.2 | 4.3 | 6.9 | 39.1 | 29.3 | 3 | 16.4 |
| Burma | 1.2 | 0.3 | 1.1 | 0.5 | 0.5 | | |
| Canada | 0.3 | 0.1 | 6.9 | 3.8 | 4.5 | 10 | 2.5 |
| China | 4.9 | ... | 16 | 35.8 | 33.7 | 1 | 18.8 |
| Czechoslovakia | ... | 0.2 | 0.2 | 0.3 | – | | |
| Germany | 0.2 | ... | 1.8 | 1.8 | – | | |
| Indonesia | 31.1 | 19.1 | 32.5 | 30.2 | 30.1 | 2 | 16.8 |
| Japan | 0.1 | 0.8 | 0.5 | – | – | | |
| Laos | 0 | 1.4 | 0.6 | 0.3 | 0.2 | | |
| Malaysia | 45.5 | 73.8 | 61.4 | 28.5 | 20.7 | 4 | 11.6 |
| Mexico | 0.2 | 0.5 | 0.1 | – | – | | |
| Mongolia | 0 | 0 | 0 | 0.2 | 0.3 | | |
| Namibia | 0.1 | 1 | 1 | 0.9 | – | | |
| Nigeria | 9.4 | 8 | 2.7 | 0.2 | 0.2 | | |
| Peru | 0.1 | 0 | 1.1 | 5.1 | 6.6 | 8 | 3.7 |
| Portugal | 0.7 | 0.4 | 0.3 | 1.4 | 3.1 | | |
| Rwanda | 1.4 | 1.3 | 1.6 | 0.7 | 0.7 | | |
| South Africa | 0.5 | 2 | 2.9 | 1.1 | 1 | | |
| Spain | 0.3 | 0.4 | 0.4 | 0.1 | – | | |
| Thailand | 4.3 | 21.8 | 33.7 | 14.6 | 10.9 | 7 | 6.1 |
| USSR (former) | ... | ... | 16 | 13 | 11 | 6 | 6.1 |
| United Kingdom | 0.9 | 1.7 | 3.3 | 3.4 | 2.3 | | |
| United States | ... | ... | 16 | 0.1 | 0.1 | | |
| Vietnam | ... | ... | 0.4 | 0.8 | 0.8 | | |
| Zaire | 11.7 | 6.5 | 3.2 | 1.6 | – | | |
| Zimbabwe | 0.1 | 0.6 | 0.9 | 0.8 | 0.8 | | |

# URANIUM

*tonnes*

*metal content*

| | 1970 | 1980 | 1991 | 1992 | Rank | % |
|---|---|---|---|---|---|---|
| World | 24,000 | 52,000 | 62,000 | 60,000 | | |
| Argentina | 50 | 242 | 10 | 10 | | |
| Australia | 299 | 1,561 | 3,500 | 3,750 | 3 | 6.2 |
| Belgium | ... | ... | 40 | 20 | | |
| Bulgaria | ... | ... | 400 | 100 | | |
| Canada | 3,639 | 6,739 | 8,200 | 9,250 | 1 | 15.4 |
| China | ... | ... | 1,250 | 1,250 | 10 | 2.1 |
| Czechoslovakia | ... | ... | 1,750 | 1,500 | 8 | 2.5 |
| France | 1,476 | 2,845 | 2,500 | 2,100 | 5 | 3.5 |
| Gabon | 472 | 1,034 | 700 | 500 | | |
| Germany | 0 | 41 | 1,100 | 250 | | |
| Hungary | 0 | ... | 400 | 425 | | |
| India | 0 | 150 | 210 | 220 | | |
| Namibia | 0 | 4,036 | 2,450 | 1,500 | 8 | 2.5 |
| Niger | 54 | 4,132 | 3,000 | 3,000 | 4 | 5 |
| Portugal | 95 | 68 | 60 | 40 | | |
| Romania | ... | ... | 100 | 200 | | |
| South Africa | 3,737 | 6,186 | 1,700 | 1,750 | 6 | 2.9 |
| Spain | 60 | 167 | 200 | 175 | | |
| USSR (former) | ... | ... | 10,000 | 8,200 | 2 | 13.7 |
| United States | 11,538 | 16,800 | 3,000 | 1,750 | 7 | 2.9 |

# ZINC ORE

*thousand tonnes*

*metal content*

| | 1948 | 1970 | 1980 | 1990 | 1991 | Rank | % |
|---|---|---|---|---|---|---|---|
| World | 1,790 | 5,520 | 6,192 | 7,366 | 7,513 | | |
| Algeria | 6 | 17 | 8 | 4 | 3.5 | | |
| Argentina | 13 | 39 | 34 | 38.7 | 39.1 | | |
| Australia | 194 | 496 | 495 | 939 | 1,048 | 2 | 13.9 |
| Austria | 3 | 16 | 22 | 16.7 | 14.8 | | |
| Bolivia | 21 | 47 | 50 | 108 | 130 | | |
| Brazil | ... | 12 | 70 | 113 | 103 | | |
| Bulgaria | 9.7 | 76 | 89 | 34.7 | 29.1 | | |
| Canada | 252 | 1,239 | 1,059 | 1,203 | 1,148 | 1 | 15.3 |
| Chile | ... | 1 | 1 | 25.1 | 31 | | |
| China | ... | 106 | 180 | 619 | 710 | 4 | 9.5 |
| Czechoslovakia | ... | ... | 7 | 7.4 | 7.8 | | |
| Finland | 8 | 69 | 58 | 51.7 | 55.5 | | |
| France | 6 | 19 | 37 | 23.9 | 27.1 | | |
| Germany | 29 | 127 | 121 | 58.1 | 54 | | |
| Greece | 3 | 9 | 27 | 26.7 | 30 | | |
| Greenland | 0 | 0 | 86 | 48 | ... | | |
| Honduras | ... | 5 | 16 | 29.3 | 38.3 | | |
| India | ... | 8 | 32 | 70 | 105 | | |
| Iran | ... | 58 | 30 | 14.8 | 31.1 | | |
| Ireland | ... | 97 | 229 | 167 | 188 | 10 | 2.5 |
| Italy | 74 | 110 | 57 | 42.4 | 37.1 | | |
| Japan | 33 | 280 | 238 | 127 | 133 | | |
| Korea, North | 13 | 130 | 130 | 195 | 215 | 9 | 2.9 |
| Korea, South | ... | 23 | 56 | 22.8 | 22.6 | | |
| Mexico | 179 | 266 | 243 | 307 | 317 | 7 | 4.2 |
| Morocco | 2 | 16 | 6 | 18.4 | 23.6 | | |
| Namibia | 12 | 46 | 32 | 37.7 | 33.1 | | |
| Norway | 6 | 10 | 28 | 16.7 | 18.9 | | |
| Peru | 59 | 321 | 468 | 584 | 628 | 5 | 8.4 |
| Philippines | 0 | 3 | 9 | ... | ... | | |
| Poland | 96 | 242 | 217 | 155 | 145 | | |
| Romania | ... | ... | 40 | 35.6 | 25.9 | | |
| South Africa | ... | ... | 82 | 74.8 | 64.4 | | |
| Spain | 47 | 98 | 179 | 258 | 261 | 8 | 3.5 |
| Sweden | 36 | 93 | 167 | 160 | 158 | | |
| Thailand | ... | 0.5 | 1 | 80.8 | 86.9 | | |
| Tunisia | 2 | 12 | 9 | 7.3 | 5.1 | | |
| Turkey | 2 | 24 | 23 | 39.1 | 32.5 | | |
| USSR (former) | ... | 610 | 1,000 | 870 | 800 | 3 | 10.6 |
| United States | 572 | 485 | 349 | 543 | 547 | 6 | 7.3 |
| Vietnam | ... | ... | 10 | 10 | 15 | | |
| Yugoslavia | 37 | 101 | 95 | 76 | 74 | | |
| Zaire | 47 | 104 | 67 | 61.8 | 45 | | |
| Zambia | 23 | 66 | 43 | 35.4 | 24.8 | | |

# WORLD
# ALMANAC

# PHYSICAL DIMENSIONS

Each topic list is divided into continents and within a continent the items are listed in order of size. The sequence of the continents is Europe, Asia, Africa, Australasia, North America and South America. All major features are listed. The world top ten are shown in square brackets; in the case of mountains this has not been done because the world top 30 are all in Asia. The figures are rounded as appropriate.

## WORLD, CONTINENTS, OCEANS

| | km² | miles² | % |
|---|---|---|---|
| The World | 509,450,000 | 196,672,000 | – |
| Land | 149,450,000 | 57,688,000 | 29.3 |
| Water | 360,000,000 | 138,984,000 | 70.7 |
| Asia | 44,500,000 | 17,177,000 | 29.8 |
| Africa | 30,302,000 | 11,697,000 | 20.3 |
| North America | 24,241,000 | 9,357,000 | 16.2 |
| South America | 17,793,000 | 6,868,000 | 11.9 |
| Antarctica | 14,100,000 | 5,443,000 | 9.4 |
| Europe | 9,957,000 | 3,843,000 | 6.7 |
| Australia & Oceania | 8,557,000 | 3,303,000 | 5.7 |
| Pacific Ocean | 179,679,000 | 69,356,000 | 49.9 |
| Atlantic Ocean | 92,373,000 | 35,657,000 | 25.7 |
| Indian Ocean | 73,917,000 | 28,532,000 | 20.5 |
| Arctic Ocean | 14,090,000 | 5,439,000 | 3.9 |

## SEAS

### Pacific

| | km² | miles² |
|---|---|---|
| South China Sea | 2,974,600 | 1,148,500 |
| Bering Sea | 2,268,000 | 875,000 |
| Sea of Okhotsk | 1,528,000 | 590,000 |
| East China & Yellow | 1,249,000 | 482,000 |
| Sea of Japan | 1,008,000 | 389,000 |
| Gulf of California | 162,000 | 62,500 |
| Bass Strait | 75,000 | 29,000 |

### Atlantic

| | km² | miles² |
|---|---|---|
| Caribbean Sea | 2,766,000 | 1,068,000 |
| Mediterranean Sea | 2,516,000 | 971,000 |
| Gulf of Mexico | 1,543,000 | 596,000 |
| Hudson Bay | 1,232,000 | 476,000 |
| North Sea | 575,000 | 223,000 |
| Black Sea | 462,000 | 178,000 |
| Baltic Sea | 422,170 | 163,000 |
| Gulf of St Lawrence | 238,000 | 92,000 |

### Indian

| | km² | miles² |
|---|---|---|
| Red Sea | 438,000 | 169,000 |
| The Gulf | 239,000 | 92,000 |

## MOUNTAINS

### Europe

| | | m | ft |
|---|---|---|---|
| Mont Blanc | France/Italy | 4,807 | 15,771 |
| Monte Rosa | Italy/Switzerland | 4,634 | 15,203 |
| Dom | Switzerland | 4,545 | 14,911 |
| Weisshorn | Switzerland | 4,505 | 14,780 |
| Matterhorn/Cervino | Italy/Switzerland | 4,478 | 14,691 |
| Mt Maudit | France/Italy | 4,465 | 14,649 |
| Finsteraarhorn | Switzerland | 4,274 | 14,022 |
| Aletschhorn | Switzerland | 4,182 | 13,720 |
| Jungfrau | Switzerland | 4,158 | 13,642 |
| Barre des Ecrins | France | 4,103 | 13,461 |
| Schreckhorn | Switzerland | 4,078 | 13,380 |
| Gran Paradiso | Italy | 4,061 | 13,323 |
| Piz Bernina | Italy/Switzerland | 4,049 | 13,284 |
| Ortles | Italy | 3,899 | 12,792 |
| Monte Viso | Italy | 3,841 | 12,602 |
| Grossglockner | Austria | 3,797 | 12,457 |
| Wildspitze | Austria | 3,774 | 12,382 |
| Weisskügel | Austria/Italy | 3,736 | 12,257 |
| Balmhorn | Switzerland | 3,709 | 12,169 |
| Dammastock | Switzerland | 3,630 | 11,909 |
| Tödi | Switzerland | 3,620 | 11,877 |
| Presanella | Italy | 3,556 | 11,667 |
| Monte Adamello | Italy | 3,554 | 11,660 |
| Mulhacén | Spain | 3,478 | 11,411 |
| Pico de Aneto | Spain | 3,404 | 11,168 |
| Posets | Spain | 3,375 | 11,073 |
| Marmolada | Italy | 3,342 | 10,964 |
| Etna | Italy | 3,340 | 10,958 |
| Musala | Bulgaria | 2,925 | 9,596 |
| Olympus | Greece | 2,917 | 9,570 |
| Gerlachovka | Slovak Republic | 2,655 | 8,711 |
| Galdhöpiggen | Norway | 2,469 | 8,100 |
| Pietrosul | Romania | 2,305 | 7,562 |
| Hvannadalshnúkur | Iceland | 2,119 | 6,952 |
| Narodnaya | Russia | 1,894 | 6,214 |
| Ben Nevis | UK | 1,343 | 4,406 |

### Asia

| | | m | ft |
|---|---|---|---|
| Everest | China/Nepal | 8,848 | 29,029 |
| Godwin Austen (K2) | China/Kashmir | 8,611 | 28,251 |
| Kanchenjunga | India/Nepal | 8,598 | 28,208 |
| Lhotse | China/Nepal | 8,516 | 27,939 |
| Makalu | China/Nepal | 8,481 | 27,824 |
| Cho Oyu | China/Nepal | 8,201 | 26,906 |
| Dhaulagiri | Nepal | 8,172 | 26,811 |
| Manaslu | Nepal | 8,156 | 26,758 |
| Nanga Parbat | Kashmir | 8,126 | 26,660 |
| Annapurna | Nepal | 8,078 | 26,502 |
| Gasherbrum | China/Kashmir | 8,068 | 26,469 |
| Broad Peak | China/Kashmir | 8,051 | 26,414 |
| Gosainthan | China | 8,012 | 26,286 |
| Disteghil Sar | Kashmir | 7,885 | 25,869 |
| Nuptse | Nepal | 7,879 | 25,849 |
| Masherbrum | Kashmir | 7,821 | 25,659 |
| Nanda Devi | India | 7,817 | 25,646 |
| Rakaposhi | Kashmir | 7,788 | 25,551 |
| Kanjut Sar | India | 7,760 | 25,459 |
| Kamet | India | 7,756 | 25,446 |
| Namcha Barwa | China | 7,756 | 25,446 |
| Gurla Mandhata | China | 7,728 | 25,354 |
| Muztag | China | 7,723 | 25,338 |
| Kongur Shan | China | 7,719 | 25,324 |
| Tirich Mir | Pakistan | 7,690 | 25,229 |
| Saser | Kashmir | 7,672 | 25,170 |
| K'ula Shan | Bhutan/China | 7,543 | 24,747 |
| Pik Kommunizma | Tajikistan | 7,495 | 24,590 |
| Aling Gangri | China | 7,314 | 23,996 |
| Elbrus | Russia | 5,642 | 18,501 |
| Demavend | Iran | 5,604 | 18,386 |
| Ararat | Turkey | 5,165 | 16,945 |
| Gunong Kinabalu | Malaysia (Borneo) | 4,101 | 13,455 |
| Yu Shan | Taiwan | 3,997 | 13,113 |
| Fuji-san | Japan | 3,776 | 12,388 |
| Rinjani | Indonesia | 3,726 | 12,224 |
| Mt Rajang | Philippines | 3,364 | 11,037 |
| Pidurutalagala | Sri Lanka | 2,524 | 8,281 |

| Africa | | m | ft |
|---|---|---|---|
| Kilimanjaro | Tanzania | 5,895 | 19,340 |
| Mt Kenya | Kenya | 5,199 | 17,057 |
| Ruwenzori | Uganda/Zaïre | 5,109 | 16,762 |
| Ras Dashan | Ethiopia | 4,620 | 15,157 |
| Meru | Tanzania | 4,565 | 14,977 |
| Karisimbi | Rwanda/Zaïre | 4,507 | 14,787 |
| Mt Elgon | Kenya/Uganda | 4,321 | 14,176 |
| Batu | Ethiopia | 4,307 | 14,130 |
| Guna | Ethiopia | 4,231 | 13,882 |
| Toubkal | Morocco | 4,165 | 13,665 |
| Irhil Mgoun | Morocco | 4,071 | 13,356 |
| Mt Cameroon | Cameroon | 4,070 | 13,353 |
| Amba Ferit | Ethiopia | 3,875 | 13,042 |
| Teide | Spain (Tenerife) | 3,718 | 12,198 |
| Thabana Ntlenyana | Lesotho | 3,482 | 11,424 |
| Emi Kussi | Chad | 3,415 | 11,204 |
| Mt aux Sources | Lesotho/S. Africa | 3,282 | 10,768 |
| Mt Piton | Réunion | 3,069 | 10,069 |

| Oceania | | m | ft |
|---|---|---|---|
| Puncak Jaya | Indonesia | 5,029 | 16,499 |
| Puncak Trikora | Indonesia | 4,750 | 15,584 |
| Puncak Mandala | Indonesia | 4,702 | 15,427 |
| Mt Wilhelm | Papua New Guinea | 4,508 | 14,790 |
| Mauna Kea | USA (Hawaii) | 4,205 | 13,796 |
| Mauna Loa | USA (Hawaii) | 4,170 | 13,681 |
| Mt Cook | New Zealand | 3,753 | 12,313 |
| Mt Balbi | Solomon Is. | 2,439 | 8,002 |
| Orohena | Tahiti | 2,241 | 7,352 |
| Mt Kosciusko | Australia | 2,237 | 7,339 |

| North America | | m | ft |
|---|---|---|---|
| Mt McKinley | USA (Alaska) | 6,194 | 20,321 |
| Mt Logan | Canada | 5,959 | 19,551 |
| Citlaltepetl | Mexico | 5,700 | 18,701 |
| Mt St Elias | USA/Canada | 5,489 | 18,008 |
| Popocatepetl | Mexico | 5,452 | 17,887 |
| Mt Foraker | USA (Alaska) | 5,304 | 17,401 |
| Ixtaccihuatl | Mexico | 5,286 | 17,342 |
| Lucania | Canada | 5,227 | 17,149 |
| Mt Steele | Canada | 5,073 | 16,644 |
| Mt Bona | USA (Alaska) | 5,005 | 16,420 |
| Mt Blackburn | USA (Alaska) | 4,996 | 16,391 |
| Mt Sanford | USA (Alaska) | 4,940 | 16,207 |
| Mt Wood | Canada | 4,848 | 15,905 |
| Nevado de Toluca | Mexico | 4,670 | 15,321 |
| Mt Fairweather | USA (Alaska) | 4,663 | 15,298 |
| Mt Whitney | USA | 4,418 | 14,495 |
| Mt Elbert | USA | 4,399 | 14,432 |
| Mt Harvard | USA | 4,395 | 14,419 |
| Mt Rainier | USA | 4,392 | 14,409 |
| Blanca Peak | USA | 4,372 | 14,344 |
| Long's Peak | USA | 4,345 | 14,255 |
| Nevado de Colima | Mexico | 4,339 | 14,235 |
| Mt Shasta | USA | 4,317 | 14,163 |
| Tajumulco | Guatemala | 4,220 | 13,845 |
| Gannett Peak | USA | 4,202 | 13,786 |
| Mt Waddington | Canada | 3,994 | 13,104 |
| Mt Robson | Canada | 3,954 | 12,972 |
| Chirripó Grande | Costa Rica | 3,837 | 12,589 |
| Pico Duarte | Dominican Rep. | 3,175 | 10,417 |

| South America | | m | ft |
|---|---|---|---|
| Aconcagua | Argentina | 6,960 | 22,834 |
| Illimani | Bolivia | 6,882 | 22,578 |
| Bonete | Argentina | 6,872 | 22,546 |
| Ojos del Salado | Argentina/Chile | 6,863 | 22,516 |
| Tupungato | Argentina/Chile | 6,800 | 22,309 |
| Pissis | Argentina | 6,779 | 22,241 |
| Mercedario | Argentina/Chile | 6,770 | 22,211 |
| Huascaran | Peru | 6,768 | 22,204 |
| Llullaillaco | Argentina/Chile | 6,723 | 22,057 |
| Nudo de Cachi | Argentina | 6,720 | 22,047 |
| Yerupaja | Peru | 6,632 | 21,758 |
| N. de Tres Cruces | Argentina/Chile | 6,620 | 21,719 |
| Incahuasi | Argentina/Chile | 6,600 | 21,654 |

| | | m | ft |
|---|---|---|---|
| Ancohuma | Bolivia | 6,550 | 21,489 |
| Sajama | Bolivia | 6,542 | 21,463 |
| Coropuna | Peru | 6,425 | 21,079 |
| Ausangate | Peru | 6,384 | 20,945 |
| Cerro del Toro | Argentina | 6,380 | 20,932 |
| Ampato | Peru | 6,310 | 20,702 |
| Chimborasso | Ecuador | 6,267 | 20,561 |
| Cotopaxi | Ecuador | 5,896 | 19,344 |
| S. Nev. de S. Marta | Colombia | 5,800 | 19,029 |
| Cayambe | Ecuador | 5,796 | 19,016 |
| Pico Bolivar | Venezuela | 5,007 | 16,427 |

| Antarctica | | m | ft |
|---|---|---|---|
| Vinson Massif | | 4,897 | 16,066 |
| Mt Kirkpatrick | | 4,528 | 14,855 |
| Mt Markham | | 4,349 | 14,268 |

## OCEAN DEPTHS

| Atlantic Ocean | m | ft | |
|---|---|---|---|
| Puerto Rico (Milwaukee) Deep | 9,220 | 30,249 | [7] |
| Cayman Trench | 7,680 | 25,197 | [10] |
| Gulf of Mexico | 5,203 | 17,070 | |
| Mediterranean Sea | 5,121 | 16,801 | |
| Black Sea | 2,211 | 7,254 | |
| North Sea | 660 | 2,165 | |
| Baltic Sea | 463 | 1,519 | |
| Hudson Bay | 258 | 846 | |

| Indian Ocean | m | ft | |
|---|---|---|---|
| Java Trench | 7,450 | 24,442 | |
| Red Sea | 2,635 | 8,454 | |
| Persian Gulf | 73 | 239 | |

| Pacific Ocean | m | ft | |
|---|---|---|---|
| Mariana Trench | 11,022 | 36,161 | [1] |
| Tonga Trench | 10,882 | 35,702 | [2] |
| Japan Trench | 10,554 | 34,626 | [3] |
| Kuril Trench | 10,542 | 34,587 | [4] |
| Mindanao Trench | 10,497 | 34,439 | [5] |
| Kermadec Trench | 10,047 | 32,962 | [6] |
| Peru-Chile Trench | 8,050 | 26,410 | [8] |
| Aleutian Trench | 7,822 | 25,662 | [9] |
| Middle American Trench | 6,662 | 21,857 | |

| Arctic Ocean | m | ft |
|---|---|---|
| Molloy Deep | 5,608 | 18,399 |

## LAND LOWS

| | | m | ft |
|---|---|---|---|
| Caspian Sea | Europe | −28 | −92 |
| Dead Sea | Asia | −403 | −1,322 |
| Lake Assal | Africa | −156 | −512 |
| Lake Eyre North | Oceania | −16 | −52 |
| Death Valley | N. America | −86 | −282 |
| Valdés Peninsula | S. America | −40 | −131 |

## RIVERS

| Europe | | km | miles |
|---|---|---|---|
| Volga | Caspian Sea | 3,700 | 2,300 |
| Danube | Black Sea | 2,850 | 1,770 |
| Ural | Caspian Sea | 2,535 | 1,575 |
| Dnepr | Volga | 2,285 | 1,420 |
| Kama | Volga | 2,030 | 1,260 |
| Don | Volga | 1,990 | 1,240 |

|  |  | km | miles |
|---|---|---|---|
| Petchora | Arctic Ocean | 1,790 | 1,110 |
| Oka | Volga | 1,480 | 920 |
| Belaya | Kama | 1,420 | 880 |
| Dnister | Black Sea | 1,400 | 870 |
| Vyatka | Kama | 1,370 | 850 |
| Rhine | North Sea | 1,320 | 820 |
| N. Dvina | Arctic Ocean | 1,290 | 800 |
| Desna | Dnepr | 1,190 | 740 |
| Elbe | North Sea | 1,145 | 710 |
| Vistula | Baltic Sea | 1,090 | 675 |
| Loire | Atlantic Ocean | 1,020 | 635 |
| W. Dvina | Baltic Sea | 1,019 | 633 |

### Asia

|  |  | km | miles |
|---|---|---|---|
| Yangtze | Pacific Ocean | 6,380 | 3,960 [3] |
| Yenisey-Angara | Arctic Ocean | 5,550 | 3,445 [5] |
| Huang He | Pacific Ocean | 5,464 | 3,395 [6] |
| Ob-Irtysh | Arctic Ocean | 5,410 | 3,360 [7] |
| Mekong | Pacific Ocean | 4,500 | 2,795 [9] |
| Amur | Pacific Ocean | 4,400 | 2,730 [10] |
| Lena | Arctic Ocean | 4,400 | 2,730 |
| Irtysh | Ob | 4,250 | 2,640 |
| Yenisey | Arctic Ocean | 4,090 | 2,540 |
| Ob | Arctic Ocean | 3,680 | 2,285 |
| Indus | Indian Ocean | 3,100 | 1,925 |
| Brahmaputra | Indian Ocean | 2,900 | 1,800 |
| Syrdarya | Aral Sea | 2,860 | 1,775 |
| Salween | Indian Ocean | 2,800 | 1,740 |
| Euphrates | Indian Ocean | 2,700 | 1,675 |
| Vilyuy | Lena | 2,650 | 1,645 |
| Kolyma | Arctic Ocean | 2,600 | 1,615 |
| Amudarya | Aral Sea | 2,540 | 1,575 |
| Ural | Caspian Sea | 2,535 | 1,575 |
| Ganges | Indian Ocean | 2,510 | 1,560 |
| Si Kiang | Pacific Ocean | 2,100 | 1,305 |
| Irrawaddy | Indian Ocean | 2,010 | 1,250 |
| Tarim-Yarkand | Lop Nor | 2,000 | 1,240 |
| Tigris | Indian Ocean | 1,900 | 1,180 |
| Angara | Yenisey | 1,830 | 1,135 |
| Godavari | Indian Ocean | 1,470 | 915 |
| Sutlej | Indian Ocean | 1,450 | 900 |
| Yamuna | Indian Ocean | 1,400 | 870 |

### Africa

|  |  | km | miles |
|---|---|---|---|
| Nile | Mediterranean | 6,670 | 4,140 [1] |
| Zaïre/Congo | Atlantic Ocean | 4,670 | 2,900 [8] |
| Niger | Atlantic Ocean | 4,180 | 2,595 |
| Zambezi | Indian Ocean | 3,540 | 2,200 |
| Oubangi/Uele | Zaïre | 2,250 | 1,400 |
| Kasai | Zaïre | 1,950 | 1,210 |
| Shaballe | Indian Ocean | 1,930 | 1,200 |
| Orange | Atlantic Ocean | 1,860 | 1,155 |
| Cubango | Okavango Swamps | 1,800 | 1,120 |
| Limpopo | Indian Ocean | 1,600 | 995 |
| Senegal | Atlantic Ocean | 1,600 | 995 |
| Volta | Atlantic Ocean | 1,500 | 930 |
| Benue | Niger | 1,350 | 840 |

### Australia

|  |  | km | miles |
|---|---|---|---|
| Murray-Darling | Indian Ocean | 3,750 | 2,330 |
| Darling | Murray | 3,070 | 1,905 |
| Murray | Indian Ocean | 2,575 | 1,600 |
| Murrumbidgee | Murray | 1,690 | 1,050 |

### North America

|  |  | km | miles |
|---|---|---|---|
| Mississippi-Missouri | G. of Mexico | 6,020 | 3,740 [4] |
| Mackenzie | Arctic Ocean | 4,240 | 2,630 |
| Mississippi | Gulf of Mexico | 3,780 | 2,350 |
| Missouri | Mississippi | 3,780 | 2,350 |
| Yukon | Pacific Ocean | 3,185 | 1,980 |
| Rio Grande | Gulf of Mexico | 3,030 | 1,880 |
| Arkansas | Mississippi | 2,340 | 1,450 |
| Colorado | Pacific Ocean | 2,330 | 1,445 |
| Red | Mississippi | 2,040 | 1,270 |
| Columbia | Pacific Ocean | 1,950 | 1,210 |
| Saskatchewan | Lake Winnipeg | 1,940 | 1,205 |
| Snake | Columbia | 1,670 | 1,040 |
| Churchill | Hudson Bay | 1,600 | 990 |
| Ohio | Mississippi | 1,580 | 980 |
| Brazos | Gulf of Mexico | 1,400 | 870 |
| St Lawrence | Atlantic Ocean | 1,170 | 730 |

### South America

|  |  | km | miles |
|---|---|---|---|
| Amazon | Atlantic Ocean | 6,450 | 4,010 [2] |
| Paraná-Plate | Atlantic Ocean | 4,500 | 2,800 |
| Purus | Amazon | 3,350 | 2,080 |
| Madeira | Amazon | 3,200 | 1,990 |
| São Francisco | Atlantic Ocean | 2,900 | 1,800 |
| Paraná | Plate | 2,800 | 1,740 |
| Tocantins | Atlantic Ocean | 2,750 | 1,710 |
| Paraguay | Paraná | 2,550 | 1,580 |
| Orinoco | Atlantic Ocean | 2,500 | 1,550 |
| Pilcomayo | Paraná | 2,500 | 1,550 |
| Araguaia | Tocantins | 2,250 | 1,400 |
| Juruá | Amazon | 2,000 | 1,240 |
| Xingu | Amazon | 1,980 | 1,230 |
| Ucayali | Amazon | 1,900 | 1,180 |
| Maranón | Amazon | 1,600 | 990 |
| Uruguay | Plate | 1,600 | 990 |
| Magdalena | Caribbean Sea | 1,540 | 960 |

# LAKES

### Europe

|  |  | km² | miles² |
|---|---|---|---|
| Lake Ladoga | Russia | 17,700 | 6,800 |
| Lake Onega | Russia | 9,700 | 3,700 |
| Saimaa system | Finland | 8,000 | 3,100 |
| Vänern | Sweden | 5,500 | 2,100 |
| Rybinsk Reservoir | Russia | 4,700 | 1,800 |

### Asia

|  |  | km² | miles² |
|---|---|---|---|
| Caspian Sea | Asia | 371,800 | 143,550 [1] |
| Aral Sea | Kazakh./Uzbek. | 36,000 | 13,900 [6] |
| Lake Baykal | Russia | 30,500 | 11,780 [9] |
| Tonlé Sap | Cambodia | 20,000 | 7,700 |
| Lake Balkhash | Kazakhstan | 18,500 | 7,100 |
| Dongting Hu | China | 12,000 | 4,600 |
| Ysyk Köl | Kyrgyzstan | 6,200 | 2,400 |
| Lake Urmia | Iran | 5,900 | 2,300 |
| Koko Nur | China | 5,700 | 2,200 |
| Poyang Hu | China | 5,000 | 1,900 |
| Lake Khanka | China/Russia | 4,400 | 1,700 |
| Lake Van | Turkey | 3,500 | 1,400 |
| Ubsa Nur | China | 3,400 | 1,300 |

### Africa

|  |  | km² | miles² |
|---|---|---|---|
| Lake Victoria | E. Africa | 68,000 | 26,000 [3] |
| Lake Tanganyika | C. Africa | 33,000 | 13,000 [7] |
| Lake Malawi/Nyasa | E. Africa | 29,600 | 11,430 [10] |
| Lake Chad | C. Africa | 25,000 | 9,700 |
| Lake Turkana | Ethiopia/Kenya | 8,500 | 3,300 |
| Lake Volta | Ghana | 8,500 | 3,300 |
| Lake Bangweulu | Zambia | 8,000 | 3,100 |
| Lake Rukwa | Tanzania | 7,000 | 2,700 |
| Lake Mai-Ndombe | Zaïre | 6,500 | 2,500 |
| Lake Kariba | Zambia/Zimbabwe | 5,300 | 2,000 |
| Lake Mobutu | Uganda/Zaïre | 5,300 | 2,000 |
| Lake Nasser | Egypt/Sudan | 5,200 | 2,000 |
| Lake Mweru | Zambia/Zaïre | 4,900 | 1,900 |
| Lake Cabora Bassa | Mozambique | 4,500 | 1,700 |
| Lake Kyoga | Uganda | 4,400 | 1,700 |
| Lake Tana | Ethiopia | 3,630 | 1,400 |
| Lake Kivu | Rwanda/Zaïre | 2,650 | 1,000 |
| Lake Edward | Uganda/Zaïre | 2,200 | 850 |

### Australia

|  |  | km² | miles² |
|---|---|---|---|
| Lake Eyre | Australia | 8,900 | 3,400 |
| Lake Torrens | Australia | 5,800 | 2,200 |
| Lake Gairdner | Australia | 4,800 | 1,900 |

| North America | | km$^2$ | miles$^2$ | |
|---|---|---|---|---|
| Lake Superior | Canada/USA | 82,350 | 31,800 | [2] |
| Lake Huron | Canada/USA | 59,600 | 23,010 | [4] |
| Lake Michigan | USA | 58,000 | 22,400 | [5] |
| Great Bear Lake | Canada | 31,800 | 12,280 | [8] |
| Great Slave Lake | Canada | 28,500 | 11,000 | |
| Lake Erie | Canada/USA | 25,700 | 9,900 | |
| Lake Winnipeg | Canada | 24,400 | 9,400 | |
| Lake Ontario | Canada/USA | 19,500 | 7,500 | |
| Lake Nicaragua | Nicaragua | 8,200 | 3,200 | |
| Lake Athabasca | Canada | 8,100 | 3,100 | |
| Smallwood Reservoir | Canada | 6,530 | 2,520 | |
| Reindeer Lake | Canada | 6,400 | 2,500 | |
| Lake Winnipegosis | Canada | 5,400 | 2,100 | |
| Nettilling Lake | Canada | 5,500 | 2,100 | |
| Lake Nipigon | Canada | 4,850 | 1,900 | |
| Lake Manitoba | Canada | 4,700 | 1,800 | |

| South America | | km$^2$ | miles$^2$ |
|---|---|---|---|
| Lake Titicaca | Bolivia/Peru | 8,300 | 3,200 |
| Lake Poopo | Peru | 2,800 | 1,100 |

## ISLANDS

| Europe | | km$^2$ | miles$^2$ | |
|---|---|---|---|---|
| Great Britain | UK | 229,880 | 88,700 | [8] |
| Iceland | Atlantic Ocean | 103,000 | 39,800 | |
| Ireland | Ireland/UK | 84,400 | 32,600 | |
| Novaya Zemlya (N.) | Russia | 48,200 | 18,600 | |
| W. Spitzbergen | Norway | 39,000 | 15,100 | |
| Novaya Zemlya (S.) | Russia | 33,200 | 12,800 | |
| Sicily | Italy | 25,500 | 9,800 | |
| Sardinia | Italy | 24,000 | 9,300 | |
| N.E. Spitzbergen | Norway | 15,000 | 5,600 | |
| Corsica | France | 8,700 | 3,400 | |
| Crete | Greece | 8,350 | 3,200 | |
| Zealand | Denmark | 6,850 | 2,600 | |

| Asia | | km$^2$ | miles$^2$ | |
|---|---|---|---|---|
| Borneo | S.E. Asia | 744,360 | 287,400 | [3] |
| Sumatra | Indonesia | 473,600 | 182,860 | [6] |
| Honshu | Japan | 230,500 | 88,980 | [7] |
| Celebes | Indonesia | 189,000 | 73,000 | |
| Java | Indonesia | 126,700 | 48,900 | |
| Luzon | Philippines | 104,700 | 40,400 | |
| Mindanao | Philippines | 101,500 | 39,200 | |
| Hokkaido | Japan | 78,400 | 30,300 | |
| Sakhalin | Russia | 74,060 | 28,600 | |
| Sri Lanka | Indian Ocean | 65,600 | 25,300 | |
| Taiwan | Pacific Ocean | 36,000 | 13,900 | |
| Kyushu | Japan | 35,700 | 13,800 | |
| Hainan | China | 34,000 | 13,100 | |
| Timor | Indonesia | 33,600 | 13,000 | |
| Shikoku | Japan | 18,800 | 7,300 | |
| Halmahera | Indonesia | 18,000 | 6,900 | |
| Ceram | Indonesia | 17,150 | 6,600 | |

| | | km$^2$ | miles$^2$ | |
|---|---|---|---|---|
| Sumbawa | Indonesia | 15,450 | 6,000 | |
| Flores | Indonesia | 15,200 | 5,900 | |
| Samar | Philippines | 13,100 | 5,100 | |
| Negros | Philippines | 12,700 | 4,900 | |
| Bangka | Indonesia | 12,000 | 4,600 | |
| Palawan | Philippines | 12,000 | 4,600 | |
| Panay | Philippines | 11,500 | 4,400 | |
| Sumba | Indonesia | 11,100 | 4,300 | |
| Mindoro | Philippines | 9,750 | 3,800 | |
| Buru | Indonesia | 9,500 | 3,700 | |
| Bali | Indonesia | 5,600 | 2,200 | |
| Cyprus | Mediterranean | 3,570 | 1,400 | |
| Wrangel Is. | Russia | 2,800 | 1,000 | |

| Africa | | km$^2$ | miles$^2$ | |
|---|---|---|---|---|
| Madagascar | Indian Ocean | 587,040 | 226,660 | [4] |
| Socotra | Indian Ocean | 3,600 | 1,400 | |
| Réunion | Indian Ocean | 2,500 | 965 | |
| Tenerife | Atlantic Ocean | 2,350 | 900 | |
| Mauritius | Indian Ocean | 1,865 | 720 | |

| Oceania | | km$^2$ | miles$^2$ | |
|---|---|---|---|---|
| New Guinea | Indon./Pap. NG | 821,030 | 317,000 | [2] |
| New Zealand (S.) | New Zealand | 150,500 | 58,100 | |
| New Zealand (N.) | New Zealand | 114,700 | 44,300 | |
| Tasmania | Australia | 67,800 | 26,200 | |
| New Britain | Papua NG | 37,800 | 14,600 | |
| New Caledonia | Pacific Ocean | 19,100 | 7,400 | |
| Viti Levu | Fiji | 10,500 | 4,100 | |
| Hawaii | Pacific Ocean | 10,450 | 4,000 | |
| Bougainville | Papua NG | 9,600 | 3,700 | |
| Guadalcanal | Solomon Is. | 6,500 | 2,500 | |
| Vanua Levu | Fiji | 5,550 | 2,100 | |
| New Ireland | Papua NG | 3,200 | 1,200 | |

| North America | | km$^2$ | miles$^2$ | |
|---|---|---|---|---|
| Greenland | Greenland | 2,175,600 | 839,800 | [1] |
| Baffin Is. | Canada | 508,000 | 196,100 | [5] |
| Victoria Is. | Canada | 212,200 | 81,900 | [9] |
| Ellesmere Is. | Canada | 212,000 | 81,800 | [10] |
| Cuba | Cuba | 110,860 | 42,800 | |
| Newfoundland | Canada | 110,680 | 42,700 | |
| Hispaniola | Atlantic Ocean | 76,200 | 29,400 | |
| Banks Is. | Canada | 67,000 | 25,900 | |
| Devon Is. | Canada | 54,500 | 21,000 | |
| Melville Is. | Canada | 42,400 | 16,400 | |
| Vancouver Is. | Canada | 32,150 | 12,400 | |
| Somerset Is. | Canada | 24,300 | 9,400 | |
| Jamaica | Caribbean Sea | 11,400 | 4,400 | |
| Puerto Rico | Atlantic Ocean | 8,900 | 3,400 | |
| Cape Breton Is. | Canada | 4,000 | 1,500 | |

| South America | | km$^2$ | miles$^2$ |
|---|---|---|---|
| Tierra del Fuego | Argentina/Chile | 47,000 | 18,100 |
| Falkland Is. (E.) | Atlantic Ocean | 6,800 | 2,600 |
| South Georgia | Atlantic Ocean | 4,200 | 1,600 |
| Galapagos | Pacific Ocean | 2,250 | 870 |

# THE EARTH

The most widely accepted theory about the origins of the Earth is that it was formed from a solar cloud consisting mainly of hydrogen 4,600 million years ago. The cloud condensed, forming the planets. The lighter elements floated to the surface of the Earth, where they cooled to form a crust; the inner material remained hot and molten. The first rocks were formed over 3,500 million years ago, but the Earth's surface has since been constantly altered.

The Earth has an oblate spheroid or solid shape, with an equatorial diameter of 12,756.28 km [7,926.38 mls] and a polar diameter of 12,713.51 km [7,899.81 mls]. The equatorial circumference is 40,075.02 km [24,906.46 mls] and is divided into 360 degrees of longitude, which is measured in degrees, minutes and seconds east or west of the Greenwich meridian. North and south of the Equator, distance is measured in degrees, minutes and seconds of latitude (the Equator lies at 0°, the North Pole at 90°N, the South Pole at 90°S, the Tropic of Cancer at 23° 26'N and the Tropic of Capricorn at 23° 26'S).

The surface area of the Earth is made up of 70.92% water and 29.08% land. Beneath the surface area are three layers: the crust, the mantle and the core.

**The crust**: This accounts for about 1.5% of the Earth's volume and consists of a brittle, low-density material varying from 5–50 km [3–31 mls] in depth (it is thickest beneath the continents and thinnest beneath the oceans). The material is a combination of silica and aluminium and is known as sial. Below the sial is a denser basaltic layer, composed of silica and magnesium, known as sima. Separating the crust and the next layer, the mantle, is a boundary called the Mohorovičić Discontinuity.

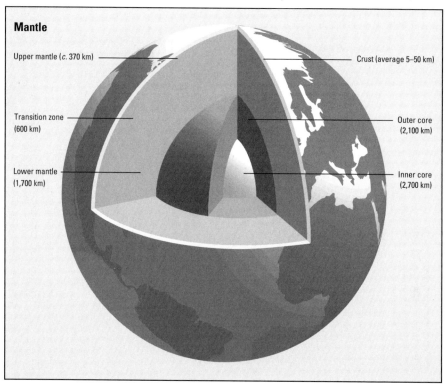

**Mantle**

Upper mantle (c. 370 km)

Transition zone (600 km)

Lower mantle (1,700 km)

Crust (average 5–50 km)

Outer core (2,100 km)

Inner core (2,700 km)

PLATE TECTONICS

EURASIAN PLATE

IRANIAN PLATE

ARABIAN PLATE

INDIAN PLATE

AFRICAN PLATE

ANTARCTIC PLATE

NORTH AMERICAN PLATE

SOUTH AMERICAN PLATE

CARIBBEAN PLATE

COCOS PLATE

NAZCA PLATE

PACIFIC PLATE

ANTARCTIC PLATE

ANTARCTIC PLATE

EURASIAN PLATE

PHILIPPINE PLATE

INDIAN PLATE

ANTARCTIC PLATE

Divergent plate boundaries (zones of construction)

Convergent plate boundaries (zones of subduction and collision)

- - - Uncertain plate boundaries

↑ Direction of plate movement

Projection: Mercator

CARTOGRAPHY BY PHILIP'S. COPYRIGHT REED INTERNATIONAL BOOKS LTD

**The mantle**: The upper mantle (including the transition zone) is about 1,000 km [600 mls] deep and is rich in iron and magnesium silicates. It is a rigid layer and temperatures can reach as much as 1,600°C [2,915°F]. Below this layer, the lower mantle is more viscous and is about 1,700 km [1,050 mls] deep. **The core**: The core has two parts. The outer core, measuring about 2,100 km [1,300 mls], consists of molten iron and nickel at between 2,100°C [3,800°F] and 5,000°C [9,000°F]. About 5,000 km [3,000 mls] below the surface is a liquid transition zone, below which is the solid inner core, about 2,700 km [1,700 mls] in depth and with rock about three times as dense as the crust, probably consisting mostly of iron. The temperature at the centre of the Earth is thought to be 5,000°C [9,000°F].

### CONTINENTAL DRIFT

The jigsaw-puzzle-like fit of the Atlantic coasts led to the theory of continental drift proposed by Alfred Wegener in 1915. He suggested that an ancient supercontinent, called Pangaea, incorporating all the Earth's land masses, gradually split up to form the six geographic continents we know today. By 180 million years ago, Pangaea had split into two major continents; a northern one, Laurasia, and a southern one, Gondwanaland, separated by a long narrow ocean known as Tethys. Gondwanaland began to break up, with India and Antarctica-Australia becoming isolated. To form today's pattern, India 'collided' with Asia (crumpling up sediments to form the Himalayas); South America rotated and moved west to connect with North America; Australia separated from Antarctica and moved north; and the familiar gap developed between Greenland and Europe.

### PLATE TECTONICS

The continental drift theory led to the idea of plate tectonics. The discovery that the continents are carried along on the top of slowly-moving crustal plates (which float on heavier liquid material – the lower mantle) provided the mechanism for the drift theories to work. There are 15 plates of various sizes (usually combining both oceanic and continental crust) which converge and diverge along margins marked by seismic and volcanic activity.

Plates diverge from mid-ocean ridges where molten lava pushes up and forces the plates apart at a rate of up to 40 mm [1.6 in] a year; converging plates form either a trench (where the oceanic plates sink below the lighter continental rock) or mountain ranges (where two continents collide). Most of the world's mountain building, earthquakes and volcanic eruptions take place along plate boundaries ■

# OCEANS

Over 360 million sq km [140 million sq mls] of the Earth's surface is covered by oceans and seas; this is equivalent to over 70% of the Earth's surface. In a strict geographical sense there are only three true oceans: the Atlantic, Pacific and Indian with an average depth of 3,900 m [12,900 ft]. The Pacific Ocean alone accounts for nearly 36% of the total surface of the Earth and almost 50% of the sea area. Gravity holds in around 1,400 million cubic km [335 million cubic mls] of water, of which over 97% is saline.

### OCEAN PROFILE

**The continental shelf**: This is geologically still part of the land mass and drops gently to about 200 m [660 ft] below sea level. This area is home to most sea life, particularly the sunlit upper layer. In this surface zone, huge energies are exchanged between the oceans and the atmosphere above. The oceans absorb large quantities of carbon dioxide and partially exchange it for oxygen, largely by way of the phytoplankton, tiny plants that photosynthesize solar energy and form the base of the marine food chain. Light and colour fade with depth and by 200 m [660 ft] there is only a dim twilight.

**The continental slope**: Here the sea bed falls away suddenly at 3° to 6°. There is then a more gradual descent to the ocean floor, known as the continental rise, with gradients between 1 in 100 and 1 in 700. At these depths temperature and light are minimal, and at a depth of about 1,000 m [3,000 ft] there occurs a temperature change almost as abrupt as the transition between the air and water above. Below this thermocline, at a near-stable 3°C [37.4°F], the waters are unmoved by the winds at the surface and circulate very slowly, often remaining in the same place for thousands of years. The pressure is immense, touching 1,000 atmospheres in the deepest trenches. Some life is supported here and the water also serves as a storehouse for heat and assorted atmospheric chemicals.

**The abyssal plains:** These are found at between 2,500 m and 6,000 m [8,200 ft and 20,000 ft]. From these plains rise volcanoes (for example, Mauna Kea on Hawaii reaches 10,203 m [33,468 ft], although only 4,205 m [13,796 ft] is visible above sea level) and underwater mountain chains up to 1,000 km [600 mls] across, whose peaks sometimes appear above sea level as islands such as Iceland and Tristan da Cunha.

Ocean trenches may cut into the sea bottom, extending the depth of the ocean. These are found particularly in the Pacific Ocean, where six trenches reach more than 10,000 m [33,000 ft] below sea level, including the Mariana Trench, at 11,022 m [36,161 ft] below sea level.

### OCEAN CURRENTS

Moving immense quantities of energy as well as billions of tonnes of water every hour, the ocean currents are a vital part of the heat engine that drives the Earth's climate. They themselves are produced by a twofold mechanism. At the surface, winds push huge masses of water before them; in the deep ocean, below the abrupt temperature gradient, density variations cause slow vertical movements. The pattern of circulation of the great surface currents is determined by the displacement known as the Coriolis effect. As the Earth turns beneath a moving object, it appears to be deflected to one side. The deflection is most obvious near the Equator, where the Earth's surface is spinning eastwards at about 1,700 km/h [1,050 mph]; currents moving polewards are curved clockwise in the northern hemisphere and anticlockwise in the southern hemisphere.

The result is a system of spinning circles known as gyres. The Coriolis effect piles up water on the left of each gyre, creating a narrow, fast-moving stream that is matched by a slower, broader returning current on the right. North and south of the Equator, the fastest currents are located in the west and in the east respectively. In each case, warm water moves from the Equator and cold water returns from it. Cold currents often bring an upwelling of old nutrients with them, supporting the world's most economically important fisheries.

Depending on the prevailing winds, some currents on or near the Equator may reverse their direction in the course of a year – a seasonal variation on which Asian monsoon rains depend, and whose occasional failure can bring disaster to millions of people ▪

# GEOLOGICAL TIME

A scheme of age classification has been evolved for geological time extending back hundreds of million of years. Geologists devised their timescale on the basis of relative, not calendar, ages. Accurate dating was impossible and estimates were often bitterly disputed, but the order in which the rocks were formed could be deduced from careful observation. The use of radioactive dating – culminating in the 1950s with the development of a mass spectrometer capable of measuring tiny quantities of isotopes – appears to have settled most of the arguments.

The years since the formation of the Earth are divided in the timescale into four great eras, further split into periods and, in the case of the most recent era, epochs. The present era is the Cainozoic (from the Greek meaning 'new life'), extending backwards through the Mesozoic ('middle life') and Palaeozoic ('ancient life') to the Pre-Cambrian, named after the Latin word for Wales, the location of some of the earliest known fossils.

Most of the Earth's geological history is encompassed by the Pre-Cambrian: though traces of ancient life have since been found (for example, algae and bacteria), it was largely the proliferation of fossils from the beginning of the Palaeozoic era onwards, some 570 million years ago, which first allowed

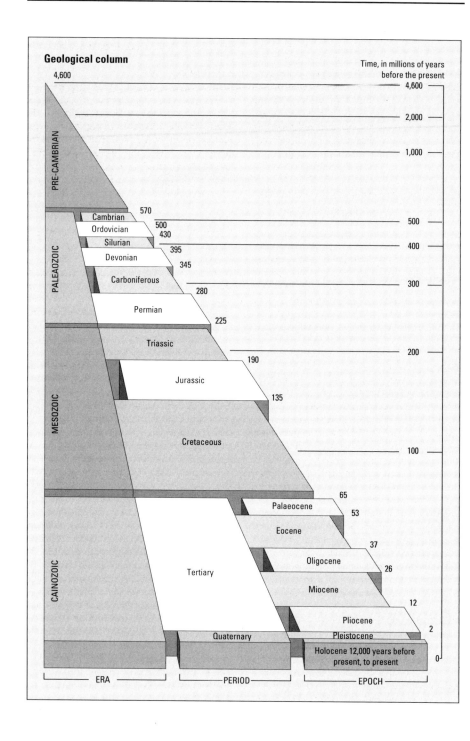

Geological column

Time, in millions of years before the present

precise subdivisions to be made. Like the Cambrian, most are named after regions exemplifying a period's geology. Others – the Carboniferous ('coal-bearing'), for example, or the Cretaceous ('chalk-bearing') – are more directly descriptive. During the Mesozoic era giant reptiles, marsupial mammals and the earliest known species of bird all appeared. Together with coniferous trees and flowering plants, the birds and mammals all survived into the next era (Cainozoic) ■

# TIME MEASUREMENT

Time is measured in terms of the rotation of the Earth about its axis (rotational time) or in terms of periodic phenomena occurring within atoms (atomic time). The various forms of rotational time and the relationship between them and atomic time are explained below.

## SOLAR TIME

The time taken for the Earth to complete one rotation on its axis, relative to the Sun, is a solar day. Because the Earth moves round the Sun in an ellipse rather than in a circle, and its speed is not constant along its orbit, the length of day or apparent solar day is not constant throughout the year (it becomes shorter than average at the equinoxes and longer at the solstices). The mean solar day averages out the differences over a period of one year. Mean solar time observed on the meridian of the telescope at the Royal Observatory at Greenwich, in England, is called Greenwich Mean Time (GMT). GMT, also known as Universal time, is the basis of standard time throughout the world and is of particular use in navigation and astronomy.

## SIDEREAL TIME

The time taken for the Earth to complete one rotation on its axis, with reference to a point in the heavens called the First Point of Aries, is a sidereal (or 'star') day. Because of the precession of the Earth's axis (which makes the length of the sidereal day shorter than the real period of rotation by 0.008 seconds) and various oscillations, astronomers use a mean sidereal time with these fluctuations evened out.

## EPHEMERIS TIME

A detailed study of the motions of the Sun, Moon and planets relative to the Earth has shown that there are irregularities in the Earth's rotation. A table giving the apparent daily positions of the Sun, planets and Moon is called an ephemeris; the method of time measurement based on bringing the ephemeris into agreement with observed values is ephemeris time.

## ATOMIC TIME

Time can be measured to a high degree of accuracy using the interval between energy changes (quantum transitions) within an atom. When an atom of a element moves from one energy level to another higher or lower one, electromagnetic radiation of a particular frequency is given out. Hydrogen, rubidium and caesium atoms have been used for this purpose. Since 1967, the SI unit of time is now the 'second' as defined in terms of a specified transition within the caesium atom. SI stands for Système International d'Unités – an international system of units devised in 1960 to meet all known needs for measurement in science and technology.

**Relationship between rotational and atomic time:** Because of variations in the speed of rotation of the Earth, the mean solar second (1/86,400 of the mean solar day) is unsatisfactory for precision measurements. In 1955 the International Astronomical Union defined the second of ephemeris time as 1/31,566,925.9747 of the tropical year for 1 January 1900 at 12 hours ephemeris time. In 1956 this definition was accepted by the General Conference of Weights and Measures. In 1964 the Conference also defined an ephemeris second as 9,192,631,770 periods of radiation of a particular transition of the caesium-133 atom. This definition was adopted as the sole definition of the SI unit of time in 1967.

## BRITISH SUMMER TIME AND BRITISH STANDARD TIME (BST)

During World War I an Act of Parliament

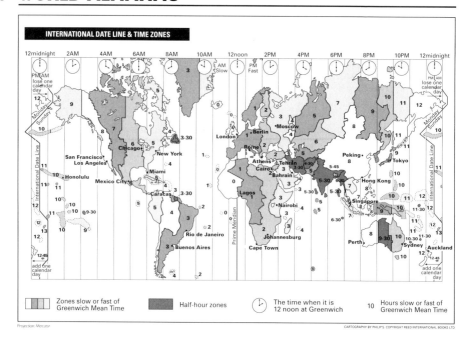

INTERNATIONAL DATE LINE & TIME ZONES

| Zones slow or fast of Greenwich Mean Time | Half-hour zones | The time when it is 12 noon at Greenwich | 10 Hours slow or fast of Greenwich Mean Time |

Projection: Mercator

CARTOGRAPHY BY PHILIP'S. COPYRIGHT REED INTERNATIONAL BOOKS LTD

decreed that during the summer months in Britain the legal time should be one hour in advance of GMT. During World War II the duration of summer time was extended, and in 1914–45 and again in 1947 double summer time (two hours in advance of GMT) was introduced. In 1968 the British

## BRITISH SUMMER TIME

| Year | Begins | Ends |
|------|--------|------|
| 1995 | 26 March | 22 October |
| 1996 | 24 March | 20 October |
| 1997 | 30 March | 19 October |

Standard Time Act put the legal time one hour ahead of GMT for the whole year to bring Britain into line with Central European Time. As from 31 October 1971 Parliament restored the concept of summer time, to operate one hour in advance of GMT between 0200 hr GMT on the day following the third Saturday in March and 0200 hr GMT on the day following the fourth Saturday in October.

## TIME AROUND THE WORLD

The Earth rotates through 360° in 24 hours, and therefore moves 15° every hour. In 1883 a system for dividing the world into separate longitudinal time zones was internationally agreed, thereby replacing local time in different areas with standard time to cover wider areas. The world was divided into 24 standard time zones (see the map above), each being approximately 15° of latitude wide, with the Greenwich meridian at the centre of the first zone. These zones are based on Greenwich Mean Time, time in each zone usually differing from GMT by a whole number of hours. All places to the west of Greenwich are one hour behind for every zone and places to the east are ahead by one hour for every zone. Some large countries have several time zones because they stretch through so many degrees of longitude; the United States, Canada and Russia, for example, are divided into zones approximately 7.5° of latitude wide on each side of central meridians. Zone boundaries are often adjusted to follow local boundaries or to avoid separating cities and towns from neighbours by a time difference. To relate work and leisure more closely to sun time or daylight, the standard zone time can be adjusted for part of the year; summer time is an example of this.

When it is 12 noon at the Greenwich meridian, 180° east the day is only just beginning. To overcome this, the International Date Line was established, an imaginary line running more or less along the 180th meridian (although the line is adjusted locally so that it does not divide countries or groups of islands). West of the date line, the date is one day ahead of that east of the line. For example, if you travelled westwards from Samoa (170° West) to Japan (140° East) you would pass from Sunday morning into Sunday night ■

# THE CALENDAR

A calendar is a method of reckoning time for regulating religious, commercial and civil life, and for dating events. Calendars have been in use from earliest times – the Ancient Egyptians had a system based on the movement of the star Sirius and on the seasons (determined by the fluctuations of the River Nile). Like all calendars this was based on the astronomical motions of the Earth, Moon and Sun. In modern times, the rotation of the Earth gives us the day, the lunar cycle the month, and the solar cycle the changing seasons and the year. The units of time used in calendar reckoning are thus the day, the month and the year.

## THE DAY

The day is the time taken for the Earth to make one complete turn on its axis. In modern calendars the day is reckoned from midnight to midnight and is divided into 24 hours. The hours are counted in two sections: the first from midnight to 12 noon (when the Sun crosses the meridian), which are known as a.m. (ante meridian), and the second from 12 noon to midnight, which are known as p.m. (post meridian). The 24-hour clock disregards a.m. and p.m. and is simply counted from 0 to 23. The hours of daylight vary throughout the year. They also vary with latitude; the further north one gets the greater is the difference between daylight hours and hours of darkness. The subdivision of the day into hours, minutes and seconds is arbitrary and only for our convenience.

## THE MONTH

The month is the time taken for the Moon to complete one full revolution around the Earth. There are different ways of defining this period; the one used in calendars is the synodic month, which is the time between successive new moons – a period of 29.53059 days. The month is used because it is a convenient number of days to count, and because the changes in the Moon's shape are easily recognized. The timing of many religious festivals, such as Easter, is based on the Moon. The week probably owes its origin to the four phases of the Moon.

**Phases of the Moon:** The Moon rises and sets as a result of the Earth's rotation and, in addition, it shows characteristic phases

## DAYS OF THE WEEK

The seven days that make up a *week* have names derived from Old English translations or adaptations of their Roman names.

| | Old English | Roman |
|---|---|---|
| **Sunday** | Sun | Sol |
| **Monday** | Moon | Luna |
| **Tuesday** | Tiw/Tbr (God of War) | Mars |
| **Wednesday** | Woden/Odin | Mercury |
| **Thursday** | Thor | Jupiter |
| **Friday** | Frigga/Freyja (Goddess of Love) | Venus |
| **Saturday** | Saeternes | Saturn |

because of its movement around the Earth. At different points in its orbit, different parts of the illuminated half are visible. At new moon the part illuminated by the Sun is hidden from the Earth and the Moon's disc is completely dark. In a lunar cycle the visible part grows (waxes) from a thin crescent, through a half moon (first quarter), to reach a full moon when the disc is completely illuminated. It then diminishes (wanes) through a second half moon (the last quarter) back to a new moon again. When the moon is between a half moon and a full moon it is said to be gibbous. The full moon nearest to the autumnal equinox (22 September) is often called a harvest moon; the following full moon, in October, is a hunter's moon.

**The tides:** The Moon and, to a lesser extent, the Sun cause tides by their gravitational pull on the water of the oceans. The effect of the Moon's attraction is to raise the water level at a point on the Earth closest to the Moon, thus distorting the Earth's water mass and producing a similar 'bulge' on the opposite side of the Earth. These places have high tide; points on the 'sides' of the Earth have low tides.

As the Earth rotates different places have high tides; most places have two tides every day separated by approximately 12 hours. The precise times of tides depend on the relative positions of the Moon and the Sun, and also on ocean currents. Each month there are two particularly high tides occurring at full and new moon, where the Sun and the Moon are acting in the same direction. These are known as spring tides. Midway between these two are the neap tides, with lowest rise and fall, when the Sun and Moon act in opposite directions.

### THE YEAR

The year is the time taken for the Earth to complete one revolution around the Sun. Again there are different ways of defining it; the one used in calendars is the tropical year, which is the time taken for the Sun to complete a full cycle of its apparent motion north and south of the Equator. The tropical year is 365.242199 days.

The seasons occur because the Earth's axis is not at right-angles to a line between the Earth and the Sun, but is tilted at a constant angle 66.5°. At one part of the orbit the

## THE SEASONS

The seasons are arbitrary divisions of the year into four periods. The generally accepted dates in Europe are:
**Spring**   21 March to 21 June
**Summer**  22 June to 22 September
**Autumn**  23 September to 22 December
**Winter**   23 December to 20 March

northern hemisphere is tilted towards the Sun. At these times it is summer in the northern hemisphere, the hours of daylight exceed the hours of darkness, and the Sun is north of the Equator. As the Earth moves to the opposite side of the orbit, six months later, the northern hemisphere is tilted away from the Sun. It is then winter, the hours of darkness exceed the hours of daylight, and the Sun is south of the Equator.

**Equinoxes and solstices:** The equinoxes occur when the Sun crosses the Equator on its apparent journey north or south. At these times the Sun is directly overhead at the Equator and the hours of daylight equal the hours of darkness at all points on the Earth. The vernal equinox occurs when the Sun is moving northwards, about 21 March. The autumnal equinox occurs on about 22 September, when the Sun is moving southwards.

Midway between the equinoxes are the solstices, which occur when the Sun is at the extremes of its apparent motion north and south of the Equator. In the northern hemisphere the summer solstice occurs on about 21 June, when the Sun is furthest north and this is the longest day of the year. The winter solstice, on about 22 December, is the shortest day in the northern hemisphere and occurs when the Sun is furthest south.

**Eclipses:** When the Moon passes between the Sun and the Earth it causes either a partial eclipse of the Sun (if the Earth passes through the Moon's outer shadow), or a total eclipse (if the inner cone shadow crosses the Earth's surface). In a lunar eclipse, the Earth's shadow crosses the Moon and, again, provides either a partial or total eclipse. Eclipses of the Sun and Moon do not occur every month because of the 5° difference between the plane of the Moon's orbit and the plane in which the Earth moves. In the 1990s only 14 lunar eclipses are possible, seven partial and seven total; each is visible only from certain, and variable, parts of the world. In the same period there are 13 solar eclipses, six partial and seven total.

## QUARTER DAYS

Quarter days are four days marking quarters of the year. They fall close to the equinoxes and solstices; note that Midsummer day is not the longest day of the year. In England, Wales and Northern Ireland, the quarter days are:

| | |
|---|---|
| **Lady day** | 25 March |
| **Midsummer day** | 24 June |
| **Michaelmas** | 29 September |
| **Christmas day** | 25 December |

In Scotland, the quarter days are:

| | |
|---|---|
| **Candlemas** | 2 February |
| **Whit Sunday** | movable |
| **Lammas** | 1 August |
| **Martinmas** | 11 November |

### THE MODERN CALENDAR

The main difficulty in compiling a calendar is that the day, the month and the year are not commensurate – the month is not an exact number of days and the year is not an exact number of months. For convenience, months and years are assigned a whole number of days, and extra days (called intercalations) are added at intervals to compensate. Thus the year, which is about 365.25 days, is taken to be 365 days. As time goes by the seasons get out of step with the dates – the solstices and equinoxes occur one day later every four years. To compensate, an extra day (29 February) is added every four years (the so-called leap years, or bissextiles in the Roman calendar).

The calendar used at the present time is the Gregorian calendar, which is a modification of the earlier Julian calendar.

**The Julian calendar:** This was introduced by Julius Caesar in the first century BC and came from an earlier Roman system based on the Moon. The Julian calendar abandoned any attempt to keep the calendar months in step with the Moon's phases; as a result, the months became arbitrary divisions of time and full moon did not occur on the same day of the month every year. The calendar was based on a year of 365.25 days with an extra day every four years added to February. The calendar was modified by Augustus, who changed the lengths of the months to the number of days they now have.

**The Gregorian calendar:** The value of 365.25 days of the Julian calendar is slightly longer (about 11 minutes) than the true value and over the years the error mounted up. By 1582 there was a difference of 10 days between the solstices and their original dates. In this year a papal bull (edict) issued by Pope Gregory XIII corrected the discrepancy by making 5 October into 15 October. The bull also modified the rule for leap years, introducing the rule that the first year of a century (1600, 1700 and so on) is a leap year only if it is divisible by 400 (thus 1600 was a leap year but 1700 was not).

The Gregorian system was not adopted immediately in all countries, in particular in Protestant countries. It was introduced in Italy, France, Spain and Portugal in 1582, but not until 1752 was it introduced in England, when it was adopted by dating the day following 2 September 1752 as 14 September. In addition the start of the year was fixed at 1 January in 1752; from the 14th century the year had been reckoned from 25 March (the feast of the Annunciation).

The Gregorian calendar is often called the New Style calendar, to distinguish it from the Julian, or Old Style, calendar. In converting dates between New and Old Styles it is necessary to subtract or add 11 days, to take into account the different starting dates for the year, and the fact that 1700 was a leap year in the Julian calendar but not in the Gregorian calendar.

**Leap years:** The modern rule for determining leap years is that leap years are divisible by four without remainder unless they are centennial years, in which case they are only a leap year if they are divisible by 400 except for the year 4000 and its multiples. These will not be leap years. Thus the year 2000 will be a leap year but 3000 and 4000 will not ∎

# RELIGIOUS CALENDARS

Religious calendars are cycles of festivals and seasons marking events or rituals of special significance. Often they are based on the Moon and do not follow the civil calendar. Nevertheless, they have a wider importance – movable feasts such as Easter and Whitsuntide, in the Christian faith, are also national holidays.

## THE CHRISTIAN CALENDAR

This developed from the Jewish calendar, which was based on a lunar cycle. The festival of Easter developed from the Jewish Passover; Christmas was introduced later to be celebrated at the time of the winter solstice, which had long been marked by such pagan festivals as the Saturnalia.

The Christian year is set by the governing bodies of individual Churches and inevitably there are differences in practice – in particular, there are differences between the Eastern and Western Churches. The festivals dated here are those currently used in the Western Roman Catholic and Anglican Churches. There are two cycles of important dates: one of saints' days and other fixed dates, the other of movable feasts based on Easter.

The dates of the principal movable festivals are calculated as follows: Shrove Tuesday is the day before Ash Wednesday; Palm Sunday is the Sunday before Easter Sunday; Maundy Thursday and Good Friday are the Thursday and Friday before Easter Sunday. Corpus Christi (RC) occurs on the Thursday after

Trinity Sunday. Rogation Sunday is five weeks after Easter. The Festival of Christ the King (RC) is the Last Sunday after Pentecost. The Baptism of Christ is the first Sunday after Epiphany (6 January).

## THE JEWISH CALENDAR

This is based on lunar and solar cycles. Years are dated from the creation, supposed to be at the time of the autumnal equinox in 3760 BC, and designated AM (anno mundi). The Jewish year runs from September to September: AD 1 January 1995 occurred in 5756 AM.

### JEWISH FESTIVALS 1995

| | |
|---|---|
| **Purim** | 16 March |
| **Passover** | 15 April |
| **Jewish New Year** | 25 September |
| **Day of Atonement** | 4 October |
| **Feast of Tabernacles** | 9 October |

Normal years (called a Common Regular year) are divided into 12 months which start at about the time of the new moon: these months have 30 and 29 days alternately, leading to a year of 354 days. In order to keep the months roughly in step with the seasons, an extra month is included in certain years and changes are also made in the number of days in some months. Jewish fasts and festivals occur on fixed dates in the Jewish calendar, which means they are movable in the civil calendar.

## THE MUSLIM CALENDAR

This is a purely lunar calendar consisting of 12 months alternating between 30 or 29 days. An extra day is added to the last month at

### MOVABLE CHRISTIAN FEASTS

| | 1995 | 1996 | 1997 | 1998 |
|---|---|---|---|---|
| **Ash Wednesday** | March | 21 February | 12 February | 25 February |
| **Easter Sunday** | 16 April | 7 April | 30 March | 12 April |
| **Ascension Day** | 25 May | 16 May | 8 May | 21 May |
| **Whit Sunday** | 4 June | 26 May | 18 May | 31 May |
| **Trinity Sunday** | 11 June | 2 June | 24 May | 7 June |
| **Advent Sunday** | 3 December | 1 December | 30 November | 29 November |

intervals to keep the months in step with the new moon, which occurs about the beginning of each month. The months do not keep in step with the seasons. The main date in the Muslim calendar is the Hejira, the flight of the Prophet Muhammed from Mecca to Medina; this corresponds to AD 16 July 622 in the Julian calendar. Hejira years (AH) are used in Iran, Turkey, Egypt, some Arab countries and in some parts of India and Malaysia.

**THE HINDU CALENDAR**

This is also a lunar calendar, consisting of 12 months of 29 days, 12 hours each. Each month is made up of a light fortnight and a dark fortnight, based on the waxing and waning of the Moon. The new year begins in the month of Chiatra (March/April). When necessary a 'leap' month is added to the Hindu calendar to make up the difference between the Hindu (360 days) and the solar (365 days) years ∎

# IMPORTANT DATES

The table below gives the dates of some of the main religious and secular anniversaries and festivals during the course of the year. The saints' days here marked as 'RC' are mainly celebrated in the Roman Catholic calendar; those marked 'Ang' are in the Anglican Book of Common Prayer; unmarked saints are common to both. The saints' days are always fixed – that is, they invariably fall on the designated date irrespective of the day of the week.

In the majority of countries, Independence Day (otherwise known as National Day) is also fixed, although sometimes a government moves it to avoid it falling on a particular day (such as a Sunday) ∎

## IMPORTANT DATES

| RELIGIOUS | | SECULAR |
|---|---|---|
| **January** | | |
| 1 | Circumcision: Solemnity of the BV Mary (RC) | Sudan: Independence Day |
| 3 | St Genevieve (RC) | |
| 6 | Twelfth Night | |
| 7 | St John the Baptist (RC); Orthodox Christmas | |
| 8 | St Lucian (Ang) | |
| 10 | St Gregory (RC) | |
| 17 | St Anthony (RC) | |
| 18 | St Prisca (Ang) | |
| 20 | St Fabian (Ang) | |
| 21 | St Agnes | |
| 22 | St Vincent | |
| 24 | St Francis de Sales (RC) | |
| 25 | Conversion of St Paul | |
| 26 | SS Timothy and Titus (RC) | Australia: Australia Day; India: Republic Day |
| 27 | St Devoté (Monaco) | |
| 28 | St Thomas Aquinas (RC) | |
| 30 | St Basil (RC) | |
| 31 | St John Bosco (RC) | |
| **February** | | |
| 2 | Purification of the Virgin Mary | |
| 3 | St Blasius (Ang) | |

| RELIGIOUS | | SECULAR |
|---|---|---|
| 5 | St Agatha | |
| 6 | | New Zealand: Treaty of Waitangi |
| 10 | St Scholastica (RC) | |
| 14 | St Valentine; SS Cyril and Methodius (RC) | |
| 24 | St Matthias | |
| 29 | | Leap Year Day |
| **March** | | |
| 1 | St David | |
| 2 | St Chad (Ang) | |
| 3 | | Bulgaria: End of Ottoman Rule; Morocco: Accession of Hassan II |
| 7 | St Perpetua (Ang) | |
| 12 | St Gregory (Ang) | |
| 15 | | Hungary: National day |
| 17 | St Patrick (RC) | Ireland: St Patrick's Day |
| 18 | St Edward (Ang) | |
| 19 | St Joseph (RC) | |
| 20 | | Tunisia: Independence Day |
| 21 | St Benedict (Ang) | Vernal equinox |
| 23 | | Pakistan: Republic Day |
| 25 | The Annunciation of the Virgin Mary | Greece: Independence Day; Lady Day (Quarter Day) |
| 26 | | Bangladesh: Independence Day |
| **April** | | |
| 1 | | All Fool's Day; Iran: Islamic Republic Day |
| 3 | St Richard (Ang) | |
| 4 | St Ambrose (Ang) | |
| 5 | | Fiscal year ends |
| 16 | | Denmark: Birthday of HM Queen |
| 17 | | Syria: National day |
| 18 | | Zimbabwe: Independence Day |
| 19 | St Alphege (Ang) | |
| 21 | St Anslem (RC) | |
| 23 | St George | |
| 25 | St Mark | |
| 27 | | Afghanistan: Anniversary of Saur Revolution |
| 29 | St Catherine | |
| 30 | | Netherlands: National Day |
| **May** | | |
| 1 | SS Philip and James | |
| 3 | St Athanasius (RC); Invention of the Cross | |
| 6 | Martyrdom of St John the Evangelist (RC) | |
| 14 | St Matthias (RC) | |
| 17 | | Norway: Independence Day |
| 19 | St Dunstan (Ang) | |
| 20 | | Cameroon: National Day |
| 24 | | Commonwealth Day |
| 25 | St Bede | |

| RELIGIOUS | SECULAR |
|---|---|

**RELIGIOUS**

| | | |
|---|---|---|
| 26 | St Philip Neri (RC); St Augustine (Ang) | |
| 27 | St Augustine (RC); St Bede (Ang) | |
| 31 | The Visitation of our Blessed Lady (RC) | South Africa: Republic Day |
| **June** | | |
| 1 | St Justine (RC); St Nicomede (Ang) | |
| 2 | | Italy: Republic Day |
| 3 | SS Charles Lwanga and Companions (RC) | |
| 5 | St Boniface (Ang) | |
| 6 | | Sweden: National day |
| 10 | | Portugal: National day |
| 11 | St Barnabas | |
| 13 | St Anthony (RC) | |
| 17 | St Alban (Ang) | |
| 20 | St Alban (RC) | |
| 21 | St Aloysius (RC) | Summer solstice: longest day |
| 22 | SS John Fisher and Thomas More (RC) | |
| 24 | St John the Baptist | Midsummer Day (Quarter Day) |
| 25 | | Mozambique: Independence Day |
| 28 | St Irenaeus (RC) | |
| 29 | St Peter and Paul (RC); St Peter (Ang) | |
| **July** | | |
| 1 | | Canada: National day |
| 2 | Visitation of the Blessed Virgin Mary (Ang) | |
| 4 | | USA: Independence Day |
| 10 | | Argentina: Independence Day |
| 11 | St Benedict (RC) | |
| 14 | | France: Fall of the Bastille |
| 15 | St Bonaventure (RC); St Swithian | |
| 17 | | Iraq: Military Revolution |
| 20 | St Margaret (Ang) | Colombia: Independence Day |
| 21 | | Barbados: Independent Kingdom Day |
| 22 | St Mary Magdalene | Poland: National Day |
| 23 | | Egypt: Anniversary of Revolution |
| 25 | St James | |
| 26 | SS Joachim and Anne (RC); St Anne (Ang) | |
| 28 | | Peru: Independence Day |
| 29 | St Martha (RC) | |
| **August** | | |
| 1 | St Alphonsus (RC); Lammas Day | Switzerland: National Day |
| 4 | St John Vianney (RC) | |
| 6 | Transfiguration of Jesus | |
| 7 | Name of Jesus | |
| 8 | St Dominic (RC) | |
| 9 | | Singapore: Independence Day |
| 10 | St Laurence | |
| 11 | St Clare (RC) | Chad: Independence Day |
| 15 | The Assumption of Mary (RC) | North Korea, South Korea: Independence Day |
| 20 | St Bernard | |
| 24 | St Bartholomew | |

| RELIGIOUS | SECULAR |
|---|---|
| **RELIGIOUS** | **SECULAR** |
| 27    St Monica (RC) | |
| 28    St Augustine of Hippo (Ang) | |
| 29    St John the Baptist | |
| 31 | Malaysia: Independence Day |
| **September** | |
| 1    St Giles (Ang) | |
| 3    St Gregory (RC) | |
| 7    St Evurtius (Ang) | Brazil: Independence Day |
| 8    Nativity of the Virgin Mary | |
| 12 | Ethiopia: People's Revolution Day |
| 13    St John Chrysostom (RC) | |
| 14    Holy Cross Day | |
| 15    Our Lady of Sorrows (RC) | El Salvador: Independence Day |
| 16    SS Cornelius and Cyprian (RC) | Mexico: National Day |
| 17    St Lambert (Ang) | |
| 18 | Chile: Independence Day |
| 21    St Matthew | |
| 22 | Autumnal equinox |
| 23 | Saudi Arabia: Unification of the Kingdom |
| 26    St Cyprian (Ang) | |
| 27    St Vincent de Paul (RC) | |
| 29    SS Michael, Gabriel and Raphael (RC); St Michael and all Angels (Ang) | Michaelmas Day (Quarter Day) |
| 30    St Jerome | Botswana: Independence Day |
| **October** | |
| 1    St Teresa of the Child Jesus (RC); St Remigius (Ang) | China: Proclamation of People's Republic; Nigeria: Republic Day |
| 4    St Francis (RC) | |
| 6    St Faith (Ang) | |
| 9    St Denys (Ang) | |
| 10 | Taiwan: Republic Day |
| 12    Our Lady Fiesta Day (Spain) | Spain: Discovery of America Day |
| 13    St Edward the Confessor | |
| 15    St Teresa of Avila (RC) | |
| 17    St Ignatius (RC); St Ethelreda (Ang) | |
| 18    St Luke | |
| 25    St Crispin | |
| 26 | Austria: Proclamation of Neutrality |
| 28    SS Simon and Jude | |
| 29 | Turkey: Republic Day |
| 31    Hallowe'en | |
| **November** | |
| 1    All Saints' Day | Algeria: Revolution Day |
| 2    All Souls' Day | |
| 4    St Charles (RC) | |
| 5 | UK: Guy Fawkes' Day |
| 10    St Leo (RC) | |
| 11    St Martin | Angola: Independence Day |
| 13    St Britius (Ang) | |

| RELIGIOUS | | SECULAR |
|---|---|---|
| 15 | St Machutus (Ang) | |
| 17 | St Elizabeth of Hungary (RC) | |
| 18 | St Hugh (Ang) | |
| 20 | St Edmund (Ang) | |
| 22 | St Cecilia | |
| 23 | St Clement (Ang) | |
| 24 | | Zaïre: Anniversary of Second Republic; USA: Thanksgiving Day |
| 25 | St Catherine (Ang) | |
| 28 | | Albania: Independence Day |
| 30 | St Andrew | |
| **December** | | |
| 3 | St Francis Xavier (RC) | |
| 6 | St Nicholas (Netherlands) | |
| 7 | St Ambrose | |
| 8 | Immaculate Conception | |
| 12 | | Kenya: Independence Day |
| 13 | St Lucy (Lucia) | |
| 14 | St John of the Cross (RC) | |
| 21 | St Thomas | |
| 22 | | Winter solstice: shortest day |
| 23 | | Japan: the Emperor's Birthday |
| 25 | Christmas Day | Quarter Day |

# INTERNATIONAL ORGANIZATIONS

## ARAB LEAGUE

Founded in 1945 to promote economic, social, political and military co-operation between its members. (Also known as League of Arab States.)

**Members**: Algeria, Bahrain, Comoros, Djibouti, Egypt, Iraq, Jordan, Kuwait, Lebanon, Libya, Mauritania, Morocco, Oman, Palestine Liberation Organization, Qatar, Saudi Arabia, Somalia, Sudan, Syria, Tunisia, United Arab Emirates, Yemen.

## ASSOCIATION OF SOUTH-EAST ASIAN NATIONS (ASEAN)

Founded in Thailand in 1967 to hasten the development (economic, social and cultural) of member countries and to encourage co-operation and unity between them.

**Members**: Brunei, Indonesia, Malaysia, Philippines, Singapore, Thailand.

## CARIBBEAN COMMUNITY AND COMMON MARKET (CARICOM)

Founded in 1973, the aim of CARICOM is to strengthen economic co-operation through the Caribbean Common Market, to co-ordinate foreign policy and encourage functional co-operation in common services, such as education, health and industrial relations.

**Members**: Antigua and Barbuda, Bahamas, Barbados, Belize, Dominica, Grenada, Guyana, Jamaica, Montserrat, St Christopher and Nevis, St Lucia, St Vincent and the Grenadines, Trinidad and Tobago.

## COLOMBO PLAN

Founded in 1950 as the Colombo Plan for Co-operative Economic and Social Development in Asia and the Pacific to aid developing countries in the region.

**Members**: Afghanistan, Australia, Bangladesh, Bhutan, Burma, Cambodia, Canada, Fiji, India, Indonesia, Iran, Japan, Laos, Malaysia, Maldives, Nepal, New Zealand, Pakistan, Papua New Guinea, Philippines, Singapore, South Korea, Sri Lanka, Thailand, UK, USA.

## COMMONWEALTH OF INDEPENDENT STATES (CIS)

Formed in 1991, the CIS co-ordinates foreign defence and economic policies in its member states and provides a forum for addressing matters arising from the break-up of the USSR, which formally ceased to exist on 26 December 1991.

**Members**: Armenia, Azerbaijan, Belarus, Georgia, Kazakhstan, Kyrgyzstan, Moldova, Russia, Tajikistan, Turkmenistan, Ukraine, Uzbekistan.

## COMMONWEALTH OF NATIONS

Evolved from the British Empire, with foundations in the 1926 Imperial Conference, the Commonwealth is a free grouping of the UK and most of its former dependencies. It was formed to further international co-operation and strengthen economic, technical and educational links. The countries in the Commonwealth comprise 16 nations recognizing the British monarch as head of state, 30 republics and five indigenous monarchies.

**Members**: Antigua and Barbuda, Australia, Bahamas, Bangladesh, Barbados, Belize, Botswana, Brunei, Canada, Cyprus, Dominica, The Gambia, Ghana, Grenada, Guyana, India, Jamaica, Kenya, Kiribati, Lesotho, Malawi, Malaysia, Maldives, Malta, Mauritius, Namibia, Nauru (special member), New Zealand, Nigeria, Pakistan, Papua New Guinea, St Christopher and Nevis, St Lucia, St Vincent and the Grenadines, Seychelles, Sierra Leone, Singapore, Solomon Islands, South Africa, Sri Lanka, Swaziland, Tanzania, Tonga, Trinidad and Tobago, Tuvalu (special member), Uganda, UK, Vanuatu, Western Samoa, Zambia, Zimbabwe.

## CONFERENCE ON SECURITY AND CO-OPERATION IN EUROPE (CSCE)

Formed in 1975 under the Helsinki Final Act, the CSCE is a group of countries with the common aim of strengthening co-operation and security in Europe. It also covers co-operation on scientific, technological and environmental matters. In November 1990 a Charter of Paris for a New Europe was signed, following the demise of the Cold War. The charter covers human rights, democracy and a rule of law. In July 1992 the member nations set up an armed peace-keeping force.

**Members**: Albania, Armenia, Austria, Azerbaijan, Belgium, Belarus, Bosnia-Herzegovina, Bulgaria, Canada, Croatia, Cyprus, Czech Republic, Denmark, Estonia, Finland, France, Georgia, Germany, Greece, Hungary, Iceland, Ireland, Italy, Kazakhstan, Kyrgyzstan, Latvia, Liechtenstein, Lithuania, Luxembourg, Malta, Moldova, Monaco, Netherlands, Norway, Poland, Portugal, Romania, Russia, San Marino, Slovak Republic, Slovenia, Spain, Sweden, Switzerland, Tajikistan, Turkey, Turkmenistan, Ukraine, UK, USA, Uzbekistan, Vatican City, Yugoslavia (suspended since July 1992).

## EUROPEAN UNION (EU)

Formed in three separate stages: the European Coal and Steel Community was founded in 1951 by the Treaty of Paris, followed by the European Economic Community (the EEC) and the European Atomic Energy Community in 1957 by the Treaty of Rome. The executive and decision-making bodies of these three merged in 1967 to form the European Community. In 1992 the Single European Market was established, removing duties, tariffs and quotas on trade between member countries and allowing a freer movement of people, money and goods within the community. Economic and monetary union may happen sometime in the future. The Maastricht Treaty, which came into effect on 1 November 1993, established the European Union, composed of three pillars: the European Community; a pillar concerned with foreign and security policy; and a pillar to co-ordinate justice and interior affairs. On 1 January 1995, Austria, Finland and Sweden joined the EU following referenda.

**Members**: Austria, Belgium, Denmark, Finland, France, Germany, Greece, Ireland, Italy, Luxembourg, Netherlands, Portugal, Spain, Sweden, UK.

## EUROPEAN FREE TRADE ASSOCIATION (EFTA)

Formed in 1960 to eliminate tariffs between members on industrial goods, enabling free trade. Part of the aim was to achieve a single West European market and increase world trade; to this end, most internal tariffs on industrial goods were abolished by the end of 1966 and the EC and EFTA created a European Economic Area in 1993. Denmark and Britain left EFTA in 1972 to join the EC, Portugal in 1986 and Austria, Finland and Sweden in 1995, leaving only four members.

**Members**: Iceland, Liechtenstein, Norway, Switzerland.

## LATIN AMERICAN INTEGRATION ASSOCIATION (LAIA)

Replaced the Latin American Free Trade Association in 1980, to continue working towards a Latin American common market, centred around the removal of tariffs and the encouragement of trade.

**Members**: Argentina, Bolivia, Brazil, Chile, Colombia, Ecuador, Mexico, Paraguay, Peru, Uruguay, Venezuela.

Costa Rica, Cuba, Dominican Republic, El Salvador, Guatemala, Honduras, Italy, Nicaragua, Panama, Portugal and Spain have observer membership.

## NORTH ATLANTIC TREATY ORGANIZATION (NATO)

Formed in 1949 as a collective defence alliance, where an attack against one member country is seen as an attack against them all. It has continued despite the winding up in 1991 of the Warsaw Pact (Eastern European Mutual Assistance Treaty), the former Eastern bloc's equivalent of NATO.

**Members**: Belgium, Canada, Denmark, France, Germany, Greece, Iceland, Italy, Luxembourg, Netherlands, Norway, Portugal, Spain, Turkey, UK, USA.

## ORGANIZATION OF AFRICAN UNITY (OAU)

Formed in 1963 to promote unity and co-operation, and to eliminate colonialism and apartheid from Africa. Its 53 members represent over 94% of Africa's total population.

**Members**: Algeria, Angola, Benin, Botswana, Burkina Faso, Burundi, Cameroon, Cape Verde, Central African Republic, Chad, Comoros, Congo, Djibouti, Egypt, Equatorial Guinea, Eritrea, Ethiopia, Gabon, The Gambia, Ghana, Guinea, Guinea-Bissau, Ivory Coast, Kenya, Lesotho, Liberia, Libya, Madagascar, Malawi, Mali, Mauritania, Mauritius, Mozambique, Namibia, Niger, Nigeria, Rwanda, São Tomé and Príncipe, Senegal, Seychelles, Sierra Leone, Somalia, South Africa, Sudan, Swaziland, Tanzania, Togo, Tunisia, Uganda, Western Sahara, Zaïre, Zambia, Zimbabwe.

## ORGANIZATION OF AMERICAN STATES (OAS)

Founded in 1948 to promote unity and co-operation between the developed nations of North America and the developing nations of Latin America, and to defend the sovereignty of its members.

**Members**: Antigua and Barbuda, Argentina, Bahamas, Barbados, Belize, Bolivia, Brazil, Canada, Chile, Colombia, Costa Rica, Cuba (suspended since 1962), Dominica, Dominican Republic, Ecuador, El Salvador, Grenada, Guatemala, Guyana, Haiti, Honduras, Jamaica, Mexico, Nicaragua, Panama, Paraguay, Peru, St Christopher and Nevis, St Lucia, St Vincent and the Grenadines, Surinam, Trinidad and Tobago, USA, Uruguay, Venezuela.

## ORGANIZATION FOR ECONOMIC CO-OPERATION AND DEVELOPMENT (OECD)

Founded in 1961 as a replacement for the Organization for European Economic Co-operation (OEEC). The OECD aims to stimulate progress in member countries and direct aid to developing countries.

**Members**: Australia, Austria, Belgium, Canada, Denmark, France, Finland, Germany, Greece, Iceland, Ireland, Italy, Japan, Luxembourg, Mexico, Netherlands, New Zealand, Norway, Portugal, Spain, Sweden, Switzerland, Turkey, UK, USA, Yugoslavia (suspended since 1992).

The 'G7' (Group of Seven) is its 'inner group', comprising Canada, France, Germany, Italy, Japan, UK and USA, whose heads of government meet to discuss economic, monetary and political matters.

## ORGANIZATION OF PETROLEUM EXPORTING COUNTRIES (OPEC)

Founded in 1960 in Iraq to co-ordinate the production and sale of petroleum by its member countries. It controls about three-quarters of the world's oil supply.

**Members:** Algeria, Gabon, Indonesia, Iran, Iraq, Kuwait, Libya, Nigeria, Qatar, Saudi Arabia, United Arab Emirates, Venezuela.

## UNITED NATIONS

Formed in 1945 to promote peace, international co-operation and security, and to help solve economic, social, cultural and humanitarian problems. Other aims include the promotion of human rights and freedom. There were 51 original members; this has now risen to 185. The UN is the world's largest political organization and has six principal organs:

**The General Assembly:** The forum at which member nations discuss moral and political issues affecting world development, peace and security. The Assembly meets every September under a newly-elected President.

**The Security Council:** The primary instrument for maintaining international peace, by attempting to settle disputes between nations.

**The Economic and Social Council:** The largest UN executive, it instructs the many UN agencies to implement Assembly decisions and co-ordinates their work.

**The Secretariat:** The staff of the UN, who administer the policies and programmes.

**The Trusteeship Council:** Administers trust territories with the aim of promoting their advancement. The Council remains despite the fact that its last charge, the Trust Territory of the Pacific Islands (Palau), became fully independent (of the US) in 1994.

**The International Court of Justice:** The judicial organ of the UN. (Also known as the World Court.)

Examples of some of the UN social and humanitarian programmes include:

**United Nations Development Programme (UNDP):** Plans and funds projects to help developing countries make better use of resources and raw materials.

**United Nations International Children's Fund (UNICEF):** Created in 1945 to help children after World War II, it now provides basic healthcare and aid worldwide.

**Food and Agriculture Organization (FAO):** Aims to raise living standards and nutrition levels in rural areas by improving food production and distribution.

There are also agencies involved in many aspects of international trade, safety and security. These include:

**International Labour Organization (ILO):** Seeks to improve labour conditions and promote productive employment with the aim of raising living standards.

**International Maritime Organization (IMO):** Promotes unity amongst merchant shipping, especially in regard to safety, marine pollution and standardization.

**World Trade Organization (WTO):** Replaced the General Agreement on Tariffs and Trade (GATT) on 1 January 1995. It sponsores negotiations on international trade and advocates a common code of conduct.

The **World Bank** comprises three UN agencies:

**International Monetary Fund (IMF):** cultivates international monetary co-operation and the expansion of trade.

**International Bank for Reconstruction and Development (IBRD):** Provides funds and assistance to developing countries.

**International Finance Corporation (IFC):** Encourages the growth of productive private enterprise in less developed countries.

Recent additions to the United Nations include Andorra, Bosnia-Herzegovina, Moldova, Palau, San Marino and the Slovak Republic. There are seven independent states which are not members — Kiribati, Nauru, Switzerland, Taiwan, Tonga, Tuvalu and the Vatican City ∎

## UN CONTRIBUTIONS

In 1994, the top ten contributors to the UN budget, which in 1994–5 was $2.6 billion, were as follows:

| | | |
|---|---|---|
| 1 | **USA** | 25.0 % |
| 2 | **Japan** | 12.5 % |
| 3 | **Germany** | 8.9 % |
| 4 | **Russia** | 6.7 % |
| 5 | **France** | 6.0 % |
| 6 | **UK** | 5.0 % |
| 7 | **Italy** | 4.3 % |
| 8 | **Canada** | 3.1 % |
| 9 | **Spain** | 2.0 % |
| 10 | **Brazil** | 1.6 % |

# INDEX

*The number in bold type which follows each name in the index refers to the number of the map page where that feature or place will be found. This is usually the largest scale on which the place or feature appears. Rivers have been indexed to their mouth or to where they join another river. All river names are followed by the symbol → . A solid square ■ follows the name of a country, while an open square □ refers to a first-order administrative area. The geographical co-ordinates which follow the place name are sometimes only approximate, but are close enough for the place name to be located.*